Lecture Notes in Computer Science   9279

Commenced Publication in 1973
Founding and Former Series Editors:
Gerhard Goos, Juris Hartmanis, and Jan van Leeuwen

More information about this series at http://www.springer.com/series/7412

Vittorio Murino · Enrico Puppo (Eds.)

Image Analysis and Processing – ICIAP 2015

18th International Conference
Genoa, Italy, September 7–11, 2015
Proceedings, Part I

Springer

Editors
Vittorio Murino
PAVIS - Pattern Analysis
  and Computer Vision
Istituto Italiano di Tecnologia (IIT)
Genoa
Italy

Enrico Puppo
Università di Genova
Genoa
Italy

and

Department of Computer Science
University of Verona
Verona
Italy

ISSN 0302-9743   ISSN 1611-3349 (electronic)
Lecture Notes in Computer Science
ISBN 978-3-319-23230-0   ISBN 978-3-319-23231-7 (eBook)
DOI 10.1007/978-3-319-23231-7

Library of Congress Control Number: 2015946761

LNCS Sublibrary: SL6 – Image Processing, Computer Vision, Pattern Recognition, and Graphics

Springer Cham Heidelberg New York Dordrecht London

Printed on acid-free paper

Springer International Publishing AG Switzerland is part of Springer Science+Business Media
(www.springer.com)

Preface

The 2015 International Conference on Image Analysis and Processing, ICIAP 2015, was the 18th edition of a series of conferences promoted biennially by the Italian Member Society (GIRPR) of the International Association for Pattern Recognition (IAPR). The conference traditionally covers both classic and the most recent trends in computer vision, pattern recognition, and image processing, addressing both theoretical and applicative aspects.

ICIAP 2015 (www.iciap2015.eu) was held in Genova, during September 7–11, 2015, in Palazzo della Borsa (the former Stock Exchange Building) conveniently located in the very center of the city, and was organized by the Pattern Analysis and Computer Vision (PAVIS) department (www.iit.it/pavis) of the Istituto Italiano di Tecnologia (IIT), with the valuable support of the University of Genova and University of Verona. Moreover, ICIAP 2015 was endorsed by the International Association for Pattern Recognition (IAPR), the Italian Member Society of IAPR (GIRPR), and the IEEE Computer Society Technical Committee on Pattern Analysis and Machine Intelligence (TCPAMI) and received the institutional support of Regione Liguria and Comune di Genova. Notable sponsorships came from several industrial partners such as Datalogic, Google, Centro Studi Gruppo Orizzonti Holding, Ansaldo Energia, EBIT Esaote, Softeco, eVS embedded Vision Systems, 3DFlow, Camelot Biomedical Systems, as well as Istituto Italiano di Tecnologia, University of Genova, and University of Verona.

ICIAP is traditionally a venue to discuss image processing and analysis, pattern recognition, computer vision, and machine learning, from both theoretical and applicative perspectives, promoting connections and synergies among senior scholars and students, universities, research institutes, and companies. ICIAP 2015 followed this trend, and the program was subdivided into seven main topics, covering a broad range of scientific areas, which were managed by two area chairs per each topic. They were: Video Analysis and Understanding, Multiview Geometry and 3D Computer Vision, Pattern Recognition and Machine Learning, Image Analysis, Detection and Recognition, Shape Analysis and Modeling, Multimedia, and Biomedical Applications.

Moreover, we hosted several prominent companies as well as start-ups to show their activities while assessing them with respect to the cutting-edge research in the respective areas: Datalogic, eVS embedded Vision Systems, 3DFlow, Camelot Biomedical Systems.

ICIAP 2015 received 234 paper submissions coming from all over the world, including Algeria, Brazil, Canada, China, Colombia, Czech Republic, Egypt, Finland, France, Germany, Italy, Japan, Korea, Lebanon, Morocco, New Zealand, Pakistan, Poland, Qatar, Romania, Russia, Saudi Arabia, Spain, Switzerland, Thailand, The Netherlands, Tunisia, Turkey, UK, USA and, Vietnam. The paper review process was managed by the program chairs with the invaluable support of 14 area chairs, together with the Program Committee and a number of additional reviewers. The peer-review selection process was carried out by three distinct reviewers in most of the cases. For the accepted papers, authors were asked to include in the final version a list of the revisions carried out on the paper, underlining the changes made according to the reviewers' comments. This ultimately led to the selection of 129 high quality manuscripts, 27 orals, and 102 posters, with an overall acceptance rate of about 55 % (about 11 % for orals). The ICIAP 2015 proceedings are published as volumes of the *Lecture Notes in Computer Science* (LNCS) series by Springer.

The program also included six invited talks by distinguished scientists in computer vision pattern recognition and image analysis. We enjoyed the plenary lectures of Arnold Smeulders, University of Amsterdam (The Netherlands), Michal Irani, Weizmann Institute of Science (Israel), Bernt Schiele, Max Planck Institute for Informatics (Germany), Kristen Grauman, University of Texas at Austin (USA), Xiaogang Wang, The Chinese University of Hong Kong (China), and Samy Bengio, Google Inc. (USA), who addressed very interesting and recent research approaches and paradigms such as deep learning, big data, search and retrieval, semantic scene understanding, visual cognition, and image enhancement.

While the main conference was held during September 9–11, 2015, ICIAP 2015 also included several tutorials and workshops, held on Monday, September 7 and Tuesday, September 8, 2015, on a variety of topics.

The organized tutorials were: "Life Long Learning in Computer and Robot Vision" by Barbara Caputo (Italy), "Structure from Motion: Historical Overview and Recent Trends" by Andrea Fusiello (Italy), "Probing Human Brain Network Architecture and Dynamics Using MRI" by Maria Giulia Preti (Switzerland), and "Deep Learning in Computer Vision" by Xiaogang Wang (China).

ICIAP 2015 also hosted seven half- or full-day satellite workshops: "International Workshop on Recent Advances in Digital Security: Biometrics and Forensics (BIO-FOR 2015)," organized by Modesto Castrilln Santana, Matthias Kirchner, Daniel Riccio, and Luisa Verdoliva; "Color in Texture and Material Recognition (CTMR 2015)," organized by Claudio Cusano, Paolo Napoletano, Raimondo Schettini, and Joost van de Weijer; "Medical Imaging in Rheumatology: Advanced Applications for the Analysis of Inammation and Damage in the Rheumatoid Joint (RHEUMA 2015)," organized by Silvana Dellepiane, Marco A. Cimmino, Gianni Viano; "Image-Based Smart City Application (ISCA 2015) by Giuseppe Pirlo, Donato Impedovo, and Byron Leite Dantas Bezerra; "First International Workshop on Multimedia Assisted Dietary Management (MADiMa 2015), organized by Stavroula Mougiakakou, Giovanni Maria Farinella, and Keiji Yanai; "Scene Background Modeling and Initialization (SBMI 2015)," organized by Lucia Maddalena and Thierry Bouwmans; "Workshop on Image and Video Processing for Quality of Multimedia Experience," organized by Nicu Sebe, Ben Herbst, and Dubravko Culibrk. Also the workshop papers were all collected in a separate volume of the LNCS series by Springer.

We thank all the workshop organizers and tutorial speakers who made possible such an interesting pre-conference program.

Several awards were conferred during ICIAP 2015. Two student support grants were provided by the International Association for Pattern Recognition (IAPR). The "Eduardo Caianiello" award was attributed to the best paper authored or co-authored by at least one young researcher (PhD student, Post Doc, or similar); a Best Paper award was also assigned after a careful selection made by an *ad hoc* appointed committee.

Unfortunately, just a few months ago, Stefano Levialdi, an eminent scientist and one of the "founders" of the Italian Chapter of the IAPR, passed away. ICIAP 2015 commemorated this scientist, colleague, and friend dedicating the Best Paper award to his memory with the aim of celebrating his pioneering activities in the early stages of Image Analysis and Pattern Recognition in Italy.

The organization and the success of ICIAP 2015 were made possible thanks to the cooperation of many people. First of all, special thanks should be given to the area chairs, who made a big effort for the selection of the papers, together with all the members of the Program Committee. Second, we also would like to thank the industrial, special session, publicity, publication, and Asia and US liaison chairs, who, operating in their respective fields, made this event a successful forum of science. Special thanks go to the workshop and tutorial chairs, as well as all workshop organizers and tutorial lecturers for making richer the conference program with notable satellite events. ASAP S.r.l., the agency that supported the registration process and the financial aspects of the conference, among many other issues, should be acknowledged for all the work done. Last but not least, we are indebted to the Local Committee, mainly colleagues from IIT-PAVIS, who covered almost every aspects of the conference when necessary and the day-to-day management issues of the ICIAP 2015 organization, notably Sara, Diego, Matteo.

Thanks very much indeed to all the aforementioned people since without their support we would have not made it.

We hope that ICIAP 2015 will serve as a basis and inspiration for the future ICIAP editions.

September 2015   Vittorio Murino
                                                     Enrico Puppo

Organization

Organizing Institution

Pattern Analysis and Computer Vision (PAVIS)
Istituto Italiano di Tecnologia (IIT), Genova, Italy
http://www.iit.it/pavis

General Chair

Vittorio Murino — Istituto Italiano di Tecnologia, Italy
University of Verona, Italy

Program Chairs

Enrico Puppo — University of Genova, Italy
Gianni Vernazza — University of Genova, Italy

Workshop Chairs

Marco Cristani — University of Verona, Italy
Carlo Sansone — University of Napoli Federico II, Italy

Tutorial Chair

Alessio Del Bue — Istituto Italiano di Tecnologia, Italy

Special Sessions Chairs

Giuseppe Boccignone — University of Milan, Italy
Giorgio Giacinto — University of Cagliari, Italy

Finance and Industrial Chairs

Sebastiano Battiato — University of Catania, Italy
Luigi Di Stefano — University of Bologna, Italy

Publicity/Web Chair

Manuele Bicego — University of Verona, Italy
Umberto Castellani — University of Verona, Italy

Publications Chairs

Ryad Chellali   Istituto Italiano di Tecnologia, Italy
Diego Sona   Istituto Italiano di Tecnologia, Italy

US Liaison Chair

Silvio Savarese   Stanford University, USA

Asia Liaison Chair

Hideo Saito   Keio University, Japan

Steering Committee

Virginio Cantoni   University of Pavia, Italy
Luigi Cordella   University of Napoli Federico II, Italy
Alberto Del Bimbo   University of Firenze, Italy
Marco Ferretti   University of Pavia, Italy
Fabio Roli   University of Cagliari, Italy
Gabriella Sanniti di Baja   ICIB-CNR, Italy

Area Chairs

Video Analysis and Understanding

Rita Cucchiara   University of Modena e Reggio Emilia, Italy
Jordi Gonzàlez   Universitat Autònoma de Barcelona, Spain

Multiview Geometry and 3D Computer Vision

Andrea Fusiello   University of Udine, Italy
Michael Goesele   TU Darmstadt, Germany

Pattern Recognition and Machine Learning

Marcello Pelillo   University of Venice, Italy
Tiberio Caetano   NICTA, Australia

Image Analysis, Detection and Recognition

Raimondo Schettini   University of Milano-Bicocca, Italy
Theo Gevers   University of Amsterdam, The Netherlands

Shape Analysis and Modeling

Leila De Floriani   University of Genova, Italy
Gunilla Borgefors   Uppsala University, Sweden

Multimedia

Nicu Sebe   University of Trento, Italy
Cees Snoek   University of Amsterdam, The Netherlands

Biomedical Applications

Silvana Dellepiane   University of Genova, Italy
Dimitri Van De Ville   EPFL and University of Genève, Switzerland

Program Committee

Lourdes Agapito, UK
Jake Aggarwal, USA
Albert Ali Salah, Turkey
Edoardo Ardizzone, Italy
Sebastiano Battiato, Italy
Stefano Berretti, Italy
Silvia Biasotti, Italy
Manuele Bicego, Italy
Elisabetta Binaghi, Italy
Giuseppe Boccignone, Italy
Alfred Bruckstein, Israel
Joachim Buhmann, Switzerland
Francesco Camastra, Italy
Barbara Caputo, Italy
Umberto Castellani, Italy
Chen Change Loy, China
Rama Chellappa, USA
Xin Chen, UK
Carlo Colombo, Italy
Marco Cristani, Italy
Maria De Marsico, Italy
Alessio Del Bue, Italy
Adrien Depeursinge, Switzerland
Luigi Di Stefano, Italy
Aykut Erdem, Turkey
Francisco Escolano, Spain
Giovanni Farinella, Italy
Mario Figueiredo, Portugal
David Fofi, France
Ana Fred, Portugal
Giovanni Gallo, Italy
Giorgio Giacinto, Italy
Mehmet Gonen, USA
Shaogang Gong, UK

Marco Gori, Italy
Costantino Grana, Italy
Edwin Hancock, UK
Anders Hast, Sweden
Francesco Isgrò, Italy
Walter Kropatsch, Austria
Claudia Landi, Italy
Laura Leal-Taixé, Switzerland
Ales Leonardis, UK
Giosué Lo Bosco, Italy
Marco Loog, The Netherlands
Lucia Maddalena, Italy
Angelo Marcelli, Italy
Gloria Menegaz, Italy
Greg Mori, USA
Michele Nappi, Italy
Ram Nevatia, USA
Ko Nishino, USA
Francesca Odone, Italy
Pietro Pala, Italy
Alfredo Petrosino, Italy
Massimo Piccardi, Australia
Julien Prados, Switzerland
Andrea Prati, Italy
Maria Giulia Preti, Switzerland
Daniel Riccio, Italy
Jonas Richiardi, Switzerland
Bodo Rosenhahn, Germany
Samuel Rota Bulò, Italy
Amit Roy-Chowdhuri, USA
José Ruiz-Shulcloper, Cuba
Gabriella Sanniti di Baja, Italy
Carlo Sansone, Italy
Ali Shokoufandeh, USA

Patricio Simari, USA
Cees Snoek, The Netherlands
Domenico Tegolo, Italy
Massimo Tistarelli, Italy
Andrea Torsello, Italy
Francesco Tortorella, Italy
Stefano Tubaro, Italy
Andrea Vedaldi, UK

Mario Vento, Italy
Alessandro Verri, Italy
Alessandro Vinciarelli, UK
Kenneth Weiss, USA
Richard Wilson, UK
Marcel Worring, The Netherlands
Tony Xiang, UK
Ramin Zabih, USA

Additional Reviewers

Patrizia Boccacci, Italy
Moazzam Butt, Germany
Alessandro Crimi, Italy
Marco Crocco, Italy
Claudio Cusano, Italy
Nikolas De Giorgis, Italy
Efstratios Gavves, The Netherlands
Fabio Ganovelli, Italy
Laura Gemme, Italy
Andrea Giachetti, Italy
Stefan Guthe, Germany
Roberto Henschel, Germany
Jian Hou, China
Federico Iuricich, USA
Mihir Jain, The Netherlands
Giuseppe Lisanti, Italy
Zhigang Ma, USA
Francesco Malapelle, Italy

Farid Melgani, Italy
Pascal Mettes, The Netherlands
Sadegh Mohammadi, Italy
Nicoletta Noceti, Italy
Elisa Ricci, Italy
Stefano Rovetta, Italy
Marco San Biagio, Italy
Enver Sangineto, Italy
Alberto Signoroni, Italy
Fabio Solari, Italy
Marco Tarini, Italy
Federico Tombari, Italy
Philipp Urban, Germany
Sebastiano Vascon, Italy
Roberto Vezzani, Italy
Radu-Laurentiu Vieriu, Italy
Michael Waechter, Germany
Pietro Zanuttigh, Italy

Local Committee

Sara Curreli   Istituto Italiano di Tecnologia
Matteo Bustreo   Istituto Italiano di Tecnologia
Nicholas Dring   Istituto Italiano di Tecnologia
Carlos Beltran   Istituto Italiano di Tecnologia

Endorsing Institutions

International Association for Pattern Recognition (IAPR)
Italian Group of Researchers in Pattern Recognition (GIRPR)
IEEE Computer Society's Technical Committee on Pattern Analysis and Machine
Intelligence (IEEE-TCPAMI)

Institutional Patronage

Istituto Italiano di Tecnologia
University of Genova
University of Verona
Regione Liguria
Comune di Genova

Sponsoring and Supporting Institutions

Istituto Italiano di Tecnologia, Italy
Datalogic, Italy
Google Inc., USA
Centro Studi Gruppo Orizzonti Holding, Italy
EBIT Esaote, Italy
Ansaldo Energia, Italy
Softeco, Italy
eVS embedded Vision Systems S.r.l., Italy
3DFlow S.r.l., Italy
Camelot Biomedical Systems S.r.l.
University of Genova, Italy
University of Verona, Italy
Camera di Commercio di Genova, Italy

Acknowledgments

We kindly acknowledge Camera di Commercio of Genova for the availability of the conference location of "Sala delle Urla" in the Stock Exchange building and for the related services.

Contents – Part I

Shape Analysis and 3D Computer Vision

Biomedical Applications

Multimedia

Contents – Part II

Video Analysis

Pattern Recognition and Machine Learning

Transfer Learning Through Greedy Subset Selection

Ilja Kuzborskij[1,2], Francesco Orabona[3], and Barbara Caputo[1,2,4]([✉])

[1] Centre du Parc, Idiap Research Institute, Rue Marconi 19,
1920 Martigny, Switzerland
ilja.kuzborskij@idiap.ch
[2] École Polytechnique Fédérale de Lausanne (EPFL), Lausanne, Switzerland
[3] Yahoo! Labs, 229 West 43rd Street, New York, NY 10036, USA
francesco@orabona.com
[4] Department of Computer, Control and Management Engineering,
University of Rome La Sapienza, Rome, Italy
caputo@dis.uniroma1.it

Abstract. We study the binary transfer learning problem, focusing on how to select sources from a large pool and how to combine them to yield a good performance on a target task. In particular, we consider the transfer learning setting where one does not have direct access to the source data, but rather employs the source hypotheses trained from them. Building on the literature on the best subset selection problem, we propose an efficient algorithm that selects relevant source hypotheses and feature dimensions simultaneously. On three computer vision datasets we achieve state-of-the-art results, substantially outperforming transfer learning and popular feature selection baselines in a small-sample setting. Also, we theoretically prove that, under reasonable assumptions on the source hypotheses, our algorithm can learn effectively from few examples.

1 Introduction

It is a truth universally acknowledged that learning algorithms perform better when trained on a lot of data. This is even more true when facing noisy or "hard" problems such as large-scale visual recognition [7]. However, considering object detection tasks, access to training data might be restricted. As noted in [23], the distribution of real-world objects is highly skewed, with few objects occurring very often, and many with few instances. Moreover, learning systems are often not trained from scratch: usually they can be build on previous knowledge acquired over time on related tasks [21]. The scenario of learning from few examples by *transferring* from what is already known to the learner is collectively known as Transfer Learning. The target domain usually indicates the task at hand and the source domain the prior knowledge of the learner.

Most of the transfer learning algorithms proposed in the recent years assume access to the training data coming from both source and target domains [21]. While featuring good practical performance [11], and well understood theoretical

© Springer International Publishing Switzerland 2015
V. Murino and E. Puppo (Eds.): ICIAP 2015, Part I, LNCS 9279, pp. 3–14, 2015.
DOI: 10.1007/978-3-319-23231-7_1

guarantees [2], they often demonstrate poor scalability w.r.t. number of sources. An alternative direction, known as a Hypothesis Transfer Learning (HTL) [3,15], consists in transfering from the *source hypotheses*, that is classifiers trained from them. This framework is practically very attractive [1,16,25], as it treats source hypotheses as black boxes without any regard of their inner workings.

The goal of this paper is to develop an HTL algorithm able to deal effectively and efficiently with a large number of sources. To this end, we cast Hypothesis Transfer Learning as a problem of *efficient selection* and *combination* of source hypotheses from a large pool. We pose it as a subset selection problem and build on results from the literature [6,28]. We develop a greedy algorithm, GreedyTL, which attains the state of art performance given a very limited amount of data from the target domain, while able to scale well over the large number of sources. Our key contribution is a $L2$-regularized variant of the Forward Regression algorithm [13]. Since our algorithm can be viewed both as feature selection and hypothesis transfer learning algorithm, we extensively evaluate it against popular feature selection and transfer learning baselines. We empirically demonstrate that all baselines but GreedyTL, fail in most small-sample transfer learning scenarios, thus proving the critical role of regularization in our formulation. Experiments over three datasets show the power of our approach: we obtain state-of-the-art results in tasks with up to 1000 classes, totalling 1.2 million examples, with only 11 to 20 training examples from the target domain. We back our experimental results by proving generalization bounds showing that, under reasonable assumptions on the source hypotheses, our algorithm is able to learn effectively with a very limited data.

2   Related Work

In the literature there are several transfer learning settings [2,11,21,22]. We focus on the Hypothesis Transfer Learning framework (HTL, [3,15]). There, it is required to have access only to *source hypotheses*, that is classifiers or regressors trained on the source domains. No assumptions are made on how these source hypotheses are trained, on the independence of their underlying distribution from that of the target, or about their inner workings: they are treated as "black boxes", in spirit similar to classifier-generated visual descriptors such as Classemes [4] or Object-Bank [17]. Several works proposed HTL for visual learning [1,20,24], some exploiting more explicitly the connection with classemes-like approaches [14], demonstrating an intriguing potential. Although offering scalability, HTL-based approaches proposed so far have been tested on problems with less than a few hundred of sources [25], already showing some difficulties in selecting informative sources.

Recently, the growing need to deal with large data collections [5,7] has started to change the focus and challenges of research in transfer learning. Scalability with respect to the amount of data and the ability to identify and separate informative sources from those carrying noise for the task at hand have become critical issues. Some attempts have been made in this direction [18,26]. However, all these approaches assume access to all source training data. Moreover, in many of these works the use of richer sources of information has been supported by an increase in the information available in the target domain as well. From an intuitive point of view, this corresponds to having more data points than dimensions. Of course, this makes the learning and selection process easier, but in many applications it is not a reasonable hypothesis. Also, none of the proposed algorithms has a theoretical backing. On the other hand, HTL-based approaches proposed so far have been tested only on problems with less than a few hundred of sources [25], already showing some difficulties in selecting informative sources.

3   Transfer Learning Through Subset Selection

Definitions. We will denote with small and capital bold letters respectively column vectors and matrices, e.g. $\boldsymbol{\alpha} = [\alpha_1, \alpha_2, \ldots, \alpha_d]^T \in \mathbb{R}^d$ and $\boldsymbol{A} \in \mathbb{R}^{d_1 \times d_2}$. The subvector of $\boldsymbol{a}$ with rows indexed by set S is $\boldsymbol{a}_S$, while the square submatrix of $\boldsymbol{A}$ with rows and columns indexed by set S is $\boldsymbol{A}_S$. For $\boldsymbol{x} \in \mathbb{R}^d$, the *support* of $\boldsymbol{x}$ is $\mathrm{supp}(\boldsymbol{x}) = \{i : x_i \neq 0, i \in \{1, \ldots, d\}\}$. Denoting by $\mathcal{X}$ and $\mathcal{Y}$ respectively the input and output space of the learning problem, the training set is $\{(\boldsymbol{x}_i, y_i)\}_{i=1}^m$, drawn i.i.d. from the probability distribution p defined over $\mathcal{X} \times \mathcal{Y}$. We will focus on the binary classification problem so $\mathcal{Y} = \{-1, 1\}$, and, without loss of generality, $\mathcal{X} = \{\boldsymbol{x} : \|\boldsymbol{x}\|_2 \leq 1, \boldsymbol{x} \in \mathbb{R}^d\}$.

To measure the accuracy of a learning algorithm, we have a non-negative *loss* function $\ell(h(\boldsymbol{x}), y)$, which measures the cost incurred predicting $h(\boldsymbol{x})$ instead of y. In particular, we will focus on the square loss, $\ell(h(\boldsymbol{x}), y) = (h(\boldsymbol{x}) - y)^2$, for its appealing computational properties. The *risk* of a hypothesis h, with respect to the probability distribution p, is then defined as $R(h) := \mathbb{E}_{(\boldsymbol{x},y) \sim p}[\ell(h(\boldsymbol{x}), y)]$, while the *empirical risk* given a training set $\{(\boldsymbol{x}_i, y_i)\}_{i=1}^m$ is $\hat{R}(h) := \frac{1}{m} \sum_{i=1}^m \ell(h(\boldsymbol{x}_i), y_i)$. Whenever the hypothesis is a linear predictor, that is, $h_{\boldsymbol{w}}(\boldsymbol{x}) = \boldsymbol{w}^\top \boldsymbol{x}$, we will also use risk notation as $R(\boldsymbol{w}) = R(h_{\boldsymbol{w}})$ and $\hat{R}(\boldsymbol{w}) = \hat{R}(h_{\boldsymbol{w}})$.

Source Selection. Assume, that we are given a finite source hypothesis set $\{h_i^{\mathrm{src}}\}_{i=1}^n$ and the training set $\{(\boldsymbol{x}_i, y_i)\}_{i=1}^m$. As in previous works [14,19,25], we consider the target hypothesis to be of the form

$$h_{\boldsymbol{w},\boldsymbol{\beta}}^{\mathrm{trg}}(\boldsymbol{x}) = \boldsymbol{w}^\top \boldsymbol{x} + \sum_{i=1}^n \beta_i h_i^{\mathrm{src}}(\boldsymbol{x}), \tag{1}$$

where $\boldsymbol{w}$ and $\boldsymbol{\beta}$ are found by the learning procedure. The essential parameter here is $\boldsymbol{\beta}$, that is the one controlling the influence of each source hypothesis. Previous works in transfer learning have focused on finding $\boldsymbol{\beta}$ such that minimizes the error on the training set, subject to some condition on $\boldsymbol{\beta}$. In particular, [25] have proposed to minimize the leave-one-out error w.r.t. $\boldsymbol{\beta}$, subject to $\|\boldsymbol{\beta}\|_2 \leq \tau$, which is known to improve generalization for the right choice of τ [15]. A slightly different approach is to use $\|\boldsymbol{\beta}\|_1 \leq \tau$ regularization for this purpose [25], which is known to prefer β with the most coefficients equal to 0, thus assuming that the optimal β is sparse. Nonetheless, it is not clear whether transfer learning tasks are always truly sparse in practice.

In this work we embrace a weaker assumption, namely, there exist up to k sources that collectively improve the generalization on the target domain. Thus, we pose the problem of the Source Selection as a minimization of the regularized empirical risk on the target training set, while constraining the number of selected source hypotheses.

k**-Source Selection.** *Given the training set* $\left\{ \left([\boldsymbol{x}_i^\top, h_1^{src}(\boldsymbol{x}_i), \ldots, h_n^{src}(\boldsymbol{x}_i)]^\top, y_i \right) \right\}_{i=1}^m$ *we have the optimal target hypothesis* $h_{\boldsymbol{w}^\star, \boldsymbol{\beta}^\star}^{trg}$ *by solving,*

$$(\boldsymbol{w}^\star, \boldsymbol{\beta}^\star) = \arg\min_{\boldsymbol{w}, \boldsymbol{\beta}} \left\{ \hat{R}(h_{\boldsymbol{w}, \boldsymbol{\beta}}^{trg}) + \lambda \|\boldsymbol{w}\|_2^2 + \lambda \|\boldsymbol{\beta}\|_2^2 \right\},$$

$$\text{s.t } \|\boldsymbol{w}\|_0 + \|\boldsymbol{\beta}\|_0 \le k. \tag{2}$$

Notably, the problem (2) is a special case of the *Subset Selection* problem [6]: choose a subset of size k from the n observation variables, which collectively give the best prediction on the variable of interest. However, the Subset Selection problem is **NP**-hard [6]. In practice we can resort to algorithms generating approximate solutions, for many of which we have approximation guarantees. Hence, due to the extensive practical and theoretical results, we will treat the k-Source Selection as a Subset Selection problem, building atop of existing guarantees.

We note that our formulation, (2), differs from the classical subset selection for the fact that it is $L2$-regularized. This technical difference practically and theoretically makes an essential difference and it is the crucial part of our algorithm. First, $L2$ regularization is known to improve the generalization ability of empirical risk minimization. Second, we show that regularization also improves the quality of the approximate solution in situations when the sources, or features, are correlated. At the same time, the experimental evaluation corroborates our theoretical findings: Our formulation substantially outperforms standard subset selection, feature selection algorithms, and transfer learning baselines.

4   Greedy Algorithm for k-Source Selection

In this section we state the algorithm proposed in this work, GreedyTL[1].

GreedyTL. *Let* $\boldsymbol{X} \in \mathbb{R}^{m \times d}$ *and* $\boldsymbol{y} \in \mathbb{R}^m$ *be the standardized training set,* $\{h_i^{src}\}_{i=1}^n$, *source hypothesis set, and* k *and* λ, *regularization parameters. Then, denote* $\boldsymbol{C} = \boldsymbol{Z}^\top \boldsymbol{Z}$ *and* $\boldsymbol{b} = \boldsymbol{Z}^\top \boldsymbol{y}$, *where* $\boldsymbol{Z} = \begin{bmatrix} \boldsymbol{X} & \begin{smallmatrix} h_1^{src}(\boldsymbol{x}_1) & \cdots & h_n^{src}(\boldsymbol{x}_1) \\ \cdots & \cdots & \cdots \\ h_1^{src}(\boldsymbol{x}_m) & \cdots & h_n^{src}(\boldsymbol{x}_m) \end{smallmatrix} \end{bmatrix}$, *and select set* S *of size* k *as follows: (I) Initialize* $S \leftarrow \varnothing$ *and* $U \leftarrow \{1, \ldots, n+d\}$. *(II) Keep populating* S *with* $i \in U$, *that maximize* $\boldsymbol{b}_S^\top ((\boldsymbol{C} + \lambda \boldsymbol{I})_S^{-1})^\top \boldsymbol{b}_S$, *as long as* $|S| \le k$ *and* U *is non-empty.*

---

[1] Source code is available at http://idiap.ch/~ikuzbor/

Derivation of the Algorithm. We derive `GreedyTL` by extending the well known Forward Regression (FR) algorithm [6], which gives an approximation to the subset selection problem, the problem of our interest. FR is known to find good approximation as far as features are uncorrelated [6]. In the following, we build upon FR by introducing a Tikhonov ($L2$) regularization into the formulation. The purpose of regularization is twofold: first, it improves the generalization ability of the empirical risk minimization, and second, it makes the algorithm more robust to the feature correlations, thus opting to find better approximate solution.

First, we briefly formalize the subset selection problem. In a subset selection problem one tries to achieve a good prediction accuracy on the *predictor* random variable Y, given a linear combination of a subset of the *observation* random variables $\{X_i\}_{i=1}^n$. The least squares subset selection then reads as

$$\min_{|S|=k, w \in \mathbb{R}^k} \mathbb{E}\left[(Y - \sum_{i \in S} w_i X_i)^2\right].$$

Now denote the covariance matrix of zero-mean unit-variance observation random variables by C, and the covariances between Y and $\{X_i\}_{i=1}^m$ as b. By virtue of the analytic solution to least-squares and using the introduced notation, we can also state the equivalent *Subset Selection problem*: $\max_{|S|=k} b_S^\top (C_S^{-1})^\top b_S$. However, our goal is to obtain the solution to (2), or a *L2-regularized* subset selection. Similarly to the unregularized subset selection, it is easy to get that (2) is equivalent to $\max_{|S|=k} b_S^\top ((C_S + \lambda I)^{-1})^\top b_S$. As said above, the Subset Selection problem is **NP**-hard, however, there are number ways to approximate it in practice [13]. We choose FR for this task for its simplicity, appealing computational properties and provably good approximation guarantees. Now, to apply FR to our problem, all we have to do is to provide it with normalized $(C + \lambda I)^{-1}$ instead of C^{-1}.

In the basic formulation, FR requires to invert the covariance matrix at each iteration of a greedy search. Clearly, this naive approach gets prohibitive with the growth of both the number of variables and desired subset size, since its computational complexity would be in $\mathcal{O}(k(d+n)^4)$. However, we note that in transfer learning one typically assumes that training set is much smaller than sources and feature dimension. For this reason we apply rank-one updates w.r.t. the dual solution of regularized subset selection, so that the size of the inverted matrix does not change. The computational complexity then improves to $\mathcal{O}(km^2(d+n)^2)$.

Theoretical Guarantees. We now focus on the analysis of the generalization properties of `GreedyTL` for solving k-Source Selection problem (2). Throughout this paragraph we will consider a truncated target predictor $h_{w,\beta}^{\text{trg}}(x) := \text{T}\left(w^\top x + \sum_{i=1}^n \beta_i h_i^{\text{src}}(x)\right)$, with $\text{T}(a) := \min\{\max\{a, -1\}, 1\}$. First we state the bound on the risk of an approximate solution returned by `GreedyTL`.[2]

---

[2] Proofs for theorems can be found in the supplementary material.

Theorem 1. *Let* `GreedyTL` *generate the solution* $(\hat{\boldsymbol{w}}, \hat{\boldsymbol{\beta}})$, *given the training set* $(\boldsymbol{X}, \boldsymbol{y})$, *source hypotheses* $\{h_i^{src}\}_{i=1}^n$ *with* $\tau_\infty^{src} := \max_i\{\|h_i^{src}\|_\infty^2\}$, *hyperparameters* λ *and* k. *Then with high probability,*

$$R\left(h_{\hat{\boldsymbol{w}},\hat{\boldsymbol{\beta}}}^{trg}\right) - \hat{R}\left(h_{\hat{\boldsymbol{w}},\hat{\boldsymbol{\beta}}}^{trg}\right) \leq \tilde{\mathcal{O}}\left(\frac{1+k\tau_\infty^{src}}{\lambda m} + \sqrt{\hat{R}^{src}\frac{1+k\tau_\infty^{src}}{\lambda m}}\right),$$

where $\hat{R}^{src} := \frac{1}{m}\sum_{i=1}^m \ell\left(y_i, \mathrm{T}\left(\sum_{j\in\mathrm{supp}(\hat{\boldsymbol{\beta}})} \hat{\beta}_j h_j^{src}(\boldsymbol{x}_i)\right)\right).$

This results in a generalization bound which tells us how close the performance of the algorithm on the test set will be to the one on the training set. The key quantity here is $\hat{R}^{src}$, which captures the quality of the sources selected by the algorithm. To understand its impact, assume that $\lambda = \mathcal{O}(1)$. The bound has two terms, a fast one of the order of $\tilde{\mathcal{O}}(k/m)$ and a slow one of the order $\tilde{\mathcal{O}}(\sqrt{\hat{R}^{src}k/m})$. When m goes to infinity and $\hat{R}^{src} \neq 0$ the slow term will dominate the convergence rate, giving us a rate of the order of $\tilde{\mathcal{O}}(\sqrt{\hat{R}^{src}k/m})$. If $\hat{R}^{src} = 0$ the slow term completely disappears, giving us a so called fast rate of convergence of $\tilde{\mathcal{O}}(k/m)$. On the other hand, for any finite m if $\hat{R}^{src}$ is small enough, in particular of the order of $\tilde{\mathcal{O}}(k/m)$, we still have a rate of the order of $\tilde{\mathcal{O}}(k/m)$. Hence, the quantity $\hat{R}^{src}$ will govern the finite sample and asymptotic behavior of the algorithm, predicting a faster convergence in both regimes when it is small. In other words, when the source and target tasks are similar, TL facilitates a faster convergence of the empirical risk to the risk. A similar behavior was already observed in [3,15].

However, one might ask what happens when the selected sources are providing bad predictions? Since $\hat{R}^{src} \leq 1$, due to truncation, the empirical risk converges to the risk at the standard rate $\tilde{\mathcal{O}}(\sqrt{k/m})$, the same one we would have without any transfering from the sources classifiers.

We now present another result that upper bounds the difference between the risk of solution of the algorithm and the empirical risk of the optimal solution to the k-Source Selection problem.

Theorem 2. *In addition to conditions of Theorem 1, let* $(\boldsymbol{w}^\star, \boldsymbol{\beta}^\star)$ *be the optimal solution to* (2). *Given a sample covariance matrix* $\hat{\boldsymbol{C}}$, *assume that* $\hat{C}_{i,j\neq i} \leq \gamma < \frac{1+\lambda}{6k}$, *and* $\epsilon := \frac{16(k+1)^2\gamma}{1+\lambda}$. *Then with high probability,*

$$R\left(h_{\hat{\boldsymbol{w}},\hat{\boldsymbol{\beta}}}^{trg}\right) - \hat{R}\left(h_{\boldsymbol{w}^\star,\boldsymbol{\beta}^\star}^{trg}\right) \leq (1+\epsilon)\hat{R}_\lambda^{src} + \tilde{\mathcal{O}}\left(\frac{1+k\tau_\infty^{src}}{\lambda m} + \sqrt{\hat{R}_\lambda^{src}\frac{1+k\tau_\infty^{src}}{\lambda m}}\right),$$

where $\hat{R}_\lambda^{src} := \min_{|S|\leq k}\left\{\frac{\lambda}{|S|} + \frac{1}{|S|}\sum_{i\in S}\hat{R}(h_i^{src})\right\}.$

To analyze the implications of Theorem 2, let us consider few interesting cases. Similarly as done before, the quantity $\hat{R}_\lambda^{src}$ captures how well the source hypotheses are aligned with the target task and governs the asymptotic and finite sample regime. In fact, assume for any finite m that there is at least one source hypothesis with small empirical risk, in particular, in $\tilde{\mathcal{O}}(\sqrt{k/m})$, and set $\lambda = \tilde{\mathcal{O}}(\sqrt{k/m})$. Then we have that $R(h_{\hat{w},\hat{\beta}}^{\mathrm{trg}}) - \hat{R}(h_{w^*,\beta^*}^{\mathrm{trg}}) = \tilde{\mathcal{O}}\left(\sqrt{k/m}\right)$, that is we get the generalization bound as if we are able to solve the original **NP**-hard problem in (2). In other words, if there are useful source hypotheses, we expect our algorithm to perform similarly to the one that identifies the optimal subset. This might seem surprising, but it is important to note that we do not actually care about identifying the correct subset of source hypotheses. We only care about how well the returned solution is able to generalize. On the other hand, if not even one source hypothesis has low risk, selecting the best subset of k sources becomes meaningless. In this scenario, we expect the selection of any subset to perform in the same way. Thus the approximation guarantee does not matter anymore.

We now state the approximation guarantees of `GreedyTL` used to prove Theorem 2. In the following Corollary we show how far the optimal solution to the regularized subset selection is from the approximate one found by `GreedyTL`.

Corollary 1. *Let* $\lambda \in \mathbb{R}^+$ *and* $k \leq n$. *Denote* OPT $:= \min_{\|w\|_0 = k} \left\{ \hat{R}(w) + \lambda\|w\|_2^2 \right\}$. *Assume that* $\hat{C}$ *and* $\hat{b}$ *are normalized, and* $\hat{C}_{i,j \neq i} \leq \gamma < \frac{1+\lambda}{6k}$. *Then, FR algorithm generates an approximate solution* $\hat{w}$ *to the regularized subset selection problem that satisfies* $\hat{R}(\hat{w}) + \lambda\|\hat{w}\|_2^2 \leq \left(1 + \frac{16(k+1)^2\gamma}{1+\lambda}\right)$ OPT $- \frac{16(k+1)^2\gamma\lambda}{(1+\lambda)^2}$.

Apart from being instrumental in the proof of Theorem 2, this statement also points to the secondary role of regularization parameter λ: unlike in FR, we can control the quality of approximate solution even if the features are correlated.

5   Experiments

In this section we present experiments comparing `GreedyTL` to several transfer learning and feature selection algorithms. As done previously, we considered the object detection task and, for all datasets, we left out one class considering it as the target class, while the remaining classes were treated as sources [25]. We repeated this procedure for every class and for every dataset at hand, and averaged the performance scores. In the following, we refer to this procedure as *leave-one-class-out*. We performed the evaluation for every class, reporting averaged class-balanced recognition scores.

We used subsets of Caltech-256 [12], Imagenet [7] and SUN09 [5]. The largest setting considered involves 1000 classes, totaling in 1.2M examples, where the number of training examples of the target domain varies from 11 to 20. Our experiments aimed at verifying two claims: (I) the importance of regularization when using greedy feature selection as a transfer learning scheme; (II) in a small-sample regime `GreedyTL` is more robust than alternative feature selection approaches, such as $L1$-regularization.

Datasets and Features. We used the whole Caltech-256, a public subset of Imagenet containing 10^3 classes and all the classes of SUN09 that have more than 1 example, which amounts to 819 classes. For Caltech-256 and Imagenet, we used as features the publicly-available 1000-dimensional SIFT-BOW descriptors, while for SUN09 we extracted 3400-dimensional PHOG descriptors.

We composed a negative class by merging 100 held-out classes (*surrogate* negative class). We did so for each dataset, and we further split it into the *source* negative and the *target* negative class as 90% + 10% respectively, for training sources and the target. The training sets for the target task were composed by $\{2, 5, 10\}$ positive examples, and 10 negative ones. Following [25], the testing set contained 50 positive and 50 negative examples for Caltech-256 and Imagenet. For the skewed SUN09 dataset we took one positive and 10 negative training examples, with the rest left for testing. We drew each target training and testing set randomly 10 times, averaging the results over them. This procedure, commonly used in the literature, helps us avoiding cases of overfitting when building the source hypotheses.

Algorithms. We chose a linear SVM to train the source classifiers [10]. This allows us to compare fairly with relevant baselines (like Lasso) and is in line with recent trends in large scale visual recognition and transfer learning [8]. The source classifiers were trained for each class in the dataset, combining all the positive examples of that class and the source negatives. On average, each source classifier was trained using 10^4 examples for the Caltech-256, 10^5 for Imagenet and 10^3 for the SUN09 dataset. The models were selected by 5-fold cross-validation having regularization parameter $C \in \{10^{-4}, 10^{-3}, \cdots, 10^4\}$. In addition to trained source classifiers, for the Caltech-256, we also evaluated transfer from Classemes [4] and Object Bank [17], which are very similar in spirit to source classifiers. At the same time, for Imagenet, we evaluated transfer from DeCAF convolutional neural network [8].

We divided the baselines into two groups - the linear transfer learning baselines that do not require access to the source data, and the feature selection baselines. We included the second group of baselines due to GreedyTL's resemblance to a feature selection algorithm. We focus on the linear baselines, since we are essentially interested in the feature selection in high-dimensional spaces from few examples. In that scope, most feature selection algorithms, such as Lasso, are linear. In particular, amongst TL baselines we chose: *No transfer*: Regularized Least Squares (RLS) algorithm trained solely on the target data; *Best source*: indicates the performance of the best source classifier selected by its score on the testing set. This is a pseudo-indicator of what an HTL can achieve; *AverageKT*: obtained by averaging the predictions of all the source classifiers; *RLS src+feat*: RLS trained on the concatenation of feature descriptors and source classifier predictions; *MultiKT* $\| \cdot \|_2$: HTL algorithm by [25] selecting β in (1) by minimizing the leave-one-out error subject to $\|\beta\|_2 \leq \tau$; *MultiKT* $\| \cdot \|_1$: similar to previous, but applying the constraint $\|\beta\|_1 \leq \tau$; *DAM*: An HTL algorithm by [9], that can handle selection from multiple source hypotheses. It was shown to perform better than a well known and similar ASVM [27] algorithm. For the feature selection baselines we selected well-established algorithms involving sparsity assumption: *L1-Logistic*: Logistic regression with $L1$ penalty [13]; *Elastic-Net*: Logistic regression with mixture of $L1$ and $L2$ penalties [13]; *Forward-Reg*: Forward regression – a classical greedy feature selection algorithm.

Results. Figure 1 shows the leave-one-class-out performance w.r.t. all considered datasets. In addition, Figures 1b, 1c, 1f show the performance when transferring from off-the-shelf classemes, object-bank feature descriptors, and DeCAF neural network activations.

Whenever any baseline algorithm has hyperparameters to tune, we chose the ones that minimize the leave-one-out error on the training set. In particular, we selected the regularization parameter $\lambda \in \{10^{-4}, 10^{-3}, \ldots, 10^4\}$. MultiKT and DAM have an additional hyperparameter that we call τ with $\tau \in \{10^{-3}, \ldots, 10^3\}$. Kernelized algorithms were supplied with a linear kernel. Model selection for GreedyTL involves two hyperparameters, that is k and λ. Instead of fixing k, we let GreedyTL select features as long as the regularized error between two consecutive steps is larger than δ. In particular, we set $\delta = 10^{-4}$, as in preliminary experiments we have not observed any gain in performance past that point. The λ is fixed to 1. Even better performance could be obtained tuning it.

We see that GreedyTL dominates TL and feature selection baselines throughout the benchmark, rarely appearing on-par, especially in the small-sample regime. In addition, on two datasets out of three, it manages to identify the source classifier subset that performs comparably or better than the Best source, that is the single best classifier selected by its performance on the testing set. The significantly stronger performance achieved by GreedyTL w.r.t. FR, on all databases and in all settings, confirms the importance of the regularization in our formulation.

Notably, GreedyTL outperforms RLS src+feat, which is equivalent to GreedyTL selecting all the sources and features. This observation points to the fact that GreedyTL successfully manages to discard irrelevant feature dimensions and sources. To investigate this important point further, we artificially add 10, 100 and 1000 dimensions of pure noise sampled from a standard distribution. Figure 2 compares feature selection methods to GreedyTL in robustness to noise. Clearly, in the small-sample setting, GreedyTL is tolerant to large amount of noise, while $L1$ and $L1/L2$ regularization suffer a considerable loss in performance. We also draw attention to the failure of $L1$-based feature selection methods and MultiKT with $L1$ regularization to match the performance of GreedyTL.

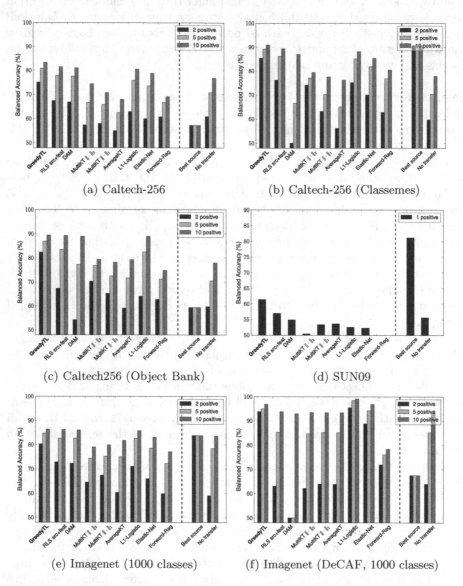

(a) Caltech-256

(b) Caltech-256 (Classemes)

(c) Caltech256 (Object Bank)

(d) SUN09

(e) Imagenet (1000 classes)

(f) Imagenet (DeCAF, 1000 classes)

Fig. 1. Performance on the Caltech-256, subsets of Imagenet (1000 classes) and SUN09 (819 classes). Averaged class-balanced accuracies in the leave-one-class-out setting.

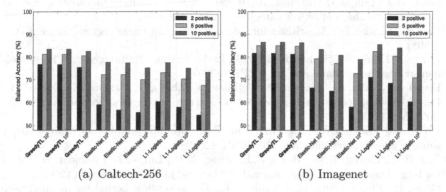

(a) Caltech-256   (b) Imagenet

Fig. 2. Baselines and number of additional noise dimensions sampled from a standard distribution. Averaged class-balanced recognition accuracies in the leave-one-class-out setting.

6 Conclusions

In this work we studied the transfer learning problem involving hundreds of sources. The kind of transfer learning scenario we consider assumes no access to the source data directly, but through the use of the source hypotheses induced from them. In particular, we focused on the efficient source hypothesis selection and combination, improving the performance on the target task. We proposed a greedy algorithm, `GreedyTL`, capable of selecting relevant sources and feature dimensions at the same time. We verified these claims by obtaining the best results among the competing feature selection and TL algorithms, on the Imagenet, SUN09 and Caltech-256 datasets. At the same time, comparison against the non-regularized version of the algorithm clearly show the power of our intuition. We support our empirical findings by showing theoretically that under reasonable assumptions on the sources, the algorithm can learn effectively from few target examples.

Acknowledgments. I.K. is supported by the Swiss National Science Foundation Sinergia project Ninapro and Idiap Research Institute.

References

1. Aytar, Y., Zisserman, A.: Tabula rasa: model transfer for object category detection. In: ICCV (2011)
2. Ben-David, S., Blitzer, J., Crammer, K., Kulesza, A., Pereira, F., Vaughan, J.: A theory of learning from different domains. Machine Learning (2010)
3. Ben-David, S., Urner, R.: Domain adaptation as learning with auxiliary information. In: New Directions in Transfer and Multi-Task - Workshop @ NIPS (2013)
4. Bergamo, A., Torresani, L.: Classemes and other classifier-based features for efficient object categorization. IEEE Transactions on Pattern Analysis and Machine Intelligence (2014)

5. Choi, M.J., Lim, J.J., Torralba, A., Willsky, A.S.: Exploiting hierarchical context on a large database of object categories. In: CVPR (2010)
6. Das, A., Kempe, D.: Algorithms for subset selection in linear regression. In: STOC (2008)
7. Deng, J., Dong, W., Socher, R., Li, L.J., Li, K., Fei-Fei, L.: Imagenet: A large-scale hierarchical image database. In: CVPR (2009)
8. Donahue, J., Jia, Y., Vinyals, O., Hoffman, J., Zhang, N., Tzeng, E., Darrell, T.: Decaf: A deep convolutional activation feature for generic visual recognition. In: ICML (2014)
9. Duan, L., Tsang, I.W., Xu, D., Chua, T.S.: Domain adaptation from multiple sources via auxiliary classifiers. In: ICML (2009)
10. Fan, R.E., Chang, K.W., Hsieh, C.J., Wang, X.R., Lin, C.J.: Liblinear: A library for large linear classification. Journal of Machine Learning Research (2008)
11. Gong, B., Shi, Y., Sha, F., Grauman, K.: Geodesic flow kernel for unsupervised domain adaptation. In: CVPR (2012)
12. Griffin, G., Holub, A., Perona, P.: Caltech-256 object category dataset. Tech. rep, Caltech (2007)
13. Hastie, T., Tibshirani, R., Friedman, J.: The Elements Of Statistical Learning. Springer (2009)
14. Jie, L., Tommasi, T., Caputo, B.: Multiclass transfer learning from unconstrained priors. In: ICCV (2011)
15. Kuzborskij, I., Orabona, F.: Stability and hypothesis transfer learning. In: ICML (2013)
16. Kuzborskij, I., Orabona, F., Caputo, B.: From N to N+1: multiclass transfer incremental learning. In: CVPR (2013)
17. Li, L., Su, H., Xing, E., Fei-Fei, L.: Object bank: a high-level image representation for scene classification & semantic feature sparsification. In: NIPS (2010)
18. Lim, J.J., Torralba, A., Salakhutdinov, R.: Transfer learning by borrowing examples for multiclass object detection. In: NIPS (2011)
19. Mansour, Y., Mohri, M., Rostamizadeh, A.: Domain adaptation with multiple sources. In: NIPS (2009)
20. Oquab, M., Bottou, L., Laptev, I., Sivic, J.: Learning and transferring mid-level image representations using convolutional neural networks. In: CVPR (2014)
21. Pan, S.J., Yang, Q.: A survey on transfer learning. IEEE Transactions on Knowledge and Data Engineering (2010)
22. Saenko, K., Kulis, B., Fritz, M., Darrell, T.: Adapting visual category models to new domains. In: Daniilidis, K., Maragos, P., Paragios, N. (eds.) ECCV 2010, Part IV. LNCS, vol. 6314, pp. 213–226. Springer, Heidelberg (2010)
23. Salakhutdinov, R., Torralba, A., Tenenbaum, J.: Learning to share visual appearance for multiclass object detection. In: CVPR (2011)
24. Tommasi, T., Caputo, B.: The more you know, the less you learn: from knowledge transfer to one-shot learning of object categories. In: BMVC (2009)
25. Tommasi, T., Orabona, F., Caputo, B.: Learning categories from few examples with multi model knowledge transfer. IEEE Transactions on Pattern Analysis and Machine Intelligence (2013)
26. Vezhnevets, A., Ferrari, V.: Associative embeddings for large-scale knowledge transfer with self-assessment. In: CVPR (2014)
27. Yang, J., Yan, R., Hauptmann, A.: Cross-domain video concept detection using adaptive SVMs. In: ACMM (2007)
28. Zhang, T.: Adaptive forward-backward greedy algorithm for sparse learning with linear models. In: NIPS (2008)

MEG: Multi-Expert Gender Classification from Face Images in a Demographics-Balanced Dataset

Modesto Castrillón-Santana[1], Maria De Marsico[2]($\boxtimes$),
Michele Nappi[3], and Daniel Riccio[4]

[1] Universidad de Las Palmas de Gran Canaria, Las Palmas, Spain
mcastrillon@siani.es
[2] Sapienza University of Rome, Rome, Italy
demarsico@di.uniroma1.it
[3] University of Salerno, Fisciano, Italy
mnappi@unisa.it
[4] University of Naples Federico II, Naples, Italy
daniel.riccio@unina.it

Abstract. In this paper we focus on gender classification from face images, which is still a challenging task in unrestricted scenarios. This task can be useful in a number of ways, e.g., as a preliminary step in biometric identity recognition supported by demographic information. We compare a feature based approach with two score based ones. In the former, we stack a number of feature vectors obtained by different operators, and train a SVM based on them. In the latter, we separately compute the individual scores from the same operators, then either we feed them to a SVM, or exploit likelihood ratio based on a pairwise comparison of their answers. Experiments use EGA database, which presents a good balance with respect to demographic features of stored face images. As expected, feature level fusion achieves an often better classification performance but it is also quite computationally expensive. Our contribution has a threefold value: 1) the proposed score level fusion approaches, though less demanding, achieve results which are rather similar or slightly better than feature level fusion, especially when a particular set of experts are fused; since experts are trained individually, it is not required to evaluate a complex multi-feature distribution and the training process is more efficient; 2) the number of uncertain cases significantly decreases; 3) the operators used are not computationally expensive in themselves.

1 Introduction

Demographic data is widely used in marketing for customer profiling, to implement both marketing strategies and personalized recommendation systems. The most commonly studied demographics for that purpose are ethnicity, age and gender. However, the same information can be useful in forensic and security-related applications too. The work in [1] discusses how the preliminary determination of those demographics, though being considered soft biometrics, can

V. Murino and E. Puppo (Eds.): ICIAP 2015, Part I, LNCS 9279, pp. 15–26, 2015.
DOI: 10.1007/978-3-319-23231-7_2

significantly improve identity recognition performance by strong traits, e.g., face. In this paper, we focus on the gender classification (GC) problem from face images.

Within the context of the Computer Vision literature related to automatic GC, the face appearance attracts the main efforts, as reflected by most recent works [2]. However, additional elements of interest have been employed to tackle the problem, such as the face local context, the whole human body, the hair, or the clothes [3]. It is to notice that the influence of demographics on human appearance cannot be sharply identified. For instance, age and ethnicity can also affect the difference between male and female appearance. Therefore, despite the specific demographics under investigation, the benchmark dataset should be fairly balanced with respect to each factor [4]. This especially holds if a training phase is required. This motivated our choice of EGA (Ethnicity, Gender and Age) dataset [5] where this aspect is especially cared of. Its images are annotated with corresponding demographics information. In the present study, such annotations represent the ground-truth for assessing demographic classification performance.

In the present work, we propose to address the problem of GC from face images by a multi-expert approach. We chose a number of local operators able to capture different aspects of images, and able to possibly provide gender-discriminative information. Then, we investigated the most appropriate way to combine them in order to obtain gender-discriminative information. We tested expert combination using either feature-level or score level fusion. The former is expected to provide more accurate classification, yet at the expense of extra computational resources and of a most demanding training process. In score-level fusion approach, experts are trained individually, and this makes the training process much more feasible and parallelizable, since it is not required to evaluate a complex multi-feature distribution. If this allows to achieve only slightly worse results, we can accept this as a good compromise between accuracy and cost.

It is to underline that we did not plan to demonstrate the performance of either new operators or new fusion strategies. Our contribution has a threefold value. 1) The achieved performance demonstrates that, when suitably applied, score fusion can provide results that are comparable to those obtained by feature fusion. However, in the former case we have a vector with size equal to the number of experts, while in the latter the size is the sum of sizes provided by the single experts, unless a further expensive step of feature selection/learning is performed. 2) Even when the accuracy is quite similar, the number of uncertain cases significantly decreases, i.e., we have less situations that possibly require manual intervention. Therefore, the obtained system is overall more efficient. 3) These outcomes hold notwithstanding the use of quite light/popular operators, and we consider this a further added value.

2   The Pool of Experts

In this work, we consider the following set of local descriptors, that have already been applied in different scenarios of facial analysis: 1) Local Binary Patterns

(LBP) [6]; 2) Local Gradient Patterns (LGP) [7]; 3) Local Ternary Patterns (LTP) [8]; 4) Local Derivative Patterns (LDP) [9]; 5) Weber Local Descriptor (WLD) [10]; and 6) Local Phase Quantization (LPQ) [11].

LBP. Since the work by Ahonen et al. [12], LBP is used as descriptor for facial images. In the original definition each pixel in turn is the center of a 3×3 window and is encoded by comparing its value with each of the neighboring ones. A pixel in the neighborhood is assigned a 1 if its value is greater than the value of the central pixel (local threshold value for a kind of window binarization), and a 0 otherwise. The code for the central pixel is produced by concatenating the 1s and 0s of the neighborhood into a binary number. A histogram of the resulting codes is used to represent the texture. LBP are therefore computed easily, and have proven their capacity of discrimination in different real world texture classification problems, while exhibiting a notorious robustness to monotonic gray-scale changes. Their definition has been extended to arbitrary circular neighborhoods of radius R with P neighbors. To achieve higher robustness, the image is divided into a predefined grid. The final feature vector is obtained by concatenating the histograms of the single cells of the grid, following a Bag of Words scheme.

LGP. LBP technique has inspired a number of variations based on similar measurements of characteristics in a pixel neighborhood of possibly varying size. LGP operator uses the gradient values of the eight neighbors of a given central pixel. These are computed as the absolute value of intensity difference between each pixel and its neighboring one. Gradient values substitute pixel values, and their average is assigned to the given central pixel and is used as the threshold value for LGP encoding, which is performed as for LBP. Also the LGP operator is extended in a way similar to LBP to use different sizes of neighborhoods.

LTP. LTP extend LBP to 3-valued codes. Gray levels in a intensity range of width $\pm t$ around g_c are quantized to zero, those above this are quantized to $+1$ and those below it to -1. The binary LBP code is replaced by a ternary LTP code. Since t is a user-specified threshold, LTP codes can be made resistant to noise, but no longer invariant to gray level transformations as LBP codes are. When using LTP for matching one could compute 3^n valued codes. However, an alternative coding scheme suggested by the authors splits each ternary pattern into its positive and negative parts (Upper Pattern and Lower Pattern respectively). These are treated as two separate channels of LBP descriptors, for which separate histograms and similarity metrics are computed, and finally combined.

LDP. LBP can be considered to represent a kind of first-order circular derivative pattern of images, i.e., a micropattern generated by the concatenation of the binary gradient directions. LDP increases the detail of coded information since it represents a high-order local pattern descriptor, by encoding directional pattern features based on local derivative variations. The nth order LDP encode the

$(n-1)^{th}$ order local derivative direction variations. While basic LBP encode the relationship between the central point and its neighbors in a 3×3 window, the LDP templates are more complex and extract high-order local information by encoding various distinctive spatial relationships contained in a given local region. Given an image I, the first-order derivatives are denoted as I'_α where $\alpha=0°$, $45°$, $90°$ and $135°$. Given g_c a point in I, and g_p, $p = 0, \ldots, P-1$ its neighbors, the four first-order derivatives at g_c can be written as:

$$LDP^1(g_c) = \left\{ \begin{array}{l} I'_{0°}(g_c) = I(g_c) - I(g_3), I'_{45°}(g_c) = I(g_c) - I(g_2), \\ I'_{90°}(g_c) = I(g_c) - I(g_1), I'_{135°}(g_c) = I(g_c) - I(g_0) \end{array} \right\} \tag{1}$$

The second-order directional LDP, LDP^2_α, in direction α is defined as:

$$LDP^2_\alpha(g_c) = \left\{ \begin{array}{l} f(I'_\alpha(g_c), I'_\alpha(g_0)), f(I'_\alpha(g_c), I'_\alpha(g_1)), \ldots \\ \ldots, f(I'_\alpha(g_c), I'_\alpha(g_7)) \end{array} \right\} \tag{2}$$

where $f(.,.)$ is a binary function which determines the type of local pattern transition, and encodes the co-occurrence of two derivative directions at different neighboring pixels as:

$$f(I'_\alpha(g_c), I'_\alpha(g_p)) = \left\{ \begin{array}{l} 0, if I'_\alpha(g_c) \cdot I'_\alpha(g_p) > 0 \\ 1, if I'_\alpha(g_c) \cdot I'_\alpha(g_p) \leq 0 \end{array} \right. \tag{3}$$

Finally, the second order Local Derivative Pattern $LDP^2(I)$ is the concatenation of the codes according to the different directions. Higher order derivatives are computed in a similar way. For more details, see [9].

WLD. Differences of pixel intensity within a local neighborhood are also encoded by WLD. It is inspired by Weber's Law, stating that human perception of a pattern depends both on the change of a stimulus and also on its original intensity. Therefore, WLD consists of two components: differential excitation and orientation. The former one is a function of the ratio between the relative intensity differences of a current pixel against its neighbors, and the intensity of the current pixel itself. The orientation component is the gradient orientation of the current pixel, and computed as in [13]. For a given image, both components make up a concatenated WLD histogram. For further details see [10].

LPQ. The codes produced by the LPQ operator are insensitive to centrally symmetric blur (e.g., due to motion, or out of focus). Even the LPQ operator is computed locally at every pixel location and the resulting codes is summarized in a histogram. The method is based on the blur invariance property of the Fourier phase spectrum. It uses the local phase information extracted using the short-term Fourier transform (STFT) computed over a $M \times M$ neighborhood at each pixel position x. For details see [11].

Feature Vectors vs Feature Images. Given the image I, the application of the local operator O (LBP, LDP, LGP, etc.) will produce either a feature vector V or a feature image F. In the first case, the operator returns either a single histogram from the frequency of the extracted codes, or the concatenation of histograms corresponding to the cells of a square grid. In our system, all operators but LDP divide the 64×100 original image in a 5×5 grid, therefore producing a vector of size 6400. When a feature image F is returned instead, each pixel in the original image is substituted by the corresponding code assigned to it by O. All operators considered assign a 8 bit code to each pixel in I, which can be interpreted as a gray level. Figure 1 shows an example of the feature images corresponding to an image, with LTP Upper and Lower patterns fused together.

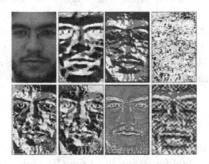

Fig. 1. From top left, original and coded images (LBP, LGP, LTP, LDP, WLD, LPQ)

2.1 Score Generation by Likelihood Ratio (LR)

The Likelihood Ratio (LR) was introduced in biometrics to evaluate the membership of a submitted probe either to the class of genuine users (those enrolled in the system), or to that of impostors (unregistered users). In accordance with the Neyman-Pearson lemma, the authors of [14] experimentally assess that the LR test represents the optimal test to assign the score vector X to either genuine or impostor users, if, when False Acceptance Rate (FAR) is fixed at Ψ, we find a constant η which maximizes Genuine Acceptance Rate (GAR). However, optimality is constrained by the precision of genuine and impostor score distributions estimates. In this work, given a face image in input, the LR is used to produce a gender-discriminative (*male/female*) score; comparing that score with a threshold properly fixed in advance, the system decides if the input face belongs either to the class *male* or *female*. A training phase is needed to estimate $f_{male}(x)$ and $f_{female}(x)$ distributions, and test performances depends on the quality of such training.

All the experts in the system that exploit LR for score generation execute the same operation pipeline, the only difference being the local operator O, among those discussed above, that each of them uses to extract relevant features from I and transform it into a feature image F. For each pixel (x, y) in the image F the training phase learns two probability distributions Pr_{male} and Pr_{female} using a training set of images of faces, whose gender male/female is obviously known. Of course, training and testing sets have no intersection. During matching, each pixel in the feature image F contributes to the calculation of the final score by voting by its own partial score $s(x, y)$. This is computed according to the learned distributions using the standard formula defined for LR:

$$s(x, y) = 2 \cdot \frac{log(f_{female}(F(x, y)))}{log(f_{male}(F(x, y)))} \tag{4}$$

The partial score produced by Eq. 4 generally has a negative value if the pixel votes for the class male and positive otherwise. The greater is the confidence of the pixel when voting for a class, the higher is the absolute value of the assigned partial score. There is an area of uncertainty in the interval around the 0, for which the partial score can be considered noise, rather than a really useful contribution for the calculation of the final score s. For this reason, we fix a threshold th_p for the partial score (here it has been experimentally set to $th = 1.3$) . The final score is calculated as:

$$s = \frac{1}{S} \sum \delta(s(x, y)) \cdot s(x, y) \tag{5}$$

where δ is the Dirac function returning 1 only if $|s(x, y)| \geq th_p$ and $S = \sum_{x,y} \delta(s(x, y))$. Similar considerations hold for the global score, if it is too close to the border between classes. Here, we deal with ambiguity of fused scores too. The first column of Table 1 summarizes the results for the single operators.

2.2 Score Generation by Support Vector Machines (SVM)

The second column of Table 1 summarizes the accuracy for experts when using a SVM classifier. For each expert we evaluated both linear and RBF kernels. The Table includes the best performance achieved, that was provided by a linear kernel for LBP, LPQ, WLD and LTP, while a RBF was better for LDP and LGP. The trade-off between margin and error, i.e., parameter C, was always fixed at $C = 1$, while for the RBF kernel, the gamma value was fixed at $gamma = 0.07$. In both columns the best achieved values are in bold. Those results are reported considering a decision threshold of 0 (negative vs. positive values). A SVM-based classifier outputs a score that also indicates the sample proximity to the threshold, and thus might be further used to evaluate the individual classification quality or ambiguity.

3   Fusion Strategies

Fusion can occur either at feature, matching score, or decision level. The first one retains the most information, but it is usually computationally more demanding. The last one looses too much information before the final result. The best

Table 1. Gender classification accuracy of the single experts using either SVM on feature vectors or LR on feature images. As for SVM, the best performance was provided by a linear kernel for LBP, LPQ, WLD and LTP, and by RBF for LDP and LGP.

Protocol	LR Accuracy	SVM Accuracy (# features)
LBP	86.36%	91.36% (6400)
LGP	90.005%	88.18% (6400)
WLD	91.36%	92.27% (6400)
LPQ	85.00%	90.45% (6400)
LTP^{low}	90.45%	91.36% (6400)
LTP^{high}	89.55%	**93.18%** (6400)
LDP	**93.19%**	86.36% (16384)

compromise is usually achieved at score level. In this work we investigate and compare multi-expert systems using three different fusion protocols.

F-SVM performs feature level fusion and is based on Support Vector Machines (SVM): a single linear SVM is trained on the compound feature vectors, which are obtained here by stacking the histograms produced by the above described methods; given the set of experts, $\Omega = E_1, E_2, ..., E_n$, the protocol combines the whole set of feature vectors $\Phi_{E_{i,k}} = f_1, f_2, ..., f_{m_{E_{i,k}}}$ extracted by individual experts E_i for a given image I_k in the new compound vector.

S-SVM is based on SVM too but uses score level fusion: more first stage SVMs are trained on the different features vectors, which are represented here by histograms produced by the above methods; the protocol then feeds the responses of individual experts E_i for a given image I_k to a second stage SVM classifier; given Ω, a set of experts, and their respective scores s_i, a new feature vector is composed as $\Sigma = s_1, s_2, ..., s_n$, and fed to a preliminary trained linear SVM.

S-LR uses score level fusion after the single experts have used LR to compute their individual scores using the feature images produced by the adopted operators; the S-LR protocol combines the responses of individual experts E_i for a given image I_k by examining them in pairs and selecting the best pair. More in detail, given Ω, a set of experts, each of which produces a score s_i, for each possible pair (E_i, E_j) with $i \neq j$, S-LR checks if both experts have voted for the same class (male, female), or $sign(s_i, s_j)$. If this is true, the pair of experts is assigned a value of $s_{i,j} = sign(s_i) \cdot \sqrt{s_i \cdot s_j}$, which represents the fused score. Otherwise, the protocol assigns the value $s_{i,j} = 0$ to the pair. At the end, the protocol S-LR selects the pair of experts that provides the maximum $s_{i,j}$ in absolute value, or $s_{global} = Max_{i,j}(|s_{i,j}|)$.

Ambiguous Answers. All protocols presented provide a score as the final result. The sign of this final score depends on the class (male, female), to which the input face was assigned by the system. Here, the males have a negative score, while females have a positive score. Some face images, produce a score which is very close to the value 0, which indicates a high degree of uncertainty of the response. It is possible to set a threshold th_s such that the response of the system is considered reliable if $abs(s_{global}) \geq th_s$ and ambiguous otherwise. The ambiguous answers are not necessarily discarded; they can be considered as particularly complex cases for the system, that need to be treated separately, for example with the interrogation of a further group of experts. In the experimental results, we present the curves that show the number of ambiguous answers and the performance of different indexes of accuracy adopted for the evaluation of the system versus variations of this threshold. It is worth underlining that strategies producing a similar genuine accept rate can differ by the number of ambiguous responses: of course, the lower this number, the better.

4   The Image Dataset

EGA (Ethnicity, Gender and Age face database) has been designed and implemented to provide demographics balance among dataset images as well as flexibility even along time. It integrates into a single dataset face images from different databases. Many of such databases are available or will be available for research. Images are drawn from publicly available ones to create a more heterogeneous and representative dataset. In particular, in order to avoid copyright infringement, EGA has been conceived as a set of links to files previously processed by appropriate scripts, and of annotations, which are provided to organize images according to individual features such as ethnicity, gender and age. Each user can ask and obtain on her/his own the original datasets with the images needed to build EGA. The scripts will reorganize and rename all requested images, according to the structure that was devised for EGA. In this way, it is possible to easily reconstruct the whole dataset, but even to expand it, as new datasets become available and after they are annotated. At present, images are taken from CASIA-Face V5 [15], FEI [16], FERET [17], FRGC [18], JAFFE [19], and the Indian Face Database [20]. Not all images from the above databases are included in EGA, but subsets allowing an overall good balance in demographics percentages and a lower influence of factors different from demographics (e.g., pose, illumination and expression - PIE). EGA includes 469 subjects from five ethnicities: a) African-American (53), b) Asian (111), c) Caucasian (162), d) Indian (65), e) Latinos (68). For each of them, subjects are chosen aiming at the best possible balance to represent the two genders male and female. These two subgroups are further divided into three age ranges: a) young, b) adult and c) middle-aged, with adult being much more represented due to the composition of the original datasets. More details on EGA composition can be found in [5].

5   Experiments and Results

As described above, EGA includes 469 subjects. The training set for both LR and SVM was chosen to be balanced with respect to demographics, therefore we included the first half of male subjects and the first half of female subjects for each ethnicity, resulting in 124 male and 111 female subjects in the training set.

Table 2. Gender Classification accuracy of the fusion approaches.

Fusion protocol	ALL	LDP WLD	LTP^{low} LTP^{high} WLD	LTP^{low} LTP^{high} WLD LBP	LTP^{low} LTP^{high} WLD LDP	LTP^{low} LTP^{high} WLD LBP LPQ	LTP^{low} LTP^{high} WLD LBP LPQ LDP
F-SVM	93.20%	92.27%	92.27%	93.63%	**94.09%**	**94.09%**	**94.09%**	93.18%
S-SVM	93.20%	92.27%	92.73%	**94.55%**	**94.55%**	**94.55%**	93.18%	93.18%
S-LR	91.16%	**92.08%**	90.08%	90.93%	90.443%	**92.08%**	89.96%	90.99%

All the remaining subjects were included in the test set. As for the latter, the first image for each subject was used for gallery, and the second for test.

Accuracy is defined as the number of correct classifications in relation to the total number of samples analyzed, $Acc = \frac{(TM+TF)}{M+F}$, where TM and TF stand for the number of correct male and female classifications, while M and F indicate the number of total male and female samples tested.

We remind that when exploiting feature level fusion, for all operators except LDP, histograms are extracted after dividing the image in a 5×5 grid and then chained in the final vector. As for LDP, the whole image is used. When exploiting score level fusion, feature images are used, with each pixel of the original image replaces by the code in $[0, 255]$ produced by the operator at hand. Table 2 shows the results, with best ones reported in bold. F-SVM and S-SVM reported similar results, but the first approach is particularly slow with limited possibilities of parallelization. It is also interesting to notice that the combination of operators providing the best results with all three fusion approaches is $\{LTP^{low}, LTP^{high}, WLD, LDP\}$, suggesting that the addition of LBP and LPQ only introduces redundant information if not noise. In any case, the accuracy achieved shows a rather limited improvement of feature or score level fusion compared to some single experts. Indeed, the best multi-expert fusion achieved 94.55 using S-SVM vs. 93.19 with LDP and LR-based classification. However, there is a positive effect too that is not shown by those results. As a matter of fact, it is important to give the appropriate focus to the ability of the compound system to reduce ambiguous cases.

In Figure 2 we show the accuracy improvement with respect of ambiguous responses (see Section 3), i.e., responses which are too close to the threshold dividing the two classes and therefore might produce errors.

In order to compute the improvement produced by setting apart ambiguous responses, we do not count them in the denominator of the expression for Accuracy. Those responses that are farther from the classification border present a better classification rate. Therefore, we can notice the compromise achieved: a slightly lower number of useful responses vs. an increased classification precision.

It is worth further underlining two observations: first, we should consider the curves obtained with respect to two thresholds, the one used for classification

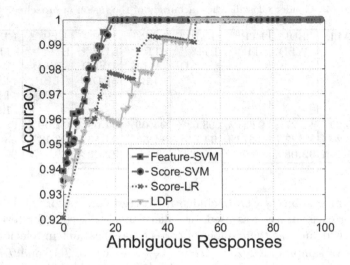

Fig. 2. Number of ambiguous cases vs. accuracy achieved for the remaining responses.

M/F and the one set for ambiguity. However, since the former distributions are normalized, the threshold is fixed and is 0 (negative vs. positive values) therefore this threshold is fixed and left implicit in the graphics; second, as mentioned before, discarding the ambiguous responses improves the accuracy of classification but has a cost, represented by the lower number of useful responses (accuracy is computed considering unambiguous responses only). The second observation implies that, since the accuracy is computed as a proportion with respect to the useful responses, the lower the number of ambiguous responses the better the system, even when producing the same accuracy value.

The advantage of the fusion approaches is evident in Figure 2, which shows that the multi-expert approach reduces the number of errors due to ambiguous cases. In order to maintain the figure readable, we only reported the curves corresponding to the best single classifier and to the fusion of all operators for the different protocols. SVM approaches report a better performance, behaving in a quite similar way for both F-SVM and S-SVM. However, the latter, even if it reported a slightly worse accuracy, would be preferred as it is more flexible in terms of usability and cost. We can notice that the curve for the single operator LDP starts better, but the fusion significantly improves the performance when a higher number of ambiguous responses is accepted, and this is a further advantage of the multi-expert approach.

6   Conclusions

We analyzed the behavior of a number of local operators, namely LBP, LGP, LTP, LDP, WLD and LPQ, in addressing the problem of gender classification. Our proposal deals with fusing the results of such operators, in order to achieve an improvement of performance in terms of both accuracy and reliability (possible ambiguity of classification results). The benefits of adopting a fusion approach are confirmed by experimental results both in terms of accuracy and in terms of robustness to ambiguous samples. In particular, the identification of ambiguous cases allows to get better relative performance by discarding the corresponding responses. The cost to pay is a lower number of useful responses. However, a further advantage achieved by fusion is that such number increases (ambiguity decreases) with all presented fusion approaches. As a consequence, the same accuracy is achieved in conjunction with higher overall rate of classified images.

References

1. Klare, B.E., Burge, M.J., Klontz, J.C., Jain, A.K., Jain, A.K.: Face recognition performance: Role of demographic information. IEEE Trans. on Information Forensics and Security **7**(6), 1789–1801 (2012)
2. Bekios-Calfa, J., Buenaposada, J.M., Baumela, L.: Robust gender recognition by exploiting facial attributes dependencies. Pattern Recognition Letters **36**, 228–234 (2014)
3. Ng, C.B., Tay, Y.H., Goi, B.-M.: Recognizing human gender in computer vision: a survey. In: Anthony, P., Ishizuka, M., Lukose, D. (eds.) PRICAI 2012. LNCS, vol. 7458, pp. 335–346. Springer, Heidelberg (2012)
4. Torralba, A., Efros, A.A.: Unbiased look at dataset bias. In: Computer Vision and Pattern Recognition (2011)
5. Riccio, D., Tortora, G., De Marsico, M., Wechsler, H.: EGA - ethnicity, gender and age, a pre-annotated face database. In: 2012 IEEE Workshop on Biometric Measurements and Systems for Security and Medical Applications (BIOMS), pp. 1–8 (2012)
6. Pietikäinen, M., Hadid, A., Zhao, G., Ahonen, T.: Computer Vision Using Local Binary Patterns. Springer (2011)
7. Jun, B., Kim, D.: Robust face detection using local gradient patterns and evidence accumulation. Pattern Recognition **45**(9), 3304–3316 (2012)
8. Tan, X., Triggs, B.: Enhanced local texture feature sets for face recognition under difficult lighting conditions. In: Zhou, S.K., Zhao, W., Tang, X., Gong, S. (eds.) AMFG 2007. LNCS, vol. 4778, pp. 168–182. Springer, Heidelberg (2007)
9. Zhang, B., Gao, Y., Zhao, S., Liu, J.: Local derivative pattern versus local binary pattern: Face recognition with high-order local pattern descriptor. IEEE Trans. on Image Processing **19**(2), 533–544 (2010)
10. Chen, J., Shan, S., He, C., Zhao, G., Pietikainen, M., Chen, X., Gao, W.: Wld: A robust local image descriptor. IEEE Transactions on Pattern Analysis and Machine Intelligence **32**(9), 1705–1720 (2010)
11. Ojansivu, V., Heikkilä, J.: Blur insensitive texture classification using local phase quantization. In: Elmoataz, A., Lezoray, O., Nouboud, F., Mammass, D. (eds.) ICISP 2008 2008. LNCS, vol. 5099, pp. 236–243. Springer, Heidelberg (2008)
12. Ahonen, T., Hadid, A., Pietikäinen, M.: Face description with local binary patterns: Application to face recognition. IEEE Transactions on Pattern Analysis and Machine Intelligence **28**(12), December 2006
13. Lowe, D.G.: Distinctive image features from scale-invariant keypoints. International Journal of Computer Vision **60**(2), 91–110 (2004)

14. Ulery, B., Hicklin, A.R., Watson, C., Fellner, W., Hallinan, P.: Studies of biometric fusion. Technical Report IR 7346, NIST (2006)
15. CASIA-FaceV5. http://biometrics.idealtest.org/
16. The FEI face database. http://www.fei.edu.br/~cet/facedatabase.html
17. Phillips, P.J., Wechsler, H., Huang, J., Rauss, P.: The FERET Database and Evaluation Procedure for Face-Recognition Algorithms. J. Image and Vision Computing **16**(5), 295–306 (1988)
18. Phillips, P., Flynn, P., Scruggs, T., Bowyer, K.W., Chang, J., Hoffman, K., Marques, J., Min, J., Worek, W.: Overview of the face recognition grand challenge. In: Proc. IEEE Conf. on Computer Vision and Pattern Recognition (CVPR) (2005)
19. Lyons, M.J., Akamatsu, S., Kamachi, M., Gyoba, J.: Coding facial expressions with gabor wavelets. In: Proceeding of the IEEE International Conference on Automatic Face and Gesture Recognition, pp. 200–205 (1998)
20. Jain, V., Mukherjee, A.: The Indian Face Database. http://vis-www.cs.umass.edu/~vidit/IndianFaceDatabase/

An Edge-Based Matching Kernel Through Discrete-Time Quantum Walks

Lu Bai[1]([✉]), Zhihong Zhang[2], Peng Ren[3], Luca Rossi[4], and Edwin R. Hancock[5]

[1] School of Information, Central University of Finance and Economics, Beijing, China
bailu69@hotmail.com, lu@cs.york.ac.uk
[2] Software School, Xiamen University, Xiamen, Fujian, China
zhihong@xmu.edu.cn
[3] College of Information and Control Engineering, China University of Petroleum
(Huadong), Qingdao, Shandong Province, People's Republic of China
pengren@upc.edu.cn
[4] School of Computer Science, University of Birmingham, Birmingham, UK
l.rossi@cs.bham.ac.uk
[5] Department of Computer Science, University of York, York, UK
erh@cs.york.ac.uk

Abstract. In this paper, we propose a new edge-based matching kernel for graphs by using discrete-time quantum walks. To this end, we commence by transforming a graph into a directed line graph. The reasons of using the line graph structure are twofold. First, for a graph, its directed line graph is a dual representation and each vertex of the line graph represents a corresponding edge in the original graph. Second, we show that the discrete-time quantum walk can be seen as a walk on the line graph and the state space of the walk is the vertex set of the line graph, i.e., the state space of the walk is the edges of the original graph. As a result, the directed line graph provides an elegant way of developing new edge-based matching kernel based on discrete-time quantum walks. For a pair of graphs, we compute the h-layer depth-based representation for each vertex of their directed line graphs by computing entropic signatures (computed from discrete-time quantum walks on the line graphs) on the family of K-layer expansion subgraphs rooted at the vertex, i.e., we compute the depth-based representations for edges of the original graphs through their directed line graphs. Based on the new representations, we define an edge-based matching method for the pair of graphs by aligning the h-layer depth-based representations computed through the directed line graphs. The new edge-based matching kernel is thus computed by counting the number of matched vertices identified by the matching method on the directed line graphs. Experiments on standard graph datasets demonstrate the effectiveness of our new kernel.

1 Introduction

Graph kernels are powerful tools for graph structure analysis in pattern recognition and machine learning [1]. The main advantage of using graph kernels is that

© Springer International Publishing Switzerland 2015
V. Murino and E. Puppo (Eds.): ICIAP 2015, Part I, LNCS 9279, pp. 27–38, 2015.
DOI: 10.1007/978-3-319-23231-7_3

they characterize graph features in a high dimensional space and thus better preserve graph structures. Generally speaking, a graph kernel is a similarity measure between a pair of graphs [1]. To extend the large spectrum of kernel methods from the general machine learning domain to the graph domain, Haussler [2] has proposed a generic way, namely the R-convolution, to define a graph kernel. For a pair of graphs, an R-convolution kernel is computed by decomposing each graph into smaller subgraphs and counting the number of isomorphic subgraph pairs between the two original graphs. Thus, a new type of decomposition of a graph usually results in a new graph kernel. Following this scenario, Kashima et al. [3] introduced the random walk kernel, which is based on the enumeration of common random walks between two graphs. Borgwardt et al. [4], on the other hand, proposed a shortest path kernel by counting the numbers of matching shortest paths over the graphs. Aziz et al. [5] introduced a backtrackless kernel using the cycles identified by the Ihara zeta function [6] in a pair of graphs. Shervashidze et al. [7] developed a fast subtree kernel by comparing pairs of subtrees identified by the Weisfeiler-Lehman algorithm. Some other alternative R-convolution kernels include a) the segmentation graph kernel developed by Harchaoui and Bach [8], b) the point cloud kernel developed by Bach [9], and c) the (hyper)graph kernel based on directed subtree isomorphism tests [10].

Unfortunately, R-convolution kernels tend to neglect the relative locations of substructures. This is because R-convolution kernels add an unit value to the kernel function by roughly identifying a pair of isomorphic substructures, i.e., any pair of isomorphic substructures will contribute an unit kernel value. As a result, the R-convolution kernels cannot establish reliable structural correspondences between the substructures. This drawback limits the precise kernel-based similarity measure for graphs.

To overcome the problem arising in existing R-convolution kernels, in our previous work [11,12], we have developed a new depth-based matching kernel for graphs. The depth-based matching kernel is based on aligning the h-layer depth-based representations around vertices of graphs (i.e., aligning the vertices of the graphs), and is computed by counting the number of matched vertex pairs. In [11], the depth-based matching kernel can be seen as an aligned subgraph kernel that encapsulates location correspondence information between pairwise inexact isomorphic h-layer expansion subgraphs. As a result, the depth-based matching kernel overcomes the shortcoming of neglecting location correspondences between substructures arising in R-convolution kernels.

In this work, we aim to develop our previous work in [11,12] one step further. We develop a new edge-based matching kernel for graphs based on discrete-time quantum walks. For a graph, we commence by transforming the graph into a directed line graph [6]. The reason of using the directed line graph is that the line graph is a dual representation of the original graph [6], i.e., the vertex of the directed line graph represents a corresponding edge of the original graph. Moreover, we show that the discrete-time quantum walk can be seen as a walk on the line graph and the state space of the walk is the vertex set of the line graph, i.e., the state space of the walk is the edges of the original graphs (See details in Section 2). Finally, the directed line graph may expose richer graph characteristics than the original graph [6]. As a result, the directed line graph provides an elegant way of developing new edge-based matching kernel based on discrete-time quantum walks, which not only reflects quantum-based information but also encapsulates richer characteristics of graphs. For a pair of graphs, we compute the h-layer depth-based representation for each vertex of their directed line graphs by computing entropic signatures (computed from discrete-time quantum walks on the line graphs) on the family of K-layer expansion subgraphs rooted at the vertex, i.e., we compute the depth-based representations for edges of the original graphs through their directed line graphs. Based on the new representations, we define an edge-based matching method for the pair of graphs by aligning the h-layer depth-based representations computed through the directed line graphs. The new edge-based matching kernel is thus computed by counting the number of matched vertices identified by the matching method on the directed line graphs. Experiments on standard graph datasets demonstrate the effectiveness of our new edge-based matching kernel.

2 Preliminary Concepts

2.1 Directed Line Graphs

In this subsection, we commence by introducing the concept of directed line graphs. The reasons of using the line graphs are threefold. First, for a graph, its directed line graph is a dual representation and each vertex of the line graph represents a corresponding edge in the original graph. Second, the required discrete-time quantum walk used in this work can be seen as a walk on the line graph and the state space of the walk is the vertex set of the line graph, i.e., the state space of the walk is the edges of the original graphs (see details in Section 2.3). Third, the directed line graph may expose richer graph characteristics than the original graph [6]. As a result, the directed line graph provides a way of developing new edge-based matching kernel based on discrete-time quantum walks, which not only reflects quantum-based information but also encapsulates richer characteristics of graphs (see details in Section 3).

Based on the definition of Ren et al. in [6], for a sample graph $G(V, E)$, the directed line graph $G_D(V_D, \overrightarrow{E}_D)$ is a dual representation of $G(V, E)$. To obtain $G_D(V_D, \overrightarrow{E}_D)$, we first construct the associated symmetric digraph $SDG(V, E_d)$ of $G(V, E)$, by replacing every edge $e(u, w) \in E(G)$ by a pair of reverse arcs, i.e., directed edges $e_d(u, w) \in E_d(G)$ and $e_d(w, u) \in E_d(G)$ for $u, w \in V$. The directed line graph $G_D(V_D, \overrightarrow{E}_D)$ is the directed graph with vertex set V_D and arc set $\overrightarrow{E}_D$ defined as

$$\begin{aligned} V_D &= E_d(SDG), \\ \overrightarrow{E}_D &= \{(e_d(u, v), e_d(v, w)) \in E_d(SDG) \times E_d(SDG) \mid u, v, w \in V, u \neq w\}. \end{aligned} \tag{1}$$

The Perron-Frobenius operator $\boldsymbol{T} = [T_{i,j}]_{|V_L| \times |V_L|}$ of $G(V, E)$ is the adjacency matrix of the associated directed line graph $G_D(V_D, \overrightarrow{E}_D)$.

2.2   Discrete-Time Quantum Walks

The discrete-time quantum walk is the quantum counterpart of the discrete-time classical random walk [13]. To simulate the evolution of a discrete-time quantum walk on a graph $G(V, E)$, we first replace each edge $e(u, v) \in E$ with a pair of directed arcs $e_d(u, v)$ and $e_d(v, u)$. This in turn ensures the reversibility of the quantum process. Let us denote the new set of arcs as E_d. Then, the state space for the discrete-time quantum walk is E_d, and we denote the state corresponding to the walker being on the arc $e_d(u, v)$ as $|uv\rangle$. A general state of the walk is

$$|\psi\rangle = \sum_{e_d(u,v) \in E_d} \alpha_{uv} |uv\rangle, \tag{2}$$

where the quantum amplitudes α_{uv} are complex, i.e., $\alpha_{uv} \in \mathbb{C}$. The probability that the walk is in the state $|uv\rangle$ is given by $\Pr(|uv\rangle) = \alpha_{uv} \alpha_{uv}^*$, where α_{uv}^* is the complex conjugate of α_{uv}.

The evolution of the state vector between the steps t and $t+1$ is determined by the transition matrix U. The entries of U determine the transition probabilities between states, i.e., $|\psi_{t+1}\rangle = U|\psi_t\rangle$. Since the evolution of the walk is linear and conserves probability, the matrix U must be unitary, i.e., $U^{-1} = U^{\dagger}$, where $U^{\dagger}$ denotes the Hermitian transpose of U.

It is usual to adopt the Grover diffusion matrix [14] as the transition matrix. Using the Grover diffusion matrices, the transition matrix U has entries

$$U_{(u,v),(w,x)} = \begin{cases} \frac{2}{d_x} - \delta_{ux}, & v = w; \\ 0, & \text{otherwise}, \end{cases} \tag{3}$$

where $U_{(u,v),(w,x)}$ gives the quantum amplitude for the transition $e_d(u, v) \rightarrow e_d(w, x)$ and δ_{ux} is the Kronecker delta, i.e., $\delta_{ux} = 1$ if $u = x$ and 0 otherwise. Given a state $|u_1 v\rangle$, the Grover matrix assigns the same amplitudes to all transitions $|u_1 v\rangle \rightarrow |vu_i\rangle$, and a different amplitude to the transition $|u_1 v\rangle \rightarrow |vu_1\rangle$, where u_i denotes a neighbour of v. Finally, note that although the entries of U are real, they can be negative as well as positive. It is important to stress that, as a consequence of this, negative quantum amplitudes can arise during the evolution of the walk. In other words, the definition in Eq.(3) allows *destructive interference* to take place.

In quantum mechanics, a pure state can be described as a single ket vector. A quantum system, however, can also be in a mixed state, i.e., a statistical ensemble of pure quantum states $|\psi_i\rangle$, each with probability p_i. The density matrix (or density operator) of such a system is defined as

$$\rho = \sum_i p_i |\psi_i\rangle \langle \psi_i| \tag{4}$$

Assume a sample graph $G(V, E)$. Let $|\psi_t\rangle$ denote the state corresponding to a discrete-time quantum walk that has evolved from the step $t = 0$ to the step $t = T$. We define the time-averaged density matrix ρ_G^T for $G(V, E)$ as

$$\rho_G^T = \frac{1}{T+1} \sum_{t=0}^{T} |\psi_t\rangle \langle \psi_t|. \tag{5}$$

Since $|\psi_t\rangle = \boldsymbol{U}^t |\psi_0\rangle$, where $\boldsymbol{U}$ is the transition matrix of the discrete-time quantum walk, Eq.(5) can be re-written in terms of the initial state $|\psi_0\rangle$ as

$$\rho_G^T = \frac{1}{T+1} \sum_{t=0}^{T} (\boldsymbol{U})^t |\psi_0\rangle \langle\psi_0| (\boldsymbol{U}^\top)^t. \tag{6}$$

As a result, the density matrix ρ_G^T describes a quantum system that has an equal probability of being in each of the pure states defined by the evolution of the discrete-time quantum walk from step $t = 0$ to step $t = T$. Note that, in fact, for a graph $G(V, E)$ the state space of the discrete-time quantum walk is the set of vertices of its directed line graph $G_D(V_D, \overrightarrow{E}_D)$ (see details in Section 2.3). As a result, based on the definitions in this Section, the time-averaged probability of the discrete-time quantum walk to visit a vertex $v_D \in V_D$ at time T is

$$P_{DQ}^T(v_D) = \rho_G^T(v_D, v_D). \tag{7}$$

where v_D corresponds to an arc $e_d(u, v)$ $(u, v \in V)$ residing on an edge $e \in E$.

2.3   The Relation to Perron-Frobenius Operators

The Perron-Frobenius operator (i.e., the adjacency matrix of the directed line graph) can be represented in terms of the transition matrix of discrete-time quantum walks. To show this connection, we first introduce the definition of the positive support of a matrix. The positive support $S^+(\boldsymbol{M}) = [s_{i,j}]_{m \times n}$ of the matrix $\boldsymbol{M} = [M_{i,j}]_{m \times n}$ is defined to be a matrix with entries

$$s_{i,j} = \begin{cases} 1, & M_{i,j} > 0, \\ 0, & \text{otherwise}, \end{cases} \tag{8}$$

where $1 \leq i \leq m, 1 \leq j \leq n$. Based on the definition in [15], we can re-define the Perron-Frobenius operator defined in Eq.(1) in terms of the unitary matrix of the discrete-time quantum walk. Let $G(V, E)$ be a sample graph and $\boldsymbol{U}$ be the unitary matrix associated with the discrete-time quantum walk on $G(V, E)$. The Perron-Frobenius operator $\boldsymbol{T}$ of $G(V, E)$ is

$$\boldsymbol{T} = \boldsymbol{S}^+(\boldsymbol{U}^\top). \tag{9}$$

Eq.(1), Eq.(8) and Eq.(9) show us how the discrete-time quantum walk and the Perron-Frobenius operator (i.e., the directed line graph) are co-related. For a graph $G(V, E)$ and its directed line graph $G_D(V_D, \overrightarrow{E}_D)$, V_D is just the state space of the discrete-time quantum walk on $G(V, E)$, i.e., each vertex in $G_D(V_D, \overrightarrow{E}_D)$ corresponds to a unique directed arc residing on the corresponding edge in $G(V, E)$. Moreover, if there is a directed edge from a vertex $v_D \in V_D$ to a vertex $u_D \in V_D$, the transition of the quantum walk on $G(V, E)$ is allowed from the arc corresponding to v_D to the arc corresponding to u_D, and vice versa. As a result, the discrete-time quantum walk on a graph can also be seen as a walk performed on its directed line graph. The state space of the walk is the vertex set of the line graph, and the transition of the walk relies on the connections between pairs of vertices in the line graph.

Discussions. As we have stated, the directed line graph possesses some interesting properties that are not available on the original graph. For instance, compared to the original graph the line graph spans a higher dimensional feature space and thus exposes richer graph characteristics. This suggests that the discrete-time quantum walk may reflect richer graph characteristics than the continuous-time quantum walk on the original graph [21]. Finally, the discrete-time quantum walk can be seen as a walk on the line graph and the state space of the walk is the vertex set of the line graph, we propose to use the rooting of the in-degree distribution of the line graph as the initial state of the walk.

2.4 Depth-Based Representations Based on Quantum Walks

For $G(V, E)$, let P_{DQ}^T be the probability distribution of discrete-time quantum walks visiting vertices of the directed line graph $G_D(V_D, \vec{E}_D)$. For G_D and a vertex $v_D \in V_D$, let a vertex set $N_{v_D}^K$ be defined as $N_{v_D}^K = \{u_D \in V_D \mid S_G(v_D, u_D) \leq K\}$, where $S_G(v_D, u_D)$ is the shortest path length between v_D and u_D. For G_D, the K-layer expansion subgraph $\mathcal{G}_{v_D}^K(\mathcal{V}_{v_D}^K; \vec{\mathcal{E}}_{v_D}^K)$ around v_D is

$$\begin{cases} \mathcal{V}_{v_D}^K = \{u_D \in N_{v_D}^K\}; \\ \vec{\mathcal{E}}_{v_D}^K = \{u_D, w_D \in N_{v_D}^K, \ (u_U, w_D) \in \vec{E}_D\}. \end{cases} \tag{10}$$

For G_D, the h-layer directed DB representation around $v_D \in V_D$ is defined as

$$\vec{DB}_{G_D}^h(v_D) = [H_E(\mathcal{G}_{v_D}^1), \cdots, H_E(\mathcal{G}_{v_D}^K), \cdots, H_E(\mathcal{G}_{v_D}^h)]^\top, \tag{11}$$

where $H_E(\mathcal{G}_{v_D}^K)$ is the Shannon entropic signature of $\mathcal{G}_{v_D}^K$ defined as

$$H_E(\mathcal{G}_{v_D}^K) = - \sum_{v_D \in \mathcal{V}_{v_D}^K} P_{DQ}^T(v_D) \log P_{DQ}^T(v_D), \tag{12}$$

where $P_{DQ}^T(v_D)$ defined in Eq.(7) is the probability of the discrete-time quantum walk visiting the vertex v_D in the directed line graph G_D. Note that, the Shannon entropic signature $H_E(\mathcal{G}_{v_D}^K)$ is not a strict Shannon entropy measure, since it is not computed by using all the probabilities of the discrete-time quantum walk visiting all the vertices in G_D. Finally, note that, since the vertices in G_D correspond to corresponding edges in G, the h-layer depth-based representations of vertices in G_D can be seen as the depth-based representations of edges in G.

3 An Edge-Based Matching Kernel for Graphs

3.1 Edge-Based Matching Through Discrete-Time Quantum Walks

As we have stated in Section 2.1, the directed line graph provides a way of defining an edge-based matching method for graphs based on discrete-time quantum walks. Because, for an original graph and its directed line graph, each vertex of the line graph represents a corresponding edge in the original graph. Moreover, the discrete-time quantum walk can be seen as a walk on the line graph. For a pair of graphs G_p and G_q, we commence by computing the h-layer depth-based representations of the vertices in their directed line graphs $G_{D;p}(V_{D;p}, \overrightarrow{E}_{D;p})$ and $G_{D;q}(V_{D;q}, \overrightarrow{E}_{D;q})$, based on the discrete-time quantum walks on the line graphs. These representations can be seen as the vectorial signatures of corresponding edges of G_p and G_q. We compute the Euclidean distance between the h-layer depth-based representations $\overrightarrow{DB}^h(v_i)$ and $\overrightarrow{DB}^h(v_j)$ as the distance measure of the pairwise vertices v_i and u_j of the directed line graphs $G_{D;p}$ and $G_{D;q}$, respectively. The affinity matrix element $R(i,j)$ is defined as

$$R(i,j) = \parallel \overrightarrow{DB}^h(v_i) - \overrightarrow{DB}^h(u_j) \parallel_2 . \tag{13}$$

where R is a $|V_{D;p}| \times |V_{D;q}|$ matrix. The element $R(i,j)$ represents the dissimilarity between vertex v_i in $G_{D;p}$ and vertex u_j in $G_{D;q}$. The rows of $R(i,j)$ index the vertices of $G_{D;p}$, and the columns index the vertices of $G_{D;q}$. If $R(i,j)$ is the smallest element both in row i and in column j, there is a one-to-one correspondence between vertex v_i of $G_{D;p}$ and vertex u_j of $G_{D;q}$. We record the state of correspondence using the correspondence matrix $C \in \{0,1\}^{|V_{D;p}||V_{D;q}|}$ satisfying

$$C(i,j) = \begin{cases} 1 \text{ if } R(i,j) \text{ is the smallest element} \\ \quad \text{both in row } i \text{ and in column } j; \\ 0 \text{ otherwise.} \end{cases} \tag{14}$$

Eq.(14) implies that if $C(i,j) = 1$, the vertices v_i and v_j are matched. Note that, like the depth-based matching previously introduced in our previous work [12], for a pair of directed line graphs a vertex from a line graph may have more than one matched vertex in the other line graph. In our work, we assign each vertex from a line graph at most one vertex in the other line graph. To achieve this, we propose to randomly assign each vertex an unique matched vertex through the correspondence matrix C. We observe that, compared to the depth-based matching associating Hungarian algorithm [17] for the assignment, our strategy will not influence the effectiveness of the resulting kernel in Section 3.2, and the kernel will be more efficient.

3.2   An Edge-Based Matching Kernel

Definition 3.1 (The edge-based matching kernel) Consider G_p and G_q as a pair of sample graphs, $G_{D;p}(V_{D;p}, \overrightarrow{E}_{D;p})$ and $G_{D;q}(V_{D;q}, \overrightarrow{E}_{D;q})$ are their directed line graphs. Based on the definitions in Eq.(11), Eq.(13) and Eq.(14), we compute the correspondence matrix C. The edge-based matching kernel $k_{DQEB}^{(h,T)}$ using the h-layer depth-based representations of the line graphs that is computed based on discrete-time quantum walks evolved from time 0 to time T is

$$k_{DQEB}^{(h,T)}(G_p, G_q) = k_{DQEB}^{(h,T)}(G_{D;p}, G_{D;q}) = \sum_{i=1}^{|V_{D;p}|} \sum_{j=1}^{|V_{D;q}|} C(i,j). \tag{15}$$

which counts the number of matched vertex pairs between $G_{D;p}$ and $G_{D;q}$. Intuitively, the edge-based matching kernel $k_{DQEB}^{(h,T)}$ is positive definite. Because $k_{DQEB}^{(h,T)}$ counts pairs of matched vertices over the correspondence matrix C. $\square$

Discussions. Clearly, like our previous depth-based matching kernel [12], the edge-based matching kernel is also related to the depth-based representation defined in [18]. However, there are three significant differences. First, the depth-based representations in [18] are computed on original graphs. By contrast, the h-layer depth-based representations for graphs required in this work are computed based on discrete-time quantum walks on directed line graphs transformed from original graphs. Second, in [18], we only compute the depth-based representation rooted at a centroid vertex of an original graph which is identified by evaluating the variance of the shortest path lengths between vertices. By contrast, in this work, we compute the h-layer depth-based representation rooted at each vertex of the directed line graph. Third, the depth-based representation from the centroid vertex is a vectorial signature of an original graph, i.e., it is an embedding vector for the graph. Embedding a graph into a vector tends to approximate the structural correlations in a low dimensional space, and thus leads to information loss. By contrast, the edge-based matching kernel aligning the h-layer depth-based representation represents directed line graphs in a high dimensional space and thus better preserves graph structures.

Moreover, as we have stated, the directed line graph may expose richer graph characteristics. Since the cardinality of the vertex set for the directed line graph is much greater than, or at least equal to, that of the original graph. Moreover, the h-layer depth-based representations based on discrete-time quantum walks on directed line graphs encapsulate quantum information relying on the walks. As a result, the new edge-based matching kernel can not only encapsulate the correspondence information between edges of original graphs, but also reflect richer graph characteristics and quantum information through discrete-time quantum walks on directed line graphs. Finally, like our previous depth-based matching kernel [11], the new edge-based matching kernel can also be seen as an aligned subgraph kernel (details of the discussion can be found in [11]). Differently, the edge-based matching kernel identifies the locational correspondence between pairwise h-layer expansion subgraphs of the directed line graphs transformed from the original graphs. By contrast, our previous depth-based matching kernel identifies the locational correspondence between pairwise h-layer expansion subgraphs of the original graphs.

4   Experimental Results

We demonstrate the performance of our new kernel on standard graph datasets from computer vision databases. These datasets include BAR31, BSPHERE31, GEOD31, and SHOCK. Details of these datasets can be found as follows.

BAR31, BSPHERE31 and GEOD31. The SHREC 3D Shape database consists of 15 classes and 20 individuals per class, that is 300 shapes [19].

This is an usual benchmark in 3D shape recognition. From the SHREC 3D Shape database, we establish three graph datasets named BAR31, BSPHERE31 and GEOD31 datasets through three mapping functions. These functions are a) ERG barycenter: distance from the center of mass/barycenter, b) ERG bsphere: distance from the center of the sphere that circumscribes the object, and c) ERG integral geodesic: the average of the geodesic distances to the all other points. The number of maximum, minimum and average vertices for the three datasets are a) 220, 41 and 95.42 (for BAR31), b) 227, 43 and 99.83 (for BSPHERE31), and c) 380, 29 and 57.42 (for GEOD31), respectively.

Shock. The Shock dataset consists of graphs from the Shock 2D shape database. Each graph is a skeletal-based representation of the differential structure of the boundary of a 2D shape. There are 150 graphs divided into 10 classes. Each class contains 15 graphs. The number of maximum, minimum and average vertices for the dataset are 33, 4 and 13.16 respectively.

Experimental Setup. We evaluate the performance of our new edge-based matching kernel through discrete-time quantum walks (DQMK), on graph classification problems. We also compare our kernel with several alternative state-of-the-art graph kernels. These graph kernels include 1) the depth-based matching kernel (DBMK) [11,12], 2) the Weisfeiler-Lehman subtree kernel (WLSK) [7], 3) the shortest path graph kernel (SPGK) [4], 4) the graphlet count graph kernel [20] with graphlet of size 4 (GCGK) [20], 5) the un-aligned quantum Jensen-Shannon kernel (UQJS) [21], and 6) the Jensen-Shannon graph kernel (JSGK) [22]. For the WLSK kernel, we set the highest dimension (i.e., the highest height of subtrees) of the Weisfeiler-Lehman isomorphism (for the WLSK kernel) as 10. For the DQMK kernel and the DBMK kernel, we set the highest layer of the required depth-based representation as 20 and 10 respectively. The reason for this is that the 10-layer or 20-layer expansion subgraph rooted at a vertex of an original graph (for the DBMK kernel) or a directed line graph (for the DQMK kernel) usually encapsulates most vertices of the original graph or the line graph. Moreover, for our DQMK kernel, we set the largest time T as 25. This is because when $T > 20$ the probabilities of discrete-time quantum walks visiting vertices on directed line graphs (i.e., edges in original graphs) tend to be stable. Finally, note that, some kernels (i.e., the WLSK kernel and the SPGK kernel) can accommodate vertex labels, we use the degree of a vertex as the label of the vertex. For each kernel, we compute the kernel matrix on each graph dataset. We perform 10-fold cross-validation using the C-Support Vector Machine (C-SVM) Classification to compute the classification accuracy, using LIBSVM [23]. We use nine samples for training and one for testing. All the C-SVMs were performed along with their parameters optimized on each dataset. We report the average classification accuracy ($\pm$ standard error) and the runtime for each kernel in Table 1 and Table 2, respectively. The runtime is measured under Matlab R2011a running on a 2.5GHz Intel 2-Core processor (i.e. i5-3210m).

Experimental Results. In terms of the classification accuracy from the C-SVM, we observe that our DQMK kernel can easily outperform all the alternative graph kernels excluding the DBMK kernel, on any dataset. The reasons

Table 1. Classification Accuracy (In % ± Standard Error) Using C-SVM.

Datasets	DQMK	DBMK	WLSK	SPGK	GCGK	UQJS	JSGK
BAR31	67.93 ± .57	**69.40 ± .56**	58.53 ± .53	55.73 ± .44	23.40 ± .60	30.80 ± .61	24.10 ± .86
BSPHERE31	**58.16 ± .67**	56.43 ± .69	42.10 ± .68	48.20 ± .76	18.80 ± .50	24.80 ± .61	21.76 ± .53
GEOD31	41.76 ± .47	**42.83 ± .50**	38.20 ± .68	38.40 ± .65	22.36 ± .55	23.73 ± .66	18.93 ± .50
Shock	**47.00 ± .55**	30.80 ± .93	36.40 ± .99	37.88 ± .93	27.06 ± .99	40.60 ± .92	21.73 ± .76

Table 2. Runtime of Computing the Kernel Matrix.

Datasets	DQMK	DBMK	WLSK	SPGK	GCGK	UQJS	JSGK
BAR31	198"	682"	30"	11"	1"	630"	1"
BSPHERE31	171"	720"	25"	14"	1"	828"	1"
GEOD31	97"	649"	15"	11"	1"	519"	1"
Shock	8"	7"	3"	1"	1"	14"	1"

for the effectiveness are threefold. First, the DQMK kernel can be seen as a vertex matching kernel through discrete-time quantum walks on directed line graphs transformed from original graphs. By contrast, other kernels are defined on original graphs. As we have stated in Section 2.1, the directed line graph transformed from an original graph can reflect richer characteristics than the original graph. As a result, the DQMK kernel defined on line graphs can encapsulate more information than other kernels defined on original graphs. Second, compared to the WLSK, SPGK and GCGK kernels that require decomposing graphs into substructures, our DQMK kernel can establish the substructure location correspondences in directed line graphs transformed from original graphs. By contrast, the WLSK, SPGK and GCGK kernels do not consider the location correspondence between pairwise substructures in the original graphs. Third, compared to the JSGK and UQJS kernels that rely on the similarity measure between original global graphs in terms of the classical or quantum JSD, our DQMK kernel can identify the correspondence information between both the vertices and the substructures of directed line graphs, and can thus reflect richer interior topological characteristics. By contrast, the JSGK and QJSK kernels only reflect the global graph similarity information of original graphs.

Finally, our DQMK kernel outperforms the DBMK kernel on the Shock and BSPHERE31 datasets. Especially, the classification accuracy of our new DQMK kernel on the Shock dataset is much better than that of the DBMK kernel. On the GEOD31 and BAR31 datasets, the classification accuracies of our DQMK kernel are a little lower than those of the DBMK kernel. Overall, our DQMK kernel outperforms or is competitive to the DBMK kernel. The effectiveness for this is that the DQMK kernel defined through discrete-time quantum walks on directed line graphs can reflect richer characteristics and quantum information than the DBMK kernel defined on original graphs.

5   Conclusion

In this paper, we develop a new edge-based matching kernel for graphs through discrete-time quantum walks on directed line graphs. Experiments demonstrate the effectiveness of the new kernel.

Acknowledgments. This work is supported by program for innovation research in Central University of Finance and Economics. Edwin R. Hancock is supported by a Royal Society Wolfson Research Merit Award.

References

1. Bai, L., Rossi, L., Bunke, H., Hancock, E.R.: Attributed graph kernels using the jensen-tsallis q-differences. In: Calders, T., Esposito, F., Hüllermeier, E., Meo, R. (eds.) ECML PKDD 2014, Part I. LNCS, vol. 8724, pp. 99–114. Springer, Heidelberg (2014)
2. Haussler, D.: Convolution kernels on discrete structures. In: Technical Report UCS-CRL-99-10, Santa Cruz, CA, USA (1999)
3. Kashima, H., Tsuda, K., Inokuchi, A.: Marginalized kernels between labeled graphs. In: Proceedings of ICML, pp. 321–328 (2003)
4. Borgwardt, K.M., Kriegel, H.P.: Shortest-path kernels on graphs. In: Proceedings of the IEEE International Conference on Data Mining, pp. 74–81 (2005)
5. Aziz, F., Wilson, R.C., Hancock, E.R.: Backtrackless walks on a graph. IEEE Transactions on Neural Networks and Learning Systems **24**, 977–989 (2013)
6. Ren, P., Wilson, R.C., Hancock, E.R.: Graph characterization via ihara coefficients. IEEE Transactions on Neural Networks **22**, 233–245 (2011)
7. Shervashidze, N., Schweitzer, P., van Leeuwen, E.J., Mehlhorn, K., Borgwardt, K.M.: Weisfeiler-lehman graph kernels. Journal of Machine Learning Research **12**, 2539–2561 (2011)
8. Harchaoui, Z., Bach, F.: Image classification with segmentation graph kernels. In: Proceedings of CVPR (2007)
9. Bach, F.R.: Graph kernels between point clouds. In: Proceedings of ICML, pp. 25–32 (2008)
10. Bai, L., Ren, P., Hancock, E.R.: A hypergraph kernel from isomorphism tests. In: Proceedings of ICPR, pp. 3880–3885 (2014)
11. Bai, L.: Information Theoretic Graph Kernels. University of York, UK (2014)
12. Bai, L., Ren, P., Bai, X., Hancock, E.R.: A graph kernel from the depth-based representation. In: Fränti, P., Brown, G., Loog, M., Escolano, F., Pelillo, M. (eds.) S+SSPR 2014. LNCS, vol. 8621, pp. 1–11. Springer, Heidelberg (2014)
13. Emms, D., Severini, S., Wilson, R.C., Hancock, E.R.: Coined quantum walks lift the cospectrality of graphs and trees. Pattern Recognition **42**, 1988–2002 (2009)
14. Grover, L.K.: A fast quantum mechanical algorithm for database search. In: Proceedings of ACM Symposium on the Theory of Computation, pp. 212–219 (1996)
15. Ren, P., Aleksic, T., Emms, D., Wilson, R.C., Hancock, E.R.: Quantum walks, ihara zeta functions and cospectrality in regular graphs. Quantum Information Process **10**, 405–417 (2011)
16. Escolano, F., Hancock, E., Lozano, M.: Heat diffusion: Thermodynamic depth complexity of networks. Physical Review E **85**, 206236 (2012)
17. Munkres, J.: Algorithms for the assignment and transportation problems. Journal of the Society for Industrial and Applied Mathematics **5** (1957)
18. Bai, L., Hancock, E.R.: Depth-based complexity traces of graphs. Pattern Recognition **47**, 1172–1186 (2014)
19. Biasotti, S., Marini, S., Mortara, M., Patané, G., Spagnuolo, M., Falcidieno, B.: 3D shape matching through topological structures. In: Nyström, I., Sanniti di Baja, G., Svensson, S. (eds.) DGCI 2003. LNCS, vol. 2886, pp. 194–203. Springer, Heidelberg (2003)

20. Shervashidze, N., Vishwanathan, S., Petri, T., Mehlhorn, K., Borgwardt, K.: Efficient graphlet kernels for large graph comparison. Journal of Machine Learning Research **5**, 488–495 (2009)
21. Bai, L., Rossi, L., Torsello, A., Hancock, E.R.: A quantum jensen-shannon graph kernel for unattributed graphs. Pattern Recognition **48**, 344–355 (2015)
22. Bai, L., Hancock, E.R.: Graph kernels from the jensen-shannon divergence. Journal of Mathematical Imaging and Vision **47**, 60–69 (2013)
23. Chang, C.C., Lin, C.J.: Libsvm: A library for support vector machines. Software (2011). http://www.csie.ntu.edu.tw/cjlin/libsvm

Implicit Boundary Learning for Connectomics

Tobias Maier and Thomas Vetter[✉]

Department of Mathematics and Computer Science, University of Basel,
Basel, Switzerland
{tobias.maier,thomas.vetter}@unibas.ch

Abstract. Segmentation of complete neurons in 3D electron microscopy images is an important task in Connectomics. A common approach for automatic segmentation is to detect membrane between neurons in a first step. This is often done with a random forest. We propose a new implicit boundary learning scheme that optimizes the segmentation error of neurons instead of the classification error of membrane. Given a segmentation, optimal labels for boundary between neurons and for non-boundary are found automatically and are used for training. In contrast to training random forests with labels for membrane and intracellular space, this novel training method does not require many labels for the difficult to label membrane and reduces the segmentation error significantly.

1 Introduction

Connectomics studies the structure and function of neuronal circuits. One approach to obtain these circuits is to reconstruct neuronal networks from 3D electron microscopy (3DEM) images. These 3D images are obtained by stacking 2D images. An example of such an image is given in Figure 1. With serial block face scanning electron microscopes [1] and focus ion beam scanning electron microscopes (FIB-SEM) the resolution in all three dimensions is high enough for an analysis in 3D. With FIB-SEM even isotropic resolution is possible. With these microscopes the acquisition is almost completely automated while for reconstruction the state of the art is still manual reconstruction. Skeleton tracings are made by hundreds of undergraduate students [2] or supervoxels are merged in the online game EyeWire[1] from more than 80 000 people.

Various approaches are proposed for the automatic reconstruction of 3DEM data. Some methods use segmentations from 2D slices and merge them to a consistent segmentation in 3D [3,4]. Laptev et al. [5] do a segmentation per slice and use neighboring slices to enrich the features for the slice. Andres et al. [6] presented a method that is working truly in 3D. All these methods have different approaches for the segmentation but all start with a random forest to detect membranes in 3DEM images.

Liu et al. proposed a hierarchical segmentation method [7] that uses learned membrane probability maps. In their experiments they use probability maps

---

[1] http://eyewire.org

© Springer International Publishing Switzerland 2015
V. Murino and E. Puppo (Eds.): ICIAP 2015, Part I, LNCS 9279, pp. 39–49, 2015.
DOI: 10.1007/978-3-319-23231-7_4

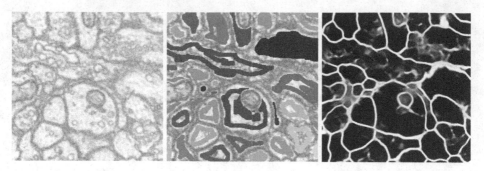

Fig. 1. From left to right: input image, rough labels of the intracellular regions overlayed on the input data, predicted probability map. Examples of the probability map on test data are shown in Figure 6.

learned with cascaded hierarchical models [8] and a deep neuronal network (DNN) from Ciresan et al. [9]. The drawback of DNNs is their requirement for much training data and long training time often on special hardware clusters. In contrast, random forests can be trained on normal workstations in a reasonable time.

Other approaches try to learn the segmentation directly. Turaga et al. [10] presented an online learning scheme for convolutional neuronal networks (CNN) that optimize the Rand index. Similarly Jain et al. [11] introduced the "warping error" and traind a CNN to optimize for this error. A supervised learning of image partitioning is proposed in [12]. A decision tree is learned in a greedy manner by selecting the split that maximizes the Matthews correlation coefficient.

When using a random forest for segmentation, the usual approach is to train a two class random forest with one class for membrane and one for intracellular space (including organelles like vesicles and mitochondria). The labels are given in advance or obtained interactively with the feedback of the prediction (e.g. with ilastik [13]). The random forest training optimizes the classification error given the training data. It is up to the user to select a set of labeled data that is appropriate for the segmentation. Therefore, labels where the output of the random forest leads to segmentation errors are important. These regions are also often difficult to label for a human. Cell membranes are thin elongated structures, sometimes only single pixels wide and occupy only a small fraction of the space. This makes it hard to get many accurate labels especially where the membrane is blurred, close to another membrane or touching organelles like mitochondria.

We introduce a new method to automatically select and label training data for a random forest. Instead of labels for membrane a rough segmentation of intracellular space as shown in Figure 1 is used. In an iterative process, a random forest is trained, the boundary prediction is analyzed in respect of the segmentation and optimal points for boundary and non-boundary are added to the training data. The segmentation error is reduced significantly compared to training with dense membrane labels or ilastik. In Figure 1 an example of the input data, labels used for our method, and the predicted boundary is shown.

In Section 2 we describe the details of the implicit boundary learning scheme. An evaluation and comparison to training with other methods is given in Section 3. Conclusion follows in Section 4.

2 Method

To learn a random forest for predicting a boundary that optimizes a segmentation we go for a hybrid approach. Using some initial labels, a two-class random forest is trained to detect an initial boundary. After training, it is applied to the complete training volume. New training samples are selected where segmentation errors occur. Then the random forest is retrained with the additional training data. This is repeated until convergence. The most important and difficult task is to get new training samples that improve the segmentation. In active learning samples close to the decision boundary are selected and the user is asked to label them. But these samples are not necessarily critical for the segmentation. In ilastik [13], the user searches for regions where the prediction is unsatisfying and adds new labels there. This is where membrane has low membrane probabilities or intracellular space is detected as membrane. In difference to that, our method automatically identifies regions where segmentation errors occur and adds labels there.

2.1 Finding Labels to Optimize Segmentation

For the reconstruction of neuronal circuits there are two important types of segmentation errors: *false mergers* and *false splits*. A false merger erroneously connects two regions to a common segment. A false split erroneously divides a region in two segments. To evaluate these errors a segmentation model is needed to transform the predicted probability into a segmentation. We use a threshold segmentation. All pixels with a boundary probability above a threshold are removed. The remaining connected components build the segmentation.

We define a path γ from a pixel x_s to another pixel x_e on the pixel grid (2D or 3D) as

$$\gamma(x_s, x_e) = \{x_s, x_a, x_b, \ldots, x_e\}, \tag{1}$$

where $x_s, x_a, \ldots$ are unique neighboring pixels, i.e. the edges $(x_s, x_a), (x_a, x_b), \ldots$ are edges in the neighborhood graph. The path of all paths from x_s to x_e for which the maximum pixel value on the path is minimal we define as minimax path:

$$\gamma^*(x_s, x_e) = \arg \min_{\gamma \in \Gamma(x_s, x_e)} \left(\max_{x \in \gamma} p(x) \right), \tag{2}$$

where $\Gamma(x_s, x_e)$ is the set of all paths from x_s to x_e, and $p(x)$ is the pixel value.

Using the threshold segmentation model, two points are in the same segment if and only if there exists a path in the boundary probability map with all pixels on the path below or equal a threshold. We can formulate the following conditions for false mergers and splits. A false merger occurs if

$$\max_{x \in \gamma^*(x_s, x_e)} p(x) \leq \text{threshold}, \tag{3}$$

where x_s and x_e are from different segments. A false split is induced if

$$\max_{x \in \gamma^*(x_s, x_e)} p(x) > \text{threshold}, \tag{4}$$

with x_s and x_e from the same segment.

The false split and false merge both happen at the maximum of the minimax path:

$$x^*(x_s, x_e) = \arg\max_{x \in \gamma^*} p(x). \tag{5}$$

This point can be found efficiently. We define the weight of the edges between neighboring pixels x_i, x_j as:

$$w_{ij} = \max(p(x_i), p(x_j)), \tag{6}$$

and use Kruskal's algorithm to find the minimum spanning tree (MST). From [14] it is known that for any edge (x_i, x_j) that is not part of the MST it is $w_{ij} \geq \max(w_{ia}, w_{ab}, \ldots, w_{dj})$. With our definition of the edge weight, the maximal edge weight on the path equals the maximal pixel value on the path. From that follows that $\gamma^*(x_s, x_e)$ is part of the MST. x^* can then be found by searching the maximum on the unique path between between x_s and x_e in the MST. This is illustrated in Figure 2.

To label new data and add it to the training data, pairs (x_s, x_e) are sampled. For x_s and x_e from different segments, x^* is labeled as "membrane". For x_s and x_e from the same segments, x^* is labeled as "intracellular". The points x^* are added to the training data regardless of their value $p(x^*)$. This means no threshold has to be specified for training.

For many pairs (x_s, x_e) the point x^* is the same. For example, in Figure 2 all points from the red and blue segment share the same maximum x^* on their minimax path. Sampling x_s and x_e spatially close and restricting the region of interest where the minimax path is searched gives more unique training data. To keep the labels and training balanced, the same number of new training data is added for boundary and non-boundary.

For the false mergers it can easily be seen that adding the maximum of the minimax path to the training data is reasonable. For false splits this is not that obvious. The path $\gamma^*(x_s, x_e)$ is the path with the lowest maximum between x_s and x_e, why should a new training label be taken from this path? Let's compare it to other methods to obtain a subset of training data from a segmentation.

(a) Randomly sample n points in the intracellular area. This is the simplest method but gives no control to select a subset of informative labels.
(b) Choose n worst classified points that are labeled as intracellular space. While this may reduce the classification error of the intracellular space, it is not known if a better classification of these points improves the segmentation.

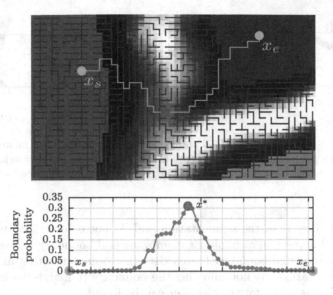

Fig. 2. Illustration of the minimax path $\gamma^*(x_s, x_e)$ (green). The corresponding probabilities for boundary on this path are plotted below. The point with the highest boundary probability is the minimax point x^*. All minimax paths in this region are part of the minimum spanning tree (blue). Segment labels are shown as red, green and blue regions. Note that for all paths between the red and blue segment, the shown minimax point x^* is the same.

(c) Randomly sample n pairs of points, with each pair within the same segment, choose a point from the minimax path between the points. This selection gives the only points that are known to be critical for the segmentation. Choosing a point from another path, such as a random path, a minimal (spatial) path, gives no such information.

To initialize the method an initial prediction for boundary is required. For this we use a random forest that is trained with a few labeled pixels for membrane and non-membrane. The method is robust against the initialization. Even the intensity of the (inverted) input image can be used as initial boundary prediction.

After the selection of additional training data a new random forest is trained. The procedure is repeated until no more improvement in the segmentation is obtained or a maximum number of iterations is reached. The required number of iterations depends on the number of new training samples that are added in each iteration.

2.2 Difference to Learn Membrane

In neuronal tissue neurons are enclosed by a cell membrane that is visible in 3DEM images. Often a classifier is trained to detect this membrane and use it for segmentation. This is not the same as the boundary in our approach. We

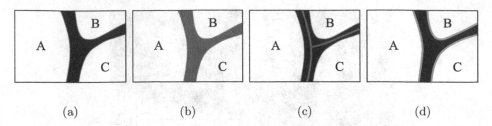

(a)   (b)   (c)   (d)

Fig. 3. (a) shows three segments A, B and C that are separated by a membrane. (b) shows a labeling for membrane in blue. It is also a valid boundary that separates the three segments. (c) and (d) show other possible boundaries that separate the segments correctly.

learn the boundary from the segmentation and do not enforce it to match the membrane. In Figure 3 an example for membrane and boundary is given. While the membrane is a valid boundary there exist other boundaries that also lead to a correct segmentation. By not enforcing the boundary to match the membrane a boundary that is easier for the classifier can be found.

3   Experiments and Results

We evaluate the proposed method on a FIB-SEM stack of the olfactory bulb from zebrafish larvae. The data is isotropic with a resolution of 6 nm. For training and testing we use two non overlapping regions of size $512 \times 512 \times 256$ and $300 \times 300 \times 300$ respectively. For both volumes we have a gold standard segmentation that is obtained by manual labeling with the interactive method from [15].

For all random forests the same implementation and the same set of features from the 3D rotation invariant Harmonic filters [16] in multiple scales are used. With these features we get good results. However, cell membranes and the membrane from mitochondria can not be differentiated. This results in mitochondria becoming segments within the neurons. Special designed features and segmentation methods for mitochondria [17,18] allow to detect and process them in a later step. We leave mitochondria and its membrane unlabeled for all experiments. This does neither enforce mitochondria to become segments of its own, nor being part of the neurons segment.

For anisotropic data the resolution in the z-direction is often insufficient leading to gaps between the membrane of consecutive slices. This allows an analysis only within the high resolution slice. With isotropic data like the FIB-SEM data the analysis can be done in 3D. We test if there is an advantage with this method working in 3D. Two random forests are trained with different sampling schemes. For the first, the pairs of points are sampled in a volume and the minimax paths between these points are calculated in 3D. For the second, the pairs of points are sampled within a slice parallel to the xy-, xz-, or yz-plane. The minimax path is then calculated only in this slice. In 2D we use a 4-connected neighborhood, in 3D a 6-connected neighborhood. While the training with the

Training and test error

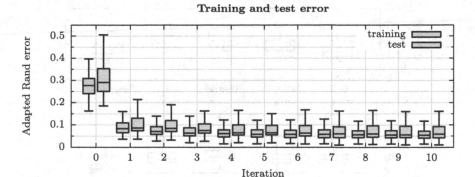

Fig. 4. Adapted Rand error for random forest trained with the given number of iterations. Iteration 0 is from the initial random forest trained with a few strokes for membrane and intracellular space. The segmentation error is evaluated for each slice and the distribution over the stack is shown.

Table 1. Segmentation errors on the test data. Each slice is evaluated with the same threshold and the error is calculated over all slices. For each method the optimal threshold is used.

	Pixel error	Warping error	Adapted Rand error
BEL[19]	0.123	0.00112	0.271
MSANN[20]	0.130	0.00111	0.176
ilastik	0.144	0.00128	0.227
dense labels	0.138	0.00081	0.177
implicit	**0.121**	**0.00050**	**0.106**

method working in 3D takes much longer than working only in-plane, there is no difference in the segmentation error. Therefore, we use in-plane sampling also for isotropic 3D data.

To analyze the convergence in training and the generalization to the test data we evaluate the segmentation in each iteration. In each iteration 5 000 new labels for boundary and non-boundary are added. This parameter depends on the size of the training stack but is not critical for the resulting random forest. More iterations are required for smaller values, for larger values more point pairs must be sampled to get new unique labels. The adapted Rand error is calculated for each slice individually and the distribution is shown in Figure 4. The largest improvement is gained in the 1st iteration. The next iterations show a further reduction of the adapted Rand error and the improvement converges rapidly. The test error is slightly higher than the training error with a larger variance. On the test data the adapted Rand error also converges after a few iterations. It is sufficient to train only a few iterations, what keeps the training time short. With further iterations the test error does not increase and no overfitting to the training data is visible.

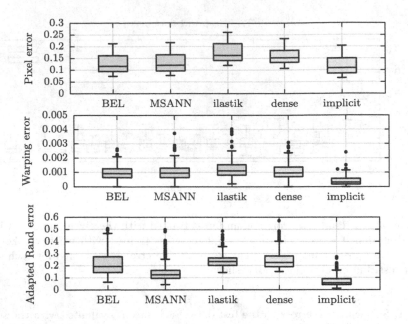

Fig. 5. Distribution of pixel error, warping error and adapted Rand error, evaluated for each slice in the test data. The methods used are BEL [19], MSANN [20], and random forests trained with labels obtained interactively with ilastik, dense labels and our proposed method.

We compare our method to random forests trained with labels from interactive labeling using ilastik and dense labels as well as boosted edge learning (BEL) [19] and multi-scale contextual model (MSANN) [20]. The dense membrane labels are obtained from the gold standard segmentation and used for BEL, MSANN and random forest training. The implicit boundary learning uses the segmentation labels directly. With ilastik an expert collected 9110 labels for membrane and 9104 labels for the intracellular space. For balanced training of the random forest with dense labels a subset of 50 000 labels per class is taken randomly. Training is done for 10 iterations with 5 000 new points for boundary and non-boundary in each iteration. If more than 50 000 labels per class are present only a subset, like for the training with dense labels, is used. The segmentation errors are calculated for the threshold that gives the lowest error. For BEL the output is filtered with a Gauss kernel ($\sigma = 1$) what gives better results than using it directly. The pixel error, warping error [11] and adapted Rand error of the test volume are given in Table 1. Additionally, the errors are calculated per slice (each with the optimal threshold) and the distribution is shown in Figure 5. Note that the pixel error is for the segment labels and not for classification of membrane. When evaluated per slice, BEL and MSANN give similar warping errors than the random forest with dense labels, but if the error is calculated with a common threshold over the volume the random forest

raw/gold   BEL   MSANN   ilastik   dense   implicit

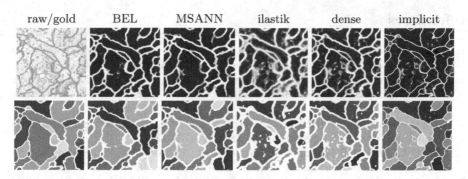

Fig. 6. The first column shows the input slice and the gold standard segmentation. In the next columns the probability maps for membrane / boundary and the corresponding segmentations are shown for the different methods.

gives better results. For the adapted Rand error MSANN seems better than the random forest with dense labels (but note that there are many outliers). If the error is evaluated over the volume they have almost the same error. With all error measures the proposed implicit boundary learning has the lowest error. For warping error and adapted Rand error the error was reduced about 40% compared to a random forest trained with dense labels and even more compared to a random forest trained with labels from ilastik. The interactive labeling with ilastik has the largest segmentation errors, but the labeling effort is the smallest.

We focus on the training of the random forests, not on segmentation. Therefore, only thresholding is used to get a segmentation. This approach is limited in practical use. Tiny holes in the boundary can produce huge errors in the segmentation. But we think that segmentation methods like [3,4,6] can also benefit of using random forests trained with our method. In Figure 6 the predicted probability maps for membrane / boundary and the resulting segmentation are shown. The output from our method shows sharp lines with high probability for boundary at the membranes and very low probabilities in the remaining regions. The output from the random forest trained with ilastik or dense labels are less distinct and blurry. The smaller regions in the upper left corner are hardly visible in the output from ilastik while they are clearly visible with the proposed method. BEL and MSANN have clear boundaries. But where the membrane is not detected correctly it gets almost deleted, leading to holes in the boundary.

4   Conclusion

We have presented a new method to train a random forest for segmentation where the boundaries are learned implicitly from a given segmentation. The segmentation error with a threshold segmentation of the boundary probability is reduced significantly compared to supervised learning with dense labels or labels from interactive labeling with ilastik. Methods that use membrane probability maps [3,4,6,7] can be used with the boundary probability maps and improve the segmentation accuracy further.

References

1. Denk, W., Horstmann, H.: Serial block-face scanning electron microscopy to reconstruct three-dimensional tissue nanostructure. PLoS Biol 2(11) (2004)
2. Helmstaedter, M., Briggman, K.L., Turaga, S.C., Jain, V., Seung, H.S., Denk, W.: Connectomic reconstruction of the inner plexiform layer in the mouse retina. Nature 500(7461) (2013)
3. Vazquez-Reina, A., Gelbart, M., Huang, D., Lichtman, J., Miller, E., Pfister, H.: Segmentation fusion for connectomics. In: ICCV (2011)
4. Funke, J., Andres, B., Hamprecht, F., Cardona, A., Cook, M.: Efficient automatic 3D-reconstruction of branching neurons from EM data. In: CVPR (2012)
5. Laptev, D., Vezhnevets, A., Dwivedi, S., Buhmann, J.M.: Anisotropic ssTEM image segmentation using dense correspondence across sections. In: Ayache, N., Delingette, H., Golland, P., Mori, K. (eds.) MICCAI 2012, Part I. LNCS, vol. 7510, pp. 323–330. Springer, Heidelberg (2012)
6. Andres, B., Kroeger, T., Briggman, K.L., Denk, W., Korogod, N., Knott, G., Koethe, U., Hamprecht, F.A.: Globally optimal closed-surface segmentation for connectomics. In: Fitzgibbon, A., Lazebnik, S., Perona, P., Sato, Y., Schmid, C. (eds.) ECCV 2012, Part III. LNCS, vol. 7574, pp. 778–791. Springer, Heidelberg (2012)
7. Liu, T., Jones, C., Seyedhosseini, M., Tasdizen, T.: A modular hierarchical approach to 3d electron microscopy image segmentation. Journal of Neuroscience Methods 226 (2014)
8. Seyedhosseini, M., Sajjadi, M., Tasdizen, T.: Image segmentation with cascaded hierarchical models and logistic disjunctive normal networks. In: 2013 IEEE International Conference on Computer Vision (ICCV), pp. 2168–2175, December 2013
9. Ciresan, D.C., Giusti, A., Gambardella, L., Schmidhuber, J.: Deep neural networks segment neuronal membranes in electron microscopy images. In: NIPS (2012)
10. Turaga, S.C., Briggman, K.L., Helmstaedter, M., Denk, W., Seung, H.S.: Maximin affinity learning of image segmentation. In: NIPS (2009)
11. Jain, V., Bollmann, B., Richardson, M., Berger, D., Helmstaedter, M., Briggman, K., Denk, W., Bowden, J., Mendenhall, J., Abraham, W., Harris, K., Kasthuri, N., Hayworth, K., Schalek, R., Tapia, J., Lichtman, J., Seung, H.: Boundary learning by optimization with topological constraints. In: CVPR (2010)
12. Straehle, C., Koethe, U., Hamprecht, F.A.: Weakly supervised learning of image partitioning using decision trees with structured split criteria. In: ICCV (2013)
13. Sommer, C., Straehle, C., Koethe, U., Hamprecht, F.A.: Ilastik: Interactive learning and segmentation toolkit. In: ISBI (2011)
14. Hu, T.C.: The Maximum Capacity Route Problem. Operations Research 9(6) (1961)
15. Straehle, C.N., Köthe, U., Knott, G., Hamprecht, F.A.: Carving: scalable interactive segmentation of neural volume electron microscopy images. In: Fichtinger, G., Martel, A., Peters, T. (eds.) MICCAI 2011, Part I. LNCS, vol. 6891, pp. 653–660. Springer, Heidelberg (2011)
16. Schlachter, M., Reisert, M., Herz, C., Schlurmann, F., Lassmann, S., Werner, M., Burkhardt, H., Ronneberger, O.: Harmonic filters for 3d multichannel data: Rotation invariant detection of mitoses in colorectal cancer. IEEE Transactions on Medical Imaging 29(8) (2010)
17. Smith, K., Carleton, A., Lepetit, V.: Fast ray features for learning irregular shapes. In: ICCV (2009)

18. Lucchi, A., Smith, K., Achanta, R., Knott, G., Fua, P.: Supervoxel-Based Segmentation of Mitochondria in EM Image Stacks With Learned Shape Features. IEEE Transactions on Medical Imaging **31**(2), 474–486 (2012)
19. Dollar, P., Tu, Z., Belongie, S.: Supervised learning of edges and object boundaries. In: 2006 IEEE Computer Society Conference on Computer Vision and Pattern Recognition, vol. 2 (2006)
20. Seyedhosseini, M., Kumar, R., Jurrus, E., Giuly, R., Ellisman, M., Pfister, H., Tasdizen, T.: Detection of neuron membranes in electron microscopy images using multi-scale context and radon-like features. In: Fichtinger, G., Martel, A., Peters, T. (eds.) MICCAI 2011, Part I. LNCS, vol. 6891, pp. 670–677. Springer, Heidelberg (2011)

A Parzen-Based Distance Between Probability Measures as an Alternative of Summary Statistics in Approximate Bayesian Computation

Carlos D. Zuluaga$^{(\boxtimes)}$, Edgar A. Valencia,
Mauricio A. Álvarez, and Álvaro A. Orozco

Faculty of Engineering, Universidad Tecnológica de Pereira,
Pereira, Colombia 660003
{cardazu,evalencia,malvarez,aaog}@utp.edu.co

Abstract. Approximate Bayesian Computation (ABC) are likelihood-free Monte Carlo methods. ABC methods use a comparison between simulated data, using different parameters drawn from a prior distribution, and observed data. This comparison process is based on computing a distance between the summary statistics from the simulated data and the observed data. For complex models, it is usually difficult to define a methodology for choosing or constructing the summary statistics. Recently, a nonparametric ABC has been proposed, that uses a dissimilarity measure between discrete distributions based on empirical kernel embeddings as an alternative for summary statistics. The nonparametric ABC outperforms other methods including ABC, kernel ABC or synthetic likelihood ABC. However, it assumes that the probability distributions are discrete, and it is not robust when dealing with few observations. In this paper, we propose to apply kernel embeddings using a sufficiently smooth density estimator or Parzen estimator for comparing the empirical data distributions, and computing the ABC posterior. Synthetic data and real data were used to test the Bayesian inference of our method. We compare our method with respect to state-of-the-art methods, and demonstrate that our method is a robust estimator of the posterior distribution in terms of the number of observations.

1 Introduction

Many Bayesian applications use inference for nonlinear stochastic models, where it is expensive or difficult to evaluate the likelihood; or the normalization constant in Bayesian modelling is also intractable. Approximate Bayesian Computation (ABC) are likelihood-free Monte Carlo methods. ABC methods can be employed to infer posterior distributions without having to evaluate likelihood functions [16,17]. It simulates data from a model with different parameter values and compare summary statistics of the simulated data with summary statistics of the observed data. There are many problems associated to how to choose the summary statistics with the goal of obtaining accepted samples. The choice of these summaries is frequently not obvious [8] and in many cases it is difficult or

© Springer International Publishing Switzerland 2015
V. Murino and E. Puppo (Eds.): ICIAP 2015, Part I, LNCS 9279, pp. 50–61, 2015.
DOI: 10.1007/978-3-319-23231-7_5

impossible to construct a general method for finding such statistics [4]. According to [12], the selection of the summary statistics is an important stage in ABC methods that is still an open question.

Different algorithms for choosing or constructing summary statistics have been proposed in the literature. In the state-of-the-art, we can find linear regression [4]. Another option is to use a minimum entropy criterion for choosing the summary statistics [2,3,11]. [12] propose a fully nonparametric ABC that avoids to select manually the summary statistics, using kernel embeddings [5]; they employ a two-step process: the first step is to compare the empirical data distributions using dissimilarity distance based on Reproducing Kernel Hilbert Spaces (RKHS). This distance is determined by Maximum Mean Discrepancy (MMD), which is denominated as $\gamma_k^2(P,Q)_{\mathrm{MMD}}$. In the second stage, they use another kernel that operates on probability measures. This nonparametric ABC outperforms other methods, ABC, kernel ABC or synthetic likelihood ABC, for more details see [12]. However this nonparametric ABC assumes that the probability distributions are discrete and is not robust when there are few observations.

In this paper, we propose a new metric for comparing two data distributions in a RKHS with application to ABC simulation. The difference with respect to Park et al. in [12] is the assumption that the probability density functions, for corresponding probability distributions in RKHS, are continuous probability functions, estimated using an smoother density estimator or Parzen estimator. This fact allows us to obtain a biased estimator of the dissimilarity distance between two empirical data distribution P and Q that we denote by $\gamma_k^2(P,Q)_{\mathrm{Parzen}}$ and that can be written as $\lambda f + (1-\lambda)\gamma_k^2(P,Q)_{\mathrm{MMD}}$, where $f \in \mathcal{H}$ ($\mathcal{H}$ is a Hilbert space), and $0 \leq \lambda < 1$. It is possible to demonstrate that our estimator presents a lower root mean squared error, between true parameter and estimated parameter, than the MMD estimator, for any value of λ, see [10]. The difficulty of calculating dissimilarity metrics for empirical distributions in RKHS is to compute integrals, these integrals are usually difficult to solve analytically. In this paper, we use Gaussian kernels for estimating these probability density functions.

We compare ABC based in our metric in RKHS with the ABC and K2ABC proposed by [12]. We also show how to use these methods in combination with sequential Monte Carlo methods.

Experimental results obtained include the application of the different methods described above over a synthetic dataset and a real dataset. The synthetic data was created from an uniform mixture model. We demonstrate that our method is a robust estimator of the parameter vector in terms of the number of observations. The real data corresponds to the change of adult blowfly population during a period of time, as explained by [18].

2 Approximate Bayesian Computation Based on Kernel Embeddings

In this section, we briefly expose the different ABC methods. We then define the metrics based on kernel embeddings employed with the ABC methods, including the MMD metric and the metric that we propose in this paper.

2.1   Short Summary on ABC Methods

Approximate Bayesian Computation (ABC) are likelihood-free Monte Carlo methods. In practical Bayesian models, exact inference may be intractable due to different reasons: the likelihood function is expensive or intractable; or the normalization constant in Bayesian modelling is also intractable. ABC methods can be employed to infer posterior distributions without having to evaluate likelihood functions [16,17]. These likelihood-free algorithms simulate data using different parameters drawn from prior distribution and compare summary statistics of the simulated data $(s\,(\mathcal{D}'))$ whit summary statistics of the observed data $(s\,(\mathcal{D}))$. For this comparison it is necessary to define a tolerance threshold that determines the accuracy of the algorithm, and a distance measure $\rho\,(s\,(\mathcal{D})\,,s\,(\mathcal{D}'))$, for example Euclidean distance, etc. If $\rho\,(s\,(\mathcal{D})\,,s\,(\mathcal{D}'))\leq\epsilon$, we then accept the parameters θ drew from $p\,(\theta)$, otherwise, it is rejected.

According to [17], there are different open questions around the ABC algorithm including how to choose the measure function ρ; what should be the value of ϵ?; how to select the summary statistics s? ρ and ϵ are experimental and implementation issues. With respect to s, it is difficult to define a methodology for choosing or constructing the summary statistics [12].

2.2   Metrics between Probability Measures by Using Kernels

The embedding of distributions in a Reproducing Kernel Hilbert Space (RKHS) is a methodology that allows us to compute distances between distributions by using kernel functions [1]. According to [15], a metric $\gamma_k^2(P,Q)$ over the probability measures P and Q can be defined through a characteristic kernel[1] $k(x,x')$ as,

$$\gamma_k^2\,(P,Q) = \left\|\int_M k\,(\cdot,x)\,dP\,(x) - \int_M k\,(\cdot,y)\,dQ\,(y)\right\|_{\mathcal{H}}^2.$$

In this study, we use a Gaussian kernel as the characteristic kernel. More examples of characteristic kernels can be found in [15].

If the distributions $P(x)$, and $Q(y)$ admit a density, then we have $dP(x) = p(x)dx$, and $dQ(y) = q(y)dy$, and an alternative expression for $\gamma_k^2\,(P,Q)$ can be written as

$$\gamma_k^2\,(P,Q) = \int_M\int_M k\,(x,z)\,p\,(x)\,p\,(z)\,dxdz + \int_M\int_M k\,(z,y)\,q\,(z)\,q\,(y)\,dzdy \\ - 2\int_M\int_M k(x,y)p(x)q(y)dxdy. \tag{1}$$

---

[1]   A characteristic kernel is a reproducing kernel for which $\gamma_k(P,Q) = 0 \iff P = Q$, $P,Q \in \mathcal{P}$, where $\mathcal{P}$ denotes the set of all Borel probability measures on a topological space $(M,\mathcal{A})$.

2.3 Kernel Embeddings as Summary Statistics for ABC

Let us assume that we have two random samples $X = \{x_i\}_{i=1}^{N_x}$, and $Y = \{y_j\}_{j=1}^{N_y}$. In ABC, one of those samples would correspond to the real data ($\mathcal{D}$), whereas the other sample would correspond to simulated data ($\mathcal{D}'$) from the model we wish to estimate. As mentioned before, we need a way to define if accepting the simulated data. A key idea introduced by [12] was to assume that the random samples X, and Y are drawn from probability measures P, and Q, respectively, and instead of comparing the distance between samples X, and Y, they propose to compare the distance between the probability measures P and Q.

The authors in [12] assume empirical distributions for P, and Q, this is $p(x) = \frac{1}{N_x} \sum_{i=1}^{N_x} \delta(x - x_i)$, and $q(y) = \frac{1}{N_y} \sum_{j=1}^{N_y} \delta(y - y_j)$. With these expressions for $p(x)$, and $q(y)$, the distance $\gamma_k^2(P, Q)$ is given by

$$\gamma_k^2(P, Q) = \frac{1}{N_x^2} \sum_{i,j=1}^{N_x} k(x_i, x_j) + \frac{1}{N_y^2} \sum_{i,j=1}^{N_y} k(y_i, y_j) - \frac{2}{N_x N_y} \sum_{i,j=1}^{N_x, N_y} k(x_i, y_j).$$

$$(2)$$

We refer to this distance as $\gamma_k^2(P, Q)_{\text{MMD}}$, since it is rooted in the Maximum Mean Discrepancy (MMD) concept developed in [6,7]. After obtaining $\gamma_k^2(P, Q)_{\text{MMD}}$, Park et al. in [12] apply a second kernel that operates on probability measures, as follows

$$k_\epsilon(P_{\mathcal{D}}, Q_{\mathcal{D}'}) = \exp\left(-\frac{\gamma_k^2(P_{\mathcal{D}}, Q_{\mathcal{D}'})_{\text{MMD}}}{\epsilon}\right),$$

$$(3)$$

where ϵ is a positive parameter for the second kernel. $P_{\mathcal{D}}$ is the distribution associated to $\mathcal{D}$, and $Q_{\mathcal{D}'}$ is the distribution associated to $\mathcal{D}'$. In [12], the authors use an unbiased estimate for $\gamma_k^2(P, Q)_{\text{MMD}}$ in which the factors $1/N_x^2$, and $1/N_y^2$ are replaced for $1/(N_x(N_x - 1))$, and $1/(N_y(N_y - 1))$, respectively. Also, the innermost sum in each of the first two terms does not take into account the terms for which $i = j$.

Instead of assuming a discrete distribution for $p(x)$, and $q(y)$, in this paper we propose to use a smooth estimate for both densities based on the Parzen-window density estimator. We assume that the densities $p(x)$, and $q(x)$ can be estimated using

$$\widehat{p}(x) = \frac{1}{N_x} \sum_{m=1}^{N_x} \frac{1}{(2\pi h_p^2)^{D/2}} \exp\left(-\frac{\|x - x_m\|^2}{2h_p^2}\right),$$

$$\widehat{q}(y) = \frac{1}{N_y} \sum_{n=1}^{N_y} \frac{1}{(2\pi h_q^2)^{D/2}} \exp\left(-\frac{\|y - y_n\|^2}{2h_q^2}\right),$$

where h_p and h_q are the kernel bandwidths, and D is the dimensionality of the input space. If we use a Gaussian kernel with parameter Σ for $k(x, x')$, and the estimators $\widehat{p}(x)$, and $\widehat{q}(y)$, a new distance between the distributions P and Q is easily obtained from expression (2) as follows

$$\gamma_k^2(P,Q) = \frac{1}{N_x^2} \sum_{i,j=1}^{N_x} \hat{k}\left(x_i, x_j; 2\Sigma_p\right) + \frac{1}{N_y^2} \sum_{i,j=1}^{N_y} \hat{k}\left(y_i, y_j; 2\Sigma_q\right) \qquad (4)$$

$$- \frac{2}{N_x N_y} \sum_{i,j=1}^{N_x, N_y} \hat{k}\left(x_i, y_j; \Sigma_p + \Sigma_q\right),$$

where

$$\hat{k}\left(x, x'; S\right) = \frac{|\Sigma|^{1/2}}{|\Sigma + S|^{1/2}} \exp\left(-\frac{\left(x - x'\right)^\top \left(\Sigma + S\right)^{-1} \left(x - x'\right)}{2}\right).$$

In expression (4), $\Sigma_p = h_p^2 \mathbf{I}$ and $\Sigma_q = h_q^2 \mathbf{I}$. We refer to the metric in (4) as $\gamma_k^2(P,Q)_{\mathrm{Parzen}}$.

As a distance measure $\gamma_k^2(P_\mathcal{D}, Q_{\mathcal{D}'})$ we can use $\gamma_k^2(P_\mathcal{D}, Q_{\mathcal{D}'})_{\mathrm{MMD}}$ or $\gamma_k^2(P_\mathcal{D}, Q_{\mathcal{D}'})_{\mathrm{Parzen}}$. The algorithm proposed by [12] that employs kernel embeddings of probability measures in ABC using MMD is shown in Algorithm 1. If we use the metric $\gamma_k^2(P_\mathcal{D}, Q_{\mathcal{D}'})_{\mathrm{MMD}}$ on line 6 for the algorithm, we refer to the method as K2ABC. If we use the metric $\gamma_k^2(P_\mathcal{D}, Q_{\mathcal{D}'})_{\mathrm{Parzen}}$ instead, we refer to the method as PABC.

Algorithm 1. ABC based on Kernel Embeddings

1: **Input:** Observed data $\mathcal{D}$, prior distribution, threshold ϵ.
2: **Output:** Empirical posterior $\sum_{i=1}^{N_s} \tilde{w}_i \delta_{\theta_i}$.
3: **for** $i = 1, \ldots, N_s$ **do**
4: Draw θ_i from $p(\theta)$
5: Simulate $\mathcal{D}'$ using $p(\cdot \mid \theta_i)$
6: Compute $\tilde{w}_i = \exp\left(-\frac{\gamma_k^2(P_\mathcal{D}, Q_{\mathcal{D}'})}{\epsilon}\right)$
7: **end for**
8: Normalize $\tilde{w}_i$

According to [15], the estimators $\gamma_k^2(P_\mathcal{D}, Q_{\mathcal{D}'})_{\mathrm{MMD}}$ and $\gamma_k^2(P_\mathcal{D}, Q_{\mathcal{D}'})_{\mathrm{Parzen}}$ of $\gamma_k^2(P_\mathcal{D}, Q_{\mathcal{D}'})$ have some properties, such as: both estimators are consistent. The former is considered an asymptotic unbiased estimator; on the other hand, the latter is a biased estimator of the distance $\gamma_k^2(P,Q)$, however if $\Sigma_p = \Sigma_q$, we can obtain $\gamma_k^2(P_\mathcal{D}, Q_{\mathcal{D}'})_{\mathrm{Parzen}} = \lambda \gamma_k^2(P_\mathcal{D}, Q_{\mathcal{D}'})_{\mathrm{MMD}}$, where $\lambda^2 = |\Sigma| / |\Sigma + 2\Sigma_p|$. If $\Sigma_p = \Sigma_q = 0$, $\gamma_k^2(P_\mathcal{D}, Q_{\mathcal{D}'})_{\mathrm{MMD}}$ is a particular case of $\gamma_k^2(P_\mathcal{D}, Q_{\mathcal{D}'})_{\mathrm{Parzen}}$.

2.4 Extension to ABC SMC

The disadvantages of ABC, such as: the selection of ϵ, the choice of summary statistics or accepted samples with low probability, it can be avoided using an

ABC algorithm based on sequential Monte Carlo methods (ABC SMC) proposed by [14]. The goal of ABC SMC is to obtain an approximation of true posterior using a series of sequential steps, expressed by $p(\theta| \rho(\mathcal{D}, \mathcal{D}') \leq \epsilon_t)$, for $i = 1, \cdots, T$, where ϵ_t is a threshold that decreases in each step ($\epsilon_1, >, \ldots, \epsilon_t, >$ $,\ldots, > \epsilon_T$), thus it refine the approximation towards the target distribution.

ABC SMC has a first stage based on ABC rejection. We can replace this stage with K2ABC or PABC, leading to what we call in the paper as the K2ABC SMC, and PABC SMC methods. Details of the ABC SMC method can be found in [16].

3 Experimental Setup

We first describe the synthetic dataset and the real dataset used for our experiments. Finally, we explain the procedure for applying the ABC methods over synthetic and real datasets.

3.1 Datasets

We follow the experiments described in [12]. Synthetic data is created from an uniform mixture model. The real dataset correspond to a time series of an adult blowfly population [18].

Toy Problem. The synthetic dataset was generated by an uniform mixture model, $p(\mathcal{D}| \theta) = \sum_{k=1}^{K} \pi_k \mathcal{U}(k, k-1)$, where $\mathcal{D}$ are the observed data; π_k are the mixing coefficients; and K is the number of components. The model parameters θ correspond to the mixing coefficients $\pi = [0.25, 0.04, 0.33, 0.04, 0.34]^{\top}$. The prior distribution for θ is a symmetric Dirichlet distribution.

Noisy nonlinear ecological dynamic system For the real dataset example, we would like to infer the parameters of a non-linear ecological dynamic system [9] represented through $N_{t+1} = P N_{t-\tau} \exp\left(-\frac{N_{t-\tau}}{N_0}\right) e_t + N_t \exp(\delta\varepsilon_t)$, where N_t is the adult population at time t, and P, N_0, δ and τ are parameters. Variables e_t and ε_t are employed to represent noise, and they are assumed to follow Gamma distributions $e_t \sim \mathcal{G}\left(1/\sigma_p^2, 1/\sigma_p^2\right)$, and $\varepsilon_t \sim \mathcal{G}\left(1/\sigma_d^2, 1/\sigma_d^2\right)$. The parameter vector we want to infer is given by $\theta = [P, N_0, \delta, \tau, \sigma_p, \sigma_d]^{\top}$. The observed data that we use in the experiments correspond to a time series of the adult population of sheep blowfly, with 180 observations. The data was provided by the authors of [18].

3.2 Validation

We perform a comparison between ABC, K2ABC, PABC, SMCABC, K2ABC SMC, and PABC SMC. The comparison is made in terms of the root-mean-squared error (RMSE) between the true parameters (when known) and the estimated parameters by the different methods. For the real dataset, we compute the cross-correlation coefficient (ρ) between the real time series and the time series generated by the different simulation methods.

3.3   Procedure

For the toy problem, the observed data $\mathcal{D}$ is sample once from the mixture of uniform densities with the mixture coefficients $\boldsymbol{\theta}$ described above. The observed data contains 400 observations. To generate the simulated data $\mathcal{D}'$, we sample from the Dirichlet prior, and with that sample, we then generate 400 observations from the mixture model. We then apply the ABC, K2ABC, PABC, ABC SMC, K2ABC SMC and PABC SMC to the observed data, and the simulated data, and compute the RMSE over the true and estimated parameters. For all the ABC methods, the procedure for generating simulated data is repeated 1000 times. For ABC, we use $\epsilon = 0.002$, and compute the mean and standard deviation as summary statistics. For K2ABC and PABC, we use $\epsilon = 0.001$, this value was chosen as mentioned in [12]. For ABC SMC, K2ABC SMC and PABC SMC, we employ $\{\epsilon_t\}_{t=1}^{T} = (0.5, 0.01, 0.005, 0.001, 0.0005)$. For the ABC SMC type of algorithms, we need to specify what is known as a perturbation kernel. For this, we use a spherical multivariate Gaussian distribution, with parameter 0.0001.

For the noisy nonlinear ecological dynamic system, we apply all the ABC methods and calculate the cross-correlation coefficient between the observed data $(\mathcal{D})$, and the simulated data $(\mathcal{D}')$, using each method. We adopt similar priors to the ones used by [9]: $\log P \sim \mathcal{N}(3, 0.2)$, $\log \delta \sim \mathcal{N}(-1.5, 0.1)$, $\log N_0 \sim \mathcal{N}(6, 0.2)$, $\log \sigma_d \sim \mathcal{N}(-0.1, 0.01)$, $\log \sigma_p \sim \mathcal{N}(0.1, 0.01)$ and $\tau \sim \mathcal{P}(6)$.

For ABC, we use $\epsilon = 0.35$, and compute 8 summary statistics used in [9]: 4 statistics using the log of the mean of all 25% quantiles of $\left\{\frac{N_t}{1000}\right\}_{t=1}^{180}$, 4 statistics employing the mean of 25% quantiles of the first-order differences of $\left\{\frac{N_t}{1000}\right\}_{t=1}^{180}$, and we also compute the maximum and minimum value of $\left\{\frac{N_t}{1000}\right\}_{t=1}^{180}$. For K2ABC and PABC, we use $\epsilon = 0.12$. For ABC SMC, K2ABC SMC and PABC SMC, we employ $\{\epsilon_t\}_{t=1}^{T} = (2, 1, 0.5, 0.35, 0.25, 0.2, 0.15)$; we also specify what is known as a perturbation kernel. For this, we use a spherical multivariate Gaussian distribution, with parameter 0.0001.

For K2ABC and PABC, in both experiments, we use a kernel bandwidth optimization approach based on minimizing the mean integrated square error (MISE) between the observed data and simulated data, to define the values of Σ, h_x and h_y. For more details about this kernel bandwidth optimization approach, see [13]. We also use a sampling-importance-resampling approach to obtain a empirical posterior distribution of parameters.

4   Results and Discussion

The ABC, K2ABC, PABC, ABC SMC, K2ABC SMC, PABC SMC were evaluated and compared over the synthetic data set and the real data set described in section 3.

4.1   Results from Synthetic Data

All ABC methods were applied over vectors of 400 observations obtained from the uniform mixture model described in section 3. Fig. 1 shows a comparison

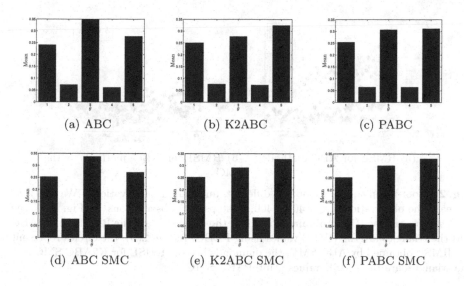

Fig. 1. Estimated posterior mean of model parameters for the uniform mixture model, using all ABC methods. The integer number in the x axis represents the subindex i in the parameter θ_i.

among the evaluated methods. The figure presents the estimated $\mathbb{E}\left[\theta | \mathcal{D}'\right]$ for each method.

For K2ABC, PABC, K2ABC SMC and PABC SMC the estimated parameters are close to the true posterior mean of the parameters (see section 3 for the true parameters). ABC and ABC SMC do not correctly estimate to θ_3 and θ_5. To observe the quality of the prediction using each method, we varied the number of observations and compute the RMSE between the true parameter vector and the estimated posterior mean of the parameter vector. We increase the observations from 40 to 400, in steps of 5 observations. For each step, we ran all methods and computed the RMSE. Fig. 2 presents the RMSE when the number of observations is increased.

Comparing Figs. 2(a) and 2(b) show that the RMSE obtained by PABC is the most steady and present the lowest variability, indicating a robust estimator of the parameter vector in terms of the number of observations. The mean and one standard deviations for the RMSE for PABC was 0.0696 ± 0.0006. The PABC SMC also present a low variability for this metric, the RMSE value was 0.0716 ± 0.0022. RMSE obtained by ABC was 0.0879 ± 0.0050, for K2ABC was 0.0733 ± 0.0031, for ABCSMC was 0.0755 ± 0.0032 and for K2ABCSMC was 0.0747 ± 0.0041. For ABC, K2ABC, ABC SMC and K2ABC SMC, notice how the RMSE decreases when the number of observations increases.

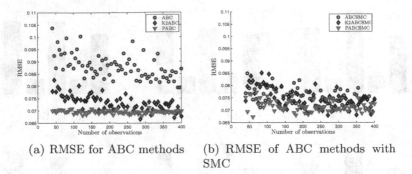

(a) RMSE for ABC methods

(b) RMSE of ABC methods with SMC

Fig. 2. Root-mean-square error for different number of observations. We start to increase the observations from 40 to 400, in steps of 5 observations. In Fig. 2(a), the circles represent the RMSE obtained by ABC, the diamonds are the RMSE for K2ABC and the triangles are the RMSE values using PABC. In Fig. 2(b), the circles represent the RMSE obtained by ABC SMC, the diamonds are the RMSE for K2ABC SMC and the triangles are the RMSE values using PABC SMC.

4.2 Results from Nonlinear Ecological Dynamic System

In Fig. 3, we present the posterior distribution for the parameters, obtained for the different methods when applied to the blowfly dataset of section 3. Figs. 3(a), 3(b), 3(c), 3(d), 3(e) and 3(f) illustrate the posterior of P, δ, N_0, σ_d. σ_p and τ, respectively. In these figures, the black dashed line corresponds to the posterior of the each parameter using K2ABC, the blue dashed line is the posterior obtained by PABC, the red dashed line is the posterior employing ABC, the posterior obtained by K2ABC SMC is the cyan dashed line, the magenta dashed line is the posterior using PABC SMC and the green dashed line is the posterior obtained by ABC SMC. The posterior distributions obtained by using all ABC methods for δ, σ_d. σ_p and N_0 are similar. For P and τ, the posterior obtained by K2ABC SMC, PABC SMC and ABC SMC are not similar with respect to the posterior using K2ABC, PABC and ABC; it is due to the parameter values, since this nonlinear model has a specific dynamical range from stable equilibrium to chaos.

To quantify the performance of all methods over the estimated parameters, we compare the time series obtained using the posterior means of the parameter and the observed data. For this comparison, we use a cross-correlation coefficient (ρ) between simulated data $\mathcal{D}'$ and observed data $\mathcal{D}$. The cross-correlation coefficient measures the similarity between two signals. We drew 100 subsets of parameters, we then apply all ABC methods, obtaining 100 estimated posterior mean for the parameters, with these estimated parameters we obtained 100 time series for these sets of signals, we compute ρ, we then sort ρ in descending order and choose the 50 first values, for all methods. Fig. 4 contains a box plot for the cross-correlation coefficient (ρ) using the different methods.

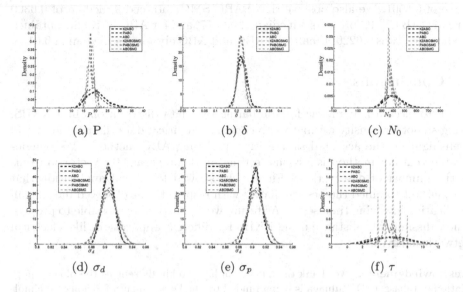

(a) P   (b) δ (c) N_0

(d) σ_d (e) σ_p (f) τ

Fig. 3. Posterior distribution for parameters of the nonlinear ecological dynamic system using ABC, K2ABC, PABC, ABC SMC, K2ABC SMC and PABC SMC.

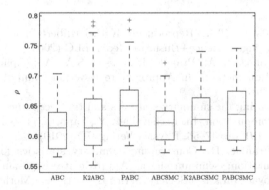

Fig. 4. Boxplots of the 25th and 75th percentiles of the cross-correlation coefficient, using all ABC methods. We drew 100 subsets of parameters, we then apply all ABC methods, obtaining 100 estimated posterior mean for the parameters, with these estimated parameters we obtained 100 time series for these sets of signals, we compute ρ, we then sort ρ in descending order and choose the 50 first values, for all methods.

From Fig. 4, notice that PABC presents the highest median for ρ, with a value of 0.6501. We also observe that PABC SMC obtained a median of 0.6360 for ρ. K2AB CSMC presents a median of 0.6277, and for ABC SMC the obtained median for ρ was 0.6220. Finally, K2ABC and ABC obtained a median of 0.6138.

5 Conclusions

We introduced a new metric for comparing two data distributions in a RKHS, using smoother density estimators to compare empirical data distributions, and then highlight the accepted samples by employing ABC methods. We demonstrated that our method is a robust estimator of the parameter vector in terms of the number of observations. Finally, we showed for a real application that our method obtained the best similarity with respect to the observed data, in an application involving time-series. As future work, it would be possible to propose a new dissimilarity distance using RKHS for different applications like electrical networks analysis.

Acknowledgments. We thank the authors of [9] who kindly sent us the blowfly population database. C.D. Zuluaga is being funded by the Department of Science, Technology and Innovation, Colciencias. E.A. Valencia is being partly funded by Universidad Tecnológica de Pereira. M.A. Álvarez would like to thank to Colciencias and British Council for funding under the research project "Hilbert Space Embeddings of Autoregressive Processes". Finally, we would like to thank to the anonymous reviewers, their suggestions have been very helpful to improve the quality of the draft.

References

1. Berlinet, A., Christine, T.A.: Reproducing Kernel Hilbert Spaces in Probability and Statistics. Springer Science+Business Media, LLC (2004)
2. Blum, M.G.B., Nunes, M.A., Prangle, D., Sisson, S.A.: A comparative review of dimension reduction methods in Approximate Bayesian Computation. Stat. Sc. **28**(2), 189–208 (2013)
3. Blum, M.G.: Choosing the summary statistics and the acceptance rate in approximate bayesian computation. In: Lechevallier, Y., Saporta, G. (eds.) Proceedings of COMPSTAT'2010, pp. 47–56. Physica-Verlag HD (2010)
4. Fearnhead, P., Prangle, D.: Constructing summary statistics for Approximate Bayesian Computation: semi-automatic Approximate Bayesian Computation. Journal of the Royal Statistical Society: Series B (Statistical Methodology) **74**(3), 419–474 (2012)
5. Gretton, A., Borgwardt, K.M., Rash, M.J., Schölkopf, B., Smola, A.: A kernel approach to comparing distributions. In: 22nd AAAI Conference on Artificial Intelligence, pp. 1637–1641. AAAI Press (2007)
6. Gretton, A., Borgwardt, K.M., Rash, M.J., Schölkopf, B., Smola, A.: A kernel method for the two-sample problem. In: Advances in Neural Information Processing Systems 15, pp. 513–520. MIT Press (2007)
7. Gretton, A., Borgwardt, K.M., Rash, M.J., Schölkopf, B., Smola, A.: A Kernel Two-Sample Test. Journal of Machine Learning Research **13**, 723–773 (2012)

8. Joyce, P., Marjoram, P.: Approximately Sufficient Statistics and Bayesian Computation. Statistical Applications in Genetics and Molecular Biology **7**(1), August 2008
9. Meeds, E., Welling, M.: GPS-ABC: Gaussian Process Surrogate Approximate Bayesian Computation. arXiv:1401.2838 (2014)
10. Muandet, K., Fukumizu, K., Sriperumbudur, B.K., Gretton, A., Schölkopf, B.: Kernel mean estimation and stein's effect. CoRR abs/1306.0842 (2013)
11. Nunes, M.A., Balding, D.J.: On optimal selection of summary statistics for Approximate Bayesian Computation. Statistical Applications in Genetics and Molecular Biology **9**(1) (2010)
12. Park, M., Jitkrittum, W., Sedjdinovic, D.: K2-ABC: Approximate Bayesian Computation with infinite dimensional summary statistics via kernel embeddings. arXiv:1502.02558 (2015)
13. Shimazaki, H., Shinomoto, S.: Kernel bandwidth optimization in spike rate estimation. J. Comput. Neurosci. **29**(1–2), 171–182 (2010)
14. Sisson, S.A., Fan, Y., Tanaka, M.M.: Sequential Monte Carlo without likelihoods. Proceedings of the National Academy of Sciences **104**(6), 1760–1765 (2007)
15. Sriperumbudur, B., Gretton, A., Fukumizu, K., Schölkopf, B., Lanckriet, G.: Hilbert space embeddings and metrics on probability measures. Journal of Machine Learning Research **11**, 1517–1561 (2010)
16. Toni, T., Welch, D., Strelkowa, N., Ipsen, A., Stumpf, M.P.H.: Approximate Bayesian Computation scheme for parameter inference and model selection in dynamical systems (2009)
17. Wilkinson, R.D.: Approximate Bayesian Computation (ABC) gives exact results under the assumption of model error. arXiv/0811.3355 (2008)
18. Wood, S.N.: Statistical inference for noisy nonlinear ecological dynamic systems. Nature **466**(5), 1102–1104 (2010)

Unsupervised Classification of Raw Full-Waveform Airborne Lidar Data by Self Organizing Maps

Eleonora Maset[✉], Roberto Carniel, and Fabio Crosilla

Dipartimento di Ingegneria Civile e Architettura (DICA),
Università degli Studi di Udine, Via delle Scienze, 206, 33100 Udine, Italy
eleonora.maset.1@gmail.com,
{roberto.carniel,fabio.crosilla}@uniud.it

Abstract. The paper proposes a procedure based on Kohonen's Self Organizing Maps (SOMs) to perform the unsupervised classification of raw full-waveform airborne LIDAR (Light Detection and Ranging) data, without the need of extracting features from them, that is without any preprocessing. The proposed algorithm allows the classification of points into three classes ("grass", "trees" and "road") in two subsequent stages. During the first one, all the raw data are given as input to a SOM and points belonging to the category "trees" are extracted on the basis of the number of peaks that characterize the waveforms. In the second stage, data not previously classified as "trees" are used to create a new SOM that, together with a hierarchical clustering algorithm, allows to distinguish between the classes "road" and "grass". Experiments carried out show that raw full-waveform LIDAR data were classified with an overall accuracy of 93.9%, 92.5% and 92.9%, respectively.

Keywords: Airborne LIDAR data · Full-waveform · Unsupervised classification · Self organizing maps

1 Introduction

The aerial laser scanner is an instrument used to survey the ground level morphology and the size and shape of natural and man-made objects, that exploits the time of flight of a reflected very short laser pulse (4 ns for the sensor used in this study), usually of wavelength between 0.8 and 1.55 μm. During its path, the laser ray can be reflected by more than one surface, placed at different heights. The earliest laser scanners could register just one return echo for each emitted one, later instruments allowed the use of 5/6 reflections for each emitted pulse. Since 2004, a new category of instruments are available on the market, the so called full-waveform airborne laser scanners, that are finally able to record the entire waveform of the reflected signal. The shape and size of the received waveform is related to the reflectance characteristics of the surface. Recording the complete waveform of the incoming pulse means that it is possible to obtain more information about geometrical and

© Springer International Publishing Switzerland 2015
V. Murino and E. Puppo (Eds.): ICIAP 2015, Part I, LNCS 9279, pp. 62–72, 2015.
DOI: 10.1007/978-3-319-23231-7_6

physical characteristics of the target hit by the laser ray, that can be useful for the classification of the 3D sampled points.

Over the last years, several classification methods have been proposed in the literature using full-waveform data and the features extracted from them [6]. Among these, we mention decision trees [5] or simple thresholds both set up manually [18] and automatically [1]. These methods exploit features extracted from the waveforms, such as amplitude, pulse width and number of pulses, and they have the advantage of not requiring assumptions regarding the distribution of input data. Other methods are based on statistical learning classifiers like Support Vector Machines (SVM, [11]), which belong to non-parametric methods and perform non-linear classification. This algorithm is well suited for high dimensional problems with limited training set. Höfle et al. [8] use instead an artificial neural network classifier consisting of a single hidden layer of neurons and trained by back propagation.

The present paper proposes the application of Kohonen's Self Organizing Maps (SOMs), a kind of neural networks introduced in the 80s of the last century by Kohonen [10] as a method for clustering and visualization of high dimension datasets. The basic principle of SOMs is that a higher level knowledge organization can be carried out by learning using algorithms that perform a self-organization in a spatial order. A SOM consists of a bi-dimensional grid of a predetermined number of equally spaced nodes, that can vary from few units to few thousand, according to the nature of the data set. Each node, also known with the term "neuron", is represented by a vector (the so called "code vector") with the same size of the vectors that constitute the data of the sample to be analyzed and is connected with the other neurons to form the network. During the training process the SOM evolves by changing the neurons' vector values as the data vectors sequentially enter into the process [2].

In the past, Self Organizing Maps found application in multispectral imagery classification and, more recently, in the Earth sciences ([9], [4]). However, methods based on the SOM concept have not been yet extensively exploited for the classification of LIDAR point clouds. Salah et al. [16] apply Self Organizing Maps for building detection from LIDAR data and multispectral aerial images. Zaletnyk et al. [19] exploit the SOM algorithm to investigate in particular the correlation between the shape of the LIDAR waveforms, using various statistical parameters (amplitude, standard deviation, skewness and kurtosis), and the properties of the reflecting surface. Toth et al. [17] and Molnar et al. [12] apply a 2x2 neural grid SOM to classify four different features types (trees, grass, roof and pavement).

In all these works, some features have been preliminary extracted from the original full-waveform data and submitted to the SOM procedure. On the contrary, in this paper the raw full wave data vectors have been directly analyzed and classified. Although Molnar et al. [12] stated in their paper the impracticability to directly use the original waveforms as input for a classification procedure, this paper shows a successful result thanks to the implementation of a SOM with a number of neurons much greater than the number of the required classes.

In [12] a network with a number of nodes equal to the number of classes is used. Tests carried out in this work have shown that presenting the raw waveform data to a SOM of small dimensions leads to a high error in the classification. Large networks, instead, allow to use the original signal for the classification procedure, despite the waveforms can be different for each reflection.

On the other hand, considering a number of nodes much greater than the number of classes, implies the necessity to successively apply a proper algorithm for clustering the nodes.

2   Methodology

As mentioned before, the classification method proposed in this paper is based on the SOM algorithm. SOMs are a particular kind of unsupervised artificial neural networks that promote self-organization of data vectors in a spatial order by suitable learning algorithms. The first stage is the so called global initialization, in which a map of predefined size, not organized at all, is considered. At the beginning, a first set of random values - usually extracted from the experimental data - is assigned to each node vector. Successively, three iterative processes are repeated for all the data vectors until a global convergence is reached ([2], [3]).

The first one is the *competitive process*, that aimed at finding the neuron whose code vector is nearest to the input vector in the n-dimensional space, where n is the dimensionality of input data. The winning neuron (Best Matching Unit, BMU) determines the spatial location of a topological neighbourhood of excited neurons on the map. To carry out the *competitive process*, it is necessary to introduce a discriminant function able to measure the similarity between the input vector $x_i(t)$ at the t-th iteration and each neuron of the map. The winning neuron at the t-th iteration is the one having the greatest similarity with the input vector $x_i(t)$. It has been demonstrated [7] that various similarity criteria of two functions, $f(y)$ and $g(y)$, including the sum of squared differences and the correlation coefficient, are related to the cross-correlation function $R_{f,g}(\tau)$ at $\tau = 0$:

$$R_{f,g}(\tau) = \int f(y)\, g(y+\tau)\, dy \tag{1}$$

Thus, they cannot provide any information about patterns that are shifted relatively to each other. In this work, a generalized expression for similarity [7], $S_{f,g}(\tau)$, is used, which is based on a weighted cross-correlation function, a weighting function $z(\tau)$ normalized with the product of the two weighted autocorrelation functions, that is:

$$S_{f,g}(\tau) = \frac{\int z(\tau)\, R_{f,g}(\tau)\, d\tau}{\sqrt{\int z(\tau)\, R_{f,f}(\tau)\, d\tau \int z(\tau)\, R_{g,g}(\tau)\, d\tau}} \tag{2}$$

where $z(\tau)$ is a triangular weighting function of width defined as $z(\tau) = 1 - |\tau|/h$ if $|\tau| < h$ and $z(\tau) = 0$ if $|\tau| \geq h$. The BMU is then the neuron $w_c(t)$ that maximizes the value of the function $S_{f,g}(\tau)$. Once the *competitive process* has selected the BMU, the next step is the so called *cooperative process*. During this stage, a neighbouring function, $h_{c(x),j}(t)$, determines how strongly the various neurons are connected to the winner at a certain iteration t. A typical choice of $h_{c(x),j}(t)$ is the Gaussian function [13].

The last process is the *adaptive* one. During the adaptive process an adjustment of the neuron vector values is carried out in order to minimize the distance of each data input from the corresponding neuron of the map and to slowly allow the map to be partitioned into relevant clusters at the end of the process. Usually the model applied is the following [13]:

$$w_j(t+1) = w_j(t) + \alpha(t) h_{c(x),j}(t) [x_i(t) - w_j(t)] \tag{3}$$

where $w_j(t+1)$ is the j-th updated neuron vector at iteration $t+1$, $\alpha(t) = \alpha_0 \cdot \exp(-t/T)$ is the learning-rate factor parameter and τ is a new time constant.

The three steps process just presented is applied at each iteration to the entire data set and the entire learning process is stopped when no more substantial changes to the code vectors are observed.

As pointed out before, the purpose of the proposed method here is to classify LIDAR data into three categories: "trees", "grass" and "road". Each input data is the entire waveform of the reflected signal, i.e. a vector whose components are the amplitude values registered and stored by the instrument at a certain sampling interval. No preprocessing procedure is applied to the data. More details about the structure of the data to be classified will be given in Sec. 3.

First of all, the extraction of the waveforms reflected from trees is performed, exploiting the fact that waveforms belonging to this class are generally characterized by the presence of two or more echoes, unlike those of the road and grass, which include only one echo. Nevertheless, as highlighted in [11], waveforms recorded by the receiver are affected by the "ringing effect", i.e. after the peak corresponding to a reflecting surface, a small secondary maximum due to the effects of the hardware waveform processing chain can be seen. So it is not possible to distinguish between trees and the other two classes only on the basis of the number of peaks of each raw signal, without first dealing with the "ringing" problem. As suggested in [15], the "ringing effect" can be recognized and removed if its amplitude is smaller than a certain fraction of the amplitude of the first peak and if the second peak is closer than a certain distance to the first one. The experiments carried out during this work have shown that, due to the variability of the waveforms reflected, it is difficult to identify a single threshold value to be applied to the raw data, which allows to eliminate only false peaks. For this reason, the SOM algorithm, described above, is used a first time, performing the training of the map with all the data set. A threshold value is then applied to the code vectors of the map, rather than directly to the raw data, in order to remove the "ringing effect". Since the code vectors of the SOM are a sort of "abstraction" of the data, the great variability of the waveforms is smoothed, and a more reliable threshold value can be identified.

At the end of this stage, the data associated with the code vectors that still have more than one peak after the application of the threshold, are labeled as trees. The remaining, i.e. those characterized by a single peak, are not classified. Tests have shown that using the SOM algorithm for this purpose can significantly reduce the error in the classification of the points belonging to the class "road" and increase the overall accuracy of the classification. In fact, if the "ringing effect" is removed applying the threshold value directly to the raw waveforms, even taking into account the fact that the second false peak occurs between 10 and 12 ns after the first one, the overall accuracy is reduced by 10%.

Once the points belonging to the category "trees" have been separated, it is possible to classify waveforms reflected by grass and roads. A new network of the same size of the previous one is created and only the waveforms that have not been labeled in the previous stage are used as input. As suggested in [16], the chosen size of the map is high (e.g. 15x15). In fact, small networks result in some unrepresented classes, while large networks lead to an improvement in the overall classification accuracy. After each piece of data has been associated with one neuron on the new map, a hierarchical clustering procedure, performed by the *agnes* function (R environment [14], *cluster* package), is applied. Each code vector is initially considered a small one-node cluster [3], that is then progressively merged with similar clusters, until only a unique cluster, containing all the code vectors, is formed. At each stage the two most similar clusters are combined. The result is a graph called "dendrogram", where the clustering process described above can be seen proceeding from bottom to top (Fig. 1). The clustering procedure can be interrupted at any vertical level by establishing an appropriate threshold. In this work, the threshold is chosen in order to determine two clusters on the map: one is associated with the class "grass" and the other with the class "road". Finally, the two obtained clusters need to be "labelled"; an automatic way to perform the interpretation of the clusters can be based on the maximum value of the average vector that represents the cluster. Surfaces covered with grass have higher reflectivity than the road; for this reason, the cluster represented by the average vector that has the highest value of amplitude is labeled as grass. It is important to underline that the information related to the amplitude is exploited only to label the two classes obtained at the end of the clustering procedure; the entire process that leads to the separation between waveforms belonging to the category "road" and waveforms belonging to the category "grass" is totally independent from this feature. Figure 2 shows the identification of the two clusters on the map.

3   Experiments and Results

The proposed method has been validated for three test areas in Horn, Austria. The data set was acquired by the company RIEGL Laser Measurement System GmbH with the sensor RIEGL LMS-Q680i during a flight at the altitude of 800 m. The emitted laser pulse has a length of 4 ns and each return waveform is composed of 60 samples, with 1 ns sampling interval. The data format used as input in the proposed procedure is amplitude vs. time series samples.

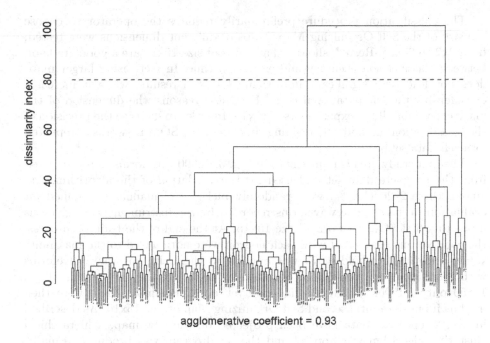

dissimilarity index
0
20
40
60
80
100
agglomerative coefficient = 0.93

Fig. 1. Dendrogram summarizing the clustering of nodes of the SOM performed during the second stage of the classification algorithm.

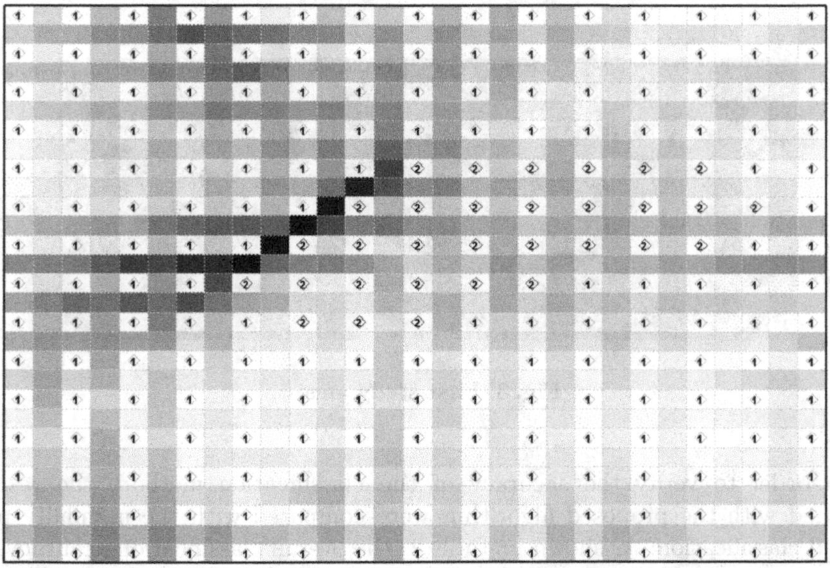

Fig. 2. SOM showing the nodes assigned to each of the clusters. Cells which do not contain a number use a gray scale to show the similarity of the nearby neurons code vectors: light gray indicates a strong similarity and vice versa.

The classification procedure preliminarily requires the operator to choose the size of the Self Organizing Map. Maps of different dimensions were tested, from 2x2 to 25x25. Results showed that maps of size 15x15 are a good trade-off between classification accuracy and execution time. In fact, using larger maps does not lead to a significant improvement of the results, while it increases considerably the computational costs. For these reasons, the dimension of the maps chosen for all the experiments is 15x15. In order to increase the precision of the classification method, the training process of the SOM networks is repeated for each data set.

The first study area is represented in Fig. 3. 15000 waveforms were extracted from the complete data set and used for the validation of the algorithm, and among these 2926 (19.5%) were randomly picked and manually classified for evaluation purposes. The waveforms recorded by the instrument were given as input to a first SOM network of size 15x15. At the end of the training process, the code vectors associated with each neuron were normalized to the maximum value, and the threshold 0.075 was applied to them. In this way, waveforms with more than one peak were classified as trees. At the end of this stage, 12850 out of 15000 waveforms had not yet been classified. These were then used as input data for a second Self Organizing Map of size 15x15. As described in Sec. 2, once the data have been projected on the new map, a hierarchical clustering algorithm was applied and the dendrogram was produced. Finally, the two clusters obtained through the dendrogram were interpreted on the basis of the maximum amplitude value of the average code vector related to each cluster and the classes "road" and "grass" were identified.

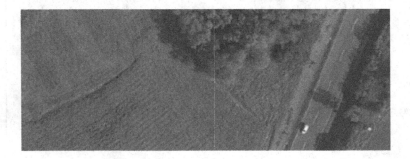

Fig. 3. First study area.

In order to verify the accuracy of the classification method, the results obtained with the proposed algorithm were compared with the manually performed classification. As shown in Table 1, the overall classification accuracy for this study area is 93.9%. The error matrix highlights that the proposed method allows to classify the data belonging to the "road" and "grass" categories with very high accuracy, respectively 97.6% and 98.6%. However, the algorithm shows more difficulty in discriminating waveforms relating to trees. This may be due to the fact that some waveforms reflected from the trees can present only one peak, or secondary peaks have low amplitude and they are not distinguished from the noise. In these cases, the method is not able to correctly establish the class, and these data are erroneously assigned to the categories "road" or "grass".

Table 1. Error matrix for the first study area, computed with 2926 manually classified points.

	Grass	Trees	Road	Total	User's accuracy
Grass	1451	86	7	1544	94.0%
Trees	13	595	3	611	97.4%
Road	22	48	701	771	90.9%
Total	1486	729	711	2926	
Producer's accuracy	97.6%	81.6%	98.6%		93.9%

Figure 4 represents the second test area. In this case 10000 waveforms were extracted from the complete data set and among these 1086 (10.9%) were randomly picked and manually classified. A new SOM of size 15x15 was trained, using this second data set. At the end of the first stage, carried out as described in the previous experiment, 8870 out of 10000 waveforms had not yet been classified. These were then used as input data for the second stage of the algorithm, which led to the results reported in Table 2.

Fig. 4. Second study area.

In this case, the overall accuracy is equal to 92.5%, while the producers accuracy related to each category is 93.9% for the class "grass", 91.9% for the class trees and 89.4% for the class "road". Unlike the previous example, the results of this experiment show that also the points belonging to the class trees are identified with high accuracy, more than 90%.

The third test area is shown in Fig. 5. 12000 waveforms were used in this experiment and among these 1588 (13.2%) were randomly picked and manually classified. The classification procedure was carried out as described above, creating a first SOM network of size 15x15 that led to the identification of 1688 points belonging to the class "trees", and a second map of dimension 15x15 for

Table 2. Error matrix for the second study area, computed with 1086 manually classified points.

	Grass	Trees	Road	Total	User's accuracy
Grass	559	15	24	598	93.5%
Trees	2	226	2	230	98.3%
Road	34	5	220	259	84.9%
Total	595	246	246	1086	
Producer's accuracy	93.9%	91.9%	89.4%		92.5%

the distinction between the class "grass" and the class "road". Table 3 shows the confusion matrix, computed from the comparison between the results obtained with the proposed algorithm and the manually performed classification.

Fig. 5. Third study area.

Table 3. Error matrix for the third study area, computed with 1588 manually classified points.

	Grass	Trees	Road	Total	User's accuracy
Grass	801	3	42	846	94.7%
Trees	27	344	8	379	90.8%
Road	27	5	331	363	91.2%
Total	855	352	381	1588	
Producer's accuracy	93.7%	97.7%	86.9%		92.9%

The overall accuracy achieved is 92.9%, which is a value similar to the previous cases. The accuracy with which points belonging to the classes grass and road were identified, 93.7% and 86.9% respectively, is similar to the second experiment, while the accuracy related to the class trees is very high, equal to 97.7%.

4   Discussion and Conclusion

The goal of this work was to implement a method for the classification of data acquired with a full-waveform airborne laser scanner, based on Kohonen's Self

Organizing Map. The algorithm proposed in this paper uses the entire waveform recorded by the instrument, without any pre-processing, in order to distinguish the data into three categories: "trees", "grass" and "road". Although Molnar et al. [12] stated in their paper the impracticability to directly use the original raw data as input for a classification procedure, since the waveforms can be really different for each reflection, this paper shows a successful result thanks to the implementation of a SOM with a number of neurons much greater than the number of the required classes. In fact, large networks manage to overcome the problem of the variability of the waveforms and the classification is then made possible by the subsequent application of the hierarchical clustering algorithm to the nodes of the map. One may argue about the necessity to pass through a SOM procedure and not directly to the clustering of the original data. In this regard, applying a clustering algorithm to the nodes of the grid and not directly to the original data vectors, is surely much more reliable since neuron's values are in some way "averaged" values.

The experiments carried out to validate this method showed that, on average, the overall accuracy provided by the proposed algorithm is 93.1%, and the three categories "grass", "trees" and "road" can be distinguished with an average producer's accuracy of 95.1%, 90.4% and 91.6%, respectively, and an average user's accuracy of 94.1%, 95.5% and 89%, respectively. It is important to emphasize that the method is almost fully automatic, and the user needs only to choose the threshold for the elimination of the "ringing effect". Unlike other methods ([5], [17], [19]), it is not required to extract features from the waveforms of the data set.

Moreover, since the SOM is a tool that realizes an unsupervised classification, any manual pre-classification of a subset of data is not necessary, as instead required by methods that perform a supervised classification.

If the user is interested only in a particular category of points, this method can be very useful because it allows to extract preliminarily some classes of data and then to process only the waveforms of interest and not the entire data set.

At the time the method is applicable to the classification of points belonging to areas without buildings. Further research is being carried out in order to extend the applicability of the algorithm.

References

1. Alexander, C., Tansey, K., Kaduk, J., Holland, D., Tate, N.J.: Backscatter coefficient as an attribute for the classification of full-waveform airborne laser scanning data in urban areas. ISPRS Journal of Photogrammetry and Remote Sensing **65**(5), 423–432 (2010)
2. Carniel, R., Barbui, L., Jolly, A.D.: Detecting dynamical regimes by Self-Organizing Map (SOM) analysis: an example from the March 2006 phreatic eruption at Raoul Island, New Zealand Kermadic Arc. Boll. Geof. Teor. Appl. **54**(1), 39–52 (2013)
3. Carniel, R., Jolly, A.D., Barbui, L.: Analysis of phreatic events at Ruapehu volcano, New Zealand using a new SOM approach. J. Volc. Geoth. Res. **254**, 69–79 (2013)

4. Carniel, R.: Characterization of volcanic regimes and identification of significant transitions using geophysical data: a review. Bull. Volc. (2014) (in press)
5. Ducic, V., Hollaus, M., Ullrich, A., Wagner, W., Melzer, T.: 3D vegetation mapping and classification using full-waveform laser scanning. In: Workshop on 3D Remote Sensing in Forestry, Vienna, Austria, February 14–15, pp. 222–228 (2006)
6. Fieber, K.D., Davenport, I.J., Ferryman, J.M., Gurney, R.J., Walker, J.P., Hacker, J.M.: Analysis of full-waveform LiDAR data for classification of an orange orchard scene. ISPRS Journal of Photogrammetry and Remote Sensing 82, 63–82 (2013)
7. de Gelder, R., Wehrens, R., Hageman, J.A.: A generalized expression for the similarity spectra: application to powder diffraction pattern classification. Journal of Computational Chemistry 22(3), 273–289 (2001)
8. Höfle, B., Hollaus, M., Hagenauer, J.: Urban vegetation detection using radiometrically calibrated small-footprint full-waveform airborne LiDAR data. ISPRS Journal of Photogrammetry and Remote Sensing 67, 134–147 (2012)
9. Klose, C.D.: Self organizing maps for geoscientific data analysis: geological interpretation of multidimensional geophysical data. Computational Geosciences 10(3), 265–277 (2006)
10. Kohonen, T.: Self-organised formation of topologically correct feature map. Biological Cybernetics 43, 56–69 (1982)
11. Mallet, C., Bretar, F., Roux, M., Soergel, U., Heipke, C.: Relevance assessment of full-waveform lidar data for urban area classification. ISPRS Journal of Photogrammetry and Remote Sensing 66(6), S71–S84 (2011)
12. Molnar, B., Laky, S., Toth, C.: Using full waveform data in urban areas. International Archives of Photogrammetry, Remote Sensing and Spatial Information Sciences 38(Part3/W22), 203–208 (2011)
13. Ortiz, A., Górriz, J.M., Ramírez, J., Salas-González, D., Llamas-Elvira, J.M.: Two fully-unsupervised methods for MR brain image segmentation using SOM-based strategies. Applied Soft Computing 13(5), 2668–2682 (2013)
14. R Development Core Team: R: A Language and Environment for Statistical Computing. R Foundation, Austria 3–900051-07-0 (2014). www.R-project.org
15. Reitberger, J., Krzystek, P., Heurich, M.: Full waveform analysis of small footprint airborne laser scanning data in the bavarian forest national park for three species classification. In: Workshop on 3D Remote Sensing in Forestry, Vienna, Austria, February 14–15, pp. 229–238 (2006)
16. Salah, M., Trinder, J., Shaker, A.: Evaluation of the Self-Organizing Map classifier for building detection from Lidar data and multispectral aerial images. Journal of Spatial Science 54(2), 15–34 (2009)
17. Toth, C., Laky, S., Zaletnyik, P., Grejner-Brzezinska, D.: Compressing and classifying LIDAR waveform data. International Archives of the Photogrammetry Remote Sensing and Spatial Information Sciences XXXVIII (1), Paper 130 (2010)
18. Wagner, W., Hollaus, M., Briese, C., Ducic, V.: 3D vegetation mapping using small-footprint full-waveform airborne laser scanners. International Journal of Remote Sensing 29(5), 1433–1452 (2008)
19. Zaletnyik, P., Laky, S., Toth, C.: LiDAR waveform classification using self-organizing map. In: ASPRS, San Diego, CA, April 26–30 (2010)

Fitting Multiple Models via Density Analysis in Tanimoto Space

Luca Magri[1](✉) and Andrea Fusiello[2]

[1] Dipartimento di Matematica, Università di Milano, Via Saldini, 50, Milano, Italy
`luca.magri@unimi.it`
[2] DIEGM, Università di Udine, Via Delle Scienze, 208, Udine, Italy

Abstract. This paper deals with the extraction of multiple models from noisy, outlier-contaminated data. We build on the "preference trick" implemented by T-linkage, weakening the prior assumptions on the data: without requiring the tuning of the inlier threshold we develop a new automatic method which takes advantage of the geometric properties of Tanimoto space to bias the sampling toward promising models and exploits a density based analysis in the conceptual space in order to robustly estimate the models. Experimental validation proves that our method compares favourably with T-Linkage on public, real data-sets.

Keywords: Multi-model fitting · Segmentation · Clustering

1 Introduction

The extraction of multiple models from noisy or outlier-contaminated data is an important and challenging problem that emerges in many Computer Vision applications. With respect to single-model estimation in presence of noise and outliers, this problem is even more difficult since it must tolerate both true outliers and *pseudo-outliers* ("outliers to the structure of interest but inliers to a different structure" [15]). Among the wide variety of approaches developed for multi-model fitting, it is possible to identify two mutually orthogonal strategies: *consensus analysis* and *preference analysis*.

The consensus set of a model is defined as the set of data points that are close to the model within a certain threshold. Consensus analysis can be traced back to the popular RANSAC paradigm and its variants [17] and gave rise also to algorithms tailored for the case of multiple structures estimation, e.g. [22]. Consensus-oriented methods generate a pool of putative model hypotheses by random sampling, then retain the models that explain better the data by inspecting their consensus sets. The same idea can be found in the popular Hough transform [20] and its generalization, where multiple models are revealed as peaks in the hypothesis space after it has been adequately quantized. Maximizing the consensus set of models can be also encountered as the foundation of optimization algorithms [9] for geometric fitting.

On the contrary, preference analysis reverses the role of data and models: rather than considering models and examining which points match them, the

© Springer International Publishing Switzerland 2015
V. Murino and E. Puppo (Eds.): ICIAP 2015, Part I, LNCS 9279, pp. 73–84, 2015.
DOI: 10.1007/978-3-319-23231-7_7

residuals of individual data points are taken into account [21]. In this way it is possible to exploit the residual information for building a *conceptual space* in which points are portrayed by the *preferences* they have accorded to provisional models. For example in [16] data points are represented as characteristic functions taking values on the set of hypothesized models, whereas in [2] a data point is represented in a Reproducing Kernel Hilbert Space by the permutation that arranges the models in order of ascending residuals. T-Linkage [12] extends the ideas beyond [16] and is mainly composed by two steps:

1. *Conceptual representation*: given an inlier threshold, points are represented in the m-dimensional unitary cube endowed with the Tanimoto distance, according to the preferences they grant to a set of m random hypotheses. We will refer to this metric space as *Tanimoto space*.
2. *Segmentation*: data are segmented via a tailored version of average linkage.

It is worth to observe that a similar *first-represent-then-clusterize* approach is also adopted by many state-of-the-art algorithms [7,11,14] for multiple subspaces estimation that relies on sparse representation of points.

In this paper we elaborate both the conceptual representation and the segmentation step introduced by T-Linkage, conceiving a new automatic method aimed at multi-model extraction resistant to noise and outliers. In particular we present an embedding in Tanimoto space of data points which does not require the tuning of the inlier threshold and we enhance the generation of tentative hypotheses capitalizing the geometric information embodied in the conceptual space. In addition we describe how a density based analysis of the Tanimoto space can be used to simultaneously cluster point and identify outliers. The main goal of this work is to gain some insights on the key advantages provided by the use of Tanimoto distance in preference analysis.

2   Method

In this section we explore the geometrical properties of Tanimoto space, introducing a new method for clustering of multi-model data. We motivate and formulate the algorithm using a working example (Fig. 1a) taken from [19]. In this dataset three objects move independently each giving rise to a set of points correspondences in two uncalibrated images: points belonging to the same object are described by a specific fundamental matrix. Outlying correspondences are present.

2.1   Preference Trick

The first step of our method, like T-Linkage, consists in building a conceptual representation of data points $X = \{x_1, \ldots, x_n\}$ in the Tanimoto space $\mathcal{T} = ([0,1]^m, d_{\mathcal{T}})$, given a set of putative models $H = \{h_1, \ldots, h_m\}$. We will denote the Tanimoto distance, defined for every $p, q \in [0,1]^m$ as

$$d_{\mathcal{T}}(p,q) = 1 - \frac{\langle p, q \rangle}{(\|p\|^2 + \|q\|^2 - \langle p, q \rangle)} \,, \tag{1}$$

whereas $d\colon X \times H \to \mathbb{R}$ indicates a suitable distance for computing the residual between a point and a model. This step can be thought as a sort of *"preference trick"*. Echoing the celebrated "kernel trick", which lifts a non linear problem in an higher dimension space in which it becomes easier, the Tanimoto representation, shifts the data points from their ambient space to a conceptual one, revealing the multiple structures hidden in the data as groups of neighbouring points. The preference trick can be formalized by defining a vector map

$$\Phi\colon X \to \mathcal{T} = ([0,1]^m, d_{\mathcal{T}}) \quad x \mapsto (\exp(-r_1), \ldots, \exp(-r_m)) , \qquad (2)$$

where r_j are the standardized residuals of data points with respect to H:

$$r_j = \frac{d(x, h_j)}{\sigma}, \quad \sigma = \mathrm{var}\{d(x_i, h_j), \ i = 1, \ldots, n, \ j = 1, \ldots, m\} . \qquad (3)$$

The rationale behind this construction is that $\Phi(x)$ expresses the preference granted by x to the model h_j with a vote in $[0,1]$ according to its residual. The Tanimoto distance $d_{\mathcal{T}}$ measures the agreement between the preferences of two points. In particular this distance ranges in $[0,1]$ and achieves its minimum for points sharing the same preferences, whereas $d_{\mathcal{T}} = 1$ when points have orthogonal preferences.

Observe that Φ differs from the embedding Φ_τ proposed in T-Linkage in which the inlier threshold τ is needed in order to cut off the preference of points too distant from the models:

$$\Phi_{\tau,j}(x) = \begin{cases} \exp\left(\frac{-d(x,h_j)}{5\tau}\right) & \text{if } d(x, h_j) < \tau \\ 0 & \text{if } d(x, h_j) \geq \tau . \end{cases} \qquad (4)$$

In this formulation τ plays a crucial role: it implicitly controls the final number of models because it affects the orthogonality between the conceptual representation of points and T-Linkage connects points until they are orthogonal in $\mathcal{T}$.

On the contrary our segmentation step does not rely on orthogonality in $\mathcal{T}$, but exploits other geometric properties of Tanimoto space, such as densities and concentrations. For this reason we do not require a correct estimate of the threshold, which indeed can be a difficult parameter to tune.

Biased Random Sampling in Tanimoto space. The pool of tentative hypotheses is generated instantiating a model on minimal sample sets (MSS), i.e. a subsets of data points having the minimum cardinality (henceforth denoted by k) necessary to estimate the model. Different sampling strategies can be used for generating these models. If uniform sampling is employed, a large number of trials is required for reaching a reasonable probability of hitting at least a *pure* (i.e., outlier free) MSS per model, as explained in [16]. Hence, many strategies have been proposed in order to guide sampling towards promising models both in the case of one model [4,5] and in the multiple models scenario [3].

With localized sampling [10] neighbouring points are selected with higher probability, thereby reducing the number of hypotheses that have to be generated. However, depending on the application, introducing a local bias can be difficult since different structures may obey different distributions of data in the ambient space (think for example to the case of motion segmentation of moving object with very different shapes).

In order to overcome this difficulty we propose to sample the hypotheses directly in the conceptual space. This can be easily done performing a preliminary uniform sampling of hypotheses, representing the data in the Tanimoto space according to these putative models and then doing a biased sampling in $\mathcal{T}$.

In particular if a point x has already been selected, then a point y such that $x \neq y$ has the following probability of being drawn:

$$P(x|y) = \frac{1}{Z} \exp \frac{d_{\mathcal{T}}\left(\Phi(x), \Phi(y)\right)^2}{\alpha^2} \ . \tag{5}$$

where Z is a normalization constant and α controls the local bias.

Tanimoto distances are then updated on the fly based on the hypotheses already sampled.

We illustrate the effectiveness of this sampling strategy on the *biscuitbookbox* sequence. In Fig. 1 we compare our biased sampling in Tanimoto space with respect to uniform sampling, localized sampling, and Multi-GS a method proposed in [3]. All these methods can be lead back to the conditional sampling scheme presented here, substituting $d_{\mathcal{T}}$ in (5) with an appropriate distance function: $d_U \equiv 1$ for uniform sampling, $d_L = \| \cdot \|$ for localized sampling and the intersection kernel d_{GS}. We run these methods with different values of α; in particular we set $\alpha = q_w$ as the w-th quantile of all these distances, varying $w \in [0.1, 1]$. Our biased sampling provides results comparable with localized sampling for more values of α (Fig. 1b) and produces many pure MSS per model (Fig. 1c).

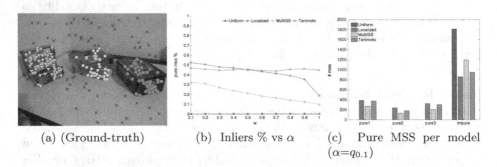

(a) (Ground-truth)   (b) Inliers % vs α (c)   Pure MSS per model
                                                                 ($\alpha = q_{0.1}$)

Fig. 1. Comparison of guided sampling methods on *biscuitbookbox* sequence. Model membership is colour coded; black crosses are outliers.

2.2   Density Based Analysis for Model Extraction

In this section we will see how to cluster the high dimensional cloud of points $Y = \Phi(X)$ originated by the preference trick in order to extract the models that explain the data. The desired segmentation is obtained by exploiting the geometric properties of the discrete set of points Y induced by the topology defined in $\mathcal{T}$. In particular the notion of *density-connected component* will serve as the geometric counterpart of the statistical notion of cluster. An analysis of points density is performed using OPTICS [1], producing a *reachability plot* from which density-connected components can be identified.

Geometric Insight. We recall that the Tanimoto distance measures the agreement between the preferences of points: data sharing the same preferences, i.e. belonging to the same models, are close according to $d_{\mathcal{T}}$. As can be appreciated from Fig. 2a, points belonging to the same model are clustered in high density region whereas outliers occupy region with low density.

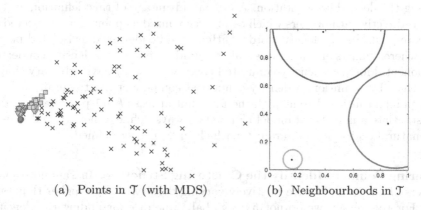

(a) Points in $\mathcal{T}$ (with MDS)   (b) Neighbourhoods in $\mathcal{T}$

Fig. 2. Insights on the geometry of Tanimoto space. (a) the *biscuitbookbox* data in Tanimoto space are projected using Multi-Dimensional Scaling for visualization purposes. Outliers (x) are recognized as the most separated points. (b) Tanimoto neighbourhoods with the same radius in $[0,1]^2$ have smaller Euclidean diameter if the centre lies near the origin.

Some insight into this property of Tanimoto space can be reached considering a system of neighbourhoods: Fixed some $\epsilon \in (0,1)$ and some $y \in \mathcal{T}$ the Tanimoto ball of radius ϵ and centre y is denoted by $N_\epsilon(y)$.

As illustrated in Fig. 2b, the Euclidean diameter of N_ϵ changes accordingly to the position of the centre y. In particular this quantity tends to be smaller for points lying near the origin of $\mathcal{T}$, that corresponds to the region of $\mathcal{T}$ prevalently occupied by outlying points. In fact outliers grant their preferences to very few sampled hypotheses, they have small Euclidean norm and consequently tend to lie near the origin. Hence the probability that two outliers live in the same ball of radius ϵ is significant lower than the probability that two inliers (with higher

Euclidean norm) are contained in a ball with the same radius. For this reason outliers can be recognized as the most separated points in $\mathfrak{I}$.

With this perspective as guide, we tailor the definition of density-connected component [8] to Tanimoto space:

Definition 1. *Given $p, q \in \mathfrak{I}$, the cardinality k of MSS and $\epsilon \in (0, 1)$*

- *p is said a* core point *if $|N_\epsilon(p)| > k$;*
- *p is* directly density-reachable *from q with respect to ϵ if $p \in N_\epsilon(q)$ and q is a core point;*
- *p is* density reachable *from q with respect to ϵ if there is a chain of points $p_1, \ldots, p_\ell$ s.t. $p_1 = p, p_\ell = q$ and p_{i+1} is directly density reachable from p_i;*
- *p is* density-connected *to point q with respect to ϵ if there is a point o such that both p and q are density reachable from o.*
- *a* density-connected component *is a maximal set of density-connected points.*

Density-connectivity is an equivalence relation hence all the points reachable from core points can be factorized into maximal density-connected components yielding the desired segmentation. A crucial advantage of this definition is that it deals directly with outliers which can be recognized as points not connected to any core point. In topological words, outliers can be identified as isolated points of Y, whereas inliers are either internal or boundary points of a density-connected component. Moreover density-connected components may have arbitrary shape. Note that, by definition, a density-connected component must contain at least $k + 1$ points; this is coherent with the fact that at least $k + 1$ points are needed to instantiate a non-trivial model (k points always define a model), and gives a very natural choice of this parameter which in [8] is user defined.

Ordering Points to Identify the Clustering Structure. In Tanimoto space clusters of inliers could have relatively varying density, though higher than outliers. For this reason we do not fix a global value of ϵ for finding the density-connected components. Instead we adopt the multi-scale approach offered by OPTICS (Ordering Points to Identify the Clustering Structure) [1]. OPTICS is a density-based technique which frame the geometry of the data in a reachability plot thanks to the notion of reachability distance.

Definition 2. *Given the cardinality k of MSS,*

- *if p is a core point, the* core-distance *of p refers to the distance between p and its k-nearest neighbour.*
- *if p is a core point, the* reachability-distance *of a point p with respect to a point q is the maximum between the core distance of p and the distance $d_\mathfrak{I}(p, q)$.*

After the data have been ordered so that consecutive points have minimum reachability distance, OPTICS produces a special kind of dendrogram, called reachability plot, which consists of the reachability values on the y-axis of all the ordered points on the x-axis. The valleys of this plot represent the density-connected regions: the deeper the valley, the denser the cluster.

Figure 3, where the *biscuitbookbox* reachability plot is shown, illustrates this. Outliers have high reachability values, on the contrary genuine clusters appears as low reachability valley and hence are density-connected components in $\mathcal{T}$.

The points ordering originated by OPTICS resembles the classical single Linkage clustering, in which at each iteration the closest points are linked together, however the use of reachability distance, which exploits local density information, mitigates the so-called chain effect.

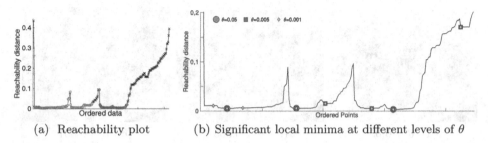

(a) Reachability plot   (b) Significant local minima at different levels of θ

Fig. 3. Output of OPTICS. (a) The reachability plot of *biscuitbookbox* shows the reachability distance of ordered points (model membership is colour coded according to the ground truth). (b) Significant local minima are marked according to the θ at which they are found.

Flooding. The final step of our method is aimed at automatically find the valleys in the reachability plot produced by OPTICS in order to robustly extract clusters and hence models. For this purpose we adapt the Meyer flooding algorithm [13], originally developed for Watershed segmentation, to deal with the 1D reachability plot:

1. Local minima of the reachability plot are found.
2. Those minima that are at least θ below their adjacent maxima are retained as significant.
3. The reachability plot is flooded starting from the basin of significant local minima.
4. The flooding of a basin stops when different water sources meet.
5. Points flooded with water coming from the same source are clustered together, whereas points untouched by the water are labelled as outliers.

Once data points are segmented, models are fitted via least square regression on points belonging to the same cluster, and outliers are reassigned to their nearest model – if they have distance smaller than the furthest inlier. Finally, models are re-estimated according to this new segmentation. Optionally, a final outlier rejection, as the one proposed in [12], could be performed.

The threshold θ controls the significance of critical points in the reachability plot, allowing us to dichotomize between significant minima and spurious ones due to noise. It is found empirically that $\theta = 0.05$ provides good local minima in several applicative scenarios, consequently the generality of the preference trick is not affected by the use of this fixed threshold.

Nevertheless it is interesting to investigate how θ affects the quality of clustering. In Fig. 3b the sets of significant minima are shown for $\theta = 0.05, 0.005, 0.001$. It is readily seen that as θ decreases the induced segmentation becomes finer, creating a hierarchy of models, which allows multiple levels of details to be captured, as can be appreciated in Fig. 4, where points that at level $\theta = 0.05$ obey a single fundamental matrix are split in clusters described by homographies.

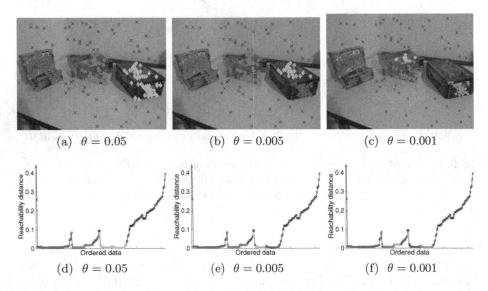

(a) $\theta = 0.05$ (b) $\theta = 0.005$ (c) $\theta = 0.001$

(d) $\theta = 0.05$ (e) $\theta = 0.005$ (f) $\theta = 0.001$

Fig. 4. Hierarchy of models at different levels of θ. Model membership is colour coded, black crosses are outliers.

3   Experimental Evaluation

This section is devoted to validate our methodology (henceforth called T-OPTICS) in several real multi-model fitting problems. All the code is implemented in Matlab on a personal computer with 2.6 GHz Intel Core i7 processor. We use the OPTICS implementation of [6] to produce reachability plots and the Matlab function `peakfinder`[1] for finding significant minima. A quantitative measure of the attained segmentation is obtained using the misclassification error (ME), that counts the percentage of misclassified points.

---

[1] www.mathworks.com/matlabcentral/fileexchange/25500-peakfinder

Video Motion Segmentation. Given a video taken by a moving camera, motion segmentation tries to identify moving object across the video. This aim is pursued by fitting subspace of dimension at most 4 to the set of features trajectories in $\mathbb{R}^{2F}$, where F is the number of frames in the video.

We use three video sequences taken from the Hopkins 155 dataset [18], *1RT2TC* from the chequerboard sequences, *cars5* which belongs to the traffic ones and *people1* which is an example of articulated motion. All the trajectories are outlier free. The *cars5* and *people1* videos, which are properly segmented by T-Linkage, are correctly segmented also by our method. The *1RT2TC* dataset is more challenging for T-Linkage, as confirmed by the experiments conducted in [12]. The tuning of a global inlier threshold τ turns out to be a thorny problem, since the subspace describing the background (red) and the one representing the moving box (blue) are close to each other with respect to their distances to the subspace of the moving glass (as can be also deduced by the reachability plot in Fig. 5d, where a small jump separates the first two valleys and an higher one separates the last object). This difficulty affects also T-linkage, which, indeed, under-segments the data (see Fig. 8b in [12]). On the contrary, as presented in Fig. 5, our methods is able to distinguish correctly the three moving objects.

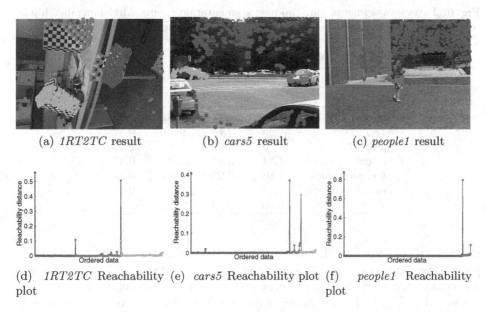

(a) *1RT2TC* result   (b) *cars5* result   (c) *people1* result

(d) *1RT2TC* Reachability (e) *cars5* Reachability plot (f) *people1* Reachability plot

Fig. 5. Video motion segmentation. Top row: segmentation results. Model membership is colour coded, no outliers. Bottom row: reachability plots.

Two Views Segmentation. In these experiments we are given a set of correspondences across two uncalibrated images. When the scene is dynamic, as in *biscuitbookbox* and in *breadcubechips*, we want to identify the moving objects by fitting fundamental matrices. If the scene is static our purpose is to identify

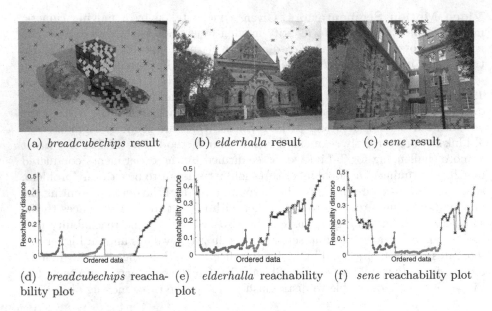

(a) *breadcubechips* result   (b) *elderhalla* result   (c) *sene* result

(d) *breadcubechips* reacha- (e) *elderhalla* reachability (f) *sene* reachability plot
bility plot   plot

Fig. 6. Two views segmentation. Top row: segmentation results. Model membership is colour coded, black crosses are outliers. Bottom row: reachability plots.

Table 1. Segmentation result: comparison between T-Linkage and T-Optics

	T-Linkage		T-Optics	
	ME (%)	Time (s)	ME (%)	Time (s)
cars5	0	11.50	0	1.09
1RT2TC	31.39	3.76	0.32	0.51
people1	0	23.92	0	2.35
biscuitbookbox	1.54	3.17	2.70	0.37
breadcubechips	0.86	2.20	3.09	0.25
elderhalla	7.51	1.65	5.14	0.15
sene	0.40	2.43	2.12	0.25

the points belonging to 3D planar surfaces by estimating multiple homographies. The latter is the case of *elderhalla* and *sene* datasets. All these datasets are contaminated by the presence of gross outliers. Segmentation results are presented in Fig. 6. In motion segmentation T-Optics succeeds in extracting the correct fundamental matrices and outliers are correctly detected after the flooding step. As plane segmentation is concerned the two dominant planes are correctly identified both in *sene* and in *elderhalla*. In the latter two additional models are detected composed by outliers which happen to lies in homographic configurations.

For each tested sequence the corresponding ME is reported in Tab. 1, where T-Optics is compared to T-Linkage, showing that in some cases T-Optics increases the performances of T-Linkage without requiring the tuning of the inlier threshold. By collating the time elapsed (in seconds) for the clustering steps of these two algorithms it is evident that T-OPTICS attains the best trade-off between accuracy and computational time. In fact, in T-Linkage every time two clusters are merged, Tanimoto distances need to be updated, whereas in OPTICS distances in $\mathcal{T}$ are computed only once, considerably reducing the computational load.

4   Conclusion

We have presented a novel approach to multi model fitting based on density analysis in Tanimoto Space. We leverage the property of Tanimoto space at different levels: at first to guide sampling towards promising models, then to recognize clusters as density-connected components in $\mathcal{T}$ and finally in order to robustly extract models from the reachability plot of the data. With respect to T-Linkage, T-OPTICS produces reliable segmentations in less time.

References

1. Ankerst, M., Breunig, M.M., Kriegel, H.P., Sander, J.: Optics: ordering points to identify the clustering structure. In: ACM Sigmod Record, pp. 49–60 (1999)
2. Chin, T., Wang, H., Suter, D.: Robust fitting of multiple structures: the statistical learning approach. In: Int. Conf. on Computer Vision, pp. 413–420 (2009)
3. Chin, T.J., Yu, J., Suter, D.: Accelerated hypothesis generation for multistructure data via preference analysis. IEEE Trans. Pattern Anal. Mach. Intell., 533–546 (2012)
4. Chum, O., Matas, J.: Randomized ransac with $T_{d,d}$ test. Image and Vision Computing **22**, 837–842 (2002)
5. Chum, O., Matas, J.: Matching with PROSAC - progressive sample consensus. In: Int. Conf. on Computer Vision and Pattern Recognition, pp. 220–226 (2005)
6. Daszykowski, M., Walczak, B., Massart, D.L.: Looking for natural patterns in analytical data, 2. Tracing local density with OPTICS. Journal of Chemical Information and Computer Sciences **3**, 500–507 (2002)
7. Elhamifar, E., Vidal, R.: Sparse subspace clustering: Algorithm, theory, and applications. IEEE Trans. Pattern Anal. Mach. Intell. **35**(11), 2765–2781 (2013)
8. Ester, M., Kriegel, H.P., Sander, J., Xu, X.: A density-based algorithm for discovering clusters in large spatial databases with noise. In: Second International Conference on Knowledge Discovery and Data Mining, pp. 226–231 (1996)
9. Isack, H., Boykov, Y.: Energy-based geometric multi-model fitting. International Journal of Computer Vision **97**(2), 123–147 (2012)
10. Kanazawa, Y., Kawakami, H.: Detection of planar regions with uncalibrated stereo using distribution of feature points. In: British Machine Vision Conf., pp. 247–256 (2004)
11. Liu, G., Lin, Z., Yan, S., Sun, J., Yu, Y., Ma, Y.: Robust recovery of subspace structures by low-rank representation. IEEE Trans. Pattern Anal. Mach. Intell, 171–184 (2013)

12. Magri, L., Fusiello, A.: T-linkage: a continuous relaxation of J-linkage for multi-model fitting. In: Conf. on Computer Vision and Pattern Recognition, June 2014
13. Meyer, F., Beucher, S.: Morphological segmentation. Journal of Visual Communication and Image Representation 1(1), 21–46 (1990)
14. Soltanolkotabi, M., Elhamifar, E., Candès, E.J.: Robust subspace clustering. Ann. Statist. 42(2), 669–699 (2014)
15. Stewart, C.V.: Bias in robust estimation caused by discontinuities and multiple structures. IEEE Trans. Pattern Anal. Mach. Intell. 19(8), 818–833 (1997)
16. Toldo, R., Fusiello, A.: Robust multiple structures estimation with J-linkage. In: Forsyth, D., Torr, P., Zisserman, A. (eds.) ECCV 2008, Part I. LNCS, vol. 5302, pp. 537–547. Springer, Heidelberg (2008)
17. Torr, P.H.S., Zisserman, A.: MLESAC: A new robust estimator with application to estimating image geometry. Comp. Vis. and Image Underst. 1, 138–156 (2000)
18. Tron, R., Vidal, R.: A benchmark for the comparison of 3D motion segmentation algorithms. In: Conf. on Computer Vision and Pattern Recognition (2007)
19. Wong, H.S., Chin, T.J., Yu, J., Suter, D.: Dynamic and hierarchical multi-structure geometric model fitting. In: Int. Conf. on Computer Vision (2011)
20. Xu, L., Oja, E., Kultanen, P.: A new curve detection method: randomized Hough transform (RHT). Pattern Recognition Letters 11(5), 331–338 (1990)
21. Zhang, W., Kosecká, J.: Nonparametric estimation of multiple structures with outliers. In: Vidal, R., Heyden, A., Ma, Y. (eds.) WDV 2005/2006. LNCS, vol. 4358, pp. 60–74. Springer, Heidelberg (2007)
22. Zuliani, M., Kenney, C.S., Manjunath, B.S.: The multiRANSAC algorithm and its application to detect planar homographies. In: Int. Conf. on Image Processing (2005)

Bag of Graphs with Geometric Relationships Among Trajectories for Better Human Action Recognition

Manel Sekma[1]([⊠]), Mahmoud Mejdoub[1,2], and Chokri Ben Amar[1]

[1] REGIM: Research Groups on Intelligent Machines, University of Sfax,
National School of Engineers (ENIS), Sfax 3038, Tunisia
manel_sekma@ieee.org
[2] Department of Computer Science, College of AlGhat, Majmaah University,
P.O. BOX 445, Al Majmaah, Riyadh 11914, Kingdom of Saudi Arabia

Abstract. This paper presents a new video representation that exploits the geometric relationships among trajectories for human action recognition. Geometric relationships are provided by applying the Delaunay triangulation method on the trajectories of each video frame. Then, graph encoding method called bag of graphs (BOG) is proposed to handle the geometrical relationships between trajectories. BOG considers local graph descriptors to learn a more discriminative graph-based codebook and to represent the video with a histogram of visual graphs. The graph-based codebook is composed of the centers of graph clusters. To define graph clusters, a classification graph technique based on the Hungarian distance is proposed. Experiments using the human action recognition datasets (Hollywood2 and UCF50) show the effectiveness of the proposed approach.

1 Introduction

Recognizing human actions in realistic uncontrolled video is a challenging problem in computer vision due to the numerous applications such as video-surveillance [1], human computer interaction [2], video indexing and retrieving [1,3,4]. In these years, many methods have been proposed on the recognition of human actions in video. Local features, coupled with the bag-of-words model (BOW), have recently become a very popular video representation for action recognition [5–19]. The BOW model [20–23] use a codebook to create a descriptor based on the visual content of a video, where the codebook is a set of visual words that represents the distribution of local features of all video. This concept can be summarized on two successive steps: coding, which assigns the local descriptors according to a codebook; and spatial pooling, which aggregates the assigned words into a single feature vector. The standard BOW model encodes only the global distribution of features, by computing a disordered histogram of occurrences of visual words, which ignore the local structural organization of features. While it is obvious that using such local structure of features should help in video action classification.

© Springer International Publishing Switzerland 2015
V. Murino and E. Puppo (Eds.): ICIAP 2015, Part I, LNCS 9279, pp. 85–96, 2015.
DOI: 10.1007/978-3-319-23231-7_8

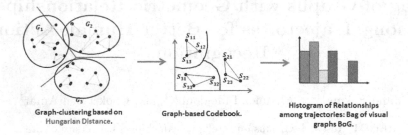

Graph-clustering based on   Graph-based Codebook.   Histogram of Relationships
Hungarian Distance.   among trajectories: Bag of visual
                                                                 graphs BoG.

Fig. 1. Visual graph quantization.

To overcome this limitation and to provide the spatial relationships between local features, we propose in this paper an approach that exploits the relationships among video trajectories based on graph encoding. To build the graphs, we apply Delaunay triangulation method [24] to link spatially near trajectories. Each graph vertex is labeled by four low level descriptors computed for its corresponding trajectory shape. Then, a graph descriptor is defined by the set of descriptors that label the graph vertices. Afterwards, to handle the relationships between trajectories, we propose a graph encoding method called bag of graphs (BOG). The BOG as illustrated in Figure 1, is an extension of the traditional BOW method that represents the video using a codebook of visual graphs instead of a visual words one.

In the first step, we quantize the graph descriptors of the video into graph clusters based on the Hungarian distance [25]. Then, the graph-based codebook is formed by the centers of the graph clusters named as visual graphs. In the next step, to describe the video we build a histogram that counts the occurrences of each visual graph of the graph-based codebook (See Figure1).

The contribution of this work can be summarized as follows: we exploit the geometric relationships of trajectories by presenting them as graph descriptors, and then using the BOG model, we build a graph-based codebook by quantifying these graph descriptors. We show how the rich information embedded in graph descriptors can improve performance over standard histogram encoding method. The rest of this paper is structured as follows.

Section 2 reviews related work. In section 3 we briefly introduce the dense trajectories that we will consider through this paper. Section 4 we give a detailed description of our approach. The experimental results are given in section 5. Finally, we conclude in section 6.

2   Related Work

Related to our work, more works perform temporal tracking of local patches and encode the temporal trajectories of frame-level local patches [8, 13, 15, 16, 26] whose performance highly depends on the performance of the local descriptors of trajectories. As has been shown in the mentioned works, when local descriptors are computed over trajectories, the performance improved considerably compared to when computed over spatio-temporal features [6]. Trajectories are widely used as features to construct the codebook of visual words. Wang et al. [8] proposed a method for trajectory shape extraction by tracking densely sampled points using the optical flow fields. To encode the shape of the trajectory, the local motion and appearance around a trajectory, four types of descriptors are computed, namely *TrajectoryShape* [8], Histograms of Optical Flow (HOF) [5], Motion Boundary Histograms (MBH) [27] and Histograms of Oriented Gradients (HOG) [28]. To encode features, the standard BOW is used. A codebook for each descriptor was built using K-means to assign each feature to the closest visual word. Based on trajectories extraction methods, several extensions to the standard BOW model have been proposed in order to build a more compact codebook. Vig et al. [29] and Mathe et al [30] have proposed to use saliency-mapping algorithms to prune background features and they focus on BOW spatio-temporal computer-based action recognition pipelines. This results in a more compact video representation. Jain et al. [16] have proposed to decompose visual motion into dominant and residual motions both for extracting trajectories and computing descriptors. They have designed a motion Divergence-Curl-Shear descriptor (DCS) to capture additional information on the local motion patterns. To encode features, they have applied the vectors of locally aggregated descriptors (VLAD) [31].

More recently, Wang et al. [26], improve dense trajectories performance [8] by taking into account camera motion to correct them. A human detector is employed to remove the inconsistent matches generated by human motion. Then, given the estimated camera motion, trajectories consistent with it are removed. To encode features, they use two features encoding methods: the standard BOW and the Fisher vector (FV) [32]. These approaches mentioned above, improve action recognition accuracy using trajectory shape methods but do not take into account the relationships between trajectories. Indeed, in order to model the relationships between trajectories, pairing techniques have been proposed. Among approaches modeling the relationships between features of dense trajectories [8], Matikainen et al. [13] have presented a method for expressing pairwise relationships between quantized features obtained by the application of the K-means algorithm. Jiang et al. [15] have proposed an approach to model the motion relationships among moving objects and the background. Their method consists in clustering the dense trajectories, and then using the cluster centers as reference points. Afterwards, the pairwise trajectory relationships are encoded by pairs of reference points.

The major problem of these methods [13,15] is that pairing visual words can leads to a quadratic number of possible pairs of visual words. Our work is different from the above techniques in that we apply quantification in the joint feature space of local graph descriptors. Then a compact graph-based codebook can be built by discovering clusters that encode the relationships between spatially close descriptors. Besides, we model more higher order spatial relationships of the video trajectories by presenting them as graph descriptors using a multi-scales triangulation.

3   Trajectory Extraction

We adopt in our approach the dense trajectory descriptors [8,26] since they showed to be an efficient video representation for action recognition. The trajectories are obtained by densely tracking sampled points using optical flow fields. First, feature points are sampled from a dense grid. Then, each feature point P_t = (x_t, y_t) at frame t is tracked to the next frame by median filtering in a dense optical flow field $F = (ut, v_t)$ as equation 1.

$$P_{t+1} = (x_{t+1}, y_{t+1}) = (x_t, y_t) + F \times \omega|_{(\bar{x}_t, \bar{y}_t)} \tag{1}$$

where F is the kernel of median filtering and $(\bar{x}_t, \bar{y}_t)$ is the rounded position of (x_t, y_t). The tracking is limited to $L = 15$ frames to avoid any drifting effect.

To encode the shape of the trajectory, the local motion and appearance around a trajectory, four types of descriptors are computed: Trajectory Shape, HOF, MBH and HOG. The Trajectory Shape descriptor encodes the shape of the trajectory represented by the normalized relative coordinates of the successive points forming the trajectory. It directly depends on the dense flow used for tracking points. HOF is computed using the orientations and magnitudes of the flow field. HOG encodes the appearance by using the intensity gradient orientations and magnitudes. MBH is designed to capture the gradient of horizontal and vertical components of the flow. The motion boundaries encode the relative pixel motion and therefore eliminate the movement of the camera, but only to some extent. Wang et al. [26] have recently improved trajectories performance by taking into account camera motion. A human detector is used to remove the inconsistent matches generated by human motion.

4   Description of the Proposed Approach

A trajectory is the path that a person moves as a function of time. The trajectory of a tracked person in a scene is often used to analyze the action or activity of the person. We propose to use graphs to encode geometric relationships among the trajectories obtained as described in section 3. The premise is that things (person or object) that are related spatially are usually dependent on each other. For instance, in the Figure 2.1, by taking into consideration the relationship between the person and the car door, we can incorporate useful scene context information in our description. For "Eat action" (Figure 2.2), by considering the relationship between the motion of the hand and the head of the person, we can enhance the person motion description. Figure 2 (b) represents the dense trajectories extraction and Figure 2 (c) represents the feature trajectories as a set of connected graphs of trajectories. In the rest, we present the overview of our proposed approach (Figure 3).

Firstly, for each video, low level descriptors (i.e., HOG, HOF, MBH and Trajectory Shape) are extracted. Afterwards, these descriptors are used to model the input video with graph descriptors. After graph extraction, a graph encoding method called bag of graphs (BOG) is performed. Finally, for classification a

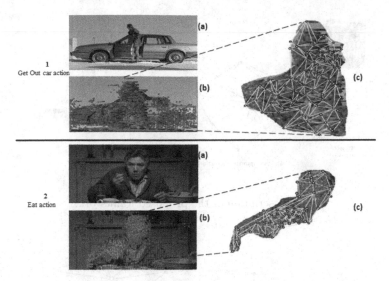

Fig. 2. Graph trajectories extraction (a) The current video frame (b) Dense trajectories; red dots indicate the trajectory shape positions in the current frame. (c) Graph of trajectories.

linear support vector machine (SVM) is used. The extraction of graph descriptors and BOG encoding method are detailed in the next subsections.

4.1   Extraction of the Graph Descriptors

The geometric relationships are provided by applying the Delaunay triangulation method [24] on the start points of the trajectories. Indeed, for each trajectory shape start point, Delaunay triangulation is applied to link neighbour trajectory points (See Figure 4). Delaunay triangulation is invariant with regard to affine transformations of image plane preserving angles: scaling, rotation and translation [33]. A collection of local graph of trajectories is constructed. Each graph vertex is labeled by the low level descriptors (i.e., HOG, HOF, MBH and Trajectory Shape) computed for its corresponding trajectory. The graph edges reflect the geometric relationships between the trajectories. A graph descriptor is defined by the set of descriptors that label the graph vertices. We notice that for each kind of low level descriptor we build a corresponding graph descriptor. Thus we obtain four graph descriptors i.e., HOG graph descriptor, HOF graph descriptor, MBH graph descriptor and Trajectory Shape graph descriptor. In this work, we adopt a multi-scale graph descriptor construction, where each scale adds more structural information. Each scale has his own set of trajectories neighbours around each given trajectory shape and then the triangulation is run separately on each scale. One scale will always contain the trajectories of all the lower scales (See Figure 4). The number of trajectories added from one scale to the upper one is fixed to three. Therefore, we define three scales, the bottom one containing only the three-nearest neighbours graph, the median

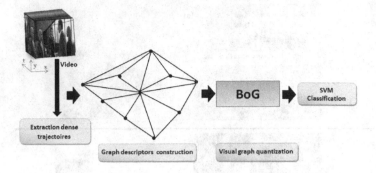

Fig. 3. Description of the proposed framework.

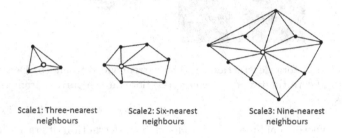

Scale1: Three-nearest   Scale2: Six-nearest   Scale3: Nine-nearest
neighbours   neighbours   neighbours

Fig. 4. The multi-scales graphs of trajectories construction: for each trajectory start point (white node), Delaunay triangulation is applied to link neighbour trajectory points (Neighbours are in black).

containing the six-nearest neighbours graph and the top one containing a graph built upon nine-nearest neighbours (See Figure 4), resulting in a more complete local structure.

4.2   Bag of Graphs

The bag of graphs (BOG) is based on the quantification of the graph descriptors using k-means clustering method. Each obtained graph cluster represents a group of similar spatial structures of trajectories. The centers of the graph clusters correspond to the visual graphs forming the graph-based codebook. The process to generate the video description uses the graph-based codebook to compute a histogram, which counts the occurrences of the visual graphs within the video (Figure 1). For either assignment or clustering, to measure the distance of each candidate graph of a video to the visual graphs of the codebook, we consider a graph matching method based on Hungarian distance [25]. The Hungarian method is an algorithm which finds an optimal assignment between two graphs, running in $O(n^3)$ time [25], where n is the size of the graph. It is used in this work to compute the distance between two graph descriptors.

Firstly, the distances between every pair of vertices in the two graph descriptors are computed. These distances form a cost matrix which defines a vertex-to-vertex assignment for a pair of graph descriptors. Then the assignment problem is solved by the Hungarian method. Considering two graph descriptors Gi and Gj, the distance $D_{Hungarian}$ between them is given by the equation 2.

$$D_{Hungarian}(Gi, Gj) = \frac{\overline{C}}{|C|} \tag{2}$$

where $\overline{C}$ is the cost of the optimum graph matching of two graph descriptors, and $|C|$ is a normalization constant that refers to the number of matching vertices. The optimum matching cost $\overline{C}$ of a pair of graph descriptors is computed by applying the Hungarian method on the distance matrix, where each element of this matrix corresponds to the distance between two vertices of graph descriptors (described in section 4.1). For instance, in the case of three sized graphs, the distance matrix is given by the equation 3, $d(v_1^i, v_2^j)$ represent the distance between vertex 1 of the graph descriptor G_i and vertex 2 of the graph descriptor G_j. This distance is computed in terms of the euclidean distance.

$$C = \begin{pmatrix} d(v_1^i, v_1^j) \ d(v_1^i, v_2^j) \ d(v_1^i, v_3^j) \\ d(v_2^i, v_1^j) \ d(v_2^i, v_2^j) \ d(v_2^i, v_3^j) \\ d(v_3^i, v_1^j) \ d(v_3^i, v_2^j) \ d(v_3^i, v_3^j) \end{pmatrix} \tag{3}$$

The procedure of clustering algorithm based on graph matching method is summarized as follows: 1) Defining from candidate graph descriptors initial graphs as graph centers of the graph clusters. 2) Assigning each graph descriptor to a given graph center by applying the Hungarian distance to compute the distance between the candidate and the center of the graph cluster. 3) Updating the graph centers by averaging the assigned descriptors with the Hungarian method to each graph center vertex 4) Repeating Steps 2) and 3) until the graph centers no longer move. We note that for each low level trajectory descriptor (HOG, HOF, MBH and Trajectory Shape) and for each graph scale, we apply the BOG pipeline. Thus, 12 final graph descriptor histograms are generated derived from the 4 kinds of low level descriptors and the 3 kinds of graph scales. We apply sum pooling and L_1 normalization for each histogram, and then we horizontally concatenate them to form the final histogram.

5   Experimental Study

In our experiments, we adopt the well-performing trajectory features used in [26]. To implement the BOG model, we train a codebook for each type of low level descriptor and for each type of graph scales separately using $100,000$ randomly selected training graphs. The size of the codebook is set to 4000. The resulting histograms of visual graphs occurrences are used as video sequence representation. An SVM with RBF χ^2 kernel is used for classification.

5.1   Action Recognition Datasets

The **Hollywood2 dataset** [34] was collected from 69 different Hollywood movies. There are 12 action classes. In total, there are 1707 action samples divided into a training set and a testing set.

The **UCF50 dataset** [35] has 50 action categories, consisting of real-world videos taken from YouTube. The actions range from general sports to daily life exercises. For all 50 categories, the videos are split into 25 groups. For each group, there are at least 4 action clips. In total, there are 6, 618 video clips.

5.2   Results

In this section we present the experimental results using Hollywood2 and UCF50 datasets. Performance values are reported as recommended by the dataset authors using the already predefined training and test split, Mean Average Precision (MAP) for Hollywood2 dataset and Average Accuracy (AA) obtained by leave-one-group-out cross-validation for UCF50 dataset.

Comparison with Different Methods of Trajectory Extraction. We evaluate the performance of our approach using different methods of trajectory extraction and using BOG and BOW models. We report the results in Table 1. *Dense Traj* shows the results using basic dense trajectories [8]. Whereas *Improved Traj* shows the results of improved trajectories [26] without human detection and *Improved Traj+HD* corresponds to the results with the human detection. We denote by *combined* the results obtained by combining BOW and BOG models.

On Hollywood2, using basic dense trajectories, we obtain a MAP equal to 58.3% with BOW model and a MAP equal to 59.6% with BOG model. We can see that this result is improved by combining BOG and BOW models, thus we achieve 60%. BOW can be considered as a specific zero scale of the BOG model where none neighbour trajectories are used. Combining BOW with BOG add richer information in the representation. This performance gain mainly owns to complementarity of these two encoding methods.

With *Improved Traj* and combination of BOW with BOG, we achieve on UCF50 89.8% and 62.8% on Hollywood2. *Improved Traj* improves the dense tra-

Table 1. Influence of different methods of trajectory extraction. (Performance values are reported in the form of MAP percentages for Hollywood2 dataset and AA percentages for UCF50 dataset.)

Trajectory methods	Hollywood2	UCF50
Dense Traj+BOW	58.3	84.8
Dense Traj+BOG	59.6	86.9
Dense Traj+combined	60	87.7
Improved Traj+combined	62.8	89.8
Improved Traj+HD+combined	64.1	90.5

jectories using camera motion estimation method, which consists to remove trajectories generated by camera motion by thresholding the displacement vectors of the trajectories in the warped flow field. If the displacement is too small, the trajectory is considered to be too similar to camera motion, and thus removed.

The results are more improved by *Improved Traj+HD* on these two datasets i.e., 64.1% and 90.5% respectively. These improvements are due to the stabilized trajectories obtained using the human detector (HD), which is employed to remove the inconsistent matches generated by human motion.

Comparison with the State-of-the Art Methods. Table 2 compare our results to the state of the art approaches. On Hollywood2 dataset, Chakra et al. [36] have introduced a spatial interest points (SIP) feature. Only distinctive SIP features are kept by suppressing unwanted background features and imposing local and temporal constraints. Their approach follows a spatial pyramid based BOW improved by a vocabulary compression technique. They have reached a MAP equal to 58.46%. Cho et al. [37] have proposed a method that selects a small number of descriptors corresponding to local motion using group sparsity and emphasizes them by the multiple kernel method. This method gives 60.5%. Wang et al. [8] have reached a MAP equal to 58.3% using the dense trajectories coupled with the BOW model. In [38] the Spatio-Temporal Pyramid (STP) representation is applied on the dense trajectories giving a MAP equal to 59.9%. The presented results [15,16,26,29,30] improve basic dense trajectories [8] in different ways. Both Vig et al. [29] and Mathe et al. [30] prune background features based on saliency-mapping algorithms, they has achieved respectively 59.4% and 61%. Jiang et al. [15] have achieved 59.5% by modeling the relationship between dense trajectory clusters. Jain ct al. [16] have given 62.5% using VLAD representation to encode the dense trajectories. Wang et al. [26] have improved dense trajectories by removing the camera motion in video to correct basic trajectories. They have reached 62.2% with the BOW model and

Table 2. Comparison with the state-of-the-art. (Performance values are reported in the form of MAP percentages for Hollywood2 dataset and AA percentages for UCF50 dataset.)

Hollywood2	MAP	UCF50	AA
Chakra et al. [36]	58.46	Kliper et al. [39]	72.7
Vig et al. [29]	59.4	Solmaz et al. [40]	73.7
Jiang et al. [15]	59.5	Reddy et al. [35]	76.9
Wang et al. (BOW) [8]	58.3	Shi et al. [42]	83.3
Cho et al. [37]	60.5	Wang et al. [38]	85.6
Mathe et al. [30]	61	Wang et al. (BOW)[26]	87.2
Jain et al. [16]	62.5	Wang et al. (FV)[26]	91.2
Wang et al. [38]	59.9		
Wang et al. (BOW)[26]	62.2		
Wang et al. (FV)[26]	64.3		
Our	**64.1**	Our	**90.5**

64.3% with FV model. The improved dense trajectories coupled with FV model outperforms BOW-based techniques. The FV is based on fitting the Gaussian Mixture Model (GMM) to the features. The obtained representation records, for each Gaussian component, mean and variance statistics along each dimension. Thus, more information is stored per visual word. But, the major inconvenient of the FV encoding method is that it provides a very large histogram ($2 \times k \times d$, where d, where d is the descriptor dimension and k is the number of Gaussian components). Despite that, we have obtained a comparable results (64.1%).

The obtained result proves that tackling the relationships between trajectories can significantly enhance the action recognition performance and thus BOG can be a good alternative to the BOW model usually used in the action recognition methods. Besides, this can encourage the investigation in future works of the possible FV encoding scheme extension by considering the topological relationships between trajectories.

On UCF50 dataset, Kliper-Gross et al. [39] have reported 72.7% by designing descriptors that capture local changes in motion directions. Solmaz et al. [40] have reached 73.7% with a GIST3D video descriptor which is an extension of the GIST descriptor [41] to video. Reddy and Shah. [35] have given 76.9% by combining the MBH descriptor with scene context information. Shi et al. [42] have reported 83.3% using randomly sampled HOG, HOF, HOG3D and MBH descriptors. Wang et al. [38] have reached 85.6% using the dense trajectories and the BOW model coupled with the STP representation. Using the improved dense trajectories method, Wang et al. [26] have reached 87.2% with the standard BOW and 91.2% with the FV encoding. As shown in table 2, our approach (90.5%) outperforms the approaches proposed in [35,38–42] by a significant margin and gives close result to Wang et al. method [26] (91.2%) which is based on FV encoding.

6   Conclusion

In this work, we have presented a new video representation that exploits the structural information from features for human action recognition. Our approach models more higher order spatial relationships of the video trajectories by presenting them as graph descriptors using a multi-scales triangulation. We have applied the BOG encoding method in order to build a compact graph-based codebook by quantifying graph descriptors. Our experimentation on two challenging datasets shows that exploiting the relationships between trajectories is important to enhance the BOW models. In future works, we expect to further improve our approach by incorporating the spatial constraints between trajectories in the encoding process of the more sophisticated FV method.

References

1. Ben Aoun, N., Elghazel, H., Ben Amar, C.: Graph modeling based video event detection. In: IIT, pp. 114–117 (2011)
2. Bouchrika, T., Zaied, M., Jemai, O., Ben Amar, C.: Neural solutions to interact with computers by hand gesture recognition. MTA, 1–27 (2013)

3. Mejdoub, M., Fonteles, L., Ben Amar, C., Antonini, M.: Embedded lattices tree: An efficient indexing scheme for content based retrieval on image databases. JVCI **20**, 145–156 (2009)
4. Ben Aoun, N., Elghazel, H., Hacid, M.-S., Ben Amar, C.: Graph aggregation based image modeling and indexing for video annotation. In: Real, P., Diaz-Pernil, D., Molina-Abril, H., Berciano, A., Kropatsch, W. (eds.) CAIP 2011, Part II. LNCS, vol. 6855, pp. 324–331. Springer, Heidelberg (2011)
5. Laptev, I., lek, M.M., Schmid, C., Rozenfeld, B.: Learning realistic human actions from movies. In: CVPR (2008)
6. Wang, H., Ullah, M.M., Klaser, A., Laptev, I., Schmid, C.: Evaluation of local spatio-temporal features for action recognition. In: BMVC (2010)
7. Klaser, A., Marsza lek, M., Schmid, C.: A spatio-temporal descriptor based on 3Dgradients. In: BMVC (2008)
8. Wang, H., Klaser, A., Schmid, C., Liu, C.L.: Action recognition by dense trajectories. In: CVPR (2011)
9. Uemura, H., Ishikawa, S., Mikolajczyk, K.: Feature tracking and motion compensation for action recognition. In: BMVC (2008)
10. Messing, R., Pal, C., Kautz, H.: Activity recognition using the velocity histories of tracked keypoints. In: ICCV (2009)
11. Wang, F., Jiang, Y.G., Ngo, C.W.: Video event detection using motion relativity and visual relatedness. In: ACM MM (2008)
12. Raptis, M., Soatto, S.: Tracklet descriptors for action modeling and video analysis. In: Daniilidis, K., Maragos, P., Paragios, N. (eds.) ECCV 2010, Part I. LNCS, vol. 6311, pp. 577–590. Springer, Heidelberg (2010)
13. Matikainen, P., Hebert, M., Sukthankar, R.: Representing pairwise spatial and temporal relations for action recognition. In: Daniilidis, K., Maragos, P., Paragios, N. (eds.) ECCV 2010, Part I. LNCS, vol. 6311, pp. 508–521. Springer, Heidelberg (2010)
14. Sun, J., Wu, X., Yan, S., Cheong, L.F., Chua, T.S., Li, J.: Hierarchical spatiotemporal context modeling for action recognition. In: CVPR (2009)
15. Jiang, Y.-G., Dai, Q., Xue, X., Liu, W., Ngo, C.-W.: Trajectory-based modeling of human actions with motion reference points. In: Fitzgibbon, A., Lazebnik, S., Perona, P., Sato, Y., Schmid, C. (eds.) ECCV 2012, Part V. LNCS, vol. 7576, pp. 425–438. Springer, Heidelberg (2012)
16. Jain, M., Jou, H., Bouthemy, P.: Better exploiting motion for better action recognition. In: CVPR (2013)
17. Dammak, M., Mejdoub, M., Ben Amar, C.: Feature Vector Approximation Based on Wavelet Network. ICAART, 394–399 (2012)
18. Mejdoub, M., Ben Amar, C.: Classification improvement of local feature vectors over the KNN algorithm. Multimedia Tools and Applications, 197–218 (2013)
19. Sekma, M., Mejdoub, M., Ben Amar, C.: Human action recognition using temporal segmentation and accordion representation. In: Wilson, R., Hancock, E., Bors, A., Smith, W. (eds.) CAIP 2013, Part II. LNCS, vol. 8048, pp. 563–570. Springer, Heidelberg (2013)
20. Sivic, J., Zisserman, A.: Video google: a text retrieval approach to object matching in videos. In: ICCV, vol. 2, pp. 1470–1477 (2003)
21. Sekma, M., Mejdoub, M., Ben Amar, C. Spatio-temporal pyramidal accordion representation for human action recognition. In: ICASSP, pp. 1270–1274 (2014)
22. Mejdoub, M., Fonteles, L., Ben Amar, C., Antonini, M.: Fast indexing method for image retrieval using tree-structured lattices. In: CBMI, pp. 365–372 (2008)

23. Mejdoub, M., Fonteles, L., Ben Amar, C., Antonini, M.: Fast algorithm for image database indexing based on lattice. In: EUSIPCO, pp. 1799–1803 (2007)
24. Hashimoto, M., Cesar Jr., R.M.: Object Detection by Keygraph Classification. In: Torsello, A., Escolano, F., Brun, L. (eds.) GbRPR 2009. LNCS, vol. 5534, pp. 223–232. Springer, Heidelberg (2009)
25. Jouili, S., Mili, I., Tabbone, S.: Attributed graph matching using local descriptions. In: Blanc-Talon, J., Philips, W., Popescu, D., Scheunders, P. (eds.) ACIVS 2009. LNCS, vol. 5807, pp. 89–99. Springer, Heidelberg (2009)
26. Wang, H. Schmid, C.: Action recognition with improved trajectories. In: ICCV (2013)
27. Dalal, N., Triggs, B., Schmid, C.: Human detection using oriented histograms of flow and appearance. In: Leonardis, A., Bischof, H., Pinz, A. (eds.) ECCV 2006. LNCS, vol. 3952, pp. 428–441. Springer, Heidelberg (2006)
28. Dalal, N., Triggs, B.: Histograms of oriented gradients for human detection. In: CVPR, June 2005
29. Vig, E., Dorr, M., Cox, D.: Space-variant descriptor sampling for action recognition based on saliency and eye movements. In: Fitzgibbon, A., Lazebnik, S., Perona, P., Sato, Y., Schmid, C. (eds.) ECCV 2012, Part VII. LNCS, vol. 7578, pp. 84–97. Springer, Heidelberg (2012)
30. Mathe, S., Sminchisescu, C.: Dynamic eye movement datasets and learnt saliency models for visual action recognition. In: Fitzgibbon, A., Lazebnik, S., Perona, P., Sato, Y., Schmid, C. (eds.) ECCV 2012, Part II. LNCS, vol. 7573, pp. 842–856. Springer, Heidelberg (2012)
31. Jgou, H., Douze, M., Schmid, C., Prez, P.: Aggregating local descriptors into a compact image representation. In: CVPR (2010)
32. Sanchez, J., Perronnin, F., Mensink, T., Verbeek, J.: Image classification with the Fisher vector: Theory and practice. IJCV, 222–245 (2013)
33. Mahboubi, A., Benois-P, J., Barba, D.: Joint tracking of polygonal and triangulated meshes of objects in moving sequences with time varying content. In: ICIP, vol. 2, pp. 403–406 (2001)
34. Marszalek, M., Laptev, I., Schmid, C.: Actions in context. In: CVPR (2009)
35. Reddy, K., Shah, M.: Recognizing 50 human action categories of web videos. In: MVA, pp 1–11 (2012)
36. B. Chakraborty, M.B. Holte, T.B. Moeslund, J. Gonzàlez, "Selective Spatio-Temporal interest points", In CVIU, pp 396–410, 2012
37. Cho, J., Lee, M., Chang, H., Oh, S.: Robust action recognition using local motion and group sparsity. Pattern Recognition, pp 1813–1825 (2014)
38. Wang, H., Klaser, A., Schmid, C., Liu, C.-L.: Dense trajectories and motion boundary descriptors for action recognition. IJCV, 60–79 (2013)
39. Kliper-Gross, O., Gurovich, Y., Hassner, T., Wolf, L.: Motion interchange patterns for action recognition in unconstrained videos. In: Fitzgibbon, A., Lazebnik, S., Perona, P., Sato, Y., Schmid, C. (eds.) ECCV 2012, Part VI. LNCS, vol. 7577, pp. 256–269. Springer, Heidelberg (2012)
40. Solmaz, B., Assari, S.M., Shah, M.: Classifying web videos using a global video descriptor. MVA, 1–13 (2012)
41. Oliva, A., Torralba, A.: Modeling the shape of the scene: A holistic representation of the spatial envelope. IJCV 42(3), 144–175 (2001)
42. Shi, F., Petriu, E., Laganiere, R.: Sampling strategies for real-time action recognition. In: CVPR (2013)

Have a SNAK. Encoding Spatial Information with the Spatial Non-alignment Kernel

Radu Tudor Ionescu[✉] and Marius Popescu

University of Bucharest, No. 14 Academiei Street, Bucharest, Romania
{raducu.ionescu,popescunmarius}@gmail.com

Abstract. The standard bag of visual words model model ignores the spatial information contained in the image, but researchers have demonstrated that the object recognition performance can be improved by including spatial information. A state of the art approach is the spatial pyramid representation, which divides the image into spatial bins. In this paper, another general approach that encodes the spatial information in a much better and efficient way is described. The proposed approach is to embed the spatial information into a kernel function termed the Spatial Non-Alignment Kernel (SNAK). For each visual word, the average position and the standard deviation is computed based on all the occurrences of the visual word in the image. These are computed with respect to the center of the object, which is determined with the help of the objectness measure. The pairwise similarity of two images is then computed by taking into account the difference between the average positions and the difference between the standard deviations of each visual word in the two images. In other words, the SNAK kernel includes the spatial distribution of the visual words in the similarity of two images. Furthermore, various kernel functions can be plugged into the SNAK framework. Object recognition experiments are conducted to compare the SNAK framework with the spatial pyramid representation, and to assess the performance improvements for various state of the art kernels on two benchmark data sets. The empirical results indicate that SNAK significantly improves the object recognition performance of every evaluated kernel. Compared to the spatial pyramid, SNAK improves performance while consuming less space and time. In conclusion, SNAK can be considered a good candidate to replace the widely-used spatial pyramid representation.

Keywords: Kernel method · Spatial information · Bag of visual words

1 Introduction

Computer vision researchers have recently developed sophisticated methods for object class recognition, image retrieval and related tasks. Among the state of the art models are discriminative classifiers using the *bag of visual words* (BOVW) representation [18,20] and spatial pyramid matching [12], generative models [6] or part-based models [11]. The BOVW model, which represents an image as a

© Springer International Publishing Switzerland 2015
V. Murino and E. Puppo (Eds.): ICIAP 2015, Part I, LNCS 9279, pp. 97–108, 2015.
DOI: 10.1007/978-3-319-23231-7_9

histogram of local features, has demonstrated impressive levels of performance for image categorization [20], image retrieval [15], or related tasks. The standard bag of words model ignores spatial relationships between image features, but researchers have demonstrated that the performance can be improved by including spatial information [12,16,19].

This work presents a novel approach to include spatial information in a simple and effective manner. The proposed approach is to embed the spatial information into a kernel function termed the *Spatial Non-Alignment Kernel*, or SNAK for short. The proposed kernel works by including the spatial distribution of the visual words in the similarity of two images. For each visual word in an image, the average position and the standard deviation is computed based on all the occurrences of the visual word in that image. These statistics are computed with respect to the center of the object, which is determined with the help of the objectness measure [1]. Then, the pairwise similarity of two images can be computed by taking into account the distance between the average positions and the distance between the standard deviations of each visual word in the two images. This simple approach has two important advantages. First of all, the feature space increases with a constant factor, which means that it uses less space than other state of the art approaches [12]. Second of all, the SNAK framework can be applied to various kernel functions, thus being a rather general approach. Object recognition experiments are conducted in order to assess the performance of different kernels based on the SNAK framework versus the spatial pyramid framework, on two benchmark data sets of images, more precisely, the Pascal VOC data set and the Birds data set. The performance of the kernels is evaluated for various vocabulary dimensions. In all the experiments, the SNAK framework shows a better recognition accuracy compared to the spatial pyramid.

The paper is organized as follows. Related work on frameworks for including spatial information is discussed in Section 2. The Spatial Non-Alignment Kernel is described in Section 3. All the experiments are presented in Section 4. Finally, the conclusions are drawn in Section 5.

2   Related Work

Several approaches of adding spatial information to the BOVW model have been proposed [9,10,12,16,19]. The spatial pyramid [12] is one of the most popular frameworks of using the spatial information. In this framework, the image is gradually divided into spatial bins. The frequency of each visual word is recorded in a histogram for each bin. The final feature vector for the image is a concatenation of these histograms. To reduce the dimension of the feature representation induced by the spatial pyramid, researchers have tried to encode the spatial information at a lower level [9,16]. Spatial Coordinate Coding scheme [9] applies spatial location and angular information at descriptor level. The authors of [10] model the spatial location of the image regions assigned to visual words using Mixture of Gaussians models, which is related to a soft-assign version of the spatial pyramid representation. A similar approach is proposed in [16], but the change is made at the low level feature representation, enabling the model to be extended to other encoding methods. It is worth mentioning that in [10], the spatial mean and the variance of image regions associated with visual words are used to define a Mixture of Gaussians model. In the SNAK framework, the spatial mean and the standard deviation of visual words are also used, but in a completely different way, by embedding them into a kernel function. Another way of using spatial information is to consider the location of objects in the image, which can be determined either by using manually annotated bounding boxes [19] or by using the objectness measure [8,16].

3 Spatial Non-Alignment Kernel

A simple yet powerful framework for including spatial information into the BOVW model is presented next. This framework is termed *Spatial Non-Alignment Kernel* (SNAK) and it is based on measuring the spatial non-alignment of visual words in two images using a kernel function. In the SNAK framework, additional information for each visual word needs to be stored first in the feature representation of an image. More precisely, the average position and the standard deviation of the spatial distribution of all the descriptors that belong to a visual word are computed. These statistics are computed independently for each of the two image coordinates. The SNAK feature vector includes the average coordinates and the standard deviation of a visual word together with the frequency of the visual word, resulting in a feature space that is 5 times greater than the original feature space corresponding to the histogram representation. The size of the feature space is identical to a spatial pyramid based on two levels, but it is roughly 4 times smaller than a spatial pyramid based on three levels.

Let U represent the SNAK feature vector of an image. For each visual word at index i, U will contain 5-tuples as defined below:

$$u(i) = \left(h^u(i), m_x^u(i), m_y^u(i), s_x^u(i), s_y^u(i) \right).$$

The first component of $u(i)$ represents the visual word's frequency. The following two components ($m_x(i)$ and $m_y(i)$) represent the mean (or average) position of the i-th visual word on each of the two coordinates x and y, respectively. The last two components ($s_x(i)$ and $s_y(i)$) represent the standard deviation of the i-th visual word with respect to the two coordinates x and y. If the visual word i does not appear in the image ($h^u(i) = 0$), the last four components are undefined. In fact, these four values are not being used at all, if $h^u(i) = 0$.

Using the above notations, the SNAK kernel between two feature vectors U and V can be defined as follows:

$$k_{\text{SNAK}}(U, V) = \sum_{i=1}^{n} \exp\left(-c_1 \cdot \Delta_{mean}(u(i), v(i))\right) \cdot \exp\left(-c_2 \cdot \Delta_{std}(u(i), v(i))\right),$$

$$(1)$$

where n is the number of visual words, c_1 and c_2 are two parameters with positive values, $u(i)$ is the 5-tuple corresponding to the i-th visual word from U, $v(i)$ is the 5-tuple corresponding to the i-th visual word from V, and Δ_{mean} and Δ_{std} are defined as follows:

$$\Delta_{mean}(u, v) = \begin{cases} (m_x^u - m_x^v)^2 + (m_y^u - m_y^v)^2, & \text{if } h^u, h^v > 0 \\ \infty, & \text{otherwise} \end{cases}$$

$$\Delta_{std}(u, v) = \begin{cases} (s_x^u - s_x^v)^2 + (s_y^u - s_y^v)^2, & \text{if } h^u, h^v > 0 \\ \infty, & \text{otherwise} \end{cases}$$

where m_x, m_y, s_x, and s_y are components of the 5-tuples u and v. If a visual word does not appear in at least one of the two compared images, its contribution to k_{SNAK} is zero, since Δ_{mean} and Δ_{std} are infinite.

It can be easily demonstrated that SNAK is a kernel function. Indeed, the proof that k_{SNAK} is a kernel comes out immediately from the following observation. For a given visual word i and two 5-tuples u and v, the equations below represent two RBF kernels:

$$\exp\left(-c_1 \cdot \Delta_{mean}(u(i), v(i))\right)$$
$$\exp\left(-c_2 \cdot \Delta_{std}(u(i), v(i))\right),$$

and their product is also a kernel. By summing up the RBF kernels corresponding to all the 5-tuples inside the SNAK feature vectors U and V, the k_{SNAK} function is obtained. From the additive property of kernel functions [17], it results that k_{SNAK} is also a kernel function.

An interesting remark is that k_{SNAK} can be seen as a sum of separate kernel functions, each corresponding to a visual word that appears in both images. This is a fairly simple approach, that can be easily generalized and combined with many other kernel functions. The following equation shows how to combine SNAK with another kernel k^* that takes into account the frequency of visual words:

$$k_{SNAK}^*(U, V) = \sum_{i=1}^{n} k^*(h^u(i), h^v(i)) \cdot \tag{2}$$
$$\cdot \exp\left(-c_1 \cdot \Delta_{mean}(u(i), v(i))\right) \cdot \exp\left(-c_2 \cdot \Delta_{std}(u(i), v(i))\right).$$

Equation (2) can be used to combine SNAK with other kernels at the visual word level, individually. Certainly, using the above equation, SNAK can be combined with kernels such as the linear kernel, the Hellinger's kernel, or the intersection kernel. Moreover, being a kernel function, SNAK can be combined with any other kernel using various approaches specific to kernel methods, such as multiple kernel learning [7].

3.1   Translation and Size Invariance

Intuitively, the SNAK kernel measures the distance between the average positions of the same visual word in two images. SNAK can be used to encode spatial information for various classification tasks, but some improvements based on

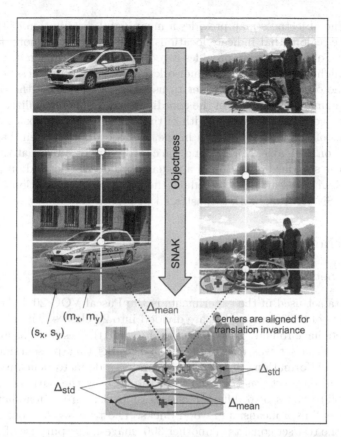

Fig. 1. The spatial similarity of two images computed with the SNAK framework. First, the center of mass is computed according to the objectness map. The average position and the standard deviation of the spatial distribution of each visual word are computed next. The images are aligned according to their centers, and the SNAK kernel is computed by summing the distances between the average positions and the standard deviations of each visual word in the two images.

task-specific information are possible. One such example is object class recognition. If the objects appear in roughly the same locations, the SNAK approach would work fine. However, this restriction may be often violated in practice. Any object can appear in any part of the image, and a visual word describing some part of the object can therefore appear in a different location in each image. Due to this fact, SNAK is not invariant to translations of the object. If the object's location in each image is known a priori, the average position of the visual word can be computed with respect to the object's location, by translating the origin of the coordinate system over the center of the object. The exact location of the object is not known in practice, but it can be approximated using the *objectness* measure [1]. This measure quantifies how likely it is for an image window to contain an object. By sampling a reasonable number of windows and by accumulating their probabilities, a pixelwise objectness map of the image can be produced. The objectness map provides a meaningful distribution of the (interesting) image regions that indicate locations of objects. Furthermore, the center of mass of the objectness map provides a good indication of where the center of the object might be. The SNAK framework employs the objectness measure to determine the object's center in order to use it as the origin of the coordinate system of the image. The range of the coordinate system is normalized by dividing the x-axis coordinates by the width of the image and the y-axis coordinates by the height of the image. For each image, the coordinate system has a range from -1 to 1 on each axis. Normalizing the coordinates ensures that the average position or the standard deviation of a visual word do not depend on the image size, and it is a necessary step to reduce the effect of size variation in a set of images. The SNAK framework is illustrated in Figure 1.

4   Experiments

4.1   Data Sets Description

The first data set used in the experiments is the Pascal VOC 2007 data set [5], which consists of 9963 images that are divided into 20 classes. The training and validation sets have roughly 2500 images each, while the test set has about 5000 images. This data set was also used in other works that present methods to encode spatial information [10,16], thus becoming a de facto benchmark.

The second data set was collected from the Web by the authors of [11] and consists of 600 images of 6 different classes of birds: egrets, mandarin ducks, snowy owls, puffins, toucans, and wood ducks. The training set consists of 300 images and the test set consists of another 300 images. The purpose of using this data set is to assess the behavior of the SNAK framework in the context of fine-grained object recognition. The Birds data set is available at http://www-cvr.ai.uiuc.edu/ponce_grp/data/.

4.2   Implementation and Evaluation Procedure

In the BOVW model used in this work, features are detected using a regular grid across the input image. At each interest point, a SIFT feature [14] is computed. This approach is known as dense SIFT [3,4]. Next, SIFT descriptors are vector quantized into visual words and a vocabulary (or codebook) of visual words is obtained. The vector quantization process is done by k-means clustering [13], and visual words are stored in a randomized forest of k-d trees [15] to reduce search cost. The frequency of each visual word is then recorded in a histogram which represents the final feature vector of the image. A kernel method is used for training.

Three kernels are proposed for evaluation, namely the L_2-normalized linear kernel, the L_1-normalized Hellinger's kernel, and the L_1-normalized intersection kernel. The norms of the kernels are chosen such that the γ-homogeneous kernels are L_γ-normalized. It is worth mentioning that all these kernels are used in the dual form, that implies using the *kernel trick* to directly build kernel matrices of pairwise similarities between samples. An important remark is that the intersection kernel was particularly chosen because it yields very good results in combination with the spatial pyramid, and it might work equally well in the SNAK framework. The kernels proposed for evaluation are based on four different representations, three of which include spatial information. The goal of the experiments is to compare the bag of words representation with a spatial pyramid based on two levels, a spatial pyramid based on three levels, and the SNAK feature vectors. The spatial pyramid based on two levels combines the full image with 2×2 bins, and the spatial pyramid based on three levels combines the full image with 2×2 and 4×4 bins. In the SNAK framework, the linear kernel, the Hellinger's kernel, and the intersection kernel are used in turn as k^* in Equation (2). Note that SNAK can also be indirectly compared with the approach described in [10], since the results reported in [10] are very similar to the spatial pyramid based on three levels.

The training is always done using Support Vector Machines (SVM). In the second experiment, the SVM classifier based on the *one versus all* scheme is used for the multi-class task. The objectness measure is trained on 50 images that are neither from the Pascal VOC data set nor from the Birds data set. The objectness map is obtained by sampling 1000 windows using the NMS sampling procedure [2].

The experiments are conducted using 500, 1000, and 3000 visual words, respectively. The evaluation procedure for the first experiment follows the Pascal VOC benchmark. The qualitative performance of the learning model is measured by using the classifier score to rank all the test images. In order to represent the retrieval performance by a single number, the mean average precision (mAP) is often computed. The mean average precision as defined by TREC is used in the Pascal VOC experiment. This is the average of the precision observed each time a new positive sample is recalled. For the second experiment, the classification accuracy is used to evaluate the various kernels and spatial representations.

4.3   Parameter Tuning

The SNAK framework takes both the average position and the standard deviation of each visual word into account. In a set of preliminary experiments performed on the Birds data set, the two statistics were used independently to determine which one brings a more significant improvement. The empirical results demonstrated that they roughly achieve similar accuracy improvements, having an almost equal contribution to the proposed framework. Consequently, a decision was made to use the same value for the two constants c_1 and c_2 from Equation (1). Only five values in the range 1 to 100 were chosen for preliminary evaluation. The best results were obtained with $c_1 = c_2 = 10$, while choices like 5 or 50 were only $2-3\%$ behind. Finally, a decision was made to use $c_1 = c_2 = 10$ in the experiments reported next, but it is very likely that better results can be obtained by fine-tuning the parameters c_1 and c_2 on each data set. An important remark is that c_1 and c_2 were tuned on the Birds data set, but the same choice

Table 1. Mean AP on Pascal VOC 2007 data set for different representations that encode spatial information into the BOVW model. For each representation, results are reported using several kernels and vocabulary dimensions. The best AP for each vocabulary dimension and each kernel is highlighted in bold.

Representation	Vocabulary	Linear L_2	Hellinger's L_1	Intersection L_1
Histogram	500 words	28.59%	39.06%	39.11%
Histogram	1000 words	28.71%	42.28%	42.99%
Histogram	3000 words	28.96%	45.23%	46.97%
Spatial Pyramid (2 levels)	500 words	31.17%	44.21%	45.17%
Spatial Pyramid (2 levels)	1000 words	31.38%	46.94%	48.27%
Spatial Pyramid (2 levels)	3000 words	31.85%	49.21%	50.78%
Spatial Pyramid (3 levels)	500 words	38.49%	45.20%	47.66%
Spatial Pyramid (3 levels)	1000 words	39.59%	47.87%	49.85%
Spatial Pyramid (3 levels)	3000 words	40.97%	50.37%	51.87%
SNAK	500 words	**42.56%**	**47.39%**	**49.75%**
SNAK	1000 words	**44.69%**	**49.54%**	**51.99%**
SNAK	3000 words	**45.95%**	**52.49%**	**54.05%**

was used on the Pascal VOC data set, without testing other values. Good results on Pascal VOC might indicate that c_1 and c_2 do not necessarily depend on the data set, but rather on the normalization procedure used for the spatial coordinate system. It is interesting to note that the two coordinates are independently normalized according to Section 3.1, resulting in small distortions along the axes. Two other methods of size-normalizing the coordinate space without introducing distortions were also evaluated. One is based on dividing both coordinates by the diagonal of the image, and the other by the mean of the width and height of the image. Perhaps surprisingly, these have produced lower average precision scores on a subset of the Pascal VOC data set. For instance, size-normalizing by the mean of the width and height gives a mAP score that is roughly 0.5% lower than normalizing each axis independently by the width and height.

In the Pascal VOC experiment, the validation set is used to validate the regularization parameter C of the SVM algorithm. In the Birds experiment, the parameter C was adjusted such that it brings as much regularization as possible, while giving just enough room to learn the entire training set with 100% accuracy.

4.4   Pascal VOC Experiment

The first experiment is on the Pascal VOC 2007 data set. For each of the 20 classes, the data set provides a training set, a validation set and a test set. After validating the regularization parameter of the SVM algorithm on the validation set, the classifier is trained one more time on both the training and the validation sets, that have roughly 5000 images together.

Table 1 presents the mean AP of various BOVW models obtained on the test set, by combining different spatial representations, vocabulary dimensions, and kernels. For each model, the reported mAP represents the average score on all the 20 classes of the Pascal VOC data set. The results presented in Table 1 clearly indicate that spatial information significantly improves the performance of the

BOVW model. This observation holds for every kernel and every vocabulary dimension. Indeed, the spatial pyramid based on two levels shows a performance increase that ranges between 3% (for the linear kernel) and 6% (for intersection kernel). As expected, the spatial pyramid based on three levels further improves the performance, especially for the linear kernel. When the 4×4 bins are added into the spatial pyramid, the mAP of the linear kernel grows by roughly $7 - 8\%$, while the mAP scores of the other two kernels increase by $1 - 2\%$. Among the three kernels based on spatial pyramids, the best mAP scores are obtained by the intersection kernel, which was previously reported to work best in combination with the spatial pyramid [12].

The best results on the Pascal VOC data set are obtained by the SNAK framework. Indeed, the results are even better than the spatial pyramid based on three levels, which uses a representation that is more than 4 times greater than the SNAK representation. The mAP scores of the Hellinger's and the intersection kernels based on SNAK are roughly 2% better than the mAP scores of the same kernels combined with the spatial pyramid based on three levels. On the other hand, a $4 - 5\%$ growth of the mAP score can be observed in case of the linear kernel. Among the three kernels, the best results are obtained by the intersection kernel. When the intersection kernel is combined with SNAK, the best overall mAP score is obtained, that is 54.05%. This is 2.18% better than the intersection kernel combined with the spatial pyramid based on three levels.

Overall, the empirical results indicate that the SNAK approach is significantly better than the state of the art spatial pyramid framework, in terms of recognition accuracy. Perhaps this comes as a surprising result given that the images from the Pascal VOC data set usually contain multiple objects, and that SNAK implicitly assumes that there is a single relevant object in the scene, due to the use of the objecteness measure. The SNAK framework also provides a more compact representation, which brings improvements in terms of space and time over a spatial pyramid based on three levels, for example.

4.5   Birds Experiment

The second experiment is on the Birds data set. Table 2 presents the classification accuracy of the BOVW model based on various representations that include spatial information. The results are reported on the test set, by combining different vocabulary dimensions and kernels.

The results of the SNAK framework on this data set are consistent with the results reported in the previous experiment, in that the SNAK framework outperforms again the spatial pyramid representation. The spatial pyramid based on two levels improves the classification accuracy of the standard BOVW model by $3 - 4\%$. On top of this, the spatial pyramid based on three levels further improves the performance. Significant improvements can be observed for the linear kernel and for the intersection kernel.

The spatial pyramid based on two levels shows little improvements over the histogram representation for the vocabulary of 3000 words, and more significant improvements for the vocabulary of 500 words. The certain fact is that the

Table 2. Classification accuracy on the Birds data set for different representations that encode spatial information into the BOVW model. For each representation, results are reported using several kernels and vocabulary dimensions. The best accuracy for each vocabulary dimension and each kernel is highlighted in bold.

Representation	Vocabulary	Linear L_2	Hellinger's L_1	Intersection L_1
Histogram	500 words	59.67%	72.00%	70.00%
Histogram	1000 words	64.67%	78.33%	71.00%
Histogram	3000 words	69.33%	80.33%	74.67%
Spatial Pyramid (2 levels)	500 words	62.67%	75.67%	74.00%
Spatial Pyramid (2 levels)	1000 words	66.67%	79.33%	74.33%
Spatial Pyramid (2 levels)	3000 words	69.67%	81.00%	77.00%
Spatial Pyramid (3 levels)	500 words	68.33%	76.67%	76.00%
Spatial Pyramid (3 levels)	1000 words	70.33%	**80.67%**	78.00%
Spatial Pyramid (3 levels)	3000 words	**73.00%**	82.67%	79.67%
SNAK	500 words	**69.33%**	**79.00%**	**76.33%**
SNAK	1000 words	**71.67%**	80.33%	**78.67%**
SNAK	3000 words	72.33%	**83.67%**	**81.33%**

spatial information helps to improve the classification accuracy on this data set, but the best approach seems to be the SNAK framework. With only two exceptions, the SNAK framework gives better results than the spatial pyramid based on three levels. Compared to the spatial pyramid based on two levels, which has the same number of features, the SNAK approach is roughly $3 - 5\%$ better. An interesting observation is that the intersection kernel does not yield the best overall results as in the previous experiment, but it seems to gain a lot from the spatial information. For instance, the accuracy of the intersection kernel grows from 71.00% with histograms to 78.67% with SNAK, when the underlying vocabulary has 1000 words. The best accuracy (83.67%) is obtained by the Hellinger's kernel combined with SNAK, using a vocabulary of 3000 visual words. When it comes to fine-grained object class recognition, the overall empirical results on the Birds data set indicate that the SNAK framework is more accurate than the spatial pyramid approach.

5 Conclusion and Future Work

This paper described an approach to improve the BOVW model by encoding spatial information in a more efficient way than spatial pyramids, by using a kernel function. More precisely, SNAK includes the spatial distribution of the visual words in the similarity of two images. Object recognition experiments were conducted to compare the SNAK approach with the spatial pyramid framework, which is the most popular approach to include spatial information into the BOVW model. The empirical results presented in this paper indicate that the SNAK framework can improve the object recognition accuracy over the spatial pyramid representation. Considering that SNAK uses a more compact representation, the results become even more impressive. In conclusion, SNAK has all the ingredients to become a viable alternative to the spatial pyramid approach.

In this work, the objectness measure was used to add some level of translation invariance into the SNAK framework. In future work, the SNAK framework can be further improved by including ways of obtaining scale and rotation invariance. Ground truth information about an object's scale can be obtained from manually annotated bounding boxes. A first step would be to use such bounding boxes to determine if it helps to compare objects at the same scale with the SNAK kernel. Another direction, is to extend the SNAK framework to use the valuable information offered by objectness [1], which is only barely used in the current framework.

Acknowledgments. The work of Radu Tudor Ionescu was supported from the European Social Fund under Grant POSDRU/159/1.5/S/137750.

References

1. Alexe, B., Deselaers, T., Ferrari, V.: What is an object?. In: Proceedings of CVPR, pp. 73–80 (June 2010)
2. Alexe, B., Deselaers, T., Ferrari, V.: Measuring the objectness of image windows. IEEE Transactions on Pattern Analysis and Machine Intelligence **34**(11), 2189–2202 (2012)
3. Bosch, A., Zisserman, A., Munoz, X.: Image Classification using random forests and ferns. In: Proceedings of ICCV, pp. 1–8 (2007)
4. Dalal, N., Triggs, B.: Histograms of oriented gradients for human detection. In: Proceedings of CVPR, vol. 1, pp. 886–893 (2005)
5. Everingham, M., van Gool, L., Williams, C.K., Winn, J., Zisserman, A.: The Pascal Visual Object Classes (VOC) Challenge. International Journal of Computer Vision **88**(2), 303–338 (2010)
6. Fei-Fei, L., Fergus, R., Perona, P.: Learning generative visual models from few training examples: An incremental Bayesian approach tested on 101 object categories. Computer Vision and Image Understanding **106**(1), 59–70 (2007)
7. Gonen, M., Alpaydin, E.: Multiple Kernel Learning Algorithms. Journal of Machine Learning Research **12**, 2211–2268 (2011)
8. Ionescu, R.T., Popescu, M.: Objectness to improve the bag of visual words model. In: Proceedings of ICIP, pp. 3238–3242 (2014)
9. Koniusz, P., Mikolajczyk, K.: Spatial coordinate coding to reduce histogram representations, dominant angle and colour pyramid match. In: Proceedings of ICIP, pp. 661–664 (2011)
10. Krapac, J., Verbeek, J., Jurie, F.: Modeling spatial layout with fisher vectors for image categorization. In: Proceedings of ICCV, pp. 1487–1494 (November 2011)
11. Lazebnik, S., Schmid, C., Ponce, J.: A maximum entropy framework for part-based texture and object recognition. In: Proceedings of ICCV, vol. 1, pp. 832–838 (2005)
12. Lazebnik, S., Schmid, C., Ponce, J.: Beyond bags of features: spatial pyramid matching for recognizing natural scene categories. In: Proceedings of CVPR, vol. 2, pp. 2169–2178 (2006)
13. Leung, T., Malik, J.: Representing and Recognizing the Visual Appearance of Materials using Three-dimensional Textons. International Journal of Computer Vision **43**(1), 29–44 (2001)
14. Lowe, D.G.: Object recognition from local scale-invariant features. In: Proceedings of ICCV, vol. 2, pp. 1150–1157 (1999)

15. Philbin, J., Chum, O., Isard, M., Sivic, J., Zisserman, A.: Object retrieval with large vocabularies and fast spatial matching. In: Proceedings of CVPR, pp. 1–8 (2007)
16. Sánchez, J., Perronnin, F., de Campos, T.: Modeling the spatial layout of images beyond spatial pyramids. Pattern Recognition Letters **33**(16), 2216–2223 (2012)
17. Shawe-Taylor, J., Cristianini, N.: Kernel Methods for Pattern Analysis. Cambridge University Press (2004)
18. Sivic, J., Russell, B.C., Efros, A.A., Zisserman, A., Freeman, W.T.: Discovering objects and their localization in images. In: Proceedings of ICCV, pp. 370–377 (2005)
19. Uijlings, J., Smeulders, A., Scha, R.: What is the spatial extent of an object?. In: Proceedings of CVPR, pp. 770–777 (2009)
20. Zhang, J., Marszalek, M., Lazebnik, S., Schmid, C.: Local Features and Kernels for Classification of Texture and Object Categories: A Comprehensive Study. International Journal of Computer Vision **73**(2), 213–238 (2007)

Convolved Multi-output Gaussian Processes for Semi-Supervised Learning

Hernán Darío Vargas Cardona[✉], Mauricio A. Álvarez, and Álvaro A. Orozco

Department of Electrical Engineering, Universidad Tecnológica de Pereira,
Pereira, Colombia
{hernan.vargas,malvarez,aaog}@utp.edu.co

Abstract. Multi-output learning has become in a strong field of research in machine learning community during the last years. This setup considers the occurrence of multiple and related tasks in real-world problems. Another approach called semi-supervised learning (SSL) is the middle point between the case where all training samples are labeled (supervised learning) and the case where all training samples are unlabeled (unsupervised learning). In many applications it is difficult or impossible to access to fully labeled data. At these scenarios, SSL becomes a very useful methodology to achieve successful results, either for regression or for classification. In this paper, we propose the use of kernels for vector-valued functions for Gaussian process multi-output regression in the context of semi-supervised learning. We combine a Gaussian process with process convolution (PC) type of covariance function with techniques commonly used in semi-supervised learning like the Expectation-Maximization (EM) algorithm, and Graph-based regularization. We test our proposed method in two widely used databases for multi-output regression. Results obtained by our method exhibit a better performance compared to supervised methods based on Gaussian processes in scenarios where there are not available a good amount of labeled data.

Keywords: Gaussian processes · Multi-output learning · Semi-supervised learning

1 Introduction

Gaussian processes (GP) have become the natural choice for non-linear regression in machine learning. Thanks to their flexibility they have been used also for classification, and in different areas of semi-supervised and unsupervised learning [1]. Extending the Gaussian process framework to the setup of vector-valued functions has been a theme of recent interest within the Gaussian process machine learning community. This interest has been triggered due to the development of a closely related area known as multi-task learning [2]. The aim in multi-task learning is to develop models capable of capturing the similarity between tasks (or outputs) and hence leverage any information transfer between them [3], [4].

© Springer International Publishing Switzerland 2015
V. Murino and E. Puppo (Eds.): ICIAP 2015, Part I, LNCS 9279, pp. 109–118, 2015.
DOI: 10.1007/978-3-319-23231-7_10

Initial attempts to extend Gaussian processes to the multiple-output setting assumed that the outputs were conditionally independent given a kernel matrix. For including correlations between the outputs, a common prior over the kernel parameters would need to be imposed [5,6]. More recently, the focus has been in developing suitable covariance or kernel functions for multiple outputs. Among these type of covariances, the linear model of corregionalization (LMC) and the process convolutions (PC) are powerful alternatives [7], being the LMC a particular case of the PC [7].

The LMC and the PC have been used successfully for multi-output regression [4,8], and multi-output classification [9,10], spanning a broad spectrum of the supervised learning field. However, the framework of multi-output Gaussian processes has been less studied in the context of semi-supervised learning. In these situations, getting labels for each observation point may required an skilled human expert or the cost of a complex experiment, so in a practical setting, we only have access to some labeled data, and plenty of unlabeled data. Also, an important issue is under what conditions unlabeled data can be used to improve the performance. The authors of [11,12] showed that when the assumed probabilistic model matches the data generating distribution, the reduction in variance leads to an improved accuracy. Nevertheless, when the assumed probabilistic model does not match the true data generating distribution, unlabeled data can be detrimental to accuracy. To avoid this problem, [13,14] presented approaches to perform semi-supervised versions of classical linear discriminant analysis and nearest mean classifier, where no additional assumptions are made to link information coming from labeled and unlabeled data together.

In this paper, we propose the use of kernels for vector-valued functions for Gaussian process multi-output regression in the context of semi-supervised learning. We combine a Gaussian process with PC-type of covariance function with techniques commonly used in semi-supervised learning like the Expectation-Maximization (EM) algorithm, and Graph-based regularization [15,16].

Although different multi-task learning methods have been developed for the semi-supervised setting [17,18], the idea of using Gaussian processes in this context has received less attention. To our knowledge, the only papers dealing with Gaussian processes for multi-outputs in semi-supervised learning are [19] and [20]. Our proposed model is different to [19] because we truly use a kernel for vectorial data, whereas [19] uses a common prior for the parameters of the kernel matrix of conditionally independent GPs. We are different to [20] because our interest is in doing multi-output regression, whereas [20] performs multi-output classification. Also, in this paper we use the process convolutions to build the multi-output Gaussian process, while [20] uses the intrinsic model of corregionalization, which is a particular version of process convolutions.

We perform experiments over two commonly used multi-task regression datasets, namely, the school score prediction dataset, and the SARCOS dataset. Our model performs better than a supervised single output regressor (SOR) and a supervised multi-output regressor (SMOR), both based on Gaussian processes. Finally, we compare favorably when looking at the results reported in [19].

2   Multi-output Gaussian Processes

A general method for multiple output Gaussian processes describes D outputs or tasks $\{f_d(\mathbf{x})\}_{d=1}^D$, by convolution integrals of latent functions $\{u_q^i(\mathbf{x})\}_{q=1,i=1}^{Q,R_q}$, with smoothing kernels $\{G_{d,q}^i(\mathbf{x} - \mathbf{z})\}_{d=1,q=1,i=1}^{D,Q,R_q}$,

$$f_d(\mathbf{x}) = \sum_{q=1}^{Q} \sum_{i=1}^{R_q} \int G_{d,q}^i(\mathbf{x} - \mathbf{z}) u_q^i(\mathbf{z}) d\mathbf{z}.$$

Assuming that the latent functions $u_q^i(\mathbf{x})$ are independent Gaussian processes with covariance functions $k_q(\mathbf{x}, \mathbf{x}')$,[1] the outputs $f_d(\mathbf{x})$ form a joint Gaussian process with covariance function $k_{f_d, f_d'}(\mathbf{x}, \mathbf{x}')$ with $d, d' = 1, \ldots, D$, given by

$$k_{f_d, f_d'}(\mathbf{x}, \mathbf{x}') = \sum_{q=1}^{Q} \sum_{i=1}^{R_q} \int \int G_{d,q}^i(\mathbf{x} - \mathbf{z}) G_{d',q}^i(\mathbf{x}' - \mathbf{z}') k_q(\mathbf{z}, \mathbf{z}') d\mathbf{z} d\mathbf{z}'.$$

The kernel construction above is sometimes refer to as a process convolution [21]. We call this covariance function the Convolved Multiple Output Covariance or CMOC.

For constructing the CMOC, we use Gaussian kernels for $G_{d,q}^i(\mathbf{x} - \mathbf{z})$, and $k_q(\mathbf{x}, \mathbf{x}')$, leading to a closed form solution for $k_{f_d, f_d'}(\mathbf{x}, \mathbf{x}')$, that we will refer to as the **gg** kernel. The details for this construction can be found in [8]. We can also use a Gaussian kernel for each $G_{d,q}^i(\mathbf{x} - \mathbf{z})$, and a Dirac delta function for $k_q(\mathbf{x}, \mathbf{x}')$,[2] which also leads to a closed form solution for $k_{f_d, f_d'}(\mathbf{x}, \mathbf{x}')$. We refer to this alternative as the **gw** kernel. The details for this construction can be found in [22].

In a regression setting, we assume that the actual data that we observe $\{y_d(\mathbf{x})\}_{d=1}^D$ is contaminated with noise,

$$y_d(\mathbf{x}) = f_d(\mathbf{x}) + w_d(\mathbf{x}),$$

where the processes $\{w_d(\mathbf{x})\}_{d=1}^D$ are white Gaussian noise processes, with covariance functions $\sigma_d^2 \delta(\mathbf{x}, \mathbf{x}')$.

We use $\boldsymbol{\theta}$ to refer to the parameters of the kernel function $k_{f_d, f_d'}(\mathbf{x}, \mathbf{x}')$, $\forall\, d$, and d', and to the values of σ_d^2, $\forall\, d$.

3   Semi-Supervised Learning for Multi-output GPs

In a supervised learning setting, a dataset $\{\mathbf{X}_d, \mathbf{y}_d\}_{d=1}^D$ for each output is available. We assume that each $\mathbf{X}_d = \{\mathbf{x}_{n_d}^d\}_{n_d=1}^N$, and $\mathbf{y}_d = \{y_d(\mathbf{x}_{n_d}^d)\}_{n_d=1}^N$. We also

---

[1] The latent functions $u_q^i(\mathbf{x})$ share the same covariance $k_q(\mathbf{x}, \mathbf{x}')$, irrespectively of the value of i

[2] This is the same to say that each latent process $u_q(\mathbf{x})$ corresponds to a white noise process.

use $\mathbf{X} = \{\mathbf{X}_d\}_{d=1}^D$, and $\mathbf{y} = [\mathbf{y}_1^\top, \ldots, \mathbf{y}_D^\top]^\top$. The marginal likelihood for $\mathbf{y}$ is given by [8]

$$p(\mathbf{y}|\mathbf{X}, \boldsymbol{\theta}) = \mathcal{N}(\mathbf{0}, \mathbf{K}),$$

where the elements of $\mathbf{K}$ are computed using $k_{f_d, f_{d'}}(\mathbf{x}, \mathbf{x}')$, including the covariance term for the noise processes.

In semi-supervised learning, the elements in $\mathbf{X}$ are split between those for which there are labels available, $\mathbf{X}_l$, and those for which there are not labels available, $\mathbf{X}_u$. We refer to the known labels as $\mathbf{y}_l$. Our unknown variables will be the labels for $\mathbf{X}_u$, that we will call $\mathbf{y}_u$, and the hyperparameters of the multi-task Gaussian process, $\boldsymbol{\theta}$. We use $\mathbf{f}_l$, and $\mathbf{f}_u$ for the versions without noise of $\mathbf{y}_l$, and $\mathbf{y}_u$. We also use $\widetilde{\mathbf{y}}$ as the vector that concatenates $\mathbf{y}_l$, and $\mathbf{y}_u$, this is, $\widetilde{\mathbf{y}} = [\mathbf{y}_l^\top \ \mathbf{y}_u^\top]^\top$. It is important to highlight the difference between the vectors $\mathbf{y}$, and $\widetilde{\mathbf{y}}$. While the elements in $\mathbf{y}$ are organized by stacking the vectors $\mathbf{y}_d$ one on top of the other, the elements in $\mathbf{y}_l$ have no particular order and are indexed according to the elements in $\mathbf{X}_l$. The unknown elements $\mathbf{y}_u$ will also be indexed according to the elements in $\mathbf{X}_u$.

3.1 Graph Regularization

We follow one of the ideas used in semi-supervised learning to exploit the geometric structure between the labeled and the unlabeled data, this is, to add a Graph regularizer or Laplacian matrix to the kernel matrix. The new marginal likelihood $\mathbf{y}$ given the Laplacian matrix is similar to the one obtained by [19,20], and is given by

$$p(\mathbf{y}|\mathbf{X}, \boldsymbol{\theta}, \alpha,) = \mathcal{N}(\mathbf{0}, (\mathbf{K}^{-1} + \alpha\mathbf{L})^{-1}),$$

where $\mathbf{L}$ is the normalized Laplacian matrix, and α is a parameter that weights the contribution of the Laplacian matrix. We define $\widetilde{\mathbf{K}} = (\mathbf{K}^{-1} + \alpha\mathbf{L})^{-1}$. Using the matrix inversion lemma, we can also write $\widetilde{\mathbf{K}} = \mathbf{K} - \mathbf{K}(\alpha^{-1}\mathbf{I} + \mathbf{L}\mathbf{K})^{-1}\mathbf{L}\mathbf{K}$.

For computing the normalized Laplacian matrix, we follow the method proposed in [23]. We first define a parameter K, representing the K-th nearest neighbor to each data point $\mathbf{x}_i$ in $\mathbf{X}$. For each data point $\mathbf{x}_i$, $\rho_{i,K}$ represents the Euclidean distance from $\mathbf{x}_i$ to its K-th nearest neighbor, call it $\mathbf{x}_{i,K}$. An important difference with [19] is that in our method, the nearest neighbor can be a data point from the same or from a different output. In [19], the nearest neighbor is strictly from the same output. We then compute a similar matrix $\mathbf{S}$, with elements given by

$$S_{ij} = \exp\left(-\frac{\|\mathbf{x}_i - \mathbf{x}_j\|^2}{\rho_{i,K}\rho_{j,K}}\right).$$

The elements S_{ii} in $\mathbf{S}$ are always zero. We then compute the diagonal matrix $\mathbf{D}$, with elements $D_{ii} = \sum_{\forall j} S_{ij}$. The normalized Laplacian matrix is then computed as $\mathbf{L} = \mathbf{D}^{-1/2}\mathbf{S}\mathbf{D}^{-1/2}$. Notice that we compute the matrix $\mathbf{L}$ taking into account the complete matrix $\mathbf{X}$, which contains the inputs $\mathbf{X}_d$ for all the different outputs.

3.2   The EM Algorithm

We need now an inference procedure to estimate $\mathbf{y}_u$, and the parameters $\boldsymbol{\theta}$, and α. For accomplishing both tasks, we use an Expectation-Maximization algorithm. We assume that both $\mathbf{y}_l$, and $\mathbf{y}_u$ follow a joint Gaussian process. This is

$$\begin{bmatrix} \mathbf{y}_l \\ \mathbf{y}_u \end{bmatrix} \sim \mathcal{N}\left(\begin{bmatrix} \mathbf{0} \\ \mathbf{0} \end{bmatrix}, \begin{bmatrix} \widetilde{\mathbf{K}}_{l,l} & \widetilde{\mathbf{K}}_{l,u} \\ \widetilde{\mathbf{K}}_{u,l} & \widetilde{\mathbf{K}}_{u,u} \end{bmatrix} \right),$$

where $\widetilde{\mathbf{K}}_{l,l}$ is the part of $\widetilde{\mathbf{K}}$ that includes the covariance between $\mathbf{y}_l$, and $\mathbf{y}_l$; $\widetilde{\mathbf{K}}_{l,u}$ is the part of $\widetilde{\mathbf{K}}$ that includes the covariance between $\mathbf{y}_l$, and $\mathbf{y}_u$; and $\widetilde{\mathbf{K}}_{u,u}$ is the portion of $\widetilde{\mathbf{K}}$ that includes the covariance between $\mathbf{y}_u$, and $\mathbf{y}_u$.

In our EM algorithm, the hidden variables are the values of $\mathbf{y}_u$. In the E step of the algorithm we compute the posterior for $\mathbf{y}_u$ given $\mathbf{y}_l$ and some parameters $\widetilde{\boldsymbol{\theta}}$.[3] Since $\mathbf{y}_l$, and $\mathbf{y}_u$ are jointly Gaussian, the posterior for $\mathbf{y}_u$ is given as

$$p(\mathbf{y}_u | \mathbf{y}_l, \widetilde{\boldsymbol{\theta}}) = \mathcal{N}(\mathbf{y}_u | \widetilde{\mathbf{K}}_{u,l} \widetilde{\mathbf{K}}_{l,l}^{-1} \mathbf{y}_l, \widetilde{\mathbf{K}}_{u,u} - \widetilde{\mathbf{K}}_{u,l} \widetilde{\mathbf{K}}_{l,l}^{-1} \widetilde{\mathbf{K}}_{l,u}).$$

In the M step, we use the posterior above to compute

$$Q(\widetilde{\boldsymbol{\theta}}^{\text{new}}, \widetilde{\boldsymbol{\theta}}) = \mathbb{E}_{p(\mathbf{y}_u | \mathbf{y}_l, \widetilde{\boldsymbol{\theta}})} \left[\log p(\mathbf{y}_l, \mathbf{y}_u | \widetilde{\boldsymbol{\theta}}^{\text{new}}) \right].$$

It can be shown that $Q(\widetilde{\boldsymbol{\theta}}^{\text{new}}, \widetilde{\boldsymbol{\theta}})$ is given as

$$-\frac{(N_l + N_u)}{2} \log 2\pi - \frac{1}{2} \log |\boldsymbol{\Sigma}| - \frac{1}{2} \mathbf{y}_l^{\top} \mathbf{M} \mathbf{y}_l + \frac{1}{2} \text{trace}\left(\mathbb{E}[\mathbf{y}_u] \mathbf{y}_l^{\top} \mathbf{M} \widetilde{\mathbf{K}}_{l,u} \widetilde{\mathbf{K}}_{u,u}^{-1} \right)$$

$$+ \frac{1}{2} \mathbf{y}_l^{\top} \mathbf{M} \widetilde{\mathbf{K}}_{l,u} \widetilde{\mathbf{K}}_{u,u}^{-1} \mathbb{E}[\mathbf{y}_u] - \frac{1}{2} \text{trace}\left(\mathbb{E}[\mathbf{y}_u \mathbf{y}_u^{\top}] \mathbf{B} \right),$$

where $\mathbf{M} = \left(\widetilde{\mathbf{K}}_{l,l} - \widetilde{\mathbf{K}}_{l,u} \widetilde{\mathbf{K}}_{u,u}^{-1} \widetilde{\mathbf{K}}_{u,l} \right)^{-1}$, $\mathbf{B} = \widetilde{\mathbf{K}}_{u,u}^{-1} + \widetilde{\mathbf{K}}_{u,u}^{-1} \widetilde{\mathbf{K}}_{u,l} \mathbf{M} \widetilde{\mathbf{K}}_{l,u} \widetilde{\mathbf{K}}_{u,u}^{-1}$, and $\boldsymbol{\Sigma}$ is the covariance for $\widetilde{\mathbf{y}} = [\mathbf{y}_l^{\top} \ \mathbf{y}_u^{\top}]^{\top}$.

Also, for the M step, we estimate the parameter vector $\widetilde{\boldsymbol{\theta}}^{\text{new}}$, by maximizing the function $Q(\widetilde{\boldsymbol{\theta}}^{\text{new}}, \widetilde{\boldsymbol{\theta}})$ through a gradient-like optimization procedure. We find the partial derivatives of $Q(\widetilde{\boldsymbol{\theta}}^{\text{new}}, \widetilde{\boldsymbol{\theta}})$ with respect to $\widetilde{\boldsymbol{\theta}}^{\text{new}}$. For this, we first find the partial derivatives of $Q(\widetilde{\boldsymbol{\theta}}^{\text{new}}, \widetilde{\boldsymbol{\theta}})$ with respect to $\mathbf{M}, \mathbf{B}, \widetilde{\mathbf{K}}_{l,l}, \widetilde{\mathbf{K}}_{l,u}, \widetilde{\mathbf{K}}_{u,u}$, and the partial derivatives of $\mathbf{M}$ and $\mathbf{B}$, with respect to $\widetilde{\mathbf{K}}_{l,l}, \widetilde{\mathbf{K}}_{l,u}, \widetilde{\mathbf{K}}_{u,u}$. We then combine those derivatives with the respective partial derivatives $\frac{\partial \widetilde{\mathbf{K}}_{l,l}}{\partial \widetilde{\theta}_i}, \frac{\partial \widetilde{\mathbf{K}}_{l,u}}{\partial \widetilde{\theta}_i}$ and $\frac{\partial \widetilde{\mathbf{K}}_{u,u}}{\partial \widetilde{\theta}_i}$, where $\widetilde{\theta}_i$ is an element of the parameter vector $\widetilde{\boldsymbol{\theta}}^{\text{new}}$. All these derivative can be computed analytically following a similar procedure to [8].

4   Experimental Setup

In this section we describe the databases used in experiments. Also, we specify the experimental procedure, the partitions of databases, relevant parameters in the model and the metric employed to test the methods.

---

[3] We use $\widetilde{\boldsymbol{\theta}}$ to refer to both $\boldsymbol{\theta}$ and α.

4.1 Databases

- **Learning Inverse Dynamics:** The data set relates to an inverse dynamics problem for a seven degrees-of-freedom SARCOS anthropomorphic robot arm [24]. The task is to map from a 21-dimensional input space (7 joint positions, 7 joint velocities, 7 joint accelerations) to the corresponding 7 joint torques. We present results for just one of the seven mappings, from the 21 input variables to the first of the seven torques.
- **Predicting Student Performance:** This data set contains examinations scores belonging to several schools in London during the years 1985, 1986 and 1987. The full database have 15362 scores from students of 139 secondary schools. Each school corresponds to a separate task. Therefore, there are 139 learning tasks in total. The input data consists of the year of the examination, four school-specific and three student specific attributes.

4.2 Procedure

We compare several methods based in Gaussian processes, namely: a Single-Output Regressor (SOR), a Supervised Multi-Output Regressor (SMOR), the method proposed here for Semi-Supervised Multi-Output Regression using an EM algorithm (SSMOR-EM) and SSMOR-EM including the normalized Laplacian matrix (SSMOR-L-EM). For constructing the Convolved Multiple Output Covariance (CMOC) we use two different kernels: a Gaussian kernel (gg) and a gaussian white noise kernel (gw). Inside the EM algorithm, we repeat 10 times and 20 times the E-step and M-step respectively.

We employ two data sets, first a data base of inverse dynamics problem for a seven degrees-of-freedom SARCOS anthropomorphic robot arm, and second the student performance in terms of examination scores (see subsection 4.1). We treat each output as a different learning task. For the SARCOS dataset we randomly select 5000 data points independently for each task. Then, we partition the whole data set into three subsets, with 1% as labeled data, 10% as unlabeled data and the rest as validation set. For student performance data we select 2% of the data as labeled data, 20% as unlabeled data, and the rest as validation data. For evaluating the performance of each method, we use the normalized mean squared error (nMSE), which is defined as the mean squared error divided by the variance of the test labels.

We report two kinds of errors. First, the error in the semi-supervised learning stage. Here, we obtain surrogate labels for the unlabeled data belonging to training set. We call this error the transition error. Second, the error in a validation stage. Here, we test the generalization capability of all methods using the surrogate labels as the true labels for a supervised learning stage for all the models. We call this error: Generalization error. Finally we apply a Kruskal-Wallis test to model selection. This test finds if two or more models have statistical differences in their performance [25].

5   Results and Discussion

We repeat each experiment ten times selecting random data for training and validation. Results of normalized mean squared error (nMSE) for the methods applied in both data sets are shown in tables 1 and 2.

Table 1. nMSE results on predicting student performance. All methods are based in Gaussian processes. SOR: Single-Output Regression, SMOR: Supervised Multi-Output Regression, SSMOR-EM: Semi-Supervised Multi-Output Regression with Expectation-Maximization (SSMOR-L-EM: including normalized Laplacian matrix).

Method	Kernel	Transition Error	Generalization Error
SOR	gg	1.334 ± 0.123	1.392 ± 0.155
SMOR	gg	1.190 ± 0.143	1.212 ± 0.139
SSMOR-EM	gg	0.902 ± 0.043	1.045 ± 0.015
SSMOR-EM	gw	0.996 ± 0.050	1.167 ± 0.021
SSMOR-L-EM	gg	$\mathbf{0.885 \pm 0.045}$	$\mathbf{1.040 \pm 0.012}$
SSMOR-L-EM	gw	0.995 ± 0.051	1.167 ± 0.021

Table 2. nMSE results on learning inverse dynamics (SARCOS dataset).

Method	Kernel	Transition Error	Generalization Error
SOR	gg	1.114 ± 0.220	1.134 ± 0.213
SMOR	gw	0.621 ± 0.151	0.688 ± 0.146
SSMOR-EM	gg	0.111 ± 0.063	0.445 ± 0.043
SSMOR-EM	gw	0.110 ± 0.029	0.308 ± 0.013
SSMOR-L-EM	gg	0.110 ± 0.055	0.440 ± 0.043
SSMOR-L-EM	gw	$\mathbf{0.099 \pm 0.027}$	$\mathbf{0.302 \pm 0.013}$

We synthesize the discussion in the following paragraphs:

– From the results of tables 1 and 2, is clear that Semi-Supervised Multi-Output Regression obtains much better performance than the other methodologies. The nMSE in SSMOR-L-EM and SSMOR-EM is considerably lower in comparison to the supervised scheme, either Multi-Output or Single-Output. This performance is explained because the method proposed here mixes unlabeled data together with a small number of labeled samples to train the model more robustly.
– The transition error is related to the prediction of unlabeled data within the training set. This is a measure of local learning in the algorithm. In the case of semi-supervised algorithm, the transference of information is better compared to the classical supervised approach. This is a key advantage, due to Semi-Supervised algorithms extract an additional information hidden in the unlabeled data. In contrast, the supervised methods only can learn from labeled data.

- The standard deviation of the method proposed in this paper is much smaller than the other supervised methods. This means that the SSMTL-L-EM algorithm is more stable respect to modifications in the training data. Furthermore, when we performed a statistical analysis of Kruskal-Wallis test, we find that differences SSMTL-L-EM and supervised methods are statistically significant.
- Generalization error concerns the generalization capability of a method. That is, the accuracy in predicting new data that are not taken into account in the training stage. In both databases, we observe that Semi-Supervised Multi-Output methods greatly improve the results of traditional approaches. In this case, we can determine that the proposed method has a better generalization capability than the supervised learning scheme.
- In relation to the selection of an appropriate kernel, we cannot establish which one is the best. If we observe the results in both tables, in student prediction database the **gg** kernel obtains better outcomes than **gw**. However, in Sarcos database the **gw** kernel outperforms to **gg**. This means that kernel choosing depends strongly of the data nature. Also, it is important a good initialization of kernel hyperparameters.
- Best results in both databases were obtained with SSMOR-L-EM. The inclusion of the normalized Laplacian matrix makes more robust the semi-supervised learning stage of the proposed EM algorithm. This matrix regularizes the covariance function of the model. Although, the difference in nMSE between SSMOR-L-EM and SSMOR-EM is not very large, we can see that Laplacian matrix allows a better information transference during the training process.
- We consider the proposed method has some advantages as less variance in mean square error, stability to changes in the training data, excellent accuracy in predicting new data and it improves the performance of supervised learning schemes in scenarios where there are not available a good amount of labeled data.

6   Conclusions and Future Work

In this paper, we tested our proposed method to perform semi-supervised learning in multi-output Gaussian processes using an EM algorithm and Graph-based regularization. We test our proposed method in two widely used databases for multi-task regression. Results obtained by our method exhibit a better performance compared to supervised multi-output methods based in Gaussian processes. As a future work, we would like to develop alternative algorithms to reduce computational complexity in the training stage. Also, we want to compare different ways to construct LMC kernels against PC kernels.

Acknowledgments. H.D. Vargas Cardona is funded by Colciencias under the program: *formación de alto nivel para la ciencia, la tecnología y la innovación - Convocatoria 617 de 2013*. This research has been developed under the project: *Estimación de los parámetros de neuro modulación con terapia de estimulación cerebral profunda en* *pacientes con enfermedad de Parkinson a partir del volumen de tejido activo planeado,* financed by Colciencias with code $1110 - 657 - 40687$.

References

1. Rasmussen, C.E., Williams, C.K.I.: Gaussian Processes for Machine Learning. MIT Press, Cambridge (2006)
2. Vijayakumar, S.: DSouza, A., Schaal, S.: Multitask learning. Machine Learning **28**, 41–75 (1997)
3. Argyriou, A., Evgeniou, T., Pontil, M.: Convex multi-task feature learning. Machine Learning **73**, 243–272 (2008)
4. Bonilla, E., Agakov, F., Williams, C.: Kernel multi-task learning using task-specific features. In: Proceedings of the 11th International Conference on 345 Artificial Intelligence and Statistics (AISTATS) (2007)
5. Lawrence, N.D., Platt, J.C.: Learning to learn with the informative vector machine. In: Proceedings of the 21st International Conference on Machine Learning (ICML 2004), pp. 512–519 (2004)
6. Yu, K., Tresp, V., Schwaighofer, A.: Learning Gaussian processes from multiple tasks. In: Proceedings of the 22nd International Conference on Machine Learning, ICML 2005, pp. 1012–1019 (2005)
7. Álvarez, M.A., Rosasco, L., Lawrence, N.D.: Kernels for vector-valued functions: a review. Foundations and Trends ® in Machine Learning **4**(3), 195–266 (2012)
8. Alvarez, M., Lawrence, N.: Computationally efficient convolved multiple output gaussian processes. Journal of Machine Learning Research **12**, 1459–1500 (2011)
9. Skolidis, G., Sanguinetti, G.: Bayesian multitask classification with Gaussian process priors. IEEE Transactions on Neural Networks **22**(12), 2011–2021 (2011)
10. Chai, K.M.A.: Variational multinomial logit Gaussian processes. Journal of Machine Learning Research **13**, 1745–1808 (2012)
11. Cohen, I., Cozman, F., Sebe, N., Cirelo, M., Huang, T.: Semisupervised learning of classifiers: Theory, algorithms, and their application to human-computer interaction. IEEE Transactions on Pattern Analysis and Machine Intelligence **26**, 1553–1566 (2004)
12. Cohen, I., Cozman, F.: Semi-Supervised learning: Chapter 4: Risks of semi-supervised learning. MIT press (2006)
13. Loog, M.: Semi-supervised linear discriminant analysis through moment-constraint parameter estimation. Pattern Recognition Letters **37**, 24–31 (2014)
14. Loog, M., Jensen, A.: Semi-supervised nearest mean classification through a constrained log-likelihood. IEEE Transactions on Neural Networks and Learning Systems **29**, 995–1006 (2015)
15. Chapelle, O., Schlkopf, B., Zien, A.: Semi-Supervised Learning. MIT press, Massachusetts (2006)
16. Zhu, X., Goldberg, A.B.: Introduction to Semi-Supervised Learning. Synthesis Lectures on Artificial Intelligence and Machine Learning. Morgan & Claypool (2009)
17. Qi, Y., Tastan, O., Carbonell, J., Klein-Seetharaman, J., Weston, J.: Semi-supervised multi-task learning for predicting interactions between hiv-1 and human proteins. Bioinformatics, 1–7 (2010)

18. Dhillon, P., Sundararajan, S., Keerthi, S.: Semi-supervised multi-task learning of structured prediction models for web information extraction. In: Proceedings of the 20th ACM International Conference on Information and Knowledge Management, pp. 957–966 (2011)
19. Zhang, Y., Yeung, D.-Y.: Semi-Supervised multi-task regression. In: Buntine, W., Grobelnik, M., Mladenić, D., Shawe-Taylor, J. (eds.) ECML PKDD 2009, Part II. LNCS, vol. 5782, pp. 617–631. Springer, Heidelberg (2009)
20. Skolidis, G., Sanguinetti, G.: Semisupervised multitask learning with Gaussian processes. IEEE Transactions on Neural Networks and Learning Systems 24(12), 2101–2112 (2013)
21. Higdon, D.M.: Space and space-time modelling using process convolutions. In: Anderson, C., Barnett, V., Chatwin, P., El-Shaarawi, A. (eds.) Quantitative Methods For Current Environmental Issues, pp. 37–56. Springer (2002)
22. Álvarez, M.A., Luengo, D., Titsias, M.K., Lawrence, N.D.: Variational inducing kernels for sparse convolved multiple output Gaussian processes. Technical report, School of Computer Science, University of Manchester, UK and Departamento de Teoría de la Señal y Comunicaciones, Universidad Carlos III, Spain (2009). http://arxiv.org/pdf/0912.3268
23. Zelnik-Manor, L., Perona, P.: Self-Tuning spectral clustering. In: Advances in Neural Information Processing Systems (NIPS), pp. 1601–1608 (2005)
24. Vijayakumar, S., D'Souza, A., Schaal, S.: Incremental online learning in high dimensions. Neural Computation 17, 2602–2634 (2005)
25. Pizarro, J., Guerrero, E., Galindo, P.: Multiple comparison procedures applied to model selection. Neurocomputing 48, 155–173 (2002)

Volcano-Seismic Events Classification Using Document Classification Strategies

Manuele Bicego[1]([✉]), John Makario Londoño-Bonilla[2],
and Mauricio Orozco-Alzate[3]

[1] Dipartimento di Informatica, Università degli Studi di Verona,
Ca' Vignal 2, Strada le Grazie 15, 37134 Verona, Italia
manuele.bicego@univr.it
[2] Observatorio Vulcanológico y Sismológico de Manizales, Servicio Geológico
Colombiano, Avenida 12 de Octubre 15–47, Manizales 170001, Colombia
[3] Departamento de Informática y Computación,
Universidad Nacional de Colombia - Sede Manizales,
km 7 vía al Magdalena, Manizales 170003, Colombia

Abstract. In this paper we propose a novel framework for the classification of volcano-seismic events, based on strategies and concepts typically employed to classify documents – subsequently largely employed also in other fields. In the proposed approach, we define a dictionary of "seismic words", used to represent a seismic event as a "seismic document" (i.e. a collection of seismic words). Given this representation, we exploit two well-known models for documents (Bag-of-words and topic models) to derive signatures for seismic events, usable for classification. An empirical evaluation, based on a set of seismic signals from Galeras volcano in Colombia, confirms the potentialities of the proposed scheme, both in terms of interpretability and classification accuracies, also in comparison with standard approaches.

Keywords: Bag-of-words · Mel frequency cepstral coefficients · Seismic volcanic signal classification · Topic models

1 Introduction

The analysis and the classification of seismic signals play a vital role in volcano monitoring. In the literature, several techniques have been proposed to address this challenge, each one using different representations and exhibiting different interpretability features, performances and computational requirements – see [21] for a comprehensive review of the literature.

In this paper a novel approach to the classification of volcano-seismic events is proposed, based on a set of tools and concepts introduced in the text processing community. In particular, our framework is based on two effective and largely applied tools, namely the bag-of-words approach [13,17] and the topic models [5]: after their introduction in the text mining community, such models have been successfully exported to many other scenarios, such as — just to cite a few — Computer Vision [7,22], Bioinformatics [4,8,23], and Audio Analysis [11,14,16]. To the

© Springer International Publishing Switzerland 2015
V. Murino and E. Puppo (Eds.): ICIAP 2015, Part I, LNCS 9279, pp. 119–129, 2015.
DOI: 10.1007/978-3-319-23231-7_11

best of our knowledge, their usefulness in the seismic scenario has never been investigated: this paper represents a first effort in this direction. It seems very appealing to investigate the capabilities of these models — which, in many applications, demonstrated powerful classification characteristics as well as interesting interpretation properties [4,7,8,11,14,16,22,23] — in the seismic scenario: we can interpret every event as a "document", which employs particular "words", and which can focus on one or more "topics". The same topic can be present in different classes of events, maybe because it is related to a shared geophysical cause; going further with our reasoning, two events can "speak" about the same set of topics, but using a different dictionary, maybe only because the signals have been acquired from different stations.

Clearly, in order to apply such models, we should define the concept of "seismic documents" and "seismic words". The first step is therefore to define a dictionary of words, containing the constituting elements of a document: in our approach, similarly to what is done in other contexts — e.g. image analysis [25] or audio processing [14,16] — the dictionary is built by first extracting some meaningful features from all the signals, subsequently applying a vector quantization / clustering approach to derive the words. As features we used the classical Mel Frequency Cepstral Coefficients (MFCCs), extracted from subsequent frames of the seismic signals – this represents a standard preprocessing in seismic event recognition [2,10]. Given the dictionary, every event is now characterized as a sequence of words, which is encoded using either the bag-of-words (BoW) approach or a topic model – here we employ the Latent Dirichlet Allocation (LDA – [6]).

For classification, we fed the BoW representation directly to a classifier; for topic models, we made an extra-step: actually, we set up a hybrid generative-discriminative classification scheme [12,15], in particular by following the so-called generative embedding strategy: the trained topic model is used to map the signals into a feature space, in which a discriminative classifier is employed. Different mappings have been proposed in recent years (see [22] and the references therein included): in our approach we employed the recent FESS scheme [22], which has been proven to be a highly informative description in different applications.

The proposed framework has been thoroughly tested with a set of pre-triggered signals (divided into 4 classes) coming from Galeras volcano in Colombia, investigating the effect of different parameters. A comparison with reference approaches showed that the proposed method represents a valid alternative to standard seismic classification techniques.

2   The Proposed Approach

In this section we discuss how to construct the dictionary, how to characterize seismic events as documents, and how to classify them. Schemes of the first two phases are shown in Fig. 1.

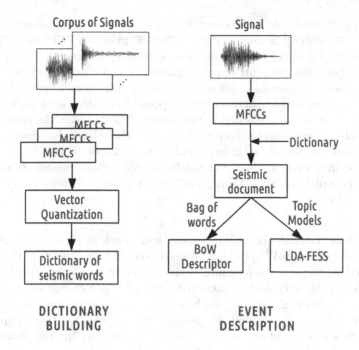

Fig. 1. Block diagram of the proposed approach.

2.1 Dictionary Building

Before applying text mining tools to seismic events, we should define what documents and words are in the specific context. Intuitively, we can associate a seismic document to a seismic event: the seismic document represents a collection of seismic words. To define seismic words, we take inspiration from the audio modelling community [14,16], adopting the following strategy: seismic signals are parametrized with the conventional MFCCs, and the seismic words are then derived using Vector Quantization. As done by [14], we use a frame-based analysis —with a fixed length— in order to represent the time varying properties of the seismic signal. MFCCs are a popular choice in the seismic community [2,10], able to provide a spectral parametrization of the signal considering human auditory properties. In this work we used frames of 256 sample values (2.5 s) with overlap of 50%, considering 13 coefficients together with their derivatives (as in [2,10]).

2.2 Event Description

Once given the dictionary, every event can be described as a sequence of words, namely a document. In order to characterize the documents, here we employed two techniques: the bag-of-words and the LDA topic model.

Bag-of-Words. The Bag-of-words approach represents a straightforward description of a document, still being really descriptive and useful. In particular, given a dictionary of W words, the BoW descriptor of a document d is a vector of length W which, in the entry j, measures the number of times the j-th word appears in such document. Therefore, every event is described by a vector of length W. It is important to note that this representation (as well as the one derived from the LDA model) does not consider the order in which the words appear in the document. This is a well known problem of this class of approaches, which are known to somehow destroy the structure of the object (the order of the words, in this case). Even if alternatives have been recently proposed (e.g. [9]), these basic descriptors are still widely and successfully applied in many fields [4, 7, 8, 11, 14, 16, 22, 23], due to their excellent discriminative capabilities: actually, the vectorial representation permits to completely exploit powerful discriminative vector-based classifiers, such as Support Vector Machines.

Topic Models: Latent Dirichlet Allocation. Topic models represent a powerful extension of the BoW approach, able to take into consideration the context in order to disambiguate the meaning of the words. In particular, these methods aim at characterizing each document with the presence of one or more topics (e.g. economics, fashion, finance), each one inducing the presence of some particular words. From a probabilistic perspective, we can see the document as described via a mixture of topics, each one giving a probability distribution over words. Such distributions are learnt by analysing word co-occurrences in the training data. The characterization of documents and words with these probabilistic technique allows the individual interpretability of each topic, since it provides a probability distribution over words that extracts a coherent group of correlated terms. In our approach we employed the Latent Dirichlet Allocation (LDA - [6]), one of the first and most famous topic models[1].

Given a set of V different words, the LDA mediates the observation of a particular word w_i in a document t through a latent topic variable $z, z \in Z = \{z_1, \ldots, z_Z\}$, which is picked from a multinomial distribution $p(z \mid t) = \theta^t$. The multinomial θ^t represents the topic proportions, peculiar for every document t: intuitively, the θ^t variable describes "how much each topic is spoken in such document". Without entering too much into the details (interested readers are referred to [6]), we can simply say that the probability of observing a given word w_i in a document t is:

$$p(w_i^t) = p(\theta^t \mid \alpha) \sum_k p(z_k \mid \theta^t) p(w_i^t \mid z_k)$$

$$= p(\theta^t \mid \alpha) \sum_k \theta_{z_k}^t \cdot \beta_{w_i, z_k} \tag{1}$$

where β_{w_i, z_k} expresses how much a word w_i is related to the topic z_k: roughly speaking, this distribution describes "how probable is to use the word w_i when

---

[1] Even if many complex topic models have been proposed, here we decided to use this simple – yet powerful – model, in order to investigate the suitability of the coding technique.

the document is speaking about topic z_k". Finally, $p(\theta^t \mid \alpha)$ is a Dirichlet prior over the possible topics' assignments.

As better detailed in [6], the various distributions of the model are learned using a variational Expectation-Maximization (EM), a technique that maximizes the log-likelihood (or its tractable lower bound called Free Energy) by iterating between two steps: the E-step, which computes the posterior over the topics (i.e. θ^t), given the current estimate of the model; the M-step, where the parameters of the models (α and β) are re-estimated, given the current θ^t. Once the model has been trained, it is possible to use the learned parameters α and β to perform inference, estimating the topic proportion $\theta^{t_{new}}$ of an unseen document t_{new}. Since the EM algorithm converges to a local optimum, a proper initialization of the LDA model is of crucial importance to guarantee the convergence to a proper local optima [18]. In our framework the initialization issue has been faced in a standard way, by repeating several times the training procedure, each starting from different random parameters, finally retaining the configuration which leaded to the highest likelihood.

2.3 From Documents to Feature Vectors

Whereas the BoW of a document is already a vectorial representation, for LDA we made an extra step. In particular, we employed a hybrid generative-discriminative classification scheme [12,15], which aims at merging together the best characteristics of both the generative and the discriminative paradigms: the first step is to learn a generative model – suitable to describe the problem at hand – from the data; then the learnt generative model is exploited to define a mapping which projects every object of the problem in a feature space (typically called generative embedding space), in which a discriminative classifier can be used.

In our approach we trained a single LDA model on the whole encoded training set, performing inference to get distributions also on the testing set. Then we employed the very recent Free Energy Score Space (FESS) approach [22] to derive a feature space: without going too much into the details – interested readers are referred to [22] – we can briefly state that the FESS vector is able to capture how well each object of problem fits the different parts of the generative model, modelled via the variational free energy (which represents a lower bound of the negative log-likelihood). It has been shown in [22] that such representation is highly informative for classification, permitting to reach state-of-the-art results in different bioinformatics and computer vision problems.

2.4 Document Classification

In the obtained feature space (the BoW or the LDA-FESS spaces), any classic discriminative classifier can be used. In our experiments we employed the standard k nearest neighbor (kNN) and the linear support vector machine (SVM) classifiers.

3   Experiments

In this section the proposed approach is evaluated. After describing the experimental details, we report some classification accuracies, also in comparison with some other standard techniques. Then, we investigate the impact of the parameters on the performances; finally, we present some intuitions about the interpretability potentialities.

3.1   Experimental Details

A data set of seismic signals from Galeras volcano (Colombia) has been used to test the proposed framework. Galeras is a stratovolcano situated in the Andes mountains, near (7 km W) to the city of Pasto[2]. After around 40 years of silence, such volcano started again its activity in 1988, with several ash and gas emissions as well as some eruptions: the most relevant were on May 1989, on July 1992, on the first semester of 1993 (many different eruptions), on the second semester of 2004, at the end of 2005 and more recently in January 2008, during the whole 2009, and in January and August 2010.

Data used in our experimentation have been gathered with a seismic network composed by seven short-period seismic stations – here we employed the Anganoy station, which is the highest station (4227 m.a.s.l) and the closest to the active crater (0.8 km). After acquisition, signals are telemetered by radio to the Observatory, where they are pre-processed using a 12-bit analog-to-digital converter with a sampling rate of 100.16 samples/s; after that, interesting events are obtained using an automatic detection/segmentation stage; finally, segmented events are stored on a series of servers as files using the Seismic Unified Data System protocol.

To test the classification potentialities of the proposed framework we used two different classification problems. The first task is composed by 300 signals, divided into three classes: Volcano-tectonic (VT) earthquakes, long-period (LP) events, and tremors (TR), which represent the most important volcano-induced earthquakes. The second classification task is definitely more challenging, since it includes the class of hybrid (HB) events: actually it has been shown in many studies [1,2] that distinguishing between LP and HB earthquakes is challenging; however, this discrimination is rather crucial in the specific application scenario.

In all the experiments, the seismic events were characterized as described before. Bag-of-words and LDA-FESS descriptors were extracted. We made dictionaries of different sizes taking the values 32, 64, 128, 256 and 512, while for LDA we made the number of topics varying from 2 to 20 (step 2). In the generative embedding space we used as classifiers the kNN and linear SVM. In the kNN case, k was automatically estimated with Leave One Out cross validation on the training set. For the SVM, after some preliminary trials, C has been fixed

---

[2] Further details about Galeras volcano activity are at the institutional web site of the Observatory: http://www.sgc.gov.co/Pasto/Volcanes/Volcan-Galeras/Generali dades.aspx

to 1. In all experiments, classification accuracies were computed using Averaged Holdout CV, with results averaged over 20 repetitions. In order to assess of the statistical significance of the results, we computed for every different set of experiments the standard errors of the mean. For the 3-class problem, they were all less than 0.0050, whereas for the 4-class problem they were all less than 0.0025.

3.2 Results and Comparison with other Methods

To have a quick summarizing view of the behaviour of the proposed scheme, in this part we show the accuracies obtained from the best configuration of parameters, leaving comments on the impact of the parameter choice to the following section. We compare our approach with some other well established seismic classification strategies: (a) the same classifiers employed in our tests on the averaged MFCCs (MFCCs averaged over all the frames of a given event – the baseline results); (b) a set of descriptive spectral parameters [24], classified using Back Propagation Neural Network (BP-NNet), Levenberg-Marquardt (LM-NNet) and the SVM with rbf kernel. The topology of the networks has been set as in [24], whereas the σ and C parameter of SVM have been optimized with cross-validation on the training set; (c) a Bayesian approach based on Continuous Gaussian Hidden Markov Models (HMMs) trained on event spectrograms [3] – being HMMs the most widely applied approach in this context. In such case we performed experiments varying the number of states in a proper range, reporting the best result obtained.

Table 1. Comparative classification accuracies.

Method	3-class	4-class
Averaged MFCC + kNN	0.8580	0.7925
Averaged MFCC + linSVM	0.9050	0.8122
Time-frequency feat + BP-NNet	0.9343	0.7082
Time-frequency feat + LM-NNet	0.9277	0.7215
Time-frequency feat + rbf SVM	0.9367	0.6963
Spectrograms + HMMs	0.9150	0.8348
Bag-of-Words (best)	0.9187	0.8177
Topic Model (best)	**0.9410**	**0.8375**

From Table 1, it is evident that the proposed approach represents a valid alternative to other standard and well established classification approaches, well comparing also with advanced tools as those based on HMM + spectrograms (in such case, almost equivalent accuracies were obtained for the 4-class problem).

3.3 Effect of the Parameters

The two most crucial parameters in our framework are the size of the dictionary and the number of topics for topic models. In the former case, even if some clever strategies and studies have recently appeared in some specific community (e.g. [19]), the problem still remains unsolved, and the typical solution is to make different trials (as done in [14]). In Table 2 we study the different results while varying this parameter (taking the best number of topics): it seems evident that the BoW approach prefers small size dictionaries, with deteriorating performances while increasing the size. On the contrary, when using FESS features extracted from the LDA, this problem is less present.

Table 2. Results when varying the dictionary size (dS).

dS	BoW+kNN	BoW+SVM	TM+kNN	TM+SVM
3-class Problem				
32	0.9187	0.9160	0.9440	0.9360
64	0.9057	0.8937	0.9390	0.9383
128	0.8760	0.9053	0.9400	0.9380
256	0.8327	0.9017	0.9370	0.9410
512	0.7477	0.9057	0.9387	0.9397
4-class Problem				
32	0.7960	0.8177	0.8193	0.8290
64	0.7800	0.7882	0.8303	0.8315
128	0.7765	0.7735	0.8305	0.8375
256	0.7410	0.7790	0.8090	0.8282
512	0.6540	0.7848	0.7975	0.8223

The choice of the second parameter (number of topics) represents a classic model selection problem, for which some techniques already appeared in the literature: hold-out likelihood [23], cross-validation, a priori knowledge or general probabilistic model selection methods. Another option, which has been used in the microarray scenario [4], appeared to be a straightforward but effective rule to select such number. Actually, authors in [4] started from the consideration that topic models have originally been designed to perform clustering, i.e. to discover groups of documents; therefore, fixing the number of topics to be proportional to the number of classes seems reasonable. Despite the simplicity of this rule-of-thumb, obtained results were very satisfactory. In Fig. 2(a) we plot the classification accuracies of the LDA-FESS descriptor when varying the number of topics (linear SVM as classifier, best dictionary size). In the figure, the two dashed horizontal lines represent the baseline results, obtained with linear SVM on the averaged MFCCs. The dotted vertical lines highlight the number of topics corresponding to two times the number of classes. From the figure, it can be seen that i) there is a quite large range of values for which the accuracies are over the baseline and ii) selecting two times the number of classes represents a reasonable choice.

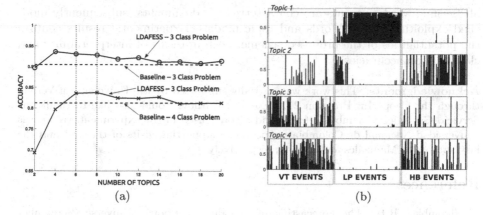

Fig. 2. (a) Results varying the number of topics for the two problems. (b) Interpretation of Seismicity.

3.4   Interpretability

In order to illustrate the interpretation capabilities of these tools – shown in many different contexts [4, 8] – we trained a LDA with 4 topics on a dataset composed by VT, LP and HB events. Topic proportions for all the events belonging to the different classes are displayed in Fig. 2(b). From the plot we can firstly observe that the topics which are more representative for the LP events (the first and the second) are mainly different from those related to the VT events (the third, the fourth – and, partially, the second). This is expected, since it is a well-known fact in volcano seismology [20] that LP events have in general spectral energies concentrated at lower frequencies, whereas VT events display a relatively high-frequency spectral content. Topic models capture co-occurrences of words, which, for the two classes of events, are reasonably different. An even more interesting observation derives by considering the HB events: from a theoretical point of view, we know that such events are defined as a mixture between VT and LP events. Actually this is partially reflected in the plots: HB events are "active" mainly in topics 2, 3 and 4. The last two are the topics mainly "spoken" in VT events, whereas the second topic explains those LP events which are not explained by the first. From these plots we can: i) confirm that HB events are a mixture of VT and LP events; ii) hypothesise that in Galeras volcano, HB events are mainly dominated by features of VT events at the Anganoy station; this can be attributed either to a dominant fracture process related with the local geology at Anganoy station, or to a site effect related with the local geology at the Anganoy station. Further tests by using other stations are needed to clarify this issue.

4   Conclusions

This paper represents a first step towards the application of document classification tools for the classification of seismic events. After defining a dictionary of "seismic words", events are characterized as documents, subsequently modelled exploiting Bag-of-Words and topic models. Experimental results confirm the potentialities of the proposed scheme, both in terms of interpretability and classification accuracies.

Acknowledgments. This work was partially supported by the University of Verona through the CooperInt Program 2011 Edition. Authors would also like to thank the Servicio Geológico Colombiano for providing data used in the experiments as well as Universidad Nacional de Colombia for partially supporting visits of the first and the last authors to Manizales and Verona, respectively.

References

1. Trombley, R.B.: The Forecasting of Volcanic Eruptions. iUniverse (September 2006)
2. Benítez, M.C., Ramírez, J., Segura, J.C., Ibáñez, J.M., Almendros, J., García-Yeguas, A., Cortés, G.: Continuous HMM-based seismic-event classification at Deception Island, Antarctica. IEEE Transactions on Geoscience and Remote Sensing 45(1), 138–146 (2007)
3. Bicego, M., Acosta-Muñoz, C., Orozco-Alzate, M.: Classification of seismic volcanic signals using hidden-Markov-model-based generative embeddings. IEEE Transactions on Geoscience and Remote Sensing 51(6), 3400–3409 (2013)
4. Bicego, M., Lovato, P., Perina, A., Fasoli, M., Delledonne, M., Pezzotti, M., Polverari, A., Murino, V.: Investigating topic models' capabilities in expression microarray data classification. IEEE/ACM Transactions on Computational Biology and Bioinformatics 9(6), 1831–1836 (2012)
5. Blei, D.M.: Probabilistic topic models. Communications of the ACM 55(4), 77–84 (2012)
6. Blei, D.M., Ng, A.Y., Jordan, M.I.: Latent Dirichlet allocation. Journal of Machine Learning Research 3, 993–1022 (2003)
7. Bosch, A., Zisserman, A., Muñoz, X.: Scene classification via pLSA. In: Leonardis, A., Bischof, H., Pinz, A. (eds.) ECCV 2006. LNCS, vol. 3954, pp. 517–530. Springer, Heidelberg (2006)
8. Brelstaff, G., Bicego, M., Culeddu, N., Chessa, M.: Bag of peaks: interpretation of NMR spectrometry. Bioinformatics 25(2), 258–264 (2009)
9. Du, L., Buntine, W., Jin, H., Chen, C.: Sequential latent Dirichlet allocation. Journal of Knowledge and Information Systems 31, 475–503 (2012)
10. Ibáñez, J.M., Benítez, C., Gutiérrez, L.A., Cortés, G., García-Yeguas, A., Alguacil, G.: The classification of seismo-volcanic signals using Hidden Markov Models as applied to the Stromboli and Etna volcanoes. Journal of Volcanology and Geothermal Research 187(3–4), 218–226 (2009)
11. Ishiguro, K., Yamada, T., Araki, S., Nakatani, T., Sawada, H.: Probabilistic speaker diarization with bag-of-words representations of speaker angle information. IEEE Transactions on Audio, Speech, and Language Processing 20(2), 447–460 (2012)
12. Jaakkola, T.S., Haussler, D.: Exploiting generative models in discriminative classifiers. In: Kearns, M.S., Solla, S.A., Cohn, D.A. (eds.) Advances in Neural Information Processing Systems (NIPS), vol. 11, pp. 487–493 (1999)
13. Joachims, T.: Text categorization with support vector machines: learning with many relevant features. In: Nédellec, C., Rouveirol, C. (eds.) ECML 1998. LNCS, vol. 1398, pp. 137–142. Springer, Heidelberg (1998)

14. Kim, S., Georgiou, P., Narayanan, S.: Latent acoustic topic models for unstructured audio classification. APSIPA Transactions on Signal and Information Processing **1**, 1–15 (2012)
15. Lasserre, J.A., Bishop, C.M., Minka, T.P.: Principled hybrids of generative and discriminative models. In: Proc. of Int. Conf. on Computer Vision and Pattern Recognition (CVPR06), vol. 1, pp. 87–94, June 2006
16. Lee, K., Ellis, D.P.W.: Audio-based semantic concept classification for consumer video. IEEE Transactions on Audio, Speech, and Language Processing **18**(6), 1406–1416 (2010)
17. Lodhi, H., Saunders, C., Shawe-Taylor, J., Cristianini, N., Watkins, C.: Text classification using string kernels. Journal of Machine Learning Research **2**, 419–444 (2002)
18. Lovato, P., Bicego, M., Murino, V., Perina, A.: Robust initialization for learning latent dirichlet allocation. In: Proc. Int. Workshop on Similarity-Based Pattern Analysis and Recognition (2015)
19. Mairal, J., Bach, F., Ponce, J.: Task-driven dictionary learning. IEEE Transactions on Pattern Analysis and Machine Intelligence **34**(4), 791–804 (2012)
20. McNutt, S.R.: Volcanic seismology. Annual Review of Earth and Planetary Sciences **33**(1), 461–491 (2005)
21. Orozco-Alzate, M., Acosta-Muñoz, C., Londoño-Bonilla, J.M.: The automated identification of volcanic earthquakes: concepts, applications and challenges. In: D'Amico, S. (ed.) Earthquake Research and Analysis - Seismology, Seismotectonic and Earthquake Geology, chap. 19, pp. 345–370. InTech, Rijeka (2012)
22. Perina, A., Cristani, M., Castellani, U., Murino, V., Jojic, N.: Free energy score spaces: Using generative information in discriminative classifiers. IEEE Transactions on Pattern Analysis and Machine Intelligence **34**(7), 1249–1262 (2012)
23. Rogers, S., Girolami, M., Campbell, C., Breitling, R.: The latent process decomposition of cDNA microarray data sets. IEEE/ACM IEEE/ACM Transactions on Computational Biology and Bioinformatics **2**(2), 143–156 (2005)
24. Ibs-von Seht, M.: Detection and identification of seismic signals recorded at Krakatau volcano (Indonesia) using artificial neural networks. Journal of Volcanology and Geothermal Research **176**(4), 448–456 (2008)
25. Zhang, J., Marszałek, M., Lazebnik, S., Schmid, C.: Local features and kernels for classification of texture and object categories: A comprehensive study. International Journal of Computer Vision **73**(2), 213–238 (2007)

Unsupervised Feature Selection
by Graph Optimization

Zhihong Zhang[1], Lu Bai[2(✉)], Yuanheng Liang[3], and Edwin R. Hancock[4]

[1] Software School, Xiamen University, Xiamen, Fujian, China
[2] School of Information, Central University of Finance and Economics, Beijing, China
bailu69@hotmail.com
[3] School of Mathematical Sciences, Xiamen University, Xiamen, Fujian, China
[4] Department of Computer Science, University of York, York, UK

Abstract. Graph based methods have played an important role in machine learning due to their ability to encode the similarity relationships among data. A commonly used criterion in graph based feature selection methods is to select the features which best preserve the data similarity or a manifold structure derived from the entire feature set. However, these methods separate the processes of learning the feature similarity graph and feature ranking. In practice, the ideal feature similarity graph is difficult to define in advance. Because one needs to assign appropriate values for parameters such as the neighborhood size or the heat kernel parameter involved in graph construction, the process is conducted independently of subsequent feature selection. As a result the performance of feature selection is largely determined by the effectiveness of graph construction. In this paper, on the other hand, we attempt to learn a graph strucure closely linked with the feature selection process. The idea is to unify graph construction and data transformation, resulting in a new framework which results in an optimal graph rather than a predefined one. Moreover, the $\ell_{2,1}$-norm is imposed on the transformation matrix to achieve row sparsity when selecting relevant features. We derive an efficient algorithm to optimize the proposed unified problem. Extensive experimental results on real-world benchmark data sets show that our method consistently outperforms the alternative feature selection methods.

Keywords: Graph learning · Laplacian · Unsupervised feature selection

1 Introduction

Recently, graph-based methods, such as spectral embedding [2], spectral clustering [1], and semi-supervised learning [3] [4], have played an important role in machine learning due to their ability to encode the similarity relationships among data. Various applications of graph-based methods can be found in clustering [1] [5], data mining [6], manifold learning [7] [8], subspace learning [9] and speech recognition [10]. A preliminary step for all these graph-based methods

© Springer International Publishing Switzerland 2015
V. Murino and E. Puppo (Eds.): ICIAP 2015, Part I, LNCS 9279, pp. 130–140, 2015.
DOI: 10.1007/978-3-319-23231-7_12

is to establish a suitable graph over the training data. Data samples are represented as vertices of the graph and the edges represent the pairwise similarity relationships between them.

In feature selection, a particularly attractive feature of graph representations is that they provide a universal and flexible framework that reflects the underlying manifold structure and the relationships between feature vectors. A frequently used criterion in graph-based feature selection methods is to select the features which best preserve the data similarity or a manifold structure derived from the entire feature set. The best known methods are the Laplacian score (LapScore) [9], spectral feature selection (SPEC) [11], multicluster feature selection (MCFS) [12] and minimum redundancy spectral feature selection (MRSF) [13]. However, a common problem in the aforementioned methods is that the graph constructing process is independent of the subsequent feature selection task. For example, MCFS [12] uses a graph to characterize the manifold structure and performs locality preserving projection (LPP) in the first-step. In the second step, MCFS performs spectral regression using a single eigenvector at a time to estimate element sparsity. Finally, a new score rule is designed to rank the goodness of the features using element sparsity. MRSF [13], on theother hand, uses the $\ell_{2,1}$-norm regularizer to replace the ℓ_1-norm regularizer in MCFS which leads to row sparsity. The row sparsity used in MRSF is better fitted for feature selection than the element sparsity used in MCFS. LapScore [9] uses a k-nearest neighbor graph to model the local geometric structure of the data and then selects the features that are most consistent with the graph structure. The SPEC [11] algorithm is an extension of LapScore aimed at making it more robust to noise.

Compared with traditional unsupervised feature selection approaches, the above methods have been in many cases been demonstrated to perform better. Nevertheless, their performance can also be further improved since they each separate the problems of estimating or learning a similarity graph and feature selection. Once the graph is determined so as to characterize the data sample similarity and underlying manifold structure, it remains fixed in the subsequent feature ranking or regression steps. As a result, the feature selection performance is largely determined by the effectiveness of graph construction. Instead, a recently proposed unsupervised feature selection algorithm called joint embedded learning and sparse regression (JELSR)[14] attempts to learn a graph embedding and a corresponding sparse transformation matrix simultaneously in one single objective function, which result in an automatically-updated graph embedding. Compared with the alternative method MCFS [12], which is to first compute the low dimensional embedding and then, regress each sample to its low dimensional embedding by adding ℓ_1-norm regularization, JELSR has been demonstrated to have superior performance by unifying two objective of MCFS. This is because the objective of sparse transformation matrix regression has also affected the derivation of low dimensional embedding. However, the optimal graph embedding in JELSR depends heavily on the transformed data, without making the best use of the original data information and the data similarity is also not learned by the algorithm. This easily leads to the instability performance, especially when encountering a "bad" transformation matrix.

To address this problem, in this paper, we propose a novel unsupervised feature selection approach via graph optimization (referred to as UFSGO), which incorporates graph construction into the data transformation, and thus obtains a simultaneous learning framework for graph construction and transformation matrix optimization. More concretely, by adding the $\ell_{2,1}$-norm regularization to the transformation matrix, our new model simultaneously learns the data similarity matrix and sparse transformation matrix to achieve optimal feature selection results. Moreover, in order to fully utilise information in the original data, a square Frobenius divergence term between a predefined graph and its updated realization is added to the objective function. As a result, we formulate an elegant graph update formula which naturally fuses the original and transformed data information. We also provide an effective method to solve the proposed problem. Compared with traditional unsupervised feature selection approaches, our method integrates the merits of graph learning and sparse regression. Experimental result are provided to demonstrate the utility of the method.

2   A Brief Review of Graph-Based Unsupervised Feature Selection Methods

In this section, we review some well-known algorithms for learning-based unsupervised feature selection, all of which are closely related to our proposed method.

. 1) MCFS and MRSF: MCFS and MRSF are learning based feature selection methods that first compute an embedding and then use regression coefficients to rank each feature. In the first step, both methods compute a low dimensional embedding represented by the co-ordinate matrix Y. One simple way in deriving low dimensional embedding is to use Laplacian Eigenmap (LE) [8], a well known dimensionality reduction method. Denote $\mathbf{Y} = [y_1, y_2, \ldots, y_n]$ and $\hat{y}_i$ as transpose of the i-th row of $\mathbf{Y}$. The idea common to both MCFS and MRSF is to regress all x_i to $\hat{y}_i$. Their differences are used to determine sparseness constraints. MCFS uses ℓ_1-norm regularization and can be regarded as solving the following problems in sequence:

$$arg \min_{\mathbf{Y}\mathbf{Y}^T=I} tr(\mathbf{Y}\mathbf{L}\mathbf{Y}^T)$$
$$arg \min_{\mathbf{W}} \|\mathbf{W}^T\mathbf{X} - \mathbf{Y}\|_2^2 + \alpha\|\mathbf{W}\|_1 \tag{1}$$

Similarly, MRSF first computes the embedding by Eigen decomposition of graph Laplacian and then regress with $\ell_{2,1}$-norm regularization. In other words, MRSF can be regarded as solving the following two problems in sequence:

$$arg \min_{\mathbf{Y}\mathbf{Y}^T=I} tr(\mathbf{Y}\mathbf{L}\mathbf{Y}^T)$$
$$arg \min_{\mathbf{W}} \|\mathbf{W}^T\mathbf{X} - \mathbf{Y}\|_2^2 + \alpha\|\mathbf{W}\|_{2,1} \tag{2}$$

MCFS and MRSF employ different sparseness constraints, i.e., ℓ_1 and $\ell_{2,1}$, in constructing a transformation matrix which is used for selecting features. Nevertheless, the low dimensional embedding, i.e., $\mathbf{Y}$, is determined in the first step and remains fixed in the subsequent ranking or regression step. In other words, we do not consider the later requirements of feature selection in deriving the embedding $\mathbf{Y}$. If it cannot only characterizes the manifold structure, but also indicates the requirements of regression, these methods would perform better.

2) JELSR [14]: Instead of simply using the graph Laplacian to characterize high dimensional data structure and then regression, JELSR (joint embedding learning and sparse regression) unifies embedding/learning and sparse regression in constructing a new framework for feature selection:

$$arg \min_{\mathbf{W},\mathbf{Y}\mathbf{Y}^T=I} tr(\mathbf{Y}\mathbf{L}\mathbf{Y}^T) + \beta(\|\mathbf{W}^T\mathbf{X} - \mathbf{Y}\|_2^2 + \alpha\|\mathbf{W}\|_{2,1}) \qquad (3)$$

where α and β are balance parameters. The objective function in Eq.(3) is convex with respect to $\mathbf{W}$ and $\mathbf{Y}$. $\mathbf{W}$ and $\mathbf{Y}$ can be updated in an alternative way. As we can see from Eq.(29) in [14], the objective of sparse regression, i.e. the value of $\mathbf{W}$, has also affected the low dimensional embedding, i.e., $\mathbf{Y}$. Alternative methods, such as MCFS and MRSF, minimize $tr(\mathbf{Y}\mathbf{L}\mathbf{Y}^T)$ merely. Although JELSR performs better in many cases, the optimal graph embedding in JELSR depends heavily on the transformed data, without making the best use of the original data information and the data similarity $\mathbf{S}$ is also not learned by the algorithm. This easily leads to the instability performance, especially when encountering a "bad" transformation matrix.

3) LPP [18]: LPP (locality preserving projection) constructs a graph by incorporating neighborhood information derived from the data. Using the graph Laplacian, a transformation is computed to map the data into a subspace by optimally maintaining the local neighborhood information. LPP optimizes a linear transformation $\mathbf{W}$ according to

$$arg \min_{\mathbf{W}} \sum_{i,j=1}^{n} \|\mathbf{W}^T x_i - \mathbf{W}^T x_j\|^2 s_{ij} \qquad (4)$$

The basic idea underlying LPP is to find a transformation matrix W, which transforms the high-dimensional data $\mathbf{X}$ into a low-dimensional matrix $\mathbf{XW}$, so as to maximally preserve the local connectivity structure of $\mathbf{X}$ with $\mathbf{XW}$. Minimizing (4) ensures that, if x_i and x_j are close, and as a result $\mathbf{W}^T x_i$ and $\mathbf{W}^T x_j$ are close too.

As described above, LPP seeks a low-dimensional representation with the purpose of preserving the local geometry in the original data. However, such "locality geometry" is completely determined by the artificially constructed neighborhood graph. As a result, its performance may drop seriously if given a "bad" graph. Therefore, it is better to optimize graph and learn the transformation simultaneously in a unified objective function.

3   Unsupervised Feature Selection by Graph Optimization

As reported by many researchers [14–17], graph construction plays a crucial role in the success of graph-based learning methods. Typically, to construct a graph, we define neighborhood based on the k nearest neighbors(kNN) method to determine the connectivity of the graph. In general, the size of the neighborhood needs to be specified in advance and fixed throughout the entire learning process. In real-world applications, it is hard to estimate the neighborhood size and different data points have a different optimal neighborhood size. As a result, some undesirable edges and weights are unavoidable. In our study, we incorporate graph construction into the LPP objective function, and thus obtains a simultaneous learning framework for graph construction and transformation optimization. Moreover, in order to perform feature selection, it is desirable to have some rows of the transformation matrix set to be all zeros. This leads us to use the $\ell_{2,1}$-norm on the transformation matrix $\mathbf{W}$, and this leads to row-sparsity of $\mathbf{W}$. The learning problem can be formulated as the following optimization problem:

$$\min_{\mathbf{S},\mathbf{W}} \sum_{i,j=1}^{n} (\|\mathbf{W}^T x_i - \mathbf{W}^T x_j\|_2^2 s_{ij}) + \alpha\|\mathbf{S} - \mathbf{S}^0\|_F^2 + \mu\|\mathbf{W}\|_{2,1}$$

$$s.t. \quad \forall_i, s_i^T \mathbf{1} = 1, 0 \le s_i \le 1, \mathbf{W}^T S_t \mathbf{W} = I \tag{5}$$

Let the transformation matrix be $\mathbf{W} \in \Re^{d \times m}$ with $m < d$ and the total scatter matrix be $S_t = \mathbf{X}^T H \mathbf{X}$, where $H = I - \frac{1}{n}\mathbf{1}\mathbf{1}^T$ is the centering matrix. We constrain the subspace with $\mathbf{W}^T S_t \mathbf{W} = I$ such that the data in the subspace are statistically uncorrelated. The predefined graph is $\mathbf{S}^0$ graph, $\|\cdot\|_F^2$ is the squared Frobenius divergence, and α and μ are trade-off parameters.

The first term of the objective function in (5) is similar to LPP in (4), which is designed for preserving local structure, such that if x_i and x_j are "close" then the transformed data $\mathbf{W}^T x_i$ and $\mathbf{W}^T x_j$ are also close. The second term of the objective function uses the squared Frobenius divergence to measure the fitting error of the learned graph similarity $\mathbf{S}$ to the predefined graph similarity $\mathbf{S}^0$. It constrains $\mathbf{S}$ to be close to $\mathbf{S}^0$ in order to make use of original data information.

4   Optimization Algorithm for Problem (5)

To obtain the global minimal solution of (5), we use an iterative and interleaved optimization process, which is summarized in Algorithm 1. At each iteration step, the sparse matrix $\mathbf{W}$ is updated by (9). After obtaining $\mathbf{W}$, we then update U using Eq.(6). Finally, we update s_{ij} by solving the problem given in (11) and obtain the optimal solution using Eq.(12).

Note that $\|\mathbf{W}\|_{2,1}$ is convex. Nevertheless, its derivative does not exist when $\hat{w}_i = 0$ for $i = 1, 2, \ldots, d$. Therefore, we use the definition $tr(\mathbf{W}^T U \mathbf{W}) = \|\mathbf{W}\|_{2,1}/2$ in [14] when $\hat{w}_i$ is not equal to 0. The matrix $U \in \Re^{d \times d}$ is diagonal with i-th diagonal element is where

$$U_{ii} = \frac{1}{2\|\hat{w}_i\|_2} \tag{6}$$

We can then rewrite the proposed method in Eq.(5) as the following problem:

$$\min_{\mathbf{S},\mathbf{W},U} tr(\mathbf{W}^T\mathbf{X}^T\mathbf{L}_S\mathbf{X}\mathbf{W}) + \alpha\|\mathbf{S} - \mathbf{S}^0\|_F^2 + \mu tr(\mathbf{W}^T U\mathbf{W})$$

$$s.t. \quad \forall_i, s_i^T\mathbf{1} = 1, 0 \le s_i \le 1, \mathbf{W}^T S_t\mathbf{W} = I \tag{7}$$

where $\mathbf{L}_S$ is the Laplacian matrix and $\mathbf{L}_S = \mathbf{D} - \mathbf{S}$. $\mathbf{D} \in \Re^{n\times n}$ is a diagonal matrix with the i-th diagonal element as $D_{ii} = \sum_{j=1}^n s_{ij}$.

We first fix $\mathbf{S}$ and solve for $\mathbf{W}$ and U, then the problem (7) becomes

$$\min_{\mathbf{W},U} tr(\mathbf{W}^T\mathbf{X}^T\mathbf{L}_S\mathbf{X}\mathbf{W}) + \mu tr(\mathbf{W}^T U\mathbf{W})$$

$$s.t. \quad \mathbf{W}^T S_t\mathbf{W} = I \tag{8}$$

which can be rewritten as the following problem

$$\min_{\mathbf{W},U} tr(\mathbf{W}^T(\mathbf{X}^T\mathbf{L}_S\mathbf{X} + \mu U)\mathbf{W})$$

$$s.t. \quad \mathbf{W}^T S_t\mathbf{W} = I \tag{9}$$

When U is fixed, the optimal solution to the problem in (9) is the spectral decomposition of $S_t^{-1}(\mathbf{X}^T\mathbf{L}_S\mathbf{X} + \mu U)$, i.e., the optimal solution $\mathbf{W}$ is formed by the k eigenvectors of $S_t^{-1}(\mathbf{X}^T\mathbf{L}_S\mathbf{X} + \mu U)$ corresponding to the k smallest eigenvalues (we assume the null space of the data $\mathbf{X}$ is removed, i.e., S_t is invertible). After that, we fix $\mathbf{W}$ and update U by employing the formulation in (6) directly.

When $\mathbf{W}$ and U are fixed, the proposed method given in Eq.(7) can be rewritten as

$$\min_{\mathbf{S}} tr(\mathbf{W}^T\mathbf{X}^T\mathbf{L}_S\mathbf{X}\mathbf{W}) + \alpha\|\mathbf{S} - \mathbf{S}^0\|_F^2$$

$$s.t. \quad \forall_i, s_i^T\mathbf{1} = 1, 0 \le s_i \le 1 \tag{10}$$

Since $\|\mathbf{S} - \mathbf{S}^0\|_F^2 = tr((\mathbf{S} - \mathbf{S}^0)^T(\mathbf{S} - \mathbf{S}^0))$, then Eq.(10) can be rewritten as

$$\min_{\mathbf{S}} \sum_{i,j=1}^n (\|\mathbf{W}^T x_i - \mathbf{W}^T x_j\|_2^2 s_{ij}) + \alpha\left[\sum_{i,j=1}^n s_{ij}^2 - 2\sum_{i,j=1}^n s_{ij}s_{ij}^0 + tr(s^{0T}s^0)\right]$$

$$s.t. \quad \forall_i, s_i^T\mathbf{1} = 1, 0 \le s_i \le 1 \tag{11}$$

Taking derivative with respect to s_{ij} and setting it to zero, we have

$$\frac{\partial}{\partial s_{ij}}\left[(\|\mathbf{W}^T x_i - \mathbf{W}^T x_j\|_2^2 s_{ij}) + \alpha\left[\sum_{i,j=1}^n s_{ij}^2 - 2\sum_{i,j=1}^n s_{ij}s_{ij}^0 + tr(s^{0T}s^0)\right]\right] = 0$$

$$\Rightarrow \|\mathbf{W}^T x_i - \mathbf{W}^T x_j\|_2^2 + 2\alpha s_{ij} - 2\alpha s_{ij}^0 = 0 \tag{12}$$

$$\Rightarrow s_{ij} = s_{ij}^0 - \frac{1}{2\alpha}\|\mathbf{W}^T x_i - \mathbf{W}^T x_j\|_2^2$$

From Eq.(12), it is clear that the similarity s_{ij} is not only updated by the initial graph similarity s_{ij}^0 in the original input space, but also updated gradually in the different transformed progressive spaces by current $\mathbf{W}$ until the algorithm converges. In fact, when α tends to $+\infty$, s_{ij} approaches s_{ij}^0. That is, the learned $\mathbf{S}$ reduces to the predefined $\mathbf{S}^0$. Intuitively, our algorithm will give better discriminative power than typical unsupervised feature selection methods. i.e. JELSR, since it simultaneously learns both the similarity matrix $\mathbf{S}$ and the sparse transformation matrix $\mathbf{W}$.

In summary, we solve the optimization problem in (5) in an iterative and interleaved way. More concretely, we first fix $\mathbf{S}$ and U, thus employing (9) to update $\mathbf{W}$, whose columns are the m eigenvectors of $S_t^{-1}(\mathbf{X}^T \mathbf{L}_S \mathbf{X} + \mu U)$ corresponding to the m smallest eigenvalues. We then fix $\mathbf{W}$ and update U using Eq.(6). Finally, we update s_{ij} by solving the problem in (11) and obtain the optimal solution as Eq.(12).

After the optimal $\mathbf{W}$ is obtained, we then sort all the original d features according to the ℓ_2-norm values of the d rows of $\mathbf{W}$ in descending order, and select the top features.

Algorithm 1. Unsupervised Feature Selection by Graph Optimization (UFSGO)

Input: $\mathbf{X} \in \Re^{n \times d}$, parameter α and μ, $\mathbf{S}^0$.
Output: the optimal sparse transformation matrix $\mathbf{W} \in \Re^{d \times m}$
1: while not converge do
2:     Update $\mathbf{w}$ by (9) whose columns are the k eigenvectors of $S_t^{-1}(\mathbf{X}^T \mathbf{L}_S \mathbf{X} + \mu U)$ corresponding to the k smallest eigenvalues;
3:     Update U by Eq.(6);
4:     We update s_{ij} by solving the problem (11) and obtain the optimal solution as Eq.(12).
5: end while

---

5   Experiments and Comparisons

To demonstrate the effectiveness of the proposed approach, we conduct experiments on five image data sets, i.e., three face image data set AR, YaleB and ORL, one hand written digit data set MNIST and one shape image data set MPEG-7. Table. 1 summarizes the extents and properties of the four image data-sets.

Table 1. Summary of four benchmark image data sets

Data-set	Sample	Features	Classes
AR	1680	2000	120
MPEG-7	1400	6000	70
YaleB	2414	1024	38
MNIST	2000	784	10

Table 2. The best result of all unsupervised methods and their corresponding size of selected feature subset (MEAN ± STD).

Dataset	AR	MPEG-7	YaleB	MNIST
SPEC	80.8% ± 2.23 (180)	72.8% ± 1.88(180)	76% ± 1.88 (140)	80.9% ± 1.91 (200)
JELSR	82.2% ± 1.77 (170)	70% ± 2.98 (190)	81.9% ± 2.34 (180)	77% ± 1.21 (140)
MCFS	78.7% ± 2.89 (120)	73.2% ± 1.03 (190)	77.4% ± 3.66 (200)	76.4% ± 2.56(170)
LapScore	76.9% ± 3.32 (130)	72.3% ± 2.51 (200)	78.7% ± 4.33(200)	76.1% ± 1.73(130)
UFSGO	**89.9% ± 2.38(130)**	**75.6% ± 1.45(180)**	**86.7% ± 1.67(140)**	**81.6% ± 2.03(140)**

Since our proposed model (see Eq.5) can be interpreted as more generalized version of LPP with additional graph similarity preservation and sparse feature selection capabilities, we begin with evaluating the classification performance based on the proposed method (UFSGO) on the above four publicly available image datasets, compared with LPP. Then, we compare the classification results from UFSGO with four representative unsupervised feature selection algorithms. These methods are LapScore [9], SPEC [11], MCFS [12], JELSR [14]. A 10-fold cross-validation strategy using the nu-Support Vector Machine (nu-SVM) [19] is employed to evaluate the classification performance. The parameters in feature selection algorithms as well as the nu-SVM classifier are tuned via cross-validation on the training data. Specifically, the entire sample is randomly partitioned into 10 subsets and then we choose one subset for test and use the remaining 9 for training, and this procedure is repeated 10 times. The final accuracy is computed by averaging of the accuracies from all experiments.

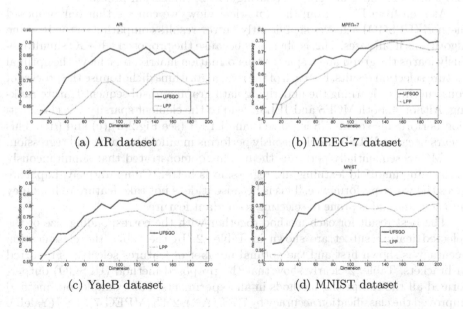

(a) AR dataset   (b) MPEG-7 dataset

(c) YaleB dataset   (d) MNIST dataset

Fig. 1. Accuracy rate vs. the variation of dimension on four benchmark image datasets by LPP and UFSGO.

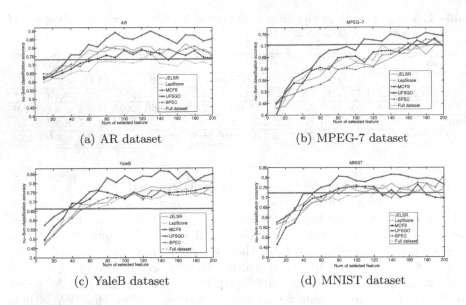

(a) AR dataset

(b) MPEG-7 dataset

(c) YaleB dataset

(d) MNIST dataset

Fig. 2. Accuracy rate vs. the number of selected features on four benchmark image datasets by nu-SVM.

From Fig.1, we observe that UFSGO can consistently outperform LPP on all the used datasets. This states that UFSGO is more discriminative than LPP, and really benefits from graph updating and optimization process.

As seen from Fig.2, from the statistical view, we can see that our proposed method (UFSGO) achieves significantly better results comparing to the baseline algorithms in all cases. This is obviously because the proposed UFSGO simultaneously learns the graph and a sparse transformation matrix, to achieve the optimal feature selection results, but each of the rival algorithms dichotomise the process of constructing or learning the underlying data graph and subsequent feature ranking. Although both MCFS and JELSR lead to the element sparsity, the classification performance of MCFS is worse than JELSR (see Fig.2(a),(c) and (d)). This occurs because JELSR simultaneously performs manifold learning and regression, but MCFS sequentially performs them. This demonstrated that simultaneously performing manifold learning and regression is better. Comparatively, LapScore gives the worst performance. This is because it does not take feature redundancy into account and is prone to selecting redundant features.

The best result for each method together with the corresponding size of the selected feature subset are shown in Table. 2. In the table, the classification accuracy is shown first and the optimal number of features selected is reported in brackets. Table. 2 clearly show that the proposed method (UFSGO) outperformed all the competing methods in all experiments. For example, our method improved the classification accuracy by 7.7% (AR), 2.4%(MPEG-7), 4.8%(YaleB), 0.7%(MNIST), respectively, compared to the best performances among the competing methods. Based on these results, we argue that the proposed joint graph optimization and feature selection method help enhance the classification performance. Although JELSR performs better in many cases, the optimal graph embedding in JELSR depends heavily on the transformed data, without making the best use of the original data information and the data similarity S is also not learned by the algorithm. This easily leads to the instability performance, especially when encountering a "bad" transformation matrix. Comparatively, our proposed method UFSGO simultaneously learns the data similarity matrix and sparse transformation matrix to achieve optimal feature selection results, while the original data information is also embedded into the graph optimization.

6   Conclusion

In this paper, we proposed a novel unsupervised feature selection algorithm. The approach not only investigates a graph optimization method by learning the data similarity matrix but also presents a simultaneously learning of the sparse matrix for feature selection. As a result, the graph in UFSGO is adjustable instead of predefined as in alternative graph based feature selection methods. Moreover, a square Frobenius divergence term between a predefined graph and its updated realization is added to the objective function which can fully utilize information in the original data. Experimental results from unsupervised feature selection cases demonstrate the effectiveness and efficiency of the proposed UFSGO framework.

Acknowledgments. This work is supported by National Natural Science Foundation of China (Grant No.61402389). Edwin R. Hancock is supported by a Royal Society Wolfson Research Merit Award.

References

1. Shi, J., Malik, J.: Normalized cuts and image segmentation. IEEE Transactions on Pattern Analysis and Machine Intelligence **22**(8), 888–905 (2000)
2. Belkin, M., Niyogi, P.: Laplacian eigenmaps and spectral techniques for embedding and clustering. Advances in neural information processing systems **14**, 585–591 (2001)
3. Kulis, B., Basu, S., Dhillon, I., Mooney, R.: Semi-supervised graph clustering: a kernel approach. In: Proceedings of The 22nd International Conference on Machine Learning, vol. 74, no. 1, pp. 457–464 (2005)
4. Chung, F.: Spectral Graph Theory. American Mathematical Society (1992)
5. Jain, V., Zhang, H.: A spectral approach to shape-based retrieval of articulated 3D models. Computer-Aided Design **39**(5), 398–407 (2007)
6. Jin, R., Ding, C., Kang, F.: A probabilistic approach for optimizing spectral clustering. Advances in Neural Information Processing systems, vol. 18. MIT Press, Cambridge (2005)
7. Zhu, X., Ghahramani, Z., Lafferty, J.: Semi-supervised learning using gaussian fields and harmonic functions. Proceedings of the Twentieth International Conference on Machine Learning **20**(2), 912–919 (2003)

8. Belkin, M., Niyogi, P.: Laplacian eigenmaps for dimensionality reduction and data representation. Neural computation **15**(6), 1373–1396 (2003)
9. He, X., Cai, D., Niyogi, P.: Laplacian score for feature selection. In: Advances in neural information processing systems, pp. 507–514 (2005)
10. Bach, F., Jordan, M.: Learning spectral clustering, with application to speech separation. The Journal of Machine Learning Research **7**, 1963–2001 (2006)
11. Zhao, Z., Liu, H.: Spectral feature selection for supervised and unsupervised learning. In: Proceedings of the 24th International Conference on Machine Learning, pp. 1151–1157 (2007)
12. Cai, D., Zhang, C., He, X.: Unsupervised feature selection for multi-cluster data. In: Proceedings of the 16th ACM SIGKDD international conference on Knowledge discovery and data mining, pp. 333–342 (2010)
13. Zhao, Z., Wang, L., Liu, H.: Efficient spectral feature selection with minimum redundancy. In: Proceedings of AAAI, pp. 673–678 (2010)
14. Hou, C., Nie, F., Yi, D., Wu, Y.: Joint embedding learning and sparse regression: A framework for unsupervised feature selection. IEEE Transactions on Cybernetics **44**(6), 793–804 (2014)
15. Liu, X., Wang, L., Zhang, J., Liu, H.: Global and local structure preservation for feature selection. IEEE Transactions on Neural Networks and Learning Systems **25**(6), 1083–1095 (2014)
16. Nie, F., Wang, X., Huang, H.: Clustering and projected clustering with adaptive neighbors. In: Proceedings of the 20th ACM SIGKDD International Conference on Knowledge Discovery and Data Mining, pp. 977–986 (2014)
17. Zhang, L., Qiao, L., Chen, S.: Graph-optimized locality preserving projections. Pattern Recognition **43**(6), 1993–2002 (2010)
18. He, X., Niyogi, P.: Locality preserving projections. Neural information processing systems. MIT Press, Cambridge (2003)
19. Chang, C., Lin, C.: LIBSVM: a library for support vector machines. ACM Transactions on Intelligent Systems and Technology (2011)

Gait Recognition Robust to Speed Transition Using Mutual Subspace Method

Yumi Iwashita[1](✉), Hitoshi Sakano[2], and Ryo Kurazume[1]

[1] Kyushu University, Fukuoka, Japan
yumi@ieee.org
[2] NTT Data Corporation, Tokyo, Japan
sakanoh@nttdata.co.jp

Abstract. Person recognition from gait images is not robust to speed changes. To deal with this problem, generally existing methods have focused on training a model to transform gait features from various speeds into a common walking speed, and the model was trained with gait images with a variety of speeds. However in case that a subject walks with a speed which is not trained in the model, the performance gets worse. In this paper we introduce an idea that an image set-based matching approach, which omits walking speed information, has a potential to solve the problem. This is based on the assumption that speed information may not be critical information to gait recognition, since speed variations are universal phenomena. To prove the proposed idea, we apply a mutual subspace method to gait images and show the effectiveness of the proposed idea with the OU-ISIR gait speed transition database.

Keywords: Gait recognition · Speed transition · Subspace method

1 Introduction

Gait-based person recognition has received an increasing amount of attentions for monitoring and surveillance applications, thanks to the advantages that gait does not require interaction with a subject and can be obtained from a distance. Person identification methods that extract features from gait images taken by a camera have been used with good results. Existing methods using appearance-based gait features, such as gait energy image (GEI) [1], active energy image (AEI) [2] and frame difference frieze pattern (FDFP) [3], reported good performance with publicly available gait databases [4] [5] [6] [7].

However, there are several causes which make the performance of gait recognition worse, and one of them is walking speed change. The walking speed change causes variations in pitch and stride, which result in non-invariant gait features. To address this problem existing methods focused on transforming the gait features from various speeds into a common walking speed [8] or extraction of speed-invariant gait feature [9]. However, since the existing methods assumed

© Springer International Publishing Switzerland 2015
V. Murino and E. Puppo (Eds.): ICIAP 2015, Part I, LNCS 9279, pp. 141–149, 2015.
DOI: 10.1007/978-3-319-23231-7_13

that the walking speed is constant in one gait cycle, the performance of gait recognition is low in cases in which the subject accelerates or decelerates. The speed transition can happen in daily life, such as acceleration after a ticket gate at a station and deceleration before stop at red traffic signal, and the speed transition problem was firstly reported by Mansur et al. [10]. They proposed a method which synthesized constant-speed gait images based on a cylindrical manifold, which was based on a mapping function trained with an auxiliary training set including gait images under various speeds. Then experimental evaluations of the proposed method was done with a newly released database for speed transition.

As we mentioned above, most of existing methods assumed to have auxiliary training sets to train models. However, in case that a subject walks with a speed which is not included in the auxiliary training set, the performance gets worse. In this paper, we introduce a new idea as follows. Since speed variations are universal phenomena, there is a possibility that speed information does not have to be regarded as critical information to gait recognition. Based on this assumption, we obtain an idea that an image set-based matching approach can solve the gait recognition problem. To show the effectiveness of this idea, in this paper we apply a mutual subspace method (MSM) [14] [15] to gait images under speed transition. Subspace-based methods have been popularly used in face recognition, and the effectiveness of MSM is demonstrated in [16]. Advantages of the use of the image set-based matching approach to gait recognition are as follows: (i) we can directly apply gait images/gait features to the image set-based matching approach without any process such as constant-speed gait image generation [10], and (ii) we do not need any auxiliary training sets. We conducted experiments with the database which Mansur et. al used in [10], and we obtained results with higher performance compared with [10].

There are some existing gait recognition methods using subspace techniques. Liu et al. proposed a gait recognition method which was robust in subject's walking direction changes with respect to a camera [11]. In [11], GEI, which is one of popular gait features, was extracted from gait images at each walking direction. A subspace method was applied to a set of GEI from multiple walking directions, and then a weighted subspace distance was used for person identification. Connie et al. proposed a gait recognition method which formulated a gait subspaces on the Grassmann manifold [12]. This method can be applied to either gait images with walking direction changes or gait images with speed changes, and it also used GEI which was extracted from gait images at each condition (e.g. at each walking direction/speed).

These existing methods need training datasets which include gait images at multiple conditions, such as gait images under multiple walking directions/speeds. We agree that gait images at multiple walking directions are necessary for gait recognition robust to changes in walking direction. However, as we mentioned above, speed information may not be critical information to gait recognition, and thus the proposed image set-based matching approach, which ignores speed information, has a big potential to be efficient to speed changes.

The remainder of the present paper is organized as follows. Section 2 describes gait recognition using the mutual subspace method. Section 3 describes experiments performed to demonstrate the efficiency of the proposed idea using the OU-ISIR gait speed transition database, and Section 4 presents our conclusions.

2 Gait Recognition Using Mutual Subspace Method

In this section we briefly review the mutual subspace method, and then we explain the way how we apply the mutual subspace method as an image set-based matching.

2.1 Mutual Subspace Method

The Mutual Subspace method (MSM) is regarded as one of powerful image set - image set matching techniques. The MSM models template images of each class in gallery dataset and input images in probe dataset as subspaces, and images are embedded to the subspaces. The similarity measure in the MSM is calculated as a canonical angle between template subspace and input subspace.

Let us assume C class pattern recognition problem. Patterns in class c are represented in d dimensional vectors $x^c{}_1$, ..., $x^c{}_{n^c}$, where n^c is the number of training samples in class c. Bases of the class c template subspace are given by the following eigenequation;

$$\Gamma^c \phi^c = \lambda^c \phi^c, \tag{1}$$

where λ^c and ϕ^c are eigenvalue and eigenvector, respectively. Γ^c is autocorrelation matrix of class c training samples,

$$\Gamma^c = \frac{1}{n^c} \sum_{i=1}^{n^c} \sum_{j=1}^{n^c} x_i^c x_j^{cT}. \tag{2}$$

Similarly input images $x_1, \ldots, x_n$ are represented by eigenvector of autocorrelation matrix ψ. The similarity measure in the MSM is canonical angle between two subspaces, which are calculated as eigenvalues of following matrix [17].

$$Z^c = (\zeta_{ij})^c = \sum_{m=1}^{M} (\phi_i^c \cdot \psi_m)(\phi_j^c \cdot \psi_m), \tag{3}$$

where M is dimensionality of input subspace. Dimensionalities of training and input images are influential parameters. Roughly speaking the dimensionality is proportional to variation of training and input images. However when the dimensionality increase too large, recognition accuracies are worse, because of the increasing amount of intersections among subspaces. Generally such dimensionalities are defined by cross validation experiments. Finally, class c is chosen, in case that the maximum eigenvalue of Z^c is the highest one among all classes.

2.2   Gait Recognition Using an Image Set-Based Matching

Assume that there are gait images of a subject and silhouette images are obtained as shown in Fig. 1 (a). As a baseline method of the image set-based approach, we directly use intensity values of each silhouette image as a feature vector, and we apply the mutual subspace method to a set of feature vectors from silhouette images. Fig. 1 (b) shows examples of visualizations of principal components. We projected silhouette images to first, second, and third principal components as shown in Fig. 2. Fig. 2 (a) shows projected results of gait image to 1st-2nd principal components, and images of frame ID 1 to 37 are for the duration of the first half gait cycle (one step) and those of frame ID 38 to 74 are for the duration of the last half gait cycle (one step). Fig. 2 (b) shows projected results of gait image to 2nd-3rd principal components.

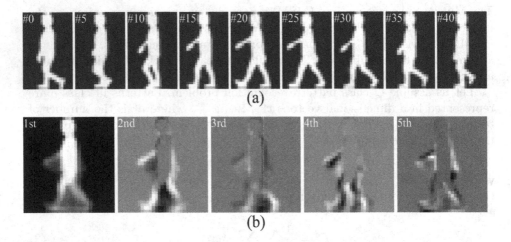

Fig. 1. (a) Examples of gait images and (b) visualization of each principal component (color information is scaled in the range from 0 to 255, for the purpose of visualization).

3   Experiments

In this section, we implement the mutual subspace method and evaluate its performance on the OU-ISIR gait speed transition database [10].

3.1   Experimental Settings

Datasets. The OU-ISIR gait speed transition dataset is the only one dataset which includes gait datasets with speed transition within an image sequence. The dataset consists of two different datasets, dataset 1 and dataset 2. In the dataset 1 the probe set consists of speed transited gait sequences recorded from 26 subjects. More specifically, each subject gradually decreased walking speed and finally stop, and the final gait period of each subject was selected as the

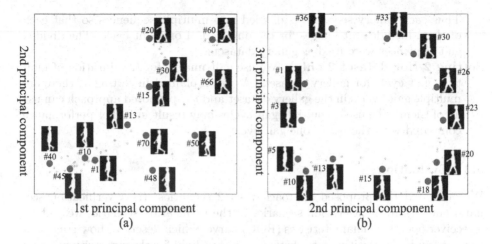

Fig. 2. Projection of gait images to 1st-2nd principal components (a) and 2nd-3rd principal components (b). Frame ID 1 to 37 are for the duration of the first half gait cycle and frame ID 38 to 74 are for the duration of the last half gait cycle.

probe dataset, which contains significant change in stride. The gallery dataset consists of gait sequences from 179 subjects, which include the 26 probe subjects, and the subjects walked at the constant speed (4 km/h) for a few seconds.

In the dataset 2 the probe set consists of 25 subjects and each subject walked twice on the treadmill under the following conditions: (i) accelerations from 1 km/h to 5 km/h and (ii) decelerations from 5 km/h to 1 km/h. For gallery dataset, there are 154 subjects, which include the 25 probe subjects, and each subject walked at a constant speed (4 km/h) for six seconds.

In addition to the two datasets we explained above, the OU-ISIR gait speed transition dataset has an auxiliary training set, which includes 24 subjects under various walking speeds (2, 3, 4, an 5 km/h). It is worth to be pointed out that in [10] the auxiliary training set was used for learning a mapping function to synthesize constant-speed gait images. However, in case that the subject walks with a speed which is not included in the auxiliary training set, the performance gets worse. On the other hand, the proposed approach does not need the auxiliary training set, and thus it can work with subjects walking with arbitrary speeds.

Evaluation Setting. We evaluated the proposed approach with the following two settings.

Setting 1: In general gait features are obtained from a set of images for the duration of one gait cycle. Thus we use gait images for the duration of one gait cycle for both probe and gallery datasets. This is the same evaluation setting of [10]. In [10], GEI was extracted from each gait sequence which includes gait images for the duration of one gait cycle. As we mentioned above, each gallery sequence of dataset 2 is for six seconds and this means the gallery sequences have images for the duration of multiple gait cycles.

Thus each gallery sequence is divided into multiple sequences so that each of them include gait images for the duration of one gait cycle. The divided gait sequences were used as gallery datasets.

Setting 2 (for dataset 2 only): We use gait images for the duration of multiple gait cycle for gallery datasets. As we explained in setting 1, there are multiple gait cycles in the gallery dataset and the proposed approach can use all of them. The use of multiple gait cycles may result in higher performance compared with the use of one gait cycle.

3.2 Evaluation

We evaluated the proposed approach with 2 scenarios: (i) a verification scenario and (ii) an identification scenario. In the verification scenario, we plotted a receiver operating characteristics (ROC) curve, which describes how true positive rate and false positive rate changes as a threshold for the similarity measure changes. In the identification scenario, we plotted a cumulative matching characteristics (CMC) curve (i.e., rank-n identification rates).

Table 1. EER, rank-1 and rank-5 identification rates for dataset 2 (acceleration).

	Mansur et. al [10]	*Proposed (setting1)*	*Proposed (setting2)*
EER [%]	8.0	7.0	1.0
Rank-1 [%]	72.0	92.0	96.0
Rank-5 [%]	96.0	92.0	100.0

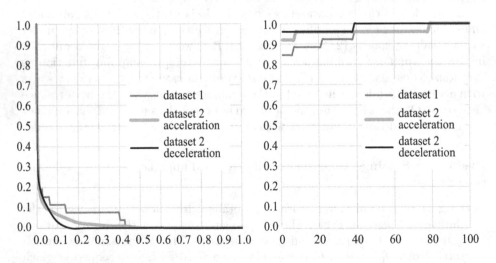

Fig. 3. ROC (left) and CMC curves (right) for dataset 1, dataset 2 (acceleration), and dataset 2 (deceleration) with the setting 1.

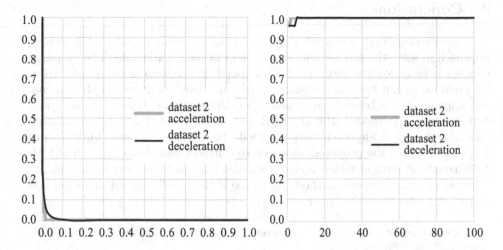

Fig. 4. ROC (left) and CMC curves (right) for dataset 2 (acceleration) and dataset 2 (deceleration) with the setting 2.

We first evaluated the proposed approach with setting 1. Figure 3 shows ROC curves and the CMC curves of the dataset 1, dataset 2 (acceleration), and dataset 2 (deceleration). These results show much higher performance compared to those of [10] (please refer to [10]). These results show higher performance than the existing method [10]. The results of dataset 1 show lower performance compared with those of dataset 2. As the reason is explained in [10], the dataset 1 is more challenging since it contains significant gait fluctuation and very short stride lengths.

Next we evaluated the proposed approach with setting 2. Figure 4 shows the ROC curves and CMC curves of the dataset 2 (acceleration) and dataset 2 (deceleration). Compared with the results of Fig. 3 at setting 1, the results of 4 at setting 2 significantly improved the performance, thanks to the use of all gait cycles in dataset.

Tables 1 and 2 show equal error rate (EER) and rank-1 and rank-5 identification rates of the proposed approach and [10]. These results show the proposed approach outperformed the existing method [10].

Table 2. EER, rank-1 and rank-5 identification rates for dataset 2 (deceleration).

	Mansur et. al [10]	*Proposed (setting1)*	*Proposed (setting2)*
EER [%]	8.0	6.0	3.0
Rank-1 [%]	84.0	96.0	96.0
Rank-5 [%]	92.0	96.0	100.0

4   Conclusions

This paper described a new idea of the use of the image set-based matching approach to solve the gait recognition problem in speed variations. The proposed concept is based on the assumption that speed information may not be critical information to gait recognition, since speed variations are universal phenomena. We implemented a baseline approach using the mutual subspace method, and experimental results with the OU-ISIR gait speed transition database showed that the proposed approach outperformed the existing method. Future work includes applying the proposed approach to different gait datasets, such as OU-ISIR treadmill dataset which includes various speeds. Moreover, we will utilize a kernel mutual subspace method [13] to see if the non-linear subspace method can work better than the linear one.

Acknowledgments. This work is supported by a Grant-in-Aid for Exploratory Research (26630099).

References

1. Han, J., Bhanu, B.: Individual Recognition using Gait Energy Image. IEEE Trans. on Pattern Analysis and Machine Intelligence, 28(2) (2006)
2. Zhang, E., Zhao, Y., Xiong, W.: Active energy image plus 2DLPP for gait recognition. Signal Processing 90(7), 2295–2302 (2010)
3. Shinzaki, M., Iwashita, Y., Kurazume, R., Ogawara, K.: Gait-based person identification method using shadow biometrics for robustness to changes in the walking direction. In: IEEE Winter Conf. on Applications of Computer Vision, pp. 670–677 (2015)
4. Iwashita, Y., Baba, R., Ogawara, K. Kurazume, R.: Person identification from spatio-temporal 3D gait. In: Int. Conf. Emerging Security Technologies (EST), pp. 30–35 (2010)
5. Iwashita, Y., Ogawara, K., Kurazume, R.: Identification of people walking along curved trajectories. Pattern Recognition Letters 46, 60–69 (2014)
6. CASIA Gait Database. http://www.sinobiometrics.com
7. Iwama, H., Okumura, M., Makihara, Y., Yagi, Y.: The OU-ISIR Gait Database Comprising the Large Population Dataset and Performance Evaluation of Gait Recognition. IEEE Trans. on Information Forensics and Security 7(5), 1511–1521 (2012)
8. Tanawongsuwan, R., Bobick, A.: Modelling the effects of walking speed on appearance-based gait recognition. Computer Vision and Pattern Recognition (2004)
9. Liu, Z., Sarkar, S.: Improved gait recognition by gait dynamics normalization. IEEE Trans. on Pattern Analysis and Machine Intelligence 28 (2006)
10. Mansur, A., Makihara, Y., Aqmar, R., Yagi, Y.: Gait Recognition under Speed Transition. In: IPSJ Trans. on Computer Vision and Applications, Computer Vision and Pattern Recognition (2014)
11. Liu, N., Lu, J., Tan, Y., Li, M.: Set-to-set gait recognition across varying views and walking conditions. In: IEEE Int. Conf. on Multimedia and Expo, pp. 1–6 (2011)

12. Connie, T., Go, M., Teoh, A.: A Grassmann graph embedding framework for gait analysis. EURASIP Journal on Advances in Signal Processing (2014)
13. Sakano, H., Mukawa, N.; Kernel mutual subspace method for robust facial image recognition. In: Int. Conf. on Knowledge-Based Intelligent Engineering Systems and Allied Technologies, vol. 1, pp. 245–248 (2000)
14. Maeda, K., Watanabe, S.: Pattern matching method with local structure. Trans. on IEICE (D) (Japanese Edition) **68–D**(3), 345–352 (1985)
15. Maeda, K.: From the Subspace Methods to the Mutual Subspace Method. Computer Vision **285**, 135–156 (2010)
16. Yamaguchi, O., Fukui, K., Maeda, K.: Face recognition using temporal image sequence. In: IEEE Int. Conf. on Face and Gesture Recognition, pp. 318–323 (1998)
17. Chatelin, F.: Veleurs propres de matrices. Masson (1988) (In French)

Path-Based Dominant-Set Clustering

Eyasu Zemene$^{(\boxtimes)}$ and Marcello Pelillo

DAIS, Università Ca' Foscari di Venezia,
via Torino 155, 30172 Venezia Mestre, Italy
eyasu.zemene@unive.it, pelillo@dais.unive.it

Abstract. Although off-the-shelf clustering algorithms, such as those based on spectral graph theory, do a pretty good job at finding clusters of arbitrary shape and structure, they are inherently unable to satisfactorily deal with situations involving the presence of cluttered backgrounds. On the other hand, dominant sets, a generalization of the notion of maximal clique to edge-weighted graphs, exhibit a complementary nature: they are remarkably effective in dealing with background noise but tend to favor compact groups. In order to take the best of the two approaches, in this paper we propose to combine path-based similarity measures, which exploit connectedness information of the elements to be clustered, with the dominant-set approach. The resulting algorithm is shown to consistently outperform standard clustering methods over a variety of datasets under severe noise conditions.

1 Introduction

Consider the data points shown in Figure 1(a). Despite the heavy background noise, we seem to have no difficulty in extracting a few "natural" clusters representing the letters of a familiar word. Unfortunately, standard clustering algorithms, such as those based on spectral graph theory, while doing a pretty good job in the noise-free case, perform rather poorly in such situations, as shown in Figure 1(c-d). The main reason behind this disappointing behavior is that they are typically all based on the idea of partitioning the input data, and hence the clutter points as well, into coherent classes.

In the last few years, dominant sets have emerged as a powerful alternative to spectral-based and similar methods [8], and are finding applications in a variety of different application domains such as computer vision, bioinformatics, medical image analysis, etc. Motivated by intriguing graph- and game-theoretical interpretations they try to capture the very essence of the notion of a cluster, namely their being maximally homogenous groups. By focusing on the question "what is a cluster?" dominant sets overcome some of the classical limitations of partition-based approaches such as the inability to extract overlapping clusters and the need to know the number of clusters in advance [9]. A typical problem associated to dominant sets, however, is that they tend to favor compact clusters. The problem therefore remains as to how to deal with situations involving arbitrarily-shaped clusters in a context of heavy background noise.

© Springer International Publishing Switzerland 2015
V. Murino and E. Puppo (Eds.): ICIAP 2015, Part I, LNCS 9279, pp. 150–160, 2015.
DOI: 10.1007/978-3-319-23231-7_14

(a)   (b)

(c)   (d)

Fig. 1. Results of extracting characters from clutter (a) Characters with uniformly distributed clutter elements which do not belong to any cluster (Original dataset to be clustered) (b) Result of our method (PBD) (c) The result of Path-based Spectral Clustering (PBS) (d) NJW's algorithms result.

In this paper we propose a simple yet effective approach to solve this problem, which is based on the idea of feeding the dominant-set algorithm with a path-based similarity measure proposed earlier in a different context [1][3][4][5]. This takes into account connectivity information of the elements being clustered, thereby transforming clusters exhibiting an elongated structure under the original similarity function into compact ones. Recently, an approach which combines path-based similarities with spectral clustering has been introduced [1]. It improves the robustness of a spectral clustering algorithm by developing robust path-based similarity based on M-estimation from robust statistics. Instead of applying the spectral analysis directly on the original similarity matrix, they first modify the similarity matrix in such a way that the connectedness information is allowed for and at the same time checking if the sample is an outlier. However, the method is robust only against small number of thinly scattered outliers and, being based on spectral partition-based methods, it cannot safely extract elements from heavy background noise. Indeed, dominant sets and spectral clustering seem to exhibit a complementary features. On the one hand, spectral-based methods do typically a good job at extracting elongated clusters but perform poorly in the presence of clutter noise, on the other hand the dominant-set algorithm prefers compact structures but is remarkably robust under heavy background noise. With our simple approach we are able to take the best of the two approaches, namely the ability to extract arbitrarily complex clusters and, at the same time, to deal with clutter noise. A similar attempt, though with different objectives, was done in [2]. Several experiments conducted over both toy and standard datasets have shown the effectiveness of the proposed approach.

2   Path-Based Dominant Sets

2.1   Dominant Set Clustering

We represent the data to be clustered as an undirected edge-weighted graph with no self-loops $G = (V, E, w)$, where $V = \{1, ..., n\}$ is the vertex set, $E \subseteq V \times V$ is the edge set, and $w : E \to R_+^*$ is the (positive) weight function. Vertices in G correspond to data points, edges represent neighborhood relationships, and edge-weights reflect similarity between pairs of linked vertices. As customary, we represent the graph G with the corresponding weighted adjacency (or similarity) matrix, which is the $n \times n$ nonnegative, symmetric matrix $A = (a_{ij})$ defined as $a_{ij} = w(i, j)$ if $(i, j) \in E$, and $a_{ij} = 0$ otherwise. Since in G there are no self-loops, note that all entries on the main diagonal of A are zero.

In an attempt to formally capture this notion, we need some notations and definitions. For a non-empty subset $S \subseteq V$, $i \in S$, and $j \notin S$, we define

$$\phi_S(i, j) = a_{ij} - \frac{1}{|S|} \sum_{k \in S} a_{ik} . \tag{1}$$

This quantity measures the (relative) similarity between nodes j and i, with respect to the average similarity between node i and its neighbors in S. Note that $\phi_S(i, j)$ can be either positive or negative. Next, to each vertex $i \in S$ we assign a weight defined (recursively) as follows:

$$w_S(i) = \begin{cases} 1, & \text{if } |S| = 1, \\ \sum_{j \in S \setminus \{i\}} \phi_{S \setminus \{i\}}(j, i) w_{S \setminus \{i\}}(j), & \text{otherwise} . \end{cases} \tag{2}$$

Intuitively, $w_S(i)$ gives us a measure of the overall similarity between vertex i and the vertices of $S \setminus \{i\}$ with respect to the overall similarity among the vertices in $S \setminus \{i\}$. Therefore, a positive $w_S(i)$ indicates that adding i into its neighbors in S will increase the internal coherence of the set, whereas in the presence of a negative value we expect the overall coherence to be decreased. Finally, the total weight of S can be simply defined as

$$W(S) = \sum_{i \in S} w_S(i) . \tag{3}$$

A non-empty subset of vertices $S \subseteq V$ such that $W(T) > 0$ for any non-empty $T \subseteq S$, is said to be a *dominant set* if:

a. $w_S(i) > 0$, for all $i \in S$.
b. $w_{S \cup i}(i) < 0$, for all $i \notin S$.

It is evident from the definition that a dominant set satisfies the two basic properties of a cluster: internal coherence and external incoherence. Condition 1 indicates that a dominant set is internally coherent, while condition 2 implies that this coherence will be destroyed by the addition of any vertex from outside. In other words, a dominant set is a maximally coherent data set.

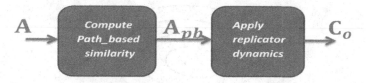

Fig. 2. Block diagram of the framework, where '**A**' is the original similarity, '**A**$_{pb}$' is the path_based similarity and **C**$_o$ is the cluster outputs

Now, consider the following linearly-constrained quadratic optimization problem:

$$\max \quad x^T A x \quad \text{s.t.} \quad x \in \Delta \tag{4}$$

where $\Delta = \{x \in R^n : \sum_i x_i = 1, \text{ and } x_i \geq 0 \text{ for all } i = 1 \ldots n\}$ is the standard simplex of R^n. [8] established a connection between dominant sets and the local solutions of (4). In particular, they showed that if S is a dominant set then its "weighted characteristics vector" x^S, which is the vector of Δ defined as

$$x_i^S = \begin{cases} \frac{w_S(i)}{W(s)}, & \text{if } i \in S, \\ 0, & \text{otherwise} \end{cases}$$

is a strict local solution of (4). Conversely, under mild conditions, it turns out that if x is a strict local solution of program (4) then its "support" $S = \{i \in V : x_i > 0\}$ is a dominant set. By virtue of this result, we can find a dominant set by first localizing a solution of program (4) with an appropriate continuous optimization technique, and then picking up the support set of the solution found. In this sense, we indirectly perform combinatorial optimization via continuous optimization.

A simple and effective optimization algorithm to extract a dominant set is given by the so-called *replicator dynamics* developed and studied in evolutionary game theory:

$$x_i^{(t+1)} = x_i^{(t)} \frac{(Ax^{(t)})_i}{x^{(t)\prime} A x^{(t)}}$$

for $i = 1, \ldots, n$. It is also possible to use a more efficient dynamics developed recently by [11] which has a computational complexity per step that grows linearly in the number of vertices. After extracting a dominant set, we remove its vertices from the graph and repeat the process until all elements are clustered. Using this "peel-off" strategy, the number of clusters is automatically determined and the resulted clusters satisfy the constraint of high intra-cluster and low inter-cluster similarity (see [14][12] for procedures to extract overlapping clusters). This makes dominant sets a flexible clustering notion, thereby making it especially attractive for the problem at hand.

2.2 Using Path-Based Similarity

The notion of path based technique, as shown in figure 3, is a simple but very effective way to capture elongated structures. It considers the connectedness

Fig. 3. Point 'i' and point 'k', even-though they are very far from each other, are more similar than point 'i' and point 'j' as they are connected by a path with denser region.

information to transform elongated structures into compact ones. A path in a graph is a sequence of distinct edges which connects the vertices of the graph. Let the similarity between object 'i' and object 'j' is denoted as $s_{i,j}$, and suppose that two vertices have been connected by a number of different possible paths, which forms a set denoted by $\mathcal{P}_{i,j}$. What we set out to do here, to make objects connected by a path following dense regions, is to define an effective similarity for all the possible paths. The effective similarity between object 'i' and object 'j' along the path $p \in \mathcal{P}$ is set as the minimum edge weight among all the edges contained by the path p. The final best similarity measure between the two objects is chosen as the maximum of all the minimum computed edge weights.

$$s_{i,j}^p = \max_{p \in \mathcal{P}} \left\{ \min_{(1 \leq h < |p|)} s_{o[h],o[h+1]} \right\} \tag{5}$$

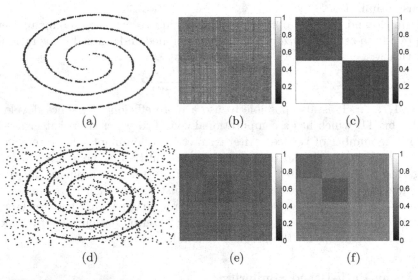

Fig. 4. Distance matrices of two spiral datasets with and without noise. (a) input spiral data without any noise; (b) original distance matrix of (a); (c) Path-Based dissimilarity matrix of (a); (d) Input spiral data with noise (e) original distance matrix of (d); (f) Path-Based dissimilarity matrix of (d)

Where $o[h]$ indicates the object at the hth position along the path p and $|p|$ is the number of objects along the path.

To observe how path-based technique is suitable for dominant set clustering, the (dis)similarity measures of the different transitions, for the spiral data set, are displayed as gray scale image. As shown from the figure 4, the framework transforms the data well in such a way that the points of the spiral data set forms two block on the diagonal as a representative of the two clusters. The clusters of the data with out noise forms a clear diagonal block as shown on the first row of figure 4 which imply that any simple clustering algorithms such as K-Means can extract the clusters easily. When we come to the second case, it is clear to see, from the second row of figure 4, that the two cluster representatives do not form a very clear blocks on the diagonal which can be extracted with simple clustering algorithms. No existing methods are as accurate as our algorithm in extracting the two spirals from the clutter noise. While our algorithm uses dominant set as it easily identifies and extracts the two spirals as two dominant sets leaving the noise as non-dominant sets, other existing algorithms forces the clutter to one of the clusters.

3 Experiments

In this section we report a number of experimental results that are done on both toy and real datasets from UCI repository [6]. The experiments were conducted in two different ways. The first way of the experiments tests the performance of the different techniques without any clutter noise added. The second approach, which is done by adding a clutter noise samples to the datasets, is performed to see how much the algorithms are robust against background noise. In the first part of the experiment, we applied all algorithms to synthetic datasets of different manually designed structures while in the last part they are tested against real-world datasets.

Our approach was tested against three different approaches: One of the most successful spectral clustering algorithms (Ng-Jordan-Weiss (NJW) algorithm) [7], Path-based Spectral Clustering and Robust Path-based Spectral clustering (RPBS) [1] which outperformed the Path-based Clustering improving its robustness to noise. We compared against the above existing methods as they address similar problems: the problem of clustering algorithms to handle complex separable and elongated structures, and the robustness of clustering algorithms to noisy environments. All the algorithms, as opposed to our method, require the number of clusters. As of the standard clustering algorithms, all the methods also require choosing the scaling parameter σ which has been optimally selected for all the approaches. We also assigned the correct number of clusters for those approaches which require it in advance.

3.1 Synthetic Data Clustering

In this part of the experiment, we applied our algorithm to eight different manually designed datasets which have been used by most of the existing algorithms

Fig. 5. Clustering results of NJW algorithm, Path-based Spectral Clustering, Robust Path-based Spectral Clustering, and Path-based Dominant Set clustering. All of the four algorithms perform equally in extracting all the clusters

for testing purpose. As can be seen from figure 8, the test had been done on complex separable structures. It has been shown that, classical clustering techniques such as K-means and Spectral Clustering can't solve the clustering problem in most of the data presented here [1]. However, extended version of the classical spectral clustering techniques and our proposed approach, as shown, in figure 8 are able to extracts all the clusters.

The robustness of our algorithm against noisy background is shown, using synthetic dataset, here. Similar works have been done to make clustering algorithm robust to noise [1] [15]. Our algorithm, as it uses dominant set framework,

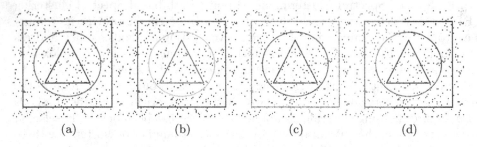

(a)   (b)   (c)   (d)

Fig. 6. Results on three shapes with uniformly distributed clutter elements which do not belong to any cluster (a) Original dataset to be clustered (b) The result of our method (c) The result of Path-based Spectral Clustering (d) NJW's algorithms result. Observe that only our approach is efficient in extracting all the shapes from the background noise

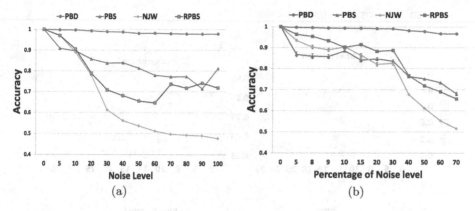

Fig. 7. Performance of extracting three shapes (a) and letters (b), as of figure 6 and 1, from noisy background where the noise level is increased starting from zero.

has the capability of extracting the best dominant sets leaving the clutter. However, other existing methods consider the background noise as part of the data to be partitioned.

It is clear to see that the existing approaches are vulnerable to applications where data is affected by clutter elements which do not belong to any cluster (as in figure/ground separation problems). Indeed, the only way to get rid of outliers is to group them in additional clusters. However, since outliers are not mutually similar and intuitively they do not form a cluster, the performance of all the approaches but ours drop drastically as the percentage of noise level increases.

Figure 6 shows three shapes (Triangle,Square and Circle) together with uniformly distributed background noise. As we have described above, other methods are not able to extract the right clusters, the three shapes. For the same data of the figure, we have performed an experiment by increasing the level of noise starting from zero. Zero noise implies that we have only the three shapes with

Table 1. Accuracy on UCI datasets (Without noise)

Data	Instances	Attributes	PBD	PBS	NJW	RPBS
Ionosphere	351	33	**0.8746**	0.8689	0.8718	0.8632
Haberman	306	3	**0.7582**	0.7451	0.7288	**0.7582**
Spect Heart	267	8	**0.7978**	0.7790	0.7940	0.7940
Blood Trans.	748	10	0.7620	0.7673	**0.7674**	0.7634
Pima	768	8	**0.6628**	0.6536	0.6615	0.6523
Breast	683	9	**0.9678**	0.9502	**0.9678**	**0.9678**
Glass	214	10	0.7664	**0.7804**	0.7523	0.7523
Liver	345	6	**0.6145**	0.5884	0.5739	0.5855

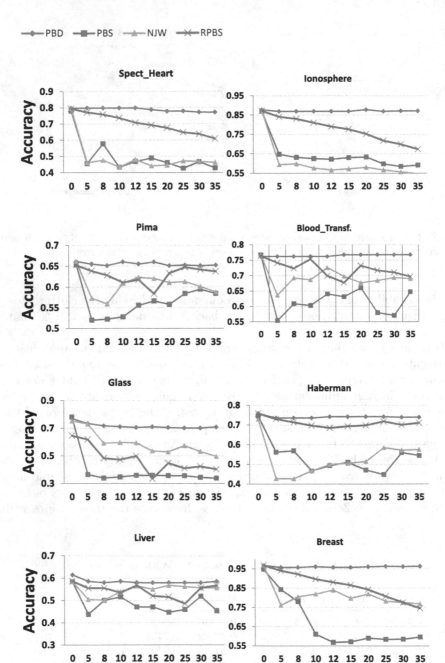

Fig. 8. Clustering performance of the algorithms when a clutter noise is added to the dataset. Observe that, in most of the cases, the performance of all the approaches but ours drop as the clutter noise is added.

out any clutter with which all the four clustering algorithms extract the right clusters. A noise level 'N' implies that a uniformly distributed noise of size of N% of the size of the data is added as an outlier. Figure 7 (a) shows that at the zero noise level the accuracy of all the methods is 100 %, however, the performance of all the methods but ours drop drastically as the noise level increases.

Figure 7 (b) shows a similar experiment but the noise level which was done on extracting different characters from clutter. A noise level 'n' in this case mean a uniformly distributed n*5 samples put together with the data as a clutter. The result from this experiment also confirms that our approach outperforms all the other approaches.

3.2 Experiments on Real-World Data

We also tested the algorithm on eight commonly used real-world datasets from UCI repository [6]. All the datasets incorporate cluster structures of complex separable, and most of them are with multiple scales. The performance of all the methods tested on the original dataset, refer table 1, is almost comparable.

An experiment has been conducted to show how much our method is robust to clutter noise added to the real-world datasets.

The experimental results, as can be referred from figure 8, consistently show that the existing approaches are vulnerable to applications where data is affected by clutter elements which do not belong to any cluster. It is easy to see, from figure 8, that the performance of all the approaches but ours drop drastically as noise is added to the datasets.

4 Conclusion

In this paper we have proposed a simple yet effective scheme to deal with the problem of extracting arbitrarily complex clusters under severe noise conditions. As is well known, dominant-sets clustering is remarkably good at dealing with cluttered situations but, on the other hand, it tends to favor compact structures. By feeding the algorithm with a path-based similarity measure, which takes into account connectedness information of the elements to be clustered, we have shown that the resulting algorithm is capable of consistently outperform standard approaches. Future work will focus on extending this idea to directed graphs [13] as well hypegraphs [10], and to investigate alternative path-based measures

References

1. Chang, H., Yeung, D.: Robust path-based spectral clustering. Pattern Recognition **41**(1), 191–203 (2008)
2. Chehreghani, M.H.: Information-Theoretic Validation of Clustering Algorithms. Ph.D. thesis, ETH ZURICH (2013)

3. Fischer, B., Buhmann, J.M.: Bagging for path-based clustering. IEEE Trans. Pattern Anal. Mach. Intell. **25**(11), 1411–1415 (2003a)
4. Fischer, B., Buhmann, J.M.: Path-based clustering for grouping of smooth curves and texture segmentation. IEEE Transactions on Pattern Analysis and Machine Intelligence **25**(4), 513–518 (2003b)
5. Fischer, B., Buhmann, J.M.: Path-based clustering for grouping of smooth curves and texture segmentation. IEEE Transactions on Pattern Analysis and Machine Intelligence **25**(4), 513–518 (2003c)
6. Lichman, M.: UCI machine learning repository (2013). http://archive.ics. uci.edu/ml
7. Ng, A.Y., Jordan, M.I., Weiss, Y.: On spectral clustering: analysis and an algorithm. In: Advances in Neural Information Processing Systems, pp. 849–856. MIT Press (2001)
8. Pavan, M., Pelillo, M.: Dominant sets and pairwise clustering. IEEE Trans. Pattern Anal. Machine Intell. **29**(1), 167–172 (2007)
9. Pelillo, M.: What is a cluster? perspectives from game theory. In: Proc. of the NIPS Workshop on Clustering Theory (2009)
10. Rota Bulò, S., Pelillo, M.: A game-theoretic approach to hypergraph clustering. IEEE Trans. Pattern Anal. Machine Intell. **35**(6), 1312–1327 (2013)
11. Rota Bulò, S., Pelillo, M., Bomze, I.M.: Graph-based quadratic optimization: A fast evolutionary approach. Computer Vision and Image Understanding **115**(7), 984–995 (2011)
12. Rota Bulò, S., Torsello, A., Pelillo, M.: A game-theoretic approach to partial clique enumeration. Image Vision Comput. **27**(7), 911–922 (2009)
13. Torsello, A., Rota Bulò, S., Pelillo, M.: Grouping with asymmetric affinities: a game-theoretic perspective. In: Proc. IEEE Conf. Computer Vision and Pattern Recognition (CVPR), pp. 292–299 (2006)
14. Torsello, A., Rota Bulò, S., Pelillo, M.: Beyond partitions: allowing overlapping groups in pairwise clustering. In: 19th International Conference on Pattern Recognition (ICPR 2008), December 8–11, 2008, Tampa, Florida, USA, pp. 1–4 (2008)
15. Zelnik-manor, L., Perona, P.: Self-tuning spectral clustering. In: Advances in Neural Information Processing Systems 17, pp. 1601–1608. MIT Press (2004)

Global and Local Gaussian Process
for Multioutput and Treed Data

Jhouben J. Cuesta$^{(\boxtimes)}$, Mauricio A. Álvarez, and Álvaro Á. Orozco

Faculty of Engineering, Universidad Tecnológica de Pereira, Pereira, Colombia
{jycuesta,malvarez,aaog}@utp.edu.co

Abstract. We propose a novel Multi-Level Multiple Output Gaussian Process framework for dealing with multivariate and treed data.We define a two-layer hierarchical tree with parent nodes on the upper layer and children nodes on the lower layer in order to represent the interaction between the multiple outputs.Then we compute the Multiple Output Gaussian Process (MGP) covariance matrix as a linear combination of a global multiple output covariance matrix (using the total number of outputs) and a set of local matrices (only using the outputs belonging to each parent node). With this construction of the covariance matrix and the tree we are capable to do interpolation using the MGP framework. To improve the results, we also test different ways of computing the Intrinsic Model of Coregionalization covariance matrix that uses the input space. Results over synthetic data, Motion Capture data and Wireless data shows that the proposed methodology makes a better representation of treed multiple output data.

1 Introduction

Gaussian Processes (GP) [7] are widely used for Bayesian regression and classification. Recently, they have been used more often in different disciplines due to its powerful prediction abilities, and the availability of GP implementations in different programming languages. GP provides a framework for non-linear interpolation and uncertainty quantification for single output problems (e.g., modeling the stock exchange), and multiple output problems (e.g, modeling a temperature map over a complete area) [4]. In the latter case, the GP are usually known as multiple output Gaussian processes (MGP). A MGP makes possible to include the correlation of the outputs, improving predictions while maintaining a positive definite covariance matrix.

In this paper, we are interested in modeling multiple-output data with a hierarchical relationship between the outputs (e.g.,the relationship between femur, tibia and the foot in the skeleton) in order to keep improve the predictions by exploiting the hierarchical correlation of the outputs. There are some methodologies that have made predictions for one output treed data, either by dividing the input space and computing classification and regression Trees [9]; making partitions over the input data and defining independent GP for each partition [8], [14]; or putting a prior over the inputs [11].

© Springer International Publishing Switzerland 2015
V. Murino and E. Puppo (Eds.): ICIAP 2015, Part I, LNCS 9279, pp. 161–171, 2015.
DOI: 10.1007/978-3-319-23231-7_15

To the best of our knowledge, the papers [5] [10] are the only two dealing with a multiple output treed data configuration. [10] proposes a Multivariate Bayesian treed Gaussian process to model the cross-covariance function and the nonstationarity of a set of multivariate outputs defining partitions over the input space. In [5] is proposed a multiple output framework for uncertainty quantification based on a construction of a correlation tree using a multi-element method, but assuming a constant relationship between outputs for a fast computing. In this paper, we propose a MGP modification (GLMGP) that includes Global and Local relationship between multiple output data and stores it into a covariance matrix. Despite of needing a prior knowledge of the hierarchy of the data, the proposed model improves the prediction performance and conserves the classical tractability of the GP framework. We made predictions over real hierarchical multiple output data applications: motion capture data-set[1], where the angular position and the hierarchical structure of the bones and a wireless spatial network configuration with sectors located within cells. Furthermore we improve even more the predictions by changing the way of computing the covariance matrix given the application.

This paper is organized as follows: in Section 2 we explain the way to go from a GP passing through a MGP in order to define the proposed GLMGP in Section 2.3. Later in Section 3 we made a comparison of the results of the MGP and the proposed methodology; we first explain the validation measures used to compare the models (Section 3.1), then we compare and analyze the results over simulated and real data. Finally on Section 4 conclusions are made.

2   Materials and Methods

In this section, we remark the basics of a GP regression. Later, we explain the multiple output framework with the two common approaches for covariance matrix computation: the linear model of coregionalization and the process convolution. Finally in Section 2.3 we introduce the proposed methodology and the proposed modification to the multiple output approach.

2.1   Gaussian Process

A Gaussian Process (GP) is a possible infinite collection of scalar random variables indexed by an input space such that for any finite set of inputs $\mathbf{X} = \{\mathbf{x}_1, \mathbf{x}_2, \cdots, \mathbf{x}_n\}$, the random variables $\mathbf{f} \triangleq [f(\mathbf{x}_1), f(\mathbf{x}_2), \cdots, f(\mathbf{x}_n)]$ are distributed according to a multivariate Gaussian distribution. A GP is completely specified by a mean function $m(\mathbf{x}) = \mathbb{E}[f(\mathbf{x})]$ and a covariance function $k_f(\mathbf{x}, \mathbf{x}') = \mathbb{E}[(f(\mathbf{x}) - m(\mathbf{x}))(f(\mathbf{x}') - m(\mathbf{x}'))^\top]$ [12]. This formulation takes the form

$$\mathbf{f}(\mathbf{x}) \sim \mathcal{GP}\left(m(\mathbf{x}), k(\mathbf{x}, \mathbf{x}')\right).$$

---

[1] CMU Graphics Lab Motion Capture Database, available on: http://mocap.cs.cmu.edu/

Without loss of generality, the mean function is assumed to be equal to zero. A covariance function is a positive semi-definite function that measures the similarity between pairs of points over the input space $\mathcal{D}$. Such functions are used to compute the so-called Gram matrix o kernel matrix. Examples of covariance functions are the Squared Exponential (RBF kernel) expressed as

$$k(\mathbf{x}, \mathbf{x}') = \exp\left(-\frac{||\mathbf{x} - \mathbf{x}'||^2}{2\ell^2}\right), \tag{1}$$

where ℓ corresponds to the length-scale; and the Màtern Class given by:

$$k(r) = \frac{2^{1-\nu}}{\Gamma(\nu)}\left(\frac{\sqrt{2\nu}r}{\ell}\right)^{\nu} K_{\nu}\left(\frac{\sqrt{2\nu}r}{\ell}\right), \tag{2}$$

where $r = ||\mathbf{x} - \mathbf{x}'||$, ν and ℓ are positive parameters and K_{ν} is a modified Bessel function as in [7]. Common cases of ν are $\frac{1}{2}, \frac{3}{2}, \frac{5}{2}$ In the case of a $\nu = 1/2$ and $\mathcal{D} = 1$ this kernel function is called Ornstein Uhlenbeck kernel (OU-kernel).

Using $\mathcal{N}(\mathbf{0}, \mathbf{K})$ as GP prior over the functions $f(\mathbf{x})$ and a likelihood distribution given by $y(\mathbf{x}) = f(\mathbf{x}) + \epsilon$ (where $\epsilon \sim \mathcal{N}(0, \sigma_n^2)$) and using Bayes theorem, it is possible to obtain a predictive distribution for a set of new inputs $\mathbf{X}_*$,

$$\mathbf{f}_*|\mathbf{X}, \mathbf{y}, \mathbf{X}_* \sim \mathcal{N}(\bar{\mathbf{f}}_*, \mathrm{cov}(\mathbf{f}_*)), \tag{3}$$

where $\bar{\mathbf{f}}_* \triangleq \mathbb{E}[\mathbf{f}_*|\mathbf{X}, \mathbf{y}, \mathbf{X}_*] = \mathbf{K}(\mathbf{X}_*, \mathbf{X})[\mathbf{K}(\mathbf{X}, \mathbf{X}) + \sigma_n^2 I]^{-1}$ and the covariance $\mathrm{cov}(\mathbf{f}_*) = \mathbf{K}(\mathbf{X}_*, \mathbf{X}_*) - \mathbf{K}(\mathbf{X}_*, \mathbf{X})[\mathbf{K}(\mathbf{X}, \mathbf{X}) + \sigma_n^2 I]^{-1}\mathbf{K}(\mathbf{X}, \mathbf{X}_*)$, here $\mathbf{K}(\mathbf{X}, \mathbf{X})$ is the covariance function evaluated on the training set $\mathbf{X}$, $\mathbf{K}(\mathbf{X}_*, \mathbf{X})$ is the covariance of the training and test sets, $\mathbf{K}(\mathbf{X}_*, \mathbf{X}_*)$ is the covariance of the new inputs and the parameter σ_n^2 represents the variance of the noise.

The estimation of the covariance function parameters is performed by maximizing the log marginal likelihood by a gradient-descent algorithm [6] [13]. The log marginal likelihood is given as in [7]

$$\log p(\mathbf{y}|\mathbf{X}, \phi) = -\frac{1}{2}\mathbf{y}^{\top}\Sigma^{-1}\mathbf{y} - \frac{1}{2}\log|\Sigma| - \frac{N}{2}D\log(2\pi), \tag{4}$$

where D is the dimension of $\mathbf{x}$, N is the number of training inputs, $\mathbf{y}$ is the vector of outputs corresponding to the total of inputs $\mathbf{X}$, ϕ represents the parameters, and $\Sigma = \mathbf{K}(\mathbf{X}, \mathbf{X}) + \sigma_n^2 \mathbf{I}$.

2.2 Multiple Output Gaussian Process

The Multiple Output Gaussian Process (MGP) framework starts by defining a set of latent Gaussian processes which are then linearly combined to represent the different outputs, and thus modeling correlations between them. The key point in such framework is the definition of a suitable covariance function, in a mathematical sense, i.e., the covariance function for multiple outputs has to be positive semi-definite. See [3] for a review of different kernel functions for vector-valued data. Once the covariance funcion is defined, the predictive distribution follow a similar form to Equation (3). The parameters of the covariance funtion can be estimated by maximizing a marginal log-likelihood similar to (4).

In what follows, we briefly review the linear model of corregionalization, which is a common choice to build valid covariance functions for multiple outputs [2], and that we use for building the multi-level multi-output covariance function.

Linear Model of Coregionalization: In the linear model of coregionaliza-tion (LMC) the covariance function is formed by a sum of separable kernels. Under this LMC assumption, the outputs are expressed as linear combinations of independent random functions, ensuring a valid positive semi-definite covari-ance matrix [3]. Over a set of outputs $\{f_d(\mathbf{x})\}_{d=1}^{D}$ with $\mathbf{x} \in \mathbb{R}^p$, each component f_d is expressed as

$$f_d(\mathbf{x}) = \sum_{q=1}^{Q}\sum_{i=1}^{R_q} a_{d,q}^i u_q^i(\mathbf{x}),$$

where Q represents the groups of latent functions $u_q^i(\mathbf{x})$ and R_q are represents the number of functions in a group that share the same covariance; and the functions $u_q^i(\mathbf{x})$, with $q = 1, ..., Q$ and $i = 1, ..., R_q$ have mean equal to zero and covariance $\mathrm{cov}[u_q^i(\mathbf{x}), u_{q'}^{i'}(\mathbf{x}')] = k_q(\mathbf{x}, \mathbf{x}')$ if $q = q'$ and $i = i'$. The cross-covariance between any two functions $f_d(\mathbf{x})$ and $f_d'(\mathbf{x}')$ is given in terms of the covariance functions for $u_q^i(\mathbf{x})$

$$\mathrm{cov}[f_d(\mathbf{x}), f_{d'}(\mathbf{x}')] = \sum_{q=1}^{Q}\sum_{q'=1}^{Q}\sum_{i=1}^{R_q}\sum_{i'=1}^{R_q} a_{d,q}^i a_{d',q'}^{i'} \mathrm{cov}[u_q^i(\mathbf{x}), u_{q'}^{i'}(\mathbf{x}')].$$

Due to independence of the latent functions, the kernel matrix can now be expressed as

$$\mathbf{K}(\mathbf{x}, \mathbf{x}') = \sum_{q=1}^{Q} \mathbf{B}_q k_q(\mathbf{x}, \mathbf{x}'), \tag{5}$$

where Q represents the number of latent functions, each $\mathbf{B}_q \in \mathbb{R}^{D \times D}$ is known as a *coregionalization matrix* and the rank R_q of each matrix $\mathbf{B}_q$ is determined by the number of latent functions that share the same covariance function.

When $Q = 1$ in Eq. (5), the LMC approach is known as the Intrinsic Core-gionalization Model (ICM). The kernel matrix for multiple outputs becomes $\mathbf{K}(\mathbf{x}, \mathbf{x}') = k(\mathbf{x}, \mathbf{x}')\mathbf{B}$ [1], and for an entire data set $\mathbf{X}$ takes the form

$$\mathbf{K}(\mathbf{X}, \mathbf{X}) = \mathbf{B} \otimes k(\mathbf{X}, \mathbf{X}), \tag{6}$$

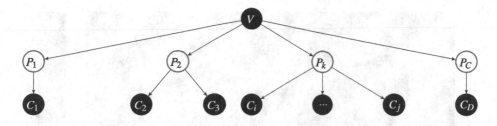

Fig. 1. Representation of a Global-Local or Parent-Child treed structure. V represents the variable of interest. The red nodes represent the C parents and the lower D nodes represent the total number of children (equal to the total number of outputs of a single MGP approach).

where the operator $\otimes$ represents the Kronecker product. There are different ways in which $\mathbf{B}$ can be parameterized. One of them is using a Cholesky decomposition, $\mathbf{B} = \mathbf{L}\mathbf{L}^{\top}$, or using a kernel matrix computed from a valid kernel function, like the ones in Eqs. (1) and (2).

2.3   Global and Local Multi Output Treed GP

In this paper, we propose the Global and Local Treed Multiple Output Gaussian Process (GLMGP) as a multiple output GP that computes the correlations of multiple-output data with a parent-child- type of configuration.

We first define the tree T as a vector of parent indexes for every child output. With this information we compute a global covariance matrix $\mathbf{K}_g$ defined as a Multi GP covariance for all the outputs (using, for example, the LMC) and later we compute the contribution of the children as a block-diagonal matrix formed by a set of C local matrices $\mathbf{K}_\ell^i$ (where C is equal to the number of parents of the global layer and $i = 1, ..., C$). Each local matrix $\mathbf{K}_\ell^i$ is computed again as a multiple output covariance matrix, but in this computation the outputs are equivalent to the group of children associated to the ith parent (again this covariance is computed using, for example, LMC). The resulting covariance matrix $\mathbf{K}$ takes the form

$$\mathbf{K} = \mathbf{K}_g + \text{blockdiag}(\{\mathbf{K}_\ell^i\}_{i=1}^C),$$

where C is the number of parents, and each matrix $\mathbf{K}_g$ and $\mathbf{K}_\ell$ is computed as in Equations 5 or 6.

The Figure 1 shows a general treed structure with a two layer (parent-child) representation. A real-life example of a tree structured data is Mocap data. Here we have measures of the spatial position of different body parts while a subject is performing a motion. Here, the tree is represented by the body that has a hierarchical inner structure i.e the femur, tibia and the foot of the left leg. We can exploit a parent-children relation where the femur is the parent and the tibia and the foot that will include information of the skeletal structure. Now, the position data of the leg can be interpreted as multiple output because of the influence of the femur, tibia and foot on the motion of a subject.

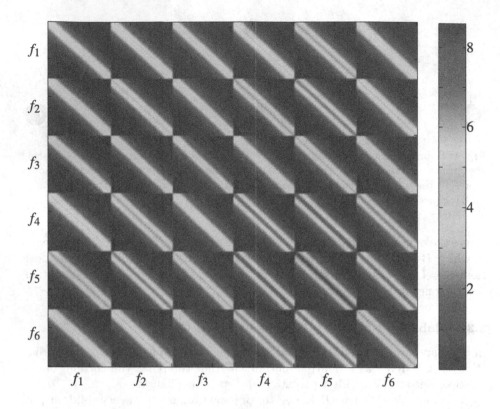

Fig. 2. MultiGP Covariance Matrix Block Structure for a set of 6 outputs f

Figures 2 and 3 show both a MGP and GLMGP covariance matrices for
a configuration of six outputs and the same six outputs plus a tree structure
conformed by three parents for the GLMGP (these two configuration will be
explained in detail on Section 3.2). We see that our proposed covariance represents the children contribution as a non uniform increment of the values of
the diagonal block. The increment value depends on the contribution that the
children do to each parent. The proposed modification of the covariance matrix
is flexible in the way that we can define different covariance functions, number
of latent functions or rank for the coregionalization matrices for each part of
the tree, this means we can define a different configuration per each Multi-GP
covariance matrix to be computed. Asides this modification does not represent
any change on the marginal likelihood expressed before in Equation 4.

In the proposed methodology, we compute the covariance matrices using the
ICM. The ICM matrix was computed using two approaches: using a Cholesky
decomposition (called ICM-L) and a covariance function (called ICM-K). The
use of ICM-L or ICM-K depends on the context and will be explained further
in the results on Sec. 3.

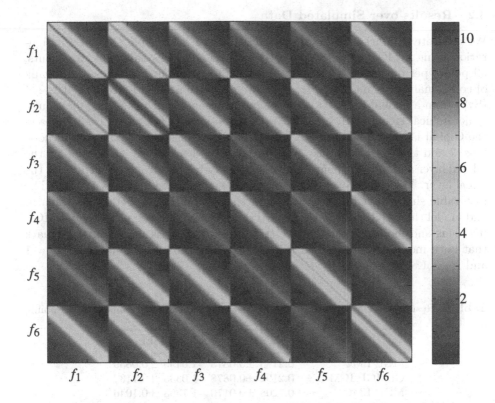

Fig. 3. GMLGP Covariance Matrix Block Structure for a set of 6 outputs f

3   Results

In this section we compare the results obtained after comparing the MGP LMC methods against the GLMGP ICM-L and ICM-K over synthetic and real data. First in Section 3.1 we describe the Validation and Error Measures. Later we report the results over synthetic and real data in Sections 3.2 and 3.3 respectively. All the algorithms were trained using 70% of the data and validated with remaining 30%. We used the the kernels OU, Squared Exponential and Màtern 3/2 covariance functions as expressed on Equations 1 and 2 on section 2.2. We repeated the experiment 10 times in order to report a standard deviation of the error measures.

3.1   Validation and Error Measures

The proposed GLMGP methodology and the MGP LMC were compared using the Standardized Mean Square Error (SMSE) and the Mean Standardized Log Loss (MSLL) measures [7] via hold-out validation (see [6]) and computed as in [2]. It is important to remark that a lower SMSE error implies a better interpolator and a lower negative MSLL implies that the model is more adequate to the data.

3.2   Results over Simulated Data

We generate a first synthetic data-set (Sy1) from a Multiple Output Configuration using a MGP model (composed by a one-dimensional input, 6 outputs, 30 points per output, a màtern 3/2 kernel, $Q = 1$ latent functions and a rank of coregionalization matrix of $R_q = 1$). We generate a second synthetic data-set (Sy2) from a Global Local Treed Configuration model with the same 6 outputs, a hierarchical tree $T = [1, 1, 1, 2, 2, 3]$ (this tree means that there are 3 nodes in the Global layer and the first node have 3 outputs associated, the second node have 2 and the third node just 1 output), a $Q = 1$ a màtern 3/2 kernel for the Global layer and [OU,OU,màtern32] respectively to each group of outputs on the Local layer. The results over Sy1 and Sy2 are summarized in tables 1 and 2. The first table shows that on the MGP data the GLMGP is as better interpolator and model than MGP, but in the second table we see that the proposed GLMGP performs and model better the tree structured data. It is important to remark that both methods were trained using just a màtern32 kernel and using $Q = 1$ and $R_q = 1$.

Table 1. Results Over Sy1 Data. Methods with a ∗ used both the same training points

Model	SMSE	MSLL
MGP LMC	0.2185 ±0.0813	-1.0499 ±0.0839
GLMGP ICM-L	0.2192 ±0.0878	-1.0335 ±0.1132
MGP LMC*	0.1208 ±0.0176	-1.1398 ±0.1046
GLMGP IMC-L*	**0.1173±0.0183**	**-1.1406±0.1310**

Table 2. Results Over Sy2 treed Data. Methods with a ∗ used both the same training points

Model	SMSE	MSLL
MGP LMC	0.2156 ±0.0357	-1.3623 ±0.1061
GLMGP ICM-L	0.1245 ±0.0302	-1.4918 ±0.0916
MGP LMC*	0.1480 ±0.0419	-1.4175 ±0.0948
GLMGP ICM-L*	**0.0881±0.0143**	**-1.6910±0.0718**

3.3   Results over Real Data

In this section we show examples of interpolation for real data. Firstly we use Mocap data-set (Online Available http://mocap.cs.cmu.edu/) as a time series regression example. Later a Colombian Network Wireless data is used for a spatio-temporal interpolation (this database is not available due to copyright).

Mocap Dataset. For Mocap data we worked with the Subject eight - trial two of a walk motion. We selected the bone structures of the right leg and left leg as Global layer parents; and the femur, tibia, foot and toes as the children for each parent (with reference to Figure 1). The time interval t of the motion was taken as the input $\mathbf{X}$ while the angles $\theta_x, \theta_y, \theta_z$ were taken as the outputs. There was a total of 8 outputs because we remove 4 angles that had no significant variation $(1e-7)$ and a tree $T = [1, 1, 1, 1, 2, 2, 2, 2]$. With this data we did interpolation using the MGP LMC and the GLMGP. Table 3 shows the results of the MGP against the two proposed methodologies. We see that GLMGP ICM is slightly better than MGP on SMSE, but has a better interpretation for Mocap treed data. In this one dimensional case we used the Cholesky decomposition for computing the coregionalization matrix (ICM-L) instead of a covariance function (ICM-K). This is done because because of using ICM-K was not ensuring a positive definite covariance matrix.

Table 3. Results over Mocap Data

Model	SMSE	MSLL
MGP ICM	0.2880 ±0.0186	-0.8839 ±0.0551
GLMGP ICM-L	**0.2533±0.0166**	**-1.2894±0.0780**

Wireless Treed Data. The Wireless data used in this paper is conformed by 30 daily measurements of a Traffic Key Performance Indicator (KPI) of a network of 32 sectors placed in 11 different spatially located cells. Using the information of the cell-sector relationship we treated the cells as a parent and the sectors as the children and defined the tree as $T = [1, 1, 2, 2, 2, 3, 3, 3, \cdots, 11, 11, 11]$. We take the spatial coordinates $[x_{x_i}, x_{y_i}]$ and the day t_i as the inputs, and the KPI value as the output y. We tested different configurations of MGP LMC and GLMGP and reported the best results on Table 4. The best LMC model was a configuration of a màtern32 kernel with $Q = 2$ and $R_q = 1$; the best ICM-L was a configuration of màtern32 for Global layer and OU for local layer with $R_q = 1$ for all the MGP covariances computed. The best ICM-K model had the same kernel configuration of ICM-L. Despite of this we see on the results table that ICM-K improves the results considerably, even for the SMSE.

Table 4. Results over Wireless Treed (Cell-Sector) Data.

Model	SMSE	MSLL
MGP LMC	0.2885 ±0.0390	-0.9147 ±0.0789
GLMGP ICM-L	0.4744 ±0.2720	-0.6850 ±0.4064
GLMGP ICM-K	**0.1602±0.0149**	**-1.1726±0.3011**

4   Conclusions

We have presented GLMGP as a model that takes into account a parent-child relationship between data outputs and represents it in a covariance matrix. Instead of modifying the prior, we defined a tree with global indexes over the inputs that remains unchanged the tractability of the model. This model proved to be better than the MGP in capturing the information and interpretation of the structured data . Despite of the fact that the model can not learn or define a proper tree by its own, it is very useful in applications when we know the interaction of the output variables previously like the cell-sector relationship, skeletal structures of the body, etc.

We also tested two ways of computing the coregionalization matrix in order make a more flexible model the ICM-L and the ICM-K. In the case of the ICM-L it had a good performance for synthetic and mocap data and the ICM-K performed better on the wireless data-set. In the future, we expect to improve this model in order to include more than a Global and Local layers and also a modification that can estimate a tree structure that improves the interpolation results. In addition, for the one-dimensional case, we expect to find a parametrization of the outputs under the ICM-K framework to ensure a positive definite covariance matrix.

Acknowledgments. JJC thanks to the research project *Análisis de Fallas en Redes de Telefonía Móvil usando reconocimiento estadístico de patrones* in the program of Jóvenes Investigadores "Virginia Gutiérrez de Pineda". JJC and MAA thank to Universidad Tecnológica de Pereira for the support under the research projects *Procesos Gaussianos Jerárquicos de Múltiples Salidas Para el Análisis y Expansión de Redes de Telefonía Móvil*, and the research project *Human motion synthesis through physically-inspired machine learning models*, with code $6 - 15 - 3$. The authors would also like to acknowledge the project *Estimación de los parámetros de neuro modulación con terapia de estimulación cerebral profunda en pacientes con enfermedad de Parkinson a partir del volumen de tejido activo planeado*, financed by Colciencias with code $1110 - 657 - 40687$.

References

1. Álvarez, M.A.: Convolved Gaussian Process Priors for Multivariate Regression With Applications to Dynamical Systems. Ph.D. thesis, School of Computer Science, University of Manchester (2011)
2. Álvarez, M.A., Lawrence, N.D.: Computationally efficient convolved multiple output Gaussian processes. Journal of Machine Learning Research **12**, 39 (2011)
3. Álvarez, M.A., Rosasco, L., Lawrence, N.: Kernels for Vector-Valued Functions: A Review. Now Publishers Incorporated (2012). http://books.google.com.co/books?id=2A5hLwEACAAJ
4. Álvarez, M.A., Lawrence, N.D.: Sparse convolved multiple output gaussian processes for multi-outptut regression. In: NIPS 2008, pp. 57–64 (2009)

5. Bilionis, I., Zabaras, N.: Multi-output local gaussian process regression: Applications to uncertainty quantification. J. Comput. Physics **231**(17), 5718–5746 (2012). http://dblp.uni-trier.de/db/journals/jcphy/jcphy231.html#BilionisZ12
6. Bishop, C.M.: Pattern Recognition and Machine Learning (Information Science and Statistics). Springer (2007). http://www.openisbn.com/isbn/9780387310732/
7. Carl Edwards Rasmussen, C.W.: Gaussian Processes for Machine Learning. The MIT Press (2006)
8. Fox, E.B., Dunson, D.B.: Multiresolution gaussian processes. In: Bartlett, P.L., Pereira, F.C.N., Burges, C.J.C., Bottou, L., Weinberger, K.Q. (eds.) NIPS, pp. 746–754 (2012). http://dblp.uni-trier.de/db/conf/nips/nips2012.html#FoxD12
9. Gramacy, R.B., Lee, H.K.H.: Bayesian treed gaussian process models with an application to computer modeling. Journal of the American Statistical Association (2007)
10. Konomi, B., Karagiannis, G., Sarkar, A., Sun, X., Lin, G.: Bayesian treed multivariate gaussian process with adaptive design: Application to a carbon capture unit. Technometrics, 145–158, May 2014
11. Lawrence, N.D., Moore, A.J.: Hierarchical gaussian process latent variable models. In: Proceedings of the 24th International Conference on Machine Learning, pp. 481–488 (2007)
12. Liutkus, G., Badeau, R.: Multi-dimensional signal separation with gaussian processes. In: IEEE Statistical Signal Processing Workshop (SSP), pp. 401–404 (2011)
13. Murphy, K.P.: Machine Learning: A Probabilistic Perspective (Adaptive Computation and Machine Learning Series). The MIT Press (2012). http://www.openisbn.com/isbn/9780262018029/
14. Park, S., Choi, S.: Hierarchical gaussian process regression. In: JMLR: Workshop and Conference Proceedings 13, pp. 95–110 (2010)

BRISK Local Descriptors
for Heavily Occluded Ball Recognition

Pier Luigi Mazzeo, Paolo Spagnolo$^{(\boxtimes)}$, and Cosimo Distante

INO-Consiglio Nazionale delle Ricerche, Via della Liberta', 3,
73010 Arnesano, Lecce, Italy
paolo.spagnolo@cnr.it

Abstract. This paper focuses on the ball detection algorithm that analyzes candidate ball regions to detect the ball. Unfortunately, in the
time of goal, the goal-posts (and sometimes also some players) partially occlude the ball or alter its appearance (due to their shadows
cast on it). This often makes ineffective the traditional pattern recognition approaches and it forces the system to make the decision about the
event based on estimates and not on the basis of the real ball position
measurements. To overcome this drawback, this work compares different descriptors of the ball appearance, in particular it investigates on
both different well known feature extraction approaches and the recent
local descriptors BRISK in a soccer match context. This paper analyzes
critical situations in which the ball is heavily occluded in order to measure robustness, accuracy and detection performances. The effectiveness
of BRISK compared with other local descriptors is validated by a huge
number of experiments on heavily occluded ball examples acquired under
realistic conditions.

1   Introduction

In last decade sport video analysis has created great interest in the computer
vision and multimedia technologies research communities [7]. This allowed to
develop applications dealing with the analysis of different sports such as tennis,
golf, American football, baseball, basketball, and hockey. Due to its worldwide
viewership there has been an explosive growth in the research area of soccer video
analysis [1], [6], and many different possible applications have been considered
[4],[10],[12].

The main issue of any kind of the most important sport automatic systems
is the detection of the ball; it is very difficult when images are taken from fixed
or broadcast cameras with a large Field of View since the ball is represented by
a small number of pixels and it can have different scales, textures and colors.
Hence, automatic detection and localization of the ball in images is challenging as
a great number of problems have to be managed: occlusions, shadowing, presence
of very similar objects both near the field lines and on player's bodies (shoulders,
legs, heads, ...), appearance modifications (for example when the ball is inside
the goal it is faded by the net and it also experiences a significant amount of

© Springer International Publishing Switzerland 2015
V. Murino and E. Puppo (Eds.): ICIAP 2015, Part I, LNCS 9279, pp. 172–182, 2015.
DOI: 10.1007/978-3-319-23231-7_16

deformation during collisions), unpredictable motion (for example when the ball is shot by players), and so on.

Most of the approaches proposed in literature use, at first, weak global information (size, color, shape) to detect the most likely ball regions and then motion hypotheses or template matching are introduced to filter candidates ([19],[22]. These approaches experience difficulties in ball candidate validation when many moving entities are simultaneously in the scene (the ball is not isolated) or when the ball abruptly changes its trajectory (for example in the case of rebounds or shots).

D'Orazio at al. [3] focus on ball pattern extraction and recognition: a neural architecture is proposed to discriminate the wavelet coefficients extracted from ball candidates and non-ball candidates previously selected by a modified version of the directional circular Hough transform (CHT). This approach fails to validate ball candidates in case of textured (invariance to rotation, scaling and illumination changes is limited) and occluded balls (wavelet description needs a large visible ball portion to supply significant coefficients). Moreover neural based classifier requires a rigorous selection of training examples and network parameters.

In [16] we have compared different local descriptors in order to face the ball recognition problem. Starting from these results we propose in this paper the novel local BRISK descriptors in order to deal with the heavily occluded balls.

Established leaders, in the field of the keypoints extractor, are the *SIFT* and *SURF* algorithms which exhibit great performance under a variety of image transformations. In [9] authors explored the use of scale-invariant feature transform (*SIFT*) to encode local information of the ball and to match it between ball instances. Experimental results point out some difficulties in detecting distinctive points on the ball and to make a decision by counting the number of correct point matches. Recently, Leutenegger [11] proposed a novel method for keypoints detection, description and matching called BRISK (Binary Robust Invariant Scalable Keypoints). BRISK, in contrast to well known algorithms with proven high performance, such as SIFT and SURF, offer a dramatically faster alternative at comparable matching performance. Considering these interesting peculiarities of BRISK, in this work we present a comparison of different features extraction approaches (Wavelet Transform - WT, Principal Component Analysis - PCA), and keypoints detectors and descriptors algorithms (SIFT and BRISK), in order to recognize soccer ball patterns.

The considered approaches were tested on a huge number of real ball images acquired in presence of translation, scaling, rotation, illumination changes, local geometric distortion, clutter, partial and heavy occlusion.

In the rest of the paper, section 2 gives a resume of the evaluation framework we use, including a short description of the implemented methodologies, whereas section 3 presents the experimental results, together with their comparison and discussion. Finally, in section 4, conclusions and future enhancement are drawn.

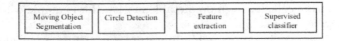

| Moving Object Segmentation | Circle Detection | Feature extraction | Supervised classifier |

Fig. 1. A schematic diagram of the processing steps executed by each Node

2   Ball Recognition Evaluation

We have created an evaluation framework based on a GLT vision system which is able to detect the ball in an acquired soccer video sequences. The schematic diagram of whole processing path of vision system is shown in figure 1. The ball detection processing is composed by four main blocks: in the first one a background subtraction technique *[Moving Object Segmentation block]* is combined with a circle detection approach *[Circle detection block]* to extract ball candidate regions. Then a features extraction scheme is used to represent image patterns *[Feature extraction block]* and finally data classification is performed by using a supervised learning scheme *[Supervised Classifier block]*.

2.1   Moving Object Segmentation

At the beginning of the image acquisition a background model has to be generated and later continuously updated to include lighting variations in the model. Then, a background subtraction algorithm distinguishes moving points from static ones. The implemented algorithm uses the mean and standard deviation to give a statistical model of the background. Detection is then performed by comparing the pixel current intensity value with its statistical parameters, as explained in several works on this topic (a good review can be found in [18]). Details about the implemented approach can be found in [20]. Finally, after the detection of moving pixels, a connected components analysis detects the blobs in the image by grouping neighboring pixels. After this step, regions with an area less than a given threshold are considered as noise and removed, whilst remaining regions are evaluated in the following blocks.

2.2   Circle Detection

The Circle Hough Transform (CHT) aims to find circular patterns of a given radius R within an image. Each edge point contributes a circle of radius R to an output accumulator space. The peak in the output accumulator space is detected where these contributed circles overlap at the center of the original circle. In order to reduce the computational burden and the number of false positives typical of the CHT, a number of modifications have been widely implemented in the last decade. The use of edge orientation information limits the possible positions of the center for each edge point. This way only an arc perpendicular to the edge orientation at a distance R from the edge point needs to be plotted. The CHT and also its modifications can be formulated as convolutions applied to an edge

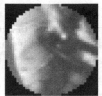

Fig. 2. Images of the training set: negative (first two) and positive examples of the ball

magnitude image (after a suitable edge detection). More details on this approach can be found in [16].

2.3   Feature Extraction

In this block the candidate ball regions are processed by different feature extraction methodologies in order to represent them only by coefficients containing the most discriminant information. A secondary aim is also to characterize the images with a small number of features in order to gain in computational time. Object recognition by using a learning-from-examples technique is in fact related to computational issues. In order to achieve real time performances the computational time to classify patterns should be small. The main parameter connected to high computational complexity is certainly the input space dimension. A reduction of the input size is the first step to successfully speed up the classification process. This requirement can be satisfied by using a feature extraction algorithm able to store all the important information about input patterns in a small set of coefficients. Wavelet Transform (WT), Principal Component Analysis (PCA), Scale Invariant Feature Transform (SIFT), Binary Robust Invariant Scalable Keypoints (BRISK) are different approaches allowing to significantly reduce the dimension of the input space, because they capture the significant variations of input patterns in a smaller number of coefficients. In the following four subsections we briefly review WT, PCA, SIFT, and BRISK approaches.

WT: Wavelet Transform. The WT is an extension of the Fourier transform that contains both frequency and spatial information [15]. Numerous filters can be used to implement WT: we have chosen Haar and Daubechies filters for their simplicity and orthogonality.

PCA: Principal Component Analysis. Principal component analysis (PCA) provides an efficient method to reduce the number of features to work with [8]. It transforms the original set of (possibly) correlated features into a small set of uncorrelated ones. In particular, PCA determines an orthogonal basis for a set of images involving an eigen analysis of their covariance matrix.

SIFT: Scale Invariant Feature Transform. The scale Invariant Feature Transform is a method for extracting distinctive invariant features from the images that can be used to perform reliable matching between different views of an object or a scene [13]. The features are invariant to image scale and rotation and they provide robust matching across a substantial range of affine distortion, change in 3D viewpoint, addition of noise, and change in illumination. The features are highly distinctive, in the sense that a single feature can be correctly matched with high probability against a large database of features from many different images.

BRISK: Binary Robust Invariant Scalable Keypoints. It is a novel method for keypoints detection, description and matching [11], based on an application of a novel scale-space FAST-based detector in combination with the assembly of a bit-string descriptor from intensity comparison obtained by dedicated sampling of each keypoint neighborhood. BRISK uses a easily configurable circular sampling pattern from which it computes brightness comparisons to form a binary descriptor string. This detector can be useful for a wide spectrum of applications, in particular for tasks with hard real-time constraints or limited computational resources. In figure 3 are highlighted some matches among BRISK descriptors using the Hamming distance applied to the two balls extracted by the CHT showed in the second row of the figure 2.

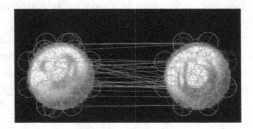

Fig. 3. BRISK descriptor matching

2.4   Supervised Classifier

The following step in the proposed framework aims at introducing an automatic method to distinguish between ball and no-ball instances on the basis of the feature vector extracted by one of the previous mentioned pre-processing strategies. To accomplish this task a probabilistic approach has been used. Probabilistic methods for pattern classification are very common in literature as reported by [21]. So-called *naive* Bayesian classification is the optimal method of supervised learning if the values of the attributes of an example are independent given the class of the example. Although this assumption is almost always violated in practice, recent works have shown that naive Bayesian learning is remarkably effective in practice and difficult to improve upon systematically. On many real-world example datasets naive Bayesian learning gives better test set accuracy than any other known method [2], [17]. In general a Naive Bayes classifier is also preferable for its computational efficiency.

Probabilistic approaches to classification typically involve modelling the conditional probability distribution $P(C|D)$, where C ranges over classes and D over descriptions, in some language, of objects to be classified. Given a description d of a particular object, the class $argmaxcP(C = c|D = d)$ is assigned. A Bayesian approach splits this posterior distribution into a prior distribution $P(C)$ and a likelihood $P(D|C)$:

$$argmax_c P(C = c|D = d) = argmax_c \frac{(P(D = d|C = c)P(C = c))}{P(D = d)} \quad (1)$$

The key term in Equation1 is $P(D = d|C = c)$, the likelihood of the given description given the class (often abbreviated to $P(d|c)$). A Bayesian classifier estimates these likelihoods from training data. If the assumption that all attributes are independent given the class:

$$P(A_1 = a_1, ..., A_n = a_n|C = c) = \prod_{i=1}^{n} P(A_i = a_i|C = c) \quad (2)$$

then a Naive Bayesian Classifier (often abbreviated to *Naive Bayes*) is introduced. This means that a Naive Bayes classifier ignores interactions between attributes within individuals of the same class. We use a Gaussian Kernel as Naive Bayes likelihood with the attribute space size depending of the dimensions of the feature vectors.

Further details and discussions about the practical consequences of this assumption can be found in [5].

2.5 Experimental Setup

Here we, briefly, describe how many features were extracted from each of the different pre-processing techniques explained in 2.3. For the SIFT and BRISK methodologies the codebook of visual words (known as Bag of word representation) was built by quantizing (using K-means algorithm [14]) the 128-long feature vectors relative to the detected points of interests in the patches containing fully visible balls under good light conditions. The pre-processing strategies reduce the number of the coefficients that are the input of the Bayesian classifier. For the SIFT and BRISK local descriptors we used 20 coefficients that were the results of the k-means clustering algorithms. This because after many experiments we found that the descriptors length, with the best ball detection rate, was 20. For the Wavelet 'HAAR' and 'Daubechies3' methods we used the approximation coefficient at the second level of decomposition; this reduces the input coefficient to a vector of 64 (8x8) elements for 'HAAR' and to a vector of 121 (11x11) elements for 'Daubechies3'. In the PCA strategy we used the Single Value Decomposition (SVD) technique to solve the eigenstructure decomposition problem; the covariance matrix was evaluated on the entire set of training images, by obtaining 30 coefficients.

3   Experimental Results

Experiments were carried out on image sequences acquired in a real soccer stadium by a *Mikroton EOSens MC1362 CCD camera*, equipped with a 135 mm focal length. The camera has the area around the goal in its field of view. Using this experimental setup the whole image size was 1280x1024 pixels whereas the ball corresponded to a circular region with radii in the range $[R\_MIN = 21, R\_MAX = 24]$ depending on the distance of the ball with respect the optical center of the camera. The camera frame rate was 200 fps with an exposure time of 1 msec in order to avoid blurring effect in the case of very high ball speed.

During the data acquisition session a number of shots on goal were performed: the shots differed in ball velocity and direction with respect to the goalmouth. This way, differently scaled (depending on the distance between the ball and the camera), occluded (by the goal posts) and faded (by the net) ball appearances were experienced. Moreover some shots hit a rigid wall placed on purpose inside the goal in order to acquire some instances of deformed ball and then to check the sensitiveness of the ball recognition system in the case of ball deformation. Figure 4 reports images acquired during the experimental phase and corresponding to two goal events; the first one refers to a goal event during the Free Shot session: the fading effect due to the presence of the Net is evident, but no occlusions and deformations are present. The second one was performed in presence of an Impact Wall: in this experiments, the ball is faded by the net, occluded by the goal posts, and deformed by the impact with the rigid wall.

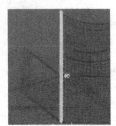   

Free shot - fading   Impact wall - deformation

Fig. 4. Some images acquired during experimental phase

During the acquisition session about *5,6M* of images where collected. Each image was processed to detect candidate ball regions by finding circular arrangement in the edge magnitude map: edge point contributes a circle to an output accumulator space and the peak in the output accumulator space is detected where these contributed circles overlap at the center of the original circle.

The main benefits of this method are the low computational cost and the high detection rate when the ball is visible in the image. The main drawback lies in the impossibility of detecting occlusions and ball absence in the image. The circle detection algorithm determines in every situation the highest peaks in the accumulator space. Then it is difficult to differentiate between images containing and not containing the ball. To reduce negative effects due to occlusions, we introduce BRISK feature descriptors and compare them with the other ones.

For each image a candidate ball region (of size $(2*R\_MAX+1)x(2*R\_MAX+1)$ i.e 42x42) was then extracted around the position corresponding to the highest value in the accumulator space.

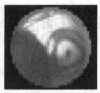

Fig. 5. Examples of occluded balls, respectively due to goal post, net, player's arm and head

After this preliminary step 3975 candidate ball regions were selected and manually labelled to form a test ground truth. This dataset has been built with the goal of provide about all possible appearances for the ball. This way, it contains balls acquired in both good and bad lighting conditions, in presence of both partial and heavy occlusions, and also in presence of cast shadows that strongly modify the ball appearance. In the acquired images these challenging conditions (occlusions and shadows) occurred either while the ball crosses the goal mouth appearing behind the goal posts or when a person interposes himself between the ball and the camera (some examples of occluded and shadowed balls are shown in figure 5).

Table 1. Ball Recognition results on the whole data set

Ball Descriptors	TP	FN	TN	FP	Detection Rate (%)
Wavelet HAAR	1890	95	1654	336	89.16%
Wavelet DB3	1870	117	1700	287	89.81%
BRISK	1027	930	1749	269	69.83%
SIFT	992	992	1702	289	67.77%
PCA	1595	383	1430	567	76.10%

Table 1 summarizes the ball recognition results obtained by comparing different feature descriptors on the whole data set. In the first column of the table 1 are itemized the used feature descriptors. From the second to fifth columns are presented respectively: the values of correct detection of the ball (TP:True Positive), the values of the errors in the ball detection (FN: False Negative), the values of correct detection of no-ball (TN: True Negative) and finally the values of errors in detection of ball in the candidate regions in which it does not exist (FP: False Positive). In the last column of the table 1 the overall detection performance of each methodology is shown. For all of the compared feature extraction methodologies we have used a Naive Bayes Classifier with the same training set composed of 50 examples of fully visible balls, and 50 examples which did not contain the ball. All the training patches are extracted at the beginning of the acquisition session, with good lighting conditions. The proposed results are very encouraging: the detection rate is always very high, with the best results obtained by using Wavelet decomposition (in particular Daubechies family slightly better than Haar family). On the other hand, the detection rate of BRISK is good but not comparable with Wavelet. In this test, all training examples consisted only of patches extracted from images acquired under good light conditions, while the test images contained patches extracted from images acquired in different and challenging conditions (poor light condition, ball occluded or deformed). However, the selected descriptors were able to well characterize the ball patches, even in critical conditions. At the same time no-ball patches were well classified, avoiding a huge number of false ball validation.

Table 2. Occluded balls recognition results

Ball Descriptors	TP	FN	Detection Rate (%)
Wavelet HAAR	114	86	114/200 (57.00%)
Wavelet DB3	90	110	90/200 (45.00%)
BRISK	157	43	157/200 (78.50%)
SIFT	148	52	148/200 (74.00%)
PCA	69	131	69/200 (34.50%)

In the second experiment, we focus our attention on a subset of the whole ground truth dataset, specifically the subset composed by partially and heavily occluded balls. The final goal of our system, as remarked in section 1, is the detection of goal events during football matches. So, it is reasonable to highlight performance of the ball detection algorithms in presence of occlusions: a goal event surely happens very close to the goalposts, probably in presence of a goal-keeper, so, before crossing the line, the ball will be likely occluded by goalposts or player's body part. For these reasons we have analyzed performance of feature descriptors on a test subset consisting of *200* examples (only partially/heavy occluded balls). In table 2 the obtained results are outlined. As evident, SIFT and BRISK methodologies give the best results in terms of ball recognition rate in these critical situations. This can be explained by considering the character-istics of these features: they are local descriptors (differently from Wavelet and PCA that are global), so they are able to better represent local (both geometrical and textural) features of the balls.

In addition, considering the computational aspects, it results that BRISK is faster than SIFT. So, we can conclude that, in very critical situations, BRISK and SIFT outperform other approaches in terms of recognition rate, and com-putational issues encouraging the use of BRISK for the detection of the ball finalized to the goal event detection in real football contexts.

The results obtained in the experiments reported in section 3 deserve a thor-ough analysis because they open up new ways to further improve the system aimed at automatically detecting goal events by using video inputs. From Table 1 it is clear that the traditional methods, which consider global features, are essential to recognize the ball in cases where it is clearly visible as well as free of external disturbances, such as shadows which substantially alter its appearance. In contrast, methods based on local descriptors are less reliable in case of coherent appearance but are much less sensitive to occlusions and to changes in lighting. That said, the results presented in this work, although preliminary and worthy of further investigation, allow us to see the possibility of introducing a substantial improvement to the traditional approaches used to recognize the ball in football images. In particular, they suggest to move from a single-step approach to a multi-step one in which different ball recognition strategies are used depending on the operative status of the system. Under this new point of view, global approaches like wavelet could be used to alert the system to the presence of the ball in the scene (since they have a higher recognition rate for not corrupted ball occurrences). Once the ball has been detected in the scene it can be tracked and, frame by frame, a double validation could be performed by using both global and local descriptors, especially when the ball is close to the goal post. This way, the 3D ball position can be retrieved on the basis of a more robust classification in each processing unit (a lower number of false negative occurrences is expected). This should increase the precision in 3D ball estimation and then in the number of correctly evaluated controversial situations about goal events.

4   Conclusion and Future Work

This paper investigated different feature descriptors to be used, as a part of a more complex system, in order to recognize football ball patterns. Experimental results on real ball examples under challenging conditions and a comparison with some of the more consolidated feature extraction methodologies demonstrated the suitability of the local descriptor (like SIFT and BRISK) to recognize ball pattern even in presence of occlusions of strong changes in appearance due to cast shadows. Future works will address computational aspects of the use of multi-step ball recognition strategies and an evaluation of the whole system after the integration of this new processing strategies.

References

1. Choi, K., Seo, Y.: Automatic initialization for 3d soccer player tracking. Pattern Recogn. Lett. **32**(9), 1274–1282 (2011)
2. Colas, F., Brazdil, P.: Comparison of SVM and some older classification algorithms in text classification tasks. In: Bramer, M. (ed.) Artificial Intelligence in Theory and Practice. IFIP AICT, vol. 217, pp. 169–178. Springer, Heidelberg (2006)
3. D'Orazio, T., Guaragnella, C., Leo, M., Distante, A.: A new algorithm for ball recognition using circle hough transform and neural classifier. Pattern Recognition **37**(3), 393–408 (2004)

4. Ekin, A., Tekalp, A.M.: Automatic soccer video analysis and summarization. IEEE Trans. on Image Processing **12**, 796–807 (2003)
5. Flach, P.A., Lachiche, N.: Naive bayesian classification of structured data. Machine Learning **57**(3), 233–269 (2004)
6. Gao, X., Niu, Z., Tao, D., Li, X.: Non-goal scene analysis for soccer video. Neuro-computing **74**(4), 540–548 (2011)
7. Hung, M.-H., Hsieh, C.-H., Kuo, C.-M., Pan, J.-S.: Generalized playfield segmentation of sport videos using color features. Patt. Recogn. Lett. **32**(7), 987–1000 (2011)
8. Jolliffe, I.T.: Principal Component Analysis. Springer (2002)
9. Leo, M., D'Orazio, T., Spagnolo, P., Mazzeo, P.L., Distante, A.: SIFT based ball recognition in soccer images. In: Elmoataz, A., Lezoray, O., Nouboud, F., Mammass, D. (eds.) ICISP 2008. LNCS, vol. 5099, pp. 263–272. Springer, Heidelberg (2008)
10. Leo, M., Mosca, N., Spagnolo, P., Mazzeo, P., D'Orazio, T., Distante, A.: A visual framework for interaction detection in soccer matches. International Journal of Pattern Recognition and Artificial Intelligence **24**(04), 499–530 (2010)
11. Leutenegger, S., Chli, M., Siegwart, R.Y.: Brisk: binary robust invariant scalable keypoints. In: 2011 IEEE International Conference on Proceedings of Computer Vision (ICCV), ICCV 2011, pp. 2548–2555 (2011)
12. Liu, J., Tong, X., Li, W., Wang, T., Zhang, Y., Wang, H.: Automatic player detection, labeling and tracking in broadcast soccer video. Pattern Recognition Letters **30**(2), 103–113 (2009)
13. Lowe, D.G.: Distinctive image features from scale-invariant keypoints. Int. J. Comput. Vision **60**(2), 91–110 (2004)
14. MacQueen, J.B.: Some methods for classification and analysis of multivariate observations. In: Proc. of the 5th Berkeley Symposium on Mathem. Stat. and Prob., vol. 1, pp. 281–297. Univ. of Calif. Press (1967)
15. Mallat, S.: A Wavelet Tour of Signal Processing. AP Professional, London (1997)
16. Mazzeo, P.L., Leo, M., Spagnolo, P., Nitti, M.: Soccer ball detection by comparing different feature extraction methodologies. Adv. in Art. Int. (2012)
17. Petrović, N.I., Jovanov, L., Pižurica, A., Philips, W.: Object tracking using naive bayesian classifiers. In: Blanc-Talon, J., Bourennane, S., Philips, W., Popescu, D., Scheunders, P. (eds.) ACIVS 2008. LNCS, vol. 5259, pp. 775–784. Springer, Heidelberg (2008)
18. Piccardi, M.: Background subtraction techniques: a review. In: IEEE SMC 2004 International Conference on Systems, Man and Cybernetics (2004)
19. Ren, J., Orwell, J., Jones, G.A., Xu, M.: Tracking the soccer ball using multiple fixed cameras. Computer Vision and Image Understanding **113**(5), 633–642 (2009)
20. Spagnolo, P., Mosca, N., Nitti, M., Distante, A.: An unsupervised approach for segmentation and clustering of soccer players. In: IMVIP Conference, pp. 133–142 (2007)
21. Tosic, I., Frossard, P.: Dictionary learning: What is the right representation for my signal? IEEE Signal Processing Magazine **28**(2), 27–38 (2011)
22. Yu, X., Leong, H., Xu, C., Tian, Q.: Trajectory-based ball detection and tracking in broadcast soccervideo. IEEE Transaction on Multimedia **8**(6), 1164–1178 (2006)

Neighborhood Selection
for Dimensionality Reduction

Paola Campadelli, Elena Casiraghi, and Claudio Ceruti[✉]

Dipartimento di Informatica, Università Degli Studi di Milano,
Via Comelico 39-41, 20135 Milano, Italy
{paola.campadelli,elena.casiraghi,claudio.ceruti}@unimi.it

Abstract. Though a great deal of research work has been devoted to
the development of dimensionality reduction algorithms, the problem is
still open. The most recent and effective techniques, assuming datasets
drawn from an underlying low dimensional manifold embedded into an
high dimensional space, look for "small enough" neighborhoods which
should represent the underlying manifold portion. Unfortunately, neighborhood selection is an open problem, for the presence of noise, outliers,
points not uniformly distributed, and to unexpected high manifold curvatures, causing the inclusion of geodesically distant points in the same
neighborhood. In this paper we describe our neighborhood selection algorithm, called ONeS; it exploits both distance and angular information to
form neighborhoods containing nearby points that share a common local
structure in terms of curvature. The reported experimental results show
the enhanced quality of the neighborhoods computed by ONeS w.r.t. the
commonly used k-neighborhoods solely employing the euclidean distance.

Keywords: Dimensionality reduction · Manifold learning · Neighborhood selection

1 Introduction

When developing automatic solutions to problems in the pattern recognition field,
most researchers are confronted with intrinsically low dimensional data lying in a
very high dimensional space. This requires dimensionality reduction (dr) as the
first and fundamental processing step, to reduce the data dimensionality without
losing important information.

To this aim, several dr techniques have been proposed in the past, such
as Multidimensional Scaling (MDS) algorithms [14], [9], [15], the mostly used
Principal Component Analysis (PCA [8]), Curvilinear Component Analysis
(CCA) [3], ISOMAP [16], Local Linear Embedding (LLE [12]), Local Tangent Space
Alignment (LTSA [23]) and its variants [17], [21], [20], [18], [22], and the CycleCut
algoritm [5].

Among them, the most recent and effective methods assume that the input
points are uniformly drawn from an underlying locally smooth manifold $\mathcal{M} \subseteq \Re^d$

© Springer International Publishing Switzerland 2015
V. Murino and E. Puppo (Eds.): ICIAP 2015, Part I, LNCS 9279, pp. 183–191, 2015.
DOI: 10.1007/978-3-319-23231-7_17

embedded into an higher D-dimensional space $\mathcal{M} \subseteq \Re^d \subset \Re^D (d \leq D)$, where d is the `intrinsic dimension` (`id`) of $\mathcal{M}$. This leads to the consideration that, though the manifold local smoothness guarantees that "small enough" manifold neighborhoods can be well approximated by their local tangent spaces, the embedding map might produce unexpected folds in $\mathcal{M}$, that should be properly accounted for when trying to discover the underlying manifold geometry.

Practically, most `dr` algorithms pursue the following steps:

1) `Id estimation`: the `id` of the embedded manifold $\mathcal{M}$ is a fundamental information, usually unknown. However, reliable estimates of its value can be computed by one of the `id` estimators recently proposed [10], [2], [6], [11], [13] , [1]

2) **Neighborhoods selection**: it is based on the fact that "small enough" neighborhoods may reliably approximate the underlying manifold's neighborhoods. Two strategies are commonly applied to select the neighborhoods of each point $\mathbf{x}$: one takes the k nearest neighbors of $\mathbf{x}$, the other selects the points in the D-dimensional ball centered in $\mathbf{x}$ and having radius ϵ (both k and ϵ are parameters to be set).

3) **Dimensionality reduction**: a reduction function is found, that preserves neighborhoods relations.

Among the `dr` techniques applying these steps, we consider `LTSA` and its variants. Assuming that point neighborhoods (approximating the underlying manifold's portions) are "smooth enough" to be well approximated by a linear tangent space, `LTSA` firstly applies local `SVD` to estimate the local tangent spaces approximating them; secondly, it computes the global mapping by finding the point coordinates that produce the best alignment among all the local tangent spaces. It must be noted that an accurate global mapping is obtained only if the point neighborhoods are "large enough" to guarantee a good overlap among nearby neighborhoods; unfortunately, the required overlap causes too large neighborhoods, that often include noise, outliers, points not uniformly distributed, or points belonging to geodesically distant regions, due to unexpected folds generated by high manifold curvatures. In this cases the assumptions of `LTSA` are violated since the approximation of the neighborhoods via local tangent spaces is not accurate. For this reason, different variants of `LTSA` have been proposed [17], [21], [20], [18], [22], which mainly modify the neighborhood selection and the local tangent space construction.

Though these variants are theoretically sound and the reported experiments seem promising, it is quite difficult to objectively compare them since none of them has been tested on standard databases; besides, they are mostly tested on classical manifolds, such as the Swiss Roll, and results are only visually presented. Though other `dr` works [19], [7], [4] are also focusing on the "bottleneck" of neighborhoods selection, the problem is still crucial and open.

For this reason in this paper we present our proposal, called `Optimal Neighborhood Selection` (`ONeS`). Based on the reliable results obtained by the `id` estimator employing both distance and angular information [1], `ONeS` builds the point neighborhoods by analyzing not only pairwise distances but also angular informations.

This paper is organized as follows: in Sect. 2 we outline ONeS; in Sect. 3 we describe the obtained results and report future works.

2   Algorithm

In this section we describe ONeS, which exploits the local angular distribution to improve the construction of the local point neighborhoods, each describing the local structure of the underlying manifold portion.

More formally, given a D-dimensional dataset $\mathbf{X}_n = \{\mathbf{x}_i, \cdots, \mathbf{x}_n\} \subset \Re^D$ composed by points sampled from a locally smooth d-dimensional manifold $\mathcal{M} \subset \Re^d$ (with $d \leq D$), we define the distance based k-neighborhoods of a point, $\mathbf{x}_i \in \mathbf{X}_n$, as the set containing the k nearest points in terms of euclidean distance, and we indicate it as $\mathcal{N}_{dist}(\mathbf{x}_i, k)$.

This k-neighborhood is commonly used by most of the manifold learning and dr techniques; we also exploit this structure to discover the local angular distribution describing the curvature of the manifold portion underlying each neighborhood. Precisely, for each sample $\mathbf{x}_i \in \mathbf{X}_n$, $\mathcal{N}_{dist}(\mathbf{x}_i, k)$ is firstly centered in $\mathbf{x}_i$; we then measure the angle between each point $\mathbf{x}_j \in \mathcal{N}_{dist}(\mathbf{x}_i, k)$ and each of the D axis of the canonical base of $\Re^D$, $\mathbf{e}_d$ with $d \in \{1, \cdots, D\}$ ($\mathbf{e}_d \in \Re^D$ is a vector composed by zeros, except for the value 1 in the position d). In this way, given the k neighbors $\mathbf{x}_j \in \mathcal{N}_{dist}(\mathbf{x}_i, k)$ of $\mathbf{x}_i$, we obtain for each $\mathbf{e}_d$ ($d = 1, \cdots, D$), the k angles:

$$\alpha_j = acos \left(\frac{< \mathbf{x}_j, \mathbf{e}_d >}{\|\mathbf{x}_j\|} \right) \qquad (1)$$

where $acos$ is the inverse of the cosine function. Afterwards, for each axis $\mathbf{e}_d$ we take the computed k angles α_j and we build an histogram of their distribution. More precisely, we split the interval $[0, \pi]$ in a fixed number of equal bins (which we experimentally set to 8), and we count the numbers of angles that fall inside each of them. As a result, we obtain D histograms, $\{h_1(\mathbf{x}_i), \cdots, h_D(\mathbf{x}_i)\}$ for the point $\mathbf{x}_i$, one for each axis; their concatenation produces a single histogram $\mathbf{h}(\mathbf{x}_i) = [h_1(\mathbf{x}_i), \cdots, h_D(\mathbf{x}_i)]$.

Having computed the histograms $\mathbf{h}(\mathbf{x}_i)$ for all the dataset points $\mathbf{x}_i \in \mathbf{X}_n$, we assign to each point $\mathbf{x}_i$ the average of the k histograms $\mathbf{h}(\mathbf{x}_j)$ computed for its k neighbors:

$$\bar{\mathbf{h}}(\mathbf{x}_i) = \frac{\mathbf{h}(\mathbf{x}_i) + \sum_{j=1}^{k} \mathbf{h}(\mathbf{x}_j)}{k+1} \qquad where \qquad \mathbf{x}_j \in \mathcal{N}_{dist}(\mathbf{x}_i, k) \qquad (2)$$

This reduces the variability between histograms of nearby points, which could be influenced by the presence of outliers, noise and variation in the density of the points sampled from the underlying manifold.

Finally, we are ready to build neighborhoods based on the similarity between the average local angular distribution of each point. In particular, we use the χ^2 distance for measuring the similarity between histograms. It is defined as:

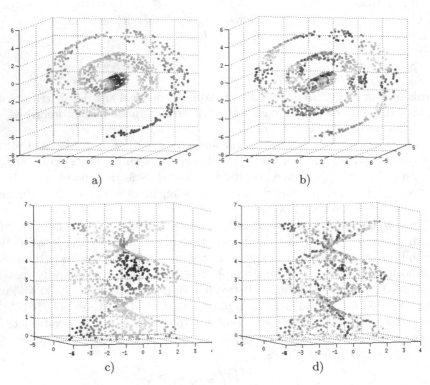

Fig. 1. Reported figures depict the distances from a given point, circled in red, measured by means of the euclidean distance and the χ^2 histogram distance of angular distribution (blue points are the closest ones, whilst the red points are the farthest): a) Swiss Roll with Euclidean distance b) Swiss Roll with histogram distance c) Helix with Euclidean distance d) Helix with histogram distance

$$\chi^2(h_1, h_2) = \sum_{n=1}^{bins} \frac{(h_1(n) - h_2(n))^2}{h_1(n)} \tag{3}$$

Taking for each $\mathbf{x}_i \in \mathbf{X}_n$ the k closest points in terms of the χ^2 histogram distance, we get the angular based neighborhood $\mathcal{N}_{ang}(\mathbf{x}_i, k)$. By doing so, for each point we build two different neighborhoods which embody two different informations: the distance based neighborhood $\mathcal{N}_{dist}(\mathbf{x}_i, k)$, which is based on the proximity between points on the underlying manifold, and the $\mathcal{N}_{ang}(\mathbf{x}_i, k)$ neighborhood, which is based on local angular distribution and allows to select as neighbors those points that share a common local structure in terms of curvature (see Figure 1). A joint use of these two structures allows to obtain local neighborhoods that not only have small radius, but are also less affected by the curvature due to the manifold embedding.

Algorithm 1. ONeS

Require: Dataset $\mathbf{X}_n, k, \hat{k}$
  return Neighborhood set $\mathcal{N}_{final}(\mathbf{x}_i, k)$ for each $\mathbf{x}_i \in \mathbf{X}_n$
  for $i = 1, \cdots, n$ **do**
    $\mathcal{N}_{dist}(\mathbf{x}_i, k) = \text{Find\_nn\_euclid}(\mathcal{X}_n, \mathbf{x}_i, k)$
    [The function $\text{Find\_nn\_euclid}(\mathcal{X}_n, \mathbf{x}_i, k)$ finds the k neighbors of the point $\mathbf{x}_i$ in $\mathbf{X}_n$
    using Euclidean distance.]
    $\tilde{\mathcal{N}}_{dist}(\mathbf{x}_i, k) = \mathcal{N}_{dist}(\mathbf{x}_i, k) - \mathbf{x}_i$
    for $d = 1, \cdots, D$ **do**
      for $\mathbf{x}_j \in \tilde{\mathcal{N}}_{dist}(\mathbf{x}_i, k)$ **do**
        $\alpha_j = \angle \mathbf{x}_j, \mathbf{e}_d$
      end for
      $h_d(\mathbf{x}_i) = \text{Histogram}(\{\alpha_j\})$
    end for
    $\mathbf{h}(\mathbf{x}_i) = [h_1(\mathbf{x}_i), \cdots, h_D(\mathbf{x}_i)]$
  end for
  for $i = 1, \cdots, n$ **do**
    $\overline{\mathbf{h}}(\mathbf{x}_i) = (1/(k+1))\mathbf{h}(\mathbf{x}_i) + \sum_{j=1}^{k} \mathbf{h}(\mathbf{x}_j)$ where $\mathbf{x}_j \in \mathcal{N}_{dist}(\mathbf{x_i}, k)$
  end for
  for $i = 1, \cdots, n$ **do**
    $\mathcal{N}_{ang}(\mathbf{x}_i, \hat{k}) = \text{Find\_nn\_}\chi^2(\mathcal{H}_n, \overline{\mathbf{h}}(\mathbf{x}_i), \hat{k})$
    [$\mathcal{H}_n$ is the collection of the mean histogram for each point of the dataset $\mathbf{X}_n$. The
    function $\text{Find\_nn\_}\chi^2$ is the analogue of Find_nn_euclid using χ^2 histogram distance
    instead of the Euclidean distance.]
    $\mathcal{N}_{dist}(\mathbf{x}_i, \hat{k}) = \text{Find\_nn\_euclid}(\mathcal{X}_n, \mathbf{x}_i, \hat{k})$
    $\mathcal{N}_{final}(\mathbf{x}_i, k) = \text{Borda\_count}(\mathcal{N}_{dist}(\mathbf{x}_i, \hat{k}), \mathcal{N}_{ang}(\mathbf{x}_i, \hat{k}), k)$
    [The Borda_count function is the method Borda Count as described in this section].
  end for

Table 1. Brief description of the synthetic datasets employed in our experiments, where d is the intrinsic dimension and D is the embedding space dimension.

Name	d	D	Description
$\mathcal{M}_2$	3	5	Affine space.
$\mathcal{M}_3$	4	6	Concentrated figure, confusable with a $3d$ one.
$\mathcal{M}_4$	4	8	Nonlinear manifold.
$\mathcal{M}_6$	6	36	Nonlinear manifold.
$\mathcal{M}_7$	2	3	Swiss-Roll.
$\mathcal{M}_8$	12	72	Nonlinear manifold.
$\mathcal{M}_9$	20	20	Affine space.
$\mathcal{M}_{11}$	1	3	Möebius band 10-times twisted.

To perform a proper mixture of distance and angular neighborhoods we fix $\hat{k} > k$, build two new sets $\mathcal{N}_{dist}(\mathbf{x}_i, \hat{k})$ and $\mathcal{N}_{ang}(\mathbf{x}_i, \hat{k})$, as described above, and use the simple and well known Borda count method to select the k points that are the closest to $\mathbf{x}_i$ with respect to both the euclidean and the angular distance. More precisely, given two sets of size $\hat{k}$, sorted in ascending order, the Borda count method selects the points sharing the top positions between the two indexed sets; to this aim, it assigns the score $\hat{k}$ to the first element of each set, the score $\hat{k} - 1$ to the second element, and so on, till the value 1 is assigned to the last element of the sets. The algorithm then sums the scores obtained by each element in the two sets (if an element is not present in a set its score is zero), orders the elements according to the resulting scores, and takes the first k elements. In this way the neighborhood set $\mathcal{N}_{final}(\mathbf{x}_i, k)$ obtained for each point $\mathbf{x}_i$ is a combination of the two sets $\mathcal{N}_{dist}(\mathbf{x}_i, \hat{k})$ and $\mathcal{N}_{ang}(\mathbf{x}_i, \hat{k})$.

In the next section, experiments on synthetic and real datasets show that the algorithm ONeS builds local neighborhoods preserving the proximity relations between points and being less affected by the manifold curvature.

3   Experimental Results and Future Works

In order to assess the quality of ONeS, we compare the neighborhood sets it computes with the commonly used k-neighborhoods, obtained by employing the euclidean distance.

The comparison employs a measure, which we call residual, that indicates how much the point neighborhoods are affected by the manifold's folds generated by the embedding. Under the assumption that the manifold has id d, once a neighborhood is computed, its residual is obtained by building its local d-dimensional tangent space and calculating the mean distance between each neighborhood point and its projection on the tangent space, normalized by the neighborhood radius (i.e. the distance of the farthest point from the center). The residual for a given dataset is the average residual over all the neighborhoods.

Table 2. Percentage values of the relative improvement using ONeS. Since manifold $\mathcal{M}_9$ has an id of 20, we need to fix $k = 22, \hat{k} = 33$ and $k = 22, \hat{k} = 44$, in order to estimate a d-dimensional tangent space having $k > d$ points.

Name	$k = 12, \hat{k} = 18$	$k = 12, \hat{k} = 24$
$\mathcal{M}_2$	62%	57%
$\mathcal{M}_3$	69%	67%
$\mathcal{M}_4$	29%	23%
$\mathcal{M}_6$	19%	13%
$\mathcal{M}_7$	48%	32%
$\mathcal{M}_8$	9%	6%
$\mathcal{M}_9^*$	32%*	24%*
$\mathcal{M}_{11}$	47%	42%

Name	$k = 12, \hat{k} = 18$	$k = 12, \hat{k} = 24$
MNIST$_0$	5%	9%
MNIST$_1$	5%	7%
MNIST$_2$	3%	5%
MNIST$_3$	5%	8%
MNIST$_4$	3%	6%
MNIST$_5$	2%	5%
MNIST$_6$	7%	13%
MNIST$_7$	2%	5%
MNIST$_8$	3%	6%
MNIST$_9$	4%	8%

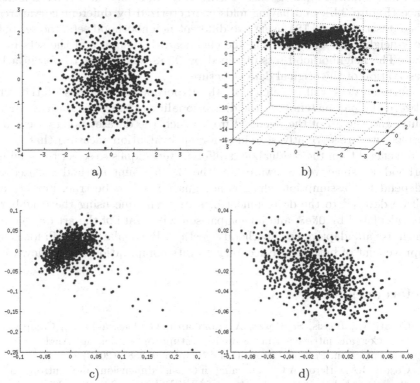

Fig. 2. a) Two dimensional dataset composed by 1000 points b) Non linear embedding in three dimensions c) Reduced dataset obtained by LTSA using Euclidean distance based neighborhood sets ($k = 12$) d) Reduced dataset obtained by LTSA using neighborhood sets calculated by ONeS ($k = 12, \hat{k} = 60$)

In order to perform experiments on datasets composed by points sampled from manifolds of both low and high id, linearly and nonlinearly embedded in an higher dimensional space (see Table 1), we use the datasets generator proposed in [6]. Besides, we test ONeS on the digit test set contained in the standard MNIST database, which contains 784-dimensional points, and has an estimated i.d. in the range $[8, \cdots, 11]$ [6]. In Table 2 we report the results obtained by fixing $k = 12$, a commonly used value in the literature, and $\hat{k} = 1.5 * k$, $\hat{k} = 2 * k$. The results are expressed as percentage values, which show the relative improvement in the reduction of the residual. Precisely, being R the residual estimated using the k-neighborhoods, and $\tilde{R}$ the residual estimated using ONeS, the percentage is obtained as $100 - \frac{\tilde{R}}{R} * 100$.

The reported results show the enhanced quality of the neighborhood set computed by OnES both on the synthetic and on the real datasets, the latter being noisy and sparse. It is notable to observe that neighborhoods built on noisy and sparse dataset may benefit by using higher values of $\hat{k}$, that is by considering more candidate neighbors. s a further visual experiment and example, we generate a two dimensional dataset (Figure 2.a) embedded in a three dimensional space (Figure 2.b), and having folds characterized by different curvatures. On this dataset we test LTSA using two different neighborhood sets, the set built by the k-neighborhoods employing the euclidean distances, and the sets built by ONeS. The neighborhood sets obtained by ONeS allow LTSA to obtain a better preservation of the original data structure.

Future works will be aimed at the experimental analysis of the relation between the parameters k, $\hat{k}$, the dimensionality of the given dataset, its cardinality, and the id of the manifold from which the dataset points are sampled. Besides, we are currently searching for an evaluation measure that could be more general than the residual, and different techniques to select the final neighborhood set since we are aware that the Borda count method is based on an independency assumption which is not guaranteed to be true. Further efforts will be devoted to the development of a dr technique using the neighborhood sets calculated by ONeS, and its comparison with state-of-the-art dr techniques, which use an adaptive neighborhood selection. Particularly, we will focus on the improvement of both the dr accuracy and its computational efficiency.

References

1. Ceruti, C., Bassis, S., Rozza, A., Lombardi, G., Casiraghi, E., Campadelli, P.: DANCo: an intrinsic Dimensionalty estimator exploiting Angle and Norm Concentration. Pattern Recognition **47**(8), 2569–2581 (2014)
2. Costa, J.A., Hero, A.O.: Learning intrinsic dimension and entropy of high-dimensional shape spaces. In: Proc. of EUSIPCO, pp. 231–252 (2004)
3. Demartines, P., Herault, J.: Curvilinear component analysis: A self-organizing neural network for nonlinear mapping in cluster analysis. IEEE Trans. on Neural Networks **8**(1), 148–154 (1997)
4. Gashler, M., Martinez, T.: Robust manifold learning with cyclecut. Connection Science, **24**(1) (2012)
5. Gashler, M., Martinez, T.: Tangent space guided intelligent neighbor finding, pp. 2617–2624 (2011)
6. Hein, M., Audibert, J.Y.: Intrinsic dimensionality estimation of submanifolds in euclidean space. In: Proc. of ICML, pp. 289–296 (2005)
7. Jing, L., Shao, C.: Selection of the suitable parameter value for isomap. Journal of Software **6**(6), 1034–1041 (2011)
8. Jollife, I.T.: Principal component analysis. Springer Series in Statistics. Springer-Verlag, New York (1986)
9. Kruskal, J.B.: Linear transformation of multivariate data to reveal clustering, vol. I. Ac. Press (1972)
10. Levina, E., Bickel, P.J.: Maximum likelihood estimation of intrinsic dimension. In: Proceedings of NIPS, vol. 1, pp. 777–784 (2004)
11. Little, A.V., Maggioni, M., Rosasco, L.: Multiscale Geometric Methods for Data Sets I: Multiscale SVD, Noise and Curvature. MIT-CSAIL-TR-2012-029 (2012)
12. Roweis, S.T., Saul, L.K.: Nonlinear Dimensionality Reduction by Locally Linear Embedding. Science **290**, 2323–2326 (2000)

13. Rozza, A., Lombardi, G., Ceruti, C., Casiraghi, E., Campadelli, P.: Novel high intrinsic dimensionality estimators. Machine Learning Journal **89**(1–2), 37–65 (2012)

14. Shepard, R.N., Carroll, J.D.: Parametric representation of nonlinear data structures. Ac. Press (1969)

15. Silva, V., Tenenbaum, J.B.: Global versus local methods in nonlinear dimensionality reduction. In: Advances in Neural Information Processing Systems, vol. 15, pp. 705–712 (2002)

16. Tenenbaum, J., Silva, V., Langford, J.: A global geometric framework for nonlinear dimensionality reduction. Science **290**, 2319–2323 (2000)

17. Wang, J.: Improve local tangent space alignment using various dimensional local coordinates. Neurocomputing **71**(1618), 3575–3581 (2008)

18. Wang, J., Jiang, W., Gou, J.: Extended local tangent space alignment for classification. Neurocomputing **77**(1), 261–266 (2012)

19. Wei, J., Peng, H., Lin, Y.S., Huang, Z.M., Wang, J.B.: Adaptive neighborhood selection for manifold learning. In: International Conference on Machine Learning and Cybernetics, pp. 380–384 (2008)

20. Zhan, Y., Yin, J.: Robust local tangent space alignment via iterative weighted PCA. Neurocomputing **74**(11), 1985–1993 (2011)

21. Zhang, P., Qiao, H., Zhang, B.: An improved local tangent space alignment method for manifold learning. Pattern Recognition Letters **32**(2), 181–189 (2011)

22. Zhang, Z., Wang, J., Zha, H.: Adaptive Manifold Learning. IEEE Transactions on Pattern Analysis and Machine Intelligence **34**(2), 253–265 (2012)

23. Zhang, Z., Zha, H.: Principal manifolds and nonlinear dimension reduction via local tangent space alignment. SIAM Journal of Scientific Computing **26**, 313–338 (2002)

Crowdsearching Training Sets
for Image Classification

Sami Abduljalil Abdulhak$^{(\boxtimes)}$, Walter Riviera, and Marco Cristani

Department of Computer Science, Cá Vignal 2, Verona, Italy
{sami.naji,walter.riviera,marco.cristani}@univr.it

Abstract. The success of an object classifier depends strongly on its training set, but this fact seems to be generally neglected in the computer vision community, which focuses primarily on the construction of descriptive features and the design of fast and effective learning mechanisms. Furthermore, collecting training sets is a very expensive step, which needs a considerable amount of manpower for selecting the most representative samples for an object class. In this paper, we face this problem, following the very recent trend of automatizing the collection of training images for image classification: in particular, here we exploit a source of information never considered so far for this purpose, that is the textual tags. Textual tags are usually attached by the crowd to the images of social platforms like Flickr, associating the visual content to explicit semantics, which unfortunately is noisy in many cases. Our approach leverages this shared knowledge, and collects images spanning the visual variance of an object class, removing at the same time the noise by different filtering query expansion techniques. Comparative results promote our method, which is capable to automatically generate in few minutes a training dataset leading to an 81.41% of average precision on the PASCAL VOC 2012 dataset.

Keywords: Image classification · Training sets · Crowdsearching · CNN · SVM

1 Introduction

Generally underestimated in favor of more appealing themes like feature design and model learning, the challenge of building effective training sets for object recognition is instead very important; an ideal training set should represent the entire visual variation of an object class, capturing all of its facets in an ensemble of representative samples. In image classification, this means to have a set of pictures which portray an object under different poses, illumination conditions, occluded or not, but also spanning all of its semantics variability. Think for example at a classifier aimed at recognizing a dog in an image: a dog could be an husky dog, a fox-terrier, bulldog, which can be running, barking, sitting etc.. All of this should be present in the pool of training images, to ensure a proper generalization.

© Springer International Publishing Switzerland 2015
V. Murino and E. Puppo (Eds.): ICIAP 2015, Part I, LNCS 9279, pp. 192–202, 2015.
DOI: 10.1007/978-3-319-23231-7_18

So far, the issue of building image datasets for training classifiers was committed to scientists [7], or, more recently, to Internet users through crowdfunding platforms like Amazon Mechanical Turk [3]. In the latter case, scientists still have to supervise the image collection, as noisy samples could be erroneously captured. All of these settings require a considerable effort, both in time and monetary terms; for this reasons, datasets are nowadays focused on few classes, depicting generic objects (dogs, cars, aeroplane etc.). A notable exception is Imagenet [5], which mirrors the taxonomy of Wordnet [15], considering circa 21841 different object classes. Anyway, many of them contain very few images ("minibike, motorbike", "tanker plane") making their use as training set unfeasible.

Another research direction looks for automatic strategies to craft image datasets [12], which obviously are faster than the human intervention, but introduce a huge number of noisy elements that cannot be removed by anyone but the human. Therefore, the challenge here is to capture as less as possible false positive images; the idea is to exploit image search engines as Google Image Search, feeding them with keywords [8] or n-grams containing the entity of interest [1], keeping the images they report and in some cases [12] perform some post processing for removing noisy pictures.

All of these automatics approaches rely on indexing methods, as the one of Google Image Search, which are not open source, meaning that one step of the collection consists in a black box, where the cues used to gather images are hidden and changing over time (due to advancements in the search engine). As a consequence, the performance of such approaches could vary considerably, with no repeatability guarantees.

In this paper, we bypass this problem, focusing on an automatic image training set collection strategy which uses social platforms for gathering the pictures (in this work Flickr[1]), exploiting the textual tags usually associated to them by the users. In this way, we produce a genuine crowdsearching algorithm where the cues to extract images are visible and not hidden. In particular, the strategy is based on the interesting mechanism of the *query expansion* [14], which first builds a statistics of the more frequent tags associated to some potentially interesting images (see for example the images resulting from the textual query "dog"); on this statistics, which mirrors the common thinking of the crowd, different filters are applied, pruning away noisy tags. The remaining tags are instead used to retrieve a second set of images, the ones which will finally form the training set.

Our strategy is simpler than the previous approaches in the literature, giving better results on diverse image classification datasets, producing a training set which is absolutely comparable to many cutting edge datasets as the PASCAL VOC and Imagenet. Most notably, the approach exploits uniquely the textual tags remaining agnostic w.r.t the visual content of the images: this shows once more time the tight connection between tags and visual content; using only the textual wisdom of crowd, our approach leads to a 81.41% of average precision on the PASCAL VOC 2012, with a dataset collected in 15 minutes. At the same

---

[1] www.flickr.com

time, our approach betters also OPTIMOL [12], which instead exploits also the visual content of the images.

The rest of the paper is organized as follows: Sec. 2 presents the few approaches for the automatic generation of image classification training set, together with some remainders for the query expansion strategy; Sec. 3 details our approach, while Sec. 4 reports its performance on several, comparative experiments. Finally, Sec. 5 concludes the paper and gives some future perspectives.

2   State of the Art

At the best of our knowledge, the only approaches dealing with the automatic generation of training sets are [1,8,13]. Prior to analyze them, it is worth noting that our goal is different from that of the standard image retrieval, where plentiful of algorithms do exist [4]. In fact, image retrieval, in its more studied form, aims at filling the semantic gap between what the user wants to see (a specific query like "my mother smiling at me when I was child") and what the system provides as output. Conversely, our approach focuses on the task of capturing for a given visual concept (like a dog, a car etc.) the most visual variation in terms of pictures. In other words, our idea is to create a system that ideally is able to select for a concept a *visual synset* [5], in the same way that ImageNet does with its content. The difference w.r.t. ImageNet is that our approach has to be dynamic, 100% customizable (no limits on the kinds of visual concepts the user may want to see, so no preconstructed structure as in ImageNet) and fast.

In [8], the authors propose an unsupervised learning approach exploiting Google Image Search. The innovation consists in the use of the Google's automatic translation tools to translate users keywords into 7 different languages and use the translated keywords for collecting images. Since the Google Image Search engine works by indexing images with the text around the images, and some textual metadata [19] the usage of multiple language enriches the visual variation one may expect. The algorithm is also capable to avoid repeated images. In our case, the adoption of multiple languages could rise linguistic issues that in our case we preferred to avoid (remaining on the English language) and postpone for future work.

The other text-based approach is that of [1], in which the starting search keyword (plus an hyperonymy specifying the context) is used to generate a set of bigrams, each one of them addressing a specific semantic aspect of the visual concept. The bigrams are produced by looking at Google Ngrams[2], individuating those additional terms that are visual adjectives (where the "visual" characteristics is found by WordNet[3]), present participles (found by Natural Language Processing basic maneuvers) and hyponymy. These bigrams, ordered by their original frequency in the Ngrams repository or uniformly weighted are used to create specific sets of images (or classifiers) that once pooled together give the final dataset (or classifier).

---

[2] See https://books.google.com/ngrams/info.
[3] See http://wordnet.princeton.edu/.

The last approach is content-based [13], and starts from a set of seed images; these images are used to train a set of image classifiers, which subsequently are employed to classify unseen pictures. Positively classified images are successively fed into the classifier as training data and the approach is iterated.

Regarding the usage of the tags associated to the images, its usage for crafting training sets represents a major novelty in this paper. Briefly speaking, textual tags put by the users may help in understanding the content of the social images[4]. In particular, the study in [18] showed that the order of appearance of the tags is related to the visual content of themselves, and in particular, that the first tags are more related with the visually dominant patterns.

3   Proposed Methodology

Our approach exploits uniquely the set of tags given by the users to social images. Unfortunately, tags associated to images are usually noisy [10], especially when single images are taken into account. The idea of the approach is to start with a search of I images in relation to a first input keyword k, where the search operates uniquely on the tags associated to the images, and not on other metadata. In this way, we can collect a statistics on the tags received (that is, each image has associated a tag list), which mirrors the intended semantics shared among the people on a given visual concept, from which the term "crowdsearching". Given the list T of all the tags, we create a dictionary D of N terms, pruning away noisy tags like stepwords and other not relevant expressions (see later). Using the tag list and the dictionary, we perform different filtering operations, which will bring to an updated list of bigrams $T_{\text{filtered}} = \{< x, k >\}$, where x is one of the M filtered tags, $M < N$. With the filtered bigrams, query expansion is performed and the final images are retrieved from the social platform, forming the training set. Naturally, the training sets are then validated using cutting edge classifiers (see the experiments, Sec. 4).

Frequency Filter: The frequency filter simply sorts the tags in the dictionary by their frequency in the tag lists of the retrieved images. The idea is then to take the first F terms in the ranking, since they presumably indicate a widely shared visual semantics that implicitly prunes away unrelated concepts (or concepts that are occasionally related by the context). For example, while looking at an image of "dog", the tag "Marie" could be present since "Marie" is the owner of the dog. When moving to a large collection of images, most probably the proper name "Marie" will be characterized by a low count of occurrences, moving low in the rank. Viceversa, the proper name "Bernardo" could be high in the rank, as it defines a dog breed. The importance of the tags by their frequency is currently employed in many applications [17,22], for example the tag cloud [9] for information visualization purposes. The output of this step will be a list T_{freq} of bigrams.

---

[4] With the term "social images" we intend those images uploaded into social platforms like Flickr.

Keyword Filter: This filter exploits the fact that the tags are organized in ordered lists and that the order in a tag list associated to an image carries some meaning [18]. In particular, the filter works by keeping all the tags that occur in the tag list associated to an image before than the keyword k. The underlying principle in that tags that occur earlier in the tag list are more important [18] and that the keyword of search k could be thought as a threshold where all the terms before of that are important. So, each tag list is filtered here, the resulting terms are organized in a dictionary, ordered by frequency and kept the first F terms, appended to the keyword k in a list of bigrams T_{ord}.

Quality Filter: The quality filter exploits a semantic oracle developed in [16], which essentially is a list of 150 terms which are "semantically rich and general". In few words, linguistic researchers in the past century individuated English terms that cover wide variety of descriptions of different entities. The quality filter analyze the N terms of the initial dictionary, keeping only those that are included in the oracle list, ordering them by frequency of usage, keeping the first F terms. This filter essentially is a specialization of the frequency filter, with output a list T_{qual} of bigrams.

Noun Filter: The last filter essentially performs the intersection of the retrieved tags with a set of nouns which are in the hyponym sets of the given keyword, or in the immediate hyperonym set (found by the help of WordNet). Even in this case, the filtered keywords are ordered by frequency and the first F terms are kept, forming the list T_{Noun} of bigrams with the keyword k.

Once we apply the filter, we basically apply the query expansion step, retrieving from Flickr I images from each of the F bigrams, and pooling together all the images so to obtain the final training dataset.

4   Experiments and Results

For testing our approach we perform two experimental sessions, one comparing against the text-based method of [1], dubbed here *Semantic Trainer* for conciseness, and the second considering the visual feature-based *Optimol* approach [13]. In both the cases we focus on the Flickr social platform. Flickr allows to look for images considering the associated text tags only, fitting perfectly our scenario. It is worth noting that the Semantic Trainer was originally tested with the Google Image Search engine, so here we apply that approach on Flickr, obtaining results which are obviously different from that of [1].

As for the visual concepts to analyze, we focus on 18 classes of the PASCAL VOC 2012 image classification challenge [6] to compare with the Semantic Trainer, and on 7 object classes to compare with Optimol. These choices have been made for the sake of fairness (the same classes have been taken into account in the original papers [1] and [13], respectively).

In both the experimental sessions, our approach is applied by first downloading $I = 500$ images for each visual concept, keeping the related tag lists. On these lists, we perform basic automatic pre-processing such as removing short strings (e.g., ab,cb,etc), non-English alphabets (e.g.,Japanes character, Chinese characters,etc), meaningless words (e.g., awsm). We then apply our four filtering techniques, keeping $F = 10$ bi-grams. Depending on the cardinality of the image classes to compare with, we divided uniformly the number of images related to each bi-gram.

4.1 Comparison Against the *Semantic Trainer*

The two experiments against the Semantic Trainer of [1] consist in evaluating the capability of a method in creating a training dataset which afterwards is exploited in the VOC 2012 image classification task. Convolutional Networks (ConvNets) are used as a feature extractor [11]; in particular, we use a feedforward multilayer perceptron, adopting publicly available pre-trained ImageNet deep learning model[20], focusing on the FC7 layer for extracting the features. We then feed the 4096-dimension sparse feature vector to learn class model using linear SVM for each class. In the details, for each image class we use 500 images, while for the negative class we consider a uniform sample from the other classes into play (see [1] for further details).

As for the figures of merit, we employ the PASCAL VOC's interpolated average precision (AP). In the first experiment, 18 classes are taken into account for the original PASCAL VOC image classification task (where an image belongs to the positive set if it contains one (or more) instances of the considered class). As for the competitor, the Semantic Trainer has 6 different versions (a basic version *basic*, a hyponym-based filter *hypo*, a verb-based filter *verb*, a visual adjective-based approach *vadj*), a combination of modules by bi-gram frequency *fcom* and a combination of classifiers *ccom*, which are all reported here. As for our approach, we report the performances of the frequency filter *freq-f*, the quality filter *qual-f*, the keyword filter *keyw-f* and the noun filter *noun-f*. In addition, we report the results using the simple Flickr (*Flickr*) for generating the training images, that is, no filtering + query expansion. The results are shown in Table 1;

As visible, all the filters are comparable with that of the Semantic Trainer, with the difference that our approach is considerably simpler. In addition, the quality filter *qual-f* betters all the other methods, having very good performances on the "tv, sofa, sheep, bird" classes, showing comparable numbers on the other ones.

To understand the quantitative results, we report some qualitative examples of the kind of images (and related bigrams) obtained by our approach and that of the Semantic Trainer (related to the fcom method), considering the classes person and cat. As visible, a higher number of false positives are produced by fcom.

4.2 Generalization Capability

Of significant interest for the practical usefulness of our approach is how well the training datasets generalize beyond the insights gathered on PASCAL VOC. One way to gain an approximate idea is by performing cross-dataset evaluations

Table 1. Comparative classification results on the PASCAL VOC 2012 dataset.

Classes	Flickr	Semantic Trainer						our techniques			
		basic	hypo	verb	vadj	fcom	ccom	freq-f	qual-f	keyw-f	noun-f
A.plane	97.7	97.3	95.2	97.4	97.1	**97.9**	97.3	97.3	96.4	97.3	93.6
bicycle	**82.8**	82.5	70.4	79.3	83.6	82.2	81.2	83.1	76.6	82.3	76.5
bird	90.7	90.4	91.5	89.9	90.2	90.1	91.7	90.7	**92.7**	89.3	92.0
boat	88.7	88.2	88.8	87.8	86.9	89.5	89.2	88.9	87.5	**89.3**	89.0
bottle	57.3	56.7	57.5	55.7	55.8	57.6	**58.3**	57.3	54.9	56.8	55.6
bus	**93.8**	93.7	87.3	94.3	93.0	94.1	93.0	93.4	91.6	93.1	92.8
car	72.6	75.6	69.8	71.9	**75.9**	71.6	74.7	73.2	74.6	73.9	73.2
cat	91.5	89.1	92.9	90.6	90.9	91.4	**93.1**	92.9	89.6	90.0	91.5
chair	70.3	69.9	73.3	71.1	72.3	67.8	**74.3**	68.9	66.5	71.0	59.5
cow	**79.0**	73.9	73.6	71.8	75.1	75.7	77.7	76.6	78.8	76.1	64.9
dog	88.9	87.3	89.5	87.3	87.1	86.1	**89.7**	88.8	88.7	86.6	87.5
horse	**85.1**	76.8	80.1	76.9	81.7	80.5	83.0	84.8	83.8	82.2	80.7
M.bike	89.1	89.4	4.7	88.9	91.0	90.7	**91.3**	89.1	89.8	85.5	79.2
person	60.4	61.5	**72.8**	60.6	58.1	63.9	68.4	57.8	71.8	66.8	58.1
sheep	84.9	84.0	85.6	82.9	85.2	84.9	87.2	84.9	**86.3**	86.2	79.5
sofa	58.0	59.6	45.7	52.7	58.7	58.2	59.0	10.6	**62.7**	49.8	39.1
train	92.8	92.4	90.6	93.1	92.2	**93.6**	93.2	89.1	92.7	91.8	91.0
tv	25.0	74.1	55.4	26.2	45.0	46.8	53.1	73.4	**77.1**	31.5	69.3
AP	78.3	80.15	73.6	76.6	78.9	79.1	80.9	77.8	**81.3**	77.8	76.3

between different benchmark datasets, and comparing the relative performance of our training sets.

Following [1], we set out to explore cross-dataset generalization, meaning to perform cross-dataset evaluations between different benchmark datasets, and comparing the relative performance of our training sets. In particular, we analyze the behavior on the "person" class, which is of particular interest for many reasons, spanning from multimedia to social robotics, from surveillance to human computer interaction. For each class, we perform 10 randomized experiments with 200 positive and 400 negative samples split into 50% for training, 25% for cross-validation and 25% for testing. As source of the negative samples, we use the "other" classes of PASCAL VOC. Results are in Table 3.

As visible, even in this case noun filter gives the best result in average among all the approaches of automatic training set generation, having the top scores when considering the Caltech 256 and PASCAL VOC. It is also worth noting that on the PASCAL VOC dataset all our filters give the best performance. Finally, it is encouraging to see that our best score is comparable to what is obtained by ImageNet.

Table 2. Qualitative analysis of our *noun-f* dataset against the 2 *fcom* based, for the classes 'person', and 'cat'.

filter	Classes	Top 10 related terms and their corresponding images
noun-f	person	human, people, guy, man, human being, subject, child, lover, artist
	cat	kitty, feline, meow, kitten, stray, tabby, pussy, lion, tiger, mammal
fcom	person	black,dead,deceased,dying,good,innocent,living ,religious,white
	cat	black, blue, domestic, gray, grey, house, orange, playing, sleeping, white

Table 3. Cross-dataset generalization on the "person" class

Train on :	Test on:				Mean others
	ImageNet	Graz	Caltech-256	PASCAL VOC	
PASCAL VOC	95.10	92.22	97.04	94.71	94.77
GRAZ	92.10	99.46	94.32	88.06	93.48
Caltech-256	96.44	90.42	99.33	92.87	94.77
ImageNet	99.14	93.59	97.88	92.39	95.75
ccom [1]	**97.61**	**97.76**	96.07	88.01	94.86
fcom [1]	95.52	94.90	94.79	87.54	93.12
freq-f	95.72	95.72	95.03	88.22	93.68
qual-f	96.48	90.53	96.22	89.85	93.27
keyw-f	96.22	94.58	96.51	90.34	94.41
noun-f	97.21	94.50	**98.00**	**91.28**	**95.25**

4.3 Comparison against OPTIMOL

A more ambitious experiment consists in comparing with the OPTIMOL [13] approach that analyzes the content of the images: in facts, our approach is agnostic with the visual information, working only on textual data. For the sake of comparison, we adopt the same experimental protocol of [13], considering a selection of classes of the Caltech-101 [7], and generating the same number of training images. As for the testing set, we consider all the images provided by the Caltech-101. As for the features, we extract 128-dimensions dense SIFT, quantizing them into a 100-visual word dictionary by applying k-means clustering provided by the Vlfeat library [21]. We then use these histograms to train a linear SVM for each class and to perform object classification.

In Table 4 the classification results are reported, showing that surprisingly all of our approaches work better than OPTIMOL. In this case, the frequency filter the best job. Other than the numbers, it is interesting to observe the nature of the images being retrieved, see Table 5. Working on the visual information, OPTIMOL is not capable of distilling basic semantic aspects that strongly penalize its images, for example the fact of having a single face in the image. More in general, it is notable that OPTIMOL retrieve more false positive samples (for more details on OPTIMOL image class sets, please see the link[5]) .

Table 4. Comparison of our techniques performances to OPTIMOL in object classification. The classification performance is better than [13] by 14.11%.

	OPTIMOL	*our techniques*			
		frequency-f	quality-f	keyword-f	noun-f
airplane	76.00	84.07	69.10	79.21	79.87
car	94.50	95.20	94.98	95.11	94.84
face	82.90	83.44	83.32	78.40	90.70
guitar	60.40	97.14	96.99	98.09	97.03
leopard	89.00	92.24	95.49	91.80	92.21
motorbike	67.30	75.83	63.67	71.77	69.03
watch	53.60	94.66	95.98	90.45	89.58
AP	74.81	**88.94**	85.65	86.40	87.61

Table 5. *Face and watch* from our prepared datasets and OPTIMOL. From our database, we show one image for each term given therein.

Filter	Classes	Top 10 related terms and their corresponding images
Frequency	face	black, city, light, mono, monochrome, people, street, vienna, white, woman
	watch	beautiful, curvy, demure, lovely, pretty, scanner, shapely, time, timepiece, woman
OPTIMOL	face	
	watch	

---

[5] Face and watch class images: http://www.cs.stanford.edu/groups/vision/projects/

5   Conclusion

The automatic generation of training sets for image classification will be for sure a hot topic in the next years, where object classifiers will be embedded into portable devices like smartphone. Recently, a 30M dollars funding to the popular applet Shazam for object recognition purposes is a valid proof of our thoughts[6]. The message of this paper is that textual tags usually associated to social images, even if noisy, represent an important source of information that taken alone may bring to expressive image datasets, not so distant from man-made repositories such as PASCAL VOC and ImageNet. In the previous work [1] we show how it is possible to use image metadata to crawl image datasets: associating metadata with textual tags will be therefore a straightforward strategy we aim to investigate, after that we will move to analyze the genuine visual content of the images, trying to understand the relation among visual features and textual features. Connecting visual, textual and metadata should be then the final move for creating visual knowledge for feeding visually intelligent systems which see and understand the world around us.

Acknowledgments. This work was supported by a Research Grant 2013, Prog. FSE cod. 1695/1/24/ 1148/2013 titled "SEMANTIC CLOUD COMPUTING" DGR 1148/2013 as part of the program "Obiettivo Competitivit Regionale e Occupazione - Asse Capitale Umano - Sviluppo del potenziale umano nella ricerca e nell'innovazione" . Any opinions, findings and conclusions or recommendations expressed in this material are those of the author(s) and do not necessarily reflect of the FSE Research.

References

1. Cheng, D.S., Setti, F., Zeni, N., Ferrario, R., Cristani, M.: Semantically-driven automatic creation of training sets for object recognition. Computer Vision and Image Understanding **131**, 56–71 (2015)
2. Carolyn, C.J.: An approach to the automatic construction of global thesauri. Information Processing & Management **26**(5), 629–640 (1990)
3. Crowston, K.: Amazon mechanical turk: a research tool for organizations and information systems scholars. In: Bhattacherjee, A., Fitzgerald, B. (eds.) Shaping the Future of ICT Research. IFIP AICT, vol. 389, pp. 210–221. Springer, Heidelberg (2012)
4. Datta, R., Joshi, D., Li, J., Wang, J.Z.: Image retrieval: Ideas, influences, and trends of the new age. ACM Comput. Surv. **40**(2), 5:1–5:60 (2008)
5. Deng, J.,Dong, W., Socher, R., Li, L.-J., Li, K., Fei-Fei, L.: Imagenet: a large-scale hierarchical image database. In: IEEE Conference on Computer Vision and Pattern Recognition, CVPR 2009, pp. 248–255. IEEE (2009)
6. Everingham, M., Van Gool, L., Williams, C.K.I., Winn, J., Zisserman, A.: The pascal visual object classes (voc) challenge. International Journal of Computer Vision **88**(2), 303–338 (2010)

---

[6] See http://goo.gl/2jNkFC.

7. Fei-fei, L., Fergus, R., Perona, P.: A bayesian approach to unsupervised one-shot learning of object categories. In: Proceedings of the 9th International Conference on Computer Vision, pp. 1134–1141 (2003)
8. Fergus, R., Fei-Fei, L., Perona, P., Zisserman, A.: Learning object categories from google's image search. In: Proceedings of the 10th International Conference on Computer Vision, Beijing, China, vol. 2, pp. 1816–1823, October 2005
9. Hassan-Montero, Y., Herrero-Solana, V., Herrero-Solana, V.: Improving tag-clouds as visual information retrieval interfaces (2006)
10. Kennedy, L.S., Chang, S.-F., Kozintsev, I.V.: To search or to label?: predicting the performance of search-based automatic image classifiers. In: Proceedings of the 8th ACM International Workshop on Multimedia Information Retrieval, MIR 2006, New York, NY, USA, pp. 249–258. ACM (2006)
11. Krizhevsky, A., Sutskever, I., Hinton, G.E.: Imagenet classification with deep convolutional neural networks. In: Pereira, F., Burges, C.J.C., Bottou, L., Weinberger, K.Q. (eds.) Advances in Neural Information Processing Systems, vol. 25, pp. 1097–1105. Curran Associates Inc (2012)
12. Li, L.-J., Fei-Fei, L.: Optimol: automatic online picture collection via incremental model learning. International journal of computer vision **88**(2), 147–168 (2010)
13. Li, L.-J., Wang, G., Fei-Fei, L.: Optimol: automatic online picture collection via incremental model learning. In: IEEE Conference on Computer Vision and Pattern Recognition, CVPR 2007, pp. 1–8, June 2007
14. Mandala, R., Tokunaga, T., Tanaka, H.: Combining multiple evidence from different types of thesaurus for query expansion. In: Proceedings of the 22nd annual international ACM SIGIR conference on Research and development in information retrieval, pp. 191–197. ACM (1999)
15. Miller, G.A.: Wordnet: a lexical database for english. Communications of the ACM **38**(11), 39–41 (1995)
16. Ogden, C.K.R.: Qualities - descriptive words. Linguistic **3**(x), x (1930)
17. Shepitsen, A., Gemmell, J., Mobasher, B., Burke, R.: Personalized recommendation in social tagging systems using hierarchical clustering. In Proceedings of the 2008 ACM Conference on Recommender Systems, RecSys 2008, New York, NY, USA, pp. 259–266. ACM (2008)
18. Spain, M., Perona, P.: Some objects are more equal than others: measuring and predicting importance. In: Forsyth, D., Torr, P., Zisserman, A. (eds.) ECCV 2008, Part I. LNCS, vol. 5302, pp. 523–536. Springer, Heidelberg (2008)
19. Sun, F., Wang, M., Wang, D., Wang, X.: Optimizing social image search with multiple criteria: Relevance, diversity, and typicality. Neurocomputing **95**, 40–47 (2012). Learning from Social Media Network
20. Vedaldi, A., Lenc, K.: Matconvnet - convolutional neural networks for matlab. CoRR, abs/1412.4564 (2014)
21. Vedaldi, A., Fulkerson, B.: Vlfeat: an open and portable library of computer vision algorithms. In: Proceedings of the International Conference on Multimedia, MM 2010, New York, NY, USA, pp. 1469–1472. ACM (2010)
22. Weinberger, K.Q., Slaney, M., Van Zwol, R.: Resolving tag ambiguity. In Proceeding of the 16th ACM international conference on Multimedia, MM 2008, New York, NY, USA, pp. 111–120. ACM (2008)

The Color of Smiling: Computational Synaesthesia of Facial Expressions

Vittorio Cuculo[1](✉), Raffaella Lanzarotti[2], and Giuseppe Boccignone[2]

[1] Dipartimento di Matematica, Università di Milano,
via Cesare Saldini 50, 20133 Milano, Italy
vittorio.cuculo@unimi.it
[2] Dipartimento di Informatica, Università di Milano,
via Comelico 39/41, 20135 Milano, Italy
{lanzarotti,boccignone}@di.unimi.it

Abstract. This note gives a preliminary account of the transcoding or rechanneling problem between different stimuli as it is of interest for the natural interaction or affective computing fields. By the consideration of a simple example, namely the color response of an affective lamp to a sensed facial expression, we frame the problem within an information-theoretic perspective. A full justification in terms of the Information Bottleneck principle promotes a latent affective space, hitherto surmised as an appealing and intuitive solution, as a suitable mediator between the different stimuli.

Keywords: Affective computing · Facial expressions · Information-bottleneck · Graphical models

1 Introduction

At the heart of non-verbal interaction between agents, either artificial or biological, is a rechannelling ability, namely the ability of gathering data from one kind of signal and instantaneously turn it into a different kind of signal. In artificial agents, such rechannelling or transcoding ability must be simulated through some form of "computational synaesthesia". Strictly speaking, synaesthesia is a neurological phenomenon in which stimulation of one sensory or cognitive pathway leads to automatic, involuntary experiences in a second sensory or cognitive pathway [31]. Here, more liberally, we adopt it as a good metaphor for such rechannelling/transcoding of information [23].

In this note, as a case study, we consider the problem of transducing a sensed facial expression into a color stimuli. Denote $\mathbf{V}$ and $\mathbf{C}$ the random variables (RVs) standing for a visible expression display and for an emitted color stimulus, respectively. Then, the transcoding $\mathbf{V} \mapsto \mathbf{C}$ can be described in probabilistic terms as that of sampling a specific color stimulus $\mathbf{c}$, when expression stimulus $\mathbf{v}$ is observed, namely

$$\mathbf{c} \sim P(\mathbf{C} \mid \mathbf{V} = \mathbf{v}), \tag{1}$$

© Springer International Publishing Switzerland 2015
V. Murino and E. Puppo (Eds.): ICIAP 2015, Part I, LNCS 9279, pp. 203–214, 2015.
DOI: 10.1007/978-3-319-23231-7_19

where $P(\mathbf{C} \mid \mathbf{V})$ is the conditional probability density function (pdf) defining the probability of generating a color stimulus $\mathbf{c}$ conditioned on the observation of expression $\mathbf{v}$. Such kind of problem is of interest for many applications in social signal processing [29], natural interaction [23], social robotics [15]. But, most important, here we discuss how a principled solution involves deep issues in spite of the apparent specificity of the problem.

An appealing way to conceive transcoding is through the mediation of some kind of latent space in particular a space of affective or emotional experience, which confers a unified semantics to the different kinds of non-verbal signals. It has been argued that this could be necessary for grounding synaesthetic cross-modal correspondences [6,25], simulation-based theory of emotion and empathy [30]. Also, the mediation of a continuous dimensional space has been advocated for analyzing many different expressive modalities and to the purpose of building affective objects [23]. To such aim, we focus on the Pleasure/Arousal/Dominance space (PAD, [22]) as a continuous latent space to support "synesthesia" of facial expressions into color.

The contribution of this note is twofold. First we discuss how a general solution to the transcoding problem behind synesthesia the can be conceived and grounded in an information-theoretic perspective, namely the Information Bottleneck (IB) framework introduced in [27] (cfr. Section 2). Second, for the specific example considered here, namely face expression $\mapsto$ color transcoding, we show how to obtain a simplified solution by drawing on results achieved in the psychological literature.

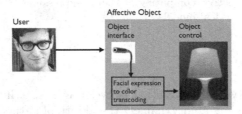

Fig. 1. The Mood Lamp: an affective "synaesthetic" object that responds to user's facial expressions by changing the color of the light emitted.

As a proof of concept we present the Mood Lamp (cfr. Fig. 1). The Mood Lamp is a kind of *affective object*, that is a "physical object which has the ability to sense emotional data from a person, map that information to an abstract form of expression and communicate that information expressively, either back to the subject herself or to another person" [23]. In particular, here a facial expression is used to convey affect states to an Ikea RGB color lamp, which will respond by changing the color of the light emitted in accordance with the affect.

Modeling computational synaesthesia as specified through Eq. 1 in the IB perspective has the advantage of providing a principled approach, characterized by a minimum of assumptions (Section 3). However there are a number of subtle difficulties to overcome that deserve being discussed (cfr. Sections 4 and 5).

2 Background and Rationales

Central to this work is the idea that the synaesthetic transduction $\mathbf{V} \mapsto \mathbf{C}$ can be performed by resorting to an affect space, say $\mathbf{E}$, as a mediating factor.

Resorting to affect for transcoding stimuli may seem *prima facie* an instrumental approach; however, two issues bear on this choice. First, the insight of an affect space as a common factor for rechanneling between kinds of information is a not new in the psychological literature. On the one hand, perception and emotion are closely linked [19]. For instance, as to the specific case of synaesthetic cross-modal correspondences, affective similarity [25] has been suggested as a contributing factor: stimuli may be matched if they both happen to increase an observer's level of alertness or arousal, or if they both happen to have the same effect on an observer's emotional state, mood, or affective state. Efficient handling of affective synesthesia has been discussed by Collier who has shown [6] that both perceptual stimuli – such as colours, shapes, and musical fragments – and human emotions can be represented in a simple multidimensional space with two or three corresponding dimensions. Clearly this idea is consistent with the framework of an underpinning continuous "affect space", which can be approximated by either two primary dimensions, e.g. valence and activity (arousal) [18], or three such as pleasure, arousal, and dominance (PAD) as proposed by Russell and Mehrabian [22] .

The second issue, which is tied in a subtle way to the previous one, grounds in the general and fundamental principle that an organism who maximizes the adaptive value of its actions given fixed resources should have internal representations of the outside world that are optimal in a very specific information-theoretic sense [2]. In a communicative action, this optimization problem is related to joint source channel coding, namely the task of encoding and transmitting information simultaneously in an efficient manner [7].

One route to do justice to both issues is the Information Bottleneck (IB), [27]. IB is an information-theoretic principle for coping with the extraction of relevant components of an "input" random variable $\mathbf{X}$, with respect to an "output" random variable $\mathbf{Y}$. This is performed by finding a *bottleneck* variable, that is a compressed, non-parametric and model-independent representation $\mathbf{T}$ of $\mathbf{X}$, that is most informative about $\mathbf{Y}$.

In our case the intuition is that the bottleneck variable $\mathbf{E}$ is suitable to capture the relevant affective aspects of the facial expression stimuli $\mathbf{V}$ that are informative about the output color stimulus $\mathbf{C}$ (cfr. Fig. 2a).

Denote $I_Q(\mathbf{X}; \mathbf{Y}) = \sum_{\mathbf{x},\mathbf{y}} Q(\mathbf{x}, \mathbf{y}) \log \frac{Q(\mathbf{x},\mathbf{y})}{Q(\mathbf{x})Q(\mathbf{y})}$ the mutual information with respect to some probability distribution $Q(\mathbf{x}, \mathbf{y})$ [7]. Following the discussion and notation provided in [10,11], the IB approach determines the auxiliary latent space $\mathbf{E}$ and related mapping $\mathbf{V} \mapsto \mathbf{E}$, such that the mutual information $I_Q(\mathbf{V}; \mathbf{E})$ is minimized (to achieve maximum compression), while relevant

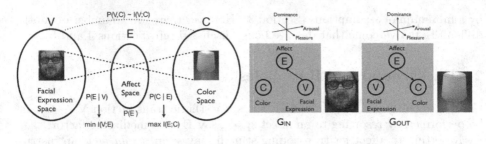

(a) The IB framework   (b) A PGM representation of IB

Fig. 2. Synesthesia of facial expression **V** into the (lamp) color **C** as an Information Bottleneck problem. The displayed expression is represented as a random vector **V**, computed on the basis of facial landmarks **L** (displayed as red dots superimposed on the face). **(a)** Transcoding $\mathbf{V} \mapsto \mathbf{C}$ is modelled as the search for a compressed representation of **V**, namely the affect space **E**, which achieves minimum redundancy while maintaining the mutual information $I(\mathbf{E}; \mathbf{C})$ about the relevant variable **C**, as high as possible. **(b)** The left graph $\mathcal{G}_{IN}$ encodes the compression process; the right graph $\mathcal{G}_{OUT}$ is the target model representing which relations should be maintained or predicted. The IB principle boils down to minimize the information maintained by $\mathcal{G}_{IN}$ and to maximize the information preserved by $\mathcal{G}_{OUT}$.

information $I(\mathbf{E}; \mathbf{C})$ is maximized. The balance between these competing goals is achieved by minimizing the Lagrangian

$$\mathcal{L}[Q] = I_Q(\mathbf{V}; \mathbf{E}) - \beta I_Q(\mathbf{E}; \mathbf{C}), \tag{2}$$

where the positive parameter β smoothly controls the tradeoff between compression and preservation of relevant information.

The optimization principle entailed by Eq. 2 is very abstract; also, no analytical solution is available. However, it has been shown by Friedman et al. [11] that the IB problem can be suitably reformulated in terms of directed Probabilistic Graphical Model (PGM, [17]) representation (cfr. Fig. 2b). A directed PGM is a graph-based representation where nodes denote RVs and arrows/arcs code conditional dependencies between RVs. Stated technically, the $\mathcal{G}$ structure encodes the set of conditional independence assumptions over the set of RVs $\{\mathbf{X}_i\}$ (called the local independencies, [17]) involved by the joint pdf $P(\{\mathbf{X}_i\})$ associated to $\mathcal{G}$. Then, the joint pdf factorizes according to $\mathcal{G}$ [17], that is P is consistent with $\mathcal{G}$, $P \models \mathcal{G}$. Given a PGM $\mathcal{G}$, $I^{\mathcal{G}} = \sum_i I(\mathbf{X}_i; Pa_i^{\mathcal{G}})$ denotes the information computed with respect to the pdf $P \models \mathcal{G}$ [11], where $Pa_i^{\mathcal{G}}$ stands for the ensemble of parents of node $\mathbf{X}_i$.

Under these circumstances, the IB principle (Eq. 2) can be shaped in the language of PGMs [10,11] by considering two directed graphs $\mathcal{G}_{IN}$ and $\mathcal{G}_{OUT}$, together with the pdfs represented by such graphs, $Q \models \mathcal{G}_{IN}$ and $P \models \mathcal{G}_{OUT}$, respectively (cfr. Fig. 2b). Thus, the information that we would like to minimize is now given by $I^{\mathcal{G}_{IN}}$ and the relevant information that we wish to preserve is specified by the *target model* $\mathcal{G}_{OUT}$, as $I^{\mathcal{G}_{OUT}}$, so that the IB Lagrangian in Eq. 2 to minimize can be rewritten in the PGM form $\mathcal{L}[\mathcal{G}_{IN}, \mathcal{G}_{OUT}] = I^{\mathcal{G}_{IN}} - \beta I^{\mathcal{G}_{OUT}}$. In turn, the latter – and thus Eq. 2 –, can be rewritten as

$$\mathcal{L}[Q, P] = I_Q(\mathbf{V}; \mathbf{E}) + \gamma D_{KL}(Q(\mathbf{V}, \mathbf{E}, \mathbf{C}) \| P(\mathbf{V}, \mathbf{E}, \mathbf{C})), \qquad (3)$$

where $D_{KL}(Q(\mathbf{X}) \| P(\mathbf{X}))$ is the Kullback-Leibler divergence between distributions Q and P [7], representing networks $\mathcal{G}_{IN}$ and $\mathcal{G}_{OUT}$, respectively.

It has been shown that the minimization of $\mathcal{L}[Q, P]$ is equivalent to the minimization of $\mathcal{L}[\mathcal{G}_{IN}, \mathcal{G}_{OUT}]$ given that $\beta = \gamma/(1 + \gamma)$ and that $I^{\mathcal{G}_{IN}} = I_Q(\mathbf{V}; \mathbf{E})$ (see [10,11] for more details). The scale parameter γ, just like β balances the above two factors. In the limit $\gamma \to 0$ we are only interested in compressing the variable $\mathbf{V}$. When $\gamma \to \infty$ we concentrate on choosing a pdf Q that is close to the distribution $P \models \mathcal{G}_{OUT}$ satisfying the independencies encoded by $\mathcal{G}_{OUT}$, namely

$$P(\mathbf{V}, \mathbf{C}, \mathbf{E}) = P(\mathbf{V} \mid \mathbf{E})P(\mathbf{C} \mid \mathbf{E})P(\mathbf{E}), \qquad (4)$$

by minimizing $D_{KL}(Q(\mathbf{V}, \mathbf{E}, \mathbf{C}) \| P(\mathbf{V}, \mathbf{E}, \mathbf{C}))$.

It has been shown that iterative approximate solutions to Eq. 2, which cycle between determining $Q(\mathbf{E})$ and $Q(\mathbf{C} \mid \mathbf{E})$ for a fixed $Q(\mathbf{E} \mid \mathbf{V})$, and computing $Q(\mathbf{E} \mid \mathbf{V})$ for fixed $Q(\mathbf{E})$ and $Q(\mathbf{C} \mid \mathbf{E})$, are a formulation of the generalized Expectation-Maximization algorithm for clustering [24]. Clearly, this holds when the latent space $\mathbf{E}$ is a discrete space. Indeed, it is readily seen that at the extreme spectrum $\gamma \to \infty$, the minimization in Eq. 3 boils down to minimize $D_{KL}(Q(\mathbf{V}, \mathbf{E}, \mathbf{C}) \| P(\mathbf{V}, \mathbf{E}, \mathbf{C}))$ which is but one instance of the Variational Bayes method for learning the generative model $P \models \mathcal{G}_{OUT}$, as represented in the target model of Fig. 2b.

When the transcoding operation relies upon a continuous latent space – as in our case – the IB approach represented in terms of $P \models \mathcal{G}_{OUT}$ is reminiscent of several latent factor models for paired data, such as Bayesian factor regression, Probabilistic Partial Least squares and Probabilistic CCA [17].

3 Methods

The IB approach provides a principled justification to the use of a mediating latent space for simulating computational synaesthesia. After the learning stage, when the distribution factors of the target joint pdf are available, transcoding in Eq. 1 can be performed via the latent space $\mathbf{E}$:

$$\mathbf{e} \sim P(\mathbf{E} \mid \mathbf{V} = \mathbf{v}), \quad \mathbf{c} \sim P(\mathbf{C} \mid \mathbf{E} = \mathbf{e}). \qquad (5)$$

It is worth remarking that learning procedures implementing optimization (2) or (3) have the goal of designing from scratch a latent space that is optimal with respect to the given constraints and the joint distribution, here $P(\mathbf{V}, \mathbf{C})$. In the case study we are considering, conditions are slightly different. First, the latent space $\mathbf{E}$ is not constructed abstractly, but it should be chosen guided by psychological theories of emotion; this somehow simplifies some machine learning issues, for instance, the dimensionality of the space is not to be learned. Second, the joint pdf is not straightforwardly available.

As to the first issue, we assume a core affect representation. Core affect is a neurophysiological state that underlies simply feeling good or bad, drowsy or energised, and it can be experienced as free-floating, or mood, or can be attributed to some cause (and thereby begin an emotional episode) [21]. Thus, it is a continuous latent space and a suitable representation is provided by the PAD space proposed by Mehrabian and Russell [22]. Such space can be described along three nearly independent continuous dimensions: Pleasure-Displeasure (measured by P), Arousal-Nonarousal (A), and Dominance-Submissiveness (D); thus, $\mathbf{E} = [PAD]^\mathsf{T}$.

Note that, under the assumption of an actual affective state $\mathbf{E} = \mathbf{e}$, it is easy to show, by using Bayes' rule and the joint pdf factorisation (4), that $P(\mathbf{V}, \mathbf{C} \mid \mathbf{E}) = P(\mathbf{V} \mid \mathbf{E})P(\mathbf{C} \mid \mathbf{E})$, thus $\mathbf{V} \perp\!\!\!\perp \mathbf{C} \mid \mathbf{E}$. That is, if the affective state is given, then $\mathbf{V}$ and $\mathbf{C}$ are conditionally independent. The very issue here is thus obtaining the "mapping" probabilities $P(\mathbf{E} \mid \mathbf{V})$ and $P(\mathbf{C} \mid \mathbf{E})$. To this end, we can make the simplifying assumption of a Gaussian IB [5]. In this case an optimal compression $\mathbf{E}$ is obtained with a noisy linear transformation of $\mathbf{V}$:

$$\mathbf{e} = \mathbf{W}_E \mathbf{v} + \xi_E, \qquad \xi_E \sim \mathcal{N}(\mathbf{0}, \Sigma_{\xi_E}), \tag{6}$$

where ξ_E is an additive noise term sampled from a zero-mean Gaussian pdf $\mathcal{N}(\mathbf{0}, \Sigma_{\xi_E})$.

Similarly, the most natural choice for color is a continuous space; e.g., in studies concerning relationships between color and emotion the HSL space – defined on Hue (H), Saturation (S) and Luminance (L) – has been used [12,15]. Thus, a generative model for mapping $P(\mathbf{V} \mid \mathbf{E})$ is

$$\mathbf{c} = \mathbf{W}_C \mathbf{e} + \xi_C, \qquad \xi_C \sim \mathcal{N}(\mathbf{0}, \Sigma_{\xi_C}). \tag{7}$$

Eqs. 6 and 7 nicely simplify the synaesthetic mapping to a pair of regressions on a joint latent space, however the second issue related to the actual availability of $P(\mathbf{V}, \mathbf{C})$ must be taken into account. Needless to say, the use of a continuous affect space brings along a number of challenges. In the psychological literature, fleeting changes in the countenance of a face are considered to be "expressions of emotion" (EEs) and have been systematically investigated by Ekman [9] in a categorical perpsective. Ekman's work has fostered a vaste amount of theoretical and empirical work, which has been particularly influent in the affective computing community [29]. Under these circumstances, finding the map $\mathbf{V} \mapsto \mathbf{E}$, has been mostly relied on a pattern recognition approach to infer emotions from expressions under the fundamental assumption of basic emotions, for example by considering the discrete set $\mathbf{E} = \{\text{joy, sadness, anger, disgust, surprise, fear}\}$. By contrast, Eq. 6 assumes a probabilistic relationship between $\mathbf{E}$ and $\mathbf{V}$ where $\mathbf{E}$ is continuously defined.

A second problem to solve is related to Eq. 7, that is to learn the mapping $\mathbf{E} \mapsto \mathbf{C}$. In the past decades, only a few researchers investigated the relationship between color and emotion [3,15,16,26,28] (and often in the sense of emotion elicited by a colors and not the vice versa). In this case, the main problem is setting up a minimal training set which we derive from data available from the psychological literature. These issues are addressed in the following sections.

4   From Face Expression to Mood

In this section we detail how we solve the problem of learning a probabilistic relationship between $\mathbf{E}$ and $\mathbf{V}$ where $\mathbf{E}$ is continuously defined according to the PAD model. To this end, we exploit results of experimental studies that have evaluated the PAD value of discrete emotion states, e.g., [13].

A very first step concerns with the facial landmark localisation, which can be summarised as follows. Denote $\mathbf{L} = \{\mathbf{l}^1, \mathbf{l}^2, \cdots, \mathbf{l}^n\}$ the locations of n landmark-ing parts of the face, and $\mathbf{F} = \{\mathbf{f}^1, \mathbf{f}^2, \cdots, \mathbf{f}^n\}$ the measured detector responses, where $\mathbf{f}^i = \phi(\mathbf{l}^i, \mathcal{I})$ is the response or feature vector provided by a local detector at location $\mathbf{l}^i$ in image or frame $\mathcal{I}$. Then, localisation can be solved by finding the value of $\mathbf{L}$ that maximises the probability of $\mathbf{L}$ given the responses from local detectors, namely $\mathbf{L}^* = \arg\max_{\mathbf{L}} P(\mathbf{L}|\mathbf{F})$. Following [8], we exploit a part-based framework that integrates an effective local representation based on sparse coding. Sparse coding has recently gained currency in face analysis (e.g., [1,14]). In particular:

$$\mathbf{L}^* = \arg\max_L \sum_{k=1}^{m} \int_t \prod_{i=1}^{n} P(\Delta \mathbf{l}_{k,t}^i) P(\mathbf{l}^i|\mathbf{f}^i) dt, \qquad (8)$$

where the prior $P(\Delta \mathbf{l}_{k,t}^i)$ accounts for the *shape* or global component of the model, and $P(\mathbf{l}^i|\mathbf{f}^i))$ for the *appearance* or local component. For what concerns the local component $P(\mathbf{l}^i|\mathbf{f}^i)$, we resort to Histograms of Sparse Codes to sample patch responses $\mathbf{f}^i$, which we learn from facial images (see [8] for details).

For each image/frame we consider 40 landmarks $\mathbf{L} = [\mathbf{l}^1 \cdots \mathbf{l}^{40}]^\mathsf{T}$ as shown in Fig. 3, and we map them into a vector of visible expression parameters $\mathbf{V}$ by measuring the landmark displacements. This step, in a vein similar to Action Units approaches [9], is aimed at capturing the expression movements within local face region, such as mouth-bent, eye-open and eyebrow-raise, etc., as detailed in Tab. 1 [4].

The extracted expression parameters $\mathbf{V} \in \mathbb{R}^7$ are put in correspondence to PAD values, $\mathbf{E} \in \mathbb{R}^3$, by using Eq. 6. In the current simulation, a multilinear ridge regression has been used, that is a penalized least squares method that adds a Gaussian prior to the parameters to encourage them to be small. Such model has interesting connection to latent variable space inference [17].

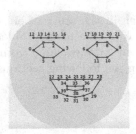

Fig. 3. The 40 facial landmarks

Table 1. Visual expression parameters (EP) via local landmark displacements

Name	EP	Definition
Eyes height	$\mathbf{v}^0$	$(l_y^0 - l_y^1) * 2$
Eyes / brows space	$\mathbf{v}^1$	$l_y^0 - l_y^{13} + \frac{(l_y^{16} - l_y^{12})}{4}$
Eyebrow's inner height	$\mathbf{v}^2$	$l_y^{12} + \mathbf{v}^1 - l_y^0$
Eyebrow's outer height	$\mathbf{v}^3$	$l_y^{16} + \mathbf{v}^1 - l_y^0$
Mouth width	$\mathbf{v}^4$	$l_x^{28} - l_x^{22}$
Mouth openness	$\mathbf{v}^5$	$l_y^{31} - l_y^{25}$
Mouth twist	$\mathbf{v}^6$	$\frac{l_y^{28} - l_y^{25}}{2} - l_y^{22}$

5   The Color of Mood

Here, we discuss some subtleties related to the mapping $\mathbf{E} \mapsto \mathbf{C}$ in order to learn the generative model of Eq. 7. Recall that we represent color as a random vector in HSL color space, i.e. $\mathbf{c} = [HSL]^{\mathsf{T}}$.

The seminal work investigating the relationship between color and emotion is that by Valdez and Mehrabian [28]. They mainly studied how saturation S and luminance L affect PAD. In [3, 16, 26] the emotions elicited by basic colors have been qualitative presented. Only recently in [15] a synthesis of these approaches has been proposed, aiming at allowing robots to express the intensity of emotions by coloring and blinking LED placed around their eyes. This work has the limit to resort to only two distinct values for both S and L, and four values for the hue H, hence leading different emotions to be represented by the same color.

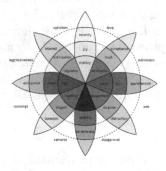

Fig. 4. Plutchik's wheel. Relationships between emotions and colors. Hue is associated to a specific emotion, while saturation and luminance determine its intensity.

Table 2. Color values of emotions according to the Plutchik's wheel and their associations to Mehrabian [22] scores of Pleasure, Arousal and Dominance.

Emotion	H	S	L	P	A	D
joy	60	67	100	0.81	0.51	0.46
ecstasy	60	67	100	0.62	0.75	0.38
fear	120	100	59	-0.64	0.60	-0.43
terror	120	100	50	-0.62	0.82	-0.43
amazement	203	100	88	0.16	0.88	-0.15
sadness	240	68	100	-0.63	-0.27	-0.33
boredom	300	22	100	-0.65	-0.62	-0.33
annoyance	0	45	100	-0.58	0.40	0.01
anger	0	100	100	-0.51	0.59	0.25
interest	29	45	100	0.64	0.51	0.17
vigilance	29	100	100	0.49	0.57	0.45

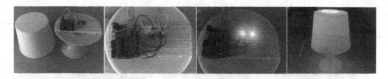

Fig. 5. Color control: the actual color stimulus is generated through a modified Ikea lamp, where the RGB LED is controlled by an Arduino UNO board.

In our study, we propose a finer correspondence model, preserving maximum representativeness of the three components HSL. More precisely, as to S and L, following [15], we invert the dependency of PAD values proposed in [28], while maintaining the obtained results. Define

$$P = 0.69L + 0.22S, \quad A = -0.31L + 0.60S, \quad D = -0.76L + 0.32S. \quad (9)$$

Then, S and L can be derived

$$\hat{\mathbf{c}} = (\mathbf{W}^\mathsf{T}\mathbf{W})^{-1}\mathbf{W}^\mathsf{T}\mathbf{e}, \quad (10)$$

where $\hat{\mathbf{c}} = [LS]^\mathsf{T}$, $\mathbf{W} = \begin{bmatrix} 0.69 & 0.22 \\ -0.31 & 0.60 \\ -0.76 & 0.32 \end{bmatrix}$, and $\mathbf{e} = [PAD]^\mathsf{T}$.

Eq. 10 provides a partial color mapping $\mathbf{E} \mapsto (S, L)$. To complete the picture we need to take into account hue values H. Unfortunately, the hue / PAD relation proposed in [28] cannot be inverted. We thus derive this component from Plutchik's psycho-evolutionary emotion theory [20]. In his work, each emotion is associated to a given hue value, while saturation and luminance vary according to the emotion intensity (Fig. 4). As we need an association between PAD and hue values, we rely on the classification made by Mehrabian [22], adopting the PAD values of a subset of corresponding affective states, as tabulated in Tab. 2.

Eventually, PAD values and the corresponding HSL values, can serve, respectively, as feature and target sets for learning the multivariate linear regression model given in Eq. 7. As in the case of Eq. 6 this is accomplished via ridge regression.

Finally, the obtained HSL values are converted into RGB space. The latter step has a practical motivation. As discussed from the beginning, the realisation of the transcoding process has been experimented through the Mood Lamp, an affective object conceived as i) a sensing interface, namely a low-cost web camera / notebook communicating via USB with ii) a modified Ikea lamp, equipped with an Arduino UNO board to control an RGB LED (see Fig. 5).

A sample of results from our preliminary experiments is presented in Fig. 6.

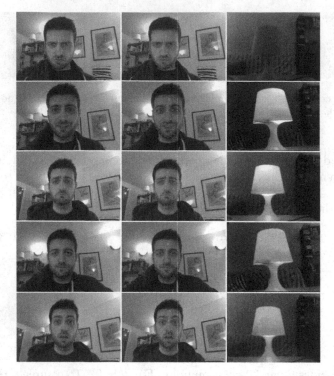

Fig. 6. Experimental results of transconding using the Mood Lamp.

6   Conclusion and Further Outlooks

In this note we have proposed to frame the general problem of synaesthetic transduction in terms of the IB principle. We have discussed how such framework is suitable to provides a parsimonious and principled account of using a latent affect space to mediate the rechanneling between different stimuli, an idea which has been informally proposed several times in the affective computing field as an intuitive and appealing solution. The specific example/case study we have been discussing here has been treated in the IB's $\gamma \to \infty$ approximation, by taking advantage of experimental results gathered in the psychological literature. However, we think it appropriate to remark that the general formalism which is expounded here admits a far wider range of applicability than that to which it has been presented in this work. The framework could be usefully adopted for current affective computing systems that more and more relying on the availability of different sensors (e.g., for monitoring autonomic activity) and brain interfaces [29]. Indeed, such systems are confronted with the issue of finding relations in high-dimensional and heterogeneous data spaces, one example being data fusion among several others which would emerge from the application of this approach to concrete instances In those specific cases the manifold structure of the latent core affect space is truly a "hidden variable", and where the IB toolbox could be fully exploited to explore the spectrum of solutions as γ varies.

As a last comment, the Mood Lamp example we have presented here was just meant to be a straightforward and practical proof of concept of synaesthetic transduction. Clearly, the preliminary and partial results reported are not to be intended as a conclusive validation of the approach. The Mood Lamp example is but one example of a Natural Interaction application: indeed, for such kind of applications, a ground-truth in the classic pattern recognition perspective is hardly available, and the ultimate validation can only be gained through an experimental user interaction study, which indeed is beyond the scope of the present note.

Acknowledgments. The research was carried out as part of the project "Interpreting emotions: a computational tool integrating facial expressions and biosignals based shape analysis and bayesian networks", supported by the Italian Government, managed by MIUR, financed by the *Future in Research* Fund.

References

1. Adamo, A., Grossi, G., Lanzarotti, R.: Local features and sparse representation for face recognition with partial occlusions. In: 20th IEEE Int. Conf. on Image Processing (ICIP), pp. 3008–3012, September 2013
2. Bialek, W., van Steveninck, R.R.R., Tishby, N.: Efficient representation as a design principle for neural coding and computation. In: IEEE International Symposium on Information Theory, pp. 659–663. IEEE (2006)
3. Birren, F.: Color Psychology and Color Therapy. Kessinger Publishing (2006)
4. Broekens, J., Brinkman, W.: Affectbutton: A method for reliable and valid affective self-report. Int. J. Hum.-Comput. Stud. **71**(6), 641–667 (2013)
5. Chechik, G., Globerson, A., Tishby, N., Weiss, Y.: Information bottleneck for gaussian variables. Journal of Machine Learning Research **6**, 165–188 (2005)
6. Collier, G.L.: Affective synesthesia: Extracting emotion space from simple perceptual stimuli. Motivation and emotion **20**(1), 1–32 (1996)
7. Cover, T., Thomas, J.: Elements of Information Theory. Wiley and Sons, New York (1991)
8. Cuculo, V., Lanzarotti, R., Boccignone, G.: Using sparse coding for landmark localization in facial expressions. In: 5th European Workshop on Visual Information Processing (EUVIP), pp. 1–6, December 2014
9. Ekman, P.: Facial expression and emotion. American Psychologist **48**(4), 384 (1993)
10. Elidan, G., Friedman, N.: Learning hidden variable networks: The information bottleneck approach. J. of Machine Learning Research **6**, 81–127 (2005)
11. Friedman, N., Mosenzon, O., Slonim, N., Tishby, N.: Multivariate information bottleneck. In: Proceedings of the Seventeenth Conference on Uncertainty in Artificial Intelligence, pp. 152–161 (2001)
12. Gao, X.P., Xin, J.: Investigation of human's emotional responses on colors. Color Research & Application **31**(5), 411–417 (2006)

13. Hoffmann, H., Scheck, A., Schuster, T., Walter, S., Limbrecht, K., Traue, H.C., Kessler, H.: Mapping discrete emotions into the dimensional space: An empirical approach. In: IEEE International Conference on Systems, Man, and Cybernetics (SMC), pp. 3316–3320. IEEE (2012)
14. Jeni, L., Girard, J., Cohn, J., De la Torre, F.: Continuous AU intensity estimation using localized, sparse facial feature space. In: 10th IEEE Int. Conf. and Workshops Automat. Face Gesture Recogn., pp. 1–7, April 2013
15. Kim, M., Lee, H., Park, J., Jo, S., Chung, M.: Determining color and blinking to support facial expression of a robot for conveying emotional intensity. In: Int'l Symposium on Robot and Human Interactive Communication, RO-MAN, pp. 219–24 (2008)
16. Mahnke, F.H.: COLOR, Environment, & Human Response. John Wiley & Sons (1996)
17. Murphy, K.P.: Machine learning: a probabilistic perspective. MIT Press, Cambridge (2012)
18. Osgood, C.E., Suci, G.J., Tannenbaum, P.H.: The measurement of meaning. University of Illinois Press (1964)
19. Pessoa, L.: On the relationship between emotion and cognition. Nature Reviews Neuroscience 9(2), 148–158 (2008)
20. Plutchik, R.: Emotion: Theory. Research and Experience. Acad. Pr. (1980)
21. Russell, J.A.: Core affect and the psychological construction of emotion. Psychological Review 110(1), 145 (2003)
22. Russell, J.A., Mehrabian, A.: Evidence for a three-factor theory of emotions. Journal of Research in Personality 11(3), 273–294 (1977)
23. Scheirer, J., Picard, R.: Affective objects. MIT Media lab Technical Rep. 524 (2000)
24. Slonim, N., Weiss, Y.: Maximum likelihood and the information bottleneck. In: Advances in Neural Information Processing Systems, pp. 335–342 (2002)
25. Spence, C.: Crossmodal correspondences: A tutorial review. Attention, Perception, & Psychophysics 73(4), 971–995 (2011)
26. Suk, H.J., Irtel, H.: Emotional response to color across media. Color Research & Application 35(1), 64–77 (2010)
27. Tishby, N., Pereira, F.C., Bialek, W.: The information bottleneck method. In: The 37th Allerton Conference on Communication, Control, and Computing (1999)
28. Valdez, P., Mehrabian, A.: Effects of color on emotions. Journal of Experimental Psychology: General 123(4), 394 (1994)
29. Vinciarelli, A., Pantic, M., Heylen, D., Pelachaud, C., Poggi, I., D'Errico, F., Schroeder, M.: Bridging the gap between social animal and unsocial machine: A survey of social signal processing 3(1), 69–87 (2012)
30. Vitale, J., Williams, M.A., Johnston, B., Boccignone, G.: Affective facial expression processing via simulation: A probabilistic model. Biologically Inspired Cognitive Architectures Journal 10, 30–41 (2014)
31. Ward, J.: Emotionally mediated synaesthesia. Cognitive Neuropsychology 21(7), 761–772 (2004)

Learning Texture Image Prior for Super Resolution Using Restricted Boltzmann Machine

Chulmoo Kang$^{(\boxtimes)}$, Minui Hong, and Suk I. Yoo

Department of Computer Science and Engineering,
Seoul National University, Seoul, Republic of Korea
{nkarma,alsdml123,sukinyoo}@snu.ac.kr

Abstract. Field of Expert (FoE) [1], which is one of the most popular probabilistic models of natural image prior, has been successfully applied to super resolution. Piecewise smoothness imposed on natural images is, however, a relatively limited model for texture image. In the field of deep learning, various approaches for texture modeling using the Restricted Boltzmann Machine (RBM) achieves or surpasses the state-of-the-art on many tasks such as texture synthesis and inpainting. In this paper, we apply the convolutional RBM (cRBM) to learning a texture prior. The maximum a posteriori (MAP) framework is proposed to utilize the probabilistic texture model well. The experiment is done on the Brodatz Dataset, and our experimental results are shown to be comparable to those using FoE and other super resolution approaches.

Keywords: Texture image prior · Restricted boltzmann machine · Super resolution · Deep learning

1 Introduction

Super Resolution is a very active research topic in the image processing community. Formally speaking, super resolution(SR) estimates a high resolution(HR) image from one or multiple low resolution(LR) images. The problem is inherently under-determined because there are many possible high resolution images given a low resolution image.

There are several means of addressing the SR problem, such as interpolation-based super resolution, reconstruction-based super resolution and learning-based super resolution. Interpolation-based super resolution attempts to interpolate the HR image from the LR input [11]. These approaches usually blur high frequency details, however. Reconstruction-based approaches estimate an SR image using multiple low resolution images or by means of patch redundancy [12,13]. Learning-based techniques estimate high frequency details from a large training set of HR images that encode the relationship between HR and LR images [14]. These approaches have shown great promise and have been applied to SR in various ways. Recently, methods which exploit natural image priors for SR have been proposed in the literature [2]. The FoE framework, which imposes piecewise

© Springer International Publishing Switzerland 2015
V. Murino and E. Puppo (Eds.): ICIAP 2015, Part I, LNCS 9279, pp. 215–224, 2015.
DOI: 10.1007/978-3-319-23231-7_20

smoothness on images, outperforms other natural image priors such as sparse coding or patch redundancy. However, the piecewise smoothness in this case is not equal to that associated with texture images; hence, the FoE framework is not suitable for modeling texture images [3]. In the field of deep learning, texture image modeling has been an active topic [4]. Following the recent exploration of the Restricted Boltzmann Machine(RBM) for texture image modeling, we choose the convolutional Gaussian Restricted Boltzmann Machine (cGRBM) [5,6]. The performance of this method is comparable to those of other modeling technique; moreover, its energy function in this case is tractable [7]. This tractable energy function is used to calculate the maximum a posteriori estimation. We explain this in detail in the following sections.

Although the modeling performance of cGRBM is acceptable, it can model only one texture image. A means of natural expansion in this case is to develop the ability to model the variety of textures seen in natural scenes. One means of addressing this problem is to train multiple texture image models individually and then to select the proper model for the given image. To do this, the implicit mixture RBM (imRBM) is used.

In this paper, exploring the implicit mixture of cGRBM, we suggest the maximum a posteriori (MAP) framework for super resolution into which a texture image prior is embedded. We investigate the mechanism how the implicit mixture of cGRBM automatically selects the correct texture among multiple cGRBMs.

The remainder of our paper is organized as follows: First, Section 2 describes the process of learning the texture image prior using the RBM; Section 3 presents details of our suggested framework. The results are presented in Section 4, and Section 5 concludes our paper with a discussion.

2   Learning Texture Image Prior

Modeling texture image prior knowledge can be understood by considering a combination of several repetitive features. Instead of hand-tuned feature selection, deep learning automatically selects the feature that captures the texture image structures. Following recent research [5,6], the convolutional Gaussian RBM matches or exceeds achieves the results of state-of-the-art method.

2.1   Modeling Individual Texture with the RBM

Boltzmann machines (Fig. 1 (a)) consider two sets of variables, the hidden unit **h**, and the visible unit **x**. They model a joint distribution of random variables with Boltzmann distribution (also called Gibbs distribution)

$$p(\mathbf{x}, \mathbf{h}) = \frac{\exp(-E(\mathbf{x}, \mathbf{h}))}{Z} \tag{1}$$

where is the energy function according to the model, and Z is a normalization constant which is also known as a partition function.

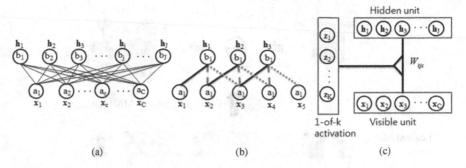

Fig. 1. (a) The undirected graph of an RBM with J hidden and C visible variables. (b) The convolutional RBM (identical color lines indeicate the same weights). (c) Schematic diagram of the implicit mixture of the RBM.

To resolve the poor scalability of the RBM, the convolutional Gaussian RBM (Fig. 1 (b)) is suggested. This model is spatially invariant and scalable to a realistic image size [8].

The energy function of cGRBM is written as

$$E_{cGRBM}(\mathbf{x}, \mathbf{h}) = \frac{1}{2\sigma^2}\mathbf{x}^T\mathbf{x} - \sum_{j \in filter} \sum_{c \in visible} h_{jc}(\mathbf{w}_j^T\mathbf{x} + b_j) \qquad (2)$$

where the σ is standard deviation of Gaussian noise. Here, $\mathbf{w}_j$ determines the interaction between pairs of visible units $\mathbf{x}_c$ and hidden units h_{jc}. Thus, $\mathbf{w}_j$ values are the filters, b_j are the biases of hidden units, and c and j are indices for all overlapping image cliques and filters.

Although cGRBM facilitates texture model learning, it also restricts the number of texture models to one. Not being able to model a variety of textures, cGRBM is naturally extended to multiple Boltzmann machines.

2.2   Implicit Mixture Modeling for Multiple Textures

One way to address the problem of cGRBM modeling one texture per cGRBM is to use an implicit mixture of RBMs (imRBM) [9]. The literal meaning of implicit mixture is that it mixes one with another; however, in our work, the underlying role of imRBM is the selection of the proper cGRBM among several learned machines *automatically*. We explain this in detail in Section 3.

The energy function of the binary visible unit is

$$E(\mathbf{x}, \mathbf{h}, \mathbf{z}) = - \sum_{k \in \{1,2,...,K\}} \sum_{j \in filter} \sum_{c \in visible} z_k h_{jc} \mathbf{w}_{jk}^T \mathbf{x}_c \qquad (3)$$

where K is the number of RBMs (Fig. 1 (c)). Eq. (3) shows that imRBM is extended by including a discrete variable z with K possible states. In addition, $\mathbf{w}_{jk}$ is the filter which determines the interaction between h_{jc} and $\mathbf{x}_c$ of the kth

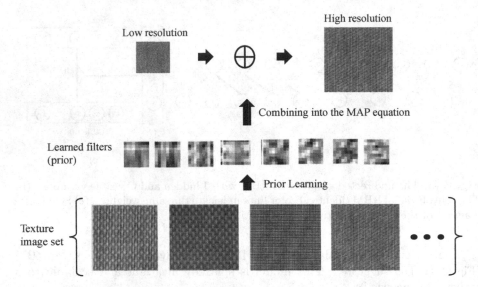

Fig. 2. A MAP framework for super resolution. In this proposed framework, we learn the filter as a prior. This prior is used to obtain the MAP solution analytically. The MAP solution is calculated using a gradient descent algorithm.

cGRBM. Eq. (3) can be adapted to a convolutional Gaussian visible unit [10]. Its energy function is given below.

$$
\begin{aligned}
E(\mathbf{x}, \mathbf{h}, \mathbf{z}) &= \frac{1}{2\sigma^2}\mathbf{x}^T\mathbf{x} - \sum_{k \in \{1,2,\dots,K\}} \sum_{j \in filter} \sum_{c \in visible} z_k \left(h_{jc} \left(\mathbf{w}_{jk}^T \mathbf{x}_c + b_j \right) \right) \\
&= \frac{1}{2\sigma^2}\mathbf{x}^T\mathbf{x} - \sum_{k \in \{1,2,\dots,K\}} \sum_{j \in filter} \sum_{c \in visible} h_{jc} \left(z_k \left(\mathbf{w}_{jk}^T \mathbf{x}_c + b_j \right) \right)
\end{aligned}
\tag{4}
$$

3   A MAP Framework for Super Resolution

To utilize the deep learning MAP framework well, we formulate probabilistic models for a priori.

3.1   Image Formation Modeling

The low resolution image, $\mathbf{y}$, the image formation process is usually modeled as the convolution of the high resolution image, $\mathbf{x}$, followed by down sampling.

$$
\mathbf{y} = \mathbf{DHx} + \mathbf{e}
\tag{5}
$$

Here, $\mathbf{D}$ is the downsampling operator, $\mathbf{H}$ is the blurring operator and $\mathbf{e}$ denotes the noise added to the low resolution image. The noise is usually modeled

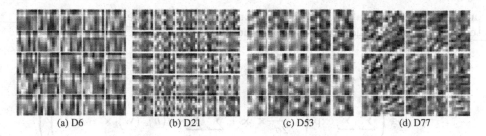

| (a) D6 | (b) D21 | (c) D53 | (d) D77 |

Fig. 3. The learned filters

as independent and identically distributed Gaussian noise. The super resolution problem, recovering **x** from **y**, is a well-known ill-posed problem. To solve the under-determined problem, it is possible to restrict the solution space by a prior knowledge.

The super resolution problem is then formulated via regularized least square regression

$$\hat{\mathbf{x}} = \arg\min_{\mathbf{x}} \|\mathbf{y} - \mathbf{D}\mathbf{H}\mathbf{x}\|^2 + \lambda' R(\mathbf{x}) \tag{6}$$

where $R(\mathbf{x})$ is the mathematical formula for a priori and λ' is a regularization parameter. The first term here serves as the log likelihood function which models the Gaussian noise. Eq. (6) can be also recognized as MAP estimation problem. To clarify this statement, we start with a reformulation of the MAP estimation equation,

$$\hat{\mathbf{x}} = \arg\max_{\mathbf{x}} p(\mathbf{y}|\mathbf{x})p(\mathbf{x}) \tag{7}$$

where $p(\mathbf{y}|\mathbf{x})$ denotes the likelihood distribution and $p(\mathbf{x})$ is the prior distribution. The likelihood distribution can be written as follows:

$$p(\mathbf{y}|\mathbf{x}) = \exp\left(-\frac{\|\mathbf{y} - \mathbf{D}\mathbf{H}\mathbf{x}\|^2}{\sigma^2}\right) \tag{8}$$

Here, σ denotes the standard deviation of the noise. The prior distribution of **x** can be represented by energy in the context of graphical models

$$p(\mathbf{y}|\mathbf{x}) = \frac{1}{Z_E} \exp\left(-E(\mathbf{x})\right) \tag{9}$$

In this equation, Z_E is the partition function. Putting Eq. (8) and Eq. (9) into Eq. (7), and taking the negative logarithm, we obtain the regularized least square formula shown in Eq. (6). At this point, we are ready to derive the prior distribution for the texture model.

3.2   Embedding Multiple Texture Prior in the MAP Framework

To obtain the probabilistic prior model, $p(\mathbf{x})$, with which to capture the structure of the texture images, we integrate the energy function shown in Eq. (4)

out of the latent variables over their domains [7]. The free energy is proportional to marginal distribution [16]. The free energy is given below.

$$
\begin{aligned}
F(\mathbf{x}) &= -\log\left(\sum_{\mathbf{z}}\sum_{\mathbf{h}}\exp\left(-E\left(\mathbf{x},\mathbf{h},\mathbf{z}\right)\right)\right)\\[2mm]
&= -\log\left(\sum_{\mathbf{z}}\sum_{\mathbf{h}}\exp\left(-\frac{1}{2\sigma^2}\mathbf{x}^T\mathbf{x}+\sum_{k}\sum_{j,c}z_k\left(h_{jc}\left(\mathbf{w}_{jk}^T\mathbf{x}_c+b_j\right)\right)\right)\right)\\[2mm]
&= -\log\left(\sum_{\mathbf{z}}\sum_{\mathbf{h}}\exp\left(-\frac{1}{2\sigma^2}\mathbf{x}^T\mathbf{x}+\sum_{k}\sum_{j,c}h_{jc}\left(z_k\left(\mathbf{W}_{kjc}\mathbf{x}+b_j\right)\right)\right)\right)\\[2mm]
&= \frac{1}{2\sigma^2}\mathbf{x}^T\mathbf{x}-\log\left(\sum_{\mathbf{z}}\sum_{\mathbf{h}}\exp\left(\sum_{k}\sum_{j,c}h_{jc}\left(z_k\left(\mathbf{W}_{kjc}\mathbf{x}+b_j\right)\right)\right)\right)\\[2mm]
&= \frac{1}{2\sigma^2}\mathbf{x}^T\mathbf{x}-\log\left(\sum_{\mathbf{z}}\prod_{j,c}\left(1+\exp\left(\sum_{k}z_k\left(\mathbf{W}_{kjc}\mathbf{x}+b_j\right)\right)\right)\right)\\[2mm]
&= \frac{1}{2\sigma^2}\mathbf{x}^T\mathbf{x}-\log\left(\sum_{k=1}^{K}\prod_{j,c}\left(1+\exp\left(\mathbf{W}_{kjc}\mathbf{x}+b_j\right)\right)\right)
\end{aligned}
$$
(10)

Here, $\mathbf{W}_{kjc}\mathbf{x}=\mathbf{w}_{jk}^T\mathbf{x}_c$, $\mathbf{W}_{kjc}$ is the tensor of the filters. In addition, $\mathbf{x}$ is the vectorized image.

The super resolution MAP framework with probabilistic texture prior is derived from combining Eq. (6) and Eq. (10).

$$
\hat{\mathbf{x}}=\arg\max_{\mathbf{x}}\left(\|\mathbf{y}-\mathbf{DHx}\|^2+\lambda\left(\frac{1}{2\sigma^2}\mathbf{x}^T\mathbf{x}-\log\sum_{k=1}^{K}\prod_{j,c}\left(1+\exp(\mathbf{W}_{kjc}\mathbf{x}+b_j)\right)\right)\right)
$$
(11)

where λ is a regularization parameter.

To get the MAP solution, the optimization is performed by gradient descent. The gradient of $F(\mathbf{x})$ w.r.t. $\mathbf{x}$ is shown in Eq. (12).

$$
\nabla F_{\mathbf{x}}=\frac{\mathbf{x}}{\sigma^2}-\log\left(\frac{\sum_{k=1}^{K}\left(AR_k\times\left(\frac{\mathbf{W}_{kjc}\times\exp(\mathbf{W}_{kjc}\mathbf{x}+b_j)}{1+\exp(\mathbf{W}_{kjc}\mathbf{x}+b_j)}\right)\right)}{\sum_{k=1}^{K}AR_k}\right)
$$
(12)

where $AR_k=\prod_{j,c}\left(1+\exp\left(\mathbf{W}_{kjc}\mathbf{x}+b_j\right)\right)$.

AR_k represents correlations between the filter of the kth RBM and the given image. Due to the product in AR_k, the correlation of each clique and filter is amplified. As a result, AR_k of the correct RBM is dominant such that the others become meaningless. This indicates that only the correct RBM which best captures the structure of the given low resolution image affects the gradient of $F(\mathbf{x})$. This gives us a good insight into the 1-of-K activation mechanism of implicit mixture model. Note that one cannot calculate AR_k directly(Under our experimental conditions, it is over $\exp(10000000)$). Because the maximum index of the AR_ks is that of the logarithm of the AR_ks, it is sufficient to determine the correct machine to sum the correlations of each clique and filter. After determining the correct machine by summing the correlations, Eq. (12) can be calcuated approximately with the filters and biases of the correct machine.

4 Experiment

The dataset used in the experiments and for the learning of the model is described in section 4.1. Section 4.2 shows the performance of the proposed algorithm as compared to that of a state-of-the-art method.

4.1 Dataset and Learning cRBM

We use a range of four texture images from the Brodatz dataset : D6, D21, D53, and D77(http://www.ux.uis.no/~tranden/brodatz.html). We apply rescaling similar to that used in earlier work in [3], in which the 640x640 textures were rescaled to 480x480 (Downscale ratio is 0.75.). We divide each image into a top half used for training and a bottom half for testing. The number of training images is 40 with the size of 76x76, which is randomly cropped in the top half image. The filter size is set to 9x9. The number of filters per cRBM is 25. The number of RBMs in the imcGRBM is 4. We learn the parameters of the models by approximate maximum likelihood, using stochastic gradient ascent based on the Persistent chains Contrastive Divergence method(PCD) [18]. The number of Markov chain transition was set to 1 (PCD-1), and the transition was done by Hybrid Monte Carlo (HMC) sampling with 30 sample steps and 20 Leapfrog steps [19]. The learning rate of the weights is 0.000005. Following the recent research [6], σ^2 is set to 0.03. Figure 3 shows the learned filters for several texture images.

To create a low resolution, we convolute the ground truth with a blur kernel for which support is 7 and sigma is 1. Down sampling operator, with a scale of 2, follows the blurred image.

4.2 Multiple Texture Super Resolution

We conduct several experiments for super resolution with a size of 60x60 for the low resolution images and a zoom factor of 2. Figure 4 shows the super resolution result compared to those of other approaches. Our result shows more visually pleasing images as compared to those of the other methods. The fifth row of Fig. 4 shows the comparison with super resolution using the natural image prior, FoE. The result with the proposed method shows a sharper image compared to the use of FoE. This may result from the piecewise smoothness of FoE, in contrast

222   C. Kang et al.

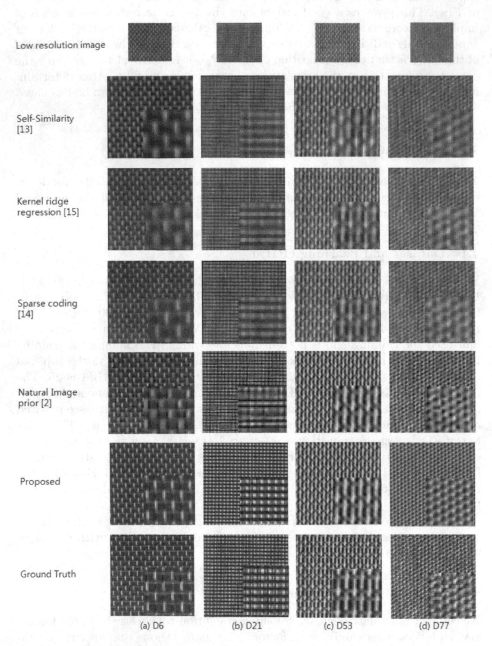

Low resolution image

Self-Similarity [13]

Kernel ridge regression [15]

Sparse coding [14]

Natural Image prior [2]

Proposed

Ground Truth

(a) D6   (b) D21   (c) D53   (d) D77

Fig. 4. Super resolution(X2) results of various approaches: Low resolution, Self-similarity, Kernel Ridge Regression, Sparse Coding, Natural Image Prior (FoE), the proposed algorithm and Ground truth (From the top row to the bottom row).

to our algorithm, which learns the image structure directly by finding the filter which is best correlated with the given low resolution image.

In addition to a qualitative comparison, we compare the result quantitatively. The well-known measure for super resolution is PSNR, which is defined as

$$PSNR = 10 \log_{10} \frac{(MaximumIntensityValue)^2}{MeanSquareError} \tag{13}$$

Another measure is the Structural Similarity Index (SSIM) [17]. As shown in Table 1, the proposed method can achieve better results than any other method such as the Self-similarity [13], Kernel Ridge Regression [15], Sparse Coding [14] and FoE [2] methods.

Table 1. Super Resolution (X2) Quality

Method		Self Similarity [13]	KRR [15]	Sparse Coding [14]	FoE [2]	Proposed
D6	PSNR	15.764	19.897	20.225	22.104	**25.201**
	SSIM	0.232	0.645	0.692	0.800	**0.913**
D21	PSNR	13.992	15.365	15.845	16.745	**22.074**
	SSIM	0.277	0.486	0.555	0.707	**0.937**
D53	PSNR	13.733	16.560	16.825	22.484	**23.136**
	SSIM	0.468	0.706	0.723	0.940	**0.955**
D77	PSNR	14.930	17.218	17.244	21.163	**21.452**
	SSIM	0.212	0.530	0.536	0.855	**0.882**

5 Conclusion

We formulate the probabilistic model for texture image prior by exploring the cGRBM. We propose a MAP framework using the texture prior learned from cGRBM for super resolution. We get the MAP solution by analytic formulation. Experimental results show that the result of the proposed algorithm is comparable with other approaches in terms of quantitative and qualitative comparison.

References

1. Schmidt, U., Gao, Q., Roth, S.: A Generative perspective on MRFs in low-level vision. In: Proc. IEEE Conference on Computer Vision and Pattern Recognition, pp. 1751–1758 (2010)
2. Zhang, H., Zhang, Y., Li, H., Huang, T.: Generative Bayesian Image Super Resolution with Natural Image Prior. IEEE Transactions on Image Processing, 4054–4067 (2012)
3. Heess, N. Williams, C., Hinton, G.: Learning generative texture models with extended fields-of-experts. In: Proc. the British Machine Vision Conference (2009)
4. Luo, H. Carrier, P.L., Couville, A., Bengio, Y.: Texture modeling with convolutional spike-and-slab RBMs and deep extensions. In: Proc. the International Conference on Artificial Intelligence and Statistics (AISTAT), pp. 415–423 (2013)

5. Kivinen, J., Williams, C.: Multiple texture Boltzmann machines. In: Proc. the International Conference on Artificial Intelligence and Statistics (AISTAT), pp. 4054–4067 (2012)
6. Gao, Qi, Roth, Stefan: Texture synthesis: from convolutional RBMs to efficient deterministic algorithms. In: Fränti, Pasi, Brown, Gavin, Loog, Marco, Escolano, Francisco, Pelillo, Marcello (eds.) S+SSPR 2014. LNCS, vol. 8621, pp. 434–443. Springer, Heidelberg (2014)
7. Ranzato, M., Mnih, V., Susskind, J., Hinton, G.: Modeling Natural Images Using Gated MRFs. IEEE Transaction on Pattern Analysis and Machine Intelligence, 2206–2226 (2013)
8. Lee, H., Grosse, R., Ranganath, R., Ng, A.Y.: Convolutional deep belief networks for scalable unsupervised learning of hierarchical representations. In: Proc. International Conference on Machine Learning, pp. 609–616 (2009)
9. Nair, V., Hinton, G.: Implicit mixtures of restricted Boltzmann machines. In: Proc. Advances in Neural Information Processing System (2009)
10. Welling, M., Rosen-Zvi, M., Hinton, G.: Exponential family harmoniums with an application to information retrieval. In: Proc. Advances in Neural Information Processing System (2008)
11. Takeda, H., Farisu, S., Milanfar, P.: Kernel Regression for Image Processing and Reconstruction. IEEE Transactions on Image Processing $12(2)$, 349–336 (2007)
12. Glasner, D., Bagon, S., Irani, M.: Super-resoluton from a single image. In: Proc. IEEE Conference on Computer Vision and Pattern Recognition (2009)
13. Freeman, G., Fattal, R.: Image and Video Upscaling from Local Self-Examples. ACM Trans. Graph. $28(3)$, 1–10 (2009)
14. Yang, J., Wang, Z., Lin, Z., Huang, T.: Coupled dictionary training for image super resolution. IEEE Transactions on Image Processing $21(8)$, 3467–3478 (2012)
15. Kim, K.I., Kwon, Y.: Single-image Super-resolution Using Sparse Regression and Natural Image Prior. IEEE Transaction on Pattern Analysis and Machine Intelligence (2008)
16. Ngiam, J., Chen, Z., Koh, P.W., Ng, A.Y.: Learning deep energy models. In: Proc. International Conference on Machine Learning (2011)
17. Wang, Z., Bovik, A.C.: Mean squared error: Love it or leave it? A New look at Signal Fidelity Measures. IEEE Signal Process. Mag. $26(1)$, 98–117 (2009)
18. Tieleman, T.: Training restricted boltzmann machines using approximations to the likelihood gradient. In: Proc. International Conference on Machine Learning (2008)
19. Neal, R.M.: MCMC using Hamiltonian dynamics (2012). arXiv:1206.1901v1

GRUNTS: Graph Representation for UNsupervised Temporal Segmentation

Francesco Battistone[1], Alfredo Petrosino[1]([✉]), and Gabriella Sanniti di Baja[2]

[1] Department of Science and Technology,
University of Naples Parthenope, Naples, Italy
alfredo.petrosino@uniparthenope.it
[2] Institute for High Performance Computing and Networking,
National Research Council, Naples, Italy

Abstract. We propose GRUNTS, a feature independent method for temporal segmentation via unsupervised learning. GRUNTS employs graphs, through skeletonization and polygonal approximation, to represent objects in each frame, and graph matching to efficiently compute a Frame Kernel Matrix able to encode the similarities between frames. We report the results of temporal segmentation in the case of human action recognition, obtained by adopting the Aligned Cluster Analysis (ACA), as unsupervised learning strategy. GRUNTS has been tested on three challenging datasets: the Weizmann dataset, the KTH dataset and the MSR Action3D dataset. Experimental results on these datasets demonstrate the effectiveness of GRUNTS for segmenting actions, mainly compared with supervised learning, typically more computationally expensive and not prone to be real time.

1 Introduction

The aim of temporal segmentation is to cut an input sequence into segments with different semantic meanings; in particular in human action recognition, some methods focus on simple primitive actions such as walking, running and jumping, without taking into account the fact that normal activity involves complex temporal patterns. In this work the problem of temporal segmentation of human behavior is formulated as a temporal clustering problem.

We propose GRUNTS, a novel graph representation that combines the result of a skeletonization algorithm with a polygonal approximation technique to obtain a structure that schematically represents the silhouette of the object of interest for each frame. The name GRUNTS (unskilled workers) describes and highlights the simple representation that the method uses for each frame. This method, taking an input sequence, allows to obtain for each frame, the graph which approximates at best the skeleton of the relative silhouette. After building all graphs, a graph matching is adopted to estimate the similarities between the graphs in order to achieve the Frame Kernel Matrix (FKM). Finally, we adopt the Aligned Cluster Analysis (ACA)[1] on the FKM to segment the sequence.

© Springer International Publishing Switzerland 2015
V. Murino and E. Puppo (Eds.): ICIAP 2015, Part I, LNCS 9279, pp. 225–235, 2015.
DOI: 10.1007/978-3-319-23231-7_21

The method possesses some advantages: (i) it captures structure information of each action by a graph representation of the silhouette; (ii) it finds an hidden structure in unlabeled data; (iii) it efficiently works on different types of datasets (2D-dataset, 3D-dataset and RGB-D dataset). GRUNTS has been tested in the framework of human action recognition on three challenging datasets: the Weizmann dataset [2], the KTH dataset [3] and the MSR Action3D dataset [4], and the obtained results prove the effectiveness of GRUNTS for segmenting actions.

Sections 2 and 3 discuss how the graph is constructed for each silhouette at each frame, while Section 4 reports the building of the Frame Kernel Matrix by graph matching and in the Section 5 how ACA works on FKM to segment a sequence is shown. Finally, in the Section 6 we report the results of GRUNTS on the three different datasets.

2   Graph Representation

The representation of the meaningful features captured at each frame has an important role in our approach. Once the skeleton of the silhouette is available, polygonal approximation is performed to identify the graph approximating the skeleton branches.

2.1   Skeleton

The skeletonization method adopted by GRUNTS [5] does not require the iterated application of topology preserving removal operations, and does not need checking a condition specifically tailored to end point detection. In fact, skeletonization is accomplished on the distance transform DT of the object, computed according to the (3,4) distance [6]. Thus, end points are automatically identified when the so called centers of maximal discs are found in DT. The skeletal pixels are all found in one raster scan inspection of DT. The set of the skeletal pixels detected in DT has all the properties expected to characterize the skeleton of the object except for unit thickness. Indeed, the set of the skeletal pixels is 2-pixel thick in correspondence of regions of the object with thickness given by an even number of pixels. Thus, a reduction to unit width is obtained by using templates able to erase the marker from suitable skeletal pixels. Finally, a pruning step is also taken into account to simplify the structure of the resulting skeleton by removing some peripheral branches corresponding to scarcely elongated regions. The elongatedness of each object region can be measured by analyzing the skeleton branch mapped into it and a threshold on elongatedness can be set depending on the specific application.

2.2   Polygonal Approximation

Several approaches exist in the literature to compute the polygonal approximation of a digital curve. We use a split type approach [7] because it is convenient when working with open curves, like the individual skeleton branches. This type of algorithm can be described as follows. The two extremes of the input open curve are taken by all means as vertices of the polygonal approximation. The Euclidean distance of all points of the curve from the straight line joining the two vertices is computed. In particular, each point of the skeleton at position (x, y) and with distance value k can be interpreted as a point in the $3D$ space with coordinates (x, y, k). Then, the Euclidean distance d of a point C in the $3D$ space from the straight line joining two points A and B, is calculated by using the following expression:

$$d^2 = \|AC\|^2 - P_{ABC} * \frac{P_{ABC}}{\|AB\|^2} \qquad (1)$$

where $\|AC\|$ is the norm of the vector AC, and P_{ABC} is the scalar product between vectors AB and AC.

The point with the largest distance is taken as a new vertex, provided that such a distance overcomes an a priori fixed threshold θ(for this work, $\theta = 1.5$, as we aim at a faithful approximation [8]). If a new vertex is detected, such a vertex divides the curve into two sub-curves, to each of which the above split type algorithm is applied. The splitting process is repeated as far as points are detected having distance larger than θ from the straight lines joining the extremes of the sub-curves to which the points belong. When the recursion is completed the points that have been detected as vertexes represent the nodes while the segments that approximate the curve represent the edges of the graph that best approximates the skeleton (see Fig. 1). Note that Fig. 1b has been cropped to the smallest area safely including the foreground once the binarized version of Fig. 1a has been obtained, so as to reduce the amount of data to process.

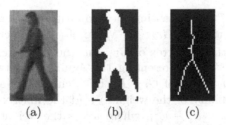

(a)   (b)   (c)

Fig. 1. A frame of the sequence (a); binary image where the foreground is the silhouette (b); the graph obtained by skeletonization and polygonal approximation (c).

2.3   Building the Graph

A graph with n vertexes and m undirected edges is represented as a 4-tuple $Gr = \{P, Q, G, H\}$, where $\mathbf{P} \in \mathbb{R}^{3 \times n}$ represent the set of vertexes that have been detected by polygonal approximation. Each vertex has three coordinates, $(x, y, DT_{(3,4)}(x, y))$, where x and y are the spatial coordinates of the vertex while

$DT_{(3,4)}(x, y)$ is the value of DT in position (x, y). The third coordinate is important because it describes the thickness of the object region in correspondence to the skeleton point; in fact, graphs with similar structure may correspond to objects with different shapes. An example is shown in Fig. 2.

$\mathbf{Q} \in \mathbb{R}^{2 \times m}$ is the set of edges represented as 2-D vector encoding the Euclidean distance between vertexes and the orientation of the c_{th} edge. The topology of the graph is represented by two binary matrices $\mathbf{G}^{n \times m}, \mathbf{H}^{n \times m}$, where $g_{ic} = h_{jc} = 1$ if the c_{th} edge starts from the i_{th} node and ends at the j_{th} node.

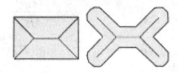

Fig. 2. Objects with different thickness and skeletons with the same geometrical structure.

3   The Frame Kernel Matrix

A Frame Kernel Matrix, $\mathbf{K} \in \mathbb{R}^{n_f \times n_f}$, where n_f is the number of frames of the input sequence, is constructed over the affinity between consecutive frames, measured as graph matching between consecutive graphs. Specifically, we adopt the algorithm of graph matching reported in [9]. A measure of similarity between graphs is achieved through the combination of the distance measures between vertexes and edges, encoded in the pairwise affinity matrix $\mathbf{A}$. Formally, given a pair of graphs $Gr_1 = \{P_1, Q_1, G_1, H_1\}$ and $Gr_2 = \{P_2, Q_2, G_2, H_2\}$, two matrices are computed:

- matrix $K_p \in \mathbb{R}^{n_1 \times n_2}$, representing the similarity between the n_1 vertexes of Gr_1 and the n_2 vertices of Gr_2. The value of $k_{i,j}^p$ is calculated as Euclidean distance between the ith vertex of Gr_1 and the jth vertex of Gr_2.
- matrix $K_q \in \mathbb{R}^{m_1 \times m_2}$, representing the similarity between the m_1 edges of Gr_1 and the m_2 edges of Gr_2. K_q is calculated as an average between the matrix A^w (affinity of the weights) and the matrix A^θ (affinity of the orientations): $A_{ij}^w = |w_i^1 - w_j^2|$, where w_i^1 is the weight of the ith edge of Gr_1 and w_j^2 is the weight of the jth edge of Gr_2, and $A_{ij}^\theta = |\theta_i^1 - \theta_j^2|$, where θ_i^1 is orientation of the ith edge of Gr_1 with respect to the z-axis and θ_j^2 is orientation of the jth edge of Gr_2 with respect to the z-axis.

Vertex and edge affinities are encoded in a symmetrical matrix $A \in \mathbb{R}^{(n_1 \cdot n_2) \times (n_1 \cdot n_2)}$, whose elements are computed as follows:

$$A_{i_1, i_2, j_1, j_2} = \begin{cases} k_{i_1, i_2}^p, & \text{if } i_1 = j_1 \text{ and } i_2 = j_2; \\ k_{c_1, c_2}^q, & \text{if } i_1 \neq j_1 \text{ and } i_2 \neq j_2 \text{ and} \\ & g_{i_1 c_1}^1 h_{j_1 c_1}^1 g_{i_2 c_2}^2 h_{j_2 c_2}^2 = 1; \\ 0, & \text{otherwise} \end{cases} \tag{2}$$

where the diagonal and off-diagonal elements encode the similarity between nodes and edges respectively. To construct the Frame Kernel Matrix, $\mathbf{K} \in \mathbb{R}^{n_f \times n_f}$, we need a single value of affinity for each graph matching, encoded in the matrix $\mathbf{A}$. This affinity is calculated as the mean of the maximum elements in each of $nb = n_{min} \cdot n_{min}$ sub-blocks $B^{n_{max} \times n_{max}}$ contained in the $\mathbf{A}$ matrix (where $n_{min} = min(n_1, n_2)$, and $n_{max} = max(n_1, n_2)$). Each entry, k_{ij}, defines the similarity between two frames, $\mathbf{x}_i$ and $\mathbf{x}_j$.

4 Aligned Cluster Analysis (ACA)

GRUNTS uses an extension of kernel k-means, ACA [1], for the temporal segmentation of human action. In contrast to k-means, dynamic time alignment kernel (DTAK) is adopted as measure of distance to establish which action is represented into a segment, defined as a set of consecutive frames. Furthermore, given a sequence $\mathbf{X} = [\mathbf{x}_1, ..., \mathbf{x}_n] \in \mathbb{R}^{d \times n}$ composed by n frames, ACA partitions $\mathbf{X}$ into m disjointed segments, each one related to a different class representing a particular action. The ith segment, $\mathbf{Y}_i \doteq \mathbf{X}_{[s_i, s_{i+1})} = [\mathbf{x}_{s_i}, ..., \mathbf{x}_{s_{i+1}-1}] \in \mathbb{R}^{d \times n}$, is composed by frames from position s_i to $s_{i+1} - 1$. The length of the segment is constrained to be $n_i = s_{i+1} - s_i \leq n_{max}$, where n_{max} is the maximum length of the segment and controls the temporal granularity of the factorization.

A matrix $\mathbf{G} \in \{0, 1\}^{k \times m}$ includes information about the assignment of each segment to a class: $g_{ci} = 1$ if $\mathbf{Y}_i$ belongs to class c, else $g_{ci} = 0$. ACA extends previous work [10] by minimizing:

$$J_{aca}(\mathbf{G}, \mathbf{s}) = \sum_{c=1}^{k} \sum_{i=1}^{m} g_{ci} \| \psi(\mathbf{X}_{[s_i, s_{i+1})}) - \mathbf{z}_c \|^2 \tag{3}$$

where k is the number of classes (which is dependent on the dataset), $\mathbf{z}_c \in \mathbb{R}^d$ is the geometric centroid of the data points for the class c and the distance is computed as follows:

$$\| \psi(\mathbf{X}_{[s_i, s_{i+1})}) - \mathbf{z}_c \|^2 = \tau_{ii} - \frac{2}{m_c} \sum_{j=1}^{m} g_{cj_1} \tau_{ij} + \frac{1}{m_c^2} \sum_{j_1, j_2 = 1}^{m} g_{cj_1} g_{cj_2} \tau_{j_1 j_2}, \tag{4}$$

where $m_c = \sum_{j=1}^{m} g_{cj}$ is the number of segments that belong to class c. The dynamic kernel function τ is defined as $\tau_{ij} = \psi(\mathbf{Y}_i)^T \psi(\mathbf{Y}_j)$ based on [11] and $\psi(\cdot)$ denotes a mapping of the sequence into a feature space. Zhou et al. in [12] presented the hierarchical version of ACA (termed HACA) that reduces the computational complexity of ACA and provides a hierarchical decomposition at different temporal scales. HACA replaces the kernel DTAK with the GDTAK (generalized DTAK) to propagate the solution at different levels, even if it does not substantially change the main idea.

5   The GRUNTS Algorithm

The main advantage of our technique surely consists in its feature independence on the input datasets. This is stressed in the detailed description of Algorithm 1 (see below). Given an input sequence, GRUNTS is performed as shown, and after the Frame Kernel Matrix is built, the aligned cluster analysis ACA is executed to obtain the temporal segmentation.

Algorithm 1 GRUNTS

1: *Take a sequence in input*
2: **for** *all frames* **do**
3:    **if** *frame is not a skeleton of the RGB − D dataset* **then**
4:       *Read each frame of a sequence;*
5:       **if** *frame is in the 2D − space* **then**
6:          **if** *frame is not binary* **then**
7:             *Background Subtraction by SOBS* [13]
8:          **end if**
9:          *Calculate* $(3 − 4)DT$
10:          *Skeletonization*
11:       **end if**
12:       **if** *frame is in the 3D − space* **then**
13:          *Skeletonization*
14:       **end if**
15:       *Polygonal Approximation*
16:    **end if**
17: **end for**
18: *Calculate FKM*
19: *Execute ACA*

---

6   Experiments

GRUNTS has been evaluated on three different types of datasets: Weizmann Dataset, KTH Dataset and MSR Action3D Dataset. We set the pruning threshold to $dist^2 = 20$ and the threshold for polygonal approximation to $\theta = 1.5$. The Frame Kernel Matrix is calculated by the Gaussian kernel, $k_{ij} = exp(-\frac{dist(\mathbf{x}_i, \mathbf{x}_j)^2}{2\sigma^2})$, where $dist(\mathbf{x}_i, \mathbf{x}_j)$ is obtained by Graph Matching as following:

$$dist(\mathbf{x}_i, \mathbf{x}_j) = 1 - (\text{similarity}_{GM}(Gr_i, Gr_j)), \tag{5}$$

where Gr_i and Gr_j are the graphs respectively related to the frames $\mathbf{x}_i$ and $\mathbf{x}_j$.

To execute ACA on a sequence, we need to set the parameters n_{min} and n_{max} that represent the minimal ad the maximal length of a segment and are adopted to control the granularity of the factorization. To evaluate the clustering accuracy, we compute the confusion matrix C and its accuracy as in [12].

6.1   Weizmann Dataset

The Weizmann dataset [2] contains 90 videos of 10 individuals performing nine different actions. In this Section we compare GRUNTS with ACA that calculates the frame kernel matrix as described in [9]. The goal of these tests is to verify that GRUNTS is characterized by the following two features: i) independence from actors and action direction, and ii) independence from length and number of actions:

Independence from Actors and Action Direction. GRUNTS, unlike ACA, is not sensitive to sequences containing the same actions performed by different actors, and especially the changes of direction in different actions do not lead to a decrease in performance. In our experiments, GRUNTS and ACA are executed on fifty sequences, of seven actions, containing some equal actions executed by different actors. We show a sample sequence to prove this:

Daria_run, Eli_walk, Denis_walk, Daria_skip, Denis_jump, Daria_jump, Eli_run.

The accuracy for this sequence was 0.90 for GRUNTS, and 0.81 for ACA. From the Frame Kernel Matrix and the segmentation of the sequence shown in Fig. 3, it is evident that ACA suffers particularly the presence of actions (especially walk, run, skip and jump) equally performed by different actors and especially with opposite directions (the gray arrow in the ground truth of the sequences shows the direction of action). Indeed, the construction of the FKM (matrix on the left) in the original ACA does not allow to identify the similarity between the two subsequences "Eli_walk" and "Denis_walk" in the example (note the differences between the FKM obtained with ACA and GRUNTS and highlighted with a blue square), which is more clear in the FKM obtained by GRUNTS (matrix on the right). This also justifies the great improvement in accuracy achieved by the proposed technique. Refer to *http://cvprlab.uniparthenope.it/GRUNTS.pdf* to compare the results obtained by GRUNTS and ACA on the fifty sequences. For both techniques the best parameters have been found for each sequence. The average accuracy achieved by GRUNTS and ACA is respectively 0.88 and 0.83, showing that GRUNTS has better performance. It is also interesting to highlight the accuracy achieved by GRUNTS on the sequences: 1, 12, 18, 29, 37, 40 and 49, shown at *http://cvprlab.uniparthenope.it/GRUNTS.pdf*, since these sequences contain actions that are performed by different actors and in different directions.

Independence from Length and Number of Actions. The performance of GRUNTS is not related to the length of the input sequences and even to the number of actions. Fig. 4 shows the graphs obtained by the experiments executed to confirm the thesis on the independence of the segmentation from the number of classes (Fig. 4a) and the length of the sequence (Fig. 4b). Looking at the first graph, it is evident that the results obtained by our method are less related to

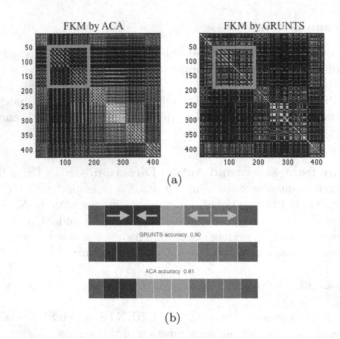

(a)

(b)

Fig. 3. (a) Frame Kernel Matrices for ACA and GRUNTS on the sample sequence; (b) Ground Truth (first row) and Temporal Segmentation by GRUNTS (second row) and ACA (third row) on the sample sequence.

the number of distinct classes, because the range of GRUNTS is smaller than that obtained by ACA. The graph on the number of frames, and therefore the length of the sequence, shows that GRUNTS obtained results always close to the average value (around 76%), while the results achieved by ACA generally differ from the average value more than those obtained by GRUNTS.

6.2   KTH Dataset

The KTH dataset [3] contains six types of human actions performed by 25 subjects in different scenarios. For this dataset, as claimed by the authors, ACA computes the FKM with a technique based on optical flow [9]. We generated 10 random testing videos for the KTH dataset and each of the videos contains 10-20 clips of different actions. The average accuracies have been: GRUNTS 0.86, ACA 0.80, HACA 0.83,Spectral Clustering (SC) [10] 0.72, setting $n_{min} = 7$ and $n_{max} = 29$ for all experiments of GRUNTS on KTH.

6.3   MSR Action3D Dataset

This dataset [4] contains twenty actions and each action was performed three times by ten subjects. GRUNTS is executed without skeletonization and polygonal approximation, since the dataset includes a skeleton already computed for

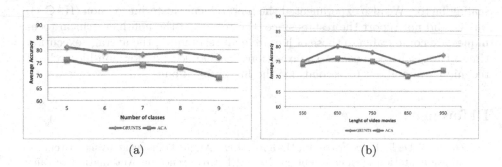

(a)   (b)

Fig. 4. Graphs of average accuracy calculated on 25 tests of 10 actions and on 25 tests containing 20 actions: (a) Graph of the average accuracy calculated on the number of classes; (b) Graph of the average accuracy on the length of the sequence.

each frame. Wang et al. [14] divide the dataset into three subsets, on which we perform GRUNTS. The results on this subsets and the average accuracy are shown in Table 1. GRUNTS does not outperform in this case, even if its accuracy is comparable with that of the two techniques with the highest accuracy values, but it is important to highlight that GRUNTS is an unsupervised method, while all other techniques are supervised.

Table 1. Performance on MSR Action3D dataset: (a) Accuracy of GRUNTS on three subsets; (b) average accuracy of GRUNTS and other approaches.

(a)

SubSet	GRUNTS
AS1	83.4
AS2	83.7
AS3	88.9
Average	85.3

(b)

Method	Accuracy
HON4D + D_{disc} [15]	88.9
Jiang et al [14]	88.2
Dollar + BOW [16]	72.4
Vieira [17]	78.2
Klaser [18]	81.4
GRUNTS	85.3

7   Conclusions

The new graph representation for unsupervised temporal segmentation of human actions reported in this paper gets surely advantage of the adopted structured representation to deal with feature independence on different datasets. It can work on different types of datasets and the achieved results are comparable with the state-of-the-art algorithms of temporal segmentation - with the specificity to be unsupervised. Indeed, we tested GRUNTS on three different datasets (Weizmann, KTH and MSR Action3D Dataset) and as clustering we have chosen the ACA clustering for its ability to be robust to noise and invariant to temporal scaling factor. We also experimented the hierarchical clustering version (HACA), but we did not report the results since: the results of the non-hierarchical techniques are comparable to those of hierarchical techniques; the average execution time of a given sequence of seven actions is 1.90 seconds for non-hierarchical techniques and about 60 seconds for the hierarchical ones.

References

1. Zhou, F., De la Torre Frade, F., Hodgins, J.K.: Aligned cluster analysis for temporal segmentation of human motion. In: IEEE Conference on Automatic Face and Gestures Recognition, September 2008
2. Gorelick, L., Blank, M., Shechtman, E., Irani, M., Basri, R.: Actions as space-time shapes. Transactions on Pattern Analysis and Machine Intelligence 29(12), 2247–2253 (2007)
3. Schuldt, C., Laptev, I., Caputo, B.: Recognizing human actions: a local svm approach. In: 17th International Conference on Proceedings of the Pattern Recognition, (ICPR 2004), vol. 3, pp.32–36. IEEE Computer Society, Washington, DC (2004)
4. Li, W., Zhang, Z., Liu, Z.: Action recognition based on a bag of 3d points (2010)
5. Sanniti di Baja, G.: Well-shaped, stable, and reversible skeletons from the (3,4)-distance transform. Journal of Visual Communication and Image Representation 5(1), 107–115 (1994)
6. Borgefors, G.: Distance transformations in digital images. Comput. Vision Graph. Image Process. 34(3), 344–371 (1986)
7. Ramer, U.: An iterative procedure for the polygonal approximation of plane curves. Computer Graphics Image Process. 1(3), 244–256 (1972)
8. Rosenfeld, A.: Digital straight line segments. IEEE Transactions on Computers 23(12), 1264–1269 (1974)
9. Zhou, F., De la Torre, F.: Factorized graph matching. In: 2012 IEEE Conference on Computer Vision and Pattern Recognition (CVPR), pp. 127–134, June 2012
10. Dhillon, I.S., Guan, Y., Kulis, B.: Kernel k-means: spectral clustering and normalized cuts. In: Proceedings of the Tenth ACM SIGKDD International Conference on Knowledge Discovery and Data Mining, KDD 2004, pp. 551–556. ACM, New York (2004)
11. Shimodaira, H., ichi Noma, K., Science, S.O.I., Nakai, M., Sagayama, S.: Dynamic time-alignment kernel in support vector machine (2001)
12. Zhou, F., De la Torre, F., Hodgins, J.: Hierarchical aligned cluster analysis for temporal clustering of human motion. IEEE Transactions on Pattern Analysis and Machine Intelligence 35(3), 582–596 (2013)
13. Maddalena, L., Petrosino, A.: A self-organizing approach to background subtraction for visual surveillance applications. Trans. Img. Proc. 17(7), 1168–1177 (2008)
14. Wang, J., Liu, Z., Chorowski, J., Chen, Z., Wu, Y.: Robust 3D action recognition with random occupancy patterns. In: Fitzgibbon, A., Lazebnik, S., Perona, P., Sato, Y., Schmid, C. (eds.) ECCV 2012, Part II. LNCS, vol. 7573, pp. 872–885. Springer, Heidelberg (2012)

15. Oreifej, O., Liu, Z.: Hon4d: histogram of oriented 4d normals for activity recognition from depth sequences. In: 2013 IEEE Conference on Computer Vision and Pattern Recognition (CVPR), pp. 716–723, June 2013
16. Dollar, P., Rabaud, V., Cottrell, G., Belongie, S.: Behavior recognition via sparse spatio-temporal features. In: Proceedings of the 14th International Conference on Computer Communications and Networks, ICCCN 2005, pp. 65–72. IEEE Computer Society, Washington, DC (2005)
17. Vieira, A.W., Nascimento, E.R., Oliveira, G.L., Liu, Z., Campos, M.F.M.: STOP: space-time occupancy patterns for 3D action recognition from depth map sequences. In: Alvarez, L., Mejail, M., Gomez, L., Jacobo, J. (eds.) CIARP 2012. LNCS, vol. 7441, pp. 252–259. Springer, Heidelberg (2012)
18. Kläser, A., Marszałek, M., Schmid, C.: A spatio-temporal descriptor based on 3d-gradients. In: British Machine Vision Conference, pp. 995–1004, september 2008

A Strict Pyramidal Deep Neural Network for Action Recognition

Ihsan Ullah and Alfredo Petrosino[✉]

Department of Computer Science, University of Milan, Milan, Italy
{ihsan.ullah,alfredo.petrosino}@uniparthenope.it

Abstract. A human action recognition method is reported in which pose representation is based on the contour points of the human silhouette and actions are learned by a strict 3d pyramidal neural network ($3DPyraNet$) model which is based on convolutional neural networks and the image pyramids concept. $3DPyraNet$ extracts features from both spatial and temporal dimensions by keeping biological structure, thereby it is capable to capture the motion information encoded in multiple adjacent frames. One outlined advantage of $3DPyraNet$ is that it maintains spatial topology of the input image and presents a simple connection scheme with lower computational and memory costs compared to other neural networks. Encouraging results are reported for recognizing human actions in real-world environments.

1 Introduction

Despite advances in image recognition, action recognition is still challenging as it contains insufficient information for proper classification of an action. Some of the well-known models [1–9] achieved 90+% accuracy on different datasets under their respective targeted scenarios. In real-world scenarios, in most of the cases, human and their surrounding changes dramatically, resulting in angle change, occlusions and interactions and performance of such approaches drop when the dataset or scenario changes.

Recent neural network based methods have been developed by going deeper for learning more discriminative and different features [10]: the functions that can be represented by a k-depth architecture might require an exponential number of computational elements to be represented by a $(k-1)$-depth architecture. This is mainly why in the last years algorithms based on deep learning approaches achieved resounding success in the community of computer vision and in the field of action recognition [11–15].

Specifically, 3D convolutional neural networks have been used to learn spatio-temporal features directly from the raw images [16,17]. They increase kernels and maps as the number of layer increases. An important aspect of convolutional deep models is the weight learning and sharing concept that reduces large number of parameters compared to conventional fully connected neural network models. Learning parameters in the convolutional models are in a kernel shape which are not specific to any neuron; rather, they are slided and shared over the

© Springer International Publishing Switzerland 2015
V. Murino and E. Puppo (Eds.): ICIAP 2015, Part I, LNCS 9279, pp. 236–245, 2015.
DOI: 10.1007/978-3-319-23231-7_22

whole image and network. It reduces the number of parameters, but increases the chance to put burden on those parameters while considering huge amounts of data from videos. Considering that the number of computational elements strongly depends on the number of training examples available for tuning the network, an insufficiently deep architecture might bring to poor generalization capabilities. So, the main limitation lies in the fact that entire images need to be used for training the network, so determining a very high computational cost which makes often unfeasible the usage of such approaches in real applications.

Our work is inspired by the idea that early models strictly pyramidal and following strict biological structure [18–20] may turn to be a possible solution. In this paper, we will be focusing on two aspects: one proposing a new model that learns features from input till output without any handcrafted features, and secondly proposing and re-utilizing such a weighting scheme that can work better and learn discriminative features for recognizing human actions in videos. In coming section we will discuss a strict pyramidal neural network known as *PyraNet* that we will utilize for designing our strict pyramidal architecture for action recognition.

The contribution of this paper is twofold. First, introducing 3D strictly pyramidal neural network (*3DPyraNet*) model that will not violate biological neural network structure and which will use a new weighting scheme that extracts discriminative spatial and temporal information. Second, the model is tailored for action recognition, demonstrating, although hard constraints are imposed on the model, it is still able to properly recognize actions.

The paper is further organized as follows. Section 2 will give slight motivational background of why we proposed such a model. Further details about existing techniques that are modified, combined and enhanced in our proposed model are given in sub-sections. Section 3 will show and discuss results achieved from proposed models. Section 4 will conclude the paper.

2   3DPyraNet

We adopted a strict 3D pyramidal architecture based on decision making pyramidal structure of a brain through feature maps. T Furthermore, to capture actions as a whole in videos, we adopted a similar weighting scheme as used in *PyraNet* that will be discussed in section 2.2. These parameters will be learned from input till output using a modified structure of traditional backpropagation algorithm. To take advantage of temporal information in videos, we adopted 3D structure by taking inspiration from 3D Convolutional Neural Network ($3DCNN$) model [14]. The aim is to show that a strict pyramidal structure can enhance performance compared to unrestricted models even with simple structure, fewer feature maps and hidden layers. In coming sub-section we will first explain existing *Pyranet* model and than the weighting scheme before going to our proposed 3D architecture.

2.1   PyraNet

The *PyraNet* model [19] was inspired by the pyramidal neural network model reported in [18] with 2D and 1D layers. The diversity from the original model presented in [18] was that the coefficients of a receptive field were adaptive and it performed feature extraction and reduction in lower 2D layers. These were followed by a 1D layer at the top for classification of an image.

This model is also similar to *CNN* if we remove pooling layers from a *CNN* [15,21]. Specifically: 1) the model is connected directly to pixels in the input image (no preprocessing holds); 2) neurons are connected only to local regions (locally connected network); and 3) layers form a reduced representation of the preceding layers (deep is the rule of thumb).

However there were two main differences. Firstly it does not perform convolution rather weighted sum (WS) operation or correlation over the receptive field. Secondly, weights are not in the form of a kernel that slides over the whole image; rather each output neuron has a local unique kernel specifically assigned to it. These kernels are based on input neurons in a receptive field and their corresponding weights in a weight matrix. This results in a unique locally connected kernel for each output neuron. This will be further discussed in next section. Further, in *PyraNet* the dimensions were reduced by the stride of the kernel at each layer.

2.2   Weighting Scheme

An important part in popular convolutional deep models is their weight-sharing concept that gives an edge over other neural network models. This property reduces large amount of learning parameters; however, it increases burden on those fewer parameters. We adopted the same weighting scheme as used in *PyraNet*. In *PyraNet* each neuron has its own unique weight. These are learned using backpropagation technique and stochastic mini-batch gradient descent approach. This unique weight scheme results in weight matrix that has same size as input image or feature map at a lower layer. At the time of computation, each output neuron gets a unique kernel based on calculated receptive field.

This approach is modified for 3D structure by using more weight matrices at a time to incorporate the temporal information from the given input frames. In order to capture further different type of features, several sets of weight matrices WS are used. We randomly initialize these weights at each layer taking care of suggested techniques stated in literature for corresponding activation functions used at those layers. Initially, feature maps produced by WS kernels were sparse as compared to convolutional kernel. But later by training the model, they become similar to smooth blurred images of the input sequences. This 3D weight matrix approach for weight-sharing is different than traditional one. The weight sharing is very minimal in this approach, i.e. in worst case $1/n$ where n is the size of the receptive field kernel. Each neuron has its weight parameter that is locally shared whenever that neuron is used in a receptive field of an output neuron.

2.3   Proposed Architecture

The basic $3DPyraNet$ model has three hidden layers in combination with pooling layer as shown in Figure 1. Unlike deep models for videos [14], no specific or sophisticated pre-processing is done and we adopt a silhoutte-based approach. In general, the temporal part gives correlation between the objects or actions in consecutive frames of a video. Therefore, the first hidden layer is a 3D weighted sum WS or correlation layer ($L1WS$) shown in Figure 1. It results in maps containing spatial as well as temporal information extracted from the given sequence of input frames at input layer. This WS layer is a pure correlation operation among the given neurons and weights in a receptive field of a frame and weight matrix as shown in equation 3.

$$y_{u,v,z}^{l} = f_l \left(\sum_{i \in R_{u,v,z}} \sum_{j \in R_{u,v,z}} \sum_{m \in R_{u,v,z}} (W_{i,j,m}^{l} \circ x_{i,j,m}^{l-1}) + b_{u,v,z}^{l} \right) \tag{1}$$

where f_l represents the activation function used at layer l, (u,v) the neuron location at z output map generated by the set of input maps m from layer $l-1$. To compute the receptive field of neuron (u,v) i.e. $R_{(u,v,z)}^{l,m}$, we use equation 2. As in our case, the input map x at layer $l-1$ and the weight matrix W for layer l have the same size, (i,j) represents the same corresponding location in matrix x and W. Equation 2 determines the local receptive field for neurons and their respective weight parameters. Concerning biases, differently from $CNNs$, we do not use one bias for each output feature map, but one bias for each output neuron in the output feature map.

$$R_{u,v,z}^{l,m} = \begin{cases} (i,j,z) \mid (u-1) \times g_l + 1 \leq i \leq (u-1) \times g_l + r_l; \\ (v-1) \times g_l + 1 \leq j \leq (v-1) \times g_l + r_l; \\ z \leq m \leq m + r_l - g_l \end{cases} \tag{2}$$

The reason behind using a correlation $\circ$ operation in equation 3 rather than a convolution is that correlation extracts and collect similarity. Since action recognition is defined as recognition of consecutive, almost similar activity or pose of a human body over a continuous time span, correlation or weighted sum operation is most suitable for recognizing similar actions in videos due to the correlation existence in consecutive frames. The WS layer has two main tunable parameters, i.e. receptive field size and stride for handling the performance. We used three sets of $3D$ weight matrix in order to extract different types of features from the actual input. The set of weights remains the same whereas their size reduces throughout the network until $1D$ layer. In addition, maps decrease by two in each set as we go deeper in the network. At each layer, after passing the feature maps through activation function, the output maps are whitened in order to allow fast convergence by regulating their saturation. To capture global as well as local discriminative features among consecutive correlated feature maps, $L1WS$ is followed by a $3D$ temporal pooling layer ($L2P$) which not only reduces spatial resolution but also, due to $3D$ pooling associated with the temporal domain, but also leads to more discriminative feature maps.

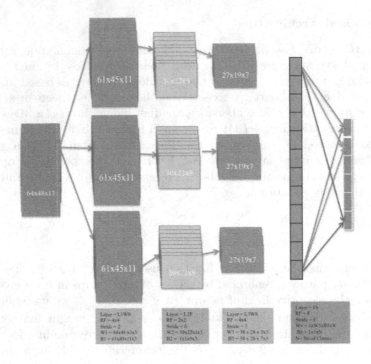

Fig. 1. Proposed model of 3DPyraNet

$$y_{u,v,z}^l = f_l(W_{u,v,z}^l \times \max_{(i,j,m)\in R_{u,v,z}} y_{i,j,m}^{l-1} + b_{u,v,z}^l) \tag{3}$$

The third layer is again a correlation layer ($L3WS$), whose output is converted to a $1D$ column feature vector that is used as a fully connected layer for classification. The overall $3DWS$ and pooling layers extract discriminative features by capturing the motion information encoded in multiple adjacent frames. Weight update is done using conventional back-propagation algorithm, where stochastic gradient descent approach is applied for weights update. We use a small learning value and reduce it by a factor of 10% after 10 epochs. Cross entropy error function is used to reduce the error. In the next section we will discuss our results achieved after experimenting on different state-of-the-art action recognition datasets.

3   Results and Discussion

The $3DPyraNet$ has been evaluated on Weizmann and KTH datasets. Weizmann is a good starting dataset for evaluating performance of a network. It is smaller in comparison to others in terms of action sequences. However, it provides ten types of quite similar human actions, i.e. walking, running, jumping, galloping sideways, bending, one-hand wave, two-hands wave, jump in place, jumping jack, and skip. Each action is done by nine actors in different scenarios that make it a complex task for recognition having only few short videos for each category which is not a good scenario rather challenging for DL models. KTH is another popular big and complex dataset that contains six actions done by 25 actors. It provides 2391 sequences in four different scenarios along with camera movement that results in different resolutions. We used a sequence of 13 consecutive frames of size 64×48 to represent an action for both datasets.

We carried out two types of experiments 1) to check the efficiency of proposed WS layers with simple activation functions and 2) later combining it with pooling and using advance rectification functions. Therefore, first we evaluated the effect of WS layer. We used a network with two WS layers and a fully connected layer to classify amongst ten classes. The output of each WS layer was passed through an activation function, i.e. sigmoid or tangent and then normalized throughout the network learning. Initial learning was not smooth and took around 450 epochs to converge. This provided an accuracy of 80% on the training set and 70% on the testing set.

As in most deep models, pooling plays an important role by providing translation invariance as well as reducing the dimensions. In addition, for faster convergence, avoidance of local minima, and improvement in performance; an extension of rectified linear unit known as leaky rectified linear units ($LReLu$) [22] is utilized. This $LReLu$ in contrast to $ReLu$ allows a small non-zero gradient when the neuron activity is less than or equal to zero. This property overcomes the limitation of $ReLU$ and updates the weights even if stuck within zeros. Therefore in our model, we adopt temporal ($3D$) pooling at ($L2P$) and $LReLu$ in combination to WS layers. This resulted in higher accuracy, i.e. 87% and 80.5% respectively for training and testing along with faster convergence i.e. within 200 epochs. Moreover, learning behaviour during training was quite smooth compared to the previous model. Furthermore, when we used voting scheme for classification of videos based on classified action sequences, the result increased by two to three percent.

We compared $3DPyraNet$ with deeper models having five to eight hidden layers. To better evaluate our model we reported the mean accuracy on 5 splits of training and testing datasets selected from same Weizmann database as adopted for evaluation of several models. Indeed, to cross validate the results, we randomized the data in same proportion keeping in mind that equal number of sequences should exist for the small number of sequences e.g. 'skip' or 'running'. So doing, no overtraining is observed. Obtained results, corresponding to 5 randomly selected training/test configurations are reported on Table 1. We achieve 90.9% accuracy considering all ten classes in the dataset as provided in Table 1 (a). However, videos containing action 'skip' were short, so letting an unbalanced dataset; this is why other approaches reported in literature did not use this category in their experiments. Our model was unable to learn and classify the 'skip' category according to our expectations, owing to lack of training data. Therefore, if we neglect the skip category, accuracy increases to 92.46% as shown in Table 1 (b.)In case of 'pjump', the same problem of having fewer training sequences arose, that

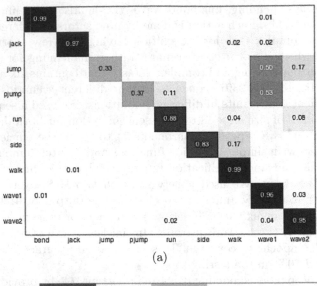

(a)

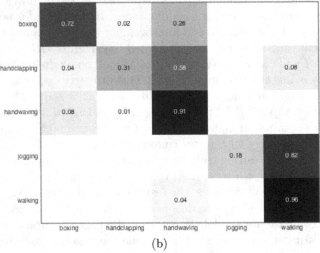

(b)

Fig. 2. Confusion matrices: (a) Weizmann without 'skip' (b) KTH without 'running'.

resulted in poor performance. However, for the rest of the categories, $3DPyraNet$ shows optimal results in both sequence and video classification shown on left of Figure 2. Results on Weizmann are comparable with the state-of-the-art model $3DCNN$, which is impressive considering fewer number of hidden layers and having no sophisticated pre-processing for extracting hard coded features.

The second dataset adopted in our experiments is KTH. The same criteria that took 9 out of 25 person's videos for testing, as stated in literature, was adopted. We randomly selected a total of 200 sequences from them of size

Table 1. (a) Mean accuracy of five random data setups, (b) Proposed Vs. Others for Weizmann and KTH datasets

(a)

SetUp	Accuracy(%)
1	90.5
2	92
3	90
4	90.5
5	91.3
Mean	90.9

(b)

Model(classes)	Weizmann (%)	KTH(%)	Layers
3DCNN	88.26[16]	90.2 [14]	6
3DPyraNet (all)	90.9	72	4
3DPyraNet (all-1)	92.46	74.23	4
ST-DBN	-	85.2	4
GRBM	-	90.0	-
Schuldt [6]	-	71.7	-
Dollar [23]	-	81.2	-
Alexandros [9](all)	90.32	-	-
Alexandros [9](all-1)	92.77	-	-

$13 \times 64 \times 48$. It should be noted that in our initial experiments we faced the same problem for 'running' class videos, i.e. having fewer frames than minimum requirement of 13 due to fast movement of the person or camera zooming scenarios. We achieved 72% accuracy over six classes. If we remove the 'running' class due to insufficient training data, the accuracy grows to 74.23% (see confusion matrix on right of Figure 2). Table 1 (b) shows the comparison of our proposed model with the state-of-the-art models reported in literature for Weizmann and KTH datasets. In case of Weizmann we overcome reported best result of 88.26% with an average of 91.07% from ten tests using the same dataset and number of consecutive input frames [16]. On the other hand for KTH dataset, $3DPyraNet$ did not show better result as provided by $3DCNN$ [14], but still it shows comparable results to some other complex models. One of the most plausible reason is that deep models need more data to have better understanding of their respective problems. $3DCNN$ [14] used ROI's sequences extracted and classified by another CNN based methodology. Unlike aforementioned, we used only silhoutte based recognition - extracted by the background subtraction model SOBS [24] in our case - and than extracted the ROI containing human. This may contain half, not centered or unaligned ROIs as input. This can greatly affect the learning process and may have high impact in reducing the classification rate compared with $3DCNN$. Despite current performance, there is room for further study. The future work can be done by using the full datasets of KTH, UT interaction dataset, UCF, TRECVID etc. to evaluate the performance of proposed network model with large number of training and testing data.

4   Conclusions

A strict pyramidal 3D neural network has been proposed that gets raw input frames from videos as input and is able to learn features in fewer layers due to its pyramid structure. It provided better results in case of Weizmann and comparable results with KTH datasets. We are verifying the generality of our model by testing it on recent larger and challenging datasets like UCF sports, Youtube action, and UT-Interaction datasets. This will help in proving benefits of using strictly pyramidal structure instead of non-pyramidal structure for learning a powerful model, since the model is aimed to obtain good performance despite the complexity and diversity of these datasets.

References

1. Schindler, K., Van Gool, L.: Action Snippets: How many frames does human action recognition require? In: 26th IEEE Conference on Computer Vision and Pattern Recognition, CVPR (2008)
2. Yang, X., Tian, Y.L.: Action Recognition using super sparse coding vector with spatio-temporal awareness. In: Fleet, D., Pajdla, T., Schiele, B., Tuytelaars, T. (eds.) ECCV 2014, Part II. LNCS, vol. 8690, pp. 727–741. Springer, Heidelberg (2014)
3. Liu, W., Wang, Z., Tao, D., Yu, J.: Hessian regularized sparse coding for human action recognition. In: He, X., Luo, S., Tao, D., Xu, C., Yang, J., Hasan, M.A. (eds.) MMM 2015, Part II. LNCS, vol. 8936, pp. 502–511. Springer, Heidelberg (2015)
4. Melfi, R., Kondra, S., Petrosino, A.: Human activity modeling by spatio temporal textural appearance. Pattern Recognition Letters 34(15), 1990–1994 (2013)
5. Efros, A.-A., Berg, A.C., Mori, G., Malik, J.: Recognizing action at a distance. In: Proceedings Ninth IEEE International Conference on Computer Vision, pp. 726–733. IEEE Computer Society (2003)
6. Schüldt, C., Laptev, I., Caputo, B.: Recognizing human actions: a local SVM approach. In: Proceedings - International Conference on Pattern Recognition, vol. 3, pp. 32–36 (2004)
7. Ballan, L., Bertini, M., Del Bimbo, A., Seidenari, L., Serra, G.: Effective codebooks for human action representation and classification in unconstrained videos. IEEE Transactions on Multimedia 14(4 PART 2), 1234–1245 (2012)
8. Wu, D., Shao, L.: Silhouette analysis-based action recognition via exploiting human poses. IEEE Transactions on Circuits and Systems for Video Technology 23(2), 236–243 (2013)
9. Chaaraoui, A.A., Climent-Prez, P., Flrez-Revuelta, F.: Silhouette-based human action recognition using sequences of key poses. Pattern Recognition Letters 34(15), 1799–1807 (2013). Smart Approaches for Human Action Recognition
10. Bengio, Y., Courville, A., Vincent, P.: Representation learning: A review and new perspectives. IEEE Trans. Pattern Anal. Mach. Intell. 35(8), 1798–1828 (2013)
11. Taylor, G.W., Fergus, R., LeCun, Y., Bregler, C.: Convolutional learning of spatio-temporal features. In: Daniilidis, K., Maragos, P., Paragios, N. (eds.) ECCV 2010, Part VI. LNCS, vol. 6316, pp. 140–153. Springer, Heidelberg (2010)
12. Freitas, N.D.: Deep learning of invariant spatio temporal features from video. In: Workshop on Deep Learning and Unsupervised Feature Learning in NIPS, pp. 1–9 (2010)
13. Le, Q.V., Zou, W.Y., Yeung, S.Y., Ng, A.Y.: Learning hierarchical invariant spatio-temporal features for action recognition with independent subspace analysis. In: Proceedings of the IEEE Computer Society Conference on Computer Vision and Pattern Recognition, pp. 3361–3368 (2011)

14. Ji, S., Yang, M., Yu, K.: 3D convolutional neural networks for human action recognition. IEEE transactions on pattern analysis and machine intelligence **35**(1), 221–31 (2013)
15. Krizhevsky, A., Sutskever, I., Hinton, G.E.: Imagenet classification with deep convolutional neural networks. In: Advances in Neural Information Processing Systems, pp. 1097–1105 (2012)
16. Baccouche, M., Mamalet, F., Wolf, C., Garcia, C., Baskurt, A.: Sequential deep learning for human action recognition. In: Salah, A.A., Lepri, B. (eds.) HBU 2011. LNCS, vol. 7065, pp. 29–39. Springer, Heidelberg (2011)
17. Ji, S., Xu, W., Yang, M., Yu, K.: 3d convolutional neural networks for human action recognition. IEEE Transactions on Pattern Analysis and Machine Intelligence **35**(1), 221–231 (2013)
18. Cantoni, V., Petrosino, A.: Neural recognition in a pyramidal structure. IEEE Transactions on Neural Networks **13**(2), 472–480 (2002)
19. Phung, S.L., Bouzerdoum, A.: A pyramidal neural network for visual pattern recognition. IEEE transactions on neural networks / a publication of the IEEE Neural Networks Council **18**(2), 329–343 (2007)
20. Fukushima, K.: Neocognitron: A hierarchical neural network capable of visual pattern recognition. Neural Networks **1**(2), 119–130 (1988)
21. Lecun, Y., Bottou, L., Bengio, Y., Haffner, P.: Gradient-based learning applied to document recognition. Proceedings of the IEEE **86**(11), 2278–2324 (1998)
22. Maas, A.L., Hannun, A.Y., Ng, A.Y.: Rectifier nonlinearities improve neural network acoustic models. In: Proc. ICML, vol. 30 (2013)
23. Dollár, P., Rabaud, V., Cottrell, G., Belongie, S.: Behavior recognition via sparse spatio-temporal features. In: Proceedings - 2nd Joint IEEE International Workshop on Visual Surveillance and Performance Evaluation of Tracking and Surveillance, VS-PETS 2005, pp. 65–72 (2005)
24. Maddalena, L., Petrosino, A.: The 3dsobs+ algorithm for moving object detection. Computer Vision and Image Understanding **122**, 65–73 (2014)

Nerve Localization by Machine Learning Framework with New Feature Selection Algorithm

Oussama Hadjerci[1]([⊠]), Adel Hafiane[1], Pascal Makris[2], Donatello Conte[2], Pierre Vieyres[3], and Alain Delbos[4]

[1] INSA CVL, Université d'Orléans, Laboratoire PRISME EA 4229, Bourges, France
oussama.hadjerci@etu.univ-orleans.fr, adel.hafiane@insa-cvl.fr
[2] Université de Francois Rabelais, Laboratoire LI EA 6300, Tours, France
{pascal.makris,donatello.conte}@univ-tours.fr
[3] Université d'Orléans, Laboratoire PRISME EA 4229, Bourges, France
[4] Clinique Medipôle Garonne, Toulouse, France

Abstract. The application of Ultrasound-Guided Regional Anesthesia (UGRA) is growing rapidly in medical field and becoming a standard procedure in many worldwide hospitals. UGRA practice requires a high training skill. Nerve detection is among the difficult tasks that anesthetists can meet in UGRA procedure. There is a need for automatic method to localize the nerve zone in ultrasound images, in order to assist anesthetists to better perform this procedure. On the other hand, the nerve detection in this type of images is a challenging task, since the noise and other artifacts corrupt visual properties of such tissue. In this paper, we propose a nerve localization framework with a new feature selection algorithm. The proposed method is based on several statistical approaches and learning models, taking advantage of each approach to increase performance. Results show that the proposed method can correctly and efficiently identify the nerve zone and outperforms the state-of-the-art techniques. It achieves 82% of accuracy (f-score index) on a first dataset (8 patients) and 61% on a second dataset (5 patients, acquired in different period of time and not used for training).

Keywords: Feature extraction · Feature selection · Supervised learning · Nerve detection · Regional anesthesia

1 Introduction

Ultrasound-Guided Regional Anesthesia (UGRA) is becoming a major technique in pain management [17]. The forearm nerve block is one of the most important blocks used in UGRA for emergent pain control and procedural anesthesia. This block targets median, radial, and ulnar nerves. Currently, the use of UGRA in clinical practice requires a high degree of training and practical skills to identify the forearm nerve block and steer the needle to it [17]. This can limit development

© Springer International Publishing Switzerland 2015
V. Murino and E. Puppo (Eds.): ICIAP 2015, Part I, LNCS 9279, pp. 246–256, 2015.
DOI: 10.1007/978-3-319-23231-7_23

and generalization of the UGRA practice. The failure to locate the nerve could lead to nerve trauma or local anesthetic toxicity [20].

The aim of this work is to provide anesthetists with a tool based on ultrasound (US) image processing to facilitate the UGRA procedure. Few accurate tool detection systems have been developed in this context. In [10], a method based on the combination of a monogenic signal and a probabilistic active contour have been proposed to detect the sciatic nerve. The technique proposed in [8] is based on the combination of Median Binary Pattern (MBP) [9] and a Gabor filter to characterize and classify pixels belonging to nerve tissues.

In this paper, we focus on the median nerve, which is visible at different positions in the forearm: elbow forearm, proximal and distal forearm, and wrist forearm [18]. Figure 1 shows different types of median nerve in ultrasound image within the region of interest (ROI) outlined by anesthetists. As the median nerve exhibits a particular texture attribute, feature extraction is a required step to enable the nerve zone identification in US images. Various feature extraction methods have been recently proposed [1,3,11,14,22]. In the context of US image, extracting these features and using them to directly train a classifier is very time-consuming and may decrease the accuracy. To reduce the computational complexity and improve the accuracy, it is necessary to eliminate the redundant features and keep significant ones.

Feature selection methods can be distinguished into three categories: filter, wrapper, and hybrid methods [2]. Wrapper methods perform better than filter methods because feature selection process is optimized for a specific classifier [13]. However, wrapper methods are very time consuming for large feature space because each feature set must evaluated, that ultimately make feature selection process slow. Filter methods have low computational cost and they are faster, but with less reliability in classification as compared to wrapper methods; they are also suitable for high dimensional data sets. Hybrid methods, recently developed, use advantages of both, filter and wrapper methods. A hybrid approach using both an independent test and a performance evaluation function of features subsets, is presented in [21]. There are many algorithms of feature selection and dimensionality reduction. While these algorithms have significantly improved performance, they are still limited by the noisy data and quality of feature extraction particularly in US image.

In this paper a new hybrid approach for feature selection is proposed to identify the median nerve zone. For that purpose, 37 textural features were extracted from each ROI. Our method is based on two main approaches: ranking technique and performance predictor to evaluate the feature subsets in terms of reducing irrelevant and redundant variables. After that, Support Vector Machine (SVM) was applied with the selected features to predict the best nerve position. As we deal with three types of median nerve (elbow, proximal and distal, wrist), three SVM models have been learned to handle such variability. This yields, three nerve positions, then, a voting strategy is applied to select the best representation.

The rest of this paper is organized as follows. Section 2 describes the overall system of nerve localization, which includes different steps from pre-processing

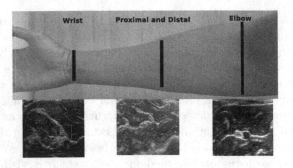

Fig. 1. Ultrasound images of the median nerve in elbow, proximal and distal, and wrist forearm.

to nerve localization. Section 3 presents experiments and results obtained from the proposed method and a comparison with other feature selection methods. Finally, conclusions are given in Section 4.

2   Nerve Detection System

In this section, we present the general framework of our system. Figure 2 shows the overall localization procedure, it consist in several image processing and machine learning techniques. First, we applied pre-processing methods to reduce the noise effect and enhance visual properties of tissues. After the pre-processing stage, feature extraction is performed to represent the texture characteristics of median nerve. In this stage 37 texture features have been obtained by several statistical measures. High number of features can inflict a heavy computational cost, and suffer from the curse of dimensionality. Furthermore, increasing the number of features may increase the risk of inclusion of irrelevant information. The aim of this stage is to select the best subset, with higher discriminative properties, from the original feature space. The optimal selected features subset, were used with SVM for learning and testing phases. Three learning SVM models were used, to handle the three median nerve positions (elbow, proximal/distal and wrist). Therefore, three candidate positions were generated. A majority vote was applied over the three candidates(ROIs), to select the best target representing the nerve.

2.1   Pre-processing

The pre-processing of US image was performed to reduce the ambiguity between the structure of nerve and epidermis. A despeckling filters was also used to reduce the degradation of the visual quality [16]. A morphological reconstruction is applied to extract the foreground region (hyperechoic tissues). Firstly, we subtract from the foreground the epidermis region, by using a skeletonization algorithm, and anatomical properties (thickness of skin (epidermis) [6]). Then

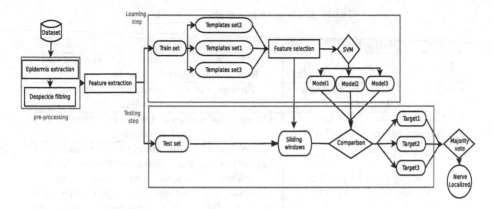

Fig. 2. Framework of median nerve localization

a despeckling filter was applied to denoise the signal of the foreground tissues. An extensive literature has recently emerged on removing the noise using different filters [12]. Most of despeckling filters are based on: linear and nonlinear filtering [16]. The linear ones showed the best result in classification and visual quality enhancement of US images [16]. In this work we adopt a linear filter that uses homogeneous mask area [19]. This filter uses two windows, the larger one is used to define the pixel neighborhood, and a moving smaller subwindow within the first main window is used to estimate the gray level homogeneity in each subwindow. The homogeneity is measured by $C = \sigma^2/\bar{M}$, where σ^2 and $\bar{M}$ are the variance and the local mean in the subwindow respectively. The center pixel value is replaced by the smallest value of C, found within the $N \times N$ search area around the center pixel. The pre-processing procedure reduce the noise and helps increasing the precision of nerve localization.

2.2   Feature Extraction

Texture information provides an important clue for nerve tissue characterization. For that purpose statistical methods were used, since they have proved to be robust in noisy data, particularly for classification of US images [16]. Hence, 37 textural features were extracted from each sliding window in US image. These features are presented in Table 1

2.3   Feature Selection

The time required for the classification increases with the number of features, and different redundant features can blur the best characterization of the nerve. Hence, this section introduces briefly some popular methods for feature selection (variable elimination), which helps to understand data, reducing computational requirements, reducing the effect of the curse of dimensionality and improving the prediction performance. Feature selection techniques can be categorized

Table 1. Feature extraction methods

Method	Extracted features
First Order Statistics (FOS)	Mean(m), median variance($\mu2$) skewness($\mu3$), kurtosis($\mu4$) and speckle index(μ/m).
Gray Level Difference Statistics (GLDS) [22]	Energy, entropy, contrast, mean and homogeneity.
Neighborhood Gray Tone Difference Matrix (NGTD) [1]	Coarseness, contrast, busyness, complexity and strength
Spatial Gray level Dependence Matrices (SGLDM) [11]	Angular second moment, contrast, correlation, sum of squares, variance, inverse difference moment, sum average, sum variance, sum entropy, entropy, difference variance, difference entropy and information measures of correlation
Statistical Feature Matrix (SFM) [3]	Coarseness, contrast, periodicity and roughness
Laws Texture Energy Measures (TEM) [14]	Average gray level (L), edges (E), spots (S), waves (W) and ripples (R).

into three classes [7]: filter based, wrapper based, and hybrid methods. Filters methods can be further separated into two groups, namely (1) feature weighting algorithms, (2) subset search algorithms. Feature weighting algorithms assign weights to features individually and rank them based on their relevance with respect to the application [23], the most used feature weighting algorithms are: mutual information, Relief, information gain, Chi-square score. Subset search algorithms use a search techniques to explore different possible feature subsets and then applies statistical measures to each subset to find their merit [15]. The most popular one and widely used subset search algorithms is the correlation feature selection algorithm. Table 2 shows equations for ranking features proposed by several algorithms. Here, we discuss the notation used in the table. Details can be found in specific literature. X and Y are two random variables and $p(\cdot)$ is the probability density function, $H(X|Y) = -\sum_j P(y_j) \sum_i P(x_i|y_i)log_2(P(x_i|y_j))$ is the the entropy of X after observing Y and $H(X) = -\sum_i P(x_i)log_2(P(x_i))$ is the entropy of X. n_{ij} is the number of samples with the ith feature value and $\mu_{i,j}$ is the mean, where $\mu_{i,j} = (n_{*j}n_{i*})/n$, n_{i*} is the number of samples with the ith value of the particular feature, n_{*j} is the number of samples in class j and n is the number of all samples. The CFS uses a correlation based heuristic (H_s) to evaluate the worth of features, H_s is the heuristic of feature subset s containing k features, $\bar{r}_{cf}$ is the mean feature class correlation, and $\bar{r}_{ff}$ is the average feature inter-correlation.

Table 2. Filter based Feature Selection methods.

Filter based feature Selection methods	Equation
Mutual information (MI)	$I(X,Y) = - \sum\limits_{x \in S_x} \sum\limits_{y \in S_y} p(x,y) \log p(x/y) \dots (2.3.1)$
ReliefF (RfF)	$\frac{1}{2} \sum\limits_{t=1}^{p} d(f_{t,i} - f_{NM(x_t),i}) - d(f_{t,i} - f_{NH(x_t),i}) \dots (2.3.2)$
Chi-square score (CS)	$\chi^2 = \sum_{i=1}^{r} \sum_{j=1}^{C} (n_{ij} - \mu_{ij})^2 / \mu_{ij} \dots (2.3.3)$
Information gain (IG)	$Ig(X,Y) = H(X) - H(X/Y)) \dots (2.3.4)$
Correlation feature selection (CFS)	$H_s = \frac{k \bar{r}_{cf}}{\sqrt{k + k(k-1)\bar{r}_{ff}}} \dots (2.3.5)$

2.4 Proposed Feature Selection Algorithm

Ultrasound images are collected and outlined by anesthetists. Features of nerve and other tissues are extracted for every location in the image inside the sliding window, with a step of 5 pixel to reduce the computational time. These feature vectors are separated into train set (TrainFSet) and test set (TestFSet). In the selection stage, only the TrainFSet are used. The TrainFSet is itself separated into two sets, 3% as the training data, and the remaining one for validation. As shown in the Algorithm 1, first the training data (R^{Train}, Y^{Train}) and validation data (R^{Val}, Y^{Val}) are extracted randomly (*line 6*).

The significance of feature for (R^{Train}, Y^{Train}) is evaluated by mutual information, Relief, information gain and Chi-square score (*lines 7-10*). The features are ranked individually in descending order. Then, we obtain four ranked lists: the mutual information ranking list MI^{List}, ReliefF ranking list RfF^{List}, information gain ranking list IG^{List}, and Chi-square ranking list CS^{List}. Then, the intersection between the features in the ordered lists are kept to form FS^{List} (*line 11*). The features intersection are those present in the same rank in the four lists. In the next stage, the CFS algorithm (see Section 2.3) uses the previous ranking process to select the most highly correlated features (*line 12*). The final ranking list is obtained by selecting features that are present in results of both weighted and correlated method. This optimal features set is used to train the SVM for classification of the validation data (R^{Val}, Y^{Val}), then the optimal features subset S is recorded, if the classification rate $fscore^t$ is higher than the $fscore^{t-1}$ obtained with the optimal features set in the previous iteration (*lines 13-15*). Then the step of the algorithm is repeated with a new random training set, the results of $(\bar{F}S^{list}, fscore^t)$ are recorded if they are better than the previous round. This procedure is repeated until the stopping criteria is true (*line 16*). In this paper the stopping criteria is true when the classification rate is stable $(fscore^t - fscore^{t-1} < \epsilon)$ or a maximum number of iterations is reached.

Algorithm 1. Random feature selection algorithm

Input: Data set of nerve ROIs and other tissues ROIs R
Label sets $Y = \{-1, +1\}$
Stopping criteria γ (Boolean Function)
Output: S_k
1 Initialization:
2 nbF; Number of subset
3 $Fscore = 0$; Classification rate
4 FS; Subset selected
5 **repeat**
6      $[(R^{Train}, Y^{Train}), (R^{Val}, Y^{Val})] = RandomSelected(R, Y)$;
7   MI^{List} Generate ranking list by Equation(2.3.1) with (R^{Train}, Y^{Train})
8   RfF^{List} Generate ranking list by Equation(2.3.2) with (R^{Train}, Y^{Train})
9   IG^{List} Generate ranking list by Equation(2.3.3) with (R^{Train}, Y^{Train})
10   CS^{List} Generate ranking list by Equation(2.3.4) with (R^{Train}, Y^{Train})
11     $FS^{List} = Intersection([MI, RfF, IG, CS]^{List})$;
12     $\bar{F}S^{List} = CFS(FS^{List})$; Generate ranking list by Equation(2.3.5)
13     $[Fscore] = Classification(\bar{F}S^{List}, (R^{Test}, Y^{Test}))$;
14   **if** $(Fscore^t > Fscore^{t-1})$ **then**
15         $S = FS^{list}$
16 **until** γ^t is true;
17 **return** S

2.5 Classification

The visual properties of nerve in US images are not necessarily consistent between different patients. Some changes in visual properties can occur. Furthermore, the position of the probe affects those properties. Several learning models are therefore required to handle such a situation. In the current work, three sets of US images were used as templates ($T1, T2, T3$) that represent different median nerves as shown in Figure 3. In the learning stage, we generated a model for each template using SVM algorithm, with a Gaussian kernel. To detect the nerve, SVM was applied in order to compare the sliding window at the position (i, j) in the input image (test) and the three templates. Then, we used the resulting SVM confidence measure with majority vote to determine the nerve position. To predict the nerve class, the distance between a sample X_p and the SVM hyperplane H_k was computed. The sample with the largest distance from the learned hyperplane is assigned with higher degree of confidence. Let be $P_{H_k} = argmax_{p=1..M} D(X_p, H_k)$, where D is the distance value assigned by the hyperplane H_k to the sample X_p, and P_{H_k} represent the largest distance. As we have three models of training, the result of the confidence measure technique yields three positions of the nerve region ($P_{H_1}, P_{H_2}, P_{H_3}$). Then, majority vote technique was applied to identify the most reliable region of the nerve between the three positions resulting from SVM. If the intersection of the three regions ($R_n = \cap_{k=1,2,3} Reg(P_{H_k})$) is at least 50 %, then the nerve is represented by this

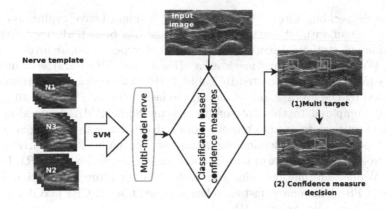

Fig. 3. Classification scheme.

intersection (R_n). Otherwise, the nerve zone is considered as the region with the highest confidence degree $P_{H_{max}} = max_{k=1,2,3}(P_{H_k})$, that is $R_n = Reg(P_{H_{max}})$.

3   Experiment Results

Sonographic video of the median nerve were obtained from 13 patients, in real conditions at the Medipôle Garonne hospital in Toulouse (France). This data are acquired in two different time periods. The first data (DS1) contains 8 patients and the second one (DS2) contain 5 patients. The probe was B-mode linear array with frequency range of 90-110 Hz for the first dataset (DS1). To evaluate the generalization of the proposed method, a second dataset (DS2) obtained from a different time period, with a frequency of 40-51 Hz, were also used for testing. To select the best frames set with different shape and texture for DS1 and DS2, 128 frames was extracted automatically by an algorithm based on the motion estimation [5]. A total of 1408 Ultrasound images of median nerve was used for the test, obtained from DS1 and DS2, and 384 ROIs obtained from DS1 was used for the training. Regional anesthesia experts validated the ground truth. The DS1 were separated into two randomly selected groups, we used one group for learning (three patients), and the remaining ones from DS1 for the tests (5 patients). DS2 were only used for testing (5 patients). For each couple of learning/testing set, the SVM algorithm has been applied to localize three ROIs per US image. For the performance measure of the proposed approach, we used the precision and recall indexes to calculate the f-score index [4]. A detected region is considered as a true positive if the intersection area of the two boxes (ground truth and detected region) divided by their union is greater than 50%. Otherwise, the detected region is considered as false positive. The false negative is incremented when it fails to give positive response, while the ground truth annotation states that there is a region of nerve. In the preprocessing stage the despeckling filter is used; therefore, a quantitative evaluation of the proposed system without feature selection stage has been performed. We have tested different statistical features with different types of linear filters: Wiener filtering (WF), homogeneous mask area (HMA) and Mean and variance local statistics (MVLS). As illustrated in Table 3, the classification performance are represented by the average and standard deviation (i.e. $\mu \pm \sigma$) over all f-scores obtained. Compared to the state-of-the art methods, HMA despeckling filter yields the best performance to remove noise. To evaluate the testing accuracies of the proposed feature selection algorithm, we compared it with other widely used approaches: t-test, sparse multinomial logistic regression (SMLR), ReliefF, Kruskal Wallis, information gain, gain index, Fisher score, correlation feature selection (CFS), Chi-square, fast correlation based filter (FCBF), Wilcoxon test, Principal Component Analysis (PCA).

Table 3. Classification results of different linear despeckling filters.

Despeckling filter\Statistical feature	WF	HMA	MVLS
FOS	0.43 ± 0.01	0.40 ± 0.008	$\mathbf{0.52 \pm 0.04}$
GLDS	0.25 ± 0.003	$\mathbf{0.39 \pm 0.02}$	0.33 ± 0.009
NGTDM	0.41 ± 0.008	$\mathbf{0.47 \pm 0.005}$	0.45 ± 0.006
SGLDM	0.59 ± 0.09	$\mathbf{0.61 \pm 0.03}$	0.48 ± 0.02
SFM	0.23 ± 0.07	$\mathbf{0.34 \pm 0.005}$	0.29 ± 0.01
TEM	0.53 ± 0.009	$\mathbf{0.42 \pm 0.08}$	0.39 ± 0.03

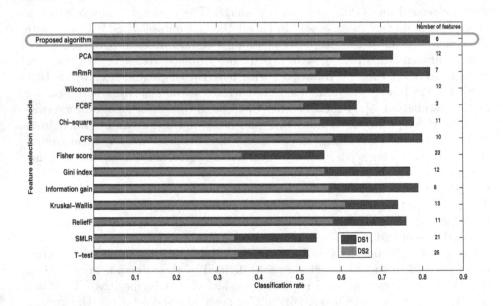

Fig. 4. Comparison of feature selection methods and the proposed algorithm

A comparison with other methods shows that the proposed method uses an equal or lower number of features to classify the median nerve with an equal or higher accuracy (see Figure 4). The highest accuracy on each dataset (DS1 and DS2) is respectively 82% and 62% and it was achieved by the proposed feature selection algorithm. The selected features in the proposed algorithm are: homogeneity, entropy, and energy derived from GLDM, strength and busyness derived from GTDM and finally the dissimilarity extracted from the SFM. The three selected statistical features can well reflect explicitly as a significant feature for classifying median nerve region and can effectively differentiate between median nerve and other tissues. Feature selection techniques show that using all information is not always good in machine learning applications. A feature selection algorithm can be chosen based on the following considerations: simplicity, stability, number of reduced features, classification accuracy, storage and computational requirements. Overall applying feature selection usually brings benefits such as providing insight into the data, better classifier model, enhance generalization and identification of irrelevant variables.

4   Conclusion

We have presented a framework based on machine learning with new feature selection algorithm to locate the nerve region for regional anesthesia application. Several texture features were extracted from ROIs, then feature selection method was used to obtain most discriminative feature set for different types of median nerve. The proposed algorithm is based on merging several feature selection approaches to improve performance. Experiments were performed in each stage of the framework, in order to evaluate the best representation of the nerve structure in ultrasound images. The proposed method can successfully identify the median nerve. These results are very helpful for the interpretation of median nerve in ultrasound images and it can increase the performance of UGRA.

Acknowledgments. This work is part of DANIEAL project supported by Region Centre-Val de Loire (France) grant 13067HPR-2013. We gratefully acknowledge Region Centre-Val de Loire for its support.1

References

1. Amadasun, M., King, R.: Textural features corresponding to textural properties. IEEE Transactions on Systems, Man and Cybernetics **19**, 1264–1274 (1989)
2. Chandrashekar, G., Sahin, F.: A survey on feature selection methods. Computer and Electrical Engineering **40**, 16–28 (2014)
3. Chung-Ming, W., Yung-Chang, C.: Statistical feature matrix for texture analysis. Graphical Models and Image **54**, 407–419 (1992)
4. Everingham, M., Van Gool, L., Williams, C.K.I., Winn, J., Zis-serman, A.: The pascal visual object classes (voc) challenge. In: IJCV, vol. II, pp. 803–806. IEEE (2010)
5. Farnebäck, G.: Two-frame motion estimation based on polynomial expansion. In: Bigun, J., Gustavsson, T. (eds.) SCIA 2003. LNCS, vol. 2749, pp. 363–370. Springer, Heidelberg (2003)

6. Frenkel, O., Mansour, K., Fischer, J.W.: Ultrasound-guided femoral nerve block for pain control in an infant with a femur fracture due to nonaccidentaltrauma. Pediatric emergency care **28**, 183–184 (2012)

7. Guyon, I.: An introduction to variable and feature selection. Journal of Machine Learning Research **3**, 1157–1182 (2003)

8. Hadjerci, O., Hafiane, A., Makris, P., Conte, D., Vieyres, P., Delbos, A.: Nerve detection in ultrasound images using median gabor binary pattern. In: Campilho, A., Kamel, M. (eds.) ICIAR 2014, Part II. LNCS, vol. 8815, pp. 132–140. Springer, Heidelberg (2014)

9. Hafiane, A., Seetharaman, G., Palaniappan, K., Zavidovique, B.: Rotationally invariant hashing of median binary patterns for texture classification. In: Campilho, A., Kamel, M.S. (eds.) ICIAR 2008. LNCS, vol. 5112, pp. 619–629. Springer, Heidelberg (2008)

10. Hafiane, A., Vieyres, P., Delbos, A.: Phase-based probabilistic active contour for nerve detection in ultrasound images for regional anesthesia. Computers in Biology and Medicine **52**, 88–95 (2014)

11. Haralick, R.M., Shanmugam, K., Dinstein, I.H.: Textural features for image classification. IEEE Transactions on Systems, Man and Cybernetics, SMC **3**(6), 610–621 (1973)

12. Joel, T., Sivakumar, R.: Despeckling of ultrasound medical images: A survey despeckling of ultrasound medical images: A survey despeckling of ultrasound medical images: A survey. Journal of image and graphic **1**(3), 161–165 (2013)

13. Kohavi, R., John, G.: Wrappers for feature selection. Artificial Intelligence **97**(1–2), 273–324 (1997)

14. Stockman, G.C., Shapiro, L.G.: Computer Vision. Prentice-Hall (2001)

15. Ladha, L., Deepa, T.: Feature selection methods and algorithms. International Journal on Computer Science and Engineering(IJCSE) **3**(5), 1787–1797 (2011)

16. Loizou, C.P., Pattichis, C.S., Christodoulou, C.I., Istepanian, R.S.H., Pantziaris, M., Nicolaides, A.: Comparative evaluation of despeckle filtering in ultrasound imaging of the carotid artery. IEEE Trans Ultrason **52**, 1653–1669 (2005)

17. Marhofer, P., Chan, V.W.S.: Ultrasound-guided regional anesthesia: current concepts and future trends. Anesth. Analg. **104**, 1265–1269 (2007)

18. McCartney, C.J.L., Xu, D., Abbas, S., Constantinescu, C., Chan, V.W.S.: Ultrasound examination of peripheral nerves in the forearm. Regional Anesthesia and Pain Medicine **32**, 434–439 (2007)

19. Nagao, M., Matsuyama, T.: Edge preserving smoothing. Comput. Graph. Image Processing **9**, 394–407 (1979)

20. Tsui, B.C., Suresh, S.: Ultrasound imaging for regional anesthesia in infants, children, and adolescents. A Review of Current Literature and Its Application in the Practice of Extremity and Trunk Blocks. Anesthesiology **112**, 473–492 (2010)

21. Veerabhadrappa, Rangarajan, L.: Bi-level dimensionality reduction methods using feature selection and feature extraction. International Journal of Computer Applications **4**, 33–38 (2010)

22. Weszka, J.C., Dyer, C.R., Rosenfield, A.: A comparative study of texture measures for terrain classification. IEEE Transactions on Systems, Man and Cybernetics **SMC–6**, 269–285 (1976)

23. Yu, L., Liu, H.: Feature selection for high-dimensional data: A fast correlation-based filter solution, pp. 856–863 (2003)

Human Tracking Using a Top-Down
and Knowledge Based Approach

Benoit Gaüzère[1]([✉]), Pierluigi Ritrovato[2], Alessia Saggese[2], and Mario Vento[2]

[1] Department of Information Engineering, Electrical Engineering and Applied
Mathematics, Via Giovanni Paolo II, 132, 84084 Fisciano, SA, Italy
benoit.gauzere@gmail.com
[2] ENSICAEN - GREYC CNRS UMR 6072, Caen, France

Abstract. In this paper, we propose a new top-down and knowledge-based approach to perform human tracking in video sequences. First, introduction of knowledge allows to anticipate most of common problems encountered by tracking methods. Second, we define a top-down approach rather than a classical bottom-up approach to encode the knowledge. The more global point of view of the scene provided by our top-down approach also allows to keep some consistency among the set of trajectories extracted from the video sequence. A preliminary experimentation has been conducted over some challenging sequences of the PETS 2009 dataset. The obtained results confirm that our approach can still achieve promising performance even with a consistent reduction in the amount of information taken into account during the tracking process. In order to show the relevance of considering knowledge to address tracking problem, we strongly reduce the amount of information provided to our approach.

Keywords: Tracking · Video surveillance · Knowledge-based approach · Expert-systems

1 Introduction

Given a video sequence, tracking problem consists in identifying the set of trajectories associated to each object present in the scene. In order to perform this task, different approaches have been proposed. A first family of methods [1,11] aims to detect objects in the scene by identifying models associated to the objects to track. The efficiency of this kind of approach depends directly on the definition of the model and its robustness to noisy situations. However, methods using this approach generally suffer from a high computational time. Another important family of tracking methods [5,8] consists in tracking objects according to a first detection step, which computes a low level abstraction of the scene. This data is then used as input data by the tracking algorithm. Most of approaches are based on a single view of the scene. In order to get a more reliable information, the information coming from multiple cameras could be combined.

The low level detection phase consists in identifying pixels composing the objects to track in the video sequence. This identification is generally made by

V. Murino and E. Puppo (Eds.): ICIAP 2015, Part I, LNCS 9279, pp. 257–267, 2015.
DOI: 10.1007/978-3-319-23231-7_24

computing the difference between the pixels of a given frame and a background model updated according to the previous acquired frames. Given the mask associated to these foreground pixels, the low level detection step consists then in identifying blobs, each blob being defined as a set of connected foreground pixels in a single frame of the sequence. The set of blobs associated to each frame corresponds to a low level abstraction of the sequence and this information is generally used as input data by tracking algorithms.

Since detection phase is computed on an imperfect video acquisition, it may suffer from some problems [12] and produce an incorrect set of blobs. First, false positive blob detection is generally due to two different causes : spurious blobs (Figure 1) are caused by foreground elements moving and ghost blobs (blob 162 in Figure 2(b)) are due to some latency when updating the background model. Second, some blobs can be missed or discarded by some heuristics defined and hard-coded within the low-level algorithm (Figure 2(a)). These errors alter the information provided to the algorithms. Moreover, avoiding such errors and considering a perfect low level detection step is impossible. Therefore, these different problems may be considered as inherent to tracking algorithms and must be taken into account by tracking algorithms to improve their robustness.

Some others issues are directly dependent on the approach used by tracking algorithms and can occur even using a hypothetical perfect detection step. On the one hand, the so-called split problem happens when a single person or object to track is split into multiple distinct blobs. This phenomenon can occur for

Fig. 1. Spurious blobs: many blobs correspond to parts of the ribbon which are moving due to the wind.

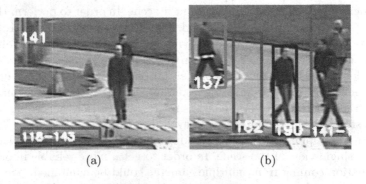

(a)   (b)

Fig. 2. Ghost and missing blobs

example when a person enters the scene or passes behind a foreground element (Figure 3(c)). Considering such cases, tracking algorithms must be able to merge the set of blobs and consider this set as a single object to track, instead of associating each blob to distinct objects, and thus distinct tracks.

On the other hand, an opposite problem of the first one, called merge problem, occurs when a single blob corresponds to a group composed of more than one single object to track. In order to keep tracks of each object in a same group, tracking algorithms must be able to identify this blob as a composition of different persons. In existing tracking algorithms, it may happen that too many (Figure 4(a)) or not enough (Figure 4(b) and 4(c)) people are associated to a same group.

In order to handle such issues, many methods [6–8,13] propose to use some heuristics. For instance, [9] uses an automaton which allows to handle some situations where problems occur. This automaton is designed to manage the uncertainty of the detection phase and to handle occlusions anywhere in the scene. However, despite the good results obtained by this approach, the extension of this automaton to resolve other problems may be a very hard task since it requires an expert to redefine the automaton and update the set of states together with their relationships. This may lead to a quite complex automaton.

In order to overcome such limitations, we propose in this paper a knowledge-based approach following a top-down model to deal with these problems in a more general way. Indeed, using such an approach instead of a hard-coded model, our knowledge approach may handle dynamically different situations occurring in the scene by taking advantage on the introduction of an expert system. Furthermore, conversely to complex expert systems, the definition of the knowledge does not require an expert. This is a very important and not negligible feature, since it allow the proposed approach to be used in real applications where unexperienced human operators can configure them.

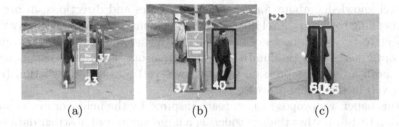

(a)   (b)   (c)

Fig. 3. Occlusions problems

2 Top-Down Approach

Approaches presented in last section follow a bottom-up approach by first identifying low level features and combining them in order to obtain a higher level

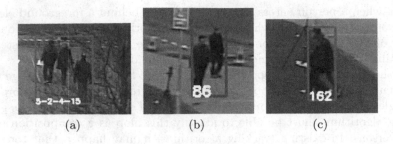

(a)   (b)   (c)

Fig. 4. Group problems

corresponding to objects to track. This bottom-up scheme is again reproduced to identify tracks from the set of objects identified in the lower level. Using such an approach, parts of each level are associated according to some heuristics defined on the data available within frames such as the position, the shape, the density of foreground pixels within blobs bounding boxes or pixel's colors.

However, existing bottom-up approaches do not include an explicit and global idea of what must be identified in the sequence, such as humans walking in the scene. Moreover, adding such knowledge into a bottom-up approach may be quite complicate since each low level part extracted from detection step can only encode a local information. This lack of information may lead to tracking errors generally encountered in classic algorithms using a bottom-up approach. For instance, those errors related to the number of people in a group, or in a more global way in the whole scene, may be avoided by considering that a human can only appear in the scene in some limited areas and can not appear suddenly in the middle of the scene. In the same way, split problems may be anticipated by knowing that blobs are included or not within an area subject to this phenomenon.

In addition, several studies [3,14] claim that human visual perception uses high level knowledge about forms, structure, colors and directions, in order to give a meaning to the low level information. Following Zhaoping [14], early vision is subject to two bottlenecks of the visual pathway: the transmission capacity of the optic nerve and the limited human attention. These two particularities impose both a data compression (at the low level) and a data deletion (at an upper level) in the visual process.

In this paper, we propose an approach inspired by the behavior of the human brain [3,4,10,14]. Rather than considering a large amount of abstract data corresponding to a sequence of pixels, we propose to limit the input data to bounding boxes of blobs identified during the detection phase. Therefore, by using such a limited information, we discard the information concerning shapes and colors of blobs. Moreover, we also restrict the input data to 1 frame per second, instead of the frame rate of 7 frames per second available in PETS 2009 dataset. By imposing this constraint, we also reduce the temporal continuity between two frames. Nonetheless, we claim that the combination of a low amount of data, which is more efficient to process, and some knowledge about (i) the task to be performed and (ii) its environment rather than a high amount of pixels may be sufficient to track trajectories of humans in a scene.

The knowledge associated to the input data may be included into our proposition using a top-down approach. Adding knowledge may allow to keep the scene consistent according to a set of constraints related to the tracking task. For instance, using a global point of view of the scene, we can encode as a knowledge piece that the number of humans in the scene is consistent according to identified exits and entries of the persons during the video sequence. Such a constraint can be satisfied using a high level model of the scene.

3   Knowledge Related to Tracking

Before defining precisely our top down approach, we briefly introduce some knowledge which can be can be profitably used to resolve tracking problems.

3.1   Scene Knowledge

First, some knowledge about the environment of the scene can be useful to understand and anticipate the behavior of human beings within a scene. This knowledge must describe the configuration of the scene in order to get a better interpretation of blobs detected during a video sequence. For example, if we consider a static point of view, the knowledge related to the scene must describe the different areas of the scene and associate them with their characteristics. For instance, one of the main information corresponds to the distance of each area from the camera. By encoding such information into our knowledge base, each blob can then be associated to the real size of the represented object. This can then be used to distinguish small objects, that we don't want to track, from objects having the size of a human or another object to track. Note that the real size of the objects can be easily extracted by using any inverse perspective mapping algorithm.

Second, it may be useful to encode special areas in the scene where unusual events may occur. In our knowledge base, we introduce two kinds of areas. First, we identify areas of the scene where people can enter into or exit from the scene. These areas correspond to borders of the frame where a path exists, doors and borders of buildings. Second, we also identify areas where people passes behind background elements. Such areas may induce split problems during the detection phase. Identifying this kind of areas allow to anticipate split problems and to consider a set of blobs in this area as a single object to track. Note that, as previously mentioned, this knowledge can be easily managed by unexperienced human operator, so making this system especially suited for working in real applications.

3.2   Human Trajectories Knowledge

The second kind of knowledge introduced into our approach corresponds to knowledge related to human behavior. Indeed, since we aim to track human trajectories in a scene, we can make some assumptions about their particularities. These assumptions correspond then to pieces of knowledge to be included into our model.

Trajectories are defined as a set of successive positions in space along time. Due to the limited moving speed of human beings, each two successive positions must be close enough according to the gap of time between them, i.e. the distance traversed by an human walking cannot exceed an upper bound according to an *a priori* walking or running maximum speed. These constraints must take into account some knowledge related to the context of the video sequence such as frame rate and real size of computed blobs.

Another particularity of human trajectories is that they can not appear or disappear suddenly and anywhere, but only in some areas identified as entry or exit areas, as discussed in the previous section. Given these assumptions, we can encode them into our model by respectively restricting begins and ends of tracks to entry and exit areas. Another important particularity of human trajectories is that they can merge to form a group. From this observation, we can induce different scenarios. First, if a human has entered into a group, either this human will leave this group in next frames or the group gets out the scene and so the trajectory. These observations can be easily extended to cases where a group already formed enters the scene. Given this simple description of an human trajectory, we can infer others assumptions which directly come from the first ones. For instance, we know that a same trajectory can not pass by the same human in a given frame. Such assumptions rely to keep a consistent number of humans populating a scene at a given frame according to number of humans and the number of entries and exits within previous frames.

3.3   From Knowledge to Model

Given the different pieces of high level knowledge discussed in the two previous sections, we now define a model both encoding and implementing this knowledge. This model is defined as a rule-based expert system where the set of rules encodes the knowledge defined in the previous section. This set of rules ensures that each set of trajectories extracted from the scene respects the set of assumptions defined in previous sections.

Our top-down model, shown in Figure 5, is designed as follows: a first high-level layer ensures that the set of tracks are compatible with each other: following assumptions stated in Section 3.2, it is impossible that two trajectories pass by a same human in a given frame. Therefore, we consider that two tracks are compatible and may belong to a same set of tracks if they do not share a same human blob in a given frame. The second layer, at the track level, ensures that each track taken separately is valid, i.e. each track starts in an entry area and finishes in an exit area. Note that we consider exceptions for the first and last frames of a sequence. Then, each track is composed by a succession of alternate sub-tracks corresponding either to a group or a human track. The connection between these sub-tracks is handled by two events, namely the entry and exit events. Going down into our model, we define a sub-track as a set of successive blobs, each pair of successive blobs corresponding to two blobs in two successive frames such as the distance in spatial space between the first and the second one is small enough to correspond to a walk of a human. Distinction between human and group sub-tracks is done using the real size of blobs, computed according to the knowledge related to the scene (Section 3.1). Finally, the lowest layer corresponds to a generalization of blobs. This generalization consists in considering the possibility that a set of initials blobs, i.e. blobs detected by detection algorithm (Section 1), can be considered as a same and unique blob. In order to handle split problems, we restrict this generalization of blobs to the set of blobs which are in the scene areas identified as occlusion areas, i.e. areas including a foreground element which may induce split problems. By doing so, we use the scene knowledge to anticipate occlusions and resolve the main cause of split problems.

Therefore, in order to implement our knowledge into a set of rules, we defined a top-down approach to identify tracks within a video sequence. By considering a first high level layer, we can ensure that all the identified tracks are coherent,

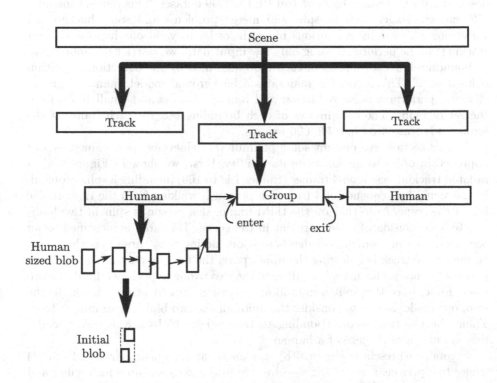

Fig. 5. Modelization of a scene to identify trajectories

thus avoiding wrong predictions about the number of humans identified in the scene or more particularly the number of persons in a given group. In addition, this assumption of the coherence of the scene can also be used to re-interpret the low-level truth. For instance, it may happen that a blob has an incorrect size due to camouflage or other problems during detection phase. By considering a global scene point of view, we can state that the first interpretation of the blob is not coherent with the set of identified tracks. Therefore, this interpretation must be modified to fulfill the defined rules. Second, the knowledge introduced into our model allows to resolve split problems by *a priori* identifying some areas of the scene where this phenomenon generally occurs. Note that the definition of knowledge requires a configuration step which must be done accordingly to each scene. However, such configuration does not require an expert but can be performed by any human operator since the encoded knowledge remains very simple. In addition, the model itself is generic enough to be adapted to any human trajectories tracking task.

4   Preliminary Results and Discussions

The model described in Section 3 has been implemented into a prototype using PROLOG. In order to test the feasibility, possibilities and capabilities of our top-down approach, we use the view 1 of PETS 2009 dataset. This dataset includes different challenges such as split and merge problems and some background variations which induces spurious blobs. In order to valid our hypothesis that tracking can be performed using only few input data, we restrict our input data to bounding box coordinates of each blob identified by the detection algorithm defined in [2]. This algorithm maintains a background model, manage lighting changes, perform a noise reduction and remove shadow and small blobs from the set of blobs. The coordinates of each bounding box for each frame of the sequence is translated into PROLOG axioms.

In this section, we present some preliminary achievements obtained by our approach in order to demonstrate its validity. First, we show in Figure 6(a), a isolated tracking result on 4 frames (frames 148 to 169) including a split problem. In this compiled sequence of 4 frames, a person is walking from the right to the left of the scene. Note that on the third frame, this person is split in two blobs due to an occlusion of a sign present in the scene. This area is identified as an occlusion area into our knowledge base. Considering this, three hypothesis can be made: the track is following the upper part, the bottom part or the two split parts of the body. Our model can discard the two wrong hypothesis thanks to two rules. First, since this split occurs in an occlusion area identified thanks to the sign, our model is able to consider the union of the two blobs as an unique blob. Then, the two tracks corresponding to two merged blobs are discard because they do not have the size of a human.

Second, we present in Figure 6(b) another isolated sequence (frames 15 to 64) where two persons are walking side by side into a same group which splits and then merges again. The two persons are followed by a third one. Four different

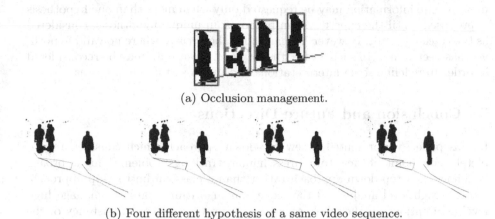

(a) Occlusion management.

(b) Four different hypothesis of a same video sequence.

Fig. 6. Tracking results obtained on challenging situations.

hypothesis have been produced by our prototype on this sequence. Two choices induce these four hypothesis. First, the two persons composing the group in the sequence do not enter the scene together, but one by one. This fact induces a first possibility when the group is splitting: either the person which has been entered first goes on top of the second person (the blue track is on top of the green one) or the first person goes above the second one (the green track is on top of the blue one). The second choice is again induced by the two persons which compose the group. Once they split, they walk side by side for two frames. Considering input data and our knowledge, it's possible that they crossed between the two frames. Hence, two hypothesis are plausible: either they crossed each other or they stayed side by side. The combination of these two hypothesis induces then four different ones. Note also that despite the fact that we have identified three tracks corresponding to the three humans in this scene, two of these tracks share a same part corresponding to a group track. In order to distinguish which of these hypothesis is the right one, we have to consider further information such as the color.

The limited input data provided to our algorithm leads to numerous hypothesis. The number of hypothesis exponentially increases as we process successive frames, causing thus a high computational time after few processed frames. In order to exclude invalid hypothesis, our approach must include further data to discriminate some hypothesis and producing an unique set of tracks. For instance, including the color into our approach may allow to discard wrong hypothesis made during the analysis of our second sequence. However, such information may be useless for simpler cases as the one described in the first sequence. Therefore, considering an adaptive level of information by an hybrid approach may be a good approach to tackle this issue. Considering an incremental processing of the sequence, i.e. frame by frame like in real case scenarios, more precise information may be requested only when more than one hypothesis is proposed, until the expert system proposes an unique hypothesis, considered as the tracking result. However, we can think about cases where no valid hypothesis has been found. In such a case, the low level input data may be reconsidered in order to redefine some interpretations and find a suitable hypothesis.

5   Conclusion and Future Directions

In this paper, we presented a new top-down approach which consider a completely new point of view to address human tracking problem. This approach is defined as a top-down approach rather than a classical bottom-up approach. Using a high level analysis of the scene, our algorithm is able to manage high level assumptions on the whole scene, hence providing some consistency of the set of identified tracks. This set of assumptions is encoded as a set of knowledge introduced into our model as PROLOG rules. In order to show the importance of knowledge, we drastically reduced the input data by reducing the frame rate and discarding the shape and color information generally taken into account by the state of the art approaches. Our claim is that the combination of a very reduced information and knowledge is sufficient to track human trajectories. Indeed, the encoded knowledge and the high level point of view of our approach allow to handle the issues generally encountered by the classical bottom-up approaches.

Despite the lack of formatted and comparable results, we shown that our prototype of an rule-based expert system is able to process complex sequences involving well known split and merge problems. Furthermore, we insist that these results have been obtained only using very few information. Further works will be devoted to the implementation of a completely functional prototype using an hybrid approach and able to process a sequence in real time.

Acknowledgement. This research has been partially supported by POR Campania FSE 2007/2013, *Bando Sviluppo di Reti di eccellenza* within the project Embedded Systems in Critical Domains.

References

1. Comaniciu, D., Ramesh, V., Meer, P.: Real-time tracking of non-rigid objects using mean shift. In: Proceedings of the IEEE Conference on Computer Vision and Pattern Recognition, vol. 2, pp. 142–149. IEEE (2000)
2. Conte, D., Foggia, P., Percannella, G., Tufano, F., Vento, M.: An experimental evaluation of foreground detection algorithms in real scenes. EURASIP Journal on Advances in Signal Processing **2010**, 7 (2010)
3. DiCarlo, P., Zoccolan, D., Rust, N.: How does the brain solve visual object recognition?. Neuron **73**(3), 415–434 (2012); cited By 120
4. Felleman, D.J., Van Essen, D.C.: Distributed hierarchical processing in the primate cerebral cortex. Cerebral Cortex **1**(1), 1–47 (1991)

5. Foggia, P., Percannella, G., Saggese, A., Vento, M.: Real-time tracking of single people and groups simultaneously by contextual graph-based reasoning dealing complex occlusions. In: 2013 IEEE International Workshop on Performance Evaluation of Tracking and Surveillance (PETS), pp. 29–36. IEEE (2013)
6. Gomez-Romero, J., Patricio, M.A., Garcia, J., Molina, J.M.: Context-Based reasoning using ontologies to adapt visual tracking in surveillance. In: 2009 Sixth IEEE International Conference on Advanced Video and Signal Based Surveillance, pp. 226–231. IEEE (September 2009)
7. Gómez-Romero, J., Patricio, M.A., Garcia, J., Molina, J.M.: Ontology-based context representation and reasoning for object tracking and scene interpretation in video. Expert Systems with Applications 38, 7494–7510 (2011)
8. Haritaoglu, I., Harwood, D., Davis, L.S.: W 4: Real-time surveillance of people and their activities. IEEE Transactions on Pattern Analysis and Machine Intelligence 22(8), 809–830 (2000)
9. Di Lascio, R., Foggia, P., Percannella, G., Saggese, A., Vento, M.: A real time algorithm for people tracking using contextual reasoning. Computer Vision and Image Understanding 117(8), 892–908 (2013)
10. Maus, G.W., Ward, J., Nijhawan, R., Whitney, D.: The perceived position of moving objects: Transcranial magnetic stimulation of area mt+ reduces the flash-lag effect. Cerebral Cortex 23(1), 241–247 (2013)
11. Tao, H., Sawhney, H.S., Kumar, R.: Object tracking with bayesian estimation of dynamic layer representations. IEEE Transactions on Pattern Analysis and Machine Intelligence 24(1), 75–89 (2002)
12. Toyama, K., Krumm, J., Brumitt, B., Meyers, B.: Wallflower: principles and practice of background maintenance. In: The Proceedings of the Seventh IEEE International Conference on Computer Vision, vol. 1, pp. 255–261. IEEE (1999)
13. Yang, J., Vela, P.A., Shi, Z., Teizer, J.: Probabilistic multiple people tracking through complex situations. In: 11th IEEE International Workshop on Performance Evaluation of Tracking and Surveillance (2009)
14. Zhaoping, L.: Theoretical understanding of the early visual processes by data compression and data selection. Network: Computation in Neural Systems (Bristol, England) 17(4), 301–334 (2006)

Shape Analysis and 3D Computer Vision

Fuzzy "Along" Spatial Relation in 3D. Application to Anatomical Structures in Maxillofacial CBCT

Timothée Evain[1,2]($\boxtimes$), Xavier Ripoche[2], Jamal Atif[3], and Isabelle Bloch[1]

[1] Institut Mines Télécom, Télécom ParisTech, CNRS LTCI, Paris, France
tevain@telecom-paristech.fr
[2] Carestream Dental, Croissy-Beaubourg, France
[3] PSL, LAMSADE CNRS UMR 7243, Université Paris-Dauphine, Paris, France

Abstract. Spatial relations have proved to be of great importance in computer vision and image understanding. One issue is their modeling in the image domain, hence allowing for their integration in segmentation and recognition algorithms. In this paper, we focus on the "along" spatial relation. Based on a previous work in 2D, we propose extensions to 3D. Starting from the inter-objects region, we demonstrate that the elongation of the interface between the objects and this region gives a good evaluation of the alongness degree. We also integrate distance information to take into account only close objects parts. Then we describe how to define the alongness relation within the fuzzy set theory. Our method gives a quantitative satisfaction degree of the relation, reliable for differentiating spatial situations. An original example on the maxillofacial area in Cone-Beam Computed Tomography (CBCT) illustrates how the proposed approach could be used to recognize elongated structures.

Keywords: Spatial relations · Fuzzy reasoning · Dental imaging

1 Introduction

Spatial relations have proved to be of great importance in numerous fields such as psychology, cartography, linguistics, and computer science [4,8,9]. They are a major concept in human reasoning for object perception, recognition, or mutual comprehension [1]. In computer vision and image understanding, spatial relations carry reliable information [6,11,15]. Many relations have been investigated in the literature [2], and several applications have been proposed, for example in brain segmentation [5]. However, while extension to 3D of simple relations is straightforward, there is still work to do for complex relations.

The alongness relation is one of these complex relations, yet important. For example, in dental practice, "along" is usually used to describe the position of the mandibular canal with respect to the mandible. Since this canal contains the very sensitive mental nerve, to avoid severe patient injury during surgery, such as dysesthetia or neuropathic pain, dental surgeons have to identify its position.

© Springer International Publishing Switzerland 2015
V. Murino and E. Puppo (Eds.): ICIAP 2015, Part I, LNCS 9279, pp. 271–281, 2015.
DOI: 10.1007/978-3-319-23231-7_25

This type of relation is intrinsically vague and its definition can benefit from fuzzy set based modeling [2, 7]. To the best of our knowledge, only few works in the literature have addressed the modeling of this relation [13, 14]. In [13], in the context of geographic information systems, the alongness is computed between a line and an object. The relation is defined as the intersection length between the line and a buffer zone around the object boundary, normalized by the length of the boundary or the length of the line. In [14], the relation is considered as an alongness degree. It is defined as the length of objects boundaries in contact with the inter-objects region, normalized by the area of this region. A way to introduce distance information is also shown, as well as methods to deal with fuzzy objects. In this paper we propose to extend this approach to deal with 3D (and possibly fuzzy) objects.

In Section 2 we present the general approach to define the along relation, which is based on inter-objects region described in Section 3 and an elongation measure, that we introduce in Section 4. The extension to fuzzy sets is then presented in Section 5. Results are discussed in Section 6.

2   General Approach to Define "Along"

In this work, we consider that two objects A and B are related by an "along" relation if at least one of them is elongated and A and B are side by side in the direction of elongation. "Side by side" implicitly means that the two objects are close to each other comparatively to their environment. Such conditions imply a specific shape for the space between A and B which should be elongated. The measure of elongation of the region between the objects can therefore be used to define the along relation, as suggested in [14].

This approach requires a definition of "betweenness" to model the inter-objects space. Another advantage is that the relation is symmetrical, considering both objects equivalently, and gives the possibility to have a satisfaction degree and not just a binary one, as already argued in [7]. Looking at the inter-objects region allows us also to compute the relation only between parts of objects, based on the distance between them. The global method to define alongness is then:

1. Compute the inter-objects region β.
2. Define the elongation of β.
3. Compute the degree of satisfaction of the relation.

3   Inter-Objects Region

Several methods exist for computing the region β between two compact objects A and B [3]. We focus on the "visibility" method [3] which is able to deal with difficult situations like concavities. It is based on admissible segments. A segment $]a, b[$ is said admissible if a and b are in A and B respectively, and if the segment is included in $A^C \cap B^C$, where the superscript C denotes the complement of the object (note that this forces a and b to be on the boundaries of objects). The region β can then be defined as:

$$\beta(A, B) = \cup\{ \,]a, b[\mid a \in A, b \in B, \,]a, b[\subseteq A^C \cap B^C\}$$

This definition does not make any assumption on the space dimensionality, and can be used directly in 3D. The two main limitations of this approach are when one of the objects is much more extended than the other one (see [3] for a definition dealing with such cases), and when the alongness relation is computed between sets of disconnected objects. These cases will not be investigated in this paper.

4   Elongation Measure

4.1   Common Definition

One common definition of elongation is to consider the inverse of compactness [10] as:

$$e_{3D}(\beta) = \frac{S^3(\beta)}{V^2(\beta)}$$

with S and V the area and volume of β, respectively. This definition is dimensionless, admits a minimum equal to 36π for spherical shapes, and increases for more elongated shapes. This definition is a good start since the measure is invariant by translation, rotation and isotropic scaling. We can now define the elongation degree as $\alpha_1 = f_a\left(e_{3D}(\beta)\right)$ where f_a is an increasing function, e.g. $\frac{1-e^{-ax}}{1+e^{-ax}}$, with $\alpha \in [0, 1]$. Normalizing the degree is important to compare different degrees with various ranges. Another way to define the degree is to normalize e_{3D} by the value for a sphere. The degree is then in $[1, +\infty[$.

4.2   Alongness Degree Based on Object Boundaries

The region β could however be elongated without A and B being along each other. An additional constraint is that β is elongated in the direction of A and B, which relies on the contact surface between $A \cup B$ and β [14]. However, in 3D, if we just consider the total area of β in contact with the objects, it is impossible to distinguish between two rectangular cuboids whose longest sides are facing each other (Figure 1 (a) first case) and two cylinders whose bases are facing each other (Figure 1 (a) second case) if the total areas of facing surfaces are equal for example.

Therefore in 3D, the inter-objects region should be elongated in only one direction. We propose the following new definition to include this constraint:

$$\alpha_2 = f_a\left(\frac{(\gamma_A S_A^c(\beta) + \gamma_B S_B^c(\beta))^3}{V(\beta)^2}\right) \quad \text{with} \quad \gamma_X = 1 - \frac{2\sqrt{S_X^c(\beta)\pi}}{P_X^c(\beta)} \quad (1)$$

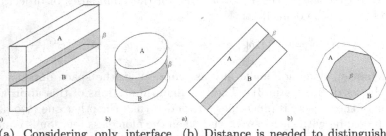

(a) Considering only interface area lead to ambiguities   (b) Distance is needed to distinguish the two configurations.

Fig. 1. Configurations possibly leading to the same elongation degree.

where $S_X^c(\beta)$ is the frontier area between β and the object X, and $P_X^c(\beta)$ the perimeter of this surface boundaries. γ_X is a measure of the elongatedness of the contact surface. When it tends to a circular shape, γ_X will tend to zero as the ratio will tend to 1 (equal to 1 in a perfect flat circle case, which is the less elongated possible shape), and increases toward 1 if the shape is more elongated, as the ratio will tend to zero. This definition takes into account the shape of both objects separately.

4.3   Including Distance Information

In some situations such as the one depicted in Figure 1 (b), the distance between the two objects can be meaningful: first configuration is closer to the intuitive "along" relation than the second one, but the α_2 score will not differentiate these two cases if the area and the volume of β are the same.

As in [14], we use the function $D_{AB}(x)$ to include distance:

$$\nu(\beta) = \int_\beta D_{AB}(x)dx \quad \text{with} \quad D_{AB}(x) = d(x, A) + d(x, B) \tag{2}$$

where $d(x, A)$ and $d(x, B)$ are the distances from x to A and B respectively, and ν is the β hyper-volume.

We can now define a new measure which includes this distance information as:

$$\alpha_3 = f_a\left(\frac{(\gamma_A S_A^c(\beta) + \gamma_B S_B^c(\beta))^2}{\nu(\beta)}\right) \tag{3}$$

One can note that exponents have changed to keep the degree dimensionless. One drawback of this degree is the loss of invariance to isotropic scaling since the distance involved in the definition is not normalized. This invariance could be obtained by normalizing the distance by its maximum value.

4.4   Using Distance to Take into Account Only Close Parts

We can examine the spatial relation only on parts of objects which are close to each other, which may be useful depending on object shapes (e.g. if two coils are next to one another, it is possible to tell if they are twisted in the same orientation or not). We reduce β by thresholding it at a distance t to keep only points which have a lower distance value, leading to β_t. This threshold can create holes so consistency should be ensured by either filling holes in each connected component of β_t or by looking for an optimal threshold around the initial one which gives only non hollow connected components when they exist. The degrees α_4 and α_5 are then defined by replacing β by β_t in (1) and (3).

5   Extension to Fuzzy Objects

The inclusion of the segment in the complement of the fuzzy objects is now modeled as a degree of inclusion [2] which can be expressed as:

$$\mu_{\text{inc}}(]a,b[) = \inf_{x \in]a,b[} \min[1 - \mu_A(x), 1 - \mu_B(x)]$$

where μ_A and μ_B are the membership functions of the two fuzzy sets (we identify in this paper a fuzzy set with its membership function, to simplify notations). Now β is the fuzzy set defined by [14]:

$$\mu_\beta(x) = \sup\{\mu_{inc}(]a,b[) \mid a \in \text{Supp}(\mu_A), b \in \text{Supp}(\mu_B), x \in]a,b[\}$$

This definition implies that the degree is equal to 1 when the segment is fully visible and equal to 0 if at least one of its points is not visible.

For a 3D fuzzy set μ, area and volume are defined as integrals of the gradient magnitude and their membership function as:

$$S(\mu) = \int_{\text{Supp}(\mu)} |\nabla \mu(x)| dx \qquad V(\mu) = \int_{\text{Supp}(\mu)} \mu(x) dx$$

which are direct extensions of definitions in [12]. To define the surface where the β region and an object μ are in contact, we now take the intersection of the support of the object and β. The frontier is then:

$$F_\mu = (\text{Supp}(\mu) \cap \text{Supp}(\mu_\beta)) \quad \text{leading to} \quad S_\mu^c = \int_{F_\mu} |\nabla \mu(x)| dx \qquad (4)$$

Equation (1) becomes:

$$F\alpha_2 = f_a \left(\frac{(S_{\mu_A}^c(\mu_\beta) + S_{\mu_B}^c(\mu_\beta))^3}{V(\mu_\beta)^2} \right) \qquad (5)$$

To add the distance information, we propose to consider the minimal length between the supports of each point rather than the length of admissible segments [14] as:

$$D_{\mu_A \mu_B}(x) = \inf\{\|\vec{ab}\| \mid a \in \text{Supp}(\mu_A), b \in \text{Supp}(\mu_B), x \in]a,b[\}$$

Equation (2) is then modified by weighting $D_{\mu_A \mu_B}(x)$ by $\mu_\beta(x)$ [14]:

$$\nu(\mu_\beta) = \int_{\mathrm{Supp}(\mu_\beta)} \mu_\beta(x) D_{\mu_A \mu_B}(x) \, dx \qquad (6)$$

A degree $F\alpha_3$ is defined by replacing the volume in (5) by (6). Using a distance threshold as suggested for α_4 and α_5 would result in a loss of the fuzzy nature of the area, so to avoid this, we use a decreasing function $g : \mathbb{R} \longrightarrow [0,1]$ of $D_{\mu_A \mu_B}$. β_t becomes a fuzzy set:

$$\mu_{\beta_t}(x) = \mu_\beta(x) g(D_{\mu_A \mu_B}(x)) = \mu_\beta(x)(1 - f_{a_1}(D_{\mu_A \mu_B}(x)))$$

where f_{a_1} is the same kind of function as f_a, i.e. a normalizing function. In order to obtain the frontier of β_t, one can simply replace β by β_t in (4). To define $F\alpha_4$ and $F\alpha_5$, β is replaced by β_t in $F\alpha_2$ and $F\alpha_3$ respectively. Table 1 summarizes the proposed definition.

Table 1. Summary of proposed degrees.

Degree	Formula	Description
α_1	$f_a\left(\frac{S^3(\beta)}{V^2(\beta)}\right)$	Inverse of compactness. Ranges from 0 for spherical shapes and tends towards 1 for vessel-like shapes
α_2	$f_a\left(\frac{(\gamma_A S_A^c(\beta)+\gamma_B S_B^c(\beta))^3}{V(\beta)^2}\right)$	Ratio taking into account only interface areas between β and the objects. The areas are weighted by an elongation score favoring elongated interfaces.
α_3	$f_a\left(\frac{(\gamma_A S_A^c(\beta)+\gamma_B S_B^c(\beta))^2}{\nu(\beta)}\right)$	Same as α_2 but the volume is weighted by the absolute minimal distance to the objects.
α_4	$f_a\left(\frac{(\gamma_A S_A^c(\beta_t)+\gamma_B S_B^c(\beta_t))^3}{V(\beta_t)^2}\right)$	Same as α_2 with a thresholded β on the distance to take into account only close parts of objects.
α_5	$f_a\left(\frac{(\gamma_A S_A^c(\beta_t)+\gamma_B S_B^c(\beta_t))^2}{\nu(\beta_t)}\right)$	Same as α_3 with a thresholded β on the distance to take into account only close parts of objects.
$F\alpha_2 - F\alpha_5$		Fuzzy versions of α_2 - α_5. Objects and β are fuzzy.

6   Experimental Results

The method has been tested with anonymized in-house clinical data. There were acquired in a dental context using 3D cone-beam computed tomography with isotropic voxels, 150 μm long on each dimension. Typical acquired volumes cover the region from the nose bottom to the chin, and from the lips to the temporo-mandibular joint. The main goal is to identify the mandibular canal which is

(a) Segmented objects overlayed on a coronal slice. (b) Segmented objects overlayed on a sagittal slice. (c) 3D facial view. (d) 3D dorsal view.

Fig. 2. Manually segmented objects of the maxillofacial area; Mandibular canals are in green, mandibular floors in red and the tooth 36 in blue.

a tubular structure running from the temporo-mandibular joint to the mental foramen through the mandible. An example image is depicted in Figure 2 (a) and (b). This is an original applicative context of spatial relations.

The proposed degrees of alongness have been evaluated on four structures, segmented manually from 3 patients: the left (LMC) and right mandibular canals (RMC), the tooth 36 (the first left-sided mandibular molar in dental classification, noted 36 after) and the left mandibular "floor" (which corresponds to the mandible bottom where the cortical bone is plain, noted LMF, and RMF for the right one, see Figure 2 (c,d)). The alongness degree using each $\alpha_i, i = 1, ..., 5$, is computed for each pair of structures. We expect the highest result between the MF and MC, for each side, as they are two elongated structures in the same direction. Comparing 36 to LMF or LMC should also show significant degrees since the tooth is being along an elongated structure. The other cases should have low degrees. A segmentation example is depicted in Figure 2 (c) and (d). Results can be seen in Figure 3. For the three patients, bar colors differentiate the patient ID (one color each). It can be seen that α_1 shows high degrees for almost all structure pairs except for the left mandibular canal and the floor, which may appear counter intuitive. This can be explained by the distance between structures giving an elongated β as discussed in Section 4.2. As predicted, this version does not fit for our purpose, and is no longer considered. In α_2 results one can observe that the degree is high when comparing the same-sided mandibular canal and the floor, which corresponds well to the intuition, and to a less extent when comparing the tooth to the canal or to the floor, which still makes sense even if the tooth is not an elongated structure. For the other comparisons, the degree is very low (<0.08). This degree appears to differentiate very well the variety of situations. Adding distance information as a distance map does not change much in these cases as α_3 shows a similar profile as α_2. However, using a threshold based on distance seems to be useful. It can be seen in α_4 that taking only the closest parts of the objects could reveal different profiles (e.g. LMF vs 36 for patients 1 and 3). This can be useful for complex-shaped objects

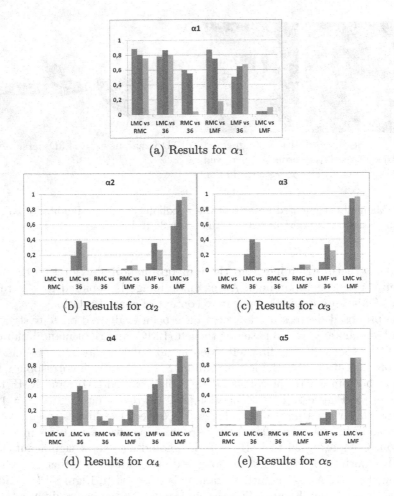

(a) Results for α_1

(b) Results for α_2 (c) Results for α_3

(d) Results for α_4 (e) Results for α_5

Fig. 3. Results obtained for crisp objects.

and/or investigating only small parts of objects. Nonetheless this version keeps significant degrees, and we can see that the highest degree is still obtained for the mandibular canal with respect to its mandibular floor. We observe the same behavior with α_5. Thresholds for these tests have been heuristically selected as the median of the distance values range.

Let us now illustrate the fuzzy case. To simulate a fuzzy segmentation of objects, manually segmented structures were considered as the core ($\mu(x) = 1$), and points were added with decreasing membership values from 1 to 0 according to the distance to the core (with 0 at 1.5mm distance). We are interested by fuzziness since it allows us to take into account inter-individual morphology variability, and potential imprecision in the segmentation, which may lead to overlapping structures (which is sometimes the case for MC and MF). Results

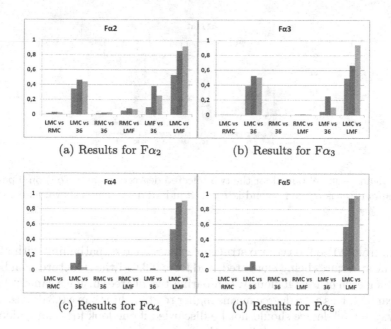

(a) Results for $F\alpha_2$ (b) Results for $F\alpha_3$

(c) Results for $F\alpha_4$ (d) Results for $F\alpha_5$

Fig. 4. Results obtained for fuzzy objects.

using $F\alpha_2$ to $F\alpha_5$ are shown in Figure 4. $F\alpha_2$ displays the same profile as α_2, with the highest degree for the MC/MF case, and quite high degrees for the LMF/36 and LMC/36 cases. Adding distance weighting does not give different results as can be seen with $F\alpha_3$. For $F\alpha_4$ and $F\alpha_5$, using the distance information allows us to pick only close structures and to perform a local analysis. For these tests, the normalizing function for β_t is the same as the one for normalizing the elongation degree (with the parameter a equal to 0.05). Fuzziness allows getting similar degrees when comparing teeth to an elongated structure, while the crisp version is much more sensitive to the tooth position and orientation.

From these results, we decided to select α_2 and $F\alpha_2$ as the best versions, since they are suited for the selected set of objects. Another advantage of selecting these versions is their lower computation cost, since the distance map does not add useful information in our cases. However for other applications, using thresholded versions of β (as α_4) should not be discarded.

The next step was to test the selected version on more data to ensure its robustness. To do so, we included three more patient data, and we also segmented the right mandibular floor to verify the behavior for two elongated structures. The results are summarized in Figure 5.

These results confirm the first tests, sorting correctly the situations depending on their spatial arrangement, and indicating a good robustness with respect to anatomical variability. Hence, we can propose a classification for the degree as follows: between 0 to 0.1 means that the two structures are not linked by an alongness

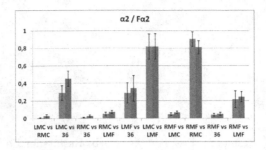

Fig. 5. Mean results obtained for the two selected degrees (α_2 and $F\alpha_2$) on 6 patients. First columns set is α_2 and second is $F\alpha_2$. Standard deviation is shown as error bars

relation, from 0.1 to 0.6 the two structures share a close spatial link with at least one of the structures being elongated, and from 0.6 to 1 the structures can be said to be along each other. Obviously, comparing two degrees inside a same "class" is still meaningful, as a 0.5 degree means higher relationship than a 0.3 degree. In the same way, a 0.58 degree should not be discarded if one look for strong alongness link just because it does not fall into the best "class".

7   Conclusion

In this paper we presented the extension of the "along" spatial relation to 3D, for crisp objects as well as for fuzzy ones, by a two-step process, based on the "between" spatial relation and elongation computation. Several versions are proposed including information such as distance, locality, or object direction, to be able to cope with a wide range of situations, and their performance is tested on clinical cases. Best versions for our precise identification goal are selected for extended tests showing good spatial configuration distinction and a satisfaction degree that can be actually used for comparisons between cases. The measure seems to be robust, but this should be further validated on larger data sets. The measures are invariant by translation and rotation, and most of them by isotropic scaling. The fact that the framework is split into two steps allows easy changes in the methods for computing the inter-objects region or the alongness degree. This paper does not investigate the case of set of disconnected objects which could be meaningful (think of row of trees being along a road for example), since the visibility approach is not designed for, nor the case of very unbalanced object sizes. Maybe the first case could be approached by considering a set of objects as a whole, and looking at its convex hull for example, or by taking a more suited β definition. For the second case, one could make use of the extension of the visibility method, called "myopic vision" and described in [3], which is able to restrain the inter-objects region to the locality of the smallest object. From an application point of view, this work aims to be a tool for automatic segmentation of mandibular canal based on dental cast to help dentists avoiding post surgery traumas, but could also be applied to other fields like structure identification in geographic information system or vessel-like pattern recognition works. Future work aims to develop other spatial relations representing the maxillofacial region, in order to create a conceptual model, able to guide precise segmentation and recognition, for dental applications.

Acknowledgments. The authors would like to thank the "Association Nationale de la Recherche et de la Technologie" (ANRT) for supporting this research through the CIFRE program.

References

1. Biederman, I.: Recognition-by-components: a theory of human image understanding. Psychological Review **94**(2), 115–147 (1987)
2. Bloch, I.: Fuzzy spatial relationships for image processing and interpretation: a review. Image and Vision Computing **23**(2), 89–110 (2005)
3. Bloch, I., Colliot, O., Cesar, R.M.: On the ternary spatial relation "between". IEEE Transactions on Systems, Man, and Cybernetics **36**(2), 312–327 (2006)
4. Clementini, E.: Qualitative representation of positional information. Artificial Intelligence **95**, 317–356 (1997)
5. Colliot, O., Camara, O., Bloch, I.: Integration of fuzzy spatial relations in deformable models—Application to brain MRI segmentation. Pattern Recognition **39**(8), 1401–1414 (2006)
6. Fouquier, G., Atif, J., Bloch, I.: Sequential model-based segmentation and recognition of image structures driven by visual features and spatial relations. Computer Vision and Image Understanding **116**(1), 146–165 (2012)
7. Freeman, J.: The modelling of spatial relations. Computer Graphics and Image Processing **4**(2), 156–171 (1975)
8. Hayward, W.G., Tarr, M.J.: Spatial language and spatial representation. Cognition **55**, 39–84 (1995)
9. Koenig, O., Reiss, L.P., Kosslyn, S.M.: The development of spatial relation representations: Evidence from studies of cerebral lateralization. Journal of Experimental Child Psychology **50**(1), 119–130 (1990)
10. Montero, R.S., Bribiesca, E.: State of the art of compactness and circularity measures. International Mathematical Forum **4**(27), 1305–1335 (2009)
11. Nempont, O., Atif, J., Bloch, I.: A constraint propagation approach to structural model based image segmentation and recognition. Information Sciences **246**, 1–27 (2013)
12. Rosenfeld, A.: The fuzzy geometry of image subsets. Pattern Recognition Letters **2**(5), 311–317 (1984)
13. Shariff, A., Egenhofer, M.J., Mark, D.M.: Natural-Language Spatial Relations Between Linear and Areal Objects : The Topology and Metric of English. International Journal of Geographical Information Science **12**(3), 215–246 (1998)
14. Takemura, C.M., Cesar, R.M., Bloch, I.: Modeling and measuring the spatial relation "along": Regions, contours and fuzzy sets. Pattern Recognition **45**(2), 757–766 (2012)
15. Vanegas, M.C., Bloch, I., Inglada, J.: Alignment and Parallelism for the Description of High-Resolution Remote Sensing Images. IEEE Transactions on Geoscience and Remote Sensing **51**(6), 3542–3557 (2013)

Compression and Querying of Arbitrary Geodesic Distances

Rosario Aiello[1], Francesco Banterle[1]([✉]), Nico Pietroni[1], Luigi Malomo[1,2],
Paolo Cignoni[1], and Roberto Scopigno[1]

[1] ISTI - CNR, Pisa, Italy
francesco.banterle@isti.cnr.it
[2] Universitá degli Studi di Pisa, Pisa, Italy

Abstract. In this paper, we propose a novel method for accelerating the computation of geodesic distances over arbitrary manifold triangulated surfaces. The method is based on a preprocessing step where we build a data structure. This allows to store arbitrary complex distance metrics. We show that, by exploiting the precomputed data, the proposed method is significantly faster than the classical Dijkstra algorithm for the computation of point to point distances. Moreover, as we precompute exact geodesic distances, the proposed approach can be more accurate than state-of-the-art approximations.

1 Introduction

Determining the shortest path between two points on a surface, geodesic, is a fundamental task of many geometry processing algorithms. Mitchell, Mount and Papadimitriou (MMP) [12] proposed the first algorithm on polygonal surfaces with a practical computational complexity. Since then, several approaches have been presented to improve specific characteristics of geodesic computation.

In this paper, we introduce a method to speed up the computation of geodesic distances over triangulated manifold surfaces. Our method is based on a precomputation step where geodesic distances between vertices of an input triangular mesh are computed and efficiently stored in a data structure that allows fast querying. Storing all possible geodesics becomes practically infeasible in the real case, as the required memory rises quadratically with the number of vertices of the input mesh. Instead, our hierarchical data structure allows to retrieve geodesic distances between arbitrary vertices in constant time and, contemporarily, the required memory rises linearly with the number of vertices of the mesh.

Differently from previous methods, which are implicitly limited to compute the plain geodesic distance, the proposed method can be used to compute the shortest paths on a surface independently by the chosen distance metric. Therefore, it can be efficiently used to integrate any kind of function/signal over a surface. Our approach introduces an approximation error in geodesic computations, but this can be bounded in the preprocessing step.

© Springer International Publishing Switzerland 2015
V. Murino and E. Puppo (Eds.): ICIAP 2015, Part I, LNCS 9279, pp. 282–293, 2015.
DOI: 10.1007/978-3-319-23231-7_26

2   Related Work

Exact Methods. The MMP algorithm, proposed by [12], is the first algorithm that allows to compute exact geodesic distances on polyhedral meshes in $\mathcal{O}(n^2 \log n)$ time (where n is the number of vertices of a mesh). This algorithm subdivides each edge into intervals or *windows*. For each window, the distance is exactly computed and then propagated in the wavefront order. Chen and Han (CH) [3] proposed uses hierarchical windows to lower the complexity to $\mathcal{O}(n^2)$ time. However, Surazhsky et al. [16] showed that in practical cases this algorithms is slower and the MMP which typically runs sub-quadratic. Xin and Wang [19] discovered that 99% of the propagated windows in the CH algorithm do not contribute to shortest distance computations. So, they proposed to filter these useless windows improving efficiency of the CH algorithm (ICH). This has been implemented in the GPU [22] and extended for handling meshes with holes [14].

Approximated Methods. Surazhsky et al. [16] presented a version of MMP (AMMP) for the approximated computation of geodesic distances. By merging adjacent windows, the AMMP algorithm gain a significative speed-up in the computation (up to an order of magnitude), introducing only a 0.1% of relative approximation error.Xin et al. [20] proposed GTU, a method based on a pre-computation step where the mesh is decomposed in triangular patches. The distance between each pair of point belonging to the same patch is precomputed and stored in a table. Geodesic distances are obtained in a two step process: first a Dijkstra shortest path computation is used to compute patch to patch distance, a second step completes the distance computation by using direct access tables. The Saddle Vertex Graph (SVG) approach recently proposed by Ying et al. [21] consists of a sparse undirected graph that encodes complete geodesic information so that every shortest path on the mesh corresponds to a shortest path on the SVG. Both GTU and SVG produce a considerable speedup in the computation, however the proposed method is limited to the computation of a specific geodesic measure. Fast Marching Method (FMM), proposed by Sethian [15] is a special case of the Level Set Method [13] for solving the *boundary value problems* of the Eikonal equation. This original method is limited to work for the case of regular grids. This method has been extended for the general case of triangular meshes [7], modified for fast computations on graphics hardware [18], or extended to work in meshes with holes [2]. Further extensions and modifications to the original algorithm were proposed in [10,11], Kirsanov's thesis [8], Martinez et al. [9], and Bertelli et al. [1]. Crane et al. [5] proposed a novel approach called *Heat Method* (HM). The main idea is to exploit the relationship between the heat kernel function $k_{t,x}(y)$ and distance function; i.e. image to touch a point x on the mesh surface with a scorching hot needle.The method is straightforward to implement and produces good approximations for relatively smooth surfaces; quality decreases in presence of fine details.

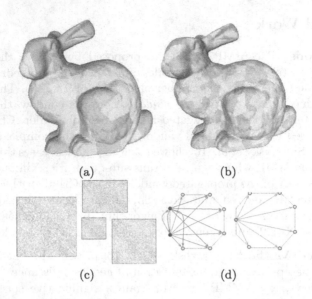

Fig. 1. Overview of the preprocessing pipeline: (a) build a Voronoi partitioning of the input mesh; (b) recursively subdivide each patch; (c) precompute for each region the geodesic distances and compress it as a set of images; (d) simplify the vertex-patch connecting graph by using a greedy pruning algorithm.

3   Algorithm

The preprocessing pipeline (see Fig. 1) to derive the hierarchical structure used to compute geodesics is composed by the following steps:

- We build a hierarchical partitioning of the input mesh. We recursively use a Voronoi-based approach using a set of uniformly sampled seeds (Fig. 1.a and 1.b). See section 3.1.
- For each region, we precompute the geodesic distances and we store them in a compressed graph based representation that allows for direct fast access (Fig. 1.c). See section 3.2.
- We simplify this graph by using a greedy pruning algorithm that minimizes the amount of introduced error (Fig. 1.c). See section 3.3.
- We assemble the graph that interconnects all the precomputed per patch information, in order to perform geodesic queries between any vertex pair.

3.1   Patch Subdivision

We want to subdivide the mesh into a set of disk-like patches that have approximately the same size. Moreover, in order to minimize the introduced error, the border between patches should be reasonably smooth and possibly convex with respect to the distance metric defined over the surface. To conform to our constraints, we used a strategy based on centroidal voronoi partitioning of the initial surface. Given a distance metric M defined over the input surface, we start from a Poisson Disk sampling of the surface under the metric M by using the algorithm proposed by [4] and choosing as seeds a subset of the mesh vertexes. Then, we perform Voronoi partitioning of the initial mesh by using the poisson samples as initial seeds; i.e. each vertex is associated to the closest seed under the distance metric M. In order to improve the partitioning, we interleave this step with a Lloyd relaxation step choosing as centroid of each patch the farthest point from boundary of the patch as in [17]. For this partitioning step when computing all the distances (for computing Voronoi partitioning and for Lloyd relaxation) we assume the use of the same distance metric of the geodesic we want to approximate.

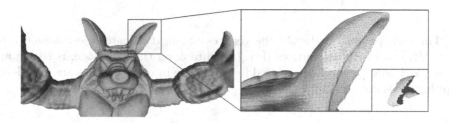

Fig. 2. A possible patching of the right ear of the ARMADILLO model. This partitioning creates a patch with two border rings.

This strategy does not guarantee that each patch is homomorphic to a disk. Indeed, it may produce patches with multiple borders. In the example shown in figure 2, the yellow patch has two border rings. This topological issue may commonly rise in correspondence of high curvature regions of the input surface (e.g. the ear of figure 2 or the tail which is also present in the ARMADILLO model). To overcome this issue, after a first partitioning step, we check each patch to have a single border. When this condition is not satisfied for a patch p_i, we re-run the Voronoi partitioning algorithm on the portion of the surface embedded by p_i. We repeat this step until every newly generated patch has exactly one single border.

This decomposition procedure is repeated in an hierarchical manner. We decompose each patch using the same Voronoi strategy, keeping tracks of the hierarchical relation between levels of subdivisions. In our experiments, we noticed that two levels of subdivision are enough to our purposes. Figure 3, on the left side, shows two examples of the patch decomposition.

The density of the patch subdivision is controlled by the number of seeds for the first level and the number of seeds used for each patch on the finest levels of the hierarchy. This constant can be set by the user at the beginning of the precomputation and it can be optimized to maximize the performance.

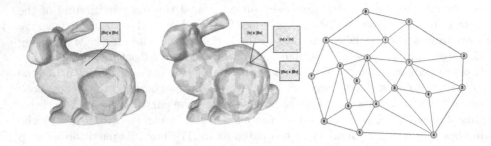

Fig. 3. On the left side, the first two levels of Voronoi decomposition of the bunny model, together with the precomputed geodesics distances. On the right side, an example of a triangulated patch. Border vertices (Bv) are shown in gray, internal vertices (Iv) are colored in yellow.

For each patch, we classify the vertices among two categories: *border* vertices (Bv) and *internal* vertices (Iv). In figure 3, on the right side, is shown an example: border vertices are colored in gray while internal vertices are in yellow. Border edges are highlighted in red.

3.2   Geodesic Precomputation

We precompute the geodesic distances by using the implementation of the MMP algorithm [12] as defined in Surazhsky [16]. This algorithm, despite the high computational cost, provides a very accurate estimation of the geodesic distance. As this is a preprocessing offline step, we are more interested in increasing the provided accuracy with respect to the time required by the process. The computation for each patch p can be summarized in the following steps:

1. For all the patches at any level, for each pair of border vertexes $v_i, v_j \in p$, we compute and store their relative distances in a $|Bv| \times |Bv|$ triangular matrix.
2. For each patch at the final level of the hierarchy, we compute the distance among border to internal vertices geodesic distance and store it in a $|Iv| \times |Bv|$ triangular matrix.
3. For each patch at the final level of the hierarchy, we compute the geodesic distances between each pair of internal vertices and store the values in a $|Iv| \times |Iv|$ triangular matrix.

These matrices represents graphs connecting various subsets of the nodes and whose arcs represents the precomputed distances. We keep these matrices as compressed images (we used ".*png*" compression), so that they can be efficiently stored to disk. We use *floats* to maintain distance values and the RGBA8888 format to encode each float value into a pixel. Intuitively, assuming 32bit (4 bytes) floating point, we map each of the 4 bytes of the float value into each channel of the RGBA image format.

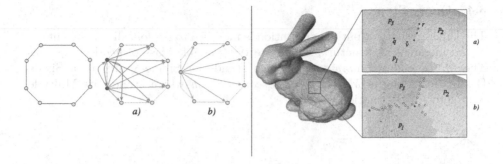

Fig. 4. Left: Pruning of two nodes: a) Two red vertices are selected for pruning. b) Pruning produces a new dummy node; Right:a) An example of a pair of nodes eligible for pruning (green) and two pairs not eligible (blue and red). b) An example of a border vertex and its $|Bv| \times |Bv|$ edges in both the patches it is contained. To have a clear picture, edges are only sketched.

As each patch has an unique border, we can sort the vertices along the border while internal vertices are sorted by considering their minimal distance to the border. Since close vertices in the patch will correspond to closer rows in the image, the produced image will vary smoothly allowing good compression ratios.

3.3   Graph Pruning

To reduce the size of the matrices described in the previous section, we simplify the graphs they represent by using a greedy pruning procedure that decreases the number of vertices actually used to generate all the pairs for which we store distances. The pruning procedure is done by iteratively merging adjacent patch boundary vertices: the intuition is that if two vertices are geometrically close (e.g. two adjacent vertices on a patch border) then their geodesics distances to other nodes will be "similar".

The error introduced by a merging operation can be estimated as the average difference of geodesic distances with respect to the other nodes of the adjacency matrices. The merging operation is shown in the left part of figure 4.a. Obviously, two nodes can be merged only if they belong to the same set of patches as shown in the right part of figure 4.

Merging operations are executed in a greedy fashion by prioritizing the operations with respect to the introduced error. The process halts when the introduced error exceeds a given threshold, δ. We express δ as a percentage of mesh bounding box diagonal. Results have shown that on small meshes (e.g. in the 70K-faces BUNNY model), a very small δ, such as $\delta = 0.01\%$, does not produce a significant pruning. In the case of high resolution meshes, the error introduced by every merging operation becomes smaller because the mesh is more densely sampled. Furthermore, the pruning becomes effective producing a considerably speedup.

3.4   Query Step

The Dijkstra shortest path computation is modified to exploit all the advantages of the hierarchical structure. There are two possible class of geodesic queries: The *SSSD geodesic computation* which stands for Single-Source to a Single-Destination and the *MSAD geodesic computation* which stands for Multiple-Source to All-Destination.

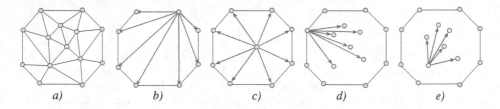

a)   b)   c)   d)   e)

Fig. 5. An overview of the different class of relations and nodes that are contained by our hierarchical structure: (a) Border and internal nodes; (b) Border to Border arcs; (c) Internal to Border Arcs; (d) Border to Internal arcs; (d) Internal to Internal arcs

Figure 5 shows an overview of the different class of relations and nodes that are contained by our hierarchical structure.

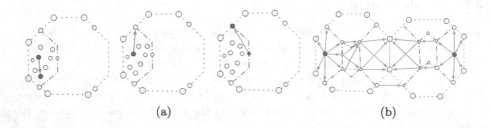

(a)   (b)

Fig. 6. a) Different cases of geodesic computation between vertices that belong to the same patch at the final level; b) The set of arcs enabled for Dijkstra shortest path computation for the general case.

SSSD Distance Computation. Given two arbitrary vertices, v_1 and v_2, we first retrieve the patches containing them along all the level of the hierarchy. If v_1 and v_2 belong to the same patch at the last level of the hierarchy p_i (as in figure 6.a left) then their distance can be simply retrieved by performing a direct access to the matrix relating internal to internal vertices of p_i.

Otherwise, when v_1 and v_2 do not belong to a common patch at the last lever we implicitly build a subset of all the arcs on which runs Dijkstra shortest path algorithm. We first retrieve the level L_{v_1,v_2} of hierarchy where v_1 and v_2 belong to a common patch. In the case there is no common patch, we consider the first level of the hierarchy. We only consider the arcs that relate each vertex and its ancestors up in the hierarchy until the level L_{v_1,v_2} is reached. We also enable all the arcs relating border to border relation at level L_{v_1,v_2}. In this way, we allow the propagation algorithm to make jumps as long as possible when the nodes are far away. Then, we execute a finer propagation when the front approach its final destination, see figure 6.b.

Moreover, we took advantage of the A* algorithm to further optimize the search. The A* algorithm requires a knowledge-plus-heuristic cost function of node v (denoted with $f(v)$) to determine the order to examine the visited nodes. The cost function $f(v)$ is a sum of two functions:

- the *past* path-cost function, which is the known distance from the starting node to the current node v (denoted with $g(v)$)
- a *future* path-cost function, which is an admissible "heuristic estimate" of the distance from v to the goal (denoted with $h(v)$).

The $h(v)$ part of the $f(v)$ function has to be an admissible heuristic; that is, it must not overestimate the distance to the goal. In our case, it is simply the Euclidean distance to the destination vertex. Therefore, we obtain a heuristic that is monotone (i.e. satisfies $h(v) \leq d(v,u) + h(u)$ for every edge (v,y)) and it is a lower bound. Indeed, the length of the shortest path between two points cannot be shorter than the norm of the vector connecting them. As exposed in [6,23], the A* algorithm achieves better timing when using admissible monotone heuristics.

MSAD Distance Computation. The MSAD distance computation algorithm is a generalization of the SSSD computation. We first use patch internal geodesic matrices to propagate all the distances to the vertices that belong to the same patch. Then, we propagate distances to the border of the patch. We use all the border to border adjacency matrices to propagate distances. Finally, we patch internal geodesic matrices to propagate the distances to the final nodes.

4   Results

We implemented our algorithm in C++ using the VCG library [1], an open source portable C++ template library for geometry processing. All our tests were performed on a machine equipped with an Intel i7 processor with 8 cores at 2.6GHz. Only the preprocessing part was parallelized.

Figure 7 shows the results of the computation of MSAD distance on different models (distance isolines are visualized). Our results are compared to those obtained by applying the MMP algorithm. We can see that our method produces smooth geodesic fields. Moreover, by checking the isolines, no artifacts are visible. The achieved accuracy in our results makes our results hardly distinguishable from those computed by the MMP algorithm.

---

[1] http://vcg.isti.cnr.it/vcglib/

Table 1. The average query time (left) and mean average error (right) statistics when varying n_1 and n_2 on the Armadillo ($173Kfaces$) Busto ($255Kfaces$) and Ramesses (826K faces) models.

	Armadillo				Busto				Ramesses		
	n_1				n_1				n_1		
n_2	100	200	300	n_2	100	150	200	n_2	950	1000	1200
5	0.01126s	0.01128s	0.01145s	5	0.01989s	0.01979s	0.01978s	5	0.06295s	0.06088s	0.06112s
10	0.01134s	0.01137s	0.01176s	10	0.01983s	0.01983s	0.01986s	10	0.06335s	0.06027s	0.06202s
15	0.01166s	0.01164s	0.01215s	15	0.01986s	0.01990s	0.01991s	15	0.65986s	0.06077s	0.06243s

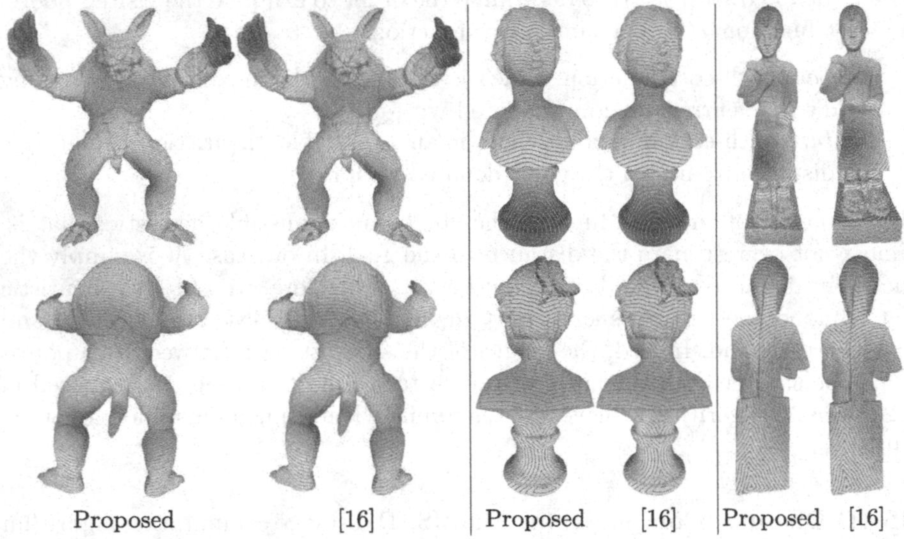

Proposed   [16]   Proposed   [16]   Proposed   [16]

Fig. 7. Comparison of geodesics computed with our method with respect to the exact MMP algorithm by Surazhsky [16].

4.1 Parameters Tuning

In our algorithm, the user needs to specify the δ parameter which controls the introduced error during the pruning phase, see section 3.3). Additionally, the user has to specify the number of patch subdivisions used for each level of the hierarchy. We noticed that two levels of hierarchy are sufficient for high quality result. We refer to n_1 and n_2 as the number of subdivisions created for the first and second level of the hierarchy.

Some statistics relating the time needed to perform a query with respect to different values of n_1 and n_2 are reported in table table 1. To estimate the time needed to perform a query, we repetitively selected randomly pairs of nodes on the mesh to perform SSSD searches. From experiments, we noticed that the optimal number of seeds is proportional to the number of faces/vertices of the input mesh.

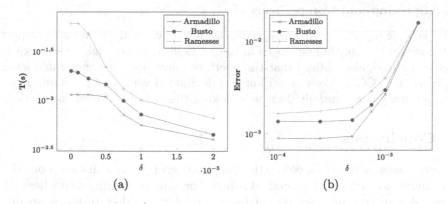

(a) (b)

Fig. 8. Effect of parameter δ on query time and introduced error. δ and ϵ are expressed as % of the diagonal of the bounding box.(a) Average query time $T(s)$ plotted for variable pruning threshold δ. (b) Average mean error ϵ plotted for variable pruning threshold δ.

In figure 8, we report the average query time when varying δ. The error ϵ is relative to the geodesic evaluated by using the exact MMP algorithm [16]. Both δ and ϵ are expressed as a percentage of the diagonal of the model bounding box. As expected, the query time is inversely proportional to δ which governs the amount of merging operation performed during the pruning. Conversely, the amount of introduced error is proportional to δ.

4.2 Preprocessing Time

We report in table 2 timings for the preprocessing step when varying n_1 and n_2. Since our implementation runs computations for each patch in parallel, the preprocessing time tends to decrease when increasing the total number of regions in the first and second layers. On the other hand, as we discussed in section 4.1, this does not necessarily imply a decrease in the query time.

A comparison of geodesics computed with our method with respect to the exact MMP algorithm by Surazhsky [16] can be found in the additional material.

Table 2. Timings for the preprocessing step when varying n_1 and n_2 on the ARMADILLO model.

	n_1		
n_2	100	200	300
5	333.4s	218.7s	182.2s
10	287.3s	197.5s	202.1s
15	264.2s	191.1s	171.5s

Table 3. Comparisons of speedups of our algorithm with respect to exact MMP algorithm by Surazhsky [16] and the algorithm for computing geodesics included in the VCG library for the case of MSAD computations.

Model	MPP	VCG	VoroGeo	Speedup
Armadillo	1.3s	0.57s	0.011s	51x
Busto	8.1s	0.82s	0.019s	44x
Ramesses	47.3s	2.73s	0.061s	45x

4.3   Speedup and Comparisons

In table 3, we report the effective speedup achieved by our algorithm with respect to the geodesic algorithm employed in the VCG library. Through several experiments, we have also noticed that time performances became comparable when applying the VCG geodesic algorithm to a decimated version of the mesh. However, accuracy exponentially decreases making these results useless in practice.

5   Conclusions

We proposed a method to speed up the computation of geodesic distances on arbitrary manifold surfaces. The method is based on a preprocessing step where the mesh is decomposed into hierarchy of disk-like regions. Geodesic distances are precomputed on subsets of the vertices of those regions and stored for a later use.

Compared to previous methods, our method is independent from the metric used to compute distances over the surface. Additionally, our method allows to control the amount of introduced error with respect to the exact value.

We successfully integrated the exact geodesic computation proposed by Surazhsky [16] within our framework. This method [16] is very accurate (close to the exact geodesic value), but it unfortunately demands high computational costs. We showed several examples how our method can be used to speed up the entire process introducing a very small approximation error.

We believe that many geometry processing algorithms may benefit from the proposed method. Furthermore, our method may be used to integrate over manifold surfaces any arbitrary point-to-point functions, independently from their complexity, and make the querying very efficient. Thanks to this flexibility, our method may be used as an essential component in various application scenarios.

References

1. Bertelli, L., Sumengen, B., Manjunath, B.S.: Redundancy in all pairs fast marching method. In: 2006 IEEE Int. Conf. on Image Processing, October 2006
2. Campen, M., Kobbelt, L.: Walking on broken mesh: Defect-tolerant geodesic distances and parameterizations. Computer Graphics Forum 30(2) (2011)
3. Chen, J., Han, Y.: Shortest paths on a polyhedron. In: Proc. of the Sixth Annual Symp. on Computational Geometry, SCG 1990. ACM, New York 1990
4. Corsini, M., Cignoni, P., Scopigno, R.: Efficient and flexible sampling with blue noise properties of triangular meshes. IEEE Trans. on Visualization and Computer Graphics 18(6) (2012)
5. Crane, K., Weischedel, C., Wardetzky, M.: Geodesics in heat: A new approach to computing distance based on heat flow. ACM Trans. Graph. 32(5), October 2013
6. Dechter, R., Pearl, J.: Generalized best-first search strategies and the optimality of a*. J. ACM 32(3), July 1985
7. Kimmel, R., Sethian, J.A.: Computing geodesic paths on manifolds. Proc. Natl. Acad. Sci., USA (1998)
8. Kirsanov, D.: Minimal Discrete Curves and Surfaces. PhD thesis, The Division of Engineering and Applied Sciences, Harvard University, September 2004

9. Martínez, D., Velho, L., Carvalho, P.C.: Computing geodesics on triangular meshes. Comput. Graph. **29**(5), October 2005
10. Mémoli, F., Sapiro, G.: Fast computation of weighted distance functions and geodesics on implicit hyper-surfaces. J. Comput. Phys. **173**(2), 730 (2001)
11. Mémoli, F., Sapiro, G.: Distance functions and geodesics on submanifolds of r and point clouds. Journal on Applied Mathematics **65**(4), August 2005
12. Mitchell, J.S.B, Mount, D.M, Papadimitriou, C.H.: The discrete geodesic problem. SIAM J. Comput. **16**(4), August 1987
13. Osher, S., Sethian, J.A.: Fronts propagating with curvature dependent speed: Algorithms based on hamilton-jacobi formulations. Journal of Computational Physics **79**(1) (1988)
14. Quynh, D.T.P., He, Y., Xin, S.-Q., Chen, Z.: An intrinsic algorithm for computing geodesic distance fields on triangle meshes with holes. Graph. Models **74**(4), July 2012
15. Sethian, J.A.: A fast marching level set method for monotonically advancing fronts. Proc. Nat. Acad, Sci. (1995)
16. Surazhsky, V., Surazhsky, T., Kirsanov, D., Gortler, S.J., Hoppe, H.: Fast exact and approximate geodesics on meshes. ACM Trans. Graph. **24**(3), July 2005
17. Valette, S., Chassery, J.-M.: Approximated centroidal voronoi diagrams for uniform polygonal mesh coarsening. In: Computer Graphics Forum, vol. 23 (2004)
18. Weber, O., Devir, Y.S., Bronstein, A.M., Bronstein, M.M., Kimmel, R.: Parallel algorithms for approximation of distance maps on parametric surfaces. ACM Trans. Graph. **27**(4), November 2008
19. Xin, S.-Q., Wang, G.-J.: Improving chen and han's algorithm on the discrete geodesic problem. ACM Trans. Graph. **28**(4), September 2009
20. Xin, S.-Q., Ying, X., He, Y.: Constant-time all-pairs geodesic distance query on triangle meshes. In: Proc. of the ACM SIGGRAPH Symp. on Interactive 3D Graphics and Games, I3D 2012. ACM, New York (2012)
21. Ying, X., Wang, X., He, Y.: Saddle vertex graph (svg): A novel solution to the discrete geodesic problem. ACM Trans. Graph. **32**(6), November 2013
22. Ying, X., Xin, S.-Q., He, Y.: Parallel chen-han (pch) algorithm for discrete geodesics. ACM Trans. Graph. **33**(1), February 2014
23. Zeng, W., Church, R.L.: Finding shortest paths on real road networks: The case for a*. Int. J. Geogr. Inf. Sci. **23**(4), April 2009

Comparing Persistence Diagrams Through Complex Vectors

Barbara Di Fabio[1]([⊠]) and Massimo Ferri[1,2]

[1] ARCES, University of Bologna, Bologna, Italy
{barbara.difabio,massimo.ferri}@unibo.it
[2] Department of Mathematics, University of Bologna, Bologna, Italy

Abstract. The natural pseudo-distance of spaces endowed with filtering functions is precious for shape classification and retrieval; its optimal estimate coming from persistence diagrams is the bottleneck distance, which unfortunately suffers from combinatorial explosion. A possible algebraic representation of persistence diagrams is offered by complex polynomials; since far polynomials represent far persistence diagrams, a fast comparison of the coefficient vectors can reduce the size of the database to be classified by the bottleneck distance. This article explores experimentally three transformations from diagrams to polynomials and three distances between the complex vectors of coefficients.

Keywords: Persistence diagram · Shape analysis · Viète formulas · Precision · Recall

1 Introduction

Persistent homology has already proven to be an effective tool for shape representation in various applications, in particular when the objects to be classified, compared or retrieved have a natural origin. The interplay of geometry and topology in persistence makes it possible to capture qualitative aspects in a formal and computable way, yet it doesn't suffer of the excessive freedom of mere topological equivalence. The privileged tool for shape comparison is the natural pseudo-distance [11], which is scarcely computable. Luckily, persistence diagrams condense the essence of the shape concept of the observer in finite sets of points in the plane [13,16]; moreover, the bottleneck distance (a.k.a. matching distance) between persistence diagrams yields an optimal lower bound to the natural pseudo-distance [9,10]. There is a problem: the bottleneck distance suffers from combinatorial explosion [8], so it becomes hard to scan a large database when it comes to retrieval. Approximations, smart organization of the database according to the metric, progressive application of different classifiers come to help, but the problem is lightened, not solved.

A paradigm shift came from an idea of Claudia Landi [15]: represent the persistence diagram as the set of complex roots of a polynomial; then comparison can be performed on coefficients. Two problems arise: one — which comes

© Springer International Publishing Switzerland 2015
V. Murino and E. Puppo (Eds.): ICIAP 2015, Part I, LNCS 9279, pp. 294–305, 2015.
DOI: 10.1007/978-3-319-23231-7_27

from the nature itself of persistence diagrams — is that in real situations there are a lot of points near the "diagonal" $\{(u,v) \in \mathbb{R}^2 : u = v\}$, due to noise so less meaningful in shape representation, but with a heavy impact on polynomial coefficients; another problem — coming from polynomial theory — is that little distance of polynomial roots implies little distance of coefficients, but the converse is false.

A completely different polynomial representation of barcodes (equivalently: of persistence diagrams) is the one through tropical algebra [17], closely adapting to the bottleneck distance.

The Contribution of the Paper. We face the first problem — the existence of points near the diagonal — by performing a plane warping which takes all the line $u = v$ to 0, so points near the diagonal actually become close together. Making noise points close and around zero diminishes their contribution to polynomial coefficients, above all to the first (and most relevant) ones: sum of roots, sum of pairwise products of roots, etc. As for the second problem — the fact that close coefficients may not mean close roots — we explore the use of polynomial comparison as a preprocessing phase in shape retrieval, i.e. as a very fast way of getting rid of definitely far objects, so that the bottleneck distance can be computed only for a small set of candidates, in the same line as [5]. The results are satisfactory: in some of our experiments the bottleneck distance even turns out to be unnecessary.

2   Preliminaries

In persistence, the shape of an object is usually studied by choosing a topological space X to represent it, and a function $f : X \to \mathbb{R}$, called a *filtering* (or *measuring*) *function*, to define a family of subspaces $X_u = f^{-1}((-\infty, u])$, $u \in \mathbb{R}$, nested by inclusion, i.e. a filtration of X. The name "persistence" is bound to the idea of ranking topological features by importance, according to the length of their "life" through the filtration. The basic assumption is that the longer a feature survives, the more meaningful or coarse the feature is for shape description. In particular, structural properties of the space X are identified by features that once born never die; vice-versa, noise and shape details are characterized by a short life. To study how topological features vary in passing from a set of the filtration into a larger one we use homology. A nice feature of this approach is modularity: The choice of different filtering functions may account for different viewpoints on the same problem (different shape concepts) or for different tasks. For further details we refer to [1,12].

Persistent homology groups of the pair (X, f) — i.e. of the filtration $\{X_u\}_{u \in \mathbb{R}}$ — are defined as follows. Given $u \leq v \in \mathbb{R}$, we consider the inclusion of X_u into X_v. This inclusion induces a homomorphism of homology groups $H_k(X_u) \to H_k(X_v)$ for every $k \in \mathbb{Z}$. Its image consists of the k-homology classes that are born before or at the level u and are still alive at the level v and is called the *kth persistent homology group of (X, f) at (u, v)*. When this group is finitely generated, we denote by $\beta_k^{u,v}(X, f)$ its rank.

The usual, compact description of persistent homology groups of (X, f) is provided by the so-called *persistence diagrams*, i.e. multisets of points whose abscissa and ordinate are, respectively, the level at which k-homology classes are created and the level at which they are annihilated through the filtration. If a homology class does not die along the filtration, the ordinate of the corresponding point is set to $+\infty$.

At the moment, our approach to convert persistence diagrams into complex vectors can be applied only when neglecting these points at infinity. Hence, we focus on the subsets of proper points of the classical persistence diagrams, known in literature as *ordinary persistence diagrams* [6]. For simplicity we still call them "persistence diagrams". We underline that this choice is not so restrictive since the number of points at infinity depends only on the homology of the space X, and persistent homology provides a finite distance between two pairs if and only if the considered spaces are homeomorphic.

We use the following notation: $\Delta^+ = \{(u, v) \in \mathbb{R}^2 : u < v\}$, $\Delta = \{(u, v) \in \mathbb{R}^2 : u = v\}$, and $\overline{\Delta^+} = \Delta^+ \cup \Delta$.

Definition 1. *Let $k \in \mathbb{Z}$ and $(u, v) \in \Delta^+$. The multiplicity $\mu_k(u, v)$ of (u, v) is the finite non-negative number defined by*

$$\lim_{\varepsilon \to 0^+} \left(\beta_k^{u+\varepsilon, v-\varepsilon}(X, f) - \beta_k^{u-\varepsilon, v-\varepsilon}(X, f) - \beta_k^{u+\varepsilon, v+\varepsilon}(X, f) + \beta_k^{u-\varepsilon, v+\varepsilon}(X, f) \right).$$

Definition 2. *The kth-persistence diagram $D_k(X, f)$ is the set of all points $(u, v) \in \Delta^+$ such that $\mu_k(u, v) > 0$, counted with their multiplicity, union the points of Δ, counted with infinite multiplicity. We call* proper points *the points of a persistence diagram lying on Δ^+.*

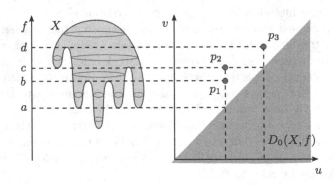

Fig. 1. Left: The height function f on the space X. Right: The associated $0th$-persistence diagram $D_0(X, f)$.

Figure 1 displays an example of persistence diagram for $k = 0$. The surface $X \subset \mathbb{R}^3$ is filtered by the height function f. $D_0(X, f)$ has three proper points p_1, p_2, p_3 since the abscissa of these points corresponds to the level at which new connected components are born along the filtration, while the ordinate identifies the level at which these connected components merge with existing ones. In terms of multiplicity, this means that $\mu_0(p_i) > 0$, $i = 1, 2, 3$, and $\mu_0(p) = 0$ for every other point $p \in \Delta^+$. To see, for example, that $\mu_0(p_1) = 2$, where $p_1 = (a, b)$, it is sufficient to observe that, for every $\varepsilon > 0$ sufficiently small, it holds that $\beta_0^{a+\varepsilon, b-\varepsilon}(X, f) = 4$, $\beta_0^{a+\varepsilon, b+\varepsilon}(X, f) = 2$, $\beta_0^{a-\varepsilon, b-\varepsilon}(X, f) = \beta_0^{a-\varepsilon, b+\varepsilon}(X, f) = 1$, and apply Definition 1. In an analogous way, it can be observed that $\mu_0(p_2) = \mu_0(p_3) = 1$.

Persistence diagrams comparison is usually carried out through the so called *bottleneck distance* because of the robustness of these descriptors with respect to it. Roughly, small changing in a given filtering function (w.r.t. the max-norm) produces just a small changing in the associated persistence diagram w.r.t. the bottleneck distance [4,7]. The bottleneck distance between two persistence diagrams measures the cost of finding a correspondence between their points. In doing this, the cost of taking a point p to a point p' is measured as the minimum between the cost of moving one point onto the other and the cost of moving both points onto the diagonal. In particular, the matching of a proper point p with a point of Δ can be interpreted as the destruction of the point p. Formally:

Definition 3. *Let D, D' be two persistence diagrams. The bottleneck distance $d_B(D, D')$ is defined as*

$$d_B(D, D') = \min_\sigma \max_{p \in D} d(p, \sigma(p)),$$

where σ varies among all the bijections between D and D' and

$$d\left((u, v), (u', v')\right) = \min\left\{ \max\left\{|u - u'|, |v - v'|\right\}, \max\left\{\frac{v - u}{2}, \frac{v' - u'}{2}\right\}\right\}$$

for every $(u, v), (u', v') \in \overline{\Delta^+}$.

3   Persistence Diagrams vs Complex Vectors

Driven by the awareness that, in the experimental framework, evaluating the bottleneck distance can be computationally expensive, making its usage not practicable on large datasets, in this work we propose a new procedure based on the preliminary idea introduced in [15]. We translate the problem of comparing directly two persistence diagrams through the bottleneck distance into the problem of comparing complex vectors associated with each persistence diagram through appropriate metrics between vectors. The components of these complex vectors are complex polynomials' coefficients obtained as follows. Firstly, we define a certain transformation taking points of persistence diagrams to the set of complex numbers. Secondly, we construct a complex polynomial having the obtained complex numbers as roots.

In this paper, we consider the three transformations below:

- $R : \overline{\Delta^+} \to \mathbb{C}$, with $R(u, v) = u + iv$,

– $S : \overline{\Delta^+} \to \mathbb{C}$, with $S(u, v) = \begin{cases} \dfrac{v - u}{\alpha\sqrt{2}} \cdot (u + iv), & \text{if } (u, v) \neq (0, 0) \\ (0, 0), & \text{otherwise} \end{cases}$,

– $T : \overline{\Delta^+} \to \mathbb{C}$, with $T(u, v) = \dfrac{v - u}{2} \cdot (\cos\alpha - \sin\alpha + i(\cos\alpha + \sin\alpha))$,

where $\alpha = \sqrt{u^2 + v^2}$.

R, S, T are continuous maps; R and S are also injective on $\overline{\Delta^+}$ and Δ^+, respectively. We define the multiplicity of a complex number in the range of R, S, T to be the sum of the multiplicities of the points belonging to its preimage (this is necessary because of the non-injectivity of T on Δ^+, although a preimage containing more than one proper point of the diagram has zero probability to occur). The main differences among these deformations are the following: the deformation R acts as the identity, just passing from $\mathbb{R}^2$ to $\mathbb{C}$; the deformation S warps the diagonal Δ to the origin, and takes points of Δ^+ to points of $\{z \in \mathbb{C} : Re(z) < Im(z)\}$; the deformation T warps the diagonal Δ to the origin, and takes points of Δ^+ to points of $\mathbb{C}$. An example showing how S and T transform a persistence diagram is represented in Figure 2. Both S and T seemed to be preferable to R because points near Δ — due to noise — have to be considered close to each other in the bottleneck distance, although they may be very far apart in Euclidean distance. Taking them to be all near the origin would then also reduce their impact in the sums and sums of products which will build the polynomial coefficients we are going to compare. In particular, T was designed to distribute the image of those noise points around zero, whereas S makes them near zero, but all on one side: in the half-plane of $\mathbb{C}$ corresponding to Δ^+. T has two drawbacks: it is not injective on Δ^+ and does not behave well with respect to simple transformations.

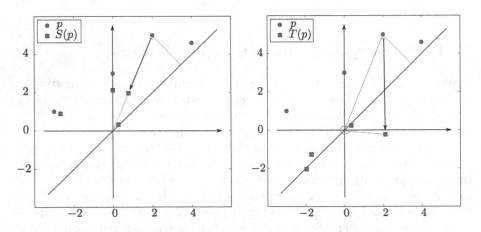

Fig. 2. A persistence diagram with its transformations S (left) and T (right). Same colors identify same lengths.

Let D be a persistence diagram, and $p_1 = (u_1, v_1), \ldots, p_s = (u_s, v_s)$ its proper points with multiplicity $r_1, \ldots, r_s$, respectively. Let now the complex numbers $z_1, \ldots, z_s$ be obtained from $p_1, \ldots, p_s$ by one of the transformations R, S or T. We associate to D the complex polynomial $f_D(t) = \prod_{j=1}^{s}(t - z_j)^{r_j}$. We are actually interested in the coefficient sequence of $f_D(t)$, which we can compute by Viète's formulas (see Algorithm 2).

Once we have the polynomials $f_D(t) = t^n - a_1 t^{n-1} + \cdots + (-1)^i a_i t^{n-i} + \cdots + (-1)^n a_n$ and $f_{D'}(t) = t^m - a'_1 t^{m-1} + \cdots + (-1)^j a'_j t^{m-j} + \cdots + (-1)^m a'_m$ corresponding to persistence diagrams D, D', we face a first problem, given by the possibly different degrees n and m ($m < n$ say). Because of their expression in terms of roots, we prefer to compare coefficients with the same index, rather than coefficients relative to the same degree of t. We manage this problem by adding $n - m$ null coefficients to $f_{D'}(t)$, i.e. multiplying $f_{D'}(t)$ by t^{n-m}, which amounts to adding the complex number zero with multiplicity $n - m$. In so doing, we can build two vectors of complex numbers $(a_1, \ldots, a_n), (a'_1, \ldots, a'_n)$ of the same length and are ready to compute a distance between them. By continuity of Viète's formulas, close roots imply close coefficients. Hence, two persistence diagrams that are close in terms of bottleneck distance have close associated polynomials. Unfortunately, the converse is not true.

Preliminary tests suggested that the first coefficients were more meaningful; therefore we experimented with different distances on two complex vectors $(a_1, \ldots, a_k), (a'_1, \ldots, a'_k)$, $k \in \{1, \ldots, n\}$, one treating all coefficients equally, two which give decreasing value to coefficients of increasing indices. The chosen metrics are the following:

$$d_1 = \sum_{j=1}^{k} |a_j - a'_j|, \quad d_2 = \sum_{j=1}^{k} \frac{|a_j - a'_j|}{j}, \quad d_3 = \sum_{j=1}^{k} |a_j - a'_j|^{1/j}.$$

Algorithms and Computational Analysis. The algorithms below resume the principal steps of our scheme. F in Algorithm 1 (line 2) and d in Algorithm 3 (line 4) correspond, respectively, to one of the transformations R, S, T and one of the metrics d_1, d_2, d_3 previously defined.

Algorithm 1: ComplexLists
Input: List A of proper points of a persistence diagram D,
$M = \max_{|A|} \{A : A \in \text{database } Db\}$
Output: List B of complex numbers associated with D

1: **for each** $(u, v) \in A$	4: **if** $|B| < M$
2: **replace** (u, v) by $F(u, v)$	5: **append** $M - |B|$ zeros to B
3: **end for**	6: **end if**

Algorithm 2: ComplexVectors

Input: M, $B = list(z_1, \ldots, z_M)$ associated with D, $k \in [0, M]$

Output: Complex vector V_k associated with D

1: **set** $V_k = list()$
2: **for** $j \in \{1, \ldots, k\}$
3:     **compute** $c_j(z_1, \ldots, z_M) = \displaystyle\sum_{1 \le i_1 < i_2 < \ldots < i_j \le M} z_{i_1} \cdot z_{i_2} \cdot \ldots \cdot z_{i_j}$
4:     **append** c_j to V_k
5: **end for**

Algorithm 3: VectorsComparison

Input: $L = \{V_k : V_k$ complex vector associated with D for each $D \in Db\}$

Output: Matrix of distances $d(V_k, V_k')$

1: **set** $M = (0_{ij})$, $i, j = 1, \ldots, |L|$ | 4:   **replace** $0_{ij}, 0_{ji}$ by $d(i, j)$
2: **for each** $i \in \{1, \ldots, |L|\}$ | 5:   **end for**
3:     **for each** $j \in \{i, \ldots, |L|\}$ | 6: **end for**

Let $N = |L| = |Db|$. It is easily seen that the computational complexities of Algorithms 1 and 3 are $C_1 = O(M \cdot N)$ and $C_3 = O(k \cdot N^2)$, respectively. The cost of Algorithm 2 depends on how we have implemented the computation of Viète formulas. Using the induction on the index j, we have $C_2 = O((2k^2 + k \cdot M) \cdot N)$.

We want to show that our approach to database classification, in general, results to be cheaper than using the bottleneck distance by a suitable choice of the number k of computed coefficients. Our comparison is realized in terms of storage locations and not in terms of running time performances since the algorithm proposed here and the one based on the bottleneck distance run on different platforms. We recall that the cost of computing the bottleneck distance $d_B(D, D')$ is $C_B = O\left((r + r')^{3/2} \log(r + r')\right)$ if A, A' are the subsets of proper points of two persistence diagrams D, D' with $|A| = r, |A'| = r'$ (see [14]). Instead, using our scheme, with $N = 2$ and $M = \max(r, r')$, we get $O((\max(r, r') + 2k^2 + k \cdot \max(r, r') + 2k)$, so $C = O(k \cdot (\max(r, r') + k))$. Since $k \le \max(r, r')$, in the worst case, we have $C = O\left((\max(r, r'))^2\right)$ which is higher than C_B, but for pre-processing we may choose a favorable k (e.g. $k = \left\lfloor \sqrt{\max(r, r')} \right\rfloor$). Also consider that, for a retrieval task, the heavy part of the computation (Viète's formulas) for the database is performed offline; in other words: if we store the coefficient vectors instead of the proper points lists, then the search can be performed by a distance computation of complexity $O\left(\max(r, r')\right)$!

4   Experimental Results

This section is devoted to validate the theoretical framework introduced in Section 3. In particular, through some experiments on persistence diagrams for 0th homology degree associated with 3D-models represented by triangle meshes, we will prove that our approach allows to perform the persistence diagrams comparison without greatly affecting (and in some cases improving) the goodness of results in terms of database classification.

To test the proposed framework we considered a database of 228 3D-surface mesh models introduced in [2]. The database is divided into 12 classes, each containing 19 elements obtained as follows: A null model taken from the Non Rigid World Benchmark [3] is considered together with six non-rigid transformations applied to it at three different strength levels. An example of the transformations and their greatest strength levels is given in Figure 3.

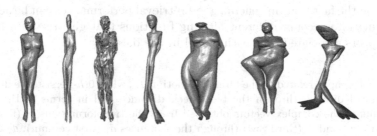

Fig. 3. The null model "Victoria0" and the 3rd strength level for each deformation.

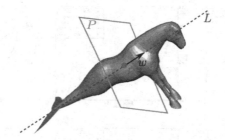

Fig. 4. The null model "seahorse0" depicted with its center of mass B and the associated vector w, which define the filtering functions f_L and f_P.

Two filtering functions f_L, f_P have been defined on the models of the database as follows: For each triangle mesh M of vertices $\{v_1, \ldots, v_n\}$, the center of mass B is computed, and the model is normalized to be contained in a unit sphere. Further, a vector w is defined as

$$w = \frac{\sum_{i=1}^{n}(v_i - B)\|v_i - B\|}{\sum_{i=1}^{n}\|v_i - B\|^2}.$$

The function f_L is the distance from the line L parallel to w and passing through B, while the function f_P is the distance from the plane P orthogonal to w and passing through B (see, as an example, Figure 4). The values of f_L and f_P are then normalized so that they range in the interval $[0, 1]$. These filtering functions are translation and rotation invariant, as well as scale invariant because of a priori normalization of the models. Moreover, the considered models are sufficiently generic (no point-symmetries occur etc...) to ensure that the vector w is well-defined over the whole database, as well as its orientation stability.

Our experimental results are synthesized in Tables 1 and 2 in terms of precision/recall (PR) graphs when the filtering functions f_L, f_P, respectively, are considered. Before going into details, we want to emphasize that our intent is not to validate the usage of persistence for shape comparison, retrieval or classification. In fact, as a reader coming from the retrieval domain will probably note, the PR graphs reported in this paper are below the state of the art. This depends on the fact that, in general, good retrieval performances can be achieved only taking into account different filtering functions that give rise to a battery of descriptors associated with each model in the database.

Table 1. PR graphs related to the filtering function f_L, when $0th$-persistence diagrams are compared directly through the bottleneck distance and in terms of the first k components of the complex vectors obtained from the transformations R (first row), S (second row) and T (third row) through the distances d_1 (first column), d_2 (second column) and d_3 (third column).

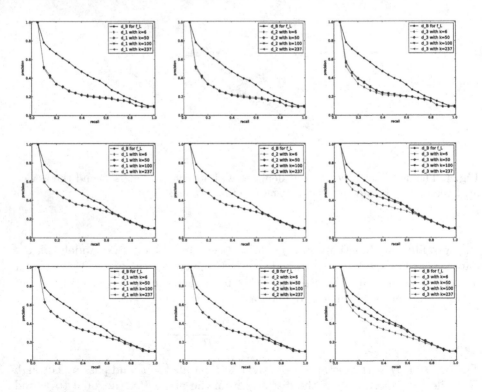

Table 2. PR graphs related to the filtering function f_P, when $0th$-persistence diagrams are compared directly through the bottleneck distance and in terms of the first k components of the complex vectors obtained from the transformations R (first row), S (second row) and T (third row) through the distances d_1 (first column), d_2 (second column) and d_3 (third column).

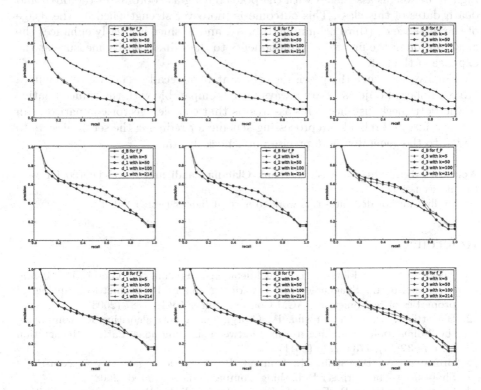

What these plots aim to show is the comparison of the performances when the database classification is carried out through the computation of the bottleneck distance d_B between persistence diagrams or the computation of the distances d_1, d_2 and d_3 between the first k components of the complex vectors obtained through the transformations R, S and T, for different values of k (see Section 3 for the definitions of R, S, T, d_1, d_2 and d_3). As it can be easily observed, increasing the value of k from the smallest to the biggest number of proper points in the persistence diagrams of our database, the PR graphs do not change so sensibly. This means that the most important information of the persistence diagram is contained in the first few vector components, the ones corresponding to the coefficients of monomials with highest degree. Moreover, we point out also that PR graphs related to vectors which are induced by transformations warping the diagonal Δ to a point (second and third rows in Tables 1 and 2) provide better results than by acting as the identity (first row). This fact depends on the properties of polynomial coefficients: Indeed roots corresponding to points of persistence diagrams farther from the diagonal weigh more than those closer to it. Hence, applying transformations S and T corresponds, in some sense, to providing points of a persistence diagram with a weight that follows the paradigm of persistence: The longer the lifespan of a homological class, the higher the weight associated with the point having as coordinates the birth and death dates of this class. This outcome is moreover strengthened by the usage of the distance d_3 (third column in Tables 1 and 2) since it greatly enhances the contribution of the first vector components to their dissimilarity measure at the expense of the last.

Finally, note that the precision values at high recall — i.e. by retrieving a large number of objects — are always fairly comparable with the values relative to the bottleneck distance. This assures us that complex vector comparison can act as a fast and reliable preprocessing scheme for reducing the set of objects to be fed to the generally more precise bottleneck distance.

Acknowledgments. We wish to thank Claudia Landi and Paweł Dłotko for very useful discussions.

The first author dedicates this work to a great fighter (Forza Vale!!!).

References

1. Biasotti, S., De Floriani, L., Falcidieno, B., Frosini, P., Giorgi, D., Landi, C., Papaleo, L., Spagnuolo, M.: Describing shapes by geometrical-topological properties of real functions. ACM Comput. Surv. **40**(4), 1–87 (2008)
2. Biasotti, S., Cerri, A., Frosini, P., Giorgi, D.: A new algorithm for computing the 2-dimensional matching distance between size functions. Pattern Recognition Letters **32**(14), 1735–1746 (2011)
3. Bronstein, A., Bronstein, M., Kimmel, R.: Numerical Geometry of Non-Rigid Shapes, 1st edn. Springer Publishing Company, Incorporated (2008)
4. Cerri, A., Di Fabio, B., Ferri, M., Frosini, P., Landi, C.: Betti numbers in multidimensional persistent homology are stable functions. Mathematical Methods in the Applied Sciences **36**(12), 1543–1557 (2013)
5. Cerri, A., Di Fabio, B., Jabłoński, G., Medri, F.: Comparing shapes through multiscale approximations of the matching distance. Computer Vision and Image Understanding **121**, 43–56 (2014)
6. Cohen-Steiner, D., Edelsbrunner, H., Harer, J.: Extending persistence using Poincaré and Lefschetz duality. Foundations of Computational Mathematics **9**(1), 79–103 (2009)
7. Cohen-Steiner, D., Edelsbrunner, H., Harer, J.: Stability of persistence diagrams. Discr. Comput. Geom. **37**(1), 103–120 (2007)
8. d'Amico, M., Frosini, P., Landi, C.: Using matching distance in size theory: A survey. Int. J. Imag. Syst. Tech. **16**(5), 154–161 (2006)
9. d'Amico, M., Frosini, P., Landi, C.: Natural pseudo-distance and optimal matching between reduced size functions. Acta. Appl. Math. **109**, 527–554 (2010)
10. Donatini, P., Frosini, P.: Lower bounds for natural pseudodistances via size functions. Archives of Inequalities and Applications **1**(2), 1–12 (2004)
11. Donatini, P., Frosini, P.: Natural pseudodistances between closed manifolds. Forum Mathematicum **16**(5), 695–715 (2004)

12. Edelsbrunner, H., Harer, J.: Computational Topology: An Introduction. American Mathematical Society (2009)
13. Edelsbrunner, H., Harer, J.: Persistent homology–a survey. In: Surveys on discrete and computational geometry, Contemp. Math., vol. 453, pp. 257–282. Amer. Math. Soc., Providence (2008)
14. Efrat, A., Itai, A., Katz, M.J.: Geometry helps in bottleneck matching and related problems. Algorithmica **31**, 1–28 (2001)
15. Ferri, M., Landi, C.: Representing size functions by complex polynomials. Proc. Math. Met. in Pattern Recognition **9**, 16–19 (1999)
16. Frosini, P., Landi, C.: Size functions and formal series. Appl. Algebra Engrg. Comm. Comput. **12**(4), 327–349 (2001)
17. Kalisnik Verovsek, S., Carlsson, G.: Symmetric and r-symmetric tropical polynomials and rational functions. arXiv preprint arXiv:1405.2268 (2014)

Pop-up Modelling of Hazy Scenes

Lingyun Zhao[✉], Miles Hansard, and Andrea Cavallaro

Centre for Intelligent Sensing, Queen Mary University of London, London, UK
lingyun.zhao@qmul.ac.uk

Abstract. This paper describes the construction of a layered scene-model, based on a single hazy image of an outdoor scene. A depth map and radiance image are estimated by standard dehazing methods. The radiance image is then segmented into a small number of clusters, and a corresponding scene-plane is estimated for each. This provides the basic structure of a 2.5-D scene model, without the need for multiple views, or image correspondences. We show that problems of gap-filling and depth blending can be addressed systematically, with respect to the layered depth-structure. The final models, which resemble cardboard 'pop-ups', are visually convincing. An HTML5/WebGL implementation is described, and subjective depth-preferences are tested in a psychophysical experiment.

Keywords: Layered scene models · Dehazing · Visualization · WebGL

1 Introduction

Impressive image-based 3D environments can now be found in many popular computer games and virtual reality tours. However, the creation of such environments remains a complicated and time-consuming process, often requiring special equipment, a large number of photographs, manual interaction, or all three. This makes it difficult for naive users to create an interactive 3D model.

This paper describes a system that can semi-automatically create a '2.5-D' model, from a single outdoor image, taken in hazy conditions. In particular, we use a *layered scene model* [19], in which the depth of each layer is estimated from the local haze-content of the images. We cannot, without other information, hope to create a full 3D model from a single view. However, we show that interactive 2.5-D models can be visually compelling.

The target application scenario is that the hazy outdoor photos would be processed rapidly, so that users would be able to browse them using ordinary web-browsers (e.g. on mobile devices). Our approach is similar to the creation of a 'pop-up' illustration in a children's book. Just like the cardboard pop-ups, our resulting 3D model is plane-based, as shown in figure 1. The foreground objects are automatically pasted onto different planes, with appropriate positions and orientations. No gaps should appear between the planes, as the viewpoint is varied. The scope of this paper is limited to outdoor scenes, in hazy conditions.

© Springer International Publishing Switzerland 2015
V. Murino and E. Puppo (Eds.): ICIAP 2015, Part I, LNCS 9279, pp. 306–318, 2015.
DOI: 10.1007/978-3-319-23231-7_28

(a)   (b)   (c)   (d)

Fig. 1. Our system constructs a plane-based 3D environment from a single hazy image, without losing any information from the original image. (a) The original photograph; (b) dehazed version of the photograph. (c) and (d): two novel views from our 3D model.

However, the visualization pipeline could easily be adapted to any other source of depth-information, including motion [19], or disparity [21].

The challenges of generating a pop-up image are as follows. Firstly, the original image does not contain explicit depth information. In order to get the depth information, we usually need multiple views, or some other source of information. This can be difficult to obtain, especially if the image-quality is poor (e.g. due to haze), or if computational resources are limited (e.g. on mobile devices). Secondly, even if depth can be estimated, it is important to resolve visibility correctly, in order to produce a convincing model. This usually requires a surface model of some kind, such as a mesh, which can again be difficult to estimate.

This work makes use of the WEBGL component of the new HTML5 standard. The final pop-up models can be rendered very efficiently, because WEBGL automatically uses GPU shaders for depth-testing and colour blending, whenever possible.

The method we propose can produce a visually pleasing 'pop-up' model, with interactive viewpoint control, based on a single hazy image. The novel contributions of this paper are as follows:

- We show that the haze-based depth information is suitable for use in 3D visualization.
- Texture-synthesis is used to fill the gaps that appear when the viewpoint is changed. Our method includes a novel preprocessing stage, which prevents 'mixed' image-regions (lying on depth boundaries) from being propagated.
- An appropriate image-blending model is introduced for depth-boundaries in the synthetic model.
- It is shown that the whole system is compatible with the WEBGL rendering model, and can be displayed interactively in any HTML5 browser.

This paper is organized as follows. In Section 2, we discuss state of the art in minimalistic 3D modelling. In Section 3, we introduce the pipeline to build up a plane-based 3D scene. In Section 4, we show the results of each step with five example images. Section 5 concludes the paper with discussion and ideas for future work.

2   Related Work

There are many different approaches in the field of image-based rendering and 3D modelling. Most systems require multiple images, or manually input information. Our system can automatically model a 3D outdoor scene — provided that a single hazy image is available.

2.1   Interactive 3D Modelling

The layered model was first proposed by Wang et al. [19]. They introduced a system for representing moving images with sets of overlapping layers. The layers are ordered by depth and they occlude each other in accord with the rules of compositing. They describe the methods for decomposing image sequences into layers using motion analysis.

Most research on full 3D reconstruction has focused on methods such as stereo vision or structure from motion. Popular urban modelling system introduced by Debevec et al. [2] and Cipolla et al. [3] require fewer images, but considerable user interaction. Other methods are able to perform user-guided modelling from a single image. Liebowitz et al. [16] and Criminisi et al. [13] demonstrate this approach, by recovering a metric reconstruction of an architectural scene, using geometric constraints. They can then compute 3D locations of user-specified points, via their distances from the ground plane. The user is also required to specify other constraints such as a square on the ground plane, a set of parallel 'up' lines and orthogonality relationships.

Most other approaches to build a metric reconstruction focus instead on producing perceptually pleasing approximations, but at the expense of quantitative accuracy. Zhang et al. [17] model free-form scenes by letting users place geometry constraints [14], such as normal directions, and then optimizing for the best 3D model to fit these constraints. Horry et al. [15] models a scene as an axis-aligned box, like a theatre stage, with floor, ceiling, backdrop and two side planes. An intuitive 'spidery mesh' interface allows the user to specify the coordinates of this box and its vanishing point. Foreground objects are manually labelled by the user and assigned to their own planes. This method produces impressive results but works only on certain scenes, since the front and back of the box are assumed to be parallel to the image plane. In our work, the positions and orientations of the planes are determined by the scene structure, rather than being limited to a pre-defined arrangement.

2.2   Automatic 3D Modelling

Hoiem et al. [4] introduced an automatic system to construct a rough 3D environment from a single image, by learning a statistical model of geometric scene-classes. Similar to our work, they limited their scope to dealing with outdoor scenes, but they also assumed that a scene is composed of a single ground plane, with piecewise planar objects sticking out of the ground at right angles and the sky. Under this assumption, they constructed a coarse, scaled 3D model from a single image by classifying each pixel as ground, vertical or sky and estimating the horizon position. Colour, texture, image location and geometric features are all useful cues for determining these labels. However, under their assumptions, crowded scenes, such as trees or people cannot be easily modelled. Additionally, their models cannot account for slanted surfaces, or scenes that contain multiple ground-parallel planes. Our system has no geometric constraints, but it does require a hazy photograph of the scene.

In recent work, Saxena et al. [6, 7] present an algorithm for predicting depth from monocular image features. However, their depth maps are not accurate enough to produce visually-pleasing 3D models. Their method also relies on good quality of image features, which makes hazy images unsuitable. More recent work proposed by Saxena et al. [8] uses a Markov Random Field (MRF) to infer a set of plane parameters that capture both the 3D position and orientation of each surface-patch. They also incorporate object-information into the MRF to improve the results. However, the resulting models are often visually incomplete.

3   Model Construction

To create a layered model of the scene, we need information about its depth-structure. Formally, our system is based on the standard image-compositing 'over' operation $\mathbf{f} \odot \mathbf{b} = \mathbf{f} + (1 - \alpha_f)\mathbf{b}$., where $\mathbf{f}$ and $\mathbf{b}$ are foreground and background layers, respectively. The opacity of each foreground pixel is determined by the alpha-map, α_f. We require a more general version of the operation $\mathbf{g} = \mathbf{f} \odot \mathbf{b}$, as used in the stereo-based model of Szeliski and Golland [21]:

$$\mathbf{g}(x,y) = \bigodot_{d=d_{\min}}^{d_{\max}} \mathbf{f}(x,y,d) \tag{1}$$

Here the operator $\odot_d$ composites each RGBA layer $\mathbf{f}$ over the current background layer, according to depth d. Note that $d_{\min}$ is the closest layer, which appears left-most in the sequence $\mathbf{f}(x, y, d_{\min}) \odot \cdots$, by analogy with the original over-operator.

Rather than using multiple views, range scanners, or complex scene-models, we use the depth information in hazy images. Meanwhile, we use the dehazed radiance image to provide the colour information for compositing. The complete pipeline is shown in figure 2, and described in the following sub-sections.

3.1   Dehazing

Atmospheric particles cause the *airlight* colour, which is effectively that of the haze, to mix with the scene radiance. This changes the observed colour distributions, and reduces the contrast of the images. Furthermore, these effects are distance dependent, which means that *dehazing* the images can produce information about scene-depth, as well as radiance. This can be seen from the Lambert-Beer law,

$$t_i = \exp(-\lambda r_i) \tag{2}$$

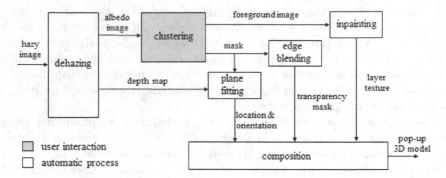

Fig. 2. Block diagram of the proposed system for creating a pop-up 3D model.

(a) Hazy image   (b) Radiance image   (c) Depth image

Fig. 3. Example of dehazing, using the dark-channel prior of He et al. [1].

where r_i is the distance of the scene along the i-th ray, λ is a weather-dependent constant, and t_i is the optical *transmission*.

We use the Dark Channel Prior (DCP) dehazing algorithm to estimate the transmission [1]. He et al. introduced the DCP, which is based on the assumption that every image patch will contain the projection of a dark or colourful (i.e. dark in one RGB channel) scene-point. Having estimated the global airlight colour, from the sky region, the transmission can be estimated from the dark-channel pixels.

3.2   Clustering and Plane-fitting

Rather than making a full 3D model, our target is to create a layered visualization. Hence it suffices to simply *cluster* the depth and radiance outputs of the dehazing process. This paper is not concerned with the details of the clustering process, so we use the semi-supervised GrabCut [18] method, to define a small number of clusters in the radiance image (usually around five).

We convert the range estimates $r_i = -\log(t_i)/\lambda$ in equation (2) to depth values d_i, (measured perpendicular to the optical axis). We then use the RANSAC algorithm [10] to fit a depth-plane to each cluster of (x, y, d) values. RANSAC is reliable even in the presence of a high proportion of outliers, which is relevant here, because the dehazing sometimes produces very bad depth-estimates (e.g. when an object has the same colour as the airlight). Note that the depths are only determined up to the overall scale-factor λ; this issue will be considered in section 4.

The clustering and fitting stage produces two outputs. Firstly, a label image, which maps each pixel to one of the layers. Secondly, a list of plane vectors, which encode the position and orientation of each layer. These outputs are stored as PNG images, and associated JSON data, which can be read by the web-browser.

3.3 Inpainting

Image inpainting is the problem of filling new colour and texture into missing parts of an image, so that the result is visually convincing. In our case, the missing parts appear at depth-boundaries, when the viewpoint changes [20]. We used Criminisi's algorithm [9] to fill the gap with patches from the surrounding region. These patches should continue the image texture into the hole, without introducing visual artifacts. Such techniques are collectively referred to as patch or examplar-based methods. Figure 4 shows the visualisation improvement after inpainting.

Two important modifications are made to the inpainting procedure. Firstly, patches should be sampled from the appropriate layer, so that the background texture grows *behind* the occluding layer. The inpainting algorithm starts computation from the edge to the centre of holes, and is therefore sensitive to the image-structure at the edge. However, we observe that this image structure is usually *not* representative of the occluded layer, because it will contain some mixture of the occluding layer (especially at complex boundaries, like foliage). Hence our second modification is to perform an erosion of each cluster, before proceeding with the inpainting process. This results in significantly more convincing textures, as shown in figure 5. The erosion radius was set to eight pixels, in all cases.

3.4 Edge Blending

The clustering process produces image-segments with hard edges. These look very unconvincing in the pop-up visualisation, especially at complex

(a) Before inpainting   (b) After inpainting

Fig. 4. Comparison between the layered model before and after inpainting.

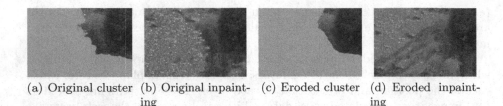

(a) Original cluster | (b) Original inpainting | (c) Eroded cluster | (d) Eroded inpainting

Fig. 5. Comparison between direct inpainting result and inpainting after erosion. The original cluster is a part of a tree with some sky region at the edge. The green region is labelled as the hole. Direct inpainting tends to propagate the edge texture, which is not representative of the foliage. A more natural inpainting is obtained after erosion.

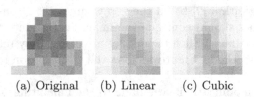

(a) Original   (b) Linear   (c) Cubic

Fig. 6. Comparison between different edge blending methods. (a) Original cluster-edge. White pixels indicate the background region. (b) Linearly-blended image. (c) Cubic blend produces a smoother transition.

depth-boundaries (e.g. due to foliage). To make the transition more natural, we add an alpha channel to each foreground layer. We then compute the distance-transform of each segment, with respect to any adjacent and *more distant* segments. This gives a scalar map $\delta(\mathbf{x})$, which encodes the image-distance from pixel $\mathbf{x}$ to the nearest occluded point. It is then straightforward to set a transition in the alpha channel $\alpha(\mathbf{x})$, based on the following rule:

$$\alpha(\mathbf{x}) = \begin{cases} \beta\big(\delta(\mathbf{x})/\epsilon\big) & \text{if } \delta(\mathbf{x}) \leq \epsilon \\ 1 & \text{otherwise} \end{cases} \tag{3}$$

where ϵ is the 'border-width' of the depth transition (set to 5 pixels in all experiments here), and $\beta(\cdot)$ is a blending function. One possibility for the latter is simply $\beta(t) = t$, which results in a linear transition. The cubic Hermite function $\beta(t) = t^2(3 - 2t)$ is more suitable, because it has zero slope at either end of the interval $t \in [0, 1]$, which results in a smoother transition. This is illustrated in figure 6. The outside edge pixels in the cubic edge blending result are softer, compared to the other results. We therefore apply cubic edge blending in our experiment.

(a)   (b)   (c)

Fig. 7. Examples of pop-up scenes, generated with our method. Column (a) shows the original hazy input images. Columns (b) and (c) show example novel views, taken from our pop-up models.

4   Results

We use the THREE JavaScript library [22], which is built on WEBGL, to display the final models. Each layer is rendered as a quadrilateral, with the corresponding RGBA texture obtained as described in section 3. The compositing procedure (1) involves *order-dependent transparency*, which can be problematic in OPENGL/WEBGL. However, in practice, we find that the layers do not have complex depth relationships, and so few artefacts are observed.

| (a) | (b) | (c) | (d) |

Fig. 8. Original hazy image (a), and 3D model (b), taken from [4]. Note the artefacts corresponding to the pedestrians in (b). Images (c) and (d) show other novel views generated from (a), using our system.

We can use either perspective or orthographic cameras to project the model. The former (used here) looks more natural, but the latter has the advantage of exactly re-creating the input image, from the appropriate viewpoint. We add interactive controls for the viewpoint and depth-scaling. The latter compensates for the unknown constant λ in equation (2), by effectively letting the user set a visually pleasing depth-range for the scene.

Figure 7 shows the qualitative results of our algorithm on several real-world images. Note that the lower region, in most outdoor photographs, is nearer to the observer than the upper region. We tested our algorithm on an image from the Hoiem et al. [4] database. The failure in their result due to overlap of vertical regions in the image is solved in our work. (Figure 8). Since we do not have the knowledge about the ground truth, the location of each plane is largely based on the accuracy of the dehazing algorithm. Some inherited problems from dehazing will also affect our result. Figure 9 shows an example of a typical failure.

4.1   Evaluation

We test viewers' subjective preferences of depth structure, in a psychophysical experiment. The evaluation system is made in a web browser, with user-interactive buttons to increase or decrease the overall depth-range of the scene (i.e. the distance between the front and back layers). Meanwhile, the entire scene undergoes a slow left-right change of viewpoint, which is not under user-control. We asked the participants to interactively adjust the depth scale, in order to

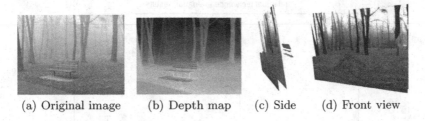

(a) Original image   (b) Depth map   (c) Side   (d) Front view

Fig. 9. Example of depth failure. The colour of the bench is similar to that of the haze, leading to an over-estimate of its depth (c). Nonetheless, the front view of the final model is visually consistent (d).

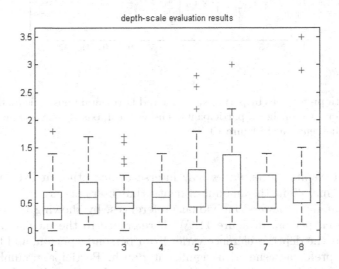

Fig. 10. Depth preferences by scene. The red horizontal lines indicate the median depth scale, for each of the eight scenes. The box edges are the 25th and 75th percentiles. The red crosses are outliers. The vertical axis is the scale factor, which is 1 for the default configuration.

achieve the most pleasing visual effect. A demonstration video for our experimental results is available online at: http://youtu.be/qKoZ5A-MvA4.

We asked 13 observers to evaluate 8 scenes, in random order, with three repetitions of each. The evaluation results are shown in figures 10 and 11. We draw the following general conclusions. Firstly, most people enjoy the experience of the virtual pop-up scene with depth information, because they do not set the depth-scale to zero. Secondly, for some specific images, such as that shown in figure 9, people prefer the trivial planar image to the pop-up. This is due to dehazing artefacts, such as missing foreground objects. Thirdly, based on the

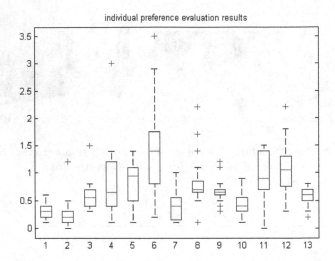

Fig. 11. Depth preferences by participant. The red horizontal lines indicate the median depth scale, for each of the 13 participants. The vertical axis is the scale factor, which is 1 for default scenes, as in figure 10.

experimental results, some planes may intersect each other at extreme depth-scales, which may limit the amount of depth that users prefer.

We also analyse viewers' individual preferences, by showing the evaluation results for each person, in figure 11. With reference to the median values, we conclude that the depth-preference varies from person to person, and that most participants prefer a scene with significant depth. Participant number 6 has much higher (and more variable) depth preferences than the others. Participants numbered 1, 2, 3, 9 and 13 are female; the other participants are male. We note that the female depth preferences appear to be more consistent across different scenes.

5   Conclusions

We have proposed a new way to model a 3D scene, based on a single hazy image. The result can be viewed interactively in an ordinary web-browser. We have shown that the problems of hole-filling and edge-blending can be addressed systematically, in relation to the layered-depth structure.

The algorithm of automatic single-view 3D reconstruction still needs to be improved. We plan to replace GrabCut with an automatic method to segment the radiance image, e.g. based on Mean Shift. This will additionally make use of the depth map, from the dehazing process, to perform RGBD clustering. It would also be interesting to study how the perceived quality of the final model depends on the number of clusters. Finally, future experiments will allow the participants to control the relative plane-depths, rather than just the overall depth scaling. It will be interesting to analyze the consistency of these judgements, and how they relate to 3D scene perception.

References

1. He, K., Sun, J., Tang, X.: Single Image Haze Removal Using Dark Channel Prior. IEEE Trans. PAMI **33**(12), 2341–2353 (2011)
2. Debevec, P.E., Taylor, C.J., Malik, J.: Modeling and rendering architecture from photographs: a hybrid geometry and image-based approach. In: Proc. ACM SIGGRAPH, pp. 11–20 (1996)
3. Cipolla, R., Robertson, D., Boyer, E.: Photobuilder - 3D models of architectural scenes form uncalibrated images. In: Proc. IEEE Conference on Multimedia Computing and Systems, pp. 25–31 (1999)
4. Hoiem, D., Efros, A., Hebert, M.: Automatic photo pop-up. In: Proc. ACM SIGGRAPH, pp. 577–584 (2005)
5. Hoiem, D., Efros, A., Hebert, M.: Putting objects in perspective. In: Proc. CVPR, pp. 3–15 (2006)
6. Saxena, A., Chuang, S.H., Ng, A.Y.: Learning depth from single monocular images. In: Proc. NIPS, vol. 18, pp. 1161–1168 (2005)
7. Saxena, A., Chuang, S.H., Ng, A.Y.: 3D depth reconstruction from a single still image. In: Proc. IJCAI, pp. 53–69 (2007)
8. Saxena, A., Sun, M., Ng, A.Y.: Learning 3D scene structure from a single still image. In: Proc. ICCV, pp. 1–8 (2007)
9. Criminisi, A.: Objecte removal by exemplar-based inpainting. In: Proc. CVPR (2003)
10. Fischler, M., Bolles, R.: Random Sample Consensus: A Paradigm for Model Fitting with Applications to Image Analysis and Automated Cartography. Communications of the ACM **24**, 381–395 (1981)
11. Schnabel, R., Wahl, R., Klein, R.: Efficient RANSAC for Point-cloud Shape Detection. Computer Graphics Forum **26**(2), 214–226 (2007)
12. Yingyang, M., Förstner, W.: Plane Detection in Point Cloud Data. Technical report, Institute of Geodesy and Geoinformation, University of Bonn (2010)
13. Criminisi, A., Reid, I., Zisserman, A.: Single View Metrology. Int. Journal of Computer Vision **40**(2), 123–148 (2000)
14. Hartley, R., Zisserman, A.: Multiple View Geometry in Computer Vision, 2nd edn. Cambridge University Press (2004)
15. Horry, Y., Anjyo, K.I., Arai, K.: Tour into the picture: using a spidery mesh interface to make animation from a single image. In: Proc. ACM SIGGRAPH, pp. 225–232 (1997)
16. Liebowitz, D., Criminisi, A., Zisserman, A.: Creating architectural models from images. In: Proc. Eurographics, vol. 18, pp. 39–50 (1999)
17. Zhang, L., Dugas-Phocion, G., Samson, J., Seitz, S.: Single view modeling of freeform scenes. In: Proc. CVPR, pp. 990–997 (2001)
18. Rother, C., Kolmogorov, V., Blake, A.: Grab-Cut: Interactive foreground extraction using iterated graph cuts. ACM Trans. Computer Graphics **23**(3), 309–314 (2004)

19. Wang, J.Y.A., Adelson, E.H.: Representing Moving Images with Layers. IEEE Trans. Image Processing **3**(5), 625–638 (1994)
20. Swirski, L., Richardt, C., Dodgson, N.A.: Layered Photo Pop-Up. SIGGRAPH Posters (2011)
21. Szeliski, R., Golland, P.: Stereo matching with transparency and matting. In: Proc. ICCV, pp. 517–524 (1998)
22. Three JavaScript Library. http://threejs.org/

3D Geometric Analysis of Tubular Objects Based on Surface Normal Accumulation

Bertrand Kerautret[1,2]([⊠]), Adrien Krähenbühl[1,2], Isabelle Debled-Rennesson[1,2], and Jacques-Olivier Lachaud[3]

[1] Université de Lorraine, LORIA, UMR 7503, F-54506 Vandoeuvre-lès-Nancy, France
{bertrand.kerautret,adrien.krahenbuhl,isabelle.debled-rennesson}@loria.fr
[2] CNRS, LORIA, UMR 7503, F-54506 Vandoeuvre-lès-Nancy, France
[3] LAMA (UMR CNRS 5127), Université Savoie Mont Blanc, F-73376
Chambéry, France
jacques-olivier.lachaud@univ-savoie.fr

Abstract. This paper proposes a simple and efficient method for the reconstruction and extraction of geometric parameters from 3D tubular objects. Our method constructs an image that accumulates surface normal information, then peaks within this image are located by tracking. Finally, the positions of these are optimized to lie precisely on the tubular shape centerline. This method is very versatile, and is able to process various input data types like full or partial mesh acquired from 3D laser scans, 3D height map or discrete volumetric images. The proposed algorithm is simple to implement, contains few parameters and can be computed in linear time with respect to the number of surface faces. Since the extracted tube centerline is accurate, we are able to decompose the tube into rectilinear parts and torus-like parts. This is done with a new linear time 3D torus detection algorithm, which follows the same principle of a previous work on 2D arc circle recognition. Detailed experiments show the versatility, accuracy and robustness of our new method.

1 Introduction

Tubular shapes appear in various image application domains. They are common in the medical imaging field. For instance, blood vessel identification and measurements are an important object of study [12,17,22]. The wall thickness in bronchial tree plays also an important role in several lung diseases [19]. Tubular shapes also occur in CT volumetric images of wood [13]: their segmentation into knots is exploited by agronomic researchers or in industrial sawmills. Outside volumetric images, tubular objects are also present in industrial context with the production of metallic pipes from bending machines. Quality assessment of such metallic pieces is generally achieved with a direct inspection by a laser scanner. Such process is also performed for calibration purpose and reverse engineering tasks.

J.-O. Lachaud—This work was partially supported by the ANR grants DigitalSnow ANR-11-BS02-009

© Springer International Publishing Switzerland 2015
V. Murino and E. Puppo (Eds.): ICIAP 2015, Part I, LNCS 9279, pp. 319–331, 2015.
DOI: 10.1007/978-3-319-23231-7_29

Geometric properties of tubular structures are extracted in different ways depending on the application domain and on the nature of input data. From unorganized set of points, Lee proposed a curve reconstruction exploiting an Euclidean minimum spanning tree with a thinning algorithm and applies it to pipe surface reconstruction [15]. Later, Kim and Lee proposed another method based on shrinking and moving least-squares [16] to improve the reconstruction of pipes with non constant radius. However, as shown by Bauer and Polthier [6], such a reconstruction method produced noisy curves in particular for data extracted from partial scans like the ones of Fig. 1 (b). Another approach estimates the principal curvatures of the set of points in order to detect cylindrical and toric parts [10]. Although promising, this approach suffers from the quality of the local curvature estimator. To overcome this limitation, Bauer and Polthier [6] proposed to recover a parametric model based on a tubular spine. Their method is able to process partial laser scans limited to one particular direction. The main steps of their method consists in first projecting the mesh points onto the spinal region of the mesh before reconstructing a spine curve and analyzing it. The method requires as parameter one radius size, and it cannot process volumetric data (voxel sets) or heightmap data.

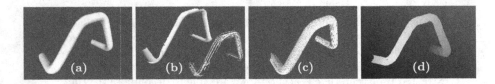

Fig. 1. Different kinds of 3D tubular data: (a) input data obtained from full laser scan, (b) partial scans from one direction, (c) digital set of voxels and (d) height map.

More generally, classic medial axis extraction looks to be a potential solution for tubular shape analysis [8]. However such extraction may be sensitive to noise or to the presence of small defaults in the volumetric discrete object (like small hole). Fig. 2 shows some results obtained with different methods available from the implementation given in the authors survey. We can clearly see that small holes in the digital object significantly degrade the result. More recently, many advances came from the field of mesh processing with approaches based on mesh contraction [3,20]. However, they are generally not adapted to surface with boundaries like the partial scan data of Fig. 1. In the same way, they are not simple to adapt to volumetric data like digital object made of voxels or height map. To process volumetric discrete objects, Gradient Vector Flow [24] was exploited by Hassouna and Farag in order to propose a robust skeleton curve extraction [11]. This method was also adapted to process gray values volumetric images used in virtual endoscopy [5]. In the field of discrete geometry we can mention a method which propose to specifically exploit 3D discrete tools to extract some medial axis on grey-level images [4]. To sum up approaches on medial axis, they are designed to process shapes defined as volumes, but they fail when processing open surfaces or partial samplings of the shape boundary. To process such data, we can refer to the work of Tagliasacchi *et al.* [21], who propose an algorithm based on surface normals. However the resulting quality depends on manual parameter tuning.

In this work, we propose a unified approach to the reconstruction and the geometric analysis of tubular objects obtained from various input data types: laser scans sampling the shape boundary with partial or complete data (Fig. 1 (a,b)), voxel sets sampling the shape (Fig. 1 (c)) or more specifically from height map data (Fig. 1 (c,d)). Potential applications of the latter datatype are numerous because of the increasing development of *Kinect*®-like devices. Our main contributions are first to propose a simple and automatic centerline extraction algorithm, which mainly relies on a surface normal accumulation image. Like other Hough transform based applications [7,23], this algorithm can handle various types of input data. We also propose to extract geometric information along the tubular object, by segmenting it into rectilinear and toric parts. This is achieved with a 3D extension of a previous work on circular arc detection along 2D curves. In the following sections, we first introduce the new method of centerline detection, then we show how to reconstruct the tubular shape and decompose it into meaningful parts. We conclude with representative experiments showing the qualities of our method.

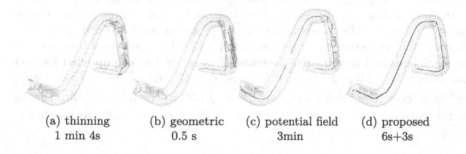

| (a) thinning | (b) geometric | (c) potential field | (d) proposed |
| 1 min 4s | 0.5 s | 3min | 6s+3s |

Fig. 2. Skeleton extraction from three different methods presented in [8] with the implementation given by the authors. Our method is presented on the right.

2   Fast and Simple Centerline Extraction on 3D Tubular Object

In this section, we present centerline extraction algorithm based on surface normal accumulation. It consists in three main steps. First, we compute a 3D accumulation image, which counts for each voxel how many faces of input data have their normal vector pointing through the voxel (i). Depending on input data, normal vectors can be defined directly from the mesh faces or estimated by a more robust and accurate estimator (in particular if we process a digital object). Then a tracking algorithm (ii) extracts an approximate centerline by following local maxima in the accumulation image. Finally, to remove digitization effects due to the 3D discrete accumulation image, we optimize the position of center points (iii) by a gradient descent method.

2.1 Accumulation Images from Normal Vectors

The first algorithm requires as input a set of faces (a mesh or a digital surface), their associated normal vectors, and a 3D digital space (the 3D grid that will store the accumulated values). If the input object is a mesh, the gridstep of the digitization grid must be specified by the user. Depending on the awaited accuracy, a default gridstep can be chosen as the median size of mesh faces (with the face size defined as its longest edge). If the input object is a digital object or a heightmap, the digitization grid just matches their resolution. Besides, this algorithm requires as parameter some approximation of the tube radius R.

The whole algorithm is detailed in Algorithm 1. It outputs for each voxel the number of normal vectors going through it as well as a vector estimating the tube local main directions (i.e. the tangent to the centerline or equivalently the direction of minimal curvature along the tube boundary). Fig. 3 illustrates the main steps of the algorithm with the 3D directional scans, starting from the face origin f_k in the direction of its normal vector $\overrightarrow{n_k}$ along a distance denoted accRadius (set to $R + \epsilon$ where ϵ is used to take into account possible small variations of the radius along the tube, see image (a) of Fig. 1). During the scan, the accumulation scores are stored for each visited voxel (image (b) of the same figure). The principal direction $\overrightarrow{p}$ of a voxel is also updated for each scan (image (c)). More precisely, if we denote by $\overrightarrow{n_j}$ and $\overrightarrow{n_k}$ the two last normal vectors intersecting a voxel V for the scans j and k, the principal direction $\overrightarrow{d_k}$ for the current scan is given by: $\overrightarrow{d_k} = \overrightarrow{d_j} + (\overrightarrow{n_k} \wedge \overrightarrow{n_j})$. In order to ignore non

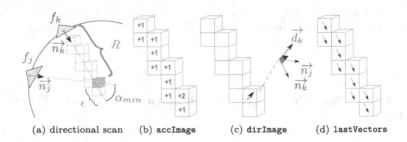

(a) directional scan   (b) accImage   (c) dirImage   (d) lastVectors

Fig. 3. Illustration of Algorithm 1, which builds an accumulation image whose peaks match the centerline of the tubular shape.

significant directions induced by near colinear vectors, we add a small constant (set by default to 0.1) to filter the norm of the resulting vector $\overrightarrow{n_k} \wedge \overrightarrow{n_j}$.

Fig. 4 illustrates the computations made in Algorithm 1 for a mesh input data, and it shows the resulting accumulation image (image (c)) and vectors $\overrightarrow{n}$ orthogonal to the tube main direction $\overrightarrow{d}$. Since centerline extraction relies on these accumulation images, we evaluate the robustness of these images with various input surface types. The first row of Fig. 5 presents the resulting 3D accumulation images obtained on partial, noisy, digital or on small resolution mesh. In all these configurations, relative maximal values are indeed well located near the center of the tubular shape. A fixed threshold was applied in order to highlight the voxels with accumulation values close to maximal ones. Such voxels are drawn in black and for a particular selected voxel, we have highlighted their scanning origin faces with blue lines. All these results confirm the robustness of the proposed algorithm. We have therefore a solid basis for the tracking algorithm presented in the following part.

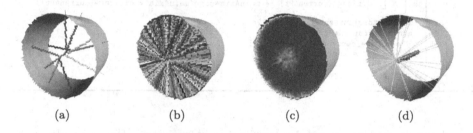

| (a) | (b) | (c) | (d) |

Fig. 4. Illustration of accumulation images generated from surface normal vectors. Image (a) (resp. (b)) illustrates some (resp. all) scanning directions defined from mesh triangles. Image (c) illustrates the values obtained in the 3D accumulation image and (d) shows some voxels having accumulation score upper than a given threshold. In the last image we also display the set of faces contributing to the accumulation score.

2.2   Centerline Tracking from Image Accumulation

Even if the maximal values obtained in the previous part are well centered on the tubular object, a
simple thresholding is not robust enough to extract
directly the centerline. Furthermore it implies the
manual adjustment of the threshold parameter. To

illustrate this point, the image on the side shows different results obtained by choosing various threshold parameters σ. A too strict threshold implies disconnected points, while a less restrictive one produces a thick line with parasite voxels.

To better approach the centerline we propose to define a simple tracking algorithm exploiting the output of Algorithm 1, i.e. the accumulation image and

---

Algorithm 1. `accumulationFromNormalVectors` : From position and normals of faces of an input mesh, this algorithm computes an accumulation image (`accImage`) by a directional scan starting from a face center in the direction of the face inward normal. It also outputs the image of vectors representing the local main axis direction of the tubular shape (`dirImage`).

```
Input    : mesh // Triangular mesh of a tube
           accRadius // Accumulation length from center of faces
           minNorm = 0.1 // Minimum norm value
Ouput    : accImage // Accumulation of normal vector number passing through a coordinate
           dirImage // Cross product of all normals passing through a coordinate
           maxAcc // Maximum number of normals passing through an (x,y,z) coordinate
           maxPt // maxAcc coordinates
Variable: lastVectors // The last considered normal for each (x,y,z) coordinate
           mainAxis // Vector contributing to the cross product of a directional vector
lastVectors = Image3D(mesh.dimensions())
maxAcc = 0
foreach face in mesh do
   currentPt = face.center
   normalVector = face.normalVector().normalized()
   while distance(currentPt, face.center) < accRadius do
      if accImage[currentPt] != 0 then
         mainAxis = lastVectors[currentPt] × normalVector
         if norm(mainAxis) > minNorm then
            dirImage[currentPt] += mainAxis*sign(mainAxis • dirImage[currentPt])

      lastVectors[currentPt] = normalVector
      accImage[currentPt]++
      if accImage[currentPt] > maxAcc then
         maxAcc = accImage[currentPt]
         maxPt = currentPt
      currentPt += normalVector
```

---

the direction vectors image. As described in Algorithm 2, the main idea is to start from a point C_0 detected as a maximal accumulation value of the 3D accumulation image. Then, from a current point C_i of the centerline, the algorithm determines next point C_{i+1} as the point having maximal accumulation value in the 2D patch image I^i_{patch} defined in the plane normal to the direction $\texttt{dirImage}(C_i)$ at distance `trackStep` (see Fig. 6 (a,b)).

2.3   Skeleton Position Optimization

Since the resulting tracking skeleton is embedded in a digital space, it suffers from digitization artefacts and is not perfectly centered within the input mesh. Moreover, depending on normal mesh quality, the tracking algorithm can potentially be influenced by perturbated normal directions, and may deviate from the expected centerline. Such perturbations can dramatically degrade the quality of upcoming geometric analysis, and hence impose some unwanted post processing tasks. To avoid such a difficulty, we propose to apply an optimization algorithm in order to obtain a perfectly centered spine line.

The idea is to model the quality of the current fitting by an error $E_s(C)$, defined as the sum of the squared difference between the known tube radius R and the distance between the tube center C and its associated input mesh points

Algorithm 2. trackPatchCenter: tracking algorithm in one direction, given a starting point and an orientation.

```
Input    : accImage // Accumulation of normal vector number passing through a coordinate
           dirImage // Cross product of all normals passing through a coordinate
           accRadius // Accumulation length from center of faces
           startPt, // Start point for tracking (must belong to the centerline)
           trackInFront // True if tracking direction is in the startPt vector direction
           trackStep // Distance between two consecutive centerline points
Output   : centerline // Point set constituting the tube centerline
Variable: continueTracking // True if tracking can continue
           patchSize // Dimension of the square patch
           currentPt, previousPt // Considered point during an iteration
           lastVect // Directional vector associated to previousPt
           centerPatch // Patch center finding from currentPt
patchImageSize = 2 * aRadius ;
centerline = emptySet()
continueTracking = true
patchSize = 2 * accRadius
currentPt = startPt
lastVect = trackInFront ? dirImage( startPt ) : - dirImage( startPt )
previousPt = startPt - lastVect * trackStep
while continueTracking do
    centerline.append( currentPt )
    dirVect = dirImage[currentPt].normalized()
    if lastVect.dot(dirVect) < 0 then
      ⌞ dirVect = -dirVect
    continueTracking = isInsideTube( accImage, currentPt, previousPt, trackStep, π/3 )
    previousPt = currentPt
    // Defined the next image patch center point
    centerPatch = currentPt + ( dirVect * trackStep )
    if not accImage.domain().contains( centerPatch ) then
      ⌞ break
    // Extract a 2D image of size 2 * accRadius from the 3D image accImage, centered on
    // centerPatch and directed along dirVect
    patchImage = extractPatch( accImage, centerPatch, dirVect, 2 * accRadius )
    maxCoords = getMaxCoords( patchImage )
    lastVect = dirVect
    previousPt = currentPt
    currentPt = patchSpaceToAccImageSpace( maxCoords)
return centerline
```

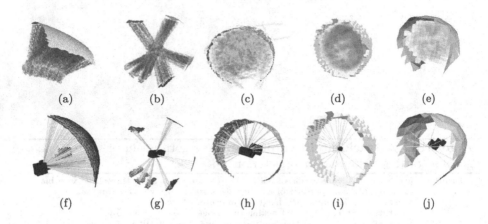

(a)   (b)   (c)   (d)   (e)

(f)   (g)   (h)   (i)   (j)

Fig. 5. Experiment of the robustness of the surface normal accumulation algorithm applied on different types of input surface: on sector filtered mesh (a,f), on partial scan mesh (b,g), on noisy mesh (c,h), on digital surface (d,i), and on small resolution mesh (e,j).

M_i. We wish to find the best position for center C that minimizes this error. Otherwise said, we look for the circle of radius R that best fits the data points M_i in the least-square sense. Hence, the error is

$$E_s(C) = \sum_{i=0}^{N-1} (\|\overrightarrow{CM_i}\| - R)^2. \tag{1}$$

This minimization problem is easily solved by a gradient descent algorithm that follows the direction of steepest descent of the error. By simple derivation, its

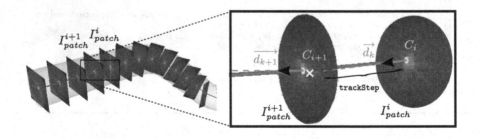

Fig. 6. Tracking algorithm step. The patch I_{patch}^{i+1} is generated from the maximum C_i of I_{patch}^i in the $\overrightarrow{d_k}$ direction at a trackStep distance before to localize the maximum C_{i+1} of this new patch.

gradient is

$$\nabla E_s(C) = 2 \sum_{i=0}^{N-1} \frac{\overrightarrow{CM_i}}{\|\overrightarrow{CM_i}\|}(R - \|\overrightarrow{CM_i}\|). \tag{2}$$

The gradient descent can also be interpreted as elastic forces acting on the center C and pulling or pushing it in the direction of data according to the current distance. Then the minimization process applies at each step of the process the sum $\overrightarrow{f}$ of theses forces on C, giving with the notations of Fig. 7: $\overrightarrow{f} = \sum_{i=0}^{N} \overrightarrow{P_iM_i}$

By this way, at each step, the total error E_S decrease and we iterate the process until convergence, i.e. the difference of errors between two iterations is below a fixed ϵ_o.

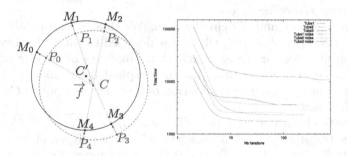

Fig. 7. (left) Illustration of the process to optimize the centerline position (point C) with elastic forces (blue arrows). Each elastic force is attached to one point of the input mesh sector (a point M_i represented in black) and oriented in the direction of the center of the virtual circle of center S. (right) evolution of the convergence speed in the optimization process.

Contrary to a simple average of neighborhood points, the optimization performs well even on partial mesh data, with missing parts or holes. Moreover, it is possible to ponder each force with its face area in order to better balance forces in presence of irregular sampling with variable density.

3   Reconstruction Results and Geometric Analysis

Reconstruction Results. Several centerline extractions and tubular shape reconstructions are shown on Fig. 8. Our input dataset contains several types of metallic tubes numerized with different acquisition tools. In each case, the centerline is always well delineated without the need to tune a special parameter. When the input data is a complete or partial mesh, the normal is simply estimated as the cross product of face edges. When the input data is a digital object or a height map, we use the digital Voronoi Covariance Measure [9] to estimate the normal vector. Parameters of this estimator are easily set since we know the radius of the tubular object; they also have little influence on the result, since the accumulation image makes the process very robust. The running time was less than 30s for each experiment. As show on image (j) and (f), few places present reconstruction errors. Small errors may be found near bent areas. These errors are less related to the reconstruction method than to the physical shape under study, since the bending machine has deformed the tube at these places.

Geometric Analysis with 3D arc Detection. We wish to segment the tubular shape into rectilinear and toric parts. This problem is equivalent to segmenting its centerline into

(a) input polygonal curve

(b) Tangent space representation

3D straight segments and 3D circular arcs. We thus extend to 3D a method presented by Nguyen *et al.* [18], which was designed to cut a 2D discrete curve into straight and circular pieces. It relies on properties of circular arcs in **the tangent space representation** that are inspired from Arkin [2] and Latecki [14]. The tangent space representation of a sequence of points $C = \{C_i\}_{i=0}^{n}$ is defined as follows :

Let l_i be the length of segment C_iC_{i+1} and $\alpha_i = \angle(\overrightarrow{C_{i-1}C_i}, \overrightarrow{C_iC_{i+1}})$. Let us consider the transformation that associates C with a polygon of $\mathbb{R}^2$ constituted by segments $T_{i2}T_{(i+1)1}, T_{(i+1)1}T_{(i+1)2}$, $0 \leq i < n$ (upper floating figure) with: $T_{02} = (0,0)$, $T_{i1} = (T_{(i-1)2}.x + l_{i-1}, T_{(i-1)2}.y)$ for i from 1 to n, and $T_{i2} = (T_{i1}.x, T_{i1}.y + \alpha_i)$ for i from 1 to $n - 1$. Moreover, let $M = (M_i)_{i=0}^{n-1}$ be the sequence of midpoints of segments $T_{i2}T_{(i+1)1}$ for i from 0 to $n - 1$. The main idea of the arc detection method is that if C is a polygon that approximates a circle or an arc of circle then $(M_i)_{i=0}^{n-1}$ is a sequence of (approximately) co-linear points [18].

In our work, the sequence $(C_i)_i$ of skeleton points obtained in Section 2.3 is considered and the representation of this sequence of points in the tangent space is computed. If the angles α_k, for k from p to q, of consecutive points of $(C_k)_{k=p}^{q}$ are close to 0, these points belong to a straight line. Otherwise, the co-linearity of the corresponding midpoints $(M_k)_{k=p}^{q}$ is tested in the tangent space by using an algorithm presented in [18]. Fig. 8 (q) shows an example of tubular shape decomposition with this 3D variant of circular arc detection. Toric and rectilinear parts are correctly identified.

4   Conclusion and Discussion

A new efficient and simple method was presented to solve the problem of delineating the centerline of 3D tubular shapes, for various types of input data approximating its boundary: mesh, set of voxels or height map. The method is robust to missing parts in input data as well as perturbations: in these situations, it still returns accurately the centerline position. To achieve this, we have decomposed

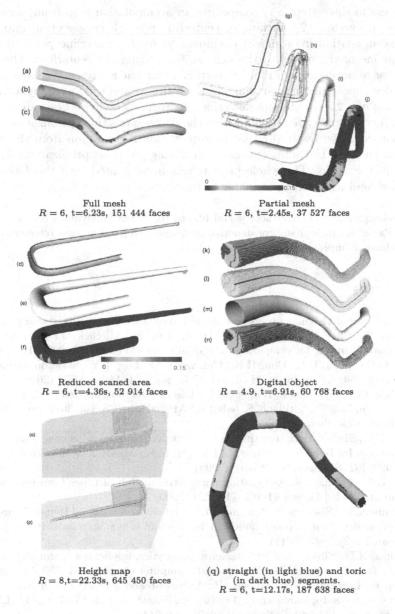

Full mesh
$R = 6$, t=6.23s, 151 444 faces

Partial mesh
$R = 6$, t=2.45s, 37 527 faces

Reduced scaned area
$R = 6$, t=4.36s, 52 914 faces

Digital object
$R = 4.9$, t=6.91s, 60 768 faces

Height map
$R = 8$,t=22.33s, 645 450 faces

(q) straight (in light blue) and toric
(in dark blue) segments.
$R = 6$, t=12.17s, 187 638 faces

Fig. 8. Result of reconstruction from various input data types. Images (a,g,l,p) show the centerline by transparency through the input surface, (k) and (o) are some input surfaces. (b,e,i,m) images are the reconstructed tubes built from the centerlines. Images (j) and (f) show the local squared distance error between the reconstructed tube and the input shape. Image (q) illustrates the decomposition of a tube into rectilinear and toric parts. For all experiments, the tracking parameter and epsilon were set respectively to R and 0.001. Running times correspond to executions on a *MacBook* computer with a 2,5 GHz *Intel Core i7* processor.

the process in three steps : 1) computing an accumulation map from faces and their normal vectors, 2) tracking of centerline through cross-section maximas of the accumulation map and 3) optimization of the centerline position by a better fitting of the model to the nearest faces along the centerline. The centerline was accurate enough to allow further geometric analysis. We have shown how to decompose the tubular shape into rectilinear and toric parts by a simple adaptation of a 2D circular arc detection algorithm. The hypothesis about constant radius parameter R only influences the skeleton position optimization. This limitation could be resolved either by direct radius estimation from the accumulation image or by radius optimization during position optimization. This is left for future works. The whole process was implemented with the *DGtal* [1] framework and will soon be available in its companion *DGtalTools*.

Acknowledgments. The authors would like to thank the anonymous reviewers and Nicolas Passat for their many constructive comments, suggestions and references that really helped to improve this paper.

References

1. DGtal: Digital Geometry tools and algorithms library. http://libdgtal.org
2. Arkin, E., Chew, L., Huttenlocher, D., Kedem, K., Mitchell, J.: An efficiently computable metric for comparing polygonal shapes. TPAMI **13**, 209–216 (1991)
3. Au, O.K.C., Tai, C.L., Chu, H.K., Cohen-Or, D., Lee, T.Y.: Skeleton extraction by mesh contraction. In: ACM SIGGRAPH, pp. 44:1–44:10. ACM (2008)
4. di Baja, G.S., Nyström, I., Borgefors, G.: Discrete 3D tools applied to 2D grey-level images. In: Roli, F., Vitulano, S. (eds.) ICIAP 2005. LNCS, vol. 3617, pp. 229–236. Springer, Heidelberg (2005)
5. Bauer, C., Bischof, H.: Extracting curve skeletons from gray value images for virtual endoscopy. In: Dohi, T., Sakuma, I., Liao, H. (eds.) MIAR 2008. LNCS, vol. 5128, pp. 393–402. Springer, Heidelberg (2008)
6. Bauer, U., Polthier, K.: Generating parametric models of tubes from laser scans. Computer-Aided Design **41**(10), 719–729 (2009)
7. Borrmann, D., Elseberg, J., Lingemann, K., Nüchter, A.: The 3d Hough Transform for plane detection in point clouds: A review and a new accumulator design. 3D Research **2**(2), 1–13 (2011)
8. Cornea, N.D., Silver, D.: Curve-skeleton properties, applications, and algorithms. IEEE Transactions on Visualization and Computer Graphics **13**, 530–548 (2007)
9. Cuel, L., Lachaud, J.-O., Thibert, B.: Voronoi-based geometry estimator for 3D digital surfaces. In: Barcucci, E., Frosini, A., Rinaldi, S. (eds.) DGCI 2014. LNCS, vol. 8668, pp. 134–149. Springer, Heidelberg (2014)
10. Goulette, F.: Automatic CAD modeling of industrial pipes from range images. In: Proc. of The ICRA 3-D Digital Imaging and Modeling, 1997, pp. 229–233 (1997)
11. Hassouna, M., Farag, A.: Variational Curve Skeletons Using Gradient Vector Flow. IEEE Transactions on Pattern Analysis and Machine Intelligence **31**(12), 2257–2274 (2009)
12. Kirbas, C., Quek, F.: A review of vessel extraction techniques and algorithms. ACM Computing Surveys (CSUR) **36**(2), 81–121 (2004)

13. Krähenbühl, A., Kerautret, B., Debled-Rennesson, I., Mothe, F., Longuetaud, F.: Knot Segmentation in 3d CT Images of Wet Wood. Pattern Recognition (2014)
14. Latecki, L., Lakamper, R.: Shape similarity measure based on correspondence of visual parts. IEEE Transactions on PAMI **22**, 1185–1190 (2000)
15. Lee, I.K.: Curve reconstruction from unorganized points. Computer aided geometric design **17**(2), 161–177 (2000)
16. Lee, I.K., Kim, K.J.: Shrinking: another method for surface reconstruction. In: Proceedings of The Geometric Modeling and Processing, 2004, pp. 259–266. IEEE (2004)
17. Lesage, D., Angelini, E.D., Bloch, I., Funka-Lea, G.: A review of 3d vessel lumen segmentation techniques: Models, features and extraction schemes. Medical Image Analysis **13**(6), 819–845 (2009)
18. Nguyen, T.P., Debled-Rennesson, I.: Arc segmentation in linear time. In: Real, P., Diaz-Pernil, D., Molina-Abril, H., Berciano, A., Kropatsch, W. (eds.) CAIP 2011, Part I. LNCS, vol. 6854, pp. 84–92. Springer, Heidelberg (2011)
19. Pare, P., Nagano, T., Coxson, H.: Airway imaging in disease: Gimmick or useful tool? Journal of Applied Physiology **113**(4), 636–646 (2012)
20. Tagliasacchi, A., Alhashim, I., Olson, M., Zhang, H.: Mean curvature skeletons. In: Computer Graphics Forum, vol. 31, pp. 1735–1744. Wiley Online Library (2012)
21. Tagliasacchi, A., Zhang, H., Cohen-Or, D.: Curve skeleton extraction from incomplete point cloud. ACM Transactions on Graphics (TOG) **28**(3), 71 (2009)
22. Tankyevych, O., Talbot, H., Passat, N., Musacchio, M., Lagneau, M.: Angiographic image analysis. In: Medical Image Processing, pp. 115–144. Springer (2011)
23. Tarsha-Kurdi, F., Landes, T., Grussenmeyer, P.: Hough-transform and extended ransac algorithms for automatic detection of 3d building roof planes from lidar data. In: ISPRS Workshop on Laser Scanning 2007 and SilviLaser 2007, vol. 36, pp. 407–412 (2007)
24. Xu, C., Prince, J.: Snakes, shapes, and gradient vector flow. IEEE Transactions on Image Processing **7**(3), 359–369 (1998)

Tongue in Cheek

George Nagy[1] and Naomi Nagy[2(✉)]

[1] Rensselaer Polytechnic Institute, ECSE, Troy, NY, USA
nagy@ecse.rpi.edu
[2] University of Toronto, Linguistics, Toronto, ON, Canada
naomi.nagy@utoronto.ca

Abstract. Differences between image processing and other disciplines in the definition and the role of shape are explored. Diverse approaches to quantifying shape are reviewed. Attention is drawn to the need for close coupling between image acquisition and shape analysis. An example of the effect of the means of observation on dynamic shape extraction is drawn from linguistics. Current instrumentation for measuring shape changes in the vocal tract are described. Advanced image processing based on emerging imaging technologies is proposed for linguistic and therapeutic applications of articulatory phonetics.

Keywords: Morphology · Morphometrics · Image processing · Computer graphics · Linguistics · Articulatory phonetics

> *Hamlet*
> Do you see yonder cloud that's almost in shape of a camel?
> *Polonius*
> By the mass, and 'tis like a camel, indeed.
> *Hamlet*
> Methinks it is like a weasel.
> *Polonius*
> It is backed like a weasel.
> *Hamlet*
> Or like a whale?
> *Polonius*
> Very like a whale.

1 Introduction

In biology, geography, geology, mineralogy and the fine arts shape is usually considered as an indication of the *origin, development* or *functionality* of the object of study. In contrast, the usual goal of quantifying shape in image processing, computer graphics and computer vision projects is to *recognize* or *label* objects or persons, to *track* targets, or to *render* natural or computer-created scenes. Another difference is that in other fields, researchers spend much effort to optimize image capture, while we often conduct experiments on large image databases with limited information about their original

© Springer International Publishing Switzerland 2015
V. Murino and E. Puppo (Eds.): ICIAP 2015, Part I, LNCS 9279, pp. 332–342, 2015.
DOI: 10.1007/978-3-319-23231-7_30

purpose and acquisition. We will elaborate these distinctions by reviewing approaches to shape within and outside our community, then focus on examples of a familiar shape in linguistics. This shape, that of the tongue, has been studied by many methods, but none provide real-time feedback during naturalistic speech. We outline the necessary parameters for a method or product to fill this lacuna, an endeavor perhaps suited to the expertise of some participants in this conference.

Consider the first sentences of a stimulating 2014 essay on *What is a Pattern*, by Eva and Godfried Toussaint, as justification of this digression from the mainline problems of image processing. Substitute *shape* for *pattern*: *The use of the word 'pattern'* ['shape'] *is ubiquitous in written and spoken discourse. Furthermore, most authors assume the intended reader knows what a pattern* [shape] *is, and hence do not define the term* [1]. Toussaint and Toussaint suggest that a *pattern* must be a sequence exhibiting some regularity, and that its opposite is *chaos* or *randomness*. It seems, however, impossible to conceive an object without any shape at all.

According to the celebrated perceptual psychologist J.J. Gibson (the second author's bio-academic great-grandfather!), *shape, figure, structure, pattern, order, arrangement, configuration, plan, outline, contour are similar terms without distinct meanings* that must be defined precisely for scientific study [2].

Dictionary definitions barely suggest the key constraint of *invariance* under certain operations or transformations, and are too abstract to serve the needs of image processing. It would also be appropriate to add the *method of observation* to any definition, because the characteristics of shape that matter depend so much on the sphere of discourse.

Shapes are often described in terms of familiar items: *egg, pear, banana, almond, peanut, pancake, gugelhupf* (an edible Teutonic truncated right cone with a central vertical cylindrical through-hole), *heart* (usually stylized), *whale, snail, butterfly, tulip, tear drop, bone, corkscrew, bottle* (wine, beer, or Klein), and *boomerang*. In engineering, *boss, chamfer, clevis, crown, driftpin, fillet, fin, flange, kerf, key, lug, camber, dowel, I-beam, hip, lintel*, and *web* have shape associations. A comprehensive survey of mathematical models of shape in geometric and topological terms is [3].

We will extend some reflections suggested by studies of the shapes of Roman and Chinese characters in the 1960s and by subsequent encounters with shape in neurophysiology, physiognomy, remote sensing and computational geometry [4]. Several notions presented in this essay are motivated by studies of variation in natural language.

In the next section, we review approaches to shape in image-processing. In Section 3, we give examples of the role of shape in some other disciplines, including mathematics. In Section 4, as a more detailed example of shape-oriented research that seems to us easily distinguishable from a computer-scientific and engineering approach, we introduce the challenging problem of dynamic characterization of the shape of the tongue in speech production.

2   Shape in Image Processing and Computer Graphics

Shape-based recognition has always played a prime role in image processing and computer vision. Although color, texture and shading all provide a direct path to image segmentation, they also offer an indirect path to shape recognition by way of *shape-from-x* [5].

Shape is equally important in computer graphics, where progress is often measured by the realism of rendering stationary or moving persons, animals and objects [6].

Some shape extraction methods mimic known psychophysical mechanisms, including gestalt perception, visual interpolation, and the interpretation of plane curves as 3-D surfaces. Other methods make use of geometry, topology and functional analysis. Physics-based modeling of deformable objects builds on optics, statics, kinematics, elasticity and plasticity. Chain codes, line-adjacency graphs, and delta-hinges preserve contour properties. Popular shape-preserving mappings include the Hu, Mellon and Zernike Moments, Medial Axis, Fourier, Haar, Radon/Hough, Hadamard/Walsh/Radamacher, Daubechies Wavelet, and Euclidian Distance transforms. Vector-space shape-feature representations can be derived from any transform coefficients, or more directly from window operations like the Histogram of Gradients (HOG) or Local Binary Patterns (LBP).

Matheron and Serra formulated *mathematical morphology* as a foundational theory for the manipulation of general geometrical structures in both continuous and discrete spaces [7]. The theory quickly found applications in image processing, first to bi-level images, then to gray-scale images, and eventually to 3-D image arrays. The expressive names of the many useful lattice operations are part and parcel of the image processing lexicon.

Tomographic volume imaging and reconstruction are based on filtered back projection (rooted in the inverse Radon transform) of a stack of 2-D sections. Direct recording methods use 3-D laser scanners (scanning range finders), ultrasound, stylus profilometers or coordinate measuring machines.

Image processing methods are often developed, tested and evaluated competitively on heterogeneous or homogenous collections of images (e.g. outdoor scenes or mug shots) without any need to derive technical or scientific information about the pictured subjects or objects. As we will see, in other fields the study of shape is generally motivated by what it reveals about the nature of the object under study.

3   Shape in Other Fields

The eighteenth century scientist Johann von Goethe coined *morphology* for the study of shape [8]. He conducted far-ranging studies of geology and mineralogy in addition to botany. He accumulated a collection of over seventeen thousand rock samples. (In his spare time he wrote novels, plays and poems, advised princes and governments, rebuilt a castle, and begat a large progeny.) *Morphometry*, the measurement and quantification of shape, is an important tool of paleontology that draws increasingly on image processing [9].

Phyllotaxis is the study, and also the configuration, of the non-structural components of plants. Some, like pine cones and sunflowers, exhibit repetitive and cylindrically symmetric spirals and logarithmic patterns. The lengths of consecutive sub-sequences of these plant organs have been linked to Fibonacci series. The extraordinary variety of beautiful yet purposeful shapes in Nature has inspired a large literature from Carl von Linné (Linnaeus) through Alexander von Humboldt, Charles Darwin and William

Jackson Hooker [10], to D'Arcy Wentworth Thompson [11] and Oliver Sacks [12]. They might have welcomed some computer help in their laborious visual quantification of organic growth and form.

Geomorphology is the study of the evolution of landforms, including the genesis and motion of the continents. *Physiography* (physical geography) tends to focus more on systematic measurement and classification of existing topographic and bathymetric features than on their formation. Most landforms are synonymous with their shape: *dome, spire, crater, escarpment, crevasse, cirque, ridge, mound, butte, knob, hummock, horn, kettle, moulin, col, saddle, mesa, berm, monadnock, cliff, canyon, cape, fjord, promontory...* However, unlike landforms, the corresponding shapes cannot be qualified by location, size or orientation.

Homology, the study of evolutionary change in organisms, was at first based exclusively on shape. However, *sequence homology*, the contemporary approach to evolutionary developmental biology, is based on the similarity of DNA sequences due to common ancestry.

Homology has a more precise meaning in mathematics. Indeed, it has several precise meanings (in different branches of mathematics), all related to homeomorphism (continuous transformations). Although *isomorphic* objects must have some kind of similarity, they need not have the same shape. Axis-parallel constraints on shape are called *isothetic*. The mathematical definition includes gridlines that meet at either of two arbitrary points.

Although symmetry in lay language is a relatively simple concept related to shape, in mathematics it is defined as invariance under some specified transformation over lattices. It is formalized in algebra via *symmetry groups*. In image processing it is usually sufficient to consider *translational, scaling, reflection* and *rotational symmetries*. *Helical symmetry* is invariance under a combination of rotation and translation along the axis of rotation. Humans and higher order animals exhibit external bilateral symmetry. Plants and micro-organisms often have rotational symmetries. At the atomic level, symmetries account for many crystallographic properties.

All five Platonic, thirteen Archimedean and four Kepler-Poinsot solids were christened long ago (e.g. *Rhombicosidodecahedron*). For an authoritative discussion of polyhedra, see Coxeter's *Regular Polytopes* [13]. Crystallography adopted the geometrical nomenclature for the shapes of crystals and their symmetries, but Gemology (perhaps more a craft than a science) has its own terminology. The overall shape of the finished stone is called the *cut*. Although the relative sizes and angles of the facets for maximum brilliance and dispersion have been known for over a century, the arbitrary shape of the raw stones often necessitates non-ideal cuts. The corresponding shapes are defined by the proportions of the *table* (flat top*)*, *crown, pavilion, girdle* and *culet*. Cuts, although often polyhedral, have less forbidding names than the 3-polytopes: *marquise, pear, brilliant, trilliant, radiant, princess, emerald, Mazarin, Peruzzi*. *Cabochon* cuts are rounded, without facets, for opaque stones. Part of a shape design spec (from the American Gem Society) reads as follows:

> *OVAL 6 Main Pavilion Length to Width 1.8:1, Table 55%, Lower Girdle Height 80%, Upper Girdle Height 64%, and 3% Girdle Thickness at the Mains Girdle Must be Faceted*

The perception of shape depends on the point of view of the observer relative to the object. In anatomy and more generally in biology and medicine, there are three principal views (and associated planes and sections). The *sagittal* (medial) plane divides the organism into left and right halves. The *coronal* plane (and frontal view) is face-on. The *transverse* (axial or horizontal) plane is perpendicular to the other two and, in humans, perpendicular to the spine. *Sinister* and *dexter, posterior* and *anterior*, and *inferior* and *superior*, refer to the two possible orientations of each plane or point of view.

Interestingly, there is a school of sculpture where the whole point is to conceal the shape of the sculpture in a specific 2-D projection thereof. These sculptures appear to be randomly twisted rods or wires which, when projected by one or more lamps onto the white wall behind the sculpture, show a familiar shape like a bicycle or a high-heeled shoe or a youth dribbling a basketball [14].

4   The Shape of the Tongue

Phonetics is the study of the sounds of speech. Its applications include language (re-)learning after brain, mouth or tongue injury, helping the deaf to speak, acquiring a new language or a new (perhaps socially privileged) dialect, and improving the articulation of opera singers. Tongue-gesture recognition has been proposed as a computer interface [15]. All of these benefit from real-time feedback showing the position of the tongue relative to the palate. In this section, we sketch the role of the tongue in speech production, describe relevant data-collection methodologies, and review an exemplary study that sets the stage for speculating about the applicability of emerging imaging modalities to this problem.

Articulatory phonetics could be an exciting opportunity for image-processing research directly related to shape extraction. The role of the tongue in speech production has long intrigued physiologists, psychologists and linguists (Latin *lingua* means 'tongue' or 'speech'), but appears to have attracted scant attention from the image processing and computer vision community. Research on the subject is more likely to appear in the *Journal of Phonetics, The Journal of the Acoustical Society of America, Clinical Linguistics & Phonetics, the International Congress of Phonetic Sciences* (ICPhS) and the *Acoustics, Speech and Signal Processing* (ICASSP) conference than at *ICPR, CVPR* or *ICIAP* (but see [16] and[17]).

Some of the obstacles to precise observation of the tongue are the following. The tongue is a highly deformable, muscular, mucous-coated organ undergoing rapid motion in multiple dimensions. Its spatial configuration must be determined with respect to the cavity which surrounds it. This cavity has moving walls and only an intermittent opening to the exterior. The internal surfaces of the cavity vary in material and optical properties. The size and shape of the tongue and the cavity vary from subject to subject, and with age and sex. The motion of the tongue relative to the other articulatory components must be synchronized with the audio stream that they generate. Data collection should not interfere with normal speech production in the course of reading, reciting or conversing. Finally, small-scale differences in target locations along multiple dimensions distinguish meaningfully different sounds.

Figure 1a illustrates the fine-grained differences among s-like sounds within languages (e.g., 'sip' vs. 'ship' in English) as well as sounds distinguishing languages (e.g., Polish has a three-way contrast between "s" as in *kasa* 'cash', post-alveolar-s as in *kasza* 'buckwheat, and palatal-s as in *Kasia* 'Katie', but no English-like "sh," while English lacks the latter two Polish sounds). Figure 1b shows slight differences in tongue position (on the left) that distinguish English vowels (plotted on the right). Figure 1c shows a tongue making a non-linguistic gesture.

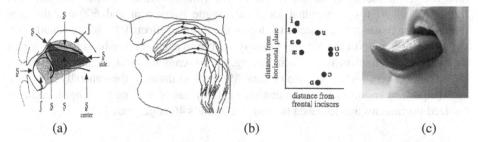

(a)   (b)   (c)

Fig. 1. (a) Tongue position for sibilant consonants (all found in the Dravidian language Toda) [17], (b) Tongue positions distinguishing American English vowels [17], (c) an ambiguous lingual gesture. Copyright 1996 by Peter Ladefoged and Ian Maddieson. Reproduced with permission.

4.1   Speech Production

Systematic study of articulatory phonetics by means of visual observation, palatography and high-speed cinematography began nearly one hundred years ago. Approximations to the position of various parts of the tongue (and therefore of its shape) have been embedded in the International Phonetic Alphabet devised in 1888.

Complete modeling systems must represent the vocal folds (two thin sheets of tissue in the larynx) that vibrate under pressure from the lungs, the velum (soft palate) that opens and closes the nasal cavity and the tongue, considered the most important speech organ, that changes the shape and size of the oral cavity (which are also affected by the lips and the uvula). Increasingly complex and accurate models of the vocal tract have been developed over the last century. Mechanical, electrical circuit, and simulation models typically consist of a fixed-frequency switchable pulse train source and a series of coupled cavities with variable resonance and attenuation.

4.2   Instrumentation

Static X-rays and X-ray cinematography are no longer acceptable for recording speech production, but a 55-minute lateral X-ray film (at 50 fps) of four subjects taken in a Quebec City hospital in 1974 has been transcribed to videodisc and is still used.

Palatography requires putting a dye (or cocoa powder) on the tongue or palate to determine the point of contact during utterance of an isolated sound. Electropalatography (EPG), a long-established but still used technique, substitutes for the dye an artificial palate with several dozen embedded electrodes. EPG provides timing information in addition to the point(s) of contact between tongue and palate.

Other non-imaging modalities are Electromagnetic Articulometry (EMA) and X-ray Microbeam (XMB). EMA records the position and orientation, relative to external transmitters, of receiver coils glued to the articulators (as a function of time). The number of transmitters required depends on whether 2-D (usually in the mid-sagittal plane) or 3-D data is wanted. XMB uses 3-4 radio-opaque pellets glued to the tongue. The tracked locations are called *fleshpoints* in both media.

Besides its widespread clinical applications, ultrasound provides non-invasive real-time images of the upper surface of the tongue (the transducer is below the chin). A frame rate of 30 fps is marginal for some tongue movement and 60fps is the new standard. The tissue-air interface at the top of the tongue reflects 99% of the sound energy, therefore the top of the tongue is clearly visible in sagittal recordings (except for its tip and root). With interactive contour tracing, spatio-temporal surfaces can be generated, but only for a very limited volume of data. Methods to improve the generally noisy images (Fig. 2) by means of head and transducer stabilization, wetting the tongue, and customized instruments are described in Maureen Stone's 46-page guide [18].

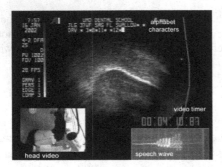 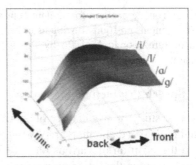

Fig. 2. Ultrasound image and generated trajectory of Subject uttering "golly" [18].

Magnetic Resonance Imaging (MRI) is even more expensive and cumbersome than ultrasound, but it provides useable images of soft tissue [19] that is invisible to ultrasound. Real-time MRI (rtMRI) captures images at up to 25 fps (e.g. Fig. 3). These images are sometimes overlaid on crisper static MRI depictions of muscles and edges in the vocal tract. Fleshpoints can be tracked with Tagged Cine-Magnetic Resonance Images (tMRI). The experimental protocol must accommodate the subject in supine confinement in a noisy cylinder, and able to communicate with the experimenter only via microphone and headset.

The speech production and articulation knowledge group (SPAN) maintains the ISC-TIMIT database of 3-D rtMRI and EMA with the same set of ten male and female speakers. The subjects read 460 sentences with statistically representative sounds and sound-transitions that were compiled fifteen years ago. The vocal tract data is interpolated from 12.5 fps 68 x 68 pixel image sequences. The SPAN also distributes free software for visualization [21].

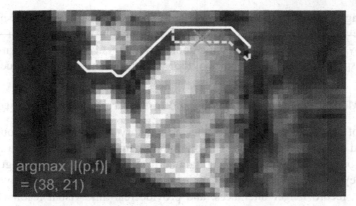

Fig. 3. Automatic location of dorsal constriction target: sagittal section of intervocalic stop [ak:o] produced by adult male Italian speaker. Cross indicates center of maximum change in locally-correlated pixel intensity over a surrounding 20-frame sequence [20].

4.3   Patterns of Tongue Movement

A fascinating study by K. Iskarous, based on the ancient X-ray movies mentioned at the beginning of the previous section, reveals a startling aspect of tongue kinematics [22]. It punctures the conjecture that the initial and final positions fix a linear trajectory of the corresponding surface points. Careful analysis of B-splines interactively superimposed on the superior edge of the tongue visible in the sagittal recordings shows that 86% of the 600 observed partitions (150 for each subject) fall into just two types: *arch* and *pivot*. Arch transitions merely raise the tongue until the tip touches the palate.

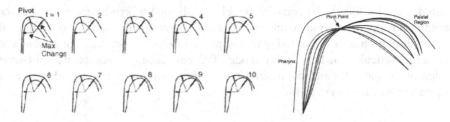

Fig. 4. Ten consecutive tongue splines for the transition [ai]. The palatal, uvular and pharyngeal locations of the vocal tract are shown on each frame. The splines are superimposed on the right to indicate the pivot point clearly [21].

The counterintuitive patterns are those of the pivots. The location of the pivot point depends on the vocal task. In Fig. 4, the middle section of the tongue is raised to narrow the distance between the tongue and the palate. On successive frames, the pivot point appears stationary, as shown by the ten superimposed frames of Fig. 4. Measurement of the squared distance (roughly proportional to the area) appears to show a stationary point on the tongue. Nevertheless, the pivot point is not a stationary point of the tongue! The whole back of the tongue passes through the uvular region. The part of the tongue that appears stationary actually moves parallel to the palate.

This finding supports a hypothesized distinction between high-level *sound-production* and low-level *articulatory* control functions. Automating the detection of shape trajectories by means of image processing could extend this type of study to many other puzzling aspects of how the dynamics of the vocal tract affect speech production.

4.4   A Modest Proposal for Imaging and Image Processing of Tongue Motion

Analysis of tongue kinematics and other articulatory phonetic studies could be improved and accelerated by wireless in-the-mouth cameras positioned on a molar and an incisor providing simultaneous sagittal and front views of both the tongue and the palate. They would have higher resolution than ultrasound and MRI, show rate of movement, record longer utterances, and provide real-time visual feedback without head restraints. They could also be combined with EPG or ultrasound recording via post-recording synchronization.

Current miniature cameras are still too large. CCD endoscopes and borescopes with a ½" diameter head have VGA resolution, 45°-67° field of view, video frame rate, and LED or fiberoptic illumination [23]. Fiberoptic endoscopes have a smaller head but a thicker cable. Either tether would interfere only moderately with speech. Intra-oral cameras are already used in orthodontics, but they require keeping the mouth open. Perhaps capsule endoscopes can be modified for this purpose. Another development on the horizon is lensless ultra-miniature CMOS computational imagers [24]. These tiny (~100μm) devices don't produce images, but images, or relevant features of images, can be reproduced, at least hypothetically, from their spectral output.

The proposed Tongue in Cheek (TIC) system has two video-cameras and a microphone, and provides real-time feedback via audio and graphics screen output. During a CAVIAR-like [25] training phase with many speakers and diverse utterances, the parameters of a kinetic articulatory model are adjusted to synthesize each speaker's mouth and tongue motion to match the audio input. In therapeutic operation, the screen displays a measure of the spatiotemporal differences between the patient's and the target articulation. In a replay mode, TIC can display a composite split-screen video of the patient's and the desired articulatory motions synchronized with either the patient's or the target audio.

5   Conclusion

The study of shape in image processing appears to be less closely tied to function than in many older disciplines. Practitioners in these disciplines tend to develop their own version of well-known image processing algorithms for specialized tasks. Articulatory phonetics is an example of opportunities for exciting multidisciplinary research using unconventional imaging technologies. In bocca al lupo!

Acknowledgments. We extend our gratitude to Alexei Kochetov and Craig Diegel, both at the University of Toronto, for sharing their wide-ranging knowledge of phonetics and photography, respectively.

References

1. Toussaint, E.R., Toussaint, G.T.: What is a pattern? In: Proceedings of Bridges 2014: Mathematics, Music, Art, Architecture, Culture, Seoul, Korea (2014). http://archive.bridgesmahart.org//brid-ges-293.pdf
2. Gibson, J.J.: What is a form? Psychological Review **58**(1951), 403–412 (2014). Cited in Toussaint & Toussaint [1]
3. Biasotti, S., De Floriani, L., Falcidieno, B., Frosini, P., Giorgi, D., Landi, C., Papaleo, L., Spagnuolo, M.: Describing shapes by geometrical-topological properties of real functions. ACM Comput. Surv. **40**(4), October 2008
4. Nagy, G.: The dimensions of shape and form. In: Arcelli, C., Cordella, L., Sanniti di Baja, G. (eds.) Visual Form. Plenum Press, New York (1992)
5. Horn, B.K.P.: Robot Vision. McGraw-Hill, NY (1986)
6. Ferwerda, J.A.: Three varieties of realism in computer graphics. In: Rogowitz, B.E., Pappas, T.N. (eds.) Human Vision and Electronic Imaging VIII, Santa Clara, CA, vol. 5007, January 20, 2003
7. Serra, J.: Image Analysis and Mathematical Morphology. Academic Press (1982)
8. Bloch, R.: Goethe, Idealistic Morphology and Science. American Scientist **40**(2), 313–322 (1952)
9. Zollikofer, C.P., Ponce de Leon, M.: Virtual Reconstruction: A Primer in Computer-Assisted Paleontology and Biomedicine. Wiley, NY (2005)
10. Jackson Hooker, W.: Exotic Flora, vol. 3, pp. 1822–1827. Bibliobazaar, Charleston (2008)
11. D'Arcy Wentworth Thompson, On Growth and Form. MacMillan, New York (1945)
12. Sacks, O.: The Island of the Colorblind. Random House Vantage Books, New York (1998)
13. Coxeter, H.S.M.: Regular Polytopes, Dover (1963)
14. Kagan, L.: Object/Shadow, Installations of Steel and Light. The Butler Institute of America, Youngstown (2009)
15. Saponas, T.S., Kelly, D., Parviz, B.A., Tan, D.S.: Optically sensing tongue gestures for computer input. In: Procs. ACM Symposium on User Interface Technology (2009)
16. Yang, Y., Guo, X.X.: Tongue visualization for a specified speech task. In: SIGGRAPH (2012)
17. Farrar, E., Balasubramanian, A., Coleman Eubanks, J.: Real-time motion capture of the human tongue. In: SIGGRAPH (2009)
18. Stone, M.: A Guide to Analyzing Tongue Motion from Ultrasound Images. Clinical linguistics & phonetics **19**(6-7), 455–501 (2005)
19. Kim, Y.-C., Proctor, M.I., Narayanan, S.S., Nayak, K.: Improved Imaging of Lingual Articulation Using Real-Time Multislice MRI. Journal of Magnetic Resonance Imaging **35**(4), 943–948 (2012)
20. Proctor, M.I., Lammert, A., Katsamanis, A., Goldstein, L., Hagedorn, C., Narayanan, S.S.: Direct Estimation of Articulatory Kinematics from Real-time Magnetic Resonance Image Sequences. Interspeech, Florence (2011)
21. Narayanan, S., Toutios, A., Ramanarayanan, V., Lammert, A., Kim, J., Lee, S., Nayak, K., Kim, Y.-C., Zhu, Y., Goldstein, L., Byrd, D., Bresch, E., Ghosh, P., Katsamanis, A., Proctor, M.: Real-time magnetic resonance imaging and electromagnetic articulography database for speech production research (TC). The Journal of the Acoustical Society of America **136**(3), 1307–1311 (2014)

22. Iskarous, K.: Patterns of tongue movement. J. Phonetics **33**, 363–391 (2005)
23. Schlegel, S., Blase, B., Brüggemann, D., Bühs, F., Dreyer, R., Kelp, M., Lehr, H., Oginski, S.: Endoscope with flexible tip and chip-on-the-tip camera. In: Long, M. (ed.) World Congress on Medical Physics and Biomedical Engineering May 26-31, 2012 Beijing, IFMBE Proceedings, vol. 39, pp. 2111–2114. Springer, Heidelberg (2013)
24. Gill, P.R., Stork, D.G.: Lensless Ultra-miniature imagers using odd-symmetry spiral phase gratings. In: Proceedings of the Computational Optical Sensing and Imaging (2013)
25. Zou, J., Nagy, G.: Visible models for interactive pattern recognition. Pattern Recognition Letters **28**, 2335–2342 (2007)

Where Is the Ground? Quality Measures for the Planar Digital Terrain Model in Terrestrial Laser Scanning

Marcin Bator, Leszek J. Chmielewski[✉], and Arkadiusz Orłowski

Faculty of Applied Informatics and Mathematics (WZIM),
Warsaw University of Life Sciences (SGGW), Poland,
ul. Nowoursynowska 159, 02-775 Warsaw, Poland
{marcin_bator,leszek_chmielewski,arkadiusz_orlowski}@sggw.pl,
http://www.wzim.sggw.pl

Abstract. In the analysis of terrestrial laser scanning (TLS) data the digital terrain model (DTM) is one of important elements. To evaluate the DTM or to find the DTM by way of optimization it is necessary to formulate the measure of DTM quality. Three parameterized measures are proposed and tested against a comparative model for a series of TLS data. The measure equal to the number of points inside a layer of specified height above the plane appeared to produce the most distinct maximum for an optimal model. The measures have been applied to the planar DTM but their use for other models is possible.

Keywords: Digital terrain model · DTM · Ground level · Planar · LIDAR · TLS · Quality measure · Robust · Optimization

1 Introduction

Measuring the parameters of forest regions with the LIDAR technique is gaining popularity due to constantly increasing quality of results of the methods of analysis of the data obtained. The data are in a form of the cloud of points in 3D space. Their analysis includes finding the location of the ground which is necessary as the reference level in the further computations. The ground level is modelled with the digital terrain model (DTM). The problem of finding the DTM from LIDAR data is still open (literature surveys can be found e.g. in [1, 2]). Until recently, the DTMs were constructed with the use of airborne laser scanning (ALS) [3]. Works on finding the DTM from terrestrial laser scanning (TLS) data emerge recently (e.g. [4]).

In this paper the simplest DTM in the form of a single plane will be used. In our opinion the planar model of terrain is still very competitive with respect to other models due to its simplicity and sufficient accuracy in the application to forest stands measured from one LIDAR position. The measurable region extends to not more than 15-20 m from the LIDAR [5]. The planar model is appropriate in geographical regions where plains dominate.

© Springer International Publishing Switzerland 2015
V. Murino and E. Puppo (Eds.): ICIAP 2015, Part I, LNCS 9279, pp. 343–353, 2015.
DOI: 10.1007/978-3-319-23231-7_31

To assess the quality of the model it is necessary to formulate a proper measure. Such a measure can be used in any optimization method. Let us consider the example of the least square error as a measure (square distance, in this case). Minimizing it leads to finding some kind of the average. In the forest data the majority of points belong to the ground, then to the tree trunks, crowns, as well as to all the other types of vegetation. The average height would encompass all these data, not only the ground points, so it would be considerably higher than the ground level due to the existence of many objects above the ground. The calculations can be further hindered by the existence of erroneous measurements. A good quality measure should operate on the data without prior selection of ground points. In this paper a number of quality measures are introduced, tested and compared.

The remainder of the paper is organized as follows. The data sets used and the problem to be solved will be described in Sect. 2. The proposed quality measures and the method of their assessment will be presented in Sect. 3 and discussed in Sect. 4. The paper will be concluded in Sect. 5.

2   Data

We have used the data chosen from the TLS data sets scanned at 15 stands near Głuchów in the Grójec Forest District, Mazovian Voivodship (Central Poland), with the terrestrial LIDAR scanner FARO LS HE880, symbolically referred to as G01-G15. A data set for each stand was collected from a single position of the LIDAR scanner. The sets contained between 12 and 22 millions of measurement points belonging to the trees, other levels of vegetation like bushes and grass, and the ground.

To illustrate the further analysis we have chosen a subset of four typical examples of data. Two of them conform to the planar model very well and two others depart from it, but the distance is at an acceptable level. As the reference value for the acceptable differences in the ground location we can use the value 0.6 m reported in [6] as the standard deviation of the error of the digital terrain model found from ALS measurements. Such large distances were not observed in our experiments.

For the analysis we have selected a number of sectors from 3D data. A sector extends between two planes marked with dash-dotted lines in Fig. 1a and is 5° wide. Such a thin sector can be easily illustrated in 2D with the projection onto its middle plane V which forms an angle φ with the plane xz. The sector extends beyond the axis Oz so the data for φ and $\varphi + 180°$ are the same data, swapped around Oz.

In this way, realistic nearly-2D data closely related to real-life data were formed. Such choice will make it possible to visualize the results conveniently for analysis, which will be explained in Sect. 3. Examples of data used and also one of those excluded from this study due to excessive terrain variation are shown in Figs. 2, 3 and in Fig. 5a. The question of choice of these data as an illustration of the presented analysis will be addressed in the following Section.

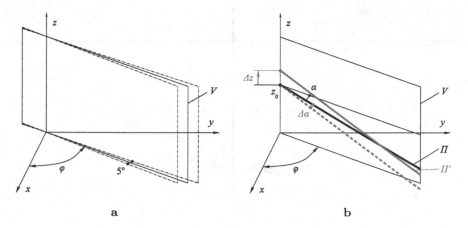

Fig. 1. (a) Sector from which the data are collected surrounds a plane V specified by angle φ. The sector extends beyond the axis Oz. See text in Sect. 2 for details. (b) Planar terrain model and its displacements. Displaced elements shown in red. See text in Sect. 3.2 for details.

3   Method

In the following we shall propose a number of quality measures for the planar terrain model. Then, these measures will be verified by examining their graphs and by comparing the model obtained by their optimization to the results calculated with the Hough transform [7]. The comparison will be made by plotting the graphs of the quality measures for a region in the parameter space surrounding the parameters of the model obtained with this comparative method. Because the data are near-2D, only one rotation and one translation of the model can be considered, so the resulting graphs will be 3D and hence will be easy to interpret. In spite of that the near-2D fragments of data are used for visualization, the comparative planes as well as the measures proposed here were calculated for the full 3D planar model (comparative model with all the points in the data set, and the proposed measures for the points belonging to the thin sector considered).

It is important to note that at this point we can not use any quantitative measure of quality of the results obtained because this is the quality measure itself that we are looking for. What is more, this measure should be used at the stage of the analysis at which the date are not yet segmented into the ground and the other classes. Therefore, the classical methods of interpolation quality assessment (cf. eg. [8]) are of little help. Due to this we shall refer to the examination of graphs which in our opinion illustrate the quality of the results in a possibly direct way. The number of graphs we can include in this paper is limited. Even in the limited set of data G01-G15 we have considered in this study the number of thin sectors is very large. From this large number of results calculated during the experiments we have tried to choose the typical ones for presentation.

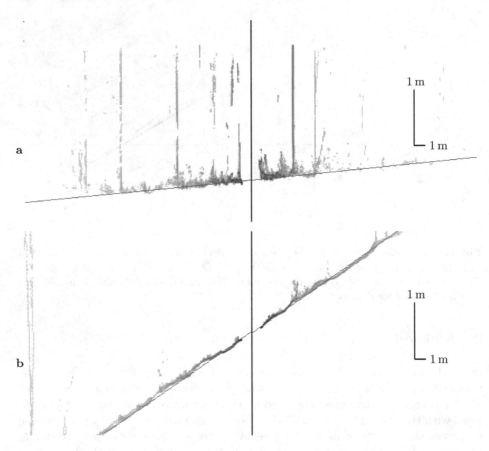

Fig. 2. Examples of good, medium, acceptably bad and excluded data (selected data sets and sectors): very good cases: (**a**) G01, $\varphi = 95°$, (**b**) G12, $\varphi = 60°$, continued in further Figs. 3 and 5. Vertical scale is 5 times denser than the horizontal one. Maximum distance from center is 20 m. Grey level (darkness) represents the number of measurements. Comparative ground level shown in red (see Sect. 3 for more details).

Besides the question of the measure itself, there is a need for the reference set with a credible golden standard for segmenting the ground measurement points from the other ones (trees, other vegetation, outliers and other artefacts). The reference sets reported in the literature are formed with the field surveys, photogrammetric measurements from the air, satellite radar imaging, or ALS, among others [2]. Their accuracy, especially in forest areas, is limited in comparison with that of the TLS, so new sets are needed. An interesting set which became available after this paper was first submitted is described in [9]. However, in this set the objects of interest are not the ground, but the trees, so the trees are segmented. For evaluation of results obtained for these data the criterion of visual inspection is proposed in [9], similarly as in our work.

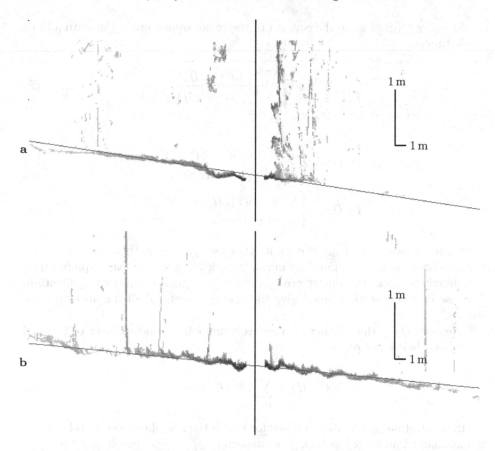

Fig. 3. Continued Fig. 2: medium cases: (a) G06, $\varphi = 55°$, (b) G15, $\varphi = 20°$.

The above considerations strongly support the need for new test data sets with reference data having appropriate accuracy for the terrestrial LIDAR measurements. However, in this study we shall resort to the data we already have.

3.1   Quality Measures Proposed

Denote an i-th measurement point by $P_i = P_i(x_i, y_i, z_i)$, $i = 1, \ldots, M$. Denote by $d(P_i, \Pi)$ the signed distance between this point and the planar model Π expressed by $Ax + By + Cz + D = 0$. Obviously,

$$d(P_i, \Pi) = \frac{A\,x + B\,y + C\,z + D}{\sqrt{A^2 + B^2 + C^2}}. \tag{1}$$

The proposed measures will be denoted by Q_i^p, where $i = 1, ..., 3$ an d p is a parameter. The upper index will be dropped if this does not lead to ambiguity.

Measure Q_1 is close to the concept of the mean square error, but with a limit on distance:

$$Q_1^l(\Pi) = \sqrt{\frac{\sum_{i=1}^{M}(d_1^l(P_i,\Pi))^2}{\sum_{i=1}^{M}N^l(P_i,\Pi)}} \; , \tag{2}$$

where

$$d_1^l(P_i,\Pi) = \begin{cases} d(P_i,\Pi) & \text{if } |d(P_i,\Pi)| < l \; , \\ 0 & \text{otherwise} \; ; \end{cases} \tag{3}$$

$$N^l(P_i,\Pi) = \begin{cases} 1 & \text{if } |d(P_i,\Pi)| < l \; , \\ 0 & \text{otherwise} \; . \end{cases} \tag{4}$$

The same measure without the limit, that is, $Q_1^{\infty}(\Pi)$ is the classical square error. The measure Q_1 should be minimized, leading to the least square error. As already written, the square error is not a good measure in this application, because its minimization would give the average height of all the measurement points.

Measure Q_2 is the number of measurement points inside a layer of height l above and below the plane:

$$Q_2^l(\Pi) = \sum_{i=1}^{M} N^l(P_i,\Pi) \; . \tag{5}$$

Its maximization should yield a plane for which the neighborhood would contain a maximum number of points. The measure Q_2^{∞} would be simply the total number of points, which is not a reasonable measure.

Measure Q_3 is the number of measurement points inside a layer of height l above the plane:

$$Q_3^l(\Pi) = \sum_{i=1}^{M} N_3^l(P_i,\Pi) \; , \text{ where} \tag{6}$$

$$N_3^l(P_i,\Pi) = \begin{cases} 1 & \text{if } 0 \leq d(P_i,\Pi) < l \; , \\ 0 & \text{otherwise} \; . \end{cases} \tag{7}$$

Its maximization should yield a plane just under the layer containing the largest number of points.

The measure $Q_3^{\infty}(\Pi)$ would be the number of all points on and above the plane. It would be maximum for any plane not extending above the ground if the data contained no points under the ground, which is not the case. Practical experience shows that among the data some points which do not represent any physical objects can appear; as an example the points located extremely far from the laser, also below the ground, can be indicated. Such data points are the errors of the measurement method. The quality measures should be insensitive to them.

In the design of the measures we have used our experience with the analysis of LIDAR data on tree stands [10–12]. However, it is apparent that the measures in which the distance limit is used can be referred to the domain of robust statistics [13]. In particular, they are close to the concept of Huber-type skipped mean, but neither of them is equivalent to it.

3.2   Assessment

The geometry is shown in Fig. 1b. As already written, the data points are located on the plane denoted as V. The intersection of the ground plane Π with V is shown with a thick black line. It is inclined versus horizon by the angle α. Quality measures will be calculated for these data points and the plane Π in a series of positions near its original position, denoted here by Π'. The plane will be displaced by rotation and translation. The rotation will be made around a horizontal axis (not shown in Fig. 1b) normal to V and passing through $(0, 0, z_0)$, by an angle $\Delta\alpha$. The translation will be made vertically, by Δz. The result is a plane whose intersection with V is Π'. The rotated plane is marked with a thick dashed red line and the rotated and translated plane with a thick solid red line.

The values of $\Delta\alpha$ and Δz were chosen so that at the practically measurable distance from the coordinate origin (15 m [5]) the change in the vertical direction due to rotation were up to ± 0.50 m and for translation up to ± 0.20 m. As it will be seen in Sect. 4 this range contained significant maxima of the quality measures proposed and was sufficient for their assessment.

To choose the initial $(\Delta\alpha, \Delta z) = (0, 0)$ position of the ground plane we have used the results from our calculations made with the Hough transform [7]. Their acceptable quality could be justified by the existence of clear maxima in the Hough space, and by visual assessment of the results (as already written, the visual inspection is unavoidable in this case).

The expected result of the present study is to find a quality measure for which a clear, global extremum of the graph $Q(\Pi)$ versus $\Delta\alpha, \Delta z$ is reached at or near the point $(0, 0)$.

4   Results and Discussion

As the limiting distance l used in Eqs. (2-6) we have used the values 0.05, 0.1 and 0.15 m which are close to the observed height of the layer corresponding to the ground in the data sets, as it can be seen in Figs. 2-3. This layer can be thought of as 'the grass'.

Examples of the measures Q_1, Q_2 and Q_3 are shown in Fig. 4. We do not show the results received for the measures Q_i^∞, according to the comments on their limited applicability to the problem made in Sect. 3.1 (for example, the minimum of the square distance Q_1^∞ for the data of Fig. 2a yields a plane located about 3.5 m above the actual ground level).

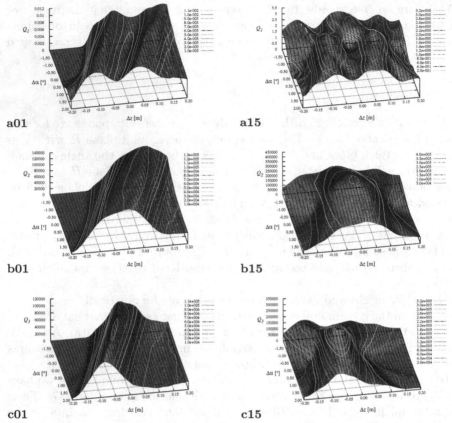

Fig. 4. Chosen quality measures for data G01 of Fig. 2a and G15 of Fig. 3b: (a) Q_1, (b) Q_2, (c) Q_3.

The shapes of the graphs of corresponding quality measures have similar shapes for all the data, so it can be attempted to draw some general conclusions from the cases shown.

The measure Q_1 has a minimum near the point $(0,0)$ in the plane $\Delta\alpha\Delta z$, but this minimum is not global and other minima can be observed in the considered region. This measure can be excluded form further considerations.

The measures Q_2 and Q_3 both have maxima near $(0,0)$ in the graphs. The maxima of Q_2 seem to be wider, but they conform with the point $(0,0)$ very well, except the case for data $G01$. In this case the result is displaced towards positive Δz by 0.05 m which is a slight difference. The maximum of the measure Q_3 is more crisp. It is displaced towards negative Δz (downwards) by $0.05 - 0.07$ m, so the plane appears slightly below the reference location. This is in conformity with the assumption made to formulate Eq. (6) that the measuring points belonging to the ground are above the terrain model.

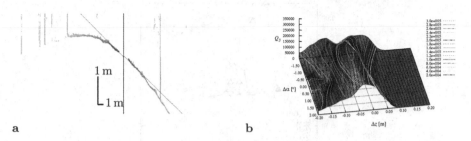

Fig. 5. (a) Continued Fig. 2: an example of an unacceptably bad case: G10, $\varphi = 20°$. In this case the ground level is curvilinear so it can not be approximated by a plane. (b) Quality measure Q_3 for data of Fig. a.

The differences in the vertical position obtained with Q_2 and Q_3 are small. It seems to be profitable to use the function having a more narrow maximum, so from the presented examples it follows that Q_3 can be suggested as a good solution, with Q_2 following quite immediately.

To investigate the influence of the parameter l on the position of the maximum of the measures Q_2 and Q_3 we have plotted them in the $O\Delta\alpha\Delta z$ coordinates for the three used values of l (Fig. 6). The measure Q_3 is stable for three from four data sets (not for G06). The measure Q_2 is stable for two from four data sets (not for G01, G06). This comparison is also in favor of Q_3.

If the traces of the plane found as a result of optimization of Q_3 were plotted in Figs. 2-3, they would be paralel to the comparative red lines, and possibly displaced down by 5 to 7 cm, which would be less than the natural variation of heights between the ground points visible in these Figures.

Let us pay attention to the graph of Q_3 for the data G10 which can not be approximated by the planar model. In spite of this, the maximum in this graph coincides with the position of the comparative ground model. This means that the measure attains its maximum for such a position of the planar ground model which encompasses the large part of measurement points (strongly concentrated around the axis Oz) and is in conformity with the model found with the compared HT method.

Finally, it should be noted that the measure Q_3, which is simply the number of points in the near vicinity above the ground model, results in a natural way from the observation that the ground is just below the most conspicuous cluster of measurement points. Such a measure is easy to implement for any DTM, irrespective of what type should it be or how many parameters should it have. Hence, it can be used in various optimization methods, including the heuristic ones.

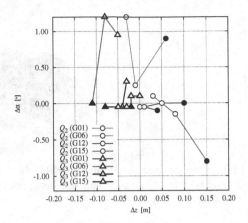

Fig. 6. Position of the minimum of measures Q_2^l, Q_3^l for three values of l, subsequently: 0.05 m, 0.10 m, 0.15 m. Evolution of Q_2^l is marked with thin lines and circles, and that of and Q_3^l with thick lines and triangles. The full symbol denotes the last used value (0.15). Results for four data sets are marked with colors: red for G01, green for G06, blue for G12 and black for G15.

5   Conclusions

The problem of finding the best plane which approximates the terrain, from the terrestrial laser scanning data, can be formulated as an optimization problem. As the criterion of optimization, some measures of quality proposed in this paper appeared to have the necessary properties related to the location of their maximum for the parameters of the DTM which can be considered as actually optimal. These measures are the number of points near to the terrain model, denoted as Q_2^l, and the number of points in the layer above the model, denoted as Q_3^l, which reflects the idea of locating the ground just under the layer in data in which the number of points is the largest. The parameter l is related to the expected thickness of the layer. The measure Q_3^l seems to perform the best in the considered application. It forms a distinct, global maximum near the optimum. The location of the maximum is relatively stable against the choice of the parameter l.

The considered measures have been applied and tested with the use of a simple planar terrain model but their application to other models is also possible.

There is the need for new test data sets provided with the reference data having appropriate accuracy and credibility to validate the methods applied to the analysis of the terrestrial LIDAR measurements. The acquisition of such a set and making it accessible is planned within the future research.

References

1. Sithole, G., Vosselman, G.: Experimental comparison of filter algorithms for bare-Earth extraction from airborne laser scanning point clouds. ISPRS J. of Photogrammetry and Remote Sensing **59**(1–2), 85–101 (2004). doi:10.1016/j.isprsjprs. 2004.05.004
2. Stereńczak, K., Zasada, M., Brach, M.: The accuracy assessment of DTM generated from LIDAR data for forest area - a case study for scots pine stands in Poland. Baltic Forestry **19**(2), 252–262 (2013)
3. Srinivasan, S., Popescu, S., Eriksson, M., Sheridan, R., Ku, N.W.: Terrestrial laser scanning as an effective tool to retrieve tree level height, crown width, and stem diameter. Remote Sensing **7**(2), 1877–1896 (2015). doi:10.3390/rs70201877
4. Puttonen, E., Krooks, A., Kaartinen, H., Kaasalainen, S.: Ground level determination in forested environment with utilization of a scanner-centered terrestrial laser scanning configuration. IEEE Geoscience and Remote Sensing Letters **12**(3), 616–620 (2015). doi:10.1109/LGRS.2014.2353414
5. Zasada, M., Stereńczak, K., Dudek, W., Rybski, A.: Horizon visibility and accuracy of stocking determination on circular sample plots using automated remote measurement techniques. Forest Ecology and Management **302**, 171–177 (2013). doi:10.1016/j.foreco.2013.03.041
6. Stereńczak, K., Kozak, J.: Evaluation of digital terrain models generated in forest conditions from airborne laser scanning data acquired in two seasons. Scandinavian Journal of Forest Research **26**(4), 374–384 (2011). doi:10.1080/02827581.2011. 570781
7. Chmielewski, L., Orłowski, A.: Ground level recovery from terrestrial laser scanning data with the variably randomized iterated hierarchical hough transform. In: Computer Analysis of Images and Patterns: Proc. Int. Conf, CAIP 2015. Lecture Notes in Computer Science. Springer (2015) (accepted for print)
8. Kozera, R., Noakes, L.: C 1 interpolation with cumulative chord cubics. Fundamenta Informaticae **61**(3–4), 285–301 (2004)
9. Gorte, B.: Tree separation and classification contest (within the IQumulus project), April 30, 2015. http://homepage.tudelft.nl/41s94/iqmulus/Contest3. html. (Online; accessed 19-May-2015)
10. Chmielewski, L.J., Bator, M., Olejniczak, M.: Advantages of using object-specific knowledge at an early processing stage in the detection of trees in LIDAR data. In: Chmielewski, L.J., Kozera, R., Shin, B.-S., Wojciechowski, K. (eds.) ICCVG 2014. LNCS, vol. 8671, pp. 145–154. Springer, Heidelberg (2014)
11. Chmielewski, L.J., Bator, M.: Hough transform for opaque circles measured from outside and fuzzy voting for and against. In: Bolc, L., Tadeusiewicz, R., Chmielewski, L.J., Wojciechowski, K. (eds.) ICCVG 2012. LNCS, vol. 7594, pp. 313–320. Springer, Heidelberg (2012)
12. Chmielewski, L.J., Bator, M., Zasada, M., Stereńczak, K., Strzeliński, P.: Fuzzy hough transform-based methods for extraction and measurements of single trees in large-volume 3D terrestrial LIDAR data. In: Bolc, L., Tadeusiewicz, R., Chmielewski, L.J., Wojciechowski, K. (eds.) ICCVG 2010, Part I. LNCS, vol. 6374, pp. 265–274. Springer, Heidelberg (2010)
13. Huber, P.: Robust Statistics. John Wiley, New York (2003)

Extending the sGLOH Descriptor

Fabio Bellavia[✉] and Carlo Colombo

Computational Vision Group, University of Florence, Florence, Italy
{fabio.bellavia,carlo.colombo}@unifi.it

Abstract. This paper proposes an extension of the sGLOH keypoint descriptor [3] which improves its robustness and discriminability. The sGLOH descriptor can handle discrete rotations by a cyclic shift of its elements thanks to its circular structure, but its performance can decrease when the keypoint relative rotation is in between two sGLOH discrete rotations. The proposed extension couples together two sGLOH descriptors for the same patch with different rotations in order to cope with this issue and it can be also applied straightly to the sCOr and sGOr matching strategies of sGLOH. Experimental results show a consistent improvement of the descriptor discriminability, while different setups can be used to reduce the running time according to the desired task.

Keywords: SGLOH · SIFT · Keypoint descriptor · Matching

1 Introduction

Keypoint descriptors are useful in many computer vision tasks, such as recognition, tracking and 3D reconstruction [10]. They encode properties of image portions extracted by a keypoint detector [11] into numerical vectors in order to evaluate local visual similarities.

Modern descriptors, such as SIFT and its variants [3,7], MROGH [6] or LIOP [12], are mainly based on histogram concatenation. Recently, despite their lower discriminability power, descriptors based on multiple binary comparisons [4], learning [5] and alternative subspace representations [13] have received a great interest too due to their characteristics of high speed and compactness.

Among the SIFT variants, the sGLOH descriptor [3] coupled with specific matching strategies achieved results comparable with the state-of-the-art LIOP and MROGH descriptors. In particular, the sGLOH descriptor uses a circular grid to incorporate more descriptor instances of the same patch at different orientations into a single feature vector, accessible by a simple cyclic shift of the feature vectors. The matching distance between two features is obtained as the minimum distance among all descriptors for the possible discrete orientations handled by sGLOH. Further improvements can be obtained by limiting the range of allowable orientations according to the scene context. Two matching strategies are derived, namely sCOr and sGOr, respectively when the orientation range constraint is defined a priori by the user or obtained without user intervention by inspecting the data.

© Springer International Publishing Switzerland 2015
V. Murino and E. Puppo (Eds.): ICIAP 2015, Part I, LNCS 9279, pp. 354–363, 2015.
DOI: 10.1007/978-3-319-23231-7_32

Although robust and efficient, the sGOR descriptor performance can degrade in the case that the true relative rotation between the two keypoint patches is equal to half sGLOH discrete rotation. In order to cope with this issue, we propose to couple together two sGLOH descriptors for the same patch, with a rotation shift equal to half sGLOH discrete rotation. A brief introduction to the sGLOH descriptor is given in Sect. 2, also providing details about the matching strategies. Next, Sect. 3 describes the proposed solution together with the different matching strategies which can rise from the proposed sGLOH extension. Evaluation results on the comparison of the proposed method against the sGLOH and other descriptors is given in Sect. 4, while an analysis of the running times in provided in Sect. 5. Conclusions and future work are discussed on Sect. 6.

2   sGLOH Description

Given a normalized image patch, so that its intensity values are affine normalized and its shape equals the unit circle, the sGLOH descriptor [3] grid is made up of $n \times m$ regions, obtained by splitting n circular rings into m sectors (see Fig. 1).

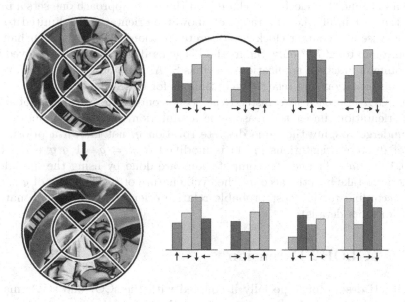

Fig. 1. Rotation of an image patch with the superimposed sGLOH grid by a factor $\frac{2\pi}{m}$ (left), which corresponds to a cyclic shift of the block histogram for each ring (right). In the example $n = 2$ and $m = 4$ (best viewed in color)

For each region, the histogram of the m quantized orientations $d_k = k\frac{2\pi}{m}$, $k = 0, \ldots, m-1$ weighted by the gradient magnitude is computed. Gaussian kernel density estimation is used for interpolation and a block histogram H_{ij} with $i = 0, \ldots, n-1$ and $j = 0, \ldots, m-1$, associated to each sGLOH region is defined by ordering the computed gradient histogram so that its first bin corresponds to the normal direction of the region and the others follow in clockwise order. The concatenation H of the block histogram, normalized using the L_1 norm, gives the final sGLOH descriptor.

As shown in Fig. 1, the rotation of the descriptor by a factor d_k, is obtained by k cyclic shifts of the block histogram for each ring, without recomputing the descriptor vector. In this sense, the sGLOH descriptor packs m different descriptors of the same patch using several discrete dominant orientations. The distance between two sGLOH features H and $\overline{H}$ is then given by

$$\widehat{\mathcal{D}}(H, \overline{H}) = \min_{k=0,\ldots,m-1} \mathcal{D}(H, \overline{H}_k) \tag{1}$$

where $\mathcal{D}(\cdot, \cdot)$ is a generic distance measure and $\overline{H}_k$ is the cyclic shift applied to the descriptor $\overline{H}$ to get the discrete rotation d_k. According to [3] setting $n = 2$ and $m = 8$, which implies that the descriptor dimension is $l = nm^2 = 128$ and the discrete orientation step is $45°$, gives the best sGLOH setup.

A further improvement on the sGLOH can be obtained by limiting the range of the handled discrete orientations, so that part of wrong matches are discarded and cannot be selected by chance. In the sCOr approach one sets a priori $k = 0, 1, m - 1$ in (1), i.e. the range of allowable orientations is limited to the first clockwise and counter-clockwise discrete rotations. Although sCOr handles rotations of up to $\pm 67.5°$ only, the method is general enough to be employed in a lot of common practical applications, such as SLAM [1] and sparse matching [9], since transformations are relatively continuous for close images.

The sGOr approach uses instead the scene context to provide a global reference orientation, under the reasonable assumption that all keypoints of the scene undergo roughly the same discrete rotation g, not known a priori. The range of discrete orientations in (1) is modified to $k = g - 1, g, g + 1$, where $g \in \{0, 1, \ldots, m - 1\}$ and the computations are done by using the modulo m arithmetic to take into the account the cyclic nature of k. The value of g is estimated according to the most probable relative orientation among all matches (see [3] for more details).

3   The sGLOH2 Extension

The sGLOH descriptor, especially if coupled with the sCOr and sGOr matching strategies, obtains results comparable with state-of-the-art descriptors [3], but can suffer performance degradations when the relative rotation between the patches approaches the one between two discrete sGLOH rotations, i.e. it is of the form $k \frac{2\pi}{m} + \frac{\pi}{m}$ for $k = 0, \ldots, m - 1$.

In order to solve this issue, we define a novel sGLOH2 descriptor $H^\star$, obtained by concatenating two sGLOH descriptors H^1 and H^2 of the same patch, where H^1 is the standard sGLOH descriptor of the patch, while H^2 is is obtained after applying a rotation of $\frac{\pi}{m}$ to the patch. This corresponds to double the number of possible discrete directions m, leaving the same histogram dimension. Note that this is not equal to double m in the sGLOH parameters, as in this case a smaller and less discriminant descriptor regions would be obtained, since the number of circular sectors would be doubled.

Assuming the sequence $\{0, \frac{\pi}{m}, \frac{2\pi}{m}, \frac{3\pi}{m}, \ldots\}$ of the $2m$ successive discrete rotations by step $\frac{\pi}{m}$, the corresponding ordered set of cyclic shifted descriptors is given by

$$Q(H^\star) = \{H_0^1, H_0^2, H_1^1, H_1^2, \ldots, H_{m-1}^1, H_{m-1}^2\} \tag{2}$$

where H_k^z is the cyclic shift applied to the descriptor H^z, $z \in \{1, 2\}$, to get the discrete rotation d_k as in Sect. 2. The distance between two sGLOH2 features $H^\star$ and $\overline{H}^\star$ becomes then

$$\widehat{\mathcal{D}}_2(H^\star, \overline{H}^\star) = \min_{K \in Q(\overline{H}^\star)} \mathcal{D}(H_0^1, K) \tag{3}$$

The sGLOH2 descriptor length is $l^\star = 2l = 256$ and different matching strategies can be obtained in analogy with the sCOr and sGOr matching. In particular, similar to the sCOr strategy, we can define several sCOr2 strategies. By limiting the rotations up to $\pm\frac{\pi}{m}$, i.e. using the subset $\{\overline{H}_0^1, \overline{H}_2^0, \overline{H}_{m-1}^2\}$ instead of $Q(\overline{H}^\star)$ in (3) we get the sCOr2.1 strategy. A wider rotation range, up to $\pm 2\frac{\pi}{m}$, could also be used resulting in the sCOr2.2 matching strategy, that uses the subset $\{\overline{H}_0^1, \overline{H}_2^0, \overline{H}_1^1, \overline{H}_{m-1}^1, \overline{H}_{m-1}^2\}$ in (3).

Similar to sGOr, the estimation of the global reference orientation g can be achieved using all the $2m$ descriptors in Q (sGOr2a strategy) or only the m descriptors belonging to the first concatenated sGLOH descriptor H^1 (sGOr2h strategy), while the relative rotation window could be constrained as above up to $\pm\frac{\pi}{m}$ or $\pm 2\frac{\pi}{m}$, obtaining 4 possible final different matching strategies (sGOr2a.1, sGOr2a.2, sGOr2h.1, sGOr2h.2).

4 Evaluation

We first evaluated sGLOH2 and the corresponding matching strategies on rotation on the same setup described in [3]. A dataset of 16 images, rotating from $0°$ to $90°$ only (due to the cyclic nature of the sGLOH descriptor) is used to measure the average percentage of correct matches for intermediate rotations. The L_1 distance is used since according to [3] it obtains better results than L_2. Plots are reported in Fig. 2.

As it can be noted, both the proposed sGLOH2 and its matching strategy improve on the original sGLOH versions when rotations are close to the worst case. In particular the results of the proposed extensions are better than SIFT and very close to the results of LIOP and MROGH. Only a negligible difference less than 2% with LIOP and MROGH exists for rotations of the form $k\frac{\pi}{m} + \frac{\pi}{2m}$ for $k = 0, \ldots, 2m - 1$, i.e. between rotations of $\frac{\pi}{m}$, in analogy with the original worst case.

Furthermore, by comparing the sCOr and sCOr2 strategies it can be observed that sCOr2.2 and sCOr can both handle angles up to $\pm67.5°$ while sCOr2.1 works with rotations up to $\pm45°$ only since it allows less rotation shifts.

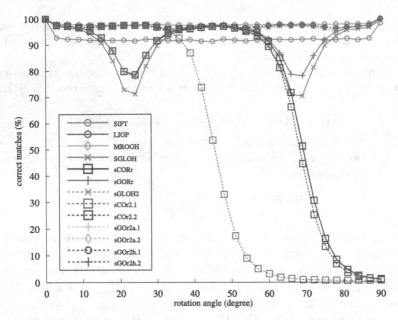

Fig. 2. Descriptor average percentage of correct matches for different rotation degrees (best viewed in color)

No relevant differences can be noted between the sGOr2a and sGOr2h matching strategies, while if we compare the sGLOH2 descriptor against sGOr2a and sGOr2h, the latter two work slightly better as they operate on a limited number of possible rotations, thus reducing the probability that two non-corresponding descriptors are matched by chance. This observation also holds for sCOr and sCOr2.2 for rotations greater than $45°$, since three rotations are checked for sCOr while five for sCOr2.2, so that in the first case there is, although minimal, less probability of wrong matches by chance.

The sGLOH2 extensions were also tested on the Oxford dataset [8], which offers a more challenging scenario since several image transformations are applied to the images, not only rotations. In order to get a fair comparison, we used the same setup described in [3] even in this case. The keypoints were extracted using the HarrisZ detector [2], while for matching the NN strategy was used for sGLOH and its variants and the NNR matching for the others, in both cases using the L_1 distance, since these parameters provide the best setup for each descriptor. Results for the first and fourth image pair for each sequence are reported in Figs. 3-4 in terms of precision versus recall (the ratio between the number of correct matches by number of total correct matches) and correspondences (the ratio between the number of correct matches by the number of total matches). The maximum achieved correspondence ratio (the ratio of the number of total correct matches by the number of total matches) is reported beside the precision, too. The sCOr and sCOr2 descriptors are not included in this evaluation, as there are image pairs with more than their allowable rotations.

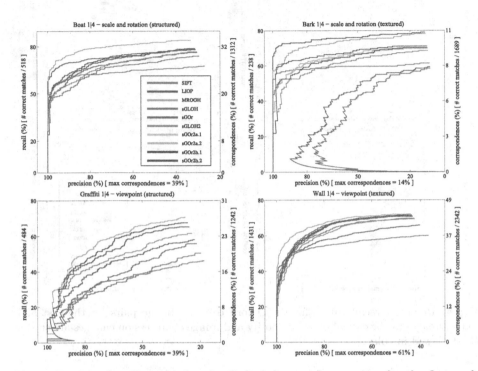

Fig. 3. Precision/recall curves for the Oxford dataset. Image pairs for the first and fourth images in the case of scale, rotation and viewpoint changes are shown (best viewed in color)

The sGLOH2, sGOr2a and sGOr2h provide a relevant improvement upon sGLOH and sGOr, especially in the case of scale, rotation and viewpoint changes, while in the case of variations of blur, luminosity and compression the improvements are less relevant. The most notable case is for the textured image rotation and scale change (Bark sequence), on which one can also note that the sGOr2a matching strategy slightly improves on the sGOr2h, while in the other cases results are the same.

Note that MROGH is introduced in the comparison as a sort of upper bound since, as noted in [3], its support regions is three times those of the other descriptors This leads to a misleading boosting in performances, especially in case of planar image transformations such as for the Oxford dataset. With respect to sGLOH and its matching strategies, the sGLOH2 extensions obtains similar or better results against LIOP in the structured image sequences with geometric transformations (the Graffiti and Boat sequences); SIFT results seem in general worse than the others.

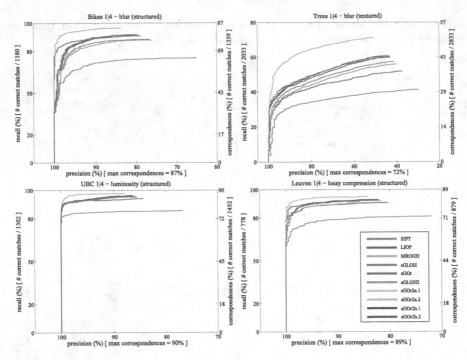

Fig. 4. Precision/recall curves for the Oxford dataset. Image pairs for the first and fourth images in the case of blur, luminosity and image compression changes are shown (best viewed in color)

Plots in Fig. 5 show the precision/recall curves with the previous setup on the first and fifth image pair of the sequences with geometrical transformations. These are more challenging image pairs with higher degree of transformations with respect to those in Fig. 3. The sGLOH2 extensions improvements upon the original sGLOH strategies are still remarkable, especially in the case of scale and rotation changes for textured images (the Bark sequence). Furthermore, it can be observed that there are no relevant difference between MROGH and the proposed descriptors for these image pairs, while LIOP and SIFT results seem more unstable.

5   Running Time

Figure 6 reports the estimated running times for the evaluated methods, together with details on the time spent by each computational step for a particular example. The estimated curves are obtained by quadratic fitting on the image pairs of the Oxford and rotation datasets, denoted by crosses. It can be noted that sGOr2a and sGLOH2 are very time consuming, while sGOr2h and sCOr2 running times are still reasonable considering the final matching results, especially up to 2000 keypoints per image. When more keypoints are used and rotations

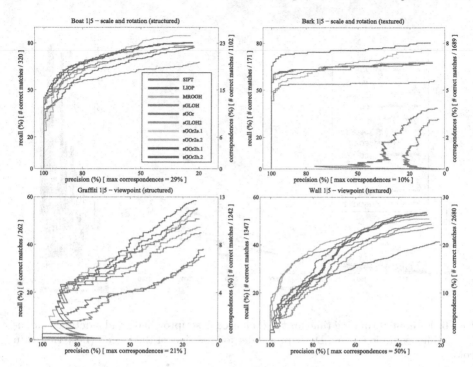

Fig. 5. Precision/recall curves for the Oxford dataset. Image pairs for the first and fifth images in the case of scale, rotation and viewpoint changes are shown (best viewed in color)

are constrained up to ±45°, only the sCOr2.1 strategy is very efficient in terms of computational speed. Note however that according to the authors' experience, in general the number of keypoints for matching are bounded to about 1500 for reducing memory issues as well as the probability of wrong matches by chance.

By inspecting the cumulative time histogram on Fig. 6(right), it can be noted that the time for computing the descriptor in the case of LIOP and sGLOH are the lowest, followed by sGLOH2, and more computational cost is required by MROGH and SIFT. The quadratic matching cost (for n features there are n^2 possible matches) makes the difference between the sGLOH and sGLOH2 methods and all the others.

In particular, setting to t the time required to compute all the matches between two images using a generic distance measure $\mathcal{D}$, which can be assumed almost equal for SIFT, LIOP and MROGH, a multiplication factor equal to the number of rotations to check should be added according to (1) so that the original sGLOH, sCOr and sGOr require respectively about mt, $3t$ and mt times for matching. Analogously, according to (3), the sGLOH2 matching required time is about $2mt$, for sCOr2.1 and sCOr2.2 respectively $3t$ and $5t$, while for sGOr2a.1, sGOr2a.2, sGOr2h.1, sGOr2h.2 the times are about $2mt$, $2mt$, mt, mt respectively, in accordance with the histogram bars.

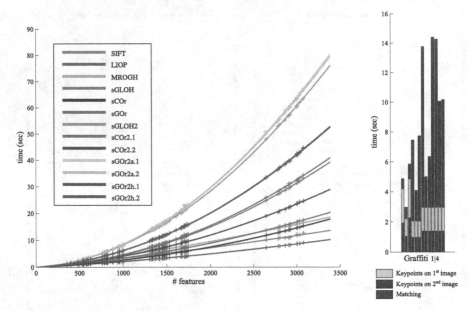

Fig. 6. Estimated running time for the evaluated descriptor (left) and a detailed cumulative time example (right). Descriptor order follows that of the legend (best viewed in color)

6   Conclusions and Future Work

This paper presents an extension to the sGLOH descriptor and the corresponding matching strategies sCOr and sGOr. According to the obtained results, these improvements are effective, through a more robust rotation handling, especially for the sGLOH worst case, but also in the general matching between descriptors. Although the computational time increases, it is still reasonable for several applications and it can be adjusted according to the required task by choosing the right matching strategy. In particular, the sCOr2.1 is the fastest among these, and can handle rotation up to ±45°, followed by sCOR2.2 with constrained rotation up to ±67.5°, and the sGOr2h.1 matching for general tasks, which differs only slightly from the more costly sGOr2a.2 matching strategy.

Future work will include more experimental evaluations, tests on descriptor binarization to reduce its dimension and to improve its running time as well as fast distance check to discard very probable bad matches.

Acknowledgments. This work has been carried out during the ARROWS project, supported by the European Commission under the Environment Theme of the "7th Framework Programme for Research and Technological Development".

References

1. Bellavia, F., Fanfani, M., Pazzaglia, F., Colombo, C.: Robust selective stereo SLAM without loop closure and bundle adjustment. In: Petrosino, A. (ed.) ICIAP 2013, Part I. LNCS, vol. 8156, pp. 462–471. Springer, Heidelberg (2013)
2. Bellavia, F., Tegolo, D., Valenti, C.: Improving Harris corner selection strategy. IET Computer Vision 5(2), 86–96 (2011)
3. Bellavia, F., Tegolo, D., Valenti, C.: Keypoint descriptor matching with context-based orientation estimation. Image and Vision Computing 32(9), 559–567 (2014)
4. Calonder, M., Lepetit, V., Ozuysal, M., Trzcinski, T., Strecha, C., Fua, P.: BRIEF: computing a local binary descriptor very fast. IEEE Transactions on Pattern Analysis and Machine Intelligence 34(7), 1281–1298 (2012)
5. Fan, B., Kong, Q., Trzcinski, T., Wang, Z., Pan, C., Fua, P.: Receptive fields selection for binary feature description. IEEE Transactions on Image Processing 26(6), 2583–2595 (2014)
6. Fan, B., Wu, F., Hu, Z.: Rotationally invariant descriptors using intensity order pooling. IEEE Transactions on Pattern Analysis and Machine Intelligence 34(10), 2031–2045 (2012)
7. Lowe, D.: Distinctive image features from scale-invariant keypoints. International Journal of Computer Vision 60(2), 91–110 (2004)
8. Mikolajczyk, K., Tuytelaars, T., Schmid, C., Zisserman, A., Matas, J., Schaffalitzky, F., Kadir, T., Van Gool, L.: A comparison of affine region detectors. International Journal of Computer Vision 65(1–2), 43–72 (2005)
9. Snavely, N., Seitz, S., Szeliski, R.: Modeling the world from internet photo collections. International Journal of Computer Vision 80(2), 189–210 (2008)
10. Szeliski, R.: Computer Vision: Algorithms and Applications. Springer (2010)
11. Tuytelaars, T., Mikolajczyk, K.: Local invariant feature detectors: a survey. Foundations and Trends in Computer Graphics and Vision 3(3), 177–280 (2008)
12. Wang, Z., Fan, B., Wu, F.: Local intensity order pattern for feature description. In: Proc. of the International Conference on Computer Vision, pp. 603–610 (2011)
13. Wang, Z., Fan, B., Wu, F.: Affine subspace representation for feature description. In: Proc. of the European Conference on Computer Vision, pp. 94–108 (2014)

Fast Superpixel-Based Hierarchical Approach to Image Segmentation

Francesco Verdoja[(✉)] and Marco Grangetto

Computer Science Department, Università degli Studi di Torino, Torino, Italy
verdoja@di.unito.it

Abstract. Image segmentation is one of the core task in image processing. Traditionally such operation is performed starting from single pixels requiring a significant amount of computations. It has been shown that superpixels can be used to improve segmentation performance. In this work we propose a novel superpixel-based hierarchical approach for image segmentation that works by iteratively merging nodes of a weighted undirected graph initialized with the superpixels regions. Proper metrics to drive the regions merging are proposed and experimentally validated using the standard Berkeley Dataset. Our analysis shows that the proposed algorithm runs faster than state of the art techniques while providing accurate segmentation results both in terms of visual and objective metrics.

Keywords: Segmentation · Superpixels · Graph partitioning · Hierarchical clustering · CIEDE2000 · Mahalanobis distance · Bhattacharyya distance

1 Introduction

Region segmentation is a key low-level problem in image processing, as it is at the foundation of many high-level computer vision tasks, such as scene understanding [7] and object recognition [8]. Traditionally regions are found by starting from single pixels and then use different approaches to find clusters of pixels. Some examples of methods include region growing [14], histogram analysis [15] and pyamidal approaches [12]; another very commonly used class of algorithms treats the image as a graph. Graph-based techniques usually consider every pixel as a node in a weighted undirected graph and then they find regions in two possible ways: by partitioning the graph using some criterion, or by merging the nodes that are most similar according to a similarity measure. Methods of the first subclass are usually based on graph-cut and its variations [18] or spectral clustering [6]. For what concerns node merging techniques, one algorithm that has been widely used is the one by Felzenszwalb-Huttenlocher [4]. The criterion proposed in this latter work aims at clustering pixels such that the resulting segmentation is neither too coarse nor too fine. The graph is initialized considering every pixel as a node; the arcs between neighboring pixels are weighted with a proper dissimilarity measure

© Springer International Publishing Switzerland 2015
V. Murino and E. Puppo (Eds.): ICIAP 2015, Part I, LNCS 9279, pp. 364–374, 2015.
DOI: 10.1007/978-3-319-23231-7_33

(e.g. minimum color difference connecting two components). At every iteration the algorithm merges pair of nodes (components) that are connected by an edge characterized by a weight that is lower than the intra-component differences. As consequence, homogeneous components that are not separated by boundaries are progressively represented by the nodes of the graph.

A recent trend in segmentation, is to start the computation from superpixels instead of single pixels [16]. As shown in Fig. 1, superpixels are perceptually meaningful atomic regions which aim to replace rigid pixel grid. Examples of algorithms used to generate these kind of small regions are Turbopixel [9] and the widely used and very fast SLIC algorithm [1]. Over-segmenting an image using one of said techniques, and the performing actual region segmentation, can be interesting both in term of reducing the complexity of the problem (i.e. starting from superpixels instead of single pixels) and improving the quality of the final result, thanks to the intrinsic properties of superpixels [10].

Fig. 1. An image divided into approximately 600 superpixels

In this study, we analyze the benefits of using a simple merging approach over a graph whose nodes are initialized with superpixels regions. The main contributions of the paper are:

- design of a local merging approach for the selection of the pair of superpixels that are likely to belong to the same image region;
- exploitation of CIELAB color space in the definition of the dissimilarity metric so as to better match human color perception;
- analysis of the performance and complexity trade-off with respect to the state of the art.

Our conclusions are that superpixels can efficiently boost merging based segmentation techniques by reducing the computational cost without impacting on the segmentation performance. In particular we show that such result can be achieved even without resorting to global graph partitioning such as graph-cut [20] or spectral clustering [10].

It's important to note that although other superpixel-based hierarical approaches have been proposed in the past, the most notable among them by Jain et al. [5], none of them have been intended as a general-use segmentation technique. The work by Jain et al., for example, has been tested only on human brain images, and its validity on standard datasets is not known. The performance of the proposed algorithm, which is intended to work on any type of image, are going to be instead objectively evaluated on a well known standard dataset for image segmentation.

The paper is organized as follows. In Sect. 2 the proposed segmentation technique is presented, whereas in Sect. 3 and Sect. 4 complexity and segmentation results are discussed, respectively.

2   The Proposed Technique

Let's start by defining an n regions segmentation of an image $I = \{x_i\}_{i=1}^{N}$ with N pixels as a partition $L = \{l_i\}_{i=1}^{n}$ of the pixels of I; more precisely, the segmented regions must satisfy the following constraints:

$$\forall x \in I, \exists l \in L \mid x \in l \; ;$$
$$\forall l \in L, \nexists l' \in L - \{l\} \mid l \cap l' \neq \emptyset \; . \tag{1}$$

Please note that in the rest of the paper the terms *region*, *label*, and *segment* are going to be used interchangeably to refer to one of the parts of the segmented image, i.e. one of the set of pixels l.

In this paper we propose to initialize the segmentation algorithm with an over-segmented partition L^m. This first segmentation can be obtained with any superpixel algorithm. Since the quality of the starting superpixels is not going to be checked by the proposed technique, the segmentation accuracy of the chosen algorithm for finding superpixels is of crucial importance in this context. In this work SLIC has been used given its known computational efficiency and segmentation accuracy [1].

Starting from an image I and a partition L^m composed of m regions, the proposed algorithm aims at merging at each iteration the pair of labels representing the most similar regions between the ones determined in the previous step. In particular at the k-th iteration the two most similar between the k segments of L^k are merged to obtain a new set L^{k-1} composed of $k-1$ segments. This process can be iterated for $k = m, m-1, \ldots, 2$; when $k = 2$ a binary segmentation L^2 is obtained, where only foreground and background are discriminated.

The proposed iterative merging algorithm generates a full dendrogram, that carries information about the hierarchy of the labels in terms of regions similarity. We can represent the merging process using a weighted graph. When the algorithm starts, an undirected weighted graph $G^m = \{L^m, W^m\}$ is constructed over the superpixel set L^m, where

$$W^m = \{w_{ij}^m\}, \ \forall i \neq j \mid l_i^m, l_j^m \in L^m \wedge A\left(l_i^m, l_j^m\right) = 1 \tag{2}$$

for some adjacency function A. Since G^m is an undirected graph we have that $w_{ij}^m = w_{ji}^m$; the weights represent the distance (or dissimilarity measure) between pair of regions $w_{ij}^m = \delta\left(l_i^m, l_j^m\right)$. The possible functions that can be used to compute the distance δ are going to be discussed in detail in Sect. 2.1.

At each iteration, the algorithm picks the pair of labels $l_p^k, l_q^k \in L^k$ having $w_{pq}^k = \min\{W^k\}$ and merges them; i.e. it generate a new partition $L^{k-1} = L^k - \{l_q^k\}$ having all the pixels $x \in l_p^k \cup l_q^k$ assigned to the label l_p^{k-1}. L^{k-1} contains now just $k-1$ segments. After that, edges and corresponding weights needs to be updated as well. W^{k-1} is generated according to the following rule:

$$w_{ij}^{k-1} = \begin{cases} \delta\left(l_p^{k-1}, l_j^{k-1}\right) & \text{if } i = p \vee i = q \ , \\ w_{ij}^k & \text{otherwise} \ . \end{cases} \tag{3}$$

Please note that w_{pq}^k is not going to be included in W^{k-1} since it doesn't exist anymore.

When $k = 2$, the algorithm stops and returns the full dendrogram $D = \{L^m, \ldots, L^2\}$ that can be cut at will to obtain the desired number of regions. An example of different cuts of the dendrogram can be seen in Fig. 2.

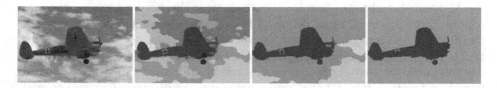

Fig. 2. A sample image and hierarchy of 3 segmentations obtained with $k = 50, 15, 2$ and δ_C metric.

2.1 Region Distance Metrics

The approach proposed here can be used in conjunction with several distance metrics capable to capture the dissimilarity between a pair of segmented regions. In the following we discuss a few alternatives that will be used in our experiments.

The first and simplest one that we have explored is color difference between the two regions. To better match human color perception, CIELAB color space and the standard CIEDE2000 color difference have been chosen [17]. Given two regions l_1 and l_2, we compute the mean values of the L*a*b* components $M_1 = (\mu_{L^*,1}, \mu_{a^*,1}, \mu_{b^*,1})$ and $M_2 = (\mu_{L^*,2}, \mu_{a^*,2}, \mu_{b^*,2})$, and we define the distance between the two labels as

$$\delta_C\left(l_i, l_j\right) = \Delta E_{00}\left(M_i, M_j\right) \tag{4}$$

where ΔE_{00} is the CIEDE2000 color difference [17].

Another possibility it to exploit the Mahalanobis distance [11] given its ability to capture statistical differences between two distributions of color component. Given a set of n_1 pixels $l_1 = \{x_i = (x_{L^*,i}, x_{a^*,i}, x_{b^*,i})\}_{i=1}^{n_1}$, we can estimate their mean $M_1 = (\mu_{L^*}, \mu_{a^*}, \mu_{b^*})$ and covariance as

$$C_1 = \frac{1}{n_1} \sum_{i=1}^{n_1} (x_i - M_1)(x_i - M_1)^T \ . \tag{5}$$

Then we compute the Mahalanobis distance of any other set of n_2 pixels $l_2 = \{y_i = (y_{L^*,i}, y_{a^*,i}, y_{b^*,i})\}_{i=1}^{n_2}$ from the estimated distribution of l_1 as

$$\Delta M\left(l_1, l_2\right) = \frac{1}{n_2} \sum_{i=1}^{n_2} (y_i - M_1)^T C_1^{-1} (y_i - M_1) \ . \tag{6}$$

Since ΔM is non symmetric, i.e. $\Delta M\left(l_1, l_2\right) \neq \Delta M\left(l_2, l_1\right)$, we compute the distance between two labels as the minimum of their relative Mahalanobis distances obtaining the following symmetric metric:

$$\delta_M\left(l_i, l_j\right) = \min\left\{\Delta M\left(l_i, l_j\right), \Delta M\left(l_j, l_i\right)\right\} \ . \tag{7}$$

Since during the iterative merging process is important to merge homogeneous regions, in particular without crossing object boundaries, we also investigate a local Mahalanobis metric that aims at detecting image segment whose adjacent borders look very different. This border variation consists in evaluating the Mahalanobis distance just for the pixels near the border between the two regions. More precisely, let us define b_{ij} the portion of common border between two adjacent image segments. Then we can define a subset of pixels whose location is across the two adjacent regions $c_{ij} = \{x \in I \mid r_1 < d\left(x, b_{ij}\right) < r_2\}$, where d is the Euclidean spatial distance and r_1 and r_2 are proper ranges. Now we can introduce function $B\left(l_i, l_j\right)$ that returns two new set of pixels $l'_i = l_i \cap c_{ij}$ and $l'_j = l_j \cap c_{ij}$ that represent the pixels of l_i and l_j respectively that are located close to the common border. Finally, the distance metric is defined as:

$$\delta_B\left(l_i, l_j\right) = \min\left\{\Delta M\left(l'_i, l'_j\right), \Delta M\left(l'_j, l'_i\right)\right\} \tag{8}$$

where l'_i and l'_j are the two outputs of $B\left(l_i, l_j\right)$.

Finally, we investigate a fourth metric based on the color histogram distance. One possible solution to measure histogram difference is the Bhattacharyya distance [3], which is the general case of the Mahalanobis distance. Given two histograms h_1 and h_2 composed each by B bins, the Bhattacharyya distance is defined as

$$\Delta H\left(h_1, h_2\right) = \sqrt{1 - \frac{1}{\sqrt{\bar{h}_1 \bar{h}_2 B^2}} \sum_{i=1}^{B} \sqrt{h_1\left(i\right) \cdot h_2\left(i\right)}} \tag{9}$$

where $h(i)$ is the number of pixels in the bin i, while $\bar{h} = \frac{1}{B} \sum_{i=1}^{B} h\left(i\right)$. Since images in the L*a*b* color space have three channels, ΔH is going to be computed on each channel independently, and then the maximum value of the three is going to be used as dissimilarity measure; this has been chosen over other possibility, like taking the mean of the three distances, as it yields higher discriminating power in finding differences just on one of the channels. In conclusion, the last dissimilarity measure between two regions l_i and l_j having respectively histograms $H_i = \{h_{L^*,i}, h_{a^*,i}, h_{b^*,i}\}$ and $H_j = \{h_{L^*,j}, h_{a^*,j}, h_{b^*,j}\}$ is defined as:

$$\delta_H(l_i, l_j) = \max \left\{ \begin{array}{l} \Delta H\left(h_{L^*,i}, h_{L^*,j}\right), \\ \Delta H\left(h_{a^*,i}, h_{a^*,j}\right), \\ \Delta H\left(h_{b^*,i}, h_{b^*,j}\right) \end{array} \right\} . \tag{10}$$

3 Complexity

In this section the complexity of the proposed algorithm is going to be discussed. We will start by analyzing the complexity of the distance metrics presented in Sect. 2.1. To this end let us consider any two regions l_1 and l_2 with a total number of pixels $n = |l_1 \cup l_2|$. The complexity of the different distance metrics is discussed in the following.

δ_C Computing the color mean of both regions requires $O(n)$ time while computation of distance between the mean values has unitary cost.

δ_M All the operations required to compute Mahalanobis distance (mean and color covariance estimates) are in the order of $O(n)$.

δ_B Since the computation is going to be performed on the $n' = |l'_1 \cup l'_2|$ pixels in the border area, the complexity is again $O(n')$, with $n' < n$.

δ_H The dominant cost is assigning every pixel to a bin; then, the cost of calculating the actual distance is negligible. Therefore the overall complexity is $O(n)$ also in this case.

To recap, computing any of the distances we proposed is linear to the number of pixels in the considered segments. Then, according to (1) computing all distances for a whole partition L of an image of N pixels will require $O(N)$ time.

Finally, we can discuss the overall complexity of all the algorithm steps:

1. The starting step of the algorithm is to compute the m superpixels. For that purpose, using SLIC, $O(N)$ time is required [1];
2. Next, the graph G^m needs to be constructed. The time required for this task is in the order of $O(N)$, as all the weights needs to be computed once;
3. Then, the m merging iterations are performed. At every iteration just a small number of the weights is going to be updated, and since all the regions are going to be merged once, the overall complexity is once again $O(N)$.

In conclusion, the overall time required by the algorithm is linear to the size of the image.

We can conclude that the proposed technique exhibits lower complexity than both merging techniques that works on pixels, like the Felzenszwalb-Huttenlocher algorithm which has complexity of $O(N \log N)$ [4], and other widely used techniques that works on superpixels, like SAS [10] and ℓ_0-sparse-coding [20], which both have complexities higher than linear.

To verify our claims, in Fig. 3 the running times of the different components of the algorithm are shown. It can be noted that the time needed by both SLIC and the clustering algorithm using all the different distance measures here proposed are growing linearly to the size of the input.

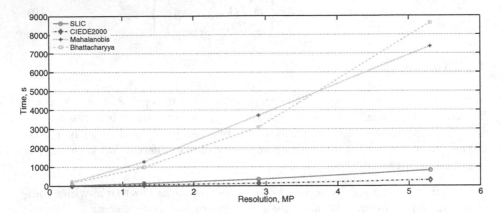

Fig. 3. Mean running times of SLIC and the proposed clustering algorithm using the different distance measures; these results are computed on three 5.3MP images scaled at different smaller resolutions.

4   Performance Evaluation

In this section the performance of the proposed algorithm is validated both visually and using objective metrics. To this end the standard Berkeley Dataset BSDS500 [2] has been used. This latter, although originally constructed for boundaries evaluation, has become a well recognized standard for evaluation of regions segmentation in images.

The discussion on objective metrics for an effective evaluation of the segmentation performance is still open [2]; still the usage of a standard set of images makes our results easier to reproduce and compare with past and future research.

In this work we have selected as benchmarks for performance evaluation two well known superpixel-based algorithms, namely SAS [10] and ℓ_0-sparse-coding [20]. Moreover, the Felzenszwalb-Huttenlocher algorithm [4] has been selected as representative of a merging approach that starts from individual pixels.

4.1   Metrics

Two common metrics have been used to evaluate the performance over the dataset. They have been chosen because results using these metrics are available for all the algorithms that have been cited in this work. For the Felzenszwalb-Huttenlocher algorithm they can be found in [2], while for ℓ_0-sparse-coding and SAS they can be found directly in the respective papers.

Probabilistic Rand Index. The Probabilistic Rand Index is a variation of the Rand Index, proposed for dealing with multiple ground-truths [19]. It is defined as:

$$PRI\left(S, \{G_k\}\right) = \frac{1}{T} \sum_{i<j} \left[c_{ij}p_{ij} + (1 - c_{ij})(1 - p_{ij})\right] \tag{11}$$

where c_{ij} is the event that pixels i and j have the same label while p_{ij} is its probability. T is the total number of pixel pairs. To average the Rand Index over multiple ground-truths, p_{ij} is estimated from the ground-truth dataset.

Variation of Information. The Variation of Information (VoI) metric allows one to compare two different clusterings of the same data [13]. It measures the distance between two segmentations in terms of their conditional entropy, given as:

$$VoI\left(S, S'\right) = H\left(S\right) + H\left(S'\right) - 2I\left(S, S'\right) \tag{12}$$

where H represents the entropy and I the mutual information between two clusterings of data, S and S'. In the case presented here, these clusterings are the segmentations performed by the algorithms to be tested and the ground-truths.

4.2   Results

First of all in Fig. 2 and Fig. 4 we show some segmentation results obtained using the simple color metric difference δ_C; every segmented region is filled with its mean color. Figure 2 reports different segmentations of the same image obtained by stopping the hierarchical clustering at progressively lower numbers of regions showing that the proposed solution can achieve different levels of segmentation granularity down to the separation into foreground and background. The images shown Fig. 4 are obtained selecting the value of k that yields the best overlap with ground-truth segmentations in the BSDS500 dataset. It can be observed that the proposed solution is able to effectively segment images; the boundary accuracy clearly depends on the starting superpixel technique, e.g. in our case SLIC, whereas the proposed hierarchical merging criterion can group the main image regions very effectively.

We do not show images segmented using the other similarity metrics proposed in Sect. 2.1 since they yields similar visual results.

In Tab. 1 objective segmentation metrics computed on the BSDS500 dataset are shown. In particular, we report PRI and VoI results yielded by our method with the four different similarity metrics proposed in Sect. 2.1 and other benchmarks in the literature. We started with 600 superpixels, then for the calculation of boundary-based metric δ_B we have set $r_1 = 3$ and $r_2 = 11$ respectively, while for δ_H we have set $B = 20$. From the obtained results it can be noted that all the techniques we compare exhibits about the same value of PRI. Moreover, it can be noted that the proposed solution yields better VoI results than the Felzenszwalb-Huttenlocher pixel based algorithm and competing superpixel based ℓ_0-sparse-coding [20]. Only the SAS [10] algorithm exhibits a lower value

Fig. 4. Sample images from BSDS500 (top) and their best corresponding segmentation outputs (bottom) using δ_C metric.

Table 1. Results obtained by the proposed technique in all its variations compared to other state-of-the-art techniques over the BSDS500

Algorithm	PRI	VoI
SAS [10]	0.83	1.68
ℓ_0-sparse-coding [20]	0.84	1.99
Felzenszwalb-Huttenlocher [4]	0.82	1.87
Ours (using δ_C)	0.83	1.78
Ours (using δ_M)	0.83	1.71
Ours (using δ_B)	0.82	1.82
Ours (using δ_H)	0.81	1.83

for VoI. At the same time, it is worth recalling that the proposed technique is by far the cheapest in terms of computational cost with respect to the other benchmarks.

We can also note that color and Mahalanobis metric provides the same segmentation accuracy. On the other hand the histogram and boundary based metrics are slightly less effective. This slight difference in performance can be explained by considering that superpixel over-segmentation is able to i) retain very homogeneous areas; ii) accurately follow image boundary. The first feature makes the advantage of a more statistically accurate metric for the description of intra-pixel color variation, such as Mahalanobis distance, negligible with respect to simple color distance in L*a*b* space. Finally, the fact that superpixels does not cut image edges makes the usage of a boundary based criterion ineffective.

In Fig. 5 we conclude the analysis of our results by showing the precision/recall curves yielded by the four proposed region distance metrics. The curves have been obtained by comparing the segmentation generated by our algorithm setting different values for k with ground-truth data in BSDS500 dataset. It can be observed that δ_C and δ_M appears to be slightly superior to both δ_B and δ_H also in terms of precision/recall trade-off.

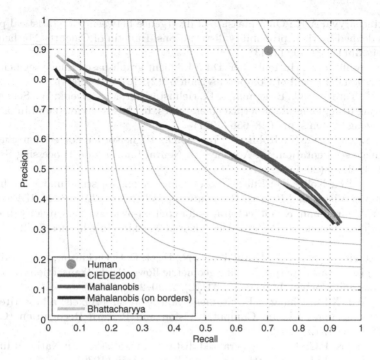

Fig. 5. Precision and recall of the proposed technique, using δ_C, δ_M, δ_B and δ_H

5 Conclusions

In this paper a new approach to image segmentation has been presented. The proposed approach is based on iterative merging of nodes in a graph initialized with an over-segmentation of an image performed by a superpixel algorithm. The algorithm employs proper distance metrics to select regions to be merged. We have shown that both CIEDE2000 and Mahalanobis color distances are very effective in terms of segmentation accuracy. Our experimentation worked out on the BSDS500 dataset shows that the proposed tool yields competitive results with respect to other state of the art techniques that segments starting both with superpixels and single pixels. Finally, one of the most important achievements is that the overall complexity of the proposed method is kept linear to the dimension of the image as opposed to the other techniques we compare to.

References

1. Achanta, R., Shaji, A., Smith, K., Lucchi, A., Fua, P., Süsstrunk, S.: SLIC superpixels compared to state-of-the-art superpixel methods. IEEE Transactions on Pattern Analysis and Machine Intelligence **34**(11), 2274–2282 (2012)
2. Arbeláez, P., Maire, M., Fowlkes, C.C., Malik, J.: Contour detection and hierarchical image segmentation. IEEE Transactions on Pattern Analysis and Machine Intelligence **33**(5), 898–916 (2010)

3. Bhattacharyya, A.K.: On a measure of divergence between two statistical populations defined by their probability distributions. Bulletin of Calcutta Mathematical Society **35**(1), 99–109 (1943)
4. Felzenszwalb, P.F., Huttenlocher, D.P.: Efficient graph-based image segmentation. International Journal of Computer Vision **59**(2), 167–181 (2004)
5. Jain, V., Turaga, S.C., Briggman, K.L., Helmstaedter, M.N., Denk, W., Seung, H.S.: Learning to agglomerate superpixel hierarchies. In: Advances in Neural Information Processing Systems, pp. 648–656 (2011)
6. Kim, S., Nowozin, S., Kohli, P., Yoo, C.D.: Higher-order correlation clustering for image segmentation. In: Advances in Neural Information Processing Systems, pp. 1530–1538 (2011)
7. Kumar, M.P., Koller, D.: Efficiently selecting regions for scene understanding. In: Computer Vision and Pattern Recognition (CVPR), pp. 3217–3224. IEEE (2010)
8. Lee, Y.J., Grauman, K.: Object-graphs for context-aware visual category discovery. IEEE Transactions on Pattern Analysis and Machine Intelligence **34**(2), 346–358 (2012)
9. Levinshtein, A., Stere, A., Kutulakos, K.N., Fleet, D.J., Dickinson, S.J., Siddiqi, K.: Turbopixels: Fast superpixels using geometric flows. IEEE Transactions on Pattern Analysis and Machine Intelligence **31**(12), 2290–2297 (2009)
10. Li, Z., Wu, X.M., Chang, S.F.: Segmentation using superpixels: a bipartite graph partitioning approach. In: Computer Vision and Pattern Recognition (CVPR), pp. 789–796. IEEE (2012)
11. Mahalanobis, P.C.: On the generalized distance in statistics. In: National Institute of Sciences of India, Calcutta, India, vol. 2, pp. 49–55 (1936)
12. Marfil, R., Molina-Tanco, L., Bandera, A., Rodrguez, J.A., Sandoval, F.: Pyramid segmentation algorithms revisited. Pattern Recognition **39**(8), 1430–1451 (2006)
13. Meilă, M.: Comparing clusterings: an axiomatic view. In: Proceedings of the 22nd International Conference on Machine Learning, pp. 577–584. ACM (2005)
14. Nock, R., Nielsen, F.: Statistical region merging. IEEE Transactions on Pattern Analysis and Machine Intelligence **26**(11), 1452–1458 (2004)
15. Ohlander, R., Price, K., Reddy, D.R.: Picture segmentation using a recursive region splitting method. Computer Graphics and Image Processing **8**(3), 313–333 (1978)
16. Ren, X., Malik, J.: Learning a classification model for segmentation. In: Proceedings of Ninth IEEE International Conference on Computer Vision, 2003, pp. 10–17. IEEE (2003)
17. Sharma, G., Wu, W., Dalal, E.N.: The CIEDE2000 color-difference formula: Implementation notes, supplementary test data, and mathematical observations. Color Research and Application **30**(1), 21–30 (2005)
18. Shi, J., Malik, J.: Normalized cuts and image segmentation. IEEE Transactions on Pattern Analysis and Machine Intelligence **22**(8), 888–905 (2000)
19. Unnikrishnan, R., Pantofaru, C., Hebert, M.: Toward objective evaluation of image segmentation algorithms. IEEE Transactions on Pattern Analysis and Machine Intelligence **29**(6), 929–944 (2007)
20. Wang, X., Li, H., Bichot, C.E., Masnou, S., Chen, L.: A graph-cut approach to image segmentation using an affinity graph based on l0-sparse representation of features. In: IEEE International Conference on Image Processing 2013 (ICIP 2013), Melbourne, Australia, pp. 4019–4023, September 2013

Supertetras: A Superpixel Analog for Tetrahedral Mesh Oversegmentation

Giulia Picciau[1]([✉]), Patricio Simari[2], Federico Iuricich[3],
and Leila De Floriani[1]

[1] Università Degli Studi di Genova, Genova, Italy
giulia.picciau@dibris.unige.it
[2] The Catholic University of America, Washington, DC, USA
[3] University of Maryland College Park, College Park, USA

Abstract. Over the past decade, computer vision algorithms have transitioned from relying on the direct, pixel-based representation of images to the use of *superpixels*, small regions whose boundaries agree with image contours. This intermediate representation improves the tractability of image understanding because it reduces the number of primitives to be taken under consideration from several million to a few hundred. Despite the improvements yielded in the area of image segmentation, the concept of an oversegmentation as an intermediate representation has not been adopted in volumetric mesh processing. We take a first step in this direction, adapting a fast and efficient superpixel algorithm to the tetrahedral mesh case, present results which demonstrate the quality of the output oversegmentation, and illustrate its use in a semantic segmentation application.

1 Introduction

Over the past decade, computer vision algorithms have gained many benefits from the introduction of the concept of *superpixels*, which are obtained from an oversegmentation of an image, comprising possibly millions of pixels, into just a few hundred small regions that become the new primitives on which image processing algorithms work. These regions are well aligned with the semantic boundaries of the image, and their relatively low number greatly improves the tractability of the segmentation problem while also allowing for the consideration of mid-level elements such as texture information.

Some approaches have been introduced to extend the idea of superpixel oversegmentation to surface meshes [26], but, to our knowledge, the extension to the volumetric case has not yet been investigated. These models, often used in tasks such as medical data analysis and simulation, usually consist of a very large number of primitives, often in the tens of millions. For this reason, we believe that an intermediate representation of these models obtained by means of an oversegmentation could prove greatly beneficial to semantic segmentation.

We take a first step towards the application of an oversegmentation as a preprocessing step for tetrahedral meshes, extending a state of-the-art superpixel

© Springer International Publishing Switzerland 2015
V. Murino and E. Puppo (Eds.): ICIAP 2015, Part I, LNCS 9279, pp. 375–386, 2015.
DOI: 10.1007/978-3-319-23231-7_34

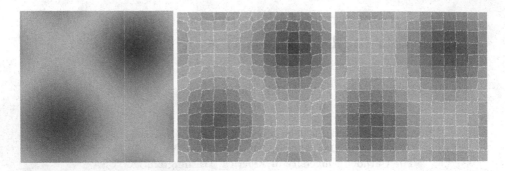

Fig. 1. Field value $f(x, y, z) = sin(x) + sin(y) + sin(z)$, with $x, y, z \in [-\pi, \pi]$ (left), and supertetrahedral segmentation with $w = 0.5$ (center) and $w = 1.5$ (right). Note how the lower w results in regions more aligned with field features, while higher w results in a more regular distribution.

algorithm [1]. The k-means based approach is efficient in time and memory making it suitable for tetrahedral meshes with several million elements for which graph-based methods would not be suitable.

2   Related Work

2.1   Superpixels in Image Processing

Superpixels are often used in Computer Vision as a representation to lower the number of primitives under consideration, thus improving the tractability of the segmentation task [12,14,16,17,24]. *Supervoxels* are the 3D equivalent of superpixels, and have been applied to the segmentation of medical images [19,32] and video sequences [23,36].

Superpixel algorithms use various strategies, including graph-cuts [10,25], watershed [31], mean and medoid shift [7,30], hill-climbing [3], geodesic k-means [33], and reciprocal nearest neighbors [20].

The approach most relevant to our method is the *Simple Linear Iterative Clustering* (SLIC) algorithm [1]. It is a k-means based approach which limits the expansion of each centroid by a constant proportional to the desired superpixel size. This limited expansion results in a complexity which is linear in the image size and is independent of the number of superpixels. The distance metric used is a weighted sum of a Euclidean term to account for the position of a pixel in the image and an intensity term. This formulation yields compact superpixels which adhere well to image contours while being significantly faster than other state-of-the-art methods. The method's low time and space complexity make it an ideal candidate to scale to high-resolution tetrahedral models.

The idea of limited region expansion has been adopted also in the approach of Papon et al. [22], which is an extension of the superpixel concept to point clouds: after initializing the segmentation superimposing a regular grid to the

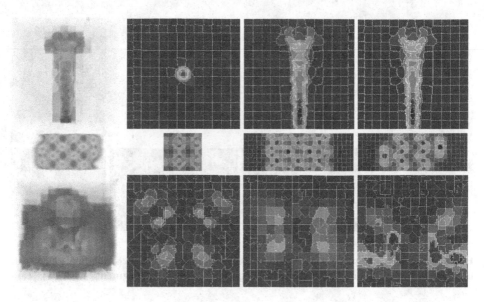

Fig. 2. Volumetric visualization and central x, y, and z slices of physical simulation of a fuel jet (top), silicium material (center), and electron orbit (bottom) segmented into 2000 supertetrahedra with $w = 1.5$.

cloud, they iteratively alternate between a classification step and a centroid update step, until convergence is reached.

2.2 Tetrahedral Domain

Much of the work in the area of tetrahedral mesh research focuses on the quality tetrahedralization of a given volume. This is a difficult task since the regular tetrahedron does not tile 3D space, and state-of-the-art methods usually rely on a Delaunay-based process to tetrahedralize the interior of an object. Tetrahedral meshes are usually computed from point samples [9], regular volume data [8,29], from a set of calibrated images [27], or tetrahedralizing the interior of a triangle mesh [13].

Many techniques have been applied for segmenting a tetrahedral mesh, including traditional unsupervised clustering techniques such as Gaussian mixture models [21], max flow [4], region growing [15], and iterative merging [8], as well as methods based on mathematical concepts such as stable manifolds [2,9], separatrix persistence [11], topological-equivalence regions [6] and discrete Morse theory [35]. Last but not least, many of the best-performing techniques from a semantic point of view apply graph cut methods [27–29].

All of the above methods are designed to produce a segmentation of the input model into a relatively low number of segments, each of relatively large size. To obtain an oversegmentation, applying these techniques would be less than ideal.

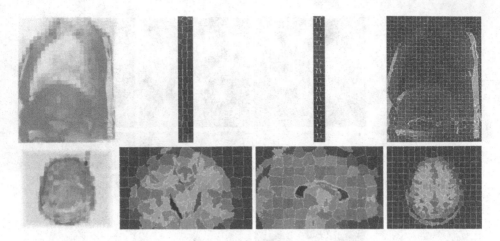

Fig. 3. Volumetric representation and central x, y, and z slices of medical data of a human thorax (top) and brain (bottom) segmented into 2000 segments with $w = 1.5$.

Techniques such as watershed, region merging, and their mathematically-related extensions allow for little control over the variance in size and shape of the resulting segments, usually producing irregular and unevenly-sized regions that are less than ideal as intermediate representations in the style of super-pixels. Graph-cut algorithms, on the other hand, require quadratic storage for an all-pairs affinity matrix, and so do not scale well to the case of graphs with millions of nodes. This makes them inappropriate since the size and resolution of the tetrahedral datasets used in practical applications is increasing. In contrast, as previously mentioned, our adaptation of the SLIC approach [1] produces semantically accurate results while keeping the complexity linear in the number of primitives.

It should be emphasized that our approach is not meant to replace the previously-mentioned tetrahedral segmentation algorithms, but rather to be used as a pre-processing step to enable their execution on a domain consisting of much fewer, well-shaped primitives conforming to semantic boundaries.

3   Algorithm

Our aim is to develop an adaptation of the SLIC algorithm [1] from the image domain to 3D scalar fields defined over the vertices of a tetrahedral mesh, considering tetrahedra rather than pixels. The concept of oversegmentation has already been extended to triangle meshes in [26], but the domain presents several differences with respect to the tetrahedral one: first, only the surface of the object is considered, and therefore every distance calculation has to be constrained to lie on the surface. Second, triangle meshes do not have a scalar field defined on them. Rather, information about the angle between adjacent faces is added to the spatial information given by the vertices as a "curvature" term. Given that in the case of the tetrahedral mesh the field is defined over vertices rather than tetrahedra, we consider the centroids of the latter, assigning as a field value the average field value at the tetrahedron's vertices. While pixels lie on a regular grid and adjacencies are implicitly given, in the tetrahedral mesh case we must encode and use adjacency information explicitly during the clustering process. To store the mesh, we use a structure that stores information about tetrahedra and their vertices together with the adjacency relations between them [5]. The segmentation process is based on the k-means algorithm, and thus consists of an initialization step followed by centroid update and a classification steps, with the latter two steps repeated until convergence. We describe each one of these steps more in detail below.

Field Normalization Preprocess: To be robust across models with varying ranges of field values, we normalize the scalar field defined over the vertices to have unit variance, taking the field $\bar{f}_i = f_i/\sigma_f$, where f_i is the field value of the i-th tetrahedron (taken as the mean field value of its vertices) and σ_f is the standard deviation of the set of all field values of the model.

Initialization: We superimpose a virtual regular grid on the domain with cells of width $S = \sqrt[3]{v/k}$, where v is the total volume of the mesh's 3D domain and k is the number of desired regions. Each tetrahedron is assigned to its corresponding discrete cell taking the integer division of its 3D coordinates and cell width S.

Centroid Update: Each supertetrahedral region's centroid is calculated as the volume-weighted average of the barycenters of the tetrahedra belonging to said region. This centroid need not fall exactly on any of the region's barycenters, and is free to lie within the continuous 3D domain.

Tetrahedral Re-Classification This step assigns each tetrahedron to the region associated with the nearest region centroid using a breadth-first expansion that starts from the tetrahedron closest to the centroid. The metric used to evaluate the distance is described in Section 3.1. Limiting the expansion to $2S$ allows the complexity of this step to remain linear in the number of tetrahedra regardless of the number of regions.

3.1   Distance Metric

The distance metric we use is an adaptation of the formula presented in SLIC [1] to the case of scalar field defined over the vertices of a tetrahedral mesh. As a consequence, it consists of the weighted sum of a term which carries spatial information and a term for the field value. The spatial term is the Euclidean distance between the 3D barycenters of tetrahedra i and j: $||c_i - c_j||$. Since the fields we consider are scalar, we define the field term as $|\bar{f}_i - \bar{f}_j|$. So that these terms are robust to variations in mesh scale and scalar field intensity across models, they are normalized and combined as follows:

$$d_{i,j} = (\bar{f}_i - \bar{f}_j)^2 + \left(w \frac{||c_i - c_j||}{S} \right)^2 \qquad (1)$$

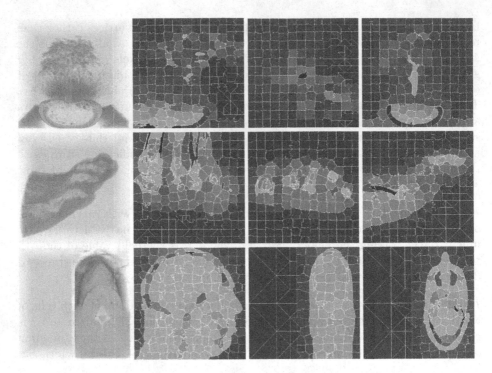

Fig. 4. Volumetric representation and central x, y, and z slices of meshes with non-regular domains segmented into 2000 segments with $w = 1.5$.

where S is the previously-defined supertetrahedral diameter, and w is a user-specified weight. Lower values of w will give more importance to the field values, and will favor more irregular regions that better adapt to the field's features. In contrast, higher values of w will result in more regularly-shaped regions. This effect can be observed in Figure 1. We have found experimentally that a good range of values for w is $[0.5, 2.0]$.

3.2 Notes on Time and Space Complexity

Analogously to the original SLIC algorithm, the complexity of the expansion step is linear in the number of tetrahedra, because the expansion of each region is limited by a constant proportional to the region size. Achieving this complexity in the tetrahedral case requires a regular spatial grid to which all tetrahedral elements register, resulting in a constant number of tetrahedra in each grid cell. With such a spatial index, the tetrahedron closest to each supertetrahedral region's centroid can be found in constant time during the reclassification step. A k-d tree or octree can be used instead, with a very modest reduction in performance with respect to the previous alternative.

The supertetrahedral representation is effective for compactly encoding simplicial meshes. In our experiments we compare the latter with another compact

Table 1. IA and supertetra comparison and running times for the latter.

Model	#V	#T	#ST	#Arcs	IA (MB)	ST (MB)	ST (s)	Ncut (s)
Silicium	113K	634K	2.1K	12.2K	22.80	13.22	21.76	245.43
Neghip	129K	728K	2.2K	11.3K	26.14	15.12	47.22	284.93
Fuel	262K	1.5M	2.2K	9K	53.78	30.96	40.49	332.15
Thorax	768K	4.1M	2.7K	14.7K	149.08	86.37	137.80	712.81
Brain	860K	5M	2K	12.4K	178.54	102.49	451.40	480.15
Trigonom.	1M	5.8M	2.1K	13.6K	208.18	119.45	193.18	591.52
Bonsai	4.5M	25.8M	2.2K	13.2K	926.18	531.92	4613.90	1774.81
VisMale	4.9M	28M	1.6K	8.8K	1,007.11	578.70	6,529.66	1,712.95
Foot	5.3M	31.2M	2.1K	12.5K	1,115.44	638.90	5,788.87	2,054.03

encoding for simplicial meshes: the IA data structure [5]. For the sake of clarity, we distinguish among the three types of entities encoded in the IA data structure: the geometry, which is represented by the vertex coordinates, the connectivity, which encodes the relations between tetrahedra and vertices, and the dual graph. Considering a tetrahedral mesh Σ, its dual graph is the graph $G = (N, A)$ where the nodes N are in one-to-one correspondence with the tetrahedra in Σ. An arc in A connects two nodes if and only if the corresponding tetrahedra are face-adjacent (i.e. they share a triangle).

In our IA implementation, vertices are indexed in a single array containing, for each of them, their coordinates and an additional scalar value, thus storing $4v$ float values, where v is the number of vertices in Σ. Tetrahedra are also indexed in a single array. Connectivity information is encoded by storing, for each tetrahedron, the four indices of its boundary vertices, thus encoding $4t$ indexes in total, where t is the number of tetrahedra in Σ. Lastly, the dual graph can be efficiently represented exploiting the regularity of the tetrahedra adjacencies. Since each tetrahedron has at most four adjacent tetrahedra, we can use a constant-size array of length $4t$ storing, for each tetrahedron, the four indices of the adjacent tetrahedra. The resulting overall storage cost of the IA structure is then $4v + 8t$.

The information represented in the supertetra structure can be conceptually subdivided as we have done for the IA representation. The geometric and combinatorial information still consists of three coordinates per vertex plus a scalar field value and $4t$ indexes, which reference each tetrahedron's vertices. However, adjacency relations are now considered between supertetra regions rather than tetrahedra. The dual graph $G = (N, A)$ now encodes one node for each supertetra region and one arc for each adjacency relation between two supertetra. Thus, each supertetra encodes the list of adjacent regions as a list of pointers to the latter. Since each adjacency relation is referred twice (i.e. a pointer is encoded on both the adjacent regions) the total number of pointers is $2|A|$. As a consequence, the storage cost of this representation becomes $4v + 4t + 2|A|$.

We have estimated the spatial occupation of the two data structures encoding real datasets and we show the obtained results in Table 3.2. We are assuming a storage cost of 8 bytes for each coordinate and scalar value and a storage cost of 4 bytes for each pointer or index over an array. We note that the supertetra representation is approximately 40% more compact than the IA representation.

4   Results

In the following, we show the results of applying our oversegmentation algorithm to sample datasets. Figure 1 illustrates the effect of the w parameter on the resulting regularity, Figure 2 shows results on models of physical simulations, and Figure 3 illustrates results on anatomical data. Lastly, Figure 5 demonstrates the application of our supertetrahedral representation to a semantic segmentation. Since the objects are volumetric, we visualize the slices obtained by cutting the mesh along its central axes. Please refer to figure captions for more details. In each case, note how the "empty space" (marked by constant field values) is divided into an approximately regular grid, while in detailed areas the supertetrahedral boundaries follow the contours of the field's features. Most of the meshes we use are regular, but our approach also work on non-regular or semi-regular meshes, as illustrated in Figure 4.

4.1   Enabling Normalized Cuts on Large Datasets

Usually, the results of an oversegmentation are computed as a preprocess, the results of which are fed as input to some subsequent algorithm, improving its results and/or efficiency. Here, we apply the Normalized Cuts algorithm of Shi and Malik [25]. This graph cut method produces high quality results, but its drawback are its $O\left(n^{\frac{3}{2}}\right)$ complexity and quadratic storage costs. The latter, in particular, would make the application of the normalized cuts approach to one of these high resolution models completely intractable. Let us consider the all-pairs distances storage cost assuming we use 32-bit single-precision floating point and only store the upper triangle of the symmetric distance matrix (something which the implementation of Shi and Malik does not currently allow for). The brain dataset, comprising approximately five million tetrahedra, would require $\frac{1}{2}(5M)^2 \times 4$ bytes ≈ 50 terabytes to store the distance matrix alone.

The oversegmentations we produce, illustrated in Figure 5, are composed of approximately 2000 regions, and therefore it is possible to perform a normalized cut considering the regions as nodes of the graph. We use the same distance metric defined in equation (1), computing it between the centroids of adjacent supertetrahedral regions, and then find all-pairs shortest path distances over the adjacency graph of these regions. Finally, we apply Normalized Cuts. Figure 5 illustrates the results of this procedure on regular and irregular tetrahedral domains respectively. The supertetrahedral representation is what enables graph-cut results such as these at this resolution.

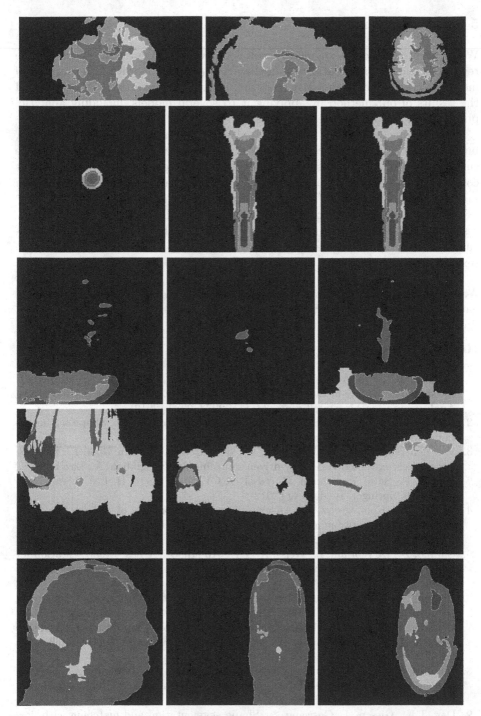

Fig. 5. Results of applying Normalized Cuts on our supertetrahedral representation. A direct application of such a graph-cut algorithm would be completely intractable due to the prohibitive storage costs of the all-pairs distance matrix.

5   Future Work

We have introduced a tetrahedral mesh segmentation algorithm, which can be regarded as an extension of a state-of-the-art superpixel algorithm to tetrahedral mesh representations with scalar fields defined over their vertices. We illustrated the results of our method by applying it to several models, including analytic, physical simulation, and medical datasets.

Since oversegmentation is not a final aim in image and mesh processing, but rather an intermediate step applied to improve the tractability of some subsequent task, we demonstrated the utility of our approach by showing how it could be used to enable the application of a graph cut approach to high resolution models, a task which would have been intractable otherwise.

Future work will focus on exploring other uses of the supertetrahedral representation, as well as extending the approach to higher-dimensional and time-varying meshes, and augmenting the regions with feature vectors that encode texture and other mid-level perceptual cues.

Acknowledgments. This work was supported in part by the National Science Foundation under grant number IIS-1116747.

References

1. Achanta, R., Shaji, A., Smith, K., Lucchi, A., Fua, P., Susstrunk, S.: Slic superpixels compared to state-of-the-art superpixel methods. IEEE Transactions on Pattern Analysis and Machine Intelligence **34**(11), 2274–2282 (2012)
2. Alexa, M., Rusinkiewicz, S., Dey, T.K., Giesen, J., Goswami, S.: Shape segmentation and matching from noisy point clouds
3. Van den Bergh, M., Boix, X., Roig, G., de Capitani, B., Van Gool, L.: SEEDS: Superpixels extracted via energy-driven sampling. In: Fitzgibbon, A., Lazebnik, S., Perona, P., Sato, Y., Schmid, C. (eds.) ECCV 2012, Part VII. LNCS, vol. 7578, pp. 13–26. Springer, Heidelberg (2012)
4. Boykov, Y., Kolmogorov, V.: An experimental comparison of min-cut/max-flow algorithms for energy minimization in vision. IEEE Trans. Pattern Anal. Mach. Intell. **26**(9), 1124–1137 (2004)
5. Canino, D., De Floriani, L., Weiss, K.: IA*: An adjacency-based representation for non-manifold simplicial shapes in arbitrary dimensions. Computer and Graphics **35**(3), 747–753 (2011)
6. Chiang, Y.J., Lu, X.: Progressive simplification of tetrahedral meshes preserving all isosurface topologies. Comput. Graph. Forum **22**(3), 493–504 (2003)
7. Comaniciu, D., Meer, P., Member, S.: Mean shift: A robust approach toward feature space analysis. IEEE Transactions on Pattern Analysis and Machine Intelligence **24**, 603–619 (2002)
8. Cuadros-vargas, A.J., Nonato, L.G., Tejada, E., Ertl, T.: Generating segmented tetrahedral meshes from regular volume data for simulation and visualization applications. In: Proceedings of CompIMAGE. Taylor and Francis Group (2006)
9. Dey, T.K., Giesen, J., Goswami, S.: Shape segmentation and matching with flow discretization. In: Dehne, F., Sack, J.-R., Smid, M. (eds.) WADS 2003. LNCS, vol. 2748, pp. 25–36. Springer, Heidelberg (2003)

10. Felzenszwalb, P.F., Huttenlocher, D.P.: Efficient graph-based image segmentation. Int. J. Comput. Vision **59**(2), 167–181 (2004)
11. Gunther, D., Seidel, H.P., Weinkauf, T.: Extraction of dominant extremal structures in volumetric data using separatrix persistence. Computer Graphics Forum **31**(8), 2554–2566 (2012)
12. He, X., Zemel, R.S., Ray, D.: Learning and incorporating top-down cues in image segmentation. In: Leonardis, A., Bischof, H., Pinz, A. (eds.) ECCV 2006, Part I. LNCS, vol. 3951, pp. 338–351. Springer, Heidelberg (2006)
13. Jimenez, J.J., Segura, R.J.: Collision detection between complex polyhedra. Comput. Graph. **32**(4), 402–411 (2008)
14. Kim, S., Nowozin, S., Kohli, P., Yoo, C.D.D.: Higher-order correlation clustering for image segmentation. In: Shawe-Taylor, J., Zemel, R., Bartlett, P., Pereira, F., Weinberger, K. (eds.) Advances in Neural Information Processing Systems, vol. 24, pp. 1530–1538 (2011)
15. Kurita, T.: An efficient agglomerative clustering algorithm for region growing (1994)
16. Levinshtein, A., Sminchisescu, C., Dickinson, S.: Optimal contour closure by superpixel grouping. In: Daniilidis, K., Maragos, P., Paragios, N. (eds.) ECCV 2010, Part II. LNCS, vol. 6312, pp. 480–493. Springer, Heidelberg (2010)
17. Levinshtein, A., Stere, A., Kutulakos, K.N., Fleet, D.J., Dickinson, S.J., Siddiqi, K.: Turbopixels: Fast superpixels using geometric flows. IEEE Transactions on Pattern Analysis and Machine Intelligence **31**(12), 2290–2297 (2009)
18. Liu, M.Y., Tuzel, O., Ramalingam, S., Chellappa, R.: Entropy rate superpixel segmentation. In: Proceedings of the 2011 IEEE Conference on Computer Vision and Pattern Recognition, CVPR 2011, pp. 2097–2104. IEEE Computer Society, Washington, DC (2011)
19. Lucchi, A., Smith, K., Achanta, R., Knott, G., Fua, P.: Supervoxel-Based segmentation of EM image stacks with learned shape features. Tech. rep, EPFL (2010)
20. LV, J.: An approach for superpixels using uniform segmentation and reciprocal nearest neighbors clustering. Journal of Theoretical and Applied Information Technology **47**(3) (2013)
21. kay Ng, S., Mclachlan, G.J.: On some variants of the em algorithm for fitting finite mixture models. Australian Journal of Statistics (2003)
22. Papon, J., Abramov, A., Schoeler, M., Worgotter, F.: Voxel cloud connectivity segmentation - supervoxels for point clouds. In: IEEE (ed.) CVPR, pp. 2027–2034 (2013)
23. Vazquez-Reina, A., Avidan, S., Pfister, H., Miller, E.: Multiple hypothesis video segmentation from superpixel flows. In: Daniilidis, K., Maragos, P., Paragios, N. (eds.) ECCV 2010, Part V. LNCS, vol. 6315, pp. 268–281. Springer, Heidelberg (2010)
24. Ren, X., Malik, J.: Tracking as repeated figure/ground segmentation. In: Conference on Computer Vision and Pattern Recognition (CVPR). IEEE Computer Society (2007)
25. Shi, J., Malik, J.: Normalized cuts and image segmentation. IEEE Transactions on Pattern Analysis and Machine Intelligence **22**, 888–905 (1997)
26. Simari, P., Picciau, G., De Floriani, L.: Fast and scalable mesh superfacets. Computer Graphics Forum **33**(7), 181–190 (2014)
27. Sinha, S.N., Mordohai, P., Pollefeys, M.: Multi-view stereo via graph cuts on the dual of an adaptive tetrahedral mesh. In: ICCV, pp. 1–8. IEEE (2007)
28. Sondershaus, R., Straßer, W.: View-dependent tetrahedral meshing and rendering using arbitrary segments. Journal of WSCG **14**(1–3), 129–136 (2006)

29. Takahashi, S., Takeshima, Y., Fujishiro, I.: Topological volume skeletonization and its application to transfer function design. Graphical Models **66**(1), 24–49 (2004)
30. Vedaldi, A., Soatto, S.: Quick shift and kernel methods for mode seeking. In: Forsyth, D., Torr, P., Zisserman, A. (eds.) ECCV 2008, Part IV. LNCS, vol. 5305, pp. 705–718. Springer, Heidelberg (2008)
31. Vincent, L., Soille, P.: Watersheds in digital spaces: an efficient algorithm based on immersion simulations. IEEE Transactions on Pattern Analysis and Machine Intelligence **13**(6), 583–598 (1991)
32. Wang, H., Yushkevitch, P.A.: Multi-atlas segmentation without registration: A supervoxel-based approach. Medical image computing and computer-assisted intervention **16**(3), 535–542 (2013)
33. Wang, P., Zeng, G., Gan, R., Wang, J., Zha, H.: Structure-Sensitive superpixels via geodesic distance. International Journal of Computer Vision **103**, 1–21 (2012)
34. Wang, S., Lu, H., Yang, F., Yang, M.H.: Superpixel tracking. In: Metaxas, D.N., Quan, L., Sanfeliu, A., Gool, L.J.V. (eds.) International Conference on Computer Vision (ICCV), pp. 1323–1330. IEEE (2011)
35. Weiss, K., Iuricich, F., Fellegara, R., De Floriani, L.: A primal/dual representation for discrete Morse complexes on tetrahedral meshes. In: Proceedings of the 15th Eurographics Conference on Visualization, vol. 32(3), pp. 361–370 (2013)
36. Xu, C., Xiong, C., Corso, J.J.: Streaming hierarchical video segmentation. In: Fitzgibbon, A., Lazebnik, S., Perona, P., Sato, Y., Schmid, C. (eds.) ECCV 2012, Part VI. LNCS, vol. 7577, pp. 626–639. Springer, Heidelberg (2012)
37. Zhang, Y., Hartley, R.I., Mashford, J., Burn, S.: Superpixels via pseudo-boolean optimization. In: Metaxas, D.N., Quan, L., Sanfeliu, A., Gool, L.J.V. (eds.) International Conference on Computer Vision (ICCV), pp. 1387–1394. IEEE (2011)

Extraction of Successive Patterns in Document Images by a New Concept Based on Force Histogram and Thick Discrete Lines

Isabelle Debled-Rennesson[1,2]($\boxtimes$) and Laurent Wendling[3]

[1] Université de Lorraine, LORIA, UMR 7503, F-54506 Vandoeuvre-lès-nancy, France
debled@loria.fr
[2] CNRS, LORIA, UMR 7503, F-54506 Vandoeuvre-ls-nancy, France
[3] Université Paris Descartes, LIPADE, 45, Rue des Saints-Pères, 75270 Paris, France

Abstract. The problematic of automatically searching series of broad patterns in technical documents is studied. Such series can be assumed to ordered information useful for the understanding of documents. The proposed methodology is able to extract successive patterns of different natures without a priori information. To make this, we consider the spatial location of triplets of similar connected components using force histogram and the recognition is performed by considering surrounding discrete lines. This new model is fast and it allows a good extraction of occulted patterns in presence of noise while requiring only few thresholds, which can be automatically set from data.

Keywords: Spatial relations · Thick discrete lines · Patterns

1 Introduction

Graphic recognition has an extremely rich state-of-the-art literature in symbol recognition and localization. Numerous applications require an accurate recognition of symbols such as automatic recognition and understanding of circuit diagrams [13], engineering drawings [16] and architectural drawings [9,15]. Due to the specificity of documents, methods are often targeted towards isolated line symbols [4,10], etc. Basically, a symbol can be defined as a graphical entity with a common meaning in the context of a specific domain.

It is well-known that successive basic patterns (e.g. dot and dashed lines, circle lines) bring precious information for the understanding of the document (e.g. separating parts, associated text boxes.) [1,8]. In many recognition systems, it is important to have an accurate and powerful operator related to the retrieval of such series of patterns. Due to document specificity, structural methods are widely studied from representation such as Attributed Relational Graphs (ARG) [2,3], Region Adjacency Graphs (RAG) [9] etc. Their common drawback comes from error-prone raster to vector conversion which can increase the confusion among close symbols and variability of the size of graphs leads to computational complexity in matching. Furthermore they are suitable in our context due

© Springer International Publishing Switzerland 2015
V. Murino and E. Puppo (Eds.): ICIAP 2015, Part I, LNCS 9279, pp. 387–397, 2015.
DOI: 10.1007/978-3-319-23231-7_35

to the extensibility of pattern series. However the repetitiveness of structural model may lie in a grammar representation considering both equal distance and spatial relations between patterns.

For instance, in the specific case of dashed line extraction, a powerful approach has been proposed by [7]. It is based on a search area whose width is the double of the current key width, and whose length is the maximal distance allowed between two segments belonging to a same dashed line. Dosch *et al.* [8] has proposed some improvements to the basic method by studying connection points and the merging dashed segments by propagating them following a distance threshold. Even if results are satisfying in many cases, methods depend on well-known raster-to-vector method drawbacks especially in presence of noise. Furthermore distortions imply the delicate location of patterns to be found. As a consequence, numerous thresholds are generally manually set while depending both on the scale of documents and on the structure of patterns to be handled. Finally it is not easy to assess the accuracy of extracted primitives from data without human parameter setting. Previous works [6] showed the interest of combining spatial relations and discrete line to provide a powerful method dedicated to the special case of dashed line problematic. The aim of our study is to extend this model by considering the problem of complex symbol localization in broad documents, composed of individual parts with no a priori knowledge about the shape but ordered following a direction and constrained by spatial relations. To make this, we consider the spatial location of triplets of similar connected components by using force histogram, integrating in its composition both distance and spatial location. Surrounding discrete lines refine the series of pattern extraction. This new model is fast and it allows a extraction of occulted patterns in most of the cases even in presence of noise while requiring only few thresholds, which can be automatically set from data.

2   Main Frameworks

2.1   Force Histogram Background

The histogram of forces allows to assess the spatial relation between two binary objects [11,12]. The attraction between two points at a distance d between is given by:

$$\forall d \in R_+^*, \ \varphi_r(d) = 1/d^r$$

with r, the kind of force processed, e.g. $r = 0$ for constant forces and $r = 2$ for gravitational ones. The handling of segments is considered to decrease the computation time instead of directly studying any pair of points between the two patterns. Let I and J be two segments beared by a line of angle θ from the frame, D_{IJ}^{θ} the distance between them and $|.|$ the length of a segment. The calculation of the attraction force f_r of a segment with regard to another is given by:

$$f_r(|I|, D_{IJ}^{\theta}, |J|) = \int_{D_{IJ}^{\theta}+|J|}^{|I|+D_{IJ}^{\theta}+|J|} \int_{0}^{|J|} \varphi_r(u - v) dv du$$

Considering two objects A and B, following a direction θ they can be entirely described by the set of segments beared by a pencil of parallel lines of angle θ. Let us take one line, denoted $\mathcal{D}_\eta^\theta$. The two sets of segments correspond to: $A_\theta(\eta) = \cup\{I_i\}_{i=1,n}$ and $B_\theta(\eta) = \cup\{J_j\}_{j=1,m}$ and the mutual attraction of these segments is given by:

$$F(\theta, A_\theta(\eta), B_\theta(\eta)) = \sum_{i \in 1..n} \sum_{j \in 1..m} f_r(|I_i|, D_{I_i J_j}^\theta, |J_j|)$$

All the pencils of lines $\mathcal{D}_\theta^\eta$ which entirely describe A and B are then considered. The histogram corresponds to a set of angles and the calculation of $F^{AB}(\theta)$ remains to an assessment of the forces exerted by an object with regard to another one in the direction θ. Finally the calculation of F^{AB} onto a set of angles θ_i ($\theta_i \in [-\pi, +\pi]$) defines a spatial relational descriptor, denoted $\mathcal{F}^{AB}$. By axiomatic definitions of the function F, the following properties, useful to characterize the series of similar patterns, can be easily checked: **translation** as objects are processed independently of their location in the image, **symmetry** considering opposite directions, **scale factor** if the histograms are normalized and **rotation** (after circular shifts), because the approach is isotropic.

2.2 Discrete Line Background

The arithmetical definition of discrete lines [5] is used in our method to embed successive patterns : a **discrete line** $\mathcal{D}(a, b, \mu, \omega)$, whose main vector is (b, a), lower bound μ and thickness ω (with a, b, μ and ω being integer such that $gcd(a, b) = 1$) is the set of integer points (x, y) verifying $\mu \le ax - by < \mu + \omega$.

In this work, we consider sequences of points, corresponding to series of patterns, and we find the thinnest discrete lines, possibly thick, containing all the points of the sequences.

More precisely, let us consider a sequence of points $\mathcal{S}_b$, with $|a| \le |b|$ to simplify the writing. A discrete line $\mathcal{D}(a, b, \mu, \omega)$ is said **bounding** for $\mathcal{S}_b$ if all points of $\mathcal{S}_b$ belong to $\mathcal{D}$.

Moreover a bounding discrete line of $\mathcal{S}_b$ is said **optimal** (see Fig. 1) if its vertical distance (i.e. $\frac{\omega - 1}{max(|a|, |b|)}$) is minimal, i.e. if its vertical distance is equal to the vertical distance of the convex hull of $\mathcal{S}_b$. A linear algorithm was proposed

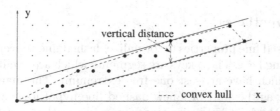

Fig. 1. $\mathcal{D}(2, 7, -8, 11)$ is the optimal bounding line (vertical distance $= \frac{10}{7} = 1.42$) of the sequence of points.

in [5] to incrementally obtain the characteristics of the optimal bounding discrete line of a sequence of points. It relies on the linear and incremental computation of the convex hull of the scanned point sequence as well as on the arithmetical and geometrical properties of discrete lines.

2.3   Overall System Description

The aim of our system is to consider spatial relations between regions as well as their organization. Spatial relations and global characteristics rely on force histogram and organization is processed with thick discrete lines. Force histogram is adapted here to process with several connected components during the image scan instead of handling one pair of objects. A matrix of force histograms is calculated and a set of kernels composed of series of similar patterns is achieved. Discrete line models are used to detect the optimal bounding lines of the selected kernels. Local mask area are defined from these bounded lines and series of similar patterns are assessed by kernel propagation. Figure 2 shows the main steps of our system. Each part is described in the further sections.

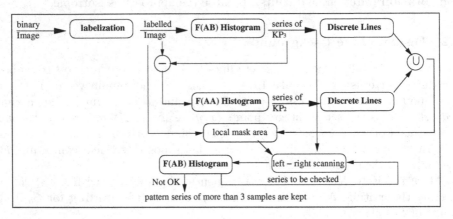

Fig. 2. Main description of the System.

3   Extraction of Successive Patterns

3.1   Model Hypotheses

Dori al. [7] proposed fine properties to formalize dashed line concept. The method starts by extracting keys. These keys are segments which are smaller than a given threshold and which have at least one free extremum. The main loop consists in choosing a key as the start of a new dashed line hypothesis, and in trying to extend this hypothesis in both directions, by adding other segments belonging to the same virtual line. This search is done in a search area whose width is the double of the current key width, and whose length is the maximal distance allowed between two segments belonging to a same dashed line. That induced numerous geometric conditions and manually set-up thresholds due to the scale and the quality of the document under consideration. However considering one application, most of the documents rely on the same building protocol. So the method [7] is really efficient after a good setting from the study of few samples. In our study we want to consider broad documents and we do not focus especially on segments but **on any kind of patterns**. On the whole, dashed lines rely on segments that can be considered as specific patterns. We consider here series of patterns of similar natures. Main hypotheses become:

- H_1 Minimum number of patterns having approximately the same length.
- H_2 Patterns are regularly spaced.
- H_3 Patterns follow a virtual line.

We also add other hypotheses to take into account more cases as occluded pattern and series of different patterns:

- H_4 Virtual line can embed occulted connected components.
- H_5 Series of patterns can be composed with patterns of different natures.

3.2 Kernel Pattern Definition

To ensure the hypotheses previously described, three successive connected components are assumed to be the minimal series of consecutive patterns to be achieved. Pattern lengths (H_1) are taken into account by the calculation and the matching between associated force histograms. The regular spacing (H_2) between patterns also relies on the principle of force histogram that directly integrates distance and spatial location. The calculation of surrounding discrete lines is made to model the third hypothesis dedicated to virtual line (H_3). Symmetric property can be useful to easily integrate a serie of two alternated patterns as, in this case, histograms are defined from opposite directions (H_5).

First the extraction of the set L of connected components is performed on a binary image to label regions. Then, the computation of histogram forces is performed as follows:

- $\forall (A, B) \in L^2$, $A \neq B$, computation of $\mathcal{F}^{AB}$ with φ_2
- $\forall A \in L$, computation of $\mathcal{F}^{AA}$ with φ_0

Let u, v, w be in L. Kernel patterns of cardinality 2 or 3: KP_2, KP_3 are extracted as follows.

- $(u, v, w) \in KP_3$ if v is the middle segment closest to u and w and $\mathcal{F}^{uv} \cong \mathcal{F}^{vw}$
- $(u, v) \in KP_2$ if $(u, v, w) \notin KP_3$ and if $\mathcal{F}^{uu} \cong \mathcal{F}^{vv}$

KP_3 corresponds to suitable series of three disconnected similar patterns and KP_2 is set to consider the presence of occluded patterns in further processing (H_4).

3.3 Optimal Bounding Mask Area

The optimal bounding discrete line of each kernel pattern is computed from associated sets of pixels. The characteristics of these discrete lines are recorded. At this step, we obtained a set of local thick line masks surrounding patterns to be applied on the initial images. However close kernels in the same direction can belong to the same series of patterns. Consequently several key kernels can constitute a large serie of pattern lines. If we consider all the associated discrete lines, this may not overlap exactly. We propose to merge intersecting discrete lines to provide local looking up area around kernels in order to be more robust to noise and to distortion. Let us consider D_i, and D_j the optimal bounding lines of two different kernels, a new discrete optimal area is defined if they largely intersect as follows.

$$\Delta_{ij} = D_i \cup D_j \text{ if } |D_i \cap D_j| \geq \frac{min(|D_i|, |D_j|)}{2}.$$

And so on for each close kernel. Finally all the achieved optimal bounding mask areas are labelled to ensure a local kernel propagation processing and to avoid to process with other directions due to possible intersection with other mask area.

3.4 Kernel Propagation

The propagation of each key kernel to the left and to the right is performed by considering its associated local mask area as follows. All the patterns of the image included in the local mask area are considered, even occulted parts (H_4). The computation of the force histogram is done between the new basic pattern candidate and the extremity basic component of the propagated key kernel. A test of equality, considering the previous global threshold, is made with the force histogram of the previous couple of components. If the test is right, the basic candidate is added to the series (H_2) and the process is run again. Finally series of achieved basic similar patterns greater than three are kept (H_1).

If the images contained several series of patterns, it is possible to regroup them following their structure. To make this, the variation between mean normalized histograms of each series is compared out to extract level map of series of patterns. The aim is just to show the potential aspect of this approach and this clustering can be improved using well-known methods based on Dunn or Davies-Bouldin indexes which can be used here considering large database of technical drawings [14].

4   Experimental Results

4.1 Setting

Our approach has been tested on real binary documents coming from different sources (and resolution) like architectural drawing, electric area networks, electronic drawing... We present here the study of mostly encountered pattern line configurations (disconnected, occulted and symmetry). First a classical connected components labelling is performed on the binary image. Due to the typical structure of graphical documents $\mathcal{F}^{AB}$ can be calculated considering four close connected components to limit processing time. Moreover $\mathcal{F}^{BA}$ is directly deduced from $\mathcal{F}^{AB}$ (property of symmetry). It is easy to show that the complexity of force histogram is in $O(pn\sqrt{n})$ with n the number of points of the image. But it is rather in $O(pn)$ considering the process of closer components in a labelled document. p is set to 128 directions. Experimental studies[12] have shown that more processed directions have low influence on the global shape of the histogram. Regarding the matching, a basic similarity ratio (min over max) is used to compare force histograms and a recognition threshold is experimentally set at 0.9 to take into account both noise effects and few pattern distortions.

4.2   Simple Case: Disconnected Patterns

Figures 3 and 4 show the processing of disconnected patterns. First image of the series represents the processed document. Second image relies on the bounding area obtained using thick lines merging. A set of lines were processed from similar number of kernels to define area masks. They are given in the second image for visualization as well as superimposed information coming from initial image. They are considered alone in the processing to avoid intersected area problematic. The last image of the series presents extracted pattern lines, showing the good behaviour of our approach. Most of the rates are greater than 0.95. Patterns included little end dashed segments in Figure 4 reached a rate close to 0.91. They can eventually be omitted.

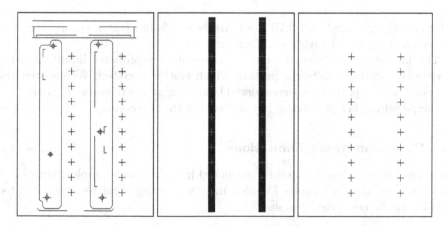

Fig. 3. Main extraction steps (Sample 1).

4.3   Complex Cases: Occulted Patterns and Symmetry

The figures 5 and 6 show more complex cases having occulted patterns. We can directly remark that such patterns are taken into account during the propagation step whereas they are not too distorted. In Figure,6, four areas were defined from 31 thick lines. We can remark that two largely occulted windows are missing

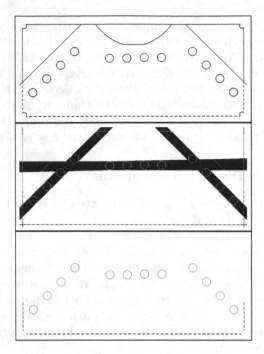

Fig. 4. Series of patterns (Sample 2).

in figures 5 (rates: 0.82 and 0.75) and circles not found (rates around 0.86) in figures 6 as they are distorted and further.

The last example shows the interest of symmetry property handling alternated series with one different pattern which can be occulted. We can remark that two additive patterns are considered belonging rather to corner shapes. This case required further processing (for instance corner detection).

4.4   Discussion About Limitations

The table 1 summarized the results presented in this paper: Samples, number of mask area, number of clusters founded in a same image and recognition rates considering the connected regions.

Fig. 5. Occulted Patterns (Sample 3).

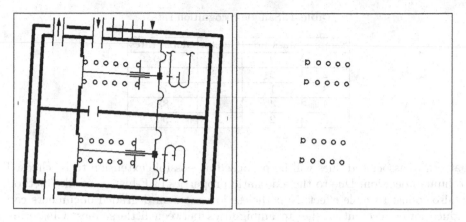

Fig. 6. Occulted patterns (Sample 4).

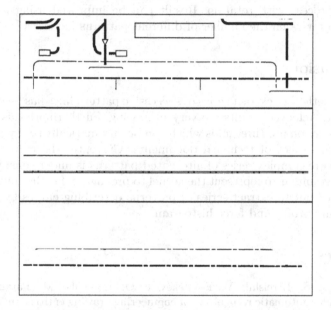

Fig. 7. Occluded and alternated patterns (Sample 5).

Rates consider any missing part due to occulted or noisy regions. We can remark that recognition rates decrease by considering little shape (as segments) due to the impact of noise on the whole representation of the shape. As said before a threshold is set at 0.9. However it is not the "best" threshold. A tuning can easily provides a 100 percent of recognition (that is using a threshold set at 0.73) on the whole set. However we consider this as having no sense because new retrieved shapes will be highly distorted and can refer to another object. Structure based approaches can be an help to dissociate them. Another idea is to provide a map of confidence pattern and less confident ones. In this case end

Table 1. Sample recognition rates.

Samples	Mask area	Cluster	Global rates
1	2	1	100
2	6	2	98
3	1	1	78
4	4	1	83
5	2	2	94

pattern of associated lines will be proposed as possible extension to be checked to human decision. Due to the axiomatic properties of F-histogram the method is also robust to scale effect. Nonetheless low scale on degraded documents can induce lower recognition due to ambiguities between little shapes. Clustering is done here considering normalized mean, and histogram shifts are taken into account to process with rotation. Result can be improved using for instance shape descriptor when the number of different patterns increases.

5   Conclusion

An original method to extract series of successive pattern lines has been proposed in this paper. Achieved results are very promising. Furthermore this method is robust and relies on few thresholds which can be automatically set by considering the particular aspect of technical documents. Currently the extension of the method to more complex series of alternated patterns is under consideration by introducing grammar to represent the kernel to propagate. Further investigations will be carried out to extract series of patterns describing curves by combining both curvature profile and force histogram.

References

1. Ablameyko, S., Bereishik, V., Frantskevich, O., Homenko, M., Paramonova, N.: A system for automatic recognition of engineering drawing entities. In: ICCP 1998, vol. 2, pp. 1157–1159 (1998)
2. Bunke, H., Messmer, B.: Efficient attributed graph matching and its application to image analysis. In: Braccini, C., Vernazza, G., DeFloriani, L. (eds.) ICIAP 1995. LNCS, vol. 974, pp. 45–55. Springer, Heidelberg (1995)
3. Conte, D., Foggia, P., Sansone, C., Vento, M.: Thirty years of graph matching in pattern recognition. International Journal of Pattern Recognition and Artificial Intelligence **18**(3), 265–298 (2004)
4. Cordella, L.P., Vento, M.: Symbol recognition in documents: a collection of techniques. International Journal on Document Analysis and Recognition **3**(2), 73–88 (2000)
5. Debled-Rennesson, I., Feschet, F., Rouyer-Degli, J.: Optimal blurred segments decomposition of noisy shapes in linear time. Computers & Graphics **30**(1), 30–36 (2006)

6. Debled-Rennesson, I., Wendling, L.: Combining force histogram and discrete lines to extract dashed lines. In: ICPR 2010, p. 4p (2010)
7. Dori, D., Wenyin, L., Peleg, M.: How to win a dashed line detection contest. In: Kasturi, R., Tombre, K. (eds.) Graphics Recognition 1995. LNCS, vol. 1072, pp. 286–300. Springer, Heidelberg (1996)
8. Dosch, P., Tombre, K., Ah-Soon, C., Masini, G.: A complete system for analysis of architectural drawings. International Journal on Document Analysis and Recognition 3(2), 102–116 (2000)
9. Llados, J., Mart, E., Villanueva, J.: Symbol recognition by error-tolerant subgraph matching between region adjacency graphs. IEEE Transactions on Pattern Analysis and Machine Intelligence 23(10), 1137–1143 (2001)
10. Lladós, J., Valveny, E., Sánchez, G., Martí, E.: Symbol recognition: current advances and perspectives. In: Blostein, D., Kwon, Y.-B. (eds.) GREC 2001. LNCS, vol. 2390, pp. 104–128. Springer, Heidelberg (2002)
11. Matsakis, P.: Relations spatiales structurelles et interprtation dimages. In: PhD Thesis. Université Paul Sabatier, Toulouse (1998)
12. Matsakis, P., Wendling, L.: A new way to represent the relative position between areal objects. IEEE Transactions on Pattern Analysis and Machine Intelligence 21(7), 634–643 (1999)
13. Okazaki, A., Tsunekawa, S., Kondo, T., Mori, K., Kawamoto, E.: An automatic circuit diagram reader with loop-structure-based symbol recognition. IEEE Transactions on Pattern Analysis and Machine Intelligence 10(3), 331–341 (1988)
14. Santosh, K., Lamiroy, B., Wendling, L.: Integrating vocabulary clustering with spatial relations for symbol recognition. International Journal on Document Analysis and Recognition (2013)
15. Valveny, E., Mart, E.: A model for image generation and symbol recognition through the deformation of lineal shapes. Pattern Recognition Letters 24(15), 2857–2867 (2003)
16. Wenyin, L., Zhang, W., Yan, L.: An interactive example-driven approach to graphics recognition in engineering drawings. International Journal on Document Analysis and Recognition 9(1), 13–29 (2007)

Hierarchical Mesh Segmentation Editing Through Rotation Operations

Federico Iuricich[1]([✉]) and Patricio Simari[2]

[1] Department of Computer Science and UMIACS,
University of Maryland, College Park, USA
iuricich@umiacs.umd.edu
[2] Department of Electrical Engineering and Computer Science,
The Catholic University of America, Washington DC, USA
simari@cua.edu

Abstract. Hierarchical and multi-resolution models are well known tools used in may application domains for representing an object at varying levels of detail. In the case of segmentations computed on a mesh, a hierarchical model can be structured as a binary tree representing the hierarchy of the region merging operations performed on the original segmentation for reducing its resolution. In this paper, we address the problem of modifying a hierarchical segmentation in order to augment its expressive power. We adapt two well-known operators defined for modifying binary trees, namely left and right rotation, to the case of hierarchical segmentations. Such operators are then applied to modifying a given hierarchy based on a user-defined function and based on a user-defined segmentation.

1 Introduction

The area of mesh segmentation algorithms research is a mature one, having inherited and adapted many of its approaches from the area of image segmentation. In the many years since its inception, segmentation algorithms have proliferated, each based on various distinct approaches and metaphors, including watershed, graph-cut, and hierarchical methods, to name a few. In all cases, once a segmentation is produced by the algorithm, it remains static and the client application must use the obtained result. If a different segmentation is desired, for example a refinement based on new objectives, an entirely new segmentation must be computed.

What if, rather than remaining static, a segmentation could be automatically refined in a principled way? By having segmentation-editing operations at our disposal, we could conceive of each segmentation as living in a space of candidate solutions, each connected to its neighbors by an edit operation application. In this fashion, we could start from a candidate segmentation obtained through the application of well-known and efficient algorithms. From here, with the algorithmically-guided application of edit operations, we could explore the space of nearby segmentations, i.e., the "segmentation neighborhood", in search

V. Murino and E. Puppo (Eds.): ICIAP 2015, Part I, LNCS 9279, pp. 398–409, 2015.
DOI: 10.1007/978-3-319-23231-7_36

of a result that better conforms to an objective that is new or more nuanced than the first algorithm was suited to optimizing.

The above motivates a "black box" approach to segmentation, decoupling the segmentation algorithm from the segmentation metric or objective function. This effectively allows us to cast the segmentation problem into the effective *meta-heuristic search* framework that has been successfully applied in the Artificial Intelligence and Optimization communities. This brings a number of advantages. On the one hand, it enables research into effective domain-specific objective functions, which users are free to collect into libraries and reuse as needed. Simultaneously, the decoupled nature of the framework allows research into metaheuristic search algorithms in a domain-independent way. Any theoretical and practical improvements can then be "swapped in", immediately translating into improved performance across domains in a way that will be effortless and transparent to most users.

In this paper, we take a first step into the area of algorithmic segmentation editing. Our proposal focuses on hierarchical segmentations and the guarded application of rotation operations analogous to those applied for the rebalancing of binary trees. After introducing our framework, we demonstrate its use by applying it to two use case: the modification of a segmentation hierarchy based on a changed objective function, and based on a segmentation outside the space of segmentations encoded in the hierarchy.

2   Related Work

Hierarchical models for geometrical objects support the representation and processing of spatial entities at different levels of detail (*LOD*) [13,4]. Such representations are especially interesting because of their potential impact on applications such as terrain modeling in Geographic Information Systems (GIS) and scientific data visualization.

The basic ingredients of a hierarchical model for a spatial object are a *base complex*, that defines the coarsest representation of the object, a set of *updates* that provide variable resolution representations of the base complex when applied to it, and a *dependency relation* among updates which allow them to be combined to extract consistent intermediate representations.

The process of building a hierarchical model depends on the simplification of a cell complex. Usually, such an operation is time consuming because sophisticated techniques are required to optimize the shape of the cells and to bound the approximation error. However, such structure-building operations can be performed off-line so that the structure can then be efficiently queried on-line.

Hierarchies and multi-resolution models have been applied in a plethora of areas, including geometric modeling [6,4], morphological analysis of 2D and 3D images [11], and shape analysis [2]. Within the are of shape analysis, mesh segmentation algorithms cover a huge area of this field [16,19].

Among the existing segmentation methods, we are particularly interested in those which are often used to create an oversegmentation as a preprocessing step. These include mean-shift clustering [18], normalized cuts [10,9,22,14,21], and, recently, an iterative approach which scales to high resolution meshes [20].

Complementary to the above algorithms is the idea of obtaining a hierarchical clustering of elements. The construction of this hierarchy can be driven by an error metric defined over the edges of the dual graph [7], or on fitting primitives of the regions [2], for example.

The hierarchical organization can provide a representation of the functional or semantic structure of a shape while reducing the emphasis on geometric details. We find various examples of these kinds of hierarchies which differ in the nature of the error function used in their construction. The hierarchy defined in [8] and applied to triangulated meshes is based on the diffusion distance on surfaces. In [17] a mesh partitioning and the corresponding hierarchy is built based on combining the well known Shape Diameter Function and the k-way graph-cut algorithm to include local geometric properties of the mesh. In [15] Reuter introduced a method to hierarchically segment articulated shapes into meaningful parts and to register these parts across populations of near-isometric shapes. The hierarchical relation applies the notion of persistent homology [5] for the elimination of topological noise.

Recently, in [12], the notion of co-hierarhical analysis has been applied to shapes. At the base of the method is the construction of a family of hierarchies for each single object. Among these hierarchies only the most representative ones are selected and studied in order to identify similarities between objects.

3   Update Operators

A tree rotation is an update operator used for changing the shape of a binary tree without changing the resulting in-order traversal of its elements. Two symmetric operators have been defined in the literature, right rotation and left rotation, which we will indicate as $rotationR(\cdot)$ and $rotationL(\cdot)$, respectively.

Let p be a node of the binary tree and q the left child of p, denoted $l(p)$. The $rotationR(p)$ operator changes the structure of the tree as follows:

- q becomes the new parent of p,
- p is the new right child of q,
- the old right child of q, denoted $r(q)$, becomes the new left child of p.

The latter can be seen as a clockwise rotation of the root p using the node q as pivot. The left rotation $rotationL(\cdot)$ is entirely dual and can be seen as a counter-clockwise rotation. These two operators are at the base of the definition of efficient data structure such as AVL, red-black, and splay trees.

Recall that working with a hierarchy of segmentations we can efficiently represent such a hierarchy as a proper binary tree T (i.e. a binary tree in which internal nodes have always two children) having the leaf nodes in one-to-one correspondence with the regions of the segmentation at finest resolution. Each internal node of T represents a merging operation between two regions (i.e. the regions represented by the left and right child) and consequently it represents the new created region. Moreover, this structure also guarantees that, given two nodes with the same parent, the corresponding regions are adjacent in the segmentation extracted at such a level. In terms of the nodes of a tree, we will say that two nodes n_1 and n_2 are *adjacent* ($n_1 \diamond n_2$) if there exists one region in the n_1 subtree that is adjacent to at least one region in n_2 subtree.

Given the above, the rotation operators defined for general binary trees could potentially bring about two inconsistent representations when applied to a segmentation hierarchy. The two cases are shown in Figure 1b. Applying *rotationL(p)*, pivoting on node 3, two internal nodes are created (nodes 3 and p) having only one child. The second problem is generated applying *rotationR(p)* pivoting on node q. The rotation applied is valid from the point of view of the node's connections. However, it results in an inconsistent representation of the segmentation. In particular, the merging between nodes 1 and 3 cannot be applied to the segmentation (see Regions 1 and 3 in Figure 1a).

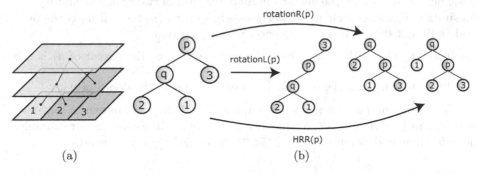

Fig. 1. (a) Binary tree and related segmentations extracted at different resolution levels. (b) Binary tree rotations resulting in invalid hierarchies and proper binary tree obtained after applying $HRR(p)$.

Thus, we have adapted the rotation operators in order to guarantee two invariants. (1) A rotation maps a proper binary tree into a proper binary tree with a different structure and, (2) for each internal node p, the left and right children are adjacents ($l(p) \diamond r(p)$).

Let q be the left child of an internal node p. The Hierarchical segmentation Right Rotation of p (denoted as $HRR(p)$), is a valid rotation if q is an internal node. Let $u = l(q)$, $v = r(q)$ and $s = r(p)$. As a consequence of $HRR(p)$, q becomes the parent of p. If v is adjacent to the region represented by s, then v becomes the left child of p. Otherwise u and v are swapped (along with the related subtrees) and u becomes the new left child of p. Note that at least one of the two regions represented by u and v is adjacent to the region represented by s since they have a common ancestor. When both u and v are adjacent to s the best node to be moved can be chosen based on application-dependent criteria. In Figure 1b we show the result of $HRR(p)$ performed on the tree depicted in

Figure 1a. The Hierarchical segmentation Left Rotation operator, indicated in the following as $HLR(\cdot)$ is performed in a dual fashion.

In contrast to the classical rotation operators, HRR and HLR rotations maintain invariant (1) as a consequence of the fact that node q, chosen as pivot, is, by definition, an internal node with non-empty subtrees.

Considering other modification operators for proper binary trees, the deletion and insertion of a single node is forbidden since it would make the binary tree not proper. The swap of two subtrees is a modification operator that could be considered in addition to rotations. Since the ordering between the left and right children of a node is irrelevant for the hierarchy, the swap of two nodes sharing the same parent, used in the rotation operators, is not a true update operator (i.e. it does not change the space of segmentations represented). Swapping two subtrees (not sharing the same parent) may cause inconsistencies in the hierarchical structure in general.

Before distinguishing between valid and non-valid swaps we introduce some basic definitions. Given the lowest common ancestor of two nodes n_1 and n_2 and its subtree T, we say that n_1 *uniquely depends* on n_2 ($n_1 \triangleright n_2$) if n_2 is the only node adjacent to n_1. As a consequence, we can say that:

- if $n_1 \triangleright n_2$ then either they share the same parent, or the parent of n_1 is the root of T,
- if $n_1 \triangleright n_2$, then the depth of n_1 is lower or equal to the depth of n_2.

The second property in particular implies that there does not exist a sequence of rotations (HRR or HLR) for moving n_2 above n_1. In Figure 2a, for example, node 5 uniquely depends on node 2 ($5 \triangleright 2$) since 2 is the only node adjacent to 5.

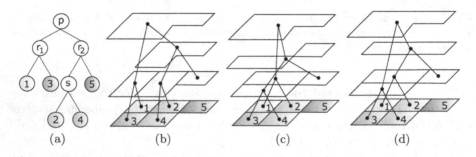

Fig. 2. (a) Binary tree representing the space of segmentations depicted in (b). (c) Inconsistent hierarchy resulting from the non-valid swap of nodes 2 and 3. (d) Hierarchy resulting from the valid swap of nodes 1 and 4

In the following, we define the conditions necessary to identify a valid swap. Let p be the common ancestor of two nodes n_1 and n_2. Let s_1 and s_2 be the siblings of n_1 and n_2 respectively. Let T_1 and T_2 be the left and right subtrees of p, rooted at r_1 and r_2 respectively.

A swap between n_1 and n_2 is a *valid swap* if $n_1 \diamond s_2$ and $n_2 \diamond s_1$. Moreover, let U be the set of nodes $n \in T_1$ such that $n \triangleright n_1$. The swap is valid if either:

i - U is empty, or

ii - for each $n \in U$, $n \diamond n_2$. (Conditions for T_2 and n_2 are dual.)

In Figure 2a for example, the swap between 1 and 4 is valid because $1 \diamond 2$, $3 \diamond 4$, and none of the nodes in the subtree of r_2 uniquely depend on 4 (condition i), while the node in the subtree of r_1 that uniquely depends on 1 (i.e. 3) is also adjacent to 4 (condition ii). In Figure 2d, the resulting hierarchy is shown.

Recalling the properties of $\diamond$ and $\triangleright$, we observe that if either condition i or condition ii are not satisfied, there does not exist a sequence of rotations for moving one node in place of the other. This leads us to conjecture that a valid swap can always be represented as a sequence of HRR and HLR rotations. In this case the rotation operators here defined would form a minimal complete set of modification operators for a segmentation hierarchy.

4 Implementation and Preliminary Results

We have studied the rotation operators HRR and HLR in the context of hierarchies built from the segmentation of triangular meshes. In our naive implementation we are encoding both the binary tree structure and the mesh. Given a triangle mesh Σ, we are indexing vertices and triangles in two separate arrays. For each vertex, we store its coordinates while, for each triangle, we store the indexes to its three vertices and the indexes to its three adjacent triangles. Let $|\Sigma_0|$ the total number of vertices and $|\Sigma_2|$ the total number of triangles the whole mesh representation takes $3|\Sigma_0| + 6|\Sigma_2|$.

Considering the proper binary tree implementation, each node encodes a pointer to its right and left children and an application-dependent value (generally a float). Differently from a binary search tree, the time complexity for finding a node in the hierarchical segmentation is linear in the number of nodes in the hierarchy. Thus, for each node, we are also encoding a pointer to its parent in order to improve the navigation efficiency. If N is the number of nodes in the binary tree, we are encoding $3N$ pointers and N float values in total.

Leaf nodes encode additional information. The set of top simplices (triangles) belonging to the corresponding region and an adjacency list pointing to the adjacent regions in the segmentation at finest resolution. If A is the set of pairs of adjacent regions we encode $2|A|$ pointers and $|\Sigma_2|$ indexes in total.

We have conducted our experiments on four benchmark meshes. All the results have been obtained on a MacBook Pro with 2.8Ghz Quad-core Intel Core i7 processor and 16GB of RAM. For all cases, the storage cost required by the hierarchy is at least two orders of magnitude smaller than the storage cost required by the triangle mesh. The FEMALE dataset is composed of 4K vertices and 9K triangles and its over segmentation is formed by 100 regions. Hierarchies are built on this dataset in about 0.26s. The VASE daset is composed by 14K vertices, 29K triangles and 200 regions, as is the case for the ARMADILLO dataset, which is composed of 25K vertices and 50K triangles. Hierarchies on these datasets are built in 1.7 and 2.8 seconds respectively. The NEPTUNE dataset is formed by 250K vertices, 500K triangles and 300 regions. The entire encoding for the mesh and the hierarchy requires approximately 18MB and building the hierarchy takes 42.1 seconds.

4.1   Hierarchy Update Based on an Input Function

For our first application, we have considered the possibility of modifying a pre-built hierarchy based on a function given as input. Specifically, we are aiming at constructing a hierarchy that adaptively combines different functions together. The first function involved computes the volume of the axis-aligned bounding box of the region resulting from the merging operation. Regions whose composition results in a small bounding box are merged before regions creating a larger bounding box. The second function evaluates the concavity along the border of two regions using the distance function described in [20]. Regions having an almost flat behavior along their boundary are the first to be merged.

In all of our experiments our starting segmentation is produced with the superfacets algorithm presented in [20]. The hierarchy is then the result of the simplification sequence created based on the function computing the bounding box volume. Based on this sequence of merging operations, nodes are created starting from the leaves and ending with a single node (the root) representing the single region obtained at the end.

Segmentations are extracted from the latter hierarchy using a threshold value indicating the desired resolution. Let t be the threshold value. The resulting segmentation is the one obtained navigating from the root and considering only those nodes having associated value greater than or equal to t. In our experiments we have always chosen a value of t resulting in a limited number of nodes (and thus a low number of regions) in order to help the visual comparison between the methods.

Once the first hierarchy is obtained, a new hierarchy is computed based on the simplification sequence created by the concavity function. The resulting hierarchy is then balanced using the bounding box function. New values for each node are computed based on the latter function. Nodes are then considered in a post-order sequence. Given a node q and its parent p, a rotation is applied on p pivoting on q if the value of p after the rotation will be lower with respect to the value of q before the rotation. After the rotation, a depth-first visit is recursively performed on the subtree of q in order to search for new rotations that could be triggered by the latter. Note that the only values changed during a rotation are the value of p and q. The aim of the rotations in this case is to minimize the increase of the function values navigating toward the root, thus simulating the hierarchical structure that would result using the bounding box function from the beginning.

At this point we have performed extractions on both hierarchies comparing the segmentations obtained. In Figures 3a-3b we show the segmentation for the ARMADILLO dataset, extracted from the original hierarchy, splitting the root only. The segmentation at the finest resolution is composed of 300 regions. The leg is last to be merged with the body since its expansion is in the opposite direction. In Figure 3c we show the segmentation obtained from the second hierarchy. Since the two legs are connected by a flat area (under the body) the influence of the concavity function makes those two parts become a single component in the first level of the hierarchy, thus improving the semantic of the result.

(a)   (b)   (c)

Fig. 3. (a-b) Segmentations for the ARMADILLO dataset obtained from the hierarchy based on the bounding box function and (c) the segmentation obtained combining two functions. Rotations are applied in 1.03 seconds

In Figure 4 we show three other examples were the semantic segmentation obtained from the first hierarchy (on the left) is improved by composing the two functions. In Figure 4a, the handles of the VASE dataset are better separated from the body. In Figure 4b, instead, the head of the FEMALE dataset is distinguished from the body while legs and calves are treated as single objects. For the NEPTUNE dataset shown in Figure 4c, the head of the trident is correctly treated as a single object in the early levels. However this is still a delicate operation. The legs in 4c or the torso of 4b, for example, are less well segmented using our framework.

The study of more complex state-of-the-art functions will be at the center of future developments.

4.2   Hierarchy Update Based on an Input Segmentation

For our second application we have considered the possibility of adapting a hierarchy to an input segmentation. For our preliminary investigations we have restricted our problem. The building blocks of the input segmentation are the same as those of the original regions on which the hierarchy has been built. This means that a leaf node in the hierarchy is always contained in only one region of the input segmentation (for general purpose implementations, building the hierarchy starting from the triangles guarantees that any segmentation defined on the same dataset respects this condition). The second restriction is given by the number of regions composing the segmentation given as input. We are using input segmentations with only two regions. However any segmentation could be treated with the same algorithm grouping the regions in two main sets and then calling the algorithm recursively on their subsets.

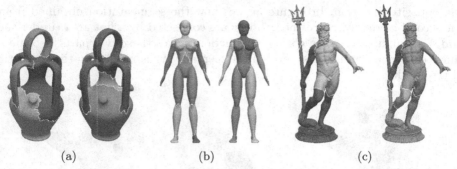

(a)   (b)   (c)

Fig. 4. Comparison of the results obtained with the two hierarchies for (a) the VASE, (b) FEMALE and NEPTUNE datasets. Rotations take 0.9, 0.1 and 10.3 seconds, respectively

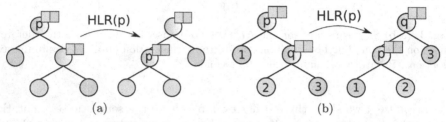

(a)   (b)

Fig. 5. (a) Rotation $HRR(p)$ reducing the number of undetermined nodes. (b) The same operation is useless if regions corresponding to nodes 1 and 3 are not adjacent. Leaf nodes are colored with red or blue depending on the region to which they belong. Colored squares over internal nodes distinguish between determined nodes (having the same color) and undetermined nodes (having both colors).

In this case the value associated with each leaf node corresponds to an index (1 or 2), indicating the region in the input segmentation to which the node belongs. The value associated with each internal node is then the set of labels of its children (such a set can be $\{1\}$, $\{2\}$ or $\{1,2\}$). We will call *determined* a node having only one label and *undetermined* the node having both labels.

Once the values have been computed, a post-order visit on the tree is performed. The objective of the algorithm is to reduce the number of undetermined nodes by means of rotations. The input binary segmentation is successfully encoded in the hierarchy when the root is the only node undetermined.

A rotation is applied to a node p if the number of undetermined nodes decrease after the rotation (see Figure 5a). Note that the nodes the state of which can change are limited to p and $l(p)$ for an HRR rotation and to p and $r(p)$ for an HLR rotation. When a rotation is performed the subtree of the new root is visited in post-order sequence, but subtrees of determined nodes are never visited twice.

There are degenerate configurations in which the latter criterion is not sufficient. An example of this configuration is depicted in Figure 5b. The adjacency relation between the regions actually obstructs some rotations that would reduce the number of undetermined nodes thus resulting in a "stuck" configuration. To overcome this problem, when at the end of the visit either one of the children of the root is still undetermined, we do the following on that respective subtree: using a depth-first visit, the deepest undetermined node is identified and, with a sequence of rotations, it is brought to the root of the subtree. Intuitively, we can think about the distance of a node from the root as the scope of the node with respect to the other regions. The nearer a node is to the root, the higher the number of regions with which it can be merged through rotations. This corresponds to augmenting the scope of the node, thus enabling new rotations.

(a)   (b)

Fig. 6. From left to right, binary segmentation encoded in the hierarchy, input segmentation and binary segmentation obtained by adapting the hierarchy for the NEPTUNE (a) and VASE (b) datasets.

After that, a new visit is triggered on the entire tree. Note that a subtree of a determined node does not need to be visited. In Figure 6, we show some of the results obtained mapping with different colors the regions of the input segmentation and the one obtained after training the hierarchy.

5   Conclusions

In this paper we have addressed the problem of modifying the structure of a hierarchical segmentation, allowing for an expansion of said hierarchy into a space of related segmentations.

We have defined two update operators related to the well known rotation operators devised for binary trees. We have applied these operators for modifying a hierarchical segmentation based on an input function and on an input binary segmentation.

Our future work will concentrate on testing our framework with different kinds of functions, also combining the modifications triggered by a new objective function with the modifications triggered by a new objective segmentation. We would like to apply the framework also to scalar fields, typically represented as triangle meshes with a scalar value defined on each vertex, where the combination of functions computed on the shape with functions computed based on the scalar values could bring new insights in this area.

Even though here we have described our implementation based on triangle meshes, our framework can be applied to any simplicial mesh, including, for example, tetrahedral meshes discretizing 3D volumes.

Acknowledgments. Datasets used are courtesy of the Princeton Mesh Segmentation Benchmark [3] (FEMALE, VASE and ARMADILLO datasets) while the NEPTUNE dataset is courtesy of the aim@shape repository [1]. This work has been partially supported by the National Science Foundation under grant number IIS-1116747. The authors wish to thank professor Leila De Floriani for the fruitful discussions.

References

1. AIM@Shape. http://visionair.ge.imati.cnr.it/ontologies/shapes/
2. Attene, M., Falcidieno, B., Spagnuolo, M.: Hierarchical mesh segmentation based on fitting primitives. The Visual Computer **22**(3), 181–193 (2006)
3. Chen, X., Golovinskiy, A., Funkhouser, T.: A benchmark for 3D mesh segmentation. ACM Transactions on Graphics (Proc. SIGGRAPH) **28**(3), 73:1–73:12 (2009)
4. De Floriani, L., Kobbelt, L., Puppo, E.: A survey on data structures for level-of-detail models. In: Dodgson, N., Floater, M., Sabin, M. (eds.) Advances in Multiresolution for Geometric Modelling. Mathematics and Visualization, pp. 49–74. Springer, Heidelberg (2005)
5. Edelsbrunner, H., Letscher, D., Zomorodian, A.: Topological persistence and simplification. Discrete & Computational Geometry **28**(4), 511–533 (2002)
6. Garland, M.: Multiresolution modeling: Survey and future opportunities (1999)
7. Garland, M., Willmott, A., Heckbert, P.S.: Hierarchical face clustering on polygonal surfaces. In: Proceedings of the 2001 Symposium on Interactive 3D Graphics, I3D 2001, pp. 49–58. ACM, New York (2001)
8. de Goes, F., Goldenstein, S., Velho, L.: A hierarchical segmentation of articulated bodies. In: Proceedings of the Symposium on Geometry Processing, SGP 2008, pp. 1349–1356. Eurographics Association, Aire-la-Ville (2008)
9. Hu, R., Fan, L., Liu, L.: Co-segmentation of 3d shapes via subspace clustering. Comput. Graph. Forum **31**(5), 1703–1713 (2012)
10. Huang, Q.X., Koltun, V., Guibas, L.J.: Joint shape segmentation with linear programming. ACM Transactions on Graphics **30**(6), 125 (2011)
11. Iuricich, F.: Multi-resolution shape analysis based on discrete Morse decompositions. Ph.D. thesis, University of Genova - DIBRIS, Italy (2014)
12. van Kaick, O., Xu, K., Zhang, H., Wang, Y., Sun, S., Shamir, A., Cohen-Or, D.: Co-hierarchical analysis of shape structures. ACM Trans. Graph. **32**(4), 69:1–69:10 (2013)
13. Magillo, P.: Spatial Operations on Multiresolution Cell Complexes. Ph.D. thesis, PhD thesis, Department of Computer Science-University of Genova (1998)
14. Meng, M., Xia, J., Luo, J., He, Y.: Unsupervised co-segmentation for 3D shapes using iterative multi-label optimization. Computer-Aided Design **45**(2), 312–320 (2013)
15. Reuter, M.: Hierarchical shape segmentation and registration viatopological features of laplace-beltrami eigenfunctions. International Journal of Computer Vision **89**(2–3), 287–308 (2010)

16. Shamir, A.: A survey on mesh segmentation techniques. Computer Graphics Forum **27**, 1539–1556 (2008)
17. Shapira, L., Shamir, A., Cohen-Or, D.: Consistent mesh partitioning and skeleton-isation using the shape diameter function. Vis. Comput. **24**(4), 249–259 (2008)
18. Sidi, O., van Kaick, O., Kleiman, Y., Zhang, H., Cohen-Or, D.: Unsupervised co-segmentation of a set of shapes via descriptor-space spectral clustering. ACM Transactions on Graphics **30**(6), 126:1–126:9 (2011)
19. Simari, P.D.: Algorithms in 3D Shape Segmentation. Ph.D. thesis, Toronto, Ont., Canada, Canada, aAINR61094 (2009)
20. Simari, P.D., Picciau, G., De Floriani, L.: Fast and scalable mesh superfacets. Comput. Graph. Forum **33**(7), 181–190 (2014)
21. Wu, Z., Shou, R., Wang, Y., Liu, X.: Interactive shape co-segmentation via label propagation. Computers and Graphics **38**(C), 248–254 (2014)
22. Wu, Z., Wang, Y., Shou, R., Chen, B., Liu, X.: Unsupervised co-segmentation of 3D shapes via affinity aggregation spectral clustering. Computers and Graphics **37**(6), 628–637 (2013)

Local Feature Extraction in Log-Polar Images

Manuela Chessa$^{(\boxtimes)}$ and Fabio Solari

Department of Informatics, Bioengineering, Robotics and System Engineering - DIBRIS, University of Genoa, Via All'Opera Pia 13, 16145 Genova, Italy
manuela.chessa@unige.it

Abstract. We propose two different strategies to compute edges in the log-polar (cortical) domain. The space-variant processing is obtained by applying local operators (e.g. local derivative filters) directly on the log-polar images, or by embedding the same operators into the log-polar mapping, thus obtaining a cortical representation of the Cartesian features. The two approaches have been tested by taking into consideration three standard algorithms for edge detection (Canny, Marr-Hildreth and Harris), applied onto the BSDS500 dataset. Qualitative and quantitative comparisons show a first indication of the validity of the proposed approaches.

Keywords: Space-variant processing · Foveated images · Edge detection · Corner detection · Cortical representation · Bio-inspired visual processing

1 Introduction

The computation of local image features such as edges and corners is at the basis of many approaches for matching and recognition, which are important in image processing, computer vision and robotics applications.

In the literature, several edge or contour detection methods, based on local operators applied in the Cartesian domain, are described. Among them, some algorithms detect edges by convolving a grayscale image with local derivative filters (e.g. the Roberts, Sobel and Prewitt operators), the Marr and Hildreth method uses zero crossings of the Laplacian of Gaussian operator, and the Canny operator defines edges' detection and localization criteria based on first derivatives of a Gaussian [5]. A combined edges and corners detector operator, based on local derivatives, has been proposed by Harris [8]. More recent local approaches take into account color and texture information and make use of learning techniques for cue combination [11]. Recently, a contour detector method that combines multiple local cues into a globalization framework, based on spectral clustering, is described in [1], and a multi-scale Harris corner detector is proposed in [7].

Though a great effort in improving edge detectors in the Cartesian domain has been done, few works address the same problem in the log-polar (cortical) domain [14]. The space-variant images are promising for many image processing

© Springer International Publishing Switzerland 2015
V. Murino and E. Puppo (Eds.): ICIAP 2015, Part I, LNCS 9279, pp. 410–420, 2015.
DOI: 10.1007/978-3-319-23231-7_37

and robotics applications, since they provide a high spatial resolution in the region of interest, i.e. the fovea, and a reduction of the amount of data to be processed, similarly to what happens in the mammals' visual system. Indeed, the distribution of the photoreceptors in the primates' retina is space-variant (i.e. denser in the center, the fovea, and sparser in the periphery), and the projection of such photoreceptors into the primary visual cortex can be described by a log-polar mapping [14]. However, the processing of the log-polar images is a challenging task, due to the image distortions generated by the retino-cortical transform, which often require a specific adaptation of the algorithms, in order to properly work. Primal feature extraction [10] in log-polar images has been addressed by some authors in the literature, which propose ad-hoc solutions designed to work in the cortical domain. In [12], the authors present a mechanism for computing operators such as edge detection and Hough transform directly in foveated images; in [6] the authors present an approach to extract edges, bars, blobs and ends from log-polar images, based on neural networks that learn the feature's class; and a comparison of several strategies for gradient detection in log-polar images is presented in [18].

In this paper, we propose two approaches that allow standard algorithms to work in the log-polar domain, without specific adaptation. Thus, we do not propose a new method for feature detection, but we analyze how well known state-of-the-art methods for edges and corners extraction work in the log-polar domain. In particular, the aim of the paper is to show the performances, also in terms of accuracy of the feature detection, of the two considered approaches: (i) the local operator for edge detection (i.e. derivative of Gaussian, and Laplacian of Gaussian) is applied on the cortical image, i.e. on the image that has been transformed into the log-polar image through low-pass Gaussian filters; (ii) the local operator is embedded into the log-polar transform, thus producing a cortical representation of the Cartesian derivatives of the image, on which to compute edges. Moreover, we assess the two proposed approaches by using the metrics and the BSDS500 dataset presented in [1].

2   Log-Polar Mapping

The log-polar mapping is a non linear transformation that maps each point of the Cartesian domain (x, y) into a cortical domain described by the coordinates (ξ, η). In the literature, several log-polar mapping models are described [2,4,9]. We consider the central blind-spot model, since it is characterized by scale and rotation invariance [17].

The log-polar transformation is described by the following equations:

$$\begin{cases} \xi = \log_a \left(\frac{\rho}{\rho_0} \right) \\ \eta = q\theta, \end{cases} \tag{1}$$

where a parameterizes the non-linearity of the mapping, q is related to the angular resolution, ρ_0 is the radius of the central blind spot, and

$(\rho, \theta) = (\sqrt{x^2 + y^2}, \arctan(y/x))$ are the polar coordinates derived from the Cartesian ones. All points with $\rho < \rho_0$ are ignored, thus ρ_0 has to be small, with respect to the size of the image.

In order to deal with digital images, given a Cartesian image of $M \times N$ pixels, and defined $\rho_{max} = 0.5 \min(M, N)$, we obtain an $R \times S$ (rings $\times$ sectors) discrete cortical image of coordinates (u, v) by taking:

$$\begin{cases} u = \lfloor \xi \rfloor \\ v = \lfloor \eta \rfloor, \end{cases} \tag{2}$$

where $\lfloor \cdot \rfloor$ denotes the integer part, $q = S/(2\pi)$, and $a = \exp(\ln(\rho_{max}/\rho_0)/R)$. Figure 1 shows the transformations through the different domains. The retinal area (i.e. the log-polar pixel) that refers to a given cortical pixel defines its *receptive field* (RF). By inverting Eq. 1 the centers of the RFs can be computed, and these points present a non-uniform distribution through the retinal plane, as in Figure 2a (green crosses). The optimal relationship between R and S is the one that optimizes the log-polar pixel aspect ratio γ, making it as close as possible to 1. It can be shown that, for a given R, the optimal rule is $S = 2\pi/(a - 1)$ [15, 17].

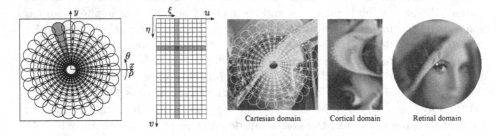

Fig. 1. Left: the cyan circle and the green sector in the Cartesian domain (x, y) map to vertical and horizontal stripes, respectively, in the cortical domain (ξ, η). The red area represents a RF that is mapped in the corresponding cortical pixel. Right: an example of image transformation from the Cartesian to the cortical domain, and backward to the retinal domain. The RFs (yellow circles) are overlapping the Cartesian image. The specific choice of the mapping parameters is: $R = 80$, $S = 131$, $\rho_0 = 3$, and $\rho_{max} = 256$. The cortical image is scaled to improve the visualization.

The shape of the RFs affects both the quality of the transformation and its computational burden. In [3] the authors analyze four techniques, each characterized by a different shape for the RFs: nearest pixel, bilinear interpolation, adjacent RFs, and overlapping circular RFs. The overlapping circular RFs [2,13] are the most biological plausible technique and they allow a better preservation of the image information [3], thus we consider this solution in the paper.

To implement the log-polar mapping, the Cartesian plane is divided in two regions: the *fovea* and the *periphery*. The periphery is defined as the part of the plane in which the distance between the centers of two RFs on the same radius is greater than 1 pixel (undersampling). To obtain the cortical image we use overlapping Gaussian RFs, as shown in Figure 2a. The fovea (in which we have an oversampling, i.e. the distance between two consecutive RFs is less than 1 pixel) is handled by using fixed size RFs, whereas in the periphery the size of the RFs grows. The standard deviation of the RF Gaussian profile is a third of the distance between the centers of two consecutive RFs, and the spatial support is six times the standard deviation. As a consequence of this choice, adjacent RFs overlap. A cortical pixel C_i is computed as a Gaussian weighted sum of the Cartesian pixels P_j in the i-th RF: $C_i = \sum_j w_{ij} P_j$, where the weights w_{ij} are the values of a normalized Gaussian centered on the i-th RF. A similar approach is used to compute the inverse log-polar mapping that produces the *retinal image*, where the space-variant effect of the log-polar mapping is observable.

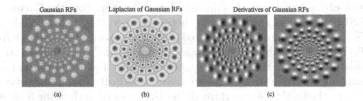

Fig. 2. The RFs considered to obtain the cortical representation of the image. (a) Gaussian RFs, used to obtain the cortical image (log-polar transform). (b) Laplacian of Gaussian RFs and (c) Derivative of Gaussian RFs (along horizontal and vertical axes, respectively), used to obtain the cortical representation of the derivatives of the image.

3   Feature Detection in the Log-Polar Domain

The cortical representation $R(\xi, \eta)$ of a space-variant processed Cartesian image $I(x, y)$ is described as follows:

$$R(\xi, \eta) = \langle g(x - x_0(\xi, \eta), y - y_0(\xi, \eta)), I(x, y) \rangle, \tag{3}$$

where $\langle \cdot \rangle$ denotes the inner product, $g(x, y)$ is the local operator that defines the weights of the log-polar mapping, and $(x_0(\xi, \eta), y_0(\xi, \eta))$ is the center of each RF.

Figure 2 shows several operators, which are used to obtain $R(\xi, \eta)$. In particular, Gaussian RFs (Fig.2a) are used to obtain the cortical image, i.e. the log-polar transform of the Cartesian image, Laplacian of Gaussian and derivatives of Gaussian (Fig.2b-c) are used to obtain the cortical representation of the image derivatives. The choice of the RFs is at the basis of the two approaches described in the following paragraphs, and summarized in Figure 3. In particular, in the following we show that the two cortical approaches can approximate the corresponding Cartesian processing.

414   M. Chessa and F. Solari

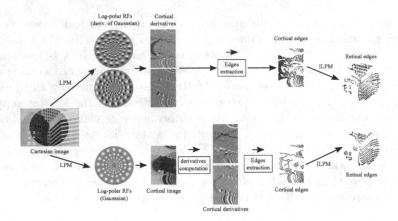

Fig. 3. Sketch of the two approaches described in the paper. Top: the Cartesian image (from the BSDS500 dataset, see Section 4) is transformed (LPM) by considering overlapping RFs embedding one of the considered local operators (in figure, the derivative of Gaussian filters) to obtain the cortical representation of the Cartesian derivatives, from which edges are extracted, thus obtaining cortical edges. Finally, through the inverse log-polar mapping (ILPM) retinal edges are computed. Bottom: the Cartesian image is transformed into the cortical image through the Gaussian RFs, then the derivatives are computed directly on the cortical image, by applying one of the considered local operators, and cortical edges are extracted. Finally, through the inverse log-polar mapping retinal edges are computed.

3.1   Direct Feature Detection in the Log-Polar Domain

To obtain a cortical representation, i.e. a cortical image, of a Cartesian image, we consider Gaussian filters as local operators that describe the RFs used to perform the log-polar mapping (see Fig.2a):

$$g(x,y) = \frac{1}{2\pi\sigma^2} \exp\left(-\frac{x^2 + y^2}{2\sigma^2}\right),$$ (4)

where σ is the standard deviation. Then, standard edge and corner differential local operators are applied onto the cortical image, by following the design strategies devised in [15]. In particular, to apply standard edge detection algorithms we define:

$$R_\xi(\xi,\eta) = \frac{\partial}{\partial \xi} R(\xi,\eta),$$ (5)

where $R_\xi(\xi,\eta)$ is the partial derivative (along ξ axis) of the cortical image, similarly for η axis.

Eq. 5 can be approximated through *derivatives of Gaussian*, to implement the Canny edge detector in the log-polar domain (Canny$_d$), which is equivalent to implement it in the Cartesian domain if the following rules are satisfied:

- Local filtering operations in the log-polar domain are a good approximation of the same filtering done in the Cartesian domain, when log-polar mapping is performed by considering the pixel aspect ratio γ close to 1, and the spatial support of the filters is small with respect to the size of the cortical image (e.g. less than 10%) [15].

- The gradients in the cortical domain are related to the ones in the Cartesian domain by the following relationship [16]:

$$\begin{bmatrix} R_\xi \\ R_\eta \end{bmatrix} = \frac{1}{\rho_0 a^\xi \ln(a)} \begin{bmatrix} \cos\eta & \sin\eta \\ -\sin\eta & \cos\eta \end{bmatrix} \begin{bmatrix} I_x \\ I_y \end{bmatrix}, \tag{6}$$

where I_x and I_y are the partial derivatives of the Cartesian image. Eq. 6 represents a rotation and a magnitude change of the Cartesian image gradient, thus cortical gradients R_ξ and R_η have the same properties of the Cartesian ones, and they can be used for edge detection (see Fig. 3 bottom).

The Marr-Hildreth edge detector (MH_d) is based on the Laplacian of Gaussian, which can be directly applied in the cortical domain, following the previously explained rules.

The Harris corner and edge detector ($Harris_d$) is based on derivatives of Gaussian that yield the cortical image structure tensor, and can be described as follows:

$$M(\xi,\eta) = w(\xi,\eta) * \begin{bmatrix} R_\xi^2(\xi,\eta) & R_\xi(\xi,\eta)R_\eta(\xi,\eta) \\ R_\xi(\xi,\eta)R_\eta(\xi,\eta) & R_\eta^2(\xi,\eta) \end{bmatrix}, \tag{7}$$

where $w(\xi,\eta)$ are Gaussian weights, and $*$ is the convolution operator. The edge and corner features are then derived, by computing:

$$H(\xi,\eta) = \det(M(\xi,\eta)) - k\mathrm{tr}^2(M(\xi,\eta)), \tag{8}$$

where k is a scalar, whose values are in the interval $[0.04, 0.15]$ [7], $\det(\cdot)$ and $\mathrm{tr}(\cdot)$ are the determinant and the trace operators, respectively.

By considering a small spatial support for the Gaussian weights $w(\xi,\eta)$, and the relationship between the cortical and the Cartesian gradients (see Eq. 6), the Harris detector in log-polar domain is a good approximation of the one in the Cartesian domain. Indeed, the cortical image structure tensor can be written in terms of a rotation of the Cartesian gradients, multiplied by a term that can be considered constant within the small spatial support of the Gaussian weights:

$$M(\xi(x,y),\eta(x,y)) = w(\xi(x,y),\eta(x,y)) * \frac{1}{\rho_0 a^{\xi(x,y)} \ln(a)} \begin{bmatrix} I_x^{\eta 2} & I_x^\eta I_y^\eta \\ I_x^\eta I_y^\eta & I_y^{\eta 2} \end{bmatrix}, \tag{9}$$

with $I_x^\eta = I_x(x,y)\cos\eta + I_y(x,y)\sin\eta$, and $I_y^\eta = -I_x(x,y)\sin\eta + I_y(x,y)\cos\eta$.

It is worth noting that the two coordinates' axes in the log polar domain have different meanings and range of values with respect to the Cartesian ones, and this affects the structure tensor. Nevertheless, by considering the design rules previously explained the error between the processing in the two domains is negligible.

3.2 Feature Detection Based on Embedded Processing in the Log-Polar Transform

By following the biological evidence, the visual processing is performed by networks of neurons described by their RFs. The RFs can be approximated by a filter bank that performs the desired visual processing. Thus, in this paper we propose to modify the log-polar transform by using as cortical mapping weights specific filters that perform the desired feature computation, in particular we consider as weights Laplacian of Gaussian and derivatives of Gaussian (see Fig. 2b-c).

The cortical representation $R_x(\xi, \eta)$ of the Cartesian derivative $I_x(x, y)$ (computed through derivatives of Gaussian filters), along x axis, of the image is obtained as follows:

$$R_x(\xi, \eta) = \langle g_x(x - x_0(\xi, \eta), y - y_0(\xi, \eta)), I(x, y) \rangle, \tag{10}$$

where $g_x(x, y)$ is the x-axis derivative of Gaussian operator, and $(x_0(\xi, \eta), y_0(\xi, \eta))$ is the center of each RF, similarly for the y-axis.

The Canny edge detector (Canny_{RF}) can be thus implemented by using the cortical representation of the Gaussian derivatives (see Fig. 3 top). It is worth noting that this approach does not require any approximation of the filtering stage, since $R_x(\xi, \eta)$ and $R_y(\xi, \eta)$ are the actual values of the image derivatives, represented in the log-polar domain. The same principle holds for the Marr-Hildreth (MH_{RF}) edge detector, by using the Laplacian of Gaussian as weights of the log-polar mapping.

The Harris corner and edge detector ($\text{Harris}_{\text{RF}}$) is now based on the following equation:

$$M(\xi, \eta) = w(\xi, \eta) * \begin{bmatrix} R_x^2(\xi, \eta) & R_x(\xi, \eta)R_y(\xi, \eta) \\ R_x(\xi, \eta)R_y(\xi, \eta) & R_y^2(\xi, \eta) \end{bmatrix}. \tag{11}$$

By considering a small spatial support for $w(\xi, \eta)$, edges and corners can be computed by using Eq. 8, since the image structure tensor is now defined in terms of the Cartesian image derivatives (mapped into the log-polar domain).

Figure 4 shows the cortical derivatives, the cortical edges, and the corresponding retinal edges for a sample image, by considering the two described approaches, and the three considered algorithms. In Section 4, we will further analyze the performance of the proposed approaches.

4   Results

The qualitative and quantitative analysis of the approaches described in this paper have been performed by using the Berkeley Segmentation Data Set and Benchmarks 500 (BSDS500), described in [1]. This dataset is an extension of the BSDS300, where the original 300 images are used for training/validation and

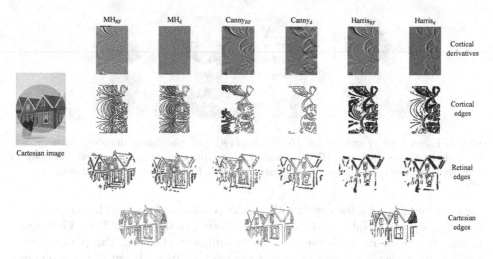

Fig. 4. Edges computed for an image of the BSDS500 dataset. The columns represent the different approaches and algorithms. First row: cortical image derivatives. Secomd row: cortical edges. Third row: retinal edges (computed from the cortical one through the inverse log polar mapping). Fourth row: edges computed in the Cartesian domain for comparison. Only the highlighted part of the Cartesian image is mapped into the cortical domain and analyzed (the shadow part is not considered).

200 fresh images, together with human annotations, are added for testing. Each image was segmented by five different subjects on average. In this paper, we only use and present results for the testing images. The log-polar mapping is performed by setting the transform's parameters as follow: $R = 100$, $S = 155$, $\rho_0 = 3$, and $\rho_{max} = 320$, which correspond to a compression ratio of about 10 times. Edges are computed by setting the following parameters:

- Marr-Hildreth (MH_d and MH_{RF}): the threshold of the slope of the zero-crossing values is 40. The spatial support of the Laplacian of Gaussian for MH_d is 3×3 pixels.
- Canny ($Canny_d$ and $Canny_{RF}$): the spatial support of the derivatives of Gaussian for $Canny_d$ is 9×9 pixels, and the standard deviation is 1.4. The non-maximum suppression and an hysteresis threshold (whose lower and upper bound are set to 0.3 and 0.7 of the maximum gradient value, respectively) have been considered.
- Harris ($Harris_d$ and $Harris_{RF}$): the spatial support of the derivatives of Gaussian for $Harris_d$ is 3×3 pixels. The weighting function $w(\xi, \eta)$ is a Gaussian function with spatial support 3×3 pixels and standard deviation 0.5, and k is 0.05.

A qualitative comparison of edge computation is presented in Figure 4. The approaches based on direct feature detection in the log-polar domain, and the ones based on feature detection using embedded processing in the log-polar transform perform in a similar manner. This suggests that the approximation errors

Fig. 5. Edges (green) and corners (red) computed with the Harris detector, by considering derivative of Gaussian RFs embedded in the log-polar transform (first row), and directly on the cortical image (second row). Images from the BSDS500 dataset.

between computing a feature directly in the cortical domain and by embedding the local operators into the log-polar transform are negligible. The differences among the three methods are due to the different choice of the parameters, but a systematic comparison of edge detection algorithms is out of the scope of this paper. The Harris method provides us both edges and corners, as Figure 5 shows for 4 sample images of the BSDS500 dataset. Also in this case, $Harris_d$ and $Harris_{RF}$ perform very similarly. In addition to the qualitative evaluation, we have tested the performances of the implemented algorithms in terms of precision, the fraction of true positives, and recall, the fraction of ground-truth

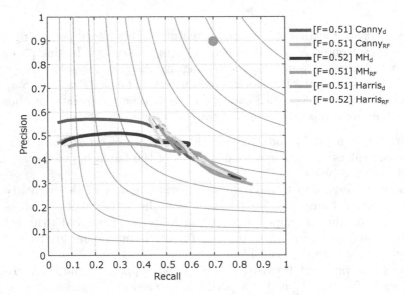

Fig. 6. Boundary benchmark on the BSDS500 dataset. Our implemented methods, working in the log-polar domain, have been compared with respect to the human ground-truth provided by the dataset. The precision-recall curves have been computed by using the code available from http://www.eecs.berkeley.edu/Research/Projects/CS/vision/grouping/resources.html. The *F-measure* for each method is shown in the legend.

boundary pixels detected [11]. We have also computed the *F-measure*, or harmonic mean of precision and recall at the optimal detector threshold, which
provides a score, useful to evaluate the methods. It is worth noting that it is not
possible to compare the proposed approaches with the state-of-the art algorithm
for edge detection, this is due to the following reasons. First, we compute edges
only in the part of the images covered by RFs (see Fig. 2). In particular, for the
BSDS500 dataset the part of the images transformed into the log-polar domain is
the highlighted one (e.g. see Fig. 4). The ground-truth edges have been masked,
accordingly. Moreover, working in the cortical domain yields a loss of details
in the image periphery (due to the high compression ratio that is achieved),
thus the comparison with respect to methods that work at full resolution is
unfair.

The precision-recall graphs are reported in Figure 6. The F-measures when
choosing an optimal scale for the entire dataset have almost the same values
for all the algorithms, whereas F-measures per images show that Harris$_{RF}$ has
slightly a better performance ($F = 0.54$). For the sake of clarity, it is worth
noting that on the same dataset Canny algorithm (in the Cartesian domain at
full resolution) has a better F-measure ($F = 0.60$).

5   Conclusion

In this paper, we have proposed two approaches for edge detection in the log-
polar domain, which allow us to apply well-known and established techniques,
previously developed in the Cartesian domain, without the need of adapting
them to the cortical domain. We have presented the theoretical basis on which
this is possible, by following two distinct approaches: one in which features are
directly computed working on the log-polar images, the other in which the local
differential operators at the basis of the considered algorithms are embedded
into the log-polar mapping, thus allowing us to obtain a cortical representation
of the Cartesian image processing.

The results confirm the validity of the approaches and suggest that they could
be promising for achieving feature detection in space-variant images. Nevertheless, some issues are still open and will be further investigated. From one hand,
a parametric analysis of the considered edge detectors should be performed, in
order to find the optimal set of parameters, and more recent state-of-the art algorithms for edge detection should be analyzed in order to describe them in the
cortical domain. From the other hand, it is necessary to consider multiple log-
polar mapping of the same image, by moving the *fovea* in several image points,
in order to build a full-resolution representation of edges, thus mimicking the
shifting focus of attention of the human visual system.

References

1. Arbelaez, P., Maire, M., Fowlkes, C., Malik, J.: Contour detection and hierarchical image segmentation. IEEE Trans. Pattern Anal. Mach. Intell. **33**(5), 898–916 (2011)
2. Bolduc, M., Levine, M.D.: A review of biologically motivated space-variant data reduction models for robotic vision. Computer Vision and Image Understanding **69**(2), 170–184 (1998)
3. Chessa, M., Sabatini, S.P., Solari, F., Tatti, F.: A quantitative comparison of speed and reliability for log-polar mapping techniques. In: Crowley, J.L., Draper, B.A., Thonnat, M. (eds.) ICVS 2011. LNCS, vol. 6962, pp. 41–50. Springer, Heidelberg (2011)
4. Florack, L.M.J.: Modeling foveal vision. In: Sgallari, F., Murli, A., Paragios, N. (eds.) SSVM 2007. LNCS, vol. 4485, pp. 919–928. Springer, Heidelberg (2007)
5. Forsyth, D.A., Ponce, J.: Computer Vision: A Modern Approach. Prentice Hall Professional Technical Reference (2002)
6. Gomes, H.M., Fisher, R.B.: Primal sketch feature extraction from a log-polar image. Pattern Recognition Letters **24**(7), 983–992 (2003)
7. Gueguen, L., Pesaresi, M.: Multi scale harris corner detector based on differential morphological decomposition. Pattern Recognition Letters **32**(14), 1714–1719 (2011)
8. Harris, C., Stephens, M.: A combined corner and edge detector. In: Proceedings of the 4th Alvey Vision Conference, pp. 147–151 (1988)
9. Jurie, F.: A new log-polar mapping for space variant imaging. Application to face detection and tracking. Pattern Recognition **32**, 865–875 (1999)
10. Marr, D.: Vision: A Computational Investigation into the Human Representation and Processing of Visual Information. Henry Holt and Co., Inc., New York (1982)
11. Martin, D., Fowlkes, C., Malik, J.: Learning to detect natural image boundaries using local brightness, color, and texture cues. IEEE Trans. Pattern Anal. Mach. Intell. **26**(5), 530–549 (2004)
12. Nattel, E., Yeshurun, Y.: Direct feature extraction in a foveated environment. Pattern Recognition Letters **23**(13), 1537–1548 (2002)
13. Pamplona, D., Bernardino, A.: Smooth foveal vision with gaussian receptive fields. In: 9th IEEE-RAS International Conference on Humanoid Robots (2009)
14. Schwartz, E.: Spatial mapping in the primate sensory projection: Analytic structure and relevance to perception. Biological Cybernetics **25**, 181–194 (1977)
15. Solari, F., Chessa, M., Sabatini, S.P.: Design strategies for direct multi-scale and multi-orientation feature extraction in the log-polar domain. Pattern Recognition Letters **33**(1), 41–51 (2012)
16. Solari, F., Chessa, M., Sabatini, S.P.: An integrated neuromimetic architecture for direct motion interpretation in the log-polar domain. Computer Vision and Image Understanding **125**, 37–54 (2014)
17. Traver, V., Pla, F.: Log-polar mapping template design: From task-level requirements to geometry parameters. Image Vision Computing **26**(10), 1354–1370 (2008)
18. Wallace, A., McLaren, D.: Gradient detection in discrete log-polar images. Pattern Recognition Letters **24**(14), 2463–2470 (2003)

Scale-Space Techniques for Fiducial Points Extraction from 3D Faces

Nikolas De Giorgis$^{(\boxtimes)}$, Luigi Rocca, and Enrico Puppo

Department of Informatics, Bio-engineering, Robotics and System Engineering,
University of Genova, Via Dodecaneso 35, 16146 Genova, Italy
{nikolas.degiorgis,rocca,puppo}@dibris.unige.it

Abstract. We propose a method for extracting fiducial points from human faces that uses 3D information only and is based on two key steps: multi-scale curvature analysis, and the reliable tracking of features in a scale-space based on curvature. Our scale-space analysis, coupled to careful use of prior information based on variability boundaries of anthropometric facial proportions, does not require a training step, because it makes direct use of morphological characteristics of the analyzed surface. The proposed method precisely identifies important fiducial points and is able to extract new fiducial points that were previously unrecognized, thus paving the way to more effective recognition algorithms.

Keywords: Scale-space · Multi-scale · Curvature · 3D computer vision · Shape analysis · Fiducial points extraction

1 Introduction

Face recognition has been widely studied and addressed in the literature, mainly in the image processing field. It can be described as the task of extracting descriptors, from images depicting human faces, which can be used to discriminate if two such images are obtained from the same face.

Many works have been presented dealing with color and gray-scale images, among which the most famous are *PCA* [9], *LDA* [7] and *EBGM* [22]. Recognition from 2D images, though, suffers from several known problems, such as a strong dependency on consistent illumination and pose. Moreover, it is straightforward to see that images cannot carry all the original information about a face's structure. Despite these shortcomings, work on 3D face recognition has been less investigated in the past, because complex and exotic hardware were needed for the extraction of 3D data and because of the consequent lack of publicly available datasets with good enough resolution. In the last few years, the hardware landscape improved and the growth in available computational power not only unlocked usage of more complex software techniques during processing steps, such as surface reconstruction and meshing, cleaning and smoothing, but also enabled novel extraction techniques of 3D raw data, such as photogrammetry.

Existent methods that extract fiducial points from 3D data can be roughly subdivided into *appearance based* and *feature based*; the first class is made of

V. Murino and E. Puppo (Eds.): ICIAP 2015, Part I, LNCS 9279, pp. 421–431, 2015.
DOI: 10.1007/978-3-319-23231-7_38

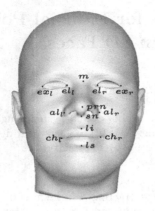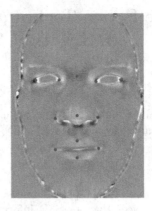

Fig. 1. On the left: names and positions of fiducial points; on the right: the same points, as extracted from a range image with our scale-space method.

methods that are typically modified versions of 2D algorithms extended to work with range images. The second class contains methods that work by extracting local relevant features. The method we propose falls into the latter category, of which we are going to give a brief overview. Lu and Jain [11] proposed a method that combines 2D and 3D techniques to extract a small set of facial features: they use *a priori* knowledge to detect the tip of the nose, and then detect the mouth and eye corners using the shape index from the range image. Colbry et al. [12] use shape index to detect a similar set of features. Gupta et al. [8] developed a method which detects a set of 10 points combining curvature information, *a priori* information and 2D techniques. Perakis et al. [18] developed a method which aims at detection of facials landmarks in presence of large yaw and expression variations using shape index and spin images. Conde et al. [5] developed a 3D method based on spin images which obtains a high accuracy but gets only three points on the faces. Segundo et al. [16] use curvature information combined with depth values from range images to detect a small set of points (nose tip, nose and eye inner corners). Shin and Sohn [20] use ten facial landmarks for face recognition, but they do not give details about how these points are extracted. Sukno et al. [21] detect a set of fiducial landmarks using spin images as described in [10] but then use statistical models to filter out outliers and infer missing features. Bockeler and Zhou [3] detect a set of ten points with strong 2D information and antrophometric constraints. A work by Berretti et al. [1] computes DoG of a mean curvature scalar field and extracts a variable number of keypoints that are not necessarily located in meaningful parts of the face. Some works by Novatnack et al. [14], [13] [15] use mesh parameterization with a distortion-adapted Gaussian scale-space to extract features using image analysis techniques (edge and corner detection) on the 2D plane.

Our method extends the family of techniques based on curvature and on prior knowledge of anthropometric features' locations. However, it makes use of the 3D surface only, without need for color or light intensity information, and it does not need any kind of learning or training phases. The input of the extraction algorithm is a range image; the core ingredient employed is a sequence of curvature fields, computed at different scales, which sets up a scale-space of differential properties of the original surface. We select fiducial points among curvature's critical points, using information computed from the scale-space as a guide. The 13 fiducial points we identify (shown in figure 1) are a subset of the 25 points presented in [6], and more precisely the 10 points that are found by the method developed in [8], plus the points named *sn*, *ls* and *li*.

2   Extraction of Morphological Features

Our goal is to extract all interesting morphological features from a 3D surface representing a human face. It seems intuitive that those features should occur where the surface varies the most, thus making the computation of curvature a very useful tool in this endeavor. Most methods for fiducial point extraction that use curvature compute it using discrete methods, which tend to highlight features at the finest scales and to be prone to noise. Moreover, it is accepted knowledge in the geometry processing field that these disadvantages tend to be exacerbated, instead of being reduced, as the resolution and size of datasets grow. We rather adopt a multi-scale curvature analysis method based on surface fitting [17]. The scale parameter is the size of the local surface around a vertex that contributes to the computation of curvature at the vertex itself, with the size measured as the radius of a sphere.

For the purposes of our scale-space analysis we use the *Gaussian curvature,* a scalar field which provides a good characterization of surface features. Our claim is that fiducial points occur at "important" maxima and minima of Gaussian curvature. Therefore, reliable criteria are needed, which can discriminate critical points of Gaussian curvature worth keeping from others caused by noise or depicting irrelevant features.

In order to measure the importance of critical points, we employ a scale-space based approach. Since their introduction, scale-space methods have been widely used in computer vision and image processing; the general idea is to build a one parameter family of images from an input signal. This is usually done by applying a filter repeatedly, thus building a discrete sequence. The main goal of scale-space methods is to highlight features at different levels of detail and importance. One of the classic approaches to this end is the computation of the *deep structure,* i.e., the tracking of critical points of the signal as they change across the scale-space. Classic approaches to deep structure computation are prone to noise and tracking errors; we adopt a virtually continuous scale-space technique, introduced in [19], which solves many of those problems. This method, which is filter agnostic and relies on piece-wise linear interpolation across scales, provides a fine-grained and reliable tracking of critical points of two dimensional signals. After this last preprocessing step, the main identification phase starts: fiducial points are chosen among critical points using the importance criteria computed during the scale-space analysis and prior knowledge based on anthropometric constraints.

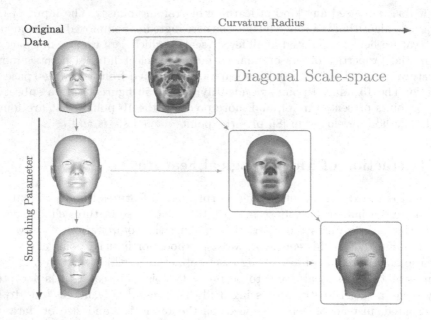

Original
Data

Curvature Radius

Diagonal Scale-space

Smoothing Parameter

Fig. 2. The diagonal scale-space is composed by a sequence of curvature fields, obtained by computing curvature at increasing scales on increasingly smoothed surfaces.

2.1   Precomputation Phase

The main preprocessing steps consist in the computation of a scale-space which effectively encodes curvature information, and in the computation of the importance measures of critical points.

Diagonal Scale-Space. Computation of differential properties is severely affected by the presence of noise. This makes the most straightforward combination of the concepts outlined in Section 2 – a scale-space of curvature where the discrete levels were computed with radii of increasing size – a inadequate solution, because the number of critical points does not decrease fast enough as the curvature method's scale parameter increases, and, as a consequence, tracking them does not provide meaningful information. We thus propose a new type of scale-space that combines multi-scale curvature with a Gaussian scale-space, called *diagonal scale-space*.

The diagonal scale-space is made up by scalar fields representing Gaussian curvature at increasing scales, but it is generated by employing both a smoothing filter on the original 3D surface and by varying at the same time the parameter of the multi-scale curvature computation method. We initially compute a linear scale-space of the original surface, with consecutive samples generated by repeated smoothing with variances of increasing size. We then compute curvature

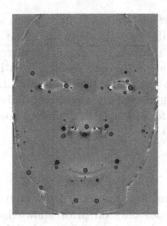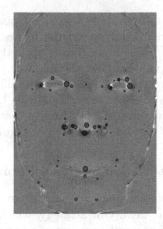

Fig. 3. Maxima (red) and minima (blue) of Gaussian curvature scaled by *life* (on the left) and *strength* (on the right).

on each level, with a correspondingly larger radius. A graphical account of this arrangement is depicted in Figure 2.

In this work, we process range images through a Gaussian smoothing filter, but the general idea of increasing two different scale parameters together, one for the amount of surface smoothing and the other for curvature computation, should be equally effective when processing full 3D data in the form of triangle meshes through a Laplacian smoothing filter. The end result is that noise is discarded in a more effective way, and the number of features decreases faster through scale. We are therefore able to achieve a meaningful tracking of the critical points of the Gaussian curvature through the scales.

Importance Measures: Life and Strength. After generation of the diagonal scale-space, we extract all the critical points in the original signal (which, in our case, is the curvature at the smallest radius computed on the original surface) and we track them through scales, using the virtually continuous scale-space method described in [19]. The output of the tracking algorithm is a data structure which encodes every critical point present in the scale-space, along with detailed information about their changes as scale grows. In particular, the data structure memorizes the moment each critical point disappears, because the feature it describes has been smoothed out and does not exist anymore. This death event marks the lifetime of a critical point in the scale-space, and we use this *life* value as our main importance measure. The life value of a critical point effectively measures the frequency of the signal that point corresponds to; critical points associated to information at higher frequencies will disappear faster than others.

Life is not the only importance measure that the proposed method employs; there is also a *strength* value that is used as a secondary criterion. Its aim is to assess the relative strength of the scalar field's maxima and minima, compared to the local trend on the surrounding surface. For each maximum, we compute the average of the curvature field at the pixels that are below its value in a growing area around it, and return the highest difference between its value and that average; the same algorithm is applied to minima by taking into account only the surface values above the minimum. The radius of the local area is capped at a value related to the scale of its life in the scale-space. The resulting value corresponds to a sort of variable-scale Laplacian of the surface at a given point. Critical points scaled according to their life and strength values for one of the faces in our test bed are shown in Figure 3.

2.2 Identification of Fiducial Points

Fiducial points are selected among maxima and minima of the Gaussian curvature scalar field. Our strategy, which relies only on prior knowledge and on the *life* and *strength* measures, is based on a hierarchical search. We start by identifying the most prominent features and then seek out other features in narrowed down areas, found by displacements relative to previously found ones. In particular, we identify fiducial points that characterize the nose and compute a symmetry axis that separates the left and right parts of the face. We then proceed to identification of the eyes' corners and of peculiar points on the mouth.

The Nose. Five fiducial points characterize this area (see Figure 4a):

- The nose tip, prn. This is a very prominent feature which is characterized by a high Gaussian curvature, a long life in the scale-space and by having the highest vertical value. The best strategy is simple: search is restricted to a wide rectangular area around the center of the range image, and the maximum of Gaussian curvature with the highest vertical value is selected.
- The sides of the nose, al_l and al_r. Those two points are saddles on the surface, which means they are minima of Gaussian curvature. To detect them the areas to the left and to the right of the nose tip, are considered, and the minima (one on the left and one on the right) with the highest life value in those areas are selected.
- The upper nose saddle, m. This is one of the most prominent saddles on a face's surface. In order to locate a rectangle located high above the nose tip is scanned, and the minimum which survives the longest is selected.
- The lower limit of the nose, sn. This point, located on the saddle where the nose ends, is a minimum of Gaussian curvature. We have discovered that this point is more reliably characterized by strength; in order to find it the search is narrowed down to an area located below the tip of the nose, and the point with the highest strength is selected.

Symmetry Axis and the Eyes. After points around the nose are identified, we use them to compute a vertical symmetry axis. The goal is to take advantage the intrinsic symmetry of the human face during the next phases. The axis is computed as the average of the line that fits the points m, prn, sn and the line orthogonal to the one connecting the two points identified as al. Most of the other fiducial points that still need to be detected are symmetric pairs with respect to this axis. From now on, when we seek a pair of left and right points, their fitness is evaluated together by requiring them to be almost symmetric, within a given tolerance, on top of any other criteria that may be necessary in order to identify them. Moreover, the line connecting al_l and al_r is considered as the dividing line between the upper half and the lower half of the face. An example is shown in Figure 4b.

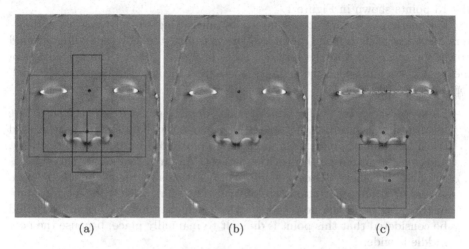

(a)   (b)   (c)

Fig. 4. (a): The first five points and the bounding boxes used to find them. (b): The horizontal line across al_l and al_r divides the face in an upper half and a lower half; the vertical line represents the symmetry axis computed on the given face. (c): Remaining points located through symmetric search, connected by a yellow dashed line, plus bounding boxes for points ls and li.

We employ the aforementioned strategy in order to find the pairs of fiducial points that characterize the eyes, as shown in the upper half of Figure 4c: the external corners, ex_l and ex_r, and the internal corners, en_l and en_r. These points are in pit regions, which means they have high Gaussian curvature. We wish to extract the two symmetric pairs in the upper half of the image that have the highest strength value. We perform this by selecting all possible symmetric pairs of maxima (a, b), with strength values (s_a, s_b); the two pairs that have the highest $s_a \cdot s_b$ value are selected.

The Mouth. This area contains four fiducial points (see lower half of Figure 4c): the pair that represents the corner of the mouth, and the two points representing the tip of the higher lip and the tip of the lower lip. The corners of the mouth, ch_l and ch_r, are identified with the same strategy employed for the eyes' corners, applied to the lower half of the face. The upper lip, ls, and the lower lip, li, are identified as the two maxima of Gaussian curvature with the highest life in the area below sn delimited by ch_l and ch_r.

3   Experiments and Results

Experiments were run on Face Warehouse dataset [4], using meshes representing faces with neutral expressions, frontally projected in order to extract range images, for a total of 111 different faces. The dataset does not provide a ground truth for fiducial points, so we created one by manually selecting on every face the 13 points shown in Figure 1.

The method's results are evaluated by measuring the distance in millimeters between each fiducial point we extract and the corresponding ground truth, for every mesh in the test set. Plots in figure 5 shows the percentage of meshes (Y axis) on which the distance is less than the given millimeters (X axis), for each fiducial point.

- Figure 5a shows results for fiducial points depicting features on the nose. The localization accuracy in this area is high: when the distance from the ground truth for fiducial point reach 4mm, prn is localized on 99% of the dataset, and sn is localized on 94% of the dataset. As far as we know, this work is the first to achieve 3D detection of this particular fiducial point. At 7mm, a_l and a_r reach a detection rate of 90%. The point with worst performance in this area is m, the nose saddle, which achieves 90% at 11mm. It should be considered that this point is difficult to manually place, because the nose saddle is wide.
- Figure 5b shows results for the eyes' corners. Our method performs with good accuracy for these fiducial points. All four point already attain a detection rate above 90% within a 3mm distance.
- Figure 5c shows results for fiducial points located around the mouth. Features depicted by these points are subtle, and extraction is easily affected by noise. In fact, only a few works have tried to detect the mouth corner, ch_l and ch_r ([8], [3], [2], [18] and [21]) and they always use also 2D information. In our case, extraction suffers because a lot of points along the mouth tend to have similar curvature values. 90% accuracy is reached at 14mm. To the best of our knowledge, this work is the first one that performs 3D detection of fiducial points on the upper and lower lip, ls and li. Detection of this points achieves a 90% rate at 8mm.

Our prototype software was designed as a proof-of-concept to test the approach, by patching together previously existing packages that compute curvature and the scale-space. The resulting software is currently slow, especially in the preprocessing phase, because such packages were not optimized and also because they compute much more information than needed by our method. For a single face, building the diagonal scale-space and performing tracking on a commodity PC takes on average 50 seconds; while identifying the 13 fiducial points takes 3.75 seconds. We believe that an optimized implementation, also exploiting parallel computing, can easily achieve a speedup of two orders of magnitude.

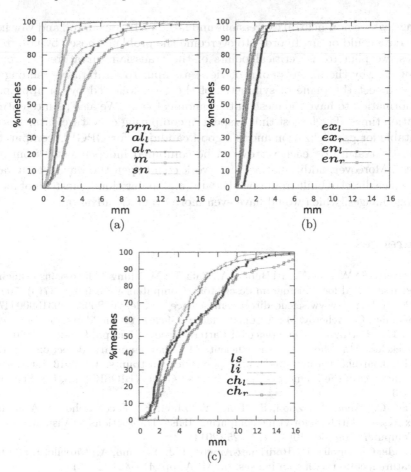

Fig. 5. Localization accuracy for fiducial points: (a) points in the nose area; (b) the corners of the eyes; (c) points around the mouth.

4 Conclusions

We presented a novel technique for extraction of fiducial points on human faces which makes use of 3D data only. Since the proposed method relies on the surface's morphological information only, no training is needed. Fiducial points that were already extracted using 2D+3D techniques in previous works are detected with a performance that is at least as good, and identification of three new, previously undetected, fiducial points is achieved. Results are promising and we plan to extend the method and test it on a wider range of datasets. In particular, we are currently working on a version that uses triangle meshes and a Laplacian filter. We plan to experiment with meshes with different facial expressions, and with range images taken from a lateral point of view (or 3D meshes with occlusions and missing pieces), in order to test for robustness in unstaged settings, where non-neutral expressions and large variations in roll and yaw in the range data could occur. In order to overcome the problems posed by non-frontal images, we plan to use critical points of the Gaussian curvature (a property not affected by the image's point of view) as input to an iterative refining process to detect the plane of symmetry of the face, followed by an appropriate transformation to have the mesh in the canonical view. We also plan to optimize execution times. The largest time is spent in computing curvature data; this task is suitable for parallelization and is a good candidate for GPGPU computation, because curvature on each vertex can be computed independently from other vertices. Moreover, additional research work could open the way to a curvature scale-space directly built from raw 3D data (e.g., point clouds) instead of meshes or range images, which would have even more dramatic advantages.

References

1. Berretti, S., Werghi, N., del Bimbo, A., Pala, P.: Matching 3d face scans using interest points and local histogram descriptors. Computers & Graphics **37**(5), 509–525 (2013). http://www.sciencedirect.com/science/article/pii/S0097849313000447
2. Beumier, C., Acheroy, M.: Automatic face verification from 3d and grey level clues. In: 11th Portuguese Conference on Pattern Recognition, pp. 95–101 (2000)
3. Bockeler, M., Zhou, X.: An efficient 3d facial landmark detection algorithm with haar-like features and anthropometric constraints. In: 2013 International Conference of the Biometrics Special Interest Group (BIOSIG), pp. 1–8, September 2013
4. Cao, C., Weng, Y., Zhou, S., Tong, Y., Zhou, K.: Facewarehouse: A 3d facial expression database for visual computing. IEEE Transactions on Visualization and Computer Graphics **20**(3), 413–425 (2014)
5. Conde, C., Cipolla, R., Rodríguez-Aragón, L.J., Serrano, Á., Cabello, E.: 3d facial feature location with spin images. In: MVA, pp. 418–421 (2005)
6. Farkas, L., Munro, I.: Anthropometric facial proportions in medicine. Thomas (1987)
7. Friedman, J.H.: Regularized discriminant analysis. Journal of the American Statistical Association **84**(405), 165–175 (1989)
8. Gupta, S., Markey, M.K., Bovik, A.C.: Anthropometric 3d face recognition. Int. J. Comput. Vision **90**(3), 331–349 (2010)
9. Hesher, C., Srivastava, A., Erlebacher, G.: A novel technique for face recognition using range imaging. In: Proceedings of the Seventh International Symposium on Signal Processing and Its Applications, 2003, vol. 2, pp. 201–204 (2003)
10. Johnson, A., Hebert, M.: Using spin images for efficient object recognition in cluttered 3d scenes. IEEE Transactions on Pattern Analysis and Machine Intelligence **21**(5), 433–449 (1999)
11. Lu, X., Jain, A.K.: Automatic feature extraction for multiview 3d face recognition. In: Proceedings of the 7th International Conference on Automatic Face and Gesture Recognition, FGR 2006, pp. 585–590. IEEE, Washington, DC (2006)
12. Lu, X., Jain, A.K., Colbry, D.: Matching 2.5d face scans to 3d models. IEEE Trans. Pattern Anal. Mach. Intell. **28**(1), 31–43 (2006)
13. Novatnack, J., Nishino, K.: Scale-dependent 3d geometric features. In: IEEE 11th International Conference on Computer Vision, ICCV 2007, pp. 1–8. IEEE (2007)

14. Novatnack, J., Nishino, K.: Scale-dependent/invariant local 3d shape descriptors for fully automatic registration of multiple sets of range images. In: Forsyth, D., Torr, P., Zisserman, A. (eds.) ECCV 2008, Part III. LNCS, vol. 5304, pp. 440–453. Springer, Heidelberg (2008)
15. Novatnack, J., Nishino, K., Shokoufandeh, A.: Extracting 3d shape features in discrete scale-space. In: Third International Symposium on 3D Data Processing, Visualization, and Transmission, pp. 946–953. IEEE (2006)
16. Segundo, M.P., Silva, L., Bellon, O., Queirolo, C.: Automatic face segmentation and facial landmark detection in range images. IEEE Transactions on Systems, Man, and Cybernetics **40**, 1319–1330 (2010)
17. Panozzo, D., Puppo, E., Rocca, L.: Efficient multi-scale curvature and crease estimation. In: Proceedings Workshop on Computer Graphics, Computer Vision and Mathematics, September 2010
18. Perakis, P., Passalis, G., Theoharis, T., Kakadiaris, I.A.: 3d facial landmark detection under large yaw and expression variations. IEEE Transactions on Pattern Analysis and Machine Intelligence **35**(7), 1552–1564 (2013)
19. Rocca, L., Puppo, E.: A virtually continuous representation of the deep structure of scale-space. In: Petrosino, A. (ed.) ICIAP 2013, Part II. LNCS, vol. 8157, pp. 522–531. Springer, Heidelberg (2013)
20. Shin, H., Sohn, K.: 3d face recognition with geometrically localized surface shape indexes. In: 9th International Conference on Control, Automation, Robotics and Vision, ICARCV 2006, December 2006
21. Sukno, F.M., Waddington, J.L., Whelan, P.F.: 3d facial landmark localization using combinatorial search and shape regression. In: Fusiello, A., Murino, V., Cucchiara, R. (eds.) ECCV 2012 Ws/Demos, Part I. LNCS, vol. 7583, pp. 32–41. Springer, Heidelberg (2012)
22. Uchida, S., Sakoe, H.: A survey of elastic matching techniques for handwritten character recognition. IEICE - Trans. Inf. Syst. **E88-D**(8), August 2005

Filtering Non-Significant Quench Points Using Collision Impact in Grassfire Propagation

Dakai Jin[1(✉)], Cheng Chen[1], and Punam K. Saha[1,2]

[1] Department of Electrical and Computer Engineering, University of Iowa, Iowa City, USA
{dakai-jin,heng-chen,punam-saha}@uiowa.edu
[2] Department of Radiology, University of Iowa, Iowa City, USA

Abstract. The skeleton of an object is defined as the set of quench points formed during Blum's grassfire transformation. Due to high sensitivity of quench points with small changes in the object boundary and the membership function (for fuzzy objects), often, a large number of redundant quench points is formed. Many of these quench points are caused by peripheral protrusions and dents and do not associate themselves with core shape features of the object. Here, we present a significance measure of quench points using the collision impact of fire-fronts and explore its role in filtering noisy quench points. The performance of the method is examined on three-dimensional shapes at different levels of noise and fuzziness, and compared with previous methods. The results have demonstrated that collision impact together with appropriate filtering kernels eliminate most of the noisy quench voxels while preserving those associated with core shape features of the object.

1   Introduction

Skeletonization provides a compact yet effective representation of an object while preserving its important topological and geometrical features; see [1,2] for through surveys. Most of the popular skeletonization algorithms [2,3] are based on simulation of Blum's grassfire propagation [4], where quench points are formed when two or more fire fronts collide and the skeleton is constructed from the set of these quench points.

A well-known challenge with skeletonization is that small protrusions and dents on an object boundary create noisy quench points leading to noisy skeletal branches. This challenge is further intensified for fuzzy objects, because local maxima as well as ridges on the membership function create additional noisy quench points. Thus, the skeleton formed by the initial set of quench points consists of a large amount of redundant structures most of which carry little information related to core shape features of the object. Therefore, it is imperative to filter and remove less significant or noisy quench points to produce meaningful skeletons. This paper presents a new filtering algorithm to remove noisy quench points using the collision impact of Blum's grassfire-fronts.

Quench points have been defined and popularly used in skeletonization in the form of centers of maximal balls (CMB) [5]. CMB can be effectively identified in digital objects as the singularity points [5-7] in the distance transform (DT) map [8,9]. Arcel-

© Springer International Publishing Switzerland 2015
V. Murino and E. Puppo (Eds.): ICIAP 2015, Part I, LNCS 9279, pp. 432–443, 2015.
DOI: 10.1007/978-3-319-23231-7_39

li and Sanniti di Baja [5] introduced a criterion to detect the centers of maximal balls (CMBs) from a 3×3 neighborhood in integer-weighted distance transform, and Borgefors [7] extended it to $5 \times 5 \times 5$ neighborhood. Saha and Wehrli [10] generalized the CMB for fuzzy objects, which was further studied by Svensson [11] where the fuzzy distance transform (FDT) [12] is used instead of DT to locate CMBs. Although, a few works [13-16] have been reported in literature to detect noisy or less significant quench points, a comprehensive theoretical formulation for characterization of significance of quench points is yet to emerge. Saha et al. [13] characterized surface- and curve-like shape points and recommended different support kernels to distinguish between noisy and significant quench points. Borgefors and Nyström [14] proposed a CMB reduction algorithm, where a CMB is marked as redundant if the maximal ball centered at it is covered by the union of some other maximal balls. Németh et al. [15] used an iterative boundary smoothing approach to reduce the set of quench points. Recently, Arcelli et al. [16] suggested to a feature-based approach to locate core, relevant and locally convex CMBs as significant ones in skeletonization.

The quench points, i.e., the locations of colliding fire-fronts, have been well-explored in the context of skeletonization in the form of CMBs. However, the measure of collision impact of meeting fire-fronts at quench points has been surprisingly overlooked in both continuous and digital approaches of skeletonization. In this paper, we formulate a new theoretical framework to characterize the significance of a quench point using the collision impact of fire-fronts and explore its role in filtering noisy quench points. The proposed algorithm is uniformly applicable to both binary and fuzzy objects. It uses local characterization of surface and curve quench points to determine the appropriate support kernels and to compute the average collision impact over the support kernel determining the significance of quench points. The new filtering algorithm has been applied to three-dimensional (3-D) binary and fuzzy objects and its performance under different levels of noise and fuzziness is examined. Also, the performance of this is compared with other DT-based methods of distinguishing between noisy and significant quench points [17-20].

2   Theory and Algorithms

In this section, we define the collision impact and describe the intuitive idea behind its relation with skeletal features of an object in the continuous space. A simple expression of collision impact is presented for digital objects. Finally, a filtering algorithm is described using the measure of collision impact to eliminate noisy quench points while preserving those associated with core shape features of the object.

2.1   Collision Impact and Its Relations with Skeletal Features

Distance transform (DT) [8,9,12] defines the time when a fire-front reaches at a given point during Blum's grassfire propagation, and a level set of DT gives a snapshot of the entire fire-front at one time instance. Note that the DT function is not differentiable everywhere (e.g., it is not differentiable at ridge points), but it is *semi-differentiable*. Thus, we can compute one-sided directional derivative of DT as follows:

$$\partial_{\mathbf{v}} DT(\mathbf{p}) = \lim_{\Delta \to 0^+} \frac{DT(\mathbf{p} + \Delta \cdot \mathbf{v}) - DT(\mathbf{p})}{\Delta}, \qquad (1)$$

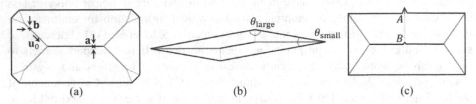

(a)   (b)   (c)

Fig. 1. Collision-impacts at different skeletal points during grassfire propagation on binary shapes. (a) The fire-fronts make head-on collision at the point **a** with the maximum collision-impact of '1'. At the point **b**, the fire-fronts collide obliquely generating a weaker collision-impact. (b) The collision impact along a skeletal branch, originated from a polygonal vertex with a small interior angle, e.g., θ_{small}, is higher than that along a skeletal branch generated from a vertex with a large interior angle, e.g., θ_{large}. (c) The collision-impact along the skeletal branch-segment AB connecting a small protruding structure to the central skeleton, shown by the dotted line, is low.

where $\mathbf{v} \in R^3$ is a direction vector. The uniform speed assumption of Blum's grassfire propagation leads to the following equality for the *speed function* τ at a point $\mathbf{p}$ through which a fire-front passes:

$$\tau(\mathbf{p}) = \max_{\mathbf{v}} \partial_{\mathbf{v}} DT(\mathbf{p}) = 1. \qquad (2)$$

The above equality is violated only at *singular* or *quench point*s where multiple fire-fronts collide forming skeletal structures. Although, colliding fire-fronts stop at quench points, their collision strength or impact may vary depending upon the angle between them. The *collision impact* ξ of colliding fire-fronts at a point $\mathbf{p}$ in a binary object is defined as follows:

$$\xi(\mathbf{p}) = 1 - f_+\big(\tau(\mathbf{p})\big) = 1 - f_+ \Big(\max_{\mathbf{v}} \partial_{\mathbf{v}} DT(\mathbf{p})\Big), \qquad (3)$$

where the function $f_+(x)$ returns the value of x if $x > 0$ and '0' otherwise.

The intuitive idea behind the formulation of collision impact is explained in Fig. 1 in two-dimension (2-D). Consider the octagonal shape of Fig. 1 (a) and the head-on collision of fire-fronts at the point **a**. At the vicinity of **a**, since, there is no point with its DT value greater than that of **a**, the maximum value of $\partial_{\mathbf{v}} DT(\mathbf{a})$ is zero. Thus, the collision impact $\xi(\mathbf{a})$ takes the highest-possible value of '1'. Now, let us consider the situation at the point **b** where the fire-fronts collide obliquely. Although, the colliding fire-fronts are stopped at **b**, there are increasing DT values at its vicinity. It can be shown that the maximum value of $\partial_{\mathbf{v}} DT(\mathbf{b})$ is achieved along the direction $\mathbf{u}_0$ lying on the tangent space of the skeleton at point **b**. Since, $\partial_{\mathbf{v}} DT(\mathbf{b})$ along $\mathbf{u}_0$ has a finite positive value, the collision impact $\xi(\mathbf{b}) < 1$. As shown in Fig. 1 (b), for a polygonal shape, the collision impact along a skeletal branch originated from a vertex with a small interior angle θ_{small} is large as compared to the collision impact along a skeletal branch originated from a vertex with a large interior angle θ_{large}. Another important observation on collision-impact is illustrated in Fig. 1 (c). The collision-impact along the skeletal branch-segment AB on the skeletal branch connecting a small protrusion to the central skeletal branch is low. Thus, collision impact assigns a significance measure to individual skeletal or quench points, and an effective algorithms for filtering noisy quench points using collision impact is presented in Section 2.3.

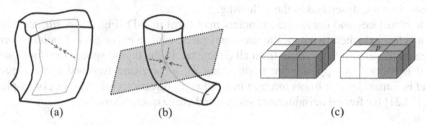

Fig. 2. (a,b) Illustration of surface- (a) and curve-like (b) quench points. (c) Two example support kernels to filter a surface quench voxel. Voxels colored in green are used for average collision impact computation. Four geometrically similar support kernels are constructed from each of these two examples.

2.2   Collision Impact for Digital Objects

In this section, we present a generalized formulation quench points that is applicable to both fuzzy and binary digital objects. Here, a 3-D *cubic grid*, denoted as Z^3, where Z is the set of integers, is used as the image space. Each grid element $p = (p_x, p_y, p_z) \in Z^3$ is referred to as a *voxel*. Traditional definitions of α-*adjacent* or α-*neighborhood* [1] between two voxels $p, q \in Z^3$, where $\alpha \in \{6,18,26\}$, are followed in this paper. $N_{26}(p)$ is used to denote the set of 26-neighbors of a voxel p including p itself while $N_{26}^*(p)$ is used for the set of all voxels of $N_{26}(p)$ excluding the central voxel p. Moreover, the traditional definitions of α-*path*, α-*connectedness*, *and* α-*components* [1] are followed in this paper.

A fuzzy digital object $\mathcal{O} = (O, f_O)$, is a fuzzy set of Z^3, where $f_O: Z^3 \to [0,1]$ is the *membership function* and $O = \{p \in Z^3 | f_O(p) > 0\}$ is its support. Here, 26-adjacency is used for object voxels in O, while 6-adjacency is used for background voxels, i.e., voxels in $\bar{O} = Z^3 - O$. A binary object $\mathcal{B}$ is defined similarly except that the membership function $f_{\mathcal{B}}: Z^3 \to \{0,1\}$ takes the value of '1' for object voxels and '0' for background voxels. A voxel p is a CMB in a fuzzy object $\mathcal{O}$, if the following inequality holds for every $q \in N_{26}^*(p)$ [10],

$$FDT(q) - FDT(p) < \frac{1}{2}\Big(f_O(p) + f_O(q)\Big)|p - q|. \tag{4}$$

Following the formulation of the collision impact in the continuous space in Eq. 3, the collision impact at any voxel p in fuzzy object $\mathcal{O}$, denoted by $\xi_D(p)$, is defined as follows:

$$\xi_D(p) = 1 - \max_{q \in N_{26}^*(p)} \frac{f_+\big(FDT(q) - FDT(p)\big)}{\frac{1}{2}\big(f_O(p) + f_O(q)\big)|p - q|}. \tag{5}$$

2.3   The Filtering Algorithm for Noisy Quench Voxels

The new algorithm for filtering noisy quench points works in the following steps – (1) detect surface- and curve-type quench voxels, (2) determine support kernels for each quench voxel depending on its type, and (3) analyze the collision impact over the support kernels and determine the significance of the quench voxel, and (4) remove quench voxels with their significance measure falling below a predefined threshold. These steps are described in the following.

Both surface- and curve-quench points may form in 3-D (Fig. 2). A *surface quench point* is formed when two opposite fire fronts meet, while a *curve quench point* is formed when co-planar fire fronts meet from all directions. In the digital space, a *surface-quench voxel* is formed by opposite fire fronts along x-, y- or z-direction and a *curve-quench voxel* is formed by fire fronts meeting from all eight directions on xy-, yz-, or zx-planes. See [13,21] for formal definitions of surface and curve quench voxels.

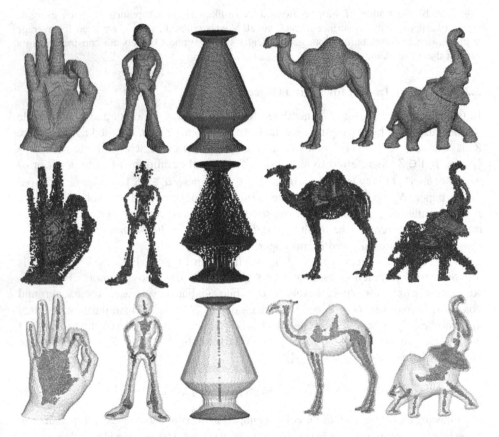

Fig. 3. Results of the collision impact and filtering method on 3-D objects. The top row shows the original binary objects, while the second and third rows show the initial and filtered quench voxels with color-coded collision impacts. The fourth and fifth rows present the initial and filtered quench voxels in fuzzy objects generated by down-sampling.

Fig. 3. (*Continued*)

To determine the significance of a surface-type quench voxel, a support kernel on a 3×3 digital surface orthogonal to the surface-normal direction is constructed and the significance is determined as the average collision impact over the support kernel (Fig. 2 (c)). For a curve-type quench voxel with the horizontal cutting plane, its significance is defined as the maximum collision impact over the support kernels of 3×3 digital surfaces on either side of the cutting plane. These processes are defined in the following. Let $p = (p_x, p_y, p_z)$ be an x-surface quench voxel. To compute the support for p, first, a projection of three voxels $\{q_{i,j}^+ = (p_x - 1, p_y + i, p_z + j), q_{i,j} = (p_x, p_y + i, p_z + j), q_{i,j}^- = (p_x + 1, p_y + i, p_z + j)\}$, for some $i, j \in \{-1, 0, 1\}$, is computed to generate a 3×3 field of significance map $M_p^x(i, j)$ as follows:

$$M_p^x(i, j) = \max\{\xi_D(q_{i,j}^+), \xi_D(q_{i,j}), \xi_D(q_{i,j}^-)\}.$$

The average significance value m_i^x over each of eight different support nels $D_i \mid i = 1, \cdots, 8$ (see Fig. 2 (c)) is computed. An x-surface-quench voxel p is referred to as *x-significant surface-quench* voxel, if any of the average values $m_i^x \mid i = 1, \cdots, 8$ is greater than a preset threshold. A voxel p is referred to as a *significant surface-quench* voxel if it is an x-, y-, or z-significant surface-quench voxel. An xy-curve-quench voxel $p = (p_x, p_y, p_z)$ is an xy-significant curve-quench voxel if the largest collision impact value in either of the two 3×3 planar cliques $C_z^+ = \{(p_x + i, p_y + j, p_z + 1) \mid i, j \in \{-1, 0, 1\}\}$ and $C_z^- = \{(p_x + i, p_y + j, p_z - 1) \mid i, j \in \{-1, 0, 1\}\}$ is greater than a preset threshold. An xy-, yz-, or zx-significant curve-quench voxel is referred to as a *significant curve-quench* voxel. A significant surface- or curve-quench voxel is referred to as a *significant quench voxel*. In this paper, a constant threshold of 0.5 and 0.75 are used for the significance of surface- and curve-quench voxels, respectively.

3   Experiments and Results

Results of the filtering algorithm on a 3-D shape of dinosaur are presented in Fig. 4. Online shapes were constructed at 512×512×512 arrays, which were down-sampled by a window of 4×4×4 voxels to generate test phantoms. The binary objects (top row) were generated by thresholding test phantoms at 0.5, while the test phantoms were directly used as fuzzy objects (not shown in the figure). The initial set of quench voxels for binary objects with color-coded collision impact values (blue = 0.0, cyan = 0.25, green = 0.5, yellow = 0.75, and red = 1.0) are illustrated on the second row of the figure, while the filtered quench voxels are shown on the third row. It is observed that that the filtering algorithm has removed visually evident noisy quench voxels while preserving the ones capturing the core skeletal shapes of individual objects. Initial quench voxels and the filtered ones for fuzzy objects are presented on the last two rows. It is observed that the initial sets of quench voxels for fuzzy objects are larger than that of binary objects. Despite the additional initial quench voxels for fuzzy objects, the filtering algorithm produced satisfactory results. The visual agreement among the filtered significant quench voxels for binary and fuzzy objects is highly encouraging that suggests that the algorithm is robust in the presence of partial voluming in fuzzy objects.

Fig. 4. An example of the collision impact and the filtering results on a 3-D shape. (a) The original binary object; (b) initial quench voxels with color-coded collision impact; (c,d) quench voxels after thresholding at the collision impact using of 0.6 (c) and 0.7 (d); (e) significant quench voxels after filtering; (f) final skeleton.

Results of the filtering algorithm on a 3-D shape of dinosaur are presented in Fig. 3 and its performance is compared with simple thresholding on collision impact. Although, a thresholding on collision impact partially works in the sense that most

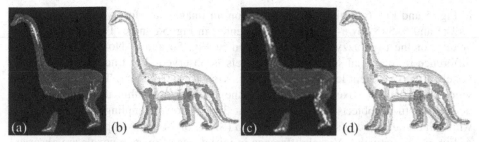

Fig. 5. Results of the collision impact and the filtering algorithm on dinosaur shape at two down-samplings of 3×3×3 and 5×5×5 voxels. (a, c) 2-D slice showing the distribution of quench voxels along with their collision impacts values. (b, d) 3-D results of the filtered quench voxels using the proposed method.

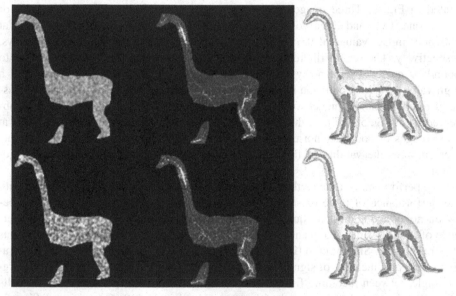

Fig. 6. Results of the collision impact and filtering algorithm on dinosaur shape under two levels of membership noises, at SNR24 (top row) and SNR6 (bottom row), respectively. Left column shows a 2-D slices from noisy object. Middle column shows the distribution of quench voxels along with their collision impact values. Right column displays the result of the filtered quench voxels by the proposed method in 3-D.

peripheral and noisy quench voxels are removed and most of the core quench voxels are preserved, the performance is still suboptimal. At the threshold of 0.6, several isolated noisy quench voxels have survived, while an over-deletion of quench voxels has occurred at the threshold of 0.7. On the other hand, the filtering algorithm has removed all visually evident noisy quench voxels while avoiding over-deletion. Finally, note that the quench voxels get connected in the final skeleton due to the topology preservation criterion [22,23] during a thinning process. The performance of the filtering algorithm under different levels of fuzziness and membership noise are presented in Fig. 5 and Fig. 6. Initial quench voxels on an image slice for two fuzzy objects at 3×3×3 and 5×5×5 down-sampling are presented in Fig. 5a and c. The filtered quench voxels for the two fuzzy objects are shown in Fig. 5b and d. No visually apparent difference in the initial sets of quench voxels is observed. The filtered set of quench voxels at two different levels of fuzziness is visually satisfactory. To study the behavior of the quench voxel generation and the filtering algorithm under membership noise, two fuzzy objects were generated at 3×3×3 down-sampling and then adding white Gaussian noise at signal to noise ratio (SNR) of 24 and 6 (top and bottom rows of Fig. 6, respectively). Visual difference in initial sets of quench voxels are observed at two different levels of noise. Despite the presence of high membership noise, the filtering method successfully eliminated noisy quench voxels while preserving the significant ones.

The performance of the algorithm under different levels of boundary noise is presented in Fig. 7. Three images were generated by randomly adding noisy balls of radius one, two, and three voxels. The sets of quench voxels after thresholding at collision impact values of 0.6 and 0.7 are shown on the second and the third rows, respectively. The sets of filtered quench voxels are presented on the last row. Due to boundary noise, several noisy quench voxels survived even after thresholding at a high value of 0.7 for collision impact. In contrast, the filtering algorithm has successfully removed noisy quench voxels, while preserving the core ones. Finally, as observed from Fig. 5 to Fig. 7, the filtered set of quench is visually similar and stable at wide ranges of boundary noise, down-sampling as well as membership noise. It further enforces the validity of the principle of our noisy quench voxel filtering algorithm.

The performance of the method at different boundary noise levels is compared with the performance of three existing DT-based methods [17-20] on distinguishing between noisy and significant quench voxels. Gagvani and Silver [17] used the difference of the DT value of a quench voxel from the average DT value of its neighbors as its significance. Siddiqi et al.[20] computed the average outward flux of the DT gradient field as a measure of significance of a quench voxel. Shah [18,19] used the largest angle between incoming fire-fronts as the significance of quench voxels. Results of applications of the three methods are presented in Fig. 8. Gagvani and Silver's method failed to remove several visually noisy quench voxels while discontinuities on meaningful skeletal segments become apparent. Shah's method fail to locate quench voxels in the neck, tail, or the legs of the dinosaur. The performance of Siddiqi et al. is more comparable to ours at low noise. However, the performance deteriorated at higher levels of noise where it failed to clean a significant number of noisy voxels.

Fig. 7. Results of the collision impact and the filtering algorithm on a binary dinosaur shape under three levels of boundary noises. The top row shows the 3-D volume of binary objects. The second and third row show the quench voxels thresholded at collision impact values of 0.6 and 0.7, respectively. The bottom row displays the filtered quench voxels by the proposed method.

Fig. 8. Results of applications of the DT-based noisy quench voxel filtering methods by Gag-vani and Silver [17] (top row), Siddiqi et al. [20] (middle row), and Shah [18,19] (bottom row) on the binary dinosaur shape under three different levels of boundary noise used in Fig. 7.

4   Conclusions

This paper has presented a new theoretical framework to characterize the significance of a quench point using the collision impact of Blum's grassfire-fronts. Its role in filtering noisy quench points, prevalent in the skeletonization of real objects, has been explored. Experimental results have demonstrated the effectiveness of method in removing noisy quench voxels while preserving the significant ones capturing core shape features in both binary and fuzzy objects. Initial results has suggested that the method is stable over wide ranges of boundary noise, down-sampling, and membership noise and generates visually satisfactory results despite significant image artifacts. Our method offers a unified solution for both binary and fuzzy objects, while existing methods are applicable to binary objects, only. Also, the initial results suggests that the current method may perform better as compared to existing ones, especially, at higher levels of noise. Currently, we are conducting quantitative analysis of its performance and exploring its role in improving the results of skeletonization.

Acknowledgements. This work was supported by the NIH grant R01-AR054439.

References

1. Saha, P.K., Strand, R., Borgefors, G.: Digital topology and geometry in medical imaging: a survey. IEEE Trans. Med. Imag. (in press)
2. Saha, P.K., Borgefors, G., Sanniti di Baja, G.: A survey on skeletonization algorithms and their applications. Pat. Reog. Lett. (in press)
3. Siddiqi, K., Pizer, S.M.: Medial representations: mathematics, algorithms and applications. Springer (2008)
4. Blum, H.: A transformation for extracting new descriptors of shape. Model. Percep. Speech Vis. Form **19**, 362–380 (1967)
5. Arcelli, C., Sanniti di Baja, G.: Finding Local Maxima in a Pseudo-Euclidean Distance Transform. Comp. Vis. Grap. Im. Proc. **43**, 361–367 (1988)
6. Borgefors, G., Ragnemalm, I., di Baja, G.S.: The Euclidean distance transform: finding the local maxima and reconstructing the shape. In: Proc 7th Scand. Conf. Imag. Anal., vol. 2, 974–981 (1991)
7. Borgefors, G.: Centres of maximal discs in the 5-7-11 distance transform. In: 8th Scandinavian Conference on Image Analysis, Tromsø, Norway, pp. 105–111 (1993)
8. Borgefors, G.: Distance transform in arbitrary dimensions. Comp. Vis. Grap. Im. Proc. **27**, 321–345 (1984)
9. Borgefors, G.: Distance transformations in digital images. Comp. Vis. Grap. Im. Proc. **34**, 344–371 (1986)
10. Saha, P.K., Wehrli, F.W.: Fuzzy distance transform in general digital grids and its applications. In: 7th Joint Conference on Information Sciences, pp. 201–213. Research Triangular Park, NC (2003)
11. Svensson, S.: Aspects on the reverse fuzzy distance transform. Patt. Recog. Lett. **29**, 888–896 (2008)
12. Saha, P.K., Wehrli, F.W., Gomberg, B.R.: Fuzzy distance transform: theory, algorithms, and applications. Comp. Vis. Imag. Und. **86**, 171–190 (2002)
13. Saha, P.K., Chaudhuri, B.B., Majumder, D.D.: A new shape preserving parallel thinning algorithm for 3D digital images. Pat. Recog. **30**, 1939–1955 (1997)
14. Borgefors, G., Nyström, I.: Efficient shape representation by minimizing the set of centres of maximal discs/spheres. Pat. Recog. Lett. **18**, 465–471 (1997)
15. Németh, G., Kardos, P., Palágyi, K.: Thinning combined with iteration-by-iteration smoothing for 3D binary images. Graph. Mod. **73**, 335–345 (2011)
16. Arcelli, C., Sanniti di Baja, G., Serino, L.: Distance-driven skeletonization in voxel images. IEEE Trans. Patt. Anal. Mach. Intell. **33**, 709–720 (2011)
17. Gagvani, N., Silver, D.: Parameter-controlled volume thinning. Graph. Mod. Imag. Proce. **61**, 149–164 (1999)
18. Shah, J.: Gray skeletons and segmentation of shapes. Comp. Vis. Imag. Und. **99**, 96–109 (2005)
19. Shah, J.: Skeletons of 3D shapes. In: Kimmel, R., Sochen, N.A., Weickert, J. (eds.) Scale-Space 2005. LNCS, vol. 3459, pp. 339–350. Springer, Heidelberg (2005)
20. Siddiqi, K., Bouix, S., Tannenbaum, A., Zucker, S.W.: Hamilton-Jacobi Skeletons. International Journal of Computer Vision **48**, 215–231 (2002)
21. Jin, D., Saha, P.K.: A new fuzzy skeletonization algorithm and its applications to medical imaging. In: Petrosino, A. (ed.) ICIAP 2013, Part I. LNCS, vol. 8156, pp. 662–671. Springer, Heidelberg (2013)
22. Saha, P.K., Chaudhuri, B.B.: Detection of 3-D simple points for topology preserving transformations with application to thinning. IEEE Trans. Patt. Anal. Mach. Intell. **16**, 1028–1032 (1994)
23. Saha, P.K., Chaudhuri, B.B.: 3D digital topology under binary transformation with applications. Comp. Vis. Image. Und. **63**, 418–429 (1996)

Robust and Efficient Camera Motion Synchronization via Matrix Decomposition

Federica Arrigoni[1]([✉]), Beatrice Rossi[2], and Andrea Fusiello[1]

[1] DIEGM, Università di Udine, Via Delle Scienze, 208, Udine, Italy
arrigoni.federica@spes.uniud.it
[2] AST Lab, STMicroelectronics, Via Olivetti, 2, Agrate Brianza, Italy

Abstract. In this paper we present a structure-from-motion pipeline based on the synchronization of relative motions derived from epipolar geometries. We combine a robust rotation synchronization technique with a fast translation synchronization method from the state of the art. Both reduce to computing matrix decompositions: low-rank & sparse and spectral decomposition. These two steps successfully solve the motion synchronization problem in a way that is both *efficient* and *robust* to outliers. The pipeline is global for it considers all the images at the same time. Experimental validation demonstrates that our pipeline compares favourably with some recently proposed methods.

Keywords: Structure from motion · Synchronization · Low-rank decomposition

1 Introduction

Structure from Motion (SfM) is a crucial problem in Computer Vision. The goal is to recover both 3D structure, namely 3D coordinates of scene points, and motion parameters, namely attitude (rotation) and position of the cameras, starting from image point correspondences.

For many years, most practical SfM pipelines have adopted either *sequential* or *hierarchical* approaches. Sequential methods, such as [20], incrementally increase a partial reconstruction by iteratively adding new cameras and 3D points, whereas hierarchical ones, such as [22], organize images in a binary tree and progressively merge smaller reconstructions into larger ones. Although being highly accurate, these approaches suffer from two main disadvantages: on one hand they require computationally-expensive intermediate bundle adjustment minimizations to contain error propagation, on the other hand the final reconstruction may depend on the order in which cameras are added or on the choice of the initial pair.

Recently, *global* SfM pipelines, such as [1,15,17–19], have gained increasing attention in the community. Such methods start from the relative motions, i.e. epipolar geometries computed from point matches among the images, compute the angular attitude and position of the cameras with respect to an absolute coordinate frame, and then recover the 3D structure. Here the term global means

V. Murino and E. Puppo (Eds.): ICIAP 2015, Part I, LNCS 9279, pp. 444–455, 2015.
DOI: 10.1007/978-3-319-23231-7_40

that such techniques take into account the entire relative motion information at once, or, in other terms, they consider the whole *epipolar graph*, which has a vertex for each camera and edges in correspondence of view pairs having consistent matching points. Global methods have the advantage of fairly distributing errors among the cameras, and thus they need bundle adjustment refinement only at the end, thereby performing faster than the other methods.

The core of global methods is the so-called *motion synchronization problem* (a.k.a *motion registration* or *motion averaging*), i.e. computing *absolute* positions and attitudes starting from *relative* measurements. Formally, the goal is to compute n rotation matrices $R_i \in SO(3)$ and n translation vectors $\mathbf{t}_i \in \mathbb{R}^3$ such that the projection matrix of the i-th camera is expressed as $P_i = K_i [R_i \ \mathbf{t}_i]$, where $K_i \in \mathbb{R}^{3 \times 3}$ are the internal calibration matrices, assumed known. It is inherent to the problem that the motion parameters can be recovered up to a roto-translation and a single scaling factor. Most techniques split such a problem in two stages: first they compute the absolute attitude of each camera, and then they recover camera positions.

The first stage is known as *rotation synchronization* (or *rotation registration* or *multiple rotation averaging*) and a thorough overview of the theory behind it can be found in [12]. Several approaches have been proposed to solve this problem, both within SfM pipelines and in stand-alone works. Non-robust methods, such as [1,17,18], suffer from the presence of inconsistent/outlier pairwise information, i.e. skewed epipolar geometries caused by mismatches, and thus they need a computationally-expensive preliminary step devoted to detect and remove such outliers. On the contrary, robust techniques, such as [2,8,11], are inherently resilient to outliers and hence they are more efficient.

The position recovery stage (a.k.a. *translation synchronization* or *translation registration*) can use only constraints derived from relative translation directions, such as [4,9,17,19], or additionally exploit point correspondences among the images, such as [1,15,24]. In practical SfM pipelines, methods from the former category should be preferred: besides being more consistent with the structure *from* motion paradigm – where structure comes into play only *after* motion has been computed – they are potentially more efficient, since they reduce memory usage.

Contribution. In this paper we combine the rotation synchronization technique in [2] with the translation synchronization method in [4]. The resulting global pipeline successfully solves the motion synchronization problem, while ensuring at the same time both *efficiency* and *robustness* to outliers. More precisely, motion synchronization is reduced to computing two matrix decompositions, involving matrices of dimension $3n \times 3n$: first a low-rank & sparse decomposition, then a spectral factorization. Experimental validation demonstrates that our pipeline compares favourably with some recently proposed methods.

1.1 Overview

The proposed SfM pipeline is organized as follows.

Step 1: Computing Relative Motions. First, a collection of reliable correspondences for each image pair is obtained by extracting and matching SIFT features. After expressing these image points in normalized coordinates (i.e. left-multiplying by the inverse of the calibration matrices), the essential matrices are computed through RANSAC in combination with the 8-point algorithm. The *epipolar graph* is then built with an edge linking two views for which a sufficient number of inliers have been found. For each edge the relative motion is computed from the essential matrix, and it is subsequently refined through Bundle Adjustment (BA). The X84 rejection rule [10] is introduced at each step of BA, removing image points with the highest reprojection error.

Step 2: Motion Synchronization. The first step synchronizes relative rotations in a robust manner, and it is at the same time efficient, thanks to the usage of a faster alternative to singular value decomposition for computing low-rank projections (Section 2). The second step (Section 3) reduces translation recovery to a graph embedding problem, which is equivalent to computing the smallest eigenvector of a data matrix, which does not involve corresponding points, resulting in an extremely fast method. The relative translation directions are refined through Iteratively Reweighted Least Squares (IRLS).

Step 3: Final Refinement. The correspondences are tracked through the images and 3D coordinates of scene points are computed by triangulation. The structure and absolute translations are refined with a partial BA with fixed rotations. Then, a global BA is applied to improve the quality of structure and motion estimation. The idea of using a two-stage BA is inspired by [17, 18] and it is motivated by the fact that rotations are more reliable in general. As in Step 1, at each iteration of BA the X84 rejection rule singles out outliers, based on the reprojection error.

2   Rotation Synchronization

The rotation synchronization step in a global structure-from-motion pipeline takes as input the observed pairwise rotations $\widehat{R}_{ij} \in SO(3)$ and returns the absolute rotations of the cameras $R_i \in SO(3)$ such that the latter are "compatible" with the former, i.e. $R_i R_j^{\mathsf{T}} \approx \widehat{R}_{ij}$. In this paper we use the hat accent to denote noisy measurements. The notion of compatibility can be formalized by considering the chordal distances between the estimated and unknown relative rotations, resulting in the following rotation synchronization problem

$$\min_{R_i \in SO(3)} \sum_{(i,j) \in \mathcal{E}} \left\| \widehat{R}_{ij} - R_i R_j^{\mathsf{T} } \right\|_F^2 . \tag{1}$$

where $\mathcal{E} \subseteq \{1, \ldots, n\} \times \{1, \ldots, n\}$ is the edge set of the epipolar graph.

More precisely, we use the R-GoDec Algorithm introduced in [2] which solves a regularized version of (1) in order to cope with outlying relative rotations. In Section 2.1 we describe such an algorithm in a general scenario, while in Section 2.2 we explain how to apply this method to find camera absolute rotations.

2.1 The R-GoDec Algorithm

The *matrix completion* problem [5, 7, 14] consists in completing a low-rank matrix $\widehat{X}$ starting from an incomplete subset of its entries $\mathcal{P}_\Omega(\widehat{X})$ possibly corrupted with a low level of noise. Here Ω denotes the sampling set and $\mathcal{P}_\Omega$ is the projection onto the space of matrices that vanish outside Ω. The goal of *low-rank and sparse matrix decomposition* [6, 25] is to find a low-rank term L, a sparse term S representing outlier measurements, and a noise term N such that a data matrix $\widehat{X}$ can be written as

$$\widehat{X} = L + S + N. \tag{2}$$

On one hand, matrix completion techniques are able to guess missing entries, but they are not robust to outliers. On the other hand, matrix decomposition techniques handle sparse errors of large intensity but they do not deal with missing data. There is a small fraction of methods (including [2, 13, 23]) addressing this double problem simultaneously, i.e. performing robust matrix completion or equivalently matrix decomposition with missing entries.

The R-GoDec Algorithm [2] is a combination of matrix completion and matrix decomposition techniques, and was derived by properly modifying the GoDec Algorithm [25] in order to handle outliers and missing entries simultaneously. More precisely, the sparse term S in (2) is replaced by the sum of two terms S_1 and S_2 having dual supports: S_1 is a sparse matrix over the sampling set Ω which is nonzero in correspondence of the outlier entries only; S_2 has support on Ω^C (the complementary of Ω) and it is an approximation of $-\mathcal{P}_{\Omega^C}(L)$, representing recovery of missing entries. This results in the following model

$$\widehat{X} = L + S_1 + S_2 + N. \tag{3}$$

Assuming that the rank r of the low-rank term is known in advance, the associated minimization problem is

$$\min_{L, S_1, S_2} \frac{1}{2} \left\| \widehat{X} - L - S_1 - S_2 \right\|_F^2 + \lambda \|S_1\|_1 \tag{4}$$
$$\text{s.t. } \operatorname{rank}(L) \le r, \quad \operatorname{supp}(S_1) \subseteq \Omega, \quad \operatorname{supp}(S_2) = \Omega^C$$

where $\lambda \ge 0$ is a regularization parameter, and $\|S_1\|_1$ denotes the ℓ^1-norm of its argument considered as a vector. Since the ℓ^1-norm is a sparsity-inducing norm, it is expected to separate sparse outliers from non corrupted low-rank data by minimizing the cost function in (4).

In order to solve problem (4), R-GoDec alternatively minimizes the cost function with respect to each optimization variable, keeping constant the others. In other words, the following steps are iterated until convergence.

- The rank-r approximation of $\widehat{X} - S_1 - S_2$ is assigned to L;
- The minimizer of the cost function in (4) with respect to S_1 is assigned to S_1, i.e. the result of applying entry-wise *Soft Thresholding* [3] with parameter λ to the matrix $\mathcal{P}_\Omega(\widehat{X} - L)$;
- The quantity $\mathcal{P}_{\Omega^c}(\widehat{X} - L - S_1) = -\mathcal{P}_{\Omega^c}(L)$ is assigned to S_2.

The low-rank projection is computed through *Bilateral Random Projections* (BRP) [25] instead of Singular Value Decomposition (SVD) in order to reduce the computational cost. More details can be found in [2].

2.2 Robust Rotation Synchronization

Let us introduce the following notation:

$$R = \begin{bmatrix} R_1 \\ R_2 \\ \cdots \\ R_n \end{bmatrix} \in \mathbb{R}^{3n \times 3}, \quad X = \begin{pmatrix} I & R_{12} & \cdots & R_{1n} \\ R_{21} & I & \cdots & R_{2n} \\ \cdots & & & \cdots \\ R_{n1} & R_{n2} & \cdots & I \end{pmatrix} \in \mathbb{R}^{3n \times 3n}. \tag{5}$$

As observed in [1], it follows from the compatibility constraint $R_{ij} = R_i R_j^\mathsf{T}$ that the block matrix X admits the factorization $X = RR^\mathsf{T}$ and hence it has rank 3. Let $\widehat{X}$ be an estimate of X, constructed by replacing R_{ij} with $\widehat{R}_{ij}$ in (5). Matrix completion is required here since not all $\widehat{R}_{ij}$ are available in practice, i.e. the epipolar graph is not complete. Moreover, matrix decomposition is required since some pairwise rotations may be wrong due to repetitive patterns and symmetries in the images. Indeed, these structures generate false essential matrices, namely two-view geometries which do not agree with the real 3D geometry, even if they are satisfied by the majority of point matches. Thus, in order to handle both missing and outlier blocks in $\widehat{X}$, in addition to a diffused noise, a decomposition of the form (3) is required, and it can be computed through the R-GoDec Algorithm with $r = 3$.

Formally, computing the low-rank & sparse matrix decomposition of $\widehat{X}$ is equivalent (up to a relaxation) to solve the rotation synchronization problem (1) in a robust manner. We now briefly explain this connection, more details can be found in [2]. By using the notation in (5), it is straightforward to see that problem (1) can be expressed equivalently as

$$\min_X \frac{1}{2} \left\| \mathcal{P}_\Omega(\widehat{X} - X) \right\|_F^2 \tag{6}$$
$$\text{s.t. } X = RR^\mathsf{T}, \ R \in SO(3)^n$$

which, if all the requirements on X are ignored but the rank constraint, reduces to

$$\min_L \frac{1}{2} \left\| \mathcal{P}_\Omega(\widehat{X} - L) \right\|_F^2 \tag{7}$$
$$\text{s.t. rank}(L) \leq 3.$$

The notation L instead of X highlights that L will not coincide with X in general, due to the rank relaxation, i.e. L will not be symmetric positive semidefinite and composed of rotations. Problem (7) is a matrix completion problem [7], and it can be written in an equivalent form as follows

$$\min_{L, S_2} \frac{1}{2} \left\| \widehat{X} - L - S_2 \right\|_F^2$$
$$\text{s.t. } \text{rank}(L) \leq 3, \quad \text{supp}(S_2) = \Omega^C \tag{8}$$

where the additional variable S_2 is introduced to handle missing entries and the projection operator $\mathcal{P}_\Omega$ is not required. Finally, if robustness is introduced in (8) through ℓ^1-regularization, then problem (4) is obtained.

Once problem (4) is solved by means of the R-GoDec Algorithm, the optimal L is used to estimate the absolute rotations. Since the solution of rotation synchronization is defined up to a global rotation, any block-column of L – after projection onto $SO(3)$ – can be viewed as an estimate of R. The absolute rotations computed in this way are resilient to outliers, since the cost function in (4) naturally includes the outliers in its definition through the sparse matrix S_1. However, *a posteriori* outlier detection is useful for the subsequent step of translation synchronization. Rogue relative rotations correspond to non-zero entries in the sparse matrix S_1. Thus a rotation $\widehat{R}_{ij}$ is classified as outlier if the number of non-zero entries in the associated 3×3 block in S_1 is greater than a given threshold θ, with $\theta \in \{1, \ldots, 9\}$. In this case, the edge (i, j) is removed from $\mathcal{E}$, since the entire epipolar geometry associated to (i, j) is likely to be wrong.

3   Translation Synchronization

The translation synchronization step in a global structure-from-motion pipeline takes as input either a set of corresponding points or the relative translation directions, and returns the absolute translations of the cameras $\mathbf{t}_i \in \mathbb{R}^3$, or equivalently the camera positions (centers) $\mathbf{c}_i = -R_i^\mathsf{T} \mathbf{t}_i$. Accordingly, there are several ways to define a suitable cost function for the problem. A possibility is to constraint camera locations to be linear combinations of rays emanating from their neighbours, with known directions and unknown coefficients. This concept is formalized in [4] where a fast spectral solution is developed. In Section 3.2 we describe such algorithm, while in Section 3.1 we explain how to refine the translation directions in an accurate way, based on the knowledge of absolute rotations and corresponding points.

3.1   Refining the Relative Translation Directions

First, the relative rotations are updated by using the compatibility constraint $R_{ij} = R_i R_j^\mathsf{T}$, where R_i are the absolute rotations returned by R-GoDec. Then, the epipolar constraint with *known* rotation becomes a linear equation in the unknown $\mathbf{t}_{ij} \in \mathbb{R}^3$ for each pair of point matches.

Let $\{\mathbf{p}_i^k, \mathbf{p}_j^k\}_{k=1}^{N_{ij}}$ denote a set of N_{ij} corresponding points for the pair $(i,j) \in \mathcal{E}$ expressed in normalized coordinates. By using the invariance to permutation of a triple product (up to sign), the epipolar constraint of this image pair can be expressed equivalently as

$$(\mathbf{p}_i^k \times R_{ij}\mathbf{p}_j^k)^\mathsf{T}\mathbf{t}_{ij} = 0. \tag{9}$$

By stacking all these equations, a homogeneous system is obtained, whose solution is the desired estimate of the relative translation direction $\mathbf{t}_{ij}/\|\mathbf{t}_{ij}\|$. In order to cope with rogue point correspondences we apply *Iteratively Reweighted Least Squares* (IRLS) to the residuals e_k of the linear system (9). The weights w_k are computed by using Mosteller and Tukey's weight function [16], namely $w_k = (1 - (e_k/s)^2)^2$ if $e_k \leq s$, $w_k = 0$ otherwise.

3.2   A Fast Spectral Method

Let $\mathbf{c}_{ij} = \mathbf{c}_i - \mathbf{c}_j = -R_i^\mathsf{T}\mathbf{t}_{ij}$ denote the baseline of the pair (i,j) and let $\mathbf{d}_{ij} = \mathbf{c}_{ij}/\|\mathbf{c}_{ij}\| = -R_i^\mathsf{T}\mathbf{t}_{ij}/\|\mathbf{t}_{ij}\|$ denote its direction. Let $\widehat{\mathbf{d}}_{ij}$ be an estimate of $\mathbf{d}_{ij}$, computed as explained in the previous section. The goal is to find a realization of the locations $\mathbf{c}_i \in \mathbb{R}^3$ starting from the measurements $\widehat{\mathbf{d}}_{ij}$. In [4] camera positions are recovered by imposing that camera-to-camera displacements $(\mathbf{c}_i - \mathbf{c}_j)$ are maximally "consistent" with the constraint directions $\widehat{\mathbf{d}}_{ij}$. The notion of consistency is expressed as a minimum-squared-error problem where the components of the displacements that are orthogonal to the constraints are minimized. This results in the following problem

$$\min_{\mathbf{c}_i \in \mathbb{R}^3} \sum_{(i,j)\in\mathcal{E}} \left\| (\mathbf{c}_i - \mathbf{c}_j)^\mathsf{T} \widehat{K}_{ij} \right\|_F^2 \tag{10}$$

where $\widehat{K}_{ij}$ is an orthonormal basis for the kernel of $\widehat{\mathbf{d}}_{ij}$. Optionally, weights can be included in (10) to reflect the uncertainty of the estimates $\widehat{\mathbf{d}}_{ij}$ (see [4] for details).

If $\mathbf{c} = [\mathbf{c}_1^\mathsf{T}, \ldots, \mathbf{c}_n^\mathsf{T}]^\mathsf{T} \in \mathbb{R}^{3n}$ denotes the stack of the unknown locations $\mathbf{c}_i$, then the following equalities hold for the cost function in (10)

$$\sum_{(i,j)\in\mathcal{E}} \left\| (\mathbf{c}_i - \mathbf{c}_j)^\mathsf{T} \widehat{K}_{ij} \right\|_F^2 = \sum_{(i,j)\in\mathcal{E}} (\mathbf{c}_i - \mathbf{c}_j)^\mathsf{T} \widehat{K}_{ij}\widehat{K}_{ij}^\mathsf{T}(\mathbf{c}_i - \mathbf{c}_j) =$$
$$\sum_{(i,j)\in\mathcal{E}} \mathbf{c}_i^\mathsf{T}\widehat{D}_{ij}\mathbf{c}_i + \mathbf{c}_j^\mathsf{T}\widehat{D}_{ij}\mathbf{c}_j - \mathbf{c}_i^\mathsf{T}\widehat{D}_{ij}\mathbf{c}_j - \mathbf{c}_j^\mathsf{T}\widehat{D}_{ij}\mathbf{c}_i = 2\mathbf{c}^\mathsf{T}\widehat{H}\mathbf{c} \tag{11}$$

where $\widehat{D}_{ij} = I_3 - \widehat{\mathbf{d}}_{ij}\widehat{\mathbf{d}}_{ij}^\mathsf{T} = \widehat{K}_{ij}\widehat{K}_{ij}^\mathsf{T} \in \mathbb{R}^{3\times3}$ is the orthogonal projector onto $\mathrm{Ker}(\widehat{\mathbf{d}}_{ij})$, $\widehat{D} \in \mathbb{R}^{3n\times3n}$ is constructed by placing $\widehat{D}_{ij}$ in each 3×3 block (and zero blocks in correspondence of missing edges), and $\widehat{H} = \mathrm{blockdiag}(\widehat{D}(\mathbf{1}_n \otimes I_3)) - \widehat{D}$. Here $\mathbf{1}_n$ denotes the vector in $\mathbb{R}^n$ with 1 at each entry, and $\otimes$ denotes the

Kronecker product. Thus problem (10) is equivalent to minimize the following quadratic form

$$\min_{\|\mathbf{c}\|=1} \mathbf{c}^{\mathsf{T}} \widehat{H} \mathbf{c}. \tag{12}$$

Problem (12) admits a closed-form solution which is the eigenvector of $\widehat{H}$ with minimum eigenvalue. However, $\mathbf{c}_i = \mathbf{c}_j$ for all i,j is a trivial solution to problem (10), that corresponds to mapping all the cameras to a single point in $\mathbb{R}^3$. This trivial subspace is spanned in $\mathbb{R}^{3n}$ by the vectors $[1\,0\,0\dots1\,0\,0]^{\mathsf{T}}$, $[0\,1\,0\dots0\,1\,0]^{\mathsf{T}}$, $[0\,0\,1\dots0\,0\,1]^{\mathsf{T}}$ which can be concatenated to form the matrix $\mathbf{1}_n \otimes I_3 \in \mathbb{R}^{3n \times 3}$. Thus the kernel of $\widehat{H}$ will have (exactly or approximately) dimension 4, and the sought solution must belong to $\mathrm{Ker}(\widehat{H})$ and be orthogonal to $\mathbf{1}_n \otimes I_3$ at the same time, in order to avoid the trivial solution. To compute it, it is sufficient to project $\widehat{H}$ onto an orthogonal basis $Q \in \mathbb{R}^{3n \times 3n-3}$ of $\mathrm{Ker}(\mathbf{1}_n \otimes I_3)$, compute the eigen-decomposition of the reduced problem and then back project the eigenvectors.

This method has the advantage of being both simple and extremely fast, as translation synchronization is cast to an eigenvalue decomposition of a matrix whose size does not depend on the number of matching points. More details about this technique can be found in [4], including problem pathologies that appear where the data are insufficient or inconsistent.

4   Experiments

In this section we evaluate our pipeline on publicly available datasets [21] where the number of cameras varies from 8 to 30 and ground-truth motions are available. All the experiments are carried out in MATLAB on a dual-core 1.3 GHz machine.

To define the epipolar graph, we consider only image pairs having more than 500 inlier correspondences. As for rotation averaging, we perform at most 100 iterations of R-GoDec, using the value $\lambda = 0.05$, and we choose the value $\theta = 3$ for outlier detection. In order to compare our results with ground-truth absolute rotations, we find the optimal rotation that aligns them by performing *single* rotation averaging [11]. As for camera positions, we find the scale and translation of the optimal alignment by solving the associated linear system in the least-square sense. We use the angular distance and the euclidean norm as distance measures for rotations and positions respectively. The results of our simulations are reported in Tables 1, 2 and 3, where our pipeline is compared with the global methods described in [17,19]. As for [19], the online code concerns motion averaging only, thus we used our pipeline for the remaining steps. The results of Moulon et al. reported in Table 2 are taken from their original paper [17], where only translation errors are disclosed. We also include in the comparison the hierarchical approach of [22], whose binary code is available online. To evaluate the execution times, we consider the largest datasets, i.e. HerzJesu-P25 and Castle-P30, and MATLAB implementations.

Table 1. Mean angular errors [degrees] on the absolute rotations.

	Our Pipeline		Ozyesil et al. [19]		SAMANTHA [22]
	before BA	after BA	before BA	after BA	
Castle-P30	0.78	0.05	1.97	0.05	0.06
Castle-P19	1.57	0.05	3.69	0.05	0.09
Entry-P10	0.44	0.03	0.56	0.04	0.05
Fountain-P11	0.03	0.03	0.03	0.03	0.06
HerzJesu-P25	0.13	0.04	0.14	0.04	0.03
HerzJesu-P8	0.04	0.03	0.06	0.03	0.04

Table 2. Mean errors [meters] on the absolute positions.

	Our Pipeline		Ozyesil et al. [19]		Moulon et al. [17]	SAMANTHA [22]
	before BA	after BA	before BA	after BA	after BA	
Castle-P30	1.123	0.030	1.393	0.030	0.022	0.033
Castle-P19	1.493	0.036	1.769	0.032	0.026	0.046
Entry-P10	0.433	0.009	0.203	0.010	0.006	0.022
Fountain-P11	0.006	0.003	0.004	0.003	0.003	0.006
HerzJesu-P25	0.038	0.009	0.065	0.009	0.005	0.031
HerzJesu-P8	0.009	0.004	0.007	0.005	0.004	0.007

Table 3. Execution times [seconds] of motion synchronization.

	Our pipeline		Ozyesil et al. [19]	
	Rotation	Translation	Rotation	Translation
Castle-P30	0.05	0.05	0.15	0.80
HerzJesu-P25	0.04	0.04	0.13	1.32

Tables 1 and 2 show that our pipeline is able to recover camera motion accurately, achieving results which are comparable to the other analysed techniques, and within the accuracy of the ground truth [21]. We obtain an average angular error less than 0.1 degrees and an average location error of the order of millimeters, after the final Bundle Adjustment (BA), confirming that motion synchronization provides a good initialization. In some cases the result is more than an initialization, being already very close to the BA optimum. In some other cases (namely, Castle-P*), the difference with BA is higher. Nevertheless, the angular errors obtained with our pipeline before BA are lower than those obtained with [19], confirming the effectiveness of low-rank & sparse decomposition for outlier handling.

As concerns the execution cost, our method outperforms the technique in [19]. Indeed, the method used in our pipeline, is one of the fastest translation synchronization techniques present in the literature as it finds camera positions by eigenvalue-decomposition of a $3n \times 3n$ matrix. Also the rotation synchronization is very efficient, as the R-GoDec Algorithm is based on fast BRP. We cannot directly compare the performances of [17], as the code is in C++, but we draw the attention of the reader on the outlier removal step, which consists in performing Bayesian inference on cycles within the epipolar graph, analysing the deviation from the identity. The number of cycles analysed must be high in order to make meaningful statistical inference, resulting in a computationally expensive technique.

Finally, in Figure 1 we report the 3D point cloud obtained with our system in the case of the Castle-P30 sequence. Even if these images contain repetitive windows, resulting in outlying two-view geometries, we are able to recover the 3D structure accurately.

Fig. 1. Left: sample images of the Castle-P30 dataset. Right: sparse 3D reconstruction obtained with our pipeline. The root-mean-squared reprojection error (RMSE) is 0.1681 pixels.

5 Conclusion

In this paper we proposed a global SfM pipeline, based on the synchronization of relative motions. We combined a robust rotation synchronization technique with a fast translation synchronization method from the state of the art. Absolute rotations are computed through low-rank & sparse matrix decomposition (R-GoDec), while absolute locations are recovered through eigenvalue decomposition. The resulting system inherits robustness from R-GoDec and efficiency from both matrix decompositions. Thus it is able to recover camera motion accurately, even in the presence of outliers, achieving low computational cost, as demonstrated by the experiments.

References

1. Arie-Nachimson, M., Kovalsky, S.Z., Kemelmacher-Shlizerman, I., Singer, A., Basri, R.: Global motion estimation from point matches. In: International Conference on 3D Imaging, Modeling, Processing, Visualization and Transmission, pp. 81–88 (2012)

2. Arrigoni, F., Rossi, B., Magri, L., Fragneto, P., Fusiello, A.: Robust absolute rotation estimation via low-rank and sparse matrix decomposition. In: International Conference on 3D Vision, pp. 491–498 (2014)
3. Beck, A., Teboulle, M.: A fast iterative shrinkage-thresholding algorithm for linear inverse problems. SIAM Journal on Imaging Sciences 2(1), 183–202 (2009)
4. Brand, M., Antone, M., Teller, S.: Spectral solution of large-scale extrinsic camera calibration as a graph embedding problem. In: Pajdla, T., Matas, J.G. (eds.) ECCV 2004. LNCS, vol. 3022, pp. 262–273. Springer, Heidelberg (2004)
5. Cai, J., Candes, E.J., Shen, Z.: A singular value thresholding algorithm for matrix completion. SIAM Journal on Optimization 20(4), 1956–1982 (2008)
6. Candès, E.J., Li, X., Ma, Y., Wright, J.: Robust principal component analysis? Journal of the ACM 58(3), 11:1–11:37 (2011)
7. Candès, E.J., Tao, T.: The power of convex relaxation: near-optimal matrix completion. IEEE Transactions on Information Theory 56(5), 2053–2080 (2010)
8. Chatterjee, A., Govindu, V.M.: Efficient and robust large-scale rotation averaging. In: International Conference on Computer Vision, pp. 521–528 (2013)
9. Govindu, V.M.: Combining two-view constraints for motion estimation. In: Conference on Computer Vision and Pattern Recognition, pp. 218–225 (2001)
10. Hampel, F., Rousseeuw, P., Ronchetti, E., Stahel, W.: Robust Statistics: the Approach Based on Influence Functions, 2nd edn. John Wiley & Sons (1986)
11. Hartley, R., Aftab, K., Trumpf, J.: L1 rotation averaging using the Weiszfeld algorithm. In: Conference on Computer Vision and Pattern Recognition pp. 3041–3048 (2011)
12. Hartley, R.I., Trumpf, J., Dai, Y., Li, H.: Rotation averaging. International Journal of Computer Vision 103, 267–305 (2013)
13. He, J., Balzano, L., Szlam, A.: Incremental gradient on the Grassmannian for online foreground and background separation in subsampled video. In: Conference on Computer Vision and Pattern Recognition, pp. 1568–1575 (2012)
14. Keshavan, R.H., Montanari, A., Oh, S.: Matrix completion from a few entries. IEEE Transactions on Information Theory 56(6), 2980–2998 (2010)
15. Martinec, D., Pajdla, T.: Robust rotation and translation estimation in multiview reconstruction. In: Conference on Computer Vision and Pattern Recognition, pp. 1–8 (2007)
16. Mosteller, F., Tukey, J.: Data Analysis and Regression: A Second Course in Statistics. Addison-Wesley series in behavioral science. Addison-Wesley (1977)
17. Moulon, P., Monasse, P., Marlet, R.: Global Fusion of Relative Motions for Robust, Accurate and Scalable Structure from Motion. In: International Conference on Computer Vision, pp. 1568–1575 (2013)
18. Olsson, C., Enqvist, O.: Stable structure from motion for unordered image collections. In: Heyden, A., Kahl, F. (eds.) SCIA 2011. LNCS, vol. 6688, pp. 524–535. Springer, Heidelberg (2011)
19. Ozyesil, O., Singer, A., Basri, R.: Stable camera motion estimation using convex programming. SIAM Journal on Imaging Sciences 8(2), 1220–1262 (2015)
20. Snavely, N., Seitz, S.M., Szeliski, R.: Photo tourism: Exploring photo collections in 3D. ACM Transactions on Graphics 25(3), 835–846 (2006)
21. Strecha, C., von Hansen, W., Gool, L.J.V., Fua, P., Thoennessen, U.: On benchmarking camera calibration and multi-view stereo for high resolution imagery. In: Conference on Computer Vision and Pattern Recognition, pp. 1–8 (2008)
22. Toldo, R., Gherardi, R., Farenzena, M., Fusiello, A.: Hierarchical structure-and-motion recovery from uncalibrated images. Computer Vision and Image Understanding (2015)

23. Waters, A.E., Sankaranarayanan, A.C., Baraniuk, R.G.: SpaRCS: recovering low-rank and sparse matrices from compressive measurements. In: Neural Information Processing Systems, pp. 1089–1097 (2011)
24. Wilson, K., Snavely, N.: Robust global translations with 1DSfM. In: Fleet, D., Pajdla, T., Schiele, B., Tuytelaars, T. (eds.) ECCV 2014. LNCS, vol. 8691, pp. 61–75. Springer, Heidelberg (2014)
25. Zhou, T., Tao, D.: GoDec: randomized low-rank & sparse matrix decomposition in noisy case. In: International Conference on Machine Learning, pp. 33–40 (2011)

Novel View-Synthesis from Multiple Sources for Conversion to 3DS

Francesco Malapelle[1]([✉]), Andrea Fusiello[1],
Beatrice Rossi[2], and Pasqualina Fragneto[2]

[1] Università di Udine - DIEGM, Via Delle Scienze 208, Udine, Italy
francesco.malapelle@uniud.it
[2] STMicroelectronics - AST Lab, Via Camillo Olivetti 2, Agrate Brianza (MB), Italy

Abstract. In this paper we confront the problem of uncalibrated view synthesis, i.e. rendering novel images from two, or more images without any knowledge on camera parameters. The method builds on the computation of planar parallax and focuses on the application of converting a monocular image sequence to a 3D stereo video, a problem that requires the positioning of the virtual camera outside the actual motion trajectory. The paper addresses both geometric and practical issues related to the rendering. We validate our method by showing both quantitative and qualitative results.

Keywords: Image-based rendering · View-synthesis · 3DS video

1 Introduction

View Synthesis (VS) or *Image Based Rendering* (IBR) is the generation of novel images as if they were captured from virtual viewpoints, starting from a set of actual images or frames. Applications include the generation of a 3D stereo (3DS) video from a monocular one [3,14,24,26] and the upsampling of video sequences in order to achieve slow-motion effects (e.g., [4,17]).

The rendering of virtual images requires some geometry information, either explicit (depth) or implicit (depth-proxies), and suitable warping functions. When cameras are *calibrated*, i.e. when both internal and external parameters are available, given the depth of an image point, it is straightforward to compute the position of the point in virtual image from any viewpoint. Techniques based on this paradigm, known as *Depth Image Based Rendering* (DIBR), have been extensively studied and several solutions are available in the literature ([27] and references therein).

When dealing with the 3DS conversion problem, calibration data is hardly available. Despite this, many works addressing this application ([3,14,24,26]) assume some knowledge on the camera parameters, and fall within the DIBR family described above. The *uncalibrated* view synthesis (UVS) is less explored and more challenging for several reasons.

© Springer International Publishing Switzerland 2015
V. Murino and E. Puppo (Eds.): ICIAP 2015, Part I, LNCS 9279, pp. 456–467, 2015.
DOI: 10.1007/978-3-319-23231-7_41

First of all, depth cannot be used in uncalibrated situations, and suitable depth-proxies must be defined, together with proper warping functions based on fundamental matrices [16], trilinear tensors [2], or plane-parallax representation [13,22].

Second, specifying the external *orientation* (position and attitude) of virtual views is unnatural, since they are embedded in a projective frame, linked to the Euclidean one by an *unknown* projective transformation. Only few works address this problem. In [7] an automatic method based on the planar parallax as a geometry proxy is presented: given two or more reference images, the possible uncalibrated orientations describe a 1-parametric trajectories obtained interpolating or extrapolating the relative motion among reference images. This approach is expanded in [10] by extending to 3-parametric trajectories, thus allowing additional positions along and orthogonally the line of sight, and in [6] by defining a 1-parametric rectified trajectory that, when derectified, is compatible with the one in [7], and is more resilient to errors induced by poor epipolar geometry estimation. In the upsampling of video sequences the virtual views are always very close to the reference view, hence simple interpolation along motion vectors is widely used.

Finally – but this issue is shared with DIBR technique, several sub-problems have to be addressed when applying warping functions: *folding*, which occurs when two or more pixels in the reference image are warped to the same pixel in the virtual image, *holes*, which may be caused either by occlusions or by missing geometric information, and *resampling*, due to the discrete nature of digital images.

Contributions. In this paper we present a fully automatic UVS pipeline which addresses most of the critical problems arising in uncalibrated scenarios. The method takes inspiration from the pipeline presented in [8], but instead of transferring points directly from the reference image to the novel one (forward), we use a *backward mapping* strategy which yields finer results. Moreover, we combine information coming from *multiple reference images*, blending several parallax maps into one. At last, we propose a simple and suitable method to fill holes in the final virtual image and cope with resampling artefacts.

2 Background

In this section we cover some of the background notions that are needed to understand the method. In Subsection 2.1 we introduce planar parallax as an uncalibrated proxy for the depth. In Subsection 2.2 we describe the theory of the uncalibrated camera orientation specification, based on [7].

2.1 Planar Parallax

Planar parallax represents the displacement in the apparent position of objects imaged from different points of view with respect to a reference plane, and can be computed from stereo correspondences.

Let us consider a 3D point $\mathbf{M}$ belonging to some plane Π and its projection $(\mathbf{m}_r, \mathbf{m}_i)$ onto the image planes I_r and I_i respectively. There exists a non–singular linear transformation, or homography, that maps $\mathbf{m}_r$ onto $\mathbf{m}_i$, i.e.

$$\mathbf{m}_i \simeq H_\Pi \mathbf{m}_r \tag{1}$$

where H_Π is the homography induced by plane Π and $\simeq$ means equality up to a scale factor. For 3D points $\mathbf{M}$ not belonging to plane Π, the following more general relation holds:

$$\mathbf{m}_i \simeq H_\Pi \mathbf{m}_r + \mathbf{e}_i \gamma \tag{2}$$

where $\mathbf{e}_i$ is the epipole in I_i and γ is the *planar parallax* (or, simply, *parallax* if the context is clear) of $\mathbf{M}$, which can be interpreted as the displacement between the point $H_\Pi \mathbf{m}_r$ mapped via the homography H_Π and its actual corresponding point $\mathbf{m}_i$. With a little abuse of notation, the term parallax is also used to denote the magnitude γ of this displacement (the direction is always towards the epipole $\mathbf{e}_i$).

Note that, when two image planes are coplanar (i.e., motion is along X axis, up to coordinates change) and the reference plane is at infinity, then H_Π is the identity and the epipole is $\mathbf{e}_i = \begin{bmatrix} 1 & 0 & 0 \end{bmatrix}^\top$, thus parallax γ in Eq. (2) results to be proportional to binocular disparity.

Given point correspondences and a plane homography H_Π, parallax values can be obtained for each pixel of the reference frame by solving for γ in Eq. (2):

$$\frac{1}{\gamma} = \frac{(\mathbf{e}_i \times \mathbf{m}_i)^T (\mathbf{m}_i \times H_\Pi \mathbf{m}_r)}{\|\mathbf{m}_i \times H_\Pi \mathbf{m}_r\|^2}. \tag{3}$$

It can be demonstrated that i) γ is proportional to the inverse of the depth of points, and ii) γ depends only on the orientation of I_r and the plane Π, and not on the orientation of I_i. For this reason we will call I_r the *reference* image and I_i the *auxiliary* image. Hence, parallax maps computed with multiple pairs (I_r, I_i) - where i varies - are commensurate, provided the reference plane is fixed.

Please note that this is not true for disparity. Since disparity is proportional to the reciprocal of the depth and the depth is defined with respect to the focal plane, there must be a common focal plane in order for disparities to be commensurate. This can always be achieved for $N \leq 3$ cameras by rectification (rotating the focal planes around the optical centres until they coincide with the plane defined by the three centres), but cannot be guaranteed for more cameras, unless camera centres lies on a plane (see [18] for more details).

In summary, the parallax can be seen as a useful generalization of the depth in the uncalibrated case, and as a generalization of disparity to unrestricted camera configurations. In the case where camera calibration is unavailable and the camera undergoes a general motion, *planar parallax* [21], can be profitably employed as a depth-proxy.

2.2   Uncalibrated Motion Description

If the parallax γ is known, since it does not depend on the auxiliary image, it is possible to exploit Eq. (2) in order to map points from the reference image I_r onto a virtual image I_v. Specifically, one must substitute H_Π with the homography of the plane Π between I_r and I_v, namely H_Π^{rv}, and and $\mathbf{e}_i$ with the epipole in I_v, namely $\mathbf{e}_v$.

In [8] it is described how to specify the so-called *uncalibrated motions*

$$D_{rv} = \begin{bmatrix} H_\Pi^{rv} & \mathbf{e}_v \\ 0 & 1 \end{bmatrix} \tag{4}$$

when the reference plane Π is the plane at infinity (i.e. $H_\Pi = H_\infty$) and D_{rv} is the orientation of the virtual camera.

Let us consider the uncalibrated motion of the reference image wrt the auxiliary one:

$$D_{ri} = \begin{bmatrix} H_\Pi^{ri} & \mathbf{e}_i \\ 0 & 1 \end{bmatrix}. \tag{5}$$

It can be noticed that D_{ri} resembles a rigid transformation matrix

$$G_{ri} = \begin{bmatrix} R_{ri} & \mathbf{t}_{ri} \\ 0 & 1 \end{bmatrix} \in SE(3, \mathbb{R}). \tag{6}$$

Specifically D_{ri} and G_{ri} are related by $D_{ri} = \hat{K} G_{ri} \hat{K}^{-1}$ with K being the unknown matrix of the internal parameters of the camera and $\hat{K} = \begin{bmatrix} K & 0 \\ 0 & 1 \end{bmatrix}$. Thanks to this identification (actually it is an isomorphism), and since $SE(3, \mathbb{R})$ is a Lie group, it is possible to continuously parametrize the uncalibrated motion of the virtual camera as:

$$D_{rv} := D_{ri}^t := \exp\left(t \log(D_{ri})\right) \quad t \in \mathbb{R}. \tag{7}$$

Varying the value of t, we obtain a 1-parameter family orientations which naturally interpolates/extrapolates the orientations of the of reference and the auxiliary cameras along a geodesic path.

The infinite plane homography H_Π^{rv}, along with the epipole $\mathbf{e}_v$ needed in Eq. (2) for the view synthesis can be extracted from D_{rv} according to Eq. (4).

3   Proposed Method

In this section we describe the steps of our method. The input is a set of reference images I_r and a set (not necessarily disjoint) of auxiliary images I_i. For each of the reference images one or more parallax maps are computed with the support of auxiliary images I_i (the ones with the highest overlap with I_r). For example, in the 3DS application there is a single reference image and typically two auxiliary images (previous and subsequent frame). In the upsampling case there are two reference images (the two frames that are to be interpolated) which – in turn – play the role of the auxiliary ones (see Fig. 1). These parallax maps are transferred (forward) to the virtual image I_v and merged together. The resulting map is then used to synthesize I_v by (backward) mapping to the "right" pixel in the "right" source image.

Please note that the use of parallax instead of disparity is crucial to allow the fusion of multiple parallax maps, as discussed in Sec. 2.

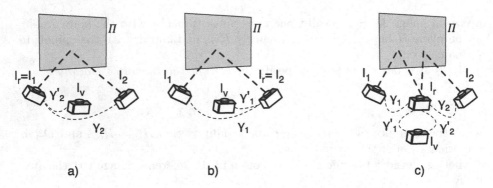

Fig. 1. a) and b) represent the interpolation scheme, with I_1 and I_2 exchanging the role of reference and auxiliary image. c) is the 3DS scenario where there is one reference frame and the neighbours are the auxiliary images. In both cases the the parallax map for I_v results from the fusion of γ_1' and γ_2'.

3.1 Virtual Camera Orientation

In the upsampling application the orientation of the virtual camera interpolates between two actual ones, hence it can be specified by computing D_{rv} using Eq. (7) and selecting $t \in [0, 1]$.

In the 3DS conversion application, on the contrary, the virtual camera position is alongside the actual one, i.e., outside its trajectory. Assuming that the video has been shot with zero roll angle, i.e., the image rows are parallel to the horizon, H_Π^{rv} and $\mathbf{e}_v$ can be specified as follows. Since there is no rotation between the reference image and the virtual one (images are coplanar), the infinite plane homography H_Π^{rv} is the identity matrix. As for the epipole, $\mathbf{e}_v = \begin{bmatrix} t\ 0\ 0 \end{bmatrix}^T$ with $t \in \mathbb{R}^+$, since the virtual viewpoint is displaced horizontally. Thus the orientation of the virtual camera can be computed as

$$D_{rv} = \begin{bmatrix} 1\ 0\ 0\ t \\ 0\ 1\ 0\ 0 \\ 0\ 0\ 1\ 0 \end{bmatrix}, t \in \mathbb{R}^+. \tag{8}$$

3.2 Stereo Processing

The purpose of this block of the algorithm is to compute the parallax value γ for each pixel of the reference image I_r, with the support of an auxiliary image to constitute a stereo pair.

First the image pair is rectified. Since the internal parameters are unknown, we use the uncalibrated procedure described in [9], which relies on sparse correspondences. To this end, first SIFT features are extracted in both images and descriptors are matched, and then a RANSAC estimation of the fundamental matrix is performed in order to discard outlier matches. Uncalibrated rectification seeks the homographies T_2 and T_1 that make the original matching points satisfy the epipolar geometry of a *normal* stereo pair. Stereo matching produces two disparity maps, one referred to I_r and the other to I_i.

At this point we perform some post-processing on the disparity maps. First we use a simple hole-filling technique as the one suggested in [20]. Afterwards, we use anisotropic diffusion [19] to smooth out the maps without compromising the edges. At last we run a left-right consistency check to gather precious occlusion (i.e., visibility) information. The disparity maps are used to obtain a set of dense correspondences that are then derectified using the inverse rectifying homographies.

Ultimately, parallax values are computed using Eq. (3) for each pixel: the dense set of correspondences $\mathbf{m}_r^k \leftrightarrow \mathbf{m}_i^k$ on the pair of images (I_r, I_i) is known from the stereo matching step; the collineation is $H_\Pi^{ri} = T_2^{-1}T_1$ and epipole $\mathbf{e}_i$ is estimated from epipolar geometry. As a by-product of the rectification method [9], H_Π approximates the homography of the plane at infinity.

3.3   Forward Mapping of Parallax Maps

Starting from a parallax map for the reference image I_r, we want to obtain a map referred to the virtual I_v instead.

First we generate a set of corresponding points between I_r and I_v by instantiating Eq. (2) as

$$\mathbf{m}_v \simeq H_\Pi^{rv}\mathbf{m}_r + \mathbf{e}_v\gamma \qquad (9)$$

where H_Π^{rv} is the infinite plane homography between the reference image I_r and the virtual one I_v and $\mathbf{e}_v$ is the epipole of I_v. Quantities H_Π^{rv} and e_v are specified through the parameter t in Eq. (7) which encodes the inter-ocular separation.

This process is a *forward mapping*: points in the original image are mapped forward, to the virtual image. Once we obtain the set of corresponding points among the reference image and the novel image we can compute parallax values with respect to our novel image using Eq. (3).

As it is well known, forward mapping raises some problems, for it is necessary to deal with small holes in the destination images due to the non-surjectivity of the map and to cope with its non-injectivity, causing the *folding* effect.

Probabilistic Splatting. In order to deal with the non-surjectivity issue, we developed a randomized technique that account for the quantization inherent to the forward mapping.

First, we generate noise in the form of random values drawn from the standard uniform distribution on the open interval $(-0.5, 0.5)$ (the amplitude of the interval is chosen to be equal to the maximum error introduced by the coordinates rounding). The noise is added to the non-integer coordinates $\mathbf{m}_v$ in Eq. (9) which are then rounded to their closest integer value. The procedure is repeated for n times (we choose $n = 100$) and all the perturbed parallax maps are merged into the final one by averaging them. This approach has two main advantages: i) as n increases, the process will tend to approximate a proper linear interpolation between the neighbouring pixels, based on the distance from the integer values (i.e. the decimal parts of the coordinates) ii) this procedure fills holes in the map, since pixels with undefined value are likely to be filled with the value of the neighbouring valid ones.

Folding. Folding occurs when different source pixels are mapped to the same destination pixel. This phenomenon is due to the modification of the viewpoint, when two points that were visible in the original image fall along the same line of sight in the new image. As most approaches in literature, we deal with this problem by selecting the pixel with the greater disparity which, by definition will be occluding the one with a smaller disparity value.

3.4   Merging of Parallax Maps

At this point we have a collection of independent parallax maps for I_v and the purpose of this step is to merge these maps into one, in order to reduce noise and fill holes.

Observe that even though these maps are commensurable, they differ by a global scale factor s. However, due to noise and outliers, the factor will not be unique for the entire image, thus we estimate it from the distribution of the pixel-wise ratios in a robust way using the Median Absolute Deviation and the x84 rejection rule [11].

Once the maps are brought to the same scale we merge them into a final one by keeping the highest parallax value in each pixel, where holes have conventionally assigned $-\infty$.

This fused parallax map is accompanied by a *source map* that records for each element of the parallax map, which of the reference images it originates from (in case of multiple I_r). Together they define a mapping from I_v to the reference images that will be exploited in the actual rendering of I_v, described in the next section.

3.5   Backward Mapping of Colour

In the final stage of the method, the pixel grid of the virtual image is used as a reference to determine corresponding point in the reference images.

This process is a *backward mapping*, since points in the virtual image are mapped (backward), to points in the reference images to get a colour assigned. Again, we rely on Eq. (2) and we rewrite it as

$$\mathbf{m}_r \simeq H_H^{vr}\mathbf{m}_v + \mathbf{e}_r\gamma \tag{10}$$

Where H_H^{vr} and $\mathbf{e}_r$ are obtained according to Eq. (4), but this time from matrix D_{rv}^{-1}, where D_{rv} is the one defined in Eq. (7).

The formula is applied pixels-wise using as the reference image the one specified in the source map. Bilinear interpolation is used to assign values to non-integer coordinates.

Occlusion Filling. There can be points that are visible in the novel image, but for which a parallax value could not be computed, because they are not visible in the reference images or because of failure of the stereo matching. Such holes can only be filled heuristically. In our method, we build a binary map that estimates local foreground/background segmentation: on the disparity map, for each unassigned pixel we compute the variance of its neighbourhood. A high variance indicates the presence of multiple depth layers, thus it is likely that an object in the foreground is occluding the background and the pixel is marked as background. Otherwise it is marked as foreground. This procedure is based on the idea presented in greater details in [20]. Once the binary map is built, we use it to fill holes on the virtual view, using the average colour of the neighbours that fall within the same class.

4   Experiments

We report two sets of experiments that validate our approach. The first set focuses on the forward vs backward mapping issue, and shows quantitative results by comparing our rendered images against ground truth images. The second set of experiments shows the visual results of the rendering of a virtual frames in a 3DS conversion scenario, where the position of the virtual camera is set alongside the actual one.

First we validate the choice of the backward mapping (BWM) approach – described in Sec. 3.5 and previous ones – against the forward mapping (FWM). FWM, used e.g. in [8], is the fusion of two virtual images obtained from the reference images. Both approaches are evaluated before the hole filling post-processing step.

In order to factor out the inaccuracies of the stereo matching we used the Middlebury 2006 dataset ([12]) which provides ground truth disparity maps. Each sequence of the dataset is composed by seven frames, we used the second and the sixth frame as the reference pair to synthesize the middle frame, which corresponds to the fourth frame. We then compared the ground truth image with the virtual one and obtained the results reported in Tab. 1. As figures of merit we considered the structure similarity index (SSIM) [23], the signal-to-noise ration (SNR) and the absolute error rate (ABS) where pixels that differ from the true value for more than 1 pixel and unassigned ones are counted as errors. The result is that BWM consistently outperforms FWM showing its better ability to recreate the virtual image.

Finally, we report some qualitative results of the 3DS conversion in Fig. 3. The images are taken from [25] and from [12]. Stereo matching have been carried out with the implementation of [15] available in OpenCV; maps are reported in Fig. 2. Despite a few artefacts – mainly due to failures of the stereo matching – the results are convincing and visually plausible.

Fig. 2. Parallax maps obtained from the stereo matching.

Table 1. Comparison of performances of our BWM approach against the FWM employed in [8]. SSIM: and SNR the higher the better. ABS: the lower the better. See text for further explanations.

	BWM				FWM		
Sequence	SSIM	SNR	ABS		SSIM	SNR	ABS
Aloe	0.77	-33.59	33.74		0.72	-34.15	37.25
Baby1	0.89	-30.48	33.83		0.87	-30.80	34.79
Baby2	0.90	-26.91	31.67		0.88	-27.04	33.75
Baby3	0.88	-25.80	21.73		0.86	-26.45	23.35
Bowling1	0.88	-31.80	46.56		0.87	-31.90	46.99
Bowling2	0.87	-30.81	37.62		0.85	-31.23	39.04
Cloth1	0.96	-20.94	39.59		0.93	-19.77	40.74
Cloth2	0.91	-27.83	42.95		0.86	-28.75	44.66
Cloth3	0.91	-26.37	37.21		0.87	-27.20	39.08
Cloth4	0.88	-31.44	35.91		0.82	-32.17	39.33
Flowerpots	0.89	-28.56	28.45		0.87	-28.73	30.23
Lampshade1	0.83	-33.99	24.36		0.82	-34.41	25.04
Lampshade2	0.84	-33.92	22.90		0.83	-34.36	23.33
Midd1	0.91	-29.85	26.57		0.89	-30.10	28.56
Midd2	0.90	-30.01	44.92		0.89	-30.24	46.03
Monopoly	0.86	-34.04	90.35		0.83	-34.33	89.11
Plastic	0.94	-25.85	29.51		0.92	-26.54	29.49
Rocks1	0.92	-21.67	27.82		0.88	-22.76	31.11
Rocks2	0.93	-21.22	33.51		0.89	-22.32	35.77
Woods1	0.92	-27.89	40.22		0.90	-27.76	42.10
Woods2	0.94	-25.05	28.45		0.92	-25.05	29.70

misprint

Fig. 3. Examples of the 3DS output. From left to right: reference image (left eye), virtual image (right eye), red-cyan anaglyph.

5   Conclusions

We presented a pipeline for uncalibrated view-synthesis of novel images. Our method is fully automatic and geometrically sound. We tested it on the conversion to 3DS, where the method produces promising results.

Future work will address the limitations of this work. Hole filling in the virtual image needs to be improved; where no information is available in the source images inpainting techniques (e.g. [5]) should be adopted. The probabilistic splatting step could also be improved by the working on superpixels (e.g.[1]). Heuristics to mitigate the effects of matching failures will be also investigated.

References

1. Achanta, R., Shaji, A., Smith, K., Lucchi, A., Fua, P., Süsstrunk, S.: SLIC Superpixels Compared to State-of-the-art Superpixel Methods. IEEE Trans. on Patt. Analysis and Machine Intell. **34**(11), 2274–2282 (2012)

2. Avidan, S., Shashua, A.: Novel view synthesis by cascading trilinear tensors. IEEE Trans Vis. and Comp. Graph. **4**(4), 293–306 (1998)
3. Cheng, C.C., Li, C.T., Huang, P.S., Lin, T.K., Tsai, Y.M., Chen, L.G.: A block-based 2D-to-3D conversion system with bilateral filter. In: Int. Conf. on Consumer Electronics, pp. 1–2 (2009)
4. Choi, B.T., Lee, S.H., Ko, S.J.: New frame rate up-conversion using bi-directional motion estimation. IEEE Trans. on Consumer Electronics **46**(3), 603–609 (2000)
5. Criminisi, A., Pérez, P., Toyama, K.: Region filling and object removal by exemplar-based image inpainting. IEEE Trans. on Image Proc. **13**(9), 1200–1212 (2004)
6. Fragneto, P., Fusiello, A., Magri, L., Rossi, B., Ruffini, M.: Uncalibrated view synthesis with homography interpolation. In: 2nd Joint 3DIM/3DPVT Conf., pp. 270–277 (2012)
7. Fusiello, A.: Specifying virtual cameras in uncalibrated view synthesis. IEEE Trans. on Circuits and Systems for Video Technology **17**(5), 604–611 (2007)
8. Fusiello, A., Irsara, L.: An uncalibrated view-synthesis pipeline. In: Proc. Int. Conf. on Image Analysis and Proc., pp. 609–614 (2007)
9. Fusiello, A., Irsara, L.: Quasi-euclidean epipolar rectification of uncalibrated images. Machine Vis. and Appl. **22**(4), 663–670 (2011)
10. Gigengack, F., Jiang, X.: Improved uncalibrated view synthesis by extended positioning of virtual cameras and image quality optimization. In: Zha, H., Taniguchi, R., Maybank, S. (eds.) ACCV 2009, Part II. LNCS, vol. 5995, pp. 438–447. Springer, Heidelberg (2010)
11. Hampel, F.R., Ronchetti, E.M., Rousseeuw, P.J., Stahel, W.A.: Robust statistics: the approach based on influence functions, vol. 114. John Wiley & Sons (2011)
12. Hirschmuller, H., Scharstein, D.: Evaluation of cost functions for stereo matching. In: IEEE Conf. on Comp. Vis. and Patt. Rec., pp. 1–8 (2007)
13. Irani, M., Anandan, P.: Parallax geometry of pairs of points for 3d scene analysis. In: Buxton, B.F., Cipolla, R. (eds.) ECCV 1996. LNCS, vol. 1064, pp. 17–30. Springer, Heidelberg (1996)
14. Jung, Y.J., Baik, A., Kim, J., Park, D.: A novel 2D-to-3D conversion technique based on relative height-depth cue. In: IS&T/SPIE Electronic Imaging, pp. 72371U–72371U (2009)
15. Kolmogorov, V., Monasse, P., Tan, P.: Kolmogorov and Zabihs Graph Cuts Stereo Matching Algorithm. Image Processing on Line **4**, 220–251 (2014)
16. Laveau, S., Faugeras, O.: 3-d scene representation as a collection of images and foundamental matrices. In: Proc. Int. Conf. Patt. Rec., 1, pp. 689–691 (1994)
17. Lee, S.H., Kwon, O., Park, R.H.: Weighted-adaptive motion-compensated frame rate up-conversion. IEEE Trans. on Consumer Electronics **49**(3), 485–492 (2003)
18. Malapelle, F., Fusiello, A., Rossi, B., Piccinelli, E., Fragneto, P.: Uncalibrated dynamic stereo using parallax. In: Proc. Int. Symp. on Image and Signal Proc. and Analysis (2013)
19. Perona, P., Malik, J.: Scale-space and edge detection using anisotropic diffusion. IEEE Trans. on Patt. Analysis and Machine Intell. **12**(7), 629–639 (1990)
20. Ramachandran, G., Rupp, M.: Multiview synthesis from stereo views. In: Int. Workshop on Systems, Signals and Image Proc., pp. 341–345 (2012)
21. Sawhney, H.S.: 3D geometry from planar parallax. In: IEEE Conf. on Comp. Vis. and Patt. Rec., pp. 929–934 (1994)
22. Shashua, A., Navab, N.: Relative affine structure: Canonical model for 3D from 2D geometry and applications. IEEE Trans. on Patt. Analysis and Machine Intell. **18**(9), 873–883 (1996)

23. Wang, Z., Bovik, A.C., Sheikh, H.R., Simoncelli, E.P.: Image quality assessment: from error visibility to structural similarity. IEEE Trans. on Image Proc. **13**(4), 600–612 (2004)
24. Zhang, G., Hua, W., Qin, X., Wong, T.T., Bao, H.: Stereoscopic video synthesis from a monocular video. IEEE Trans. on Vis. and Comp. Graph. **13**(4), 686–696 (2007)
25. Zhang, G., Jia, J., Wong, T.T., Bao, H.: Consistent depth maps recovery from a video sequence. IEEE Trans. on Patt. Analysis and Machine Intell. **31**(6), 974–988 (2009)
26. Zhang, L., Vázquez, C., Knorr, S.: 3D-TV content creation: automatic 2D-to-3D video conversion. IEEE Trans. on Broadcasting **57**(2), 372–383 (2011)
27. Zhu, C., Zhao, Y., Yu, L., Tanimoto, M.: 3D-TV System with Depth-image-based Rendering. Springer (2014)

Dynamic Optimal Path Selection
for 3D Triangulation with Multiple Cameras

Mara Pistellato, Filippo Bergamasco, Andrea Albarelli[✉], and Andrea Torsello

Dipartimento di Scienze Ambientali, Informatica e Statistica,
Università Ca' Foscari Venezia, via Torino 155, Venice, Italy
albarelli@unive.it

Abstract. When a physical feature is observed by two or more cameras, its position in the 3D space can be easily recovered by means of triangulation. However, for such estimate to be reliable, accurate intrinsic and extrinsic calibration of the capturing devices must be available. Extrinsic parameters are usually the most problematic, especially when dealing with a large number of cameras. This is due to several factors, including the inability to observe the same reference object over the entire network and the sometimes unavoidable displacement of cameras over time. With this paper we propose a game-theoretical method that can be used to dynamically select the most reliable rigid motion between cameras observing the same feature point. To this end we only assume to have a (possibly incomplete) graph connecting cameras whose edges are labelled with extrinsic parameters obtained through pairwise calibration.

Keywords: Game theory · 3D reconstruction · Extrinsic calibration

1 Introduction

Two points of view are in general enough to reconstruct 3D information from 2D projections. Nevertheless, in many practical scenarios, the adoption of multiple independent cameras is the preferred choice. This is the case, for instance, when people have to be tracked within large areas [1] and strong resilience to occlusion is sought [2].A collection of different points of view can also result from dynamic scenarios, where cameras are mounted on drones [3] or images are collected by different users on social networks and online services [4]. Camera grids can also be very helpful when the phenomenon to be studied is difficult to analyze from a single point of view. This happens with many Computer Vision tasks, ranging from human action recognition [5] to video surveillance [6] and tracking [7]. The adoption of multiple cameras could finally lead to improved accuracy with image-based surface reconstruction [8], especially when dealing with complex artifacts [9]. Of course, for any of these applications to be feasible, the geometry of the cameras must be known, at least to some extent. For this reason, a lot of calibration methods that can be used to recover intrinsic and extrinsic parameters have been proposed. Classic approaches use artificial

© Springer International Publishing Switzerland 2015
V. Murino and E. Puppo (Eds.): ICIAP 2015, Part I, LNCS 9279, pp. 468–479, 2015.
DOI: 10.1007/978-3-319-23231-7_42

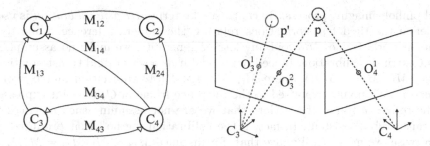

Fig. 1. Overview of the addressed scenario. Multiple cameras are loosely registered through a partially incomplete graph of extrinsic transformation. A physical point is observed by different cameras through an imaging process afflicted by random positional noise and a possibly wrong labelling.

targets with known geometry [10] to compute intrinsic parameters and simultaneously assess the relative pose of each camera [11]. Other methods perform pairwise calibrations that can be subsequently made consistent with respect to a reference world [12]. It is also very common to exploit the scene itself to obtain simultaneous extrinsic calibration ad structure reconstruction [13]. Finally, many techniques have been proposed to calibrate a whole camera network at the same time [14,15]. Regardless of the method of choice, any calibration procedure will result in some degree of inaccuracy. In addition, even very accurate calibrations could deteriorate over time, as a consequence of movements of the cameras, slight changes in the network topology or drift of intrinsic parameters. With this paper we are not proposing a new calibration method. Neither are we interested in how the calibration has been performed. We are just assuming that a (possibly large) set of cameras are available and that some process assessed their extrinsic position up to its best accuracy. Within this scenario, our goal is not to enhance the calibration or to correct its precision. Rather we are proposing a consensus-based approach to select the more reliable set of extrinsic parameters that can be used to perform triangulation given the current calibration. This happens dynamically and depends on several factors, including the position of the material points to be triangulated, the quality of the observations on the image plane and the quality of initial extrinsic estimate.

2   General Scenario and Main Contributions

The general scenario we are working with is well represented in Fig. 1. We are dealing with a network of cameras $C = \{C_1, C_2 \ldots C_n\}$, each referred by a unique label C_i. The typical size of such network can range from a few to several tenths of independent devices. The cameras have been previously calibrated for both intrinsic and extrinsic parameters. Within this paper, we are using the term *intrinsic calibration* to refer to all the parameters needed to convert the image acquired by the cameras to normalized image planes, as captured by an ideal pinhole imaging process. By contrast, the term *extrinsic calibration* is used to define the rigid transformations relating the camera reference frame to a common world frame. To avoid any loss of generality, we make no assumption about extrinsic calibration. Indeed, we model it as a set of rigid transformations $M = \{M_{11}, M_{12} \ldots M_{nn}\}$ where M_{ij} is a 4×4 roto-translation matrix which transforms 3D points expressed in the reference frame of C_j to point expressed in the reference frame of C_i. Note that we are not assuming such matrices to be transitively consistent. In fact, if the calibration method that produced M is pairwise, we might easily have that, for instance $M_{13} \neq M_{12}M_{23} \neq M_{14}M_{43}$. Differently, if the calibration method is global, all the elements of M will be consistent with respect to the same world, still this does not mean that they exhibit the same accuracy, since it really depends on how they are built. For instance, if they are built by incrementally chaining pairwise registrations, errors can easily add up. Note that, although we are assuming $M_{ii} = I$, we are not pretending $M_{ij} = M_{ji}$ to be true, since this property also depends on how the extrinsic calibration was performed. Most of current literature aims to enforce consistency in the calibration graph $G = \{C, M\}$. This usually happens by means of some averaging process or by a-priori selection of optimal paths in G. With this paper we take quite the opposite approach. In fact, we propose to maintain the whole graph G and to select the optimal weighted subset of paths (extracted from $\mathcal{P}(M)$) for every triangulation to be performed. To this end we assume that two or more cameras from C are able to observe the same physical point p (see the right half of Fig. 1). This will result in a number of points on the image planes, which are subject to random observation uncertainty (usually modeled as zero-mean Gaussian additive noise). In addition, since a scene can comprise several physical points, the labelling process that identifies the same feature throughout all the observing cameras could fail, resulting in outliers related to wrongly labelled observations. In the following we will refer to observation a from camera i as O_i^a. An example is shown in Fig. 1. Here, cameras C_3 and C_4 are observing material point p. A single observation, labelled O_4^1 is reported by camera C_4. Differently, two observation are available from camera C_3, being O_3^2 generated by the correct point of interest p, and O_3^1 resulting from a wrong labelling of the p'. In order for the position of p to be recovered from its projections, four elements must be selected: two observations and two paths connecting the observing cameras to the global reference. For instance, if we assume C_1 to be the world reference for our example, two feasible triangulation hypotheses for p could be $(M_{14}M_{43}, O_3^2, M_{14}, O_4^1)$ and $(M_{13}, O_3^1, M_{12}M_{24}, O_4^1)$.

The ultimate goal of our method is to find the best way to triangulate p. This happens by modeling each possible pair of paths and observations as strategies in a non-cooperative game and by letting them play together until a consistent weighted subset emerges. Key advantages of this approach include the ability to select different paths for different regions for the Euclidean space. This makes sense, since, out of geometrical considerations, is easy to observe that different type of calibration errors will result in non-isotropic inaccuracies throughout the space. Moreover, calibration quality could change over time due to physical changes, making it desirable to dynamically select the optimal paths. Also our method works equally well if extrinsic calibration are consistent with a common space (i.e. transitively closed) and when only loosely related pairwise transformations are available. Finally, by properly defining the compatibility between alternative labelling, we automatically filter outliers from the final solution.

3   Game-Theoretical Optimal Path Selection

Game Theory was introduced in the early 40's by J. von Neumann to model the behavior of entities with competing objectives, and was further developed by J. Nash in the postwar period [16] through the introduction of the Nash equilibrium. According to this view, the emphasis shifts from the search for an optimum shared by the population, to the definition of equilibria between opposing forces. The main intuition is that competitive behavior between agents can be modeled as a *game* where a number of predefined *strategies* are available, and a fixed *payoff* is gained by two individuals when they play a given pair of strategies against each other. Evolutionary Game Theory [17] considers a scenario where pairs of individuals, each pre-programmed with a given strategy, are repeatedly drawn from a large population to play a game, and a selection process allows "fit" individuals to thrive, while driving "unfit" ones to extinction. The idea underlying the adoption of Evolutionary Game Theory for selection is to model each hypothesis as a strategy and let them be played one against the other, until a stable population emerges. We will cast this idea within our context by using paths and observations as hypotheses and the consistence of the related triangulations as their mutual payoff.

3.1   Hypotheses

We define $H = \{H_1, H_2, \cdots, H_n\}$ be the set of n available hypotheses. Each hypothesis is a possible triangulation. To this end, it must include exactly two observations and the two paths connecting the observing cameras to the world frame. Without any loss of generality we can assume the world frame aligned with C_1, this way each hypothesis is a quadruple $(M_{1x} \ldots M_{yi}, O_i^a, M_{1w} \ldots M_{vj}, O_j^b)$. Here $M_{1x} \ldots M_{yi}$ and $M_{1w} \ldots M_{vj}$ are paths that combine a sequence of rigid transformation matrices connecting cameras C_i and C_j to C_1. The accuracy of such paths can vary according to the accuracy of the calibration. O_i^a and O_j^b are two observations of the (hopefully) same physical point on the image planes of camera C_i and C_j. Each hypotesis must include by construction two different cameras, each path must not comprise cycles and must be shorter to a maximum value $maxpath$. Accuracy of observations depends on several sources of noise, usually distributed as a zero-mean Gaussian. In addition, each wrong labelling could result in a totally misplaced point. Given these factors, the correctness of each triangulation depends on both calibration-related and observation-related error sources. It is very difficult, in general, to assess the quality of each hypothesis by looking just at the single 3D point obtained.

3.2   Payoff

As a matter of fact, we are not really interested in the reliability of each hypothesis alone. Rather, our focus is on the definition of a measure of how well two hypotheses play together. This measure is called payoff and should be high if the two hypotheses reliably converge on the same 3D point and low otherwise. The payoff is usually expressed as a function $\pi(i,j) : H \times H \to \mathbb{R}_{\geq 0}$, where i and j are labels to hypotheses H_i and H_j. Since payoffs are defined between all the pairs, an alternative notation is the payoff matrix $\Pi = (\pi_{ij})$, where $(\pi_{ij}) = \pi(i,j)$. Our goal is to define a payoff that can account for both the consensus between reconstruction and their reliability. From each hypothesis H_i it is possible to obtain a 3D point by means of triangulation. We call such point $\boldsymbol{x}(H_i)$. Our method is not affected by the actual triangulation technique used, as long as, in addition to the 3D points, it also return a *skewness* value $s(H_i)$ which measures the distance between the two rays used to recover the material point. The position of the point $\boldsymbol{x}(H_i)$ and the triangulation skewness $s(H_i)$ can be used to build a proper payoff function. In fact, two hypotheses can be deemed to be compatible if the associated 3D points are close. Moreover, each one of them can contribute to the overall reliability measure according to its skewness. Albeit these two error sources are not really independent, we can still reasonably approximate them as a bidimensional Gaussian function:

$$\pi'(i,j) = e^{-\frac{1}{2}(\frac{(|\boldsymbol{x}(H_i)-\boldsymbol{x}(H_j)|)^2}{\sigma_p^2} + \frac{max(s(H_i),s(H_j))^2}{\sigma_s^2})} \tag{1}$$

Where σ_p and σ_s are two parameters that represent respectively the expected standard deviation of point position and of skewness. Note that $(|\boldsymbol{x}(H_i) - \boldsymbol{x}(H_j)|)^2$ is a pairwise measure that is defined between pairs of hypotheses. Differently, $s(H_i)$ and $s(H_j)$ are independent one from the other, thus the *max* operator is needed to account for them within the pairwise function π'.

While π' expresses the degree of consensus between hypothesis, we must also account for special cases where two hypotheses are not compatible regardless of the quality of triangulation. This is the case when the hypotheses include two different observations from the same camera. Indeed this is not possible since we are tracking a single material point, thus one of the two observations must be a wrong labelling. The other unfeasible case consists in the presence of two different paths to the same camera. In fact, while different transformations might be optimal for different points, it makes no sense to use two alternative paths to the same camera for the same point, since it would break the reference to the common world. These constraint can be enforced by explicitly setting a value of zero in the final payoff function.

$$\pi(H_i, H_j)) = \pi((P_\alpha^u, O_\alpha^a, P_{\alpha'}^{u'}, O_{\alpha'}^{a'}), (P_\beta^v, O_\beta^b, P_{\beta'}^{v'}, O_{\beta'}^{b'})) \tag{2}$$

$$= \begin{cases} 0 & \text{if} & \alpha = \beta \wedge (u \neq v \vee a \neq b) \\ & & \alpha' = \beta' \wedge (u' \neq v' \vee a' \neq b') \\ & & \alpha' = \beta \wedge (u' \neq v \vee a' \neq b) \\ & & \alpha = \beta' \wedge (u \neq v' \vee a \neq b') \\ \pi'(i,j) & \text{otherwise} \end{cases}$$

where P_α^u represents a path connecting camera C_α to the world frame.

3.3   Evolution

With the set of hypotheses and payoff at hand, we can perform the evolutionary process needed to select mutually consistent triangulations. To this end we need to define the concept of *population*. That is a discrete probability distribution $x = (x_1, \dots, x_n)^T$ over the available strategies H. Any population vector is bound to lie within the n-dimensional standard simplex $\Delta^n = \{x \in \mathbb{R}^n : x_i \geq 0 \text{ for all } i \in 1 \dots n, \sum_{i=1}^n x_i = 1\}$ The *support* of a population $x \in \Delta^n$, denoted by $\sigma(x)$, is defined as the set of elements chosen with non-zero probability: $\sigma(x) = \{i \in O \mid x_i > 0\}$. In order to find a set of mutually coherent hypotheses, we are interested in finding configurations of the population maximizing the average payoff. Since the total payoff obtained by hypothesis i within a given population x is $(\Pi x)_i = \sum_j \pi_{ij} x_j$, the (weighted) average payoff over all the considered hypotheses is exactly $x^T \Pi x$. Unfortunately, it is not immediate to find the global maximum for $x^T \Pi x$, however local maxima can be obtained using a rather wide class of evolutionary dynamics called *Payoff-Monotonic Dynamics*. A quite common evolutionary process starts by setting an initial population x near the barycenter of the simplex and then proceeds by evolving it through the discrete-time replicator dynamic [18]:

$$x_i(t+1) = x_i(t) \frac{(\Pi x(t))_i}{x(t)^T \Pi x(t)} \tag{3}$$

where x_i is the i-th element of the population and Π the payoff matrix. This family of dynamics are guaranteed to converge to an equilibrium where the support does not include strategies with mutual payoff zero. This means that the constraints expressed in equation (2) are actually guaranteed to be enforced. This approach, while novel within the scenario covered by this paper, has shown to be very successful in addressing a wide range of problems, including feature-based matching [19], medical images segmentation [20] and registration [21], rigid [22] and non-rigid [23] 3D object recognition.

To give to the reader a better understanding of how the process works we illustrate a complete case in Fig. 2. While the example is kept intentionally simple, out of practical reasons, the evolution has been performed actually using the shown payoff matrix and the replication dynamic described by equation (3). Here, we are assuming the netwotk topology and observations shown in Fig. 1. We are also assuming that all the pairwise extrinsic calibrations have been performed with good accuracy, with the exception of M_{14} which is afflicted by a larger error (for whatever reason). Observations O_3^2 and O_4^1 are correctly labeled, albeit subject to measurement error. Observation O_3^1 is an outlier and results from a wrong labeling. We are considering two cameras (i.e. $C = \{C_3, C_4\}$) and a total of four paths, two for each camera (i.e. $M = \{M_{13}, M_{14}M_{43}, M_{14}, M_{12}M_{24}\}$). This result in a total of eight hypotheses, shown in figure. The payoff matrix is shown with color coded entries. Namely we used red to highlight entries

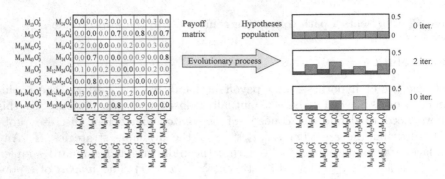

Fig. 2. Example of the selection process applied to the instance of the problem shown in Fig. 1. Please note that this is a very simplified example with a non perfectly accurate payoff matrix (albeit the sown evolution has been computed accurately). See the text for an explanation of this specific example.

that are zero due to the constraints expressed by equation (2). For instance hypotheses $(M_{13}O_3^1, M_{14}O_4^1)$ and $(M_{13}O_3^2, M_{14}O_4^1)$ are not compatible since they include different observations from the same camera. Differently, hypotheses $(M_{13}O_3^1, M_{14}O_4^1)$ and $(M_{13}O_3^1, M_{12}M_{24}O_4^1)$ have zero mutual consensus since they are connecting camera C_4 to the world frame through two different paths. Hypotheses that receive low mutual payoff due to geometrical inconsistencies are highlighted in purple. Basically, they include all the pairs afflicted by the wrong labeling of O_3^1. Other pairwise payoffs are assigned according to the coherence between reconstructions. Blue payoffs are slightly lower than green ones due to the fact that they include the rigid transformation M_{14}, which we assumed to be less accurate. In the right part of the figure we show the actual evolution. The process starts from an uniform distribution, where every hypothesis has the same probability to thrive. After just 2 iterations of equation (3), hypotheses related to outliers start to decrease, due to they low average payoff. After just 10 iteration, only feasible hypotheses survived. Note that paths including the slightly inaccurate transformation M_{14} are less represented in the final population. Indeed, the final distribution can be used to produce a weighted average of the 3D point, rather than just selecting the hypothesis with higher score.

4   Experimental Evaluation

To test our proposed optimal path selection approach we designed a set of synthetic camera networks resembling typical real-world topologies. Testing with a synthetic case allows us to factorize out all the unpredictable error sources and properly analyze the behavior with respect to erroneous observations and inaccurate positioning of the cameras.

We started by generating 3 different network topologies, namely: grid, hemisphere and line. The first is composed by a regular grid of 15 cameras spanning an area of 20×12 centered at the origin and lying onto the xy-plane (Fig 3,

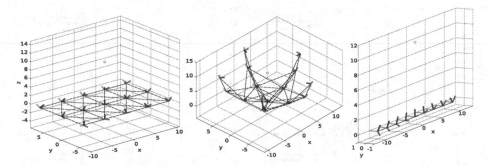

Fig. 3. The 3 generated graph topologies used for experimental evaluation: grid (left), hemisphere (center) and line (right).

left). All the cameras were rotated so that the z-axis points toward the network center $c = (0, 0, 10)^T$. We generated the exact relative motion between couple of cameras whose distance is less than 10, for a total of 88 graph edges. The second (hemisphere) is composed by 16 cameras disposed in a semi-sphere with center c and radius $r = 10$ (Fig 3, center). We placed the cameras reference frame origins with an uniformly distributed angular azimuth and elevation and pointed all the optical axes toward the center. Also in this case, a total of 90 edges describe the relative motions of camera pairs that are less than 10 units apart. Finally, we generated the line network topology as a set of 9 cameras lying on the x-axis, uniformly spaced around the origin and oriented toward c (Fig 3, right). A set of 30 edges links together adjacent cameras. For all the three topologies, camera intrinsic parameters were set with unitary focal length and principal point lying at the origin. Furthermore, we placed the first camera C_1 so that its frame coincides with the world reference frame. From this ground truth, many different perturbed instances of such topologies were generated by means of a normally-distributed additive angular error (with zero mean and standard deviation σ_r) to the rotation matrix of rigid motions associated to each edge.

In our first test we analyze the sensitivity of the proposed method wrt. payoff parameters σ_p and σ_s. In Figure 5 (left) we show the spatial distance, varying σ_p and σ_s, between a reconstructed 3D point and the generated ground truth for a grid topology instance with $\sigma_r = 9.1*10^{-3}$. As expected, there exists a large area around $\sigma_p = 0.08, \sigma_s = 0.12$ in which the interplay between the two parameters leads to satisfactory results. This also give us a clue that the skewness, even if is not a quantity directly measuring the final reconstruction error, can help the effectiveness of the payoff function.

In the second experiment (Fig. 4) we compared the reconstruction accuracy of our approach against "dual-quaternions" [12] and "SBA" [13]. The first method exploits properties of dual-quaternions to diffuse the camera network error and creates a new set of coherent motions to a common reference frame. The latter is commonly used in structure-from-motion applications to simultaneously optimize extrinsic camera parameters and the reconstructed 3D points given their observations on each image plane. Reconstruction error is evaluated for grid,

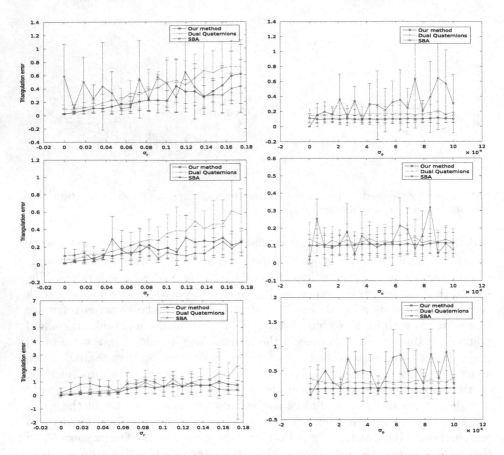

Fig. 4. Comparison between our method, dual-quaternions [12] and SBA [13]. Triangulation error is evaluated while perturbing the graph edges (left col.) and observations (right col.) for grid, hemisphere and line graph topologies (top to bottom).

hemisphere and line topologies (top to bottom row) varying the network graph error σ_r (first column) and observation error σ_o (second column) by means of an additive zero-mean Gaussian error with variance σ_o^2. All the tests were performed by reconstructing a structure of 10 points. For [12], we considered the best triangulation in terms of re-projection error between all the graph paths with less than 3 vertices whereas, for [13], all the structure points were optimized at the same time. We can observe that SBA, even if it has the advantage of recomputing the camera poses while triangulating, mostly suffers from the observation errors. On the contrary, our proposed approach dynamically discards incoherent observations producing structures that are less noisy and more reliable. A similar behaviour can be observed for [12] varying the network graph error σ_r. Since [12] can only diffuse errors without discarding any edge, it suffers from large relative motion displacements that may happen during graph calibration. Overall, our method can deliver the best of the two worlds, being either able to

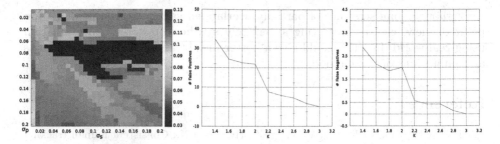

Fig. 5. Left: triangulation error varying σ_p and σ_s. Right: false positives and negatives wrt. inlier/outlier distance ratio K.

smooth the errors by averaging the triangulation among many cameras while still being very effective when selecting a small set of reliable paths and observations. Finally, we tested the behaviour of our method in case of observation outliers. To this extent, we computed the number of false positives (wrong observations still involved in the point triangulation) and false negatives (number of good observations wrongly discarded) in the winning population for many different triangulation attempts varying the observations outlier distribution for the grid network topology. Specifically, we generated exactly one inlier observation (with a random uniform uncertainty of $\sigma_o = 10^{-3}$) and one outlier displaced from the ground truth observation by $K\sigma_o$. The more K is increased, the more the distance on the image plane between inlier and outlier observations increase. As we can observe from Figure 5 (right), both the number of false positive and false negatives decrease proportionally with K. With just 3 times σ_o, the number of wrongly selected observations is almost 0. In a real-case scenario, we expect wrong observations being either close to the correct one, so that they should not hinder the triangulation, or more than 3 times the standard deviation apart and thus discarded from the winning population.

5   Conclusions and Future Work

In this paper we introduced a dynamic path selection method that can be used to perform robust 3D reconstructions when using multiple cameras characterized by inaccurate extrinsic calibrations. Reconstruction is performed point-wise by dynamically selecting the best possible set of camera poses and observations that maximize the consistency of each pairwise triangulation. The ability to locally exclude part of the graph or observations from the final triangulation makes our method particularly effective in all the scenarios when either a precise calibration or a reliable localization of the target cannot be provided. Finally, it should be noted that the presented study is preliminary and our future goal is to complete it with respect to both theoretical aspects and evaluation. From a theoretical standpoint, the current solution works well only when the cameras are well overlapped. Suitable techniques should be introduced to obtain a transitive closure throughout a long sequence of partially overlapped cameras. From a validation point of view, we are presenting an entirely synthetic test set. An evaluation using real-world data [24] could give a better insight about the practical merits and limitations of the method.

References

1. Lee, K.H., Chu, C.T., Lee, Y., Fang, Z., Hwang, J.N.: Consistent human tracking over self-organized and scalable multiple-camera networks. In: Distributed Embedded Smart Cameras, pp. 189–209. Springer (2014)
2. Raman, R., Sa, P.K., Majhi, B.: Occlusion prediction algorithms for multi-camera network. In: 2012 Sixth International Conference on Distributed Smart Cameras (ICDSC), pp. 1–6. IEEE (2012)
3. Hoppe, C., Wendel, A., Zollmann, S., Pirker, K., Irschara, A., Bischof, H., Kluckner, S.: Photogrammetric camera network design for micro aerial vehicles. Computer vision winter workshop (CVWW) **8**, 1–3 (2012)
4. Agarwal, S., Furukawa, Y., Snavely, N., Simon, I., Curless, B., Seitz, S.M., Szeliski, R.: Building rome in a day. Communications of the ACM **54**, 105–112 (2011)
5. Ramagiri, S., Kavi, R., Kulathumani, V.: Real-time multi-view human action recognition using a wireless camera network. In: Distributed Smart Cameras (ICDSC), pp. 1–6. IEEE (2011)
6. Wang, X.: Intelligent multi-camera video surveillance: A review. Pattern recognition letters **34**, 3–19 (2013)
7. Morye, A., Ding, C., Song, B., Roy-Chowdhury, A., Farrell, J.: Optimized imaging and target tracking within a distributed camera network. In: American Control Conference (ACC), 2011, pp. 474–480. IEEE (2011)
8. Furukawa, Y., Ponce, J.: Accurate, dense, and robust multi-view stereopsis. IEEE Trans. on Pattern Analysis and Machine Intelligence **32**, 1362–1376 (2010)
9. Alsadik, B., Gerke, M., Vosselman, G.: Optimal camera network design for 3d modeling of cultural heritage. ISPRS Annals of the Photogrammetry, Remote Sensing and Spatial Information Sciences **3** (2012)
10. Zhang, Z.: A flexible new technique for camera calibration. Pattern Analysis and Machine Intelligence **22**, 1330–1334 (2000)
11. Heikkila, J., Silvén, O.: A four-step camera calibration procedure with implicit image correction. In: CVPR, pp. 1106–1112. IEEE (1997)
12. Torsello, A., Rodola, E., Albarelli, A.: Multiview registration via graph diffusion of dual quaternions. In: 2011 IEEE Conference on Computer Vision and Pattern Recognition (CVPR), pp. 2441–2448. IEEE (2011)
13. Lourakis, M.I., Argyros, A.A.: Sba: A software package for generic sparse bundle adjustment. ACM Transactions on Mathematical Software (TOMS) **36**, 2 (2009)
14. Svoboda, T., Martinec, D., Pajdla, T.: A convenient multicamera self-calibration for virtual environments. Teleoperators and Virt. Environments **14**, 407–422 (2005)
15. Barreto, J., Daniilidis, K.: Wide area multiple camera calibration and estimation of radial distortion. In: Proceedings of the 5th Workshop on Omnidirectional Vision, Camera Networks and Non-Classical Cameras, Prague, Czech Republic (2004)
16. Nash, J.: Non-cooperative games. Annals of mathematics, 286–295 (1951)
17. Weibull, J.: Evolutionary Game Theory. MIT Press (1995)
18. Taylor, P., Jonker, L.: Evolutionarily stable strategies and game dynamics. Mathematical Biosciences **40**, 145–156 (1978)

19. Albarelli, A., Rota Bulò, S., Torsello, A., Pelillo, M.: Matching as a non-cooperative game. In: Proc. ICCV, pp. 1319–1326 (2009)
20. Ibragimov, B., Likar, B., Pernus, F., Vrtovec, T.: A game-theoretic framework for landmark-based image segmentation. Medical Imaging **31**, 1761–1776 (2012)
21. Banerjee, J., Klink, C., Peters, E.D., Niessen, W.J., Moelker, A., van Walsum, T.: 4D liver ultrasound registration. In: Ourselin, S., Modat, M. (eds.) WBIR 2014. LNCS, vol. 8545, pp. 194–202. Springer, Heidelberg (2014)
22. Albarelli, A., Rodolá, E., Bergamasco, F., Torsello, A.: A non-cooperative game for 3d object recognition in cluttered scenes. In: 2011 International Conference on 3D Imaging, Modeling, Processing, Visualization and Transmission, 3DIMPVT 2011, pp. 252–259 (2011)
23. Rodolà, E., Bronstein, A., Albarelli, A., Bergamasco, F., Torsello, A.: A game-theoretic approach to deformable shape matching. In: CVPR, pp. 182–189 (2012)
24. Joo, H., Park, H.S., Sheikh, Y.: Map visibility estimation for large-scale dynamic 3d reconstruction (2014)

Smartphone-Based Obstacle Detection for the Visually Impaired

Alessandro Caldini, Marco Fanfani$^{(\boxtimes)}$, and Carlo Colombo

Computational Vision Group, University of Florence, Florence, Italy
alecaldini@gmail.com, {marco.fanfani,carlo.colombo}@unifi.it

Abstract. One of the main problems that visually impaired people have to deal with is moving autonomously in an unknown environment. Currently, the most used autonomous walking aid is still the white can. Though in the last few years more technological devices have been introduced, referred to as electronic travel aids (ETAs). In this paper, we present a novel ETA based on computer vision. Exploiting the hardware and software facilities of a standard smartphone, our system is able to extract a 3D representation of the scene and detect possible obstacles. To achieve such a result, images are captured by the smartphone camera and processed with a modified Structure from Motion algorithm that takes as input also information from the built-in gyroscope. Then the system estimates the ground-plane and labels as obstacles all the structures above it. Results on indoor and outdoor test sequences show the effectiveness of the proposed method.

Keywords: Elettronic Travel Aid (ETA) · Visually impaired people · Smartphone-based vision · Gyroscope · Depth · Obstacle · Structure from motion

1 Introduction

One of the main problems that a person with visual disabilities has to deal with is the difficulty of moving in an unknown environment. More precisely, the most urgent problem is related to avoiding obstacles along the path. Currently, visually impaired people still rely almost exclusively on the white can to help themselves to detecting obstacles and finding a safe path.

Recently, more technological solutions have been developed to support the autonomous mobility of visually impaired people [2]. Yet currently, proposed methods tend to not completely fulfill all the user requirements, so that visually impaired people are usually skeptical about them, and not keen to replace traditional solutions. ETAs, to be fully accepted by the users, should be reliable, affordable, light and their usage should not be an evident mark of disability. Moreover, they should be designed so that hands and ears remain free, thus allowing users to manipulate objects and acoustically perceive their surroundings.

© Springer International Publishing Switzerland 2015
V. Murino and E. Puppo (Eds.): ICIAP 2015, Part I, LNCS 9279, pp. 480–488, 2015.
DOI: 10.1007/978-3-319-23231-7_43

In the last few years an ever increasing diffusion of mobile devices, such as smartphones and tablets, has been observed. These devices are characterized by relatively high computational resources and limited dimensions. Equipped with visual and inertial sensors, they offer an optimal platform for the development of computer vision mobile applications [15]. In particular such devices can support the development and use of effective yet inconspicuous vision-based ETAs for the visually impaired [5].

In this paper, a novel vision-based ETA is proposed. Exploiting both the inertial gyroscope and the camera, nowadays available in any consumer smartphone, our system is able to compute the depth of the scene in front of the user and detect the presence of near obstacles. Next Section (Sect. 2) briefly describes related work on ETA. Then in Sect. 3 the proposed method is described. Section 4 discusses experimental results obtained on indoor and outdoor sequences, and Sect. 5 concludes the paper.

2   Related Work

To solve the problem of autonomous mobility for the visually impaired, solutions based on the Global Positioning System (GPS) cannot be considered due to their lack of accuracy and the impossibility to work in indoor scenarios. Hesch and Roumeliotis [8] propose a system that includes a pedometer and a laser scanner mounted on the white cane: While the authors show its validity, the additional hardware and the need of a precomputed map of the environment decrease the usability of this approach. In [1,4] the authors propose systems that visually detect known makers placed into the scene so to guarantee accurate localization of the user: Though effective, these approaches are limited to work only in previously structured environments. Zhang et al. [18] developed a smartphone-based system to visually localize the user. A drawback of this method is that images of the environment have to be previously collected and mapped, and heavy 3D computations must be run on a remote server. Other ETAs based on vision can provide localization information though object detection and optical character recognition (OCR) softwares, such as [17], or by exploiting visual and depth information to train a conditional random field (CRF) framework [14]. In [5] a smartphone-based application to detect and recognize bus line numbers have been developed to help visually impaired people to use public transport services.

Several systems were proposed to provide users with navigational aids and to detect obstacles exploiting a stereo camera pair. Leung and Medioni [9] propose an odometry system using stereo images and an inertial measurement unit (IMU) to reduce drift errors. Papers [11–13] describe methods focused on obstacle detection and safe path estimation, that employ a stereo pair to improve estimation accuracy. However, stereo cameras are currently quite expensive, bulky and showy, as compared to a standard mobile device.

In [10,16] ETAs based on single camera systems are introduced. In particular, Tapu et al. [16] develop a smartphone-based method for obstacle detection by computing homography relations and exploiting HOG descriptors for obstacle classification.

3   Method Description

Our method is designed to work with generic obstacles in both indoor and outdoor environments. Given an image sequence $\mathcal{I}$ captured by a calibrated smartphone camera attached to the user chest, the presented method implements a modified Structure from Motion (SfM) algorithm by taking advantage of the gyroscope installed on the mobile device. For each acquired image the system read the angular velocity $(\dot{\theta}_x, \dot{\theta}_y, \dot{\theta}_z)$ registered by the gyroscope; then by temporal integration, the rotation angles $(\theta_x, \theta_y, \theta_z)$ can be retrieved. With this information we can compute an estimation for the incremental rotation R_{ij} between two subsequent images $I_i, I_j \in \mathcal{I}$. Once the measurements have been acquired, the gyroscope status is re-initialized to limit the drift error.

3.1   Scene Reconstruction

Our modified SfM algorithm takes as input both a pair of images I_i, I_j and their relative rotation matrix R_{ij}.

At first point correspondences between I_i, I_j are computed using the FAST corner detector and the ORB feature descriptor. Once obtained the matching set, we exploit the relation on the essential matrix E [7], i.e.

$$\mathbf{x}_j^\top K^{-\top} E_{ij} K^{-1} \mathbf{x}_i = 0 \tag{1}$$

where $\{\mathbf{x}_i, \mathbf{x}_j\}$ is a match between I_i and I_j, and K is the calibration matrix. Then, since the essential matrix can be decomposed as $E = [\mathbf{t}]_\times R$, by substitution in Eq. 1 we obtain

$$\mathbf{x}_j^\top K^{-\top} [\mathbf{t}_{ij}]_\times R_{ij} K^{-1} \mathbf{x}_i = 0 \tag{2}$$

where R_{ij} is the rotation matrix and $[\mathbf{t}_{ij}]_\times$ the skew-symmetric matrix of the translation vector $\mathbf{t}_{ij}$. $\mathcal{T}_{ij} = [R_{ij}|\mathbf{t}_{ij}]$ describes the relative transformation between I_i and I_j.

Since R_{ij} is supposed to be known from gyroscope readings, we can define $\hat{\mathbf{x}}_j = K^{-1}\mathbf{x}_j$ and $\tilde{\mathbf{x}}_i = R_{ij}K^{-1}\mathbf{x}_i$ and Eq. 2 becomes

$$\hat{\mathbf{x}}_j^\top [\mathbf{t}_{ij}]_\times \tilde{\mathbf{x}}_i = 0 \tag{3}$$

Now Eq. 3 can be rewritten as a linear homogeneous equation on the elements of $\mathbf{t}_{ij}$. With at least three correspondences—or just two if the translation scale factor is fixed a priori— we can solve a linear system to estimate $\mathbf{t}_{ij}$. However, wrong matches are always present, and to avoid the introduction of outliers, we wrap the estimation process into a RANSAC framework [3]. Once the maximum consensus set is found, $\mathbf{t}_{ij}$ is refined minimizing the error on all the inlier correspondences.

Similarly to what happens with the decomposition of the essential matrix, the solution of Eq. 3 has a two-fold ambiguity on the sign of the translation. To select the correct vector, we triangulate [6] all inlier correspondences with both candidate solutions and we retain the 3D map satisfying the positive depth constraint on most points (i.e. the 3D points must lie in front of both cameras). The computed 3D of the scene is then exploited for the detection of obstacles.

3.2 Obstacle Detection

To detect obstacles and evaluate their proximity to the user, our algorithm estimates first the scene ground-plane, and simultaneously identifies 3D points that lie on it.

The system selects a 3D point set $S_\pi = \{\mathbf{X}_p\}$ related to matched correspondences detected in the bottom part of the images (under the hypothesis that such points belong to the ground-plane). Then a robust plane estimation algorithm is executed over S_π by randomly choosing three points for each RANSAC iteration k.

In each iteration, a plane equation $\pi_k(\mathbf{n}_k, d_k)$ is evaluated, where $\mathbf{n}_k$ is the plane π_k normal vector and d_k its distance w.r.t. the origin of the coordinate frame. A 3D point $\mathbf{X}_p \in S_\pi$ is considered as inlier if $\mathbf{n}_k^\top \mathbf{X}_p + d_k < \epsilon_1$. In our experiments we set ϵ_1 to a low value (e.g. $\epsilon_1 = 0.1$) in order to perform a strict selection of inliers. Note that to evaluate inliers we use an algebraic criterion instead of a geometric point/plane distance: while the latter approach is typically more correct, in this case, since we don't have the metric scale factor of the scene, the definition of the right threshold for the geometric distance can be misleading.

Once obtained the maximum inlier set $\widetilde{S}_\pi$, the 2D correspondence set associated to $\widetilde{S}_\pi$ is used to estimate the homography transformation H_{ij} between the planar regions of I_i and I_j. Then all matches that don't already have the associated 3D point in $\widetilde{S}_\pi$ are tested: If the distance $\mathcal{D}(\mathbf{x}_i, \mathbf{x}_j)$ defined as

$$\mathcal{D}(\mathbf{x}_i, \mathbf{x}_j) = \|H_{ij}\mathbf{x}_i - \mathbf{x}_j\| \tag{4}$$

is less than ϵ_2, then the 3D point relative to the correspondence $\{\mathbf{x}_i, \mathbf{x}_j\}$ is considered as a point on the ground-plane.

Finally, all 3D points that don't belong to the ground plane are labeled as obstacles and their relative depth can be exploited to assign different *warning level*—higher for closer objects, lower for distant ones.

In order to better evaluate obstacle distances and proximity of collision, a bird's-eye view of the scene is produced. To this aim, all 3D points are at first registered with a coordinate frame with the X and Z axes aligned with the ground-plane; then all obstacle 3D points are projected onto the ground-plane.

4 Evaluation

All images that have been used in the tests have a resolution of 320×240 pixels. Processing is carried out on an Android LG Nexus 5 smartphone, equipped with a Qualcomm Snapdragon 800 quad-core processor at 2.3GHz. With this setup, the method works at about 2 seconds per frame, which is suitable for use at standard walking speed.

Fig. 1 reports the results of an indoor test. The test sequence was recorded by moving the smartphone over a table where objects simulated a cluttered environment. For each original frame the system produced a sparse depth map and a bird's-eye view of the scene showing the ground-plane and the detected obstacles.

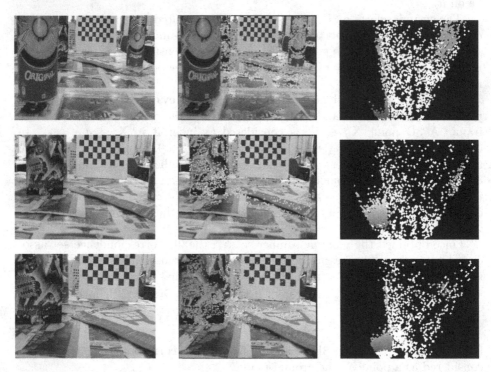

Fig. 1. Example frames of the indoor test sequence. In the first column the original images, in the second column the spare depth map computed, and finally the bird's-eye view with in white the ground-plane and obstacle colored from red to blue to represent their proximinty to the user. (Best viewed in color)

In Fig. 2 and Fig. 3 results on two different outdoor tests (respectively named *pilon* and *parking*) are reported. The tests were carried out with a walking person equipped with the smartphone held in front of his chest. Also in this case the algorithm computes correct depth values and produces a coherent bird's-eye view where ground-plane and obstacles are clearly visible.

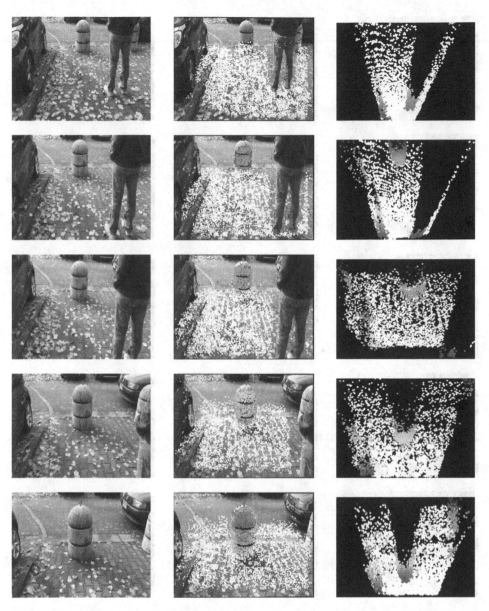

Fig. 2. Example frames of the *pilon* sequence. Again we present the original images (first column), the sparse depth map with ground-plane points in white (second column), and the bird's-eye view (third column). (Best viewed in color)

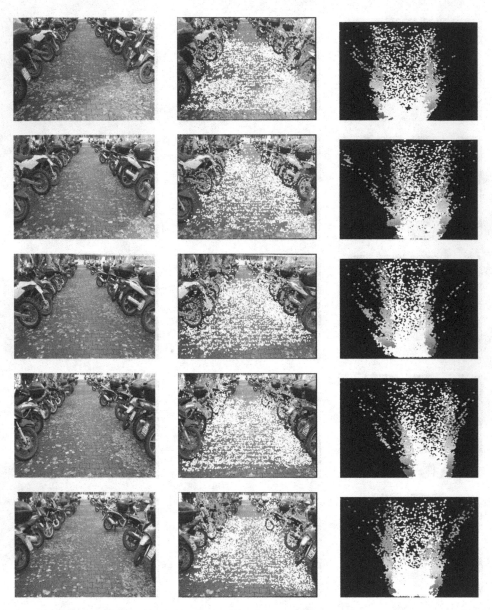

Fig. 3. Original images, depth map and bird's-eye view representation for some frame of the *parking* sequence. (Best viewed in color)

5 Conclusions and Future Work

In this paper we have presented a smartphone-based obstacle detection vision system to help visually impaired people to move autonomously in unknown indoor and outdoor environments. The developed algorithm exploits both visual information from the camera and inertial measurements registered from the gyroscope. A sparse depth map is computed with a modified Structure from Motion approach, and obstacles are detected as they pop out the ground-plane. Results show the good performance of our method.

Future work will address the development of a tactile/acoustic interface to provide feedback to visually impaired people and alert them regarding obstacles on their path. An extensive evaluation/refinement process carried out with the help of blind users is planned, aimed at improving system performance and usefulness.

References

1. Coughlan, J., Manduchi, R., Shen, H.: Cell phone-based wayfinding for the visually impaired. In: 1st International Workshop on Mobile Vision (2006)
2. Dakopoulos, D., Bourbakis, N.: Wearable Obstacle Avoidance Electronic Travel Aids for Blind: A Survey. IEEE Transactions on Systems, Man, and Cybernetics, Part C: Applications and Reviews **40**(1), 25–35 (2010)
3. Fischler, M.A., Bolles, R.C.: Random sample consensus: a paradigm for model fitting with applications to image analysis and automated cartography. Commun. ACM **24**(6), 381–395 (1981)
4. Gallo, P., Tinnirello, I., Giarr, L., Garlisi, D., Croce, D., Fagiolini, A.: ARIANNA: pAth recognition for indoor assisted navigation with augmented perception. CoRR (2013)
5. Guida, C., Comanducci, D., Colombo, C.: Automatic bus line number localization and recognition on mobile phones—a computer vision aid for the visually impaired. In: Maino, G., Foresti, G.L. (eds.) ICIAP 2011, Part II. LNCS, vol. 6979, pp. 323–332. Springer, Heidelberg (2011)
6. Hartley, R., Sturm, P.: Triangulation. Computer Vision and Image Understanding **68**(2), 146–157 (1997)
7. Hartley, R.I., Zisserman, A.: Multiple View Geometry in Computer Vision, 2nd edn. Cambridge University Press (2004)
8. Hesch, J.A., Roumeliotis, S.I.: Design and Analysis of a Portable Indoor Localization Aid for the Visually Impaired. Int. J. Rob. Res. **29**(11), 1400–1415 (2010)
9. Leung, T.S., Medioni, G.: Visual navigation aid for the blind in dynamic environments. In: Proceedings of the 2014 IEEE Conference on Computer Vision and Pattern Recognition Workshops, CVPRW 2014, pp. 579–586 (2014)
10. Lin, Q., Han, Y.: Safe path estimation for visual-impaired people using polar edge-blob histogram. In: Proc. of The World Congress on Engineering and Computer Science (2013)
11. Pradeep, V., Medioni, G., Weiland, J.: Robot vision for the visually impaired. In: 2010 IEEE Computer Society Conference on Computer Vision and Pattern Recognition Workshops (CVPRW), pp. 15–22 (2010)
12. Rodríguez, A., Yebes, J.J., Alcantarilla, P.F., Bergasa, L.M., Almazn, J., Cela, A.: Assisting the Visually Impaired: Obstacle Detection and Warning System by Acoustic Feedback. Sensors **12**(12), 17476–17496 (2012)
13. Saez Martinez, J.M., Escolano Ruiz, F.: Stereo-based aerial obstacle detection for the visually impaired. In: Workshop on Computer Vision Applications for the Visually Impaired (2008)

14. Schauerte, B., Koester, D., Martinez, M., Stiefelhagen, R.: Way to go! Detecting open areas ahead of a walking person. In: Agapito, L., Bronstein, M.M., Rother, C. (eds.) ECCV 2014 Workshops. LNCS, vol. 8927, pp. 349–360. Springer, Heidelberg (2015)
15. Tanskanen, P., Kolev, K., Meier, L., Camposeco, F., Saurer, O., Pollefeys, M.: Live metric 3d reconstruction on mobile phones. In: 2013 IEEE International Conference on Computer Vision (ICCV), pp. 65–72 (2013)
16. Tapu, R., Mocanu, B., Bursuc, A., Zaharia, T.: A smartphone-based obstacle detection and classification system for assisting visually impaired people. In: The IEEE International Conference on Computer Vision (ICCV) Workshops (2013)
17. Tian, Y., Yang, X., Yi, C., Arditi, A.: Toward a computer vision-based wayfinding aid for blind persons to access unfamiliar indoor environments. Machine Vision and Applications 24(3), 521–535 (2013)
18. Zhang, D., Lee, D.J., Taylor, B.: Seeing Eye Phone: a smart phone-based indoor localization and guidance system for the visually impaired. Machine Vision and Applications 25(3), 811–822 (2014)

Efficient Moving Point Handling for Incremental 3D Manifold Reconstruction

Andrea Romanoni[✉] and Matteo Matteucci

DEIB, Politecnico di Milano, Via Ponzio 34/5, 20133 Milano, Italy
{andrea.romanoni,matteo.matteucci}@polimi.it

Abstract. As incremental Structure from Motion algorithms become effective, a good sparse point cloud representing the map of the scene becomes available frame-by-frame. From the 3D Delaunay triangulation of these points, state-of-the-art algorithms build a manifold rough model of the scene. These algorithms integrate incrementally new points to the 3D reconstruction only if their position estimate does not change. Indeed, whenever a point moves in a 3D Delaunay triangulation, for instance because its estimation gets refined, a set of tetrahedra have to be removed and replaced with new ones to maintain the Delaunay property; the management of the manifold reconstruction becomes thus complex and it entails a potentially big overhead. In this paper we investigate different approaches and we propose an efficient policy to deal with moving points in the manifold estimation process. We tested our approach with four sequences of the KITTI dataset and we show the effectiveness of our proposal in comparison with state-of-the-art approaches.

1 Introduction

Incremental 3D reconstruction from a sparse point cloud is gaining interest in the computer vision community as incremental Structure from Motion algorithms are consolidating [18]. This is clearly true for those applications where a rough, but dense, surface represents a sufficient and effective representation of the scene, e.g, for traversability analysis in unmanned vehicle navigation. Furthermore, in real-time applications, the map of the environment needs to be updated online, and the surface has to be estimated incrementally.

Most of the existing algorithms [10,13,8,9] bootstrap the reconstruction of a mesh surface from the 3D Delaunay triangulation of a sparse point cloud. Indeed, the 3D Delaunay triangulation is very powerful: the Delaunay property, i.e., no point of the triangulation is inside the sphere circumscribing any tetrahedron, avoids as much as possible the resulting tetrahedra to have a degenerate shape [11]; it is self-adaptive, i.e., the more the points are dense the more the tetrahedra are small; it is very fast to compute, and to update against point removal or addition; off-the-shelf libraries, such as CGAL [16], enable a very simple and efficient management of it.

As soon as a Delaunay triangulation is available, several approaches exist to extract a surface taking into account the visibility of each point. The simplest

© Springer International Publishing Switzerland 2015
V. Murino and E. Puppo (Eds.): ICIAP 2015, Part I, LNCS 9279, pp. 489–499, 2015.
DOI: 10.1007/978-3-319-23231-7_44

algorithm is the Space Carving [6]: it initializes all the tetrahedra as *matter*, then it marks as *free space* the tetrahedra intersected by the camera-to-point *viewing rays*, i.e., the lines from the camera center to the observed 3D points in the triangulation. The boundary between free space and matter represents the final surface of the scene. Pan et al. [13] improve upon this simple procedure by proposing an online probabilistic Space Carving, but this is not an incremental approach: they start from scratch every time new points are added. Lovi et al. [10] present the first incremental Space Carving algorithm which runs real-time, but, as for the previous methods, the estimated surface is not guaranteed to be manifold.

Several reasons lead to enforce the manifold property as explained in [7]. Most Computer Graphics algorithms need the manifold property, for instance smoothing with Laplace-Beltrami operator [12], or the linear mesh parametrization [15]. Moreover the manifold property enables surface evolution in mesh-based Multi-View Stereo, as in [17,1].the manifold property enables a photometric refinement by surface evolution such as with the high accurate Multi-View Stereo mesh-based algorithm as in [17,1]. With these approaches is hard to estimate the surface evolving flow in the presence of non manifold vertices: indeed they compute for each vertex the gradient minimizing the reprojection error, by summing-up the contribution of the incident facets; if the vertex is not manifold, this gradient does not converge. As a further proof of this, [17] needs to manually fix the surface estimated via s-t cut. As in [17], it is possible to fix the mesh as a post-processing step, but reconstructing directly a manifold as in the proposed paper, enables the design of a fully automatic pipeline which do not need human intervention.

In literature, the only algorithm reconstructing a manifold incrementally was proposed by Litvinov and Lhuiller [8,9]. In their work, the authors bootstrap from the Space Carving procedure and, by taking into account the number of intersections of each tetrahedron with the viewing rays, they reconstruct a surface keeping the manifold property valid. The main limitation is that Litvinov and Lhuiller insert a point into the Delaunay triangulation only when its position is definitive, then they cannot move the point position anymore even in the case they could refine their estimate. The main reason of Litvinov and Lhuiller design choice has to be ascribed to the computational cost of updating the visibility information along the viewing rays incident to each moved point, and the computational cost of updating part of the Delaunay triangulation, which in turn induces a new manifold reconstruction iteration step.

Indeed, the very common approach to deal with a point moving in the triangulation, is to remove it and add it back in the new position [16] (Fig. 1). When we remove a point (the point A in Fig. 1(a)) and we want to keep the Delaunay property, we have to remove all the tetrahedra incident to that point (light red triangles in Fig. 1(b)); then, we add a new set of tetrahedra to triangulate the resulting hole (dark green triangles in 1(c)). When we add a new point into the triangulation (the point B in Fig. 1(d)), a set of tetrahedra would conflict with it, i.e., the Delaunay property is broken (light red triangles in Fig. 1(d)); so,

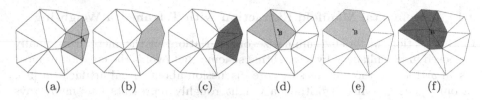

(a)   (b)   (c)   (d)   (e)   (f)

Fig. 1. Example of point removal in 2D case. Light red triangles depict are removed and replaced with the new dark green ones.

we remove this set of tetrahedra again (red triangles in Fig. 1(e)) and we add a new connected set that re-triangulate the hole (dark green triangles in Fig. 1(f)). Whenever a set of tetrahedra is replaced, we have to transfer conveniently the information about the visibility (matter or free space) of the removed tetrahedra to the new one. In addition to this, we have to update the visibility of the tetrahedra crossed by a visibility ray from one camera to the moved point. For these reasons the update of the point position is computational demanding.

To complete the overview of the incremental reconstruction methods from sparse data, we mention here another very different approach was proposed by Hoppe et al. [5] who label the tetrahedra with a random field, and extract the surface via graph-cuts by minimizing a visibility-consistent energy function. This incremental algorithm is effective and handles the moving points, but the manifold property of the reconstructed surface is not yet guaranteed.

In this paper we propose, to the best of our knowledge, the first manifold 3D reconstruction algorithm from sparse data which deals with dynamic point changes. In particular, we show that in this setting the algorithm by Lovi et al. [10] provides a feasible solution, but it is very inefficient and we propose a novel efficient policy to handle the visibility update of Delaunay tetrahedra with moving points.

In Section 2 we summarize a slightly modified version of the approach of [8] we use to reconstruct a manifold surface. In Section 3 we describe Lovi's approach [10] and our proposal to deal with moving points, together with a complexity analysis that explains why our approach is more efficient. In Section 4 we show the experimental results on the publicly available dataset KITTI [3], while, in Section 5 we point out some future works and in the conclusion of the paper.

2 Manifold Reconstruction

In this paper we reconstruct a manifold surface that represents the observed scene. A surface is manifold if and only if the neighborhood of each point is homeomorphic to a disk. In the discrete case, the points are the vertexes of a mesh, and the neighborhood is represented by the incident triangles (or polygons); a surface is manifold if each vertex v is *regular*, i.e., if and only if the edges opposite to v form a closed path without loops (see [8] for more details).

2.1   Incremental Manifold Extraction with Tetrahedra Weighting

In this section we briefly summarize our variation on the method originally proposed in [8] enhanced by a weighting scheme that avoids the creation of most visual artifact in the final mesh (more discussion about visual artifacts in [9]). In our Space Carving algorithm, a weight roughly represents how many rays intersect a tetrahedron, and in the following, a tetrahedron belongs to *free space* if its weight w is higher than a threshold T_w (in our case $T_w = 1.0$).

Sparse Point Cloud.   The input of our algorithm is a sparse 3D point cloud, estimated incrementally by assuming the camera poses to be known. For each keyframe, i.e., every $K = 5$ frames, we extract Edge-point features, i.e. 2D points laying on the image edges [14]; these points represent measurements of 3D points. Frame-by-frame we track these features with the Kanade-Lucas-Tomasi tracker, and, at each keyframe, we estimate the new positions of the 3D points with the new measurements available from the tracking. New estimates are obtained by triangulating the 2D tracked points and by minimizing the reprojection error with a Gauss-Newton algorithm. Once a new estimate of a 3D point is available, we add it to the Delaunay triangulation, i.e., to the reconstruction; then we update its position according to the new measurements: this update induces the motion of the points inside the triangulation.

3D Reconstruction.   The reconstruction of the surface bootstraps from the manifold partitioning the 3D triangulation between the set O of *outside* tetrahedra, i.e., the manifold subset of the free space (not all the free space tetrahedra will be part of the manifold), and the complementary set I of inside tetrahedra, i.e. the remaining tetrahedra that represent the matter together with the free space tetrahedra which would invalidate the manifold property.

Let $\delta(O_{t_{\mathrm{init}}})$ be the initial manifold. This initial manifold is obtained with the following steps. *Point Insertion*: add all the 3D points estimated up to time t_{init} and build thir 3D Delaunay triangulation. *Ray tracing and tetrahedra weighting*: for each viewing ray, the algorithm traverses the triangulation and adds a weight $w_1 = 1.0$ to the intersected tetrahedra, a weight $w_2 = 0.8$ to the neighbors and a weight $w_2 = 0.2$ to the neighbors of their neighbors. Such weighting scheme acts as a smoother of the visibility and avoids the creation of visual artifacts; it is the main difference between our algorithm and the algorithms proposed in [8,9]. *Growing*: initialize a queue Q starting from the tetrahedron with the higher weight. Then: (a) pick the tetrahedron with highest weight from Q and add it to $O_{t_{\mathrm{init}}}$ only if the resulting surface between $O_{t_{\mathrm{init}}}$ and $I_{t_{\mathrm{init}}}$ remains manifold; (b) if inserted add the neighboring tetrahedra to the queue Q, otherwise discard it; continue iteratively until Q is empty.

Once the system is initialized, a new set of points P_{t_k} is estimated at each $t_k = t_{\mathrm{init}} + k * T_k$ frame, named keyframes, where $k \in \mathbb{N}^+$ and T_k is the inverse of the keyframe rate. The insertion of a point $p \in P_{t_k}$ causes the removal of the set D_{t_k} of tetrahedra breaking the Delaunay property, and, the surface $\delta(O_{t_k}) =$

$\delta(O_{t_{k-1}} \setminus D_{t_k})$ is not guaranteed to be manifold anymore. To avoid this, the authors in [8] define a list of tetrahedra $E_{t_k} \supset D_{t_k}$ and apply the *Shrinking* procedure, i.e., the inverse of Growing: they subtract iteratively from $O_{t_{k-1}}$ the tetrahedra $\Delta \in E_{t_k}$ keeping the manifoldness valid. After this process, it is likely that $D_{t_k} \cap O_{t_k} = \emptyset$. Whenever $D_{t_k} \cap O_{t_k} \neq \emptyset$ the point p is not added to the triangulation, i.e., is dropped. Once all points in P_{t_k} have been added (or dropped), the growing process runs similarly to the initialization procedure, but the queue Q is initialized with the tetrahedra $\Delta \in T \setminus O$ such that $\Delta \cap \delta O \neq \emptyset$.

3   Reconstructing a Manifold with Moving Points

As previously described, Litvinov and Lhuiller [8] algorithm adds points to the triangulation only when their 3D position is completely defined; by doing this, there are no changes in the Delaunay triangulation, induced by moving points. This results in a restriction if we would like to refine the estimation of the position of a point 3D position after its insertion.

Only Lovi et al. [10] presents an incremental Space Carving algorithm which deals with moving points, but their method does not enforce the manifold property. In this paper we verify the approach of Lovi et al. [10] to be very inefficient for manifold reconstruction, and we present a different approach to deal with moving points that leads to a significant faster computation.

3.1   The Straightforward Approach

The simplest way to deal with moving points while reconstructing a manifold surface, is to apply a straightforward modification to the so called *Refinement Event Handler* by Lovi et al. in [10]. The Refinement Event Handler algorithm assumes that, for each tetrahedron in the Delaunay triangulation a list of the intersecting viewing rays is stored. In our voting schema an intersecting ray is each ray that increase the weight of the tetrahedron.

Let p_{old} be a point that moves to position p_{new}, the algorithm in [10] moves the point by removing point p_{old} and adding p_{new} as a new point, according to the classical approach of [2], then for each point they apply the following steps. *Rays collection*: collect in a set U all the rays stored into the tetrahedra incident to p_{old}, i.e., those affected by the p_{old} removal (e.g., the light red triangle in Fig. 1(a)). *Vertex removal*: remove the vertex p_{old} and its neighboring tetrahedra from the triangulation (Fig. 1(b)); then re-triangulate the hole left by the deleted tetrahedra (Fig. 1(c)). *New point insertion*: insert the new point p_{new} into the triangulation and add to the set U all the rays stored in the conflicting tetrahedra (Fig. 1(d-f)). *Rays removal*: for each tetrahedron of the entire triangulation remove the rays ending in p_{old}. *Ray casting*: cast one ray for each ray in U.

In our case, whenever the 3D estimate of a point moves, we apply the Refinement Event Handler, before point addition and region growing, if and only if the point is inside the shrinked volume D_{t_k} (see Section 2), otherwise we do not move the point (this second case happens very rarely [8]).

Table 1. Complexity analysis; "-" means not existing step.

Step	straightforward algorithm	K heuristic	proposed algorithm	window heuristic
Rays collection	$O(F \cdot N^2)$	$O(N)$	-	-
Weight collection	-	-	$O(N)$	$O(N)$
Vertex Removal	$O(N)$	$O(N)$	$O(N)$	$O(N)$
New points insertion	$O(F \cdot N^2 \cdot N)$	$O(N)$	$O(F \cdot N^2 \cdot N)$	$O(N)$
Rays removal	$O(N^2 \cdot F \cdot N^2)$	$O(N^2)$	-	-
Weight Update	-	-	$O(N)$	$O(N)$
Backward ray casting	-	-	$O(N^2 \cdot F)$	$O(N)$
Ray casting	$O(N^2 \cdot F)$	$O(1)$	$O(N^2 \cdot F)$	$O(1)$
Overall complexity	$O(N^4 \cdot F)$	$O(N^2)$	$O(N^3 \cdot F)$	$O(N)$

Complexity. The number of rays involved in space carving algorithms is $O(F \cdot N^2)$ where F and N represent respectively the number of frames and the number of points in the triangulation [10], and the number of tetrahedra in a 3D triangulation grows quadratically with the number of points ($O(N^2)$). In Table 1 we reported the complexities for each of the previous stage; since our implementation exploits the CGAL [16] 3D triangulation data structure, the complexity of a single Ray casting, i.e., a cast of a single ray, is $O(N)$ in the general case, but we bound the size of the viewing ray, to avoid to include too far uncertain 3D points estimates, so the final complexity becomes $O(1)$ (see [19, p.94]).

From the analysis in the table is quite clear that this straightforward solution is not scalable, especially for the dependence between the number of rays and the number of processed frames.

Forgetting Heuristic. Lovi et al. [10] proposed a *forgetting* heuristic to limit the number of rays stored in each tetrahedron to a fixed number K, thus making the complexity independent from the number of the processed frames. However, we show in Section 4 that, when the points are moving, the reconstruction is very inefficient even with this heuristic.

3.2   The Efficient Approach

Our contribution in this paper is an approach to deal with moving points, different from the straightforward variation of [10]. Indeed in our proposal, we avoid storing the list of rays inside each tetrahedron, and we just store the weight associated with it. This allows the incremental reconstruction algorithm of Section 2.1, and, at the same time, we are able to bound the temporal complexity.

The main difficulty in the proposed approach is updating coherently the weights whenever a point moves, i.e., when the point is removed from the triangulation and added as a new point. As soon as the point is removed from the triangulation, we perform a backward ray casting with negative weights for each viewing camera such that the influence of the point is neglected. Then we remove

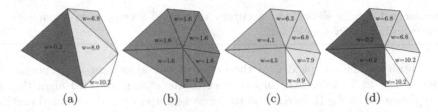

Fig. 2. 2D example of moving point addition in the new position after point removal (a brighter region corresponds to a higher weight, i.e., higher probability to be carved).

the point, and we add a new vertex in the new position. Finally, we perform the ray casting from each viewing camera to the new point.

During both point removal and addition, we have to remove a set of connected tetrahedra from the triangulation and add a new one. Let $R = \{\Delta_1^R, \Delta_2^R, \ldots, \Delta_{n_R}^R\}$ be the set of removed off tetrahedra and $A = \{\Delta_1^A, \Delta_2^A, \ldots, \Delta_{n_A}^A\}$ the set of the new ones; their associated weights are respectively $W_R = \{w_1^R, w_2^R, \ldots, w_{n_R}^R\}$ and $W_A = \{w_1^A, w_2^A, \ldots, w_{n_A}^A\}$. The weights W_R are known, while W_A are those to be computed for the new tetrahedra, without recasting the visibility rays related to those tetrahedra.

Different approaches are possible: *Mean value*: $w_i^A = \frac{1}{n_A} \sum_{k=1}^{n_R} w_k$; *Weighted mean*: let $d_{i,j}$ be the Euclidean distances between the centroids of the i-th tetrahedron of A and the j-th of R; then $w_i^A = \frac{\sum_{k=1}^{n_R} d_{i,k}^{-1}}{\sum_{k=1}^{n_R} d_{i,k}^{-1}}$; *Minimum distance*: $w_i^A = w_{\bar{j}}^R$ such that $\bar{j} = \arg\min_{j \in 1 \ldots n_R}(d_{ij})$.

Among these, the third solution gives a non-smooth outcome and, even if this seems counter-intuitive, it results to be more suitable for our purposes. The main reason is that it preserves the discontinuity between matter and free space. For instance in Fig. 2(a) we depict a 2D triangulation where we want to add a new point position; in Fig. 2 (b), (c) and (d) we show the results of weights update after point addition with, respectively, Mean value, Weighted Mean value and Minimum distance approaches. It is clear that only Fig. 2(d) preserved the discontinuity, while in other cases becomes hard to distinguish between matter (lower weights) and free space (higher weights).

In case of very sparse data, the centroids of big tetrahedra, together with the associated visibility information, can be far from the newly added or moved points, and our update policy might lead to results far from the ideal solution, i.e., the straightforward approach discussed in Section 3.1. Our algorithm overcomes this issue thanks to the use of the (so called) Steiner points added to the triangulation before the actual reconstruction is performed; this idea was already introduced in [8]. We add Steiner points to the Delaunay triangulation every 5m along each axis so that they cover all the space that can be represented. The use of Steiner points limits the creation of very big tetrahedra, the visibility information becomes always local, and the update policy avoids drifts. Indeed, experimental results show good accuracy on varied scenes, even when lack of textures induces very sparse data.

Complexity. The complexity of the steps of our algorithm are reported in Table 1. The main difference with respect to the straightforward algorithm is the replacement of the Rays removal to the weight update and backward casting which are the key of the gaining in computational complexity. The proposed algorithm is thus $O(F \cdot N^2)$, so, in principle, the dependence with F still remains and results in a non scalable solution.

Window Heuristic. We are able to bound the complexity of our algorithm to $O(N^2)$ thanks to the following heuristic: instead of backward casting all the rays connecting the moving point to all the viewing cameras, we consider only the most recent cameras. In this case the complexity of the ray casting becomes $O(W \cdot N^2)$, where W is the (constant) size of the window (in our case $W = 15$), so the final complexity is $O(N^2)$.

4   Experimental Validation

To evaluate our approach, we tested the system on four different sequences of the KITTI dataset [3] on a 4 Core i7-2630QM CPU at 2.2Ghz (6M Cache), with 6GB of DDR3 SDRAM. The video stream was captured by a Point Grey Flea 2, which records 1392x512 gray scale images at 10 fps. The vehicle pose are estimated through a RTK-GPS and they are the initial input of our system together with the video stream.

Among all the sequences we choose the 0095 (268 frames) and 0104 (313 frames) since they depict two different urban scenarios: the former shows a narrow environment where the building façades are close to the camera, the latter captures a wide road. We also tested our approach on sequences 03 (801 frames) and 04 (271 frames) from the odometry dataset: these videos provide a varied landscape mixing natural (trees and bushes) and man-made (houses, cars) features.

To provide a quantitative evaluation we compared the reconstructed meshes with the very accurate point clouds measured by the Velodyne HDL-64E sensor in the KITTI dataset through the CloudCompare tool [4]. This tool computes the reconstruction error as the average of the distances between each Velodyne point and the nearest triangle in the reconstructed mesh.

We evaluated the performance and the accuracy of the Lovi's approach against our three different updating policy. As explained previously, no manifold incremental reconstruction approach deals with moving points, so a fair comparison results to be between the straightforward approach of Lovi, applied to manifold reconstruction (Section 3.1) and our updating policies. In Fig. 3 we show an example of the reconstruction results before and after the red points has been moved in the Delaunay triangulation (see also the video at http://youtu.be/_-q9sKjcOC0).

Fig. 3. Incremental reconstruction example. From up left to bottom right: original frame, before point positions update, points moved in the scene (red dots) and manifold updated.

Fig. 4 shows the results of the comparison where we applied the window heuristic (Section 3.2) to all the algorithms. In the case of Lovi's algorithm we applied the forgetting heuristic with $K = 5$ and $K = 1$, where K is the number of viewing rays stored for each tetrahedron. Fig. 4(a) shows that the accuracy of the proposed approach, i.e, moving point management through minimum distance weight updates, is comparable with respect to Lovi's proposal outcomes, where the algorithm with $K = 5$ stores more information, so it performs better. We compared our approach with respect to Lovi's method instead of the other incremental reconstruction algorithm presented in [8]; the reasons are twofold. In [8] Litvinov and Lhuiller does not deal with moving points, which is the main point addressed in this paper. Moreover, Litvinov and Lhuiller point out in [9] that the ideal solution for a manifold reconstruction algorithm is represented by the manifold including as much as free space tetrahedra as possible. Since the solution provided by Lovi et al. coincides with the (non-manifold) mesh containing all the free space tetrahedra, a reconstruction accuracy similar to Lovi's suggests that the reconstruction is near to the ideal solution. In some cases our algorithm reaches even better accuracy, this is due to the smoothing effect induced by our heuristic.

Fig. 4(a) shows that the Minimum Distance always outperforms the other two updating schema as expected (see the Section 3.2).

In Fig. 4(b) we report the time performance of the algorithms. Let T_{mov} and $T_{non\text{-}mov}$ be the overall processing time with and without moving points, and N_{mov} be the number of the total points moves, e.g., if one point moves three times, $N_{mov} = 3$. The overhead introduced in the whole reconstruction process for each move of each point has been computed as $\frac{T_{mov} - T_{non\text{-}mov}}{N_{mov}}$. The performance of the different update schema we presented in Section 3.2 is very similar since the steps involved are basically the same: for each update on the Delaunay data structure, we iterate over the old tetrahedra to collect the weights, then we iterate over the new tetrahedra to set the new weights. As expected by Section 3.2, our algorithm clearly outperforms Lovi's approach. Our updating schema is very efficient for two reasons. First, we only need to update locally the visibility, while Lovi's approach casts a ray for each visibility ray stored

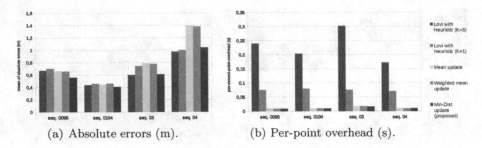

(a) Absolute errors (m).   (b) Per-point overhead (s).

Fig. 4. Experimental evaluation of the proposed approach with respect to Lovi's [10].

inside the tetrahedra. Second, when we remove a point (first step of moving point management), we perform a ray casting backward to update only the convenient tetrahedra, instead of iterating over the whole triangulation to remove the visibility rays involving the point moved as in [10].

5   Conclusion and Future Work

In this paper we have shown that manifold reconstruction from sparse data with moving points is not a trivial task. To keep the Delaunay property valid when a point moves inside the Delaunay triangulation, we have to remove it and add a new point in the new position. This induces the removal of a set of tetrahedra, with the associated visibility information; then, we have to add a new set of tetrahedra with coherent visibility information; finally we have to update the visibility information in all the tetrahedra affected by the point move.

Existing solutions successfully applied for classic Space Carving, result to be inefficient and slow when applied in the manifold reconstruction setting. In this setting, we investigated different approaches to handle visibility information propagation, by updating the weight for each tetrahedron, which roughly represents the number of ray intersections, and we proposed an efficient algorithm to conveniently update it. We tested our system with the KITTI dataset and it clearly outperforms the existing approach of Lovi et al. [10] for incremental manifold reconstruction.

Future works would include a photometric refinement of the manifold extracted incrementally, and an evaluation of the manifold quality on-the-fly, relying on the uncertainty information carried by the estimation of 3D points. A natural extension could also deal with the reconstruction of non-rigid shapes whose 3D points are moving.

Acknowledgments. This work has been partially funded by the SINOPIAE project, from the Italian Ministry of University and Research and Regione Lombardia, and the MEP: Maps for Easy Paths project funded by Politecnico di Milano under the POLISOCIAL program.

References

1. Delaunoy, A., Prados, E., Piracés, P.G.I., Pons, J.P., Sturm, P.: Minimizing the multi-view stereo reprojection error for triangular surface meshes. In: BMVC 2008- British Machine Vision Conference, pp. 1–10. BMVA (2008)
2. Devillers, O., Teillaud, M.: Perturbations and vertex removal in a 3d delaunay triangulation. In: 14th ACM-Siam Symp. on Algorithms, pp. 313–319 (2003)
3. Geiger, A., Lenz, P., Urtasun, R.: Are we ready for autonomous driving? the kitti vision benchmark suite. In: 2012 IEEE Conference on Computer Vision and Pattern Recognition (CVPR), pp. 3354–3361. IEEE (2012)
4. Girardeau-Montaut, D.: Cloud compare (access March 22, 2015). http://www. cloudcompare.org/
5. Hoppe, C., Klopschitz, M., Donoser, M., Bischof, H.: Incremental surface extraction from sparse structure-from-motion point clouds. In: Proc. BMVC (2013)
6. Kutulakos, K.N., Seitz, S.M.: A theory of shape by space carving. International Journal of Computer Vision **38**(3), 199–218 (2000)
7. Lhuillier, M.: 2-manifold tests for 3d delaunay triangulation-based surface reconstruction. Journal of Mathematical Imaging and Vision, 1–8 (2014)
8. Litvinov, V., Lhuillier, M.: Incremental solid modeling from sparse and omnidirectional structure-from-motion data. In: BMVC (2013)
9. Litvinov, V., Lhuillier, M.: Incremental solid modeling from sparse structure-from-motion data with improved visual artifacts removal. In: International Conference on Pattern Recognition (ICPR) (2014)
10. Lovi, D.I., Birkbeck, N., Cobzas, D., Jagersand, M.: Incremental free-space carving for real-time 3d reconstruction. In: Fifth International Symposium on 3D Data Processing Visualization and Transmission (3DPVT) (2010)
11. Maur, P.: Delaunay triangulation in 3d. Tech. rep., Dep. of Computer Science and Engineering. University of West Bohemia, Pilsen, Czech Republic (2002)
12. Meyer, M., Desbrun, M., Schröder, P., Barr, A.H.: Discrete differential-geometry operators for triangulated 2-manifolds. In: Visualization and Mathematics III, pp. 35–57. Springer (2003)
13. Pan, Q., Reitmayr, G., Drummond, T.: Proforma: probabilistic feature-based on-line rapid model acquisition. In: BMVC, pp. 1–11 (2009)
14. Rhein, S., Lu, G., Sorensen, S., Mahoney, A.R., Eicken, H., Ray, G.C., Kambhamettu, C.: Iterative reconstruction of large scenes using heterogeneous feature tracking. In: 2013 IEEE Conference on Computer Vision and Pattern Recognition Workshops (CVPRW), pp. 407–412. IEEE (2013)
15. Saboret, L., Alliez, P., Lévy, B.: Planar parameterization of triangulated surface meshes. In: CGAL User and Reference Manual. CGAL Editorial Board, 4.4 edn. (2000)
16. The CGAL Project: CGAL User and Reference Manual. CGAL Editorial Board, 4.5 edn. (2014)
17. Vu, H.H., Labatut, P., Pons, J.P., Keriven, R.: High accuracy and visibility-consistent dense multiview stereo. IEEE Transactions on Pattern Analysis and Machine Intelligence **34**(5), 889–901 (2012)
18. Wu, C.: Towards linear-time incremental structure from motion. In: 2013 International Conference on 3D Vision-3DV 2013, pp. 127–134. IEEE (2013)
19. Yu, S.: Automatic 3d modeling of environments: a sparse approach from images taken by a catadioptric camera. Ph.D. thesis, Université Blaise Pascal-Clermont-Ferrand II (2013)

Volumetric 3D Reconstruction and Parametric Shape Modeling from RGB-D Sequences

Yoichi Nakaguro[1], Waqar S. Qureshi[2]([✉]), Matthew N. Dailey[2],
Mongkol Ekpanyapong[2], Pished Bunnun[1], and Kanokvate Tungpimolrut[1]

[1] National Electronics and Computer Technology Center,
Klong Luang, Pathum Thani 12120, Thailand
[2] Asian Institute of Technology, Klong Luang, Pathum Thani 12120, Thailand
waqar.shahid@gmail.com, waqar.shahid.qureshi@ait.asia

Abstract. The recent availability of low-cost RGB-D sensors and the maturity of machine vision algorithms makes shape-based parametric modeling of 3D objects in natural environments more practical than ever before. In this paper, we investigate the use of RGB-D based modeling of natural objects using RGB-D sensors and a combination of volumetric 3D reconstruction and parametric shape modeling. We apply the general method to the specific case of detecting and modeling quadric objects, with the ellipsoid shape of a pineapple as a special case, in cluttered agricultural environments, towards applications in fruit health monitoring and crop yield prediction. Our method estimates the camera trajectory then performs volumetric reconstruction of the scene. Next, we detect fruit and segment out point clouds that belong to fruit regions. We use two novel methods for robust estimation of a parametric shape model from the dense point cloud: (i) MSAC-based robust fitting of an ellipsoid to the 3D-point cloud, and (ii) nonlinear least squares minimization of dense SIFT (scale invariant feature transform) descriptor distances between fruit pixels in corresponding frames. We compare our shape modeling methods with a baseline direct ellipsoid estimation method. We find that model-based point clouds show a clear advantage in parametric shape modeling and that our parametric shape modeling methods are more robust and better able to estimate the size, shape, and volume of pineapple fruit than is the baseline direct method.

Keywords: Volumetric reconstruction · Parametric shape modeling · Fruit health monitoring · RGB-D sensors

1 Introduction

Vision-based simultaneous localization and mapping (SLAM) has come to the point of maturity in coping with large-scale environments, gradually imposing fewer assumptions on sensors. The PTAM algorithm [9] performs motion estimation and mapping in parallel based on efficient bundle adjustment (BA) of sparse point features. Along the same lines, SVO-SLAM [6] applies sparse point-based direct alignment [5,8] to localize micro aerial vehicles (MAVs) flying in

© Springer International Publishing Switzerland 2015
V. Murino and E. Puppo (Eds.): ICIAP 2015, Part I, LNCS 9279, pp. 500–516, 2015.
DOI: 10.1007/978-3-319-23231-7_45

outdoor environments. In contemporary work, LSD-SLAM [4] applies semi-dense direct alignment to monocular camera sequences and has been successfully used to map large-scale outdoor environments containing challenging scale changes. While the work mentioned above builds accurate maps represented as sparse 3D point clouds, for near-range scene mapping, we can obtain more dense representations of the environment using modern portable and inexpensive RGB-D sensors such as the Microsoft Kinect. The seminal KinectFusion algorithm [12] demonstrated real-time dense mapping of indoor scenes with weighted signed distance functions assigned to fixed voxel grids. However, its critical reliance on GPU hardware and heavy memory demands due to a non-adaptive voxel grid representation pushed the development of more optimized solutions. The TUM Computer Vision Group released a series of RGB-D methods that cover direct motion estimation [7,8], benchmarking [18], and large-scale surface reconstruction using a memory-efficient octree data structure [16]. More recently, an even more carefully optimized version of the octree-based surface reconstruction algorithm was introduced as FastFusion, which requires only a single CPU [17].

The availability of low-cost RGB-D sensors and the maturity of machine vision algorithms for motion estimation and large-scale surface reconstruction have provided opportunities to automate monitoring and inspection tasks in applications as diverse as surveillance, medical diagnostics, remote sensing, industrial quality control, and precision agriculture. Automation in agricultural monitoring and inspection can help farmers to increase their efficiency and productivity as well as optimize crop yield. Crops bearing fruit, such as pineapples, mangoes, apples, oranges, and guavas have attracted researchers' attention due to the high demand for and value of the crops. Fruit crops require monitoring at regular intervals across different stages of growth to acquire information regarding pest infestation, fruit health, and predicted yield. One aspect of fruit health monitoring for such crops is to estimate the size and volume of individual fruits in the pre-harvest stage.

An autonomous fruit crop inspection system incorporating one or more mobile camera sensors and a host processor able to analyze the video sequences in detail could help farmers to monitor fruit health and growth trajectories over time and predict crop yield. The first step is to retrieve images containing fruits through an RGB-D sensor. Then we must segment the fruit regions from the background and track the fruit regions over time. The segmented fruit regions can then be used to generate volumetric 3D models to estimate the size and volume of the fruit.

In this paper, we perform a case study on the application of 3D dense volumetric reconstruction and shape modeling to pineapple fruit. Pineapple is a high-value crop that is grown by many farmers and on a large scale in Thailand. Chaivivatrakul and colleagues [1,11] describe a method for 3D reconstruction of pineapple fruits based on sparse keypoint classification, fruit region tracking, and structure from motion techniques. The method finds sparse Harris keypoints, calculates SURF descriptors for the keypoints, and uses a SVM classifier trained offline on hand-labeled data to classify the local descriptors. Morphological closing is used to segment the fruit using the classified features. Fruit regions are tracked from frame to frame. Frame-to-frame keypoint matches within putative fruit regions are filtered using the nearest neighbor ratio, symmetry test, and epipolar geometry constraints, then the surviving matches are used to obtain a 3D point cloud for the fruit region. An ellipsoid model is fitted to the point cloud to estimate the size and orientation of each fruit. The main limitation of the method is the use of sparse features with SURF descriptors to segment fruit regions. Filling in the gaps between sparse features using morphological operations is efficient but leads to imprecise delineation of the fruit region boundaries. To some extent, robust 3D reconstruction methods can clean up these imprecise boundaries, but the entire processing stream would be better served by an efficient but accurate classification of *every pixel in the image*, and then a dense 3D reconstruction using the classified fruit pixels. Qureshi et al. [13] present a texture-based dense fruit segmentation method for pineapples that uses super-pixel over-segmentation, dense SIFT (scale invariant feature transform) descriptors that characterize the local gradient field of an image around a keypoint, and a bag-of-visual-word histogram classifier within each super-pixel. This enables classification of every pixel in the image as a member of a fruit or non-fruit region.

In this study, we present a new method for volumetric reconstruction and shape modeling of quadric objects, with the ellipsoidal shape of a pineapple as a special case in cluttered outdoor environments typical of agricultural fields using an RGB-D sensor. We first estimate the camera trajectory, then we perform volumetric reconstruction of the scene. We segment out the point cloud that belongs to the fruit regions. We then use two novel methods to estimate a parametric shape model for the dense point cloud. We compare our shape modeling methods with direct fitting of an ellipsoid to the segmented point cloud. We find that our methods are better able to estimate the size, shape, and volume of pineapple fruit than is the baseline direct method.

2   Methodology

In order to obtain volumetric 3D models of objects in a scene captured by an RGB-D camera, we execute four consecutive processes: (i) camera motion estimation, (ii) 3D reconstruction given the estimated motion sequence, (iii) 2D segmentation of the objects of interest, and (iv) parametric shape modeling. We use the DVO-SLAM algorithm [7] for motion estimation and the FastFusion algorithm [17] for volumetric model reconstruction. With DVO-SLAM, we obtain an estimated camera trajectory based on a sequence of RGB-D image data. We then apply FastFusion with the DVO-SLAM trajectory as input. FastFusion fuses the observed color and geometry data to acquire a volumetric model from which a high-quality mesh can be generated. Although the general approach to parametric shape modeling is applicable to any kind of object whose shape can be expressed parametrically, in the case study developed in this paper, we focus on modeling pineapple fruit as ellipsoidal volumes. For dense segmentation of pineapple fruit from RGB-D point clouds, we use pixel classification based on super-pixel over-segmentation, clustering of dense SIFT (Scale Invariant Feature Transform) features into visual words, and bag-of-visual-word super-pixel classification using SVMs (Support Vector Machines). The implementations of the DVO-SLAM and FastFusion algorithms are open source and freely available [20,21].

2.1   Motion Estimation

Camera tracking is the task of estimating, at any point in a sequence of images, a frame-to-frame transformation

$$G_{4 \times 4} = \begin{bmatrix} R & t \\ 0 & 1 \end{bmatrix}, \tag{1}$$

consisting of a rotation matrix $R \in SO(3)$ and a translation vector $t \in \mathbb{R}^3$. Since G expresses an element of the group $SE(3)$, G can be parameterized by a 6-vector $\xi = [\omega_{3 \times 1}^\mathsf{T}, v_{3 \times 1}^\mathsf{T}]^\mathsf{T} \in \mathbb{R}^6$, which is an element of the Lie algebra $\mathfrak{se}(3)$, where ω and v are the angular and linear displacements. We write $G(\xi)$ to indicate the transformation matrix corresponding to ξ. Using the exponential map $\exp(\cdot)$ from $\mathfrak{se}(3)$ to $SE(3)$, we can calculate $G(\xi)$ as

$$G(\xi) = \exp \left(\begin{bmatrix} \hat{\omega} & v \\ 0 & 1 \end{bmatrix} \right), \tag{2}$$

where $\hat{\omega}$ is the skew-symmetric matrix form of ω.

Let T and T' be the 4×4 transformation matrices relating points in the world coordinate system to camera frames F and F'. We define the camera projection π of a point $p = [p_1, p_2, p_3, 1]^\mathsf{T}$ in the camera frame as

$$\pi(p) = \left[\frac{f_u p_1}{p_3} - c_u, \frac{f_v p_2}{p_3} - c_v \right]^\mathsf{T}, \tag{3}$$

where f_u and f_v are the focal lengths and $[c_u, c_v]^\mathsf{T}$ is the principal point of the camera. Using π, the projected image points $x = \pi(T p_w)$ and $x' = \pi(T' p_w)$ of a world point p_w, along with the relationship $T' = GT$, we can obtain a warping function τ explicitly written as a function of ξ:

$$\begin{aligned} \tau(x, \xi) &= x' \\ &= \pi(T' p_w) \\ &= \pi(G(\xi) T p_w) \\ &= \pi(G(\xi) \pi^{-1}(x, Z(x))). \end{aligned} \tag{4}$$

The inverse of π is calculated from a pixel $x = [u, v]^\mathsf{T}$ and $Z(x)$ (the observed depth of x) as

$$\pi^{-1}(x, Z(x)) = \left[\frac{u + c_u}{f_u} Z(x), \frac{v + c_v}{f_v} Z(x), Z(x), 1 \right]^\mathsf{T}. \tag{5}$$

We use DVO-SLAM to find the frame-to-frame transformations $\mathsf{G}(\boldsymbol{\xi})$ that optimally align the observed intensity and depth images. More specifically, DVO-SLAM attempts to minimize the combined error $\boldsymbol{r} = [r_I, r_Z]^\mathsf{T}$ consisting of the photometric residue r_I and the depth residue r_Z, which are defined as

$$r_I = I'(\tau(\boldsymbol{x}, \boldsymbol{\xi})) - I(\boldsymbol{x}), \tag{6}$$
$$r_Z = Z'(\tau(\boldsymbol{x}, \boldsymbol{\xi})) - Z(\boldsymbol{x}), \tag{7}$$

where I, I', Z, and Z' are the intensity images and depth images captured from camera frames F and F', respectively. To obtain an optimal robust estimate of $\mathsf{G}(\boldsymbol{\xi})$, we seek the motion vector $\boldsymbol{\xi}$ that minimizes the sum of the weighted squares of $\boldsymbol{r}$ over all valid pixel indices i in I:

$$\boldsymbol{\xi}^* = \underset{\boldsymbol{\xi}}{\operatorname{argmin}} \sum_i w_i \boldsymbol{r_i}^\mathsf{T} \Sigma_r^{-1} \boldsymbol{r_i}, \tag{8}$$

where $w_i = (\nu + 1)/(\nu + \boldsymbol{r_i}^\mathsf{T} \Sigma_r^{-1} \boldsymbol{r_i})$ is a pixel-wise weight and Σ_r is a scale matrix. DVO-SLAM assumes that the bivariate random variable $\boldsymbol{r}$ follows a t-distribution $p_t(\boldsymbol{\mu_r}, \Sigma_r, \nu)$ with mean $\boldsymbol{\mu_r} = \boldsymbol{0}$ and $\nu = 5$ degrees of freedom. Nonlinear least squares estimation of $\boldsymbol{\xi}$ is performed iteratively using the Gauss-Newton algorithm with the following linearized normal equations:

$$\sum_i w_i \mathsf{J}_i^\mathsf{T} \Sigma_r^{-1} \mathsf{J}_i \Delta\boldsymbol{\xi} = -\sum_i w_i \mathsf{J}_i^\mathsf{T} \Sigma_r^{-1} \boldsymbol{r_i}, \tag{9}$$

where $\Delta\boldsymbol{\xi}$ is an unknown increment vector and $\mathsf{J}_i = \partial\boldsymbol{r_i}/\partial\boldsymbol{\xi}$ is the 2×6 Jacobian matrix of the residual vector $\boldsymbol{r_i}$ evaluated at $\boldsymbol{\xi} = \boldsymbol{0}$. On each Gauss-Newton iteration, w_i and Σ_r are re-estimated using an expectation-maximization algorithm.

To reduce the accumulated drift across the estimated frame-to-frame transformations, DVO-SLAM uses a key-frame based pose SLAM method. A new key-frame is selected as the uncertainty of motion estimation relative to the last key-frame grows. To obtain an optimized camera trajectory, we construct and optimize a pose graph of the key-frames where the edges between adjacent key-frames are weighted by the uncertainty of the corresponding motion estimation. For further details, we refer the reader to [7].

2.2   Model Reconstruction

As previously mentioned, we use the FastFusion algorithm for volumetric 3D reconstruction. FastFusion is based on three main concepts: implicit surface representation, an efficient octree data structure, and mesh generation.

Surface Representation via Signed Distance Function. After motion estimation, we have the estimated trajectory of the camera $\mathsf{T}_1, \cdots \mathsf{T}_t$. In FastFusion [17], following Curless and Levoy [2], a 3D surface is implicitly expressed as a collection of signed distances assigned to the centers of voxels in the space.

Let p be the center of a voxel in the world coordinate frame. For a given camera frame with estimated world-to-camera transformation T_t at time t, the center point p_c in the camera coordinate frame is

$$p_c = \mathrm{T}_t p. \tag{10}$$

On the other hand, using the image projection function $\pi(p_c)$ and the depth map Z_t, an observed point p_{obs} along the ray from the camera center through p_c can be calculated as

$$p_{obs} = \pi^{-1}(\pi(p_c), Z_t(\pi(p_c))). \tag{11}$$

$Z_t(\pi(p_c))$ can be interpolated from neighboring pixel depth measurements. The signed distance function d_t is defined as

$$d_t(p_c, Z_t) = \max(\min(|p_c - p_{obs}|, \Phi), -\Phi), \tag{12}$$

where $|\cdot|$ is the Euclidean norm with a sign indicating which side of the surface containing p_{obs} the voxel center p_c lies, and $\Phi(> 0)$ is a cut-off threshold set to twice the voxel scale. Along with d_t, FastFusion also defines a weight function

$$w_t = \begin{cases} 1 & \text{if } d_t < \delta \\ \frac{\Phi - d_t}{\Phi - \delta} & \text{if } \delta < d_t < \Phi \\ 0 & \text{if } d_t > \Phi, \end{cases} \tag{13}$$

where δ is set to one tenth of the voxel resolution. This weight gives linearly decreasing confidence when the voxel center is behind the surface (the sign of $|p_c - p_{obs}|$ is positive).

When a new observation for a previously observed voxel is obtained at time t, again following Curless and Levoy, the previously assigned weight W_{t-1} and signed distance D_{t-1} are updated according to the following rules:

$$W_t = w_t + W_{t-1}, \tag{14}$$

$$D_t = \frac{D_{t-1}W_{t-1} + d_t w_t}{w_t + W_{t-1}}. \tag{15}$$

Similarly, the previously stored RGB color vector $C_{t-1} = [C_{R,t-1}, C_{G,t-1}, C_{B,t-1}]^\mathsf{T}$ is updated as

$$C_t = \frac{C_{t-1}W_{t-1} + I_t^C(\pi(p_c))w_t}{w_t + W_{t-1}}, \tag{16}$$

where $I_t^C = [I_{R,t}, I_{G,t}, I_{B,t}]^\mathsf{T}$ is the observed RGB pixel at time t.

Multi-resolution Octree Representation of Surfaces. To store observed surfaces in a memory efficient manner, FastFusion uses a novel octree-based surface representation with the previously explained signed distance function.

Associated with every branch and leaf in the octree is a set of $8 \times 8 \times 8$ voxels that equally partition its volume. Each tree level represents a 3D model at a particular resolution, and we only allocate voxels within the vicinity of observed 3D points, making the data structure sparse and memory efficient.

When a new observation is obtained, we first determine the resolution of the observed surface points based on their depth values, then we conduct a depth-first-search to find a bounding volume in the level corresponding to that resolution. Finally, we allocate a new set of voxels if the corresponding volume is empty, or otherwise, update the signed distances and color information based on Equations 14, 15, and 16.

Mesh Generation with Marching Cubes. Now, given the signed distance associated with each voxel in the the multi-resolution grid, we apply the well-known marching cubes algorithm to extract an explicit surface representation from the grid. Since voxels near to and in front of an observed surface will have negative signed distances, and voxels near to and behind an observed surface will have positive signed distances, an excellent estimate of the surface would be a 3D triangle mesh corresponding to the 0 level set of the grid. The well-known marching cubes algorithm is ideal for obtaining such a mesh.

The mesh extraction is thus straightforward when the voxels being considered are all at the same level of resolution in the octree. With multi-resolution voxels, however, we have to solve for border cases where voxels at a higher and lower resolution are adjacent to each other. FastFusion proposes a recursive algorithm capable of solving this problem as follows.

Suppose a branch B^s at scale s is divided into eight subbranches $B_i^{s+1}, i \in \{1, \cdots, 8\}$ at scale $s + 1$. We can categorize voxels $V_{i,j}^{s+1}, j \in \{1, \cdots, 8^3\}$ belonging to each of the eight subbranches into four types: interior, face, edge, and corner. An interior voxel is a voxel, when considered as the origin of a group of eight neighboring voxels considered for mesh generation, whose seven higher voxels are all within the same subbranch. A face voxel is a voxel having neighbor voxels belonging to one other subbranch. An edge voxel is a voxel having neighbors belonging to three other subbranches. Finally, a corner voxel is a voxel having neighbors belonging to seven other subbranches. If any of the subbranches affecting meshing of $V_{i,j}^{s+1}$ are subdivided into a higher scale $s + 2$, the voxels in the higher resolution neighboring subbranches could themselves be either interior, face, edge, or corner voxels depending on the situation. Therefore, we can construct a recursive algorithm to perform meshing of the entire tree. When a marching cube contains voxels with lower resolution than other voxels, we perform interpolation to break the lower resolution voxels into corresponding higher resolution voxels.

2.3 Fruit Segmentation

For dense segmentation of fruit regions in images, we need to classify each pixel into fruit and non-fruit regions. Color-based dense classification fails when the objects of interest have coloration similar to that of the background, such as pineapple fruits in the field. Chaivivatrakul et al. [1] note the limitations of color and shape cues for recognition of green fruit on trees and plants and propose texture-based classification instead. Qureshi et al. [13] describe a texture-based classification method that selects fruit regions using a dense pixel segmentation method. The method performs over-segmentation into super-pixels, extracts Dense-SIFT descriptors for the pixels in a super-pixel, maps SIFT descriptors to clusters, constructs a bag-of-visual-words histogram for the clusters appearing in the super-pixel, and then classifies the histogram for a super-pixel as fruit or non-fruit using a support vector machine (SVM). Dense-SIFT is a type of gradient orientation histogram descriptor that captures the distribution of local gradients in a pixel's neighborhood. Clustering local gradient descriptor improves sensitivity to noise, then the bag-of-visual-words histogram characterizes the differing distribution of gradient descriptors within a superpixel. Finally, since local histograms based on a small number of pixels in a region with uniform coloration can be quite sparse, augmenting each histogram by including the histograms of neighboring super-pixels. Put together, these techniques enable us to create a unique signature of a region for classification. The classifier requires off-line training prior to runtime utilization of the classifier model. Training requires a set of training images along with ground truth data. Ground truth labeling (assigning a label of "fruit" or "non-fruit" to each pixel) is performed manually.

To segment an input point cloud into fruit and non-fruit regions, we first obtain a 2D image mask indicating likely fruit regions, then we segment the point cloud by filtering out 3D points in correspondence with non-fruit regions in the 2D mask. To obtain the 2D mask, we use the method described by Qureshi et al. [13].

For the experiments reported upon in this paper, we used the same parameters (quick-shift variables, dense-SIFT bin size, size of the dictionary for the k-means clustering of SIFT descriptors, scale at which to compute SIFT features, number of neighbors used to construct super-pixel histograms, and conditional random field (CRF) post-processing) as reported by Qureshi et al. [13].

At runtime, segmenting a new image using the trained model requires super-pixel over-segmentation, dense SIFT descriptor computation, visual word histogram calculation, SVM classification, and CRF post-processing. The classifier outputs a confidence for each super-pixel; a super-pixel is classified as a fruit region if the confidence is higher than a threshold. The threshold, determined by the SVM training algorithm, is that which best separates the fruit super-pixels from the non-fruit super-pixels in its training set.

As already mentioned, once a 2D mask for likely fruit regions is obtained, we use the mask to filter the 3D point cloud (raw or generated through volumetric reconstruction) according to the label assigned to each 3D point's 2D correspondence.

2.4   Parametric Fruit Modeling

A pineapple fruit shape can be best described by an ellipsoid [1]. An ellipsoid is a special case of the general quadric, which is the set of homogeneous 3D points p such that

$$p^T Q p = 0, \tag{17}$$

with Q a 4×4 symmetric homogeneous matrix.

When the quadric is a centered, axis-aligned ellipsoid, the diagonal terms of Q must have the same sign to be characterized as ellipsoids. Enforcing this constraint constrains the parameters of the general quadric, reducing sensitivity to errors. One method to estimate an ellipsoid from a 3D point cloud is Li and Griffiths' [10] direct least squares method. However, when we use an RGB-D sensor in the field, it is not in general possible to move slowly around every fruit, so we typically obtain only a partial view. Also, the raw or FastFusion-based point clouds we obtain as previously described contain noise from the RGB-D sensor as well as small non-fruit regions arising due to false positives in the 2D image segmentation method. We find that the direct least squares method for estimating ellipsoids from sparse point clouds does not work well for dense point clouds containing false fruit regions and other noise. Therefore, robust estimation of an ellipsoid requires eliminating outliers (false positive fruit points) that would otherwise affect the ellipsoid model estimate. Moonrinta et al. [11] present a robust ellipsoid estimator using RANSAC and the direct least squares method with sparse samples of 3D points from the fruit surface. Here, we present an extension of their parametric shape modeling method to dense point clouds that is more robust to noise and false fruit regions. Then we present a new nonlinear optimization method for finding the parameters of an ellipsoid that minimizes the dense SIFT descriptor distance between pixels in correspondence according to the hypothesized ellipsoid.

Robust Parametric Shape Fitting. Prior to shape fitting, to eliminate noisy and non-fruit points far from the target point cloud, we perform clustering of the points in the 3D point cloud using k-means. In the experiments reported upon in this paper, we manually set k to be one more than the number of actual fruits observed in the point cloud. In future work, we plan to automate the selection of k (using, for example, the Bayesian Information Criterion (BIC)). After performing k-means, we remove the points belonging to the smallest cluster on the assumption that it contains only noise.

After k-means and noise removal, we perform robust estimation of the ellipsoid model with Li and Griffiths' direct least squares method as the basic estimator. Following the general approach of random sample consensus (RANSAC), we alternate between estimation of a model from a randomly selected minimum sample from the data set and checking the size of the "consensus" or inlier set for the estimated model. The sample-and-test process is terminated after a fixed number of iterations.

When testing an estimated model in this procedure, we use Torr et al.'s [19] ranking of the consensus set. The original RANSAC method simply maximizes the count of the number of points in the consensus set CS:

$$r(CS) = \sum_i |CS|. \tag{18}$$

Following Torr et al., this can also be written as minimization of a cost function

$$r(CS) = \sum_i \rho(e_i^2), \tag{19}$$

where e_i^2 is the orthogonal distance between point i and the estimated model, and

$$\rho_{RANSAC}(e_i^2) = \begin{cases} 0 & e_i^2 < T \\ 1 & \text{otherwise,} \end{cases} \tag{20}$$

where T in our case is a threshold on the allowable distance of each 3D point to the ellipsoid model's surface.

Torr et al. propose, rather than a hard threshold and inlier count, an alternative cost function inspired by M-estimation:

$$\rho_{MSAC}(e_i^2) = \begin{cases} e_i^2 & e_i^2 < T \\ T & \text{otherwise.} \end{cases} \tag{21}$$

In MSAC, outliers are given a fixed penalty as in RANSAC, but inliers are graded by how fit they are for the model. This sample ranking method results in better estimates than the original RANSAC ranking criterion. We use Zuliani's implementation of MSAC [24]. The complete estimation procedure can be summarized as follows:

1. Randomly select 10 points from the point cloud.
2. Estimate the ellipsoid Q best fitting the selected points [10].
3. Translate and rotate the 3D point set into the ellipsoid's coordinate system.
4. Find the orthogonal distance of each point to the surface of the ellipsoid [3].
5. Find the inlier consensus set, i.e., the set of points lying within the distance threshold from the ellipsoid surface.
6. Find the MSAC cost of the sample [19]. If it is the lowest-cost sample seen so far, save the model.
7. Repeat from step 1 until a maximum number of iterations is reached.

Nonlinear Optimization. Here we present a new iterative nonlinear optimization method for estimating an ellipsoid parametric shape model from RGB-D point cloud data. We aim to find the parameters of the ellipsoid that minimizes the dense SIFT descriptor distance between pixels in correspondence according to the hypothesized ellipsoid. We use two key-frames to find the optimized ellipsoid. We first eliminate noisy and non-fruit 3D points far from the target point cloud by k-means as explained in Section 2.4. We use the Levenberg-Marquardt (LM) algorithm to find the best Q. We initialize LM with the ellipsoid estimated from the 3D point cloud using Li and Griffiths' [10] direct least squares method. Mathematically we can state the problem as follows:

Given a set of 2D points $\boldsymbol{x}_i \in \mathbb{P}^2$ in image I with $i \in 1 \cdots n$ and $n \geq 10$ and a second image I', find a 4×4 symmetric homogeneous matrix Q that minimizes the cost function

$$\chi = \sum_{i=1}^{n} d(D_{\boldsymbol{x}_i}, D_{\boldsymbol{x}'_i})^2, \tag{22}$$

subject to

$$\boldsymbol{p}_i^{\mathsf{T}} \mathsf{Q} \boldsymbol{p}_i = 0.$$

In the equation, $d(\cdot)$ is Euclidean distance, $D_{\boldsymbol{x}_i}$ and $D_{\boldsymbol{x}'_i}$ are SIFT descriptors of $\boldsymbol{x}_i$ and $\boldsymbol{x}'_i$ in image I and I', respectively, $\boldsymbol{p}_i$ is the back projection of $\boldsymbol{x}_i$ onto Q, and $\boldsymbol{x}'_i$ is the reprojection of $\boldsymbol{p}_i$ into image I'.

For lack of space, we omit the derivation of how to find $\boldsymbol{x}'$ from $\boldsymbol{p}$ and Q.

To compute SIFT descriptors for the reprojected 2D points $\boldsymbol{x}'$ with subpixel accuracy, we first compute a dense SIFT descriptor for each pixel in image I', then we use spline interpolation to interpolate the SIFT descriptors of the reprojected 2D points.

Whenever the ray back-projected from point $\boldsymbol{x}_i$ in image I does not intersect with the hypothesized quadric, there is no corresponding 3D point $\boldsymbol{p}_i$, in which case we assign a cost ϱ in place of $d(D_{\boldsymbol{x}_i}, D_{\boldsymbol{x}'_i})$ in Equation 22.

Pineapple fruit can be modeled by ellipsoids (nearly spheroids) that have a major-axis to minor-axis ratio in the range of 1.0 to 2.0. To encourage LM to traverse only the family of ellipsoids that have a major-axis to minor-axis ratio of r such that $1 < r < 2$, we add another penalty σ in the cost function given in Equation 22 penalizing extreme ratios. As a final modification, since the point cloud from the RGB-D sensor is dense, and since the depths of the points in the point cloud give reasonable estimates of the location of the ellipsoid in the z-direction, we further constrain LM by adding a penalty ζ discouraging changes in the average depth of the hypothesized quadric by more than $\pm 1.0\%$.

The new cost function, after adding penalties ϱ, σ, and ζ, becomes

$$\chi = \sum_{i \in 1 \cdots n | \boldsymbol{x}'_i \text{exists}} d(D_{\boldsymbol{x}_i}, D_{\boldsymbol{x}'_i})^2 + \sum_{i \in 1 \cdots n | \boldsymbol{x}'_i \neg \text{exists}} \varrho + \sigma + \zeta. \tag{23}$$

A summary of the steps of the LM optimization of Q is as follows:

1. Find the 3D points lying on Q back-projected from the fruit points in image I.
2. Find the re-projections of the back-projected 3D points into image I'.
3. Compute SIFT descriptors of fruit pixels in image I and I'.
4. Compute SIFT descriptors of re-projected pixels in I' using spline interpolation.

5. Compute the L2 distances between SIFT descriptors of corresponding fruit pixels in image I and I'.
6. For each back-projected 2D point that does not intersect Q, add a penalty ϱ instead of the SIFT descriptor distance.
7. Find the ratio of major-axis to minor axis of the hypothesized ellipsoid.
8. If the ratio r is in the range $1 < r < 2$, then $\sigma = 0$, else $\sigma = 5$.
9. If the mean depth of the back-projected 2D points is within 1% of the point cloud's average depth, then then $\zeta = 0$ else $\zeta = 5$.

3   Experimental Evaluation

We performed a real-world experiment involving a case study on 3D reconstruction of pineapple fruits as an empirical evaluation of the feasibility of our approach. We captured video data from an outdoor scene containing two fruits then applied the modeling method to the resulting RGB-D image sequence. In this section we detail the experimental design then present the experiment's results.

3.1   Experimental Methods

To simulate conditions in a pineapple field, we placed two pineapple fruits (Fruit A and Fruit B) on top of other plants with long leaves that resemble real pineapple leaves. The horizontal distance between the two pineapples was approximately 2m. The entire volume needed for this small-scale mock pineapple field was approximately 4m × 2m × 0.5m. To record an RGB-D sequence of the mock field, we used the Apple Primesense Carmine 1.09 short-range sensor, which has an operational range of 0.35m–1.4m. Since this device requires only a standard USB connection to operate, we can use it with a laptop computer in both indoor and outdoor environments. In the case of an outdoor environment, however, the scene illumination should not substantially exceed typical indoor illumination, or the depth sensor fails. Therefore, in this experiment, we enforced this weak lighting constraint by recording in the late afternoon. We recorded an RGB-D sequence of 400 frames while manually moving the sensor over the pineapples with the camera facing toward the fruits. The frame rate for both RGB and depth image acquisition was set to 30 fps. After acquiring the RGB-D sequence, we applied DVO-SLAM to obtain an estimated trajectory for the sequence of camera frames. With the trajectory and RGB-D data as input, we then applied FastFusion to incrementally build a volumetric model of the scene. After completing the fusion of all 400 RGB-D frames, we exported a textured triangle mesh of the final model into our OpenGL-based custom software. Fig. 1 shows the entire view of the final model along with the estimated camera trajectory.

Based on the FastFusion mesh, we used OpenGL to render a new sequence of 100 RGB and 100 depth images corresponding to every four camera frames in the original trajectory. At this point, we had 100 synthetic RGB and depth images rendered in OpenGL relative to a sequence of estimated camera frames. Fig. 2 shows a pair of synthetic RGB and depth images of Fruit A. For each

Fig. 1. Reconstruction of a mock pineapple field with the estimated camera trajectory.

resulting synthetic RGB image, we applied the 2D fruit region mask obtained from dense segmentation of the corresponding original image. Finally, we generated a 3D point cloud from the masked synthetic RGB-D image. For purposes of experimental comparison, in addition to these 100 synthetic point clouds, we also generated 100 corresponding 3D point clouds based on the raw RGB-D sensor data using the same fruit mask.

(a)   (b)   (c)

Fig. 2. Sample data for Fruit A. (a) Original RGB image. (b) Synthetic RGB image rendered from volumetric model at the same camera position as (a). (c) Depth buffer corresponding to (b).

For parametric shape modeling, we compare three methods of estimating an ellipsoid from the segmented 3D-point cloud data, where the point cloud is either the raw RGB-D sensor based point cloud or the point cloud synthesized from the volumetric model. The first estimation method is direct least squares [10], the second is MSAC, and the third is SIFT differences, which were discussed in section 2.4. For the direct estimation we perform k-mean clustering to remove potential false fruit regions similar to the steps. For method two and three we follow the steps mentioned in and respectively.

We tuned the penalty parameters experimentally. For each of the two fruits in the experimental sequence, we extracted point clouds based on two manually selected key-frames. Fig. 3 shows the dense segmentation of the four key-frames

<table>
<tr><td>(a)</td><td>(b)</td><td>(c)</td><td>(d)</td></tr>
</table>

Fig. 3. Segmented Fruit A and Fruit B. (a) Segmented Fruit A in frame 1. (b) Segmented Fruit A in frame 2. (c) Segmented Fruit B in frame 3. (d) Segmented Fruit B in frame 4.

used to segment the point clouds for fruits A and B. The segmentations of the fruit A images contain several non-fruit false positive regions connected to the true positive region, while the segmentation of fruit B is more accurate, with one false positive region not connected to the true positive region in Fig. 3(d).

3.2   Results

Results for the application of three parametric shape modeling methods (Direct, MSAC, and SIFT differences) to two types of point clouds (raw and synthetic model-based) are given in Table 1. We obtained ground truth geometries of Fruit A and Fruit B by manual measurements. Parametric shape modeling was performed on segmented point clouds corresponding to synthetic models and raw sensor observations, respectively. Fig. 4 shows shape models of fruit B projected onto an original RGB image.

(a)   (b)   (c)   (d)

Fig. 4. Shape models of fruit B. (a) Original RGB image. (b) Direct method (failure). (c) MSAC method. (d) SIFT differences method.

There is a clear advantage to model-based point clouds. Except for the divergence of the direct method applied to model-based point clouds of fruit B, the error rates for all shape modeling methods are smaller due to the higher accuracy of model-based point clouds than raw point clouds from the sensor.

The baseline direct method shows instability when it is applied to model Fruit B due to false fruit regions. We used non-connected fruit region for direct method, MSAC and LM. The k-mean was not able to remove the non connected path. We assume the same steps for each. Parametric shape modeling using other two methods however successfully converged to the approximate shape and size of the fruits.

The performance comparison between MSAC and SIFT differences is less clear. Although SIFT differences uses the richer information contained in the SIFT descriptors as constraints, it does not show any clear performance gain over the MSAC method.

Table 1. Point cloud types vs. shape modeling methods.

| Point Cloud | Parameters | Ground Truth | | Observations | | | | | |
| | | | | Direct | | MSAC | | SIFT differences | |
		Fruit A	Fruit B	Fruit A	Fruit B	Fruit A	Fruit B	Fruit A	Fruit B
Model	Major	8.9	7.8	10.5	30.7	9.2	7.7	9.2	7.9
	Minor 1	5.1	5.2	4.8	24.8	5.9	5.2	5.9	5.3
	Minor 2	5.1	5.2	5.1	20.9	5.6	5.8	5.6	5.9
	Volume	969.2	883.0	1079.0	66431.7	1257.7	974.9	1268.8	1047.6
	Major/Minor	1.75	1.50	2.12	1.35	1.61	1.41	1.61	1.41
	Major error	–	–	18.0%	294.0%	**3.3%**	**-0.7%**	3.6%	1.7%
	Minor 1 error	–	–	**-5.5%**	376.3%	14.8%	**0.3%**	15.2%	2.8%
	Minor 2 error	–	–	**-0.2%**	301.0%	9.4%	**10.9%**	9.7%	13.5%
	Volume error	–	–	**11.3%**	7423.3%	29.8%	**10.4%**	30.9%	18.6%
	Major/Minor error	–	–	21.5%	-10.2%	**-7.8%**	**-6.0%**	-7.9%	**-5.9%**
Raw	Major	8.9	7.8	11.1	23.1	9.8	8.5	9.8	8.5
	Minor 1	5.1	5.2	6.6	14.9	6.1	5.6	6.1	5.6
	Minor 2	5.1	5.2	7.2	13.6	7.3	4.8	7.3	4.9
	Volume	969.2	883.0	2183.1	19510.5	1815.4	965.8	1814.1	971.3
	Major/Minor	1.75	1.50	1.61	1.62	1.47	1.62	1.47	1.62
	Major error	–	–	24.6%	195.6%	**10.1%**	**8.7%**	10.1%	8.9%
	Minor 1 error	–	–	28.8%	186.3%	**19.3%**	**8.0%**	19.3%	8.2%
	Minor 2 error	–	–	**40.4%**	161.1%	42.6%	-6.8%	42.5%	**-6.6%**
	Volume error	–	–	125.3%	2109.5%	87.3%	**9.4%**	87.2%	10.0%
	Major/Minor error	–	–	**-7.5%**	**8.0%**	-16.0%	8.1%	-15.9%	8.1%

4 Conclusion

In this paper, we have presented a new method for volumetric reconstruction and shape modeling of quadric objects using an RGB-D sensor. We first estimate the camera's trajectory, then we perform volumetric reconstruction of the scene. We segment out point clouds belonging to object regions. We then use two novel methods for robust estimation of a parametric shape model for the extracted dense point cloud. We compare our shape modeling methods with direct fitting of an ellipsoid to the segmented point cloud.

The main limitations of the experimental setup are (i) the small scale of the mock pineapple field (4 m × 2 m × 0.5 m, with only two fruit), (ii) the limited operational range of the sensor (0.35 m–1.4 m), (iii) the limited resolution of the RGBD camera (640 × 480), (iv) the requirement for diffuse lighting, and (v) the requirement for sufficient fruit surface visibility given the camera angles. In future work, we will attempt to mitigate these limitations.

We find that model-based point clouds show a clear advantage over raw depth sensor point clouds for parametric shape modeling. Also, our methods are more robust and better able to estimate the size, shape, and volume of pineapple fruit than is the baseline direct method. Although we hypothesized that LM optimization of dense SIFT descriptor distances would perform better than MSAC, we did not observe a clear difference in the performance of the two algorithms. One reason for this may be the noise due to false positive fruit pixels around the segmented fruit boundaries (see Fig. 3).

In the future, we plan to investigate possible improvements, for example constraining the parametric model to spheroids rather than general ellipsoids. We also plan to improve the SIFT difference method's sensitivity at object boundaries. We also plan to investigate the possibility of obtaining similarly high accuracy without the RGB-D sensor and volumetric modeling, instead estimating the camera trajectory using structure from motion (SfM) based techniques similar to those of Wu et al. [23]. After obtaining monocular camera positions, we can perform SIFT difference optimization to estimate the parametric shape model by initializing it with a quadric estimated from the sparse set of 3D points estimated through SfM. We also plan to test our methods on a large scale real fruit crop in Thailand. Efficient fitting of quadric shapes to unstructured point clouds or triangle meshes is an important component of many reverse engineering systems [15,22]. Up till now, the use of ellipsoid shapes has been limited, but ellipsoids have proven useful for body-part modeling in the past [14]. Our methods (MSAC and SIFT differences) could both be used in a general framework for quadric surface modeling to point-cloud data. Although most objects are not purely quadratic, an extension to piecewise-quadratic surface estimation would enable efficient and accurate modeling of a large class of real-world objects more compactly than the current polygon mesh based approaches.

References

1. Chaivivatrakul, S., Moonrinta, J., Dailey, M.N.: Towards automated crop yield estimation: detection and 3D reconstruction of pineapples in video sequences. In: International Conference on Computer Vision Theory and Applications (2010)
2. Curless, B., Levoy, M.: A volumetric method for building complex models from range images. In: Proceedings of the 23rd Annual Conference on Computer Graphics and Interactive Techniques, SIGGRAPH 1996, pp. 303–312. ACM, New York (1996)
3. David Eberly: Distance from a Point to an Ellipsoid (2008). http://www.geometrictools.com/
4. Engel, J., Schöps, T., Cremers, D.: LSD-SLAM: large-scale direct monocular SLAM. In: Fleet, D., Pajdla, T., Schiele, B., Tuytelaars, T. (eds.) ECCV 2014, Part II. LNCS, vol. 8690, pp. 834–849. Springer, Heidelberg (2014)
5. Engel, J., Sturm, J., Cremers, D.: Semi-dense visual odometry for a monocular camera. In: IEEE International Conference on Computer Vision (ICCV). Sydney, Australia, December 2013
6. Forster, C., Pizzoli, M., Scaramuzza, D.: Svo: fast semi-direct monocular visual odometry. In: Int. Conf. on Robotics and Automation, pp. 15–22 (2014)
7. Kerl, C., Sturm, J., Cremers, D.: Dense visual SLAM for RGB-D cameras. In: Proc. of the Int. Conf. on Intelligent Robot Systems (IROS), pp. 2100–2106 (2013)
8. Kerl, C., Sturm, J., Cremers, D.: Robust odometry estimation for RGB-D cameras. In: Proc. of the IEEE Int. Conf. on Robotics and Automation (ICRA), May 2013

9. Klein, G., Murray, D.: Parallel tracking and mapping for small AR workspaces. In: Proc. Sixth IEEE and ACM International Symposium on Mixed and Augmented Reality (ISMAR 2007), Nara, Japan, November 2007

10. Li, Q., Griffiths, J.G.: Least squares ellipsoid specific fitting. In: Proceedings of the Geometric Modeling and Processing, 2004, pp. 335–340. IEEE (2004)

11. Moonrinta, J., Chaivivatrakul, S., Dailey, M.N., Ekpanyapong, M.: Fruit detection, tracking, and 3d reconstruction for crop mapping and yield estimation. In: IEEE International Conference on Control, Automation, Robotics and Vision (2010)

12. Newcombe, R.A., Izadi, S., Hilliges, O., Molyneaux, D., Kim, D., Davison, A.J., Kohli, P., Shotton, J., Hodges, S., Fitzgibbon, A.: Kinectfusion: real-time dense surface mapping and tracking. In: Proceedings of the 2011 10th IEEE International Symposium on Mixed and Augmented Reality. ISMAR 2011, pp. 127–136. IEEE Computer Society, Washington, DC (2011)

13. Qureshi, W.S., Satoh, S., Dailey, M.N., Ekpanyapong, M.: Dense segmentation of textured fruits in video sequences. In: 9th International Conference on Computer Vision Theory and Applications (VISAPP 2014), pp. 441–447 (2014)

14. Sarris, N., Strintzis, M.G.: 3D modeling and animation: Synthesis and analysis techniques for the human body. IGI Global (2005)

15. Shamir, A.: A survey on mesh segmentation techniques. In: Computer Graphics Forum, vol. 27, pp. 1539–1556. Wiley Online Library (2008)

16. Steinbruecker, F., Kerl, C., Sturm, J., Cremers, D.: Large-scale multi-resolution surface reconstruction from RGB-D sequences. In: IEEE International Conference on Computer Vision (ICCV), Sydney, Australia, pp. 3264–3271 (2013)

17. Steinbruecker, F., Sturm, J., Cremers, D.: Volumetric 3D mapping in real-time on a CPU. In: Int. Conf. on Robotics and Automation, Hongkong, China, pp. 2021–2028 (2014)

18. Sturm, J., Engelhard, N., Endres, F., Burgard, W., Cremers, D.: A benchmark for the evaluation of RGB-D SLAM systems. In: Proc. of the International Conference on Intelligent Robot Systems (IROS), October 2012

19. Torr, P.H., Zisserman, A.: MLESAC: A new robust estimator with application to estimating image geometry. Computer Vision and Image Understanding **78**(1), 138–156 (2000)

20. TUM Computer Vision Group: Dense Visual Odometry and SLAM (2013). https://github.com/tum-vision/dvo_slam

21. TUM Computer Vision Group: Volumetric 3D Mapping in Real-Time on a CPU (2014). https://github.com/tum-vision/fastfusion

22. Varady, T., Martin, R.R., Cox, J.: Reverse engineering of geometric modelsan introduction. Computer-Aided Design **29**(4), 255–268 (1997)

23. Wu, C.: Towards linear-time incremental structure from motion. In: 2013 International Conference on 3D Vision-3DV 2013, pp. 127–134. IEEE (2013)

24. Zuliani, M.: Ransac for dummies. Tech. rep., November 2008

Biomedical Applications

Efficient Resolution Enhancement Algorithm for Compressive Sensing Magnetic Resonance Image Reconstruction

Osama A. Omer[1,2]([✉]), M. Atef Bassiouny[3], and Ken'ichi Morooka[1]

[1] Graduate School of Information Science and Electrical Engineering,
Kyushu University, 744 Motooka, Nishi-Ku, Fukuoka 819-0395, Japan
omer.osama@gmail.com
[2] Department of Electrical Engineering, Aswan University, Aswan 81542, Egypt
[3] Arab Academy for Science, Technology and Maritime Transport, Aswan, Egypt

Abstract. Magnetic resonance imaging (MRI) has been widely applied in a number of clinical and preclinical applications. However, the resolution of the reconstructed images using conventional algorithms are often insufficient to distinguish diagnostically crucial information due to limited measurements. In this paper, we consider the problem of reconstructing a high resolution (HR) MRI signal from very limited measurements. The proposed algorithm is based on compressed sensing, which combines wavelet sparsity with the sparsity of image gradients, where the magnetic resonance (MR) images are generally sparse in wavelet and gradient domain. The main goal of the proposed algorithm is to reconstruct the HR MR image directly from a few measurements. Unlike the compressed sensing (CS) MRI reconstruction algorithms, the proposed algorithm uses multi measurements to reconstruct HR image. Also, unlike the resolution enhancement algorithms, the proposed algorithm perform resolution enhancement of MR image simultaneously with the reconstruction process from few measurements. The proposed algorithm is compared with three state-of-the-art CS-MRI reconstruction algorithms in sense of signal-to-noise ratio and full-with-half-maximum values.

Keywords: MRI · Wavelet transform · Sparsity · Resolution enhancement

1 Introduction

Sparsity has been demonstrated to be a powerful tool in several problems in last years [1]. It has been recognized that it is possible to make a good reconstruction of medical images by exploring sparsity and redundancy of these images. Also, it is known that sparsity is an important structure in MR images. As a good feature of sparse signals, it is well known that sparse signals require fewer samples than required by the Shannon-Nyquist sampling theorem. Therefore, to shorten magnetic resonance imaging (MRI) scanning time, compressed sensing is widely applied in the MRI reconstruction.

On the other hand, there are several approaches for increasing the resolution of MR images. Among these approaches, the problem of super-resolution (SR) reconstruction

© Springer International Publishing Switzerland 2015
V. Murino and E. Puppo (Eds.): ICIAP 2015, Part I, LNCS 9279, pp. 519–527, 2015.
DOI: 10.1007/978-3-319-23231-7_46

has been studied by many researchers in recent years. The SR problem is defined as restoring a high-resolution (HR) image from a sequence of low-resolution (LR) images [6]. The SR approaches have the feature that they don't require high magnetic field's strength which affects human bodies [6]. Nowadays, most MRI scanners used for medical purposes have magnetic field value of 1.5 or 3 Tesla. Most of the super-resolution approaches are formulated as a post-acquisition image processing techniques.

Although there is doubt that SR is not achievable in MRI [7, 8, 9], since the Fourier encoding scheme excludes aliasing in frequency and phase encoding directions, simulation results show that SR techniques can achieve resolution enhancement in MRI [10-14].

Reconstruction of HR MR image from a few samples is still challenging task in MRI reconstruction. This paper proposes a new method for enhancing the resolution for MRI using resolution enhancement technique using multi-sparse measurements. Like the work done in [12], the resolution enhancement is done simultaneously with the reconstruction process rather than being done as a post-process. However, in this paper the simultaneous resolution enhancement and reconstruction is adopted with the compressed sensing which combines wavelet sparsity with the sparsity of image gradients, where the magnetic resonance images are generally sparse in wavelet and gradient domain.

2   Sparsity of MRI Reconstruction

Compressed sensing focuses on reconstructing an unknown signal from a very limited number of samples. Because information such as boundaries of organs is very sparse in most MR images, compressed sensing makes it possible to reconstruct the same MR image from a very limited set of measurements while significantly reducing the MRI scan duration. In the literature, compressed sensing MRI algorithms minimize a linear combination of total variation and wavelet sparsity constrains [3, 4, 5].

TVCMRI: In [3], Ma et al. proposed the method jointly minimizing the L1 norm of the image, total variation (TV) of the wavelet coefficients, and the least squares of the error as a solution for CS-MRI. This algorithm is based upon an iterative operator-splitting framework. The cost function proposed in [3] is formulated as

$$J(y) = \left\| \mathbf{R}y - b \right\|_2^2 + \alpha \left\| \mathbf{\Phi}y \right\|_{TV} + \beta \left\| y \right\|_1 \tag{1}$$

where $\mathbf{R}$ is a matrix representing the partial Fourier transform, y is the MR image to be reconstructed, b is the measured data in k-space, $\mathbf{\Phi}$ is a matrix representing the wavelet transformation β, α are positive weighting parameters and $\|y\|_{TV} = \sum_i \sum_j \sqrt{\left(\nabla_1 y_{ij} \right)^2 + \left(\nabla_2 y_{ij} \right)^2}$, where ∇_1, ∇_2 are the forward difference operators, of a variable y, on the first and second coordinates, respectively.

FCSA: In [4], Huang et al. proposed to jointly minimizes the L1 norm of the wavelet coefficients, total variation (TV) of the image, and a least squares of the error as a solution the for CS-MRI. The cost function proposed in [4] is formulated as

$$J(y) = \|\mathbf{R}y - b\|_2^2 + \alpha\|y\|_{TV} + \beta\|\Phi y\|_1 \tag{2}$$

The minimization of TV(y) leads to sparsity of the gradient of y, which is the case of MR images, while minimizing $\|y\|_1$ leads to sparsity of y, which is not the case of MR images. Therefore, minimization of (2), which leads to sparsity of image gradient and sparsity of wavelet coefficients of the image, leads to better results compared to minimization in (1), which leads to sparsity of gradients of wavelet coefficients and sparsity of images values, as will be shown in simulation results.

WaTMRI: In [5], the quad-tree sparsity constraint is combined with the sparsity of wavelet coefficients and sparsity of gradient image. The cost function of this algorithm is formulated as

$$J(y) = \|\mathbf{R}y - b\|_2^2 + \alpha\|y\|_{TV} + \beta\left(\|\Phi y\|_1 + \sum_{g\in G}\|\Phi y_g\|_2 \right)$$

where G indicates the set of all parent-child groups and y_g is the data belonging group G.

CS-MR imaging is interested in low sampling ratio. In [3,4,5], authors follow the sampling strategy that is randomly choose more Fourier coefficients from low frequency and less on high frequency.

3   Sparsity-Based HR MRI Reconstruction

Inspired by the success of the minimization of L1-norm and TV in CS-MRI reconstruction, we design the reconstruction of HR CS-MRI by fusing multi measurements in the proposed HR CS-MRI reconstruction model. In the proposed model called CS-MRISR, we propose to penalize the least square of error measure, sparsity of wavelet coefficients and sparsity of gradient image. The proposed cost function is formulated as

$$J_2(y) = \sum_{k=1}^{N}\left[\|\mathbf{RDBF}_k y - b_k\|_2^2\right] + \alpha\|y\|_{TV} + \beta\|\Phi y\|_1 \tag{3}$$

where **D** is the sampling operator, **B** is the blurring operator and $\mathbf{F}_k$ is the warping operator for k-th image. It is commonly assumed that the point spread function (PSF) induced by the MRI acquisition process is space-invariant, so that we used the same operator *B for all images*.

To fasten the proposed algorithm, we utilize the composite splitting algorithm [15]; 1) Splitting variable y into two variables x and z, 2) Performing operator splitting over each of the two variables independently, and 3) Obtaining the solution y by linear combination of z and x. Therefore, the optimization problem can be divided into three sub-problems that alternatively solved;

1. Minimize least square problem:

$$\hat{y} = \arg\min_{y} \sum_{k=1}^{N} \frac{1}{2} \left[\left\| \mathbf{RDBF}_k \, y - b_k \right\|_2^2 \right] \tag{4}$$

2. De-noising:

$$\hat{x} = \arg\min_{x} \left\{ \frac{1}{2} \left\| x - \hat{y} \right\|_2^2 + \alpha \left\| x \right\|_{TV} \right\} \tag{5}$$

3. Sparsity constraint in the wavelet domain

$$\hat{z} = \arg\min_{z} \left\{ \frac{1}{2} \left\| z - \hat{y} \right\|_2^2 + \beta \left\| \Phi z \right\|_1 \right\} \tag{6}$$

The reconstructed MR image is the weighted sum of the de-noised term and the constrained wavelet coefficients

$$y = \frac{\hat{z} + \hat{x}}{2} \tag{7}$$

Finally, at each iteration, values of y are projected in the reasonable range of MR images which is [0,255] for 8-bit MR images. The convergence of the proposed algorithm is guaranteed as the cost function is convex. Note: even if the MR imaging is dominated by Rician noise, other types of noise appear while fusing multiple LR measurements, including shifting error and blurring operator modelling error. The shifting error is modelled in the literature by Laplacian noise [16], while the blurring operator modelling error is better modelled by Gaussian noise, therefore, we implicitly modelled the overall contaminating noise by Gaussian noise.

4   Simulation

4.1   Setup

In the simulation, we used 4 low-resolution (LR) measurement data that are sensed from 128 × 128 positions. The resolution enhancement factor is used as 2 in each direction. The relative shift of the simulated object to generate LR measurements is assumed to be known. The fewer measurements we samples, the less MR scanning time is need. So MR imaging is always interested in low sampling ratio cases. The sampling ratio is fixed to be approximately 20%. We follow the sampling strategy of previous works [3, 4, 5]. All measurements are mixed with 0.01 white Gaussian noise. We conduct experiments on two images, namely, "Synthetic Image" and "Brain Image". For fair comparison, the comparison with other algorithms is done with the same forward imaging operator.

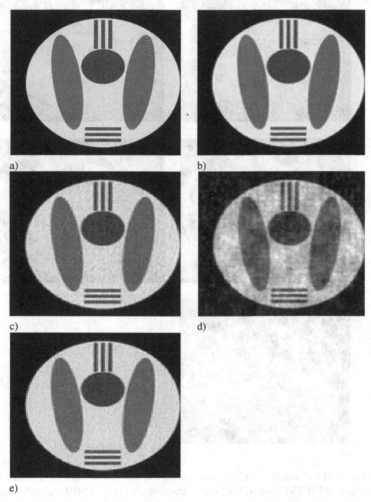

Fig. 1. Original test image #1, b) Proposed CS-MRI reconstruction c) LR FCSA-based MRI reconstruction, d) LR TVC -based MRI reconstruction, e) LR WaTMRI reconstruction

4.2   Simulation Results

The proposed CS-MRISR is compared with the following methods; 1) total variation L1 Compressed MRI (TVCMRI [3]), 2) Fast Composite Splitting Algorithm (FCSA [4]) and 3) Wavelet Tree Sparsity MRI (WaTMRI [5]). To evaluate these algorithms SNR, full-width-half-maximum (FWHM) and visual results are used.

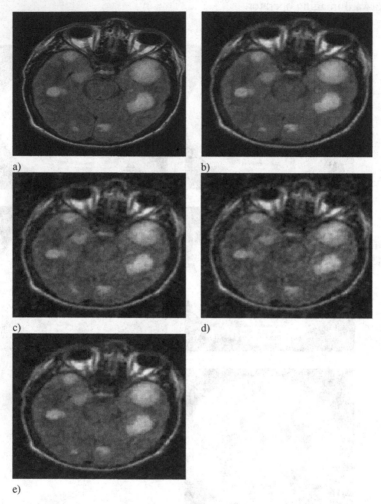

Fig. 2. a) original test image #2, b) Proposed CS-MRI reconstruction c) LR FCSA-based MRI reconstruction, d) LR TVC -based MRI reconstruction, e) LR WaTMRI reconstruction

4.3   Visual Comparisons

Figure 1a shows the original phantom image. The reconstructed MR image using the proposed algorithm is shown in Fig. 1b. The reconstructed MR images using algorithms FCSA, TVCMRI and WaTMRI are shown in Figs. 1c, 1d and 1e, respectively.

From these figures we can see that the proposed resolution enhancement algorithm improves the quality of the CS- MR image (see Fig. 1b) compared to the conventional CS-MRI algorithms (see Figs. 1d and 1e).

The results of the other experiment are shown in Fig. 2. This example confirm the results in the first example, that is the proposed algorithm can enhance the quality of the CS-MRI compared to the reconstructed LR MR images using algorithms FCSA, TVCMRI and WaTMRI.

4.4   Objective Results

The FWHM values for the PSF function of the reconstructed MR images is shown in Fig. 3. From this figure it can be shown that the proposed algorithm results in low FWHM value which indicate higher resolution compared CS-MRI reconstruction algorithms proposed in [3,4,5].

Another measure for the quality that can demonstrate the efficiency of the proposed algorithm is shown in Table 1. This table can show the higher SNR for the proposed algorithm compared to CS-MRI algorithms. For fair comparison, the reconstructed MR images by using algorithms in [3], [4] and [5] are interpolated to be compared with the original HR images. The plot of cost function versus iteration number is shown in Fig. 4 which can show the convergence of the proposed algorithm. In this figure, the maximum number of iteration is used as the stopping criteria.

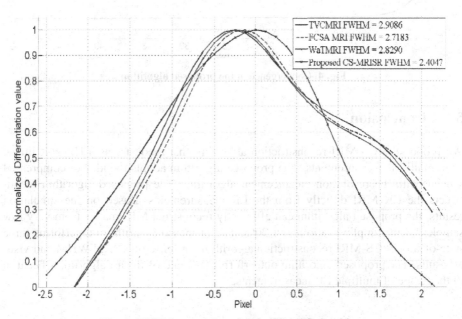

Fig. 3. FWHM comparison for the CS-MRI algorithms

Table 1. SNR comparison for different CS-based MRI reconstruction algorithms

	TVCMRI [3]	FCSA [4]	WaTMRI [5]	**Proposed**
IMAGE#1	12.0783	15.7975	15.9910	**16.3744**
IMAGE#2	10.3166	11.4029	11.9797	**12.4043**

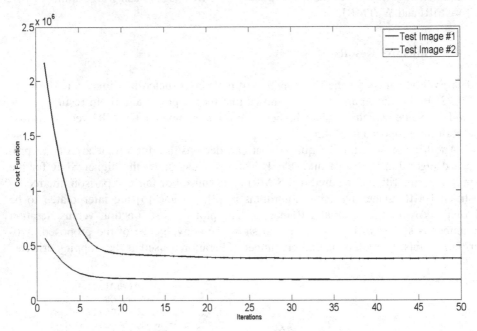

Fig. 4. Convergence of the proposed algorithm

5   Conclusion

We proposed a CS-MRI reconstruction algorithm that reconstructs a HR MR image from multi LR measurements. The proposed algorithm adopts the idea of compressed sensing with the resolution enhancement algorithm. The proposed algorithm reconstructs the HR MRI directly from the LR measurements. Based on the simulation results, the proposed algorithm can efficiently reconstruct MR images from very low samples, with sampling ratio about 20%. The proposed algorithm outperforms three state-of-the-art CS-MRI reconstruction algorithms in sense of SNR, FWHM and visual results. The proposed algorithm outperforms the state-of-the art algorithms because of the fusion of multiple LR measurements.

References

1. Donoho, D.: Compressed sensing. IEEE Trans. on Information Theory **52**(4), 1289–1306 (2006)
2. Lustig, M., Donoho, D., Pauly, J.: Sparse MRI: The application of compressed sensing for rapid MR imaging. Magnetic Resonance in Medicine **58**(6), 1182–1195 (2007)
3. Ma, S., Yin, W., Zhang, Y., Chakraborty, A.: An efficient algorithm for compressed MR imaging using total variation and wavelets. In: Proc. of the IEEE Computer Society Conf. on Computer Vision and Pattern Recognition (2008)
4. Huang, J., Zhang, S., Metaxas, D.: Efficient MR Image Reconstruction for Compressed MR Imaging. Medical Image Analysis **15**(5), 670–679 (2011)
5. Chen, C., Huang, J.: Compressive sensing MRI with wavelet tree sparsity. In: Proc. of the 26th Annual Conference on Neural Information Processing Systems (NIPS), Nevada, USA, December 2012
6. Van Reeth, E., Tham, I.W.K., Tan, C.H., Poh, C.L.: Super-resolution in magnetic resonance imaging: A review. Concepts in Magnetic Resonance Part A **40A**(6), 306–325 (2012)
7. Scheffler, K.: Superresolution in MRI? Magnetic Resonance in Medicine **48**, 408 (2002)
8. Peled, S., Yeshurun, Y.: Superresolution in MRI – Perhaps sometimes. Magnetic Resonance in Medicine **48**, 409 (2002)
9. Uecker, M., Sumpf, T.J., Frahm, J.: Reply to: MRI resolution enhancement: how useful are shifted images obtained by changing the demodulation frequency? Magnetic Resonance in Medicine **66**, 1511–1512 (2011)
10. Tieng, Q.M., Cowin, G.J., Reutens, D.C., Galloway, G.J., Vegh, V.: MRI resolution enhancement: how useful are shifted images obtained by changing the demodulation frequency? Mag. Res. in Medicine **65**, 664–672 (2011)
11. Peled, S., Yeshurun, Y.: Superresolution in MRI: Application to human white matter fiber tract visualization by diffusion tensor imaging. Magnetic Resonance in Medicine **45**, 29–35 (2001)
12. Omer, O.A.: High Resolution Magnetic Resonance Image Reconstruction in K-Space. ICIC Express Letters, Part B: Applications **5**(6), 1659–1666 (2014)
13. Plenge, E., Poot, D.H.J., Bernsen, M., Kotek, G., Houston, G., Wielopolski, P., et al.: Super-resolution reconstruction in MRI: better images faster?. In: Haynor, D.R., Ourselin, S., (eds.) SPIE Medical Imaging, vol. 8314. SPIE Press, Bellingham, P83143V (2012)
14. Scherrer, B., Gholipour, A., Warfield, S.K.: Superresolution reconstruction to increase the spatial resolution of diffusion weighted images from orthogonal anisotropic acquisitions. Medical Image Analysis **16**, 1465–1476 (2012)
15. Beck, A., Teboulle, M.: A fast iterative shrinkage-thresholding algorithm for linear inverse problems. SIAM Journal on Imaging Sciences **2**(1), 183–202 (2009)
16. Farsiu, S., Robinson, M.D., Elad, M., Milanfar, P.: Fast and Robust Multiframe Super-resolution. IEEE Trans. on Image Processing **13**(10), 1327–1344 (2004)

Towards Accurate Segmentation of Fibroglandular Tissue in Breast MRI Using Fuzzy C-Means and Skin-Folds Removal

Mohammad Razavi[1], Lei Wang[1(✉)], Albert Gubern-Mérida[2],
Tatyana Ivanovska[3], Hendrik Laue[1], Nico Karssemeijer[2], and Horst K. Hahn[1]

[1] Fraunhofer MEVIS - Institute for Medical Image Computing, Bremen, Germany
lei.wang@mevis.fraunhofer.de
[2] Radboud University Medical Centre, Nijmegen, The Netherlands
[3] Ernst-Moritz-Arndt University Greifswald, Greifswald, Germany

Abstract. Breast density measuring the volumetric portion of fibroglandular tissue is considered as an important factor in evaluating breast cancer risk of women. Categorizing breast density into different levels by human observers is time-consuming and subjective, which may result in large inter-reader variability. In this work, we propose a fully automated fibroglandular tissue segmentation technique aiming to assist automatic breast density measurement in magnetic resonance imaging (MRI). Firstly, a bias field correction algorithm is applied. Secondly, the breast mask is segmented to exclude air background and thoracic tissues, such as liver, heart and lung. Thirdly, the segmentation is further refined by removing the skin-folds that are normally included in the breast mask and mimic the fibroglandular tissue, leading to incorrect density estimation. Finally, we apply a fuzzy c-means approach to extract the fibroglandular tissue within the breast mask. To quantitatively evaluate the proposed method, a total of 50 MR scans were collected. By comparing the volume overlap between manually annotated fibroglandular tissue with the results of our method, we achieved an average Dice Similarity Coefficient (DSC) of 0.84.

Keywords: Breast · MRI · Fibroglandular · Skin-folds

1 Introduction

Breast density is classified into four groups in the standardized report of Breast Imaging-Reporting and Data System (BI-RADS) proposed by American College of Radiologists (ACR) [5]. Dense breasts classified into groups 3 and 4 have more fibrous and glandular tissue that may obscure small masses and thus lower the sensitivity of mammography (MG). Women with dense breasts have been shown to have a four to six-fold increased risk of developing breast cancer [6]. However, the classification of an individual breast depends on the opinion of radiologists, which leads to higher inter-reader variability. Automated density quantification based on breast MG and magnetic resonance imaging (MRI)

© Springer International Publishing Switzerland 2015
V. Murino and E. Puppo (Eds.): ICIAP 2015, Part I, LNCS 9279, pp. 528–536, 2015.
DOI: 10.1007/978-3-319-23231-7_47

allows for fast and reproducible assessment and thus decreases variability. As a better imaging modality to measure breast density, breast MRI scans the entire breast volumes in 3D without any tissue overlapping or projection. Therefore, density measurement in MRI tends to be more accurate than MG [4].

Several works were published aiming to segment fibroglandular tissue in breast MRI. Most algorithms used intensity-based approaches, such as fuzzy c-means (FCM) or Gaussian mixture (GM) models. Gubern-Mérida et al. developed a fibroglandular tissue segmentation using a GM model based on an atlas-based approach [2] . The overall average Dice Similarity Coefficient (DSC) reported was 0.80. Nie et al. proposed a FCM based method which was applied on a semi-automatically segmented breast mask, which requires users interactions to identify important landmarks [8]. Wu et al. adopted an atlas-aided FCM approach to segment fibroglandular tissue, which requires again large training set for atlas construction and might encounter difficulties to cope with new testing images acquired from other sites with different imaging protocols [13]. Moreover, the best average DSC achieved from their experiments was 0.69. Most recent work published by Ivanovska et al. used level-set based gradual method which simultaneously corrects bias field and segments fibroglandular tissue [3]. The method processed input images in 2D slice-by-slice and achieved DSC of 0.83 on average.

In this work, we propose a fully automated fibroglandular tissue segmentation framework based on robust breast segmentation and a skin-folds removal procedure. The entire work flow consists of four major steps which are illustrated in Fig. 1. First, a bias field correction algorithm is applied to alleviate intensity inhomogeneity of each tissue type. Second, breast region is extracted to exclude air background and irrelevant thoracic tissue, such as lung, liver and heart. Third, the breast segmentation is further refined by removing skin-folds which are typical false positive structures mimicking fibroglandular. Finally, we adopt a FCM algorithm to classify breast volume into fatty and fibroglandular classes. The performance of the proposed method is tested on 50 MR scans acquired from 50 different subjects. The volumetric overlap between manual annotations and segmented results is measured.

2   Material and Method

2.1   Material

For this study, we used a set of 50 coronal T1-weighted MR breast volumes from 50 different patients collected within the years 2003 and 2009 from Radboud University Medical Center. Patients were scanned in prone position. The age of screened women ranged from 23 to 76 years (45.84 ± 11.97 on average). The breast MRI examinations were performed on either a 1.5 or 3 Tesla Siemens scanner (Magnetom Vision, Magnetom Avanto and Magnetom Trio), with a dedicated breast coil (CP Breast Array, Siemens, Erlangen). The clinical imaging parameters varied; matrix size: 256×128 or 256×96; slice thickness: 1.3 mm; slice spacing: 0.625 - 1.25 mm; flip angle: 8, 20 or 25 degrees; repetition time: 7.5

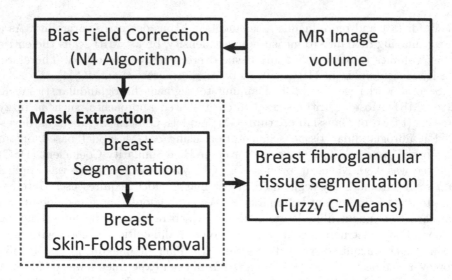

Fig. 1. General overview of the process for fibroglandular tissue segmentation in breast MRI.

- 9.8 ms; echo time: 1.7 - 4.76 ms. Each MRI exam in the test set was manually segmented into 7 tissue classes by an experienced expert which are used as the reference image to compare the quality of segmentation. A detailed description of the annotation is given in [2].

2.2   Method

Bias field Correction. Intensity inhomogeneity in MRI can attribute to the imperfection in radio-frequency coils or to the problems associated with acquisition protocols. It results in a slowly varying intensity change over the image that can produce errors with conventional intensity-based methods to distinguish different tissue types. The N4 bias field correction algorithm which is used in this work is a variant of the popular non-parametric nonuniform intensity normalization (N3) algorithm introduced by Sled et al. [9]. By assuming that the corruption of low frequency bias field can be modeled as a convolution over the intensity histogram by a Gaussian kernel, the algorithm iterates the following steps: de-convolving the intensity histogram by a Gaussian; re-mapping the intensities; spatially smoothing the result by a B-spline model[10]. By removing such artifacts, segmenting different tissue types in MR images can be done more accurately (see Fig. 2).

Breast Segmentation. Breast mask extraction separates the breast area from the other body parts such as lung, heart, pectoral muscle as well as air background presented in MRI scans. We previously implemented a fully automatic segmentation method specially designed for processing non-fat suppressed breast

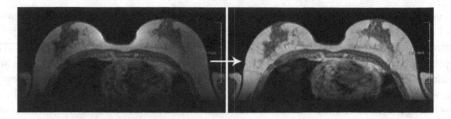

Fig. 2. (**Left**) The original breast MR image with the bias field artifacts from magnetic coil. (**Right**) The bias field corrected MR image using N4 algorithm.

MRI [12]. The key observation of this method is that the pectoral muscle and the breast-air boundaries exhibit as smooth sheet-like surfaces in 3D, which can be simultaneously enhanced by a Hessian-based sheetness filter [11]. The method consists of four major steps: enhancing sheet-like structures, segmenting the pectoral muscle boundary which defines the lower border of breast region, segmenting the breast-air boundary which delimits the upper border of the breast region, and extracting the region between the upper and lower borders that finally captures the area of breast tissue.

Skin-folds Removal. Skin-folds artifact could appear due to either large breasts do not entirely fit in the coils [2] or MRI technician's fault as breasts are not pulled perfectly into the coils while taking images [7]. Since the voxels of skin-folds have similar intensity levels with the fibroglandular tissue, normally they are included in the breast mask obtained in segmentation step (see Fig. 3), which will be erroneously recognized as the fibroglandular tissue in subsequent steps. Therefore, skin-folds need to be removed from the breast mask.

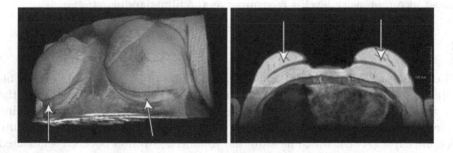

Fig. 3. On the **left**, the skin-folds artifact in 3D view. On the **right**, skin-folds which are usually included in the breast segmentation mask (red overlay area).

Based on the fact that skin-folds have lower intensity level compared to fatty tissue, we applied a first stage of FCM on entire MR volume to classify all the voxels into two classes i.e. dark and bright structures, which yields a binary image. As shown in Fig. 4(c) skin-folds, air background, fibroglandular tissue and other thoracic tissues are classified into one class. Considering the 3D spatial connectivity of the skin-folds and the background, we then carry out a 3D region growing procedure on the binary images starting from the seeds in the background and propagating to the skin-folds. Although in 2D transversal view, the skin-folds might be partially surrounded by fatty tissue and not corrected to the background in several slices, the 3D region growing process guarantees these parts will be reached. For the cases where the fibroglandular tissue connects to the background near the nipples, region growing might leak into the fibroglandular tissue. To prevent the leakage near the nipple, we cut a small patch on the top of the segmented breast mask (see Fig. 4(b)) and paste it to the corresponding location in the binary images resulted from the first stage of FCM (see Fig. 4(c)). More specifically, the patch is obtained by cutting the breast mask through a cutting-line placed in the middle distance of the peak point (i.e., the closest point of the breast mask to the top border of image in transversal view) and concavity point (i.e., the first intersection of the breast mask with the center line) automatically detected on the breast mask (see Fig. 4(b)). After blocking the leakage, the region growing procedure results in a union of connected dark structures, such as background, skin-folds, lungs etc, but except fibroglandular tissue (see Fig. 4(d)). Hence, a subtraction between the breast mask and the region growing results will produce a refined breast mask excluding the skin-folds (see Fig. 4(e)).

Fibroglandular Tissue Segmentation. In the previous pre-processing steps, intensity inhomogeneity is corrected, and a breast mask excluding air background and skin-folds artifact is obtained. Within the breast mask, a second stage of FCM is carried out. The class number is set to three, to capture the fatty tissue, the fibroglandular tissue and any transition structures resulting from either partial volume effect or imperfect inhomogeneity correction. The class with the lowest mean intensity level is recognized as the fibroglandular tissue.

3   Evaluation

To evaluate our approach, automatic segmentation of 50 MRI scans were compared to the reference masks created manually. The agreement between the reference annotations and the segmented results was measured by calculating Dice Similarity Coefficient (DSC) and Jaccard Coefficient (JC) and Absolute Volume Error (AVE), which measure the volumetric overlap between segmented and reference volumes. The definitions of the volumetric metrics are given in the following equations:

$$DSC(V_{Ref}, V_{Seg}) = \frac{2 \times |V_{Ref} \bigcap V_{Seg}|}{|V_{Ref}| + |V_{Seg}|} \tag{1}$$

$$JC(V_{Ref}, V_{Seg}) = \frac{|V_{Ref} \bigcap V_{Seg}|}{|V_{Ref} \bigcup V_{Seg}|} \tag{2}$$

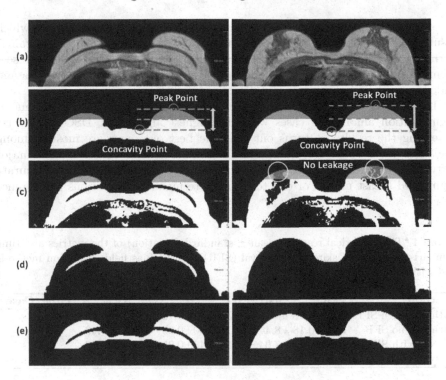

Fig. 4. Skin-folds removal and leakage prevention procedures applied on two representative slices (left: the skin-folds are present; right: the fibroglandular tissue near the nipples are connecting to the background). (**a**) results of bias field correction; (**b**) the segmented breast masks and the obtained patches (red overlay) by identifying the cutting-lines between the peak and concavity points. (**c**) the binary masks achieved from the first stage FCM with overlay of the patches that block the leakage near the nipples (see right figure). (**d**) the results of region growing. (**e**) the refined breast masks without the skin-folds (labeled as background) by subtracting (**b**) and (**d**).

$$AVE(V_{Ref}, V_{Seg}) = |V_{Seg}/V_{Ref} - 1| * 100 \qquad (3)$$

where V_{Seg} and V_{Ref} represent the segmentation and reference volumes. Additionally, average symmetric Root Mean Square Distance (asRMSD) between the boundary surfaces of the two volumes is computed [1]. First, the boundary voxels of segmentation and reference are determined. For each voxel in one set, the closest voxel in the other set is determined (using RMSD). All these distances are stored for boundary voxels from both reference and segmentation. The average of all these distances gives the averages symmetric distance.

The evaluation results are summarized in Table 1, which shows how the skin-folds removal and the N4 bias field correction influence the accuracy of the results. As seen in the first row, the best results were achieved by using a combination of both steps, since typical false positive segmentation in terms of skin-folds and inhomogeneous fatty tissue are removed. By combining both, an average DSC of 0.84 with a standard deviation of 0.08 was achieved, which resulted in the best volumetric overlap and lowest boundary surface distance. Although taking advantage of each steps adds up more time to the whole segmentation process, we finally managed to optimize the computing process and ended up with an average computation time of 39.78 seconds per case.

In Fig. 5, a comparison is made between the references and the automated segmentation among the cases with the highest and lowest DSC values. By observing the results, it turns out that the best outcomes are mostly among the cases with dense breasts and the worst are among the ones with major fatty tissues. The remaining errors in the results are either due to inaccurate segmented breast masks, or due to incomplete manual annotations in reference images.

Table 1. The statistical results (mean ± standard deviation) of the metrics and time comparison using the skin-folds removal (SFR) and N4 bias field correction methods and without using them.

Method	DSC	asRMSD	JC	AVE	Time/Case
with N4, with SFR	0.84±0.08	4.22±2.82	0.73±0.12	18.61±14.48	39.78 s
with N4, no SFR	0.72±0.18	8.44±3.26	0.60±0.20	18.83±16.43	28.38 s
no N4, with SFR	0.61±0.25	7.04±2.54	0.48±0.25	44.84±23.66	24.58 s
no N4, no SFR	0.57±0.24	8.38±2.12	0.44±0.23	50.09±26.83	13.78 s

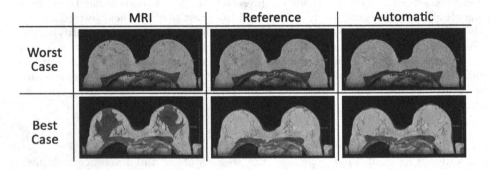

Fig. 5. Comparison of reference and automated segmentation of one axial slice from the worst case (**top**) with DSC of 0.4 and best case (**bottom**) with DSC of 0.95.

4   Conclusion and Future Works

The presented framework for automatic fibroglandular tissue segmentation shows high quality results in most of the testing cases. By incorporating skin-folds removal and bias filed correction steps, the method is more robust against intensity inhomogeneity and skin-folds artifacts. The experiments proved the importance of these pre-processing steps. Compared to previous works, we achieved slightly higher overall average DSC (0.84) than the work reported by Gubern-Mérida et al. [2] (0.80) by using the same datasets. In addition, our results showed higher accuracy than the work by Wu et al. [13] with DSC of 0.69. Our method is comparable to the work reported by Ivanovska et al. [3], who achieved an average DSC of 0.83 using different datasets comprising 37 MRI scans. Nevertheless, we find that FCM is quite sensitive to the remained inhomogeneity that is not fully recovered by the bias field correction. Therefore, an advanced multi-dimensional FCM, which classifies the voxels not only based on their intensity similarities but also spatial connectivity, will be considered to further improve the segmentation quality in the future works.

Acknowledgments. This research leading to these results has received funding from the European Unions Seventh Framework Programme FP7 under grant agreement No. 306088.

References

1. Gerig, G., Jomier, M., Chakos, M.: Valmet: a new validation tool for assessing and improving 3d object segmentation. In: Niessen, W.J., Viergever, M.A. (eds.) MICCAI 2001. LNCS, vol. 2208, pp. 516–523. Springer, Heidelberg (2001)
2. Gubern-Merida, A., Kallenberg, M., Mann, R., Marti, R., Karssemeijer, N.: Breast segmentation and density estimation in breast MRI: a fully automatic framework. IEEE Journal of Biomedical and Health Informatics **19**(1), 349–57 (2015)
3. Ivanovska, T., Laqua, R., Wang, L., Liebscher, V., Völzke, H., Hegenscheid, K.: A Level set based framework for quantitative evaluation of breast tissue density from MRI data. PloS One **9**(11), November 2014
4. Lee, N.A., Rusinek, H., Weinreb, J., Chandra, R., Toth, H., Singer, C., Newstead, G.: Fatty and fibroglandular tissue volumes in the breasts of women 20–83 years old: comparison of X-ray mammography and computer-assisted MR imaging. AJR. American journal of roentgenology **168**(2), 501–506 (1997)
5. Liberman, L., Menell, J.H.: Breast imaging reporting and data system (BI-RADS). Radiologic Clinics of North America **40**(3), 409–430 (2002)
6. McCormack, V.A., dos Santos Silva, I.: Breast density and parenchymal patterns as markers of breast cancer risk: a meta-analysis. Cancer epidemiology, biomarkers, prevention **15**(6), 1159–1169 (2006)
7. Morris, E.A., Liberman, L.: Pitfalls in analysis of carcinomas. Breast MRI: Diagnosis and Intervention, pp. 488–501 (2005)
8. Nie, K., Chen, J.H., Chan, S., Chau, M.K.I., Yu, H.J., Bahri, S., Tseng, T., Nalcioglu, O., Su, M.Y.: Development of a quantitative method for analysis of breast density based on three-dimensional breast MRI. Medical Physics **35**(12), 5253–5262 (2008)
9. Sled, J.G., Zijdenbos, A.P., Evans, A.C.: A nonparametric method for automatic correction of intensity nonuniformity in MRI data. IEEE Transactions on Medical Imaging **17**(1), 87–97 (1998)
10. Tustison, N.J., Avants, B.B., Cook, P.A., Zheng, Y., Egan, A., Yushkevich, P.A., Gee, J.C.: N4itk: improved N3 bias correction. IEEE Transactions on Medical Imaging **29**(6), 1310–1320 (2010)

11. Wang, L., Filippatos, K., Friman, O., Hahn, H.: Fully automated segmentation of the pectoralis muscle boundary in breast MR images. In: SPIE Medical Imaging, pp. 796309–796309 (2011)
12. Wang, L., Platel, B., Ivanovskaya, T., Harz, M., Hahn, H.K.: Fully automatic breast segmentation in 3D breast MRI. In: IEEE International Symposium on Biomedical Imaging (ISBI), pp. 1024–1027 (2012)
13. Wu, S., Weinstein, S.P., Conant, E.F., Kontos, D.: Automated fibroglandular tissue segmentation and volumetric density estimation in breast MRI using an atlas-aided fuzzy C-means method. Medical Physics **40**(12), 122302 (2013)

Robust and Fast Vessel Segmentation via Gaussian Derivatives in Orientation Scores

Jiong Zhang[1](✉), Erik Bekkers[1], Samaneh Abbasi[1], Behdad Dashtbozorg[1], and Bart ter Haar Romeny[1,2]

[1] Department of Biomedical Engineering, Eindhoven University of Technology, Eindhoven, The Netherlands
{J.Zhang1,E.J.Bekkers,S.Abbasi,B.Dasht.Bozorg,B.M.TerHaarRomeny}@tue.nl
[2] Department of Biomedical and Information Engineering, Northeastern University, Shenyang, China

Abstract. We propose a robust and fully automatic matched filter-based method for retinal vessel segmentation. Different from conventional filters in 2D image domains, we construct a new matched filter based on second-order Gaussian derivatives in so-called orientation scores, functions on the coupled space of position and orientations $\mathbb{R}^2 \rtimes S^1$. We lift 2D images to 3D orientation scores by means of a wavelet-type transform using an anisotropic wavelet. In the domain $\mathbb{R}^2 \rtimes S^1$, we set up rotation and translation invariant second-order Gaussian derivatives. By locally matching the multi-scale second order Gaussian derivative filters with data in orientation scores, we are able to enhance vessel-like structures located in different orientation planes accordingly. Both crossings and tiny vessels are well-preserved due to the proposed multi-scale and multi-orientation filtering method. The proposed method is validated on public databases DRIVE and STARE, and we show that the method is both fast and reliable. With respectively a sensitivity and specificity of 0.7744 and 0.9708 on DRIVE, and 0.7940 and 0.9707 on STARE, our method gives improved performance compared to state-of-the-art algorithms.

Keywords: Retinal vessel segmentation · Matched filter · Gaussian derivatives · Orientation scores · Crossing preservation · Micro-vasculature

1 Introduction

The analysis of retinal images, especially retinal blood vessels, provide useful information for the early diagnosis of systematic and eye-related diseases, such as diabetes, hypertension, and arteriosclerosis [1]. The changing geometric properties of vessels need to be quantified as important biomarkers (as humans are not good at this), and then analyzed to assist the ophthalmologists. To this end, a vascular tree needs to be segmented from the retinal image to support clinical diagnosis and treatment planning. In this work, we propose a robust, efficient and unsupervised vessel segmentation approach. Our method provides a sound basis for the quantitative analysis of large data sets, e.g. in a screening setting.

© Springer International Publishing Switzerland 2015
V. Murino and E. Puppo (Eds.): ICIAP 2015, Part I, LNCS 9279, pp. 537–547, 2015.
DOI: 10.1007/978-3-319-23231-7_48

In a general sense, conventional segmentation approaches can be divided into three categories: classifier-based [2,3], tracking-based [4] and filter-based [5–7]. Classifier-based methods rely on a prior labor-intensive process to label training samples, which are pixels with given feature vectors and known answers for learning a model. E.g., Soares et al. [2] extract a feature vector for a supervised classification from the pixel intensity and matched filter responses. Tracking based methods iteratively expand connected vessel models starting from detected seed points. These methods heavily rely on both the correct detection of seed points, and robustness of the iterative tracking scheme [4,8].

Other algorithms [5–7,9–11], including ours, are based on maximizing the filter response of the gray-level profile of the vessel cross-section. These approaches are generally faster and simpler than supervised methods. A Gaussian cross-section model was firstly proposed by Chaudhuri et al. [12] to describe the intensity variations of a vessel profile. Mendonca and Campilho [13] employed differential filters to detect vessel centerlines followed by morphological operators for vessel segmentation. Krause et al. [9] proposed a fast and accurate retinal vessel segmentation method in a higher dimension, in which vessels are detected through convolution with the second-order differential operator of the local Radon transform. In our work, we follow a similar approach of processing image data in a higher dimensional domain, but instead of using the local Radon transform, we rely on the formal group-theoretical frame-work of orientation scores [4,14,15]. Additionally, we exploit a multi-scale approach using rotation invariant Gaussian derivatives.

The theory of invertible orientation scores is inspired by the orientation-selective property of cortical hypercolumns in the primary visual cortex [16]. Invertible orientation scores are constructed by lifting 2D images to 3D functions on the roto-translation group $SE(2)$, an extended Lie-group domain of positions and orientations $\mathbb{R}^2 \rtimes S^1$. In the additional third orientation dimension, elongated structures of 2D images are disentangled into different orientation planes separately without tampering data-evidence, see Fig. 1. Here, we will develop multi-scale matched filters that live in the domain of an orientation score. By locally matching the vessel profile to the second order Gaussian differential operator perpendicular to the corresponding orientation, the vessel intensity can be enhanced accordingly. In the validation phase, we show that the proposed method not only gives improved performance on the major parts of the retinal vasculature with a competitive speed, but also is capable of dealing with difficult cases such as strong central arterial reflex, crossings, highly curved vessel parts, closely parallel and tiny vessels.

The remainder of this article is organized as follows: In Section 2 we provide the theory of invertible orientation scores on $SE(2)$, the left-invariant Gaussian derivatives and the constructed multi-scale matched filters. In Section 3 we validate the performance of our method with special attention on handling difficult structures. We conclude our paper in Section 4.

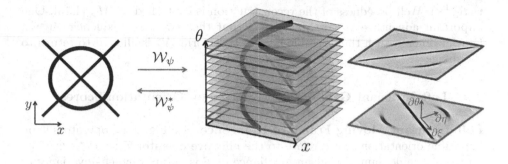

Fig. 1. Exemplary image with circle and cross, and corresponding orientation score.

2 Theory

In this section, we will firstly give details of the domain where we exploit left-invariant operators. Then we will explain why we need to keep left-invariance on that domain, and how to build Gaussian derivatives with left-invariance property.

2.1 Invertible Orientation Scores on SE(2)

The Euclidean Motion Group $SE(2)$. The domain $\mathbb{R}^2 \rtimes S^1$ of an orientation score can be identified with the group $SE(2)$, equipped with group product

$$gg' = (\mathbf{x}, \theta)(\mathbf{x}', \theta') = (\mathbf{x} + \mathbf{R}_\theta \cdot \mathbf{x}', \theta + \theta'), \quad \text{for all} \quad g, g' \in SE(2), \qquad (1)$$

with $\mathbf{R}_\theta = \begin{pmatrix} \cos\theta & -\sin\theta \\ \sin\theta & \cos\theta \end{pmatrix}$ a counter clockwise rotation over angle θ.

Invertible Orientation Scores. An orientation score $U_f : SE(2) \to \mathbb{C}$ is defined on the group $SE(2)$. The transform from an image f to an orientation score $U_f := \mathcal{W}_\psi f$ is achieved via an anisotropic convolution kernel $\psi \in \mathbb{L}_2(\mathbb{R}^2)$:

$$U_f(\mathbf{x}, \theta) = (\mathcal{W}_\psi[f])(\mathbf{x}, \theta) = \int_{\mathbb{R}^2} \overline{\psi(\mathbf{R}_\theta^{-1}(\mathbf{y} - \mathbf{x}))} f(\mathbf{y}) d\mathbf{y}, \qquad (2)$$

where $\mathcal{W}_\psi$ denotes the transform between image f and orientation score U_f. Here we choose cake wavelets[1] [4] for ψ. Exact reconstruction is obtained by

$$f(\mathbf{x}) = (\mathcal{W}_\psi^*[U_f])(\mathbf{x}) = \left(\mathcal{F}_{\mathbb{R}^2}^{-1} \left[M_\psi^{-1} \mathcal{F}_{\mathbb{R}^2} \left[\frac{1}{2\pi} \int_0^{2\pi} (\psi_\theta * U_f(\cdot, \theta)) d\theta \right] \right] \right)(\mathbf{x}), \quad (3)$$

for all $\mathbf{x} \in \mathbb{R}^2$, where $\mathcal{F}_{\mathbb{R}^2}$ is the unitary Fourier transform on $\mathbb{R}^2$ and M_ψ is given by $M_\psi(\boldsymbol{\omega}) = \int_0^{2\pi} |\hat{\psi}(\mathbf{R}_\theta^{-1}\boldsymbol{\omega})|^2 d\theta$ for all $\boldsymbol{\omega} \in \mathbb{R}^2$, with $\hat{\psi} := \mathcal{F}_{\mathbb{R}^2}\psi$, $\psi_\theta(\mathbf{x}) =$

---

[1] They are called 'cake' kernels, as they are constructed by dividing the Fourier domain in equal angular segments from the origin, like pieces of a cake.

$\psi(R_\theta^{-1}\mathbf{x})$. Well-posedness of the reconstruction is controlled by M_ψ [4,15]. One important advantage of cake wavelets is that they cover all frequencies in the Fourier domain such that a stable inverse transform $\mathcal{W}_\psi^*$ is allowed to return to the image f.

2.2   Left-Invariant Gaussian Derivatives on Orientation Scores

Left-Invariant Moving Frame of Reference. See Fig. 2, all operators Φ on invertible orientation scores relate to the effective operator $\Upsilon := \mathcal{W}_\psi^* \circ \Phi \circ \mathcal{W}_\psi$ on the image domain. Euclidean-invariance of Υ is ensured by left-invariance of Φ. This is a desirable property since we can keep all operations invariant with respect to translation and rotation. The left-invariance can be preserved if the operator Φ on orientation scores satisfies $\Phi \circ \mathcal{L}_g = \mathcal{L}_g \circ \Phi$ for all $g \in SE(2)$, with group representation $g \mapsto \mathcal{L}_g$ given by $\mathcal{L}_g U_f(g') = U_f(R_\theta^{-1}(\mathbf{x}'-\mathbf{x}), \theta'-\theta)$, for all $g = (\mathbf{x}, \theta), g' = (\mathbf{x}', \theta') \in SE(2)$. Therefore we should rely on the following frame of left-invariant derivatives acting on the domain $SE(2)$ of orientation scores:

$$\{\partial_\xi, \partial_\eta, \partial_\theta\} = \{\cos\theta\partial_x + \sin\theta\partial_y, -\sin\theta\partial_x + \cos\theta\partial_y, \partial_\theta\}, \qquad (4)$$

where we use short hand notation $\partial_i = \frac{\partial}{\partial_i}$.

Left-Invariant Gaussian Derivatives. Suitable combinations of derivatives have been widely used to pick up geometric invariant structures/features like edges, ridges, corners and so on. However, obtaining derivatives directly is an ill-posed problem. Therefore, we regularize the orientation scores via convolutions with Gaussian kernels $G_{\sigma_s, \sigma_o}(\mathbf{x}, \theta) = G_{\sigma_s}(\mathbf{x}) G_{\sigma_o}(\theta)$, with a d−dimensional Gaussian given by $G_\sigma(\mathbf{x}) = (2\pi\sigma^2)^{-d/2} e^{-\frac{\|\mathbf{x}\|^2}{2\sigma^2}}$, and where σ_s and σ_o are used to define the spatial scale $\frac{1}{2}\sigma_s^2$ and orientation scale $\frac{1}{2}\sigma_o^2$ of the Gaussian kernel. Note that $G_{\sigma_s} : \mathbb{R}^2 \to \mathbb{R}^+$ the spatial Gaussian distribution *must be isotropic* to preserve commutator relations of the $SE(2)$ group for scales $\sigma_s > 0$, i.e., to preserve left-invariance.

2.3   Scale-Invariant Matched Filters

It is well-known that the second-order Gaussian derivatives can be used to match vessel profiles for enhancement [9,17]. Here, based on the local coordinates system $\{\xi, \eta, \theta\}$ in the orientation score domain, we propose the second-order operator $\Phi_\eta^{\sigma_s, \sigma_o}(U_f) := \partial_\eta^2(G_{\sigma_s, \sigma_o} * U_f)$ perpendicular to the orientation of elongated structures for vessel detection. By applying isotropic Gaussian blurring spatially in ξ and η directions, as well as a small Gaussian blurring angularly in θ direction, we enforce structure smoothness on different orientation planes and information propagation along the vessel directions. Moreover, the variation of retinal vessel calibers requires a proper scale selection of second-order operators to match different vessel profiles. As studied by Lindeberg [18], the response of a derivative of Gaussian filter decreases as σ increases. Therefore, a scale normalization factor

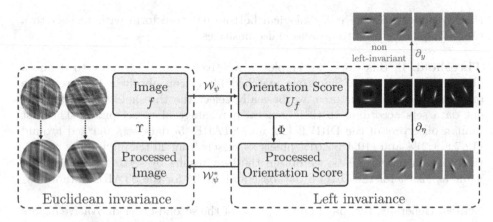

Fig. 2. Image processing via invertible orientation scores. Operators Φ on the invertible orientation score robustly relate to operators Υ on the image domain. Euclidean-invariance of Υ is obtained by left-invariance of Φ. We show the relevance of left-invariance of ∂_η acting on an image of a circle (as in Fig. 1) compared to action of the non-left-invariant derivative ∂_y on the same image.

$\mu = \sigma_o/\sigma_s$ with physical unit 1/length is required to make the filter responses dimensionless and truly scale invariant. The angular scale σ_o is a kept constant over all spatial scales and therefore does not affect extrema response. Thus our scale-normalized second-order matched filter can be written as:

$$\Phi^{\sigma_s,\sigma_o}_{\eta,\mathrm{norm}}(U_f) := \mu^{-2}\Phi^{\sigma_s,\sigma_o}_{\eta}(U_f) = \mu^{-2}\partial_\eta^2(G_{\sigma_s,\sigma_o} * U_f). \tag{5}$$

In the $SE(2)$-generalizations, the final image reconstruction from the multi-scale filtered orientation scores is obtained via

$$\Upsilon^{\sigma_s,\sigma_o}_{\eta}(f))(\mathbf{x}) := \max_{\theta_i \in \{1,2,...N_o\}} \{\sum_{\sigma_s \in \mathcal{S}} \Phi^{\sigma_s,\sigma_o}_{\eta,\mathrm{norm}}(U_f)(\mathbf{x},\theta_i)\}, \tag{6}$$

where N_o and $\mathcal{S}$ represents the number of orientations and the set of spatial scalings respectively, and the maximum filter response is calculated over all orientations per position.

3   Validation and Experimental Results

3.1   Settings

Preprocessing. Retinal images very often suffer from non-uniform illumination and varying contrast, which may affect the later detection process. Therefore we use the luminosity and contrast normalization proposed by Foracchia et al. [19]. The normalization radius for creating a disk-shaped filter is set as $r_{LC} = \frac{l_h}{30}$, where l_h is the height of an image. Moreover, the strong brightness of the optic disk and pathologies in RGB retinal images will cause erroneous detection of their boundary. So the morphological bottom-hat transform with respect to a range-7 square is used to decrease false positives.

Threshold. In this work, we employ a relatively simple strategy to define a global threshold value. Since our matched filters can obtain a high response only in vessel-like structures, we basically select the threshold value of different data sets according to their general percentage of vessel pixels. The first human observers of the DRIVE [20] and STARE [5] data sets marked around $(12.7 \pm 1.2)\%$ and $(10.4 \pm 2.0)\%$ pixels as vessels from 20 testing images respectively. In our experiments, we obtain the best results by setting the threshold value as 12.4% for the DRIVE database and 10.7% for the STARE database.

Scales. Generally, the maximum response of the second-order derivative occurs at $\sigma = r/\sqrt{2}$, where r represents the radius of the vessel caliber [18]. The vessel calibers of the DRIVE and STARE data sets roughly range from 2 to 14 pixels. In our experiments, we sample the spatial scales σ_s for both data sets as $S = \{0.7, 1.0, 1.5, 2.0, 2.5, 3.5, 4.5\}$ with a small angular blurring $\sigma_o = \pi/5$. For the orientation score transformation we use $N_o = 36$ orientations sampled from 0 to π. In Fig. 3, we give segmentation examples on the DRIVE and STARE data sets based on our proposed method.

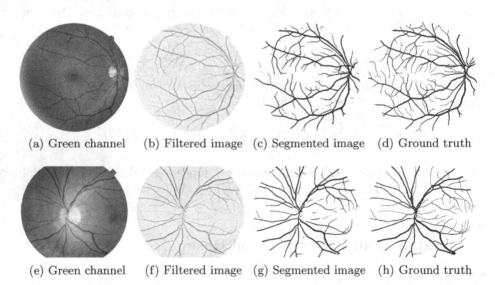

(a) Green channel   (b) Filtered image   (c) Segmented image   (d) Ground truth

(e) Green channel   (f) Filtered image   (g) Segmented image   (h) Ground truth

Fig. 3. Examples of automatic vessel segmentation on two images by the proposed approach. (a)-(d): An image from the DRIVE data set ($Sen = 0.8308$, $Spc = 0.9824$ and $Acc = 0.9635$). (e)-(h): An image from the STARE data set ($Sen = 0.8587$, $Spc = 0.9806$ and $Acc = 0.9676$).

3.2   Difficult Structures Preservation

Retinal vessel segmentation often suffers from difficult cases such as strong central reflex, crossings/bifurcations, highly curved vessel parts, closely parallel and tiny vessels. In order to investigate the influence of our proposed vessel enhancement in $SE(2)$, we compare this to multi-scale Frangi vesselness filtering in $\mathbb{R}^2$ [17], a frequently used method in vessel segmentation tasks. For the sake of equal comparison we substitute the filter $\Upsilon_\eta^{\sigma_s,\sigma_o}$ in our implementation with the Frangi vesselness filter, with the same preprocessing steps and scale settings as our approach. The best performance of the Frangi vesselness filter is obtained based on the $F_1 - score$ measure, which is the mean of precision and recall. As shown in Fig. 4 (a)-(c), the Frangi vesselness filter performs well on picking up parallel vessel structures, however, it has limitations to connect the low intensity vessel profiles of crossings and highly curved vessel parts. Missing of the central vessel parts due to the central reflex and partially merging segmentation of two closely parallel vessels can be seen in the results of the supervised segmentation method by Soares et al. [2], as shown in Fig. 4 (e) and (f). From Fig. 4 (g) and (h) we can see that the recently proposed B-COSFIRE filter [11] also suffers from difficult crossing cases. The proposed orientation score based multi-scale matched filters show much better structure preservation ability on these special cases, as illustrated in Fig. 4 (j)-(l). Quantitative results are tabulated in Table 1, and further discussed in Section 3.4.

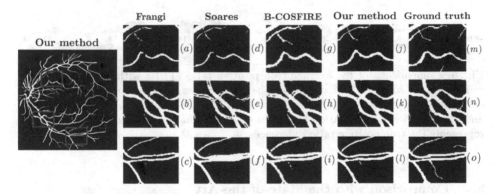

Fig. 4. Vessel segmentation results of our method in comparison with state-of-the-art methods on an image of the DRIVE database. (a)-(c), (d)-(f) and (g)-(i) respectively show the vessel segmentation results by the methods of Frangi et al. [17], Soares et al. [2] and B-COSFIRE filter [11] on 3 difficult cases: (a) high curvature change on low intensity vessel part and tiny crossing, (b) artery and vein crossing with central reflex and (c) closely parallel vessels; (j)-(l) show the results of our method, and (m)-(o) give the corresponding ground truth annotations by the human observer [20].

3.3   Validation of Vessel Calibers

To show the performance of our vessel detection approach on vessels of different calibers, particularly on small vessel width with 2-3 pixels, we validate the vessel width distribution on the detected true positive pixels. The basic procedure is as follows: we assign to each ground truth pixel a vessel caliber value based on the vessel caliber of the closest centerline point. Caliber of centerline pixels are found via thinning and a distance transform on the ground truth segmentation.

In Fig. 5, we show the comparisons of true positive ratio (TPR) with respect to different vessel calibers on the STARE database. In order to make an equal comparison, we move along the ROC curves of the proposed matched filter approach such that we can compare the sensitivity at the same specificity level where other methods [2,11,17] achieve their best performance. In general, we can see that our method can not only outperform the others on large vessel calibers, but also can detect more tiny vessels with caliber 2-3 pixels. Although the supervised segmentation approach by Soares et al. [2] performs slightly better on vessel calibers with 8-10 pixels, our method gives a large increase in performance on small calibers with 2-5 pixels.

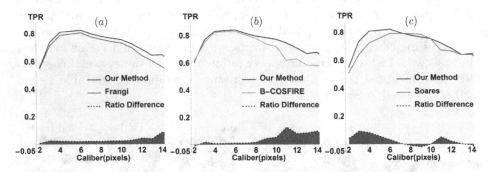

Fig. 5. Comparisons of the average true positive ratio (TPR) with respect to vessel calibers on the whole STARE database. The three figures show the comparison between our proposed method with (a) Frangi-vesselness filter [17], (b) B-COSFIRE filter [11], and (c) supervised segmentation by Soares et al. [2]. The bottom region with red color represents the true positive ratio differences.

3.4   Comparison with the State-of-the-Art

We validate our method on the public DRIVE and STARE data sets according to the aforementioned parameter settings from Section 3.1. In order to compare our method with other vessel segmentation algorithms, we use the performance measures: *Sensitivity (Sen)*, *Specificity (Spc)* and *Accuracy (Acc)* to evaluate the classified pixels within the field of view (FOV). Table 1 shows the experimental results of different algorithms evaluated on the DRIVE and STARE data sets. The performance measures of the methods we compare come from their respective references.

We can see that our method leads to very good and competitive results in comparison to other supervised and unsupervised methods from the literature. Particularly, our method achieves a higher sensitivity level compared to other algorithms. For the sake of equal comparison on sensitivity, we move along the ROC curves in order to validate the performance of our approach with respect to the best results achieved by other algorithms. As can be seen from Table 1, the two highest sensitivities on the DRIVE database are reported by B-COSFIRE filter [11] ($Sen = 0.7655$ and $Spc = 0.9704$) and Krause et al. [9] ($Sen = 0.7517$ and $Spc = 0.9741$). Our method can achieve a better sensitivity of 0.7761 and 0.7587 for the same specificity of the two methods respectively. Similarly, we can see from Table 1 that the two highest sensitivities for the STARE database are obtained by B-COSFIRE filter [11] ($Sen = 0.7716$ and $Spc = 0.9701$) and Frangi vesselness [17] ($Sen = 0.7540$ and $Spc = 0.9744$). Here based on our method we can reach to a significantly better result with sensitivities 0.7980 and 0.7743 for the same specificity of the two algorithms respectively.

Table 1. Segmentation results on the DRIVE and STARE data sets.

Method	DRIVE			STARE		
	Sen	Spc	Acc	Sen	Spc	Acc
Our Method	**0.7744**	**0.9708**	**0.9446**	**0.7940**	**0.9707**	**0.9511**
2nd human observer	0.7761	0.9725	0.9473	0.8949	0.9390	0.9354
Matched filter [12] (1989)	0.6168	0.9741	0.9284	0.6134	0.9755	0.9384
Frangi [17] (1998)	0.7460	0.9719	0.9418	0.7540	0.9744	0.9503
Mendonca [13] (2006)	0.7344	0.9764	0.9452	0.6996	0.9730	0.9440
Soares [2] (2006)	0.7332	0.9782	0.9466	0.7207	0.9747	0.9480
MF-FDOG [10] (2010)	0.7120	0.9724	0.9382	0.7177	0.9753	0.9484
Marin [3] (2011)	0.7067	0.9801	0.9452	0.6944	0.9819	0.9526
MPMF [7] (2012)	0.7154	0.9716	0.9343	0.7191	0.9687	0.9407
Krause[9] (2013)	0.7517	0.9741	0.9468	-	-	-
B-COSFIRE [11] (2015)	0.7655	0.9704	0.9442	0.7716	0.9701	0.9497

Table 2. Comparative analysis of running time for processing a DRIVE/STARE image.

Method	Running time
Our Method (Sequential Mode)	15 s
Mendonca [13] (2006)	2.5 min
Soares [2] (2006)	3 min
Marin [3] (2011)	1.5 min
B-COSFIRE [11] (2015)	10 s

3.5 Speed Comparison

The proposed orientation score based multi-scale matched filters have the advantage of time-efficiency for real applications. The *Mathematica* implementation we used for experiments takes less than 15s for segmenting an entire image from the DRIVE (565×584 pixels) and STARE data sets (700×605 pixels), on a personal computer with a 2 GHz processor. However, the computational speed can still be improved if we use a parallel mode to process multiple scales simultaneously. Comparative analysis of running time can be seen in Table 2.

4   Conclusion

In this paper, we have proposed a robust and efficient multi-scale and multi-orientation matched filter approach for retinal vessel segmentation. The filter is constructed by the left-invariant second-order Gaussian derivatives in the orientation score domain, where the vessel-like structures are disentangled into different orientations accordingly. With proper scale selection and simple parameter settings, the newly proposed method can match the vessel profile and maximize the filter response on multiple vessel calibers. After that, a global threshold value is defined to segment the filtered retinal image according to the general percentage of vessel pixels. The validation results show that the proposed matched filter not only gives improvement on global performance compared to most of the state-of-the-art segmentation schemes, but is also capable of dealing with generally difficult vessel structures. Last but not the least, the high computational efficiency of our method gives the potential of applying vessel segmentation on large data sets.

Acknowledgments. The research leading to these results has received funding from the China Scholarship Council (CSC) No. 201206300010. This work is also part of the NWO-Hé Programme of Innovation Cooperation 2013 No. 629.001.003 and the European Foundation for the Study of Diabetes/Chinese Diabetes Society/Lilly project.

References

1. Ikram, M.K., Ong, Y.T., Cheung, C.Y., Wong, T.Y.: Retinal vascular caliber measurements: clinical significance, current knowledge and future perspectives. Ophthalmologica **229**(3), 125–136 (2013)
2. Soares, J.V.B., Leandro, J.J.G., Cesar Jr., R.M., Jelinek, H.F., Cree, M.J.: Retinal vessel segmentation using the 2D Gabor wavelet and supervised classification. IEEE Trans. Med. Imag. **25**(9), 1214–1222 (2006)
3. Marin, D., Aquino, A., Gegundez-Arias, M.E., Bravo, J.M.: A new supervised method for blood vessel segmentation in retinal images by using gray-level and moment invariants-based features. IEEE Trans. Med. Imag. **30**, 146–158 (2011)
4. Bekkers, E.J., Duits, R., Berendschot, T., ter Haar Romeny, B.: A multi-orientation analysis approach to retinal vessel tracking. Journal of Mathematical Imaging and Vision, pp. 1–28 (2014)
5. Hoover, A., Kouznetsova, V., Goldbaum, M.: Locating blood vessels in retinal images by piecewise threshold probing of a matched filter response. IEEE Trans. Med. Imag. **19**(3), 203–211 (2000)
6. Al-Rawi, M., Qutaishat, M., Arrar, M.: An improved matched filter for blood vessel detection of digital retinal images. Comput. Biol. Med. **37**, 262–267 (2007)

7. Li, Q., You, J., Zhang, D.: Vessel segmentation and width estimation in retinal images using multiscale production of matched filter responses. Expert Systems with Applications **39**(9), 7600–7610 (2012)
8. Al-Diri, B., Hunter, A., Steel, D.: An active contour model for segmenting and measuring retinal vessels. IEEE Trans. Biomed. Eng. **29**(9), 125–1497 (2009)
9. Krause, M., Alles, R., Burgeth, B., Weickert, J.: Fast retinal vessel analysis. J. Real-Time Image Process, 1–10 (2013). doi:10.1007/s11554-013-0342-5
10. Zhang, B., Zhang, L., Zhang, L., Karray, F.: Retinal vessel extraction by matched filter with first-order derivative of Gaussian. Computers in Biology and Medicine **40**, 438–445 (2010)
11. Azzopardi, G., Strisciuglio, N., Vento, M., Petkov, N.: Trainable COSFIRE filters for vessel delineation with application to retinal images. Med. Image Anal. **19**, 46–57 (2015)
12. Chauduri, S., Chatterjee, S., Katz, N., Nelson, M., Goldbaum, M.: Detection of blood-vessels in retinal images using two-dimensional matched-filters. IEEE Trans. Med. Imag. **8**, 263–269 (1989)
13. Mendonca, A.M., Campilho, A.: Segmentation of retinal blood vessels by combining the detection of centerlines and morphological reconstruction. IEEE Trans. Med. Imag. **25**, 1200–1213 (2006)
14. Zhang, J., Duits, R., Sanguinetti, G., ter Haar Romeny, B.M.: Numerical Approaches for Linear Left-invariant Diffusions on SE(2), their Comparison to Exact Solutions, and their Applications in Retinal Imaging. Accepted by Numerical Mathematics: Theory, Methods and Applications (NM-TMA) **40**, 1–49 (2015). Preprint. arxiv.org/abs/1403.3320
15. Duits, R., Felsberg, M., Granlund, G., ter Haar Romeny., B.M.: Image analysis and reconstruction using a wavelet transform constructed from a reducible representation of the Euclidean motion group. International Journal of Computer Vision **79**(1), 79–102 (2007)
16. Hubel, D.H., Wiesel, T.N.: Receptive fields of single neurons in the cat's striate cortex. The Journal of Physiology **148**, 574–591 (1959)
17. Frangi, A.F., Niessen, W.J., Vincken, K.L., Viergever, M.A.: Multiscale vessel enhancement filtering. In: Wells, W.M., Colchester, A.C.F., Delp, S.L. (eds.) MICCAI 1998. LNCS, vol. 1496, pp. 130–137. Springer, Heidelberg (1998)
18. Lindeberg, T.: Scale-space theory: A basic tool for analysing structures at different scales. Journal of Applied Statistics **21**(2), 224–270 (1994)
19. Foracchia, M., Grisan, E., Ruggeri, A.: Luminosity and contrast normalization in retinal images. Med. Image Anal. **9**(3), 179–190 (2005)
20. Staal, J., Abramoff, M.D., Niemeijer, M., Viergever, M.A., van Ginneken, B.: Ridge-based vessel segmentation in color images of the retina. IEEE Trans. Med. Imag. **23**(4), 501–509 (2004)

Information-Based Cost Function
for a Bayesian MRI Segmentation Framework

David Cárdenas-Peña[1]([✉]), Alvaro A. Orozco[2],
and Germán Castellanos-Dominguez[1]

[1] Universidad Nacional de Colombia, Manizales, Colombia
dcardenasp@unal.edu.co
[2] Universidad Tecnológica de Pereira, Pereira, Colombia

Abstract. A new information-based cost function is introduced for learning the conditional class probability model required in the probabilistic atlas-based brain magnetic resonance image segmentation. Aiming to improve the segmentation results, the α-order Renyi's entropy is considered as the function to be maximized since this kind of functions has been proved to lead to more discriminative distributions. Additionally, we developed the model parameter update for the considered function, leading to a set of weighted averages dependant on the α factor. Our proposal is tested by segmenting the well-known *BrainWeb* synthetic brain MRI database and compared against the log-likelihood function. Achieved results show an improvement in the segmentation accuracy of $\sim 5\%$ with respect to the baseline cost function.

Keywords: Magnetic resonance imaging · Atlas-based segmentation · Entropy-based optimization

1 Introduction

Techniques of Brain Magnetic Resonance (MR) imaging play a significant role in many medical applications like: *i*) Identification of differences among functional brain structures along the time or space, which may help to model evolution of pathologies (as dementia, Alzheimer, and schizophrenia) [1], *ii*) Building realistic conductivity head models enhancing activity reconstruction accuracy [2,3], *iii*) Extraction of spatial characteristics (as size, shape, and place) allowing to build representative anatomical models of populations [4]. Since most of the above applications demand quantitative analysis and objective interpretation of the properties of brain structures, a reliable and accurate segmentation of the brain regions of interest has to be carried out from the MRIs.

However, region segmentation tasks are far from being an easy task due to the presence of image artifacts and inherent magnetic properties of each structure [5]. In order to overcome these problems, the atlas-based segmentation is usually employed. Here, an intensity template is registered to a target image, in such a way that the resulting spatial transformation allows to propagate information to the coordinates of the target image space [6]. Commonly, this information

© Springer International Publishing Switzerland 2015
V. Murino and E. Puppo (Eds.): ICIAP 2015, Part I, LNCS 9279, pp. 548–556, 2015.
DOI: 10.1007/978-3-319-23231-7_49

is provided in the form of probabilistic atlases for structures like white matter, gray matter, and cerebrospinal fluid. Subsequently, the Atlas information is combined with tissue classification approaches, where voxels are assigned to a tissue class according to their intensity. To this end, each tissue distribution has to be accurately modeled, for instance by single or a mixture of Gaussians, but using tissue probability maps to weigh the classification according to the Bayes rule.

In general, to map the atlas information and to find the tissue model parameters, a maximum likelihood estimation is carried out by minimizing an introduced cost function. The most common employed function is the negative log-likelihood of the entire voxel set joint probability while expecting each tissue class model to measure the density of voxels within an intensity range [7]. Then, class conditional distribution can be used as a voxel-wise discriminant function so that the classification is performed using the maximum likelihood principle. Nevertheless, the above cost function relies upon the assumption that tissue properties do not overlap significantly; this supposition is far from being realistic.

Bearing the above in mind, this work discusses the use of the Renyi's α entropies as a new cost function for learning each tissue parameters. This sort of function has been proved to lead to more discriminative distributions while maximizing the information entropy inside the provided target image [8]. Additionally, we develop the model update of the tissue parameter for the considered function. Finally, our proposal is tested by segmenting the well-known *BrainWeb* synthetic brain MRI database. For the purpose of comparison, we also use the baseline log-likelihood function as a cost function. As a result, obtained results of segmentation accuracy, measured in terms of the Dice index similarity, show that our proposal outperforms the log-likelihood ($\sim 5\%$).

2   Materials and Methods

Let $\boldsymbol{X}=\{x_r \in \mathbb{R}: r \in \Omega\}$ be a scalar image, where the value r indexes the spatial elements (spels). The probability of obtaining a spel with intensity x_r, given that it belongs to the class $c \in C$, can be written as $P(x_r|l_r=c, \theta)=f_{rc}(\theta)$, where $l_r \in [1, C]$ is the label associated to the r-th spel, f_{rc} is a predefined probability model for the class c and evaluated at x_r, s.t. $\int f_{rc}(\theta)dr=1; \forall c \in [1, C]$, and θ is the set of the model parameters. In practice, $f_{rc}(\theta)$ is assumed as either parametric (Gaussian or Mixture of Gaussians) or non-parametric (Parzen-based) model. Moreover, the prior probability of any spel belonging to the c-th class, regardless of its intensity, can be provided by a spatial varying probability atlas as $P(l_r = c)=b_{rc} \in [0, 1]$, s.t. $\sum_{c=1}^{C} b_{rc}=1$.

As a result, the probability of x_r, given set of model parameters, can be obtained by the Bayes theorem as follows:

$$P(x_r) = \sum_{c=1}^{C} P(x_r, l_r = c) = \sum_{c=1}^{C} P(x_r|l_r = c, \theta)P(l_r = c)$$
$$= \sum_{c=1}^{C} f_{rc}(\theta)b_{rc} \tag{1}$$

Consequently, evary image can be segmented into C classes using the *maximum a posteriori* (MAP) criterion, expressed as $l_r^* = \arg\max_{\forall c} P(l_r = c|x_r)$.

In the most common scheme, the set of model parameters θ is found by maximizing the probability of the entire set of voxels under the assumption of having just independent voxels, yielding:

$$P(\boldsymbol{X}) = \prod_{r \in \Omega} \sum_{c=1}^{C} f_{rc}(\theta) b_{rc} \tag{2}$$

The probability defined in Equation (2) is equivalent to minimize the cost function, known as the negative log-likelihood of the entire voxel set joint probability, as follows:

$$\mathcal{L}(\boldsymbol{X}) = - \sum_{r \in \Omega} \log \left(\sum_{c=1}^{C} f_{rc}(\theta) b_{rc} \right) \tag{3}$$

2.1 Information-Based Cost Function

Instead of using the common log-likelihood as the cost function, we introduce the amount of information contained in the image $\boldsymbol{X}$. To this end, we consider maximizing the α-order Renyi's entropy with respect to the set of parameters θ as follows:

$$\max_{\theta} \mathcal{H}_\alpha(\boldsymbol{X}) \equiv \min_{\theta} \frac{-1}{1-\alpha} \log \left(\int_\Omega P^\alpha(x_r) \right) \tag{4}$$

Since the aim of the current work is to evaluate the cost function for estimating the model parameter, we will assume that each tissue class is described by the normal distribution, $\mathcal{N}(,)$, that is:

$$f_{rc}(\theta) = \gamma_c \mathcal{N}(x_r|\mu_c, \sigma_c^2), \tag{5}$$

where μ_c and σ_c^2 are the class mean and variance, respectively. $\gamma_r \in [0,1]$ is the prior probability of any voxel, irrespective of its intensity, to belong to the c-th tissue, and it is subject to $\sum_{c=1}^{C} \gamma_c = 1$. Consequently, the parameter set becomes $\theta = \{\gamma_r, \mu_r, \sigma_c^2\}_{c=1}^{C}$.

2.2 Optimization Framework

For the optimization, we use the Expectation-Maximization (EM) algorithm that attempts to minimize a given energy function $\mathcal{E}$ w.r.t. the parameters θ and a newly introduced distribution $Q = \{q_{rc} \in [0,1]; \forall r \in \Omega, c \in [1, C]\}$:

$$- \mathcal{H}_\alpha \leq \mathcal{E} = -\mathcal{H}_\alpha + \sum_{c=1}^{C} \mathcal{D}_\alpha (q_{rc} || P(l_r = c|x_r)) \tag{6}$$

This new energy function works as an upper bound on the proposed cost function and it is composed of two terms. The first one consider only the α-order

Renyi's entropy, while the second term, $\mathcal{D}_\alpha(\|)$, is the α-order Renyi's divergence between the posterior probability and the introduced distribution Q. Therefore, the problem in Equation (6) can be rewritten as:

$$\min_{\{\theta,Q\}} \mathcal{E} = \frac{-1}{1-\alpha} \log \left(\int_\Omega p^\alpha(x_r) \right) + \sum_{c=1}^{C} \int_\Omega \frac{1}{\alpha-1} \log \left(\frac{q_{rc}^\alpha}{P^{\alpha-1}(l_r = c|x_r)} \right) \quad (7)$$

For the M-step, the α-divergence is minimized w.r.t. Q as:

$$\min_Q \mathcal{E} \equiv \min_Q \sum_{c=1}^{C} \int_\Omega \frac{1}{\alpha-1} \log \left(\frac{q_{rc}^\alpha}{P^{\alpha-1}(l_r = c|x_r)} \right)$$

that yields to the solution:

$$q_{rc} = P^{(\alpha-1)/\alpha}(l_r = c|x_r), \quad (8)$$

under the assumption that the following restriction holds: $\sum_{c=1}^{C} q_{rc}^{\alpha/(\alpha-1)}=1$.

For the E-step, the energy function $\mathcal{E}$ is minimized w.r.t. the parameters θ. Given the result of the M-step, the second term in the cost function is at minimum zero whenever relation in Equation (8) holds. Additionally, given the following expression:

$$P(x_r) = \frac{P(x_r, l_r = c)}{P(l_r = c|x_r)} = \sum_{c=1}^{C} q_{rc}^{\alpha/(\alpha-1)} \frac{P(x_r, l_r = c)}{P(l_r = c|x_r)},$$

then, the optimization for the E-step is rewritten as:

$$\min_\theta \frac{-1}{1-\alpha} \log \left(\sum_{c=1}^{C} \sum_{r \in \Omega} \frac{P^\alpha(x_r|l_r = c)}{q_{rc}^\alpha} \right)$$

yielding,

$$\min_\theta \frac{-1}{1-\alpha} \log \left(\sum_{c=1}^{C} \sum_{r \in \Omega} \frac{f_{rc}^\alpha b_{rc}^\alpha}{q_{rc}^\alpha} \right) \quad (9)$$

Taking into account that $\alpha \in [0, 1]$, the minimization of the function in Equation (9) is equivalent to maximize the argument of the log function as follows:

$$V(\theta) = \sum_{c=1}^{C} \sum_{r \in \Omega} \left(\frac{f_{rc}(\theta) b_{rc}}{q_{rc}} \right)^\alpha \quad (10)$$

Finally, the M-step assigns new parameter values θ, in such a way that the derivatives of V with respect to parameters are zero:

$$\frac{dV(X)}{d\theta} = \alpha \sum_{r \in \Omega} \left(\frac{b_{rc}}{q_{rc}} \right)^\alpha f_{rc}^{(\alpha-1)} \frac{df_{rc}}{d\theta}$$

By differentiating Equation (10) with respect to the means μ_c, we obtain the following expression:

$$\frac{dV(\boldsymbol{X})}{d\mu_c} = \alpha \sum_{r \in \Omega} \left(\frac{b_{rc} f_{rc}}{q_{rc}}\right)^\alpha \frac{(x_r - \mu_c)}{\sigma_c}, \tag{11}$$

that is solved for $dV/d\mu_c = 0$, resulting in the next updating rule:

$$\mu_c^{(n+1)} = \frac{\sum\limits_{r \in \Omega} \left(\frac{b_{rc} f_{rc}}{q_{rc}}\right)^\alpha x_r}{\sum\limits_{r \in \Omega} \left(\frac{b_{rc} f_{rc}}{q_{rc}}\right)^\alpha} \tag{12}$$

Likewise, the derivative of V with respect to the variance parameters obtained is follows:

$$\frac{dV(\boldsymbol{X})}{d\sigma_c^2} = \frac{\alpha}{2} \sum_{r \in \Omega} \left(\frac{b_{rc} f_{rc}}{q_{rc}}\right)^\alpha \left(\frac{(x_r - \mu_c)^2}{\sigma_c^2} - 1\right). \tag{13}$$

Hence, the variance is updated in accordance to the following rule:

$$(\sigma_c^2)^{(n+1)} = \frac{\sum\limits_{r \in \Omega} \left(\frac{b_{rc} f_{rc}}{q_{rc}}\right)^\alpha \left(x_r - \mu_c^{(n+1)}\right)^2}{\sum\limits_{r \in \Omega} \left(\frac{b_{rc} f_{rc}}{q_{rc}}\right)^\alpha} \tag{14}$$

Following the above derivative scheme, the attained updating function for the prior parameter γ_c is given by:

$$\gamma_c^{(n+1)} = \frac{\sum\limits_{r \in \Omega} \left(\frac{b_{rc} f_{rc}}{q_{rc}}\right)^\alpha \mathcal{N}(x_r | \mu_c, \sigma_c^2)}{\sum\limits_{r \in \Omega} \left(\frac{b_{rc} f_{rc}}{q_{rc}}\right)^\alpha} \tag{15}$$

3   Experimental Setup

3.1   Image Database Description

A simulated MRI set was used as test data that had been generated with the Internet connected MRI Simulator at the McConnell Brain Imaging Centre in Montreal publicly available at [1]. The pre-computed simulated MRI volumes for normal brain database was employed with the following parameters: $T1$ image modality, $1\,mm \times 1\,mm \times 1\,mm$ voxel size, $\{0, 1, 3, 5, 7, 9\}\%$ noise (relative to the brightest tissue in the images), and intensity non-uniformity (INU) values of 40%. The $T1$ image was simulated as a spoiled FLASH Figure 1.

---

[1] http://brainweb.bic.mni.mcgill.ca/brainweb/ [9].

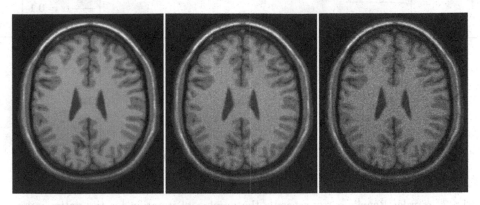

Fig. 1. Simulated MRI sample for the different noise intensities (left: 1%, center: 5%, right: 9%) for two different coronal slices

3.2   Evaluation of Performed Segmentation

Our proposed information-based cost function is employed for segmenting the images of the dataset into five regions. Namely, white matter (WM), gray matter (GM), cerebrospinal fluid (CSF), skull (SK), and scalp (SC). To this end, we make use of the prior probability atlas provided by the SPM software [7]. Since the scope of the work is to evaluate only the cost function for improving MRI partitioning, we will consider only a fixed affine atlas mapping to the target images. Though it is important noting that there are iterative deformable mapping schemes for enhancing the image segmentation. The resulting segmentation is attained using the MAP criterion at each voxel. The accuracy is measured in terms of the average dice index similarity index ($\kappa \in [0, 100]\%$), expressed as follows:

$$\kappa = \frac{1}{C} \sum_{c=1}^{C} \frac{2 \times TP_c}{2 \times TP_c + FP_c + FN_c}, \tag{16}$$

being TP_c the number of true positives, FP_c false positives, and FN_c false negatives, for the c-th tissue.

Firstly, we analyze the influence of the α factor in the optimization process. In Figure 2, the introduced information-based cost function versus the number of iterations is depicted for several α values. As expected, the relation between the entropy order is $\mathcal{H}_\alpha(\boldsymbol{X}) < \mathcal{H}_\beta(\boldsymbol{X}); \forall 0 < \beta < \alpha < 1$. This inequation means that the larger the entropy order, the smaller the entropy value. Moreover, we get that the EM algorithm converges faster for the case of smaller orders.

The evaluation of the influence of the entropy on the segmentation accuracy is given in the Figure 3 showing the curves of DI versus α for the considered noise intensities. As seen, the α factor leads the segmentation results so that for very small or very large values the amount of misclassifications is greater

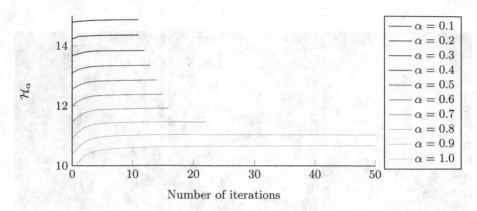

Fig. 2. α-order Renyi's entropy versus the number of iteration for the optimization procedure, for several α values and a given image in the dataset

than for values of the mid range. Moreover, the highest segmentation accuracy is achieved at α=0.5. It is also important noting that the algorithm performance decreases as the noise level increases. This result may be explained mainly due to variations in the tissue distribution because of the high noise intensity.

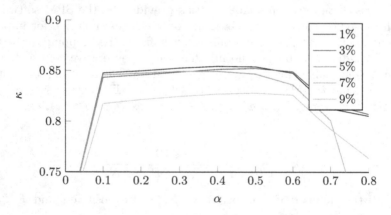

Fig. 3. Average Dice similarity index versus the entropy order for available image noise intensities.

Finally, we compare attained results against the well-known log-likelihood cost function in Equation (3). The achieved segmentation accuracy is computed for optimal α=0.5 for each considered structure. As shown in Table 1, the proposed Renyi's entropy outperforms the other compared cost function – the baseline log-likelihood.

Table 1. Dice index for each structure at optimal $\alpha = 0.5$

	Proposed Entropy					Baseline Log-likelihood				
Noise	1%	3%	5%	7%	9%	1%	3%	5%	7%	9%
Average	85.38	85.22	84.66	84.69	82.78	81.08	80.25	79.94	79.73	77.88
SC	88.61	89.28	86.86	86.92	88.11	84.43	84.97	82.17	82.87	83.15
SK	67.73	67.90	68.40	68.46	68.46	63.16	63.28	64.17	64.26	63.65
CSF	73.03	73.15	71.66	71.57	68.59	68.52	68.60	67.30	67.28	64.35
GM	89.60	88.50	89.73	89.72	84.15	84.88	84.18	85.39	84.89	79.27
WM	90.22	89.12	90.51	90.53	85.77	85.72	85.08	85.85	86.11	80.99

4 Concluding Remarks

In the current paper, we have discussed the use of information-based measures into the parameter optimization scheme for MRI segmentation. In particular, we introduce the α-order Renyi's entropy as a new cost function for finding the tissue distribution parameters under the assumption of normally distributed classes. Additionally, we have developed the model of updating equations for an EM-based optimization using the considered function. As a result, parameters are updated from weighted averages (see Equations (12), (14) and (15)), where the influence of the r-th voxel for each parameter is $(b_{rc}f_{rc}/q_{rc})^{\alpha}$.

As seen in Figure 2, we have proved the relationship between two different entropy orders. We show that in the range $[0, 1]$, the larger the order, the smaller the information measure. In fact, the maximum possible value for the Renyi's entropy is achieved when $\alpha = 0$, corresponding to $\mathcal{H}_0 = -\log\left(\frac{1}{|\Omega|}\right)$. Additionally, we found a proportional relationship between the order and the algorithm convergence iterations. The above is due to the influence of α in the probability values. As α tends to zero, the entropy tends to weight all the events more evenly, regardless their probability, i.e., $(b_{rc}f_{rc}/q_{rc})^{\alpha} \to 1; \forall r \in \Omega, c \in [1, C]$. On the other hand, for large α values, the entropy is determined by events with higher probabilities.

Regarding the segmentation accuracy, from Figure 3, we found the optimal order at $\alpha = 0.5$. Additionally, we show that the larger the noise intensity, the larger the number of misclassifications. Here, it has to be highlighted that Parzen-based estimation of the class conditional probability distribution may overcome this issue. Nevertheless, such a test is out of the scope of the current paper. Then, we compared our proposal against the log-likelihood as the baseline approach. Achieved results for the optimal entropy order, in Table 1, show that our scheme outperforms the baseline, since the obtained parameters for the entropy function are more discriminative than those for the log-likelihood.

Finally, as future work two main research lines are proposed. As there are iterative schemes integrating the mapping parameters of the prior image distribution atlases into the optimization process, we plan to extend the entropy cost function for finding a proper model update for such mapping parameters. Next, we have performed all of the experiments under the assumption of normally distributed classes. Therefore, we will test our approach for the class conditional models as mixture of Gaussians or Parzen.

Acknowledgments. This work was supported by *Programa Nacional de Formación de Investigadores "Generación del Bicentenario"*, 2011/2012 funded by COLCIEN-CIAS and the research project number 111065740687, both funded by COLCIENCIAS.

References

1. Lao, Z., Shen, D., Xue, Z., Karacali, B., Resnick, S.M., Davatzikos, C.: Morphological classification of brains via high-dimensional shape transformations and machine learning methods. NeuroImage **21**(1), 46–57 (2004)
2. Valdés-Hernández, P.A., von Ellenrieder, N., Ojeda-Gonzalez, A., Kochen, S., Alemán-Gómez, Y., Muravchik, C., Valdés-Sosa, P.A.: Approximate average head models for EEG source imaging. Journal of neuroscience methods **185**(1), 125–32 (2009)
3. Strobbe, G., Cárdenas-Peña, D., Montes-Restrepo, V., Van Mierlo, P., Castellanos-Dominguez, G., Vandenberghe, S.: Selecting volume conductor models for EEG source localization of epileptic spikes: preliminary results based on 4 operated epileptic patients. In: First International Conference on Basic and Clinical multimodal Imaging (BaCI), vol. c (2013)
4. Ericsson, A., Aljabar, P., Rueckert, D.: Construction of a patient-specific atlas of the brain: application to normal aging. In: 2008 5th IEEE International Symposium on Biomedical Imaging: From Nano to Macro, 480–483. IEEE, May 2008
5. Cardenas-Pena, D., Martinez-Vargas, J.D., Castellanos-Dominguez, G.: Local binary fitting energy solution by graph cuts for MRI segmentation. In: Conference Proceedings : ... Annual International Conference of the IEEE Engineering in Medicine and Biology Society. IEEE Engineering in Medicine and Biology Society, Conference, vol. 2013(2), 5131–5134, January 2013
6. Lötjönen, J.M., Wolz, R., Koikkalainen, J.R., Thurfjell, L., Waldemar, G., Soininen, H., Rueckert, D.: Fast and robust multi-atlas segmentation of brain magnetic resonance images. NeuroImage **49**(3), 2352–2365 (2010)
7. Ashburner, J., Friston, K.J.: Unified segmentation. NeuroImage **26**(3), 839–851 (2005)
8. Erdogmus, D., Xu, D., Hild, Kenneth, I.: Classification with EEC, divergence measures, and error bounds. In: Information Theoretic Learning, pp. 219–261 (2010)
9. Cocosco, C.A., Kollokian, V., Kwan, R.K.S., Pike, G.B., Evans, A.C.: BrainWeb: Online Interface to a 3D MRI Simulated Brain Database. NeuroImage **5**, 425 (1997)

Learning by Sampling for White Blood Cells Segmentation

Cecilia Di Ruberto, Andrea Loddo, and Lorenzo Putzu[✉]

Department of Mathematics and Computer Science,
University of Cagliari, via Ospedale 72, 09124 Cagliari, Italy
lorenzo.putzu@gmail.com

Abstract. The visual analysis and the counting of white blood cells in microscopic peripheral blood smears is a very important procedure in the medical field. It can provide useful information concerning the health of the patients, e.g., the diagnosis of Acute Lymphatic Leukaemia or other important diseases. Blood experts in clinical centres traditionally use these methods in order to perform a manual analysis. The main issues of the traditional human analysis are certainly related to the difficulties encountered during this type of procedure: generally, the process is not rapid and it is strongly influenced by the operator's capabilities and tiredness. The main purpose of this work is to realize a reliable automated system based on a multi-class Support Vector Machine in order to manage all the regions of immediate interests inside a blood smear: white blood cells nucleus and cytoplasm, erythrocytes and background. The experimental results demonstrate that the proposed method is very accurate and robust being able to reach an accuracy in segmentation of 99%, indicating the possibility to tune this approach to each couple of microscope and camera.

Keywords: Automatic detection · Biomedical image processing · Segmentation · Machine learning · White blood cell analysis

1 Introduction

The main purpose of this work is to develop an automatic system able to extract appropriate information from blood cell images taken by microscopes in order to easily perform a useful activity on them, e.g., white blood cells count. Ideally, there are several useful operations for what this method can be used for: essentially, identify, analyse, classify or count the white blood cells held in one or more microscopic images. Nevertheless we can say that the most important and key step of the entire automatic process is, certainly, the image segmentation, which differentiates meaningful objects from the background. It is a crucial step because its accuracy greatly affects both the computational speed and the overall accuracy of the whole system. However, it is also a very difficult problem to manage because of the complex nature of the cells, low resolution of microscopic images and the presence of complex scenes, e.g. cells can overlap each other or

V. Murino and E. Puppo (Eds.): ICIAP 2015, Part I, LNCS 9279, pp. 557–567, 2015.
DOI: 10.1007/978-3-319-23231-7_50

cells can have different sizes or shapes. On the other hand, the colour and the contrast between the cells and the background can vary very often according to the frequent, inconsistent staining technique, thickness of smear and illumination. Although a standardization is useful to avoid superfluous differences in the features of similar images, a robust segmentation approach can cope with the described issues. One natural way for colour image segmentation is to perform pixels clustering or classification in colour space. Unsupervised and supervised schemes [1], such as k-means, neural network et al., have been widely used for this purpose even if there are many disadvantages to deal with. Generally, the biggest problem of an unsupervised clustering scheme is how to determine the number of clusters, which is known as cluster validity. And as for a colour image, the selection of colour space is quite critical. The supervised scheme needs training. The training set and initialization may affect the results, and overtraining should be avoided. So a supervised clustering/classification algorithm with good generalization property is most appealing. Our method aims to solve the segmentation problem in a non-linear feature space obtained by kernel methods in order to overcome the non-linearity of data distribution and the shift/offset of colour representing the different regions of interest inside a blood sample: mature erythrocytes, nuclei and cytoplasm of white blood cells. We want to develop an automatic machine learning to perform image segmentation of blood and bone marrow cells images. SVM (Support Vector Machines) and ANN (Artificial Neural Network) are machine learning models with excellent performances in classification, but their main drawbacks are that a training phase is absolutely necessary to make them work and the training phase could be computationally hard with large datasets.Our solution has been developed following the suggestions of [2–4]. We have used the ALL-IDB dataset [5], a public and free dataset that contains microscopic images of blood samples, specifically designed for the evaluation and the comparison of algorithms for segmentation and image classification. Our idea is to use a part of this dataset as a training set for our learning by sampling algorithm. The first step of the algorithm is to apply a classic segmentation method to obtain pure samples related to the regions of white blood cells nucleus and cytoplasm, mature erythrocytes and background. As a comparison, we have also realized a method based on three Mean Shift procedures in order to search the clustering modes corresponding to the colour of the above defined three regions. Then we prepared the training samples by adapting sampling from the regions obtained from the classic segmentation phase so as to perform the training process of a multi-class SVM in order to correctly classify all the pixels of a given image. Finally, the SVM is used to segment the image for extracting whole white cells, using a classification phase by means of a classification model. Since the size of training set could be controlled and reduced in sampling, SVM training is really fast. Section 2 introduces a brief summary about the classic segmentation methods, known in literature. Section 3 describes Mean Shift theory and its application to image segmentation. Section 4 presents SVM basis theory and how it can be used for our purposes. Section 5 shows the proposed solution and some experimental results and comparisons with other methods. Discussions, conclusions and future aspects are given in Section 6.

2 Background and Related Works

A typical blood image usually consists of three components: red blood cells or erythrocytes, white blood cells (WBCs) or leukocytes, and platelets. Leukocytes are easily identifiable, as their nucleus appears darker than the background. However, the analysis and the processing of data related to the WBCs are complicated due to wide variations in cell shape, dimensions and edges. The generic term leukocyte refers to a set of cells that are quite different from each other (Fig. 1). Leukocytes containing granules are called granulocytes, and they include neutrophils, basophils and eosinophils. Cells without granules are called mononuclear, and they include lymphocytes and monocytes. Furthermore, lymphocytes suffering from ALL, called lymphoblasts, have additional morphological changes that increment with increasing severity of the disease. In particular, lymphocytes are regularly shaped and have a compact nucleus with regular and continuous edges, whereas lymphoblasts are irregularly shaped and contain small cavities in the cytoplasm, termed vacuoles, and spherical particles within the nucleus, termed nucleoli. In Fig. 1 some examples of healthy and sick WBCs belonging to the ALL-IDB database [5] are showed. The ALL-IDB is a public image dataset of peripheral blood samples from normal individuals and leukaemia patients. These samples were collected by the experts at the M. Tettamanti Research Centre for childhood leukaemia and haematological diseases, Monza, Italy. The ALL-IDB database has two distinct version (ALL-IDB1 and ALL-IDB2). The ALL-IDB1 can be used both for testing segmentation capability of algorithms, as well as the classification systems and image pre processing methods. This dataset is composed of 108 images captured with an optical laboratory microscope coupled with an Olympus Optical C2500L camera or a Canon PowerShot G5 camera. All images are in JPG format with 24-bit colour depth. The first 33 have 1712×1368 resolution, the remaining have 2592×1944 resolution. The images are taken with different magnifications of the microscope ranging from 300 to 500 which brings the colour differences that we managed grouping the images with same brightness characteristics together. The ALL-IDB2 is a collection of cropped area of interest of normal and blast cells extracted from the ALL-IDB1 dataset. It contains 260 images and the 50% of them represent lymphoblasts. According to the literature, few examples of automated systems are able to analyse and classify WBCs from microscopic images, and the existing systems are only partially automated. In particular, a considerable amount of work has been performed to achieve leukocytes segmentation. For example, Madhloom [7] developed an automated system to localise and segment WBC nuclei based on image arithmetical operations and threshold operations. Sinha [8] and Kovalev [9] attempted to differentiate the five types of leukocytes in cell images. Sinha used k-means clustering on the HSV colour space for WBCs segmentation and different classification models for cell differentiation. Kovalev first identified the nuclei and then detected the entire membrane by region growing techniques. Few papers sought to achieve robust segmentation performance under uneven lighting conditions. However, a study by Scotti [10], used a low-pass filter to remove background, different threshold operations and image clustering to segment WBCs. Moreover, other authors proposed methods for automated disease classification. In particular, Piuri [11] proposed an approach based on edge detection for WBC segmentation, and used morphological features to train a neural network to recognise lymphoblasts. Halim [12] proposed an automated blast counting method to detect acute leukaemia in blood microscopic images that identifies WBCs through a thresholding operation performed on the S component of the HSV colour space, followed by morphological erosion for image segmentation. Although the results of this study seem very encouraging, there is no method to determine the optimum threshold for segmentation, and no feature or classifiers were presented. Mohapatra [13] investigated the use of an ensemble classifier system for the early diagnosis of ALL in blood microscopic images. The identification and segmentation of WBCs is realised through image clustering followed by the extraction of different types of features, such as shape, contour, fractal, texture, colour and Fourier descriptors, from the subimage. Finally an ensemble of classifiers is trained to recognise ALL. The results of this method were good, but they were obtained by using a proprietary dataset, so the reproducibility of the experiment and comparisons with other methods are not possible.

3   On Mean Shift Technique

Mean Shift technique was originally proposed in 1975 by Fukunaga [2], then adapted by Chen [1] and generalized for image analysis purposes. More recently it have been extended to low-level vision problems [14], including segmentation, adaptive smoothing and visual tracking. Basically, it is used as a non-parametric technique for the estimation of the density gradient in image analysis field, even if it was developed in order to perform mode finding on clustering procedures. In contrast to the classic K-means clustering approach, there are neither a priori assumptions about the point distribution nor the number of modes and clusters:

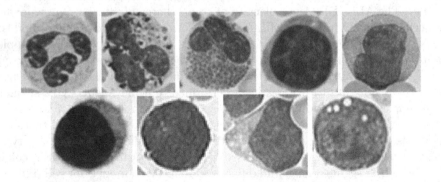

Fig. 1. (Top) A comparison between different types of WBCs: neutrophils, basophils, eosinophils, lymphocytes and monocytes. (Bottom) A comparison between lymphocytes suffering from ALL: a healthy lymphocyte, followed by lymphoblasts classified as L1, L2 and L3, respectively, according to the FAB [6].

they are computed by the Mean Shift procedure itself. Furthermore, Mean Shift has been adapted to become a very effective image segmentation technique, even if it was born as a clustering method of data analysis. It allows to attenuate shape or colour differences between the objects inside the considered images; for these reasons it works as a local homogenization technique. Considering its operating principles, the objective is to substitute every single pixel value with the mean of the sampled pixel values in a certain neighbourhood, within a certain radius R and a certain colour distance D; both of them are usually input defined by the user which generally has a deep knowledge about the context or uses some pre-processing technique to obtain the best values of R and D. Typically, Mean Shift requires at least three basically information to gain the best results; first of all, we have to define a certain kernel, which uses a distance function, to measure the pixel distance in every single iteration of the procedure: examples are the Gaussian kernel and the Epanechnikov kernel. Secondly, it needs two distance values: an R radius and a D colour distance. Then, iteratively, the procedure finds the modes of an input given image and calculates new values for every single pixel, according to the chosen kernel function and the distance parameters. It is worth mentioning that Mean Shift algorithm is not well defined at the boundaries, because it does not consider the non-existent neighbour pixels. Consequently, a strategy to handle them is necessary. For example, we have studied a padding of the image to process boundary pixels correctly.

4 SVM for Segmentation

Remembering that our starting objective was to segment blood cells images, now we explain how this classification method can be used to reach our segmentation purposes and targets. Support Vector Machine (SVM) has been chosen in order to perform a classification of every single pixel belonging to the images we have to segment, according to the method proposed in [1]. Once the Mean Shift has been performed on a certain training set, we use a set of these produced images to train the different SVM we realized. As a comparison, we also segment every single dataset image with classic segmentation methods. It is done to execute a more in-depth analysis of our study. The **first strategy** works as a normal binary SVM classifier, hence we have exactly two classes in which the pixels will be classified: the positive class groups together the white blood cell nuclei and cytoplasm pixels, instead the negative class represents pixels belonging to erythrocytes or background. Fig. 2 shows the segmentation result using this solution, in which the WBC is exactly recognized and segmented, but the lighter region of erythrocytes is misclassified as WBC region. The **second strategy** substantially works like the first one, with the main difference that we exclude from the training samples all the pixels belonging to the cytoplasm, in order to avoid misclassification due to similarities with the lighter region of erythrocytes. Fig. 2 shows the segmentation result using this solution. Again the nucleus is well detected but for determined classes of WBCs the cytoplasm is not well detected. The **third strategy** is based on the results obtained with the two previous versions. In fact the classifier needs more valid training samples for cytoplasm only.

So, in last version we perform a three-class SVM, using both the pixels belonging from WBCs nuclei (class 1) and both pixels belonging to the WBCs cytoplasm (class 2). Thus, pixels belonging to erythrocytes or background are labelled with class 3. Note that for this approach only classic segmentation have been used to produce pure samples for the SVM, because Mean Shift segmentation merge together both WBC nucleus and cytoplasm. A Mean Shift alteration could be done to adapt it for our purposes, but we have chosen to use classic method for simplicity. Fig. 2 shows the segmentation result using this solution in which both nucleus and cytoplasm are well detected.

5   System Implementation

For each strategy, the training set is formed by sampling pixels from the images belonging to the ALL-IDB2 presenting healthy WBCs chosen to make part of the available training images. On the other hand, the test set is formed of the first 33 images of ALL-IDB1, acquired in the same lighting conditions and with the same camera.

5.1   First Step

According to the prior knowledge defined about Mean Shift and classic segmentation methods, we have used two strategies to perform the first phase of our algorithm. Both of them are focused to offer the SVM a sufficient set of possible training samples. We have used either classic methods or Mean Shift to obtain this training set. The main objective is to train the SVM with the most accurate pixels related to white blood cell nuclei and cytoplasm. Once the pre processing strategy has been used, the next step is the classic or Mean Shift segmentation method. As said before, we have used both the approaches to experiment their

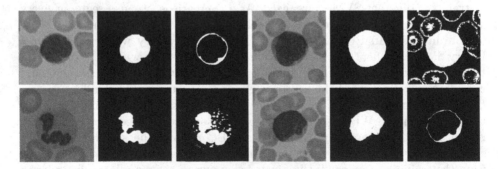

Fig. 2. (Top) From left to right: training original image from ALL-IDB2, manually segmented nucleus and cytoplasm; test original image, segmentation result for nucleus and cytoplasm with the first strategy. (Bottom) From left to right: test original image, segmentation result for nucleus and cytoplasm with the second strategy; test original image, segmentation result for nucleus and cytoplasm with the third strategy

behaviour in relation to the SVM training set building. With the classic segmentation methods, we have obtained two binary masks. The first one contains the white blood cells segmented in their entirety while the second one contains only the white blood cells nuclei. From these images, the segmented cytoplasm region could be easily obtained performing a difference operation between the first image and the second one and remembering that the cytoplasm region is always placed around the white blood cell nucleus. Thanks to this process we can easily perform the training of the SVM in the next phase, according to a defined strategy. Overall, we have obtained, in both cases, a certain set of images in which the regions have been pointed out. Mean Shift method, instead, produces only a set of images in which the regions of interest are marked with different colours, obtained by finding the dominant colour modes of the three main regions: erythrocytes, white blood cell and background. It is important to note that this phase is crucial to detect pure candidate pixels to perform the SVM training in the next phase, therefore we make a comparison between the results obtained in our method, realized without using Mean Shift, and the method inspired to the theory expressed in literature.

5.2   Second Step

Now our interest is to perform a properly training phase over the given pixels obtained in phase one. The chosen pixels must be the most various possible all over the regions obtained in phase one, in order to realize a proper classification model during SVM training phase. According to our implementation, we have chosen to use classic segmentation to perform phase one, and Mean Shift to realize a secondary implementation to show and compare the obtained results. Note that Mean Shift technique can be easily adapted to our purposes, but the final method should be adapted to be a three phases method, as long as Mean Shift does not directly offer pixels belonging to cytoplasm. They could only be obtained performing a two-phase SVM training. Now, we show a strategy to train the SVM in order to produce a classification model. Once we have obtained pixels belonging to cytoplasm, white blood cell nucleus and red blood cells regions, the remaining step to perform is to accurately choose these pixels with a uniform sampling, in order to consider every single image available in the group of images given for the training set. Thus, four different regions form candidates of training set for SVM. We mark nucleus pixels of white blood cells with class label I_1, cytoplasm pixels with class label I_2, instead mature erythrocyte and non-cell region pixels are marked with I_3. To avoid uncertainty, the following property has been set:$I_1 \cap I_2 \cap I_3 = \emptyset$ (empty set). SVM implements a classification strategy that exploits a margin-based ?geometrical? criterion rather than a purely ?statistical? criterion. It does not estimate the statistical distributions of classes for classification, while defines the classification model by exploiting the concept of margin maximization. There are two types of margin in SVM. Hard margin classifier works well in no-noise cases, but fails with noisy data due to overfitting. Soft margin classifier may achieve much better generalization results by relaxing the hard margin and ignoring the noisy data. So, removing noisy samples from the training set may benefit to training; for this reason we have produced pure samples of the three classes. Statistics theory has revealed that, through uniform, or Monte Carlo sampling, a subset could be produced to represent the entire data set approximately while retaining the distribution of data effectively [17]. The essential steps of this phase can be summarized as follows:

- sample N pixels from I_1, I_2, I_3 regions. There are N/4 pixels sampled respectively from four regions (cytoplasm, nucleus, mature erythrocytes and background region) to keep the size of the training set balanced;
- train a SVM online, taking the reduced training set defined at point one and a RBF kernel and generate a classifier model;
- use this model to classify the image pixels which are represented by $(R, G, B)^T$.

We have performed two main experiments. The first one has been realised to verify our implementation performances over single WBCs and in order to identify the most suitable parameters for the SVM. Thus, through a 10 fold cross-validation each time we have divided the original training set in two subsets, the first one to train the SVM and the second one to test the obtained model. An ideal average accuracy value has been reached by choosing the parameters c and γ as 1e3 and 1e1 respectively. The second and final experiment have been realised to verify the segmentation performances of the proposed method. Thus the whole original training set has been used to create the SVM model. The first 33 native resolution images has been used as test set and to check the method applied to a natural image composed of several white blood cells of many different classes.

5.3   Third Step

Once the first (visual) results have been obtained we have started experimenting with various features that can be used to train the classifier. In fact, even though we are talking of a segmentation technique, pixels are used as features for the SVM classifier. Until now the only descriptors used are the colour values. Although in many cases these features are enough to reach a good segmentation result, in other cases a poor feature set like this is not able to discriminate pixels belonging to regions with wide variations in colours. Thus the first intuition has been to add the average colour values of each pixel neighbourhood. These average values have been tested for neighbourhood of size 3×3, 5×5 and 7×7. For the same neighbourhood we have also computed other statistical features that are often used for segmentation purposes: standard deviation, uniformity and entropy. While the segmentation accuracy highly benefits from the use of these new features, the overall system became to slow, both in training and segmentation phase. Furthermore, the step of samples selection, used to train the classifier, became too complex, due to a higher number of samples with different values. For all these reasons the features previously mentioned have been extracted only for neighbourhood of size 3×3, showing excellent performances

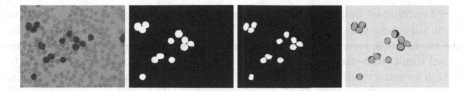

Fig. 3. Original images from the ALL-IDB1 database, ground-truth for whole leukocyte, ground-truth for leukocyte nuclei and final segmentation result.

Table 1. Segmentation performances.

	Otsu	Zack	Our Approach
Accuracy	77.67 ± 0.6	74.76 ± 3.6	97.61 ± 1.7
Sensitivity	76.70 ± 8.3	85.43 ± 6.8	98.45 ± 0.3
Specificity	85.62 ± 4.6	81.27 ± 5.4	97.56 ± 1.2
Precision	53.55 ± 12.8	79.12 ± 8.6	70.45 ± 5.8
F-measure	45.18 ± 5.3	55.15 ± 3.3	82.13 ± 2.3

as showed in fig. 3, outperforming previous results. After the segmentation, all the images have been automatically cleaned, as we have already proposed in [18], in order to remove small artefacts from the background and to give to the reader an idea about the goodness of the results. In order to evaluate the segmentation performances of the proposed method, a subset of images (10 random samples) belonging to the ALL-IDB1 have been manually segmented by skilled operators, creating two ground-truth images for each sample. These images display respectively each blood cell present in the image and the white blood cell nuclei. Fig. 3 shows some images belonging to the ALL-IDB1 and their relative ground-truth images. Finally, the ground-truth images previously described have been compared with the automated segmented images in order to calculate the most common metrics for segmentation evaluation, that are: accuracy, sensitivity, specificity, precision and F-measure. Our segmentation approach has been compared with some well know segmentation algorithms like Otsu [19] and Zack [20]. Table 1 shows the average performances obtained with the ten tested samples. As it can be seen the most important values obtained with our approach are higher than the other segmentation approaches.

6 Conclusions

This work proposed and investigated a new automated white blood cell recognition method that can be applied to support some existing medical methods, like the WBCC, White Blood Cells Counting. It is realized using lots of notions already known in literature but combining them to build an essentially brand new method in which the major innovation is brought by the use of multi class SVM. Whereas the aim of a fully automated cell analysis and diagnosis of white blood cell has not yet reached, many important steps in the image segmentation using Learning by Sampling method have been realized. We proposed a segmentation approach using several variations in the schemes. One of these variation consists in using classic segmentation methods or the Mean Shift. The experimental results demonstrate that the new approach is very accurate and robust in relation to some traditional methods such as the already mentioned Mean Shift combined with two-phase SVM training method. The performances achieved with the ALL-IDB often reaches the 99% of accuracy, but in particular we want to highlight the possibility to tune this approach to each couple of microscope and camera using only few image samples. Despite the good results, we do not consider the development of our project totally concluded. Our purposes and hopes are certainly to continue the work in order to experiment several new investigations that could potentially bring to better results. Among the future works we can indicate the extension to different colour spaces in which segmentation process could be achieved easily and more effectively. A further step will include analysis and recognition of the different types of healthy and blasted white blood cells. Finally, our idea is to export the whole procedure to bone marrow images, in which the first segmentation phase is more difficult than in the peripheral blood images, since the brightness conditions could be very different and large clusters of cells can exist.

Acknowledgments. This work has been funded by Regione Autonoma della Sardegna (R.A.S.) Project CRP-17615 DENIS: Dataspace Enhancing Next Internet in Sardinia. Lorenzo Putzu gratefully acknowledges Sardinia Regional Government for the financial support of his PhD scholarship (P.O.R. Sardegna F.S.E. Operational Programme of the Autonomous Region of Sardinia, European Social Fund 2007-2013 - Axis IV Human Resources, Objective l.3, Line of Activity l.3.1.

References

1. Pan, C., Lu, H., Cao, F.: Segmentation of blood and bone marrow cell images via learning by sampling. In: Huang, D.-S., Jo, K.-H., Lee, H.-H., Kang, H.-J., Bevilacqua, V. (eds.) ICIC 2009. LNCS, vol. 5754, pp. 336–345. Springer, Heidelberg (2009)
2. Fukunaga, K., Hostetler, L.: The estimation of the gradient of a density function, with applications in pattern recognition. IEEE Transactions on Information Theory **21**(1), 32–40 (1975)
3. Shapiro, L.G., Stockman, G.C.: Computer Vision, chap. 12, pp. 279–325. Prentice Hall, New Jersey (2001)
4. Gonzalez, R.C., Woods, R.E.: Digital Image Processing, 3rd edn. Prentice Hall Pearson Education Inc., New Jersey (2008)
5. Donida Labati, R., Piuri, V., Scotti, F.: ALL-IDB: the acute lymphoblastic leukemia image database for image processing. In: Macq, B., Schelkens, P. (eds.) Proceedings of the 18th IEEE ICIP International Conference on Image Processing, pp. 2045–2048. IEEE Publisher, Brussels (2011)
6. Bennett, J.M., Catovsky, D., Daniel, M.T., Flandrin, G., Galton, D.A., Gralnick, H.R., Sultan, C.: Proposals for the classification of the acute leukemias. French-American-British (FAB) co-operative group. British Journal of Hematology **33**(4), 451–458 (1976)

7. Madhloom, H.T., Kareem, S.A., Ariffin, H., Zaidan, A.A., Alanazi, H.O., Zaidan, B.B.: An Automated White Blood Cell Nucleus Localization and Segmentation using Image Arithmetic and Automated Threshold. Journal of Applied Sciences **10**(11), 959–966 (2010)
8. Sinha, N., Ramakrishnan, A.G.: Automation of differential blood count. In: Chockalingam, A. (ed.) Proceedings of the Conference on Convergent Technologies for the Asia-Pacific Region, vol. 2, pp. 547–551. IEEE Publisher, Taj Residency (2003)
9. Kovalev, V.A., Grigoriev, A.Y., Ahn, H.: Robust recognition of white blood cell images. In: Kavanaugh, M.E., Werner, B. (eds.) Proceedings of the 13th International Conference on Pattern Recognition, pp. 371–375. IEEE Publisher, Vienna (1996)
10. Scotti, F.: Robust segmentation and measurements techniques of white cells in blood microscope images. In: Daponte, P., Linnenbrink, T. (eds.) Proceedings of the IEEE Instrumentation and Measurement Technology Conference, pp. 43–48. IEEE Publisher, Sorrento (2006)
11. Piuri, V., Scotti, F.: Morphological classification of blood leucocytes by microscope images. In: Proceedings of the IEEE International Conference on Computational Intelligence for Measurement Systems and Applications, pp. 103–108. IEEE Publisher, Boston, July 14–16, 2004
12. Halim, N.H.A., Mashor, M.Y., Hassan, R.: Automatic Blasts Counting for Acute Leukemia Based on Blood Samples. International Journal of Research and Reviews in Computer Science **2**(4), August 2011
13. Mohapatra, S., Patra, D., Satpathy, S.: An Ensemble Classifier System for Early Diagnosis of Acute Lymphoblastic Leukemia in Blood Microscopic Images. Journal of Neural Computing and Applications (article in press, 2013)
14. David, J.F., Comaniciu, D., Meer, P.: Computer-assisted discrimination among malignant lymphomas and leukemia using immunophenotyping, intelligent image repositories, and telemicroscopy. IEEE Transaction on Information Technology in Biomedicine **4**(4), 12–22 (2000)
15. Lezoray, O., Elmoataz, A., Cardot, H., Gougeon, G., Lecluse, M., Elie, H., Revenu, H.M.: Segmentation of Color Images from Serous Cytology for Automated Cell Classification. Journal of Analytical and quantitative cytology and histology/the International Academy of Cytology [and] American Society of Cytology **22**(4), 311–322 (2000)
16. Vapnik, V.N., Vapnik, V.: Statistical learning theory, vol. 1. Wiley, New York (1998)
17. Caflisch, R.E.: Monte Carlo and quasi-Monte Carlo methods. In: Acta Numerica, vol. 7, pp. 149. Cambridge University Press (1998)
18. Putzu, L., Di Ruberto, C.: Investigation of different classification models to determine the presence of Leukemia in peripheral blood image. In: Petrosino, A. (ed.) ICIAP 2013, Part I. LNCS, vol. 8156, pp. 612–621. Springer, Heidelberg (2013)
19. Otsu, N.: A Threshold Selection Method from Gray-Level Histograms. IEEE Transactions on Systems, Man, and Cybernetics **9**(1), 62–66 (1979)
20. Zack, G., Rogers, W., Latt, S.: Automatic Measurement of Sister Chromatid Exchange Frequency. Journal of Histochemistry and Cytochemistry **25**, 741–753 (1977)

Fully Automatic Brain Tumor Segmentation by Using Competitive EM and Graph Cut

Valentina Pedoia[1], Sergio Balbi[2], and Elisabetta Binaghi[3(✉)]

[1] Department of Rad. and Biomed. Imaging, University of California, San Francisco, USA
Valentina.Pedoia@ucsf.edu
[2] Department of Biotechnologies and Life Sciences, Insubria University, Varese, Italy
sergio.balbi@uninsubria.it
[3] Department of Theoretical and Applied Science, Insubria University, Varese, Italy
elisabetta.binaghi@uninsubria.it

Abstract. Manual MRI brain tumor segmentation is a difficult and time consuming task which makes computer support highly desirable. This paper
presents a hybrid brain tumor segmentation strategy characterized by the allied
use of Graph Cut segmentation method and Competitive Expectation Maximization (CEM) algorithm. Experimental results were obtained by processing in-
house collected data and public data from benchmark data sets. To see if the
proposed method can be considered an alternative to contemporary methods,
the results obtained were compared with those obtained by authors who undertook the *Multi-modal Brain Tumor Segmentation* challenge. The results obtained prove that the method is competitive with recently proposed approaches.

Keywords: MRI segmentation · Brain tumor · Graph cut · Competitive expectation maximization

1 Introduction

Gliomas are the most common primary malignant brain tumors. Their infiltrative
nature causes no clear boundary between tumor and healthy tissues, which makes
surgical resection difficult [1]. Magnetic Resonance Imaging (MRI) has a central role
in radiological assessment of Gliomas for several reasons. It represents the first
adopted exam to forward a diagnostic hypothesis, typically based on the finding of an
hyper-intensity on T2/FLAIR-weighted sequences with no or slight enhancement after
gadolinium injection [2]. High accuracy segmentation is required to evaluate and
tracing the morphological, topographical and evolutionary characteristics of Gliomas.
MRI brain tumor segmentation is fundamental in order to select the most appropriate
treatment, to plan the best surgical approach and postoperatively, to evaluate the extent of resection which constitutes, in addition to histopathology, the most important
prognostic factor [3,4]. A precise spatial distribution and volumetric computation is of
basilar relevance during the follow-up, especially for monitoring the evolution over
time of any possible residue.

© Springer International Publishing Switzerland 2015
V. Murino and E. Puppo (Eds.): ICIAP 2015, Part I, LNCS 9279, pp. 568–578, 2015.
DOI: 10.1007/978-3-319-23231-7_51

Manual brain segmentation is a difficult and time consuming task which makes computer support highly desirable. Computer-assisted segmentation plays a vital role by freeing physicians with varying degrees of automation, from the burden of total manual labeling and by providing quantitative measurements to aid in diagnosis and disease modeling. Over the last two decades, many automatic MRI brain tumor segmentation methods have been proposed in literature [5,6]. Kaus et al. [3] addressed Low Grade Gliomas and Meningioma segmentation by developing an algorithm that uses a statistical classification with atlas prior. Liu et al. [7], proposed a semi-automatic segmentation strategy based on Fuzzy Connectedness; results obtained are highly accurate, however a high level of user interaction is required by the strategy, impacting the stability and then the reproducibility of the segmentation. Other approaches, widely explored in the literature, are based on active and deformable models such as level set and Machine Learning techniques oriented to multimodal segmentations [5,6], [8].

In recent years, there has been a growing interest in Graph Cut based methods for solving segmentation tasks [9,10,11,12]. The "Tumor-Cut" method has been proved highly accurate in solving the brain tumor segmentation task [10]. The method is interactive, asking experts to provide accurate initialization information. Interactive methods can improve the accuracy by incorporating prior knowledge from the user; however, in some practical applications where a large number of images are needed to be handled, they can be laborious and time consuming. Automatic and interactive methods are often used together to improve the segmentation results. Interactive methods, for example, may start with the preliminary results from automatic segmentation as an initial segmentation.

The present paper proposes a fully automatic brain tumor segmentation strategy characterized by the allied use of Graph Cut and Competitive Expectation Maximization (CEM) algorithms [13]. The strategy synergically combines the two techniques and attempts to optimize the balancing between accuracy and stability/reproducibility of the results. In a first set of experiments we used an in-house collected volumetric MRI tumor dataset. Results obtained were evaluated through a behavioral comparison based on manually traced masks. In a second set of experiments we have used data from the public dataset collected for the Multimodal Brain Tumor Segmentation (BRATS) challenge, a satellite event of the Medical Image Computing and Computer Assisted Intervention Society (MICCAI) Conference 2012 [14]. To see whether the proposed method can be considered an alternative to contemporary methods, a comparison analysis has been developed in which our results were compared with those obtained by authors who undertook the BRATS Challenge.

2   Theoretical Background

This section briefly outlines the basic concepts of Graph Cut and CEM algorithms adopted in the proposed hybrid segmentation strategy. Of the two methods, only the ingredients   directly involved in the integration are detailed.

2.1   Graph Cut

The s/t Graph Cuts framework proposed by Boykov et al. [9], [12], offers a globally optimal object extraction method for N-dimensional images. Graph cuts optimize a segmentation energy function that combines boundary regularization with regularization of regional properties.

The aim of a volumetric, segmentation is to assign to each voxel $v \in V$ a label L_v representing the membership of the voxel to a specific region; in the case of binary segmentation aimed to subdivide the image into Object and Background, each L_v can be either *Obj* or *Bkg*.   Vector L=(L_1,...., L_v ,....,$L_{|V|}$) defines a segmentation. Each pair of adjacent voxels *(v,w)* belonging to the set *N* of pairs of neighboring voxels, has a (boundary) cost $B_{(v,w)}$. The cost $B_{(v,w)}$ is related to the type of labeling of the pair of voxels and the similarity of *v, w*. The optimal labeling is obtained by minimizing the following energy function:

$$E(L) = \lambda R(L) + B(L) \tag{1}$$

where

$$R(L) = \sum_{v \in V} R_v(L_v) \tag{2}$$

$$B(L) = \sum_{v_i, w_j \in N} B_{(v_i, w_j)} \delta_{L_i, L_j} \quad \text{with } \delta_{L_i, L_j} = \begin{cases} 0 \text{ if } L_i = L_j \\ 1 \text{ if } L_i \neq L_j \end{cases} \tag{3}$$

R(L) and *B(L)* are called Regional and Boundary terms respectively. The regional term *R(L)* assumes that the individual penalties for assigning voxel *v* to Object and

Background, correspondingly *Rv(Obj)* and *Rv(Bkg)*, are given. The coefficient $\lambda \geq$ 0 in (1) specifies a relative importance of the region properties term *R(L)* versus

the boundary properties term *B(L)*. Energy function can be encoded via *n-links* and *t-links* of the graph whose nodes represent image elements; *n-links* are edges between pixels and *t-links* are edges used to connect   nodes to *S (source)* and *T (sink)* terminal nodes representing *Obj* and *Bkg* labels. The weights assigned to *n-links* represent the distance between two neighbor nodes, and these contribute to the Boundary term $B_{(v;w)}$. Costs $B_{(v;w)}$ may be computed using local intensity gradient, Laplacian zero-crossing, gradient direction, geometric or other criteria. The weights assigned to t-link contribute to the Regional terms *Rv(Obj)* and *Rv(Bkg)*. For example, Rv(.) may reflect how the intensity of the voxel *v* fits into the given intensity models of the object and background.

The max-flow/min-cut algorithm [15] is used as optimization framework. The application of Graph Cut algorithm requires the identification of object and background prototypes with which to initialize the overall segmentation process. Usually this task is accomplished through an interactive session in which users manually select seeds on the image. Seeds constrain the search space and intensities of elements marked as seeds are used to define regional terms.

2.2   CEM Algorithm

The CEM algorithm proposed by Zhang at al. [13] is based on competitive mechanisms and is used for parameter estimation of Gaussian Mixture Model (GMM) overcoming the limitation of the classical EM algorithm.

Let x be a d-dimensional random variable whose probability distribution can be written as the composition of k components. Each component is formulated as follows:

$$p(x \mid \theta) = \sum_{m=1}^{k} \alpha_m p(x \mid \theta_m)$$

(4)

where α_m is the prior probability of the m-th component; under the assumption of Gaussian distribution, we have:

$$p(x \mid \theta_m) = \frac{1}{2\pi^{\frac{d}{2}} |\Sigma|^{\frac{1}{2}}} \exp\left(-\frac{1}{2}(x - \mu)^T |\Sigma|^{-1}(x - \mu) \right)$$

(5)

The goal of the CEM algorithm is to find the best set $\theta = [k, \alpha, \mu, \Sigma]$ with $\alpha = \{\alpha_1, ..., \alpha_k\}$, $\mu = \{\mu_1, ..., \mu_k\}$, $\Sigma = \{\Sigma_1, ..., \Sigma_k\}$. To estimate the appropriate number of components the CEM algorithm uses the criterion presented by Figueiredo et al. [49].

2.3   Graph Cut Initialisation through CEM Algorithm

Consider to achieve a set of observations X_o and X_b in a d-dimensional space of the unknown Object and Background distributions. By applying the CEM strategy on these data we obtain two sets of parameters θ_o and θ_b that fully describe the statistics of the Object and of the Background respectively. These parameters are used in the Graph Cut segmentation strategy to denote the terminal nodes of the graph.. The regions labeled *Obj* and *Bkg* are the composition of the Gaussian components of the mixture model and the corresponding components in the regional term of the Graph Cut are specified as follows:

$$R_v(Obj) = \sum_{i}^{k^o} \frac{1}{\alpha_i^o} \left(I_v - \mu_i^o \right)^T \left(\Sigma_i^o \right)^{-1} \left(I_v - \mu_i^o \right)$$

(6)

$$R_v(Bkg) = \sum_{i}^{k^b} \frac{1}{\alpha_i^b} \left(I_v - \mu_i^b \right)^T \left(\Sigma_i^b \right)^{-1} \left(I_v - \mu_i^b \right)$$

(7)

where *Iv* is the description of the voxel *v* in the d-dimensional space.

The term $B_{(v,w)}$ in the boundary term B(L) is defined as follows:

$$B_{(v,w)} \propto \exp\left(-\frac{1}{2}(I_v - I_w)^T \left|\Sigma_{v,w}\right|^{-1}(I_v - I_w)\right)$$

(8)

where $\Sigma_{(v,w)}$ is the sum of the covariance matrix Σ_i^o and Σ_i^b correspond-ing to the Object mixture component and Background mixture component to which the voxels v and w are assigned, respectively.

2.4   CEM-Graph Cut for Multicentric Brain Tumor Segmentation

In the context of MRI brain tumor segmentation,   observations X_o and X_b of the unknown Object (Tumor area) and Background (Brain) distributions can be provided by a preliminary easily done segmentation of homolateral tumor regions. Homola-teral tumors can be easily identified, in a fully automatic manner, operating in the symmetry feature space   and considering the tumor as an anomaly in the symmetry of the brain with respect to the Mid Sagittal Plane [16].   The CEM algorithm receives in input the   observations X_0 and X_b and computes the two sets of parameters θ_o and θ_b that fully describe the statistics of the   multi-centric pathological areas and of the Background respectively. The analysis is conducted in the one-dimensional image intensity space. The Graph Cut is subsequently applied with regional terms for the Object and Background specified as follows:

$$R(Obj) = \sum_v \sum_i^{k^o} \frac{1}{\alpha_i^o \sigma_i^o}\left(I_v - \mu_i^o\right)^2$$

(9)

$$R(Bkg) = \sum_v \sum_i^{k^b} \frac{1}{\alpha_i^b \sigma_i^b}\left(I_v - \mu_i^b\right)^2$$

(10)

The term $B_{(v,w)}$ in the boundary term B(L) is defined as follows:

$$B_{(v,w)} \propto \exp\left(-\frac{(I_v - I_w)^2}{2\sigma}\right)$$

(11)

Final Object/Tumor area and Background/Brain area are obtained as union of the corresponding k^o and k^b components. The CEM algorithm is integrated in the Graph Cut framework by providing initialization information. The Graph Cut is an image-based procedure that consider only intensity values as features. In this specific context formal ingredients of the CEM algorithm (probability distributions for each mixture component) reduce to the uni-dimensional case with a limited number of parameters to be estimated.

3   Experimental Results

The experiments were conducted using two datasets: one in-house collected and one public, created for the BRATS Challenge, a satellite event of the MICCAI 2012 Conference.

3.1   Evaluation Metrics

In our experiments performances were evaluate by adopting a behavioral comparison in which spatial distribution of the masks obtained by the automated segmentation were compared with spatial distribution of reference masks manually segmented by experts. Metrics adopted for the evaluation is described below according with Bouix et.al. [17]. The minimal problem of assessing the agreement between two binary maps B1 and B2, representing reference and segmented data respectively, is obtained in terms of number of voxels at which both B1 and B2 score "1" (True Positive T_p) or "0" (True Negative T_n), the number of voxels at which B1 scores "0" and B2 scores "1" (False Positive F_p) and viceversa (False Negative F_n). Starting from these concepts several similarity metrics could be defined. The most relevant measures to MR brain segmentation are the Jaccard coefficient (JC) and the Dice coefficient (DC) defined as follows:

$$JC = \frac{T_p}{T_p + F_p + F_n} \; ; \; DC = \frac{2T_p}{2T_p + F_p + F_n} \tag{12}$$

3.2   Experiments Performed on the In-House Collected Dataset

The acquired dataset is composed of twenty FLAIR MRI, gray scale, twelve bit depth, volumes acquired in a Philips 1.5T Machine. The dataset includes six "dense" and fourteen "sparse" MRI volumes considering dense volumes those in which the spacing between slice is equal to the slice thickness and sparse volumes those in which a layer of air is interposed between slices. Ten cases concern Low Grade Glioma tumors, and the remaining High Grade Glioma, Butterfly and Multi-centric Tumor manifestations. The tumor cases considered are heterogeneous in terms of shape, position and intensity level. Several configurations of the segmentation procedure were considered distinguished by different values of lambda parameter in equation (1). In the light of the results obtained, we decided to set the lambda parameter to 1 giving equal weight to regional and boundary terms. Our experience suggests that imagery, anatomical district and segmentation goals could lead to different setting. However it is worth to note that in our hybrid strategy, the description of the final object as union of different objects implies that the cut never needs to split strong gradients or tries to keep together heterogenous regions so that the method is less sensitive to the lambda parameter setting. Figure 2 shows examples of the automatic segmentation results when applied on dense FLAIR MRI volumes. Table 1 shows numerical results in terms of JC scores. The automatic segmentations were evaluated qualitatively by five medical experts through visual inspection along the axial, coronal and sagittal planes. The experts have analyzed both the source and segmented images, comparing their decisions with the automated results, exploiting critical aspects inherent to the specific cases and formulating their final qualitative judgment in the light of them. Segmentation results have been judged very satisfactory even if a slight overestimation was noticed in regions with very blurred edges or with edema infiltration (see Fig.2).

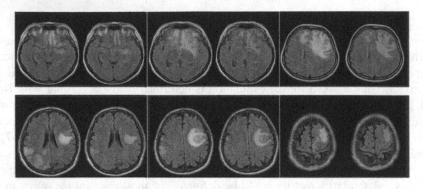

Fig. 1. Source slices of two FLAIR MRI dense volumes and superimposition of segmented masks computed by the automated procedure.

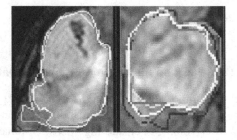

Fig. 2. Crop of two original Flair MRI slices with superimposed the contours delineated by the experts and the automated strategy (white contour)

Table 1. Mean Jaccard values obtained by comparing manual segmentations (EXP1-EXP6) and automatic segmentation (AUTO) for the cases under study

	EXP1	EXP2	EXP3	EXP4	EXP5	EXP6
AUTO						
mean	0.81	0.83	0.80	0.82	0.82	0.80
std	0.004	0.014	0.035	0.003	0.019	0.030

3.3   Experiments Performed on the MICCAI BRATS Public Dataset

The MICCAI BRATS dataset consists of multi-contrast MR scans of 30 glioma patients (both low-grade and high-grade, and both with and without resection) along with expert annotations for active tumor and edema. For each patient, T1, T2, FLAIR, and post-Gadolinium T1 MR images are available. All volumes were linearly co-registered to the T1 contrast image, skull stripped, and interpolated to 1mm isotropic resolution. The dataset contains 20 MRI volumes of real high grade glioma (BRATS HG) and 10 real low grade glioma (BRATS LG) ; moreover it also contains simulated images for 25 high-grade (BRATS SimHG) and 25 low-grade (BRATS SimLG) glioma subjects. The manual segmentations were performed in the axial plane. The CEM-Graph Cut strategy was applied to the four groups of MRI volumes included in the MICCAI dataset with the aim of segmenting the whole pathological area as in our previous experiments. The lambda parameter in equation (1) is set to the value equal to 1 as in the previous experiment.

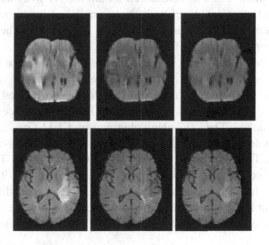

Fig. 3. From top to down: Case BRATS HG0024, Case BRATS LG0004; from left to right: source slice, source slice with reference mask superimposed, source slice with automated segmentation mask superimposed

Figures 3 shows the segmentation results obtained by applying the CEM-Graph Cut strategy to a High Grade Glioma case (BRATS HG00249) and a Low Grade Glioma case (BRATS LG0004). In both cases the qualitative evaluation of the segmentation results confirms the good behavior of the CEM-Graph Cut strategy who performs only few errors of commission. Tables 2 shows the results obtained in terms of JC scores. The performances obtained with BRATS HG and BRATS LG cases are lower than those obtained using our dataset. These results can be attributed to the high variability in the In Vivo cases included in the MICCAI BRATS dataset. Performances obtained by segmenting BRATS SimHG and BRATS SimLGare synthetic cases, are comparable with those obtained using our dataset.

Table 2. Mean Jaccard values *(JC)* obtained by segmenting the overall tumor area in MRI volumes of the BRATS dataset: BRATS HG (20 cases), BRATS LG (10 cases), BRATS SimHG (25 cases) and BRATS SimLG (25 cases)

	BRATS HG	BRATS LG	BRATS SimHG	BRATS SimLG
JC mean	0.72	0.71	0.79	0.76
std	0.07	0.09	0.008	0.003

3.4   Comparison Analysis

To see if the new method can be considered an alternative to contemporary methods, the results obtained were compared with those published by authors who undertook the BRATS challenge [14]. To make the results comparable, The CEM Graph Cut strategy has been applied to the BRATS dataset, hierarchically sub-classifying the previously segmented pathological regions into Edema and Active Tumor Area. Consistently with the metrics adopted in the challenge, we express comparison results in terms of *DC* index. In Table 3 the means of the *DC* index obtained by segmenting all the 20 High Grade Glioma cases are reported. The performances obtained by our strategy are well ranked. The *DC* value obtained by CEM-Graph Cut is higher than the average for an amount of 0.77% for the Edema and of 7.14% for the Active Tumor segmentation. The comparison between CEM-Graph Cut and Tumor-cut covers a particular interest, considering the shared theoretical framework. Tumor-Cut slightly prevails, however the comparison must take into account that, differently from our method, Tumor Cut is interactive and information provided by the users may improve performances thus reducing stability and reproducibility of the results.

Table 3. Dice scores *(DS)* obtained by the CEM-Graph Cut and methods presented by authors who undertook the Multi-modal Brain Tumor Segmentation challenge, when segmenting Edema and Active part of the tumor area in HG BRATS dataset. CEM-Graph Cut ranked for edema and tumor tissues 5/10 and 3/10 respectively

Method	DS	
	Edema	*Tumor*
Context-sensitive Classification Forests	0.70 ± 0.09	0.71 ± 0.24
Integrated Hierarchical Classif. and Reg.	0.61 ± 0.15	0.62 ± 0.27
Spatial Decision Forests	0.56 ± 0.17	0.58 ± 0.27
Tumor-cut Method	0.56 ± 0.20	0.73 ± 0.20
Prob. Gabor and Markov Random Fields	0.56 ± 0.11	0.67 ± 0.12
Coupled Global-Loc. Int. Bayesian Mod.	0.43 ± 0.28	0.55 ± 0.29
Generative Model for Brain Lesion Seg.	0.57 ± 0.14	0.56 ± 0.20
Generative-Discriminative Model	0.70 ± 0.13	0.70 ± 0.28
Multi-modal Segmentation Latent Atlas	0.60 ± 0.19	0.59 ± 0.27
CEM Graph Cut	$\mathbf{0.59 \pm 0.18}$	$\mathbf{0.70 \pm 0.21}$

4   Conclusions

The objective of the present study was to develop a fully automatic hybrid image segmentation strategy capable of exploiting and integrating in an unified framework image-based and statistical information for accurate and precise brain tumor delineation in MR imagery. The Graph Cut segmentation framework is built on the top of the CEM algorithm which serves as an effective automated initialization techniques overcoming limitations in the manual selection of initial seed points.. The use of CEM algorithm for Graph Cut initialization naturally supports an accurate   representation of the heterogeneity in the scene and this ensures   an accurate Min-Cut of   the Graph. The strategy was tested on both in-house collected data and on public data from MICCAI benchmark data set, including cases of homolateral and multi-centric glial tumors. The results prove that the allied use of CEM and Graph Cut produces high accurate segmentation of tumors present in scenes of varied complexity.

References

1. Kelly, P.J., Daumas-Duport, C., Kispert, D.B., Kall, B.A., Scheithauer, B.W., Illig, J.J.: Imaging-based stereotaxic serial biopsies in untreated intracranial glial neoplasms. J. Neurosurgery **66**(6), 865–874 (1987)
2. Duffau, H.: Lessons from brain mapping in surgery for low-grade glioma: insights into associations between tumour and brain plasticity. Lancet Neurol **4**(8), 467–487 (2005)
3. Kaus, M.R., Warfield, S.K., Nabavi, A., Black, P.M., Jolesz, F.A., Kikinis, R.: Automated segmentation of MRI of brain tumors. Radiology **218**, 586–591 (2001)
4. Clarke, L.P., Velthuizen, R., Camacho, M., Heine, J., Vaidyanathan, M., Hall, L., Thatcher, R., Silbiger, M.S.: MRI segmentation: methods and applications. Magn Reson Imaging **13**(3), 343–368 (1995)
5. Bauer, S., Wiest, R., Nolte, L.-P., Reyes, M.: A survey of MRI-based medical image analysis for brain tumor studies. Phys. Med. Biol. **58**, R97–R129 (2013)
6. Gordillo, N., Montseny, E., Sobrevilla, P.: State of the art survey on MRI brain tumor segmentation. Magn. Reson. Imaging **31**(8), 1426–1438 (2013)
7. Liu, J., Udupa, J.K., Odhner, D., Hackney, D., Moonis, G.: A system for brain tumor volume estimation via mr imaging and fuzzy connectedness. Comput. Med. Imag. Graphics **29**(1), 21–34 (2005)
8. Bauer, S., Nolte, L.-P., Reyes, M.: Fully automatic segmentation of brain tumor images using support vector machine classification in combination with hierarchical conditional random field regularization. In: Fichtinger, G., Martel, A., Peters, T. (eds.) MICCAI 2011, Part III. LNCS, vol. 6893, pp. 354–361. Springer, Heidelberg (2011)
9. Boykov, Y., Veksler, O., Zabih, R.: Fast approximate energy minimization via graph cuts. IEEE Trans. Pattern Anal. Mach. Intell. **23**, 1222–1239 (2001)
10. Hamamci, A., Kucuk, N., Karaman, K., Engin, K., Unal, G.: Tumor-Cut: segmentation of brain tumors on contrast enhanced MR images for radiosurgery applications. IEEE Trans. Medical Imaging **31**(3), 790–804 (2012)
11. Chen, V., Ruan, S.: Graph cut segmentation technique for MRI brain tumor extraction. In: 2nd International Conference on Image Processing Theory Tools and Applications (IPTA), pp. 284–287. IEEE Press, New York, 7–10 2010

12. Boykov, Y., Funka-Lea, G.: Graph cuts and efficient n-d image segmentation. Int. J. Comput. Vision **70**, 109–131 (2006)
13. Zhang, B., Zhang, C., Yi, X.Y.: Competitive EM algorithm for finite mixture models. Pattern Recognition **37**(1), 131–144 (2004)
14. Multimodal Brain Tumor Segmentation Challange (2012). http://www2.imm.dtu.dk/projects/BRATS
15. Boykov, Y., Kolmogorov, V.: An experimental comparison of min-cut/max-flow algorithms for energy minimization in vision. IEEE Transactions on Pattern Analysis and Machine Intelligence **26**(9), 1124–1137 (2004)
16. Pedoia, V., Binaghi, E., Balbi, S., De Benedictis, A., Monti, E., Minotto, R.: Glial brain tumor detection by using symmetry analysis. In: SPIE Int. Conf. Medical Imaging, pp. 831445–831445-8. SPIE (2012)
17. Bouix, S., Martin-Fernandez, M., Ungar, L., Koo, M.-S., Nakamura, M., McCarley, R.W., Shenton, M.E.: On evaluating brain tissue classifiers without a ground truth. NeuroImage **36**, 1207–1224 (2007)

An Automatic Method for Metabolic Evaluation of Gamma Knife Treatments

Alessandro Stefano[1,2(✉)], Salvatore Vitabile[3], Giorgio Russo[1], Massimo Ippolito[4], Franco Marletta[4], Corrado D'Arrigo[4], Davide D'Urso[1], Maria Gabriella Sabini[4], Orazio Gambino[2], Roberto Pirrone[2], Edoardo Ardizzone[2], and Maria Carla Gilardi[1]

[1] Institute of Molecular Bioimaging and Physiology,
National Research Council (IBFM-CNR) - LATO, Cefalù, PA, Italy
alessandro.stefano@ibfm.cnr.it
[2] Department of Chemical, Management, Information Technology and
Mechanical Engineering, University of Palermo, Palermo, Italy
[3] Department of Biopathology and Medical Biotechnologies (DIBIMED),
University of Palermo, Palermo, Italy
[4] Cannizzaro Hospital, Catania, Italy

Abstract. Lesion volume delineation of Positron Emission Tomography images is challenging because of the low spatial resolution and high noise level. Aim of this work is the development of an operator independent segmentation method of metabolic images. For this purpose, an algorithm for the biological tumor volume delineation based on random walks on graphs has been used. Twenty-four cerebral tumors are segmented to evaluate the functional follow-up after Gamma Knife radiotherapy treatment. Experimental results show that the segmentation algorithm is accurate and has real-time performance. In addition, it can reflect metabolic changes useful to evaluate radiotherapy response in treated patients.

Keywords: Segmentation · Random walk · PET imaging · Gamma Knife treatment · Biological target volume

1 Introduction

Gamma Knife (LGK; Elekta) radiosurgery is a mini-invasive technique defined as the delivery of a single, high dose of radiation to obtain a complete destruction of brain lesions. It provides a safe and effective way of treating inaccessible cerebral tumors. An examination to differentiate malign and benign tissue in brain tumors with great preciseness is the Positron Emission Tomography (PET) with the amino acid tracer 11c-methionin (MET). PET is a non-invasive functional imaging technique that shows complementary information with respect to Computed Tomography (CT) and Magnetic Resonance Imaging (MRI). In addition, metabolic changes are often faster and more indicative of the effects of the therapy with respect to anatomical imaging [1]. Numerous studies have shown that the specificity of the MET PET for marking tumor delineation and for the differentiation relapse versus radiation necrosis is higher

© Springer International Publishing Switzerland 2015
V. Murino and E. Puppo (Eds.): ICIAP 2015, Part I, LNCS 9279, pp. 579–589, 2015.
DOI: 10.1007/978-3-319-23231-7_52

compared with MRI. In the paper reported in [2], metabolic imaging was used for biological target delineation in 36 patients that showed a significantly longer median survival compared with the group of patients, in which target volume was merely defined by MRI. Nevertheless, due to the nature of PET images (low spatial resolution, high noise and weak boundary), the Metabolic Tumor Volume (MTV) varies substantially depending on the algorithm used to delineate functional lesions: the choice of a standard method for PET volume contouring is a very challenging yet unresolved step.

Visual delineation is widely used because it is easily applicable, but it is potentially inaccurate being susceptible to the window level settings and subject to both intra and inter-operator variability. In this paper an algorithm based on random walks (RW) on graphs [3] has been adapted for PET imaging. To create an automatic and operator independent method starting from previous work [4], we propose an automated seed localization method to identify RW seeds. Our framework is used in 12 patients with cervical metastases to evaluate therapeutic response in sequential scans for a total of 24 PET scans. Patients undergo MET PET examinations before and 2 months after the Gamma Knife treatment.

The paper is organized as follows: in the next section the current state of the art in PET image segmentation techniques is reviewed. In the "Materials and Methods" section, the RW algorithm adapted for PET imaging and for a clinical environment is described. In the "Results" section, our delineation method is evaluated to assess the accuracy and the Gamma Knife treatment response. We conclude with a discussion of results in the last section.

2 Related Works

Image thresholding and region growing methods are the most widely used due to their simplicity to implement but they are too sensitive to PET image noise and heterogeneity [5, 6]. Variational approaches based on gradient differences between target and background regions are mathematically efficient but sensitive to noise and subject to numerical fluctuation [7, 8]. Learning methods as artificial neural network (ANN), support vector machine (SVM), k-means algorithm, fuzzy C-means algorithm are efficient but require high computational steps and are sensitive to variability of PET radiotracer depending on study protocol, as for example scanner characteristics, radiotracer injected dose and interval between radiotracer injection and exam start, e.g. [9, 10]. In addition, supervised algorithms have limited application in PET imaging, unlike in the MRI or CT fields, due to high heterogeneity that makes the recognition of stable features in the training set very difficult. Graph based methods are used to find the globally optimal segmentation of images. The RW algorithm was developed by Grady [3] in the computer vision domain and then was extended for image segmentation [11, 12]. RW treats the segmentation as the solution to a linear system with an exact solution and it is very accurate in noisy and low contrast images, such as PET images. At last, in several works, e.g. [13, 14], the different tumor contours on PET and on CT are simultaneously segmented. Although our patients undergo a PET/CT scans, CT has strong limitations for target delineation of cervical metastases and this makes impossible to apply a PET/CT delineation in our study.

3   Materials and Methods

3.1   Phantom Studies

National Electrical Manufacturers Association International Electro-technical Commission (NEMA IEC) phantom with six spheres of different diameters (d1= 10 mm, d2 = 13 mm, d3 = 17 mm, d4 = 22 mm, d5 = 26 mm, d6 = 37 mm) is used to estimate the accuracy of the PET segmentation algorithm. Spheres, and background are filled with a ratio between measured sphere radioactivity concentration and measured background radioactivity concentration (S/B) that ranged from 3 to 7.

PET acquisitions are performed on time of flight PET/CT Discovery 690 by General Electric Medical Systems following the same protocol used in clinical routine. PET images have an in-plane resolution of 256 × 256 voxels with 1.1719x 1.1719x3.27 mm3 voxel size. The proposed segmentation method is evaluated by matching the sphere delineation with the ground truth in the CT images.

3.2   Clinical Study

Twelve patients with cervical metastases are enrolled to evaluate the metabolic response to Gamma Knife treatment, for a total of 24 PET scans. The patient fasts for 4 hours before PET exam and is intravenous injected with MET before and 2 months after the Gamma Knife treatment (see Fig.1). The PET oncological protocol begins 10 minutes after the injection.

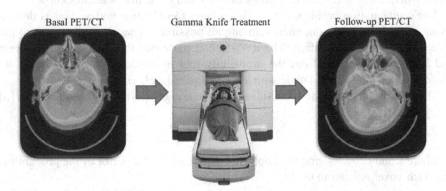

Fig. 1. Patients with cervical metastases undergo a MET PET examinations before and 2 months after the Gamma Knife treatment

The handmade segmentation is the gold standard for the clinical study. It is used to compare the results obtained with the automatic proposed method. PET/CT studies are reported by an expert nuclear medicine physician for diagnostic and staging purposes. A time-expansive slice-by-slice manual segmentation is performed on a software platform (Xeleris workstation) from General Electric Medical Systems healthcare. Due to inevitable variability of PET image visualization, the window level setting is changed by the nuclear medicine physician to obtain a clear visual appearance of MET PET positive structures. Then, the active tumor volume is defined including the tumor volume with an intense tracer uptake respect to background MET activity level.

3.3 Automatic Segmentation

3.3.1 RW Method in PET Imaging Field

RW is an efficient and accurate method in low contrast images characterized by noise and weak edges such as PET studies [15]. The graph-based segmentation method represents an image as a graph in which the voxels are its nodes and the edges are defined by a cost function which maps a change in image intensity to edge weights [3]. The weights w_{ij} between nodes are obtained using the following Gaussian function:

$$w_{ij} = \exp(-\beta(g_i - g_j)^2) \tag{1}$$

where both g_i and g_j are the image intensity values at voxels i and j; β is a free parameter (in our experiments, β is set to 1).

RW parameters have been calibrated to be suited for PET imaging modality. In (1) we replace g_i and g_j with the Standardized Uptake Value (SUV) in the voxels i and j. SUV is the ratio of lesion radioactivity concentration, and administered dose at the time of injection divided by body weight [16]. The PET image is converted into a graph where some nodes are labeled by the user and some nodes are not known.

The segmentation problem is to assign a label to unknown nodes. This is done by trying to find the minimum energy among all possible scenarios in the graph to provide an optimal segmentation. The RW method partitions the nodes into foreground and background subsets from the probability that a "random walker" starting at a source node, first reaches a node with a pre-assigned label, visiting every voxel.

The RW problem has the same solution as the combinatorial Dirichlet problem [3]:

$$D[x] = (x^T L x) / 2 \tag{2}$$

where L indicates the graph's Laplacian matrix and x the vector of the probabilities that each voxel is inner to target.

A probability array is then produced, and a threshold of 50% is chosen to discriminate the foreground from the background creating a voxel binary mask, so that:

- target voxel value = 1 if its probability $\geq 50\%$
- background voxel value = 0 if its probability $< 50\%$.

3.3.2 Automatic Detection of RW Seeds

To create an user independent method starting from previous work [4], we propose an automated seeding process of the RW algorithm. The algorithm automatically identifies the PET slice with the highest SUV (SUV_{max}) and the seeds for each slice. The n voxels with a SUV>95% of SUV_{max} are marked as target seeds. Then, the method explores the neighborhood of the voxel with SUV_{max} through searching in 8 directions to identify the background voxels with a SUV<30% of SUV_{max} (see Fig.2). Once the target and background seeds are localized, RW performs a 3D delineation (see Fig.3).

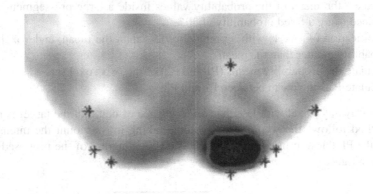

Fig. 2. Background (*) and target seeds (°) automatically identified by our method. After this step, the RW algorithm performs the lesion segmentation (red curve) to discriminate foreground from background voxels

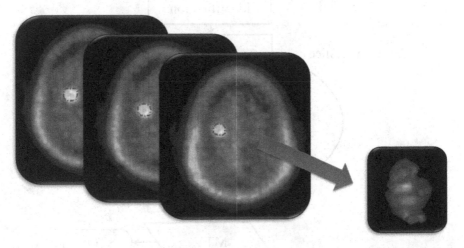

Fig. 3. A metabolic lesion in three different PET slices and the corresponding 3D rendered object derived from RW segmentation are show

3.3.3 Adaptive RW Method

RW method depends on the choice of the β-weighting factor in (1). To overcome this issue (in our experiments, β is set to 1), we change, slice after slice, the probability threshold to discriminate the target from background voxels. Using an adaptive probability, we obtain a method independent of the choice of the β-weighting factor. In fact, β influences how quickly the probability decreases with increasing intensity differences.

The probability map produced by the RW algorithm is processed to obtain an adaptive threshold value (P) using the following method:

- Calculate the mean of the probability values inside a large pre-segmented lesion obtained using a fixed probability of 20%
- Identification of voxels with a probability less than the mean, and voxels with a probability greater than the mean
- Calculate the probability means (P1 and P2) of the two voxel sets
- Calculate P as the mean between P1 and P2

In this way any voxel with less than a P% chance of being in the target is rejected. This method follows the whole lesion volume taking into account the intensity gradient of the PET lesion in different slices. The flow diagram of the proposed method is shown in figure 4.

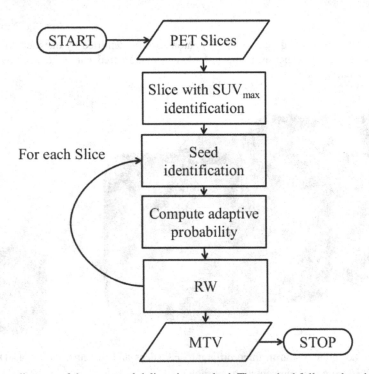

Fig. 4. Flow diagram of the proposed delineation method. The method follows the whole lesion volume taking into account the gradient of intensity and contrast changes of the PET lesion in different slices

3.4   Evaluation

The segmentation performance of the proposed method is evaluated making a comparison with manual MTV segmentation by the dice similarity coefficient (DSC), median Hausdorff distance (HD) and true positive and false positive volume fractions (TPVF and FPVF). DSC is a measurement of spatial overlap between segmented and manual MTV: a DSC of one indicates a perfect match between the two volumetric segmentations, while a DSC of zero indicates no overlap. HD is a shape dissimilarity metric measuring the most mismatched boundary pixels between automatic and manual MTV: a small median of HD values means an accurate segmentation, while a large median of HD values means no accuracy. TPVF indicates the fraction of the total amount of tissue inside the target lesion (sensitivity), and FPVF denotes the amount of tissue falsely identified (specificity=100 - FPVF) [17]. A perfect segmentation algorithm would be 100% sensitive (segmenting all voxels from the target voxels) and 100% specific (not segmenting any from the background voxels).

The average time for delineating brain metastases is recorded to assess algorithm performance.

In addition, lesion segmentation is used to evaluate therapeutic response using SUV_{max}, MTV, and Total Lesion Glycolysis (TLG) variations in sequential scans. MTV provides metabolic volumetric information of the tumors; TLG, defined as MTV x (average SUV within the MTV), combines the volumetric and SUV information, to try to obtain a better evaluation of the treatment response.

Variations (Δ) in SUV_{max}, MTV, and TLG in sequential scans are normalized to baseline:

$$\Delta(\%) = 100 \text{ x (post-treatment} - \text{baseline)/baseline} \qquad (3)$$

4   Experimental Results

4.1   Trials and Results on Phantoms

Phantom images are used to validate the proposed method. The size of the spheres is known, and the accuracy of the delineation method can be evaluated. The thresholds to identify target and background voxels in section 3.3.2 are set to 95% and 30% because there give better results among the tested values. The DSC range is found to be from 81.23% up to 99.99% (95.27±2.98%). The HD range is found to be from 1.69mm up to 3.66mm (2.10±0.79mm). The average TPVF is 98.80±2.22% (range: 95.10% - 100%). The average specificity (100 – FPVF) is ~ 100% since the sphere voxel number with respect to the background voxel number is very small.

4.2   Trials and Results on the Clinical study

24 PET studies (2 scans for each patient) are used to assess the accuracy of our method by comparing the automatic to manual segmentation. Fig. 5 shows the lesion segmentation obtained using the two different methods in three patient studies. The RW delineation is not subject to both intra and inter-operator variability.

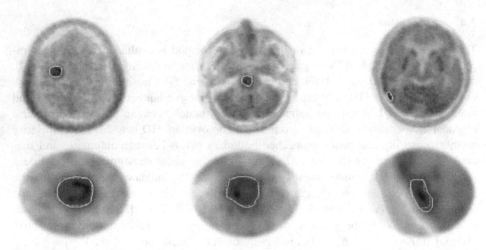

Fig. 5. Three different segmentation examples of uptake regions are shown in each column with a zoom of the lesion. RW (broken line) and manual (continuous line) lesion segmentations are overlaid

The DSC range of PET delineation using the RW algorithm is found to be from 76.35% up to 92.70% with a mean of 87.61±4.47%. The HD range is found to be from 1.00 mm up to 2.85 mm with a mean of 1.86±0.55 mm.

The average TPVF is found to be 89.40±8.09% (range: 71.20% - 100%). The average specificity (100 − FPVF) is ~ 100% since the target voxel number with respect to the background voxel number is very small (a single PET slice consists of 65536 voxels while the largest lesion in a single slice is < 50 voxels).

High DSC and TPVF, and low HD and FPVF values confirm the accuracy of method. An analysis of the time performance shows that our algorithm is fast: the segmentation time for single slice is around 0.3 seconds.

About Gamma Knife treatment response evaluation, results are shown in Table 1. Most patients show the same treatment response trend using SUV_{max}, MTV, and MTV variations in sequential scans. Differently, the third patient shows a minimal change in SUV_{max} (-1.00%) and great variation in the metabolic tumor mass and in TLG (-61.12% and -59.43%, respectively). Patients number 4, and 9 show a positive ΔSUV_{max} (+9.47% and +14.73%, respectively), and a negative ΔTLG, and ΔMTV (-16.89% and -8.50%, +49.98% and +39.74%, respectively).

The sixth patient study shows a positive ΔMTV (+24.85%), and a negative ΔSUV_{max} (-44.36%), and ΔTLG (-26.15%). At last, patients number 8 and 12 show a visual disappearance of metabolic lesions indicating a complete metabolic response (CMR) to treatment.

Table 1. Metabolic response obtained on the segmented lesions for each patient

Patients	ΔSUV_{max}	ΔMTV	ΔTLG
#1	-30.10%	-62.20%	-66.67%
#2	-26.21%	-31.53%	-43.83%
#3	-1.00%	-61.12%	-59.43%
#4	9.47%	-16.89%	-8.50%
#5	-41.83%	-81.16%	-83.86%
#6	-44.36%	24.85%	-26.15%
#7	-62.72%	-20.22%	-64.93%
#8	CMR	CMR	CMR
#9	14.73%	-49.98%	-39.74%
#10	-39.64%	-13.27%	-10.21%
#11	-37.00%	-30.95%	-56.50%
#12	CMR	CMR	CMR

5   Discussions and Future Works

Gamma Knife radiosurgery is a stereotactic treatment defined as the delivery of a single, and high dose of radiation for a precise destruction of target tissues. MRI, the commonly used imaging modality in neuro-radiosurgery, has limitations for the post-operative evaluation. We integrate PET imaging to evaluate the treatment response in 12 patients with cervical metastases. PET has, however, not yet been fully incorporated into routine Gamma Knife procedure: metabolic segmentation is a critical task due to the lack of consistency in tumor contour, low image resolution, and a relatively high level of noise and heterogeneity of uptake within a tumor. Nevertheless, an accurate automatic 3D delineation is desirable because manual segmentation is a prohibitively laborious task. In addition, automated segmentation is also important because of the need for repeatable delineation in patient studies for a proper quantification of therapy response, given the considerable variations within and across nuclear medicine physicians.

In this paper a modified RW method for PET images segmentation has been presented. We propose an extension of our previous method [4] to automatically change the probability value needful to lesion from background area discrimination and to make it fully automatic.

First, our method uses an adaptive probability value instead of a fixed one to make the segmentation performance independent of the choice of the β factor in the Gaussian weighting function (1). Second, the algorithm automatically identifies the RW seeds: our method is an operator independent method, satisfying this critical requirement in a clinical environment. Third, the method accuracy is optimal with high DSC and TPVF values and low HD and FPVF values. At last, the proposed method is very powerful in terms of time performance: the algorithm is fast (one slice in ~ 0.3 seconds) if compared against the time needed for manual segmentation.

In addition, we use our method to calculate MTV and TLG in order to reflect metabolic changes in sequential PET scans after Gamma Knife treatment throughout the entire tumor mass. These parameters should be more accurate methods of detecting global changes than a single-pixel value measurement such as SUV_{max}. The results in Table 1 show that the patient number 3, 4, and 9 could be a demonstration of this theory. On the other hand, in the literature cut-offs for SUV are reported [1, 18], instead there are no data for MTV or TLG evaluations. Analyses of receiver operating characteristic curves to estimate these cut-offs will be evaluated. In addition, MTV and TLG values depend on the delineation processes. Our segmentation approach is fully automatic, and an experienced nuclear medicine physician is considered in the manual lesion definition, to assess our method accuracy. Nevertheless, partial volume effect is one of the most important factors impacting the quality and the quantitative accuracy in PET imaging [19]. The images are blurred due to the limited spatial resolution of PET scanner and small lesions appear larger [20]. Several corrective techniques have been developed and a method of partial volume correction could be included in the algorithm, as that described in [21].

At last, the sixth patient shows a positive ΔMTV, and a negative ΔTLG that is indicative of partial response to treatment. TLG combines the volumetric (MTV) and the semi-quantitative parameter (SUV) information: it probably provides a better evaluation of the prognosis compared to MTV.

In conclusion, PET delineation in neurosurgical radiosurgery appears helpful for assessing the effects of therapy in brain metastases. The developed method could be used as a Medical Decision Support System to help clinicians in treatment response evaluation of oncological patients. Nevertheless, as this is only a preliminary study, further investigations are required with a larger number of patients in order to assess the prognostic usefulness and long-term clinical impact to correlate MTV segmentation with clinical outcomes, progression-free survival and overall survival.

Acknowledgments. This work is partially supported by CIPE1 (n. DM45602).

References

1. Wahl, R.L., et al.: From RECIST to PERCIST: Evolving Considerations for PET Response Criteria in Solid Tumors. Journal of Nuclear Medicine **50**, 122S–150S (2009)
2. Grosu, A.L., et al.: Reirradiation of recurrent high-grade gliomas using amino acid PET (SPECT)/CT/MRI image fusion to determine gross tumor volume for stereotactic fractionated radiotherapy. International Journal of Radiation Oncology Biology Physics **63**(2), 511–519 (2005)
3. Grady, L.: Random walks for image segmentation. IEEE Transactions on Pattern Analysis and Machine Intelligence **28**(11), 1768–1783 (2006)
4. Stefano, A., Vitabile, S., Russo, G., Ippolito, M., Sardina, D., Sabini, M.G., Gallivanone, F., Castiglioni, I., Gilardi, M.C.: A graph-based method for PET image segmentation in radiotherapy planning: a pilot study. In: Petrosino, A. (ed.) ICIAP 2013, Part II. LNCS, vol. 8157, pp. 711–720. Springer, Heidelberg (2013)

5. Jentzen, W., et al.: Segmentation of PET volumes by iterative image thresholding. Journal of Nuclear Medicine **48**(1), 108–114 (2007)
6. Li, H., et al.: A novel PET tumor delineation method based on adaptive region-growing and dual-front active contours. Medical Physics **35**(8), 3711–3721 (2008)
7. Geets, X., et al.: A gradient-based method for segmenting FDG-PET images: methodology and validation. European Journal of Nuclear Medicine and Molecular Imaging **34**(9), 1427–1438 (2007)
8. Wanet, M., et al.: Gradient-based delineation of the primary GTV on FDG-PET in non-small cell lung cancer: A comparison with threshold-based approaches, CT and surgical specimens. Radiotherapy and Oncology **98**(1), 117–125 (2011)
9. Hatt, M., et al.: A Fuzzy Locally Adaptive Bayesian Segmentation Approach for Volume Determination in PET. IEEE Transactions on Medical Imaging **28**(6), 881–893 (2009)
10. Zaidi, H., et al.: Fuzzy clustering-based segmented attenuation correction in whole-body PET imaging. Physics in Medicine and Biology **47**(7), 1143–1160 (2002)
11. Bagci, U., et al.: A Graph-Theoretic Approach for Segmentation of PET Images. Annual International Conference of the IEEE Engineering in Medicine and Biology Society (EMBC) **2011**, 8479–8482 (2011)
12. Onoma, D.P., et al.: 3D Random walk based segmentation for lung tumor delineation in PET imaging. In: 2012 9th IEEE International Symposium on Biomedical Imaging (ISBI), pp. 1260–1263 (2012)
13. Song, Q., et al.: Optimal Co-Segmentation of Tumor in PET-CT Images With Context Information. IEEE Transactions on Medical Imaging **32**(9), 1685–1697 (2013)
14. Xia, Y., et al.: Dual-modality brain PET-CT image segmentation based on adaptive use of functional and anatomical information. Computerized Medical Imaging and Graphics **36**(1), 47–53 (2012)
15. Zaidi, H., El Naqa, I.: PET-guided delineation of radiation therapy treatment volumes: a survey of image segmentation techniques. European Journal of Nuclear Medicine and Molecular Imaging **37**(11), 2165–2187 (2010)
16. Paquet, N., et al.: Within-patient variability of F-18-FDG: Standardized uptake values in normal tissues. Journal of Nuclear Medicine **45**(5), 784–788 (2004)
17. Udupa, J.K., et al.: A framework for evaluating image segmentation algorithms. Computerized Medical Imaging and Graphics **30**(2), 75–87 (2006)
18. Young, H., et al.: Measurement of clinical and subclinical tumour response using F-18 - fluorodeoxyglucose and positron emission tomography: Review and 1999 EORTC recommendations. European Journal of Cancer **35**(13), 1773–1782 (1999)
19. Soret, M., Bacharach, S.L., Buvat, I.: Partial-volume effect in PET tumor imaging. Journal of Nuclear Medicine **48**(6), 932–945 (2007)
20. Stefano, A., et al.: Metabolic impact of partial volume correction of 18F FDG PET-CT oncological stucies on the assessment of tumor response to treatment. Quarterly Journal of Nuclear Medicine and Molecular Imaging **58**(4), 413–423 (2014)
21. Gallivanone, F., et al.: PVE Correction in PET-CT Whole-Body Oncological Studies From PVE-Affected Images. IEEE Transactions on Nuclear Science **58**(3), 736–747 (2011)

Spinal Canal and Spinal Marrow Segmentation by Means of the Hough Transform of Special Classes of Curves

Annalisa Perasso[1]($\boxtimes$), Cristina Campi[1],
Anna Maria Massone[1], and Mauro C. Beltrametti[2]

[1] CNR–SPIN, Genova, Italy
{perasso,campi}@dima.unige.it, annamaria.massone@cnr.it
[2] Dipartimento di Matematica, Università degli Studi di Genova, Genova, Italy
beltrametti@dima.unige.it

Abstract. In this paper we present a Hough Transform-based method for the detection of the spinal district in X-ray Computed Tomography (CT) images in order to build binary masks that can be applied to functional images to infer information on the metabolic activity of the spinal marrow. This kind of information may be of particular interest for the study of the spinal marrow physiology in both health and disease.

Keywords: Hough transform · Tomographic imaging · Image segmentation · Algebraic plane curves

1   Introduction

Hough Transform (HT) [1] is a classical pattern recognition technique commonly used to recognize profiles of interest in images. Its early formulation provided a strategy to detect just straight lines but it has been first extended to ellipse and circle recognition [2], and then generalized to arbitrary shape detection by means of look-up tables [3]. Recently, an extension to special classes of algebraic plane curves has been proposed in [4], and applications of this method to real astronomical and medical data have been presented in [5]. Here we want to apply this method to the case of the human spinal marrow and spinal canal segmentation in X-ray Computed Tomography (CT) images, bearing in mind clinical applications concerned with neurological diseases. In fact, it is very interesting to study how such disorders affect the spinal marrow, i.e., the elongated central nervous system tissue, which is contained in the spinal canal. The combination of different medical imaging techniques like X-ray CT and Positron Emission Tomography (PET) provides encouraging results for the study of neurological diseases [6]. The anatomical information coming from high resolution CT images are indeed very useful to exactly identify on the low resolution PET images the regions from which to extract the metabolic information. Unlike the case of Magnetic Resonance Imaging [7,8], in CT images the main problem which is

© Springer International Publishing Switzerland 2015
V. Murino and E. Puppo (Eds.): ICIAP 2015, Part I, LNCS 9279, pp. 590–600, 2015.
DOI: 10.1007/978-3-319-23231-7_53

encountered in discriminating the spinal marrow within the spinal canal is due to the low contrast between the spinal marrow and the surrounding tissue. In [9], exploiting high local contrast between bone and spinal canal, an automated region growing algorithm is used for the spinal canal detection, while spinal cord detection is performed on the basis of geometrical arguments as the maximal inscribed circle in the polygon representing the spinal canal. In this paper we use the classical HT for ellipse detection, and its extension to special classes of algebraic plane curves, for an automated recognition of both the spinal marrow and the spinal canal in CT images, in order to build digital masks that can be applied to PET images.

The paper is organized as follows. In Section 2 we recall some basic concepts concerning the HT for algebraic plane curves, we present the family of curves we are interested in, and we study in detail the properties of the corresponding HT. Then in Section 3 we show the application to real CT images in order to identify both, the spinal marrow and the spinal canal, and we show the consequent integration with PET functional information. Finally, we offer our conclusions and comments in Section 4.

2 Background Material and Methods

We follow the notation introduced in [4,5]. Let us consider a family of irreducible polynomials in the variables X, Y,

$$F(X,Y;\lambda) = \sum_{i,j=0}^{d} g_{ij}(\lambda) X^i Y^j, \quad 0 \le i + j \le d, \tag{1}$$

where the coefficients $g_{ij}(\lambda)$ are real polynomials in the independent parameters $\lambda = (\lambda_1, \ldots, \lambda_t)$ varying in an Euclidean open set $\mathcal{U} \subseteq \mathbb{R}^t$, and with the degree, d, of $F(X,Y;\lambda)$ not depending on λ. Let $\mathcal{F}$ be the corresponding family of zero loci $\mathcal{C}_\lambda$ of $F(X,Y;\lambda)$, and assume that each $\mathcal{C}_\lambda$ is a real curve in the affine plane $\mathbb{A}^2_{(X,Y)}(\mathbb{R})$. So we want a family $\mathcal{F} = \{\mathcal{C}_\lambda\}$ of irreducible curves which share the degree.

If $P = (x_P, y_P)$ is a point of $\mathbb{A}^2_{(X,Y)}(\mathbb{R})$, then the *Hough Transform* of P (with respect to the family $\mathcal{F}$) is the locus of the affine space $\mathbb{A}^t_{(\Lambda_1, \ldots, \Lambda_t)}(\mathbb{R})$ of equation $\Gamma_P(\Lambda) : F(x_P, y_P; \Lambda) = 0$, where

$$F(x_P, y_P; \Lambda) = \sum_{i,j=0}^{d} g_{ij}(\Lambda) x_P^i y_P^j, \quad 0 \le i + j \le d,$$

is a real polynomial in the indeterminates $\Lambda = (\Lambda_1, \ldots, \Lambda_t)$. For a general point P, $\Gamma_P(\Lambda)$ is a hypersurface. Thanks to [4, Lemma 2.3], we can say that the condition

$$\mathcal{C}_\lambda = \mathcal{C}_{\lambda'} \implies \lambda = \lambda' \quad \forall \, \mathcal{C}_\lambda, \mathcal{C}_{\lambda'} \in \mathcal{F} \tag{2}$$

is equivalent to

$$\bigcap_{P \in \mathcal{C}_\lambda} \Gamma_P(\Lambda) = \{\lambda\}. \tag{3}$$

Condition (3) is easy to be translated into a discrete framework for curve recognition in images: provided that an edge detection process selects in the image a set of points of interest potentially lying on the curve to be recognized, the intersection of their HTs leads to the identification of the parameter set characterizing the curve. Thus, we look for families of curves which satisfy the above equivalent conditions. Such families are called *Hough regular*. Condition (2) provides an effective way to check condition (3). In fact, the equality $\mathcal{C}_\lambda = \mathcal{C}_{\lambda'}$ is equivalent to $F(X, Y; \lambda) = kF(X, Y; \lambda')$ for some non-zero constant k. This leads to solve a polynomial system, in the variables $\lambda = (\lambda_1, \ldots, \lambda_t)$, $\lambda' = (\lambda'_1, \ldots, \lambda'_t)$, made up of the equations $g_{ij}(\lambda) = kg_{ij}(\lambda')$ for each pair of indices i, j. Therefore, saying that a family is Hough regular simply means that such a polynomial system implies $\lambda = \lambda'$. The two families of curves we will use in the sequel meet the above Hough regularity condition (see also [5, Section 3]).

Based upon the above theoretical result, then a recognition algorithm can be implemented as described in [5, Section 4], to which we refer for more details. Here, we confine ourselves to highlight the main steps of the process. First of all, we apply to the image an edge detection technique to select $P_1, \ldots, P_\nu$ points of interest. Then, we discretize the parameter space by means of an appropriate number of cells and for each point P_i, $i = 1, \ldots, \nu$, we compute the Hough Transform $\Gamma_{P_i}(\Lambda)$ with respect to a fixed family of curves. Next, we apply an accumulator function to count how many times each cell in the parameter space is crossed (voted) by the computed HTs. Finally, we look for the cell corresponding to the maximum of the accumulator function: the parameter set associated to that cell provides the curve of the family which best approximates the profile of interest in the image.

Remark 1. The application of an edge detection algorithm to select the points that will be processed with the HT technique has two advantages. First, grey levels of the image pixels can be forgotten; second, the number of points to process is dramatically reduced.

Remark 2. The computation of the accumulator function and its maximization is the most time-consuming step of the algorithm. Further, it strongly depends on the number of parameters, since the dimension of the domain of this function exactly corresponds to the number of parameters in the game. Even though the theory, and the algorithmic aspects, presented in this section hold true in the above general framework, in practice, the computational burden associated to the accumulator function computation and optimization leads to the need of restricting to families of curves depending on a small number of parameters. Work to overcome such a restriction is in progress.

2.1   Curve with 3 Convexities

As highlighted by the results of [5] (see in particular subsection 5.1 and Figure 6) the family of curves with 3 convexities, expressed by the equation in form (5) below, looks as a suitable family of curves to optimally detect the spinal canal profile. In addition, to recognize the spinal marrow profile, ellipses in the form presented in Section 3 seem good candidate curves.

Generally speaking, we are well-aware of the fact that our approach strongly depends on the choice of a suitable family $\mathcal{F}$ of curves to optimally recognize a given profile. Work to perform an automated search of an appropriate family $\mathcal{F}$ is strictly related to the question raised in Remark 2 above. Even though in progress, it is not accomplished at the present state-of-the-art. On the other hand, let us stress how a good choice of the family $\mathcal{F}$ makes the HT-based procedure extremely robust even in presence of noise (see also [4, Section 6]).

The *curve with m convexities* is defined by the polar equation

$$\mathcal{C}_{a,b,m} : \rho = \frac{a}{1 + b\cos(m\theta)}, \tag{4}$$

where a, b are real positive numbers such that $b < 1$, and $m \geq 2$ is an integer.

The curve with m convexities is bounded. In fact, computing the derivative with respect to θ in equation (4) we find

$$\rho' = \frac{abm\sin(m\theta)}{(1 + b\cos(m\theta))^2}.$$

Therefore $\rho' = 0$ if and only if $\theta = \frac{k}{m}\pi$ for some integer k. For such values of θ, equation (4) gives

$$\rho_{\min} := \frac{a}{1+b}, \quad \rho_{\max} := \frac{a}{1-b}$$

according to whether k is even or odd, respectively. Thus, the graph of the curve is contained in the circular crown of radii $\frac{a}{1+b}$, $\frac{a}{1-b}$. The special case $m = 3$ looks of interest for us. In this case, the curve has degree 6 and a direct computation yields the cartesian equation

$$\mathcal{C}_{a,b} : (X^2 + Y^2)^3 = \left(a(X^2 + Y^2) - b(X^3 - 3XY^2)\right)^2. \tag{5}$$

The shape of the curve with 3 convexities strongly depends on the values of the parameters. In particular, a is a sort of scale factor, while, as much as the value of b increases as much the convexities of the curve are sharpened. Figure 1 shows the curve for three different values of b with a fixed to 1.

As far as the HT is concerned, fix a point $P = (x_P, y_P)$ in the image space $\mathbb{A}^2_{(X,Y)}(\mathbb{R})$. Then the HT of P with respect to the family $\mathcal{F} = \{\mathcal{C}_{a,b}\}$ is a degenerate conic $\Gamma_P(A, B) : r_- \cup r_+$ in the parameter plane $\mathbb{A}^2_{(A,B)}(\mathbb{R})$, i.e., the union of the parallel lines

$$r_{\mp} : A(x_P^2 + y_P^2) - B(x_P^3 - 3x_P y_P^2) \mp \sqrt{(x_P^2 + y_P^2)^3} = 0.$$

The fact that $\Gamma_P(A, B)$ is a degenerate conic could make the maximization of the accumulator function particularly challenging. It is then worth noting that the line

$$r_+ : A(x_P^2 + y_P^2) - B(x_P^3 - 3x_P y_P^2) + \sqrt{(x_P^2 + y_P^2)^3} = 0$$

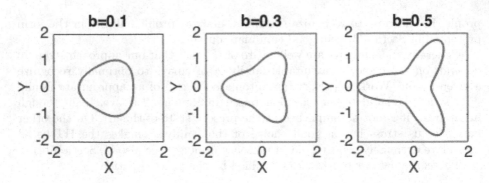

Fig. 1. Three curves with 3 convexities with $a = 1$ and, from left to right, $b = 0.1$, $b = 0.3$, and $b = 0.5$.

results in fact out of the game in our context. That is, in practice, the HT of P can be assumed to be the single line of equation

$$r_- : A(x_P^2 + y_P^2) - B(x_P^3 - 3x_P y_P^2) - \sqrt{(x_P^2 + y_P^2)^3} = 0.$$

First, note that the line r_+ intersects the negative A-axis of the parameter space $\mathbb{A}^2_{(A,B)}(\mathbb{R})$ in the point $\left(-\frac{\sqrt{(x_P^2 + y_P^2)^3}}{x_P^2 + y_P^2}, 0\right)$. Let

$$b_+ := \frac{\sqrt{(x_P^2 + y_P^2)^3}}{x_P^3 - 3x_P y_P^2}$$

be the ordinate of the point where the line r_+ intersects the B-axis. As the region of interest, $\mathcal{T}$, to be discretized is defined by the conditions $a > 0$, $1 > b > 0$, it is then enough to show the inequality

$$b_+ \geq 1, \tag{6}$$

which implies that the line r_+ doesn't cross the region $\mathcal{T}$. This follows as soon as we show that

$$(X^2 + Y^2)^3 - (3XY^2 - X^3)^2 \geq 0, \tag{7}$$

or

$$Y^6 + 9X^4Y^2 - 6X^2Y^4 = Y^2(Y^4 + 9X^4 - 6X^2Y^2) = Y^2(Y^2 - 3X^2)^2 \geq 0,$$

which is, in fact, the case. Let's also point out that all the above agrees with the fact the family $\mathcal{F}$ is Hough regular.

3   Applications

In order to study the metabolic activity of the spinal district in a human being, we have considered a stack of CT images of a control subject corresponding to

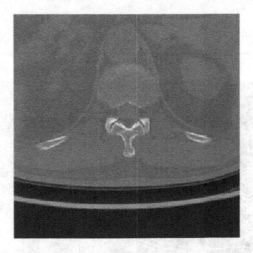

Fig. 2. Zoom of a CT image with focus on the spinal canal. It is possible to see the structure of both the spinal canal and the spinal marrow, the highlighted circular region inside the spinal canal.

a whole body acquisition. Note that the spinal marrow is situated in the upper part of the vertebral column, between the occipital bone and the first and the second lumbar vertebra. For this reason, we have limited our analysis just to the cervical and thoracic segments, for a total of 90 axial slices. In Figure 2 we show a detail of a CT image referring to a vertebra of this region, where it is possible to see the structure of both the spinal canal and the spinal marrow, i.e., the circular region inside the spinal canal, highlighted by the arrow.

For each slice, we first apply an edge detection algorithm [10] to get a set of points of interest (panel (a) in Figure 3). Then we compute the HTs of these points with respect to the family $\mathcal{F} = \{\mathcal{C}_{a,b}\}$ of curves with 3 convexities, and we take the parameters corresponding to the maximum of the accumulator function as those which identify the curve with 3 convexities best approximating the spinal canal profile in the image. The graph of such a curve (panel (b) in Figure 3) is then used to identify the region of the spinal canal. This step allows us to exclude the points outside of the canal. The points inside the graph of the curve (panel (c) in Figure 3) are the candidate points of interest for the recognition of the spinal marrow. We point out that, due to the very low local contrast between the spinal marrow and the surrounding tissue, it is hard for any edge detection algorithm to sample the whole profile of the spinal marrow. On the other hand, the HT procedure is very robust and effective in recognizing an entire profile from a few isolated pieces. Then, we compute the HTs of such points with respect to the family $\mathcal{F} = \{\mathcal{E}_{a,b,c,d}\}$ of ellipses, expressed in the cartesian form with four parameters:

$$\mathcal{E}_{a,b,c,d} : b^2(X - c)^2 + a^2(Y - d)^2 - a^2b^2 = 0,$$

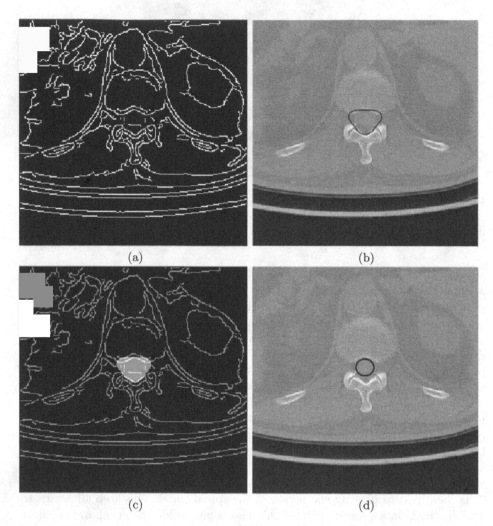

(a)   (b)

(c)   (d)

Fig. 3. First row: edge detection (a) and curve with 3 convexities (b) associated to the parameters ($a = 0.85$, $b = 0.15$) obtained by using the HT-based procedure. Second row: edge points (c) inside the region bounded by the curve with 3 convexities in (b) and the ellipse (d) detected by applying the HT-based procedure to the points highlighted in (c). The ellipse parameters are $a = 0.6$, $b = 0.65$, $c = -0.125$, $d = -0.025$.

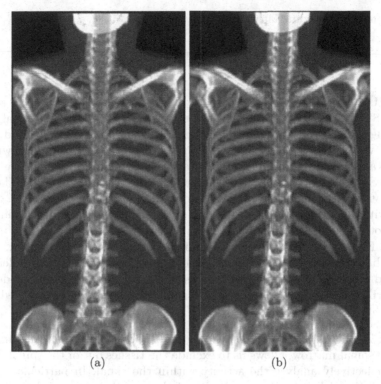

(a)   (b)

Fig. 4. PET activity of the whole spinal canal (a) and PET activity of the spinal marrow (b) for cervical and thoracic segments, superimposed to the original CT images in coronal view (color figure online).

where (c, d) is the center of the ellipse and the positive real numbers a, b play the role of semi-axes. The recognized curves (Figure 3: curve with 3 convexities in panel (b), and ellipse in panel (d)) are then used to create binary masks that can be applied to 180 PET images of the same subject, properly coregistered, each CT image corresponding to two PET images. Once the spinal canal and the spinal marrow are recognized and the corresponding binary masks are applied to the PET images, it is possible to quantitatively study the metabolic activity of the spinal district. In Figure 4 we show the activity of the whole spinal canal (panel (a)) together with the activity given just by the spinal marrow (panel (b)). Starting from the first PET image in the cervical segment and moving down to the last one in the thoracic segment, for each image we can compute the sum of the pixel values (i.e., the Standardized Uptake Value, SUV) in the spinal canal and in the spinal marrow. For the two Regions Of Interest (ROI) separately, we can compute the cumulative activity and the normalized cumulative activity

$$\text{SUV}_c(i) = \sum_{j=1}^{i} \text{SUV}(j), \qquad i = 1, \ldots, 180, \tag{8}$$

and the normalized cumulative activity

$$\mathrm{SUV}_{\mathrm{nc}}(i) = \frac{1}{i}\sum_{j=1}^{i}\mathrm{SUV}(j), \qquad i = 1,\ldots,180, \tag{9}$$

where $\mathrm{SUV}(j)$ is the metabolic activity of the ROI in the j-th slice, and, of course, $\mathrm{SUV}_{\mathrm{c}}(180)$ ($\mathrm{SUV}_{\mathrm{nc}}(180)$) is the total activity (normalized total activity) along the vertebral column. Referring to the computation of (8) and (9), in Figure 5 we compare results obtained by using the HT-based procedure with the ones obtained by using the OsiriX software [11], whereby the ROIs are drown manually by an expert user, slice by slice, and are used as ground truth. The overall behavior of the cumulative functions obtained via HT replicates the ground truth, with a good agreement in the case of the spinal canal activity evaluation. On the other hand, we can notice a slight underestimation of the spinal marrow activity. Finally, we point out that a comprehensive comparative analysis among the HT-based technique, when applied to the bone profile detection problem, and standard recognition/fitting techniques, such as the active contour model [12], the OsiriX package [11] and smoothing spline toolbox [13], is provided in [5, Section 5].

Remark 3. The use of two different recognition steps, the spinal canal first and then the spinal marrow, allows us to exclude the tissues out of the spinal district and to effectively analyze the activity within the canal. In particular, we are able to distinguish between the activity of the spinal marrow and the activity given by other tissues belonging to the spinal canal and surrounding the spinal marrow.

Remark 4. The benefit of using the curve with 3 convexities for recognizing the spinal canal is twofold. First, in [5, Section 5] it has been proved that curves from this family are able to adapt themselves to best approximate three different profiles of the spinal canal at different levels of the same vertebral column. This peculiar behavior makes the curve with 3 convexities a good candidate for the recognition of the spinal canal profiles across a whole stack of CT images. Second, the use of the curve with 3 convexities to limit the region where to search for the spinal marrow, gives us for free an upper bound for the semi-axes of the ellipse we use for the spinal marrow recognition. Accordingly, this allows us to optimize the parameter space discretization.

Remark 5. In medical imaging applications, the use of the HT-based technique leads to associate an equation to a specific bone or human tissue profile. However, the families of curves used in this paper display symmetries that are not perfectly preserved in humans. As a consequence, a more precise identification of tissue profiles would require a method to assign an appropriate piece of curve to a specific portion of the human district under investigation. To address this issue, a piecewise formulation of the HT technique is in progress (see [14]).

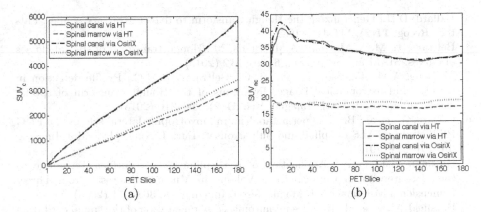

Fig. 5. The cumulative values of the SUV activity (a) and normalized SUV activity (b) across the PET slices for the spinal canal computed via HT (solid line) and via OsiriX (dash-dot line). The same quantities (again in panel (a) and (b), respectively) for the spinal marrow computed via HT (dashed line) and via OsiriX (dotted line).

4 Conclusions

In this paper we have presented a HT-based method for the segmentation of the spinal canal and spinal marrow in X-ray CT images. We have used different families of curves for the recognition of both the spinal canal and of the spinal marrow profiles, in order to separate the marrow from the surrounding tissue. Information inferred from the anatomical images has been integrated with functional information from PET images in order to quantitatively evaluate the metabolic activity of the spinal marrow with respect to the one of the whole canal. We have tested our method on a control subject, who does not present any neurological disease, before utilizing it in those cases where the knowledge of the activity of the spinal marrow is essential. In fact, its application to large datasets of neurological patients and control subjects could assess the presence of different levels of metabolic activity in the spinal canal and/or marrow and, thus, information on the nature of this kind of disease can be derived.

Acknowledgments. We wish to thank our colleague Michele Piana for many helpful discussions. We also thank Gianmario Sambuceti, Head of the Nuclear Medicine Unit of the IRCCS San Martino - IST, Genova, for providing us with the CT and PET images processed in this paper.

References

1. Hough, P.V.C.: Method and Means for Recognizing Complex Patterns. U.S. Patent 3069654 (1962)
2. Duda, R.O., Hart, P.E.: Use of the Hough transformation to detect lines and curves in pictures. Commun. ACM **15**(1), 11–15 (1972)

3. Ballard, D.H.: Generalizing the Hough transform to detect arbitrary shapes. Pattern Recog. 11(2), 111–122 (1981)
4. Beltrametti, M.C., Massone, A.M., Piana, M.: Hough transform of special classes of curves. SIAM J. Imaging Sci. 6, 391–312 (2013)
5. Massone, A.M., Perasso, A., Campi, C., Beltrametti, M.C.: Profile detection in medical and astronomical images by means of the Hough transform of special classes of curves. J. Math. Imaging Vis. 51(2), 296–310 (2015)
6. Cistaro, A., et al.: Brain hypermetabolism in amyotrophic lateral sclerosis: a FDG PET study in ALS of spinal and bulbar onset. Eur. J. Nucl. Med. Mol. Imaging 39, 251–259 (2012)
7. Hickman, S.J., et al.: Application of a B-spline Active Surface Technique to the Measurement of Cervical Cord Volume in Multiple Sclerosis From Three-Dimensional MR Images. J. Magn. Reson. Imaging 18, 368–371 (2003)
8. Horsfield, M.A., et al.: Rapid semi-automated segmentation of the spinal cord from magnetic resonance images: Application in multiple sclerosis. NeuroImage 50, 446–455 (2010)
9. Archip, N., et al.: A Knowledge-Based Approach to Automatic Detection of the Spinal Cord in CT Images. IEEE Trans. Med. Imag. 21(12), 1504–1516 (2002)
10. Canny, J.F.: A computational approach to edge detection. IEEE Trans. Pattern Anal. Mach. Intell. PAMI 8(6) 679–698 (1986)
11. Rosset, A., Spadola, L., Ratib, O.: OsiriX: an open-source software for navigating in multidimensional DICOM images. J. Dig. Imag. 17(3), 205–216 (2004)
12. Aramini, R., Brignone, M., Coyle, J., Piana, M.: Postprocessing of the linear sampling method by means of deformable models. SIAM J. Sci. Comput. 30(5), 2613–2634 (2008)
13. The MathWorks, Inc. http://www.mathworks.com/help/curvefit/cftool.html (accessed May 31, 2015)
14. Ricca, G., Beltrametti, M.C., Massone, A.M.: Piecewise recognition of bone skeleton profiles via an iterative Hough transform approach without re-voting. In: Ourselin, S., Styner, M.A. (eds.) Proc. of SPIE Medical Imaging 2015: Image Processing, vol. 9413, p. 94132M

A New Graph-Based Method
for Automatic Segmentation

Laura Gemme[✉] and Silvana Dellepiane

Università degli Studi di Genova, DITEN, via Opera Pia 11a 16145, Genova, Italy
laura.gemme@edu.unige.it, silvana.dellepiane@unige.it

Abstract. In this paper, a new graph-based segmentation method is proposed. Various Regions of Interest (ROIs) can be extracted from digital images/volumes without requiring any processing parameters. Only one point belonging to the region of interest must be given.

The method, starting from a single source element, proceeds with a specific propagation mechanism based on the graph theory, to find a Minimum Path Spanning Tree (MPST).

As compared with other existing segmentation methods, a new cost function is here proposed. It allows the process to be adaptive to both a local and global context, to be optimal and independent from the order of analysis, requiring a single iteration step. The final decision step is based on a threshold value that is automatically selected. Performance evaluation is presented by applying the method in the biomedical field, considering the extraction of wrist bones from real Magnetic Resonance Imaging (MRI) volumes.

Keywords: Unsupervised segmentation · Minimum Path Spanning Tree · Graph theory · MRI volumes

1 Introduction

Image segmentation, or rather the process of identifying regions of interest starting from a digital image or volume, has been a major problem in image processing.

According to the classical definition, the aim of segmentation is to partition an image into a set of non-overlapping regions whose union is the entire image. In the particular case of ROI segmentation, like in this work, the result is a bi-partition of the image into the so-called foreground and background. In a second time, all the single extracted ROIs could be collected together forming a partition.

More recently, the purpose of segmentation has become more oriented to the detection of image parts that are meaningful within a particular application domain.

One of the most promising segmentation approach refers to the graph-based methods. The graph cuts with respect to regional constraints is a well-studied problem, and many methods have been proposed as a solution. The minimal graph cuts [1] approach calculates how to define an appropriate cut of the graph where objects related to seed-points are separated. Usually the criterion is such that the sum of the edge weights along the cut is minimal. Another family of methods is based on the calculation of a minimum

© Springer International Publishing Switzerland 2015
V. Murino and E. Puppo (Eds.): ICIAP 2015, Part I, LNCS 9279, pp. 601–611, 2015.
DOI: 10.1007/978-3-319-23231-7_54

cost path forest. Examples of this approach include the Image Foresting Transform (IFT) [2], and the Relative Fuzzy Connectedness method [3]. The Random Walker [4] method computes cuts such that each vertex is connected to the seed-point that a "random walker", starting at the vertex, is expected to reach first. The classical watershed approach has recently been reformulated on edge-weighted graphs [5].

One of the major drawbacks in graph-based methods consists in properly taking into account spatial correlation and contextual information during the graph visit. In addition, these approaches aims to find the Minimum Spanning Tree (MST) [8]; here, a new aggregation criterion is defined: the Minimum Path Spanning Tree (MPST). More details will be explained in Section 2.2.

In the present work, a seed-based algorithm which applies a graph-based segmentation driven by the research of minimum cost paths for the analysis of digital images/volumes is described. An optimal grouping algorithm is proposed; it proves to be independent of any model, parameter, threshold, or order of analysis.

The specific tree traversal propagation mechanism, starting from a user-defined seed, adapts to the actual data content and correctly accounts for local and global connectedness relationships in terms both of spatial relation among vertices and feature information. The obtained result is a graph-based segmentation, where a cost value is associated to each analyzed pixel/voxel and represents how it relates to the starting seed-class. During the graph visit, the assignment of the cost function is computed only one time and not reconsidered at each step of the propagation process.

The cost function here proposed is known in the framework of network optimization as the Bottleneck Shortest Path Problem (BSP); its goal is to determine the limiting capacity of any path between two specified vertices of the network [10]. In the context of segmentation, this formula has not explicitly been employed before. In fact, most of the graph-based methods consider as cost function the summation of the edge weights.

The innovative aspect of this work actually regards the MPTS and the cost function previously introduced.

This paper is structured in the following way. In Section 2, the graph-based method is described: initially, some graph notations are recalled, and then the algorithm with a detailed explanation of the different steps is presented. Application cases related to the biomedical domain are shown in Section 3, dealing with MRI volumes of the hand district.[1] In Section 4, the performance of the method is quantitatively evaluated by computing some classical parameters from the confusion matrix and a similarity measure. In addition, a discussion about the choice of the value where computing the graph cut is carried out.

2   The Proposed Method

The image is mapped into a graph, where each voxel corresponds to a vertex and pairs of neighboring vertices represent the edges. The objective is to locate and segment different regions of interest from the original volume, i.e., to extract a number of

---

[1]   The MRI volumes are available thanks to the Project MEDIARE: "New methodologies of Diagnostic Imaging for rheumatic diseases". PAR FAS 2007-2013 Program 4 – Pos. N. 14.

separated connected components from the graph. In this work, the ROIs are extracted one at a time. The proposed method is an unsupervised and automatic approach, which can be applied to both 2D and 3D digital images. Let us first consider some classical graph notations [9] that will be useful in Section 2.2, followed by a detailed description of the algorithm.

2.1   Graph Notations

Starting from [6], we define a graph as a pair $G(V, E)$, where $V = \{v_1, .., v_n\}$ is the vertex set and $E \subset \{(v_i, v_j) \subseteq V \mid v_i \neq v_j\}$ is the edge set, the set of the pairs of neighboring vertices. The order of G is the number of the vertices and it is denoted by $|V|$ or $|G|$ or sometimes $n(G)$.

We define a weighted graph when the vertices and/or the edges are labelled with weights. In the former case, we call the graph a vertex-weighted graph; in the latter case, we call the graph an edge-weighted graph. The weights can be positive or negative and can be assigned by different functions and with different criteria.

We say that two vertices v_i and v_j are adjacent if an edge $e_{ij} = (v_i, v_j)$ connecting v_i with v_j exists. A graph G is undirected (or not oriented) if the pairs of the edges are not ordered, i.e., $e_{ij} = e_{ji}$.

Let $\pi(v_1, v_k) = \langle v_1, .., v_k \rangle$ be an ordered sequence of vertices. π is a path from v_1 to v_k if for any $i \in [2, k]$, v_i is adjacent to v_{i-1}. If the extremities of the path coincide, we say that π is a cycle. We define G a connected graph if any two vertices of G are linked for G.

Let $G(V, E)$ and $G'(V', E')$ be two graphs; if $V' \subset V$ and $E' \subset E$, we say that G' is a subgraph of G, i.e., $G' \subset G$. If G' is a connected graph without cycle, then G' is a tree.

A spanning tree is a tree containing all vertices of the graph. A Minimum Spanning Tree (MST) is a spanning tree for which the sum of the edges is minimal [8]:

$$c(T) = \min \left(\sum_{e=1}^{n-1} w_T(e) \right) \tag{1}$$

where T is the tree and $w_T(e)$ represents the weight assigned to edge $e \in E_T$ and E_T defines the set of edges of T.

A Shortest Path Tree (SPT) rooted at a vertex s defines a tree composed by the union of the paths between s and each of the other vertices in G such that [8]:

$$c(s, v) = \min \left(c_G(s, v) \right) \tag{2}$$

where $c_G(s, v)$ is the cost of the path, i.e., the sum of the weights of the edges belonging to the path.

2.2   Proposed Cost Function and Algorithm

In this work, the authors propose a graph-based segmentation method by defining a new cost function. This function is the formulation of bottleneck single source shortest path, which although commonly known, is not usually considered and employed in the context of graph-based segmentation methods. Unlike the classical graph notations, where the sum of the edge weights is used, the aim of the algorithm is to find the Minimum Path Spanning Tree, that is a spanning tree considering a cost function as this:

$$f_{w_s}(v_i) = \min_{\pi(s,v_i)}[\max_{x \in \pi(s,v_i)} w_s(x)] \tag{3}$$

where w is the weight associated to the vertices, $\pi(s, v_i)$ is the path from the seed s to a vertex v_i. This function minimizes the largest of the vertex weight in the path π and is equivalent to the maximum capacity path problem [11]. By this definition, the algorithm does not consider the length of the path, and consequently the dimension of the object to segment.

A digital image $I = (D, \vec{I})$ is a pair, where $D \subset \mathbb{Z}^n$ is the image domain and $\vec{I}(x) \in \mathbb{Z}^m$ is a vectorial mapping, which assigns a set of values to each $x \in D$.

The image (or volume) to be segmented can be interpreted as a graph $G(V, E)$, where $V \subseteq D$ is the vertex (or node) set, represented by the pixels (or voxels) and $E \subset D \times D$ is the set of arcs, defined by an adjacent relation, i.e., 4-connected in 2D or 6-connected in 3D space.

The graph is an undirected, vertex weighted, grid graph. In the graph-based approach, a seed-based segmentation, given a seed point s belonging to a ROI, is a partition of V into components. Here, the extracted region corresponds to a connected component in a subgraph $G'(V, E')$, containing the vertex s. This vertex encloses all connected nodes that are homogeneous with respect to some properties of the seed point. In other words, the segmentation result is induced by a subset E' of the edges in E.

Let $I: V \longrightarrow \mathbb{R}$ be the intensity map with $I(v_i)$ the intensity of the vertex v_i and L be the maximum grey level value that can be represented in the digital image/volume.

Let $w: V \longrightarrow \mathbb{R}^+$ be the weight function with $v_i \longmapsto w(v_i)$, where $w(v_i)$ is the weight of the vertex v_i with $i = 1, .., |V|$.

Chosen a seed point (source) s belonging to a ROI, the weights are assigned to the vertices following this criterion:

$$\forall v_i \in V, \qquad w_s(v_i) = |I(v_i) - I(s)| \tag{4}$$

From the previous formula, it follows that the weight function w is a function from V to the scalar domain $[0, L]$.

This vertex weight assignment takes into account the dissimilarity of the pixel as compared to the seed point, like a sort of distance. From the formula, it is possible to observe that vertices with values very close to the seed value have a weight close to zero, while vertices with values different from the seed value have a weight close to L.

To avoid a too strong influence of local noise, the value $I(s)$ has been replaced by the local average value of the 4-connected neighborhood N_4, instead of the seed intensity value itself:

$$I(s) = \frac{1}{|N_4|} \sum_{v_i \in N_4} I(v_i) \tag{5}$$

Let define the cost function f_{w_s} from V to the scalar domain $[0,L]$ as

$$f_{w_s}(v_i) = \min_{\pi(s,v_i)}[\max_{x \in \pi(s,v_i)} w_s(x)] \tag{6}$$

where $\pi(s, v_i)$ is the path from s to v_i.

The contextual segmentation problem is comparable to the single-source shortest path problem for a graph with non-negative vertex weights, producing a Minimum Path Spanning Tree. It follows that, starting from the first node, the process oriented to the correct solution moves to each neighbor by computing the cost of the new path from the starting point, taking into account all previous computations.

The purpose of the algorithm is to assign the cost function f_{w_s} to each vertex, v_i, according to the best path from the seed s. As a preliminary step, with respect to the seed point, the algorithm computes the $w_s(v_i)$ value for each seed v_i representing the dissimilarity with the seed.

The image segmentation method is implemented by performing a particular propagation process, that decides which nodes are the candidate ones to be analyzed (based on the already analyzed nodes) and selects the best paths starting from a fixed seed point. Such a mechanism, being adaptive to the image content, allows a non-iterative approach to account for contextual information.

The seed point represents the generator and the other pixels are initially considered "unvisited". We create two lists of vertices: S is the list of generators with their connected neighbors; T is the complementary set of S. During this process, S is updated with new nodes until T becomes an empty list.

In the following, the main steps of the algorithm are described:

- *Input*: a non-empty connected, undirected, vertex weighted graph $G(V, E)$.
- *Initialization*: setting the value zero for the seed ("generator") point and its direct neighbors and the value one for the others vertices. This choice is important in case the seed point is a noise pixel.

$$w_s(v_i) = \begin{cases} 0 & if\ v_i = \{s, N_4\} \\ 1 & otherwise \end{cases} \tag{7}$$

At the beginning, all the nodes are marked as "unvisited" and the generators are the seed point closed neighbourhood: $S = \{s, N_4\}, T = V \setminus S$.

- *Steps to repeat:*
  1. For each "generator" or "father", we consider its unvisited 4-connected neighbour pixels (or 6-connected neighbour voxels) and we change their status in "candidates". We choose the minimum weighted vertex considering the weighted function w.

     The new vertex, "son", is added to the generator, updating the set S, i.e. $S = S \cup \{v_{new}\}$.
  2. We consider the neighbour of this new vertex together with the previous and we choose the minimum. If the minimum weight is greater than its "father" then it maintains its weight; if the minimum weight is lower than its "father" then we assign the father value. For two contiguous nodes, v_{i-1} and the fol-

lowing v_i belonging to the best path from the seed, the cost function is given by:

$$f_{w_s}(v_i) = \begin{cases} w_s(v_i) & \text{if } w_s(v_i) > f_{w_s}(v_{i-1}) = w_s(f) \\ f_{w_s}(v_{i-1}) & \text{if } w_s(v_i) \leq f_{w_s}(v_{i-1}) = w_s(f) \end{cases} \tag{8}$$

Such a value will not be checked again; its cost as recorded is now final and will never be changed.

In the case that the minimum weight corresponds to two vertices, we choose arbitrarily one of the two nodes. All the new vertices considered are chosen so that no cycles in the path are created.

3. We continue to apply this criterion of growing and labelling until all the nodes are considered (all nodes are marked as visited), i.e., $S = V, T = \{\emptyset\}$.

• *Output*: the obtained paths are a Minimum Path Spanning Tree.

The described algorithm starts from a seed point and successively analyzes all image sites at recursion steps. The steps are organized into a sequential order dependent on the image content. This adaptive procedure performs selective propagation steps based on the computed intermediate cost vertex. The order of visited sites leads to the generation of a tree, whose root is the seed point and where a node is instantiated for each analyzed image site.

The approach proceeds selecting the best path and producing a Minimum Path Spanning Tree. In the literature, different algorithms exist for obtaining the Minimum Spanning Tree (such as Kruskal's Algorithm, Prim's Algorithm), the shortest path (such as Dijkstra's Algorithm), the shortest path tree [8]. All these methods consider the cost of the path as the sum of the edges.

The proposed method utilizes the same criterion of propagation of Prim's Algorithm, but with some differences in the intermediate steps.

The Prim's Algorithm finds a Minimum Spanning Tree from a connected weighted undirected graph, minimizing the cost of the sum of the edges.

Through the proposed approach a spanning tree is found, that is minimum with respect to the cost function defined in Equation (3). This gives to the algorithm an innovation aspect. The main advantages are that the segmentation can be obtained in one-shot and without considering the spatial information. In addition, the Equation (8) ensures that the paths from the seed to each vertex are optimal and that the method is good from a computational point of view, because after the cost value is assigned, it will never be changed during the graph visit.

2.3   Graph Cut

The algorithm generates a spanning tree, whose root is the seed point. In order to obtain the region of interest, a graph cut is applied: the image can be represented by two disjoint sets, A, B where $A \cup B = V$, $A \cap B = \emptyset$.

The figure below describes the criterion followed to identify the ROI. We start from a single source (red point) and its 4-connected neighbors. Each level corresponds to a value of the cost function f_{w_s}. For each level, the graph order (i.e., a summation of the vertices) is computed and updated according to the previous level value.

Let $n(v_{l_i})$ be the number of vertices at level i. We compute

$$\sum_{i=1}^{l_i} n(v_{l_i}) \tag{9}$$

The meaning of such a sum relates to the size of the region that can be obtained with a cut at this level.

We propose to cut the tree at a certain level, in order to cut the edges connecting these levels; thus, one connected component including the source point is obtained. The rest of the graph can consist of one or more connected components, depending on the shape of the ROI.

In particular, we define a "gap" when there is a large difference between the orders of two consecutive levels. This happens in presence of contrast or edges. When a graph cut is performed, corresponding to a gap it means that a region made of very similar voxels is extracted. On the contrary, if homogeneity property is relaxed a graph cut can be chosen after a gap. This means that the ROI expands out of a significant border if the gap is larger than the gradient value.

Such a result can be interpreted as a multi-level segmentation: with a cut just before the gap, we obtain the region of interest. After the gap there can be an enlargement of the region until the entire image is covered.

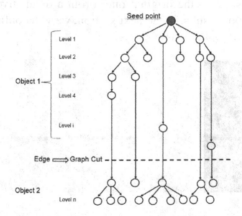

Fig. 1. Scheme of the criterion used to make the graph cut.

3   The Application Case

For the experiments five volumes of T1-weighted magnetic resonance of the hand district, affected by Rheumatoid Arthritis (RA) are considered. Rheumatic disease involves in particular the joints, the bones and the muscles. RA is one of the most common autoimmune rheumatic disease; it is a chronic and progressive inflammatory polyarthritis. According to current recommendations, MRI is used to asses three main signs of RA based on manual evaluation of MR images: synovitis, bone edema, and bone erosions [7].

The graph-based approach is applied to these volumes in order to segment the main wrist bones: capitate, trapezium, trapezoid, pisiform, scaphoid, lunate, triquetrum, hamate.

The results are compared with ground references delivered by Softeco Sismat Srl [9]. For the latter, a quantitative evaluation through statistical values of sensitivity, precision and Dice coefficient is performed.

For each volume (of size 256×256×102), starting from a seed point decided by the user, the wrist bones are extracted separately. To prove the independence of the method from the seed choice, the fuzzy graph-based approach is applied several times to the various volumes of interest.

Figure 2 shows the different phases from the original image to the final result: (a) the original image; (b) the map of the final cost function (inverted grey levels); (c) the image after the graph cut, with the identification of the region of interest in red color; (d) the binary map of the capitate bone; (e) the boundary of the bone overlapped to the original image; (f) the 3D visualization of the segmented bone.

After detecting all the bones individually, we perform a composition of the segmented images by overlapping to the original image.

Figure 3 shows the original image (on the left) and the segmented bones overlapped to the original image. It is possible to observe how the edges are very precise and accurate with respect to the original one. From a qualitative point of view, the segmentation gives good results; in the next section, we will confirm this statement by means of a quantitative evaluation.

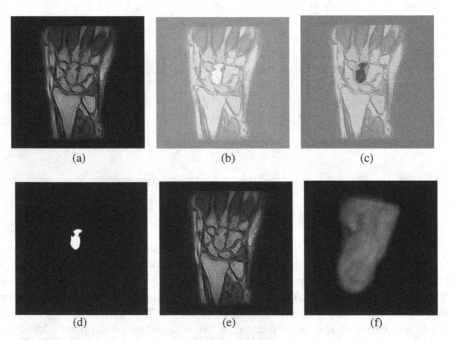

(a)   (b)   (c)

(d)   (e)   (f)

Fig. 2. Phases of graph-based method, from the original image to the bone extraction.

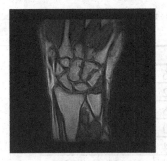 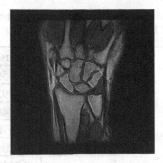

Fig. 3. The original image (on the left); the segmented bones overlapped to the image with colored boundaries.

4   Quantitative Evaluation

To establish the performance quality of the proposed segmentation, different evaluation measurements are computed, referring to the ground truth. In particular, the following parameters have been extracted for each region of interest: Sensitivity, Precision and the similarity measure, Dice Coefficient.

The indices are given by these formulae [12]:

$$Sensitivity = \frac{TP}{TP+FN}, \; Precision = \frac{TP}{TP+FP} \tag{10}$$

$$DICE = \frac{2\,TP}{(TP+FP)+(TP+FN)} \tag{11}$$

where TP are the True Positives, TN are the True Negatives, FP are the False Positives, FN are the False Negatives, P are the Positives and N are the Negatives.

Sensitivity informs about how many data are correctly evaluated as positive on the total positive observations, while precision is the proportion of the predicted positive cases that are correct. Dice coefficient is a similarity index, which measures the overlap of two sets. A value of 0 indicates no overlap; a value of 1 indicates perfect agreement. Higher numbers point out better agreement in the sets, so when we apply this index to evaluate the agreement of segmentation results, the goal is to get as close to 1 as possible.

The parameters presented in table 1 are the mean values of three patients. The evaluation shows promising results, since the method does not use a-priori knowledge or models. In particular, precision shows high values, close to 1. Sensitivity values are lower, a sign of an under segmentation. Possible post-processing steps can be applied in order to improve the results. In addition, Dice coefficient provides values ranging from 0.69 to 0.83.

As regards the graph cut phase, analyzing these five patients it is possible to note that usually the value of the cut is around 200.

The figure below represents the values of the cut for the different wrist bones, for the five patients. For each bone, there are 5 values corresponding to the patients: it is possible to observe that the values range from 180 to 250. The value of the cut has been chosen by an adaptive method, since a fixed value should have led to bad results.

Table 1. The quantitative evaluation of the method: a comparison between sensitivity, precision, and Dice Coefficient.

	Sens	Prec	DICE
Capitate	0,7056	0,9986	0,8258
Triquetrum	0,5392	0,9978	0,6952
Pisiform	0,5746	0,9962	0,7217
Scaphoid	0,6570	0,9997	0,7886
Lunate	0,6204	0,9978	0,7647
Trapezium	0,7147	0,9983	0,8320
Trapezoid	0,6905	0,9979	0,8130
Hamate	0,6605	0,9966	0,7852

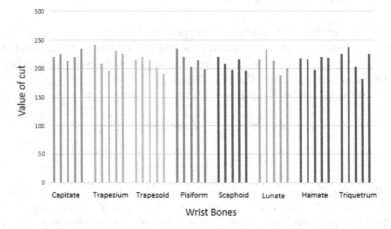

Fig. 4. Histogram of the values of the cut for the different wrist bones, for each patient.

5   Conclusions

In this work a new graph-based method has been proposed for analyzing digital volumes. An unsupervised approach that, starting from a single source, extracts the regions of interest one by one. Unlike other methods, it considers only one seed in the foreground and not in the background, with no further user interaction or a-priori model.

The aim of the algorithm is to find a Minimum Path Spanning Tree, whose root is the seed point, through the definition of a cost function. This function maximizes the minimum of the weight vertex over the path, without considering the sum of the edges like many algorithms present in literature. The innovative aspects of this work are exactly the aggregation criterion of MPST and the cost function.

The main advantage of the presented method is the independence on the image content and resolution, so it works well for any kind of image. Furthermore, this approach is simple to use and very fast. It is a robust method, since it does not depend on the choice of the seed point and it is also adaptive; in fact, the value of the graph cut is not fixed at first, but it is chosen considering the content of the image.

This approach has been applied to real RMI volumes in order to extract the wrist bones and to identify the presence of pathology in the hand, more precisely the manifestation of the rheumatoid arthritis.

The robustness of this method is investigated through the analysis of statistical parameters, and the first results are very good. The evaluation of the approach, in terms of Sensitivity, Precision and Dice coefficient produced very promising results.

At the same time, good qualitative results are obtained in the segmentation of the total volume of the hand. Other cases will be analyzed in order to make more robust the method and increase the significance of the quantitative evaluations.

References

1. Boykov, Y., Funka-Lea, G.: Graph cuts and efficient ND image segmentation. International journal of computer vision **70**(2), 109–131 (2006)
2. Falcão, A.X., Stolfi, J., de Alencar Lotufo, R.: The image foresting transform: Theory, algorithms, and applications. IEEE Transactions on Pattern Analysis and Machine Intelligence **26**(1), 19–29 (2004)
3. Udupa, J.K., Saha, P.K., Lotufo, R.D.A.: Disclaimer: "Relative fuzzy connectedness and object definition: theory, algorithms, and applications in image segmentation". IEEE Transactions on Pattern Analysis and Machine Intelligence **24**(11), I-1500 (2002)
4. Grady, L.: Random walks for image segmentation. IEEE Transactions on Pattern Analysis and Machine Intelligence **28**(11), 1768–1783 (2006)
5. Cousty, J., Bertrand, G., Najman, L., Couprie, M.: Watershed cuts: Thinnings, shortest path forests, and topological watersheds. IEEE Transactions on Pattern Analysis and Machine Intelligence **32**(5), 925–939 (2010)
6. Cousty, J., Bertrand, G., Najman, L., Couprie, M.: Watershed cuts: Minimum spanning forests and the drop of water principle. IEEE Transactions on Pattern Analysis and Machine Intelligence **31**(8), 1362–1374 (2009)
7. Włodarczyk, J., Czaplicka, K., Tabor, Z., Wojciechowski, W., Urbanik, A.: Segmentation of bones in magnetic resonance images of the wrist. International Journal of Computer Assisted Radiology and Surgery, 1–13 (2014)
8. Campos, R., Ricardo, M.: A fast algorithm for computing minimum routing cost spanning trees. Computer Networks **52**(17), 3229–3247 (2008)
9. Barbieri, F., Parascandolo, P., Vosilla, L., Cesario, L., Viano, G., Cimmino, M. A.: Assessing MRI erosions in the rheumatoid wrist: a comparison between RAMRIS and a semiautomated segmentation software. In: Ann. Rheum. Dis, **71** (2012)
10. Peinhardt, M., Kaibel, V.: On the bottleneck shortest path problem. In: Technical Report ZIB-Report 06–22, Konrad-Zuse-Zentrum für Informationstechnik Berlin (2006)
11. Turner, L.: Variants of shortest path problems. Algorithmic Operations Research **6**(2), 91–104 (2012)
12. Chang, H.H., Zhuang, A.H., Valentino, D.J., Chu, W.C.: Performance measure characterization for evaluating neuroimage segmentation algorithms. Neuroimage **47**(1), 122–135 (2009)

Color Spaces in Data Fusion of Multi-temporal Images

Roberta Ferretti$^{(\boxtimes)}$ and Silvana Dellepiane

Università degli Studi di Genova, DITEN, via Opera Pia 11a 16145, Genova, Italy
roberta.ferretti@edu.unige.it, silvana.dellepiane@unige.it

Abstract. The data fusion process is strongly recommended in biomedical applications. It allows a better detection and localization of the pathology, as well as the diagnosis and follow-up of many diseases [1], especially with multi-parametric or multi-temporal data.

The independent visualization of multiple images from large volumes is a main cause of errors and inaccuracy within the interpretation process. In this respect, the use of color fusion methods allows to highlight small details from multi-temporal and multi-parametric images.

In the present work, a color data fusion approach is proposed for multi-temporal images, in particular for images of the liver acquired through triphasic CT.

The best color association has been studied considering various data sources. Different metrics for quality assessment have been selected from the color space theory, making an interesting comparison with the human visual perception.

Keywords: Data fusion · Color · Triphasic

1 Introduction

The Data fusion technique combines data from two or more sources within a single piece of information having a high informative content. The aim of image fusion is to integrate individual two-dimensional images, three-dimensional images (volumes or video sequences), or images with larger dimensions, in order to improve visual perception, reduce uncertainty and redundancy of information and maximize the probability of localizing relevant information [2]. In this way, a broader spatial and temporal coverage, a greater reliability and a considerable reduction in the amount of data to be displayed are obtained, without significantly affecting the amount of relevant information [2].

In the medical field, image fusion simplifies the assessment of spatial relationships between images displayed side by side [3]. In this respect, it is important to consider that identical shapes and lines may appear in different sizes, depending on background shades and colors [2]. The data fusion technique is not widely used, but it can make a quantitative assessment of the images easier and help physicians to deliver an impartial and objective diagnosis in a short amount of time. Furthermore, being able to realize multi-sensor, multi-parametric and multi-temporal fusions, allows the physician to analyze different types of images with a different information content.

© Springer International Publishing Switzerland 2015
V. Murino and E. Puppo (Eds.): ICIAP 2015, Part I, LNCS 9279, pp. 612–622, 2015.
DOI: 10.1007/978-3-319-23231-7_55

In image fusion, the information content is displayed in a single image, often revealing particulars that are otherwise invisible to the human eye [4].

In the medical field, the employment of image fusion during the last twenty years has promoted the research and study of new techniques or the adoption of existing techniques in new application fields [4]. A key feature in data fusion process is the analysis and the possibility of correlating the content of the original images. The relevant information content of each source can be stored and then combined to form a new image.

By analyzing a specific case study of liver tumor, this work aims to:

- find a rule capable of associating RGB channels to the images, in order to highlight the image content at the best;
- show how human visual perception is often misleading and can cause interpretation errors;
- improve the localization and identification of the pathology, characterizing significantly the nature of a lesion.

Starting from a data fusion based on RGB color representation we have tried to demonstrate how results can be enhanced as regards information.

The aim of the proposed work is not to obtain a classification, but to improve image display and show how image details can be immediately highlighted using colors.

In the following paragraph, we analyze different color spaces and metrics necessary to evaluate the results of the color data fusion.

2   Color Space and Metrics

In literature several color spaces and metrics have been proposed, all aimed at representing color in different contexts, and evaluating the similarity between two colors in the view of the human visual perception [5].

2.1   Color Space

Digital color images are usually represented in the RGB space. However, RGB does not represent a perceptually uniform color space; this means that the color difference calculated in this space (for example, using the Euclidean distance) does not correspond to that perceived by the human eye [6]. To overcome this problem the International Committee on Colorimetry, CIE (Commission Internationale de l'Eclairage), has defined the two color spaces L*a*b* and L*u*v*[6], where color components are separated from the Luminance information. However, even though performing better than RGB space, these color spaces are not so perceptually homogeneous, as they are claimed to be. These two representations are determined through an intermediate reference space, referred to as CIE XYZ, which is derived from RGB space using the following linear transformation [7, 8].

$$\begin{bmatrix} X \\ Y \\ Z \end{bmatrix} = \begin{bmatrix} 0.4887180 & 0.3106803 & 0.2006017 \\ 0.1762044 & 0.8129847 & 0.0108109 \\ 0.0000000 & 0.0102048 & 0.9897952 \end{bmatrix} \cdot \begin{bmatrix} R \\ G \\ B \end{bmatrix} \quad (1)$$

L*a*b* and L*u*v* [7, 8] are defined by the following non-linear transformations. The L*a*b* formulae are:

$$L = 116f\left(\frac{Y}{Y_n}\right) - 16$$

$$a^* = 500\left[f\left(\frac{X}{X_n}\right) - f\left(\frac{Y}{Y_n}\right)\right]$$

$$b^* = 200\left[f\left(\frac{Y}{Y_n}\right) - f\left(\frac{Z}{Z_n}\right)\right] \quad (2)$$

where:

$$f(q) = \begin{cases} q^{1/3}, & \text{if } q > 0.008856 \\ 0.787q + 16.116, & \text{otherwise} \end{cases}$$

The L*u*v* formulae are:

$$L^* = \begin{cases} 116\sqrt[3]{y_n} - 16 & y_n > \varepsilon \\ k y_n & y_n \le \varepsilon \end{cases}$$

$$u^* = 13L^*(u' - u'_n)$$

$$v^* = 13L^*(v' - v'_n) \quad (3)$$

where:

$$y_n = {}^Y\!/_{Y_n}, \quad \varepsilon = 0.008856, \quad k = 903.3$$

$$u' = \frac{4X}{X+15Y+3Z}, \quad v' = \frac{9Y}{X+15Y+3Z}$$

$$u'_n = \frac{4X_n}{X_n+15Y_n+3Z_n}, \quad v'_n = \frac{9Y_n}{X_n+15Y_n+3Z_n}$$

For both formulae X_n, Y_n and Z_n are the reference white defined by a CIE standard illuminant, E [6], in this case.

2.2   Color Metrics

Various measures are used to calculate the difference between two colors, all developed to better reflect human perception without confusing different colors and without separating similar colors [5]. Several metrics have been created over time, because none of them seems to fully satisfy this goal.

The most relevant are briefly described as follows. They have also been used in the proposed approach.

Euclidean Distance. The Euclidean distance is frequently employed in RGB and L*a*b* spaces, see the equation (4) and (5) [9]:

$$\Delta E_{RGB} = \sqrt{(R_1 - R_2)^2 + (G_1 - G_2)^2 + (B_1 - B_2)^2} \qquad (4)$$

$$\Delta E_{ab}^* = \sqrt{(L_1^* - L_2^*)^2 + (a_1^* - a_2^*)^2 + (b_1^* - b_2^*)^2} \qquad (5)$$

CMC. The Color Measurement Committee (CMC) of the Society of Dyers and Colorists [9] defined a color difference metric called CMC (*l*:*c*) based on the CIE L*a*b*. $\Delta L^*, \Delta C_{ab}^*$, and ΔH_{ab}^* are, respectively, lightness, chroma, and hue difference. The parameters *l* and *c* are, respectively, lightness weighting, and chroma weighting. Then:

$$\Delta E_{CMC(l:c)}^* = \sqrt{\left(\frac{\Delta L^*}{lS_L}\right)^2 + \left(\frac{\Delta C_{ab}^*}{cS_C}\right)^2 + \left(\frac{\Delta H_{ab}^*}{S_H}\right)^2} \qquad (6)$$

where:

$$S_L = \begin{cases} 0.511 & L_1^* < 16 \\ \dfrac{0.040975L_1^*}{1 + 0.01765L_1^*} & L_1^* \geq 16 \end{cases}$$

$$S_C = \frac{0.0638C_1^*}{1+0.0131C_1^*} + 0.638, \quad S_H = S_C(FT + 1 - F) \quad, \quad F = \sqrt{\frac{C_1^{*4}}{C_1^{*4}+1900}}$$

$$T = \begin{cases} 0.56 + |0.2\cos(h_1 + 168°)| & 164° \leq h_1 \leq 345° \\ 0.36 + |0.4\cos(h_1 + 35°)| & otherwise \end{cases}$$

The terms S_L, S_C, and S_H are the weighting functions for the lightness, chroma, and hue components, respectively. Except for textile industry, it is usually recommended that *l*=2 and *c*=1.

CIEDE2000. The CIE has proposed another formula: CIEDE2000 [10]. which should be able to assess small color differences.. Here we have:

$$\Delta E_{00}^* = \sqrt{\left(\frac{\Delta L'}{k_L S_L}\right)^2 + \left(\frac{\Delta C'}{k_C S_C}\right)^2 + \left(\frac{\Delta H'}{k_H S_H}\right)^2 + R_T \frac{\Delta C'}{k_C S_C} \frac{\Delta H'}{k_H S_H}} \qquad (7)$$

where:

$$S_L = 1 + \frac{0.015(\bar{L}-50)^2}{\sqrt{20+(\bar{L}-50)^2}}, \quad S_C = 1 + 0.045\bar{C}', \quad S_H = 1 + 0.015\bar{C}'T$$

$$\Delta L' = L_1^* - L_2^*, \quad \Delta C' = C_1' - C_2', \quad \Delta H' = 2\sqrt{C_1'C_2'}\sin\left(\frac{\Delta h'}{2}\right)$$

$$T = 1 - 0.17\cos(\bar{H}' - 30°) + 0.24\cos(2\bar{H}') + 0.32\cos(3\bar{H}' + 6°)\,0.2\cos(4\bar{H}' - 63°)$$

$$R_T = -2\sqrt{\frac{\bar{C}'^7}{\bar{C}'^7 + 25^7}}\sin 60°\left[\exp\left(-\left[\frac{\bar{H}' - 275°}{25°}\right]^2\right)\right]$$

3   The Proposed Method

This work applies a data fusion approach based on the use of color within an innovative multi-parametric diagnostic method: triphasic CT of the liver.

3.1   Triphasic CT of the Liver

This technique is based on the acquisition of three volumes, upon the injection of a contrast agent; the first volume is the arterial phase, the second one is the portal venous phase, and the last one is the delayed phase. These acquisitions are performed respectively after 20-30 seconds, 60-70 s, and 60-180 s from the contrast material injection [11, 12].

The 75-100% of potential types of liver tumors receives blood from the hepatic artery: they are known as hypervascular tumors. Neoplasms are hypovascular tumors and represent about 25% of all tumors [11]. The venous phase is more sensitive for the detection of lesions, while the arterial and delayed phases can provide additional information on the vascularity of lesions in order to clarify their nature [13]. The combination of the arterial and venous phases reveals 92% of the lesions, the combination of the arterial and delayed phases detects 91% of the lesions, and the combination of the venous and delayed phases accounts for 80% of the lesions. The combination of all three phases detects 92% of the lesions [14].

3.2   Color Fusion

The scientific literature describes many methods for the registration phase, that is the phase preceding the actual data fusion process, but very little has been formally said about the combination of the original data, their information content, and the fusion of multi-temporal and multi-parameter information [15, 16].

The algorithm proposed in this paper should allow the fusion of images by the use of color. In a different way with respect to the classical Look-Up–Table method, the proposed process envisions the generation of an actual color image. To this end, it is necessary to specify the content of the three channels of a color image, i.e., the Red, Green and Blue channels.

Starting from the original CT phase images, a visual enhancement of their global content should be achieved through the display of a most informative color image.

In this respect, it is necessary to perform an accurate and adaptive choice of the criteria to decide which image is to be associated to each color channel RGB. In the literature, this is a novel approach since, usually, the choice of the associations is random.

To this end, a quantitative study has been carried out along with a qualitative analysis. Appropriate objective measurements have been investigated in order to evaluate the best result from among the various possibilities offered by the given data fusion procedure.

Fig.1 shows the structure of the proposed algorithm.

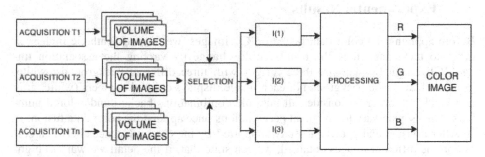

Fig. 1. Description of the algorithm fusion

The first step of the algorithm is aimed at identifying the images to be used as input to the fusion process. This is necessary in order to localize the images containing the area of interest and select them accurately in all three phases. In fact, the three volumes acquired may not have a direct correspondence between homologous slices.

The association of a color channel with a specific image may refer to the original images (8), or to new images (9) obtained from some processing algorithm applied to them. For instance, simple operators such as subtraction or average can be applied. In previous works other linear transformations were proposed, such as those derived from the PCA application [17].

$$\begin{cases} R = I(i) \\ G = I(j) \quad \text{with } i,j,k = 1,2,3 \text{ and } i \neq j \neq k \\ B = I(k) \end{cases} \tag{8}$$

$$\begin{cases} R = f_R(I(i), I(j), I(k)) \\ G = f_G(I(i), I(j), I(k)) \\ B = f_B(I(i), I(j), I(k)) \end{cases} \tag{9}$$

Once images to be used as input to the data-fusion process have been chosen, it is necessary to establish the most appropriate association with the RGB channels.

For every three images provided as input to the algorithm, it is possible to make different permutations between the RGB channels, and then get different results. Permutation of RGB channels is N!=6; this causes significant changes in the final visualization result. A study on synthetic images has been carried out in order to optimize this stage, provide the best possible result and define the rules of color association to the original images. The results have been evaluated using the metrics: ΔE_{RGB}^*, ΔE_{ab}^*, ΔE_{uv}^*, $\Delta E_{CMC(l:c)}^*$, and ΔE_{00}^*, as described above.

Then, qualitative and quantitative assessments have been conducted a posteriori also on the CT final images. The aim was to select the final image with the highest informative content from a perceptual point of view and check if the results obtained on synthetic images were verified.

All the resulting images have been submitted to several experts for a quantitative assessment. According to it, none of the distances totally reflects human judgment.

4   Experimental Results

Before applying the color data fusion on CT images, we created synthetic images in order to understand how the results could change by varying the association image/RGB channel. There are three images with three different backgrounds: white, gray and black. The background of each image displays colored numbers (white, gray and black), in order to consider all possible combinations background/colored numbers. This is necessary to obtain all permutations once applied the color data fusion.

After a visual and analytical study supported by the use of distances between colors on the different images obtained, we can state that, if the detail we want to highlight appears exclusively in one of the input images, it is advisable to associate that image to the red, or better, to the green channel. This is because the eye, under the same luminous intensity, is more sensitive to green than to red and blue lights.

Then a color data fusion approach is applied to images of the triphasic liver in order to better localize and identify the disease, as well as to significantly characterize the nature of a lesion.

To this purpose, a direct color fusion algorithm has been applied in order to compare human visual perception to the actual image information content. This new approach makes use of a maximum contrast criterion and suggests a practical rule to enhance the visualization.

The proposed algorithm has been applied to a case study regarding a Hepatocellular carcinoma (HCC) tumor after chemoembolization. In the case illustrated in Fig.2 the presence of a known sign in S8/S4 liver segments (45x33x48mm) should be underlined. Such a formation has an inhomogeneous appearance as it is characterized in part by necrotic hypodense tissue and in part by neoplastic persistent tissue, as shown respectively with the arrows in Fig. 2a. The former is free of contrastographic enhancement. The latter shows some strengthening in arterial phase and moderate washout, as compared to neighboring parenchyma in venous and delayed phases.

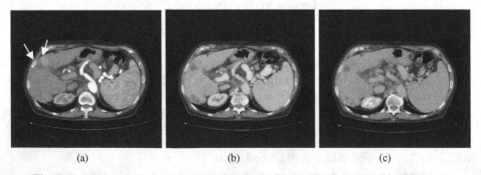

(a)   (b)   (c)

Fig. 2. Images of triphasic CT: (a) arterial phase, (b) venous phase, (c) delayed phase

Some general pre-processing steps have been applied to all the images of the tri-phasic volumes, as regards calibration, filtering and masking. The images are not perfectly registered to one another, but it is not the aim of this paper to propose a method of registration or pause on this aspect.

When visually analyzing the case, shown in Fig.2, a human expert perceives the neoplastic tissue to be lighter in the arterial phase as compared with the venous and the delayed phases. The necrotic tissue in all three phases is darker than the tumor and the liver; but also in this case it appears brighter in the arterial phase than in the other two phases.

A color fusion of the three phases is proposed using the association image/channel RGB of the formula (8) to test whether the perception is in line with the actual image content. Performing a direct association of each RGB channel with one of the original CT phases, as shown in Fig.3, it is possible to appreciate how the tumor and the necrotic tissue Hounsfield Units (HU) are not changing between phases. This can be observed by the small presence of color in the tumor and in the necrotic tissue.

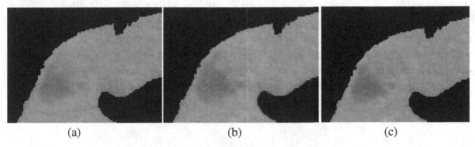

(a)   (b)   (c)

Fig. 3. RGB fusion of three phases with different permutation.

In order to highlight the pathology with respect to healthy tissue, images have been processed to each other using different algorithms. The most satisfactory result has been obtained by subtracting the phases, while the best combination is represented by the Difference-Image between arterial and delayed phases, where the tumor-to-parenchyma contrast is maximum (10).

$$\begin{cases} f_m = I(1) \\ f_n = I(3) \\ f_l = I(1) - I(3) \end{cases} \tag{10}$$

All the associations between arterial, delayed, and difference images have been performed; in Fig.4, some examples are shown. As may be seen, the color allows the tumor to stand out from the parenchyma.

All results, obtained by permutation of the direct fusion of original images and processed images, have been assessed visually and with appropriate color distance metrics. This allowed studying the results and defining the best combination.

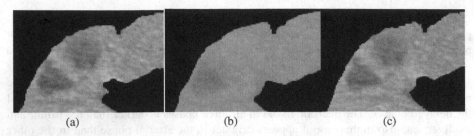

| (a) | (b) | (c) |

Fig. 4. RGB fusion of arterial phase, delayed phase and difference image between them with different permutation

The data in Fig.5 show the correlation between the results obtained from human perception and those achieved with the application of different color metrics. In particular, the abscissa axis reports the ratings from 1 to 13 (from worst to best) suggested by a sample of people who visually evaluated the images. Fig.3 shows the three worst images and Fig.4 the three best ones. On the ordinates, we can find the results from the different distances calculated, where a small result corresponds to very similar colors.

Looking at the graph it is possible to observe that not all metrics applied show the same results. The distance ΔE_{RGB} does not cause variations among the three worst and the three best results, and provides the same result starting from different colors comparisons. Another distance that does not meet the requirements is the ΔE_{00}^*. In this case, the distinction between worst and best results is not clear, and in fact, the results in both cases are very similar.

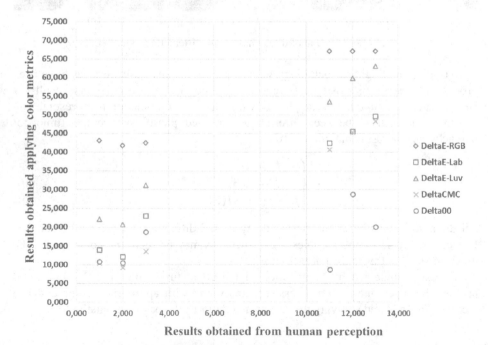

Fig. 5. Graph of the correlation.

Comparing the results obtained with the calculation of the most promising distances, we can see that in all three cases, (ΔE_{ab}^*, ΔE_{uv}^* and $\Delta E_{CMC(l:c)}^*$) there is a gap between the results considered perceptually the worst (bottom left corner) and the best (top right corner). The best results in all three cases fully reflect the results perceived by the human eye. Considering the worst results, no one of them fully reflects the order relevant to human perception, but the one that comes the closest is the $\Delta E_{CMC(l:c)}^*$.

Two of the three best results obtained visually and by a quantitative measure show in the green channel the image with the highest information content. This confirms the results previously achieved on synthetic images. The best image is shown in Fig.4a with the combination of delayed phase, difference image and arterial phase in association with RGB, respectively.

As compared with PCA-transform-based data fusion, which addresses a global analysis of input images, in this study, an analysis of multi-temporal volumes has been carried out, according to the specific local content.

5   Conclusions

Through this work a fusion algorithm supported by the color has been developed, providing the physician with a concrete support in the analysis of a large amount of images. With this method, a complete view has been obtained, showing detail enhancement and high information content preservation.

A first study on synthetic images has allowed defining the best associations between images and RGB channels, where the importance of associating the image with a high information content to the green channel has been pointed out.

The application of the algorithm on the images of the triphasic liver has emphasized the advantage of using the color to interpret the texture of the liver and tumor since the gray levels can fool the eye. The need to perform a processing of images to highlight the pathology with respect to the parenchyma has been demonstrated as well.

References

1. Baum, K.G., Helguera, M., Hornak, J.P., Kerekes, J.P., Montag, E.D., Unlu, M.Z., Feiglin, D.H., Krol, A.: Techniques for fusion of multimodal images: application to breast imaging. In: 2006 IEEE International Conference on Image Processing. IEEE (2006)
2. Goshtasby, A.A., Nikolov, S.: Image fusion: advances in the state of the art. Information Fusion 8(2), 114–118 (2007)
3. Bedi, S., Jyoti, A., Pankaj, A.: Image fusion techniques and quality assessment parameters for clinical diagnosis: A Review. International Journal of Advanced Research in Computer and Communication Engineering 2(2), 2319–5940 (2013)
4. James, A.P., Dasarathy, B.V.: Medical image fusion: A survey of the state of the art. Information Fusion 19, 4–19 (2014)

5. Pujol, A., Chen, L.: Color quantization for image processing using self information. In: 2007 6th International Conference on Information, Communications & Signal Processing. IEEE (2007)
6. Wyszecki, G., Stiles, W.S.: Color science. Wiley, New York (1982)
7. Banu, S., Sattar, S.A.: The comparative study on color Image segmentation Algorithm. International Journal of Engineering Research an Applications 2(4), 1277–1281 (2012)
8. Paschos, G.: Perceptually uniform color spaces for color texture analysis: an empirical evaluation. IEEE Transactions on Image Processing 10(6), 932–937 (2001)
9. Kim, A.-R., Kim, H.-s., Park, S.-o.: Measuring of the perceptibility and acceptability in various color quality measures. Journal of the Optical Society of Korea 15(3), 310–317 (2011)
10. Luo, M.R., Cui, G., Rigg, B.: The development of the CIE 2000 colour-difference formula: CIEDE2000. Color Research & Application 26(5), 340–350 (2001)
11. Joel Gibson, R.: Spiral CT of the Liver: is Biphasic or Triphasic Scanning the Routine in your Department? In: Advance for Imaging & Radiation Oncology (2010)
12. Tarantino, L., Sordelli, I., Nocera, V., Piscopo, A., Ripa, C., Parmeggiani, D., Sperlongano, P.: Ablation of large HCCs using a new saline-enhanced expandable radiofrequency device. Journal of ultrasound 12(2), 69–74 (2009)
13. van Leeuwen, M.S., Noordzij, J., Feldberg, M., Hennipman, A.H., Doornewaard, H.: Focal liver lesions: characterization with triphasic spiral CT. Radiology 201(2), 327–336 (1996)
14. Choi, B., Lee, H., Han, J., Choi, D., Seo, J.B., Han, M.: Detection of hypervascular nodular hepatocellular carcinomas: value of triphasic helical CT compared with iodized-oil CT. AJR. American Journal of Roentgenology 168(1), 219–224 (1997)
15. Rattanapitak, W., Udomhunsakul, S.: Comparative efficiency of color models for multi-focus color image fusion. Hong Kong (2010)
16. Tsagaris, V., Anastassopoulos, V.: Multispectral image fusion for improved RGB representation based on perceptual attributes. International Journal of Remote Sensing 26(15), 3241–3254 (2005)
17. Dellepiane, S.G., Angiati, E.: A new method for cross-normalization and multitemporal visualization of SAR images for the detection of flooded areas. IEEE Transactions on Geoscience and Remote Sensing 50(7), 2765–2779 (2012)

TRAgen: A Tool for Generation of Synthetic Time-Lapse Image Sequences of Living Cells

Vladimír Ulman[✉], Zoltán Orémuš, and David Svoboda

Centre for Biomedical Image Analysis, Masaryk University,
Botanická 68a, 602 00 Brno, Czech Republic
{ulman,xoremus,svoboda}@fi.muni.cz
http://cbia.fi.muni.cz

Abstract. In biomedical image processing, correct tracking of individual cells is important task for the study of dynamic cellular processes. It is, however, often difficult to decide whether obtained tracking results are correct or not. This is mainly due to complexity of the data that can show hundreds of cells, due to improper data sampling either in time or in space, or when the time-lapse sequence consists of blurred noisy images. This prohibits manual extraction of reliable ground truth (GT) data as well. Nonetheless, if reliable testing data with GT were available, one could compare the results of the examined tracking algorithm with the GT and assess its performance quantitatively.

In this paper, we introduce a novel versatile tool capable of generating 2D image sequences showing simulated living cell populations with GT for evaluation of biomedical tracking. The simulated events include namely cell motion, cell division, and cell clustering up to tissue-level density. The method is primarily designed to operate at inter-cellular scope.

Keywords: Biomedical imaging · Simulation · Evaluation · Cell tracking

1 Introduction

The present biomedical research increasingly relies on automated processing and analysis of large amount of image data, which are nowadays commonly produced by the vast majority of acquisition devices. Two fundamental tasks in this area are image segmentation and motion tracking. The task of segmentation is to split the image into several disjoint regions. Depending on the application, the regions can be whole cells, various intra-cellular objects (e.g., mitochondria or some proteins), cell nuclei themselves, or intra-nuclei objects (e.g., chromatin territories or individual genes). The task of motion tracking is to provide links between these regions between consecutive images in the acquired time-lapse sequence. This allows for description of events and changes in the characteristics of studied objects over a period of time. Of course, such analyses should be performed over significantly large datasets, thus in an unsupervised manner. This, however, calls for proper validation, in terms of precision and accuracy, of

© Springer International Publishing Switzerland 2015
V. Murino and E. Puppo (Eds.): ICIAP 2015, Part I, LNCS 9279, pp. 623–634, 2015.
DOI: 10.1007/978-3-319-23231-7_56

the image analysis methods prior to their use in practice. In particular, we will focus on quality examination of cell and cell nuclei tracking algorithms.

For proper evaluation one needs to possess reliable and complete ground truth data (GT), which is a sequence of labelled mask images and corresponding cell lineage trees in the case of cell and nuclei tracking. When seeking for GT for one's particular application, one may ask a human expert to annotate her existing images in order to turn them into a GT dataset. But this is often very tedious and unreliable [27], especially in the 3D case. It is also possible to use some of the existing publicly available datasets. Unfortunately, none of the popular ones [3, 8, 13, 21] offers time-lapse data, except, to the best of our knowledge, for the recent one [16]. Another, and recently becoming particularly popular, solution is to make use of a simulator, which we understand as a tool for generating pseudo-real synthetic testing images accompanied with the GT data, e.g., labelled mask images.

1.1   Current Approaches to Analysis of Tracking Performance

Dufour et al. [4] can be considered to belong among the first research groups that were creating synthetic time-lapse sequences of moving cells for evaluation of tracking performance. In their work, only two spheres were positioned randomly under constraint that they can't overlap and that they touch at least once during the sequence. The images of the spheres were then covered with noise. Later on, the same authors [5] elaborated further their idea in order to yield yet more realistic image sequences.

Other significant contributions [7, 11, 14] to the field as well as many other researchers relied on expert manual annotation of small subsets of available data. This is somewhat surprising provided that simulated data are often used for evaluating segmentation algorithms. One conclusion we may draw from it is that tracking developers lack reasonable aid for creating one's own synthetic time-lapse images.

Looking into the field of image registration, some authors [12, 26] reported recently to obtain synthetic images with elaborate non-rigid object shape changes and realistic texture. Here, the image sequences were created by iteratively preparing image transformations, that introduced various types of motion and deformations, and by applying them on a given initial real image. These methods require, therefore, a sample real image and transformations either measured from real data [26] or synthetic ones [12]. One of the first attempts to put synthetic cells to motion according to fully synthetic transformations, was drafted in [24]. The authors initially filled a mask with a procedural texture [17] to mimic a chromatin structure. The structure was then iteratively transformed with generated smooth vector fields in the course of time. Such approaches can, however, display only limited number of cells, usually only a single one, in the image sequence, which is usually short as well.

In this paper, we would like to fill the gap in the evaluation of tracking algorithms and offer researchers a tool that creates for them image data with populations of realistically living, thus moving and splitting, cells with GT.

1.2   Background on Biomedical Image Simulation

As presented in [23], every simulator can be clearly split into three principal phases: (I) digital phantom object generation, (II) simulation of signal transmission through an optical system, and (III) simulation of signal detection and image formation in an image sensor. In this paper, we introduce a tool capable of generating the appropriate phantom data accompanied with the relevant GT. In this sense, the topic covers the first phase. The remaining two phases are beyond the scope of this text. For further reading, see [15,23]. We would like to emphasize, that we use the term digital phantom instead of model. This comes from our need to avoid association with a comprehensive and the most correct description of an object of interest (that a model would be), quite often devised to have a predictive potential to discover new biology-relevant findings. Our idea is to focus only on the object properties that may influence our observation (the visual experience) in optical microscopy. In fact, the observation is subject to the last two phases. The second phase (II) typically comprises of convolution with a point spread function, often modelled with Gaussian blur, while the third phase (III) typically adds several types of noise to the image. See Ref. [23] for detailed explanation and Ref. [24] for an extension of the three-phase model for time-lapse datasets.

Unlike the majority of simulation toolboxes whose structure can be decomposed into the three consecutive phases, the learning-based approaches employ generative modelling methods or machine learning approaches. These techniques have been recently surveyed in [2].

The credibility of synthetically generated datasets comes from how closely the simulation procedures in all three phases mimic the real data and the simulated system. When creating the digital phantom of cells and cell populations, we need to deal with the following three aspects:

- mutual positions of individual cells,
- cell shape,
- and cell internal texture.

In the rest of the paper, we would like to focus on the former two aspects. These can be represented with cell masks in the synthetic time-lapse image sequence, and they can provide the complete tracking GT. The initial shape of cells, of course, depends on the simulated cell line. We were experimenting with shapes based on the idea that the z-projection of human somatic cells is topologically equivalent to a circle. Hence, the basic initial shape was generated as a slightly deformed ellipse. The fundamental ideas how to prepare a computer generated large cell population were presented by Lehmussola et al. [10]. They were placing individual cells repeatedly until suitable position and allowed overlap were established. The ideas defined in their paper influenced many other authors [15,18,22,28].

Regarding the time-lapse development of cell mask positions within the images, we propose a concept adopted from the field of crowd motion simulations (see the recent review [6]). In particular, it is extending the popular social force model [9] mainly in the three aspects. First, cells, which correspond to pedestrians in terms of their model, can split or naturally die during the simulation. Second, cells can take different shape and change its shape during simulation, in contrast to modelling all pedestrians with fixed-radius circles. Third, we have changed the semantics of the forces used in the model, some of which in their paper were artificial, not physically motivated. On the other hand, it is exactly the modelling based on forces that makes this model attractive for cell simulations. In fact, the relation between forces and pedestrian positions is in their model, perhaps not knowingly, formulated with the Langevin equation [20], which is used to model Brownian motion of particles and is also used for modeling motion of cells [25].

1.3   Contribution of This Paper

In this paper we propose a simple to use yet versatile method[1] to generate GT-enabled image sequences with vast amounts of cells which show various tracking events:

– cells move and change shape (as an inevitable property of live),
– they may have contact and can even overlap slightly (simulates dense populations),
– they split due to cell divisions (simulates mitosis),
– they disappear due to cell death (simulates starvation due to excessive forces acting on them) or as they leave the image (simulates leaving the observed field of view),
– they appear after the mitosis or enter the image again.

The method works with 2D masks of all common biomedical shapes, including those of nuclei and cells themselves. The method is primarily designed to operate at inter-cellular scope, not at the intra-cellular scope.

We leave the simulated time-lapse development of cell internal structure, the cell texture, in the first phase (I) as well as the simulation of second (II) and third (III) phases to the user — a developer of tracking algorithm for her particular application. It is precisely this application that dictates what texture should be used and how images of the cells will be further altered to simulate the image acquisition. We suggest that developers of the tracking algorithms substitute their masks with the output of the proposed method in order to obtain yet more intricate tracking tasks, for which complete tracking GT is available, see Fig. 1.

2   Method

2.1   Cell Motion

Each cell i is represented with its centre $x_i(t)$ and polarity vector $p_i(t)$, both with respect to the fixed image coordinates, and with a list of polar coordinates of

---

[1] The implementation is freely available at http://cbia.fi.muni.cz/projects/tragen.html

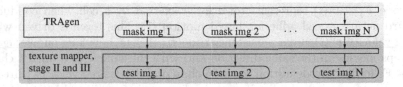

Fig. 1. Scheme of a complete image sequence generator. The output, a sequence of labelled image masks, from the proposed method is submitted to a user supplied SW that overlays the masks with proper texture, yielding a sequence of testing images.

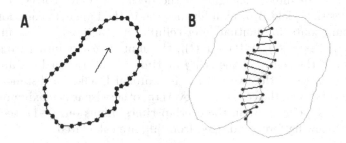

Fig. 2. A) Illustration of a 2D cell representation with emphasized boundary points and the polarity vector placed in the cell centre. Border lines between points are straight. B) Illustration of an (exaggerated) contact of two cells (gray contour) with recognized collision point pairs (solid lines) of the extended boundary. Their number $cp_{i,j}(t, \triangle_f)$ approximates the length of boundary in contact; the length of the longest pair is $-\boldsymbol{d}_{i,j}(t)$.

points representing a cell boundary. The boundary points are treated relatively to the cell centre, see Fig. 2A, and are sorted according to the angular element. The parameter t represents simulated time measured in minutes. We consider any spatial or distance parameters in units of micrometers.

The method utilizes a concept of several types of forces acting on every cell, which conducts motion as a result of it. In fact, it is a purely mechanical model of cell motion. We assume cells are rigid and forces act in their centres. The change of position of a cell is, therefore, characterized with the differential equations:

$$\frac{d\boldsymbol{x}_i(t)}{dt} = \boldsymbol{v}_i(t), \quad m_i \frac{d\boldsymbol{v}_i(t)}{dt} = \boldsymbol{F}_i(t), \tag{1}$$

where $\boldsymbol{v}_i(t)$ is an instantaneous velocity at time t, m_i is a mass of the cell, and $\boldsymbol{F}_i(t)$ is a sum of individual forces (described below) acting on it at time t. We solve this system with the standard Euler method with time step of 0.1 minutes.

In order to push cell i to move, we introduce two forces:

$$\boldsymbol{F}_i^{desired}(t) = m_i \, \boldsymbol{v}_i^d(t)/\tau_p \,, \tag{2}$$

$$\boldsymbol{F}_i^{friction}(t) = -m_i \, \boldsymbol{v}_i(t)/\tau_p \,. \tag{3}$$

The force $F_i^{desired}(t)$ represents total force exerted by a cell when conducting standard actin-induced adhesion-based motion [1]. This force is driven with a desired velocity $v_i^d(t)$ and a persistence time τ_p, that is, how long on average the cell keeps moving in the same direction and with the same speed until a change occurs. Following this definition, we keep changing the desired velocity (direction and speed) after normally-distributed random period of time; hence $v_i^d(t)$ is a function of time. To counterbalance this motion-inducing force, as in standard mechanics any object keeps accelerating as long as result of forces acting on it is not zero, we consider a friction force $F_i^{friction}(t)$. This force can be understood as a drag when cell is moving in a viscous environment; it also allows cell to decelerate when required. Changing of the desired velocity corresponds to the random terms that yield Brownian-like motion in the Langevin equation [20, 25].

To accommodate for mutual inter-cellular interactions, let us first define $n_{i,j}(t) = (x_j(t) - x_i(t))/|x_j(t) - x_i(t)|$, the unit vector pointing from the cell i centre toward the centre of the cell j at time t, and a signed distance $d_{i,j}(t)$ between boundaries of the two cells: it is minimal Euclidean distance between boundary points when the cells do not overlap, otherwise it is maximum distance of the boundary point pairs in the overlap times minus one (-1), see Fig. 2B. Finally, the following forces, adapted from [9], are calculated:

$$F_i^{repulsive}(t,j) = n_{j,i}(t) \ max(d_{i,j}(t), 0) \ A e^{-d_{i,j}(t)/B} , \qquad (4)$$

$$F_i^{body}(t,j) = n_{j,i}(t) \left(max(-d_{i,j}(t) - \triangle_o, 0) \ k + max(-d_{i,j}(t), 0) \ A \right), \qquad (5)$$

$$F_i^{sliding}(t,j) = n_{i,j}^{\perp}(t) \ max(-d_{i,j}(t), 0) \ \kappa \ n_{i,j}^{\perp}(t) \cdot (v_j(t) - v_i(t)) , \qquad (6)$$

$$F_i^{attractive}(t,j) = n_{i,j}(t) \ decay_{i,j}(t, \tau_a) \ C(1 + cp_{i,j}(t, \triangle_f)) . \qquad (7)$$

The operator $max()$ serves as a unit-less cut-off operator such that, for instance, the force $F_i^{repulsive}(t,j)$ is effective only when there is no collision between the two cells. Note that orientations of forces differ; the $n_{i,j}^{\perp}(t)$ is a unit vector perpendicular to $n_{i,j}(t)$.

The repulsive force $F_i^{repulsive}(t,j)$ corresponds to an increasing effort of an approaching cell to expel all material between the two cells so that they can touch eventually. This force can be also understood as a force to slow down the approaching cell before the contact. Once the contact occurs, the sliding force $F_i^{sliding}(t,j)$, altered with the parameter κ, is in effect. Its task is to equal velocities of the cells in contact. The counter-deformation force $F_i^{body}(t,j)$ permits a decent overlap of a distance $\triangle_o$ micrometers. If, however, the overlap of cells increases, this force increases proportionally as well. Since the overlap mimics non-rigid deformation of the cell, by adjusting the rate k, one can control cell stiffness and consequently the amount of deformation and thus overlap allowed.

The purpose of the attractive force $F_i^{attractive}(t,j)$ is to keep neighboring cells together. The strength of the connection is proportional to the length of the coinciding boundary extended by $\triangle_f$ micrometers between the cells i and j. This is expressed with $cp_{i,j}(t, \triangle_f)$, see Fig. 2B, as the number of extended boundary point pairs in the cell overlap. The extension $\triangle_f$ of the boundary corresponds to the length of cell filaments which many cells use to sense others within their close spatial vicinity. In order to allow a cell to escape from a cluster, we introduce the term $decay_{i,j}(t, \tau_a) \in \{0,1\}$ that goes to 0 whenever there is no contact between the two cells within the period of time τ_a, i.e., $\forall t' \in \langle t - \tau_a, t \rangle : cp_{i,j}(t', \triangle_f) = 0$. During this period, decent force $F_i^{attractive}(t', j) = C$ still applies, and then vanishes completely.

Last but not least, we consider the force $F_i^{boundary}(t) = Ae^{-db_i(t)/B}$ where $db_i(t)$ is the distance to the closest image boundary. The force acts perpendicularly away from it. This (artificial) force is an optional aid to keep cells within the simulated field of view.

If any of $F_i^{repulsive}(t, j)$, $F_i^{body}(t, j)$, or $F_i^{sliding}(t, j)$ keeps exceeding a threshold value F_{max} over a period of 5% of the cell cycle (the length of the mitosis), the cell is assumed not to sustain the force and is, thus, removed from simulation.

2.2   Cell Shape Changes

In order to allow for realistic simulation of long-term observations, longer than is the duration of one cell cycle of the simulated cells, we suggest to implement cell division. The cell cycle is split into several phases [19]. From the shape changes perspective, the significant ones are Telophase, Cytokinesis and G1-phase, during which a mother cell elongates before the division, the division happens, and daughter cells grow after the division, respectively. Given that the boundary points are represented in polar coordinates with respect to the cell centre, we just iteratively extend distance elements in all boundary points by a constant or by Gaussian-shaped function centered along axis of elongation to mimic cell growth or cell elongation, respectively. The elongation axis coincides with the polarity vector $p_i(t)$. For the division, we first iteratively decrease the distances by narrow Gaussian-shaped function centered along axis of division which is perpendicular to the axis of elongation, and split the boundary point list into new lists of two daughter cells in the end.

Furthermore, it is established that many cells (but not all, e.g., keratocytes) tend to maintain polarity and move along this direction. To simulate this, we smoothly rotate the cell around its centre such that the angle between the current polarity $p_i(t)$ and desired velocity $v_i^d(t)$ vectors is minimized.

To summarize the simulation, we first adjust shape of every cell in the system, then we calculate forces, and solve eq. (1) afterwards. Note that this enables a user to inject one's own cell mask instead of having the shape adjusted as described above. In this way, one can fully control the mask shapes, e.g., employ one's own complex non-rigid shape changes [5,26], while have the masks moving and interacting during the simulation.

3   Results

The parameters of the simulations are summarized in Table 1. Initial number of cells was always 64 and were spread in a 8-by-8 grid with initial desired speed of 0μm min^{-1}. The diameter of cells along the polarity vector was 20μm.

Table 1. Summary of values used in this paper. The notation $\langle a, b \rangle$ denotes uniformly distributed random value between the numbers a and b.

$m_i = 1\text{mg}$	$\tau_p \in \langle 10, 20 \rangle \text{min}$	$\boldsymbol{v}_i^d(t) \in \langle 0.0, 0.8 \rangle \mu\text{m min}^{-1}$
$A = 0.1\text{N}$	$B = 0.6\mu\text{m}$	$\boldsymbol{F}_{max} = 0.3\text{N}$
$k = 0.2\text{N}$	$\kappa = 0.3\text{N min }\mu\text{m}^{-1}$	$\delta_o = 0.5\mu\text{m}$
$C = 0.02\text{N}$	$\tau_a = 10\text{min}$	$\delta_f = 0.5\mu\text{m}$

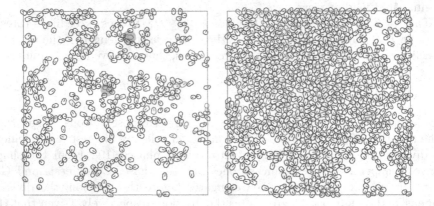

Fig. 3. Comparison of synthetic medium-dense (in the left) to dense (in the right) populations of cells. There are 418 and 955 cells displayed. The cells in red are in mitosis, those in blue are not. Note in the left image the two outlined cells that are in the process of cell division. Images were dilated by 1px for displaying purposes.

The complete cell cycle duration was set to 300min, with 0.4%, 0.4% and 50% of it allocated for the cell elongation, division, and growth, respectively. The system was computing with temporal resolution of 0.1 simulated minutes. The frequency of rendering cells into a sequence of images, the temporal sampling of the sequence, is a user parameter. Spatial resolution is limited only by machine floating-point precision as the coordinates were real-valued, presumably in units of μm. Similarly, spatial image resolution, DPI, is a user parameter as well.

We show here four snapshots of simulations, and encourage interested reader to download and try the method. The snapshots focus on the prominent problem in the tracking task: the linking of touching objects between consecutive images. Note that segmentation of images is not addressed in this paper. In Fig. 3, we compare medium-dense population of cells, where some had already formed tight clusters, to dense, tissue-like cell configuration. In this case, the force $\boldsymbol{F}_i^{boundary}(t)$ was used. The death-inducing threshold $\boldsymbol{F}_{max}$ was, however, set very high so that it effectively prohibited cells to get removed, yielding tight over-populated configuration of cells under increased stress (stress figures not shown). In Fig. 4, boundary force was not used and $\boldsymbol{F}_{max}$ was set as reported in the table. Notice relaxed packing configuration in the right image.

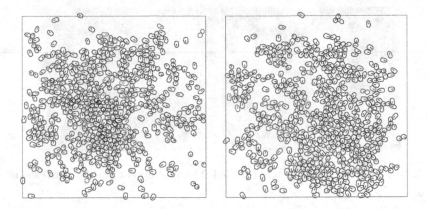

Fig. 4. Comparison of synthetic populations of 551 (in the left) and of 553 (in the right) cells with disabled (in the left) and enabled (in the right) removing of cells due to exceedingly strong forces acting on them. The black cells suffer from the excessive force. Images were dilated by 1px for displaying purposes.

The time complexity of the method when generating next image in the sequence is quadratic with respect to the number of simulated cells, because it needs to calculate mutual distances between all the cells. The most demanding operation is to compute $cp_{i,j}(t, \triangle_f)$. The time complexity is independent of the size of the generated images. Total time required to calculate positions of 300 cells in 100 frames on a standard desktop PC was less than 1 minute (single threaded implementation).

3.1   Case Study: Comparison Against Real Annotated Data

In order to demonstrate that the method can be adapted to simulate a particular and non-trivial real tracking data, we will compare generated sequences against a real sequence of Pancreatic Stem Cells on a polystyrene substrate[2]. It is a sequence of 2D images showing single-isolated motile cells to small clusters, 150–300 cells in an image, acquired in a sequence of 100 images sampled every 10 minute, and observed with the phase-contrast microscopy, see Fig. 5.

To mimic the sequence, we adjusted the initial number, initial positions and the desired speed of all cells as well as the size of the output images to meet spatial parameters, the total simulated time and sampling to meet temporal parameters, and complete cell cycle duration to meet the population growth rate, see Fig. 6. Finally, we have implemented provisional texture mapper, that used the produced masks as described earlier in this paper (e.g., Fig. 1), to obtain a visually similar sequence, see Fig. 5.

---

[2] Data was obtained with permission from the Cell Tracking Challenge web site http://www.codesolorzano.com/celltrackingchallenge/, courtesy of Dr. Tim Becker.

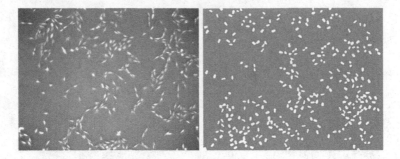

Fig. 5. Sample image from the real (in the left) and synthetic (in the right) sequence.

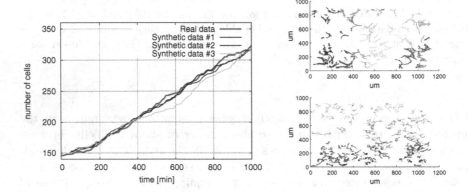

Fig. 6. In the left, comparison of the development of the number of cells over time. The growth rate of the simulated population appears to mimic the one in the real data. In the right, comparison of the cell tracks. The motility of synthetic cells (bottom) appears rather similar to the real ones (top).

4   Conclusion

We have described a method, which is both simple to use and control yet versatile in the variety of simulated aspects. It can simulate, for instance, motile isolated cells, cells preferring to form clusters, or tissue-like cell cultures during complete cell cycle including the cell division. One can control the rate of cell divisions, average speed of cells, and temporal sampling of the simulation to steer complexity of the tracking task. It is designed to provide a sequence of 2D images with labelled masks together with lineage trees that serves as a complete tracking GT data, all in the format adopted in the Cell Tracking Challenge [16]. We believe that prospective authors of next tracking algorithms may easily add appropriate textures [10,15] to these masks and tailor appearance of the obtained testing images specifically to the context of their needs, e.g., to phase-contrast or fluorescence microscopy, or to images with different SNR. The testing images obtained in this way, can become yet more realistic and thus more relevant for the evaluation.

The method is primarily designed to operate at inter-cellular scope, not at the intra-cellular scope. It is, however, possible to extend it such that it can work even with masks of particles, e.g., genes, or some smaller intra-cellular structures such as protein territories or mitochondria, provided forces are adapted appropriately or new ones are introduced, e.g., a force keeping genes within the same cell.

Given the results of this report, that the adopted force-based approach is viable for 2D time-lapse cell simulations, we plan to extend the simulations into a full 3D time-lapse including non-rigid deformations of the 3D cells. The simultaneous movement and deformation of cells should be a result of mechanical model of a viscoelastic cell after collecting various forces acting on it.

Acknowledgments. This work was supported by Czech Science Foundation — grant No. GA14-22461S.

References

1. Ananthakrishnan, R., Ehrlicher, A.: The forces behind cell movement. International Journal of Biological Sciences **3**(5), 303–317 (2007)
2. Buck, T., Li, J., Rohde, G., Murphy, R.: Toward the virtual cell: Automated approaches to building models of subcellular organization "learned" from microscopy images. Bioessays **34**(9), 791–799 (2012)
3. Coelho, L.P., Shariff, A., Murphy, R.F.: Nuclear segmentation in microscope cell images: A hand-segmented dataset and comparison of algorithms. In: ISBI, pp. 518–521 (2009)
4. Dufour, A., Shinin, V., Tajbakhsh, S., Guillen-Aghion, N., Olivo-Marin, J.C., Zimmer, C.: Segmenting and tracking fluorescent cells in dynamic 3-D microscopy with coupled active surfaces. IEEE Trans. on Image Processing **14**(9), 1396–1410 (2005)
5. Dufour, A., Thibeaux, R., Labruyere, E., Guillén, N., Olivo-Marin, J.: 3-D active meshes: fast discrete deformable models for cell tracking in 3-D time-lapse microscopy. IEEE Trans. on Medical Imaging **20**(7), 1925–1937 (2010)
6. Duives, D.C., Daamen, W., Hoogendoorn, S.P.: State-of-the-art crowd motion simulation models. Transportation Research Part C: Emerging Technologies **37**, 193–209 (2013)
7. Dzyubachyk, O., van Cappellen, W.A., Essers, J., Niessen, W.J., Meijering, E.: Advanced level-set-based cell tracking in time-lapse fluorescence microscopy. IEEE Trans. on Medical Imaging **29**(3), 852–867 (2010)
8. Gelasca, E.D., Byun, J., Obara, B., Manjunath, B.: Evaluation and benchmark for biological image segmentation. In: ICIP, October 2008
9. Helbing, D., Farkas, I., Molnar, P., Vicsek, T.: Simulation of pedestrian crowds in normal and evacuation situations. Pedestrian and Evacuation Dynamics **21**, 21–58 (2002)
10. Lehmussola, A., Ruusuvuori, P., Selinummi, J., Huttunen, H., Yli-Harja, O.: Computational framework for simulating fluorescence microscope images with cell populations. IEEE Trans. Med. Imaging **26**(7), 1010–1016 (2007)

11. Li, K., Miller, E., Chen, M., Kanade, T., Weiss, L., Campbell, P.: Cell population tracking and lineage construction with spatiotemporal context. Medical Image Analysis **12**(5), 546–566 (2008)
12. Lihavainen, E., Mäkelä, J., Spelbrink, J., Ribeiro, A.: Mytoe: automatic analysis of mitochondrial dynamics. Bioinformatics **28**(7), 1050–1051 (2012)
13. Ljosa, V., Sokolnicki, K.L., Carpenter, A.E.: Annotated high-throughput microscopy image sets for validation. Nat. Methods **9**(7), 637 (2012)
14. Magnusson, K., Jalden, J.: A batch algorithm using iterative application of the viterbi algorithm to track cells and construct cell lineages. In: 2012 9th IEEE International Symposium on Biomedical Imaging (ISBI), pp. 382–385, May 2012
15. Malm, P., Brun, A., Bengtsson, E.: Simulation of bright-field microscopy images depicting pap-smear specimen. Cytometry Part A **87**(3), 212–226 (2015)
16. Maška, M., Ulman, V., Svoboda, D., Matula, P., Matula, P., et al.: A benchmark for comparison of cell tracking algorithms. Bioinformatics, pp. 1609–1617 (2014)
17. Perlin, K.: An image synthesizer. In: SIGGRAPH 1985: Proceedings of the 12th Annual Conference on Computer Graphics and Interactive Techniques, pp. 287–296. ACM Press, New York (1985)
18. Rajaram, S., Pavie, B., Hac, N.E.F., Altschuler, S.J., Wu, L.F.: Simucell: a flexible framework for creating synthetic microscopy images. Nat. Methods **9**(7), 634–635 (2012)
19. Reece, J., Urry, L., Cain, M., Wasserman, S., Minorsky, P., Jackson, R.: Campbell Biology, 9th edn. Pearson Benjamin Cummings (2011)
20. Romanczuk, P., Bär, M., Ebeling, W., Lindner, B., Schimansky-Geier, L.: Active Brownian particles. The European Physical Journal - Special Topics **202**(1), 1–162 (2012)
21. Ruusuvuori, P., Lehmussola, A., Selinummi, J., Rajala, T., Huttunen, H., Yli-Harja, O.: Benchmark set of synthetic images for validating cell image analysis algorithms. In: Proceedings of the 16th European Signal Processing Conference, EUSIPCO (2008)
22. Svoboda, D., Ulman, V.: Towards a realistic distribution of cells in synthetically generated 3d cell populations. In: Petrosino, A. (ed.) ICIAP 2013, Part II. LNCS, vol. 8157, pp. 429–438. Springer, Heidelberg (2013)
23. Svoboda, D., Kozubek, M., Stejskal, S.: Generation of digital phantoms of cell nuclei and simulation of image formation in 3d image cytometry. Cytometry Part A **75A**(6), 494–509 (2009)
24. Svoboda, D., Ulman, V.: Generation of synthetic image datasets for time-lapse fluorescence microscopy. In: Campilho, A., Kamel, M. (eds.) ICIAR 2012, Part II. LNCS, vol. 7325, pp. 473–482. Springer, Heidelberg (2012)
25. Szabo, A., Perryn, E., Czirok, A.: Network formation of tissue cells via preferential attraction to elongated structures. Phys. Rev. Lett. **98**, 038102 (2007)
26. Tektonidis, M., Kim, I.H., Chen, Y.C.M., Eils, R., Spector, D.L., Rohr, K.: Non-rigid multi-frame registration of cell nuclei in live cell fluorescence microscopy image data. Medical Image Analysis **19**(1), 1–14 (2015)
27. Webb, D., Hamilton, M.A., Harkin, G.J., Lawrence, S., Camper, A.K., Lewandowski, Z.: Assessing technician effects when extracting quantities from microscope images. Journal of Microbiological Methods **53**(1), 97–106 (2003)
28. Xiong, W., Wang, Y., Ong, S.H., Lim, J.H., Jiang, L.: Learning cell geometry models for cell image simulation: An unbiased approach. In: ICIP, pp. 1897–1900 (2010)

Automatic Image Analysis and Classification for Urinary Bacteria Infection Screening

Paolo Andreini[1], Simone Bonechi[1($\boxtimes$)], Monica Bianchini[1],
Alessandro Mecocci[1], and Vincenzo Di Massa[2]

[1] University of Siena – Department of Information Engineering and Mathematics,
Roma 56, I-53100 Siena, Italy
simo_bone@alice.it
http://www.diism.unisi.it
[2] Diesse Ricerche S.r.l., C/o TLS via Fiorentina 1, I-53100 Siena, Italy

Abstract. In this paper, we present an automatic system for the screening of urinary tract infections. It is estimated that about 150 million infections of this kind occur world wide yearly, giving rise to roughly five billion health–care expenditures. Currently, Petri plates seeded with infected samples are analyzed by human experts, an error prone and lengthy process. Nevertheless, based on image processing techniques and machine learning tools, the recognition of the bacterium type and the colony count can be automatically carried out. The proposed system captures a digital image of the plate and, after a preprocessing stage to isolate the colonies from the culture ground, accurately identifies the infection type and severity. Moreover, it contributes to the standardization of the analysis process, also avoiding the continuous transition between sterile and external environments, which is typical in the classical laboratory procedure.

Keywords: Advanced image processing · Support vector machines · Urinoculture screening

1 Introduction

Recent technological advances in biomedical engineering and biomedicine allow the development of automated vision systems that use digital image processing techniques along with machine learning methodologies to give reliable and automatic analysis of specimens in different application fields. This is the case of urinoculture, a screening test typically done on hospitalized patients and pregnant women. In fact, the urinary tract infections, together with those of the respiratory tract, are of great clinical relevance for the high frequency with which they are found in common medical practice and because of the complications arising therefrom. They are mainly caused by Gram–negative microorganisms, with a high prevalence of *Escherichia coli* (E.Coli, 70%), even if clinical cases frequently occur where complicated infections are caused by Gram–positive or multi–resistant germs, on which the common antimicrobial agents are

V. Murino and E. Puppo (Eds.): ICIAP 2015, Part I, LNCS 9279, pp. 635–646, 2015.
DOI: 10.1007/978-3-319-23231-7_57

inevitably ineffective, leading to therapeutic failures. Actually, manual methods for urinoculture screening are work and time intensive, requiring visual inspection by a biomedical scientist for semi–quantitative scoring of each sample. This impacts on laboratory throughput and induces a poor use of qualified resources for what are predominantly negative screens. Actually, in the standard protocol, the urine sample is seeded on a Petri plate that holds a culture substrate, used to artificially recreate the environment required for the bacterial growth, and incubated at 37° C overnight. After the incubation, each plate is examined by a human expert.

Even if some interesting research has been carried out in recent years, obtaining an overview of the state–of–the–art in image processing solutions to the automatic analysis of Petri plates is difficult, since results are published in various domains — from food and beverage safety to environmental control and specific clinical analyses [1–3] —, based on different data sets, and often related to subtle variations of the core problem (like, f.i., in [4], where the colony classification problem is addressed with promising results, but with respect to a very small number of images and based only on the determination of isolated colonies).

The tool we propose, is able of handling the whole examination cycle starting from the automatic acquisition of the plate with a color camera and ending with the identification of the type of infection(s) and with the assessment of its severity through Support Vector Machines (SVMs). The system has been tested and evaluated on real samples provided by DIESSE Ricerche Srl, Siena, and acquired in real operative conditions.

The paper is organized as follows. Section 2 introduces the problem and describes the preprocessing procedure, from the image acquisition phase to the background removal. Section 3 presents the classification methods and shows experimental results, whereas Section 4 defines the procedure used to detect each single colony. Finally, conclusions are given in Section 5.

2   Automatic Image Analysis of Petri Plates

In order to correctly recognize the infection type and to precisely estimate the bacterial load, it is fundamental to grab a good quality image of the Petri plate. To avoid imperfections due to manual plate handling, the images are captured by an automatic camera setup (Fig. 1). After the acquisition, a suitable preprocessing step is applied to locate the region of interest (the Petri plate), and to grant that it is in an appropriate position inside the field of view. At this point, the image is saved along with auxiliary information. The automatic acquisition is performed as follows: a simple and fast algorithm, based on change detection [5] and morphological filtering [6], is applied and the image is acquired only when the plate is correctly positioned, the scene is well illuminated, and no movements are observed. Before saving the image, the Petri dish is isolated from the rest of the scene using a Random Hough circle transform [7] to detect the circular Region of Interest (RoI).

The acquisition setup has been used in a real application scenario at DIESSE Ricerche premises, to collect a dataset of 253 images, subsequently divided into

Fig. 1. The automatic acquisition set.

a training, a validation, and a test set, containing 154, 64, and 35 images, respectively. As a requirement, eight different classes of infection were detected, namely: E.Coli, KES (Klebsiella, Enterobacter, Serratia), Enterococcus Faecalis, Streptococcus Agalactiae, Pseudomonas, Proteus, Staphylococcus Aureus, and Candida.

2.1 Selection of the Chromatic Space

Since a chromogenic medium (Uriselect 4) is used as ground seed, the color of the pixels is the most important feature for classifying the different colonies. During preliminary studies, the background color distribution has been analyzed in four different color spaces (i.e., RGB, HSV, CIE–Lab, and YCrCb). The chromatic data relative to the background in each chromatic space have been accumulated and the Dunn's Index has been used to give a quantitative ranking (based on the Centroid Linkage distance and the Centroid Diameter dispersion [8]):

$$DI(X) = \min_{1 \leq i \leq k} \left\{ \min_{1 \leq i \leq k} \left\{ \frac{\delta(X_i, X_j)}{\max_{1 \leq s \leq k} \{\Delta(X_s)\}} \right\} \right\}$$

$$\delta(X_i, X_j) \triangleq \frac{1}{|X_i| + |X_j|} \left(\sum_{\vec{c} \in X_i} d(\vec{c}, C_{X_j}) + \sum_{\vec{c} \in X_j} d(\vec{c}, C_{X_i}) \right)$$

$$C_{X_i} \triangleq \frac{1}{|X_i|} \sum_{\vec{c} \in X_i} \vec{c}; \; C_{X_j} \triangleq \frac{1}{|X_j|} \sum_{\vec{c} \in X_j} \vec{c}$$

$$\Delta(X_i) \triangleq 2 \left(\frac{\sum_{x \in X_i} d(x, C_{X_j})}{|X_i|} \right)$$

where $\vec{c}$ is the chromatic vector (a, b) of each pixel, while the other variables have an obvious meaning. Experiments have shown that CIE–Lab has a higher ranking and also gives increased separation between the color of the eight infections and the background. CIE–Lab [9] has been selected for the chromatic description. It is known that the use of (a, b) chromaticity coordinates only, makes the histogram more stable with respect to differences in illumination and local variations caused by shadows [10]. Moreover, if only the (a, b) chromaticity components are used, the background colors concentrate in a very compact and stable region (Fig. 2).

2.2 Background Removal

The classification of infections is performed in a hierarchic way. As a preliminary step, the colonies are segregated from the background by a background–removal process based on chromatic information about the specific chromogenic medium

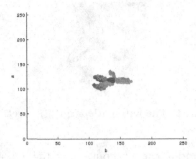

Fig. 2. Background (a,b) color distribution (marked in red) compared to the distribution of the eight infections.

used in the culture (Uriselect 4, in this study). To this end a suitable chromatic background model has been defined.

Background Modeling – To obtain a chromatic description of the background, a supervised training technique is adopted, during which a human expert selects about 40 different regions belonging to the background of different images coming from the training set. The chromatic components (a,b) of the pixels belonging to such regions are accumulated to represent the typical background chromatic values. The samples have been preliminarily filtered by a fast vector median filter [11] to reduce the effect of noisy samples. The color histogram distribution is estimated by a Parzen–window with a Gaussian shape [12].

Foreground Modeling – A similar approach has been used to model the foreground (infected) regions. Again a supervisor selects about 40 regions belonging to each different infection classes coming from the images of the training set. Again a Parzen–window approach is used to estimate the probability of the (a,b) chromatic components for each infection class. So, finally, we are left with eight estimates of the conditional probability density function relative to the eight possible infections considered. These functions are then compared with the background probability density function to define the chromatic regions that can give rise to classification uncertainty. The uncertainty region is obtained as a union of the intersections of some binary masks obtained by imposing a threshold on the probability level of the background and of the infected regions. In formulae:

$$U_M = \bigcup_{i=1}^{8} C_i$$

$$C_k = \bigcap (B_\tau, I_{\tau,k}); \ k \in [1,8]$$

$$B_\tau = \begin{cases} 1 & if \ \vec{c}_{back} \in background \ \&\& \ p(\vec{c}_{back}) \geq \tau \\ 0 & otherwise \end{cases}$$

$$I_{\tau,j} = \begin{cases} 1 & if \ \vec{c}_j \in j-region \ \&\& \ p(\vec{c}_j) \geq \tau \\ 0 & otherwise \end{cases}$$

$$\tau = \min\{t_1, t_2\}$$

$$t_1 = \min_k \left\{ \iint_{p(\vec{c}_j) \geq k} p(\vec{c}_j) d\vec{c} \geq \alpha \,\middle|\, \vec{c}_j \in I_{\tau, j}; j = 1, \dots 8 \right\}$$

$$t_2 = \iint_{p(\vec{c}_{back}) \geq t_2} p(\vec{c}_{back}) d\vec{c} \geq \alpha; \; \vec{c}_{back} \in background$$

where τ is a constant threshold imposed to be sure that a percentage of at least α (say $\alpha = 90\%$) of the background pixels belong to each set, $\vec{c}_j$ is the chromatic vector of a pixel belonging to the j–th infection type, and $\vec{c}_{back}$ is a pixel belonging to the background.

At this point the mask relative to each infected region (C_k for the k–th infected region) is intersected with the background mask to give a superposition binary mask. Finally the union U_M of the whole set of superposition masks is computed. It is easy to see that the final mask comprises all the chromatic coordinates that belong with a certain degree of probability (actually more than τ) both to the background and to one of the infected regions. The chromatic coordinates of the points belonging to the final mask are marked as uncertain and used during the subsequent classification stage.

Background Segmentation – Even if the background chromatic model is quite stable and accurate, some minor chromatic variations are still present. To accommodate for these variations, a Mean–Shift segmentation [13] algorithm is used to associate each image pixel to the corresponding modal density value in the (a, b) space (actually, as usual, the chromatic coordinates are mixed with the positional coordinates of each pixel so the Mean–Shift algorithm runs in a four–dimensional space). The modal value so obtained, is compared with the background chromatic model (by using the corresponding likelihood), to establish if the pixel belongs to the background region or not. In this way a first approximated background segment is obtained. Unfortunately such an approximation is rarely satisfying because the background slightly changes its colors according to the type of bacterium grown on the plate. To solve this problem, we use the previously defined uncertainty chromatic mask U_M. In particular, when some pixels belong to the mask (i.e., they cannot be assigned with reasonable certainty on the basis of chromatic coordinates), we assign them to a fictitious class of uncertain points. In the image space such points form a set of *uncertainty regions* and specific post–processing steps are applied to each of them.

Uncertainty regions are analyzed taking into account also local spatial properties like discontinuities (edges), that are typically present between the colonies and the background. In particular, we have considered the following five classes:

(1) Colonies (E. Coli, KES, E. Faecalis, S. Agalactiae);
(2) Background without edges (blue in Fig. 3);
(3) Background with edges (pink in Fig. 3);
(4) Uncertainty region without edges (red in Fig. 3);
(5) Uncertainty region with edges (green in Fig. 3).

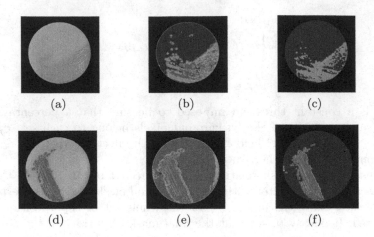

Fig. 3. Images (a) and (d) represent two dishes in which Pseudomonas and KES colonies are present; images (b) and (e) show the five different regions present on each Petri dish, and (c) and (f) the results obtained after the application of the described background segmentation procedure.

The classification procedure is the following: at first the background chromatic model is used to decide if a segment (obtained by Mean–Shift segmentation) belongs to a colony, to the background or to an uncertainty region. Thereafter, a Sobel [14] based edge enhancement is applied to distinguish class (3) and (5). Then, uncertainty regions (4) and (5) are analyzed to assign them to the background or to the colonies. During the experiments, it has been noted that if the HSV space [15] is used to describe uncertainty regions then, if the region belongs to the background, the H (hue) channel shows a peak that is near to the one obtained by taking the same histogram but relative to the region of class (2). To take advantage of this observation, the uncertainty regions of class (4) and (5) are analyzed separately by applying the same procedure, summarized in the following.

1. The Otsu method [16] is used to threshold the H values of uncertainty regions in class (4) and (5) and to segment them;
   (a) Based on the computed threshold, the considered uncertainty region is divided into two sub–regions;
   (b) The histograms of the two sub–regions are computed and compared, to establish if a significant separation exists (i.e. if the peaks of the two sub–regions are far enough in the histogram of the H channel). If the peaks are separated, the two sub–regions are identified as (6) and (7), respectively, and processed separately. If the peaks are not separated, the two sub–regions are kept together;
2. The peaks of the histogram (H channel) of the region of class (2) and of the analyzed regions ((6) and (7) separately or together, depending on the previous step) are compared;

3. If the peaks of the background and of the current region ((6) and (7) separately or together) are distant enough, the current region cannot be assigned to the background and is passed to the final classification step to assign it to the appropriate colony;
4. Instead, if the peaks are almost coincident, the uncertainty region shows a H value similar to the background, and it is assigned to it.

In other words, for both regions (4) and (5), we identify different sub–regions (if any) and, for each "homogeneous" zone, we establish its membership to the background or not.

Further problems arise when considering Candida colonies, since their color is practically the same as the culture ground. To classify this infection, an ad hoc procedure has been devised, particularly focused on analyzing segments belonging to region (3).

The performance of the background segmentation method has been evaluated on the test set comprising 33 images. The results are reported in Table 1.

Table 1. Results of the background extraction preprocessing.

Background extraction	
Total Number of background pixels	1091413
Background pixels correctly classified	1068445
Background pixels incorrectly classified	22968
Accuracy	97,9%

3   Classification

After the background removal process has been performed, the residual regions, not belonging to it, are classified. A multi–stage classification approach is used for this aim.

The classification of the bacteria grown on a Petri plate is a very difficult problem and it is usually carried out by a qualified biologist. Human experts can use their visual skills and *a priori* knowledge to solve the task. Due to the use of a chromogenic ground seed, the most important feature for recognizing different type of bacteria is color. In fact, Uriselect 4 is specifically designed to support the infections classification through the hue taken by the colonies. This is due to different bacterial enzymes whose activity produces a peculiar color:

– β–galactosidase and tryptophanase: red–pink, typical for E. Coli infections;
– β–glucosidase: turquoise blue, typical for Enterococcus Faecalis infections; the simultaneous presence of β–galactosidase turns the color to purplish blue, typical for the KES group infections;
– tryptophane désaminase: yellow/orange, typical for Proteus–Providencia–Morganella infections.

Therefore, the first step in our multi–stage classification algorithm is to recognize the previous three classes by using chromatic features. This lead to a pre–classification which can be further used to recognize subclasses among the main classes. The pre–classification step divides the infections into three main chromatic groups: red (E. Coli), blue (Enterococcus Faecalis, KES and Streptococcus Agalactiae), and yellow/orange (Pseudomonas, Proteus and Staphylococcus Aureus). Such a division is obtained by an SVM (Support Vector Machine) classifier with a Gaussian kernel, with $\gamma = 0.1$ and $C = 7.75$ (the parameters have been chosen via a trial–and–error procedure). SVMs has been implemented by using the Weka software tools (http://www.cs.waikato.ac.nz/ml/weka/). To collect the feature vectors for the classifier, we have first executed a Mean–Shift segmentation algorithm and then, for each segment, the (a,b) color components in the CIE–Lab space have been extracted. The results of this pre–classification step are reported in Table 2.

Table 2. Classification results for the three main colors based on an SVM classifier.

(a) Accuracy

SVM classifier for the three main colors		
Total Number of Segments	13292	Percentage
Incorrectly Classified Segments	36	0.2708 %
Correctly Classified Segments	13256	99.7292 %

(b) Confusion Matrix

Red	Blue	Yellow/Orange
4479	0	10
0	8691	12
14	0	86

Only E. Coli produces red colonies among the eight diverse types of infections considered, so it can be recognized in the first step. Instead, for the other classes, some more information is needed to recognize each specific kind of infection.

For the blue class (E. Faecalis, KES, St. Agalactiae), the first important issue is the presence of residual background segments not correctly identified by the background segmentation module. Even if the module is quite efficient, experimentally, it turned out that even a small amount of background badly affects the blue class classification performance. The background extractor output and the pre–tag have been used as an input for a GrabCut algorithm [17], that allows to remove the majority of the remaining background segments. Thereafter, an SVM classifier with a Gaussian kernel, with $\gamma = 0.12$ and $C = 1$ (the parameters have been chosen via a trial–and–error procedure) has been used. Results for the classification of blue infections are reported in Table 3.

Furthermore we find out unpredictable chromatic variations produced when different species of bacteria overlap on the same Petri dish. This is the case of the contemporary presence of E. Coli and E. Faecalis, that produces an overlapping region which looks like KES. Therefore, we use this a priori information to predict which colonies are probably present also in the overlapping regions, starting from the classification of segregated colonies. The colony dimension is a useful feature to discriminate Enterococcus Faecalis (small colonies, $0,5 - 1,5$ mm for the diameter) from KES ($2 - 3$mm). Taking advantage from the procedure capable to recognize isolated colonies (Section 4) we then use the dimension of a single colony as a feature to improve the classification performance. Based on both the color component (a, b) and the dimension of the colonies, we train another SVM classifier with a polynomial kernel, with degree $= 3$, $\gamma = 0.25$, and $C = 1$. Results for this classification are reported in Table 4.

A similar procedure was also implemented with respect to the yellow class (Pseudomonas, Proteus and Staphylococcus Aureus), obtaining very promising results. Anyway, such results are very preliminary, since they were achieved on a too small set of images to be actually statistically significant.

Table 3. Classification results for the blue class.

(a) Accuracy

SVM classifier for KES, Faecalis and Agalactiae		
Total Number of Segments	7122	Percentage
Incorrectly Classified Segments	1240	17.4108 %
Correctly Classified Segments	**5882**	**82.5892 %**

(b) Confusion Matrix

KES	Faecalis	Agalactiae
3021	191	12
604	2548	213
17	203	313

Table 4. Classification results for the blue class using both color and colony dimension as input features.

(a) Accuracy

SVM classifier for KES, Faecalis and Agalactiae isolated colony		
Total Number of Colonies	226	Percentage
Incorrectly Classified Colonies	30	13.2743 %
Correctly Classified Colonies	**196**	**86.7257 %**

(b) Confusion Matrix

KES	Faecalis	Agalactiae
76	0	0
24	91	1
0	5	29

Finally a distinct procedure has been developed to detect the Candida infections. This is a very difficult task because Candida looks semi–transparent, with a color which is nearly the same as the culture ground. In fact, biologists, in order to find out the presence of Candida, usually rotate and move the plate in different positions, an operation aimed at finding any additional useful feature (reflections, thickness of the colony, etc.). Since the camera catches just a frontal view of the Petri dish, a 2D image does not allow such a possibility. Therefore, Candida was revealed by detecting eventual edges inside the background (caused by the colony extrusions originating small reflections). Unfortunately, an edge can be also due to noise; therefore, in order to reduce the number of false positives, we used the shape of the colony, generally circular, as a fundamental feature to distinguish colonies from noise. Single non overlapping colonies were then searched on the edge mask and, based on their number, we were finally able to establish the presence of Candida or not (see Fig. 4).

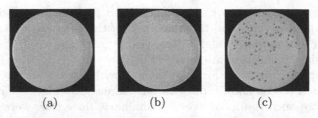

Fig. 4. In (a), the original image; in (b) the identified edges within the background, in orange; in (c), Candida colonies found on the Petri dish.

4   Colony Detection and Bacterial Count

In order to perform the bacterial count, a multistage algorithm has been developed that, at first, searches only for single, not overlapping colonies, and then tries to enucleate colonies belonging to slightly overlapping regions. A binary image is first constructed, in which the background is represented by the ground seed and the foreground by the colonies. Single colonies show a roughly circular shape and can be easily identified based on this feature. In particular, for each connected component in the binary image, we calculate the least enclosing circle and then, if the ratio between the circular area and the area of the given connected component is under a fixed threshold (chosen via a trial–and–error procedure), such a component is supposed to be a colony. Obviously, this simple approach is not effective in massive overlapping regions, where a different procedure has to be used. Therefore the convexity of each colony contour is calculated and sub–contours with convex shape are found; then, the best ellipse (in the least square sense), that fits each sub–contour, is selected. A score matrix, that takes into account both the axes rate and the ellipses' points belonging (or not) to the contour, is constructed and used to remove non–relevant ellipses (Fig. 5).

Fig. 5. In (a) the original image; in (b) contours are evidenced (blue: the concave part; red: the convex part); in (c) the ellipses, with a high score (red), and a low score (blue).

Using the dimension of the discovered single colonies, combined with the area of the infected region, our system calculates the infection severity (or the bacterial load), which is an estimate of the number of microorganisms per milliliter of urine (UFC/ml), expressed by using a logarithmic evaluation scale. The actual measurement value is obtained by multiplying the number of bacterial colonies counted on the dish by the inverse of the seeding dilution rate. Based on this procedure, we obtain an accuracy of 92,1% (our estimations agree with those of the biologists for 233 out of 253 images constituting the dataset).

5 Conclusions

In this paper, an automatic procedure to detect and classify urinary infections was described, able to obtain a good accuracy on the most common bacteria present in humans. Preliminary results were presented. It is a future matter of research to refine the classification procedure related to colonies with very similar colors and also revealing the presence of Candida. Finally, the tool will be also extended to treat diverse types of culture grounds, possibly transparent and based on the action of different enzymes (so producing different chromatic reactions).

References

1. Ogawa, H., Nasu, S., Takeshige, M., Funabashi, H., Saito, M., Matsuoka, H.: Noise-free accurate count of microbial colonies by time-lapse shadow image analysis. Journal of Microbiological Methods **91**(3), 420–428 (2012)
2. Clarke, M.L., Burton, R.L., Hill, A.N., Litorja, M., Nahm, M.H., Hwang, J.: Low-cost, high-throughput, automated counting of bacterial colonies. Cytometry Part A **77**(8), 790–797 (2010)
3. Brugger, S.D., Baumberger, C., Jost, M., Jenni, W., Brugger, U., Mühlemann, K.: Automated counting of bacterial colony forming units on agar plates. PLoS ONE **7**(3), e33695 (2012)
4. Ferrari, A., Signoroni, A.: Multistage classification for bacterial colonies recognition on solid agar images. In: Proceeding of IEEE IST 2014, pp. 101–106 (2014)
5. Ilsever, M., Unsalan, C.: Two-Dimensional Change Detection Methods: Remote Sensing Applications, pp. 7–21. SpringerBriefs in Computer, Science (2012)
6. Maragos, P., Pessoa, L.: Morphological filtering for image enhancement and detection. In: Handbook of Image and Video Processing. Academic Press (2005)
7. Mount, D., Netanyahu, N.: Efficient Randomized Algorithms for Robust Estimation of Circular Arcs and Aligned Ellipses. Computational Geometry **19**(1), 1–33 (2001)
8. Halkidi, M., Batistakis, Y., Vazirgiannis, M.: On Clustering Validation Techniques. Journal of Intelligent Information Systems **17**, 107–145 (2001)
9. Hunter, R.S.: Photoelectric color difference meter. In: Proceedings of the Winter Meeting of the Optical Society of America, vol. 38(7), p. 661. JOSA (1948)
10. Saxe, D., Foulds, R.: Toward robust skin identification in video images. In: 2nd Int. Face and Gesture Recognition Conf. (1996)
11. Smolka, B., Szczepanski, M., Plataniotis, K.N., Venetsanopoulos, A.N.: Fast modified vector median filter. In: Skarbek, W. (ed.) CAIP 2001. LNCS, vol. 2124, p. 570. Springer, Heidelberg (2001)
12. Heidenreich, N., Schindler, A., Sperlich, S.: Bandwidth selection for kernel density estimation: a review of fully automatic selectors. Adv. Stat. Anal. **97**, 403–433 (2013)
13. Comaniciu, D., Meer, P.: Mean-shift: A robust approach toward feature space analysis. IEEE Trans. Pattern Anal. Machine Intell. **24**, 603–619 (2002)

14. Gonzalez, R., Woods, R.: Digital Image Processing, pp. 414–428. Addison Wesley (1992)
15. Smith, A.R.: Color gamut transform pairs. In: SIGGRAPH 1978 - Proceedings of the 5th Annual Conference on Computer Graphics and Interactive Techniques, vol. 12(3), pp. 12–19 (1978)
16. Otsu, N.: A threshold selection method from gray-level histograms. IEEE Trans. on System, Man and Cybernetics **9**, 62–66 (1979)
17. Rother, C., Kolmogorov, V., Blake, A.: GrabCut: Interactive foreground extraction using iterated graph cuts. ACM Trans. Graph. **23**, 309–314 (2004)

LBP-TOP for Volume Lesion Classification in Breast DCE-MRI

Gabriele Piantadosi[1], Roberta Fusco[2], Antonella Petrillo[2] , Mario Sansone[1], and Carlo Sansone[1(✉)]

[1] DIETI, University of Naples Federico II, Naples, Italy
{gabriele.piantadosi,mario.sansone,carlo.sansone}@unina.it
[2] Department of Diagnostic Imaging, National Cancer Institute of Naples 'Pascale Foundation', Naples, Italy
r.fusco@istitutotumori.na.it, antonellapetrillo2@gmail.com

Abstract. Dynamic Contrast Enhanced-Magnetic Resonance Imaging (DCE-MRI) is a complementary diagnostic method for early detection of breast cancer. However, due to the large amount of information, DCE-MRI data can hardly be inspected without the use of a Computer Aided Diagnosis (CAD) system. Among the major issues in developing CAD for breast DCE-MRI there is the classification of segmented regions of interest according to their aggressiveness.

While there is a certain amount of evidence that dynamic information can be suitably used for lesion classification, it still remains unclear whether other kinds of features (e.g. texture-based) can add useful information. This pushes the exploration of new features coming from different research fields such as Local Binary Pattern (LBP) and its variants. In particular, in this work we propose to use LBP-TOP (Three Orthogonal Projections) for the assessment of lesion malignancy in breast DCE-MRI. Different classifiers as well as the influence of a motion correction technique have been considered. Our results indicate an improvement by using LPB-TOP in combination with a Random Forest classifier (84.6% accuracy) with respect to previous findings in literature.

Keywords: LBP-TOP · DCE-MRI · Lesion classification · Dynamic features · 4D Volume · Random forest

1 Introduction

In recent years Dynamic Contrast Enhanced-Magnetic Resonance Imaging (DCE-MRI) has gained popularity as an important complementary diagnostic methodology for early detection of breast cancer [12]. It has demonstrated a great potential in screening of high-risk women, both for staging newly diagnosed breast cancer patients and in assessing therapy effects [17] thanks to its minimal invasiveness and to the possibility of visualizing 3D high resolution dynamic (functional) information not available with conventional RX imaging [5,13,22]. However, due to the large amount of information, DCE-MRI data can hardly

© Springer International Publishing Switzerland 2015
V. Murino and E. Puppo (Eds.): ICIAP 2015, Part I, LNCS 9279, pp. 647–657, 2015.
DOI: 10.1007/978-3-319-23231-7_58

be inspected without the use of a computer aided support. This stimulated researchers in the last decade to develop Computer Aided Detection/Diagnosis (CAD) systems.

Among the major issues in developing CAD systems for breast DCE-MRI there are (a) detection of suspicious region of interests (ROIs), while simultaneously minimising the number of false alarms [14] and (b) the classification of each segmented ROI according to its aggressiveness.

The main focus of this study is the second issue. It is well known that both ROI detection and classification can be affected by patient movements, so that a registration phase is often required to correct motion artefacts. In this paper we do not consider this problem in detail, but we used a median filtering (detailed in Section 3.1) whose effectiveness has been previously assessed [14].

Different features have been proposed to address issue (b). They can be roughly categorized in: Clinical [9], Dynamic [6,7,9], Textural [7], Pharmacokinetic [15], Spatio-temporal [28] and Morphological [6]. The kind and the size of the chosen feature set strongly influence the CAD architecture that is usually designed to maximise accuracy or sensitivity. Some works addressed the problem by comparing or combining different kind of features. As an example, Fusco et al. [6] propose to combine dynamic and morphological features within a Multiple Classifier System (MCS) while Glaßer et al. [9] suggest to consider clinical features combined into a decision tree with other different features.

While there is a certain amount of evidence that dynamic information can improve lesion classification, it still remains unclear whether other kinds of feature (e.g. texture-based) can add useful information. This pushes the exploration of other feature coming from different research fields such as Local Binary Pattern (LBP). LBP is a very efficient texture operator which labels the pixels of an image by thresholding the neighbourhood of each pixel and considers the result as a binary number [16]. Different LBP versions have been proposed so far [2,16,26,27]. It can be used both in a spatial and spatio-temporal modality. Since DCE-MRI data lie in a spatio-temporal context, the spatio-temporal version of the LBP in three orthogonal panes (LBP-TOP) [2] seems a good candidate for the problem at hand.

In this paper we propose the use of the LBP-TOP features for the assessment of lesion malignancy in breast DCE-MRI. To the best of our knowledge, this is the first time that LBP-TOP are used in this context. Different classifiers (Random Forest, MLP and SVM), as well as the use of a motion correction technique, were evaluated. LBP-TOP were extracted from manually segmented ROIs for all patients in our database. Classification performance of LBP-TOP were assessed by using a leave-one-out cross-validation procedure. Our result were compared to previous findings in literature; the obtained results demonstrate the effectiveness of the proposed approach.

The paper is organized as follows. In Section 2 we outline the state of the art with regard to the feature for the classification of breast lesions. In Section 3 some information is given on the LBP-TOP features considered in this study. Moreover, the classification and evaluation modality are described. In Section 4 we present the results of our analysis. Finally in Section 5 we discuss the results and provide some conclusions.

2   Related Work

As far as the problem of ROI classification is concerned, different feature have been proposed up to now. *Clinical features* provide information about the patient itself such as age [1,9] and gender or can incorporate information about clinical history and parental risk indicators. Moreover, density of the breast tissue, presence of silicon implant or secondary clinical information can be considered [24]. *Dynamic features* describe Time Intensity Curve (TIC) courses. A TIC represents the temporal dynamics of the signal and reflects the absorption and the release of the contrast agent, following vascularisation characteristics of the tissue under analysis [11]. Dynamic features have the advantage that can be extracted at single voxel resolution and easily adapted to the whole ROI resolution. Due to this potentiality, they are largely used for breast pixel-by-pixel segmentation. Area under curve, relative enhancement, time to peak, wash-in, wash-out, etc. [1,6,7,9] are examples of dynamic features. *Textural features* are based on local spatial variation of voxel intensity within the image. Some base statistical approaches are used in [5,21]. Another approach proposes to analyse the texture in a different space, i.e, the frequency. These methods are based on Fourier Transform, Gabor Transform and Wavelet transform, or on filters like Kirsch and Sobel [23]. Variance, kurtosis, skewness, angular moment, contrast, correlation, entropy, etc.[7] are examples of textural features. *Morphological features* describe instead the shape of the ROI obtained during the segmentation phase, by providing geometrical indication such as: eccentricity, compactness, perimeter, area, smoothness etc. [5,6]. *Pharmacokinetic features* reflect some physiological tissue parameters and are obtained from mathematical models [10,15,20]. These parameters, such as permeability surface area, blood plasma volume and extravascular extracellular space volume, can indicate the malignity of the tissue. On the other hand, fitting such models can be quite expensive from a computational point of view. Finally, *Spatio-temporal features* model the signals in a 4D space to capture both the temporal dynamics and the spatial variations of the voxel [8]. DFT coefficient map, margin gradient, radial gradient, etc.[28] are examples of spatio-temporal features.

3   Materials and Methods

To put some notations useful in the following, let us consider that the DCE-MRI data is a 4D volume (3 spatial dimensions and 1 temporal dimension). Let T the number of time series, N the number of voxel for each 3D volume and let $I(x, y, z, t)$ be the signal intensity of the voxel (x, y, z) at the time t.

3.1   The Proposed Approach

The aim of this work is to investigate the performance of LBP-TOP features within the problem of ROI classification. For this reason a ROI classification system is proposed as depicted in Fig.1. For each patient an experienced radiologist delineated suspect ROIs as described in Section 3.4; then, in the last step, each ROI was classified according to the aggressiveness of the lesion.

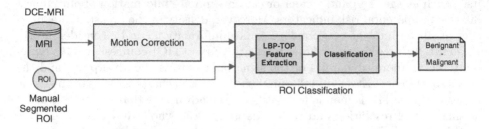

Fig. 1. Block diagram of the proposed approach.

It is well known that, before of any image analysis of the 4D MRI volume, a Motion Correction (MC) stage needs to be applied in order to reduce the effect of the motion artefact [19] and to improve the accuracy of the results. In our previous work we deeply investigate different MC techniques [14,15]. We find out that small transformations can be considered as noise superimposed on correctly aligned images. Then a median filter applied with a sliding 3D windows of 3x3x3 pixels can deal with those small shifts [14].

3.2   LBP Feature

Local Binary Pattern (LBP) [16] provides a very efficient set of features by thresholding the neighbourhood of each pixel and considers the result as a binary number. As threshold, the luminance value of the pixel in the center of the neighbourhood is considered. Then the binary numbers are interpreted as a local pattern and an histogram of the occurrences for all the patterns of the image is calculated. This simple 2D implementation provided very good performance in unsupervised texture segmentation [16]. The original LBP operator was only defined to deal with the 2D spatial information. Later, it was extended to a spatio-temporal context for dynamic texture analysis with the Volume-LBP (VLBP) [27]. The VLBP address the spatio-temporal problem handling a 3D volume with the X, Y and T axis. The neighbourhood is then considered on a 3D windows over both the spatial and temporal dimension. To make VLBP computationally simple and easy to be extended, an operator based on co-occurrences of LBP on Three Orthogonal Planes (LBP-TOP) was also introduced. LBP-TOP considers three orthogonal planes: XY, XT and YT, and concatenates LBP histograms in these three directions as shown in Figure 2.

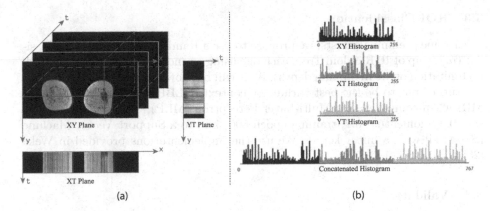

(a)   (b)

Fig. 2. LBP-TOP extraction starting from the 3D volume (a) till to the concatenated histogram (b) on the bottom-right

LBP and LBP-TOP have proved to have great potential respectively in face description [2] and visual speech recognition of moving lips [26].

In order to fit LBP-TOP feature to the 4D DCE-MRI volume (composed by X,Y,Z and T axis), we propose to calculate the histograms for each slice (coronal planes of the DCE-MRI). LBP-TOP feature were extracted only for the voxel within the ROI that need to be classified. Then the histogram of the patterns for all the slide are summed into one global histogram that refers to the whole ROI. We choose to test and implement the multi-resolution version of the LBP-TOP as proposed into [16] with a temporal radius of 1 and 2. Then, for each ROI, we obtain three histogram from temporal radius 1 (XY-1, XT-1, YT-1) and three histogram from temporal radius 2 (XY-2, XT-2, YT-2). With the aim of achieving better results we define and evaluate different feature sets, as reported in Table 1.

Table 1. Different subsets of LBP-TOP features.

	Histograms		
Feature Set	XY	XT	YT
XY	•		
XT		•	
YT			•
XYXT	•	•	
XYYT	•		•
XTYT		•	•
ALL	•	•	•

3.3   ROI Classification

After some preliminary tests, we propose to use a Random Forest (RF) [4] classifier (made up of 10 Random Trees each one using a random subset of feature with no limitation on its maximum depth). As it will be shown in the next Section, the RF turned out to be the best within the context of LBP-TOP feature on DCE-MRI when compared to a Multi-Layer Perceptron (MLP) [4] classifier (learning rate 0.3, momentum 0.2, training epoch 500) and to a Support Vector Machine (SVM) [4] with a linear kernel. We use the implementations provided in Weka [25] and LibSVM [3].

3.4   Validation

Gold Standard. An experienced radiologist delineated suspect regions of interest (ROIs) using T1-weighted and *subtractive* image series. Starting from DCE-MRI acquired data, the subtractive image series is defined by subtracting t_0 series from t_4 series. In subtractive images any tissue that does not absorb contrast agent is suppressed. Manual segmentation stage was performed in Osirix [18], that allows user to define ROIs at a sub-pixel level. Per each ROI the lesion was histopathologically proven. The evidence of malignity was used as Gold Standard (GS) for the ROI Classification problem.

Evaluation. All the result are evaluated and compared in terms of Accuracy, Sensitivity and Specificity according to the equation (1), (2) and (3).

$$ACC = \frac{TP+TN}{TP+FP+FN+TN} \tag{1}$$

$$SEN = \frac{TP}{TP+FN} \tag{2}$$

$$SPE = \frac{TN}{FP+TN} \tag{3}$$

Where TP, TN, FP, FN are respectively the True Positive, True Negative, False Positive and False Negative values for the binary voxel classification. All the results reported hereinafter have been obtained by using a leave-one-patient-out approach.

Patients. The dataset is constituted of 26 women breast DCE-MRI 3D data, (average age 41 years, in range 26-69) with benign or malignant lesions histopathologically proven: 15 lesions were malignant and 11 were benign for a total of 26 ROIs.

Data Acquisition. All patients underwent imaging with a 1.5 T scanner (Magnetom Symphony, Siemens Medical System, Erlangen, Germany) equipped with breast coil. DCE T1-weighted FLASH 3D coronal images were acquired (TR/TE: 9.8/4.76 ms; flip angle: 25 degrees; field of view 370 x 185 mm x mm; matrix:

256 x 128; thickness: 2 mm; gap: 0; acquisition time: 56s; 80 slices spanning entire breast volume). One series (t_0) was acquired before and 9 series (t_1-t_9) after intravenous injection of 0.1 mmol/kg of a positive paramagnetic contrast agent (gadolinium-diethylene-triamine penta-acetic acid, Gd-DOTA, Dotarem, Guerbet, Roissy CdG Cedex, France). An automatic injection system was used (Spectris Solaris EP MR, MEDRAD, Inc.,Indianola, PA) and injection flow rate was set to 2 ml/s followed by a flush of 10 ml saline solution at the same rate.

4   Experimental Results

Figure 3 shows (in red) a manually segmented ROI over the pre-contrast DCE-MRI image. Figure 4 shows the three LBP-TOP concatenated histograms extracted for the ROI in Fig. 3 with a temporal radius equal to 1.

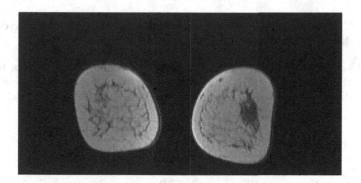

Fig. 3. Example of a manual selected ROI.

In Table 2 we report Accuracy, Sensitivity and Specificity (calculated according to Eqs. (1), (2) and (3)) per each motion correction technique and classifier. In all the experiments LBP-TOP feature was extracted using the complete feature-set (ALL). Rows are ordered according to decreasing accuracy (highest on the top row). It is worth to note that SVM and MLP show highest sensitivity; however they have very poor specificity.

For the subsequent analysis, on the basis of Table 2, we selected the combination of classifier and motion correction having the highest accuracy. In Table 3 we report the performance of such a combination (RF as classifier and median filtering with a 3px windows as motion correction technique) with different feature sets as described in Table 1 (Section 3.2).

Table 4 reports the comparison between the performance of our proposal (first row in Tab. 3) and other approaches proposed so far in the literature using different feature sets extracted from our dataset. In particular, it is worth to note that Fusco et al. [6] used both Dynamic and Morphological feature with a Multiple Classifier System (MCS), while Glaßer et al. [9] combine Clinical and Morphological feature into a Decision Tree classifier.

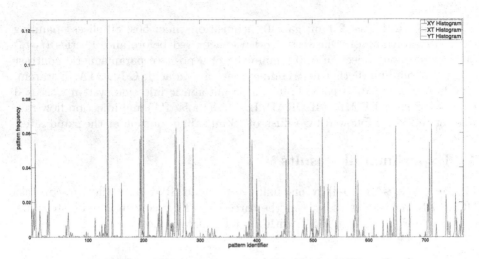

Fig. 4. LBP-TOP concatenated histograms per each orthogonal plane corresponding to the ROI showed in fig.3.

Table 2. Classification results per each combination of Motion Correction technique and Classifier. LBP-TOP were evaluated by using the complete feature-set (ALL). Rows are ordered according to decreasing accuracy (highest on the top row).

Motion Correction	Classifier	Accuracy [%]	Sensitivity [%]	Specificity [%]
Yes	RF	80.8	86.7	72.7
No	RF	76.9	80.0	72.7
No	MLP	73.1	93.3	45.5
No	SVM	69.2	100.0	27.3
Yes	MLP	61.5	93.3	18.2
Yes	SVM	61.5	93.3	18.2

5   Discussion and Conclusion

In this paper we proposed the use of LBP-TOP features for the assessment of lesion malignancy in breast DCE-MRI. Different classifiers (RF, MLP and SVM) as well as the contribution of a motion correction technique were evaluated. LBP-TOP were extracted from manually segmented ROIs for all patients in our database. Classification performance of LBP-TOP were assessed in a leave-one-out cross-validation modality.

Our results indicate that LBP-TOP features combined with Random Forest (RF) classifier and median filtering with a 3px sliding windows as motion correction technique, achieve the highest accuracy (84.6%), when only the YT histogram is used. From Table 2 it emerges that, when RF is used in combination with LBP-TOP features, motion correction improves the classification results.

Table 3. Classification results per each Feature Set using the Random Forest as classifier and the Median Filter (3px) as Motion Correction technique. Rows are ordered according to decreasing accuracy (highest on the top row).

Feature Set	Accuracy [%]	Sensitivity [%]	Specificity [%]
YT	84.6	80.0	90.9
ALL	80.8	86.7	72.7
XTYT	76.9	80.0	72.7
XY	69.2	80.0	54.5
XYXT	65.4	66.7	63.6
XYYT	61.5	66.7	54.5
XT	57.7	66.7	45.5

Table 4. Comparison among performance of our proposal and different approaches in literature on our dataset. NB: Naive Bayes; DT: Decision Tree; MCS: Multiple Classifier System; Dyn.: Dynamic features; Morph.: Morphological features.

Author	Methodology	Accuracy [%]	Sensitivity [%]	Specificity [%]
Our proposal	LBP-TOP + RF	84.6	80.0	90.9
Fusco et al. [6]	Dyn. only + NB	65.4	80.0	45.5
	Morph. only + DT	65.4	53.3	81.8
	Dyn. & Morph. + MCS	69.2	86.7	45.5
Glaßer et al. [9]	Morph. & Clinical + DT	61.5	93.3	18.2

On the other hand, for SVM and MLP it is better not to use motion correction. These last results seem in contrast with our previous findings [14]: differently from dynamic features, LBP-TOP features are not always influenced by patient movements. However, it is worth to note that our previous work with dynamic features was aimed at voxel-by-voxel ROI segmentation instead of classification.

Moreover, it is worth noting that (see Tab. 4) the proposed approach significantly outperforms the other method under comparison [6,9] in terms of overall accuracy, giving rise to a very good specificity.

One issue concerning the use of LBP in the context of DCE-MRI lies in the fact that there is no clear physiological interpretation (on the contrary of the dynamic feature having a direct physiological interpretation). Therefore, they can be difficult to understand form a radiologist point of view. Another limit of this study can be traced to the population size: our findings should be confirmed on a larger population. This will be the matter of our future research.

References

1. Abdolmaleki, P., Buadu, L.D., Naderimansh, H.: Feature extraction and classification of breast cancer on dynamic magnetic resonance imaging using artificial neural network. Cancer Lett **171**, 183–191 (2001)
2. Ahonen, T., Hadid, A., Pietikäinen, M.: Face description with local binary patterns: Application to face recognition. IEEE Transactions on Pattern Analysis and Machine Intelligence **28**, 2037–2041 (2006)
3. Chang, C.C., Lin, C.J.: LIBSVM: A Library for Support Vector Machines. ACM Transactions on Intelligent Systems and Technology **2**, 27:1–27:27 (2011)
4. Duda, R.O., Hart, P.E., Stork, D.G.: Pattern Classification. John Wiley and Sons, New York (2000)
5. El-Kwae, E.A., Fishman, J.E., Bianchi, M.J., Pattany, P.M., Kabuka, M.R.: Detection of suspected malignant patterns in three-dimensional magnetic resonance breast images. Journal of Digital Imaging: The Official Journal of the Society for Computer Applications in Radiology **11**, 83–93 (1998)
6. Fusco, R., Sansone, M., Petrillo, A., Sansone, C.: A multiple classifier system for classification of breast lesions using dynamic and morphological features in DCE-MRI. In: Gimel'farb, G., Hancock, E., Imiya, A., Kuijper, A., Kudo, M., Omachi, S., Windeatt, T., Yamada, K. (eds.) SSPR 2010, vol. 7626, pp. 684–692. Lecture Notes in Computer Science, LNCS (2012)
7. Fusco, R., Sansone, M., Sansone, C., Petrillo, A.: Segmentation and classification of breast lesions using dynamic and textural features in dynamic contrast enhanced-magnetic resonance imaging. In: 25th International Symposium on Computer-Based Medical Systems (CBMS), pp. 1–4. IEEE (2012)
8. Gilhuijs, K.G., Giger, M.L., Bick, U.: Computerized analysis of breast lesions in three dimensions using dynamic magnetic-resonance imaging. Medical physics **25**, 1647–1654 (1998)
9. Glaßer, S., Niemann, U., Preim, B., Spiliopoulou, M.: Can we distinguish between benign and malignant breast tumors in DCE-MRI by studying a tumor's most suspect region only? In: Proceedings of CBMS 2013–26th IEEE International Symposium on Computer-Based Medical Systems, pp. 77–82. IEEE (2013)
10. Hayton, P., Brady, M., Tarassenko, L., Moore, N.: Analysis of dynamic MR breast images using a model of contrast enhancement. Medical image analysis **1**(3), 207–224 (1997)
11. Kuhl, C.K., Mielcareck, P., Klaschik, S., Leutner, C., Wardelmann, E., Gieseke, J., Schild, H.H.: Dynamic breast mr imaging: Are signal intensity time course data useful for differential diagnosis of enhancing lesions? Radiology **211**(1), 101–110 (1999)
12. Lehman, C.D., Gatsonis, C., Kuhl, C.K., Hendrick, R.E., Pisano, E.D., Hanna, L., Peacock, S., Smazal, S.F., Maki, D.D., Julian, T.B., DePeri, E.R., Bluemke, D.A., Schnall, M.D.: MRI evaluation of the contralateral breast in women with recently diagnosed breast cancer. The New England journal of medicine **356**, 1295–1303 (2007)
13. Levman, J., Leung, T., Causer, P., Plewes, D., Martel, A.L.: Classification of dynamic contrast-enhanced magnetic resonance breast lesions by support vector machines. IEEE Transactions on Medical Imaging **27**, 688–696 (2008)
14. Marrone, S., Piantadosi, G., Fusco, R., Petrillo, A., Sansone, M., Sansone, C.: Automatic lesion detection in breast DCE-MRI. In: Petrosino, A. (ed.) ICIAP 2013, Part II. LNCS, vol. 8157, pp. 359–368. Springer, Heidelberg (2013)

15. Marrone, S., Piantadosi, G., Fusco, R., Petrillo, A., Sansone, M., Sansone, C.: A novel model-based measure for quality evaluation of image registration techniques in DCE-MRI. In: 27th International Symposium on Computer-Based Medical Systems (CBMS) 2014 IEEE, pp. 209–214. IEEE (2014)
16. Ojala, T., Pietikäinen, M., Mäenpää, T.: Multiresolution gray-scale and rotation invariant texture classification with local binary patterns. IEEE Transactions on Pattern Analysis and Machine Intelligence **24**, 971–987 (2002)
17. Olsen, O., Gøtzsche, P.C.: Cochrane review on screening for breast cancer with mammography. The Lancet **358**(9290), 1340–1342 (2001)
18. Rosset, A., Spadola, L., Ratib, O.: OsiriX: An open-source software for navigating in multidimensional DICOM images. Journal of Digital Imaging **17**, 205–216 (2004)
19. Tanner, C., Khazen, M., Kessar, P., Leach, M., Hawkes, D.: Does registration improve the performance of a computer aided diagnosis system for dynamic contrast-enhanced MR mammography? In: 3rd IEEE International Symposium on Biomedical Imaging: Nano to Macro, pp. 466–469. IEEE (2006)
20. Tofts, P.S., Brix, G., Buckley, D.L., Evelhoch, J.L., Henderson, E., Knopp, M.V., Larsson, H.B.W., Lee, T.Y., Mayr, N.A., Parker, G.J.M.: Others: Estimating kinetic parameters from dynamic contrast-enhanced T 1-weighted MRI of a diffusable tracer: standardized quantities and symbols. Journal of Magnetic Resonance Imaging **10**(3), 223–232 (1999)
21. Twellmann, T., Lichte, O., Nattkemper, T.: An adaptive tissue characterization network for model-free visualization of dynamic contrast-enhanced magnetic resonance image data. IEEE Transactions on Medical Imaging **24**, 1256–1266 (2005)
22. Twellmann, T., Saalbach, a., Müller, C., Nattkemper, T.W., Wismüller, A.: Detection of suspicious lesions in dynamic contrast enhanced MRI data. In: 26th Annual International Conference of the IEEE Engineering in Medicine and Biology Society (IEMBS2004), vol. 1, pp. 454–457 (2004)
23. Twellmann, T., Meyer-Baese, A., Lange, O., Foo, S., Nattkemper, T.W.: Model-free visualization of suspicious lesions in breast MRI based on supervised and unsupervised learning. Engineering Applications of Artificial Intelligence **21**, 129–140 (2008)
24. Vomweg, T.W., Buscema, M., Kauczor, H.U., Teifke, A., Intraligi, M., Terzi, S., Heussel, C.P., Achenbach, T., Rieker, O., Mayer, D., Thelen, M.: Improved artificial neural networks in prediction of malignancy of lesions in contrast-enhanced MR-mammography. Medical physics **30**, 2350–2359 (2003)
25. Witten, I.H., Frank, E., Hall, M.A.: Data Mining: Practical Machine Learning Tools and Techniques. Morgan Kaufmann (2011)
26. Zhao, G., Barnard, M., Pietikäinen, M.: Lipreading with local spatiotemporal descriptors. IEEE Transactions on Multimedia **11**, 1254–1265 (2009)
27. Zhao, G., Pietikäinen, M.: Dynamic texture recognition using local binary patterns with an application to facial expressions. IEEE Transactions on Pattern Analysis and Machine Intelligence **29**, 915–928 (2007)
28. Zheng, Y., Englander, S., Baloch, S., Zacharaki, E.I., Fan, Y., Schnall, M.D., Shen, D.: STEP: spatiotemporal enhancement pattern for MR-based breast tumor diagnosis. Medical physics **36**, 3192–3204 (2009)

Kernel Centered Alignment Supervised Metric for Multi-Atlas Segmentation

Mauricio Orbes-Arteaga[1]([✉]), David Cárdenas-Peña[1], Mauricio A. Álvarez[2],
Alvaro A. Orozco[2], and Germán Castellanos-Dominguez[1]

[1] Universidad Nacional de Colombia, Manizales, Colombia
[2] Universidad Tecnológica de Pereira, Pereira, Colombia
hmorbesa@unal.edu.co

Abstract. Recently multi-atlas based methods have been used for supporting brain structure segmentation. These approaches encode the shape variability on a given population and provide prior information. However, the accuracy on the segmentation depend on the capability of the each atlas on the dataset to propagate the labels to the target image. In this sense, the selection of the most relevant atlases becomes an important task. In this paper, a new locally-weighted criterion is proposed to highlight spatial correspondences between images, aiming to enhance multi-atlas based segmentation results. Our proposal combines the spatial correspondences by a linear weighted combination and uses the kernel centered alignment criterion to find the best weight combination. The proposal is tested in an MRI segmentation task for state of the art image metrics as Mean Squares and Mutual Information and it is compared against other weighting criterion methods. Obtained results show that our approach outperforms the baseline methods providing a more suitable atlas selection and improving the segmentation of ganglia basal structures.

Keywords: Magnetic resonance imaging · Image similarity metric · Multi-atlas segmentation · Template selection

1 Introduction

The segmentation of brain structures from magnetic resonance images (MRI) have been used in several medical applications, as pathology progression analysis and brain mapping [1]. Many automatic approaches have been proposed for performing segmentation, being the atlas-based ones the most employed. In these approaches, *a priori* knowledge about the structures of interest, e.g., shape and intensity distribution, can be correctly propagated from *atlases* to a target subject. To this end, the atlases are usually non-linearly mapped to the query image space so that they can be used as segmentation guiding references.

Recently, it has been proved that the use of multiple atlases outperforms single or averaged atlases when each labeled images is accurately aligned with the

© Springer International Publishing Switzerland 2015
V. Murino and E. Puppo (Eds.): ICIAP 2015, Part I, LNCS 9279, pp. 658–667, 2015.
DOI: 10.1007/978-3-319-23231-7_59

target image autonomously and their contributions are finally combined [2]. The most widely used combination approach is the majority voting (also known as label voting or decision fusion) since it leads to fast implementations and accurate performances when the atlases are suitable selected. The majority voting assigns to each spatial element the label agreeing the most number of atlases. For example, the STAPLE algorithm, introduced in [3], is an iterative algorithm that linearly weighs each atlas according to its performance using the expectation maximization. The approach in [4] allows to combine atlases at fine scales by weighting all atlases locally. Presented results show that their proposal outperforms the global atlas weighting in segmentation accuracy. Nevertheless, the mapping or registration of all atlases to a single query subject can be impractical for large image sets since the computational cost increases linearly with the number of atlases. Additionally, if there is a heterogeneous population in the set, the obtained results can be biased because of anatomically unrepresentative images [5].

To overcome these issues, atlas selection approaches have been included in the pipeline so that only the most appropriate candidate segmentations for a given subject are propagated and combined to produce the final result. The selection criterion is usually based on any image similarity metric, being the mutual information one the most popular. Moreover, the same metric can be used to weight the influence of a given atlas in the final segmentation. For instance, authors in [6] select a number of the atlases based on the mutual information between the query and atlas images. However, as the measure is assessed globally, it is biased towards large regions, as the background, instead of the small relevant structures, e.g. basal ganglia. On the other hand, a structure-wise atlas selection is introduced in [7] to segment brain MRIs based on the highest local mutual information. Also in [8], an adaptive method for a local combination is proposed so that a subset of templates and their weighting are estimated independently at image localities. The main drawback of these approaches lies in the requirement of a deformable registration stage for all atlases in order to measure the image similarity. That procedure is computationally more expensive than linearly mapping all the images into a common reference space.

With all the constraints in mind, we propose a new spatially weighting of well-known image metrics for supporting the atlas selection in a multi-atlas-based segmentation scheme. The considered metrics are both the mean squares (MS) and normalized mutual information (NMI), as they are the most employed ones for image registration. Our approach computes independently the metric at regular image partitions; then all partition similarity values are linearly combined to obtain a single similarity value. The combination parameters are properly tuned to match the optimal atlas selection from a pre-labeled image set, being extracted by an offline exhaustive search. Our new linear combination scheme is compared with the global metric assessment, as well as a two other state-of-the-art combination approaches, in a subcortical brain MRI segmentation task. Experiments show that our proposal outperforms the selection results for all considered metrics.

In this paper, image similarity metrics for atlas selection and linear combination criteria are initially introduced. Then, all carried out experiments to evaluate the effectiveness of the metrics for atlas selection/weighting are accurately described and discussed. In the final section, some concluding remarks and future work are considered.

2   Materials and Methods

Let $\mathscr{X} = \{ \boldsymbol{X}^n, \boldsymbol{L}^n : n = 1, \dots, N \}$ be a labeled MRI dataset that holds N image-segmentation pairs, where $\boldsymbol{X}^n = \{ x_r^n \in \mathbb{R} : r \in \Omega \}$ is the n-th MR image, the value r indexes all spatial elements, and the matrix $\boldsymbol{L}^n = \{ l_r^n \in [1, C] : r \in \Omega \}$ is the provided image segmentation into $C \in \mathbb{N}$ classes. In case of 3D volumes, matrix $\boldsymbol{L}^n$ has dimension $\Omega = \mathbb{R}^{T_a \times T_s \times T_c}$, with $\{ T_a, T_s, T_c \}$ being the Axial, Sagittal, and Coronal sizes, respectively.

2.1   Image Similarity Metrics

The similarity of a given image pair, $\{ \boldsymbol{X}^n, \boldsymbol{X}^m \}$, can be measured by using one of the following widely employed metrics:

1. *Mean Squares (MS)*: This metric is based on the average square difference along the space and is embedded into a Gaussian kernel function, so the metric can be read as a bounded similarity as follows:

$$s\{ \boldsymbol{X}^n, \boldsymbol{X}^m \} = \exp \left\{ -\frac{1}{2\sigma^2} \mathbb{E} \left\{ (x_r^n - x_r^m)^2 : \forall r \in \Omega \right\} \right\} \in [0, 1] \qquad (1)$$

   where notation $\mathbb{E} \{ \cdot \}$ stands for the expectation operator and σ is the kernel bandwidth.

2. *Normalized Mutual Information (NMI)*: The information-based similarity between image pairs can be measured by their normalized mutual information in the form:

$$s\{ \boldsymbol{X}^n, \boldsymbol{X}^m \} = \frac{\mathbb{H} \{ \boldsymbol{X}^n \} + \mathbb{H} \{ \boldsymbol{X}^m \}}{\mathbb{H} \{ \boldsymbol{X}^n, \boldsymbol{X}^m \}} - 1 \in [0, 1] \qquad (2)$$

   where the notation $\mathbb{H} \{ \boldsymbol{X}^n, \boldsymbol{X}^m \}$ stands for the joint entropy between $\boldsymbol{X}^n$ and $\boldsymbol{X}^m$.

It is worth noting that MS and NMI have been re-written from their original definition. Thus, the above-introduced metrics share the same interpretation as similarity metrics. That is, $s\{ , \} = 0$ implies a complete mismatch between images, while $s\{ , \} = 1$ means an absolute match achieved only if $\boldsymbol{X}_n = \boldsymbol{X}_m$.

2.2 Spatial Enhancement of Image Metrics

Since the considered metrics are computed over the whole image, they do not account for any local content similarity. Therefore, the measures are biased towards largely similar regions (like the background), masking the relationship between common image structures. Additionally, those similarities lack robustness to artifacts like the spatially varying bias field since this artifact affects the image intensity distribution along the space [9].

The most common approach to overcome these issues is to focus the metric calculation upon local regions and develop a suitable combination of both metrics. To this end, each image $\boldsymbol{X}$ at hand is split into P different regular blocks, Ω_p. Hence, every image is interpreted as a set of non-overlapped blocks $\boldsymbol{X} = \{\boldsymbol{\Xi}_p \in \mathbb{R}^{\rho_a \times \rho_s \times \rho_c} : p \in [1, P]\}$, with $P = \prod_v P_v$, $\rho_v = T_v / P_v$, and P_v the number of partitions along the axis v ($v \in \{a, s, c\}$). Accordingly, a P-dimensional vector of metrics holding each block-wise similarity is calculates in the form:

$$s\{\boldsymbol{X}^n, \boldsymbol{X}^m\} = \{s_p^{n,m} = s\{\boldsymbol{\Xi}_p^n, \boldsymbol{\Xi}_p^m\}; \forall p \in [1, P]\}$$

With the aim to build a new bounded scalar similarity metric, $\zeta \in \mathbb{R}[0, 1]$, we make use of the following linear combination of the block-wise measures:

$$\zeta^{n,m} = \boldsymbol{w}^\top s\{\boldsymbol{X}^n, \boldsymbol{X}^m\}$$

where $\boldsymbol{w} = \{w_p\}$, ($\boldsymbol{w} \in \mathbb{R}^P$) is the weighting combination vector, subject to $\sum_{p=1}^P w_p = 1$. Usually, each weight has to account for the influence of the corresponding region on the resulting metric $\zeta^{n,m}$. According to this, the estimation of $\boldsymbol{w}$ can be assumed dependent on the partition size, which in the case of the equally-sized blocks yields to the following computation [10]:

$$w_p = \frac{\rho_a \rho_s \rho_c}{T_a T_s T_c} = \frac{1}{P}, \tag{3}$$

In this case, the resulting similarity metric results in the average block distance, that is, $\zeta^{n,m} = \mathbb{E}\left\{s\{\boldsymbol{\Xi}_p^n, \boldsymbol{\Xi}_p^m\} : \forall p \in [1, P]\right\}$. Nevertheless, each block holds, in practice, different amount of information depending on whether its content is relevant to the considered task.

For the purpose of implementing the content-dependent weighting, we analyze the contribution of each block in terms of the following two metrics:

$$\textit{Intensity variance: } w_p = \frac{1}{\omega} \mathbb{E}\left\{\text{var}\left\{\boldsymbol{\Xi}_p^n\right\}; \forall n \in [1, N]\right\}, \tag{4a}$$

$$\textit{Information: } w_p = (-\log(\mathbb{E}\left\{s\{\boldsymbol{\Xi}_p^n, \boldsymbol{\Xi}_p^m\} : \forall m, n \in [1, N]\right\}))/\omega, \tag{4b}$$

where $\omega \in \mathbb{R}^+$ is a normalization factor.

2.3 Supervised Image Metric Learning

For improving the segmentation accuracy, we also propose to learn the combination weights grounded on the provided image set segmented from the dataset $\mathscr{X}$.

To this end, a similarity matrix $\boldsymbol{Z_w} \in \mathbb{R}^{N \times N}$ holding all pair-wise metric values, $\{\zeta\{\boldsymbol{X}^n, \boldsymbol{X}^m\} : n, m \in [1, N]\}$, is built as the following linear combination function of the weights:

$$\boldsymbol{Z_w} = \sum_{p=1}^{P} w_p \boldsymbol{S}_p, \tag{5}$$

where $\boldsymbol{S}_p = \{s_p^{n,m} : m, n = 1, \ldots, N\}$ is the similarity matrix attained for the p-th block. Since all considered metrics are bounded similarity measures, $\boldsymbol{S}_p$ as well as their linear combination $\boldsymbol{Z_w}$ are examples of a positive definite symmetric (PDS) kernel matrix.

Here,   we   make   use
of the PDS kernel matrix $\boldsymbol{K} = \{k^{n,m} : m, n = 1, \ldots, N\} \in \mathbb{R}^{N \times N}$ to learn the similarity metric ζ through the kernel centered alignment (KCA) measure. Namely, we search for optimal weight vector w_p^* maximizing the correlation between $\boldsymbol{Z_w}$ and the objective kernel matrix $\boldsymbol{K}$ as follows:

$$\boldsymbol{w}^* = \max_{\boldsymbol{w}} \frac{\langle \boldsymbol{Z'_w}, \boldsymbol{K'} \rangle_F}{\|\boldsymbol{Z'_w}\|_F \|\boldsymbol{K'}\|_F}, \tag{6}$$

where notations $\langle \cdot, \cdot \rangle_F$ and $|\cdot|$ stand for the inner product and the Frobenius norm, respectively. $\boldsymbol{Z'_w}$ and $\boldsymbol{K'}$ are the centered kernel versions of $\boldsymbol{Z_w}$ and $\boldsymbol{K}$. Here, we compute the centered version of $\boldsymbol{\Gamma}$ as $\boldsymbol{\Gamma'} = \boldsymbol{H} \boldsymbol{\Gamma} \boldsymbol{H}$, where $\boldsymbol{H} = [\boldsymbol{I} - \boldsymbol{1} \boldsymbol{1}^\top / N]$, and $\boldsymbol{1} \in \mathbb{R}^{N \times 1}$ is the all-ones vector. Generally, the solution for $\boldsymbol{w}$ in the optimization problem of ?? is as follows [11]:

$$\boldsymbol{w} = \frac{\boldsymbol{A}^{-1} \boldsymbol{b}}{\|\boldsymbol{A}^{-1} \boldsymbol{b}\|_2}, \; \boldsymbol{A} \in \mathbb{R}^{P \times P}, \boldsymbol{b} \in \mathbb{R}^{P \times 1} \tag{7}$$

where   the   buffer   arrangements   are   determined   as
$\boldsymbol{A} = \{a_{pq} = \langle \boldsymbol{S'_p}, \boldsymbol{S'_q} \rangle_F; \forall p, q \in [1, P]\}$ and $\boldsymbol{b} = \{b_p = \langle \boldsymbol{S'_p}, \boldsymbol{K'} \rangle_F\}$.

In order to achieve an image similarity function more related to the segmentation, the knowledge about the expected labels can be included within the optimization framework of ??. In particular, we learn the kernel parameters in a supervised scheme by making each one equals to the Dice Index similarity measuring the accuracy of segmentation between the atlases and defined as:

$$k^{n,m} = 2\langle \boldsymbol{L}^n, \boldsymbol{L}^m \rangle / (\|\boldsymbol{L}^n\|_1 + \|\boldsymbol{L}^m\|_1) \tag{8}$$

where notation $\|\cdot\|_1$ stands for the 1-norm.

Therefore, the attained measure can be used to select a subset of the most similar atlases to a target image so that the segmentation is improved. For accomplishing the segmentation, a weighted majority voting scheme is employed since it is the most widely used label fusion algorithm for multi-atlas-based segmentation approaches. Such a system provides a single label for each spell determined by collecting weighted votes from all the contributions over the selected templates and assigning the label with the highest vote to each voxel.

So, let $\mathscr{X}_T = \{X^t, L^t : t=1,\ldots T\}$ a set of T selected atlases and $\hat{L}^t$ be the estimated segmentation after deformable registration to the target image. Provided the similarity measure s^t between the target image and the selected atlases X^t, matrix $\hat{L}^t$ assigns the label $\hat{L}(r)$ to each spel r, the final segmentation for the spels on the target image $O(r)$ is given by:

$$O(r) = \max_{\forall c}\{O_1(r),\ldots,O_C(r),\ldots,O_C(r)\}$$

where $O_c(r) = \sum_{t=1,T} \delta_c^n(r)$ and $\delta_c^n(r) = \begin{cases} s^t, & c=\hat{L}^t(r) \\ 0, & \text{otherwise} \end{cases}$

3 Experimental Setup

We evaluate the performance of all the above-introduced metrics to measure the contribution of each atlas on a final segmentation over a selected atlas. Thus evaluation of the the used supervised similarity metric for MRI segmentation appraises the following stages: i) Image preprocessing, ii) Metric parameter learning, and iii) Evaluation of the Similarity Metric.

3.1 Database and Image Preprocessing

For experimentation, We use the dataset evaluated in the contest *MICCAI 2012-Multi-Atlas Labeling and Statistical Fusion*[1].More concretely, we employ the subset data collection, termed Open Access Series of Imaging Studies (OASIS) database, that T1-weighted structural MRI scans from 35 subjects (13 males and 22 females), aging from 18 to 90 years. Due to our research interest in Parkinson surgery, only the following structures are considered: hypothalamus (HYPO), amygdala (AMYG), putamen (PUT), caudate nucleus (CAUD), thalamus (THAL) and pallidum (PAL). figure 1 shows a sample image subject and the accessible segmentation.

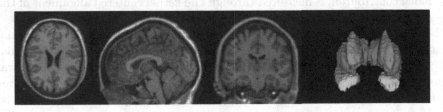

Fig. 1. Left to Right: Axial, Sagittal, Coronal views, and ground-truth segmented structures.

For the sake of comparison within a single common space, all images are spatially normalized into the Talairach space where each image is rigidly aligned to

[1] https://masi.vuse.vanderbilt.edu/workshop2012

the ICBM atlas (MNI305-template). This normalization allows properly extracting the morphological feature set from each considered image. To this end, the Advanced Normalization Tool (ANTS) is employed with a quaternion-based mapping and MI metric as parameters.

For the label propagation, every pre-labelled dataset image has to be spatially mapped into the query image spatial coordinates (*target space*) with a non-linear transformation so that query and atlas images match the best. The registration procedure is performed using the ANTS tool under default parameters: elastic deformation as the mapping function (Elast), MI as the similarity metric, and 32-bins histograms for estimating the probability density functions. In order to get a finer alignment, the registration is performed at three sequential resolution levels: *i)* the coarsest alignment with a resolution of $1/8 \times$ *Original space*, and 100 iterations, *ii)* the middle resolution $1/4 \times$ *Original space* and 50 iterations, and *iii)* the finest deformation with a resolution of $1/2 \times$ *Original space* parameter and 25 iterations, the Gaussian regularization method is employed ($\sigma=3$).

3.2   Metric Parameter Learning

Since localities of the image may provide information distinctly, each similarity metric is assessed independently in different regions of the image. To this end, the MRI volumes are regularly partitioned into $P=27$ blocks (3 partitions along each dimension). Upon this partitioned set, the metric is pair-wise computed as a weighted linear combination of all local measures.

Aiming to estimate the contribution of each block to a single metric, we consider four different approaches for computing the block weights. a) each block is assumed to have equal contribution to the similarity metric, so the resulting similarity metric becomes the averaging of local measures. b) We assume that regions with large intensity changes among the structures should provide a major contribution to the similarity metric than regions with homogeneous intensity values. Thus, the block weight is computed as the average intensity variance (equation (4a)). c) The contribution of the regions is the same as in the case b), but the block contribution is assessed by the local entropy in equation (4b). d) The block contribution is measured through the kernel centered alignment of the supervised kernel matrix.

figure 2 shows the 3D scatter plot of all resulting weights with their spatial location in the image partition, where the color and size are directly proportional to the value. It is worth noting that the larger weights are located in the central region for all metrics. This fact may be explained mainly due to the structures located in the center of the brain, namely, the basal ganglia.

3.3   Similarity Metric Evaluation

In order to assesses the images similarity measures describe above, each of them is used for select the closes atlases to a query image and the similarity values are used as weights in a weighted majority vote method. Then the quality of the segmentation for all considered structures is assessed by the Dice Index similarity

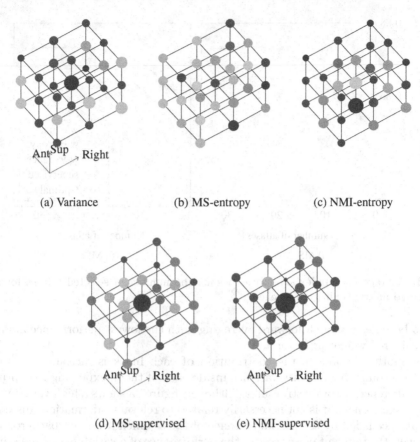

(a) Variance   (b) MS-entropy   (c) NMI-entropy

(d) MS-supervised   (e) NMI-supervised

Fig. 2. Resulting weight distribution for the variance criterion and all considered metrics. Markers are located at the center of each partition. Color and size are directly proportional to weight parameter value.

between L_c and O_c as in equation (8), comparing the c-th labeling class on the resulting segmentation, O, against the one on the provided ground-truth, L. The results for multi-atlas segmentation with all templates selected in the common space for all metrics are shown in figure 3

4   Discussion and Concluding Remarks

We propose a new spatially weighting criterion aiming to enhance image similarity metrics. Resulting metrics are used in a multi-atlas segmentation scheme for selecting a subset of the most relevant atlases and weighting their contribution to the final segmentation. For the sake of comparison, three unsupervised criteria are considered, namely, size, variance, and entropy weighting. Attained results show that the supervised scheme outperforms all of the baselines on spatially weighting mean squares a normalized mutual information metrics. Specifically for the size-based weighting, when regular partitions are considered, the resulting

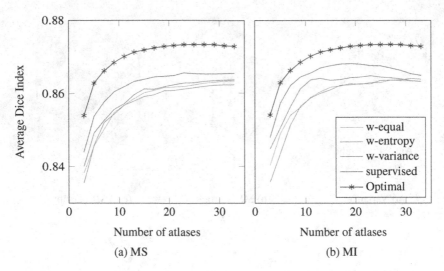

Fig. 3. Average Dice Index similarities versus the number of selected atlases for all considered metric tuning approaches.

metric becomes a straightforward averaging with the lowest performance among all considered weighting criteria.

As another approach, the contribution of each block is measured by taking into account the intensity variance inside each of them, expecting to capture shape differences in brain structures. Although figure 2a shows a high variance in some image corners, it is not necessarily related to relevant information. Instead, this variance is led by the partial presence of the scanned head and background. Moreover, the inherent noise reduces the performance of a variability-based criterion. The third approach assesses the relevance of each partition as the information provided by each block for the whole database, which is measured in terms of the entropy function. This criterion shows a different weight distribution for both, mean squares and mutual information metrics. In the case of mean squares, the computed entropy assigns similar weights for each the partitions (figure 2b). In the case of mutual information, the highest weight is assigned to the near neck region as shown in figure 2c. Although such an area has a high information due to the subcortical structures contained on it, the background presence can bias the result.

Finally, our proposal makes use of a supervised kernel matrix to learn the most appropriate combination weights so that resulting similarity metric between a pair of images is highly related to the similarity of their provided labelings. To this end, the kernel centered alignment between the supervised kernel, and the image kernel is maximized with respect to the weight values. An advantage of our proposal is that the closed form to the kernel alignment solution provides an easy implementation for weights computation, while the construction of supervised kernel matrix is carried out only once offline. As a result, we can employ the attained metric as an atlas weighting and selection criterion. Therefore, the similarity-based atlas ranking correlates accurately with the segmentation accuracy for subcortical structures. Additionally, the learned metric showed to provide a subset of atlases for each target image so that the segmentation accuracy is larger than the regular label propagation using the whole dataset. It is also important to highlight that achieved performance is close to the weighting obtained from the supervised kernel matrix.

As a future work, new similarity metric combination approaches can be considered for the introduce supervised framework, as they can take advantage of different relationships between image partitions. For instance, a gain factor for each weight can be used to span the combination weights distribution. Also, new experiments for evaluating the metric for different demographic categories as age, gender, and neurodegenerative disease, as well as, presence of tumors will be performed. This is because every morphological change will be reflected into the measure performance.

Acknowledgments. This work was supported by *Programa Nacional de Formación de Investigadores "Generación del Bicentenario"*, 2011/2012 funded by COLCIENCIAS and the research project number 111065740687, both funded by COLCIENCIAS.

References

1. Joshi, S., Davis, B., Jomier, M., Gerig, G.: Unbiased diffeomorphic atlas construction for computational anatomy. NeuroImage **23**(Suppl 1), S151–S160 (2004)
2. Rohlfing, T., Brandt, R., et al.: Quo vadis, atlas-based segmentation. In: Suri, J., Wilson, D., Laxminarayan, S. (eds.) Handbook of Biomedical Image Analysis. Topics in Biomedical Engineering International Book Series, pp. 435–486. Springer, US (2005)
3. Warfield, S.K., Zou, K.H., Wells, W.M.: Simultaneous truth and performance level estimation (staple). IEEE Trans. on Med. Imag. **23**(7), 903–921 (2004)
4. Artaechevarria, X., Munoz-Barrutia, A., Ortiz-de Solorzano, C.: Combination strategies in multi-atlas image segmentation. IEEE Trans. on Med. Imag
5. Aljabar, P., Heckemann, R., et al.: Multi-atlas based segmentation of brain images: atlas selection and its effect on accuracy. NeuroImage **46**(3), 726–738 (2009)
6. Klein, S., van der Heide, U., et al.: Automatic segmentation of the prostate in 3d mr images by atlas matching using localized mutual information. Med. Physics **35**(4), 1407–1417 (2008)
7. Wu, M., Rosano, C., et al.: Optimum template selection for atlas-based segmentation. NeuroImage
8. van Rikxoort, E.M., Isgum, I., et al.: Adaptive local multi-atlas segmentation: application to the heart and the caudate nucleus. Medical Image Analysis
9. Rivaz, H., Karimaghaloo, Z., Collins, D.L.: Self-similarity weighted mutual information: a new nonrigid image registration metric. Medical Image Analysis **18**(2), 343–358 (2014)
10. Studholme, C., Drapaca, C., et al.: Deformation-based mapping of volume change from serial brain mri in the presence of local tissue contrast change. IEEE Trans. on Med. Imag., 626–639, May 2006
11. Cortes, C., Mohri, M., Rostamizadeh, A.: Algorithms for learning kernels based on centered alignment. The Journal of Machine Learning Research **13**(1), 795–828 (2012)

Multimedia

Emotions in Abstract Art: Does Texture Matter?

Andreza Sartori[1,2]($\boxtimes$), Berhan Şenyazar[3], Alkim Almila Akdag Salah[4],
Albert Ali Salah[3], and Nicu Sebe[1]

[1] DISI, University of Trento, Trento, Italy
{andreza.sartori,sebe}@disi.unitn.it
[2] SKIL Lab, Telecom Italia, Trento, Italy
[3] Bogazici University, Istanbul, Turkey
{berhan.senyazar,salah}@boun.edu.tr
[4] University of Amsterdam, Amsterdam, The Netherlands
alelma@ucla.edu

Abstract. The classification of images based on the emotions they evoke
is a recent approach in multimedia. With the abundance of digitized
images from museum archives and the ever-growing digital production
of user-generated images, there is a greater need for intelligent image
retrieval algorithms. Categorization of images according to their emotional impact offers a useful addition to the state of the art in image
search. In this work, we apply computer vision techniques on abstract
paintings to automatically predict emotional valence based on texture.
We also propose a method to derive a small set of features (Perlin
parameters) from an image to represent its overall texture. Finally, we
investigate the saliency distribution in these images, and show that computational models of bottom-up attention can be used to predict emotional valence in a parsimonious manner.

Keywords: Abstract paintings · Emotion recognition · Perlin images ·
Saliency · Eye-tracking

1 Introduction

During the centuries various art movements and artists used different tools and
techniques to embed feelings in artworks. Art historians and artists have sought
to describe this process via theories based on intuition, observation and experiments [1,7]. These rules incorporate the understanding of experts of the domain.
It is also possible to look at this process from a reductionistic perspective and
use visual perception models to understand it as a brain process [11]. Computer
vision can be positioned between these approaches, as by virtue of descriptors of
various levels of complexity, it can reveal new rules, or help us validate or change
the existing ones. It may also be used to describe statistically what makes a painting to be perceived as emotional, or why certain parts of a painting command
more attention.

© Springer International Publishing Switzerland 2015
V. Murino and E. Puppo (Eds.): ICIAP 2015, Part I, LNCS 9279, pp. 671–682, 2015.
DOI: 10.1007/978-3-319-23231-7_60

In this work we aim at assessing the contribution of texture to the emotional perception of abstract paintings. The latter choice is motivated by a need to reduce the effect of semantics (or top-down information) as much as possible. There is no doubt that the top-down information is more prominent in creating feelings. This is, however, difficult to analyse automatically, and the information obtained from such analysis would be at a different level. The information we extract from the bottom-up, or low level feature analysis can be useful in terms of assessing and using technique, rather than content. Yanulevskaya et al. [23] have previously assessed the informativeness of colour in estimating emotions induced by artworks, and made their database available. In this study, we look at the contribution of texture, and its relation to colour.

We determine the negative and/or positive feelings induced by the artwork with a user study, and make our annotations publicly available. We use two approaches for characterizing texture in artworks. The first approach is a classifier based on SIFT descriptors. The second approach is based on a study that evaluated textures for the perception of masculinity-femininity, heaviness-lightness, and hardness-softness perception [12]. In this work, we derive texture parameters for each artwork and use the psychophysical model proposed in [12]. To obtain this parametrization, we derive MR8 texture feature descriptors of [21], and train a classifier that maps these features to Perlin texture parameters [17].

We postulate that the contribution of colour to the feelings created by the artwork is more prominent than texture, but a combination of colour and texture may improve our models. To assess texture with respect to colour, we report a second user study that replicates the first, but this time with coloured images. We illustrate that the coloured and non-coloured versions of artworks have low, but visible correlation in the feelings they invoke in their viewers.

Finally, we look at image saliency to analyse qualitatively what features people associate with positive and negative feelings. We report an eye gaze study conducted with original and gray-scale artworks, and contrast it with predictions of a computational bottom-up saliency model. The high predictive power of the computational model establishes that the bottom-up estimation is reliable, and we are justified in our usage of abstract art for reducing the top-down effects. Furthermore, it suggests that by disabling the colour in the computational model, we can predict the eye gaze patterns in non-coloured images, and perform an analysis based on this.

Our main contributions are: (1) we study the role of texture and propose an inverse-Perlin parametrization to enable a psychophysical model on feelings induced by abstract paintings; (2) we apply a bottom-up saliency model to abstract paintings and analyse the relation between its predictions and the human fixations; (3) we implement a classifier that gives positive/negative feeling decisions for the study of abstract paintings, which can be useful for image retrieval, art historians, researchers and museum curators.

2   Related Work

Abstract artists were concerned about the basic elements of visual art and how these elements and their various compositions affect the viewer. They have extensively debated and written about these elements, and tested their theories via the use of their artworks. Hence, abstract art offers a good ground if one wants to study visual fundamentals and what emotions they generate in the viewer [15].

The visual texture is an intuitive part of the human sensory input and it can influence the human perception and emotions. Indeed, texture has been subject of study in many areas including psychophysics and computer science. Simmons and Russell [19], investigated the emotional effect of ten different visual textures on colours. They reported that, depending on a certain texture class, add texture to colours change significantly the humans raking of unpleasant colours. Kim et al. [8] extracted colour, texture and pattern features from textile images to predict humans emotions. The authors show that, their proposed textile indexing system was effective for predicting human emotions based on textile images. Thumfart et al. [20] used a layered prediction model to predict the human aesthetic judgments given a computational texture feature. These and others studies aim to simulate the human perception on texture in order to improve the computational representations for classification and segmentation.

Several works in computer vision that focuses on emotion recognition has used texture as one of the features to recognize emotions in images and artworks. Yanulevskaya et al. [22] proposed an emotion categorization system, trained on the International Affective Picture System (IAPS) [9], which is based on the assessment of local image statistics followed by supervised learning of emotion categories using Support Vector Machines. In [13], low-level features were combined with concepts from psychology and art theory for categorization of emotion in affective images and artworks. They obtained better accuracy in affective categorization of semantically rich images in comparison with abstract paintings that were relatively free of semantics. In [23] a Bag-of-Visual-Words model was trained to classify abstract paintings in positive or negative emotions. With the Backprojection technique they determined which parts of the paintings evoke which emotions. Recently, [24] applied multiple kernel learning framework for affective classification of digital abstract art images. These and the other studies extensively rely on colour in predicting affective content. There are scarcely any studies that investigate texture independent of colour for this problem.

3   Texture Analysis

Texture can give the beholder a 'visual sense' of the artwork composition, which is almost multimodal, in that it can invoke tactile associations. In abstract art, feelings of hardness, softness, smoothness, etc. can be created via texture, and we postulate that texture is an integral element of the feeling induced by the artwork (regardless of the artist intentions). To analyse how texture affects feelings in abstract paintings, we have conducted a user-study of positive and negative feelings invoked by abstract paintings with no hue value.

3.1   MART Dataset: A Dataset of Abstract Paintings

We conduct our analyses on the publicly available set of 500 abstract paintings from the electronic archive of the Museum of Modern and Contemporary Art of Trento and Rovereto (MART), collected by [23]. The paintings chosen for the dataset are from 78 artists, including Wassily Kandinsky, Luigi Veronesi, and Carlo Belli. These artists are particularly distinct by their studies of abstract art and its characteristics, in terms of colour, shapes and texture. For studying texture only, we have prepared a gray-scale version of this dataset.

3.2   User Study for Assessing Feelings Induced by Abstract Paintings

To collect the ground truth of gray-scale version of MART dataset, we use the relative score method from our previous work [18] by asking people to choose the more positive painting in a pair. Our assumption is that judging between two images, placed side by side, is a relatively straightforward setting. The following instruction was provided: "Which painting in the pair looks more positive to you? Let your instinct guide you and follow your first impression of the paintings."

The method to annotate the paintings in positive and negative feeling and the scoring procedure is based on the TrueSkill ranking system [5,16]. The TrueSkill ranking system, developed by Microsoft Research for Xbox Live, identifies and ranks the skills of the players of a game and matches players with similar skills for a new game. With this method, the annotation task is more manageable, as it gives a representative annotation with only 3,750 pairs of paintings, instead of 124,750 comparisons ($500 * (500 - 1) * 0.5$) in case each painting is compared with all the remaining paintings in the dataset.

During the annotation process, we consider that all paintings initially have the same 'skills' and the painting which is chosen as more positive in a single trial wins a 'game'. Then, the rankings of the compared paintings are updated. Afterwards, the paintings with similar rankings are compared, until each painting is compared with at least 15 other paintings. The results are considered as feeling scores of the paintings, which lower values correspond to negative feelings and the higher values to positive feelings. 55 subjects participated in the annotation task, 22 females and 33 males, respectively. Each subject annotated from 5 to 334 pairs of paintings, 67 paintings on average. The subjects participated voluntarily and were free to annotate at any time they wanted.[1]

We have no overlapping annotations, as the rating system determines the annotation sampling online, and never presents the same pair of images to two different annotators. This makes the computation of an inter-annotator agreement impossible. We have, however, matched the TrueSkill ratings obtained at the end of the user study to the individual annotations of the pairs, presented to all the annotators. The results show about 79% agreement, which is effectively

---

[1] The dataset with its respective ground truth is publicly available at: http://disi.unitn.it/~sartori/datasets/

Table 1. Texture emotion scales based on Perlin parameters (from [12]). Emotion scales are MF: masculinity-femininity, HS: hardness-softness, HL: heaviness-lightness, given as a function of mean intensity (L) and parameters of Perlin noise texture (oct: octaves, freq: frequency, pers: persistence, lac: lacunarity).

Emotion Scale	Function Predicting Absolute Scale Values
MF	$101.36 + 9.27L^{0.1} - 30.06oct^{0.05} - 6.06freq^{0.3} - 53.38pers^{0.1} - 25.15lac^{0.1}$
HS	$116.12 + 6.10L^{0.1} - 32.30oct^{0.05} - 13.13freq^{0.1} - 48.81pers^{0.1} - 29.33lac^{0.1}$
HL	$42.67 + 0.064L - 12.46oct^{0.05} - 11.35freq^{0.1} - 5.84pers^{0.5} - 17.23lac^{0.05}$

the mean human performance for the valence classification task, and represents an upper bound for the automatic algorithm.

The distribution of gray-scale paintings from the most negative to the most positive annotation scores is illustrated in Fig. 1 (a). To better visualize the results, we arrange the paintings in a matrix 50×10, where the paintings are sorted in reading order from the most negative to the most positive. From the annotation results, we observe that lightness is a determinant factor of positive and negative feelings. Paintings with low value of overall intensity (nearly black) are considered as more negative. Itten [7] postulates that neutral gray is a characterless, mute, indifferent, achromatic colour, and the number of distinguishable shades of gray depends on the sensitivity of the eye. This may be the reason of the mixed distribution. Another factor effecting the ranking from negative to positive seems to be in the structural qualities of the paintings, i.e. some very dark paintings with light spots are considered positive, probably due to their composition and the way they use light colors. We also note that the ordering of the paintings is quite different compared to the ordering induced by coloured images. Compared to the distribution of coloured images, one can say that gray-scale ranking is more dependent on the composition of the paintings, whereas in coloured images colour itself plays a much more important role in determining the overall positive/negativeness of the painting.

3.3 Inverse Perlin Parametrization

A psychophysical experiment assessing the effect of texture on color emotion was conducted by Lucassen et al. [12] using Perlin images. They presented the subjects with textured image patches in varying colours and asked subjects to place those images on four emotion[2] scales: warmness-coolness, masculinity-femininity, hardness-softness and heaviness-lightness. As a result of their experiment, the authors performed a regression analysis and established parametric relations between the Perlin images and the subject classifications (Table 1).

---

[2] We use the word 'emotion' following the terminology of [12], but in general 'emotion' may be a strong word for what we are assessing, and 'feeling' is more appropriate in this context.

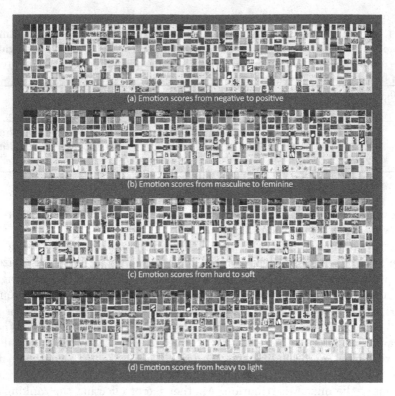

Fig. 1. MART dataset depicted as thumbnails. The paintings in (a) are ordered by TrueSkill scores from the most negative to the most positive. The paintings in (b), (c) and (d) are ordered by computing Perlin parameters and using the psychophysical model. High resolutions of these images are available at: http://disi.unitn.it/∼sartori/datasets/

Perlin images are textures created using Perlin noise, which is a method to create a parameterized, pseudo-random noise [17]. We used the same library [2] used by [12] to generate those images. They have four parameters: octave, frequency, persistence and lacunarity. The computation of these parameters for a given image can provide us with a parsimonious and informative representation of the texture features.

To determine the Perlin parameters for any given image, we developed an inverse Perlin method, which consists of extraction of texture features of Perlin images and machine learning to give us Perlin parameters from those features. To extract texture features from the raw images, we used the MR8 texture descriptors of [21]. These features are low dimensional, include rotational invariance properties, and allow us to perform parameter interpolation from a single image.

To create the MR8 texture descriptors and train our classifier, we create a gallery of Perlin images with different appearances for each parameter set used by [12], and take the convolution of the these images with the designated filter bank. The responses, called textons, are clustered using k-Means clustering algorithm, following the procedure of [21]. From a given image, the textons are extracted and their histograms are formed, then used as feature vectors in the classifiers. We used Extreme Learning Machines (ELM), a single-hidden layer feedforward network implementation for classifying the Perlin parameters [6]. Essentially, what we propose is to create a rich training set of Perlin images (i.e. the gallery), and derive the texton histograms for each such image. Then for a given probe image, we extract its texton histogram, and use it as an input to a classifier that outputs the corresponding Perlin parameters. An overview of the method is presented in Fig. 2. Using those parameters and the formulae of Table 1, we calculated the predicted emotion scores for each image.

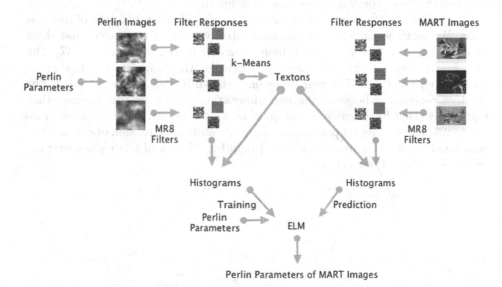

Fig. 2. Schema of the Inverse Perlin Method

Fig. 1 shows MART paintings sorted by emotion scores. The paintings sorted from heavy to light (Fig. 1(d)) follow a luminosity pattern. The distribution of hard to soft (Fig. 1(c)) has a similar pattern: in general, the darker a painting, the harder it is scored. However, 'texture' itself plays a great importance in the distribution of images from 'hard' to 'soft'. This observation is in agreement with the results of [12] which reports the hard-soft scales independency of colour and its dominance by texture. Hence the parameters that bring texture to the fore, such as brushstrokes, complexity, composition become essential elements. Paintings with chaotic structure and granular patterns are ranked as hard, whereas paintings with geometrical structure, neat lines and a look of 'matte' finish are ranked as soft. We observe a similar pattern in the distribution of masculine-feminine (Fig. 1(b)): dark and chaotic paintings seem to be more masculine, whereas light and simple designs are feminine. This observation again supports the findings of [12], when they report the effect of texture as being most influential in the hard-soft scale, followed by masculine-feminine, and then heavy-light.

3.4 Coloured vs. Gray-Scale Images

The user study we conducted produced valence ratings of paintings viewed in gray-scale. We compare these ratings with the results of our previous work [18] obtained by using the coloured version of the paintings. In [18] 25 subjects (11 females, 14 males) participated in the annotation. Each person annotated from 145 paintings on average. Even though the annotation approach is essentially the same in both studies (but with different sets of subjects performing the evaluation), we could observe that there was a low correlation between the preferences of subjects (linear correlation coefficient: 0.3674).

Fig.3 displays the relation between the results of these two sets of annotations. We sort the paintings by the annotated valence in gray-scale, and show these values in a black line that monotonically increases from 4 to 47. The scattered points are the valence annotations for the same images, but made on coloured paintings. The regression line, shown in red, shows the small but positive correlation between the two annotations. These results suggest that texture by itself has a smaller contribution for the positive and negative emotional valence of coloured paintings compared to the contribution of colour. The emotional valence of gray-scale images (including black and white photographs) should be assessed independently.

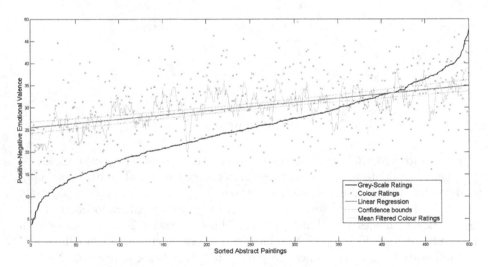

Fig. 3. Correlation between annotations of gray-scale and coloured paintings. The x axis shows the paintings index sorted by valence. The black line indicates the valence ranking on gray-scale dataset. The blue crosses are the rankings for these images on coloured dataset. The green line illustrates the mean filtered results on the coloured set, and the red line shows the linear regression fit to the ratings on the coloured set. The small positive correlation manifests itself in the slope of the red line.

4   Visual Attention and Emotional Content

When making a valence judgment, different parts of a painting may influence a subject in different ways. One way of analysing which parts are most influential in the evaluation is to track the subject's gaze while he or she looks at the painting. Another way is to use a computational model that can simulate the gaze behaviour of a subject. We have used abstract artworks in this study to minimize the effect of semantics in the attribution of positive and negative feelings. It is postulated that attention is driven by a combination of bottom-up and top-down components, the former being data-driven, and the latter depending on higher level cognitive factors like intentions, context, knowledge, and such [4]. Most computational models of attention are bottom-up, as the top-down part is extremely complex and very difficult to model. If our premises hold, we expect that the visual attention while viewing abstract paintings will mostly be a bottom-up process, especially in the absence of narratives that may direct the subject to look at an image in a particular way.

To validate this, we compare the predictions of a successful computational saliency model, implemented by Dirk and Koch [3], with the eye-tracking results we had previously obtained on the MART dataset [23]. In [23] we analysed whether people prefer to look at positive or negative parts of paintings. Guided by a user study that established ground truth of valence for coloured paintings, we have trained a valence classifier based on the Bag-of-Visual-Words approach. We used colour features described by LAB and SIFT descriptors. We have then labelled parts of images using the valence classifier. By comparing averaged pixel-wise contributions from fixated and non-fixated locations with the classifier outputs, we concluded that there is a positive attention bias when people look at abstract paintings, meaning that positive visual words have more important contribution in fixated locations, compared to non-fixated locations.

We replicate the eye-tracking study of [23] on the gray-scale version of the abstract paintings with 12 participants (8 male and 4 female). To present the stimuli we used the ASL Eye-Trac 6 software in a full-size 19 inch screen (ASUS VW192T+, 1680x1050 resolution). To collect the data we follow the same procedure of [23]. The results show positive attention bias (63%) when people look at the paintings with no colour. Only 4 paintings present neutral attention bias.

Subsequently, we believe that inspecting the distribution of saliency over the images in our study can be potentially informative. The saliency algorithm of [3] is partly a reimplementation of the iNVT toolkit, in which the colour features, intensity, edges, etc. are evaluated over the visual scene independently before being integrated into a saliency master map that shows what part of the visual scene is interesting.

We first establish whether computational models do a good job in predicting the gaze patterns of subjects on abstract paintings. We use the Fixation Analysis Software of Le Meur [10] to compare predictions of the computational model of attention (i.e. using Dirk and Koch's software) with the eye fixation ground truth data that was made available with the MART dataset for coloured paintings and the ground truth results collected for gray-scale paintings.

The Area Under the Curve (AUC), computed from the ROC curve, is the suggested method of assessing similarity of these streams. An AUC value of 0.50 indicates random performance, where 1.00 denotes a perfect match. The average AUC between eye-fixation ground truth and simulations of the computational model of attention was 0.93 for colored paintings and 0.94 for gray-scale. These results indicate that 1) the bottom-up computational approach is a good substitute for the eye-tracking study, and can be used to find the salient locations of abstract paintings; 2) there is little difference in salient locations for coloured and gray-scale paintings. While colour is the dominant modality for inducing feelings, texture dominates in guiding the attention of the subject.

5   Classifying Positive and Negative Images

In this section we describe a classification approach to automatically estimate the emotional valence of a given painting. Our approach is a standard bag-of-words paradigm based on SIFT descriptors, extracted from either a dense grid over the image, or just from salient locations. We train a Support Vector Machine with a histogram intersection kernel for supervised learning, using the fast approximation of [14]. The TrueSkill ratings are used as ground truth labels.

For testing the approach, a 5×2 cross validation setup is used, where the images are assigned to folds randomly. Table 2 shows the classification results. We have obtained a 73.0% correct classification rate when the entire images were used, which is close to the 79.0% human classification rate reported in Sect. 3.2. Using the computational saliency model described in the previous section, and extracting SIFT features from only the top 2.5% most salient locations in the image with the same experimental setup gives a classification rate of 73.9%. The difference is not significant (as established by a t-test), but a much smaller portion of the painting is evaluated for reaching this accuracy. Using the inverse Perlin coefficients, and the emotional scales of Lucassen et al. that are derived from these coefficients with a Support Vector Machine classifier directly results in an accuracy of 62.0%. The primary reason is that the latter set of descriptors are very parsimonious, compared to the SIFT-based descriptors, and while useful in qualitative evaluation, do not contain enough discriminatory power for automatic classification.

Table 2. Classification Results.

Type	Correct Classification Rate
Entire image	73.0%
Only top 2.5% most salient parts	73.9%
Emotions derived from Perlin parameters	62.0%
Human classification rate (upper bound)	79.0%

6   Conclusions

In this work we studied how texture affects the positive and negative feelings evoked by abstract paintings. To this effect, we conducted a user study to establish a ground truth of emotional valence for 500 abstract paintings with no hue value. The analysis of annotations revealed that people reacted differently to gray-scale versions of paintings when annotating the emotional content. Our experiments confirmed that colour played a greater role than texture in emotional assessment, yet the effect of texture was visible. We proposed an inverse-Perlin parametrization method to map a given image to a four-dimensional representation of its overall texture content. We have used this parametrization in a psychophysical model to depict the paintings in several emotional scales. A quantitative analysis showed that texture was especially influential in giving an impression of hardness and softness.

Existing computational models of attention use colour and texture jointly to predict where the bottom-up attention of a subject will be directed, and as we have observed via eye tracking studies, they make a good job of predicting attention in abstract paintings. It is quite interesting that these models, when used on gray-scale versions of the paintings, predict very similar saliency maps. This may be partly due to the abstract nature of the images, and partly due the prominence of texture-based channels over colour-based channels in the computational approach. However, the user study we report in this paper established that the feelings induced by gray-scale images are quite different than the feelings induced by their coloured counterparts.

References

1. Arnheim, R.: Art and Visual Perception: A Psychology of the Creative Eye. University of California Press (2004)
2. Bevins, J.: Libnoise library (2007). http://libnoise.sourceforge.net/ (accessed March 23, 2015)
3. Dirk, W., Koch, C.: Modeling attention to salient proto-objects. Neural Networks **19**, 1395–1407 (2006)
4. Frintrop, S.: Computer Analysis of Human Behavior. In: Computational Visual Attention. Advances in Pattern Recognition. Springer (2011)
5. Herbrich, R., Graepel, T.: Trueskill(tm): A bayesian skill rating system. no. MSR-TR-2006-80 (2006)
6. Huang, G., Zhu, Q., Siew, C.: Extreme learning machine: a new learning scheme of feedforward neural networks. IJCNN. **2**, 985–990 (2004)
7. Itten, J.: The Art of Color: The Subjective Experience and Objective Rationale of Color. Wiley (1974)
8. Kim, S., Kim, E.Y., Jeong, K.J., Kim, J.-I.: Emotion-based textile indexing using colors, texture and patterns. In: Bebis, G., et al. (eds.) ISVC 2006. LNCS, vol. 4292, pp. 9–18. Springer, Heidelberg (2006)
9. Lang, P.J., Bradley, M.M., Cuthbert, B.N.: International affective picture system (iaps): Technical manual and affective ratings (1999)

10. Le Meur, O., Baccino, T.: Methods for comparing scanpaths and saliency maps: strengths and weaknesses. Behavior Research Methods 45(1), 251–266 (2012)
11. Leder, H., Gerger, G., Dressler, S.G., Schabmann, A.: How art is appreciated. Psychology of Aesthetics, Creativity, and the Arts. 6(1) (2012)
12. Lucassen, M.P., Gevers, T., Gijsenij, A.: Texture affects color emotion. Color Research & Application 36(6), 426–436 (2011)
13. Machajdik, J., Hanbury, A.: Affective image classification using features inspired by psychology and art theory. In: ACM Multimedia (2010)
14. Maji, S., Berg, A.C., Malik, J.: Classification using intersection kernel support vector machines is efficient. In: CVPR (2008)
15. Moholy-Nagy, L.. In Defense of "Abstract" Art. The Journal of Aesthetics and Art Criticism 4 (1945)
16. Moser, J.: True skill library (2010). https://github.com/moserware/Skills/ (accessed March 23, 2015)
17. Perlin, K.: An image synthesizer. ACM Siggraph Computer Graphics 19(3), 287–296 (1985)
18. Sartori, A., Yanulevskaya, V., Salah, A., Uijlings, J., Bruni, E., Sebe, N.: Affective analysis of professional and amateur abstract paintings using statistical analysis and art theory. ACM Transactions on Interactive Intelligent Systems (TiiS), in press (2015)
19. Simmons, D.R., Russell, C.: Visual texture affects the perceived unpleasantness of colours. Perception 37, 146–146 (2008)
20. Thumfart, S., Jacobs, R.H., Lughofer, E., Eitzinger, C., Cornelissen, F.W., Groissboeck, W., Richter, R.: Modeling human aesthetic perception of visual textures. ACM Transactions on Applied Perception (TAP) 8(4), 27 (2011)
21. Varma, M., Zisserman, A.: A statistical approach to texture classification from single images. IJCV 62(1–2), 61–81 (2005)
22. Yanulevskaya, V., Gemert, J.V., Roth, K., Herbold, A., Sebe, N., Geusebroek, J.: Emotional valence categorization using holistic image features. In: ICIP (2008)
23. Yanulevskaya, V., Uijlings, J., Bruni, E., Sartori, A., Zamboni, E., Bacci, F., Melcher, D., Sebe, N.: In the eye of the beholder: employing statistical analysis and eye tracking for analyzing abstract paintings. In: ACM Multimedia (2012)
24. Zhang, H., Yang, Z., Gönen, M., Koskela, M., Laaksonen, J., Honkela, T., Oja, E.: Affective abstract image classification and retrieval using multiple kernel learning. In: Lee, M., Hirose, A., Hou, Z.-G., Kil, R.M. (eds.) ICONIP 2013, Part III. LNCS, vol. 8228, pp. 166–175. Springer, Heidelberg (2013)

Movie Genre Classification by Exploiting MEG Brain Signals

Pouya Ghaemmaghami[1]([☒]), Mojtaba Khomami Abadi[1,4],
Seyed Mostafa Kia[1,2,3], Paolo Avesani[1,2,3], and Nicu Sebe[1]

[1] Department of Information Engineering and Computer Science,
University of Trento, 38123 Trento, Italy
{p.ghaemmaghami,seyedmostafa.kia}@unitn.it,
{khomamiabadi,sebe}@disi.unitn.it, avesani@fbk.eu
[2] NeuroInformatics Laboratory (NILab), Bruno Kessler Foundation, Trento, Italy
[3] Centro Interdipartimentale Mente e Cervello (CIMeC), University of Trento,
Trento, Italy
[4] Semantic, Knowledge and Innovation Lab (SKIL), Telecom Italia, Trento, Italy

Abstract. Genre classification is an essential part of multimedia content recommender systems. In this study, we provide experimental evidence for the possibility of performing genre classification based on brain recorded signals. The brain decoding paradigm is employed to classify magnetoencephalography (MEG) data presented in [1] to four genre classes: Comedy, Romantic, Drama, and Horror. Our results show that: 1) there is a significant correlation between audio-visual features of movies and corresponding brain signals specially in the visual and temporal lobes; 2) the genre of movie clips can be classified with an accuracy significantly over the chance level using the MEG signal. On top of that we show that the combination of multimedia features and MEG-based features achieves the best accuracy. Our study provides a primary step towards user-centric media content retrieval using brain signals.

Keywords: Multimedia content retrieval · MEG · Genre classification · Brain decoding · Signal processing

1 Introduction

Movies are one of the most important sources for entertaining people. Nowadays, thanks to advances in technology, people have access to a large number of movies from various sources. From this fact has emerged the need for automatic movie recommendation and automatically detecting the genre of a movie is an important ingredient of a good recommender system [17,26]. So far, various automatic genre classification methods have been proposed based on audio-visual features such as average shot length, color variance, saturation, brightness, grayness, motion, and visual excitement [2,8,14,17,20,26]. However, analyzing only the audio-visual features may not be sufficient for this task as these features may fail to capture the personal preferences of the human viewer. On the other hand,

© Springer International Publishing Switzerland 2015
V. Murino and E. Puppo (Eds.): ICIAP 2015, Part I, LNCS 9279, pp. 683–693, 2015.
DOI: 10.1007/978-3-319-23231-7_61

a recommendation system that can access the viewer's perception of the movie (e.g. via psycho-physiological data), might be able to perform better.

Prior works on brain studies have shown that, in the human brain, low-level visual features are encoded in the early visual cortex and high-level visual features are encoded in inferior temporal cortex [15,21,22]. Recent papers on brain signal decoding demonstrate that some of these low-level visual features such as orientation, direction of motion and color of visual stimulus can be successfully decoded from brain signals [7,9,10]. In a typical brain decoding paradigm, different categories of stimuli are presented to the participants participating in the experiment, while their brain signal is recorded simultaneously. Then a classifier is employed to classify the recorded data into the target stimulus classes. If the classifier performs above chance on the test set, it can be concluded that the stimuli related activities are encoded in the brain signal [3,4,6].

In this paper, we address the specific problem of genre classification of movie clips using magnetoencephalography (MEG) data. Our contribution is two-fold: first, we use the correlation analysis to show that genre related information is present in the visual and temporal areas of the brain; second, we illustrate that these genre related brain signals can be decoded to target genre classes using the brain decoding paradigm. We tested our hypotheses on DECAF dataset [1] which contains 30 subjects who watched 36 movie clips. Figure 1 illustrates the overall framework used in our study.

The rest of this paper is organized as follows. In section 2 we briefly review the state of the art on genre classification in the multimedia content analysis context. Then, in section 3 we present the dataset, data preprocessing and feature extraction. Furthermore, we discuss the method used for movie genre annotation and present our correlation and classification analyses. Section 4 presents our experimental results and a brief discussion. Finally, section 5 concludes this paper by stating the future directions.

2   State of the Art

In the literature various content-based genre classification approaches have been proposed based on audio-visual features [2,8,14,17,20,26]. Rasheed, et al. [17] used four low-level visual features (average shot length, color variance, motion content and lighting key) to classify over a hundred movie previews into four broad genre categories (Comedy, Action, Drama and Horror). In a similar study [8], the authors used the same low-level visual features and slow and fast moving effects to classify movie previews into three different genres. Elsewhere, Zhou, et al. [26] represented over one thousand movie trailers using a bag-of-visual-words model with shot classes as vocabularies. Then they mapped these bag-of-visual-words models to high-level movie genres.

Apart from audio-visual features, movies can be classified into different genres based on their emotional content. In other words, movie genre can also be described via the affective content of the movie. This emotional content induces an emotional experience in the viewer [23]. In fact, the emotions that are elicited

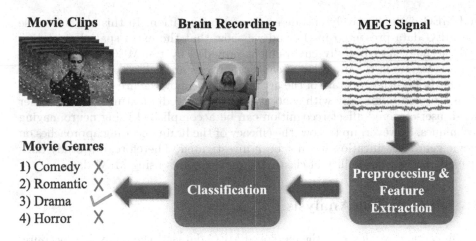

Fig. 1. The framework used in this study for movie genre classification using MEG signals.

in response to a video clip contain useful information regarding the genre of the video clip [19]. For example, in case of Horror and Action movies, it has been shown that movie segments with high emotion intensity cover the major part of the movie highlights [24].

The common approach for predicting multimedia affect is a content-centric approach, in which audio-visual features of the movie are used for affect prediction. Many researchers have investigated the affective contents of the video clips. Xu, et al. [23], analyzed the affective content of comedy and horror movies by detecting emotional segments. Soleymani, et al. [19] showed that a Bayesian classification approach can tag movie scenes into three affective classes (calm, positive excited and negative excited). They used content-based features extracted from each shot of 21 full length movies. In another study [24], a hierarchical model for analyzing movie affective contents was proposed. The proposed model, firstly, detects the emotional intensity level of the movie using fuzzy clustering on arousal features. Secondly, emotion types (Anger, Sad, Fear, Happy and Neutral) are detected using valence related features. Finally, Hidden Markov Models (HMMs) are applied to capture the context information. A similar hierarchical approach using conditional random fields (CRFs) was proposed in [25].

The second approach regarding multimedia affect prediction is a user-centric approach that aims to capture the emotion of the viewer. In [18], 64 movie scenes were shown to participants while their physiological responses were recorded. Their results showed a significant correlation between self-assessed emotional responses of the participants and the predicted affect from physiological responses. Koelstra, et al. [11] employed electroencephalogram (EEG) to record brain activity of 32 participants watching 40 music video excerpts. A similar study was done in [1] with magnetoencephalography (MEG) data, in which 30 subjects were watching 36 movie clips. These two studies suggest that EEG and MEG data effectively encode emotional information. In this study, we use the MEG data presented in [1], and we show that the extra spatial resolution and the more user-friendly environment provided by the MEG device provide positive factors in the direction of capturing the emotional response of subjects.

Our brief review of state of the art reveals that movie genre classification has been achieved so far only with content-based multimedia features. On the other hand, user-centered affect recognition can be accomplished using neuroimaging techniques. However, up to now, the efficacy of the brain decoding approaches on movie genre classification has not been investigated. Therefore, our study aims at exploring the possibility of classifying movie genres using MEG data.

3 MEG Signal Analysis

In this section, we describe the employed MEG dataset, the analysis procedure, and our experimental setup.

3.1 Dataset

In this study we used the MEG dataset reported in [1]. This dataset contains 36 movie clips cropped from Hollywood movies (see table 2 for their titles). The MEG brain signals of 30 volunteers were recorded while they were watching the movie clips. All movie clips were shown with 20 frames/second at a screen refresh rate of 60 Hz, and they were projected onto a screen placed about a meter in front of the subject inside the MEG acquisition room. The MEG data were recorded with 1KHz sampling rate in a magnetically shielded room with controlled illumination using a Electa Neuromag system, which has 306 channels via 102 triple-sensors, i.e., 102 magnetometers and 204 planar gradiometers (see [1] for more details).

3.2 MEG Feature Extraction

The MEG data preprocessing has been handled using the MATLAB Fieldtrip toolbox [16]. Following [1], after extracting the MEG trials, we preprocessed the MEG recordings as follows:

Band-pass Filtering. Upon downsampling the MEG signal to 300 Hz, in order to remove the noise generated by external perturbations such as moving vehicles or muscle activity, high-pass and low-pass filtering with cut-off frequencies of 1 Hz and 95 Hz are performed, respectively.

Time-Frequency Analysis. The spectral power of MEG data between 3 and 45 Hz was estimated using the Welch method with a window size of 300 samples. Following [1], (i) we discarded the magnetometer sensors because they are generally prone to noise and (ii) we used a standard Fieldtrip function to combine the spectral power of planar gradiometers to obtain 102 combined-gradiometer spectral power for each trial.

MEG Features Extraction. MEG features are computed by averaging the spectral power over four major frequency bands: theta (3:7 Hz), alpha (8:15 Hz), beta (16:31 Hz), and gamma (32:45 Hz). For each trial of a given subject, the output of this procedure is a 3-dimensional matrix with the following dimensions: 102 (number of the MEG combined-gradiometer sensors) $\times$ 4 (major frequency bands)$\times L$, where L is the length of a video clip in seconds.

3.3   Multimedia Content Feature Extraction

Following [1], the low-level audio-visual features (listed in Table 1) are extracted for each second of the movie clips. The extracted multimedia content analysis (MCA) features include 49 video features and 56 audio features. Hence, for each video, we have 105 (low-level multimedia features) $\times L$ features.

Table 1. Extracted audio-visual features from each movie clip (the number of features is listed in the parenthesis).

Audio features	Description
MFCC features (39)	MFCC coefficients [13], derivative of MFCC, MFCC Autocorrelation (AMFCC)
Energy (1) and Pitch (1)	Average energy of audio signal [13] and first pitch frequency
Formants (4)	Formants up to 4400Hz
Time frequency (8)	mean and std of: MSpectrum flux, Spectral centroid, Delta spectrum magnitude, Band energy ratio [13]
Zero crossing rate (1)	Average zero crossing rate of audio signal [13]
Silence ratio (2)	Mean and std of proportion of silence in a time window [13]
Video features	Description
Brightness (6)	Mean of: Lighting key, shadow proportion, visual details, grayness, median of Lightness for frames, mean of median saturation for frames
Color Features (41)	Color variance, 20-bin histograms for hue and lightness in HSV space
Motion (1)	Mean inter-frame motion [1]
VisualExcitement (1)	Features as defined in [1]

3.4   Annotating Movie Genres

In order to annotate movie genres, three human observers were asked to watch the movie clips and classify each movie into four genres: Comedy, Romantic, Drama, Horror. The movie genres were picked based on the majority voting between the observers. To evaluate the consistency of the genres across subjects, we measured the agreement between annotators' labeling using the Cohen's Kappa measurement. The average κ across observers is $77\% \pm 2\%$ ($p-value < 0.001$) that suggests a *substantial agreement* [12] between the annotators. Furthermore, we employed the Cohen's kappa to evaluate the agreement between the movie genres obtained from the majority voting, with the genres obtained from the Internet Movie Database (IMDB)[1]. The average κ across the two labels is 72% ($p-value < 0.001$) that shows a *substantial agreement* between our picked labels (sign majority voting) and the labels obtained from the IMDB. The lack of *full agreement* between these two labels is mainly due to the fact that the employed movie clips in [1] are not necessarily representing the whole movie theme. The genre labels provided by this study augment the dataset proposed in [1]. From here on we refer to the majority voting labels resulting from the annotation process as the ground-truth (see table 2 for the obtained ground-truth labels).

3.5 Correlation Analysis

We calculate the Pearson correlation between the 102 combined MEG gradiometers in each frequency band (θ, α, β, and γ) and audio-visual features extracted from movie clips. The obtained p-values were first fused over all clips and then over all subjects using the Fisher's method [5]. To correct our results for multiple comparisons, we performed the Boferroni correction before reporting significant results. The results of the correlation analysis are discussed in section 4.

3.6 Classification Procedure

In the classification experiments we used a naive Bayes classifier to decode the MEG and MCA features into four genre classes. To do this we performed the following analysis:

MEG-Based and MCA-Based Descriptors. MEG/MCA descriptor of each trial is calculated by averaging the MEG/MCA features over time. Hence, the length of each MEG/MCA descriptor is 408 (4 bands $\times$ 102 triple-sensors) and 105, respectively.

MEG-Based User-Centric Classification. The classification of the MEG-descriptors is repeated 30 times (corresponding to the 30 users) independently. For each user, the 36 MEG-descriptors of 36 movie clips are used as samples.

MCA-Based Video Classification. For the video-centric genre classification, the 36 MCA-descriptors are used as samples.

---

[1] http://www.imdb.com

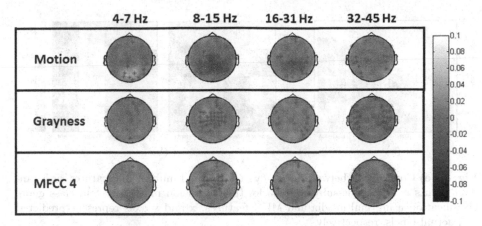

Fig. 2. Pearson correlation analysis between the MEG responses and audio-visual features. Correlation over each channel is denoted by the gray level, and significant correlations are marked with red ⋆.

MEG+MCA. The MEG descriptors of each subject are concatenated to the MCA descriptors and a feature vector of 408+105=513 features is used for genre classification.

Single-Subject Classification Scenario. We used the Naive Bayes classifier under the leave-one-clip-out cross-validation schema for each subject separately. The ground-truth labels are used as the target labels in the classification procedure.

Population Analysis. To evaluate the efficacy of MEG/MCA descriptors at the population level, for each video clip, we computed the majority vote over predictions of the single-subject classification across 30 subjects.

4   Results and Discussion

4.1   Correlation Results

The calculated Pearson correlation between 102 MEG sensors in each frequency band and audio-visual features extracted from movie clips is shown in Figure 2. This figure shows two visual features (motion and grayness) and an audio feature (the forth MFCC coefficient). As one can see, audio-visual features are significantly correlated with MEG sensors in temporal area of the brain in the γ band (32:45 Hz). This part of the brain processes the visual information as well as the audio information. Furthermore in the α band (8-15 Hz), the extracted motion feature is significantly correlated with the MEG sensors located in the posterior part of the brain, confirming previous studies [7,9].

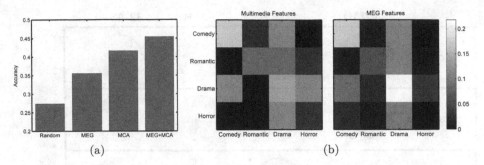

(a)   (b)

Fig. 3. (a) Comparison between accuracy of MEG and multimedia features with random inputs in the single-subject scenario. (b) Confusion matrix for four-class genre classification using multimedia and MEG features. x and y axes represent predicted and actual labels, respectively.

4.2   Classification Results

Figure 3a summarizes the results of the single-subject classification scenario. It compares the accuracy of four-class classification based on the MEG and MCA features with the chance level (27.4%). The chance level is computed by feeding random numbers with normal distribution into the classification procedure for 100 times. In the MEG case, the mean accuracy of 35.6% is obtained over 30 subjects which is significantly ($p - value < 0.001$) higher than the chance level. This significant difference suggests the existence of genre related information in the recorded brain activity. Furthermore, combining MEG features of each subject with MCA features provides higher accuracy (45.5%) than employing only MCA features (41.7%). This improvement suggests the existence of complementary genre related information in the MEG brain signal.

Figure 3b shows the confusion matrices for four-class genre classification using MCA and MEG features. To facilitate the comparison, the confusion matrices are normalized with respect to the total number of samples (30×36 in the MEG case and 36 in the MCA case). Even though the classification accuracy using MCA features is higher than using MEG features, confusion matrices show significantly similar patterns ($p - value < 2 \times 10^{-5}$). In both cases, the comedy and drama genres are predicted with higher confidence while romantic and horror genres are almost indistinguishable from other categories.

Finally we performed a population analysis on the predicted labels from the MEG signal alone and the combined MEG and MCA features. To do this, the predicted genres at the population level are computed by majority voting over the predicted labels of single-subject predictions. The results are summarized in table 2. The population level accuracy for both MEG and MEG+MCA features is 55.6% which is significantly higher than classification accuracy of only MCA features (41.7%). Despite the same performance in MEG and MEG+MCA scenarios, examining the predicted genres in table 2 shows that the combined features are more successful in predicting the romantic genre. This is mainly because the MEG features are weaker than the MCA features in classifying the romantic genre (compare the 4th and the 5th columns of table 2). This fact confirms the existence of complementary genre related information in brain signals and multimedia contents.

Table 2. Movie clip titles, ground-truth labels, and predicted labels.

ID	Titles	Ground-Truth	MCA	MEG	MEG+MCA
1	Ace-Ventura: Pet Detective	COMEDY	COMEDY	COMEDY	COMEDY
2	The Gods Must be Crazy II	COMEDY	DRAMA	COMEDY	COMEDY
3	Liar Liar	COMEDY	ROMANTIC	COMEDY	COMEDY
4	Airplane	COMEDY	COMEDY	COMEDY	COMEDY
5	When Harry Met Sally	COMEDY	COMEDY	COMEDY	COMEDY
6	The Gods Must be Crazy	COMEDY	DRAMA	COMEDY	COMEDY
7	The Hangover	COMEDY	DRAMA	COMEDY	DRAMA
8	Up	COMEDY	COMEDY	DRAMA	COMEDY
9	Hot Shots	COMEDY	DRAMA	COMEDY	DRAMA
10	August Rush	ROMANTIC	DRAMA	DRAMA	DRAMA
11	Truman Show	ROMANTIC	DRAMA	DRAMA	DRAMA
12	Wall-E	ROMANTIC	HORROR	COMEDY	DRAMA
13	Love Actually	ROMANTIC	DRAMA	DRAMA	DRAMA
14	Remember the Titans	DRAMA	HORROR	DRAMA	DRAMA
15	Legally Blonde	COMEDY	COMEDY	DRAMA	DRAMA
16	Life is Beautiful	COMEDY	COMEDY	COMEDY	COMEDY
17	Slumdog Millionaire	ROMANTIC	ROMANTIC	DRAMA	ROMANTIC
18	House of Flying Daggers	ROMANTIC	ROMANTIC	DRAMA	ROMANTIC
19	Gandhi	DRAMA	DRAMA	DRAMA	DRAMA
20	My girl	DRAMA	COMEDY	DRAMA	COMEDY
21	Lagaan	DRAMA	COMEDY	DRAMA	COMEDY
22	Bambi	DRAMA	HORROR	DRAMA	DRAMA
23	My Bodyguard	DRAMA	DRAMA	DRAMA	DRAMA
24	Up	ROMANTIC	ROMANTIC	DRAMA	DRAMA
25	Life is Beautiful	DRAMA	DRAMA	DRAMA	DRAMA
26	Remember the Titans	DRAMA	COMEDY	DRAMA	DRAMA
27	Titanic	DRAMA	HORROR	DRAMA	DRAMA
28	Exorcist	HORROR	HORROR	DRAMA	DRAMA
29	Mulholland Drive	DRAMA	COMEDY	DRAMA	COMEDY
30	The Shining	HORROR	DRAMA	DRAMA	DRAMA
31	Prestige	DRAMA	HORROR	COMEDY	DRAMA
32	Alien	HORROR	DRAMA	DRAMA	DRAMA
33	The untouchables	DRAMA	DRAMA	COMEDY	DRAMA
34	Pink Flamingos	HORROR	DRAMA	COMEDY	DRAMA
35	Crash	DRAMA	DRAMA	DRAMA	DRAMA
36	Black Swan	HORROR	DRAMA	DRAMA	DRAMA
	Accuracy		41.7%	55.6%	55.6%

5   Conclusions

In this paper, we presented an approach for classification of movie clips into four genres (Comedy, Romantic, Drama, Horror) using MEG brain signals. We experimentally illustrated that there exists a significant correlation between audio-visual multimedia features and the MEG signal. This finding opens the door of research toward prediction and reconstruction of multimedia features using brain signals, generally known as mind reading. Furthermore, a naive Bayes classifier has been used to perform the genre class prediction using the features extracted from MEG sensors. Our classification results confirm the possibility of user-centered classification of movies into four broad genres only based on brain signals. In addition, our analysis supports the hypothesis of existence of complementary genre related information in the brain signal and in multimedia contents. To the best of our knowledge, this is the first effort in the direction of user-centered movie genre classification using brain signals. We plan to extend this work by employing more effective and sophisticated brain decoding approaches in order to improve our classification results. Furthermore, in the future work, we plan to replicate the experiments using the brain signals recorded by portable brain recording devices such as the Emotiv sensors.

Acknowledgments. This work has been supported by the MIUR Cluster project Active Ageing at Home.

References

1. Abadi, M., Subramanian, R., Kia, S., Avesani, P., Patras, I., Sebe, N.: DECAF: MEG-based multimodal database for decoding affective physiological responses. IEEE Transactions on Affective Computing (2015)
2. Brezeale, D., Cook, D.J.: Using closed captions and visual features to classify movies by genre. In: International Workshop on Multimedia Data Mining (2006)
3. Carlson, T.A., Hogendoorn, H., Kanai, R., Mesik, J., Turret, J.: High temporal resolution decoding of object position and category. Journal of vision 11(10) (2011)
4. Cox, D.D., Savoy, R.L.: Functional magnetic resonance imaging (fmri) brain reading: detecting and classifying distributed patterns of fmri activity in human visual cortex. Neuroimage 19(2), 261–270 (2003)
5. Fisher, R.A.: Statistical methods for research workers. Quarterly Journal of the Royal Meteorological Society 82(351), 119–119 (1956)
6. Haxby, J.V., Gobbini, M.I., Furey, M.L., Ishai, A., Schouten, J.L., Pietrini, P.: Distributed and overlapping representations of faces and objects in ventral temporal cortex. Science 293(5539), 2425–2430 (2001)
7. Haynes, J.D., Rees, G.: Decoding mental states from brain activity in humans. Nature Reviews Neuroscience 7(7), 523–534 (2006)
8. Huang, H.Y., Shih, W.S., Hsu, W.H.: A film classifier based on low-level visual features. In: IEEE Workshop on Multimedia Signal Processing, pp. 465–468 (2007)
9. Kamitani, Y., Tong, F.: Decoding motion direction from activity in human visual cortex. Journal of Vision 5(8), 152–152 (2005)
10. Kamitani, Y., Tong, F.: Decoding the visual and subjective contents of the human brain. Nature neuroscience 8(5), 679–685 (2005)
11. Koelstra, S., Muhl, C., Soleymani, M., Lee, J.S., Yazdani, A., Ebrahimi, T., Pun, T., Nijholt, A., Patras, I.: Deap: A database for emotion analysis; using physiological signals. IEEE Transactions on Affective Computing 3(1), 18–31 (2012)
12. Landis, J.R., Koch, G.G.: The Measurement of Observer Agreement for Categorical Data. Biometrics 33(1), 159–174 (1977)
13. Li, D., Sethi, I.K., Dimitrova, N., McGee, T.: Classification of general audio data for content-based retrieval. Pattern Recognition Letters 22(5), 533–544 (2001)
14. Nam, J., Alghoniemy, M., Tewfik, A.H.: Audio-visual content-based violent scene characterization. In: International Conference on Image Processing (1998)
15. Obermayer, K., Blasdel, G.G.: Geometry of orientation and ocular dominance columns in monkey striate cortex. The Journal of neuroscience 13(10), 4114–4129 (1993)
16. Oostenveld, R., Fries, P., Maris, E., Schoffelen, J.M.: Fieldtrip: open source software for advanced analysis of MEG, EEG, and invasive electrophysiological data. Computational intelligence and neuroscience (2010)

17. Rasheed, Z., Sheikh, Y., Shah, M.: On the use of computable features for film classification. IEEE Transactions on Circuits and Systems for Video Technology **15**(1), 52–64 (2005)
18. Soleymani, M., Chanel, G., Kierkels, J.J., Pun, T.: Affective characterization of movie scenes based on multimedia content analysis and user's physiological emotional responses. In: IEEE International Symposium on Multimedia (2008)
19. Soleymani, M., Kierkels, J.J., Chanel, G., Pun, T.: A bayesian framework for video affective representation. In: International Conference on Affective Computing and Intelligent Interaction (2009)
20. Sugano, M., Isaksson, R., Nakajima, Y., Yanagihara, H.: Shot genre classification using compressed audio-visual features. In: International Conference on Image Processing (2003)
21. Tanaka, K.: Mechanisms of visual object recognition: monkey and human studies. Current opinion in neurobiology **7**(4), 523–529 (1997)
22. Wang, G., Tanaka, K., Tanifuji, M.: Optical imaging of functional organization in the monkey inferotemporal cortex. Science **272**(5268), 1665–1668 (1996)
23. Xu, M., Chia, L.T., Jin, J.: Affective content analysis in comedy and horror videos by audio emotional event detection. In: IEEE International Conference on Multimedia and Expo (2005)
24. Xu, M., Jin, J.S., Luo, S., Duan, L.: Hierarchical movie affective content analysis based on arousal and valence features. In: ACM Multimedia (2008)
25. Xu, M., Xu, C., He, X., Jin, J.S., Luo, S., Rui, Y.: Hierarchical affective content analysis in arousal and valence dimensions. Signal Processing **93**(8), 2140–2150 (2013)
26. Zhou, H., Hermans, T., Karandikar, A.V., Rehg, J.M.: Movie genre classification via scene categorization. In: ACM Multimedia (2010)

Egocentric Video Personalization in Cultural Experiences Scenarios

Patrizia Varini$^{(\boxtimes)}$, Giuseppe Serra, and Rita Cucchiara

Università degli studi di Modena e Reggio Emilia, via Pietro Vivarelli, 10,
Modena, Italy
{patrizia.varini,giuseppe.serra,rita.cucchiara}@unimore.it
http://imagelab.ing.unimore.it

Abstract. In this paper we propose a novel approach for egocentric video personalization in a cultural experience scenario, based on shots automatic labelling according to different semantic dimensions, such as web leveraged knowledge of the surrounded cultural Points Of Interest, information about stops and moves, both relying on geolocalization, and camera's wearer behaviour. Moreover we present a video personalization web system based on shots multi-dimensional semantic classification, that is designed to aid the visitor to browse and to retrieve relevant information to obtain a customized video. Experimental results show that the proposed techniques for video analysis achieve good performances in unconstrained scenario and user evaluation tests confirm that our solution is useful and effective.

Keywords: Video analysis · Video personalization · Cultural heritage

1 Introduction and Related Work

In recent years the widespreading use of wearable cameras to capture everyday life activities such as sport, education, social interactions and cultural heritage visits, has made popular egocentric videos. Typically they consist of long streams of data with a ceaseless jumping appearance, frequent changes of observer's focus and lack of hard cuts between scenes, thus requiring new methodologies for automatic analysis and understanding. There is a sharply increasing need of automated tools able to classify, search and select from these extremely long and continuous life logging streams, only the most relevant scenes according to the user preferences and to the specific purpose, eventually enriching them with customized semantically related content.

Various approaches exist for data visualization to help users navigation in the selected videos. Visualization systems based on timeline slider and on shots sequence show are the most common and easiest way to get a quick overview of video content but they suffer by lack of semantic categorization and poor scalability for large documents. Campanella *et al.* [2] propose a data visualization system to explore and annotate video sequences where contents are analyzed and displayed organized in classes and browsable in a feature distributed space

© Springer International Publishing Switzerland 2015
V. Murino and E. Puppo (Eds.): ICIAP 2015, Part I, LNCS 9279, pp. 694–704, 2015.
DOI: 10.1007/978-3-319-23231-7_62

shown in a 2D Cartesian plane, where each axis corresponds to one feature type selected by the user and each shot is represented by a little square filled by the dominant colour of the shot. Snoek *et al.* [10] present the MediaMill video search engine, and proposes, among others, Sphere Browser, that represents a novel interface for searching through semantic space using conceptual similarity. This is obtained classifying shots with a similar conceptual index clustered together into threads. The Sphere Browser shows the timeline of the current video on the horizontal axis, and for each shot from the video it displays the relevant threads on the vertical axis. It uses a linear ordering to ranking video data. The vertical axis is related to a selected concept. The horizontal one is used to visualize video program in a timeline from which a keyframes is selected.

Moving to video personalization, Wei *et al.* [11] propose a novel architecture for video personalization and caching for resource constrained environments such as mobile devices, that performs automatic video segmentation and video indexing based on semantic video content, and generates personalized videos based on client preference using a Multiple-Choice Multi-Dimensional Knapsack Problem (MMKP)-based video personalization strategy. Araujo *et al.* [1] present a system for personalization of interactive digital media in educational environment, which combines context of access, user preferences and device presentation constraints in order to provide an interactive access experience. It allows content recommendation, ranking and personalization of interactive multimedia presentations captured in an instrumented classroom. These personalization techniques however do not take into account egocentric video peculiar issue. To best of our knowledge however, no one has addressed video personalization in egocentric vision.

Recently new methodologies related to egocentric video analysis have been developed to tackle its characteristic issues. Lee *et al.* [7] proposed a egocentric video summarization method that focuses on learning importance cues for each frame, such as objects and people the camera wearer interacts with, using features related with gaze, object-like appearance and motion and likelihood of a person's face within a region. Lu and Grauman [9] handle egocentric video summarization partitioning videos into sub-shots on the basis of motion features analysis, smooth the classification with a MRF and then select a chain of sub-shots choosing the ones in which they can detect the reciprocal influence propagation between important objects and characters. Yeung *et al.* [12] present a technique to evaluate video summarization through text, by measuring how well a video summary is able to retain the semantic information contained in its original stream making use of textual summarization benchmarking tools.

In this paper we propose a method for user egocentric video personalization which associates patterns of low level features to high level concepts relevant to different semantic levels, relying on geolocalization and on web dynamically extracted knowledge. We use a cultural experience scenario as use case, choosing candidate relevant semantic dimensions such as Points Of Interest (POI), visitor's behavior and spatial information about his stops and moves. Furthermore we present a web application that classifies and makes available shots corresponding to different semantic levels, allowing the final user to select easily the relevant scenes, eventually according to his high level expressed preferences, expressed for sake of simplicity by simple groups of keywords containing names of classes (eventually with labels within the class to further filter the results, limited to the POI semantic level) belonging to one or more semantic levels. Our preliminary experimental results show that this approach is able to exploit dynamically user's preferences to obtain a personalized version of a cultural visit video.

2   Video Personalization

We propose an approach for egocentric video personalization tailored on the use case of cultural experience scenario in which a video is segmented and classified in shots according to three different classes of semantic information: camera's wearer attitude or behaviour, stops and moves in the geolocalized traveled route and the presence of relevant cultural Points Of Interest.

In order to achieve a motion based classification of camera's wearer behaviour pattern, we define the underline motion taxonomy, structured in six classes. Annotations related to presence of stops and moves in the geolocalized trajectories are detected using a spatio-temporal clustering technique based on shared nearest neighbor. Detection of cultural POI is achieved by means of image classification using sets of positive and negative samples dynamically obtained from the web.

Observer's Behavior Pattern Detection. Based on the analysis of the visitor's typical behaviours, we define a taxonomy of a set of primitive motion classes: for the class "Person motion" the sub-classes "Static" (Body and head stand still), "Walking" (Body is walking, head is approximately still), "Higher speed motion" (Body running or jumping etc. and Head in coherent motion), "On wheels" (Body and Head are still respect to a moving on wheels mean of transport), for the class "Head motion" the sub-classes "Rolling" (Body is still or in motion and head is widely rolling) and "Pitching" (Body is still or in motion and head is widely pitching). To detect these classes, we analyze frame quality assessment and motion pattern features by partitioning frames using a 3×3 grid.

In particular, blurriness is used to assess quality frame. We compute this feature by using the method proposed by Roffet *et al.* [3], assuming that the sharpness of an image is contained in its gray component and estimate the blur annoyance only on the luminance component, computing and evaluating the line and row difference between the original image and the image obtained applying to it a horizontal and a vertical strong low-pass filter. The blurriness descriptor is thus obtained by concatenating sector features.

Motion features are based on dense optic flow estimated using the Farneback's algorithm [5] and consist of optical flow and its gradient spatial histograms. Considering the optic flow computed for each couple of consecutive frames, the relative apparent velocity and acceleration of each pixel is V_x, V_y, A_x and A_y. These values are expressed in polar coordinates as in the following:

$$M_V = \sqrt{V_x^2 + V_y^2} \qquad \theta_V = \arctan(V_y/V_x) \qquad (1)$$

$$M_A = \sqrt{A_x^2 + A_y^2} \qquad \theta_A = \arctan(A_y/A_x) \qquad (2)$$

For each of the 3×3 sections of the frame, we compute a histogram by concatenating the magnitudes M_V and M_A, quantized in eight bins, with the orientations θ_V and θ_A, (quantized in eight bins) weighting them by the magnitude respectively.

In order to smooth the jumpy values of motion measures due to meaningless head motion, the feature vector descriptors have been averaged over a window of about 20 frames (when acquiring at 29 FPs) as this has been regarded to be a reasonable compromise to reduce randomness without relevant information loss. In fact, the typical interval duration of head movement in the visual fixation pattern, studied using gaze analysis, is about 330 ms but has a wide range of variation [6]. Head movements themselves, measured with our approach, have been found to have a typical duration between 1 and 1.5 second (median 1,27 sec). To speed up classification task, a linear multiclass SVM has been trained over the six identified classes.

Based on the classification of these primitive classes, we exploit Hidden Markov Model to recognize the following behavior patterns and gain classification smoothing: attention, changing point of attention, wandering around and traveling from one point to another. In particular, we estimate the transition and emission probabilities from sample sequences in a supervised approach, in order to obtain a smoothed classification frame vector. A n-states Hidden Markov Model may be completely described by the initial state probability, by transition matrix from state S_i and by *pdf* matrix of observable O_i. Once defined the model the likelihood of the hidden state variables is computed with the Baum-Welsh algorithm which uses a forward and backward recursion. A model for each pattern of behaviour is prepared where states are related to different motion states. Afterward, the models are fed with observables vector and probability of precedent state and Viterbi algorithm is used to calculate the *pdf* to be higher than current, assigning the correspondent class.

Stop and Move Detection. In cultural experience scenarios, stops are a semantically relevant part of a touristic visit, identified as places where a visitor has stayed for a minimum amount of time. Collecting the geographic locations by means of GPS sensors, trajectories are represented by movement tracks, that basically consist in the temporal sequence of the spatio-temporal points, meant as pairs compound with coordinate in space and in time $\{p_0 = (x_0, y_0, z_0, t_0), ...,$ $p_N = (x_N, y_N, z_n, t_N)\}$, where $(x_i, y_i, z_i) \in \mathcal{R}^3, t_i \in \mathcal{R}^+$ for $i = 0, 1, ..., N$ and $t_0 < t_i < t_N$. As this definition itself does not embed any insight about stops and moves semantic informations, we proposed to adopt a spatio temporal clustering algorithm.

K-means is a standard and efficient clustering algorithm, but needs to calculate the number of clusters, instead we propose the use of a Shared Nearest Neighbor (SNN) density-based algorithm [4], whose extension in 4 spatio-
temporal dimensions was first explored by [8], that is able to deal with clusters
of different densities, sizes and shapes and with noise. SNN relies on strength or
similarity concept, evaluated on the number of nearest neighbors that couples
of points, belonging to a set of N points in a metric space D, share, computed
on the basis of a metric distance: $S(p,q) = size(kNN(p) \bigcap kNN(q))$. Density
of a point p is evaluated as the number of points, within a radius Eps, defined
so that its Eps-neighborhood is $N_{Eps}(p) = \{q \in D | dist(p,q) \leq Eps\}$, assumed
that dist() is the Euclidean distance function. Then we define a cluster C as a
set of elements in which for every point p there is at least a point q in C so that
p is inside of the Eps-neighborhood of q and $N_{Eps}(q)$ contains at least a minimum number $(MinPts)$ of points (q points are defined as core or representative
points).

Thus assuming that a stop is semantically identified as the permanence of the
visitor in a location (within a given radius) for a certain period of time, the used
algorithm relies on fixing the number of nearest neighbors k, a density threshold
$MinPts$ for a core point and a fixed radius (Eps), and starts with creating
the similarity graph, reducing it to keep only the most similar nodes with their
strength over the $MinPts$ threshold, discarding noise points as non-core points
that are not within a radius Eps of a core point, and putting together in a same
cluster core points within a Eps radius. Non-core points and non-noise points
are classified as reachable points and assigned to clusters of their nearest core
point.

A specific dataset of classified ground truth points for different trajectories was prepared, and clustering parameters were experimentally set as follows:
$MinPts = \frac{1}{7}k$ and $Eps = \frac{1}{3}k$.

Points of Interest. To achieve visual recognition of cultural Points Of Interest, we build a set of specific classifiers. In particular, based on the georeferenced route of the visitor, we retrieve points of high cultural interest querying
geolocalized DBpedia for a set of four classes, chosen from main Wikipedia categories of particular interest in cultural heritage (i.e. Buildings and structures
by location, Monuments and memorials, Religious architecture, Museums), after
which we name our four corresponding classes respectevly Buildings, Monuments, Churches, Museums. In order to retrieve a sufficient number of reliable
and up to date image training samples from the web, we extract from Flickr
georeferenced images tagged with the corresponding POI for positive samples,
while negative samples are randomly chosen from georeferenced images far from
the visitor's location over a threshold.

Once collected the training set, Fisher Vectors based on local SIFT features
densely sampled (FV) are extracted. This is done in each region of the spatial
pyramid, which was set up combining regions in this configuration: 1×1, 2×2
and 3×1 and the FVs of each of these regions are concatenated for each image.

This results in a vectorial representation x of $D = M \times 2G \times R$ dimensions per image, where $M = 80$ is the local feature dimensionality (after PCA), $G = 256$ is number of Gaussians in the mixture and $R = 8$ is the number of pyramid regions. Point of Interest detection is performed on every ten frames extracted from the video.

3   VAEX System: A Web Tool for Egocentric Video Personalization

The VAEX system is a multi-layer web system for video personalization. Each uploaded user video is processed and automatically annotated on different semantic dimensions which rely on geolocalization and on web leveraged knowledge of the surrounded cultural POI, on camera's wearer behaviour and information about stops and moves.

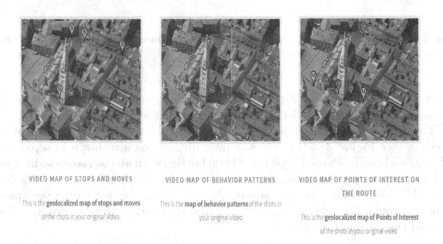

Fig. 1. VAEX Tool: Video semantic browsing. Legend for the Figure 1 on the left: spatial stop shots are marked with teal markers, red continuous line corresponds to move pattern shots. Figure 1 in center: Behavior pattern: blue continuous line = attention; cyan continuous line = wandering, red continuous line = traveling, light green continuous line=changing point of attention (head motion). Figure 1 on the right: light green markers labeled with "C" ="Church" or "Cathedral", yellow markers labeled with "M" = "Monument", red markers labeled as "S" = "Museum" or "Exhibition", cyan markers labeled as "B" = "Palaces" or "Buildings".

The interface shown in Figure 1 allows the user to browse the video according to any of the three semantic level separately by clicking the corresponding image

Fig. 2. VAEX Tool: Video semantic browsing user interface to explore video in according to a stops and moves semantic dimension.

in the main interface. Selecting a specific semantic dimension the user may easily browse along the shots labeled on that dimension as shown in Figure 2.

The VAEX system includes as the main feature the video personalization interface (see Figure 3) where the semantic dimensions are shown in separated columns and can be crossed together. Shots, labeled with all the recognizable tags within the correspondent semantic category (see for example Modena Cathedral in the POI dimension), may be specifically selected according to the user preferences through the search bar, and drag and dropped in the working timeline to build the personalized stream.

4   Experimental Results

4.1   Behavior Pattern Detection

To evaluate the performance of the proposed behavior pattern detection, we collected ten videos from head-mounted cameras captured by tourists that spend some time to visit a cultural city. Each video is about one hour long and taken in a uncontrolled setting. They show the experience visitors such as a visit of cultural interest point. The camera is placed on the tourist's head and captures a 720×576, 24 frames per second RGB image sequence. Granularity of GPS sensor is one second in time and 2 meters linear displacement in space.

Fig. 3. VAEX Tool: Video personalization general interface with search function.

A subset of 7200 annotated frames is used in order to test our methodology to recognize the high level observer's behaviors: "Attention", "Transit", "Changing point of interest", "Wandering around". First, we examine the effectiveness of our 297-dimension feature vector, based on blurriness, optical flow and acceleration spatial gradient directions weighted over magnitudes and magnitudes, on 3 × 3 grids with average pooling in time, on low-level motion pattern detection: "Static", "Walking", "High speed", "On wheels", "Head Roll" and "Head Pitch".

In Table 1 we compare our results to a similar descriptor recently proposed by Lu *et al.* [9] (25-dimension feature vector based on blurriness, optical fow directions weighted over magnitudes and magnitudes). The Figure 4 shows the performance of the two techniques per class.

Table 1. Comparison of classification accuracy.

	Lu *et al.* [9]	**Our approach**
Accuracy	62.92	**72.48**

As can be seen from Figure 4, adding feature vectors related to optical flow variations in magnitude and orientation over each of the 3 × 3 frame sections, with 8-bins quantization, we achieve a better precision as optical flow variation represents local motion thus helps distinguish the special motion of abrupt and

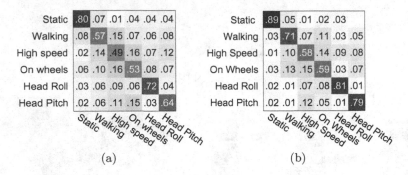

Static	.80	.07	.01	.04	.04	.04
Walking	.08	.57	.15	.07	.06	.08
High speed	.02	.14	.49	.16	.07	.12
On wheels	.06	.10	.16	.53	.08	.07
Head Roll	.03	.06	.09	.06	.72	.04
Head Pitch	.02	.06	.11	.15	.03	.64

(a)

Static	.89	.05	.01	.02	.03	
Walking	.03	.71	.07	.11	.03	.05
High Speed	.01	.10	.58	.14	.09	.08
On Wheels	.03	.13	.15	.59	.03	.07
Head Roll	.02	.01	.07	.08	.81	.01
Head Pitch	.02	.01	.12	.05	.01	.79

(b)

Fig. 4. Classification accuracy using different descriptors: a) feature vector proposed by Lu *et al.* [9]; b) our feature vector.

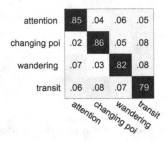

attention	.85	.04	.06	.05
changing poi	.02	.86	.05	.08
wandering	.07	.03	.82	.08
transit	.06	.08	.07	.79

Fig. 5. HMM estimated behavior pattern detection accuracy.

random camera movements, related to "Head motion" and "Head pitch", from significant motion.

Finally Figure 4.1 presents the results obtained applying to the primitive motion classification a Hidden Markov Model, to recognize the behavior patterns and gain classification smoothing, and shows that the accuracy results are quite promising. "Attention" and "Changing POI" obtain a higher performance with respect to the other two classes. This is probably due to the fact that these two last behaviors are characterized by different types of motion caused by the combination of head and body movements and the fast background changes.

4.2 Participants and Experiments

A subjective evaluational test was performed by selecting to participate 8 subjects. Seven participants were undergraduate and postgraduate students and one from technical staff, all of them ranging in age from 18 to 45. They had no previous knowledge about video personalization or video editing. Participants self-reported that they were familiar with web searches and most common programs for editing of text and images with GUI interface. The main qualifying criterion for a participant in entering the evaluation experiment was to have a strong interest in the fruition of common online video platforms for user

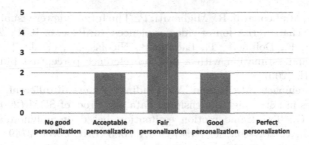

Fig. 6. User evaluation of the personalization interface.

generated video and to have a certain familiarity with text and images processors and presentation tools. The subjects were requested to produce their own personalization, working on videos belonging to our egocentric dataset. Since personalization of all 10 movies might have been burdensome for some subjects, they were randomly divided into 2 groups of 4 subjects each.

Subjects were first invited for a twenty minutes tutorial session, in which they were given instructions about the system and shown how to specify preferences to personalize videos.

Finally, a "blind taste test" was performed, in which each group had to evaluate each personalized video by the other group w.r.t the user expressed preferences. We used a Likert scale with a score between 1 and 5, where 1 was "no good personalization" and 5 "perfect personalization" w.r.t user preferences. This test, resulting in Fig. 4.2, shows that 75% of the evaluations considers the web application a useful and suitable tool for building a short and customized personal video.

5   Conclusions

In this paper we have proposed a video personalization web system designed to support tourists to personalize the egocentric captured videos of their experiences, based on shots automatic classification according to the semantic dimensions of stops and moves, POI detection and behavior pattern. The system supports the user in semantic browsing through the scenes of the video and in selecting and combining easily on the working timeline the relevant shots. The experimental assessments reported in Section 4 exhibit promising results, from the point of view of both results accuracy and usefulness of the personalization web tool.

References

1. Araújo, R.D., Brant-Ribeiro, T., Cattelan, R.G., Amo, S.A.d., Ferreira, H.N.: Personalization of interactive digital media in ubiquitous educational environments. In: Proc. of SMC (2013)

2. Campanella, M., Leonardi, R., Migliorati, P.: The future-viewer visual environment for semantic characterization of video sequences. In: Proc. of ICIP (2005)
3. Crété-Roffet, F., Dolmiere, T., Ladret, P., Nicolas, M., et al.: The blur effect: perception and estimation with a new no-reference perceptual blur metric. In: Proc. of SPIE (2007)
4. Ertöz, L., Steinbach, M., Kumar, V.: Finding clusters of different sizes, shapes, and densities in noisy, high dimensional data. In: Proc. of SDM (2003)
5. Farnebäck, G.: Two-frame motion estimation based on polynomial expansion. In: Bigun, J., Gustavsson, T. (eds.) SCIA 2003. LNCS, vol. 2749, pp. 363–370. Springer, Heidelberg (2003)
6. Henderson, J.M.: Regarding scenes. Current Directions in Psychological Science 16(4), 219–222 (2007)
7. Lee, Y.J., Ghosh, J., Grauman, K.: Discovering important people and objects for egocentric video summarization. In: Proc. of CVPR (2012)
8. Liu, Q., Deng, M., Bi, J., Yang, W.: A novel method for discovering spatio-temporal clusters of different sizes, shapes, and densities in the presence of noise. International Journal of Digital Earth 7(2), 138–157 (2014)
9. Lu, Z., Grauman, K.: Story-driven summarization for egocentric video. In: Proc. of CVPR (2013)
10. Snoek, C., Sande, K., Rooij, O.d., Huurnink, B., Uijlings, J., Liempt, M.v., Bugalhoy, M., Trancosoy, I., Yan, F., Tahir, M., et al.: The mediamill trecvid 2009 semantic video search engine. In: Proc. of TRECVID (2009)
11. Wei, Y., Bhandarkar, S.M., Li, K., Ramaswamy, L.: Video personalization in heterogeneous and resource constrained environments. Multimedia Systems Journal 17(6), 523–543 (2011)
12. Yeung, S., Fathi, A., Fei-Fei, L.: Videoset: Video summary evaluation through text. CoRR, abs/1406.5824 (2014)

Advanced Content Based Image Retrieval for Fashion

Tewodros Mulugeta Dagnew$^{(\boxtimes)}$ and Umberto Castellani

Università degli studi di Verona, via strada le grazie 15, 30172 Verona, Italy
{tewodros.dagnew,umberto.castellani}@univr.it

Abstract. In this paper we propose a new content based approach for clothing image retrieval trying to mimic the human vision understanding not only based on naive manipulation of texture and color, but also combining some recent and advanced techniques like human pose estimation, super-pixel segmentation and cloth parsing. Moreover, we exploit metric learning to improve the image matching phase by proposing a new approach to learn a distance properly designed for the analyzed application. Specially in fashion sector our work seems very helpful in obtaining more accurate categorization and naturally desirable image retrieval from a large database of images of models dressing various types of style, pattern and fashion. In particular, a drastic improvement is observed when the metric learning strategy is introduced.

1 Introduction

Content based image retrieval (CBIR) is a wide research area aiming at searching for images from a large database by exploiting visual information based on a given *query* image [6]. When the database is composed of a specific class of images, the content based retrieval strategy can be specialized in order to exploit *prior* information available in the analyzed application. For instance, if the database is composed by people, some method for people detection and pose estimation can be employed to concentrate the analysis on the part of the image containing the person [17]. Recently, a great attention is devoted to content based image retrieval for fashion [10,16]. Overall, the idea is to search for a specific cloth by exploiting *cloth parsing* [8,15,16], or garment classification [10]. These methods are very important to improve on-line cloth shopping [3,9], or to better organize the internal archives of the fashion industries. In this paper we propose a complete pipeline for content based retrieval of fashion images. We assumed that a cloth is dressed by a runway/catwalk (fashion) model. A cloth parsing procedure is employed to obtain the cloth semantic parts (i.e., labels). Then, the image retrieval can be accomplished by looking at the color or texture attributes of the region of interest only. In this way it is possible to search for a "red T-shirt" or a "squared cardigan". This problem is still challenging due to the weakness of current cloth parsing methods and the large variability of cloths patterns and styles. More in details, our pipeline is composed of: i) human body detection and pose estimation, ii) cloth parsing, iii) texture and color feature

© Springer International Publishing Switzerland 2015
V. Murino and E. Puppo (Eds.): ICIAP 2015, Part I, LNCS 9279, pp. 705–715, 2015.
DOI: 10.1007/978-3-319-23231-7_63

extraction, and iv) image matching by distance metric learning. Several work has been proposed to deal with cloth parsing and retrieval. In [16] an effective cloth parsing procedure is proposed which combines robust human pose estimation [17] with semantic super-pixel labeling using conditionally random fields (CRF). The work has been extended in [15] where a descriptor is proposed to retrieve cloth of similar style. In [10] a well defined pipeline is introduced for color-based garment segmentation and classification. A Gaussian Mixture Model (GMM) is introduced to detect the part of interest, then a new color descriptor is provided to deal with both accuracy and efficiency of the retrieval performance. In [8] authors improve the laborious and time consuming supervised cloth parsing training proposed in [16] by introducing more flexible and weakly supervised approach where labels are given at only image level rather than at super-pixel level. In the most of these works the matching phase is carried out by using standard L_2 norm on the image descriptor space. In this paper we propose to improve this step of the cloth retrieval pipeline by exploiting *metric learning* [11,14]. The idea is to provide a set of image pairs of the same class (i.e., positive examples) and a set of image pairs of different class (i.e., negative examples) [14]. Then, a proper metric is estimated in order to reduce the distance between positive examples (and vice versa)[14]. In particular, we design a new metric learning approach to learn a specific distance that is suitable for the given image descriptor. In more details we extend the *large margin* nearest neighbor metric learning paradigm [14] to work with diffusion distance [7] for histogram comparison. We evaluate our approach on a dataset provided by a company working on fashion[1]. We evaluate both color- and texture- based descriptors to make the retrieval flexible. The experiments show a clear improvement with the use of metric learning approach.

2   Learning a Proper Distance for Histogram

The overall aim of distance metric learning is to replace Euclidean distances by so-called *Mahalanobis* distances. A Mahalanobis distance metric computes the distance between two vectors X and Y as $D_L = \sqrt{(X - Y)^t L(X - Y)}$, where L is a positive semidefinite matrix. When L becomes Identity matrix, the general equation becomes standard euclidean distance equation. This matrix L can be learned using *Large margin nearest neighbor* distance metric learning [14].

$$\min_L \sum_{i,j:j->i} D_L(x_i, x_j)^2 + \mu \sum_{k:y_i \neq y_k} [1 + D_L(x_i, x_j)^2 - D_L(x_i, x_k)^2]_+$$

$[f]_+$ implies a hinge-loss $[f]_+ = \max(0, f)$. The first term pull target neighbors together. In the equation above j− >i implies i and j are neighborers. The second term pushes away differently labeled ($k : y_i \neq y_k$) instances from the target instances by a large margin so that the differently labeled instances are

---

[1] Openinnovation: http://www.openinnovation.it

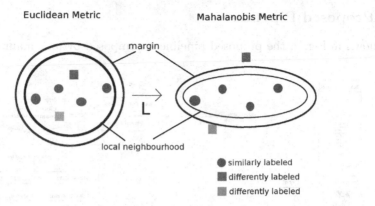

Euclidean Metric   Mahalanobis Metric

margin

L

local neighbourhood

● similarly labeled
■ differently labeled
■ differently labeled

Fig. 1. Illustration of large margin nearest neighbor distance metric learning. (left)before training and (right) after training.

located further with higher distance unit in the space (see Figure 1). μ sets the trade-off between the pulling and pushing objectives.

In this paper we propose to exploit distance metric learning for a measurement designed to compare histogram. A popular measurement is the so called diffusion distance [7] which exploits cross-bins similarities by combining several versions of the original histogram at different scales. According to [7], in order to make the connection with distance metric learning clearer, we reformulate the original diffusion distance as:

$$d(h_1, h_2) = \sum_{l=0}^{L} ||(h_1(x) * \phi(x, \sigma_l)) - (h_2(x) * \phi(x, \sigma_l))||_1, \qquad (1)$$

or in a more general definition:

$$d(h_1, h_2) = ||\hat{h}_1 - \hat{h}_2||_1, \qquad (2)$$

where $\hat{h} = [h(x)*\phi(x, \sigma_l)]_{l=0}^{L}$ and $h(x)$ is the original extracted feature . Equation 2, shows how to calculate the distance between two images. To introduce a metric learning process for histogram comparison we propose to include the Mahalanobis matrix L on Equation 2 by leading to $D_L = ||L(\hat{h}_1 - \hat{h}_2)||_2$. In practice, this method increase the dimension of the descriptor by concatenating the convolution responses from a gaussian filer (i.e $\phi(vector, \sigma)$) on the original feature $h(x)$ sequentially by down sampling to the half size (i.e $|vector|_{\downarrow 2}$) at each step until the response vector to be concatenated is less than the size of the specified gaussian kernel. We set the size of the gaussian filer 3x3. we set $\sigma=0.5$. Finally, according to [14] the new metric will be learned on the diffused features using the following objective function optimization:

$$\min_L \sum_{i,j:j \rightsquigarrow i} D_L(\hat{h}_i, \hat{h}_j)^2 + \mu \sum_{k:y_i \neq y_k} [1 + D_L(\hat{h}_i, \hat{h}_j)^2 - D_L(\hat{h}_i, \hat{h}_k)^2]_+$$

3   Proposed Pipeline

As shown in Fig. 2, the proposed pipeline is composed by four main steps.

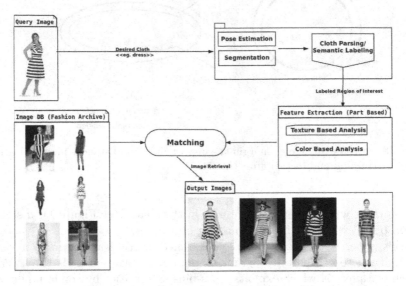

Fig. 2. The proposed pipeline Architecture.

Super-Pixel Segmentation and Pose Estimation: To obtain super-pixels, we used a recent image segmentation algorithm [2] that does hierarchical segmentation. The pose estimation component produces the location in coordinates of body parts/joints from input image of a person. The best pose $\hat{X}$ can be estimated by solving $\hat{X} \in argmax_X P(X|I)$. which is actually $(\hat{X}, \hat{T}) \in argmax_{X,T} P(X,T|I)$ where $T-> t_p$ holds information about a type label for pose mixture components for each body joint p. According to [17], the scoring function is formulated as follows:

$$ln\, P(X,T|I) \equiv \sum_p w_p(t_p)^T \Phi(x_p|I) + \sum_{p,q} w_{p,q}(t_p, t_q)^T \Psi(x_p - x_q) - ln Z$$

where, w are the model parameters, Φ and Ψ are feature functions, Z is a partition function and I is the image.

Cloth Parsing (Semantic Labeling): Once Pose configuration $\hat{X}$ are obtained, according to [16] the clothing labeling is formulated as :

$$\hat{Cl} \in argmax_{Cl}\, P(Cl|\hat{X}, I)$$

The probability distribution is modeled with second order conditional random field.

$$ln\, P(Cl|X,I) \equiv \sum_{i \in U} \Phi(cl_i|X,I) + \sum_{(i,j) \in V} \lambda_1 \Psi_1(cl_i, cl_j) + \sum_{(i,j) \in V} \lambda_2 \Psi_2(cl_i, cl_j|X, I) - ln Z$$

where
$$\Phi(cl_i|X,I) \equiv ln\,P(cl_i|\phi(s_i,X)), \qquad \Psi_1(cl_i,cl_j) \equiv ln\,P(cl_i,cl_j),$$
$$\Psi_2(cl_i,cl_j|X,I) \equiv ln\,P(cl_i=cl_j|\psi(s_i,s_j,X)), \quad \phi(s_i) \text{ is feature of a super-pixel}$$
image region s_i, $\psi(s_i,s_j)$ is feature transformation, U is the set of super-pixels, V is neighboring super-pixels and $\lambda1$, $\lambda2$ are model parameters.

Fig. 3. Super-pixel segmentation, Pose estimation and Cloth parsing (semantic labeling).

Texture and Color Feature Extraction: For color feature we used normalized HUE and VALUE histograms from the HSV color space representation of the image. For texture feature we used a binary gabor pattern texture descriptor [18] which we empirically found out that it discriminates the representative texture features well when compared to the likes of local binary pattern (LBP) [12], shift local binary pattern (SLBP) [1], local phase quantization (LPQ)[13] and Wiener's local descriptor (WLD) [4] texture descriptors in texture domain related with textiles. Finally the last step has been described in Section 2.

4   Experiments and Results

In this section we show results. The retrieval performance of our system has been evaluated under different settings using the conventional precision-recall curve plot, an evaluation method commonly used in information retrieval domain. In PR plot, The wider the curve area the better retrieval performance and vice versa.

Datasets. The whole image are provided from the company mentioned at page 2. For color based experiment we used 98 JPEG format images with models dressing red(24), blue(40) and green(34) dresses with varying mode and color intensities in varying backgrounds. the size(width and hight) of the images in the set ranges from 174x290 to 1240x1780 pixels. For texture based experiment,

Fig. 4. Sample Blue, Green & Red colored dresses with varying style and color intensities under different background settings.

we did the test on 110 JPEG format images. The set consists of models dressing dresses with 11 types of textures named (Houndstooth (Pied de poule), Flower, Zigzag, Vertical stripe, Horizontal stripe, Leopard, python, Aztec , Squares, Scottish and Dotted (Pois)) on fashion industry.

Fig. 5. 11 Sample textured Dresses with their reference name in the fashion industry.

Color Based Retrieval: In this test, Hue histogram with 256 bins from HSV(hue,saturation & value) color space values of the images has been used as a color feature to describe the images.

Comparison has been shown under different settings explained as follows,

Case A :- Extracting the color feature of the whole part of the image and matching the features directly (with out learning a proper distance metric). The dissimilarity is computed using L2-norm, χ^2 and diffusion distance [7] designed specifically for histogram comparison.

Case B :- Extracting the color feature of the whole part of the image and matching after proper distance metric learning (lmnn-L2, lmnn-χ^2 [5] and our proposed method diffusion, lmnn-diff).

Case C :- Extracting the color feature of only the segmented part (region of interest) which is semantically labeled with cloth after cloth parsing and matching the features directly (with out learning a proper distance metric). The dissimilarity is computed using L2-norm, χ^2 and diffusion distance [7].

Case D :- Extracting the color feature of only the segmented part (region of interest) after cloth parsing and matching the features by applying proper distance metric learning (lmnn-L2, lmnn-χ^2 [5] and our proposed method (lmnn-diff).

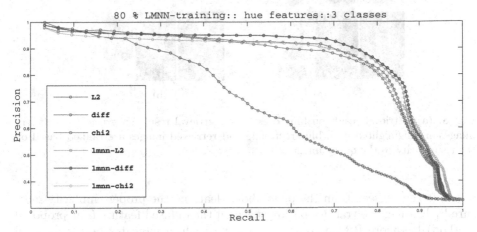

Fig. 6. PR plot on 'Models With Colored Dresses' DB. **Case A** (L2, χ^2 & diffusion distance) and **Case B** (lmnn-L2, lmnn-χ^2 and lmnn-diff).

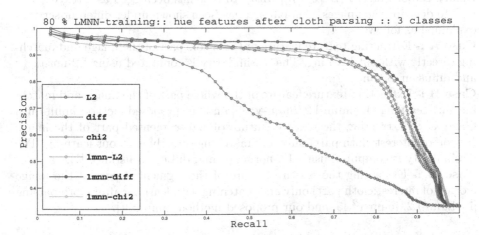

Fig. 7. PR plot on 'Models With Colored Dresses' DB. **Case C** (L2, χ^2 & diffusion distance) and **Case D** (lmnn-L2, lmnn-χ^2 and lmnn-diff).

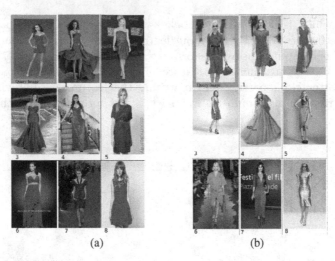

(a)   (b)

Fig. 8. (a) Retrieval result on blue dress. (b) Retrieval result on green dress. Query images are highlighted with blue rectangle and retrieved images are ranked based on their similarity to the query image.

As it can be seen from the plots above, learning the proper similarity measure by learning the transformation space on the diffused feature (our proposed method) has more PR curve area on the plot which indicates better retrieval performance. Sample qualitative result for retrieval by dress color is reported in fig. 8.

Texture Based Retrieval: In this test, a texture descriptor histogram named Binary Gabor Pattern (BGP) [18] with 216 bins has been used as a texture feature to describe the images. Comparison has been shown under different settings explained as follows,

Case A :- Extracting texture feature of the whole part of the image and matching directly with out learning. The dissimilarity is computed using L2-norm, χ^2 and diffusion distance [7].

Case B :- Extracting texture feature of the whole part of the image and matching with learning [i.e lmnn-L2, lmnn-χ^2 [5] and our proposed method lmnn-diff].

Case C :- Extracting the texture feature of the segmented part of the image (region of interest:cloth part) only and matching directly with out learning. The dissimilarity is computed using L2-norm, χ^2 and diffusion distance [7].

Case D :- Extracting the texture feature of the segmented part of the image (region of interest:cloth part) only and matching with learning after cloth parsing [i.e lmnn-L2, lmnn-χ^2 [5] and our proposed method lmnn-diff].

As it can be seen from the plots below lmnn-L2 and lmnn-diff (our method) from Case D are the best case. Sample qualitative result for retrieval by dress texture is reported in fig. 11.

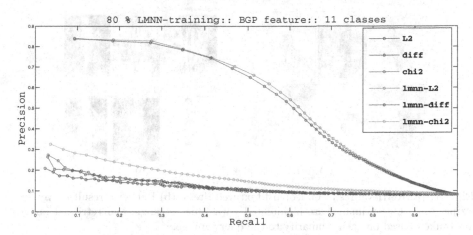

Fig. 9. PR plot on 'Models With Texture Dresses' DB. **Case A** (L2, χ^2 & diffusion distance) and **Case B** (lmnn-L2, lmnn-χ^2 and lmnn-diff).

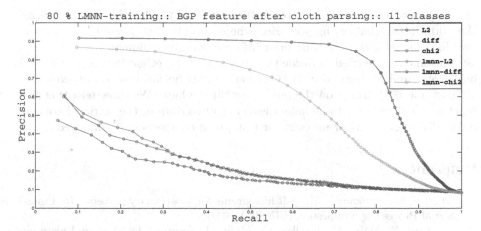

Fig. 10. PR plot on 'Models With Texture Dresses' DB. **Case C** (L2, χ^2 & diffusion distance) and **Case D** (lmnn-L2, lmnn-χ^2 and lmnn-diff).

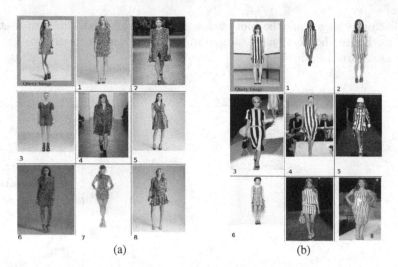

(a)   (b)

Fig. 11. (a) Retrieval result on leopard textured dress. (b) Retrieval result on vertical stripe dress. Query images are highlighted with blue rectangle and retrieved images are ranked based on their similarity to the query image.

5 Conclusion

In this paper we introduce a content based retrieval pipeline for fashion images. We address the challenging scenarios where the cloth is dressed by a runway (fashion) model and then using prior information about human detection, pose estimation e.t.c. we tried to tackle the problem. Our method is able to deal with both color and textured dresses. Our main contribution consists of exploiting distance metric learning on the image matching phase. We show how this approach is a natural way to include a learning procedure in the retrieval context, especially when a proper measure for histogram comparison is employed.

References

1. Ahonen, T., Pietikäinen, M.: Soft histograms for local binary patterns. In: Finnish Signal Processing Symposium (FINSIG) (2007)
2. Arbelaez, P., Maire, M., Fowlkes, C., Malik, J.: Contour detection and hierarchical image segmentation. IEEE Trans. Pattern Anal. Mach. Intell. **33**(5), 898–916 (2011)
3. Di, W., Wah, C., Bhardwaj, A., Piramuthu, R., Sundaresan, N.: Style finder: fine-grained clothing style detection and retrieval. In: CVPRW, pp. 8–13 (2013)
4. Chen, J., Shan, S., He, C., Zhao, G., Pietikäinen, M., Chen, X., Gao, W.: Wld: A robust local image descriptor. IEEE Transactions on Pattern Analysis and Machine Intelligence **32**(9), 1705–1720 (2010)
5. Kedem, D., Tyree, S., Weinberger, K., Sha, F., Lanckriet, G.: Non-linear metric learning. Advances in Neural Information Processing Systems **25**, 2582–2590 (2012)

6. Lew, M.S., Sebe, N., Djeraba, C., Jain, R.: Content-based multimedia information retrieval: State of the art and challenges. ACM Transactions on Multimedia Computing, Communications, and Applications **2**(1), 1–19 (2006)
7. Ling, H., Okada, K.: Diffusion distance for histogram comparison. In: CVPR, vol. 1, pp. 246–253 (2006)
8. Liu, S., Feng, J., Hui, X., Huang, J., Zhenzhen, H., Yan, S.: Fashion parsing with weak color-category labels. IEEE Transaction on Multimedia **16**(1), 253–265 (2014)
9. Liu, S., Song, Z., Liu, G., Xu, C., Lu, H., Yan, S.: Street-to-shop: cross-scenario clothing retrieval via parts alignment and auxiliary set. In: CVPR, pp. 3330–3337 (2012)
10. Manfredi, M., Grana, C., Calderara, S., Cucchiara, R.: A complete system for garmet segmentation and color classification. Machine Vision and Application **25**(4), 955–969 (2014)
11. Perina, A., Cristani, M., Castellani, U., Murino, V., Jojic, N.: Free energy score spaces: using generative information in discriminative classifiers. IEEE Transactions on Pattern Analysis and Machine Intelligence **34**(7), 1249–1262 (2012)
12. Ojala, T., Pietikäinen, M., Mäenpää, T.: Multiresolution gray-scale and rotation invariant texture classification with local binary patterns (2002)
13. Ojansivu, V., Heikkilä, J.: Blur insensitive texture classification using local phase quantization. In: Elmoataz, A., Lezoray, O., Nouboud, F., Mammass, D. (eds.) ICISP 2008 2008. LNCS, vol. 5099, pp. 236–243. Springer, Heidelberg (2008)
14. Weinberger, K.Q., Saul, L.K.: Distance metric learning for large margin nearest neighbor classification. The Journal of Machine Learning Research **10**, 207–244 (2009)
15. Yamaguchi, K., Kiapour, M.H., Ortiz, L.E., Berg, T.L.: Retrieving similar styles to parse clothing. IEEE Transaction on Pattern Analysis and Machine Intelligence. To appear
16. Yamaguchi, K., Kiapour, M.H., Ortiz, L.E., Berg, T.L.: Parsing clothing in fashion photographs. In: CVPR, pp. 3570–3577. IEEE (2012)
17. Yang, Y., Ramanan, D.: Articulated pose estimation with flexible mixtures-of-parts. In: CVPR, pp. 1385–1392. IEEE (2011)
18. Zhang, L., Zhou, Z., Li, H.: Binary gabor pattern: an efficient and robust descriptor for texture classification. In: ICIP, pp. 81–84, September 2012

Author Index

Printed in the United States
By Bookmasters